Collins

SOCIOLOGY A2
FOR AQA

Stephen Moore   Steve Chapman   Dave Aiken

ACKNOWLEDGEMENTS

William Collins' dream of knowledge for all began with the publication of his first book in 1819. A self-educated mill worker, he not only enriched millions of lives, but also founded a flourishing publishing house. Today, staying true to this spirit, Collins books are packed with inspiration, innovation and practical expertise. They place you at the centre of a world of possibility and give you exactly what you need to explore it.

Collins. Do more.

Published by HarperCollinsPublishers Limited
77–85 Fulham Palace Road
Hammersmith
London W6 8JB

Browse the complete Collins catalogue
at **www.collinseducation.com**

© HarperCollinsPublishers Limited 2009

Reprint 10 9 8 7 6 5 4 3 2

ISBN 978-0-00-728844-1

Commissioned by Charlie Evans
Consultant editor: Peter Langley, Lewes
Project managed by Hugh Hillyard-Parker, Edinburgh
Edited by Rosamund Connelly, Cambridge
Cover design by Oculus
Internal design and typesetting by Hugh Hillyard-Parker
Cartoons by Oxford Designers and Illustrators
Figures typeset by Liz Gordon, Auckland, NZ
Index compiled by Indexing Specialists (UK) Ltd
Production by Simon Moore
Printed and bound by L.E.G.O. S.p.A. Italy

Sociology A2 for AQA

CONTENTS

Sociology A2 for AQA

INTRODUCTION

Features of the textbook

The book is divided into chapters that match the AQA A2-level topics (see pp. 489–90 for more information). Each chapter contains a number of features designed to help students with learning, revision and exam-preparation.

Getting you thinking

The opening activity draws on existing knowledge and experiences to lead in to some of the main issues of the topic. The questions are usually open and, although suitable for individual work, may be more effectively used in discussion in pairs or small groups, where experiences can be shared.

AQA specification table

At the start of each chapter, a clearly laid out table shows how the topics in that chapter cover the AQA A2-specification.

Key themes

This feature encourages students to make links between the topic they are studying and key themes that run through the specification. These are **Crime and deviance, Socialization, culture and identity, Sociological theories and methods**, and **Stratification and differentiation**.

Getting you thinking

1. What role of the state is implied by this collection of images?
2. How does each of them benefit your daily life?
3. How might you use these images to suggest that the state wields too much power?
4. What state institutions do you come into contact with on a daily basis? Are these contacts mainly beneficial or harmful?

Above: the BBC series *Spooks* follows the exploits of a group of fictional MI5 intelligence officers

Above: Home Secretary Jacqui Smith shows off an example of a new identity card (September 2008)

AQA Specification	Topics	Pages
Candidates should examine:	**Candidates should examine:**	
Different theories of the nature and distribution of power.	Covered in Topics 1 and 2.	208–23
The role of the contemporary state.	Covered in Topic 3.	224–31
The nature of, and changes in, different forms of political participation, including voting behaviour, political action and protest, and membership of political organizations and movements.	Voting behaviour is covered in Topic 4. Other forms of political participation are covered in Topic 5.	232–41 242–52
The role of political parties, pressure/interest groups, new social movements and the mass media in the political process.	Political parties are covered in Topic 4. Pressure and other interest groups are covered in Topic 5.	232–41 242–52
The significance of globalization for an understanding of power and politics in the contemporary world.	Covered throughout the chapter, but see especially the pages listed on the right.	220–21 230

Key themes

Socialization, culture and identity

Weber used the concept of a theodicy of disprivilege to describe a situation whereby those who experience hardship and social disadvantage are able to endure such circumstances because they believe that they will be somehow compensated in their future lives or in the next life. Clearly, such a theodicy prevents social change as it is inclined to make individuals accept things as they are until salvation inevitably arrives. This may explain why the elderly are often more religious than the young. In the first instance, they often experience social deprivation and, second, ultimate salvation in the next life does not seem to be so far off! Similarly, women of all ages are more religious than men and are more likely than men to experience social deprivation.

Activities

At the end of each topic, there are two types of activity that will help students take their learning further:

- *Research ideas* – Suggestions for small-scale research, which could be used for class or homework activities.

- *Web tasks* – Activities using the worldwide web to develop understanding and analysis skills. This feature also serves to identify some of the key websites for each topic.

Activities

Research idea

Try to find out which countries are the Top Ten recipients of DFID aid and what their GNP is. You could do this by visiting the DFID website at **www.dfid.gov.uk**. Construct a graph showing the relationship between debt and GNP.

Web.task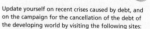

Update yourself on recent crises caused by debt, and on the campaign for the cancellation of the debt of the developing world by visiting the following sites:

- **www.debtchannel.org** – this site allows you to research debt by country. It is also excellent on the latest debt news.
- **www.jubileedebtcampaign.org.uk** – excellent site documenting British efforts to have debt cancelled.
- **www.cafod.org.uk/campaign** – excellent site documenting clearly and in detail the debt crisis and possible solutions.
- **www.makepovertyhistory.org** – the campaign to cancel the debt of developing countries that resulted in Live 8 (July 2005).

Key terms

These are simple definitions of important terms and concepts used in each topic, linked to the context in which the word or phrase occurs. Most key terms are sociological, but some of the more difficult but essential vocabulary is also included. Each key term is printed **in bold type** the first time it appears in the text.

Key terms

Anomie a breakdown in, absence of or confusion about social norms, rules, etc.

Autonomy freedom to choose one's own actions.

Boundary problem the constantly shifting nature of work makes it more difficult to draw boundaries between classes of workers.

Class fractions the recognition that the main social classes are fragmented into competing and often conflicting internal groups or fractions.

Convergence coming together, e.g. of working-class and middle-class lifestyles.

De-skilling reducing the skill needed to do a job.

Downsizing reducing the size of the permanent workforce.

Economic capital money in shares (and so on) which generates more money.

Embourgeoisement the idea that the working class is adopting the attitudes, lifestyle and economic situation of the middle classes.

Primary industries those involved in extraction of raw

materials, e.g. mining, agriculture, fishing.

Proletarianization a tendency for lower-middle-class workers to become de-skilled and hence to share the market position of members of the working class.

Proletarian traditionalist members of the working class with a strong sense of loyalty to each other because of shared community and work experience.

Routine white-collar workers clerical staff involved in low-status, repetitive office work.

Secondary industries those involved in producing products from raw materials.

Self-employed/petit-bourgeois owners of small businesses.

Social closure the process by which high-status groups exclude lower-status groups from joining their ranks.

Tertiary or service sector jobs providing services such as transport, retailing, hotel work, cleaning, banking and insurance.

Underclass termed used by Charles Murray to describe those living at the margins of society, largely reliant on state benefits to make ends meet.

Focus on research activities

This feature is usually used to draw attention to a recent piece of interesting and relevant research. Aspects of the research are summarized and questions follow that encourage evaluation of the methods used, as well as understanding of the conclusions drawn. The feature is designed to help develop the skills required to answer the methods-in-context questions appearing in Unit 4.

Check your understanding

These comprise a set of basic comprehension questions – all answers can be found in the preceding text.

Check your understanding

1 Give two examples of meta-narratives in sociology.

2 Why does the postmodernist stress on the relativity of knowledge imply criticism of positivism?

3 Explain in your own words what is meant by 'discourse'. Give an example.

4 How do postmodernists view experts and professionals?

5 What do postmodernists do when they deconstruct a concept or theory?

6 Give one example of:
   (a) a traditional subject looked at in a new way by postmodernists
   (b) a new subject brought into the domain of sociology by postmodernists.

7 What are the three key elements of feminist methodology, according to Harding?

8 Give one criticism of Harding's approach.

Focus on research

Evolution

Table 1.1 below shows the views of a sample of Americans about the evolution of humans. Two of the categories reflect the belief that a god or supreme being played the key role in creating humanity:

1 Those who believe humans have existed only in their present form subscribe to the biblical idea that 'God created man'.

2 Those who believe that evolution has occurred but think it was guided by a supreme being or higher power believe in the view that has become known as **intelligent design**.

The respondents who believe that evolution occurred through 'natural selection' accept the dominant scientific view.

Where do dinosaurs fit into different people's beliefs about creation?

1 Which religious groups subscribe most to the Bible story of creation?

2 What is the majority view in American society, according to the research?

3 Can you suggest explanations for the relationship between religion and beliefs in evolution?

4 What problems do you think the researchers faced in attempting to obtain valid data on this subject?

Exam practice

At the end of each chapter is a complete exam-style question of the type found in the relevant AQA A2-level exam paper. A candidate's 'answer' is provided, together with comments and a mark from a real AQA examiner. The comments point out where the answer scores good marks and when it fails to score.

Finally, an essay-style question is provided, together with some hints from the examiner about the best way to tackle it. Free answers are available at

www.collinseducation.com/sociologyweb

Exam Practice

1 Read **Item A** below and answer parts (a) and (b) that follow.

Item A

Functionalists, Marxists and feminists generally believe religion acts as a conservative force. Religion can be seen as conservative in two senses. First, in the sense of religion as preventing change, functionalists and Marxists both claim, in their different ways, that religion facilitates the continued existence of society in its present form. Secondly, 'conservative' may also be used to describe traditional beliefs and customs. Religion may also maintain such traditional customs and beliefs. For example, the stance of successive popes against contraception has restricted its use in Catholic countries.

However, in some circumstances, religion can support social change. This often occurs when there is a revival in 'fundamentalist' religious beliefs. Such beliefs involve a return to a group's 'fundamentals' or original beliefs of a religion, as in the case of the Islamic revolution in Iran in 1979.

Adapted from Haralambos, M. and Holborn, M. (2008) *Sociology: Themes and Perspectives* (7th edn), London: Collins Educational

(a) Identify and briefly explain **three** features of sects. *(9 marks)*

Sects are voluntary. You have to join the sect, you are not born into it, unlike a church.

They are often led by a charismatic leader, such as the Reverend Moon of the Moonies. The leader is the source of all rules and is to be obeyed without question.

Sects often reject mainstream society and its values or way of life.

7/9

(b) Using information from **Item A and elsewhere**, assess the extent to which religion forms an obstacle to social change. *(18 marks)*

Religion is often thought to be an obstacle to social change. Functionalists argue that religion helps to prevent change and maintain the status quo (Item A). They claim it does this by promoting solidarity and integration through shared values and beliefs. According to Malinowski, religion also helps individuals to cope with stresses that might disrupt social life.

Marxists also see religion as maintaining the status quo. However, they see it as serving the interests of the ruling class, whereas functionalists see it serving society as a whole by maintaining the value consensus. For Marxists, all institutions are manipulated by the ruling class in order to preserve capitalism and the status quo. Religion offers the exploited proletariat ideological comfort that they will be rewarded for their suffering. In this way, they are less likely to rebel against their capitalist bosses. Likewise, Hinduism preserves the caste system by teaching the lower castes that if they are obedient and dutiful, they will be reborn in a higher caste.

Feminists, too, see religion as a conservative force, for instance by suppressing women and maintaining a patriarchal society in the interests of men through fear of God. It legitimates their subordinate position in society and encourages them to accept it as God's will.

However, religion can also bring about change as well as prevent it. Fundamentalism is an example of this. In the Iranian revolution (Item A), fundamentalists overthrew the pro-Western monarchy and set up an Islamic republic, with strict adherence to Islamic principles. Thus, we can see that many sociologists regard religion as an obstacle to change, but it can also sometimes bring about change.

11/18

An examiner comments

All three points are correct, but the last one needs explaining, e.g. because they see society as corrupt and godless.

This answer shows reasonable knowledge of different perspectives. It makes some use of material from the Item and it has some examples of its own. However, evaluation is limited to the last paragraph and, in the example of Iran, better use could be made of the Item to distinguish between the two senses of 'conservative'. The answer could use more examples of where religion is not an obstacle to change.

One for you to try

Assess the view that religion is declining in importance in today's society. *(33 marks)*

An examiner comments

Begin by examining the different ways religion may or may not be declining, such as church attendance, membership, belief and social influence (e.g. over personal behaviour or government policy). What problems are there with these indicators? Examine different explanations, e.g. rationalization, differentiation, pluralism, individuation, as well as views that do not accept there is a decline, e.g. vicarious religion, revivals and the secularization cycle.

Answers to the 'One for you to try' are available free on **www.collinseducation.com/sociologyweb**

An eye on the exam

Data-response activities – one at the end of each topic – that reflect the AQA A2-level exam questions. These can be used to assess progress, as well as for practice of exam-type questions.

An eye on the exam — Modernist sociological theories

Item A

The functionalist method sees any system as having needs or requirements. If the system is to survive, and to continue in more or less its current form, then these needs must be met in some way. The idea of need is quite simple. A human body needs food if it is to survive; it will die without this food.

How then can functional analysis be used in the study of societies? The first step is to identify the needs of society. A society is assumed to be a relatively self-contained unit. As such it has many internal needs. These include the biological and psychological needs of its members and the need to maintain boundaries and identity. However, many needs can only be met if the society draws on resources from the external environment, for example by producing food – the economic need. Functionalists see social systems as characterized by harmony and consensus. Marx's view, on the other hand, viewed conflict and division as normal features of all societies. Social systems develop over time as a result of contradictions that arise as a result of their economic systems.

Adapted from Fulcher, J. and Scott, J. (2007) *Sociology* (3rd edn), Oxford: OUP

Assess the contribution of functionalism to an understanding of society. (33 marks)

Grade booster — Getting top marks in this question

Outline the core elements of functionalism, focusing on functional prerequisites and pattern variables, introducing them with the notion of the 'organic analogy'. You should then bring in the whole raft of criticisms made of it, including its overemphasis on consensus; the problem with the organic analogy; its failure to explain social change; the failure to look at power differences; and the way it seems to treat people like puppets. You could point out that Merton did reply to some of these criticisms, talking about dysfunctional institutions and latent functions. Finally, while functionalism is no longer fashionable in sociology, it has contributed to the development of sociological theory, raising the levels of debate and providing a theoretical counterbalance to Marxism.

CREDITS

Photographs

The publishers would like to thank the following for permission to reproduce photographs. The page number is followed, where necessary, by T (top), B (bottom), C (centre), L (left) or R (right).

Alamy/Pictor International (1); Photos.com (2L); iStockphoto (2R); Christian Darkin/Science Photo Library (5); S & R Greenhill (8L); Alamy/simo-images (8C); Alamy/Simon de Trey-White (8R); Rex Features (10T); Getty Images (10B); Rex Features (14both); Punchstock/Steve Mason (15); Getty/Time & Life Pictures (17); Empics/Stefan Rousseau (20L); Rex Features (20C); Empics (20R); Rex Features/Alisdair Macdonald (22); Rex Features/Geoff Dowen (27); Rex Features (32); Rex Features/F Sierakowski (34); Alamy/P.Gapper (39); Rex Features (44L); Roger Scruton (44R); Corbis/Reuters (47); Getty Images/AFP (53); Rex Features (54L); Getty Images/AFP (54R); Alamy/Joe Sohm (58); Rex Features/Sipa Press (64L); Science Photo Library/Rosenfield Images Ltd (64R); Still Pictures/Jorgen Schytte) (69); Alamy/Peter Bowater (76); Corbis/Thierry Orban/Sygma (80T); Alamy/Jack Sullivan (80B); Getty Images/Ami Vitale (83); iStockphoto (84); Corbis (92); Alamy (94); Omar Sobhani/Reuters (98); Still Pictures/Andreas Riedmiller (100); Still Pictures/Jotgen Schytte (102); Alamy (104, 113); Alamy/John Rensten (116); Alamy (122); Rex Features (125, 127); Getty Images (128); Rex Features (129); iStockphoto/Marjan Paliuskevic (133); iStockphoto (137); iStockphoto/Robert Billstone (141); iStockphoto/George Peters (144L); IStockphoto (144R); iStockphoto/Tammy Bryngelson (147); Rex Features (150); Flickr/Janis Krums (156); Rex Features (158); Associated Press (161); Ronald Grant Archive (168); Kobal (170 both); Advertising_Archives (178TL); Rex Features (178B); PA Archive/PA Photos (178TC); Kobal (178TR); Rex Features (181, 183, 185, 186, 188); Advertising Archives (192); Rex Features (194, 196); Getty Images (201); Rex Features (203); Corbis/Joe Mahoney (207); Rex Features (208 *Barack Obama*); Rex Features/Sipa Press (208 *Osama bin Laden*); Getty/Peter Dazeley (208 *Policewoman*); Rex Features/Richard Young (208 *Madonna*); Rex Features (208 *Simon Cowell*); Corbis/Bettmann (209); Rex Features/Ray Tang (210); John Hunt/OutRage! London ©1998 (213); PA Archive/PA Photos (216); Rex Features (220); PA Archive/PA Photos (225C); PA Wire/PA Photos (225TR); Rex Features (225BR); Rex Features (227); Getty Images/AFP (228); WENN (232); Getty Images (237); Alamy/Peter Titmuss (239); Alamy/Homer Sykes (246); Corbis/Bernard Bisson (247); Rex Features/ALF (248); Alamy (250); Getty Images (254, 255); Alamy/Robert Llewellyn (257); Courtesy Apple Corp (263); Alamy (266, 267); David Gauntlett (268); Adam Gault/Science Photo Library (270); Alamy (274); Getty/Garry Hunter (275); Punchstock/David de Lossy (278); Rex Features (281, 282); Alamy (290, 293); Alamy (296TL, 296TR); Corbis (296BL); Getty (296BR); Alamy (300); PA Archive/PA Photos (305); Alamy (313); PA Archive/PA Photos (316); Alamy (319, 325); Rex Features (329, 330, 332); PA Archive/PA Photos (334); Getty Images/Nicolas Russell (338); Rex Features (342, 343); OnAsia Images/Gerhard Jörén (345T); Rex Features (345B); Alamy (348); Rex Features (349, 350); Still Pictures (352); Corbis/Bassouls Sophie/SYGMA (353); S & R Greenhill (355); Rex Features/Dennis Stone (357); Alamy/David Sanger (359TL); Alamy/Peter Usbeck (359TR); Getty Images/Stephen Mallon (359B); Getty Images (366T); Alamy/Janine Wiedel (366B); Getty Images/Jon Gray (369); Rex Features/Image Source (374); Karen Robinson/Panos (379T); Rex Features (379B); Corbis (380); Corbis (382T); Getty Images (382B); Photofusion/Paula Solloway (387); Impact Photos/Steve Parry (395); Rex Features (399); Topfoto (401); Getty Images (402); Punchstock (407); www.JohnBirdsall.co.uk (408T); Alamy (408C); Alamy/Robert Judges (408B); Alamy/John Phillips (413); Alamy/geogphotos (416); Getty Images (421); Alamy (424L); Rex Features (Sipa Press (424R); Alamy (429); Getty Images (433TL); Rex Features (433TR); Punchstock/Flying Colours Ltd (433BL); Alamy//David Levenson (433BR); Alamy/Profimedia (437); Empics/Kim Myung Jung Kim/PA (441L); Alamy/The Photolibrary Wales (441R); Alamy/Dominic Burke (445); Alamy (449); Photofusion/Jacky Chapman (451); Alamy (455, 461); Punchstock/ImageState (464); Getty Images (466); Photofusion/David Montford (472); Getty Images (478); Rex Features (481L); PA Archive/PA Photos (481C); Getty Images (481R); Photofusion (482); Corbis (488)

Text permissions

The publishers gratefully acknowledge all those organizations that have given us permission to reproduce material from their publications. Sources are given in the text where the material is quoted.

Whilst every effort has been made to contact the copyright holders, this has not proved possible in every case.

Table 7.9 (p.449) and Key themes (p.453): The copyright and all other intellectual property rights in the material reproduced are owned by, or licensed to, the Commission for Equality and Human Rights, known as the Equality and Human Rights Commission ('the EHRC'). This includes material published by the former EOC (now the EHRC).

Beliefs in society

AQA Specification	Topics	Pages
Candidates should examine:		
Different theories of ideology, science and religion, including both Christian and non-Christian religious traditions.	Covered in Topic 1	2–7
The relationship between religious beliefs and social change and stability.	Covered in Topics 2 and 3	8–19
Religious organizations, including cults, sects, denominations, churches and New Age movements, and their relationship to religious and spiritual belief and practice.	Covered in Topics 4 and 5	20–31
The relationship between different social groups and religious/ spiritual organizations and movements, beliefs and practices.	Class is addressed in Topics 4 and 5, and gender. ethnicity and age in Topics 6 and 7	20–43
The significance of religion and religiosity in the contemporary world, including the nature and extent of secularization in a global context.	Covered in Topic 8	44–51

TOPIC 1

Religion, science and ideology

Getting you thinking

Buddhism

Buddhism is a spiritual tradition that focuses on personal spiritual development and the attainment of a deep insight into the true nature of life. Buddhism teaches that all life is interconnected, so compassion is natural and important.

- Buddhism is 2500 years old.
- There are currently 376 million followers worldwide.
- According to the 2001 census, there are around 151 816 Buddhists in Britain.
- Buddhism arose as a result of Siddhartha Gautama's quest for Enlightenment in the 6th century BCE.
- There is no belief in a personal God. It is not centred on the relationship between humanity and God.
- Buddhists believe that nothing is fixed or permanent – change is always possible.
- Buddhists can worship both at home or at a temple.
- The path to Enlightenment is through the practice and development of morality, meditation and wisdom.

Adapted from www.bbc.co.uk/religion/religions/
buddhism/ataglance/glance.shtml

1   What beliefs are shared by Paganists, Buddhists and the Amba?

2   How might these beliefs help believers deal with the 'big' questions in life – for example, about suffering and death?

3   Do you consider each of these to be religions? Explain your answers.

4   What is your definition of religion?

Beliefs of the Amba

People like the Amba and their kinsmen believe profoundly that the world is ruled by supernatural forces. … For this reason, nothing happens by chance. … Let us consider this example: Sebuya is driving his car, has an accident and dies. … That very day, all over the world, millions of cars reached their destination safely – but Sebuya had an accident and died. White people will search for various causes. For instance, his brakes malfunctioned. … But this kind of thinking leads nowhere, explains nothing. … Sebuya died because someone cast a spell on him. … Speaking in the most general terms, a wizard did it.

Adapted from Kapuscinski, R. (1998) *The Shadow of the Sun: My African Life*, London: Penguin

Paganism

Paganism describes a group of contemporary religions based on a reverence for nature. These faiths draw on the traditional religions of indigenous peoples throughout the world.

- Paganism encompasses a diverse community, including Wiccans, druids, shamans, sacred ecologists, Odinists and heathens.
- Some groups concentrate on specific traditions or practices, such as ecology, witchcraft, Celtic traditions or certain gods.
- Most Pagans share an ecological vision that comes from the Pagan belief in the organic vitality and spirituality of the natural world.
- Because of persecution and misrepresentation, it is necessary to define what Pagans are not, as well as what they are. Pagans are not sexual deviants, do not worship the devil, are not evil, do not practise 'black magic', and their practices do not involve harming people or animals.
- The Pagan Federation of Great Britain estimate that the number of Pagans in the British Isles is between 50 000 and 200 000 (2002).

Adapted from www.bbc.co.uk/religion/religions/
paganism/ataglance/glance.shtml

At some point in their lives everyone asks some 'big' questions about those things that are beyond our everyday experiences. These might include '… sleep and dreams, death, catastrophes, war, social upheaval, the taking of life, suffering and evil' (Hamilton 2001).

Berger (1971) points out that every culture across the world and throughout history has developed ways of dealing with these issues in order to prevent anxiety and social disruption. These consist of sets of beliefs that give some meaning to the world for individuals. He refers to these beliefs as a '**sacred canopy**' that gives significance to everyday life as it becomes seen as something that is part of a larger purpose. For Berger, it is religion that provides this sacred canopy.

What is religion?

Working out an acceptable definition of religion is a problem that has troubled sociologists since the earliest days of the subject. Across the world and throughout history, the nature of beliefs has varied so widely that it is very difficult to identify the kinds of common factors that allow for simple definitions. For example, should the witchcraft and **magic** of the Amba (see 'Getting you thinking' opposite) be seen as religious belief? Similarly, Buddhism, which does not include the idea of a personal God or a relationship between humans and God (see opposite)? And what about fanatically following a football team or a political view – can these be seen as religious?

Sociological approaches to defining religion can be divided into three broad categories:

1 **Substantive definitions** – These attempt to explain what religion actually is.
2 **Functional definitions** – These define religion in terms of its uses and purposes for individuals and societies.
3 **Polythetic definitions** – These define religion by creating a list of possible characteristics that make up a religion but accept that no one example will share them all.

Substantive definitions

One of the simplest definitions of religion dates from over 100 years ago. Tylor (1903) defined religion as 'belief in spiritual beings'. This definition was criticized for ignoring **religious practices** – the things people do to show their belief, for example forms of worship and ceremonies. Durkheim (1915) introduced the idea of practices into his definition. Religion, he said, is:

>> *a unified system of beliefs and practices relative to* **sacred** *things, that is to say, things set apart and forbidden – beliefs and practices which unite into one single moral community called a Church all those who adhere to them.* >> (Durkheim 1915)

Durkheim focuses on religion as a group activity and the way that certain symbols are imbued with a sacred power: they are regarded with awe and are often associated with rituals – an example might be the cross as a symbol in Christianity.

Substantive definitions of religion are dogged by the problem of which beliefs should and should not be included as 'religious'. For example, should the Amba's belief in magic be seen as religious, or should magic be a separate category as it may not include belief in god or gods or practices such as worship? And what about New Age ideas such as belief in the power of crystals, or cults such as scientology?

Functional definitions

These kinds of definitions state what religion actually does – its functions. There is an element of functionality about Durkheim's definition above, as it talks about uniting followers into 'one single moral community'. The assumption behind these definitions is that, as religion is a product of society, it needs to be defined in terms of its contributions to society. Because of this, these definitions are sometimes associated with the functionalist perspective.

An example of a functional definition is Yinger's:

>> *Religion is a system of beliefs and practices by means of which a group of people struggles with the ultimate problems of human life.* >> (Yinger 1970)

There are, however, problems with functional definitions of religion:

1 They are too broad – For example, belief systems that are specifically antireligious could be included, such as Marxism. As Scharf (1970) puts it, functional definitions are cast in such wide terms that they 'allow any kind of enthusiastic purpose or strong loyalty, provided it is shared by a group, to count as religion'. To get around this problem, the term 'civil religion' is sometimes used to describe these types of belief systems (see Topic 2, pp. 9–10).
2 Functional definitions simply assume that religion plays a useful role in society. Anything that contributes to social stability can be considered as a religion without any need for evidence.

Polythetic definitions

This approach to defining religion identifies a number of overlapping factors that most religions share. To qualify as a religion, a set of beliefs needs to exhibit a number of these factors but not necessarily all of them.

Southwold (1978) suggests the following factors:

- a concern with godlike beings and human relationships with them
- a concern with the sacred
- a focus on salvation from the ordinary world
- rituals and practices
- beliefs based on faith rather than evidence
- an ethical code based on those beliefs
- supernatural sanctions if this code is violated
- a mythology
- sacred texts or oral traditions
- priests or some other religious elite
- links with a moral community, a church
- links with an ethnic or similar group.

This approach avoids some of the problems associated with other types of definition as it does not attempt to draw a clear line between religions and non-religions, but it does bring its own problems. For example, it is not clear how many of these factors need to be shared for something to be considered a religion, and the decision about what to include in the list is itself a matter of judgement.

So, defining religion is full of problems – but where does that leave us? Is it possible to create a simple working definition that most sociologists would accept? Perhaps the closest we might get is Giddens' suggestion that:

<< *religions involve a set of symbols, invoking feelings of reverence or awe, and are linked to rituals or ceremonials engaged in by a community of believers.*>> (Giddens 2006)

Types of religion

Whichever definition of religion is used, there can be no doubt as to the bewildering array of religions that exist in societies today and in the past. The following section identifies the main types of religions.

Totemism and animism

These religions are associated with tribal societies and smaller cultures. **Totems** are animals or plants that are believed to possess supernatural powers of some kind. Ritual activities among families or tribes are associated with a particular totem. It was his study of this type of religion that led Durkheim to his conclusions about the function of religion (see Topic 2).

Animism refers to belief in ghosts or spirits. Spirits may be forces for good or evil and can have a huge influence on human behaviour, causing illness, accidents and death, for example. The beliefs of the Amba are an example of animism.

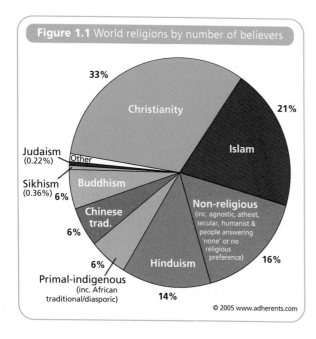

Figure 1.1 World religions by number of believers

- Christianity 33%
- Islam 21%
- Non-religious (inc. agnostic, atheist, secular, humanist & people answering 'none' or no religious preference) 16%
- Hinduism 14%
- Primal-indigenous (inc. African traditional/diasporic) 6%
- Chinese trad. 6%
- Buddhism 6%
- Sikhism (0.36%)
- Judaism (0.22%)
- Other

© 2005 www.adherents.com

Theistic religions

Theistic religions centre around belief in a sacred, higher and controlling power. This power is the source of moral codes and is worthy of great reverence. There are two types of theistic religions:

1 **Monotheistic religions** – As their name suggests, these religions believe in one divine power. They include major world religions such as Christianity and Islam.

2 **Polytheistic religions** – These religions focus on a number of separate gods. The religions of ancient Greece and Rome are examples. 'For the Greeks, Zeus ruled the spiritual world from Mount Olympus, along with other such gods as Athena, Poseidon, Hermes and Artemis' (Fulcher and Scott 2007). Hinduism, one of the world's largest religions, is a polytheistic religion.

The case of Buddhism

The status of Buddhism as a religion is sometimes questioned. Buddhism has no conception of god, as Christians, for example, would understand it. However, Buddhists do revere those who have achieved perfect enlightenment, and they are referred to as Buddhas or Bodhisattvas. Buddhism also resembles other religions in setting values and standards by which followers are directed to live their lives.

Religion, science and the Enlightenment

You can see from Fig. 1.1 that most people in the world subscribe to some kind of religious belief. However, there was a time when many believed that religion would wither away and disappear.

The Enlightenment and scientific thinking

Religious explanations of the world dominated human thinking for many hundreds of years. They were challenged, however, by the emergence of scientific ways of thinking during the period in the 18th century that has become known as the **Enlightenment**. As Bilton *et al.* (2002) put it:

<< *It was during the Enlightenment that humans crossed 'the Great Divide' and moved from ignorance, guesswork and faith to certainty and truth.*>>

The idea of science is discussed fully in Chapter 5 (see Topic 3, pp. 270–7), but the key aspects of a scientific approach can be summarized as follows:

- Knowledge must be based on empirical evidence, that is, evidence that is observable – in other words, facts.
- Scientists must ignore their personal feelings and remain objective at all times.
- Scientific thinking should be rational and logical.
- Scientists' observations and theories must be testable by other scientists.

The Enlightenment and religious thinking

These scientific ideas create problems for religion: the existence of god or gods cannot be proved, and religious belief relies on faith rather than hard scientific evidence. Some early commentators, such as Frazer (1890), believed that the growth of scientific explanations of the world would cause religion to disappear. As humanity discovered more and more about the real nature of the world, religion would decline and be replaced by solid scientific knowledge.

Religion has not disappeared, however, and there is some debate about whether or not it is even in decline. For a full account of these arguments see the debate about secularization in Topic 8.

Scientists cannot tell us how to live our lives, and science tells us little about things that matter a great deal to us: values, hopes, fears, aspirations, anxieties and so on. Science is not able to make us feel comfortable.

Science and religion

So, science and religion continue to exist side by side, but they do not do so without tensions. The United States is the most religious of the advanced industrial democracies. At the same time, American scientists are recognized to be leaders in many areas of scientific research and application. Where scientific evidence and long-held religious belief come into direct conflict, many Americans reject science in favour of the teachings of their faith tradition. While virtually all scientists agree that life on earth has evolved over billions of years, many Americans consistently reject the very idea of natural **evolution**, largely on the grounds that it conflicts with biblical accounts of creation (see 'Focus on research' on the right).

Ideology, science and religion

In the situation above, religious and scientific ideas are in conflict. Sociologists use the term **ideology** to help us understand how conflict between belief systems can occur and how belief systems relate to the distribution of power in society.

Focus on research

Evolution

Table 1.1 below shows the views of a sample of Americans about the evolution of humans. Two of the categories reflect the belief that a god or supreme being played the key role in creating humanity:

1. Those who believe humans have existed only in their present form subscribe to the biblical idea that 'God created man'.

2. Those who believe that evolution has occurred but think it was guided by a supreme being or higher power believe in the view that has become known as **intelligent design**.

The respondents who believe that evolution occurred through 'natural selection' accept the dominant scientific view.

Where do dinosaurs fit into different people's beliefs about creation?

1. Which religious groups subscribe most to the Bible story of creation?

2. What is the majority view in American society, according to the research?

3. Can you suggest explanations for the relationship between religion and beliefs in evolution?

4. What problems do you think the researchers faced in attempting to obtain valid data on this subject?

Table 1.1 Views on evolution among Americans						
Views on evolution	Total	White evangelist	Black evangelist	White mainline	Total Catholic	Secular
Human and other living things have:						
1 Existed in present form only	42	65	65	32	33	12
2 Evolved over time:	51	28	23	62	59	83
– Guided by supreme being	21	20	11	26	31	9
– Through natural selection	26	6	8	31	25	69
– Don't know how evolved	4	2	4	5	3	5
3 Don't know	7	7	12	6	8	5

All figures are percentages

Source: Pew Research Center Survey, July 2006

KEY
- *Total* = All the sample
- *White/Black evangelical* = Supporters of evangelical sects and churches
- *White mainline* = Supporters of conventional Protestant churches such as Methodism
- *Total Catholic* = Supporters of Catholicism
- *Secular* = Those with no religious views

An ideology is a set of shared views or principles that help people make sense of the world. So feminism, conservatism, Christianity or Islam might be seen as ideologies. But sociologists go further than this. They say that ideologies often legitimate, or justify, the position of powerful groups in society. Thus, the idea that kings in medieval Europe were answerable only to God – the principle known as the 'divine right of kings' – helped them justify their absolute power, as it meant that they were not accountable to any individual or group.

Marxists use the term ideology more specifically. Marx (1845) stated that, at any point in history, 'the ideas of the ruling class are … the ruling ideas'. That is, the beliefs that most people accept as 'normal' actually justify the power and dominance of the ruling class and the highly unequal society that they benefit from. For example, the idea that desiring wealth is 'only natural' helps support the capitalist system.

Science and religion as ideologies

Many sociologists have argued that both science and religion are ideological in that they work in the interests of powerful groups.

Critics of science argue that its progress and priorities reflect the interests of powerful groups, such as drug companies. For example, feminists, such as Harding (1986), argue that science reflects male assumptions and understandings about the world. See pp. 270–7 for a fuller discussion of science as an ideology.

Marxists claim that religion justifies inequalities in society and encourages passivity and acceptance of the status quo. Whether or not this is the case is the subject of the next topic.

Key themes

Socialization, culture and identity

Faith schools

Religious groups see **faith schools** as important for sustaining religion, culture, identity and language, and for maintaining continuity of belief between home and school. For parents, this means their children are more likely to grow up good Christians, Jews, Muslims or Sikhs, sharing their own deeply held beliefs, participating in community celebrations, and living moral and responsible lives. The role of the school in handing on the community identity is seen to be particularly important where a group feels under threat and marginalized by the majority culture. There is no doubt that these schools are popular with parents and often oversubscribed, partly because of their above-average achievement outcomes, which critics suggest are the result of pupil selection.

The government, however, argues that faith schools can help boost standards in deprived areas. In September 2007, Schools Secretary Ed Balls said the government would open more faith schools where there was parental demand. However, a recent coalition known as Accord, made up of religious leaders, **humanists** and teachers, have called for, not an end to, but a change to faith schools.

As well as changes to the admissions and staffing criteria, Accord wants to see faith schools follow an objective and balanced religious education syllabus covering a range of religious and non-religious beliefs. In addition to discriminatory practices, they also argue that:

● Faith schools are divisive – some argue that this type of segregation can lead to intolerance and division.
● Children may become indoctrinated into one set of beliefs, not exposed to other alternatives or encouraged to use critical judgement in relation to faith.
● Children of other faiths or of none can be excluded, reducing their choice of local schools.
● They encourage hypocrisy, whereby parents attend church solely for the purpose of getting their children into the school.
● They are disruptive to the school system as a whole – the setting-up of a new school may affect the viability of other schools in the locality.

Key terms

Animism belief in ghosts or spirits.

Enlightenment period associated with the 18th century when reason became to be seen as a guiding principle.

Evolution theory that life develops through a process of natural selection.

Faith school school based around the principles of a particular religious group.

Functional definitions of religion definitions that focus on the role religion plays for societies and individuals.

Humanist category of philosophies based on human free will and self-determination.

Ideology set of ideas that legitimate the power of a particular group.

Intelligent design the view that evolution has occurred but was guided by a supreme being or higher power.

Magic events not explained by traditional science.

Monotheistic religions based around the worship of one god.

Polytheistic religions based around the worship of many gods.

Polythetic definitions of religion those that attempt to define religion by creating a list of possible characteristics.

Religious practices rituals and rites associated with religion.

Sacred regarded with awe and reverence.

Sacred canopy Berger's term for beliefs that give meaning to the world.

Substantive definitions of religion those that attempt to explain what religion actually is.

Theistic religions that believe in sacred, higher controlling powers.

Totems objects such as animals or plants that are believed to have supernatural powers.

Check your understanding

1 Why is it important for cultures to provide answers to the 'big questions' in life?

2 How has Durkheim's definition of religion been challenged?

3 What problems are associated with functional definitions of religion?

4 What are the advantages of polythetic definitions of religion?

5 Why is Buddhism's status as a religion sometimes questioned?

6 How do the ideas associated with the Enlightenment challenge religious ways of thinking?

7 How is it possible for people in modern societies to accept both religious and scientific ideas?

8 How can religion and science both be seen as ideologies?

Activities

Research idea

Ask your friends some 'big questions' about, for example, the meaning of life, and life after death. Make sure you get informed consent from them before the interview, as this sort of questioning might upset some people. What sort of belief systems do their answers reveal? To what extent can their beliefs be described as 'religious'?

Web.tasks

1 Go to the BBC's 'religions' website at www.bbc.co.uk/religion/religions. Choose four religions and draw up a table to compare them using the categories: beliefs, customs, rites and values.

2 Visit the websites of the National Secular Society at www.secularism.org.uk and the British Humanist Association at www.humanism.org.uk. What problems does each organization believe religion causes for societies?

An eye on the exam   Religion, science and ideology

Item A

Religion and science are generally regarded as very different from one another. For example, religion is seen as dependent on faith – the members of a religion are expected to accept its teachings as true even though there may be no empirical proof of them. By contrast, according to one view of science, scientists subject everything to questioning and only accept a statement as true when evidence for it has been presented. On the other hand, not everyone accepts this view of science and numerous criticisms have been made of it. Similarly, although religions are undoubtedly belief systems, they are much more than this. Not only are they a very particular form of belief, they also have many other features.

(a) Identify and briefly explain **three** features of science other than that referred to in **Item A**.   (9 marks)

(b) Identify and briefly explain **three** features of religion (**Item A**).   (9 marks)

Grade booster   Getting top marks in this question

For both of these questions, you need to remember to explain as well as to identify the features. You should, therefore, write a short sentence for each point that identifies what it is, followed by a further sentence or two of brief explanation. Note, also, that both questions mention the Item, so you should check it for clues as to how you could answer them. You will need to check the Item carefully before you answer part (a). You will also find that there is at least one idea in the Item that you could include as one of the points in your answer to part (b).

Religion as a conservative influence on society: functionalist & Marxist approaches

Getting you thinking

Right: Members of a church meet for coffee in the vestry

Above: A funeral

Right: God can both explain poverty and offer hope of salvation from it

1 **What purpose does religion serve for the individuals in each picture?**

2 **What might happen to these individuals if religion suddenly ceased to exist?**

3 **Suggest some ways in which religion helps people in modern society to cope with destabilizing influences in their lives.**

Sociologists who have studied the role of religion in society often tend to fall into one of two broad camps:

1 Those who see religion as a **conservative** force – 'Conservative' means keeping things the way they are. These sociologists see religion as a force for stability and order. They may well favour a functionalist (see Chapter 5, pp. 255–7) or a Marxist point of view (see pp. 257–9).

2 Those who see religion as a force for social change – Supporters of this position point to the role of religion in encouraging societies to change. They may be influenced by the writings of Max Weber or by some neo-Marxist thinkers.

This first topic examines the first of these groups of thinkers.

Inhibiting change

Both functionalists and traditional Marxists adopt the view that religion inhibits change – that is, they identify a similar role for religion. However, functionalists tend to view this as a 'good' thing, while Marxists view it as a 'bad' thing.

Functionalist approaches

The key concern of functionalist writing on religion is the contribution that religion makes to the wellbeing of society – its contribution to social stability and value consensus. In his famous work, *The Elementary Forms of Religious Life*, Durkheim (1912) relates religion to the overall structure of society. He based his work on a study of **totemism** among Australian aborigines. He argued that totemism represents the most elementary form of religion.

The totem is believed to have divine properties that separate it from those animals or plants that may be eaten or harvested. There are a number of ceremonies and rituals involved in worship of the totem which serve to bring the tribe together as a group and consequently to reaffirm their group identity.

Durkheim defined religion in terms of a distinction between the **sacred** (holy or spiritual) and the **profane** (unspiritual, non-religious, ordinary). Sacred people, objects and symbols are set apart from ordinary life, and access to them is usually forbidden or restricted in some way.

Why is the totem so sacred?

Durkheim suggests that the totem is sacred because it is symbolically representative of the group itself. It stands for the values of the community, who, by worshipping the totem, are effectively 'worshipping' their society.

Durkheim's distinction between the sacred and profane, is, in effect, the distinction between society and people. The relationship between god and humans (power and dependence) outlined in most religions is a reflection of the relationship between society and humans. It is not god who makes us behave and punishes our misdemeanours, but society.

Durkheim argues that religion is rarely a matter of individual belief. Most religions involve collective worship, ceremony and rituals, during which group solidarity is affirmed or heightened. An individual is temporarily elevated from their normal profane existence to a higher level, in which they can recognize divine influences or gods. These divine influences are recognized as providing the moral guidance for the particular social group concerned. For Durkheim, however, gods are merely the expression of the influence over the individual of what he calls the '**collective conscience**' – the basic shared beliefs, values, traditions and norms that make the society work. The continual act of group worship and celebration through ritual and ceremony serves to forge group identity, creating cohesion and solidarity. God is actually a recognition that society is more important than the individual.

In maintaining social solidarity, religion acts as a conservative force; when it fails to perform this function, new ideas may emerge that effectively become the new religion. Thus, Durkheim regarded **nationalism** and **communism** as examples of the new religions of industrial society, taking over from Christianity, but performing the same essential functions. Durkheim and other functionalists are not saying that religion does not change – clearly its *form* does – but what remains unchanged is its *function*, and that, essentially, is to offer support for the status quo. Politics and its associated rituals, flag waving, parades and so on, are the new forms by which collective sentiments are symbolically expressed. Consequently, religion, in one form or another, is a necessary feature of any society.

The functions of religion in modern society

The key functions of religion can be summarized as follows.

Socialization

In modern societies, the major function of religion is to socialize society's members into a value consensus by investing values with a sacred quality. These values become 'moral codes' – beliefs that society agrees to hold in the highest regard and socialize children into. Consequently, such codes regulate our social behaviour – for example, the Ten Commandments (from the Old Testament) are a good example of a set of moral codes that have influenced both formal controls, such as the law (e.g. 'Thou shalt not kill/steal'), as well as informal controls, such as moral disapproval (e.g. 'Thou shalt not commit adultery').

Social integration and solidarity

Encouraging collective worship is regarded by functionalists as particularly important for the integration of society, since it enables members to express their shared values and strengthens group unity. By worshipping together, people develop a sense of commitment and belonging; individuals are united into a group with shared values, so that social solidarity is reinforced, deviant behaviour restrained and social change restricted. Also, religion and its associated rituals foster the development of the collective conscience or moral community, which helps people to understand the reality of social relations, communicate with others and establish obligations between people.

Civil religion

In modern societies, ritual and ceremony are common aspects of national loyalties. In the UK, street parades, swearing allegiance to Queen and country, and being part of a flag-waving crowd all remind us of our relationship to the nation.

This idea has been developed by some functionalist thinkers into the theory of '**civil religion**'. This refers to a situation where sacred qualities are attached to aspects of the society itself. Hence, religion in one form or another continues to be an essential feature of society. This is very evident in America where the concept of civil religion was first developed by Bellah (1970), himself American. America is effectively a nation of immigrants with a wide range of co-existing cultural and religious traditions. What does unite them, however, is their faith in 'Americanism'. While traditional religion binds individuals to their various communities, civil religion in America unites the nation. Although civil religion need not involve a connection with supernatural beliefs, according to Bellah, God and Americanism appear to go hand in hand. American coins remind their users 'In God we trust', and the phrase 'God bless America' is a common concluding remark to an important speech. Even the phrase 'President of the United States of America', Bellah argues, imbues the country's leader with an almost divine quality. The God that Americans are talking about, however, is not allied to a particular faith; he is, in a Durkheimian sense, the God of (or that is) America.

Bellah, however, suggests that even civil religion is in decline, as people now rank personal gratification above obligation to others and there is, in his view, a deepening cynicism about established social institutions. However, the events of 11 September 2001 and their aftermath have undoubtedly led to a reaffirmation of Americanism and its associated symbolism.

Preventing anomie

Durkheim's main fear for modern industrial society was that individuals would become less integrated and their behaviour less regulated. Should this become widespread, **anomie** (a state of confusion and normlessness) could occur whereby society could not function because its members would not know how they should behave relative to one another.

Focus on civil religion

1   To what extent can the terms 'sacred' and 'profane' be applied to the situations above?

2   How can the situations in the photos be seen to:

    (a) strengthen social solidarity?
    (b) act as a conservative influence?

3   To what extent do you agree that the concept of civil religion is helpful in understanding religion today?

4   How might Marxists argue that, like religion, football rivalry diverts the attention of the working class from the real opposition, the ruling class?

Religious and civil ceremony prevents this happening by encouraging an awareness of common membership of an entity greater than, and supportive of, the individual. Some religious movements seem to have grown in times of social upheaval when anomie may have been occurring. For example, the industrial revolution in Britain was marked by a series of revivalist movements, such as Methodism and Presbyterianism.

Coming to terms with life-changing events

Functionalist thinkers, such as Malinowski (1954) and Parsons (1965), see religion as functioning to relieve the stress and anxieties created by life crises such as birth, puberty, marriage and death. In other words, such events can undermine people's commitment to the wider society and, therefore, social order. Religion gives such events meaning, helping people come to terms with change. Most societies have evolved religious **rites of passage** ceremonies in order to minimize this social disruption. For example, the death of a loved one can cause the bereaved

to feel helpless and alone, unable to cope with life. However, the funeral ceremony allows people to adjust to their new situation. The group mourning also reaffirms the fact that the group outlives the passing of particular individuals and is there to support its members.

Criticisms of functionalism

- Church attendance is declining in most Western societies, such as the UK. It is difficult to see how religion can be functioning to socialize the majority of society's members into morality and social integration, if only a minority of people regularly attend church.
- Some have argued that Durkheim's analysis is based on flawed evidence: he misunderstood both totemism and the behaviour of the aboriginal tribes themselves.
- Religion can have a negative effect on societies – it can be dysfunctional. Rather than binding people together, many of the world's conflicts have been caused by religion, for example between Sunni and Shiite Muslims, Hindus and Muslims in India, and Christians and Muslims throughout the world. The latter situation prompted Islamic scholars in October 2007 to write to Pope Benedict XVI and other Christian leaders suggesting a joint emphasis on mutual understanding and shared aspects of the religions, such as an emphasis on 'loving your neighbour'.
- Much functionalist analysis is based upon the idea that a society has one religion, but many modern societies are multicultural, multifaith societies.
- The idea that religion can be seen as the worship of society depends on an assumption that worship is a collective act – people joining together to celebrate their god or gods. However, religious belief may be expressed individually (see pp. 23–4).

Durkheim did recognize that religion had a strong social control function, as the following quotation illustrates.

>> *Religion instructed the humble to be content with their situation, and, at the same time, it taught them that the social order is providential; that it is god himself who has determined each one's share, religion gave man a perception of a world beyond this earth where everything would be rectified; this prospect made inequalities seem less noticeable, it stopped men from feeling aggrieved.* >> (Durkheim 1912)

Marxists take this argument much further. They argue that religion, far from being an instrument of social solidarity, is an instrument of social control and exploitation.

Marxism and religion

The following quotations provide a summary of the classic Marxist position on religion.

>> *Religion is the sigh of the oppressed creature, the sentiment of a heartless world ... the soul of soulless conditions. It is the opium of the people.* >> (Marx 1844)

>> *Religion is a kind of spiritual gin in which the slaves of capital drown their human shape and their claims to any decent life.* >> (Lenin 1965)

Like Durkheim, Marx also argued that religion was a conservative force in society. However, he did not agree that this force was essentially positive and beneficial to society. Rather, Marx argues that the primary function of religion is to reproduce, maintain and justify class inequality. In other words, religion is an **ideological apparatus**, which serves to reflect ruling-class ideas and interests. Moreover, Marx describes religion as the 'opium of the people', because in his view it prevents the working classes from becoming aware of the true nature of their exploitation by the ruling class and doing anything about it. Instead, they see it all as 'God's will' and passively accept things as they are, remaining in a state of false consciousness. Religion acts as an opiate – a pacifying drug – in that it does not solve any problems people may have, but merely dulls the pain and, therefore, argued Marx, most religious movements originate in the oppressed classes.

However, as Engels pointed out:

<< The history of early Christianity has notable points of resemblance with the modern working-class movement. Like the latter, Christianity was originally a movement of oppressed people: it first appeared as the religion of slaves and emancipated slaves, of poor people deprived of all rights, of peoples subjugated or dispersed by Rome. Both Christianity and the workers' socialism preach forthcoming salvation from bondage and misery; Christianity places this salvation in a life beyond, after death, in heaven; socialism places it in this world, in a transformation of society. >>
(Marx and Engels 1975)

Religion is seen by Marx as being ideological in three ways, as outlined below (Marx and Engels 1957).

1 Legitimating social inequality

Religion serves as a means of controlling the population by promoting the idea that the existing hierarchy is natural, god-given and, therefore, unchangeable. We can particularly see this during the **feudal period**, when it was widely believed that kings had a divine right to rule. During the 18th and 19th centuries, it was generally believed that God had created both rich and poor, as reflected in the hymn 'All Things Bright and Beautiful'. This stated (in what is now a little-used verse):

<< The rich man in his castle,
the poor man at his gate,
God made them, high or lowly,
and order'd their estate. >>

2 Disguising the true nature of exploitation

Religion explains economic and social inequalities in supernatural terms. In other words, the real causes (exploitation by the ruling class) are obscured and distorted by religion's insistence that inequality is the product of sin or a sign that people have been chosen by God.

3 Keeping the working classes passive and resigned to their fate

Some religions present suffering and poverty as a virtue to be accepted – and even welcomed – as normal. It is

Key themes

Crime and deviance

Religion has a contradictory relationship to crime and deviance. On the one hand, it can be seen as encouraging conformity, while on the other, it can provide justification for deviant subcultures to challenge the status quo. In the first case, 'official' religious organizations, such as churches, or civil religions, such as the monarchy, provide a sense of collective identity and belonging to a moral community with shared goals. Deviance is inhibited as the central values of the society are continually reaffirmed through religious or civil practice and ritual. In the second case, however, religion may be used to justify criminal activity, such as the bombing of abortion clinics or murdering innocent people as in the attack on the World Trade Center in New York on 11 September 2001 and in the London bombings of July 2005.

Furthermore, religious groups are often demonized by politicians and the mass media, and some become the subject of moral panics. This has been the case with some fundamentalist groups and new religious movements both in Britain and the USA (see p. 28).

suggested that those who do not question their situation will be rewarded by a place in heaven. Such ideas promote the idea that there is no point in changing society now. Instead, people should wait patiently for divine intervention. Religion offers hope and promises happiness in a future world. The appeal to a God is part of the illusion that things will change for the better. This prevents the working class from actually doing anything which challenges the ruling class directly.

Marx was interested in industrial capitalist societies and Christianity was at the centre of his thinking. However, other religions can be seen to have the same effect, whether it is the Buddhist focus on individual meditation, or the Hindu caste system, which fixes status for this life in one caste and only allows for improvement after reincarnation.

Religion thus discourages people from attempting change, so the dominant groups can retain their power. Religion is used by the ruling class to justify their position. Church and ruling class are mutually reinforcing:

<< The parson has ever gone hand in hand with the landlord. >> Communist Manifesto (Marx 1848)

However, evidence for the traditional Marxist position is partial and tends to be of a documentary nature, looking at the nature of faith and the way in which the religion of the poor concentrates on the afterlife. Also, some traditional Marxists adopt the view that religion can bring about social change, a position also adopted by some neo-Marxists and discussed further in the next topic.

Evidence to support Marxist views

- Halevy (1927) argued that the Methodist religion played a key role in preventing working-class revolution in 19th-century Britain. Most European nations, apart from Britain, experienced some type of proletarian attempt to bring about social change in this period. Halevy argued that working-class dissatisfaction with the establishment in Britain was, instead, expressed by deserting the Church of England, which was seen as the party of the **landed classes**. Methodism attracted significant numbers of working-class worshippers, and Halevy claims Methodism distracted the proletariat from their class grievances by encouraging them to see enlightenment in spirituality rather than revolution. In this sense, religion inhibited major social upheaval and, therefore, social change.

- Leach (1988) is critical of the Church of England because it recruits from what is essentially an upper-class base (80 per cent of bishops were educated at public school and Oxbridge). The Church is also extremely wealthy. Leach argues that, as a result, the Church has lost contact with ordinary people. He suggests it should be doing more to tackle inequality, especially that found in the inner cities.

- Religion is used to support dominant groups in America. It has been suggested that modern Protestant **fundamentalist religions** in the USA support right-wing, conservative and anticommunist values. Fundamentalists (the **Christian Right**) often suggest that wealth and prosperity are a sign of God's favour, while poverty, illness and homosexuality are indicators of sin.

- Hook (1990) noted that the (then) Pope, John Paul II, had a very conservative stance on contraception, abortion, women priests and homosexuality (a stance shared by his successor, Benedict XVI). He points out that the Vatican's stance on contraception is causing problems in less developed areas of the world, such as South America. Hook also suggests that the considerable wealth of the church could be doing more to tackle world poverty.

Criticisms of Marxism

- Like functionalism, the Marxist theory of religion fails to consider **secularization**. Surely the ideological power of religion is undermined by the fact that fewer than 10 per cent of people attend church?

- Marx failed to explain the existence of religion where it does not appear to contribute to the oppression of a particular class. Nor does Marxism explain why religion continues to exist when, in theory at least, oppression has come to an end. In the USSR under communism after the 1917 revolution, the state actively discouraged religion and many places of worship were closed. The communist state placed limits on religious activity and the religious instruction of children was banned. Nevertheless, religion did not die out under communism, as Marx predicted it would.

- There are also some examples of religious movements that have brought about radical social change and helped remove ruling elites (see Topic 3). They demonstrate that religion can legitimize radical revolutionary ideas as well as ideologically conservative ones. Marx failed to recognize this. Neo-Marxists have recognized the way in which religion is sometimes used as the only means to oppose the ruling class. Recently in Britain, for example, churches have often provided safe havens for immigrant groups facing deportation by the government, enabling such groups to publicize their case further and to gain time and support.

Check your understanding

1 What is the distinction between the sacred and the profane?

2 What is Durkheim's explanation of the true nature of the 'totem' and 'god'?

3 Identify and explain four functions of religion.

4 Explain, using examples, how civil religion performs similar functions to religion as it is usually understood.

5 How have functionalist ideas about religion been criticized?

6 How, according to Marxists, does religion benefit the capitalist class?

7 What evidence is there to support such views?

8 How, according to Engels, is socialism both similar to and different from early Christianity?

9 How can Marxist views on religion be criticized?

Activities

Research idea

Interview a sample of people who participate in different religions. Find out their views on the relationship between religion and society. Do they believe that religion should get involved with politics, or is it a purely private matter?

Web.tasks

1 Go to the website of the *Guardian* newspaper at www.guardianunlimited.co.uk and, in the archive search section, key in the words 'government' and 'church'. What evidence can you find for the continuing influence of the church on politics in modern society?

2 Go to a search engine and type in the phrase 'Christian Right + USA'. Investigate the extent to which they lend support for the Republican party (an American political party with conservative views).

Key terms

Anomie a state of confusion and normlessness.

Christian Right fundamentalist and right-wing Christian groups, particularly powerful in the southern states of America.

Civil religion events or activities that involve ritualistic patterns and generate the collective sentiments usually associated with established religions.

Collective conscience beliefs, values and moral attitudes shared by members of a society that are essential to the social order.

Communism political philosophy originated by Karl Marx that advocates common ownership of land and business.

Conservative supporting things staying as they are.

Feudal period medieval period when wealth in society was based on the ownership of land.

Fundamentalist religions belief systems that argue the need to subscribe or return to traditional values and practices, usually involving the literal translation of, and belief in, a religious text.

Ideological apparatus agencies (such as religion, education and the mass media) that transmit ruling-class ideology to persuade subordinate groups (e.g. the working class) that inequality is natural and normal, thereby ensuring their consent to it.

Landed classes wealthy, land-owning aristocracy.

Nationalism patriotic feelings towards a nation; belief that your nation is superior to others

Profane ordinary, unreligious aspects of life.

Rites of passage a ceremony or event that marks an important change in a person's life

Sacred holy or spiritually significant.

Secularization a process whereby religious beliefs and practices lose their social significance.

Totemism a primitive religion involving the worship of certain objects seen to have a widespread influence over tribal life.

An eye on the exam — Religion as a conservative influence

Item A

Christian Right groups, as the name implies, consist primarily of Christians, many of them fundamentalists; some have been known to claim that their political positions are, or ought to be, the views of all Christians. In reality, American Christians hold a wide variety of political views, although many elements of the Christian Right sympathize with, support and sometimes influence the US Republican Party. For example, such support is thought to have provided considerable backing for the campaign of former US President George W. Bush.

Issues with which the Christian Right is (or is thought to be) primarily concerned include:

- banning or heavily restricting abortion
- opposition to the gay rights movement and upholding what they consider 'traditional family values'
- support for the teaching of creationism (the Bible story of creation) in schools
- support for the presence of Christianity in the public sphere
- opposing US court decisions widening the separation of church and state beyond historical tradition
- banning of books, music, television programmes, films, etc., that they view as indecent, especially pornography.

Adapted from www.nationmaster.com

(a) Identify and briefly explain **three** functions of religion. (9 marks)

(b) Using material from **Item A** and elsewhere, assess the extent to which religion can be seen as a conservative influence. (18 marks)

Grade booster — Getting top marks in this question

In answering question (b), you need to explain how and why religion is seen by some sociologists as a conservative influence. You should examine the views of functionalists, such as Durkheim, as well as those of Marxists, identifying and describing the different ways in which religion can hold back social change and act as an agent of social control. You also need to give examples of the ways in which religion acts as a conservative force. These can include the function of rituals and ceremonies, as well as of beliefs. You should also identify some of the criticisms of these views. Remember to use relevant material from the Item in your answer. Use some of the examples of policies that the American Christian Right support, such as opposition to abortion and gay rights, but note also the point that American Christians hold a variety of political views.

Religion as a force for social change: Weber and neo-Marxists

Getting you thinking

The attacks on 11 September 2001 in New York and on 7 July 2005 in London – and the American and British response (the so-called 'war on terror') – have often been presented in religious terms, as 'good versus evil', for example. Both sides have used religion to try to change the world.

Photo left: George W. Bush, US president at the time of the bombings in 2001 and 2005

Photo right: the bombers making their way to London on 7 July 2005

1 How has religion motivated the individuals in each picture?

2 How might their actions be viewed if religion did not exist?

3 To what extent do you think religion causes or justifies social change?

Both the functionalist and Marxist approaches, covered in Topic 2, suggest that religion generally plays a conservative role in society – preventing change and supporting the existing social order. This topic looks at an alternative position – that it is possible for religion to change societies.

The role of theodicies

How do people make sense of a world full of suffering, unfairness, inequality and danger? Why are some people poor, while others are rich? Why are some healthy, while others die of cancer? Why do those we love always die? What will happen to me after I die? Why does God allow such terrible things to happen?

Many sociologists see religion as a means of providing answers to such fundamental questions and these answers are sometimes called '**theodicies**'. Berger (1967) uses the metaphor of a '**sacred canopy**' to refer to the different religious theodicies that enable people to make sense of,

and come to terms with, the world. Some of these theodicies justify keeping things as they are – the **status quo** – while others encourage change.

Examples of religious theodicies

- In many Western religions, there is a belief that suffering in this life will bring rewards in the next.
- Hinduism suggests that living the 'right way' in this life will lead to a better future life on earth through **reincarnation**.
- Some theodicies include a belief in fate – people believe their lives are **predestined** and there is nothing they can do to change them. They may, however, devise ways to counter the bleakness of this perception. One way might be to be as successful as possible in order to highlight God's favour and thus reassure themselves of their ultimate place in heaven.
- Followers of some spiritual beliefs and practices, such as the reading of **tarot cards** and **astrology**, believe that life is fated or that certain things are meant to be.

Theodicy and social change

All these theodicies have social consequences. For example, Islamic fundamentalists in countries that have had **trade sanctions** imposed on them by Western countries that disapprove of their fundamentalism may gain strength from the sanctions and resulting material deprivations they suffer. One Islamic theodicy is the belief that suffering plays a role in gaining entry to heaven. Western sanctions, therefore, are seen as a means to divine salvation and so provide greater resolve.

Max Weber, in his famous work *The Protestant Ethic and the Spirit of Capitalism* (1958, originally 1905), identified one particular theodicy that may have helped to facilitate dramatic social change.

The Protestant ethic and the spirit of capitalism

Calvinists were a Protestant group who emerged in the 17th century and believed in predestination. According to them, your destiny or fate was fixed in advance – you were either damned or saved, and there was nothing you or any religious figure could do to improve your chances of going to heaven. There was also no way of knowing your fate. However, it was believed that any form of social activity was of religious significance; material success that arose from hard work and an **ascetic** life would demonstrate God's favour and, therefore, your ultimate destiny – a place in heaven.

Weber argued that these ideas helped initiate Western economic development through the industrial revolution and capitalism. Many of the early **entrepreneurs** were Calvinists. Their obsessive work ethic and self-discipline, inspired by a desire to serve God, meant that they reinvested, rather than spent, their profits. Such attitudes were ideal for the development of industrial capitalism.

The influence of religious leadership on social change

According to Weber, religious and other authority takes one of three forms:

1 *Charismatic* – People obey a religious leader because of their personal qualities. Well-known **charismatic** figures might include Jesus Christ and Hitler. Charisma has been a common feature of leadership in some religions, particularly cults and sects, which can, if the charismatic leader attracts enough followers, bring about significant changes to the societies in which they originate.

2 *Traditional* – Those who exercise authority do so because they continue a tradition and support the preservation and continuation of existing values and social ties. Those in authority give orders (and expect to be obeyed) because the office they fill gives them the right to. Though generally conservative, this kind of authority can be responsible for change in the face of modernizing regimes. The authority of the Islamic leaders in Afghanistan and Iran are recent examples.

3 *Legal–Rational* – This type of authority is not based on the personal qualities of the individual but on laws and regulations. Orders are only to be obeyed if they are relevant to the situation in which they are given. Individuals within the legal system, government and state institutions exercise this form of authority.

Social change can be caused by influential religious leaders who have challenged legal–rational authority – the form exercised by the state or government. Charismatic leaders, in particular, have been responsible for the establishment of many alternative social arrangements, often causing conflict with mainstream society or much negative publicity through the harmful influences of their leaders (see first 'Webtask', p. 18).

Criticisms of Weber

- Some countries with large Calvinist populations, such as Norway and Sweden, did not industrialize. However, as Marshall (1982) points out, Weber did not claim that Calvinism *caused* capitalism; he only suggested that it was a major contributor to a climate of change. Calvinist beliefs had to be supplemented by a certain level of technology, a skilled and mobile workforce, and rational modes of law and bureaucracy.

Key themes

Socialization, culture and identity

Theodicies of disprivilege

Weber used the concept of a theodicy of disprivilege to describe a situation whereby those who experience hardship and social disadvantage are able to endure such circumstances because they believe that they will be somehow compensated in their future lives or in the next life. Clearly, such a theodicy prevents social change as it is inclined to make individuals accept things as they are until salvation inevitably arrives. This may explain why the elderly are often more religious than the young. In the first instance, they often experience social deprivation and, second, ultimate salvation in the next life does not seem to be so far off! Similarly, women of all ages are more religious than men and are more likely than men to experience social deprivation.

- Some commentators have suggested that slavery, colonialism and piracy were more important than Calvinist beliefs in accumulating the capital required for industrialization.
- Marxists are also critical because, as Kautsky (1953) argued, capitalism predates Calvinism. He argued that early capitalists were attracted to Calvinism because it made their interests appear legitimate.
- Aldridge (2000) points out that charismatic leadership can be unstable, in that movements often disintegrate once the charismatic leader dies (see the first 'Webtask' on p. 18 for some dramatic examples). Such leadership does not, therefore, contribute significantly to long-lasting social change.

Neo-Marxist views on religion

Not all Marxists have followed the view that religion is purely 'the opium of the people' (see p. 10). Some have emphasized the revolutionary potential of religion. O'Toole (1984) has pointed out that:

<<*Marxists have undoubtedly recognized the active role that may be played by religion in effecting revolutionary social change.*>>

Writers who have tried to update the ideas of Marx to suit new developments in society are known as neo-Marxists. Some neo-Marxists have rejected the classic Marxist idea that all the cultural institutions in society, such as the media, the law and religion, are inevitably under the control of the ruling class. They argue that ruling-class domination is actually more effective if its members are not directly involved in these cultural institutions. This is because it will then appear that the media and so on are independent when, in fact, the economic power of the bourgeoisie means that no matter who fills particular roles in these institutions, they are still under ruling-class control. Neo-Marxists call this apparent independence of cultural institutions **relative autonomy**.

The Italian neo-Marxist Antonio Gramsci (1971) wrote in the 1920s and 30s. Although he was aware at the time that the church was supporting ruling-class interests, he did not believe this to be inevitable. He argued that religious beliefs and practices could develop that would support and guide challenges to the ruling class, because the church, like other cultural institutions, was not directly under their control. Members of the working class could challenge the dominant class through the distribution of more radical ideas.

Otto Maduro (1982), also argued for the relative autonomy of religion, suggesting that in situations where there is no other outlet for grievances, such as in Latin America, the clergy can provide guidance for the oppressed in their struggle with dominant groups (see 'Religion and radical change' on p. 17).

Why do some religions encourage social change?

Most sociologists today do not believe that there is any simple one-directional relationship between religion and social change. Instead, they try to identify the particular factors that influence the role of religious beliefs and institutions in specific social contexts. MacGuire (1981) and Thompson (1986) argue that there are a number of factors that determine whether or not religion promotes change.

Beliefs

Religions that emphasize strong moral codes are more likely to produce members who will be critical of and challenge social injustice. The Reverend Martin Luther King and the Southern Baptist Church were at the forefront of the Black civil rights campaign in the 1960s. King's nonviolent demonstrations were important in dismantling segregation and bringing about political and social rights for Black people. Christianity was also a powerful opponent of apartheid in South Africa. Religious beliefs that focus on this world will have more potential to influence it than those that focus on spiritual and other-worldly matters. Christianity and Hinduism, therefore, have more revolutionary potential than, for example, Buddhism, which focuses on improvement of the self rather than society.

As the 'Focus on research' demonstrates (see right), religions with 'other-worldly' beliefs are less likely to promote change than those with temporal or 'this-worldly' beliefs.

Culture

Where religion is central to the culture of a society, then anyone wishing to change that society is more likely to use religion to help them bring about that change. In India, for example, Gandhi used the Hindu concept of *sarvodaya* (welfare for all) to attack British colonial rule, inspiring rural peasants and the urban poor to turn against the British.

Social location

Where a religious organization plays a major role in political or economic life, there is wide scope for it to influence social change. In situations where the clergy come from and remain in close contact with their communities, they are more able to mobilize them against negatively perceived outside influences. An Islamic revolution led by the Ayatollah Khomeini overthrew the Shah of Iran's pro-Western regime in 1979.

Internal and external organization

Religions with a strong centralized source of authority have more chance of affecting events. The Roman Catholic church was instrumental in bringing about the collapse of communism in Poland through its support of the opposition movement known as 'Solidarity'. This same authority can, however, have the opposite effect by restraining the actions of some parts of its organization.

Focus on research

Above: US civil rights campaigner, Martin Luther King

Gary Marx (1973)
Religion: opiate or inspiration?

Gary Marx studied the role of religious belief during the Black struggle for racial equality in the USA during the 1960s. In general, for Marx's nationwide sample of Black people, the effect of **religiosity** on attitudes to protest indicated that the greater the religious involvement, the less the militancy. However, this was not always the case. Marx found that the nature of religious belief affected its capacity to inhibit or promote change.

If Black people's religious beliefs were 'other-worldly' – stressing the powerlessness of humans and the promise of salvation in the world to come – then they provided little motivation to change society. In contrast those with 'this-worldly' (or temporal) beliefs – those that focused on the importance of this world – would be encouraged to try to change the world for the better glorification of God.

Marx concludes that until such time as religion loosens its hold, or comes to embody more of a temporal or 'this-worldly' orientation, it may be seen as an important factor inhibiting Black militancy overall.

Marx, G. (1973) 'Religion: opiate or inspiration of civil rights militancy among negroes?', in B. Beit-Hallahmi (ed.) *Research in Religious Behavior: Selected Readings*, Monterey, CA: Brooks/Cole

1 Why do you think that an 'other-worldly orientation' appears to inhibit involvement in civil rights issues?

2 Why do you think that the religious conviction of figures such as Martin Luther King was so influential in increasing support for the civil rights movement?

For example, the Pope has expelled some Latin American bishops for supporting **liberation theology**.

However, in communist societies, and to some extent in Latin America, the organizational support the church receives from outside the country is an important factor in its ability to resist the authorities and criticize existing social and political arrangements. A movement without a large external organizational structure is more susceptible to repression.

Religion and radical change

Similarly, some would argue that religious organizations with a less obviously hierarchical structure are better equipped to frustrate state control, as removal or imprisonment of their leadership makes little difference. Parkin (1972) argues that political leadership of the Black population in the southern states of the USA was frequently taken on by clergymen and that churches provided an organizational focus for the civil rights movement. However, as the 'Focus on research' shows (see left) the implications of religion for protest are often somewhat contradictory.

Revolutionary movements have deliberately used religion in an attempt to change society. In some Central and South American countries, such as Guatemala, Chile and El Salvador, where the police and military have been used to crush opposition, religion has become the only remaining outlet for dissent. This fusion of Christianity and Marxism is known as 'liberation theology'. In the 1960s, various radical groups and individuals emerged from within the Catholic Church in Latin America. They argued that it was a Christian duty to be involved in action leading to economic and political liberation. Catholics collaborated with Marxists in political and social action. In 1979, Catholic revolutionaries played a part in the overthrow of the Somoza regime in Nicaragua and the new government included a number of priests.

One other aspect of this discussion involves the reactionary nature of some religions – that is, their desire to turn the clock back to a time when society and its moral order were more in line with their religious ideals. Such religions are opposed to what they consider to be the undesirable state of modern society. Christian and Islamic fundamentalists illustrate this position well.

For Islamic fundamentalists, religion provides the basis for resistance to the process of Westernization. Iran and Afghanistan are obvious recent examples, but this is not a new phenomenon. In Egypt, the Moslem Brotherhood played an important part in the revolt that deposed King Farouk in 1952; Colonel Gaddafi, in Libya in 1969 led a revolution pledged to return to an Islamic way of life; and Islamic fundamentalists were involved in the assassination of President Sadat of Egypt in 1981. Christian fundamentalists in the USA have significantly influenced the policies of the Bush administration in relation to family life and social policy.

The nature and motivations of fundamentalist religious groups is explored further in the next topic.

Focus on ...

Christian fundamentalism in the USA

The Rev W. A. Criswell: an obituary

THE REV W. A. CRISWELL, former president of the Southern Baptist Convention has died at the age of 92. Christian fundamentalists have heaped praise on a man who spent 50 highly influential years insisting that the Bible is the unerring word of God and that its historical accuracy is beyond question.

Though this may seem a fringe attitude on this side of the Atlantic, Criswell led a denomination of some 16m people, ran four radio stations and established a seminary which has turned out hundreds of young graduates to spread the same message. He paid lip service to the constitutional separation of church and state, yet he and his followers worked untiringly to ensure that their conservative social agenda dominated the US political debate.

Based in Dallas, Texas, Criswell was part of the influential network surrounding the Bush family. The Rev Billy Graham, a White House adviser for 50 years, is a leading member of the First Baptist Church, which Criswell led; the elder George Bush regularly worshipped there, and his son made strenuous efforts to retain the backing of Criswell's adherents during his own presidential election campaign.

The relentless energy of this core conservative group – drawn from such disparate fields as the oil industry and the Christian Right – led a *Washington Post* commentator to observe four weeks ago that 'for the first time since religious conservatives became a modern political movement, the president of the United States has become the movement's de facto leader' – a development for which Wallie Amos Criswell could claim much credit.

But Criswell's message, often delivered at enormous length, went back uncompromisingly to Genesis, where God created the world in six days and made man in his image. That led, quite naturally, to a repeated effort to encourage the teaching of creationism (the Bible story of creation) in American schools. It also brought such church rulings as its 1998 declaration that a woman's duty was to submit graciously unto her husband's leadership.

The Guardian, 15 Jan 2002

1 In what ways can the Rev W.A. Criswell be described as a fundamentalist?

2 How did the Rev W.A. Criswell attempt to ensure that fundamentalist Christian views were influential in American politics?

3 To what extent do you think Christian fundamentalist groups, such as those described above, are an influence for social change or a conservative influence?

Check your understanding

1 What purpose do religious theodicies serve?

2 In your own words, explain one example of a religious theodicy.

3 What does Weber mean by the 'Protestant ethic'?

4 How did Weber suggest that the Protestant ethic contributed to the development of capitalism?

5 Give an example that shows in each case how charismatic and traditional leadership have caused social change.

6 What criticisms have been made of Weber's work?

7 According to neo-Marxists, how does the relative autonomy of cultural institutions such as religion benefit the ruling class?

8 What factors may determine whether religion has a radical influence?

9 How is fundamentalism related to both conservatism and change?

Activities

Research idea

Interview (or conduct a focus group with) a small number of fellow students who attend religious events on a regular basis. Try to cover a range of religions. Ask them about their beliefs and their views about society.

- Do they argue for social change or are they content with the way things are?
- If they want change, what sort of changes are they looking for?
- How do they think these might come about?

Web.tasks

1 Look up the following examples of mass suicides arising from members unquestioning belief in their cult's charismatic leader.

- Order of the Solar Temple, Heaven's Gate, People's temple and Movement for the Restoration of the Ten Commandments of God.
- In each case, find examples that illustrate the leader's charismatic authority, i.e. what did members do because the leader told them to?

2 Search the net for examples of liberation theology. Using a search engine, type in the following names: Archbishop Oscar Romero, Camilo Torres and Dom Helder Camara.

Key terms

Ascetic self-denying.

Astrology the study of the positions and aspects of celestial bodies (stars, planets, moon) in the belief that they have an influence on the course of natural earthly events and human affairs.

Calvinists a 17th-century Protestant sect based on the thinking of John Calvin.

Charismatic leader leader with a powerful and magnetic personality.

Entrepreneurs self-made, successful business people.

Liberation theology a fusion of Christianity and Marxism that has been influential in Central and South America.

Predestination belief that an individual's destiny is fixed before their birth.

Reincarnation being reborn after death into another life.

Relative autonomy the degree of freedom that state institutions, such as religion, have from the direct control of the dominant class.

Religiosity the importance of religion in a person's life.

Sacred canopy an overarching set of religious ideas that serves to explain the meaning of life.

Status quo current state of affairs.

Tarot readings an occult practice that claims to predict the future through analysis of specific cards which are alleged to relate to the fate of the client.

Theodicies religious ideas that explain fundamental questions about the nature of existence.

Trade sanctions international boycott of the trade in key goods imposed on a country for its perceived wrongdoing.

An eye on the exam — Religion as a force for social change

Item A

John Wesley, a leader of the great Methodist movement that preceded the expansion of English industry at the close of the 18th century, wrote:

>> *For religion must necessarily produce industry and frugality, and these cannot but produce riches. We must exhort all Christians to gain what they can and to save all they can; that is, in effect to grow rich.* >> (Quoted in Weber 1958)

These riches could not be spent on luxuries, fine clothes, lavish houses and frivolous entertainment, but on the glory of God. In effect, this meant being even more successful in terms of one's calling, which in practice meant reinvesting profits in the business.

The Protestants attacked time-wasting, laziness, idle gossip and more sleep than was necessary – six to eight hours a day at the most. They frowned on sexual pleasures ... The impulsive fun and enjoyment of the pub, dance hall, theatre and gaming house were prohibited to ascetic Protestants. In fact, anything that might divert or distract people from their calling was condemned.

Adapted from: Haralambos, M. and Holborn, M. (2004) *Sociology: Themes and Perspectives*, London: Collins

Using material from **Item A** and elsewhere, assess the extent to which religion produces social change.

(33 marks)

Grade booster — Getting top marks in this question

For this question, you need to make use of a range of theories, such as Weber's views on Protestantism and the origins of capitalism. You should refer to the concept of theodicy in your account of how religion may promote social change. Remember to make use of relevant material from the Item in your answer, for example to show how Calvinist beliefs may have promoted capitalism. Evaluate Weber's claims by reference to the absence of industrial capitalism in some Calvinist countries and to the role of other (often economic or political) factors in the emergence of capitalism. You should also consider neo-Marxist views of the relative autonomy of religion and how this may enable it to promote social change, as well as the idea that certain religions may be better equipped to do so than others because of their beliefs, social location or organization.

Organized religion and religious activity

Getting you thinking

A Christian church service *(left)*, Jehovah's Witnesses preaching door to door *(centre)* and a mass wedding of 'Moonies' *(right)*

The pictures above show members of various religious organizations.

1   How does each organization acquire its members?

2   To what extent does each claim to be the only true route to spiritual salvation?

3   How much influence does each organization have on its members? What type of influence is it?

Religious organizations

Religious organizations can be broadly grouped into four main types:

● churches
● sects
● denominations
● cults.

Churches and sects

Weber (1920) and Troeltsch (1931) were the first to distinguish between churches and sects. A church is a large, well-established religious body, such as the mainstream organizations that represent the major world religions – Christian churches (such as the Roman Catholic, Anglican and Eastern Orthodox churches), Judaism, Islam, Hinduism, and so on. However, the term 'church' is particularly associated with the Christian religion and today many prefer to call religions such as Islam and Hinduism 'faiths'. A sect is a smaller, less highly organized grouping of committed believers, usually setting itself up in protest at what a church has become – as Calvinists and Methodists did in preceding centuries (they are now considered to be denominations within the Christian Church – see below). In terms of membership, churches are far more important than sects. The former tend to have hundreds of thousands or even millions of members, whereas sect members usually number no more than a few hundred. Hence, the often widespread media attention given to sects is somewhat disproportionate.

Denominations

According to Becker (1950) a denomination is a sect that has 'cooled down' to become an institutionalized body rather than an active protest group. Niebuhr (1929) argues that sects that survive over a period of time become denominations because a **bureaucratic**, non-hierarchical structure becomes necessary once the charismatic leader dies. Hence, they rarely survive as sects for more than a generation. While they initially appear deviant, sects gradually evolve into denominations and are accepted as a mere offshoot of an established church. They no longer claim a **monopoly of truth**, and tend to be tolerant and open, requiring a fairly low level of commitment. However, Bryan Wilson (1966) rejects Niebuhr's view and suggests that some sects do survive for a long time without becoming denominations and continue to require a high level of commitment.

Cults

There is some disagreement among sociologists over how to classify a cult, but most agree that it is the least coherent form of religious organization. The focus of cults tends to be on individual experience, bringing like-minded individuals together. People do not formally join cults, rather they subscribe to particular theories or forms of behaviour. Scientology, for example, is claimed to have eight million members worldwide.

The terms 'sect' and 'cult' are often used interchangeably by the media to describe new forms of religious organization and there can be considerable **moral panic** about them, as we shall see in the next topic. Recently, sociologists such as Wallis (1984) have developed the terms 'new religious movement (NRM)' and 'New Age movement (NAM)' to describe these new forms of religion (see Topic 5).

Table 1.2 below summarizes the differences between churches, denominations, sects and cults.

Postmodernity and organized religion

For some sociologists, the advent of postmodern society (see Chapter 5, pp. 266–9) has resulted in:

- previously powerful religious organizations becoming less significant
- an increase in fundamentalist factions within all major world religions
- new types of religious movements and networks, and the development of the '**spiritual shopper**'.

> **Table 1.2** The differences between churches, denominations, sects and cults
>
> This table illustrates key differences between types of religious organization. It is inevitably an oversimplification, as religious organizations do not always fit neatly into these categories.
>
> | Feature | Churches | Denominations | Sects | Cults |
> |---|---|---|---|---|
> | Scope | National (or international); very large membership; inclusive | National (or international); large membership; inclusive | Local or national. Tend to start small but can become extremely large. | Local, national or international; inclusive; vary in size |
> | Internal organization | Hierarchical; bureaucratic | Formal bureaucratic | Voluntary; tight-knit; informal | Voluntary; loose structure |
> | Nature of leadership | Professional clergy with paid officials | Professional clergy; less bureaucratic; use lay preachers | No professional clergy or bureaucratic structure; often charismatic leader | Individualistic; may be based on a common interest or provision of a service; inspirational leader |
> | Life span | Over centuries | Often more than 100 years | Sometimes more than a generation; may evolve into a denomination | Often short-lived and die with the leadership |
> | Attitude to wider society | Recognize the state and accept society's norms and values. Often seen as the establishment view | Generally accepted but not part of formal structure; seen as a basis of non-conformist views | Critical of mainstream society; often reclusive with own norms and values | May be critical or accepting of society, but have a unique approach that offers more |
> | Claims to truth | Monopoly view of truth; strong use of ritual with little arousal of strong emotional response | No monopoly on truth; less ritual but clear emphasis on emotional fervour | Monopoly view of truth; aim to re-establish fundamental truths | No monopoly; borrow from a range of sources |
> | Type of membership | Little formal commitment required; often by birth | Stronger commitment and rules, such as teetotalism or non-gambling | Exceptional commitment | Membership flexible |
> | Examples | Anglicanism, Roman Catholicism, Islam, Judaism, Hinduism, Sikhism | Baptists, Methodists, Pentecostalists | Mormons, Jehovah's Witnesses, Moonies, Branch Davidian, Salvation Army | Scientology, spiritualism, transcendental meditation, New Age ideas |

According to Lyotard (1984), postmodern society is characterized by a loss of confidence in **meta-narratives** – the 'grand' explanations provided by religion, politics, science and even sociology. The 'truths' that these subjects and belief systems claim to be able to reveal have not been forthcoming. This has led to what Bauman (1992) calls a 'crisis of meaning'. Traditional religions, in particular, seem unable to deal with this crisis. Take, for example, the social conflicts caused in the name of religion and religion's inability to reconcile this with the claim to preach love

rather than hate. Consequently, newer expressions of religiosity have become more individualistic and less socially divisive. This has enabled individuals to restore meaning to their lives without having to rely on religious institutions imposing their monopoly of truth. This can be seen in the decline of religious monopolies and the rise of NRMs and NAMs. Some established religions have attempted to respond to these changes by watering down their content – according to Herberg (1960), they have undergone a process of internal secularization. Examples of

Focus on research

Heelas et al. (2004)
The Kendal project

Kendal, a town of 28 000 people in the Lake District, has a church-attendance rate slightly above the national average, and is also something of a centre for alternative spirituality, offering the team from Lancaster University an ideal place to explore some of the key questions in current religious studies debates.

The researchers' book begins with the claim made by some commentators that traditional forms of religion appear to be declining, while new forms of alternative spirituality are growing.

The focus of the study was, therefore, on the two main types of sacred groupings:

- the 'congregational domain' (the various church congregations)
- the 'holistic milieu' (a range of activities involving the mind, body and spirit – such as yoga, tai chi, healing and self-discovery).

Between 2000 and 2002, questionnaires and interviews were conducted with members of each grouping – 26 congregations and 62 groups with a spiritual dimension, as well as a doorstep survey of over 100 households.

The researchers found that involvement in church and chapel – at 7.9 per cent of the population – still outweighs that in alternative spirituality, where only 1.6 per cent are estimated to be committed practitioners. However, alternative spirituality is catching up fast, as church congregations are in general decline (down from 11 per cent of the population in

1980) while the holistic milieu is growing. Furthermore, those churches that emphasized individuals 'in the living of their unique lives' were thriving, compared with those that subordinate all individuality to a higher good, e.g. 'the Almighty', which were contracting.

The writers see this as evidence of a 'spiritual revolution', whether Christian or alternative. What people are seeking are forms of religiosity that make sense to them, rather than those which demand that they subordinate their personal truth to some higher authority. In other words, we are witnessing a **'subjectivization'** of the sacred.

While the study reaffirmed an overall decline in total numbers involved in sacred activities, the growth in the holistic milieu, primarily by women practitioners (80 per cent), seems to reflect the 'subjective turn of modern culture', whereby people see themselves more as unique individuals with hidden depths. This is part of a general process of perceiving individuals as consumers who can express their own individuality through what they buy, or buy into. The findings also suggest that the sociology of spirituality ought to take gender more seriously.

However, the age profile of the holistic milieu was very uneven, with 83 per cent being over 40 and many who were ex-hippies who had maintained their affiliation with alternative spiritualities since the 1960s. Many in the holistic milieu also worked in people-centred, caring jobs, where personal wellbeing is a major concern. Given the relatively small number in such jobs and the other demographic and cultural factors, this would suggest that the rate of growth of the holistic milieu is likely to slow down. Nonetheless, on the basis of the Kendal research, the writers predict that holistic milieu activity will exceed church attendance within the next 20 to 30 years.

Adapted from Heelas, P., Woodhead, W., Seel, B., Tusting, K. and Szerszynski, B. (2004) *The Spiritual Revolution: Why religion is giving way to spirituality*, Oxford: Blackwell

1 What problems might the researchers have encountered when conducting a 'doorstep survey' about religious and spiritual belief and behaviour?

2 What do the researchers mean by:
   (a) 'spiritual revolution'?
   (b) subjectivization?

this include the increased acceptance of divorce, homosexuality and the ordination of women in the Christian church, and the increasing popularity of Reform Judaism and Progressive Judaism.

Fundamentalism

Other established religions have encouraged a counterresponse to internal secularization and perceived moral decline by returning to the fundamentals, or basics, of their religious roots. Hence, there has been a rise in religious fundamentalism. Examples include Zionist groups in Israel, Islamic fundamentalists in Iran, Afghanistan and elsewhere, and the Christian Right in the USA. In the past 30 years, both Islamic and Christian fundamentalism have grown in strength, largely in response to the policies of modernizing governments and the shaping of national and international politics by **globalization**. The increasing influence of Western consumerism, for example, on less developed societies may be perceived as a threat to their faith and identity, thus provoking a defensive fundamentalist response. As Bauman puts it (1992), 'fundamentalist tendencies may articulate the experience of people on the receiving end of globalization'.

According to Holden (2002), fundamentalist movements, such as Jehovah's Witnesses, offer hope, direction and certainty in a world that seems increasingly insecure, confusing and morally lost.

Fundamentalism can sometimes lead to violence, especially where fundamentalists value their beliefs above tolerance of those who do not share them. In some cases, these beliefs can be so strong as to overcome any respect or compassion for others. They can sometimes even overcome the basic human values of preserving one's own life and the lives of others. The bombing of abortion clinics in the USA, the attacks on the Pentagon and World Trade Center Towers on 11 September 2001, and the suicide bomb attacks in Madrid (March 2004) and London (July 2005) are specific examples.

Features of fundamentalist groups

Sociologists such as Caplan (1987), Hunter (1987), and Davie (1995) provide a useful summary of some of the key features of fundamentalist groups (see Table 1.3 below).

Individual choice and the postmodern world

The next topic explores the postmodernist view that society has encouraged the development of NRMs, as people assert their identity through individual consumption rather than group membership. The information explosion created by new technologies has provided an opportunity for people to pick and choose from a vast array of alternatives in a virtual 'spiritual supermarket'. Those in developed countries where this choice is greatest, act as 'spiritual shoppers', picking those beliefs and practices that suit their current tastes and identity, but dropping them or substituting them for other products if those identities change.

Table 1.3 Key features of fundamentalist groups	
What fundamentalists do	**Why they do it**
They interpret 'infallible' sacred texts literally.	They do this in order to counter what they see as the diluting influence of excessive intellectualism among more **liberal** organizations. They often use texts from scriptures selectively to support their arguments.
They reject **religious pluralism**.	Tolerance of other religious ideas waters down personal faith and consequently fundamentalists have an 'us' and 'them' mentality.
Followers find a personal experience of God's presence.	They define all areas of life as sacred, thus requiring a high level of engagement. For example, fundamentalist Christians are 'born again' to live the rest of their lives in a special relationship with Jesus.
They oppose secularization and modernity and are in favour of tradition.	They believe that accommodation to the changing world undermines religious conviction and leads to moral corruption.
They tend to promote conservative beliefs, including patriarchal ones.	They argue that God intends humans to live in heterosexual societies dominated by men. In particular, they condemn abortion and detest lesbian and gay relationships.
They emerge in response to social inequality or a perceived social crisis.	They attract members by offering solutions to desperate, worried or dejected people.
Paradoxically, they tend to make maximum use of modern technology.	To compete on equal terms with those who threaten their very existence, the Christian Right, for example, use television (in their view the prime cause of moral decay) to preach the 'Word'. Use of the internet is now widespread by all fundamentalist groups.

However, postmodernists have been criticized for overstating the extent of individual choice. Critics, such as Bruce (2002), point to the continuing influence of group membership on identities, as evidenced by the ways in which factors such as class, gender and ethnicity continue to influence the spiritual life course. This is explored further in later topics, especially Topic 6 (gender) and Topic 7 (ethnicity).

Key themes

Socialization, culture and identity

Social class and religiosity

- *Churches* – Recent research by the Christian charity Tearfund (Ashworth and Farthing 2007) demonstrates that churchgoing is associated with those of higher social classes. For both sexes, professionals and senior and middle management have an above-average frequency of churchgoers, whilst skilled, semi-skilled and unskilled manual have the lowest proportion. Many of those dependent on the state, through sickness, unemployment or old age, are open to attending, but often are unable to do so.

  The Church of England has always been seen as middle or upper class, having had a close relationship with the monarchy and state. The monarch, members of parliament and other dignitaries are frequently seen at religious ceremonies such as Remembrance Day services. This was more tolerated in the past as working-class membership went hand in hand with **deference** to the middle classes generally, and the adoption of middle-class cultural standards was expected as a mark of decency and respectability. The middle classes went to church and so 'decent' working-class people did too. The greater decline in working-class attendance may, therefore, reflect changes in the relationship between the classes, where deference is no longer expected or given.

  In addition, the middle classes tend to be more geographically mobile and this can have an impact on churchgoing. Research for *Religious Trends* showed that while churchgoing is in decline, there are pockets of growth in prosperous areas: 9.6 per cent of people in wealthier areas went to church compared to 5.9 per cent in the poorest areas. According to Brierley (1999), the church offers people new to an area an opportunity to become part of the community. The 'flip side' was that working-class people in poorer areas felt alienated from a church they perceived to be middle class.

- *Sects* – Many sects require members to donate their 'worldly goods'. The middle class tend to be rather more willing to renounce theirs, than the working classes who have never experienced such a lifestyle. On the other hand, some sects appeal to the underprivileged, offering a theodicy of ultimate salvation in a world they experience as offering few rewards. This could explain the appeal of world-rejecting sects to some members of ethnic minorities or young social 'drop-outs'.

  Relative deprivation can also explain the appeal of Islamic fundamentalism to those who have been upwardly mobile. Bruce (2002) argues that a sense of a weakening community due to the modernizing influence of Western morality, leaves some feeling relatively deprived. A return to traditional principles is an attempt to reclaim the past and redress the balance.

- *Cults* – The composition of New Age cults is overwhelmingly middle class. As Bruce (1995) argues, spiritual growth appeals mainly to those whose more pressing material needs have been satisfied but who feel there may be more to life. Bruce further maintains that New Age cults appeal specifically to 'university-educated middle classes working in the "expressive professions": social workers, counsellors, actors, writers, artists, and others whose education and work cause them to have an articulate interest in human potential'. This seems to be confirmed by the Kendal research (see 'Focus on research', p. 22).

Key terms

Bureaucratic centralized form of organization run by official representatives.

Deference Great respect or high public esteem given as a right to those perceived as superior.

Globalization a process whereby social and economic activity spans many nations with little regard for national borders.

Liberal a concern with individual freedoms.

Meta-narratives the 'grand' explanations provided by religion, politics, science and even sociology.

Monopoly of truth a view that only the viewpoint of the holder can be accepted as true.

Moral panic media-induced panic about the behaviour of particular groups.

Religious pluralism where a variety of religions co-exist, all of which are considered to have equal validity.

Spiritual shoppers a postmodern idea that people consume religion in much the same way as any other product.

Subjectivization the increasing relevance of the self and personal experiences as a dominant feature of religion in late-modern society.

Check your understanding

1 Briefly define 'church', 'denomination', 'sect' and 'cult', giving examples of each.

2 What evidence is given for the claim that previously dominant religious organizations have become less significant?

3 What does Herberg mean by the phrase 'internal secularization'?

4 In your own words, outline the key features of fundamentalism.

5 Give two possible reasons for the rising number of fundamentalist groups across the globe.

6 Give two reasons why church attendance appears to be greater among the middle class.

7 What do you understand by the term 'spiritual shopper'?

8 How does Bruce criticize the postmodern view of religion?

Activities

Research idea

Identify a small sample of students who participate in organized religious activity. Conduct semi-structured interviews with them, aiming to discover what appeals to them about that particular religious group. Do you find any differences between those who are involved in different kinds of religious organizations?

Web.task

There are many sites that represent and discuss churches, sects and cults. Many are the websites of the groups themselves. Search for some websites of churches, sects and cults. Compare some organizations using some of the criteria in Table 1.2 on p. 21. What other differences and similarities can you identify?

An eye on the exam   Organized religion

Item A

According to Gilles Kepel (1994), American fundamentalists are notable for their extraordinary skill in using the most up-to-date language and technology to disseminate their message. The electronic media have been centrally involved in changes affecting religion in the US since the 1960s. Billy Graham was the first to preach regularly across the airwaves amassing a large following ... 'The electronic church' – religious organizations that operate primarily through the media rather than local congregation meetings – has come into being. Through satellite communications, religious programmes can now be beamed across the world ... Inspirational preachers use their star quality to convert non-believers, their charismatic qualities being projected to an audience of thousands or even millions of people. The electronic preaching of religion has become particularly prevalent in Latin America where North American programmes have inspired the growth of Pentecostal protestant movements in mostly Catholic countries such as Chile and Brazil.

Adapted from Giddens, A. (2001) *Sociology* (4th edn), Cambridge: Polity Press

(a) Identify and briefly explain **three** types of religious organization.   (9 marks)

(b) Using material from **Item A** and elsewhere, examine some of the reasons for the growth of fundamentalism.   (18 marks)

Grade booster   Getting top marks in this question

In your answer to question (b), remember to make use of relevant material from the Item. You need to outline the major features of fundamentalist religious groups, such as their literal interpretation of their sacred texts, their rejection of religious pluralism and their use of modern technology (as in Item A, for example) to spread their beliefs. You need to consider a number of possible reasons for the growth of these groups, such as in reaction to the process of globalization and its impact, or as a response to secularization or to Western-style consumerism. Access to the latest technology may also have been a significant reason for the growth of fundamentalist religion, via the internet, cable television and the 'electronic church'.

New religious and New Age movements

Getting you thinking

1 Have you ever experienced strange coincidences? Do you think that there may be something more to them than mere coincidence?

2 Do you think there is something beyond the physical world that traditional religions are unable to explain?

3 Do you believe that human beings have a spiritual aspect to their nature? Explain the reasoning behind your answer.

4 Which of the following would you be more interested in and why:
(a) an alternative religion or movement that promised you greater spiritual fulfilment?
(b) an alternative movement or religion that offered you the opportunity to be more financially and romantically successful?

The Celestine Prophecy

The Celestine Prophecy by James Redfield fast became one of the top commercial publishing events of the1990s, hovering at the top of the New York Times best-seller list for several months. It has now been made into a major film. The fictional narrative centres around a search for ancient Mayan manuscripts known as the 'Nine Insights'. These insights purport to contain information and ancient wisdom about ultimate reality and man's place in it.

Essentially, according to the book, life's 'chance coincidences', strange occurrences that feel like they were meant to happen, are actually events, indicative of another plane of existence and following them will start you on your path to spiritual truth – a oneness of human spirit with the forces of the universe.

The success of the original book largely arose from the fact that many *Celestine* devotees believed the book's story to be true. The fact that Hollywood filmmakers believe that the potential interest is still sufficiently widespread to justify spending the millions of dollars involved in the making of a feature film would suggest that they, at least, believe that new religious beliefs have grown sufficiently to cross over into popular culture.

If you answered 'yes' to any of questions 1 to 3 above, you are not alone. As the Kendal project showed (see p. 22), an increasing number of people are rejecting traditional religious explanations of spirituality as well as scientific accounts of the natural world. Some are even prepared to make life-changing commitments to realize their goal of spiritual fulfilment. This process, of what some have called '**resacrilization**', has been accelerating since the 1960s.

Sociologists have adopted the concept 'new religious movements' (NRMs) as an overarching idea that embraces both cults and sects. The term was coined by Eileen Barker (1984) as a more neutral term than the highly negative meanings of the concepts 'cult' and 'sect' in popular culture. However, as Hadden and Bromley (1993) point out, the concepts of cult and sect do have precise meanings as used by sociologists (see pp. 20–1), and are free of prejudice. Nonetheless, it is true that this non-judgemental use of the word is not always understood as

such by the general public. The term 'new religious movement' is value-free, but is not without its own problems. Most significantly, many NRMs are not new, and some are not even new to a particular culture.

The emergence of new religious movements (NRMs)

As we saw in the previous topic, membership of established 'mainstream' churches has dropped dramatically. However, affiliation with other religious organizations (including Pentecostal, Seventh-Day Adventists and Christian sects) has risen just as noticeably. It is estimated that there may now be as many as 25 000 new religious groups in Europe alone, over 12 000 of whose members reside in the UK (see the 'Focus on research' on the right).

Difficulties in measuring affiliation to NRMs in the UK

There are a number of difficulties in measuring affiliation to NRMs in the UK:

- Many of the organizations listed in the 'Focus on research', right, have a large number of followers who are not formally registered in any way. It is estimated that about 30 000 people have attended meditation courses run by Brahma Kumaris, for example.
- Some groups have disbanded their organizations but still have 'devotees' – an example is the Divine Light Mission, whose followers, once initiated with 'the Knowledge', continue to practise the techniques of meditation independently.
- Many organizations are based overseas and their supporters in the UK are not traceable.
- The commitment required varies enormously between organizations. While those who devote themselves full time to their movement are generally quite visible, part-time commitment is more difficult to identify.

Affiliation through practice and belief is much higher than formal membership for both traditional and new religions.

Classifying NRMs

Sociologists have attempted to classify such movements in terms of shared features. One way is to identify their affinities with traditional mainstream religions. For example, some may be linked to Hinduism (e.g. Hare Krishnas) and others to Buddhism (various Zen groups). Some NRMs, such as the Unification Church (Moonies), mix up a number of different theologies, while others have links with the Human Potential Movement, which advocates therapies such as transcendental meditation and Scientology to liberate human potential.

Wallis (1984) identifies three main kinds of NRM:

1 world-affirming groups
2 world-rejecting groups
3 world-accommodating groups.

World-affirming groups

These are usually individualistic and life-positive, and aim to release 'human potential'. They tend to accept the world as it is, but involve techniques that enable the individual to participate more effectively and gain more from their worldly experience. They do not require a radical break with a conventional lifestyle, nor strongly restrict the behaviour of members. Research suggests that these are more common amongst middle-aged, middle-class groups – often in people who are disillusioned and disenchanted with material values and in search of new, more positive meanings. These groups generally lack a church, ritual worship or strong ethical systems. They are often more like 'therapy groups' than traditional religions. Two good examples of world-affirming groups are:

- *The Church of Scientology* founded by L. Ron Hubbard – Hubbard developed the philosophy of 'dianetics',

Focus on research

Peter Brierley
Membership of NRMs

Membership of new religious movements, UK 1980 to 2000

	1980	1990	2000
The Aetherius Society	100	500	700
Brahma Kumaris	700	900	1500
Chrisemma	–	5	50
Da free John	35	50	70
Crème	250	375	510
Eckankar	250	350	450
Elan Vital*	1200	1800	2400
Fellowship of Isis	150	250	300
Life training	–	250	350
Mahikari	–	220	280
Barry Long Foundation	–	400	–
Outlook seminar training	–	100	250
Pagan Federation	500	900	5000
The Raelian movement	100	100	100
Shinnyo-en UK	10	30	60
Sahaja Yoga	220	280	365
Solara	–	140	180
3HO	60	60	60
Hare Krishna	300	425	670
Others	50	575	1330
Total	3925	7710	14 625
% of UK population	0.007	0.014	0.028

* previously known as the Divine Light Mission

Compiled from: Brierley, P. (ed.) (2000) *Religious Trends 2000*, London: HarperCollins

1 **Assess the reliability of the figures above.**

2 **Identify key patterns in the figures and suggest explanations for them.**

which stresses the importance of 'unblocking the mind' and leading it to becoming 'clear'. His church spread throughout the world (from a base in California). Its business income is estimated at over £200 million per year through the courses members pay for, as well as through the sale of books.

- *Transcendental Meditation* (or TM) was brought to the West by the Hindu Mahareshi Mahesh Yogi in the early 1950s and was further popularized through the interest shown in it by the Beatles in the 1960s. Adherents build a personal **mantra**, which they then dwell upon for periods each day. Again, the focus is on a good world – not an evil one – and a way of 'finding oneself' through positive thinking.

World-rejecting groups

These organizations are usually sects, in so far as they are always highly critical of the outside world and demand significant commitment from their members. In some ways, they are quite like conventional religions in that they may require prayer and the study of key religious texts, and have strong ethical codes. They are exclusive, often share possessions and seek to relegate members' identities to that of the greater whole. They are often **millenarian** – expecting divine intervention to change the world. Examples include:

- The Unification Church (popularly known as the Moonies), founded in Korea by the Reverend Sun Myung Moon in 1954. The Unification Church rejects the mundane secular world as evil and has strong moral rules, such as no smoking and drinking.
- Members of Hare Krishna (Children of God, or ISKCON International Society for Krishna Consciousness) are distinguished by their shaved heads, pigtails and flowing gowns. Hare Krishna devotees repeat a mantra 16 times a day.

World-rejecting sects are the movements that have come under most public scrutiny in recent years, largely because of the public horror at the indoctrination that has even led to mass suicide. There is a growing list of extreme examples:

- the mass suicide of Jim Jones's People's Temple in Jonestown, Guyana in 1987
- the Aum Supreme Truth detonating poisonous gas canisters on a Tokyo underground train in 1995, leaving 12 dead and 5000 ill
- the suicidal death in 1997 of the 39 members of the Heaven's Gate cult in California.

Signs of cultist behaviour

Robbins (1988) identifies the following signs of cultist behaviour:

- *Authoritarianism* – Control of the organization stems from an absolute leader or a small circle of elite commanders.
- *Infallibility* – The chosen philosophy or **experiential panacea** is the only path to salvation, and all others

are worthless. Anyone who questions or challenges what the cult offers is denied access or exiled.

- *Programming* – The belief in the infallibility of the cult's philosophy, experiential panacea and leader are derived from the abandonment of critical and rational thinking.
- *Shunning* – Members are encouraged to sever communications and relationships with friends and family members.
- *Secret doctrines* – Certain teachings are 'secret' and must never be revealed to the outside world.
- *Promised ones* – Members of the cult are encouraged to believe they were chosen, or made their choice to join the cult, because they are special or superior.
- *Fire and brimstone* – Leaving the cult, or failing at one's endeavour to complete the requirements to achieve its panacea, will result in consequences greater than if one had never joined the cult in the first place.

Key themes

Crime and **deviance**

The Waco Siege

Sects, in particular, are often the subject of moral panics, particularly as they tend to attract young people from middle-class backgrounds. The integrity of leaders is usually called into question, and exaggerated accounts of either financial or sexual impropriety are common. The public reaction and that of the authorities is often amplified, sometimes leading to unanticipated consequences, as the siege of the headquarters of the Branch Davidian sect in Waco, Texas, in 1993 illustrates. The sect predicted the end of the world and separated itself from the wider society. Its leader, David Koresh, was seen to be a charismatic 'God incarnate'. Membership involved whole families as well as people who had left their families to join. The wider societies' view was that Koresh had captured and indoctrinated people and was sexually abusing them. The group had also armed themselves in preparation for the 'end' and this became the excuse for police, military and FBI involvement. A 51-day stalemate between federal agents and members of the cult ended in a fiery tragedy after federal agents botched their assault on the sect's compound. About 80 Branch Davidians, including Koresh himself and at least 17 children, died when the compound burned to the ground in a suspicious blaze in September 1993. The FBI claim that the fire was a mass-suicide attempt by members of the sect, whilst survivors claim that the FBI fired an incendiary device. Jurors in the criminal trial of surviving cult members were unable to determine who fired the first shot. Cult apologists and surviving members, many of whom still believe that Koresh will return, continue to criticise the Federal government both for its religious intolerance and for its selective application of gun controls in a state that generally defends the right to possess firearms.

Cult apologists

Cult apologists, such as Haddon and Long (1993), while not members themselves, both defend the right of such groups to exist and argue for more religious tolerance. They claim that:

● most cults are simply misunderstood minority 'religions'
● these movements only seem weird because people don't know enough about them and believe sensational media accounts
● anticult organizations and individuals misrepresent the beliefs and practices of such movements
● anticult organizations are intolerant of religious freedom.

World-accommodating groups

This final category of religious movement is more orthodox. World-accommodating groups maintain some connections with mainstream religion, but place a high value on inner religious life. The Holy Spirit 'speaks' through the Neo-Pentecostalists, for example, giving them the gift of **'speaking in tongues'**. Other examples include spiritualists who claim to be able to contact the spirits of the dead; many spiritualists draw inspiration from faiths with a deep mystical tradition, such as Sufism, the Kabbalah and Buddhism. Such religions are usually dismayed at both the state of the world and the state of organized mainstream religions. They seek to establish older certainties and faith, while giving them a new vitality.

New Age movements (NAMs)

The term 'New Age' refers to a large number of religions and therapies that have become increasingly important since the 1970s. Many New Age movements can be classed as 'world affirming' (see above) as they focus on the achievement of individual potential.

Bruce (1996) suggests that these groups tend to take one of two forms:

1   *Audience cults* involve little face-to-face interaction. Members of the 'audience' are unlikely to know each other. Contacts are maintained mostly through the mass media and the internet as well as occasional conferences. Both astrology and belief in UFOs are good examples of these. Audience cults feed a major market of 'self-help therapy' groups and books which regularly appear in best-seller lists.
2   *Client cults* offer particular services to their followers. They have led to a proliferation of new 'therapists' (from astrological to colour therapists), establishing new relationships between a consumer and a seller. Amongst the practices involved are tarot readings, **crystals** and astrology. Many bookshops devote more to these sorts of books than to books on Christianity.

NAMs seem to appeal to all age groups, but more especially to women (see also Topic 6). Bruce (1995) suggests that those affiliated, however, already subscribe to what Heelas calls the '**cultic milieu**' (Heelas 1996) or '**holistic milieu**' (Heelas *et al.* 2004) – a mish-mash of belief in the power of spirituality, ecology and personal growth, and a concern that science does not have all the answers. An annual celebration of New Age beliefs – the Festival for the Mind, Body and Spirit – takes place in London and Manchester.

The appeal of NRMs and NAMs

For sociologists, one of the most interesting questions is why people join or support NRMs.

Spiritual void

Since the decline in the importance of established religion, people have been seeking alternative belief systems to explain the world and its difficulties. In addition, as postmodernists argue, there is also an increased cynicism about the ability of science to provide solutions to these problems.

Drane (1999) argues that Western societies are turning against modern institutions and belief systems. Modern rationality is increasingly being blamed for disasters such as the World Wars, the Holocaust, numerous other bloody conflicts, weapons of mass destruction, the depletion of the ozone layer, potentially dangerous genetically modified crops and global warming. People have lost faith in institutions such as the medical profession, which is now seen as more likely to misdiagnose or even cause illness through new diseases, such as MRSA or CDiff (clostridium difficile), rather than improve the health and welfare of those they treat. Churches are considered to have done little to fill the spiritual void left by wholesale adoption of modern belief systems.

In the absence of either **grand narrative** (religion or science), people may seek to acquire a personal rationale. This can involve a process of 'spiritual shopping', trying out the various alternatives until they find a belief system that makes sense to them. People in the New Age are free to choose whatever fulfils them and have access to a huge range of spiritual and therapeutic products.

Pragmatic motives

Motivations for affiliation with world-affirming groups can be very practical – financial success and a happier life, for example. These **pragmatic motives** are not the sort that many religious people would recognize and this is probably one of the main reasons why the religious nature of many NRMs is questioned.

Marginality

Weber (1920/1963) pointed out how those marginalized by society may find status and/or a legitimizing explanation for their situation through a theodicy that offers ultimate salvation. This could explain the appeal of world-rejecting sects to some members of ethnic minorities or young social 'drop-outs'.

Relative deprivation

People may be attracted to an NRM because it offers something lacking in the social experience of the seeker – whether spiritual or emotional fulfilment. This could explain the appeal of NRMs to certain members of the middle class, who feel their lives lack spiritual meaning.

The appeal to the young of world-rejecting movements

Many young people are no longer children but lack adult commitments, such as having their own children. Being unattached is an outcome of the increasing gap between childhood and adulthood which, as Wallis (1984) has argued, has been further extended by the gradual lengthening of education and wider accessibility of higher education. It is to these unattached groups that world-rejecting movements appeal. They try to provide some certainty to a community of people who face similar problems and difficulties. What seems to be particularly appealing is the offer of radical and immediate solutions to social and personal problems.

Barker, in her famous study *The Making of a Moonie* (1984), found that most members of the Unification Church (the 'Moonies') came from happy and secure middle-class homes, with parents whose jobs involved some sort of commitment to public service, such as doctors, social workers or teachers. She argued that the sect offered a **surrogate** family in which members could find support and comfort beyond the family, while fulfilling their desire to serve a community, in the same way as their parents did in the wider society. High patterns of drop-out from NRMs suggest that the need they fulfil is temporary.

The appeal of world-affirming movements

World-affirming groups appeal to those who are likely to have finished education, are married, have children and a mortgage. There are two issues in the modern world that add to the appeal of world-affirming movements:

1 As Weber suggested, the modern world is one in which rationality dominates – that is, one in which magical, unpredictable and ecstatic experiences are uncommon.

2 There is tremendous pressure (e.g. through advertising) to become materially, emotionally and sexually successful.

According to Bird (1999), world-affirming sects simultaneously do three things that address these issues:

1 They provide a spiritual component in an increasingly rationalized world.

2 They provide techniques and knowledge to help people become wealthy, powerful and successful.

3 They provide techniques and knowledge which allow people to work on themselves to bring about personal growth.

In some ways, there are common issues that motivate both the young and old. They both live in societies where there is great pressure to succeed and hence great fear of failure. Religious movements can provide both groups with a means to deal with the fear of failure by providing techniques that lead to personal success.

Furthermore, New Age and other world-affirming movements, in particular, fit with the tendency within modern society towards greater individualism, a focus on self-improvement and personal indulgence. As Bruce 2002 suggests, people today feel more empowered to change what they are not personally happy about, by spending money upon themselves in ways which would, in relatively recent times past, have seemed selfish. Gym memberships, health spas, counselling, alternative therapies, as well as the rapidly growing number of tourism centres (e.g. yoga retreats) focusing on wellbeing and personal growth, are evidence of this trend.

Activities

Research idea

Conduct a survey or interview a sample of other students to discover the extent of New Age beliefs among your peers. Try to assess their knowledge and experience of New Age phenomena such as tarot cards, crystal healing and astrology.

Web.task

Go to the website of the Cult Information Centre at www.cultinformation.org.uk and explore some of the organizations and incidents mentioned.

Then go to the website of Inform at www.inform.ac/infmain.html and compare the attitude to NRMs, cults and sects on each site.
To what extent do you think their accounts of 'cults' are biased?

Check your understanding

1 Why are the numbers of those involved with NRMs probably much higher than membership figures suggest?

2 Briefly explain what Wallis means by the term 'world-affirming movements'. Give examples.

3 How does Bruce classify New Age movements?

4 What does Wallis mean by the term 'world-rejecting movements'? Give examples.

5 What is the response of mainstream society to world-rejecting movements?

6 What are world-accommodating movements? Give an example.

7 How have the grand narratives of science and religion failed where new religious movements are now succeeding?

8 Give three reasons for the appeal of NRMs/NAMs.

9 What is the relationship between age, social attachment and the appeal of NRMs?

Key terms

Crystals belief in the healing power of semiprecious stones.

Cult apologists non-cult members who are religiously tolerant and challenge the misinterpretation of cult practice common in the wider society.

Cultic or holistic milieu a range of activities involving the mind, body and spirit, such as yoga, tai chi, healing and self-discovery.

Experiential panacea cure-all, solution to life's ills.

Grand narrative belief system, such as religion or science, that claims to explain the world.

Mantra personal word or phrase given by a religious teacher (guru) which is used to free the mind of non-spiritual secular awareness and provide a focus for meditation.

Millenarian belief in a saviour.

Pragmatic motives desire to acquire personally beneficial practical outcomes.

Resacrilization renewed interest and belief in religion and therefore a religious revival.

Speaking in tongues the power to speak in new (but often incomprehensible) languages believed to be a gift from God.

Surrogate replacement.

An eye on the exam   New religious and New Age movements

Item A

The NAM 'is a miscellaneous collection of psychological and spiritual techniques that are rooted in Eastern mysticism, lack scientific evaluative data, and are promoted zealously by followers of diverse idealized leaders claiming transformative powers' (Langone 1993).

There are four main streams of thought within the NAM:

1 the 'transformational training' stream, represented by groups such as 'est' (Erhard Seminar Training) and Lifespring
2 the intellectual stream, represented by publications such as *The Tao of Physics*
3 the lifestyle stream, represented by publications such as *Whole Life Monthly* and organizations such as the Green Party
4 the occult stream, represented by astrology, tarot, palmistry, crystal power, and the like.

It is important to keep in mind that within this diversity, there is much disagreement. Many intellectual new agers, for example, ridicule believers in the occult stream of the new age.

The NAM is similar to traditional religions in that it subscribes to the existence of a supernatural realm, or at least something beyond 'atoms and the void'. But the NAM believer considers that spiritual knowledge and power can be achieved through the discovery of the proper techniques. These techniques may be silly, as in crystal power. But they may be very sophisticated, as in some forms of yoga. Its concepts have permeated our culture in a quiet, almost invisible way. For example, a Gallup survey of teenagers, several years ago, found that approximately one third of churchgoing Christian teenagers believed in reincarnation, a fundamental new age belief.

Dole. A. (1990) *Cultic Studies Journal*, 7(1), University of Pennsylvania

---

(a) Identify and briefly describe **three** features of New Age Movements (**Item A**).   (9 marks)

(b) Using material from **Item A** and elsewhere, examine reasons for the appeal of New Age and new religious movements.   (18 marks)

Grade booster   Getting top marks in this question

In your answer to question (b), you should briefly explain the difference between New Age and new religious movements (NAMs and NRMs) and then outline the different types of NRMs – world-affirming, world-rejecting and world-accommodating. Focus on what each one has to offer and who it is likely to appeal to, for example in terms of age groups, gender and class background. Consider the different motives people may have for joining a NAM or NRM, such as relative deprivation, marginality, etc. Remember to make use of relevant material from the Item; for example, you can use the four streams of thought within NAMs to illustrate reasons such as self-improvement (the 'transformational training' stream of NAMs).

Gender, feminism and religion

Getting you thinking

Is Buffy responsible for slaying women's church attendance?

Today's modern woman sees more relevance in TV icons who promote female empowerment, such as *Buffy the Vampire Slayer*, than in church and traditional religion, according to new research to be published in the *Church Times*.

Dr Kristin Aune, a sociologist at the University of Derby, says the church must act to halt the steep decline in female attendance at services across the country.

She says: 'In short, women are abandoning the church ... Young women tend to express egalitarian values and dislike the traditionalism and hierarchies they imagine are integral to the church.' Because of its focus on female empowerment, young women are attracted by Wicca, popularized by the TV series *Buffy the Vampire Slayer* [shown right]. While all eyes focus on women's ordination as priests and now as bishops, Dr Aune argues the church should be looking to act and do more to reach out to women.

One alarming statistic uncovered by the research, using the English Church Census, has revealed that the church (all Christian denominations) has been losing at least 50 000 women worshippers each and every year since 1989 (a total of over a million).

Source: Adapted from University of Derby Press Office 22 August 2008

Church attendance and experience in the UK, by gender					
(%)	All	Men	Women	Christian	No religion
Regular churchgoer	15	11	19	28	1
Fringe churchgoer	3	3	4	6	1
Occasional churchgoer	7	6	8	11	3
Open de-churched[1]	5	3	6	7	2
Closed de-churched[2]	28	28	27	29	31
Open non-churched[3]	1	1	1	1	1
Closed non-churched[4]	32	38	27	18	57
Other religions	6	7	6	0	0
Unassigned	2	3	2	1	3

Source: Ashworth, J. and Farthing, I. (2007) *Churchgoing in the UK: A research report from Tearfund on church attendance in the UK*, Teddington: Tearfund

1 Open de-churched: former churchgoers who may return.
2 Closed de-churched: former churchgoers unlikely to return.
3 Open non-churched: have never been churchgoers but are likely to be in future.
4 Closed non-churched: never been to church and unlikely to do so.

1 Summarize the patterns of church attendance given in the table above.

2 Using the table and the article above, as well as your wider sociological knowledge, identify reasons that can be given for the decline in women's church attendance.

3 Suggest reasons why women still appear to be more religious than men overall.

The exercise above indicates that women tend to be more religious than men. This issue is discussed in depth later in this topic. But is it also the case that, despite this, the practices and beliefs of most religious organizations reflect and justify male domination – in other words, they are **patriarchal**?

Let's start by looking at conceptions of god in different religions.

Images of God in different religions

Although there is only one god in most contemporary religions (Hinduism being an exception), men and women tend to view that god differently. Davie (1994) showed that:

- women see God more as a god of love, comfort and forgiveness
- men see God more as a god of power and control.

An implicit recognition of the female connection with spirituality can also be seen in the Jewish religion, in which a person can only automatically be Jewish if their mother is. On the other hand, though, some Orthodox Jewish men include the following words in daily prayer:

<< Blessed art thou O Lord our God that I was not born a slave. Blessed art thou O Lord our God that I was not born a woman.>>

Christianity is also inherently patriarchal, with men made in 'the image and glory of God' and women made 'for the glory of man', as the following passage from the New Testament shows:

<<Wives be subject to your husbands, as to the Lord. For the husband is the head of the wife as Christ is the head of the church.>> (Ephesians 5:22–24)

There are many female characters in the biblical texts, and some are portrayed as acting charitably or bravely, but the primary roles are reserved for males. All the most significant Old Testament prophets, such as Isaiah and Moses, are male, while in the New Testament, all the apostles are men.

The most prominent females in the Bible, Eve and Mary mother of Jesus, can be interpreted as reinforcing patriarchal ideas regarding, on the one hand, the dangers of female sexuality and, on the other, the virtues of motherhood. Similarly, the Qur'an, the sacred text of Islam, contends that 'men are in charge of women'. Even Buddhism (in which females appear as important figures in the teachings of some Buddhist orders) is dominated (like Christianity) by a patriarchal power structure, in which the feminine is mainly associated with the secular, powerless, profane and imperfect.

Sexuality and religion

Women's bodies and sexuality are also felt to be dangerous by many religions. Because women menstruate and give birth, they are considered to have a greater capacity to 'pollute' religious rituals. In addition, their presence may distract the men from their more important roles involving worship.

Bird (1999) points out that sexuality is an important issue in many religions. Roman Catholic priests are expected to be **celibate**, while (some interpretations of) Christianity and Islam (amongst others) are opposed to homosexuality.

Turner (1983) suggests that a disciplinary role with respect to sexuality is central to religion. Widespread importance is given to **asceticism**, a self-disciplined existence in which pleasure (especially physical pleasure) is repressed. This means that, in order to carry out priestly duties properly, there needs to be a degree of policing of the body – and the presence of women makes this more difficult.

Women in religious organizations

Patriarchal attitudes have meant that, until recently, women have been barred from serving as priests in many of the world's great religions, and the more traditional factions continue to bar them. Islamic groups, Orthodox Jews and the Roman Catholic church continue to exclude women from the religious hierarchy.

Although women ministers have long been accepted in some sects and denominations, the Church of England persisted in formally supporting inequalities of gender until 1992, when its General Synod finally voted to allow the ordination of women. However, Anglican churches in other countries (such as Hong Kong, the USA, Canada and New Zealand) had moved to ordain women during the 1970s.

Simon and Nadell (1995) conducted research about women in religious organizations, drawing on evidence from in-depth interviews with 32 female rabbis and 27 female members of the Protestant clergy. They concluded that the women conduct themselves in totally different ways to the male members of their religious organizations. They asked the female rabbis whether they carried out their duties differently from male rabbis of the same age and training. Almost all of the women replied 'yes'. They described themselves as less formal, more approachable, more egalitarian, and more inclined to touch and hug. Seventeen out of the 27 female members of the Protestant clergy described themselves as less formal, more people-orientated, more into pastoral care and less concerned about power struggles, than were the male clergy.

Feminism and religion

Many Christian feminists argue that there will never be gender equality in the church so long as notions of God continue to be associated with masculinity. Mary Daly (1973,1978) goes as far as to suggest that Christianity itself is a patriarchal myth. Although originally a Catholic herself, she argues that the Christian story eliminated other 'goddess' religions. She argues that Christianity is rooted in male 'sado-rituals' with its 'torture cross symbolism', and that it embodies women-hating.

Simone de Beauvoir in her pioneering feminist book, *The Second Sex* (1953), saw the role of religion in a similar way to Marx. However, she saw it as oppressive to women in particular. Religion is used by the oppressors (men) to control the oppressed group (women). It also serves as a way of compensating women for their second-class status. Like Marx's proletariat, religion gives women the false belief that they will be compensated for their suffering on earth by equality in heaven. She concludes:

<< [Religion] gives her the guide, father, lover, divine guardian she longs for nostalgically; it feeds her daydreams; it fills her empty hours. But, above all, it confirms the social order, it justifies her resignation by giving hope of a better future in a sexless heaven. >>

El Sadaawi (1980), a Muslim feminist, does not blame religion in itself for its oppressive influences on women, but blames the patriarchal domination of religion that came with the development of **monotheistic** religions. Such religions, she argues, 'drew inspiration and guidance from the patriarchal and class societies prevalent at the time'. Men wrote their scriptures, and the interpretation of them was almost exclusively male-orientated. This has, on many occasions, enabled men to use religion as an abuse of power. In the 14th century, for example, the Catholic Church declared that women who treated illnesses without special training could be executed as witches. Clearly, the traditional remedies administered by women were seen as as a threat to the authority of the emerging male-dominated medical profession.

Is religion necessarily patriarchal?

It should not be assumed that all religions are equally oppressive to women and there have been some successful challenges to the patriarchal structure of organized religion. Gender-neutral language has been introduced in many hymns and prayers, and the requirement in the Christian marriage ceremony for the bride to promise to obey her husband is now also optional.

Judaism has allowed women to become rabbis in its non-orthodox denominations since 1972, and even some Christian religions, particularly Quakerism, have never been oppressive to women. According to Kaur-Singh (1994), Sikh gurus pleaded the cause for the emancipation of Indian womanhood, fully supporting them in improving their condition in society.

Some writers highlight how there are signs of hope developing. Gross (1994) detects signs of a post-patriarchal Buddhism developing in the West, which does not differentiate roles for male and female members. Paganism, from which many New Age religions emanate, remains the most female-friendly approach to religion, with a strong feminist element in contemporary neo-paganism, where God is a mixture of male and female, and strong female leadership is common. Leila Badawi (1994) has noted aspects of Islam that are positive for women, such as being able to keep their own family name when they marry. In fact, most converts to Islam are female. Numerous writers have highlighted how veiling (the covering of the entire face and hair in the company of men outside the family), rather than being a submission to patriarchy, is in fact a means of ethnic and gender assertiveness. Leila Ahmed (1992) suggests that the veil is a means by which Muslim women can become involved in modern society while maintaining a sense of modesty and correctness. As she puts it: '[Islamic dress] is a uniform of both transition and arrival, signalling entrance into and determination to move forward in modern society.'

Why are women more religious than men?

Whatever women's influence and status may have been in religious organizations, and despite a recent drift away from mainstream Christianity, studies have consistently shown that women are more religious than men. Miller and Hoffmann (1995) report that women:

- are more likely to express a greater interest in religion
- have a stronger personal religious commitment
- attend church more often.

Until relatively recently, these patterns appeared to hold true throughout life, irrespective of the kind of religious organization (cult, sect or church) or religious belief (astrology, magic, spirits, and so on). It is only during the last 20 years or so that women have begun to leave the church at a faster rate than men. According to Brierley (2006), between 1989 and 1998, more than 65 000 women were lost from churches each year, 57 per cent of all those leaving churches. From 1998 to 2005, the figure was

---

Focus on research

Helen Watson (1994)
The meaning of veiling

According to the Qu'ran, women should exercise religious modesty or *hijab* because their seductiveness might lead men astray. Many writers, including some Islamic feminists, have argued that this has been misinterpreted by men to mean that women must cover their bodies and faces in the presence of men who are not relatives, with the patriarchal motive of controlling women. Western commentators also are critical of the practice, seeing it as evidence of repression. As Julie Burchill (2001) writing in the *Guardian* commented, 'such women carry round with them a mobile prison'.

Watson (1994), however, demonstrated that the veil also has the potential to liberate. She interviewed three Muslim women who had alternative perspectives on the practice of veiling. Nadia, a second-generation British Asian woman studying medicine at university, chose to start wearing a veil at 16. She commented, 'It is liberating to have the freedom of movement to be able to communicate without being on show'. She found that far from being invisible it made her stand out as a Muslim and also helped her to avoid 'lecherous stares or worse' from men. The second woman, Maryam, was a middle-aged Algerian living in France. Upon moving to France she felt it more appropriate to wear a veil. She commented that 'it is difficult enough to live in a big foreign city without having the extra burden of being molested in the street because you are a woman'. The third respondent, Fatima, was an older woman. She was less positive about veiling, seeing it as 'just a trend', but recognized that to turn against some of the less desirable Western values, e.g. the overemphasis on women as sex objects, was a good thing. In her opinion veiling should be a matter of choice.

Adapted from Watson (1994) 'Women and the veil: personal responses to global process', in A. Ahmed and H. Donnan (eds) *Islam, Globalisation and Postmodernity*, London: Routledge

1 **What criticisms could be made of Watson's research?**

2 **How does Watson's work serve as a caution to sociologists who interpret the practices of unfamiliar religions in simplistic terms?**

---

slightly lower (51 000 per year) but throughout this time, women were leaving churches at about twice the rate of men.

Aune *et al.* (2008) cite a number reasons for the decline in church attendance and why certain women in particular are not going to church as much as they once did:

- *Fertility levels* – Women have fewer children and so the older generation lost from the church is not being replaced.
- *Feminist values* – Feminist values began influencing women in the 1960s and 1970s, challenging traditional Christian views about women's roles and raising women's aspirations.
- *Paid employment* – At the beginning of the 20th century, a third of women were in paid work; now, a century later, two-thirds are in the labour market. Juggling employment with childcare and housework causes time pressures and attending church is one activity to suffer.
- *Family diversity* – Compared to wider society, churches include fewer non-traditional families. Family forms which are growing, such as singleness, lone-parent families and cohabitation, are underprovided for and even discouraged by churches.
- *Sexuality* – The church's ambivalence towards sexuality is driving women to leave, feeling that the church requires them to deny or be silent about sexual desire and activity.

However, an explanation for the persistence of a greater degree of religious orientation among women overall is offered by Greeley (1992). He argues that before women acquire a partner and have children, their religiosity is not dissimilar to men's (although slightly more committed). But, 'once you start "taking care" of people, perhaps, you begin implicitly to assume greater responsibility for their "ultimate" welfare'. Greeley contends that women are more involved in caring than in practical responsibilities. Caring, it seems, tends to be associated with a more religious outlook.

Miller and Hoffmann (1995) identify two main explanations for such gender differences:

1 *Differential socialization* – Females are taught to be more submissive, obedient and nurturing than males. These traits are compatible with religiosity, as such characteristics are highly esteemed by most religions. By the same token, men who internalize these norms tend to be more religious than men who do not.
2 *Differential roles* – Females have lower rates of participation in paid work and this, it is argued, gives women not only more time for church-related activities, but also a greater need for religion as a source of personal identity and commitment. They also have higher rates of participation in child-rearing, which in turn increases religiosity because it coincides with a concern for family wellbeing.

However, changes in women's roles are having an impact on their religious orientation. Linda Woodhead (2005), in attempting to explain the diversity of responses that modern women have begun to demonstrate towards religion, divides contemporary women into three groups:

1 *Home-centred women,* whose priority is their home and families, even if they engage in part-time work. They tend to be traditionally Christian because Christianity affirms their priorities.
2 *Jugglers,* who combine home and work. These women are more likely to be found in alternative spirituality because alternative spiritualities do most to help

Key themes

Sociological theories and methods

Feminism and religion

Linda Woodhead (2004) argues that the various periods of feminist writing have different emphases in their analysis of society and religion. First-wave feminism, the feminist movement in the 19th century and early 20th century, primarily focused on gaining the right of women to vote.

Second-wave feminism, originating in the 1960s, was mainly concerned with independence from men and greater political action to improve women's rights.

Third-wave feminism began in the early 1990s. Unlike second-wave feminism, which largely focused on the inclusion of women in traditionally male-dominated areas, it seeks to challenge and expand common definitions of gender and sexuality. It recognizes the impact of race, class and sexuality on the experience of both sexes. Third-wave feminists have been critical of earlier feminists for concentrating on Christianity and on the concept of patriarchy, which, they argue, is used as a blunt instrument made applicable to all women. The general assumption that all women involved in religion are in a state of false consciousness and so gain nothing from it has also been strongly criticized. Third-wave feminists have abandoned the 'sex war' stance and simple dichotomy between patriarchal male oppressors and innocent female victims and have shed light on the way in which both sexes may actually benefit from their involvement in religion.

Adapted from Fenn (2004)

women who are negotiating private/public boundaries, affirming their commitments to their families while also endorsing female **empowerment** and the search for fulfilment outside the home.

3 *Work-centred women,* who are more likely to follow male patterns of religiosity, abandoning church because it doesn't fit with their demanding work schedules and taking on a more secular outlook.

Women and NRMs

Sects

Women tend to participate more in sects than men. Although it is difficult to estimate, Bruce (1995) has suggested that the ratio of female-to-male involvement is similar to that in established religion at about 2:1.

Women are more likely than men to experience poverty, and those who experience economic deprivation are more likely to join sects. As Thompson (1996) notes: 'They may not have the economic and social standing of others in society, but sect members have the promise of salvation and the knowledge that they are enlightened.'

Glock and Stark (1969) identify a number of different types of deprivation in addition to the economic, all of which are more likely to apply to women. They suggest that people who form or join sects may have experienced one or even a number of these.

- *Social deprivation* – This may stem from a lack of power, prestige and status. For example, if people experience a lack of satisfaction or status in employment, they may seek these goals via a religious sect. Those in unsatisfying lower-middle-class jobs (mainly occupied by women) may find satisfaction in the **evangelical goals** set by **conversionist** sects, such as Jehovah's Witnesses or Mormons.
- *Organismic deprivation* – This is experienced by those who suffer physical and mental problems (again more likely among women than men). For example, people may turn to sects in the hope of being healed or as an alternative to drugs or alcohol.
- *Ethical deprivation* – People may perceive the world to be in moral decline and so retreat into an **introversionist sect** that separates itself from the world, such as Jim Jones' People's Temple. Again, women tend to be more morally conservative than men.

In the 19th century, many sects were initiated by women: Ellen White set up the Seventh Day Adventists, Mary Baker Eddy founded Christian Science, Ann Lee founded the Shakers, and the Fox sisters began the Spiritualist movement.

Cults

Cults involve a highly individual, privatized version of religious activity. This is mainly involved with promoting a notion of personal 'improvement'. Even where wider issues are addressed (such as social problems of crime, unemployment or the destruction of the environment), the solutions offered tend to be couched in personal terms (meditation, greater consciousness, etc.). This 'private sphere' of cult activity relates to traditional gender roles for women, which are based in the 'private' arena of the home. Women are also more inclined to see in themselves a need for self-improvement.

Women and NAMs

Historically, wherever nature is conceptualized, the role of women has been seen in terms of their 'essential femininity', that is, as being naturally different creatures to males – more attuned to the supposed natural rhythms of life. Thus, within the philosophies of New Age cults, women tend to be afforded a much higher status than men. This is one reason that may explain higher female involvement in NAMs, as many of them emphasize the 'natural', such as herbal and homeopathic remedies, aromatherapy and massage. Research by Glendinning and Bruce (2006) confirms that middle-class women more often than men subscribe to alternative therapies associated with NAMs, such as yoga and meditation, whereas younger working-class women more often believe in astrology and fortune-telling.

Women and fundamentalism

The resurgence of religious fundamentalism over the past decade has played a major role in attempting to reverse the trend of women's increasing autonomy and their pursuit of fulfilment beyond motherhood.

- In the USA, opposition to women controlling their fertility through abortion has sometimes ended in violence, with right-wing, religious pro-life groups adopting near terrorist tactics to close clinics down.
- Despite India's long history of reform and modernization, the rise of Hindu fundamentalism has made it difficult for governments there to intervene in family life or encourage greater freedom for women, despite their commitment to preventing the oppression of members of lower castes.
- Fundamentalist groups in Iran, Israel, Afghanistan and elsewhere similarly insist on ruthlessly conserving or reinstating women's traditional positions.

Cohen and Kennedy (2000) suggest that 'the desire to restore fundamentalist religious values and social practices is associated with the fear that any real increase in women's freedom of choice and action will undermine the foundations of tradition, religion, morality and, it could be argued, male control'.

Women's traditional roles centre around childrearing and the home. They are thus responsible for transmitting religious values from one generation to the next and upholding all that is most sacred in the lives of family members. Fundamentalism, both in the West (such as the Christian Right or the **Nation of Islam** in the USA) and elsewhere, has often emphasized the significance of protecting and defending women. The spin-off is that this re-empowers men by removing some of the **ambiguities** that have been associated with the modern world. But, as feminists assert, the apparent position of importance such women experience in upholding the faith, brings with it

Check your understanding

1 What evidence is there to show that women were not always subordinate to men in religion?

2 What caused men to dominate religion and religious practice?

3 What evidence for patriarchy is there in the world's major religions:
  (a) in terms of their scriptures?
  (b) in terms of roles in religious institutions?

4 Why is sexuality such an issue for many religions?

5 How do feminists view the role of religion?

6 What evidence is there to show that some religions are not necessarily patriarchal?

7 (a) What evidence is there for women's greater religiosity?
  (b) What explanations have been given for this?

8 What reasons are given for women's greater involvement in NRMs?

9 How has the resurgence of fundamentalism affected the role of women?

powerlessness and sometimes abuse at the hands of husbands and kinsmen.

However, not all women are unwilling victims of the return to traditional roles – as the work on Muslim women and veiling demonstrates. Research by Woodhead and Heelas (2000) shows how women converting to orthodox Judaism in the US are actually attracted by the status in the home that it provides them with. Such women can also be seen as seeking to remove the ambiguities of modernity, as they perceive them.

Key terms

Ambiguities uncertain issues, having more than one meaning.

Asceticism the practice of severe self-discipline and denial of individual pleasure.

Celibate deliberately refraining from sexual activity.

Conversionist religious groups whose aim is to convert people to their faith.

Empowerment to be given greater power and recognition.

Evangelical goals the aim of converting others to your faith.

Introversionist sect world-rejecting sect.

Monotheism belief in one god.

Nation of Islam Black, radical, American Islamic organization.

Patriarchal male-dominated.

Activities

Research idea

Using an equal sample of males and females from amongst your peers, try to assess the extent of gender differences in religiosity. Focus on formal religious practice (e.g. church attendance), belief/non-belief in God, the nature of God (compassionate or powerful) and alternative beliefs, e.g. spirituality.

Web.task

Search the web for 'the role of women in religion' using any search engine of your choice. Select an article on women in various religious organizations past and present and summarize it. Compare your reading with others in your class.

An eye on the exam   Gender, feminism and religion

Item A

Despite feminist criticisms of the prescriptive roles ascribed to women by many religions, significant numbers of women continue to be attracted to such religions. Davidman (1991) explored the reasons why culturally advantaged North American women were converting to Orthodox Judaism. Davidman's conclusion is that it is precisely because such religion maintains a clear distinction between the sexes that it becomes attractive to women who, in an increasingly dislocating world, value domesticity and their future role as wives and mothers. In contrast to the feminist goal of sexual liberation, careers and variation in family patterns, Orthodox Judaism offered clear gender norms, assistance in finding partners and explicit guidelines for family life. It legitimated their desires for the traditional identity of wives and mothers in nuclear families. Also, women are seen as central in the Jewish religious world and are given special status. In contrast to the liberal feminist goal of equality, such women seek the alternative of equity – the idea of equal but separate roles.

Adapted from Woodhead, L. and Heelas, P. (2000) *Religion in Modern Times: An Interpretive Anthology*, Oxford: Blackwell

Using material from **Item A** and elsewhere, assess the relationships between gender and religion.

(33 marks)

Grade booster   Getting top marks in this question

You should examine aspects of the relationship between gender and religion, such as the way in which different religions treat gender difference – for example, ideas about gods and goddesses, priests and priestesses, and views of the roles of men and women both within religious organizations and in wider society. You should consider the debates about whether religion is necessarily always patriarchal – for example, can aspects of religious teaching or practice, such as veiling in Islam, be seen as liberating women? You should examine women and men's participation in different kinds of religion, such as churches, sects and cults. If religion is patriarchal, how do we explain the fact that, in general, women have higher rates of participation? Remember to make use of relevant material from the Item, which offers one answer to this question.

TOPIC 7

Religion, ethnicity and youth

Getting you thinking

Group	1970	1980	1990	2000	
Christian: Trinitarian* of whom:	9272	7529	6624	5917	mainly White ethnic majority
Anglican	2987	2180	1728	1654	
Catholic	2746	2455	2198	1768	
Free Churches	1629	1285	1299	1278	
Presbyterian	1751	1437	1214	989	
Orthodox	159	172	185	235	
Christian: Non-Trinitarian**	276	349	455	533	
Buddhist	10	15	30	50	mainly ethnic minority
Hindu	80	120	140	165	
Jewish	120	111	101	88	
Muslim	130	305	495	675	
Sikh	100	150	250	400	
Others	20	40	55	85	

Membership in the UK (thousands)

Adapted from Brierley, P. (ed.) *Religious Trends 2000*, London: HarperCollins

***Trinitarian churches** are those that accept a view of God as the three eternal persons: God the Father, God the Son and God the Holy Spirit. These are the great majority of Christian churches.

****Non-Trinitarian churches** accept a range of different views of God. These include sects such as: Christian Scientists, the Church of Scientology, Jehovah's Witnesses, Mormons (Church of Jesus Christ of Latter Day Saints), Spiritualists and the Unification Church (Moonies).

1 **What is the overall trend in the membership of Trinitarian churches?**

2 **What do the figures tell us about ethnicity and religious practice?**

3 **In what ways does religion influence the way that you lead your life?**

4 **How important is it to you that children practise their faith or that they pass on their religious heritage to their children?**

5 **Does religion give you a personal motivation and strength that helps you to cope with the stresses and difficulties involved in society?**

It is likely that most White members of your class will have had little to say about the role of religion in their lives. On the other hand, non-White students from different ethnic backgrounds may have said a great deal more. The statistics above show the continuing importance of overt religious practice in the lives of many minority groups in Britain. Why this is the case is much more difficult to explain and this is even harder when you take into account differences between first-generation immigrants and their children who were born in Britain.

The United Kingdom in the 21st century is a multifaith society. Everyone has the right to religious freedom. A wide variety of religious organizations and groups are permitted to conduct their **rites** and ceremonies, to promote their beliefs within the limits of the law, to own property and to run schools and a range of other charitable activities. For the first time in the UK since 1851, the 2001 census included a question on religion. Although it was a voluntary question, over 92 per cent of people chose to answer it (see Table 1.4).

Table 1.4 People claiming religious affiliation in the UK

Religion (all people)	Number	Percentage of population
Christian	42 079 417	71.75
Buddhist	151 816	0.28
Hindu	558 810	1.06
Jewish	266 740	0.50
Muslim	1 591 126	2.71
Sikh	336 149	0.63
Other	178 837	0.30
No Religion	8 706 679	14.80
Religion not stated	4 532 646	7.70

Source: UK census 2001

Religion and community solidarity

If we compare the data in Table 1.4 with those in the table on the 'Getting you thinking' above it, we can see that the number in the census who claimed a religious affiliation is very different from the number who are active members of a religious organization. If we look at the disparity according to religious group, we can calculate that only about 14 per cent of those claiming to be Christians in the census are active members, against 42 per cent of Muslims, 33 per cent of Buddhists, 32 per cent Jews and 29 per cent of Hindus. Given that women are less likely to attend a place of religious worship within many non-Christian religions, the level of visible commitment among ethnic-minority religious groups is probably even higher. Interestingly, however, over half of all churchgoers in London are Black, yet the proportion of Black people in London is less than 20 per cent.

A lower proportion of active Christians does not, in itself, necessarily indicate lower levels of religiosity, as it is probable that the majority population value the community experience of the place of worship less than do people from ethnic minorities. However, clear evidence of greater religiosity among ethnic minorities comes from the first detailed Home Office survey of the nation's belief (O'Beirne 2004). When asked what they considered important to their identity, religion was cited tenth by White Christians behind family, work, age, interests, education, nationality, gender, income and social class. For Black people, 70 per cent of whom say they are Christian, religion was third, while Asians placed it second, only behind family. People of mixed race ranked their religion seventh.

There are various possible reasons why immigrants to Britain have placed a greater emphasis on religion than the long-established population:

- People had high levels of belief before migration and, as Weber (1920) has suggested, being members of deprived groups, they tended to be more religious. Religion provides an explanation for disadvantage and possibly offers hope of salvation, if not elsewhere on earth then in the afterlife.
- Religion helps bond new communities – particularly when under threat. As Durkheim (1912/1961) has argued, it provides members with a sense of shared norms and values, symbolized through rituals that unite them as a distinctive social group.

However, religion has also become a basis for conflicts between cultures. The dominant culture often sees minority cultures in a negative light, as there is the feeling that newcomers to British society should **assimilate**. Ethnic-minority issues, such as arranged marriages, the refusal of Sikhs to wear motorcycle helmets, and the growth in the number of religious temples and mosques (while many Christian churches have closed) suggest an unwillingness to assimilate and have created resentment from the host community. However, many second- and third-generation ethnic-minority Britons were born in the UK and their refusal to assimilate fully has led to a re-evaluation of what being British actually means.

In studying religion and ethnicity, it is clear that religions offer much more than just spiritual fulfilment. They have the power to reaffirm the ethnic identity of their adherents, albeit in uniquely different ways – as is clear from Table 1.5 on p. 40.

Religion and ethnic identity

While there are significant differences in religiosity within the Asian and African-Caribbean communities, it is possible to make some initial generalizations about them. African-Caribbeans were mainly Christian on arrival in the UK, but when they tried to join existing religious institutions, they often had to come to terms with the racism displayed by the church and its congregations, a racism pervasive in British society at the time. On the other hand, Hindus, Sikhs and Muslims (for whom religion was part of their 'difference') had virtually no existing religious organizations and places of worship in Britain to join. They had to make a collective effort to establish and practise their faith in a radically new social setting. As Modood et al. (1994) point out, for Asians their religion was intricately connected with their status as an ethnic group, but this was not the case for African-Caribbeans (see Table 1.5). Even for those who saw their Christianity as part of family tradition and culture, their religion was not significantly part of their sense of ethnic difference.

Nonetheless, distinctively African-Caribbean forms of Christian spirituality in both the mainstream churches and in the Black-led churches have mushroomed in the past 20 years, as some African-Caribbeans have sought to establish their own churches. Many have adopted an evangelical affiliation to Christianity, which stresses belief in personal conversion and the factual accuracy of the Bible alongside a commitment to seek new converts. Such Christianity, practised by the **charismatic** and **Pentecostal** movements has grown dramatically over the last decade.

An average of three new churches a week have been started since 1998 (Christian Research 2006) – half this growth is from ethnic-minority churches, especially Black churches. Quite apart from African-Caribbean Pentecostalism in the UK, evangelical movements have drawn millions of Africans to Christian churches across the continent of Africa and, since 2001, a third of all immigrants to Britain have come from Africa. There has also been a growth of Chinese, Croatian, Portuguese and

Below: Worshippers at a Pentecostal service. How do you account for the growth of Pentecostal churches in the UK?

Table 1.5 Differences in the significance of religion for first-generation Asian and African-Caribbean migrants to Britain

	African-Caribbean	Asian
Role of religion	Religion is used as a means of coping with the worries and the pressures of life through the joyful nature of prayer, as much through its immediacy and mood-affecting quality as its long-term contribution to personal development.	Asian groups tend to speak of control over selfish desires and of fulfilling one's responsibilities to others, especially family members. Prayer is seen in terms of duty, routine and the patterning of their lives.
Religion and family life	Used to develop trust, love, mutual responsibilities and the learning of right and wrong within the context of the family. African-Caribbeans express an individualistic or voluntaristic view of religion. Children should decide for themselves whether they maintain religious commitment into adulthood.	Used in a similar way, but Asians tend to adopt a collective or conformist approach. The expectation of parents is that their children will follow in adulthood the religion they have been brought up in; not to do so is to betray one's upbringing or to let one's family down.
Religion and social life	Little importance beyond fostering and maintaining a spiritual, moral and ethical outlook. The church offers opportunities to socialize and to organize social events in an otherwise privatized community of member families.	Muslims tend to see conformity to Islamic law and Islam as a comprehensive way of life, affecting attitudes to alcohol, food, dress and choice of marriage partner. The influence of religion is less extreme for most Sikhs and Hindus, but its importance for the first generation is still great.

Adapted from Modood, T., Beishon, S. and Virdee, S. (1994) *Changing Ethnic Identities*, London: Policy Studies Institute

Tamil churches, especially in London. However, at the same time, slightly more than three churches a week have closed. Changes in the composition of practising Christians is, therefore, coming mainly from an increase in ethnic-minority and Pentecostal churches. In 2005, 17 per cent of churchgoers were from non-White ethnic groups, an increase from 12 per cent in 1998. Pentecostal churches have replaced Methodist churches as the third largest Christian denomination and were the only denomination that grew in the period 1998 to 2005 (Brierley 2006). Half of Pentecostal churches are predominantly Black (ESRC Society Today 2006). While the Roman Catholic Church lost the greatest number and proportion of members of any denomination from 1998 to 2005, there has also been a growth in the membership of particular Catholic churches – for example, there appears to be revitalization of some inner-city Catholic communities as a result of migration from Eastern Europe, especially Poland (reported in Bates 2006).

Differences in styles of worship

While worship in Anglican churches is dominated by older people and women, and demands limited formal involvement of the congregation, Pentecostal church congregations comprise every age group and an equal balance of the sexes. There is a greater emphasis on religious experience than **religious dogma**, and worship is concerned with demonstrating publicly the joyous nature of religious conversion and the power of religion to heal people, both physically and mentally. Considerable involvement is required from worshippers in the form of dancing and 'call and response' between congregation and clergy.

Bird (1999) suggests that Pentecostalism has played a dual role for African-Caribbean people:

1 For some, it has enabled them to cope with and adjust to a racist and unjust society. It serves as an 'opium' for the people, as Marx has suggested. Beckford (2000) also suggests that evangelical Christianity gives Black people a sense of hope and independence.

2 For others, such as Pryce (1979), it encourages hard work, sexual morality, prudent management of finances and strong support of the family and community. In this sense, it reflects the Protestant ethic that Weber saw as essential in the development of capitalism (see Topic 2).

Evangelical churches – both Black and White – have also grown in popularity, in part due to their populist approach and innovative marketing strategies. Members preach the gospel intensely and seek converts in a way that other British Christians do not. The mainly White evangelical churches have developed the 'Alpha course', a movement that has gained two million converts in the UK and ten million worldwide. Other evangelical churches run inspirational radio and TV stations. At worship, their services are filled with popular-style music and videos aimed at the younger generation.

Young people and religiosity

When examining the position of members of ethnic minorities born in Britain, Modood *et al.* (1994) found that there appears to be an overall decline in the importance of religion for all of the main ethnic groups, and fewer said they observed the various rules and requirements. Even those who said that religion was important wished to interpret their religious traditions and scriptures flexibly. Also, fewer second-generation respondents regularly attended a place of religious worship. The least religiously committed were Sikhs. When asked how they saw themselves, virtually none of the second-generation Punjabis spontaneously said 'Sikh'. However, a decade earlier, Beatrice Drury studied a much larger sample of 16- to 20-year-old Sikh girls and found that, if prompted, all saw their Sikh identity as fundamental (reported in Drury 1991).

This reflects similar trends amongst the majority ethnic group. Aside from a growth in membership of some evangelical, mainly ethnic-minority churches, described above, attendance amongst under 20s in mainstream Christian churches has about halved since 1980. Buddhists, closely followed by Christians, are the group with the smallest percentage of young members (Christian Research 2004). There is also evidence of a general dislike of the church, especially in its institutional form. Peter Brierley (2002) found that 87 per cent of 10 to 14 year olds thought church was boring.

According to Voas and Crockett (2005), younger generations are becoming less and less religious, and it could be that 'believing without belonging' (an idea proposed by Davie (1994) that people still have religious belief but no longer choose to express it formally through church membership) is giving way to no belief at all. Older people are most likely to describe themselves as religious, middle-aged people as spiritual and young people as neither.

But despite their claims to religious indifference, some kind of belief or spirituality appears to be continuing among young people. Recent research by Mayo (2005),

Smith (2005) and Rankin (2005) seems to suggest that they are interested in spiritual matters, but that they attribute to the term 'spiritual', a wider variety of meanings, appreciated among themselves, rather than ascribe to those proposed by official religious or spiritual representatives. Rankin (2005) noted the reluctance of young people to identify aspects of their experience as spiritual, but when opportunities were offered for discussion, it became clear that the young people were engaged in the same kinds of soul searching that older people call 'spiritual'.

Young Muslims

Whilst increasing reluctance to demonstrate religiosity was apparent among most young people of all ethnic backgrounds, this trend has become less clear cut in the case of young Muslims. There appears to be a re-emphasis on Islamic identity arising in the wake of perceived injustice. In a PEW poll of 2006, 72 per cent of Muslims of all ages in the UK said they believed that Muslims have a very strong (28 per cent) or fairly strong (44 per cent) sense of Islamic identity, and 77 per cent felt that this sense of identity was increasing.

Some argue that 'Muslim' has become a new ethnicity. According to Samad (2004), 'as South Asian linguistic skills are lost, identification with Pakistan and Bangladesh – countries that young people may only briefly visit –

Focus on research

Abby Day (2007)
Believing in belonging

The 2001 census showed much higher proportions than expected stating a religious affiliation, seeming to support the view expressed by Grace Davie (1994) that religion in the UK was characterized by 'believing without belonging'. However, Day showed that the apparent high levels of religious affiliation found in surveys may be more about a sense of belonging to a community than about actual belief in a religion.

She found that most people over 18 believed in belonging 'to other people like themselves', whereas younger age groups were more **inclusive**. There tended to be an 'us' and 'them' mentality among the over 18s. The 'others' tended to fall into three main categories:

- *Ethnic others* – Respondents were careful to stress that they were not 'racist' but talked about other 'races' and religions as threateningly different.
- *Young others* – Older people talked about young people as disrespectful, rude and dangerous (to older people).
- *Bad mothers* – Women who were seen as rejecting the traditional motherhood role were seen as 'others' by both men and women.

Very few people mentioned God, Christianity or religion. Day was able to identify subsets within those describing themselves as Christian. In her sample, a little over half were what she termed adherent Christians who believed in God and in heaven, and attended church. However, of the remainder, there were a significant number who neither belonged nor believed. They fell into one of three categories:

1 *Natal Christians* saw themselves as Christians because they were born into it/baptized, and so saw themselves as part of a Christian family and place of birth.
2 *Ethnic Christians* saw Christianity in terms of Englishness and, therefore, as a way of identifying with an ethnic group.
3 *Aspirational Christians* saw Christianity as being about being good or respectable.

How far Day's finding about a sense of belonging to a community, rather than actual belief, can be applied to different religions and/or ethnic groups is clearly an area for further research.

Day, A. (2007) 'Believing in belonging: religion returns to sociology mainstream', *Network*, British Sociological Association, Summer 2007

1 What did religious affiliation really signify for many of the respondents?

2 Day's research shows that an apparent identification with a religion can, for many, really be a non-religious marker of identity. How far do you think this is true of those claiming to belong to non-Christian faiths? Explain your answer.

becomes less significant and being Muslim as an identity becomes more important'. Archer (2003) also finds that a strong Muslim identity provides an alternative to the gang and drug cultures of the 'street'. It is a way to resist stereotypes of 'weakness and passivity' and can provide a positive role model as an alternative identity that young Muslims can have pride in.

Though exaggerated by the media, the so-called radicalization of Muslim youth, where it has occurred, is due, according to Choudhury (2007), to a lack of religious literacy and education. He argues that this appears to be a common feature among those drawn to extremist groups. The most vulnerable are those who have been prompted by recent world events to explore their faith for the first time, yet are not in a position to evaluate objectively whether the radical group before them represents an accurate understanding of Islam. Akthar (2005) argued that after 9/11 and the wars in Afghanistan and Iraq, radical Islamic groups were able to exploit the view of a simple dichotomy of oppressors and oppressed – the West versus Islam, which puts the blame for all of the problems faced by Muslims under the same banner. Ironically, according to Hopkins and Kahani-Hopkins (2004), it is also those who are religiously astute as well as academically inclined who have been susceptible to radicalization. They cite how leaders of the banned extremist group Al-Muhajiroun, for example, identify young university students who suffer from a sense of blocked social mobility, as their most important recruitment pool. They suggest that it is this group that believes that they face a discriminatory system preventing them from realizing their potential. Analysis of the 2004 Home Office Citizenship survey showed that for Muslims, perceptions of discrimination, rather than socio-economic status, affect their sense of belonging and attachment to Britain.

However, according to Choudhury (2007) there are also signs of a progressive 'British Muslim' identity forming, partly as a reaction to violent radicalism, which is receptive to Western influences and demonstrates a desire to take a full part in British society.

Young Muslim women

This certainly appears to be the case with regard to young Muslim women, often commented on for their apparent submissiveness and repression, who have actually adapted well to the challenge of maintaining their cultural and religious identity, while at the same time becoming effective, well-integrated members of mainstream society. A number of studies such as that of Butler (1995) have explored this **cultural hybridity**. Recent research shows how veiling and the wearing of traditional dress may actually give Muslim girls greater freedom from patriarchal attitudes experienced by many White girls. (This was discussed further in Topic 6.) Research by Knott and Khoker (1993) and Samad (2006) suggests that many young South Asian Muslim women draw a distinction between 'religion' and 'culture', in contrast to their parents who, in their view, mistakenly confuse the two. Furthermore, they reject their parents' conformity to cultural traditions whilst at the same time fully embracing their Muslim identity. Dwyer (1999), whose research involved interviewing 35 young Muslim women, aged 13 to 18, found that, for them, their Muslim identity is a source used to resist parental opinion and challenge family prohibitions. They are able to use what is actually in the Muslim texts rather than the culturally biased, received wisdoms, to challenge their parents' attempts to restrict their behaviour. For example, by showing themselves to be 'good Muslims', they gained greater freedom to pursue other interests. Individuals were able to argue that not only should they be able to dress in a style which was both 'Western' and 'Islamic', but that they should have greater freedoms to go out, or to go on to higher education and be fully involved in the choice of marriage partner. Woodhead (2007) goes as far as to suggest that many young Muslim women have developed, as she puts it, 'a careful and often lavish attention to style, mixed with a very deliberate nod to faith', which she terms 'Muslim chic', creatively asserting their Muslim identity, whilst at the same, making a commitment to a British national identity.

Conclusion

Whilst the focus of this topic has been on the main ethnic-minority religions, there are many other religions, all of which can help to define and maintain a cultural identity, traditions and customs. Some provide direction and enable their members to cope in a racist and unjust society (e.g. **Rastafarianism**). Some religions or religious factions are antagonistic to society and the ambiguities of modernity. They offer solutions that may involve resistance and/or a return to fundamental principles felt to have been eroded through spiritual and moral decline. Such fundamentalism was discussed further in Topic 4.

Check your understanding

1 Give two reasons why immigrants to the UK have placed a greater emphasis on religion than the indigenous population.

2 (a) How did the experience of Asian and African-Caribbean groups differ when they originally came to Britain?

  (b) How did this affect their sense of identity?

3 What role does Pentecostalism play for African-Caribbean believers?

4 What are the reasons for the growing popularity of Pentecostal churches?

5 (a) What in general appears to be the trend in terms of the religiosity of young people of all ethnic groups.

  (b) How does the work of Rankin and others question such trends?

6 Why have many second-generation Asians chosen to hold on to their religious identity?

7 Give examples of how recent world events have served to reaffirm religious commitment for many ethnic-minority groups.

Key terms

Assimilate blend in and integrate.

Charismatic movements religious movements that believe that some individuals have gifts of the Holy Spirit, such as healing powers and the ability to speak in tongues.

Cultural hybridity to mix and match different cultural influences.

Inclusive all encompassing.

Pentecostal movement various fundamentalist Christian congregations whose members seek to be filled with the Holy Spirit (emulating the experience of the Apostles at Pentecost).

Rastafarianism Rastafarians worship Haile Selassie I (known as Ras [Prince] Tafari), former emperor of Ethiopia, considering him to have been the Messiah. Rastas believe that Black people are the Israelites reincarnated and have been persecuted by the White race in divine punishment for their sins.

Religious dogma rules and regulations, commandments and formal requirements of a particular religion.

Rites customary religious practices, e.g. baptism.

Activities

Research idea

Interview a number of respondents from different religious backgrounds who wear religious artefacts, such as Jewish headwear, the hijab or crucifixes.

Try to determine how important they consider this right to display religious commitment to be. Are their motivations mainly cultural or religious?

Web.task

Find the results of the The Home Office Citizenship Survey at
www.homeoffice.gov.uk/rds/pdfs04/hors274.pdf

How was the survey carried out? Choose any one aspect of the findings and summarise them as a report for the rest of your class.

An eye on the exam   Religion, ethnicity and youth

Item A

There are considerable differences in the patterns of religious observance of different ethnic groups in the UK, and in the value they place upon religion in their lives. For example, according to one survey, about three quarters of Muslims and nearly half of Sikhs and Hindus felt religion to be very important, as against only one in nine White people. Among those attending Christian churches, over one in six are non-White – a much higher proportion than in the population as a whole. Most of these are Black, and many of them attend Pentecostal churches – the only Christian denomination in the UK to be growing. However, the Catholic Church has attracted new members in parts of the country where there have been significant numbers of East European immigrants.

(a) Identify and briefly explain **three** reasons for differences in religious belief between the young and the old.   (9 marks)

(b) Using material from **Item A** and elsewhere, assess the relationship between religion and ethnicity.   (18 marks)

Grade booster   Getting top marks in this question

In your answer to question (b), remember to make use of relevant material from the Item. For example, you should consider ethnic patterns in relation to both Christian and non-Christian religions, and different Christian denominations and churches. You should consider a range of possible factors that affect the relationship between ethnicity and religion, such as the role of religion in maintaining ethnic identity, and pre-existing levels of religiosity among migrant groups. Differing levels of affluence and social and economic deprivation experienced by different ethnic groups can be linked to racism and discrimination, and also to the messages of denominations such as evangelicals, who emphasize the possibility of success and prosperity. You can also examine different styles of worship and participation among different ethnic and religious groups (e.g. the formalism of the Church of England versus the greater emphasis on religious experience among Pentecostalists).

TOPIC 8

Secularization

44

Getting you thinking

Left: The Baitul Fatuh mosque, the largest in Western Europe, built in 2003 in the south-west London suburb of Morden

Centre: a former church now housing a carpet warehouse

Right: a former cinema in Woolwich, London, now being used as an evangelical church

Variation between groups

According to the 2004 Home Office Citizenship Survey:

- Only 10 per cent of 16 to 24 year olds say they 'belong to a religion'. The equivalent for those aged 25 to 49 is 43 per cent, and for the over 50s it is 47 per cent.
- 19 per cent of women are frequent or regular churchgoers, compared with 11 per cent of men. Congregations generally reflect a 2:1 split. Among those declaring no religious affiliation the split is 2:3 (see Topic 6, p. 32).
- 16 per cent of the middle classes attend church compared with 12 per cent of the working class, yet of the non-attenders, more members of the middle class are non-believers.
- Minority-ethnic groups are generally more religious than Whites. Whites ranked religion as the 10th most important indicator of their identity, compared with Asian and Black respondents, who cited it as second and third respectively (see Topic 7).

1 How do the photographs above challenge or support the view that religion in the contemporary UK is declining in significance?

2 What types of religion in Britain appear to be declining and which thriving?

3 Suggest reasons why the variations in religiosity outlined above exist.

4 What may the implications of these patterns be for the future religiosity of British society?

It is difficult to make conclusive statements about religious commitment. The complexity of operationalizing – defining and measuring – religious belief and religious activity has long haunted sociologists, particularly those concerned with judging whether or not religion is in decline in the modern world – the process known as **secularization**. This topic outlines some of the problems faced by sociologists in assessing this process and also looks at the actual evidence for and against secularization.

In order to judge whether secularization is or is not taking place, sociologists need to define and measure key concepts, such as religion and religious belief, as well as secularization itself. This is by no means straightforward.

Whether you adopt a substantive definition of religion, which requires a belief in a supernatural force, or whether you consider that religion can be defined merely in terms of societal effect – i.e. you adopt a functional definition – will have an impact upon whether or not you believe secularization is occurring.

As Wilson (1982) has pointed out, those who define religion in substantive terms are more likely to argue that religious belief has declined as people accept other more rational explanations of the world. But those who see religion in functional terms are more likely to reject this view. If the functions of religion are essential to the smooth running of society, they argue, even though religion may change, these functions still need to be fulfilled. What we call religion must simply remain in some form or another to fulfil them.

Furthermore, as the figures in the 'Getting you thinking' opposite illustrate, patterns of religious commitment vary between groups. If certain ethnic groups are religious, but only constitute a small percentage of the population, it may be said that they have little impact on the society as a whole. But, if they are confined to a particular geographical region, then that area may appear to be much more religious and the impact of religion stronger there. If women are more religious than men, they may have more influence on young children. Though the young are generally less religiously affiliated – that is, they tend not to be members of religious organizations – how can we know whether they express religious beliefs privately at home?

Defining secularization

Wilson (1966) provides the following 'classic' definition of secularization: 'the process whereby religious thinking, practices and institutions lose social significance'. This seems a general enough catch-all statement, and is one that has been widely adopted, but problems occur straight away. What exactly is 'religious thinking'? What is meant by 'significance'? How can you measure them?

Measuring religious belief and practice

There is no clear definition of the boundaries of religious belief. Is a belief in fate or luck a religious belief? What about belief in ghosts or guardian angels? If they are, then an awful lot of people share such beliefs and may be termed 'religious'. *Most Haunted* is a British paranormal television programme based on investigating purported paranormal activity. Since 2002, it has been a popular show on the satellite and cable channels Living and Virgin 1, primarily for the UK market. Live shows every Halloween attract millions of viewers. It has a dedicated website and significant DVD sales.

There are also problems in measuring religious commitment. In the UK, 33 per cent of people say religion is very important personally (Pew Global Attitudes Project 2002). Does this mean, for example, that for a third of the population, religion has a significant impact upon behaviour? Furthermore, is such religiously influenced behaviour increasing or decreasing?

Church attendance

Declining church attendance has been used as a common indicator of secularization occurring in the UK – Sunday attendance having halved between 1967 and 2006.

However, does this necessarily indicate a reduction in the religiosity of society? Hamilton (2001) points out that the notion of an 'age of faith' in the past is an illusion partly created as a result of concentrating on the religious behaviour of the elite, about which we have more information than the vast majority of ordinary people. This may mean that the past was no more or less religious than the present, as the spiritual life of most people went unrecorded.

Until relatively recently, the religious sentiments of the religious minority restricted non-religious behaviour on Sundays. Before trading laws were relaxed in 1994, options were limited and the decision to attend church was unchallenged by the availability of significantly fewer alternatives. Nowadays, people may still believe, but have a lot more options on a Sunday. Greater levels of personal freedom and individualism may be causing people to see churches as inappropriate these days because they think that religion is a private matter. On the other hand, those who attend church may do so for reasons other than religion: to appear respectable or to make new friends or perhaps to get their child into a denominational school with a good academic reputation.

Is secularization best measured through church attendance anyway? There has undoubtedly been a decline in attendance, at least among Christians in Britain, but Britain is now a multicultural and multifaith society. To assume secularization on the basis of an analysis of the fortunes of Christianity is to dismiss the importance of other major world faiths supported in Britain. Also, at the global level, some social changes are enhancing the importance of religion. Many young Muslims have returned to Islam having been politicized by the widespread perception that Islam is under attack globally.

Glock and Stark (1968) argue that not enough attention has been paid to the detail of defining religion and religiosity, and that, because of this, the secularization thesis cannot be accurately tested. Indeed, the same empirical evidence can be used by different researchers to 'prove' both that secularization 'is' or 'is not' occurring. Martin (1978) has actually advocated the removal of the term 'secularization' from the sociological vocabulary, instead supporting the careful and detailed study of the ways in which the role of religion has changed at different times and different places.

However, despite the difficulties, a large body of sociological literature has emerged involving a debate between two groups of writers on opposite sides of the discussion who have sought to engage with the evidence on some level.

What is the evidence for secularization?

Church attendance and membership

It is likely that declining attendance is, at least to some extent, reflecting a decline in the significance of religion for many people. The growth in evangelical or non-Christian religious practice, and increased membership of New Religious movements have not countered the millions lost from the established churches.

However, the fall in numbers of those in the Christian community is not as rapid as the fall in church attenders. Figures from the 2001 census suggest that the proportion of the population who claim affiliation to Christianity remains high, at 72 per cent, though down from 76 per cent in 1980. Meanwhile, Sunday attendance has fallen from 1.2 million to 850 000 in the same period.

Table 1.6 Percentage of all churchgoers by age group 1979–98			
Age	1979	1989	1998
Under 15	26	25	19
15 to 29	20	17	15
30 to 64	36	39	41
65 and over	18	19	25

Source: Brierley, P. (ed.) (2000)

Age bias

Brierley also points out that the gross figures of decline hide a trend even more worrying for the future of organized Christianity in Britain: age bias. For each of his three English surveys (1979, 1989, 1999), he estimates the age profile of the various groups of denominations. With the exception of the Pentecostal churches, he notes the increasing percentage of the congregations in the older age groups being matched by the declining percentages of younger people – see Table 1.6. This could mean that as congregations age, and fewer and fewer young people join them, they could eventually die out altogether.

Reduced moral influence

Davies (2004) suggests that the UK population in the 21st century is no longer guided by the kinds of collective moral codes and community emphasis once promoted by the church, Sunday schools, and voluntary youth and community organizations. He points to the beginning of the 20th century as a turning point, when **individualism** progressively took over, particularly from the late 1950s onwards as the family and working-class community changed. Moral judgements, he argues, became more about minimizing personal harm than taking on board the thoughts and feelings of the wider, generally Christian community. Davies suggests that this is the reason for the increasing acceptance of divorce, illegitimacy and homosexuality, and for the dramatic increases in crime rates.

Furthermore, as Terry Sanderson (1999), a spokesman for the National Secular Society, put it, the church even seems to be losing its 'core business', that is, to 'hatch, match and dispatch' (i.e. baptize, marry and bury people):

- Weddings now only make up approximately 40 per cent of marriages compared with about 75 per cent 30 years ago (Brierley 2001).
- In the early 1930s, seven out of ten of all children were baptized into the Church of England. More than a third were still christened in the early 1980s. Latest figures (Church of England 2005) show that the proportion has fallen to 1 in 7.
- The Church of England carried out 207 300 funerals in 2005, down from 232 550 funerals in 2000, when figures were first collected, as increasing numbers opt for 'celebration-of-life' ceremonies rather than church services.

Lower status of clergy

As the number of clergy has fallen, their pay and status have declined. As Bruce (2001) states, the number of clergy is a useful indicator of the social power and popularity of religion. In 1900, there were over 45 000 clerics in Britain; this had declined to just over 34 000 in 2000, despite the fact that the population had almost doubled. In a patriarchal society, the very fact that women are now being ordained may in itself reduce the perceived status of the clergy.

Societal aspects of secularization

Bryan Wilson (1966) and others – notably, Bruce (1996) and Wallis (1984) – cite other evidence for secularization in addition to statistics. They argue that secularization is a development rooted in modernity and focus on three key processes: **rationalization**, **disengagement**, and **religious pluralism**.

Desacrilization and rationalization

This is the idea that the sacred has little or no place in contemporary Western society – the world is no longer seen as being in the control of supernatural forces. Instead, humans are viewed as in control of their own destiny, and with the advent of biotechnology, humans have the opportunity to 'play God'. Our consciousness has been secularized. This growth of **rational** or scientific thinking is seen as a clear indicator of secularization. This approach is particularly associated with Weber, who saw **desacrilization** as the 'disenchantment of the world' – the world losing its mystery and magic. It is suggested that rational thinking in the form of science has replaced religious influence in our lives, because scientific progress has resulted in higher living standards. Moreover, science has produced convincing explanations for phenomena that were once the province of religion, such as how the world was created.

Further, Berger (1973) has suggested that Christianity has ultimately been its own gravedigger. Protestantism focused attention on this life, work and the pursuit of prosperity, rather than on the domain of God and the afterlife.

Disengagement

The disengagement, or separation, of the church from wider society is an important aspect of secularization. The church is no longer involved in important areas of social life, such as politics, and has become disengaged from wider society.

People are now more concerned with their material standard of living, rather than with spiritual welfare, and are more likely to take moral direction from a variety of sources other than the church. Steve Bruce (1995) uses the term 'social differentiation' in pointing out that the church now has much less opportunity to involve itself in non-religious spheres. It has, therefore, become differentiated and assigned to more specialized roles. Religious faith and morality become less and less significant in the culture and institutions of modern societies: Hamilton (2001) has suggested that churches themselves have secularized in an attempt to compromise with those who have rejected more traditional beliefs. For example, he argues the Church of England no longer supports ideas of the Virgin Birth, Hell or even God as a real external force.

Religious pluralism

Bruce (1996) suggests that industrialization has fragmented society into a marketplace of religions and other community organizations. Wilson (1966) argues that, as a result, religion no longer acts as a unifying force in society as social life becomes more fragmented. He points to the **ecumenical movement** as an attempt by institutionalized religion to reverse secularization because such unification only occurs when religious influence is weak. In particular, the growth in the number of sects, cults and NRMs has also been seen by Wilson as evidence of secularization. He argues that sects are 'the last outpost of religion in a secular society' and are a symptom of religion's decline. Competition between religions is seen to undermine their credibility as they compete for 'spiritual shoppers' (see p. 21). Bruce (2002) also interprets the growth of sects as evidence of secularization, as they further undermine the authority of the established church on central issues of moral concern. Religious pluralism is therefore seen as evidence of religion's weakening influence. The established church, along with NRMs and new denominations in the UK, simply lacks credibility.

Religion in the USA: the Religious Economy Theory

On the other hand, the situation in the USA would seem to suggest that religious pluralism may, in fact, be responsible for the increasing appeal of religion there. In the USA, 40 per cent of the adult population regularly attend church. About 5 per cent of the US television audience regularly tune in to religious TV and 20 million watch some religious programming every week.

Scharf (1970), however, suggests American churches have developed in a secular way. They echo the American dream and religion has been subordinated to the American way of life. Churches place little emphasis on theology (belief) but stress the values of democracy, freedom, attainment and success. As Scharf notes: 'Being American includes being religious, and finding in religion a sanction for the American values of individualism and self-improvement.'

Warner (1993) puts the popularity of religion in the US down to the fundamental separation of religion from the influence of the state. The 18th-century American founders distinguished a series of principles of religious liberty, which included equality of faiths and separation of church and state. These principles encouraged religious pluralism without any centralizing influences. In the American context, the different religious traditions compete with each other equally for members. Religion has become a commodity to sell like any other product.

There can be greater specialization as the huge number of denominations (320 000 in 2007) tailor their product to meet market demand. Many advertise their unique characteristics in much the same way as schools in the UK market themselves. The result of competition in the US is a religious economy that results in more participants by expanding the base of participation, rather than a struggle for the loyalty of a fixed number of participants. This, it is suggested, is why there is a contrast between church attendance in Europe and the USA. In Europe, beliefs have not been compromised so much and the churches are empty. In the USA, the church has adapted itself to a changing society and the churches are full because they work to attract customers, free of interference from the church/state apparatus.

Evidence against secularization in the UK

While established religion may appear to be in decline in Western countries, such as Britain, the growth of their immigrant populations is causing an increase in religiosity in certain localities and regions of the UK. Islam is the fastest-growing religion in Britain and non-Trinitarian church membership has mushroomed.

However, in relation to the non-immigrant population, Grace Davie (1994) has characterized the situation in Britain as 'believing without belonging' – that is, people may admit to private religious beliefs but are less inclined to join religious groups or to attend religious services on a regular basis. Recent research by Day (2007) has cast doubt on this interpretation, suggesting religion is used as a 'public marker of identity', not necessarily highlighting an affiliation to a particular faith but to a community of other people like themselves rather than what they saw as 'others' (see 'Focus on research', p. 41).

In relation to church attendance, it could in fact be argued that this reflects 'belonging without believing'. That is, people may attend church for social or emotional reasons rather than religious commitment.

Vicarious religion

Davie also compares the UK with other European countries, such as those of Scandinavia. She suggests that religion is not practised overtly by the majority, but that most engage with religion on a **vicarious** level. In this sense, religion involves rituals and practices performed by an active minority on behalf of a much larger number, who (implicitly at least) not only understand, but also clearly approve of what the minority is doing.

Interruptions in 'normality'

One way to unravel what is happening is to observe societies when 'normal' ways of living are, for one reason or another, suspended and something far more expressive comes to the fore. Tragedy provides some examples. For example, in Sweden in 1994, the ferry *Estonia* sank with the loss of some 900 lives. Large numbers of Swedish people went to their churches, some to light candles and to mourn privately, but also to hear, articulated on their behalf (i.e. vicariously), both the sentiments of the people and the meaning of the tragedy for the country. Similarly, the death of Princess Diana in Paris in a car crash in 1997 drew large numbers of British people to church to make a similar sort of gesture. What is significant in both these examples is an awareness in the population as a whole that multiple and well-intentioned gestures of individual mourning are inadequate in themselves to mark the end of these particular lives; there is the additional need for public ritual or worship in the established church.

The *Estonia* and the Princess Diana examples are simply large-scale versions of what goes on in the life-cycles of ordinary people. People expect that they will have the right to the services of the church at critical moments in their lives, such as birth, marriage and death. Churches must exist in order to meet such demands. So churches do not belong exclusively to those who use them regularly. European populations continue to see such churches as public utilities maintained for the common good.

Religious belief

Despite very low levels of church attendance and membership, surveys show that there seems to be a survival of some religious belief. According to the 1998 British Social Attitudes survey, 21 per cent of those surveyed agreed to the statement 'I know God exists and I have no doubt about it', whereas only 10 per cent said that they did not believe in God at all. However, there may be a moral connotation attached to such surveys, such that people feel more inclined to answer 'yes', whether or not they actually believe in God.

Individuation

A number of sociologists, notably Bellah (1987), have argued that, while institutional religion is in decline, this is only one form of religion, and that other aspects of religion continue in a variety of forms in modern society. Individuation is the idea of religion as 'finding oneself' through an individual search for meaning. Rather than uncritically accepting institutionalized religion, many have embarked on what might be called 'spiritual journeys' in search of themselves. Therefore, the importance of religion has not declined, but its form of expression may have changed.

Other criticisms of the secularization thesis

There is evidence that people prefer 'religious' explanations for random events, e.g. the early death of loved ones. Many people still subscribe to the concept of 'luck' or 'fate', as evidenced by the growth of gambling opportunities, such as the National Lottery and the relaxation of gambling laws.

There can be little doubt that religion plays less of a political role than it did in earlier centuries. However, national debates about issues such as the age of homosexual consent, the family, abortion and so on are given a moral dimension by the contribution of religious leaders. The media still shows a great interest in issues such as women priests, while religious programmes like *Songs of Praise* still attract large audiences (7 to 8 million viewers). Some sociologists, notably Parsons (1965), have argued that disengagement is probably a good thing because it means that the churches can focus more effectively on their central role of providing moral goals for society to achieve.

According to Hamilton (2001), decline in religious practices may be part of a more general decline in organizational membership and increased privatization. For example, fewer people join trade unions or political parties. It may be that they still 'believe', but are more committed to spending their time with family or on individual priorities.

Thompson (1996) suggests that the influence of the new Christian evangelical churches is underestimated. In the absence of mass political campaigning, church-inspired campaigns have a high media profile, especially in the

USA. Many New Right policies on abortion, media violence and single parents are, he argues, influenced by the evangelical churches.

The secularization cycle

According to Stark and Bainbridge (1985), secularization is not an end to religion in itself but part of a dynamic cycle of secularization, innovation and religious revival (see Fig. 1.2).

From Stark and Bainbridge's perspective, Mormonism is the latest in a long series of world religions arising from sects that flourish where conventional religion has become too weak.

Stark and Bainbridge argue that religion can never disappear nor seriously decline. They see religion as meeting the fundamental needs of individuals. Whilst the privileged may have most of what they desire, individuals sometimes want rewards which are so great that the possibility of gaining them can only be contemplated alongside a belief in the supernatural – for instance, answers to our most fundamental questions, or a life after death. Only religion can answer these questions. The need for **religious compensators** is a constant whenever, wherever, and for whom, desired rewards are not obtainable. The less privileged, relatively lacking in rewards in life, may find that the increasingly secularized religions of the more privileged provide insufficient compensation and so seek alternatives, innovating as described above.

Religious pluralism as religious revival?

Rather than being seen as indicative of a weakening influence of religion on society, studies by Greeley (1972) and G.K. Nelson (1986) argue that the growth of NRMs indicate that society is undergoing a religious revival. Nelson argues that, in the 1980s, institutional religion lost contact with the spiritual needs of society because it had become too ritualized and predictable. In this sense, Nelson agrees with Wilson that established religion is undergoing secularization. The young, in particular, are 'turned-off' by such religion. However, Nelson argues that a religious revival is underway, and is being helped by the success of evangelical churches. These churches offer a

more spontaneous religion, which is less reliant on ritual and consequently more attractive to the young.

But Bruce (1996) and Wallis (1984) point out that neither NRMs nor those churches that have increased their membership have recruited anywhere near the numbers of those lost from the established churches. Brierley (1999) estimates that the growth of non-Trinitarian churches of half a million members, amounts to about only one-sixth of those lost to the main churches.

The secularization myth? A global perspective

Many writers have pointed out that secularization has tended to be seen in terms of the decline of organized established churches in Western industrialized countries. However, if one looks at the world globally, then religion is as overwhelming and dominant a force as ever. Berger (1997), one of the foremost advocates of secularization during the 1960s, has formally retracted his earlier claims, 'the world today with some exceptions is as furiously religious as it ever was and in some places more so than ever'. Religious revival among Christians in the USA, Jews in Israel and Muslims throughout the world has gone unexplained by proponents of the secularization thesis.

The postmodernist view

Postmodernists, too, see the development of New Age beliefs, what Heelas *et al.* (2004) call a '**holistic milieu**', as a rejection of science and modernity in the postmodern age. The true extent of New Age beliefs cannot be known, but the number of internet sites feeding such interests indicates that they are widespread. This new explosion of spirituality doesn't at first seem to detract from the secularization thesis because these private beliefs don't impact upon the way society runs. However, as postmodernists argue, consumption is the way society runs now, or is at least a very significant factor, so this is precisely where we should look to find openings for religious activity.

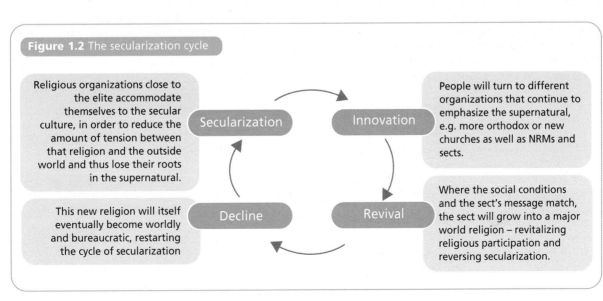

Figure 1.2 The secularization cycle

Religious organizations close to the elite accommodate themselves to the secular culture, in order to reduce the amount of tension between that religion and the outside world and thus lose their roots in the supernatural.

Secularization

Innovation

People will turn to different organizations that continue to emphasize the supernatural, e.g. more orthodox or new churches as well as NRMs and sects.

This new religion will itself eventually become worldly and bureaucratic, restarting the cycle of secularization

Decline

Revival

Where the social conditions and the sect's message match, the sect will grow into a major world religion – revitalizing religious participation and reversing secularization.

Secularization: an over-generalization?

As far as the UK is concerned, it is fairly obvious that profound changes are occurring in institutional religion. However, whether these changes can be described as secularization is difficult to ascertain. Religious participation through organized religion has declined, but the extent and nature of continuing belief still proves difficult to determine. Further, increased globalization has meant that **religio-political events** elsewhere have global significance and this is bound to have an impact upon religious influence in Britain.

Bauman (1997) and Giddens (2001), for example, argue that religion is becoming more important in the late modern/postmodern world. According to Giddens:

<< *Religious symbols and practices are not only residues from the past: a revival of religious or more broadly spiritual concerns seems fairly widespread … not only has religion failed to disappear; we see all around us the creation of new forms of religious sensibility and spiritual endeavour.* >>

Activities

Research ideas

1   Identify a small sample of students who participate in organized religious activity. Conduct semi-structured interviews with them, aiming to discover what appeals to them about that particular religious group. Do you find any differences between those who are involved in different kinds of religious organizations?

2   Conduct a survey to discover the extent of belief in a range of supernatural and spiritual phenomena among students at your school or college. To what extent do your results indicate widespread 'religious belief'? Would your conclusions be different if you used different criteria for measuring 'religious belief'?

Web.tasks

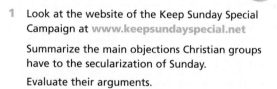

1   Look at the website of the Keep Sunday Special Campaign at **www.keepsundayspecial.net**

    Summarize the main objections Christian groups have to the secularization of Sunday.

    Evaluate their arguments.

2   Explore the website of the 'Mind, Body and Spirit' organization at **www.mindbodyspirit.co.uk**

    What do you think the success of these exhibitions tells us about secularization?

Check your understanding

1   According to Wilson, how does the definition of religion affect the way secularization is seen?

2   Why is generalizing about secularization in relation to members of British society as a whole problematic ?

3   Why, according to Hamilton, is the notion of an 'age of faith' an illusion?

4   Why is a focus on church attendance as an indicator of declining religiosity essentially flawed?

5   What evidence on religious participation does Wilson give to support the secularization thesis?

6   What is the significance of the changing age profile for the future of religion in Britain?

7   What indicators are there of a reduced status of the clergy?

8   What, according to Wilson, is the significance of rationalization and disengagement for the secularization thesis?

9   How does Bruce argue that religious pluralism is evidence of secularization?

10 Why is the USA so 'religious' relative to the UK?

11 How does Davie counter the view that religion in Britain is declining in significance?

12 How do Stark and Bainbridge explain the cycle of secularization, innovation and revival?

13 Why do they argue that religion can never truly disappear?

14 In what ways does a more global perspective demonstrate that secularization is a myth?

15 How do postmodernists view the secularization thesis?

Key terms

Desacrilization where sacred explanations give way to scientific rational explanations.

Disengagement where the religious institutions become less engaged in wider aspects of social life.

Ecumenical movement where churches come together in joint worship, each seeing the other as having something to offer.

Holistic milieu a range of activities involving the mind, body and spirit, such as yoga, tai chi, healing and self-discovery.

Individualism putting the interests of the individual before the interests of the state or social group.

Rational based on reason, logic and science.

Rationalization the use of reason and science to replace spiritual and religious thinking.

Religio-political events instances of religion coming into conflict with governments, with national and sometimes international consequences.

Religious compensators aspects of religion that provide temporary answers to fundamental queries about the nature of existence and satisfy universal needs.

Religious pluralism where a variety of religions co-exist, all of which are considered to have equal validity.

Secularization thesis belief in the declining influence of religion in society.

Vicarious religion religious practices of a socially approved of minority who symbolically represent the religious adherence of the majority.

An eye on the exam Secularization

Item A

The death of religion was the conventional wisdom in the social sciences during most of the 20th century; it has been regarded as the master model of sociological inquiry, where secularization was ranked with bureaucratization, rationalization, and urbanization as the key historical revolutions transforming medieval agrarian societies into modern industrial nations. C. Wright Mills summarized this process: 'Once the world was filled with the sacred – in thought, practice, and institutional form. After the Reformation and the Renaissance, the forces of modernization swept across the globe and secularization, a resulting historical process, loosened the dominance of the sacred. In due course, the sacred shall disappear altogether except, possibly, in the private realm.'

During the past decade, however, this thesis of the slow and steady death of religion has come under growing criticism; secularization theory is currently experiencing the most sustained challenge in its long history. Critics point to multiple indicators of religious health and vitality today, ranging from the continued popularity of churchgoing in the United States to the emergence of New Age spirituality in Western Europe, the growth in fundamentalist movements and religious parties in the Muslim world, the evangelical revival sweeping through Latin America, and the upsurge of ethno-religious conflict in international affairs.

Adapted from C. Wright Mills (1959) *The Sociological Imagination*, Oxford: Oxford University Press., pp. 32–3

Using material from **Item A** and elsewhere, assess the view that we are now living in a secular society.

(33 marks)

Grade booster Getting top marks in this question

You should begin with a brief definition of secularization that identifies some of its main aspects (such as belief, practice and institutions, including influence over other areas of life) and consider the problems of measuring these. For example, how valid and reliable are church attendance and membership statistics? Examine the processes that have been seen as causing secularization, such as rationalization and bureaucratization. In your answer, remember to make use of relevant material from the Item. For example, you can use the issues referred to there, such as the continuing popularity of churchgoing in the USA, and the growth of New Age spirituality, fundamentalism, evangelicalism, and ethno-religious conflicts, as evidence against the secularization thesis. Other aspects you could consider include Stark and Bainbridge's view that there is a cycle of secularization and revival, or whether the decline of religion will be permanent. Also, any conclusions that are reached about the extent of secularization will depend on how religion is actually defined – see Topic 1.

1 Read **Item A** below and answer parts (a) and (b) that follow.

Item A

Functionalists, Marxists and feminists generally believe religion acts as a conservative force. Religion can be seen as conservative in two senses. First, in the sense of religion as preventing change, functionalists and Marxists both claim, in their different ways, that religion facilitates the continued existence of society in its present form. Secondly, 'conservative' may also be used to describe traditional beliefs and customs. Religion may also maintain such traditional customs and beliefs. For example, the stance of successive popes against contraception has restricted its use in Catholic countries.

However, in some circumstances, religion can support social change while at the same time promoting traditional values. This often occurs when there is a revival in 'fundamentalist' religious beliefs. Such beliefs involve a return to what a group claims are the 'fundamentals' or original beliefs of a religion, as in the case of the Islamic revolution in Iran in 1979.

Adapted from Haralambos, M. and Holborn, M. (2008) *Sociology: Themes and Perspectives* (7th edn), London: Collins Educational

(a) Identify and briefly explain **three** features of sects. *(9 marks)*

Sects are voluntary. You have to join the sect, you are not born into it, unlike a church.

They are often led by a charismatic leader, such as the Reverend Moon of the Moonies. The leader is the source of all rules and is to be obeyed without question.

Sects often reject mainstream society and its values or way of life.

An examiner comments

All three points are correct, but the last one needs explaining, e.g. because they see society as corrupt and godless.

(b) Using information from **Item A** and elsewhere, assess the extent to which religion forms an obstacle to social change. *(18 marks)*

Religion is often thought to be an obstacle to social change. Functionalists argue that religion helps to prevent change and maintain the status quo (Item A). They claim it does this by promoting solidarity and integration through shared values and beliefs. According to Malinowski, religion also helps individuals to cope with stresses that might disrupt social life.

Marxists also see religion as maintaining the status quo. However, they see it as serving the interests of the ruling class, whereas functionalists see it serving society as a whole by maintaining the value consensus. For Marxists, all institutions are manipulated by the ruling class in order to preserve capitalism and the status quo. Religion offers the exploited proletariat ideological comfort that they will be rewarded for their suffering. In this way, they are less likely to rebel against their capitalist bosses. Likewise, Hinduism preserves the caste system by teaching the lower castes that if they are obedient and dutiful, they will be reborn in a higher caste.

Feminists, too, see religion as a conservative force, for instance by suppressing women and maintaining a patriarchal society in the interests of men through fear of God. It legitimates their subordinate position in society and encourages them to accept it as God's will.

However, religion can also bring about change as well as prevent it. Fundamentalism is an example of this. In the Iranian revolution (Item A), fundamentalists overthrew the pro-Western monarchy and set up an Islamic republic, with strict adherence to Islamic principles. Thus, we can see that many sociologists regard religion as an obstacle to change, but it can also sometimes bring about change.

This answer shows reasonable knowledge of different perspectives. It makes some use of material from the Item and it has some examples of its own. However, evaluation is limited to the last paragraph and, in the example of Iran, better use could be made of the Item to distinguish between the two senses of 'conservative'. The answer could use more examples of where religion is not an obstacle to change.

One for you to try

Assess the view that religion is declining in importance in today's society. *(33 marks)*

An examiner comments

Begin by examining the different ways religion may or may not be declining, such as church attendance, membership, belief and social influence (e.g. over personal behaviour or government policy). What problems are there with these indicators? Examine different explanations, e.g. rationalization, differentiation, pluralism, individuation, as well as views that do not accept there is a decline, e.g. vicarious religion, revivals and the secularization cycle.

Answers to the 'One for you to try' are available free on www.collinseducation.com/sociologyweb

Global development

AQA Specification	Topics	Pages
Candidates should examine:		
Different theories of development, underdevelopment and global inequality.	Topic 1 discusses these key terms. The main theories of development are the focus of Topics 2 and 3.	54–79
Globalization, aid and trade, and their influence on the cultural, political and economic relationships between societies.	These themes run through the chapter. Topic 8 is devoted to globalization, Topic 4 to aid and debt.	116–24 80–89
The role of transnational corporations, non-governmental organizations and international agencies in local and global strategies for development.	Strategies for development are described and evaluated throughout the chapter. The specific role of transnational corporations is covered in Topic 8. The impact of all the different types of organization is discussed in Topic 4.	116–24 80–89
Development in relation to industrialization, urbanization, the environment, war and conflict.	Topic 7 covers industrialization, urbanization and the environment. War and conflict is the focus of Topic 9.	107–15 125–31
Employment, education, health, demographic change and gender as aspects of development.	The theme of employment and education runs through the whole chapter. Demographic change is in Topic 5, gender issues in Topic 6. Health is also discussed in Topic 5.	90–106

TOPIC 1

Defining development

Getting you thinking

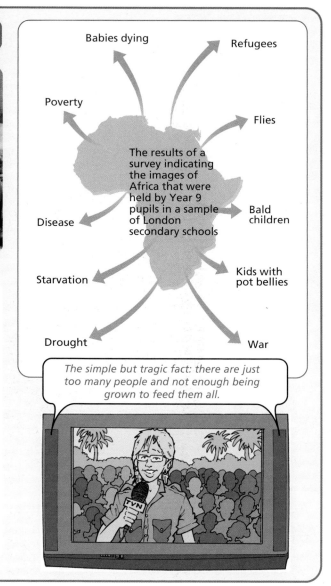

Babies dying

Refugees

Poverty

Flies

The results of a survey indicating the images of Africa that were held by Year 9 pupils in a sample of London secondary schools

Disease

Bald children

Starvation

Kids with pot bellies

Drought

War

The simple but tragic fact: there are just too many people and not enough being grown to feed them all.

1 Look at the two images of children on this page – one forced to work from a very young age and one starving.

What feelings does each picture provoke in you? Suggest reasons for the predicament of each child. How would you go about improving their lives – even their chances of survival into adulthood?

2 Examine the results of the survey into children's images of Africa (above right). Do these images reflect the dominant images in your head? What other images might you add to this list? Where do people get such images from?

3 What does the cartoon tell us about our perception of problems in the developing world?

Surveys generally indicate that the sorts of images of children used above provoke two distinct sets of feelings among young people in the UK:

● Some feel compassion and pity, and perhaps an overwhelming need to help. If you felt this way, you probably constructed a detailed list of solutions that focused on how we in the West might help these children out of poverty. In this case, you are probably the type of person who gives generously to charities that target children in the developing world, such as Make Poverty History.

● Many feel indifference. If this was true for you, the likelihood is that you have seen these types of images so many times now that you may have become immune to their emotional content. If so, you are experiencing what is known as 'compassion fatigue'. Such feelings are likely to be accompanied by nagging questions such as 'Why do we always need to put our hands in our pockets?' and 'Why don't these people sort themselves out?'

You are likely to find both these sets of feelings present in any group of young people, such as your own sociology class. Neither set is right or wrong. Both groups of people share similar characteristics in that they both hold images of places like Africa that are similar to the ones held by the children in the survey on p. 54. Note how negative these images are. They are generally images of Africa starving, Africa overpopulated with too many babies, and Africa as victim of natural disasters, such as drought, or self-inflicted disasters, such as war. Such images are the product of **value judgements** that we make about how people should live their lives. They are constructed relative to our own experience. Our standard of living in the UK generally ensures that most children in the UK survive healthily into adulthood. We should, therefore, not be too surprised that our ideas about how societies like these in Africa should change or develop are based on our own Western experiences. Moreover, some of us will quite naturally jump to the conclusion that their problems are created by their failure to adopt our way of life.

We should not underestimate the role of the mass media in constructing our perceptions of other parts of the world and the explanations and solutions available to their problems. Few of us have had actual experience of these parts of the world and, consequently, our perceptions are formed by the images we see in the media. Media analysis may be partial and selective, as the cartoon on p. 54 indicates.

It is important to understand that both our perception and media representations of developing countries reflect a wider academic and political debate about how sociologists, politicians and aid agencies should define development. As we shall see, the dominant definitions of development that exist involve the same sorts of value judgements that informed your reaction to the poverty and suffering of children in the developing world.

Affluence and destitution

World sociology is concerned with explaining the relationship between different countries and peoples of the world, and, in particular, the economic and social differences between them. World sociologists aim to explain why the nations of the world exist in a hierarchy of affluence which ranges from utter destitution to immense wealth (Harris 1989). For example, in 1997, the richest fifth of the world's population enjoyed an income 78 times as great as the poorest. Most of this wealth is concentrated in the industrialized world – North America, Western Europe, Japan and Australasia (see Fig. 2.1). Most of the destitution is concentrated in the less developed world – which consists mainly of most of Africa, South and Central America, the Indian subcontinent and most of East Asia. Evidence suggests that this wealth gap between

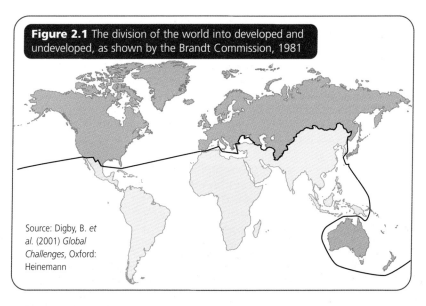

Figure 2.1 The division of the world into developed and undeveloped, as shown by the Brandt Commission, 1981

Source: Digby, B. *et al.* (2001) *Global Challenges*, Oxford: Heinemann

the developed and developing world, despite the billions of pounds given in aid over the past 50 years, is actually getting wider.

The Commission for Africa was set up by the former British Prime Minister Tony Blair in early 2004. It was composed of 17 individuals, 9 of whom were from Africa. Its aim was to identify solutions to the continent's most serious problems. Its report was published in 2005. Here is an extract from that report:

<< *We live in a world where new medicines and medical techniques have eradicated many of the diseases and ailments which plagued the rich world. Yet in Africa, some four million children under the age of five die each year, two-thirds of them from illnesses which cost very little to treat. … We live in a world where scientists can map the human genome and have developed the technology even to clone a human being. Yet in Africa we allow more than 250 000 women to die each year from complications in pregnancy or childbirth … We live in a world where rich nations spend as much as the entire income of all the people in Africa subsidising the unnecessary production of unwanted food, while in Africa hunger is the key factor in more deaths than all the continent's infectious diseases put together.* >> (pp.5–6)

This chapter will generally distinguish between the rich and poor regions of the world by using the terms 'developed world' and 'developing world'. However, these terms are themselves not without problems because world sociologists are not in total agreement as to how development should be defined and, therefore, measured. Moreover, even within these two worlds there are enormous inequalities in terms of wealth, poverty, health, education, etc.

The terminology of development

This topic area uses the terms 'developed' and 'developing' worlds but there is a confusing range of terms used by world sociologists and textbooks. Up to the

1990s, the terms 'First World' (i.e. the West), 'Second World' (i.e. communist countries) and 'Third World' (i.e. the developing world) were in common use, but the collapse of **communism** has largely rendered such terms redundant. Some sociologists also objected to such terms because they imply superiority and inferiority between the developed and developing worlds. Other sociologists divided the world into 'North' (i.e. the industrialized world) and 'South' (i.e. the developing world) after the Brandt Report (1981) on global inequality, but if you look at a map you will see this is not geographically very accurate (see Fig. 2.1). It also implies that countries within these broad categories are very much alike in their development features, which is not the case. The situation is therefore complicated by the diversity of economic and social progress found in the developing world today. For example, some sociologists have identified four broad groups of societies which make up a hierarchical global stratification system:

1 *More economically developed countries (MEDCs)* – Developed countries mainly found in the West but which also include Japan and Australia.
2 *Newly industrialized countries (NICs)* – The Asian Tiger countries, e.g. China, Singapore, Malaysia, Hong Kong, Taiwan and South Korea, which have rapidly industrialized in the past 40 years. Today, these have a large share of the global high-tech manufacturing market in computers and electronics, textiles (particularly sportswear) and plastics.
3 *Less economically developed countries (LEDCs)* – These are mainly dependent on agriculture and raw materials, although they have experienced some industrialization and fairly extensive **urbanization**, e.g. India, Brazil, Mexico. People enjoy a reasonable standard of living, but economic and social progress in these countries is impeded by massive debt and rural poverty.
4 *Least economically developed countries (LLEDCs)* – These are the poorest countries in the world, e.g. Bangladesh, Afghanistan and the sub-Saharan African countries of Niger, Ethiopia and Somalia. Despite billions of dollars of aid, **absolute poverty** is the daily norm, and social and economic conditions for the majority of their citizens have actually grown worse as a result of debt, civil war and famine.

These terms have now come into more general sociological use, but they are not entirely satisfactory, mainly because they give the impression that batches of countries experience economic and social problems in an **homogeneous** fashion. Although countries may share some characteristics in terms of lack of development, it is important to realize that there are often more differences than similarities between them. For example, people living in Mozambique in Africa and Honduras in Central America may both experience **subsistence poverty**, but in a quite different way, because of cultural differences and the specific locales in which they live. It is increasingly being recognized that countries have unique problems and needs that are the result of geographical, religious, ethnic, cultural, political, economic and social factors specific to

them. These then interact with global economics and culture in ways that may differ qualitatively from other seemingly similar societies. This, of course, makes it difficult, if not impossible, to place such countries into off-the-peg categories.

Despite these difficulties of categorization, most sociologists working in the development field are largely (but not entirely) agreed on what economic and social factors need to be present to judge a society as lacking in development (see Table 2.1).

The list of features in Table 2.1 is by no means exhaustive – there are plenty of other negative social characteristics that could be added to the list (for example, many developing nations have had some experience of war in the past 50 years). Moreover, it is also important to understand that this list is also **value-laden**, i.e. it is constructed using Western value judgements as to what is good and bad. For example, we tend to assume in the West that personal happiness, standard of living and development are bound up with our economic conditions. However, not all societies or sociologists accept this as necessarily true and they may, therefore, object to the presence or absence of the factors above as indicating a lack of development. We shall return to this theme later.

Table 2.1 The developing world: its distinguishing features

Developing countries, in contrast with the developed world, are likely to have the following features:

● a colonial past
● economies based on agriculture (especially the export of cash crops) and the extraction of raw materials, rather than manufacturing industry
● low economic growth (e.g. a large proportion of income from exports is likely to be used to service foreign debt)
● vast inequalities in ownership of and access to land
● large sections of the population may be unemployed or underemployed
● a subsistence standard of living – the World Bank estimates that 800 million people live in absolute poverty in the developing world, i.e. living on $1–$2 dollars or less a day.
● a young and fertile population that is growing rapidly
● high rates of child malnutrition
● low life expectancy
● high rates of infant mortality
● death from preventable and treatable diseases, such as measles, due to a lack of basic medical provision, e.g. the number of doctors, hospitals and clinics per head of population is low
● high levels of adult illiteracy
● lack of access to free schooling
● lack of basic infrastructure and services, including telecommunications, roads, electricity supply, clean water and sanitation
● lack of civil and human rights
● totalitarian and repressive governments
● patriarchal forms of inequality.

Measuring development 1945–80

The period 1945–80 saw the dominance of two overlapping approaches to development, especially with regard to how Western governments, multilateral agencies (such as the World Bank and International Monetary Fund) and **non-governmental organizations** (such as development charities like Oxfam) managed assistance to the developing world:

- development as economic wellbeing
- development as social wellbeing.

Development as economic wellbeing

Approaches to development in the period 1945 to 1980 tended to favour economic measurements of development, such as Gross National Product (GNP). This is the total economic value of goods and services (expressed in US dollars) produced by a country over the course of a year available for consumption in the marketplace or export to other countries. The total value of GNP is divided by the total population of a country to give a figure per head (i.e. known as 'per capita'). It is argued that GNP tells us how economically healthy a society is. A society experiencing low GNP could, therefore, be targeted with financial aid by agencies such as the World Bank and International Monetary Fund.

The use of GNP figures illustrates the enormity of the gap between the developed and developing worlds in terms of wealth and income. For example, from Table 2.2, we can see that in 2006, GNP per capita in the USA was $44 970, and in the UK it was $40 180, whilst in the Democratic Republic of Congo it was only $130, and even in China, a country that has made great economic strides in recent years, only $5890 (although if Hong Kong GNP is added, this figure increases to $28 460). Moreover, the figures in Table 2.2 show that the USA, the UK, Sweden and Japan greatly increased their GNP between 1992 and 2006, whilst the poorest countries, such as The Gambia and Congo (which has been ravaged by civil war), actually experienced a decline, thus increasing the wealth gap between the developed and undeveloped parts of the world. When economic growth does occur in the developing world, e.g. in the case of Ethiopia, the rate of increase is much lower than that of the developed world.

Table 2.2 GNP for selected countries, 1992 and 2006

Country	Per capita GNP (US$) 1992	Per capita GNP (US$) 2006
Brazil	2770	4730
The Gambia	390	310
China	370	5890
Sweden	16 200	43 580
UK	15 000	40 180
Nigeria	320	640
USA	23 120	44 970
Japan	28 220	38 410
Bhutan	199	1410
Dem. Rep Congo	1050	130
Ethiopia	130	180

Source: World Development Report, 1992 & 2008

However, GNP as a measure of development is regarded by some sociologists as unsatisfactory for the following reasons:

- There are inconsistencies in the way countries collect such data, so we cannot be sure of its reliability or its value as a comparative tool.
- Production in developing countries is often informally geared to survival rather than for consumption in the marketplace or profit (as it is in the West). GNP neglects what Black (2002) calls the 'invisible economies', such as keeping livestock or growing crops for personal use, grazing livestock on common land, trading girls into marriage, and managing assets such as fuel and water. These activities, which are mainly carried out by women in family units (and which can be the difference between life and death), are extremely difficult to value. Similarly, in order to survive, the urban poor may be immersed in a black or illegal economy that involves activities such as scavenging through rubbish tips, prostitution, begging, drug-dealing, etc. Both these invisible and illegal types of survival techniques are unlikely to be included in GNP measurements.
- GNP gives us little insight into either the standard of living of a population or how wealth and income are actually distributed within a society. Therefore, the $44 970 GNP figure for the USA quoted earlier gives a false impression because it disguises the fact that some social groups in the USA, mainly African-Americans and Native-Americans, experience disproportionate poverty. Economic growth in terms of GNP, therefore, does not necessarily result in economic development for all members of a population. In fact, GNP has actually grown in some societies whilst the majority of people in them have experienced greater levels of poverty and inequality.
- GNP may give us some idea of the wealth and prosperity of a developing society, but it fails to tell us how much of that wealth actually stays in that society.

Key themes

Stratification and differentiation

The study of global development is essentially an examination of global stratification and the inequalities of wealth, income, health and education that stem from the fact that nations are ranked in a hierarchy of affluence and destitution. Within both the developed and developing worlds, stratification systems based on status categories such as social class, gender, race/ethnicity, caste and tribe can clearly be seen.

In many developing societies, industry is controlled by transnational companies who transfer profits back to the developed world. In addition, a great deal of the 'wealth' generated by developing societies is lost in aid repayments.

- We need to recognize that the focus on production for wealth accumulation and consumption embodied in GNP probably reflects Western value assumptions that materialism and consumerism are somehow central to personal happiness and progress, and that developing societies may not share these values. A poor person in the developing world may lack personal possessions but this does not necessarily mean that they feel deprived or that they suffer hardship. Other factors, such as community or family, may be regarded as more important and compensate for material poverty. Moreover, as Foster-Carter (1985) argues, the economic prosperity represented by GNP is often accompanied by profound social problems, such as the breakdown of community, feelings of isolation, anomie and alienation, environmental and health problems, and increased rates of suicide and crime. Economic growth, therefore, may end up imposing these Western social problems on developing societies.

Development as social wellbeing

It is argued that the measurement of development should focus on social rather than economic indicators of development. This approach, which is largely based on a desire for social justice and equity, has dominated the thinking on development by organizations like Oxfam, Christian Aid and Cafod, as well as the agencies of the United Nations. For example, many charitable agencies have focused on the concept of 'basic needs'. This is a recognition that the poor need to be lifted out of subsistence poverty (i.e. living hand to mouth in order to survive) and should have the right to a nutritious diet, safe drinking water, sanitation, shelter, health and education. It is argued that people in the developing world need to experience 'social wellbeing', i.e. the right to be healthy, to be able to resist disease and to be able to live into adulthood and old age, as well as the right to be educated.

These needs and rights can be converted into statistical measurements relatively easily and without controversy, in that most of us would agree that the things listed above are worthwhile goals. Moreover, these basic needs also have economic benefits in that they produce a healthy and literate workforce. In 1990, the United Nations constructed the Human Development Index (HDI) which aims to measure aspects of human welfare, such as adult literacy, life expectancy at birth, and the number of doctors per 100 000 population. In 2008, the HDI showed that, in the USA, 99 per cent of the adult population was literate, whilst average life expectancy was 78 years. However, in Nigeria, only 69 per cent of the population was literate and average life expectancy was 46.5 years.

Evaluating development as economic and social wellbeing

Kingsbury et al. (2004) have questioned the motives behind Western sponsorship of development aimed at

Focus on research

Pakko and Pollard (2003) 'Burgernomics'

An alternative, light-hearted economic indicator of development invented by the *Economist* magazine in the 1990s is the concept of 'burgernomics'. The magazine points out that it is now possible to buy the 'Big Mac' burger in 120 countries around the world. Moreover, the Big Mac is a valued consumer commodity in most of these countries. However, the magazine noted that in many developing countries the Big Mac is not an inexpensive meal option. For example, in Thailand, the Big Mac costs over three quarters of the hourly wage of Thai consumers. Using this criteria, the *Economist* has devised a development table showing how many minutes a worker must work in any particular society to buy a Big Mac:

USA	11	Russia	30	Brazil	43
UK	15	China	30	Mexico	65
				Philippines	112

The cut-off point dividing developed from developing societies seems to be about 20 minutes.

Pakko, M. & Pollard, P. (2003) 'Burgernomics: a Big Mac guide to purchasing power parity', *Federal Reserve Bank of St. Louis Review*, 85(6), pp. 9–28

What criticisms would you make of this means of measuring development?

economic and social wellbeing. Kingsbury notes that the economic and ideological self-interest of Western governments has far outweighed any humanitarian purpose in their dealings with developing societies. The industrialized West saw the economic development of poorer countries as being in their economic interest because this increased the purchasing power of such countries, thus generating more international trade and opening up new markets for Western manufactured goods. Moreover, development was seen by both the USA and USSR as a means of increasing their sphere of influence as part of the ideological '**Cold War**'. Meeting social needs in this context was secondary to Western and Soviet strategic interests. This ideological rationale for development has continued despite the collapse of communism. Kingsbury notes that it has been recognized, particularly by the USA, that poverty can cause global conflict in the form of international terrorism and anti-Western feeling. Development aimed at economic and social wellbeing, therefore, is primarily concerned with protecting Western interests – poverty reduction is an essential component on the 'war on terror'.

Kingsbury's rather cynical view of development is challenged by the work of Maggie Black (2002) who suggests that there was originally a 'heartfelt political commitment' by politicians and general public alike in the rich nations to help the poor of the developing world in the postwar period. She argues that mass media exposure of mass hunger 'seared consciences and captured the public imagination' and led to the notion of development as a 'moral force' and as an instrument of compassion and social justice. She also notes that the motive for social justice often stemmed from the guilt felt by some progressive politicians for the wrongs committed by Britain in the colonial period. However, Black does acknowledge that the concept of development was soon soured by unrealistic expectations, the activities of **transnational corporations** and banks, as well as the fact that the humanitarian aspect of development was often neglected in favour of its strategic and political value.

Remenyi (2004) suggests that the 1980s saw a major shift in Western attitudes towards development. Concern for the needs of the poor in the developing world (i.e. poverty reduction) was downgraded as a priority as many Western governments tightened their belts following the economic recession of the 1980s. Many developed nations actually cut their aid commitments in this period, whilst World Bank development policy mainly focused on making sure that developing nations honoured their loan contracts with the major commercial banks. The International Monetary Fund meanwhile promised development assistance only if developing governments agreed to save money by cutting back or abandoning welfare policies aimed at poverty reduction. The social wellbeing of people in developing countries, therefore, was often sacrificed to ensure the wellbeing of Western economies.

Sustainable development

In 1987, the Brundtland Report was published by the United Nations and proposed the idea that socioeconomic progress had to be eco-friendly. The concept of 'sustainable development' was invented – this was based on the idea that social and economic development was important in order to assure human beings of a healthy and productive life, but it was argued that that progress should not jeopardize the right of future generations to the same, if not better, living standards.

Black (2002) argues that sustainable development aimed not only to improve the living standards of people in the developing world, it also proposed to safeguard the environment – the air, soil, water and all forms of life – from the acute pressures of population growth, modern technology and consumer demand. For example, Brundtland noted that poverty in sub-Saharan Africa was often caused by environment degradation as land was overfarmed because this led to desertification and a reduction in food production. Sustainable development therefore aimed to tackle a range of ecological worries – species loss, global warming, deforestation, toxic waste, the depletion of the world's natural resources, etc. – which had come about in the course of development. As Black notes:

<< Sustainable development was a new big idea. It brought environmentalism into poverty reduction and poverty reduction into environmentalism in a neat and simple formula. >> (p.94)

Millennium Development Goals

In 1990, the concepts of economic and social wellbeing, and sustainable development were brought together by the United Nations in eight Millennium development goals. These are outlined in Table 2.3 on p. 60.

Critique of the Millennium Development Goals

Although the Millennium Development Goals have been widely welcomed, there are some anxieties that they do not go far enough in demanding greater responsibility from those who govern developing nations. It is suggested that many of the problems discussed in this chapter have been brought about by poor governance by the elites of these developing nations who have engaged in corrupt practices and are more concerned with enriching themselves than improving the lives of their peoples. These critics argue that additional development criteria should be added to the UN's Millennium charter. These include:

- protecting human dignity through the introduction of basic human rights, e.g. the use of torture and imprisonment without trial should be banned
- the encouragement of religious tolerance and cultural maintenance, i.e. discrimination on religious and cultural grounds should be made illegal
- the freedom to participate in political affairs without fear of repression, especially the right to hold democratic, free elections.

The six recommendations of the Commission For Africa report (2005) do address some of the alleged shortcomings of the developing world. Whilst the Commission focuses on 'Investing in People' (and consequently on the need for better education, better healthcare, water and sanitation, poverty reduction, environment and climate change, as well as the need for more equitable trade conditions, more aid and debt relief), it also highlights the need for better self-governance by Africa's elites. It argues that lack of development has been caused partly by bad government policies, corruption and bureaucratic systems not open to scrutiny, as well as by military conflict that has resulted in the loss of millions of lives.

However, there are also concerns that both the Millennium Development Goals and the recommendations of the Commission for Africa reflect a desire to impose Western values and institutions on developing nations in order to persuade them that the **industrial–capitalist** development path is the best possible route to take to benefit their people. It is suggested that the real rationale behind these goals is not to bring about development but to ensure that the capitalist system continues to be dominated by the developed countries and that developing societies continue to be the source of cheap raw materials and labour markets, as well as being potential new consumer markets for Western goods.

Development or Westernization?

Western values, Western development

Kingsbury et al. (2004) suggest that the focus of the Millennium Development Goals on education and economic success highlights Western values and ways of thinking at the expense of traditional cultures, implying that the latter are deficient and have little to contribute to countries' development. This **ethnocentrism** fails to consider that Western values may have little cultural meaning in the developing world. For example, Western aid agencies often incorrectly assume that people who lack material possessions are in poverty and so are unhappy, and that men know more about the production of crops and technology than women do. Sahlins (1997) argues that people in the developing world may have few possessions but they are not poor. Poverty is a social status and, as such, it is the invention of Western civilization.

Table 2.3 Millennium Development Goals and progress towards them

Goal 1: to eradicate extreme poverty and hunger

In 2005, more than 1.4 billion people – 26 per cent of the developing world's population – lived in extreme poverty, i.e. on less than $1 a day. It is intended that the proportion of people suffering from absolute poverty and hunger should be halved by 2015, although the United Nations announced in 2008 that this target was unlikely to be met. Absolute poverty may have fallen to under 20 per cent in East Asia but in sub-Saharan Africa it has remained constant at around 50 per cent. Moreover, the UN reported in 2008 that about one quarter of all children in developing societies are suffering from malnutrition.

Goal 2: to achieve universal primary education

By 2005, most developing nations had made progress towards universal primary education, but it was estimated that 115 million children were still not in school. Some 862 million adults were estimated to be illiterate in the world in 2005. In the least developed nations, 44 per cent of their populations were illiterate in 2005. There was also a gender imbalance with regards to schooling and literacy: 53.3 per cent of females were illiterate compared with only 34.8 per cent of males, and 56 per cent of girls in the developing world are also not in school.

Goal 3: to promote gender equality & empower women

Progress towards this goal is measured by examining education, employment and political decision-making. In terms of education, females are less likely to have access to primary and secondary schooling, although progress has been made in most regions of the developing world except Southern Asia and sub-Saharan Africa. Women's access to secure paid employment, especially in sectors outside of agriculture, is still lower than men's in most of the developing world. For example, almost two-thirds of employed women in the developing world are in poorly paid and insecure paid jobs or are unpaid family workers.

Goal 4: to reduce child mortality

Each year, almost 11 million children die before the age of 5, i.e. 30 000 children a day. In some developing regions, child deaths have actually increased since 2000. However, deaths from measles fell from 750 000 in 2000 to less than 250 000 in 2006. About 80 per cent of children in developing countries now receive a measles vaccine.

Goal 5: to improve maternal health

Complications during pregnancy and childbirth are a leading cause of death and disability among women in developing countries – more than half a million women die every year and about 10 million suffer serious injuries. Most of this suffering is located in sub-Saharan Africa and Southern Asia. Most die in pregnancy and childbirth because developing countries still lack maternal healthcare systems. There is evidence that this goal is on track in most of the developing world except sub-Saharan Africa.

Goal 6: to combat HIV/AIDS, malaria and other diseases

AIDS has become the leading cause of premature death in sub-Saharan Africa and the fourth largest killer worldwide. At the end of 2004, it was estimated that 39.4 million people were living with HIV – nearly two-thirds of these live in sub-Saharan Africa. However, the number of deaths from AIDS fell from 2.2 million in 2005 to 2.0 million in 2007, and the number of people newly infected declined from 3.0 million in 2001 to 2.7 million in 2007. Malaria claims the lives of a million people a year, mostly young children. Tuberculosis is also making a comeback. However, the UN is optimistic that deaths from these diseases can be substantially reduced by 2015.

Goal 7: to ensure environmental sustainability

This goal focuses on reversing the loss of environmental resources, including forests, biological diversity and the earth's ozone layer, along with providing safe water, adequate sanitation and decent affordable housing for the world's poor. In 2008, the UN reported that some 1.6 billion people have gained access to safe drinking water since1990. However some 2.5 billion people, almost half the developing world's population, still live without improved sanitation and more than one-third of the growing urban population in developing countries live in slum conditions. The environmental record to date is mixed. The use of ozone-depleting substances has almost been eliminated and this has contributed to the effort to reduce global warming. However, carbon dioxide emissions have continued to increase.

Goal 8: to develop a global partnership for development

This is probably the most contentious goal because it involves developing nations committing themselves to addressing the human and social needs of their populations. The developed countries, in turn, have agreed to support poorer countries in achieving the previous seven goals through aid, more equitable trade relationships and debt relief. In 2005, several donor countries committed themselves to increasing their aid to the developing world, but overall the contribution of the developed world still falls far short of the amount needed to address the Millennium Goals effectively.

There has been some progress in terms of debt relief – in 2005, the major developed countries agreed to provide for the full cancellation of the $40 billion that 18 countries owed to the World Bank, the International Monetary Fund and the African Development Bank. This seems to have had some positive effect in that the share of developing countries' export earnings devoted to servicing external debt fell from 12.5 per cent in 2000 to 6.6 per cent in 2006. However, the UN ruefully noted in 2008 that developed countries' foreign aid expenditures declined for the second year running in 2007. Moreover, there are still concerns that the way world trade is organized benefits developed nations at the expense of developing nations, particularly with regard to the latter's access to technology and medicines.

This Western approach to development also fails to consider alternative models of development rooted in the religious beliefs of people in the developing world. One such alternative model of development is that adopted by Islamic societies such as Iran. Islamic societies often regard development as the need to apply Muslim principles to all aspects of their societies – government, law, education, art and so on – and as a result have adopted **fundamentalist** ways of life. Western secular values are rejected because they are seen as decadent and dangerous. However, as Said (2003) notes, Western commentators tend to regard the Islamic model of development as a product of irrational extremism and, as a result, relationships between the Islamic and Western worlds are, at best, tense.

Ironically, liberation from the consequences of Westernization, such as neo-colonialism and economic dependency on the West, is now seen by some sociologists in the developing countries as their ultimate development goal. In some countries, such as India, resistance to Western forms of development has resulted in protest movements based on violent separatist agendas, whilst globally, in recent years, we have seen a rise of an international new social movement based on a radical critique of the global capitalist economy and the Western institutions that underpin it.

Imposing Western-style democracy

The notion that developing societies should adopt Western-style **democracy** is also a contentious aspect of development. The emphasis on this up to the 1990s was very much a product of the ideological conflict between the free West and the Soviet Bloc – the Cold War. Western models of development generally tend to assume that democratic forms of development are more suitable than communist or **socialist** models of development – which are often dismissed as extremist and dangerous. There is evidence that Western governments and agencies, such as the World Bank and International Monetary Fund (IMF), distributed aid in the past on the condition that socialist/communist policies were jettisoned. In practice, this has meant that policies that have positive benefits for people in developing countries, such as collective farming cooperatives, land reform and welfare benefits, have been cut back or abandoned altogether because of the stringent political conditions attached to Western aid.

The experience of Cuba suggests that alternative socialist models of development can have positive benefits. Despite decades of enforced isolationism (the USA has imposed a trade embargo on Cuba that has made it extremely difficult for it to export its goods), Cuba has achieved literacy rates, infant-mortality rates and life expectancy comparable to those experienced in the West.

People-centred, local development

Korten (1995) argues that development strategies are too often in the hands of Western experts who fail to consult local people or take account of their local knowledge and skills. He argues that development needs to be more 'people-centred' and to focus on empowering local people

Focus on research

Defining and measuring happiness

'Happiness is inward, and not outward; and so, it does not depend on what we have, but on what we are.' So said Henry Van Dyke. A noble vision of a less materialistic world, some might say – but is it something that can be quantified?

People in the rugged and remote Asian country of Bhutan are busy trying to 'operationalize' a notion of true happiness that sounds a lot like Van Dyke's dream. One of the world's least-developed countries, Bhutan is worried about what globalization may bring, and it is determined to protect its unique culture. The country wants to safeguard its social values by entrenching them in terms that the wider world may understand and respect, that is to say, in quantifiable measures. By developing measures of progress that account properly for the country's social, cultural and environmental assets as well as its economic development, the country is following through on the 1972 declaration made by His Majesty King Jigme Singye Wangchuck: 'Gross National Happiness is more important than Gross National Product.'

Prime Minister Lyonpo Jigmi Y Thinley says: 'The four pillars of GNH are the promotion of equitable and sustainable socioeconomic development, preservation and promotion of cultural values, conservation of the natural environment, and establishment of good governance.' While these ideals are already ensconced in state policy, the Bhutanese government is increasingly interested in measuring and even quantifying its progress according to these values.

1 How would you quantify happiness?
2 What problems can you identify with regard to defining and measuring development?

to encourage them to take more responsibility for their community. Similarly, Amartya Sen (1987) argues that development needs to be about restoring or enhancing basic human capabilities and freedoms, giving people real choices and power over their daily situations.

A good example of this in recent years has been the success of 'microcredit'. This is the invention of Mohamed Yunus, a professor of economics at Dhaka University in Bangladesh who set up the Grameen Bank, which lends money in tiny amounts to landless women. These extremely poor women have no collateral and so are unable to borrow money from conventional banks. Yunus' enterprise has had considerable success: it has over 2.3 million borrowers and lends $35 million every month to fund over 500 types of economic activity. Some 98 per cent of loans are repaid. Similar banks have been set up successfully in over 50 developing countries. Microcredit has resulted in self-sufficiency, i.e. dependence on people's own resourcefulness and skill rather than dependency on Western aid agencies.

Influence of globalization

It is argued by some sociologists, such as Cohen and Kennedy, that development as a concept needs to redefined in the context of globalization, because culturally, socially, politically and economically, national and regional boundaries are less important than ever. As a result, we now have to consider definitions of development and 'consequently' the interrelationship between the developed and developing world within the context of global economics, culture and communications. This theme will be examined in depth in Topic 8.

'Post-development' school

Critics of Western models of development, such as Sachs (1992) and Esteva (1992), known as the 'post-development school', argue that development was always unjust, that it never worked and that it has now clearly failed. They suggest that development is a 'hoax' in that it was never designed to deal with humanitarian and environmental problems. Rather, it was simply a way of allowing the industrialized world, particularly the USA, to continue its dominance of the rest of the world. They point out that the poor have actually got poorer in the developing world, despite 40 years of development. As Black (2002) concludes:

<< Instead of creating a more equal world, five decades of 'development' have produced a

socioeconomic global apartheid: small archipelagos of wealth within and between nation-states, surrounded by impoverished humanity. >>

In contrast, Allen and Thomas (2001) acknowledge that development has not always succeeded but they challenge this post-development position. They point to the economic success of the Asian **tiger economies** and China. They also suggest that the evidence with regard to reductions in mortality and increases in literacy also support the view that development has, on balance, made a difference in the developing world.

So, what is 'development'?

The lesson to be learned from this topic is that the concept of development is about social change. However, we have seen that defining what form that social change should take is not an easy, straightforward process. There are now a number of models of development impacting on global inequality today; the United Nations' Millennium model; the Commission for Africa model; the Islamic model; the socialist/communist model; and the people-centred model. All have something to contribute to our understanding of global stratification.

Moreover, what is now increasingly recognized by development agencies is that these models of development may have to be individually tailored in order to reflect each country's individual circumstances whilst acknowledging the impact of global influences.

Check your understanding

1 Identify five key differences in the living standards of the developed and developing world.

2 Identify two reasons why the terms 'First World' and 'Third World' are now thought to be obsolete.

3 Why can Western models of development be seen as ethnocentric?

4 Identify three negative consequences of Western forms of development for people in the developing world.

5 Why are economic indices of development seen as unsatisfactory as measures of development?

6 What are the main characteristics of 'basic needs' development?

7 In addition to the industrial–capitalist model of development, what three alternative types of development are identified in this topic?

Activities

Research idea

Conduct a survey that investigates the general public's images and understanding of the developing world. You should ask questions about:

1 the origin of their images
2 what they think are the causes of problems in the developing world
3 how they see the developing world solving its problems
4 whether they consider the West, and especially the UK, makes a contribution in terms of causes and solutions.

What do your results tell you about which model of development the general public might subscribe to?

Web.task

The United Nations website contains detailed reviews of the Millennium Development goals. In addition, the United Nations Development Programme website: www.undp.org is particularly good and contains an impressive range of information about development projects being carried out by United Nations agencies across hundreds of countries.

Key terms

Absolute (or subsistence) poverty where an individual or family does not have enough food, clothing or shelter needed to sustain human life.

Cold War period of tension between communist countries (dominated by the then Soviet Union) and capitalist countries (dominated by the USA) between the 1950s and the fall of communism in the 1990s.

Communism a political system and set of beliefs that stresses shared ownership of property by the group or community.

Democracy a political system involving governments produced by the nation's people voting in free elections.

Ethnocentrism a set of beliefs, values, behaviours, etc. that lack objectivity in that they are based on the view that some cultures are superior whilst others are deficient.

Fundamentalism the belief, usually religious in origin, in the need to subscribe or return to traditional values and practices.

Homogeneous sharing the same or similar characteristics.

Industrial–capitalist the economic system of the West: this is based on an industrial mode of production (i.e. factory system) and is underpinned by unregulated (free-market) economic competition.

Non-governmental organizations (NGOs) organizations such as charities (e.g. Oxfam) that work independently of governments in the developing world.

Socialism general term applied to political systems where the state plays a major role in allocating resources.

Subsistence poverty see 'Absolute poverty'.

Tiger economies term used to describe fast-growing economies in south-east Asia.

They are sometimes called newly industrialized countries (NICs).

Transnational corporations (TNCs) global businesses that produce and market goods and brands across both the developed and developing worlds.

Urbanization the growth of cities.

Value judgements positive or negative statements about, for example, the behaviour of others, which are shaped by our own subjective experiences.

Value-laden bias in favour of a particular cultural point of view.

An eye on the exam — Defining development

Item A

Absolute poverty describes a situation in which people are barely existing, where the next meal may literally be a matter of life or death. The cumulative effect of malnutrition and starvation enfeebles all, particularly children, whose weakness gives them the tragic distinction of having the highest mortality rate for any group anywhere in the world. In these circumstances, poverty takes on an 'absolute' status since there is nothing beyond or 'beneath' it except death. Many in the developing world are close to this very vulnerable position, relying on aid, food relief or their own meagre returns from squatter farming, scavenging on refuse tips, prostitution, street hawking and so on. For such people, statistics about relative GNPs can have no meaning or worth.

GNP for selected countries, 1992 and 2006

Country	Per capita GNP (US$) 1992	Per capita GNP (US$) 2006
Japan	28 220	38 410
USA	23 120	44 970
Brazil	2770	4730
Nigeria	320	640
The Gambia	390	310

Source: World Development Report, 1992 & 2006

(a) Identify and briefly explain **three** criticisms of using Gross National Product (GNP) as a measure of development (**Item A**). (9 marks)

(b) Identify and briefly explain the usefulness of three non-economic measures of development. (9 marks)

Grade booster — Getting top marks in this question

For each of these questions, remember to make sure your three points are clearly different from and unconnected to each other. For example, don't state one point and then simply give its opposite or 'the other side of the same coin' as your next point. For question (a), read Item A carefully for any clues as to problems with using GNP as a measure of development. For question (b), avoid the trap of talking about other economic measures apart from GNP and stick to clearly non-economic measures.

TOPIC 2

Modernizing the world

It is very likely that you associated the image showing science and technology with the developed world. This is not surprising as you are probably aware that your rather comfortable standard of living (compared with that experienced by 17 year olds in developing societies) is underpinned by scientific discovery and constantly evolving technology. You are probably also aware, having seen countless images in the media, that parts of the developing world lack our taken-for-granted access to such technical support. It is easy to attribute this to poverty, but there are those who believe that it has more to do with beliefs, values and attitudes. In other words, aspects of the culture of developing worlds (such as religious beliefs) will, they argue, always prevent progress. As we shall see, there are those who strongly believe that it is not enough to inject aid in the form of money into the developing world, but that physical and material development can only come about if attitudinal development occurs as well. However, as the industrialized world piles increasing pressure on the environment, having the 'right' attitudes can come at a terribly expensive price.

Modernization theory

After World War II (1939–45), it became clear that many countries in Africa, Asia, Latin America and the Caribbean were remaining poor despite exposure to capitalism and the rational and scientific ways of thinking that underpinned this economic system. This observation was coupled with a concern among the leaders of wealthier countries that widespread poverty, encouraged by the strong mass appeal of communism, could lead to social unrest across the world – particularly in the ex-colonies of the European powers that had recently acquired their political independence. Crucially, such political instability was seen by US politicians as likely to limit the growth of the United States economy as communist ideology was anticapitalist and likely to impede US trade interests. In response to these potential developments, American economists, sociologists and policymakers developed the theory of modernization.

In terms of its sociological input, the roots of modernization theory lie in the work of the classical 19th-century sociologists, Durkheim and Tonnies, who both argued that societies evolve through predictable stages towards **modernity**. Durkheim (1893/1960), for example, saw traditional societies organized around what he called 'mechanical solidarity' (i.e. the sharing of similar beliefs and occupational roles and a strong sense of community) evolving into more complex societies organized around 'organic solidarity' (i.e. beliefs are less likely to be shared, roles are more likely to be specialized and **individualism** has replaced community). Tonnies (1887/1957) saw traditional societies based on 'gemeinschaft' (i.e.traditional community values reinforced by kinship and religion) giving way to modern societies based on 'gesellschaft' (i.e. community has been replaced by more rational, selfish, impersonal and superficial relationships). Sociologists who developed the modernization theory adopted this idea that societies progress through **evolutionary** stages. For example, Huntington (1993) describes modernization as an evolutionary process that brings about revolutionary change. In terms of international development, it is assumed that development should follow a similar evolutionary path as that taken by the industrialized nations of the developed world. Modernization theory made what McKay (2004) called the beguiling promise: by implementing the 'correct' policies, all nations, however poor, could achieve a modern standard of living by following exactly the same growth path as that pioneered by the Western nations.

Modernization theory, therefore, can be seen to have two major aims:

1 By focusing on the process of development, it attempts to explain why poorer countries have failed to develop. In particular, it has attempted to identify what economic and cultural conditions may be preventing a country from modernizing.

2 It aimed to provide an explicitly non-communist solution to poverty in the developing world by suggesting that economic change (in the form of capitalism) and the introduction and encouragement of particular cultural values could play a key role in bringing about modernization.

Before we begin to examine the mechanics of modernization theory, it is important to understand the profound influence this theory has had (and is still having) on the relationship between the developed and developing worlds. No other sociological theory can claim to match its influence on global affairs – not even Marxism which, of course, has steadily declined in credibility since the collapse of the Soviet Bloc in the early 1990s. Much of Western, especially American, foreign-aid policy is underpinned by the principles of modernization theory.

The process of development

Walt Rostow (1971) suggested that development should be seen as an evolutionary process in which countries progress up a development ladder of five stages. This model of development follows the pattern of development that the developed countries allegedly experienced between the 18th and 20th centuries.

- *Stage 1* – Rostow argued that at the bottom of this evolutionary ladder are traditional societies whose economies are dominated by subsistence farming (i.e. they produce crops in order to survive rather than to make profits). Consequently, such societies have little wealth to invest and thus have limited access to science, technology and industry. The LLEDCs are generally in this position today. Moreover, Rostow argued that in addition to these economic barriers to development, cultural barriers also exist in that people in traditional societies generally subscribe to traditional

values that impede modernization, e.g. religious values that stress **patriarchy** (thus preventing intelligent and skilled women from competing equally with men), **ascription** (being born into a particular position, role or trade, and consequently lacking the innovation to try new roles or ways of doing things), **particularism** (judging people and allocating them to tasks on the basis of **affective relationships** rather than what they are capable of or what they have achieved), fatalism (the view that things will never change, i.e. accepting one's lot) and **collectivism** (putting the social group before self-interest). Rostow saw traditional institutions such as the extended family, tribal systems, and religions as responsible for disseminating such values, and thus limiting the potential for social change.

- *Stage 2* – The preconditions for take-off – the stage in which Western values, practices and expertise can be introduced into the society to assist the take-off to modernization. This may take the form of science and technology to modernize agriculture, and infrastructure such as communications and transport systems, as well as the introduction of manufacturing industry. Investment by Western companies and aid from Western governments are, therefore, essential to this stage. These 'interventions' would produce economic growth and the investment required to act as the fuel for 'take-off'. As McKay notes: 'the image of take-off is particularly evocative, full of power and hope as the nation is able to launch itself into a bright new future'.

- *Stage 3* – This 'take-off' stage involves the society experiencing economic growth as these new modern practices become the norm. Profits are reinvested in new technology and infrastructure, and a new entrepreneurial and urbanized class emerges from the indigenous (native) population that is willing to take risks and invest in new industries. The country begins exporting manufactured goods to the developed world. This new wealth trickles down to the mass of the population as employment in these new industries grows, creating a demand for consumer goods as living standards rise.

- *Stage 4* – The drive to maturity involves continuing economic growth and reinvestment in both new technology and the infrastructure, i.e. particularly education, mass media and birth control. A modern, forward-thinking population takes advantage of the meritocratic opportunities available to them and, as a result, continues to benefit from ever-rising living standards. These economic benefits are reinforced through export earnings as the country strengthens its place in the international trade system.

- *Stage 5* – Finally, the society hits the ultimate stage of development – the age of high mass consumption or modernity – in which economic production and growth are at Western levels, and the majority of the population live in urban rather than rural areas, work in offices or in skilled factory jobs and enjoy a comfortable lifestyle organized around **conspicuous consumption**. Life expectancy is high and most citizens have access to a welfare state that includes healthcare and free education.

However, despite Rostow's influence on US foreign policy (he was a special adviser to the State department) and on how American aid was distributed to the developing world in the 1960s, major parts of the developing world, especially Africa and South Asia, remain desperately poor. Many of these societies have failed to progress beyond the traditional stage, despite huge injections of Western aid. Some modernization theorists have attempted to explain this persistent subsistence poverty by suggesting that cultural factors are more important than economic factors in explaining poverty in the developing world. It is argued that such countries have access to the capital and technology (via Western aid and expertise) needed to modernize but have failed to take advantage of these opportunities because of fundamental flaws in their cultural value systems.

Talcott Parsons (1964a) argued that such societies are often dominated by traditional values that act as obstacles to development. People are committed to customs, rituals and practices based firmly on past experience and consequently they are often fatalistic about their future. Inkeles (1969) noted that such people are unwilling to adjust to modern ideas and practices, i.e. to entertain the notion of social change.

Parsons was particularly critical of the extended kinship systems found in many traditional societies. He argued that these hinder **geographical** and social **mobility**, which he claimed is essential if a society is to industrialize quickly and effectively. They also encourage traditional values and norms such as ascription, particularism and collectivism which undermine modernity by discouraging individual incentive, achievement and, therefore, social change. Parsons argued that these societies needed to adopt the values that had propelled Western societies to economic success, such as **meritocracy** (i.e. rewarding effort, ability and skill on the basis of examinations and qualifications), **universalism** (applying the same standards to all members of society), individualism, competition and future orientation (i.e. seeing the future as full of possibilities). Parsons argued that the adoption of these values would lead to the emergence of an 'entrepreneurial spirit' among sections of the population, which would generate economic growth. Moreover, he argued that such societies should be strongly encouraged to replace traditional institutions, such as the extended family and political systems based on tribe, clan, caste or religion, with nuclear families and democratic political systems respectively. Parsons claimed that these traditional institutions stifled the individual initiative, free enterprise, geographical mobility and risk-taking necessary for societies to develop and modernize.

Modernization, education and social engineering

Modernization theorists, then, see the West as playing a crucial role in assisting and guiding the development of poorer countries. A number of **interventionist** 'motors' of development emanating from the West are thought to

Key themes

Stratification and differentiation

Influences on modernization theory

Modernization theory is very influenced by the functionalist theory of stratification in terms of both its explanation of global stratification and its solution to global inequalities. Parsons argued that modern societies were characterized by open social-class systems underpinned by universal meritocratic education systems, entrepreneurial values and both geographical and social mobility, whilst developing societies were characterized by closed, feudal-like systems underpinned by traditional values such as ascription and religious superstitions. Modernization theory argues that in order to develop, poorer countries need to modernize by adopting Western stratification systems that reward individualism and achievement measured by examinations and qualifications. Modernization theory, like functionalism, would argue that high rewards in the West are deserved because they reflect the more scientific measurement of achievement in contrast with unfair ascriptive practices found in the developing world.

be essential in bringing about the social organization and values necessary for development:

1   Rostow and others argued that traditional societies needed to encourage Western companies to invest in building factories and to train the local population in technical skills. Moreover, official aid programmes could supplement this process by paying for technical expertise and specialist equipment, as could borrowing from both the World Bank and the commercial banking sector. It was argued that the wages paid to the local labour force would '**trickle down**' and stimulate the economy of the developing nation by creating demand for manufactured goods.

2   Bert Hoselitz (1960) argued that the introduction of meritocratic education systems (paid for by official aid and borrowing) would speed up the spread of Western values such as universalism, individualism, competition and achievement measured by examinations and qualifications. These values are seen as essential to the production of an efficient, motivated, geographically mobile factory workforce. Similarly, Lerner (1958) argued that Western values could more effectively be transmitted to developing societies if the children of the political and economic elites of these countries were educated in Western schools, universities and military academies. It is suggested that these future leaders of the developing world could then disseminate Western values down to the mass of the population.

3   Inkeles (1969) argued that the mass media was a crucial agent in bringing about modernity because it rapidly diffused ideas about the need for geographically mobile, nuclear-family units, family planning, secular beliefs and practices and the adoption of the democratic process – all essential components of modern development.

4 Hoselitz (1960) argued that urbanization should be encouraged in the developing world because:

- it is easier to spread Western ideas and values amongst a concentrated city population than a thinly dispersed rural population
- in the city, the individual is free from the obligations and constraints found in rural areas
- cities have a cultural effect on the rest of society. Malcolm Cross (1979) notes that 'the city is the key entry point for Western values and ideas to undeveloped societies; the city is the nucleus for the cultural penetration of the modernizing society'.

Modernization theory believed that these motors of development would produce a new capitalist entrepreneurial middle-class who believed in change, and who were willing to take risks and therefore drive progress forward. As Timmons Roberts and Hite (2000) note:

<< in a traditional society, the entrepreneur is a social deviant because he is doing something new and different; in a modern society, change is routine, innovation is valued, and the entrepreneur esteemed. >>

Some general criticisms of modernization theory

Ethnocentrism

Some commentators claim that modernization theory is ethnocentric in four ways:

1 It implies that the traditional values and social institutions of the developing world have little value. Modernization theory clearly argues that Western forms of civilization are technically and morally superior and that the cultures of developing societies are deficient in important respects. Often such societies are defined as 'backward' if they insist on retaining some elements of traditional culture and belief and/or if they apply fundamentalist religious principles to the organization of their society.

This is certainly true of early modernization theorists such as Parsons but neo-modernization theory argues that capitalist culture can make use of traditions within societies in order to bring about modernization. Edwards (1992), for example, suggests that the economic success of the Asian tiger economies and China is due to a successful combination of the Chinese Confucian religion and Western rational thinking and practices. Religion in these societies has encouraged the emergence of a moral and authoritarian political leadership that demands sacrifice, obedience and hard work from its population in return for prosperity. This has paved the way for an acceptance of Western economic and cultural practices, such as widespread respect for meritocratic education for both men and women, discipline, and the acquisition of technical skills.

2 It ignores the 'crisis of modernism' in both the developed and developing worlds. In the developed world, there are problems such as inequalities in the distribution of wealth, poverty, homelessness, high rates of crime, drug abuse and suicide. In the developing world, poverty has not been eradicated and the resulting disillusion may lead to non-Western societies resisting modernization because they equate it with Western or American **cultural imperialism** or exploitation.

3 It reflects Western propaganda and ideology. Rostow's (1971) book was subtitled 'a non-communist manifesto' and in it he actually described communism as a disease. Malcolm Cross points out that Inkeles' modern man is essentially an individualized version of the **American Dream**. Western models of development generally tend to assume that democratic forms of development are more suitable than communist or socialist models of development – which are often dismissed as extremist and dangerous. There is evidence that the US government in the period 1960 to 1980 supported oppressive right-wing elites that had questionable human-rights records (especially in Central and South America, and in Iran and the Philippines), simply because such elites took an anti-communist stance. As mentioned in Topic 1, there is evidence too that Western governments and agencies such as the World Bank and International Monetary Fund (IMF) have distributed aid on the condition that socialist/communist policies were jettisoned.

However, in defence of modernization theory, one could argue that it rightly celebrates American capitalism as a success. It may be mainly interested in opening up new markets for its products, but it also genuinely believes that capitalism can bring benefits to the developing world.

4 Ethnocentric interpretations of development tend to exclude contributions from sociologists located in the developing world. Consequently, they neglect the notion that development needs to be **culture-specific** – i.e. that it needs to be adapted to the particular needs of particular societies, rather than being universally imposed in an homogeneous fashion. Carmen (1996) argues that modernization is a 'Trojan horse' because **acculturation** (i.e. the taking-over of indigenous cultures by Western culture) is 'at the heart of the development business'.

Modernization theory clearly sees development as a process initiated and implemented by outside forces. McKay (2004) suggests that this emphasis on the role of outside experts, the central role of aid and the stress on the introduction of Western values and institutions downgrades the role of local initiative and self-help. Carmen (1996) argues that such an approach is demeaning, dehumanizing and results in dangerous delusions because often the people of the developing world end up internalizing the myth that they are incapable and incompetent, and that they themselves are the problem. As Sankara (1988) notes, their minds end up being colonized with the notion that they should be dependent and should look to the West for direction. Galeano (1992) concludes 'they train you to be paralysed, then they sell you crutches'.

Questioning the benefits of education

It has been argued that education only benefits a small section of developing societies. There is evidence that educated elites monopolize top positions, restrict upward mobility and engage in human-rights abuses in their desire to hold onto power. **Neo-liberals**, such as Bauer, are particularly critical of governing elites in the developing world who, they argue, undermine development by acting as a '**kleptocracy**' (i.e. such elites are often self-seeking, interested only in lining their own pockets). They create vast inequalities in wealth through corruption and the siphoning-off of aid into their own bank accounts. Interestingly, the Commission for Africa report (2005) has also addressed this issue by suggesting that poor governance and corruption in Africa is partly to blame for the state Africa finds itself in today.

Ecological limits

Modernization also has **ecological** limits. The existing process of modernization cannot be extended to all societies because of the limits of the planet. For example, for all nations to enjoy similar standards of living would involve a six-fold increase in global consumption and result in unsustainable pollution. There are already signs in some developing societies that modernization is leading to environmental degradation. As Esteva and Austin (1987) note:

> << In Mexico, you must either be numb or very rich if you fail to notice that 'development' stinks. The damage to persons, the corruption of politics and the degradation of nature which until recently were only implicit in 'development' can now be seen, touched and smelled. >>

Social damage

There is evidence that Western models of development create problems for the populations of developing societies. For example, indigenous peoples have been forcibly removed from their homelands, aggressive advertising and marketing have created **false** (and ultimately harmful) **needs** such as smoking cigarettes, grave environmental damage has been done to rainforests and child labour has been exploited – all in the name of progress towards the industrial–capitalist model of development. Marxist and post-development sociologists refer to this process as **underdevelopment** and suggest that development strategies are essentially aimed at maintaining exploitative practices, such as ensuring cheap labour for transnational corporations and new markets for Western products. Development, therefore, may not be positive progress if it means increasing social and economic divisions and inequalities within a country.

How societies develop

Cross (1979) argues that modernization theory assumes that all societies will advance in the same way through a fixed set of changes. However, this can be challenged in two main ways.

Diversity of societies

There is no reason to assume that traditional societies share the same features or that capitalism will mould societies in the same fashion. The evidence suggests that there exists a diversity of both traditional and capitalist societies. Modernization theory has been slow to understand that value systems and institutions tend to be culture specific. For example, Ethiopia and Somalia are neighbouring countries, but their cultures are quite different from one another and they each require different development programmes.

Western domination

Traditional societies cannot develop in the same way as modern Western societies because they exist within a global economy dominated by Western interests. For example, it may not be in the industrialized world's interest to let poorer countries develop manufacturing industry that may compete with their own.

Marxist commentators have pointed out that developing nations cannot follow the same path as the developed world because the world has dramatically changed. The developing countries do not have an equal relationship with the rich and powerful developed economies. As McKay (2004) notes, the rules of global trade are rigged in favour of Western businesses and banks, and the governments of developed countries have the power to erect trade barriers, by imposing tariffs and quotas, to prevent developing countries competing with their own industries. In fact, Marxists such as Andre Gunder Frank (1971) have gone as far as insisting that the lack of development that we see in the developing world today is the direct result of the development of the West. This theme will be explored in more detail in Topic 3.

The postmodernist critique of modernization theory completely dismisses the assumption that the developing world is homogeneous and undifferentiated. They argue that the development path of a society and its choices in regards to development goals are historically conditioned and shaped by a web of power relations. Postmodernists see the process of development as a discourse shaped by disparities in power between the developed world and the developing world. This dominant discourse is **paternalistic** in that the developed world is treated 'as a child in great

---

Key themes

Crime and deviance

Deviant cultures

Modernization theory strongly implies that developing nations subscribe to traditional values that are 'deviant' because they inhibit progress towards modernity. The dominance of modernization theory in development studies and practices has meant that development models other than those based on Western lines, e.g. communist/socialist or Islamic, are often perceived as 'deviant' and hence are also often dismissed as extremist or somehow backward. A good example of this is Rostow's reference to communism as a 'disease'.

need of guidance' whilst the poor are seen as a problem to be solved by Western experts and aid. Postmodernists such as Escobar (1995) argue that the aim of development should be to escape from this trap and 'to reflect the real needs and goals' of the poor, although it is unclear how this should be achieved. Other postmodernist thinkers have focused on the modernist concept of 'progress' and suggested that this needs to be replaced with a greater sense of pessimism or an acknowledgement that the world and, therefore, development paths involve more risk than in the past.

The influence of modernization theory today

Despite these **empirical** and theoretical problems, modernization theory still exerts a considerable influence, especially on the policies of organizations such as the United Nations, the World Bank and the International Monetary Fund which 'lead' and finance much of the world's development initiatives and programmes. This is because, despite all the criticisms thrown in the direction of modernization theory, industrial–capitalist democracies are regarded as generally successful societies because they have raised the standard of life of the majority of their citizens. Subsistence poverty has been almost totally eradicated in the developed world.

The 'people first' aid policies of non-governmental agencies (which aim to help the rural poor by helping them take control of agricultural projects through training and education) are still based on the quite distinct modernization principle of 'intervention'. As Burkey (1993) notes 'the poor are seldom able to initiate a self-reliant development process without outside stimulation. An external agent must therefore be the catalyst'. Critics of this modernization approach are keen to describe it as paternalistic but they very rarely offer alternatives that are not idealistic in their view of what the poor can achieve on their own.

Neo-liberal theories

Neo-liberal theories of development, dominant in the 1990s, were strongly influenced by aspects of modernization theory. This movement gained great confidence from the collapse of communism and reasserted many aspects of modernization theory. In particular, it portrayed development as involving a straightforward path towards modernity. This depended on developing societies recognizing that traditional cultural systems (especially the system of obligations found in traditional kinship systems) impede the proper working of the free-market economy, which neo-liberals claimed could deliver the benefits of development more effectively than economies that were centrally planned or characterized by government intervention. They argued that government interference in the economy should be kept to a minimum. This idea was particularly influential in the International Monetary Fund, which often lent money to developing countries in the 1990s on the condition that

Focus on research

Inglehart and Baker (2000)
Modernization and cultural change

The assumption that cultural ideas can initiate economic growth is challenged by empirical evidence collected by Inglehart and Baker (2000) based on a study of 61 pre-industrial societies. They found that all the pre-industrial societies for which they had data placed a strong emphasis on: religion, male dominance in economic and political life, deference to parental authority and traditional gender roles, and the importance of family life. Such societies were also authoritarian, found cultural diversity threatening and were generally opposed to social change. Advanced industrial societies tended to have the opposite characteristics. However, Inglehart and Baker's data suggests that such cultural characteristics were the product of economic insecurity and low levels of material wellbeing rather than the cause of it. Culture therefore may be less important than differential access to scarce resources.

Inglehart, R. and Baker, W. (2000) 'Modernization, cultural change, and the persistence of traditional values', *American Sociological Review*, 65(1), February, pp. 19–21

Explain how Inglehart and Baker reach the conclusion described in the final sentence above.

government spending, particularly on social projects such as health, education and welfare, be cut back.

However, some neo-liberals, such as Bauer (1981), have taken this perspective into areas that challenge some of modernization theory's approaches to poverty reduction. For example, Bauer argues that foreign aid has not only encouraged the greed of the kleptocracy, who have largely controlled its 'distribution', but it has also stifled the free market – for example, food aid, in particular, often brings down local prices and makes it difficult for local producers to get a fair price for their products. These ideas will be further explored in Topic 4.

Neo-modernization, culture and conflict

The work of the neo-modernization theorist, Samuel Huntington (1993) has been very influential in recent years. He strongly affirms the importance of culture as the primary variable for both development and the conflict generated by that development. He asserts that the world is divided into eight major 'cultural zones' based on cultural differences that have persisted for centuries. These zones were shaped by religious traditions that are still powerful today, despite the forces of modernization. The zones are Western Christianity, the Orthodox world, the Islamic world, and the Confucian, Japanese, Hindu, African, and Latin American zones.

Huntington sees future world confrontations and conflicts developing between these cultural zones. He suggests that the roots of this conflict lie in the exceptional values and institutions of the West that have brought it economic success and that are lacking in the rest of the world. Huntington argues that non-Western civilizations resent this success and what they see as the West's attempts to impose its version of modernity upon them through control of institutions like the United Nations and the World Bank. Huntington concludes that resistance to Western forms of modernization are now more likely to provoke a return to fundamentalism in the Arab world and the sponsorship of international terrorism against Western interests and targets. Huntington's ideas seem particularly significant in the USA after the events of 11 September 2001.

American policy in Afghanistan and Iraq, and the 'war on terror' can be seen as a direct response to the conflict that Huntington identifies. 'Nation-building' in Iraq and Afghanistan focuses on a central aspect of modernization theory, i.e. the export of American values, particularly democracy, free trade and women's rights, in order to break the hold of what the Americans see as the tyrannical power of religion and tradition – which they view as the main cause of poverty, inequality and inhumanity in this part of the world. This view, of course, neglects the Islamic view that poverty and inequality are in fact caused by US economic and cultural imperialism – the very 'modernist' culture that the Americans are attempting to introduce in Iraq and Afghanistan.

The contribution of modernization theory

Early modernization theory can rightly be criticized for dismissing the culture of the developing world as irrelevant. However, it is often too easy and 'politically correct' to blame the problems of developing societies on colonialism, world trade, debt, global capitalism, etc. These factors are important, but modernization theory has probably been right (and certainly unpopular) in insisting that in order to reduce poverty, we need to understand culture or at least take it into account when assessing development progress. This once deeply unpopular view is again in fashion with some postmodernist accounts of development suggesting that culture is, and always has been, more important than economics in encouraging social change.

Check your understanding

1   What are the two major aims of modernization theory?

2   What are the economic characteristics of traditional, undeveloped societies according to Rostow?

3   Identify four cultural values or institutions that allegedly hold up development.

4   How are geographical mobility, kinship systems and modernization interconnected?

5   What is the role of aid in development?

6   How might the introduction of education systems help accelerate modernization?

7   Why does modernization theory regard both the mass media and urbanization as essential components of modernization?

8   Explain what is meant by the two meanings of 'crisis of modernism' in terms of their critique of modernization theory.

9   Why is modernization theory criticized for being ideological?

10 How do Inglehart and Baker challenge modernization theory?

11 What influence does modernization theory have today?

12 Why is there conflict between the West and the Islamic world, according to Huntington?

Activities

Research idea

Think about your own experience of modern society. Make a list of 'traditional' values and 'modern' values, and turn them into a list of statements that people can either agree or disagree with. Follow this up with a mini-survey of your friends and family to see how many of them subscribe to the traditional values that are so disapproved of by some modernization theorists.

Web.task

Visit **www.worldbank.org** – the World Bank website – and using the search facility, look for policy statements or documents that focus on culture, poverty, population growth, education, etc. What aspects of World Bank policy endorse the view that it supports an industrial–capitalist or modernization model of development?

Key terms

Acculturation the taking-over of indigenous cultures by Western culture.

Affective relationships relationships based on love.

American Dream a set of ideas associated with the USA suggesting that if you work hard, you can succeed regardless of your social background.

Ascription the occupying of jobs, authority within the family and political roles on the basis of inheritance or fixed characteristics such as gender and race.

Collectivism the notion that members of the family/tribal unit put the interests of the group before self-interest.

Conspicuous consumption consuming goods for status reasons, e.g. wearing designer labels.

Cultural imperialism global dominance of American culture such as McDonalds and Disney.

Culture-specific relevant to a particular culture.

Ecological concerned with the environment.

Empirical based on first-hand research.

Evolutionary gradual change or progress that is the result of natural accumulation.

False needs the outcome of intensive advertising that persuades people that a particular consumer item is vital to their social wellbeing despite it being potentially harmful in the long term.

Geographical mobility being able to move around the country easily to meet economic demands for particular skills.

Individualism the notion that individual self-interest should come before the interests of the group.

Interventionist believing in the need to take an active role to change a situation.

Kleptocracy corrupt elites in the developing world who defraud their own people by pocketing aid, taking bribes, etc.

Meritocracy system that rewards people on the basis of merit, i.e. intelligence, effort, ability, qualifications, and so on.

Modernity the state of being modern or fully developed.

Neo-liberal the view that the free market is the best way of organizing societies; against government intervention in society.

Particularism loving someone or treating someone in a certain way on the basis of them being a member of your family regardless of their level of achievement outside the family group.

Paternalistic patronizing. Not believing others are capable on their own.

Patriarchy system of male domination.

Trickle down view that wealth will 'drip' down to benefit the less well-off.

Underdevelopment term used to describe the process whereby capitalist countries have distorted and manipulated the progress of less-developed countries to their own advantage.

Universalism the idea that occupational roles be allocated on the basis of universal norms, such as achievement measured by examinations and qualifications.

An eye on the exam — Modernizing the world

Item A

According to the modernization theorist, J.A. Kahl, 'modern man' experiences a relatively low degree of contact with extended family, a high level of individualism and contact with the mass media, and a pronounced interest in urban living. 'Modern man' is stimulated by the city and urban life – 'he sees it as open to influence by ordinary citizens like himself' and he sees society as a meritocracy. Modern man reads newspapers, listens to the radio and discusses civil affairs. Kahl concludes that the more modern one's men, the more likely a society is to develop and modernize, i.e. to become like the United States.

Using material from **Item A** and elsewhere, assess the usefulness of modernization theory as an explanation for differences in the levels of development of different societies. (18 marks)

Grade booster — Getting top marks in this question

For this question, you should outline the main features of modernization theory, including aspects such as Rostow's five evolutionary stages of development, Parsons' idea of a change from traditional to modern values and institutions (such as the nuclear rather than the extended family), and the role of institutions such as the education system and the mass media in spreading 'modern' values such as meritocracy and individualism in less-developed countries. Note also the positive role assigned by modernization theory to Western investment in stimulating modernization in these countries. Remember that you need to make use of relevant information from Item A in your answer. You also need to discuss some of the criticisms of modernization theory, such as its ethnocentric assumptions about the superiority of the West as the only model of development, ecological criticisms, and so on.

Underdevelopment and dependency

Getting you **thinking**

What do you think the cartoon symbolizes about the relationship between the developed and developing worlds?

The message from the cartoon is clear: the wealthy nations of the world got rich on the backs of the poorer nations, who are still being exploited today and keeping the West's 'lavish' life style going. This is essentially the message of the Marxist-based 'dependency theory'.

The Marxist economist-sociologist, Andre Gunder Frank provided the major critique of the principles underlying modernization theory. Frank (1971) argued that developing countries have found it difficult to sustain development along modernization lines (see Topic 2) – not because of their own deficiencies, but because the developed West has deliberately and systematically underdeveloped them in a variety of ways, leaving them today in a state of **dependency**. Hence, Frank's theory is known as dependency theory.

The world capitalist system

Frank argued that since the 16th century, there has existed a world capitalist system organized in a similar fashion to the unequal and exploitative economic or class relationships that make up capitalist societies. This world capitalist system is organized as an interlocking chain

consisting of **metropolis** or **core nations** (i.e. the developed world) that benefit from the economic surplus of **satellite** or **peripheral countries** (i.e. the developing world). These peripheral countries:

<< *have low wages, enforced by coercive regimes that undermine independent labour unions and social movements. The metropolis exploits them for cheap labour, cheap minerals and fertile tropical soils.* >> (p.12)

This results in the accumulation of wealth in the developed world, and in stagnation and destitution in the developing world.

For dependency theory, then, underdevelopment in the periphery is the product of development in the centre. In turn, the elites of the developing world living in their own urban metropolis (i.e. cities) and sponsored by the core countries exploit those living in rural regions or the periphery of their own countries. Foster-Carter (1985) suggests that the ultimate satellite is a landless rural labourer, who has nothing and no one to exploit and is probably female.

The origins of dependency

Slavery

Frank argued that dependency and underdevelopment were established through slavery and **colonialism**, both of which helped kick-start Britain's industrial revolution. Over a 200-year period (1650 to 1850), the triangular slave trade (see Fig. 2.2) shipped approximately nine million Africans aged between 15 and 35 across the Atlantic to work as an exceptionally cheap form of labour on cotton, sugar and tobacco plantations in America and the West Indies, owned mainly by British settlers. This generated tremendous profits for both the British slave-traders and the plantation owners. Britain also enjoyed a virtual monopoly over raw materials such as cotton, tobacco and sugar, which benefited industrial expansion such as that found in the Lancashire/Yorkshire textile industry.

Colonialism

Colonialism locked much of Africa, Asia and Latin America even further into an exploitative relationship with the capitalist West. During the period 1650 to 1900, using their superior naval and military technology, European powers, with Britain at the fore, were able to conquer and colonize many parts of the world. As Harrison (1990) argues, this **imperial** expansion was to work the greatest transformation the human world has ever seen. The

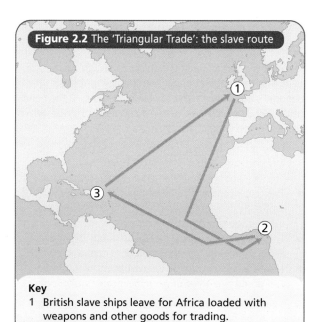

Figure 2.2 The 'Triangular Trade': the slave route

Key
1 British slave ships leave for Africa loaded with weapons and other goods for trading.
2 Goods are exchanged for slaves.
3 Slaves are exchanged for Caribbean produce and ships return to England.

principal result of this European rule was the creation of a global economy. Consequently, colonialism had a number of effects that benefited the world capitalist system:

- Colonies were primarily exploited for their cheap food, raw materials and labour.
- The most fertile land was appropriated for growing cash crops for export to the West.
- New markets were created for the industrial world's manufactured goods.
- Local industries, especially manufacturing, that attempted to compete with those of the colonial powers, were either destroyed or undermined by cheap imported manufactured goods from the West.
- Divisions and conflicts were created or reinforced between indigenous peoples as the colonial powers sponsored some tribes and social groups, giving them wealth and power as a reward for acting as their agents of social control.
- Arbitrary borders were imposed on countries (especially in Africa), which are partially the cause of civil wars and refugee problems today.

Contemporary forms of dependency: neo-colonialism

Many colonies have achieved political independence today, but dependency theory argues that their exploitation continues via **neo-colonialism**. Frank (1971) noted that new forms of colonialism have appeared that are more subtle but as equally destructive as slavery and colonialism.

Neo-colonial exploitation and world trade

World trade is one aspect of neo-colonialism. Despite political independence, the legacy of colonialism means

that the economies of developing countries are dependent for their export earnings upon a small number of commodities, i.e. agricultural cash crops or raw materials. This overconcentration on **primary products** (often a single commodity) was the result of the way that colonial powers reorganized societies after conquest in order to produce one or two particular crops or materials required by their industries. It is estimated that out of roughly 2.5 billion people engaged in agriculture in developing countries, about 1 billion receive most of their income from exports of agricultural or mineral commodities. Out of the 141 developing countries, 95 depend on commodities for at least 50 per cent of their export earnings. Approximately two-thirds of African countries derive over 80 per cent of their export earnings from one or two commodities (see Table 2.4)

- Overproduction of the primary products, or any fall in demand caused by variation in Western tastes and lifestyles, can have a severe negative effect upon their economies. This situation is made worse by the fact that their markets often consist of only a few metropolitan countries rather than many – with the main one usually being the colonial mother country. Recently, the prices of some commodities – copper, aluminium, rubber and soya beans – have risen because of soaring demand from China. China now accounts for over 15 per cent of global imports of these commodities. However, if China's economy cools, commodity prices would plummet across the board, and have a severe negative effect on the economies of many developing nations.
- Raw materials in themselves have little value. It is the processing of those raw materials into manufactured goods that adds value in terms of the costs charged to the consumer. This processing mainly occurs in Western factories and consequently it is the West that reaps the benefit. For example, we can clearly see this process with regard to cocoa and chocolate. A bar of chocolate that costs £1 in the UK will see about 77 pence going to the manufacturer, 15 pence going to the government in the form of tax and only 8 pence going to the cocoa farmer.

Table 2.4 Examples of countries reliant on a limited range of commodities in their exports, 2002

Country	Type of produce	Named produce as % of agricultural exports
Ethiopia	Coffee	75.0
Malawi	Tobacco, tea	70.0
Uganda	Coffee	63.0
Rwanda	Coffee	68.0
Zambia	Copper	61.0
Mali	Cotton	72.7

Source: Brown, O. and Gibson, J. (2006) *Boom or Bust: Developing countries' rough ride on the commodity price rollercoaster*, Winnipeg, Canada: International Institute for Sustainable Development

- Western nations can limit the amount of goods, especially manufactured goods, imported from the developing world by imposing **tariffs** (a type of import tax that results in the goods becoming more expensive than home-produced goods) and quotas. Moreover, the West can affect commodity-dependent developing societies by breaking trade agreements. Export dumping also undermines the value of exports. Developed countries may heavily subsidize a home industry that exports the product to the developing country at prices lower than the cost of production in the recipient country. This, in turn, drives prices down as local producers try to compete with the cheap imports. Food aid may also have this effect because it demotivates local farmers.
- Sometimes, the value and price of a commodity is totally out of the hands of the producer country and is set by commodity speculators located in Western organizations, such as the London Metal Exchange. In 2006, it was estimated by the bank Merrill Lynch that commodities were trading at prices 50 per cent higher than they would have been without speculators. Any fluctuation in the world's money or credit market may end up bursting this financial bubble.
- Western inflation means that, over the past 30 years, the prices of manufactured goods produced by the West have risen rapidly whilst the prices of the primary products mainly produced by the developing world have actually fallen. Hayter (1981) notes that cash crops are 'false riches' because countries have to produce more and more of them to get the same amount of manufactured goods in return. In 1960, the earnings from 25 tons of natural rubber would buy four tractors, but today it is not enough to buy one. As Hayter notes, 'in their desperate search for foreign exchange, underdeveloped countries produce more and more, thus setting up a vicious circle of overproduction and declining prices'.
- The money earned by the export of primary commodities can also be severely undermined by natural disasters, political instability and military conflict.

Commodity dependence and local elites

The exploitation of this export-orientated primary production found in developing countries is often made easier by a class alliance between the agents of the developed world, i.e. the transnational companies and the local landed elite. The power and economic interests of the latter often derived from colonialism. As Hoogvelt (2001) notes, their 'economic interests became increasingly intertwined with those of the advanced capitalist states, and their cultural lifestyles and tastes were a faithful imitation of the same'. Cardoso (1972) points out that these elites paved the way for the penetration of transnational companies into developing countries on favourable terms for Western capitalism (see Topic 8) and economically benefited themselves from the related trade and banking arrangements. In some extreme cases, these elites, often military in origin, have even removed threats to foreign interests by violence, while their repressive powers (their control of police and military) serve to assure the cooperation of the masses.

Neo-colonialism; transnational exploitation

In 1994, the World Trade Organization (WTO) was set up by the rich and powerful nations in order to reduce national trade barriers and to liberalize trade. At the heart of the WTO are the transnational companies (TNCs), which share the following characteristics:

- They usually operate in more than one country and have no clear home or national base. They therefore produce and market in a genuinely international sense.
- They seek competitive advantage and maximization of profits by constantly searching for the cheapest and most efficient production locations.
- They have geographical flexibility in that they can easily shift resources and operations across the world.
- They are responsible for three-quarters of world trade and about one-third of all global economic output.

A league table of the world's top 100 most important economic units would show that half are nation-states and half are TNCs. Approximately 130 nation-states (mainly in the developing world) have economies smaller than the top 50 TNCs. It is argued by neo-Marxists that TNCs exercise power without responsibility. Bakan (2004) refers to transnational corporations as 'institutional psychopaths', and notes that they are programmed to exploit and dehumanize people for profit. TNCs have been accused of acting immorally and illegally in their pursuit of profit in the following respects:

- Shell in Nigeria and RTZ in Angola have exploited natural resources with ruthlessness and indifference. Indigenous people have had their land forcibly seized and, despite international protests, have been removed at gunpoint from their homelands by local elites working on behalf of these TNCs.
- The sweatshop conditions of transnational factories in developing countries have been criticized, especially for their use of child labour and exploitative rates of pay. British chain stores such as Primark and Matalan have been accused of keeping their prices low because of these exploitative practices.
- TNCs have been responsible for ecological damage in countries like Nigeria. In 2003, Coca-Cola was accused of putting thousands of farmers out of work in the Indian state of Kerala by draining up to one million litres of water, which normally feeds the farmers' wells, in order to produce the soft drink for the Indian market.
- TNCs have refused to take responsibility for the welfare of local people killed or injured by their factories and plants. The explosion at Bhopal in India at the Union Carbide plant killed 2800 people and injured 28 000 people in 1984. The company has not paid a cent in compensation.
- TNCs have influenced tastes and consumption patterns in the developing world in negative ways. For example, Nestlé has been criticized for its aggressive marketing of baby-milk powder in areas without easy access to clean water. Other TNCs have been criticized for their marketing of high-tar cigarettes, drugs and pesticides;

many of the latter have been banned in the West for being dangerous to health.

- There is evidence that TNCs have interfered in the internal politics of developing countries and have even financed military coups in developing countries against political leaders they don't like. The military coup against the democratically elected socialist president of Chile, Salvador Allende in the early 1970s, was sponsored by American multinational companies unhappy at his nationalization of the copper industry. In 2003, an international boycott of Coca-Cola products was launched by the trade union movement in protest at the company's alleged use of illegal paramilitary groups to intimidate, threaten and kill those of its workers who wished to set up a trade union at its bottling plant in Colombia.

Transnational exploitation of the resources and labour of developing societies, then, is seen by dependency theorists as a crucial aspect of neo-colonial power.

Neo-colonialism, aid and debt

Dependency theory argues that official aid and the international debt crisis that has stemmed from borrowing money from Western governments and multilateral organizations such as the World Bank and IMF is the third major component of neo-colonialist exploitation. This will be examined in detail in Topic 4.

Solutions to dependency

Timmons Roberts and Hite (2000) argue that there are two sets of views when it comes to ideas for fixing these situations of dependency.

1   Breaking away from dependency

The first view argues that 'underdevelopment is not a phase but a permanent, inescapable position. In other words, the only way this situation of dependency can be escaped is to escape from the entire capitalist system' (p.13). Frank's theory of dependency suggests that the peripheral or satellite countries can never develop in a sustained way so long as they are stuck in what Paul Baran (1957) calls an 'imperialist' stage of capitalism and remain part of the world capitalist system.

One solution is 'isolation' as in the example of China (although even that country is now adopting capitalist free-market principles and trading extensively with the West). Another solution is to 'break away' at a time when the core or 'metropolis' country is weak, as in times of war or recession. This may involve a socialist revolution in order to overthrow the local elite – as in Cuba in the early 1960s. However, Frank was pessimistic about this and believes that, sooner or later, the global capitalist economy will reassert its control through denying the rogue country access to free world trade, applying sanctions to countries that attempt to trade with it and through the threat of military force. This has been Cuba's experience for the past 40 years.

Key themes

Stratification and differentiation

Marxism and dependency theory

Dependency theory is a Marxist theory of stratification and consequently it is concerned with the exploitation of a less powerful poor majority (the developing nations) by a more powerful wealthy minority (the capitalist nations of the West). Wallerstein's world systems theory can be seen as a global version of the relationship between bourgeoisie and proletariat that Marxists see as the major characteristic of capitalism. Wallerstein notes that the core capitalist nations are the global bourgeoisie, who are engaged in the exploitation of peripheral nations (or the global proletariat) in a modern world capitalist system. Marxists argue that capitalist exploitation has acquired a global character – the labour-power of factory and service workers in the West and factory/sweatshop workers and peasants in the developing world is equally exploited.

2   Associate or dependent development

The second view argues that despite dependency, there is some scope for what has been called 'associate development' or 'dependent development' through nationalist economic policies such as Import Substitution Industrialization (ISI). ISI involved industrialization aimed at producing consumer goods that would normally be imported from the developed world. ISI transformed the economies of South America, as Green illustrates (quoted in Hoogvelt (2001), p.243):

>> By the early 1960s domestic industry supplied 95 per cent of Mexico's and 98 per cent of Brazil's consumer goods. From 1950 to 1980 Latin America's industrial output went up six times. >>

However, ISI eventually failed for the following reasons:

- It neglected to address the issue of class and income distribution – that is, the existing elites controlled ISI and this led to further deepening of income and wealth inequalities in these societies.
- It was still dependent on the West for technical expertise, spare parts, oil, etc.
- The export-orientated form of industrialization adopted by the Asian tiger economies was seen as more successful.

Despite these difficulties in coming up with realistic solutions, Hoogvelt argues that the influence of dependency theory on the political ideologies of many developing countries in the 1960s and 1970s shouldn't be underestimated. She notes that political leaders, particularly in Africa, used the principles of dependency theory to argue for development as liberation from Western exploitation. Political and social movements in Africa in this period consequently stressed nationalism, self-reliance and delinking as a means of countering neo-colonialism.

Elliot and Harvey (2000)
Jamaica's plantation economy

A case study of Jamaica carried out by Elliott and Harvey (2000) supports the work of Frank. They conclude that Jamaica's development problems will never be solved by policies that ignore the vast inequalities in power arising from Jamaica's political, social and economic history. They suggest that the root of Jamaica's contemporary problems lie in the creation of the plantation economy by the British, which resulted in vast inequalities in ownership of land that persist to this day. Today, the Jamaican economy continues to serve the needs of the Jamaican ruling class rather than those of the masses.

Elliott, D.R. and Harvey, J.T. (2000) 'Jamaica: An Institutionalist perspective', *Journal of Economic Issues*, June, pp. 393–401

In what ways does Elliott and Harvey's study support the work of Frank?

Criticisms of dependency theory

A number of criticisms have been made of dependency theory.

1   Defining 'dependency'

Frank's biggest problem was that he failed to be precise in his use of terms. 'Dependency' is extremely difficult to operationalize and, therefore, test or measure empirically. Some sociologists, such as Myrdal (1968), have attempted to measure the amount of investment put into the developing world and compare it with the amount of profit taken out. However, it is generally agreed that this is a crude and imprecise method that does not necessarily measure dependency, exploitation and subordination. Similarly, it is unclear how and why Frank categorized particular societies as part of the 'metropolis' or as 'satellites'. Moreover, Frank paints the relationship between the metropolis and satellite as always negative, but some commentators have suggested this is oversimplistic. For example, it could be

argued that Canada and Taiwan are satellites of the USA because both are very dependent upon US trade. However, it is doubtful whether these relationships are exploitative. The health of the US economy depends on maintaining positive trade relationships with both countries. In other words, the interconnectedness of the global economy means that capitalist economies are often interdependent, i.e. the USA needs Canada and Taiwan as much as they need the USA.

2   Benefits to developing nations

Clearly, modernization theory would argue that Western aid and transnational corporations do bring benefits to developing nations. For example, the economic success of the Asian Tigers can be partly attributed to the role of Japanese aid and transnational investment. However, in reply, neo-Marxists point out that these societies are heavily in debt, while their industrial base is largely controlled by Japanese TNCs. Their economies have also demonstrated instability in recent years, as the Japanese economy has faltered and foreign investment has been withdrawn. In 1997, Thailand, Indonesia and South Korea had to accept Western rescue packages. Moreover, the economic success of these economies is founded on people working very long hours for very low wages. Economic growth may have been rapid but it has only benefited the top 10 per cent of these societies.

3   Role of homegrown elites

The issue of homegrown elites, however, is another aspect of exploitation not seriously addressed by dependency theory. Frank ignored the fact that Western exploitation of developing nations has often occurred with the connivance of the elites of the developing world. Such elites played a crucial role in slavery and colonialism, while today, many of them sit on the boards of the transnational companies that have invested in their countries and they have taken financial advantage of the huge sums of money being injected into their countries via aid. As the Commission for Africa (2005) notes, poor governance and corruption by this elite kleptocracy is partly responsible for the poor condition of many African countries today.

4   Creation of infrastructure

John Goldthorpe (1975) and other liberals have argued that colonialism had the positive benefits of providing developing countries with a basic infrastructure. Moreover, it provided people with wage-labour and made more efficient use of land. He also points out that those countries without colonies (such as Germany and Japan) have performed economically better than those with empires, whilst countries such as Afghanistan and Ethiopia, which were never colonized, face severe problems of development because they lack the infrastructure provided by the colonial powers.

5   Different levels of exploitation

Timmons Roberts and Hite (2000) note that Frank's version of dependency theory fails to explain why there appear to be greater levels of exploitation over time or why there are significant differences among poorer countries. Later dependency theorists, such as Gereffi (1994) and Evans (1979), have addressed these issues by noting that the influence of the core is not always homogeneous and that differences among elites in the periphery can explain different political regimes, economies and class relationships within the peripheral countries.

World systems theory

Some sociologists, notably Chase-Dunn (1975) and Gereffi (1994), argue that the overly descriptive nature of dependency theory means that it does not have much explanatory power. These sociologists subscribe instead to a variation on dependency theory called **world systems theory**, which was a response to criticisms of dependency theory. The founder of world systems theory was Wallerstein (1979). His theory has four underlying principles to it:

1 Individual countries or nation-states are not an adequate unit of sociological analysis. Rather, we must look at the overall social system that transcends (and has done for centuries) national boundaries. Capitalism is responsible for creating the world order or Modern World System (MWS) because capital from its beginning has always ignored national borders in its search for profit. At the economic level, then, the MWS forms one unified system dominated by the logic of profit and the market.

2 Wallerstein builds upon dependency theory by suggesting that the MWS is characterized by an economic division of labour consisting of a structured set of relations between three types of capitalist zone: the core, semi-periphery and periphery (see Fig. 2.3). The 'core' or developed countries control world trade and monopolize the production of manufactured goods. The 'semi-peripheral' zone includes countries like Brazil and South Africa, which resemble the core countries in terms of their urban centres but also have extremes of rural poverty. Countries in the semi-periphery are often connected to the core because the latter contract work out to them. Finally, Wallerstein identifies the 'peripheral' countries (such as much of Africa), which are at the bottom of this world hierarchy. These countries provide the raw materials, e.g. cash crops, to the core and semi-periphery, and are the emerging markets in which the core countries market their manufactured goods.

3 Wallerstein argues that countries can be upwardly or downwardly mobile in the hierarchy of the MWS although most countries have not been able to move up. This obviously partially solves one of the weaknesses of dependency theory – the tremendous economic variation in the developing world. It could be argued that the Asian Tiger economies have moved up into the semi-periphery. Some have argued that the UK may now be a semi-peripheral economic power rather than a core one. Wallerstein's model, therefore, is more flexible than Frank's because it allows us to look at the world system as a whole and to explain changes in the fortune of individual countries.

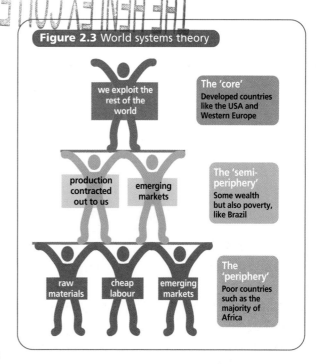

Figure 2.3 World systems theory

we exploit the rest of the world

The 'core'
Developed countries like the USA and Western Europe

production contracted out to us

emerging markets

The 'semi-periphery'
Some wealth but also poverty, like Brazil

raw materials

cheap labour

emerging markets

The 'periphery'
Poor countries such as the majority of Africa

4 The processes by which surplus wealth is extracted from the periphery are those already described by dependency theory (historically through slavery and colonialism, and contemporaneously through forms of neo-colonialism).

Wallerstein goes on to suggest that this MWS is constantly evolving in its search for profit. The signs of this are constant **commodification** (attaching a price to everything), **de-skilling**, **proletarianization** and mechanization. Wallerstein shows his Marxist roots by insisting this will lead to the **polarization** of class. It will supposedly generate so many dispossessed, excluded, marginal and poor people that in the long term they will constitute a revolutionary movement that will eventually result in the world economy being located within a socialist world economy.

Evaluation of world systems theory

The main problem with world systems theory, as with Marxism generally, is that it is too economistic. It assumes that the economy is driving all other aspects of the system (politics, culture, and so on). Bergesen (1990) argues that it was military conquest and political manipulation of local peoples that imposed economic dependency on developing nations rather than the logic of capitalism. Wallerstein has also been accused of being vague about how challenges to the established capitalist order can be mounted and how the socialist world economy will come about.

Wallerstein is also criticized by modernization theory, which accuses him of neglecting the importance of internal factors, especially cultural factors, in the failure of LDCs to develop. For example, his critics point out that he ignores the corruption of LDC elites and their wasteful spending.

The most important criticism, however, is of Wallerstein's methodology. The theory, like Frank's, is highly abstract. It is also rather vague in its definitions of concepts such as 'core', 'peripheral', etc. and many of its propositions cannot be measured or tested.

However, despite these criticisms, Wallerstein's work was one of the first to acknowledge the 'globalization' of the world (although he himself never uses the word). He drew attention to the international division of labour which some see as the basis of global inequality. Lately, however, sociologists working from a globalization perspective have noted that relationships within the world system are far from one-way. Economic interdependence can also mean that problems in the developing world (such as financial crises caused by debt) may have profound ripple effects on the economies of core countries, thereby causing unemployment and destabilization of Western currencies. These themes will be explored further in Topic 8.

Activities

Research idea

Bananas are a really interesting topic to research if you want to understand the way that world trade is loaded in favour of the developed world. A 'trade war' broke out between Europe (which supports bananas produced by a confederation of Caribbean countries) and the USA (which supports bananas produced by American transnationals in Latin America) in 2003. Find out as much as you can about this. Your school or college Geography department may have copies of the following useful books: *Global Challenges* (Digby 2001) or *Population, Resources and Development* (Chrispin and Jegede 2000). You could also visit the website of the Caribbean Banana Exporters Association – **www.cbea.org** – in order to investigate how they view their relationship with the developed world.

Your research should focus on the following:

- the role of past colonial relations
- the role of TNCs
- tariffs
- trade blocs
- the role of the World Trade Organization
- the impact on both Caribbean and South American farmers.

Web.task

Check out the websites for the following charities/pressure groups and note their comments on world trade.

- Traidcraft: **www.traidcraft.co.uk/** – click on 'factsheets'
- Christian Aid: **www.christian-aid.org.uk**
- **www.maketradefair.com/**
- World Development Movement: **www.wdm.org.uk/** – click on 'The Tricks of the Trade'
- Actionaid: **www.actionaid.org.uk**
- Oxfam: **www.org/en/campaigns/trade**

The contribution of dependency theory

Dependency theory, and particularly Frank, were probably at their most influential in the 1970s, and certainly were important in distracting attention away from the dominant modernization theory idea that lack of development was solely caused by the internal culture of developing nations. Frank was able to shift thinking away from the notion that developing societies were to blame for their situation. Instead, he focused on examining the role that Western societies played in bringing about the conditions in which developing societies found themselves after independence, along with the role of aid, trade and transnationals in maintaining global inequality. However, the fundamental weakness of dependency theory was that it offered no realistic solutions to global poverty. It was also hamstrung by the fact that capitalism as an economic system has brought tangible benefits to the world. The credibility of dependency theory was further undermined after the global collapse of the European Communist bloc in the 1990s and the apparent conversion of China to entrepreneurial capitalism in the last decade.

Check your understanding

1. Define 'underdevelopment' and 'dependency'.

2. Outline Frank's theory of the world capitalist system.

3. Who is at the very bottom of this system according to Foster-Carter?

4. How did the triangular slave trade result in a super-accumulation of capital for Britain?

5. What advantages did colonialism have for Western capitalism?

6. How are the economies of the developing world locked into and dependent upon the developed nations today?

7. What role have some elites of developing countries played in the world capitalist system?

8. Apart from world trade, what two other forms of Western intervention are described as neo-colonialist today?

9. How does dependency theory criticize the modernization view that urbanization is a catalyst of positive change in the developing world?

10. What solutions does Frank offer for dependency?

11. How does the solution of dependent development differ from that offered by Frank?

12. Identify the similarities and differences between the theories of Frank and Wallerstein.

Key terms

Colonialism the take-over and exploitation of countries, usually by means of superior military force.

Commodification applying an economic value to a range of human activities.

De-skilling breaking down expensive complex occupational skills into routine and simple tasks.

Dependency the state of being dependent on more powerful countries for investment, trade, aid, debt relief, charity, etc.

Imperial empire-building.

Metropolis or **core nations** terms used by Frank to describe the developed world.

Neo-colonialism modern forms of exploitation of poorer societies by rich societies, which are usually dressed up as beneficial, e.g. aid, world trade and transnational investment.

Polarization the Marxist idea that the experience of workers will become so alienating that they will see the need for socialist revolution.

Primary products crops and mineral extracts.

Proletarianization the process by which professional, managerial and white-collar workers experience convergence with working-class conditions of work, service, etc.

Satellite or **peripheral countries** terms used by Frank to describe countries in the developing world. The terms indicate their dependence on the 'core' nations.

Tariffs taxes on imports to protect a country's own industries.

World systems theory explains development in terms of the ever-changing economic relationships between countries in the 'modern world system'.

An eye on the exam — Underdevelopment and dependency

Item A

Colonial powers laid the foundation of the present division of the world into industrial nations on the one hand, and hewers of wood and drawers of water on the other. They wiped out indigenous industry and forced the colonies to buy their manufactures. They undermined the self sufficiency of regions like Africa and transformed it into a source of raw materials for Western industry. Sometimes they forced locals to grow the desired crops. Sometimes they bought land or just seized it to set up their plantations, drafting in cheap labour to work them. In this way the colonial powers created the world economic order that still prevails today, of industrial centre and primary producing periphery, prosperous metropolis and poverty-stricken satellites. Apologists of empire – and there are some, even today – point to the benefits it often brought; education, science and technology, the rule of law, efficient administration and so on. However, despite this, almost all the imbalances that now cripple the economies, societies and politics of the developing world had their origins in colonialism.

Adapted from Harrison, P. (1990) *Inside the Third World: The Anatomy of Poverty* (2nd edn), Harmondsworth: Penguin

Using information from **Item A** and elsewhere, assess the view that the 'less developed' countries have been systematically underdeveloped by western capitalism.

(33 marks)

Grade booster — Getting top marks in this question

To answer this question, you should begin by presenting the details of the view that it refers to, which is that of the various types of dependency or underdevelopment theory, such as Frank's or Wallerstein's. You should deal with ideas such as the capitalist world system and its origins in colonialism, and how it creates and maintains dependency through underdeveloping the 'periphery' or 'satellite' countries. You should consider the role of TNCs and neo-colonialism in perpetuating this system today. Remember that you need to make use of relevant information from Item A in your answer, which you should do when describing dependency theory.

You need to evaluate the view, for example by considering possible strategies for breaking out of underdevelopment, and by looking at alternative explanations such as modernization theory.

TOPIC 4

Aid and debt

Getting you thinking

FACT

The total cost of providing debt relief for the 20 worst affected countries would amount to between £3.25 billion and £4.54 billion. This is roughly the equivalent to the cost of building EuroDisney.

FACT

The £16 billion Britain is spending on 232 Eurofighters would cancel the entire debt of South Asia and sub-Saharan Africa.

FACT

Britons spend £5 billion a year on sweets and chocolate.

FACT

The £20 billion that Britons pocketed in 1997 in windfall payments from building societies would cancel the entire debt of the lowest income countries in the developing world.

The sieve-maker's daughter, Zenithou, has half a face, the rest has been eaten by a sickness called the Grazer or Noma which eats through the muscles, the tissues and bones. In Niger where they live, there is no war, famine or pestilence, but the Grazer is kept supplied with children by the starvation diets and a collapsing health system caused by pressure of international debt. In Niger, the poorest country in the world, they spend three times more money paying off foreign debt than on health and education. Debt means that they have no money to buy the antiseptic cream and mouthwash Zenithou needs to treat the Grazer. As a result, the World Health Organization estimates that 80 000 children will die from this very treatable disease in this region. Niger owes Britain £8 million. If we cancelled this debt, Niger could inoculate 750 000 children from measles, which kills nearly one in three children in Niger before they are 5 years old.

Adapted from 'Suffering from Plague – The Plague of Debt' by Maggie O'Kane, *The Guardian*, 11 May 1998

1 Look at the facts accompanying each of the pictures above. What is your view of the morality of the spending decisions above? Do you believe that we should take a lead in helping developing nations out of debt or even in cancelling it altogether? Try and list your reasons for and against such actions.

2 In your opinion, do we have a moral obligation to help children like Zenithou? What should the UK do about the Niger debt? How would we feel if 80 000 British kids died because of measles?

Many people believe that debt is the fault of developing countries and that Western interference, e.g. by cancelling the debt, only encourages countries to become more dependent on their help. However, in considering the questions above, you may have suggested that debt is not the fault of the debtors. You may have argued that the cause of the problem lies with the developed world (and especially the desire of Western banks to lend money in order to make profit) and the organization of world trade. The truth lies somewhere in between.

Whatever 'truth' we go with, the facts tell us that children like Zenithou are suffering early death because of debt. Imagine how people would feel if children regularly died in the UK because of debt to building societies and banks. And yet Zenithou and 80 000 other children have done so indirectly because the Niger owes the UK money. This section explores some of these issues and looks at the interconnectedness of British aid, world trade, the debt of the developing countries and children's deaths.

Aid

'Aid' refers to any flow of resources from developed countries to the developing world, which may take the form of:

- a financial grant or material gift that does not have to be paid back
- a loan with interest.

Aid mainly involves the transfer of capital (i.e. money), but may also be made up of expertise (i.e. experts are sent and their wages are paid by the donor country), science and technology, medicines and contraceptives, weapons, and so on. In 2005, the total quantity of aid provided by rich countries to the developing world topped $100 billion for the first time. Aid has virtually doubled since the $52 billion given in 2001.

Types of aid

There are essentially five broad types of aid.

1 Bilateral aid

Bilateral aid involves governments in the developed world giving aid to governments in the developing world. This is known as 'official development assistance' and in the UK is administered by a branch of the Foreign Office, i.e. the Department for International Development (DFID). In 2007/8, £2962m (57 per cent) of the DFID programme was bilateral aid, a 6 per cent increase from £2783m in 2006/7. India, Ethiopia, Tanzania and Sudan received the largest amounts of DFID bilateral aid in this period.

2 Multilateral aid

Multilateral aid involves the UK donating capital (43 per cent of the DFID budget in 2007/8 or £1990m) to agencies such as:

- the **World Bank** – set up after World War II by Western governments. Although all countries can join, US economic interests dominate its policy. It makes loans to member states at interest rates below those of commercial banks in order to finance **infrastructure** development projects, such as power plants, hydroelectric dams and roads. It is also the world's largest funding source for agricultural development. The Bank's International Development Association makes soft loans, i.e. with no or very low interest rates to the poorest countries. In 2007/8, the World Bank received £493m from the DFID
- the International Monetary Fund (IMF), although most of the funding for this organization comes from the USA
- the European Commission – the UK, along with other member states, contributes to a European aid fund that allocates grants rather than loans to developing countries. Food aid has also been an important aspect of EC aid. In 2007/8, the EC received £991m from the DFID
- the United Nations – a small proportion of the UK's aid budget is allocated to UN agencies such as UNICEF (the UN's children's educational fund). In 2007/8, the UN received £250m from the DFID.

Table 2.5 Top five recipients of DFID aid in 2004/5		
Rank	Country	Aid received (millions)
1	India	£259
2	Bangladesh	£128
3	Tanzania	£97
4	Sudan	£84
5	Afghanistan	£80

Source: Statistics on International Development (SID), DFID 2005

3 Commercial banks

These lend money to developing countries at commercial rates of interest. In 2000/1, for example, private flows from the UK to developing countries were estimated at £1.4 billion.

4 Non-governmental organizations (NGOs)

NGOs include charities such as Oxfam, the Red Cross, VSO and Save the Children Fund, which aim to raise donations from the general public by raising awareness of problems in the developing world. NGO fundraising is usually matched by donations from the DFID. However, in the past, aid raised by NGOs was minute compared with bilateral and multilateral aid. The NGOs in the UK generally raised approximately £50 million annually (of which 50 per cent was donated by the DFID), which is less than one tenth of DFID official aid. However, in 2007/8, the DFID decided to make use of the local knowledge and expertise of these organizations and channelled £317m of bilateral assistance through them. NGOs prefer to target the 'poorest of the poor' and so tend to work with voluntary groups, rather than the governments of developing countries, on small-scale aid projects such as **irrigation schemes** and well-boring, as well as rural health and education schemes.

5 Emergency aid

This is humanitarian relief that is raised in response to specific circumstances, such as natural disasters (e.g. the worldwide appeal in reaction to the tsunami that devastated South East Asia in 2004 raised $7.5 billion), famine (e.g. in Ethiopia in 1985 and Niger in 2005), and war, with its resulting refugee problems (e.g. Darfur in Sudan in 2004/5). The DFID's bilateral humanitarian assistance in 2007/8 totalled £431m, representing an increase of £47m (12 per cent) compared with 2006/7. The largest recipients of bilateral humanitarian assistance in 2007/8 were Sudan (£91m), Democratic Republic of Congo (£46m) and Iraq (£20m).

The UK government's record on aid

In 1969, a UN commission recommended that 0.7 per cent of rich countries' GNP (i.e. less than 1 per cent!) should be given in aid. This excludes both loans and **military aid**. However, very few rich countries, including the UK, have managed to meet this target. For example, the UK official aid total in 2007/8 totalled £6027 million – this sounds a lot, but is only 0.36 per cent of Gross National Income (formerly GNP). However, the DFID points out that the UK is the third largest Western donor of aid to the developing world. Most British aid (approximately 60 per cent) goes to Africa, while Asian countries receive about 30 per cent.

Overall, aid flowing from the developed world to the developing world is growing. In 2005, US$78.6 billion was given in aid and this figure was projected to rise to above US$125 billion by 2010. However, the financial crisis experienced by Western financial institutions in 2007/8 is likely to impact negatively on future aid to the developing world. Toussaint (2008) notes that in the period 2004 to 2006, Western banks increased their lending to the developing world. Furthermore, substantial credit was granted within developing countries by local or foreign banks. Other private financial groups (pension funds, insurance companies, hedge funds) gave credit to developing countries by buying the bonds that these countries issued on the leading stock exchanges. Such lending was encouraged by interest rates and risk insurance premiums which were far below those that prevailed up to the early 2000s.

However, in July 2007, these private sources of credit suddenly dried up because private Western banks became reluctant to lend money. The authorities of the US, Western Europe and Japan had to inject hundreds of billions of dollars and euros to prevent the Western financial system from collapsing. This has had a ripple effect on other sectors of Western economies, such as car manufacturing and construction.

Toussaint predicts a number of consequences of this financial crisis for the developing world:

- As manufacturing industry is affected by the credit crunch, there will be a sharp decline in demand for the primary products (e.g. cash crops and raw materials) mainly produced by the developing world. Toussaint suggests that there will be a major fall in the prices of primary products and, consequently, less export income available to repay loan interest and debt.
- As American and British banks collapse or merge, they will be less willing to take risks on extending credit into the developing world. Loans will become more difficult to come by.
- Migrant workers are often employed in insecure parts of Western economies, e.g. construction, and are more likely than indigenous workers to be laid off in recession. Toussaint argues that this will have a profoundly negative effect on cash flow into the developing world as migrant workers have less cash to send home.

Modernization and aid

As we saw in Topic 2, according to modernization theory, official aid is a crucial component required for take-off into industrialization. This was a view shared by policymakers after World War II and especially the World Bank. As a result, aid was spent by the countries receiving it on importing Western technicians and experts to develop industry and modernize agriculture. Moreover, aid aimed to change cultural attitudes by setting up meritocratic education systems focused on literacy, and family-planning programmes targeted at freeing women from the powerlessness and dependency caused by the patriarchal family system.

These early aid strategies acknowledged that elites in the developing world would be the primary beneficiaries of aid, but it was argued that the poor would benefit in the long run as wealth 'trickled down' from the better off to the local economy and stimulated local production and markets. Indeed, this modernization approach did generate some early successes, as shown by the fact that the large quantities of aid distributed in the 1950s meant that global levels of infant mortality, life expectancy, literacy levels, etc., improved slowly but surely. In the 20 years following independence, many African nations experienced economic growth.

However, the aid bubble is generally perceived to have burst in the late 1970s. Both absolute poverty and relative poverty (i.e. the gap between rich and poor) in the developing world have actually increased in the past 30 years.

Diseases of poverty, such as tuberculosis and malaria, once thought to be under control, have returned with a vengeance and today are major killers of children in the developing world. Moreover, despite fantastic amounts of aid pouring in, countries such as Bangladesh actually became poorer in the 1980s and 1990s. Such trends have led some sociologists and economists to talk about the 'poverty of aid' and 'the end of development'.

Dependency theory and aid

Neo-Marxists, in particular, argue that aid creates and sustains unequal relationships and, consequently, they have questioned the functions of official aid. They reject the view that the primary function of aid is to assist development. Rather, they suggest that it functions to bring about and sustain underdevelopment, and to benefit a Western monopoly of wealth, consumption and political power. Other critics have suggested that organizations like the World Bank and IMF have adopted inappropriate and ineffective aid strategies that have primarily served the interests of the transnational corporations that dominate global capitalism. Theresa Hayter (1981) argues that official aid is a form of neo-colonialism because the development promoted by aid is aimed at reproducing, maintaining and legitimating the interests of the capitalist metropolis.

The political agenda of aid

The allocation of UK and US aid has often depended on whether the political ideology and practices of the developing country have met with Western approval. This was most obvious during the Cold War when the regimes of developing countries were rewarded with aid for aligning themselves with the capitalist world, whilst others were punished for adopting socialist policies or for being seen as too close to the Soviet Union. The effects of the famine in Ethiopia in 1985 (which led to Band Aid, Live Aid and Comic Relief) were probably worsened by the fact that, despite extensive warnings of potential famine by the

UN, both the USA and UK refused aid on the grounds that Ethiopia had a Marxist government.

The focus on anticommunism can also be seen in the US military-aid programme. By the end of the 1950s, there was a 4:1 proportion of military to economic aid in terms of US spending. Much of this was sent to South and Central America, where it was used by right-wing governments to repress groups fighting for a more just social order. The result of such aid was often the creation of vast inequalities in wealth and land ownership between elites and the rural poor.

However, the fall of communism in the 1990s has not diluted the political character of both US and UK aid. There has merely been a shift in emphasis, as new political threats are identified. Developing countries are rewarded with aid today for supporting Western strategic interests. For example, Kenya was rewarded with aid for providing US forces with port facilities during the Gulf War in 1991, while Turkey was denied massive US aid for refusing to let the USA lease air bases during the same conflict. In 2005, developing nations were rewarded for assisting the USA's war against international Islamic terrorism. As George W. Bush stated in 2001: 'Over time it's going to be important for nations to know they will be held accountable for inactivity. You're either with us or against us in the fight against terror.' This policy will have negative economic implications for the poorest countries, who have little or no political, strategic or commercial advantages for the developed world.

The economic agenda of aid

Neo-Marxists argue that there is an economic motive at the heart of all official aid and that this is the expansion of global capitalism. Aid is aimed at opening up new markets for Western goods and services. The evidence strongly supports this argument because approximately 75 per cent of British aid is **tied** – that is, the recipient country has to spend the grant or loan in the UK. Such aid stimulates the economy of the UK in the following ways:

- A substantial number of jobs in the UK depend on the orders placed by developing nations using official aid. Oxfam suggests that the UK aid programme often appears to be more concerned with supporting ailing or inefficient sectors of British industry than the poor of the developing world.
- The DFID can also control what the money is spent on, e.g. they may insist that the aid is spent on infrastructure or technology that the UK supplies. For example, British aid to India has resulted in the purchase of millions of pounds worth of helicopters and airport-surveillance equipment. Oxfam notes that such projects very rarely benefit the poor.
- There is evidence that the British government has given aid to countries such as Indonesia and Malaysia in return for securing weapons, aircraft and construction contracts for British industry.
- Tied aid creates artificial markets because the developing country will need spare parts and technical expertise from the donor country for many years to come.

Focus on research

Aid in Sierra Leone

Even before Sierra Leone's 11-year civil war was ended in February 2002, the aid advisers from Washington and London had arrived in the capital of Freetown with their prescriptions for development and tackling poverty. Their solution to the problems of the second poorest country in the world was to privatize virtually the entire country, including, most controversially, the national water utility. The World Bank and the IMF came up with a complex aid package with lots of strings. In the long term, privatization, including water and sanitation, was a core requirement. In November 2002, Britain signed a 10-year agreement with Ahmad Tejan Kabbah's government. The UK is Sierra Leone's largest bilateral development partner, with £104.5m in aid in three years. The UK is supporting the National Commission for Privatization, which intends to privatize 24 public enterprises including shipping, roads, the airline, telecommunications, housing, the postal service, the national power authority and water. Department for International Development officials said that UK aid was conditional on 37 benchmarks this year. Privatization of water, through various forms of management contracts, is probably one of the most sensitive and disputed areas of development, dividing those who believe it is an economic good, and others who regard water provision as a human right.

Source: *The Guardian*, 24 September 200

> **How does the extract above illustrate some of the problems of aid?**

- Much of the money borrowed went to fund projects which have failed to generate the capital required to pay back both the loan and the interest on it. In the 1980s, this led to countries taking out further loans in order to repay the interest on the original loans. Capital that might have been invested in technology, healthcare, education and the eradication of absolute poverty, went straight back to the West in the form of loan repayments, e.g. it was estimated in 1993 that rich countries got back £3 in debt repayments for every £1 donated in aid.
- There is some evidence too that aid undermines indigenous markets – in particular, food aid may depress the prices of locally produced crops and throw

local farmers out of business, consequently making the country even more dependent upon the West.

In 2001, the DFID, announced that it was bringing tied aid to an end. In 2005, the UK Development Secretary, Hilary Benn, pledged that the UK would no longer provide aid on the condition that countries adopt free-market ideas. Today, both the World Bank and IMF impose these conditions on loans and debt relief. Benn has stated that the only conditions the UK will impose in the future will be transparency and tackling corruption, respect for human rights and helping the poor. However, research in 2005 showed that DFID aid is still dependent on the recipient country achieving between 40 and 50 benchmarks, many of which encourage the introduction of free-market policies or international investment, before British aid is given – for example, Guyana was told by the DFID that it must privatize its water supplies if it was to receive DFID aid.

The aid business

Dependency theory has also raised concerns about the 'aid business', which now employs hundreds of thousands of people worldwide. Hancock (1989) refers to the largely White and Western administrators of the World Bank, IMF and large charities as the 'lords of poverty', because of the amount of aid that is spent on large salaries, administrative expenses and attendance at international conferences. He further argues that these organizations are overly bureaucratic and are 'secretive, bloated and self-serving'. He suggests that they have created 'monstrous projects that, at vast expense, have devastated the environment and ruined lives'. In addition, these organizations have 'sapped the initiative, creativity and enterprise of ordinary people and substituted the superficial and irrelevant glitz of imported advice' (p.189). Hancock may be right to highlight the wasteful spending of aid organizations. Even in the UK, the DFID spent £248 million on administrative costs as part of its 2007/8 bilateral aid programme.

Yasmin Alibhai-Brown (2005) is critical of humanitarian aid initiatives such as Live Aid, Live 8 and the Make Poverty History campaign, arguing that these campaigns perpetuate the dependency culture created by colonialism and encouraged by aid, debt and unfair trade terms. She claims that Bob Geldof has 'infantilized' Africa by giving the impression that the continent is incapable of modernization without the help of White pop stars and politicians.

What are the arguments for and against campaigns such as 'Make Poverty History'?

Sociology A2 for AQA

The debt crisis

By the mid-1990s, it was apparent that a debt crisis existed in the developing world. In 1980, the developing world owed the West $600 billion, but by 1998, this had increased to $2.2 trillion. Most of the countries in real trouble are extremely poor African states, e.g. in 1998, sub-Saharan Africa owed $222 billion, which made up 71 per cent of its national earnings, whilst Mozambique and Ethiopia spent almost half their export earnings servicing their debts. Nearly a quarter of the aid African countries receive this year will be immediately given back to the West in the form of debt repayments. The problem is not unique to Africa. Mexico, Brazil and, most recently in 2002, Argentina, have struggled to repay their foreign debts, resulting in political and economic instability in these countries.

Dependency theorists argue that the debt crisis has been brought about by a number of factors:

- Colonialism resulted in the economies of developing countries being overdependent on the production of a few major cash crops or raw materials. However, the prices of such commodities, and therefore export earnings, have fallen sharply in the past two decades whilst the price of oil and manufacturing goods needed for development have risen steeply. Therefore, developing countries have needed to borrow money to make up the difference. In their search for greater profits, Western banks were happy to oblige in the belief that countries never go bust.
- Little of the money borrowed was spent on effective economic development. It generally went on oil (as prices rose again) and about 20 per cent went on weapons. Much of it was stolen by corrupt post-colonial elites or was squandered on projects such as international airports that were totally inappropriate for the needs of developing countries. Even the successful or appropriate projects, such as irrigation schemes, were too slow in generating income to match both repayments and interest. David Landes (1998) argues that too much was expected of political leadership in Africa. He notes that since it took Europe centuries to get good government, why should Africa do so in mere decades, especially after the distortions of colonialism?
- In the 1980s, recession in the West increased interest rates. The effect on the developing world was that they were forced to keep borrowing in order to pay the interest on old debts. Western banks were happy to lend, because they were making record profits through the interest charged.

The costs of debt

The overall effect on the developing world of the debt crisis has been devastating. Debt has actually increased infant-mortality rates and lowered life expectancy because essential capital that should have been used for developing healthcare has been diverted to servicing debt. According to Oxfam, more than 100 000 Ethiopian children die each year from easily preventable diseases, but debt repayments are four times more than health spending in that country.

George (1993) has identified a number of other negative consequences of the debt crisis which impact both on the developed and developing world:

- Environmental damage, such as deforestation, desertification and pollution, which may be contributing to global warming, is caused by the developing world's need to raise capital by overexploiting its natural resources.
- Farmers in some countries have turned to the production of lucrative illegal crops, such as poppies for heroin and opium (e.g. Afghanistan and Pakistan) and coca for cocaine (e.g. Colombia and Bolivia), in order to survive, thus contributing to the drug problem (and rising crimes rates) found in Western societies such as the USA.
- Poor people in developing countries are desperate to move to richer nations in search of work and improvements in their standard of living. Illegal immigration and people-trafficking have become major problems, as has an international sex-trade as women in the developing world are increasingly sold into sex-slavery for prostitution in the West.

Western solutions to the debt crisis have produced mixed results. The main lender countries wrote off or renegotiated over $300 billion worth of debt in the 1990s. However, this made little impact, as symbolized by the fact that every baby born into the developing world in 2000/1 owed $482 to the banks in the developed world. In 2005, the G8 countries agreed a $40 billion plan to write-off the debt of 38 countries, although there are some doubts about how this plan will actually be financed. In 2005, the Commission for Africa recommended a 100 per cent debt cancellation for the sub-Saharan countries. There are signs that the UK has incorporated debt relief into the DFID aid programme. In 2006/7, the DFID paid £2014 million in debt relief although only £75 million was set aside for this purpose in 2007/8. About two-thirds of the 50 per cent increase in worldwide aid between 2001 and 2005 was mainly absorbed by debt relief.

So is aid a good or a bad thing?

The case for aid

Sachs (2005) notes that 'aid works, when it is practical, targeted, science-based and measurable'. In particular, he argues that aid aimed at improving health, and especially, child mortality, has been successful because it has resulted in mass immunization for millions of children against diseases such as polio, diphtheria and measles. The Commission for Africa notes that aid 'eradicates disease – smallpox was wiped out by a little more than US$100 million worth of targeted aid' (p.103). Sachs notes that aid has been relatively successful in terms of the 'green revolution' in Asia – India, China and South East Asia have seen their rice yields rise dramatically, and have been able to use the capital generated by this to diversify into cash crops and industry. Sachs argues that the green revolution came about because of targeted aid from the Rockefeller Foundation and USAID. Similarly, the Commission for Africa notes that aid has brought about 12 per cent economic growth in Mozambique.

The case against aid

Neo-liberals such as Erixon (2005) argue that, despite billions of dollars in aid, most African countries are poorer today than they were at the time of their political independence. He observes that aid to Africa seems to have lowered rather than increased economic growth. Bauer (1981), another neo-liberal, argues that aid creates a dependency culture and discourages the entrepreneurial spirit vital to economic growth and development. He suggests that people in the developing world are actually demotivated by aid – why produce food if it is being distributed for free?

However, in criticism of this neo-liberal position, dependency theorists argue that the free market and globalization are responsible for poverty and underdevelopment because the free market shapes the world capitalist system. This makes it difficult for developing nations to industrialize and ensures that trade in cash crops and raw materials continues on unfair terms that serve Western interests.

Calderisi: debt – a self-inflicted problem?

Calderisi (2006), an ex-World Bank official, suggests that Africa's poverty and debt has been almost entirely self-inflicted. He argues that Africa has failed to use Western aid effectively and accrued massive debt because of:

- *Poor economic management* – He argues that overtaxation has led to Africa losing half of its share of the world's agricultural markets to other developing countries in Asia and Latin America between 1970 and 1990. These other nations were simply able to produce and deliver the same goods more cheaply. Calderisi estimates that Africa lost income of about $70 billion a year, which exceeds the amount of foreign aid being spent in all of Africa, Asia and Latin America combined. Another aspect of economic management is debt management. Calderisi argues that many Asian countries, such as Indonesia, have managed their debts carefully and cannot understand why African countries are receiving special treatment in terms of debt relief and outright cancellation.
- *Lack of African unity* – Tribal or border conflicts have undermined the ability of African countries to trade with each other. This has reduced potential export income, which could have been reinvested in their economies. Calderisi points out that it is difficult to attract industries and investment to countries which are not willing to share common interests, such as transport or telecommunications.
- *Corruption* – Calderisi suggests that this is endemic in everyday life at every level. He argues that petty day-to-day corruption that Africans experience hurts the poor the most because they have to pay a higher percentage of their income in bribes. He notes:

<< *They may have to hand over two weeks' wages to obtain a death certificate for burying a relative, a month's farming income to have a child admitted to school, more "tips" to the schoolteacher to have their son or daughter seated in the first few rows (important in classes of 150 or 200), and the like.>>* (p.88)

Calderisi suggests that these corrupt practices sap the energy of the poor, dull their enterprise and make them fatalistic and cynical about the possibility of change.

- *Lack of good government* – No other continent has ever experienced such prolonged dictatorships and one-party states. Moreover, African leaders tend to be the epitome of corruption. As Calderisi notes:

<< *these men spent their entire careers enriching themselves, intimidating political opponents, avoiding all but the merest trappings of democracy, actively frustrating movements towards constitutional rule, and thumbing their noses – sometimes subtly, other times blatantly – at the international community.* >> (p.59)

Calderisi notes that it is governments not people who benefit from aid; massive sums of Western aid have generally ended up in the pockets of these corrupt politicians and dictators. For example, in 2000 the newly elected government of Nigeria was prepared to let the children of the former corrupt President, General Abacha, keep $100 million as part of a settlement to recover the $2 to 3 billion that Abacha had stolen and transferred to Swiss bank accounts. However, Calderisi can be criticized for neglecting the fact that many of these leaders were sponsored by the West for strategic reasons. The West often turned a blind eye to corruption and human-rights abuses.

Calderisi takes issue with the dependency theory view that globalization has exacerbated Africa's problems; he argues that, with only a few exceptions, Africa has refused to concern itself with foreign markets. He claims that Africa's problems are not caused by terms of trade that benefit the West. Rather, he argues that 'the continent has both wittingly and unwittingly walled itself off from the rest of the world'. The economy of the whole continent is now comparatively tiny – barely the size of Argentina's. Excluding South Africa, the continent produces only as much as Belgium. Calderisi argues that African governments have not supported African farmers or attempted to attract private investment, which went instead to Asian countries such as India. He describes how investors were deterred from investing in Africa by factors such as high exchange rates, high taxes, outlandish regulations, administrative inertia, the legal system, the complicated labour code, monopolies, corruption and fraud.

Collier: 'four traps'

Collier (2008) focuses on why aid has been largely ineffective in improving the lives of the world's bottom billion people. He suggests that the inability of aid programmes to eradicate their poverty is the result of four traps:

1 *The conflict trap* – Collier notes that wars and military coups have been experienced by 73 per cent of the bottom billion. After analyzing the social and economic make-up of societies that have experienced such conflict, he observes that civil war is much more likely to break out in low-income countries that have experienced low economic growth or stagnation and decline in such growth. Furthermore, Collier's research

---

Focus on ...

The Samaritan's dilemma

The term 'the Samaritan's dilemma' refers to the inclination of the Samaritan (the helper) to offer assistance and to the reaction of the recipient. The Samaritan wishes to help and so is 'better off' no matter what the recipient does. However, once the recipient recognizes that the Samaritan will always help and exert 'high effort', they can respond by merely exerting 'low effort'. In short, the best outcome for the donor of wishing to disburse aid quickly and with high effort is not matched by an equal response from the recipient. Rather, the 'best outcome' for the recipient will be achieved by accepting the aid, but utilizing the aid funds provided with 'low effort'. This goes some way to explaining the common phenomenon of aid-funded infrastructural projects breaking down far earlier than similar non-aid-funded projects because of the lack of attention paid to planned maintenance. This shows the Samaritan's dilemma operating in practice: the recipient relies on the donor coming back to provide additional aid to repair the faulty plant.

Adapted from R. Riddell (2007) *Does Foreign Aid Really Work?* Oxford: OUP

---

estimates the cost of a typical civil war to a country and its neighbours to be around $64 billion.

2 *The natural resource trap* – Collier argues that the discovery of valuable natural resources in the context of poverty also undermines the efficient use of aid because it has social and economic consequences that slow economic growth. There is evidence that the discovery of some types of natural resources, e.g. diamonds and oil, has led to civil unrest and war as particular interest groups compete for control over these valuable commodities. Even when unrest does not occur, corruption is encouraged by the potential massive rewards generated by the resource. It is rare in these situations for the wealth generated by the commodity to filter down to ordinary people in terms of improving their living standards or the country's infrastructure.

3 *The being landlocked with bad neighbours trap* – Collier argues that in Africa in particular, geography matters. He observes:

<< *Why is Uganda poor when Switzerland is rich? It is indeed partly that Switzerland's access to the sea depends upon German and Italian infrastructure, whereas Uganda's access to the sea depends upon Kenyan infrastructure. Which do you imagine is better? If you are landlocked with poor transport links to the coast that are beyond your control, it is very difficult to integrate into global markets for any product that requires a lot of transport, so forget manufacturing – which to date has been the most reliable driver of rapid development.* >> (p.55)

4 *The bad governance trap* – Like Calderisi, Collier highlights the role of corruption in holding back development and the efficient use of aid. For example, he notes the findings of a survey that tracked money released by the government in Chad intended for rural health clinics, which discovered that less than 1 per cent of the money actually reached the clinics. He also notes that the leaders of many of the poorest countries in the world are themselves among the global super-rich. For example, when self-proclaimed emperor of the Central African Empire, Jean-Bedel Bokassa, was deposed, he was exiled to France, where he owned four chateaux, a hotel, a luxurious villa and an executive jet. He was later tried in his own country for the theft of an estimated $170 million from state coffers (*New York Times* 1993). The Commission for Africa estimated that the amount stolen by corrupt elites and held in foreign bank accounts is equivalent to more than half of Africa's external debts.

Collier notes that all of the people living in the countries of the bottom billion have been in one or another of the above traps; 73 per cent have been through civil war, 29 per cent are caught in the resources trap, 30 per cent are landlocked with bad neighbours, whilst 76 per cent have been through a prolonged period of bad governance and poor economic policies. Some countries have been in more than one trap.

However, Collier argues that some aid does make a difference, in that his research indicates that in the last 30 years it has added one percentage point to the annual economic growth rate of the bottom billion. He describes aid as a 'holding operation preventing things from falling apart', claiming that without it, the countries of the bottom billion would have become even poorer than they are today. However, Collier's evidence also indicates that the more aid is increased, the less is the return in economic growth. This is because developing countries do not share the priorities of the donor countries. The donor country may want to improve health and education services, but they cannot dictate how the aid is spent. Often the developing country will spend it on the military instead. Collier also points out that research suggests aid actually encourages military coups.

However, Collier argues that aid can also contribute to lowering the possibility of the conflict trap, particularly in post-conflict situations, which, as we saw earlier, can quickly relapse into further civil war or coups. It can do this by raising both economic growth and living standards, which are often the causes of the original conflict. Collier suggests that aid is fairly impotent with regard to the natural resource trap but can be useful in improving the infrastructure, particularly transport systems, for landlocked countries.

Aid can also be used effectively to overcome corruption and bad governance if it contains incentives, i.e. that aid depends on the politicians and officials of developing nations meeting certain conditions; if these are not met, the aid should be cut off. Collier argues such an approach is entirely legitimate – 'why should we give aid to governments that are not willing to let their citizens see how they spend it?' (p.110). Aid should also be targeted at technical assistance (which, at present, only a third of aid is aimed at), ensuring a supply of skilled people in the civil service and key infrastructure services. Finally, Collier argues that aid should be used as reinforcement – especially for economic reform (e.g. the eradication of corruption) and if developing societies demonstrate their accountability, although Collier acknowledges this would be a high-risk strategy.

Collier notes that globalization is making things harder for the bottom billion. However, this is not because of the developed world and institutions like the World Bank. It is because the export market has been dominated by countries such as India, China and the Asian Tigers, which have managed the transition to manufacturing economies much more effectively than the economies of Africa. Collier argues that aid could be used to help the bottom billion break into this global market by improving port and transport facilities, and lowering the costs of trade with the rest of the world. This progress might then attract the opportunities for private investment.

However, Collier concludes that aid is only a partial solution to the problems that the bottom billion face; he argues that other actions are just as important as aid, such as introducing international laws for both countries and global corporations as well as charters for democracy, investment, budget accountability and post-conflict situations. He suggests that there is also a need to introduce positive discrimination in trade policies.

Riddell: Donors' responsibilities for aid failure

Riddell (2007) argues that we don't really know whether aid has generally worked, because we do not have enough empirical data to judge its success or failure. At best, he argues the evidence is partial. Some of it suggests that some aid works but not nearly as well as it could. Like Calderisi and Collier, Riddell also highlights the problems of poor governance and corruption in recipient countries. However, he suggests that the donor countries also have to shoulder the blame, for several reasons:

● Donors often give aid to countries that don't really need it while denying effective aid to those countries that do. Riddell notes that less than half of all official aid is channelled to the 65 poorest countries.
● Some 60 per cent of aid is still tied, benefiting the economy of the donor country rather than the developing world. Tied aid forces poor countries to buy resources that are not a high priority in challenging poverty.
● There are too many donors, aid programmes and projects. Riddell notes that donors often compete with each other to give aid, which results in a lack of cooperation and coordination between agencies and undermines the effectiveness of aid.
● Western aid agencies often do not learn from their past mistakes, because they have insufficient local knowledge and often do not consult with local people about their needs and the particular difficulties they face.
● Aid agencies do little to promote a sense of ownership among either the political elites or the ordinary people

of developing nations. Consequently, this means that people are not committed in the long term to aid projects because they don't really understand their purpose or they misinterpret the intentions of the agency, e.g. they may see the project as an extension of Western or imperial power or as a threat to their local culture, which should be resisted.

The future of aid?

Calderisi makes 10 recommendations with regard to future aid to Africa, which he claims will help the continent more than the billions of dollars of foreign aid have done in the past:

1   There is a need to introduce mechanisms for tracing and recovering the public funds stolen by corrupt leaders.
2   All heads of state, ministers and senior officials should be required to open their bank accounts to public scrutiny and to be accountable in showing how public money is spent.
3   Direct aid to individual countries should be cut in half so that countries have to compete with each other for resources. This competition would encourage more effective management of leaner and more realistic budgets.
4   Direct aid should only be focused on four to five countries that are serious about reducing poverty. Governments that are indifferent to poverty, that cannot guarantee basic education for their citizens, or who only offer lip service to fighting HIV/AIDS, should not be helped at all.
5   All countries should be required to hold internationally supervised elections. He notes that it can be argued

that this is necessary because African governments are committing 'acts so reprehensible that past courtesies should be abandoned'.

6   Other aspects of democracy, including a free press and an independent judiciary, should be promoted. As the Commission for Africa notes, the media in Africa is not currently sufficiently free or professional to hold governments to account or to expose corruption.
7   The West should supervise the running of Africa's schools and HIV/AIDS programmes.
8   Citizen review groups should be established to oversee government policy and aid agreements.
9   More emphasis should be put on infrastructure and regional links.
10 The World Bank, the IMF and United Nations development programme should be merged to bring about greater coordination of aid projects.

Carderisi argues that it is only by the adoption of the above programme that aid can be truly effective and that Africans 'can break the cycle of terror, poverty and mediocrity that keeps them subdued'.

Riddell notes that the way aid is managed and distributed requires a new approach. He too argues that all aid should be channelled through one overall coordinating agency so that research data can be gathered to scientifically assess the success or failure of aid.

He argues that the aid and debt crisis has actually had a number of positive effects, which, he believes, will lead to major reforms in the way aid is managed by both donors and recipients. First, he notes that, in the past,

Activities

Research idea

Try to find out which countries are the Top Ten recipients of DFID aid and what their GNP is. You could do this by visiting the DFID website at **www.dfid.gov.uk**. Construct a graph showing the relationship between debt and GNP.

Web.task

Update yourself on recent crises caused by debt, and on the campaign for the cancellation of the debt of the developing world by visiting the following sites:

● **www.debtchannel.org** – this site allows you to research debt by country. It is also excellent on the latest debt news.

● **www.jubileedebtcampaign.org.uk** – excellent site documenting British efforts to have debt cancelled.

● **www.cafod.org.uk/campaign** – excellent site documenting clearly and in detail the debt crisis and possible solutions.

● **www.makepovertyhistory.org** – the campaign to cancel the debt of developing countries that resulted in Live 8 (July 2005).

Check your understanding

1   **What is the difference between bilateral and multilateral aid?**

2   **What percentage of GNP does the UN recommend should be given by developed countries to the developing world and how does the UK measure up?**

3   **How does modernization theory view the process of aid?**

4   **How might aid be used as a political weapon?**

5   **Why might aid benefit the economies of the developed world?**

6   **How has colonialism contributed to debt today?**

7   **How does debt impact on children?**

8   **What solutions have been suggested by the West to alleviate debt?**

9   **Has aid made any positive difference in the developing world?**

development and aid were relatively minor concerns of Western governments because they were seen as merely moral issues that the West felt some obligation to pay lip service to. However, since 2000, development, poverty and aid issues have become a central focus of attention of world leaders and a top agenda item in a succession of summit meetings. This is partly the result of the populations of richer countries taking a keener interest in these issues because of campaigns such as Make Poverty History. However, Riddell argues that globalization is probably the main reason – the leaders of Western donor nations see the world as increasingly characterized by global interdependence, poverty and underdevelopment and realize that this may make a significant contribution to future terrorism, conflict and global instability. Consequently, future aid is likely to be targeted more specifically at the cause of low incomes, such as poor governance, particularly the corruption of elites, and the protection of people in the developing world from the human rights abuses caused and perpetuated by extreme poverty.

Key terms

Bilateral aid official aid that goes from the government of one country to the government of another.

Infrastructure the basic services that underpin a society, such as roads, communications, electricity, gas and water supplies.

Irrigation schemes schemes that create water supplies to areas that suffer from lack of water.

Military aid aid in the form of weapons or troops.

Multilateral aid aid that is given to international agencies (such as the World Bank) to distribute.

Tied aid aid that is dependent on the recipient taking a particular course of action. i.e. usually buying products manufactured by the donor country.

World Bank set up after World War II by Western governments to make loans to member states at interest rates below those of commercial banks in order to finance development projects.

An eye on the exam Aid and debt

Item A

In the 1970s, the international community followed a developmentalist or modernization model in the developing world, and especially Africa, that effectively set up autocratic state regimes. Such state-led development intervened in the economy in order to encourage economic competitiveness, introduced subsidies on staple foods and petrol, and provided social and welfare services such as education and health, to promote 'modern' attitudes. However, all this was beyond the financial capacity of such countries and as a result a mountain of debt was built up as they were encouraged to catch up with the West. By the end of the 1970s, private lending to Africa by commercial banks outstripped bilateral and multilateral aid by 3:1. However, this 'borrowing culture' also encouraged a kleptocratic elite and corruption at all levels, and led to millions being wasted on inappropriate aid schemes. Debt continues to distort African economic development as government revenue is swallowed up by interest payments.

Using material from **Item A** and elsewhere, assess the view that debt has become the main obstacle to the development of less developed countries.

(33 marks)

Grade booster Getting top marks in this question

You could begin your answer by outlining the scale of the indebtedness of developing countries. You need to examine the causes of indebtedness, such as the legacy of colonialism, overdependence on exporting raw materials to the West and rising interest rates, as well as factors such as domestic corruption and siphoning off of funds by politicians. You should examine the consequences of indebtedness for development, for example the effects of the IMF and World Bank imposing structural adjustment programmes as a condition of loans, e.g. environmental impact, effects on the poor and children as public spending is cut. Remember to make use of relevant material from the Item in your answer, e.g. in discussing interest payments and corruption. You could link these points to perspectives such as dependency theory.

TOPIC 5

Population and consumption

Getting you thinking

Table 2.6 Statistics on population, fertility and mortality rates

Region or country	Population Total (millions) 1995	Population Total (millions) 2005	Population average annual growth rate (%) 2005–10	Crude birth rate (births per 1000 population) 2005–10	Total fertility rate (children per woman) 2005–10	Crude death rate (deaths per 100 000 population) 2005–10	Infant mortality (infant deaths per 1000 live births) 2005–10
Developed world	1175	1215	0.28	11.1	1.60	10.4	7.1
Developing world	4543	5299	1.37	22.4	2.75	8.3	54.1
Bangladesh	126	153	1.67	24.8	2.83	7.5	52.5
Brazil	162	187	1.26	19.2	2.25	6.3	23.6
China	1214	1313	0.58	13.1	1.73	7.1	23.0
Ethiopia	60	79	2.51	38.2	5.29	13.0	86.9
India	954	1134	1.46	23.0	2.81	8.2	55.0
Indonesia	197	226	1.16	18.7	2.18	6.3	26.6
Kenya	27	35	2.65	39.2	4.96	11.8	64.4
Mozambique	16	22.6	1.95	39.5	5.11	19.8	95.9
Uganda	21	29	3.24	46.6	6.46	13.4	76.9

1 What do the statistics in Table 2.6 tell us about population growth in both the developed and developing world?

2 Which countries seem to be experiencing the most rapid population growth?

3 Look closely at the figures for fertility and infant mortality. What are the trends here? Do these have any effect on the reasons why population growth in some of these countries may be so high?

4 Can you think of any cultural or religious reasons why some of these countries are experiencing rapid population growth?

It is not surprising, when we look at the statistics on population growth, that some people conclude that the developing world has a 'problem' and this may be the cause of other problems such as famine, malnutrition and shortage of resources. However, as sociologists, we should attempt to avoid making such value judgements. We hope that objective examination of other statistics above (especially infant mortality) will have alerted you to the possibility that there may be a rational context in which this population growth is taking place.

The sociological study of population change is known as '**demography**'. Sociologists believe that it is important to study demographic trends, such as those associated with birth, fertility, infant mortality, death and migration,

because they can produce insights into why societies experience social change. Table 2.7 on the next page lists some of the key indicators used by demographers.

World population growth

In 2008, the population of the world reached 6.7 billion people. There is no doubt that the world has experienced a massive rise in population. Two aspects of this rise stand out:

- Much of the increase has occurred in the past 100 years: there were only two billion people in 1925. Another way of thinking about this is to consider that the fifth billionth human born is about 12 years old,

Table 2.7 The demographer's toolkit

Indicator	What it shows
Crude birth rate	Measures the number of live births per 1000 members of a population in a given year. For example, the Kenyan rate was 53.8 in the mid-1980s compared with 15.3 in the USA.
Fertility rate	The number of live births per woman over her lifetime. The USA and Europe show very low fertility rates in the mid-1980s, i.e. approximately 1.2.
Crude death rate	This measures the number of deaths per 1000 of the population. In the USA it was 8.7 in 1987, whilst in Chad it was 44.1 in the same year.
Infant mortality rate	The number of deaths among infants aged below 1 year per 1000 of the infant population. In the USA, it is 10, whilst in Mozambique it is estimated at 96 (see Table 2.6 on p. 90).
Life expectancy	The number of years projected as remaining to an average person of a particular age. Most developed societies have life expectancy of 70+, whereas it is 41 in Malawi.

Adapted from Cohen, R. and Kennedy, P. (2000) *Global Sociology*, Basingstoke: Palgrave

the fourth billionth is about 25 years old, whilst the third billionth is approximately 40 years old. The increase in world population, then, has been phenomenally rapid.

- Most of this increase has occurred in the developing world. World population increases by about 83 million people annually. Ninety-nine per cent of this increase occurs in the less-developed regions of Africa, Asia, Latin America and the Caribbean. For example, Africa's population, despite the AIDS epidemic, tripled to 926 million between 1960 and 2005, whilst Asia's population doubled in the same period to 3.9 billion. Six countries account for half of the increase in world population: India, China, Pakistan, Nigeria, Bangladesh and Indonesia. In contrast, the population of the developed world has fallen.

Population: future projections

The United Nations forecasts that, by 2050, the world's population will hit 9.2 billion. The population of less developed countries is expected to rise from 4.9 billion in 2001 to 8.2 billion in 2050. Nine out of every ten people in 2050 will live in a developing country. In contrast, only three of the more developed countries, the United States, Russia and Japan, are expected to remain amongst the most populous by 2025. In particular, population levels in Europe are projected to decline sharply.

Sociological explanations: neo-Malthusian modernization theory

In his *Essay on the Principle of Population* in 1798, Thomas Malthus (1766–1834) argued that populations increase in size at a much faster rate than the ability of those same populations to feed themselves. He concluded that these limits on food supply would lead to natural checks on population, such as famine and malnutrition – and perhaps even war – as people fought over scarce resources. Such checks limit population because they

increase death rates. Malthus also argued, however, that we should attempt to avoid overpopulation by delaying marriage and abstaining from sex.

Malthus' ideas have been adopted by the biologist Paul Ehrlich who, in his book *The Population Bomb* (1968), argued 'the battle to feed all humanity is over' after studying the figures for birth rates and death rates and comparing them with food production and malnutrition rates. Ehrlich argues that the high birth rates of developing countries have led to a 'population explosion' that has put too much strain on their limited resources of food and energy. This, he alleges, is responsible for problems in the developing world, such as famine, malnutrition, poverty, war, **desertification** (because of overuse of land), **deforestation** (because more land is required for housing) and increasing environmental pollution. He concludes that 'the birth rate must be brought into balance with the death rate or mankind will breed itself into oblivion'.

Sociologists sympathetic to the modernization approach to development have seized upon these arguments with some relish. Overpopulation has been cited as yet another internal obstacle preventing countries from adopting Western forms of development. It is argued that the economic growth necessary for industrial development is difficult to achieve because any spare capital is unlikely to be reinvested in developing industry. Instead, it is likely to be spent feeding the population in order to avoid civil unrest and political instability. In addition, the infrastructure of such societies, especially their health and education systems (which are already basic), are stretched to the limit.

Blaming the victims

The modernization approach to development sees religions such as Islam and Roman Catholicism as responsible for the high birth rates in the developing world. Paul Harrison's *Inside the Third World* (1990) notes that 'the areas with the fastest population growth rates lie preponderantly in the Moslem belt from North Africa, through South-West Asia to Pakistan and Bangladesh, and in Roman Catholic Central and South America'. Harrison points out that the **theologians** of the Islamic world are divided about family planning, whilst the Koran does permit some forms of birth control. However, Harrison notes that ordinary Muslims are often opposed to any form of family planning because they fear that contraception will lead to 'promiscuity' and 'premarital sex'. Harrison suggests this 'could undermine the entire sexual politics of society from arranged marriages and parental authority, to fathers' control over daughters and men's control over women'. In other words, it is the patriarchal nature of Muslim societies that prevents 'progress' in the form of family planning.

Many religions in developing societies emphasize the importance of having sons rather than daughters. Sons attract dowries, earn more than daughters and are able to conduct funeral rites. As a result, men may insist on having more children in order to produce sons. In some societies, female infanticide may be practised as the marriage of daughters is expensive because their families have to pay a dowry to the family of the potential husband.

Harrison is particularly critical of the stance of the Roman Catholic Church on contraception. Pope John Paul II rigorously opposed effective family planning during his papacy (1978 to 2005) and his successor, Benedict XVI, takes a similar hard line. Harrison notes that priests in Latin America and Africa have rigidly enforced this line among the poor.

Moreover, the Church has found an ally in the 'powerful **machismo**' of the Latin male, who views contraception in all its varied forms as a threat to masculinity. As Harrison argues:

<< *The macho (South American) male wishes to prove his virility not only to himself and his wife, but also, and perhaps primarily, to other men. The only verifiable way of doing so is by getting women pregnant.* >>

Modernization theory highlights the low status of women in developing societies dominated by these belief systems, seeing this as yet another obstacle to development because women are often not allowed access to either education or employment. In many of these societies, women are denied reproductive rights – they cannot choose not to have children, when to have children or the number of children they have – because they are denied access to both contraception and abortion rights. Moreover, such women are economically dependent on men and have few opportunities to exercise the sorts of choices that Western women take for granted. Their potential talents and ability to contribute to the economies – and, therefore, the modernization – of developing nations go unrecognized and unused.

Solutions to overpopulation

Modernization theory has suggested three broad solutions to the 'problem' of overpopulation.

1   Family planning

Some countries have introduced voluntary family-planning schemes aimed at aggressively reducing population. They include China, which restricted couples to one child, and

A poster promotes the Chinese government's policy of restricting most couples to having one child. Why do you think this policy has been introduced?

Singapore, which economically rewarded those parents who chose to have fewer children. However, policies of this nature, although generally successful, are often coercive and are really only possible in societies in which authoritarian controls are accepted by a passive citizenry.

2   Western aid

Official aid from the West has been used to encourage the governments of developing countries to adopt family-planning and health-education policies. There is some evidence that this view has strongly influenced the US government and that the receipt of aid from the USA has been largely dependent on introducing such policies. A massive amount of Western aid has been pumped into family planning, e.g. introducing contraceptives into the developing world and promoting birth control through health education and media via radio and television advertising. For example, in 2006, USAID spent over $400 million on 'population stabilization' in developing nations whose birth rates are starting to fall.

However, Catley-Carlson (1994) notes that the existence and influence of religious belief systems means that family planning initiated by Western agencies in the developing world must be respectful and not offend the beliefs and convictions of those encouraged to use them. For example, there is some evidence that some Islamic societies see birth control as part of a Western plan to reduce their populations to impose control over them more easily.

3   The education of women

The education of women is seen as the most important aspect of this attempt to reduce population in the developing world. It is based on the assumption that, given the choice, women would want to have fewer children. One good reason for this is that 500 000 women a year die in pregnancy or childbirth in the developing world. It is argued that if women's educational and employment opportunities were improved, this would provide them with alternative sources of status and satisfaction beyond childbearing. Moreover, a major effect of illiteracy is the lack of access to information about contraception. Educated women are generally better able and more willing to use contraceptives.

This model is generally based upon the experience of women in Western societies. For example, in the UK, improved education has increased female aspirations and this has had the effect of delaying marriage and reducing family size. It is believed that education and literacy could have similar effects in the developing world. Education would open doors to jobs (possibly with Western transnationals) and eventually provide women with their own income and assets. This would increase the power of women to acquire reproductive rights, to make their own decisions about marriage and childbearing, and thus slow down population growth in the developing world.

The critique of neo-Malthusianism

One major problem with neo-Malthusian statistical analysis is that the statistics we have are unreliable. In the developed world, there is a legal obligation to register births, deaths and marriages. However, similar registration data in the developing world is inconsistently gathered. As Chrispin and Jegede (2000) note:

> << Those people who do register may not be representative of the whole population. Often, they are better educated, wealthier and they understand the need and procedures for vital registration. >>

In addition, Cohen and Kennedy (2000) argue 'it would be foolish to deny that there is cause for concern' with regard to world population growth. However, they suggest that neo-Malthusians may be guilty of overstating their case and distorting their statistical analysis. Cohen and Kennedy point out that predictions of population explosions and world collapse are usually based on present trends (i.e. from the period in which the author is writing). However, these are often wrong because 'people change their conduct in response to earlier plausible warnings'. The slowing-down of the annual growth rate of the world's population from 2 per cent in 1980 to 1.5 per cent in 2000 would support this view. Brian Carnell (2000) is critical of Ehrlich for similar reasons:

> << Why did Ehrlich's predictions fail to come true? Because the model he used was basically flawed. In a nutshell, what Ehrlich did was take population growth for the 1960s and **extrapolate** it out through the 1970s, but he insisted production of food and water were at their limits – both would likely decline and certainly not increase. However, food production not only increased, but increased faster than population growth because of advances in technology. >>

However, Carnell points out that, in the developed world, farmers are actually paid by governments not to produce food because in the past they have produced too much. Carnell, then, is critical of the selective bias in Ehrlich's examination of the statistics.

In defence of positivist approaches to population, they have highlighted a crucial dimension of population growth – that is, the fact that in developing countries, the majority of the population are aged under 25 years old, e.g. in Mexico, 45 per cent of the population is aged under 15. Consequently, there will be a much higher proportion of women of childbearing age than in developed countries.

Sociological explanations – dependency theory

Sociologists working from Marxist or socialist perspectives (i.e. a dependency theory perspective) are very critical of the neo-Malthusian idea that developing countries are responsible for the poverty they experience and that this is the result of their inability to control their family size.

Influence of social and economic relationships

Mamdani (2004) notes that the economic inequalities that characterize social and economic relationships within developing countries are neglected by modernization theory. These are often the legacy of colonialism and are shaped in the contemporary world by the terms of world trade, which favour the developed West. Access to land in developing nations is often controlled by local elites who were put into place by the colonial powers. For example, in South America, 47 per cent of the land is owned by just 2 per cent of the population. Land is also monopolized by Western multinationals in order to produce cash crops for export to the West. For example, Lappe and Collins (1977) note that Mexico (which experiences high rates of child malnutrition) provides the USA with most of its winter and spring vegetables. Such processes mean that the rural poor often have to make do with less efficient marginal

---

Key themes

Sociological theories and methods

Population statistics

Most of the population statistics collected by governments in the developing world use a census questionnaire that requires heads of household to complete a form. However, there are all sorts of methodological problems associated with collecting census data in the developing world. For example, nomads and the homeless may be difficult to record; there may be transport difficulties in remote rural areas; there may be language barriers (e.g. in Cameroon, over 30 languages are spoken); in some Islamic societies, male enumerators may not be allowed to interview women, and in areas with low literacy levels, people may have problems filling in forms. Many people do not have birth certificates and the enumerators may have to guess at age. People may describe themselves as being younger or older than they actually are, e.g. teenage girls and older women may shift their ages into the fertile age band, and where status is associated with age, people may give an older age.

land, which is often overfarmed and thus creates the conditions for famine, poverty, malnutrition, high infant mortality and high birth rates. Webster (1990) argues that land-reform programmes would probably be more effective in reducing birth rates and relieving world hunger than population-control policies.

The social context of fertility

Neo-Malthusians, like Ehrlich, tend to ignore the social context of fertility. Adamson (1986) argues this is because of a fundamental misunderstanding of the relationship between poverty and population. He claims that Ehrlich makes the mistake of supposing that population causes poverty. However, Adamson argues that poverty causes high population because in developing societies, children are economic assets in terms of their labour power and the extra income they can generate. For example, in Bangladesh, boys are already producing more than they can consume by the age of 10.

Moreover, in developing societies that lack a welfare infrastructure, such as pensions, children are vital for providing security and welfare in old age. The decision to have lots of children is rational in this context, especially if infant-mortality rates are high. For example, in sub-Saharan Africa, a couple have to bear 10 children in order to be certain of producing a son who will survive to the age of 38. There are signs that economic prosperity slows down birth rates because the costs of supporting a child increase and, for this reason, dependency theorists argue that birth-control programmes will always fail if poverty is not tackled. Adamson argues 'look after the population and the population will take care of itself'. There is some evidence for this from countries such as India, China and Mauritius, where high population is a norm rather than a problem. The key in these countries seems to be education. A high population can actually be an asset if it is skilled and educated, and can stimulate economic growth.

The UK experience of population change in the 19th century supports the view that development is the best contraceptive. Improved living standards and the introduction of public health had the effect of dramatically decreasing the UK death rate, especially the infant-mortality rate, as improved diet led to greater resistance to disease. The introduction of mass education and the trend towards urbanization led to a natural fall in the birth rate, as children were more likely to survive into adulthood and also became more expensive to raise.

However, dependency theory points out that there exist crucial differences between the UK experience and that of developing nations, which have led to rapid population growth in the developing world:

- Population growth in the developing world has been compressed into a shorter period of time, and population growth rates are, therefore, steeper and more dramatic.
- The impact of processed food, and advances in hygiene and medicine on infant mortality and life expectancy, have been quicker than that experienced in Europe.
- Europe was relatively wealthy before industrialization. It did not face the problems that the developing world

faces today in terms of debt and a disadvantaged position in world trade.
- There were more economic opportunities for European populations because population increased just as the industrial revolution was taking off.

However, Robey et al. (1993) question the dependency theory view that people in the developing world will have fewer babies if they become more prosperous. They note that birth rates are falling despite the persistence of poverty. They support the modernization theory line that this is due to the growing influence and scope of family-planning programmes. Some 51 per cent of women of childbearing age in the developing world now use contraception (compared with over 70 per cent of women in the developed world). The educational power of the mass media is seen as responsible for this massive cultural change, which has had the effect of reducing the number of children a woman has and hence family size. Robey and colleagues also note the growing influence of secondary education and the possibility of waged work in reducing population growth.

The relationship between health and population

There is some evidence that the birth rates in the developing world have not dramatically changed in the last 200 years, and so the argument that people in the developing world are 'having too many babies' is quite simply wrong. Instead, it is argued that high population growth is mainly due to a major decline in the death rate, especially the infant mortality rate, which ironically is mainly due to Western medical intervention. As the demographer Nick Eberstadt (quoted in Carnell 2000) observed in relation to population growth: 'It's not because people starting breeding like rabbits. It's that they stopped dying like flies.' Western-led public health education with regard to hygiene and clean water, the processing of food, medical advances in the eradication of diseases such as smallpox, and the control of disease such as measles and malaria have all contributed to a fall in the death rates of the developing world.

Moreover, Western-led educational health programmes aimed at women have also been successful in reducing

Access to safe water reduces the scourge of water-borne diseases

infant mortality rates and the need for what Cohen and Kennedy call 'insurance children'. For example, Oxfam has observed that in Ghana, the children of educated mothers are twice as likely as children of uneducated mothers to survive to their first birthday. Similarly, Swale (2004) notes that 'literate mothers are 50 per cent more likely to immunize their children, to take them to clinics for treatment and to understand the causes and treatments of common but life-threatening conditions such as diarrhoea and respiratory infections' (p.19).

However, dependency theorists also point out that there still exist major health problems in the developing world which have a profound influence on population growth:

- People in the developing world are still at grave risk of dying of diseases of poverty – 90 per cent of the world's disease burden occurs in developing countries. It is estimated that 30 000 children a day die of preventable diseases, especially communicable diseases caused by infected and polluted water supplies, particularly in sub-Saharan Africa. Thirteen million children were killed by diarrhoea alone in the 1990s. Poverty, in the form of malnutrition and poor diet, also decreases resistance to diseases such as measles. Some 800 million children are estimated by the United Nations to be malnourished.

- Aid and the debt that it generates, as well as fluctuations in the value of commodities such as cash crops and minerals (which many developing societies are overdependent on for export earnings), means that less money is available to invest in and spend on healthcare. There is evidence that the more a country pays to reduce its debt as a percentage of its earnings, the more likely its infant mortality rate will increase. Often, organizations such as the World Bank will only lend money if the developing country agrees to reduce its public spending. As a result, healthcare suffers – the country cannot afford to train and pay health professionals such as doctors and nurses. For example, the New Internationalist estimates that, whilst richer nations have on average one doctor for every 520 people, in the poorest developing countries, the ratio is one doctor for every 17 000 people. This has led to a 'brain drain' from the developing world to the West as medical staff migrate to secure better jobs. The Nursing and Midwifery Council estimates that 10 per cent of nurses employed in the UK were 'poached' from the developing world.

- Another problem faced by the developing world is the high cost of manufactured pharmaceuticals and medical technology, which are mainly produced by Western-based transnationals and which developing societies often cannot afford. Many African countries have run into severe financial difficulties raising the cash required to buy the drugs needed to control the HIV virus and AIDS. Western pharmaceutical companies have been accused of exploiting the African AIDS epidemic for profit, in that the prices they charge the developing world for these drugs is well in excess of their costs. TNCs have also been accused of creating further health problems through irresponsible and aggressive advertising of products such as babymilk powder, cigarettes and pesticides.

Dependency theory suggests, therefore, that the high death rates, particularly infant mortality rates, caused by these deficiencies in healthcare contribute to women in some developing societies continuing to bear large numbers of children in order to satisfy their perception, founded on their very real experiences, that infant mortality is a major problem.

The unequal distribution of resources

Adamson (1986) argues that by focusing on overpopulation, we run the risk of ignoring the major cause of poverty and its associated problems in the developing world, which is the unequal global distribution of resources such as food and energy between the developed and the developing world. In particular, Adamson argues that we should be focusing on the overconsumption of the world's resources by the West and the wasteful nature of Western standards of living. For example, the average American consumes 300 times as much energy as the average Bangladeshi. New Internationalist magazine points out that 'the 16 million babies born each year in the rich world will have four times as great an impact on the world's resources as the 109 million born in the poor world' (Adamson 1986). The USA, which has 6 per cent of the world's population, consumes 40 per cent of its resources.

This inequality in consumption can particularly be seen in Western taste for meat. It is argued that this is a wasteful type of nutrition because the land used for grazing cattle could be more effectively used for growing crops, whilst the cereal fed to cattle could go a long way towards reducing world hunger. In this light, the cutting down of rainforest and jungle in developing nations such as Brazil and Costa Rica, in order to graze cattle for fast food outlets in the West, is particularly problematical. As Hayter (1981) notes: 'by consuming meat, which wastes the grain that could have saved them, last year we ate the children of Ethiopia and Bangladesh. And we continue to eat them this year with undiminished appetite'. Note, too, that our pets in the developed world probably consume more food than the average African.

Moreover, Western industries, rather than the peoples of the developing world, have caused the most environmental pollution. Adamson argues that much of the neo-Malthusian concern with population is unconsciously racist because it reflects White Western concerns that Black and brown-skinned people may start to demand a fairer share of the world's resources and this may impact on White affluence. Family-planning policies, from this perspective, therefore, end up 'substituting condoms for justice'.

The world's food resources

There is little evidence that the world's food resources are running out. In fact, the opposite seems to be true. Technology has given us the means of producing more food more effectively. This has actually led to the overproduction of food in the West, leading to food either being stocked in warehouses for long periods (e.g. grain mountains) or the dumping and destruction of food, particularly fruit and vegetables. Often, excess production is fed back to farm animals. Finally, governments in the West frequently pay farmers for not producing food. It is important to understand that our attitudes to food production in the West are not shaped by the desire to eradicate world hunger – decisions to produce or destroy perfectly good food are motivated by the market. Oversupply leads to a depression in prices, possible loss in terms of profits and, consequently, the decision to stockpile or destroy.

Conclusions

The neo-Malthusian approach, despite its 'doom-and-gloom' predictions, has given us a valuable insight into the cultural context of population growth and, despite its ethnocentric judgements, it has rightly drawn our attention to problems that arise out of factors such as the patriarchal control of women. Furthermore, there is no doubt, as Jonathon Porritt (1985) argues, that family planning is important in the short term, because economic

changes with regard to standards of living can take years to take effect.

Anti-Malthusians are also important because they have drawn attention to the influence of global inequalities on population growth. They suggest that our concerns about population growth and the implication that this is deviant and irresponsible behaviour may stem from our concerns about whether we can continue to consume the world's resources at our present rates. They also point out that economic prosperity is the most powerful influence on reducing birth rates in the developing world – followed by education (especially of women), better healthcare facilities and a welfare state – rather than birth control. As Cohen and Kennedy (2000) argue:

>> Birth rates are only likely to decline if people in the developing world have the following questions answered: Where is my next meal coming from? Will my family have a future? Are my children likely to survive? >>

Activities

Research idea

Conduct a social survey to find out what view of population is held by a representative sample of people. Ask people whether they agree or disagree with the following statements, on a scale of 1 to 5, where 1 means 'strongly agree' and 5 means 'strongly disagree'.

- They have too many babies in the developing world.
- The world's population is out of control.
- We consume more than our fair share of resources in the West.
- The developing world needs more contraception.
- The world just cannot support all these extra mouths.
- High population results in more poverty.
- There are simply not enough resources to go around.
- The cause of high population in the developing world is poverty.
- The world's food resources are not fairly distributed.
- Obesity in the developed world is linked to starvation in the developing world.

Web.tasks

1 Discover the latest figures on world population at **http://esa.un.org/unpp/** – this UN site monitors the growth of world population and can therefore supply you with the latest figures.

2 Find out how you might be part of the consumption problem by accessing the ecological footprint site **www.myfootprint.org/**

Check your understanding

1 How does population change in the past 30 years compare across the developed and developing worlds?

2 What did Malthus predict with regard to population growth and the world's resources?

3 Identify six problems identified by Paul Ehrlich that are allegedly a consequence of the population explosion.

4 In what ways might the value systems of some developing countries contribute to high population growth?

5 What solutions do neo-Malthusians offer for high population growth?

6 Identify three reasons why population statistics may be unreliable.

7 What is the reason for population growth in the developing world, according to Nick Eberstadt?

8 In what ways might inequalities in wealth and access to land contribute to high population?

9 Compare and contrast the neo-Malthusian and anti-Malthusian approach to the relationship between poverty and high population.

10 Why is Adamson convinced that birth control strategies in the developing world encouraged by Western aid are essentially racist?

11 In your view, is the problem overpopulation or overconsumption? Explain your reasoning.

Key terms

Demography the sociological study of population.

Deforestation destruction of forests.

Desertification increasing spread of deserts.

Extrapolate take a pattern or idea and apply it to wider or future situations.

Machismo an exaggerated sense of masculinity, mainly found in Latin America.

Theologians religious thinkers.

Population and consumption

Item A

The more people there are, the more resources they will consume. This seems obvious – at first glance. But when I stopped to think about it, it was equally obvious that 15 people might not make any more impact than 10, if the 15 lived frugally and the 10 were big spenders. In fact, the 10 might consume far more.

Paradoxically, fewer people could make more environmental damage than many people. The key lay not in numbers but in choice: how much each person chose to consume – and how much the world at large chose to enable that person to consume. But surely, although hundreds of millions of people in the developing world are very poor, the sheer weight of their numbers would make their consumption catch up with the consumption of us few in the developed world. But the developed world consumes five-sixths of the world's resources and each person in the developed world consumes around 20 times as much as a person in the developing world. This is really a remarkable ratio. It means that 80 average people in the developing world are managing to live their lives consuming no more than my husband, my two children and I consume. Even with population in the developing world projected to double to 9 billion people, the 20:1 consumption ratio means we will always be consuming twice as much as them.

Source: Population Reference Bureau, 2001, and 'Consuming Passions' in *New Internationalist*, 235, September 1992

	Population 2008 (millions)	Births per 1000 of population	Deaths per 1000 of population	Rate of natural increase	Projected population change 2008–2050 (%)
World	6.7	21	8	1.2	29
More developed	1.2	12	10	0.2	5
Less developed	5.5	23	8	1.5	47

Source: Population Reference Bureau, 2001

Using information from Item A and elsewhere, assess the view that overconsumption is now more of a threat than overpopulation to world development. (33 marks)

Grade booster Getting top marks in this question

In answering this question, it is important that you consider overconsumption as well as overpopulation. You should consider different explanations of population growth, including Malthusian, modernization theory and dependence theory views. You also need to examine the Malthusian argument that population growth undermines development by causing environmental damage such as desertification. Remember that you need to make use of relevant information from Item A in your answer. For example, you can link the issue of population growth to overconsumption by contrasting the share of the world's resources consumed by developed and developing countries, relative to their population sizes. You can evaluate the view by considering whether current Western consumption levels are achievable in a sustainable way for the entire planet, as well as by considering different views of the relationship between underconsumption (or poverty) and population growth.

Getting you thinking

Women are the backbone of Africa's rural economy accounting for 70 per cent of food production, most of the selling of family produce and half of the animal husbandry in addition to food preparation, gathering firewood, fetching water, childcare and the care of the sick and elderly. Women spend most of the earnings they control on household needs, particularly for the children, whilst men spend a significantly higher amount on themselves. But women have fewer opportunities to generate income; they are less likely to attend school; they are subject to harassment and violence; and on widowhood lose their assets.

Source: Commission for Africa (2005)

Nasrin Akther aged 21 is from Bangladesh and until recently worked from 8am to 10pm every day in a garment factory. Around 80 per cent of the garment workers in Bangladesh are women, often producing clothes for the big Western labels, and working in appalling conditions for low wages. Nasrin says: 'there is no childcare, no medical facilities. The women don't receive maternity benefits. We have two days off a month. In my factory, it is very crowded, very hot and badly ventilated. I could not support myself with the wage I was getting. Because we have to work very long hours, seven days a week, we have no family life, no personal life, no social life … Our lives have been stolen. Any workers who attempt to get together a union are fired immediately and may be blacklisted.'

Source: Van der Gaag (2004)

1 **Compare an African woman's day with that of a Western mother. How do the lifestyles differ?**

2 **Compare the experience of Bangladeshi woman workers with that of a female factory worker in the UK. How do their experiences differ?**

3 **Why might the sorts of experiences some women face in Afghanistan and Bangladesh hold up development in these countries?**

Acid attacks and rape: growing threat to women who oppose traditional order

They were walking to school in the southern Afghan city of Kandahar, a group of teenage girls discussing a test they had coming up, when two men on a motorcycle sprayed them with a strange liquid. Within seconds a painful tingling began, and there was an unusual smell as the skin of 16-year-old Atifa Biba began to burn. Her friend rushed over to help her, struggling to wipe the liquid away, when she too was showered with acid. She covered her face, crying out for help as they sprayed her again, trying to aim the acid into her face. The weapon was a water bottle containing battery acid; the result was at least one girl blinded and two others permanently disfigured. Their only crime was attending school. It was not an isolated incident. For women and girls across Afghanistan, conditions are worsening – and those women who dare to publicly oppose the traditional order now live in fear for their lives. Afghan women who defy traditional gender roles and speak out against the oppression of women are routinely subject to threats, intimidation and assassination. An increasingly powerful Taliban regularly attacks projects, schools and businesses run by women.
In Bangladesh, more than 200 girls and young women were mutilated in acid attacks last year, leaving them scarred and blinded. Reported reasons for the acid-throwing attacks include the refusal of an offer of marriage, dowry disputes, domestic fights and arguments over property.

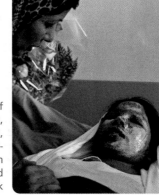

Kabul's head of education, Naziba Norstani, visits the 17-year-old victim of an acid attack

Adapted from: *The Guardian*, 22 November 2008

Women in developing countries

Despite women in the developed world lagging behind males in terms of pay, women in the West enjoy opportunities with regard to education, health, access to jobs and legal rights that suggest greater equality with men than is experienced by women in the developing world. Patriarchy is not dead and buried in the West, but it is no longer all-powerful. However, patriarchal control in the developing world can be all-consuming and exert control that can often threaten women's lives in different ways, as the three sources on p. 98 illustrate. Madeleine Leonard (1992) notes:

<< What is very striking is how different women's ordinary lives are from men's ordinary lives. No matter which country we focus on ... women are worse off than men. Women have less power, less autonomy, do more work, earn less money, and often have more responsibility. Women everywhere have a smaller share of the pie, and if the pie is very small (as it is in developing countries) than their share is smaller still. >>

Leonard argues that 'the conditions of underdevelopment – dependency, powerlessness, vulnerability and inequality of income – are experienced by women to a greater extent than men'. Steinem (1995) suggests that women in

Focus on...

Women in the developing world

WORK

- In 1995, the United Nations conducted a survey of 17 developing countries and found that women's work hours exceeded men's by approximately one third. This confirmed previous studies, which had long concluded that women do more work than men in subsistence societies. Leonard (1992) notes that in many developing countries, women grow, harvest and prepare all the food consumed by their families.
- Hay and Stichter (1984, see Leonard 1992) found in Africa that women perform 60 to 80 per cent of all agricultural work. Paul Harrison (1990) actually refers to women in developing nations as 'the poorest of the poor' because, in general, they spend eight hours or more on formal work outside the home and spend the equivalent on domestic labour. The latter is very different to that experienced by Western women and includes tasks such as fetching water and gathering firewood as well as nursing children.

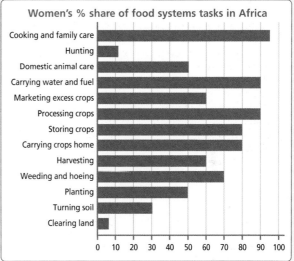

Women's % share of food systems tasks in Africa

EDUCATION

Ninety million girls receive no education at all in the developing world. Two-thirds of the 867 million illiterate people in the world are women. In developing countries, nearly one out of every five girls who enrols in primary school does not complete her primary education.

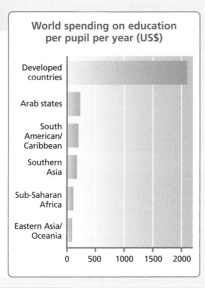

World spending on education per pupil per year (US$)

HEALTH

Half a million women die each year as a consequence of pregnancy and childbirth. Of these deaths, 99 per cent are in the developing countries, e.g. the maternal death rate in developing countries is 479 per 100 000 live births (at least one woman every minute), compared with just 27 in developed countries. This means that a woman's lifetime risk of dying from pregnancy-related causes in Africa is 1 in 16; in Asia, 1 in 65; and in Europe, 1 in 1400. Pregnancy and the complications of childbirth are the leading cause of death for young women aged between 15 and 19. Over 300 million women in the developing world suffer from short-term or long-term illness brought about by pregnancy and childbirth.

AIDS has a disproportionate effect on women; 25 million people have AIDS in Africa and 57 per cent of them are women. For example, in Zambia, females are three times more likely to be infected with the HIV virus than men. Life expectancy continues to increase for women and men in most developing regions but has decreased dramatically in Southern Africa as a result of AIDS.

Focus on ...

Women's lack of status and power

- Women often lack **reproductive rights**. They do not have the power to decide whether to have children, when to have them and how many they should have. They are often prevented from making rational decisions about contraception and abortion. Men make all these decisions. Instead, women are strongly encouraged to see their role and status as tied up with being a mother and being dependent upon the male head of household. This lack of reproductive rights is one of the main causes of high maternal death rates in the developing world.

- Both the developed and developing world have experienced a feminization of poverty – 70 per cent of the 1.5 billion people living on $1 a day or less are women. Many are denied access to credit, land and inheritance.

- Foster-Carter (1985) notes that **purdah** is practised in many Islamic countries (in West and South Asia, and North Africa). This is the custom of making women wear clothing that covers them from head to toe. This often prevents them from playing an active role in social, economic and political life. As Foster-Carter notes, 'women's participation in public life ranges from limited to non-existent. Often, even to enter the public domain (e.g. walk in the street) requires varying degrees of veiling'. Most people are now familiar with how the hardline Islamic regime of the Taliban treated women in Afghanistan, but they are unaware that these rules about women's dress codes apply in varying degrees across a range of developing societies. There is evidence that females are more likely to be subjected to violence than men. In war, rape is often used as a weapon against the female population and women prisoners are often subjected to sexual slavery. In conflicts in Africa, for example, women and children make up the majority of civilian casualties (70 per cent) as well as the majority of refugees. Seventy-two per cent of the world's 33 million refugees are women and children.

- In Africa, it is estimated that 6000 girls every day are subject to genital cutting or female circumcision (removal of the clitoris) in order to enhance their future husband's enjoyment of sex.

- There is evidence that in rural India, between five and ten women a day die because of dowry-burning, where husbands kill wives so that they become free to marry again and attract a dowry.

- The emphasis on women marrying and becoming mothers means that cultures and families may not regard the education of female children as a priority.

---

developing countries make up a 'fifth world', in that they are more at risk than men in these countries from subsistence poverty, poor healthcare and exploitation in factories and sweatshops, as well as the sex trade.

Explanations for the position of women in developing countries

Modernization theory

Modernization theory blames internal cultural factors for women's subordination in the developing world. It is argued that some cultures, and especially the religious ideas that underpin the values, norms, institutions and customs of the developing world, ascribe status on the basis of gender. In practice, this means that males are accorded patriarchal control and dominance over a range of female activities and, consequently, women have little status in many developing societies. Van der Gaag (2004) notes that these attitudes go back a long way – one verse from the Chinese Book of Songs, written 3000 years ago, says:

≪ When a son is born, let him sleep on the bed, Clothe him with fine clothes, and give him jade to play...

When a daughter is born, let her sleep on the ground, Wrap her in common wrappings, and give broken tiles to play... ≫

Van der Gaag reports that in many countries today, the birth of a boy is still something to be celebrated whilst the birth of a girl is a cause for commiseration. This can have serious consequences for their human rights. For example, although it is often technically illegal, in Asia, at least 60 million women are missing due to sex-selective abortion and the practice of killing or abandoning girl babies. Once they are born, girl babies are likely to be fed less than their brothers when food is short, leading to a permanent cycle of anaemia and undernourishment. They are also less likely to go to school. As they grow up, many young women find they cannot choose when they have sex, or who they have it with, or under what conditions. More than 70 000 teenage girls, some as young as 10, are married every day, and 14 million girls under 18 are already mothers.

Modernization theory would argue that the low status of women in developing societies is another obstacle to development, for two reasons:

- Their potential contribution to the economy is not being fully realized.
- Their status as mothers contributes to overpopulation.

Boserup (1970) called for greater educational opportunities for adolescent girls in order to break the cycle of early childbearing. This view is echoed by the Commission for Africa which argues:

> << Getting girls into school, studies show, is crucial for development. Economic productivity is raised by educating girls. Infant and maternal mortality is lowered. Nutrition and health improve. The spread of HIV is reduced. Providing girls with one extra year of education boosts their eventual wages by 10 to 20 per cent.>>

Modernization theorists believed that the creation of industrial jobs by multinational companies would encourage female economic independence from men. Moreover, family planning, health education and a sympathetic media transmitting Western values would reinforce female liberation and sexual equality, which (according to modernization theory) are essential components of the Western-industrial model of development.

Modernization theory also argues that attitudinal change needs to be promoted. In particular, fathers, husbands and brothers need to be encouraged to view their female relatives as equal to themselves. Young men must challenge the ways they have been brought up and the traditional ways in which they see themselves. It is argued that as long as women are considered second-class citizens, young women will never be able to achieve their full potential.

However, observations about cultural practices such as those above are controversial because the experiences of Western women tend to be used as the yardstick in terms of quality of life for women in developing countries. However, such views may be guilty of ethnocentrism and of imposing Western values on such societies. For example, it is often assumed by Western feminists that aspects of patriarchy in developing countries, e.g. female circumcision, are morally wrong, repressive, exploitative and barbaric. Development is often associated with bringing these cultural practices to an end. This, of course, assumes a moral superiority among Western feminists and simplistically dismisses such cultural behaviour as being the product of ignorance. However, some Muslim women argue that Islam values and empowers them – for example, wearing the **burkha** ensures that women control how men perceive their bodies.

The marginalization thesis

The marginalization perspective on development suggests that the introduction of capitalism in developing societies has led to women being increasingly excluded from economic life, restricted to the home and being forced to be dependent upon men. A number of observations can be made to support this thesis, which is similar in tone to dependency theory:

- Colonial powers and missionaries brought with them, and imposed upon indigenous peoples, traditional Western values about males and females, e.g. a woman's place is in the home. Abbott and Wallace (1997) describe how Western notions of femininity and the family have been imposed upon other models of gender, rendering them 'peculiar',

'heathen', 'unliberated' or 'sexually exotic'. Colonialism probably introduced new forms of inequality which reaffirmed the ascribed roles encouraged by religion. As Leonard (1992) argues, the colonial powers introduced a 'money economy, based on wage labour and **cash crops**, into Africa and Asia. Men were absorbed into the cash economy while women were left with all the work associated with subsistence food production'. However, there is evidence that colonialism challenged some aspects of ascribed gender roles that were harmful to women, e.g. the British made female circumcision, infanticide, *suttee* (the burning of wives after the death of their husbands) and dowries illegal.

- Leonard notes that the emphasis on exporting cash crops in the developing world today has resulted in men rather than women being employed as agricultural labourers. Moreover, many men migrate to other regions in search of such work, leaving women to subsist without male help on the smaller and poorer plots of land not taken by elites or multinational companies for cash-crop production.

- The modernization view that men's wages will trickle down to women rarely occurs in practice. Moreover, Leonard notes that in Africa many men are unused to the status of being a wage-earner and they see their wage as their own money rather than as a means of supporting their families.

- Aid projects also marginalize women. Information collected from 46 African countries showed that only 3.4 per cent of trained government workers providing agricultural advice to people in rural areas were women. The introduction of modern agricultural technology is primarily aimed at male tasks and used almost exclusively by men.

- Leonard's review of official aid programmes concludes that aid is not gender-neutral. Rather, it comes with Western values attached – values that are often male-dominated and male-orientated. Aid workers bring

Key themes

Sociological theories and methods

Feminism and development

The experience of women in developing countries can be linked to the concepts of patriarchy, subordination and exploitation focused on by feminist theories of gender stratification. Western feminists have identified a number of social areas in which women face inequality both in the West and the developing world, although they acknowledge that the experience of women in the developing world may be more extreme and potentially devastating. However, female sociologists in the developing world have argued that patriarchy and men are not the only enemy of women in the poorer parts of the world – women's experience of poverty in the developing world has a great deal in common with that of men and may have more to do with nationality, ethnicity, religion, caste and social class than gender.

with them the patriarchal prejudices about women and technology found in their own societies. For example, science and technology are considered masculine activities in the West because women are not supposed to understand technical matters. As a result, technical aid in terms of training and equipment tends to be aimed at men rather than women, despite the fact that women play a greater role in the production of food than men. Even irrigation systems are seen to be a male domain – men are trained to use pumps, wells and filtering systems despite the fact that women play the central role in supplying water to fulfil the household's needs. Moreover, aid planners tend to neglect other aspects of female work, such as domestic tasks, because they do not consider this 'real work' as it is unwaged or because they undervalue the role of women.

Focus on research

Maria Mies (1986)
A Marxist–feminist perspective

Mies's research was conducted from a Marxist–feminist perspective. She argued on the basis of her findings that capitalism could not spread in the developing world without the subordination and exploitation of women. She found that women were employed in multinational factories in the developing world, particularly in the electronics, textile and garment industries, at lower wages and in poorer conditions compared with male workers. Often women's work was regarded by management as supplementing that of the male breadwinner and, for this reason, they were paid less on casual insecure contracts. Moreover, women workers were vulnerable to a range of hazards from allergy to dyes, exposure to carcinogenic chemicals and deterioration of eyesight due to close work. Those who suffered from such problems were often dismissed without compensation and were forced into the sex trade to survive.

Mies, M., (1986) *Patriarchy and Accumulation on a World Scale: Women in the International Division of Labour*, London: Zed Books

Which aspects of Mies' work indicate that she is a Marxist feminist?

The exploitation thesis

The exploitation view is essentially a Marxist–feminist position. It suggests that modernization is about imposing an exploitative global system of capitalism on developing societies.

Many Western transnational companies (TNCs) have relocated their mass-production assembly lines producing electronic equipment, textiles, sports shoes, etc., to export-processing zones or centres (EPZs) mostly in developing countries. TNCs are attracted to these zones by governments offering benefits such as tax privileges, cheap labour, restrictions on the activities of trades unions and limited or non-existent health, safety and environmental regulations. The work exported to the EPZs is generally standardized and repetitive, calls for little technical knowledge and is labour intensive. The majority of workers in these factories (90 per cent) are young women, who are employed because the TNCs regard them as cheap, pliable and docile. The exploitation of these women takes several forms:

- Low pay – Women workers in the EPZs are paid lower rates than male workers. Wages are often only about 10 per cent of those in developed societies, and working hours are often 50 per cent higher. Consequently, women in the EPZs are producing more for less pay.
- Western owners do not invest a great deal in training female workforces. The work is generally regarded as unskilled despite high skill levels being evident. However, because girls have already learned these skills in the home (e.g. sewing), the skill is downgraded.
- TNCs take advantage of what Elson and Pearson (1981) call 'women's material subordination as a gender', i.e. the fact that women will put up with lower wages or accept oppressive working conditions. They do this because either there is no alternative or the patriarchal conditions of their society mean the job is only temporary until they achieve the cultural goal of marriage and childbearing. As a result, TNCs are able to control their female workforces socially with little protest, e.g. sacking them when they become pregnant, minimizing toilet breaks, bullying by management.

Leonard (1992) and others conclude that TNCs aim to exploit female labour rather than provide women with training, fair pay and job security. However, in criticism, we have to acknowledge that the wages earned from such work are superior to the subsistence living eked out of rural existences. Also, it does allow some escape from the powerful forms of patriarchy found in the countryside, such as arranged marriages. Such developments, alongside urban living and access to education, constitute major changes for women. Nonetheless, as Foster-Carter (1993) points out, such changes often bring with them new forms of exploitation 'in which the price of gaining some measure of autonomy and income of one's own is often submission to long hours, low wages and the advances of chauvinist male bosses'.

Solutions to gender inequalities in the developing world

Marxist–feminist approaches

Marxist–feminists argue that socialism is committed to dismantling patriarchal regimes in the developing world. Molyneux's (1981) study of societies that were both Marxist–Leninist and Islamic found that such regimes were willing to challenge traditions such as child marriage and the veil, as well as being fully committed to maximizing women's education and job opportunities. However, there was little sign of change within the home. As Elwood (*New Internationalist* 1986) said of the old Soviet Union, 'women can fly to the moon but they still have to do the ironing when they get home again'.

Radical-feminist approaches

The international feminist movement, too, has not always understood the nature of the developing world. The radical-feminist insistence that men were the enemy failed to address what women in developing nations saw as their main problem – uneven development and neo-colonial exploitation. Women's subordination only formed part of this. Feminists in these regions argued that their immediate task was to join with men to fight such exploitation and oppression. Hence, women in the developed world have different priorities to those in developing nations. Whilst women in the developed world were campaigning against the trivialization of women in the media, women in the developing world were focusing on acquiring the reproductive rights that women in the West took for granted. Moreover, women in the developing world were physically at risk from male violence for even daring to campaign for such rights. In other words, for them, nationality, social class, ethnicity and religious identity were just as important (and in some cases, more important) than gender as a source of inequality.

Postmodern-feminist approaches

Hunt (2004b) notes that postmodernists have drawn attention to how the category of 'woman' has been constructed, and particularly how specific female groups in the developing world have been perceived by Western feminists. Mohanty (1997) is critical of the way Western feminists have presented women in the developing world as 'ignorant, poor, uneducated, tradition-bound, domestic, family-orientated, victimized, etc.' compared with Western feminists, who are seen as 'educated, modern, as having control over their own bodies and sexualities, and the freedom to make their own decisions' (p.80). Mohanty suggests such views of women in the developing world smack of ethnocentric and colonial attitudes.

Cohen and Kennedy (2000) point to a form of **postmodern feminism** that appeared in the 1990s, made up of feminists from both the developed and developing worlds who share a more global agenda. It was generally agreed that the **globalization** of the world had led to common problems for women, such as the following:

- *Sex tourism and prostitution* – There has been a growth in the numbers of women and girls from the developing world being trafficked for forced sexual activities. The UN estimates that four million women a year are trafficked – as Van der Gaag (2004) notes:

  << *Traffickers exploit women's desire to make a better life for themselves with promises of jobs as waitresses, dancers, models, maids and nannies. Once they arrive, their passports are taken away and they are forced to work as prostitutes. And even if they manage to escape, their families will often not have them back as they have been 'dishonored'.* >> (p.52)

- *Environmental degradation* – **Eco-feminists** such as Shiva (1989) argue that women are more inclined towards nature than men and therefore more protective of the natural world. About 60 to 70 per cent of the world's agricultural workers are women and there are worrying signs that these women are more likely than men to be victims of environmental pollutants such as pesticides.

- *The international debt crisis* – Feminist action groups have supported the 'breaking the chains' of debt movement because they appreciate that women and children in the developing world bear the brunt of debt in terms of less spending on health and education.

Inclusion of gender in development policy

Pearson (2001) notes that, since the mid-1990s, the major development agencies have responded positively to the critique that women's issues were neglected by development policy. Consequently, gender has been incorporated into the indices of development used by multilateral aid agencies such as the UK's Department for International Development, the World Bank and United Nations. For example, the Millennium Development goals include the promotion of gender equality, the empowerment of women and the improvement of maternal health. The Gender Empowerment Measure (GEM) indicates whether or not women play an active part in economic and political life across both the developed and developing world. All these agencies now check, as a matter of course, that gender is considered across a range of projects, including civil engineering works and famine relief.

In particular, NGOs have championed a number of projects aimed at alleviating the feminization of poverty. For example, micro-credit schemes in countries such as India and Bangladesh make small amounts of credit available to the poor to cover subsistence needs, so that they can invest in livestock, equipment, fertilizer, etc. These schemes are seen particularly to empower women (who are often responsible for domestic production). For example, research by Kilby (2001) into 80 micro-credit schemes suggests that women who take part in these self-help schemes experience increased mobility, respect, dignity, assertiveness and support.

The future?

The prognosis for women in the developing world is, at best, mixed. On the plus side, the expansion of both education and family planning does constitute progress. Adamson (1986) argues that there is now a generation of women in the developing world who see education as the norm and not the exception. These women will demand more input into political and domestic decision-making, and will pass down these attitudes to their daughters.

According to Van der Gaag (2004), the advances women have made over the last 20 years cannot hide the fact that for millions of women life is still very grim. While noting the improvements in women's lives – better education, longer life span, better prospects of a career in business or politics, legislation against domestic violence and action against genital cutting – some brutal facts remain:

> ≪ The vast majority of the world's women still have very little power, at work, in their relationships at home, or in the wider social world. Worldwide, 70 per cent of those living in poverty are women, as are two-thirds of illiterate adults. One in four women is beaten by her husband or partner. Every day, 1300 still die unnecessarily in childbirth or pregnancy. ≫

Van der Gaag suggests there are signs that the rights women have won are being clawed back. She identifies five threats to the progress women have achieved:

1. *The increasingly militarization of the world* – Women are disproportionately affected by war and are often the victims of ethnic cleansing and rape. Women and their children are often forced off their land and often make up the bulk of refugees in war-torn areas of the world, particularly Africa. The values of military societies are male values – strength, aggression and domination – which disadvantage women. For example, in times of crisis, women are expected to be in the home.

2. *Disempowerment of women through economic globalization* – There is no doubt that globalization has brought some positive effects for women. For example, women are entering the workforce in unprecedented numbers. However, economic globalization has also led to women being exploited by the global pornography industry that operates through the internet. Women are being trafficked from country to country to feed the sex trade. For example, trafficking in women and girls for forced labour and sexual exploitation grew rapidly between 1995 and 2005, largely as a result of war, displacement, and economic and social inequities between and within countries. The United Nations estimates that approximately 800 000 people are trafficked across national borders annually.

   In addition, millions of victims are trafficked within their own national borders. Women are also being exploited in the developing world by transnational companies as well as British supermarkets and clothing stores. They are employed in low-paid jobs in sweatshops to meet Western demand for cheap

Focus on ... Darfur

Stark choices: in Darfur, women risk leaving their camp to collect firewood. Unprotected, they risk being raped by roaming militias, and many are. But if the men go, they risk being murdered, and if no one goes, the family will starve.

Rape as a weapon of war

Sexual violence against women is occurring on a massive scale in Darfur. Amnesty International calls these mass rapes a weapon of war. After years of pressure from women's organizations around the world, a 1998 landmark United Nations decision confirmed the concept of rape as a war crime, one that has increased during recent years. Darfur fits the pattern of Cambodia, Liberia, Peru, Bosnia, Sierra Leone, Rwanda, Somalia and Uganda, with violence against women being systematically used by warring parties. In Darfur, the Arab militia and military make a point of abusing women in front of their families or entire village. Raping a woman is such an effective weapon because it affects an entire community, for decades. French anthropologist Véronique Nahoum-Grappe calls it 'destroying the future'. Children who witness the crime are traumatized, men flee from their partners out of shame, and women become 'damaged goods', sometimes literally, if they can no longer have children because of the violence. Through raping wives and daughters, Nahoum-Grappe explains, the attackers actually target the 'real enemy': the men behind them. Having to have your enemy's baby goes one step further and turns this sexual violence into a tool for 'ethnic cleansing'. Feminists like Susan Brownmiller (2000) and Robin Morgan (2006) argue that rape is inherent in the nature of war: it is never about sex, but about power and the military culture of violence.

Source: van Zeijl, F. (2007) 'War against women', *New Internationalist, 401, June*

clothing. Many of these women are denied rights at work that Western women take for granted. Many of the jobs that women take on in factories in the developing world are bad for their health.

3. *The rise of religious extremism and fundamentalism* – This has resulted in heightened legal and social restrictions for women. Seager (2003) observed that 25 countries introduced restrictions on women's behaviour between the late 1990s and 2002. She

Key themes

Crime and deviance

Sex-trafficking

A major global problem that has been developing over the last few years is sex-trafficking. It is estimated that at least 1400 women a year are trafficked from abroad into the UK sex industry. Victims are often promised jobs in bar work or nannying but on arrival in the UK, they have their passports confiscated by criminal gangs, are kept captive and are forced to sell sex. The UK's response to victims of trafficking has been criticized because women who are released from this ordeal are usually deported as illegal immigrants and often end up being retrafficked or ostracized by their communities back home because they have sold sex.

notes that at the heart of the religious fundamentalist agenda (whether Christian, Hindu, Jewish or Muslim) is 'the control of women, of reproductive rights and of the family'. Van der Gaag notes that beliefs and practices, e.g. genital mutilation, are being dredged up from the past by Islamic fundamentalists as an 'Islamic duty', despite the fact that they have nothing to do with Islam or the Qur'an. Van der Gaag also notes an increase in the number of honour killings of women for infringing family 'honour' or because they have been raped. In India and Bangladesh, women are killed or burned with acid for not bringing enough dowry into their husband's family when they marry. Van der Gaag argues that the USA has played a role in the global subordination of women in the developing world. The Bush presidency, which was anti-abortion, refused to fund family-planning organizations in the developing world because they provided abortion services. Moreover $34 million in aid to the United Nations Fund for Population Activities and $3 million for the World Health Organization's reproductive

4   *Rejection of women's rights as a 'Western' import* – Van der Gaag notes that often Islamic fundamentalists see women's rights as the product of decadent Western thought, and for that reason oppose such rights on the back of a general anti-Western feeling. She suggests that for some Muslim women, veiling has become 'part of a wider statement against the West'. However an Afghan feminist, Zuhra Bahman argues that the burkha is a symbol of traditionally conservative Afghan society in which women are viewed as men's possessions, to be kept hidden from other men.

5   *Male backlash against women's rights* – Van der Gaag notes that, in some developing countries, it is believed that women have too many rights. In South Africa, women are experiencing high levels of violence which may be partly fuelled by a male backlash against the progress women have made. This 'neo-patriarchy' is a new attempt to exert male authority through a culture of violence.

Check your understanding

1   **Identify four aspects of patriarchal inequality experienced by women in the developing world.**

2   **What are reproductive rights and how do women in the developed and developing world differ in access to them?**

3   **What is the relationship between religion and patriarchy in the developing world?**

4   **Why might Western critiques of cultural and religious practices be ethnocentric?**

5   **What is the key to women's development according to Boserup?**

6   **What effect did colonialism have on the social status of women in the developing world?**

7   **Why is aid not gender-neutral?**

8   **What forms does exploitation of female labour by transnationals take in the developing world?**

9   **Why might exploitation of women by transnationals be acceptable for many women in the developing world?**

10 **Why has the international feminist movement not always understood the nature of the problems faced by women in the developing world?**

11 **What international problems are thought to be shared by women today?**

12 **What is the future of women in the developing world likely to be?**

Key terms

Burhka long enveloping garment worn by Muslim women in public.

Cash crops crops grown to sell rather than to use.

Crisis of masculinity the notion that masculinity is under threat because of the rapidly changing nature of work and that this has undermined men's sense of their role and power in the world.

Eco-feminists feminists who link the social position of women to environmental issues.

Globalization the increasing interconnectedness and interdependency of the world.

Postmodern feminism a branch of feminism that suggests that there is a diversity of female experience in the world and that no one feminist theory is capable of explaining the range of culture-specific patriarchal experiences that women have.

Purdah Muslim custom of keeping women in seclusion by requiring them to wear clothing that shields them from public view.

Reproductive rights rights relating to women's choice to have children and control their bodies.

Hunt (2004b) argues that women's rights and issues need to be more firmly embedded in mainstream development policies. There are signs that this is happening, as reflected in the Millennium development goals and their focus on gender (see p. 103). However, the dominance of neo-liberal policies in aid programmes and economic policy generally suggests that gender equality is viewed as a natural outcome of economic growth. Hunt points out that the gender inequality and patriarchy still apparent in the developed West suggest that this neo-liberal assumption may be overly optimistic.

Finally, there has also been a growing realization in development theory that the concentration on women in recent years has led to neglect in the understanding of men and masculinity. In the developed world, this has resulted in sociologists investigating a so-called '**crisis of masculinity**'. Researchers have now begun to focus on examining how masculinity is constructed in the developing world in order to understand the nature of patriarchal gender-relations. However, it is important to acknowledge that all these changes with regard to masculinity are still in their infancy.

Activities

Research idea

Find out how three of the major British aid agencies, e.g. Oxfam, Cafod, Christian Aid are specifically targeting women's development in the countries in which they are involved.

Web.tasks

1 Visit the *New Internationalist* website – **www.newint.org** – and access the Magazine mega index and click on 'W'. This will give you access to all the articles on women in the developing world published by the magazine in the last ten years. Their search engine is also worth using because they monitor articles on women in the developing world produced by a host of other agencies such as Amnesty International.

2 Compare the treatment of women across the world at Human Rights Watch – **www.hrw.org**

An eye on the exam   Gender in the developing world

Item A

It used to be believed that women and men in the developing world faced largely the same problems: technological and institutional backwardness, poverty, illiteracy, malnutrition and ill health. According to modernization theorists, the introduction of capitalism would benefit both sexes; at the same time, it would also liberate women from the oppression they suffered in traditional society and bring gender equality through the introduction of 'modern' values and job opportunities in capitalist enterprises.

However, critics argue that this is not necessarily true: development may benefit men without automatically benefiting women. In fact, it may make women's position even worse than before and impose increased burdens upon them.

Using material from **Item A** and elsewhere, assess the view that the introduction of capitalism into developing countries liberates women.   (33 marks)

Grade booster   Getting top marks in this question

In answering this question, you could begin by outlining the view of modernization theory in relation to capitalism. Remember to make use of relevant material from the Item in your answer, for example in explaining why modernization theorists feel capitalism is likely to 'liberate women from the oppression they suffered in traditional society', e.g. in terms of ending oppressive cultural practices, providing educational opportunities and so on. You should evaluate this view by reference to other approaches that see capitalism as compounding women's subordinate position, either by marginalizing them from development, or by exploiting their existing subordination, e.g. by allowing employers to pay them lower wages. You can also look at how globalization impacts on women in developing countries, e.g. in terms of sex tourism or migration, and you can examine some of the possible solutions, such as incorporating gender issues into development policies.

TOPIC 7

Urbanization and environment

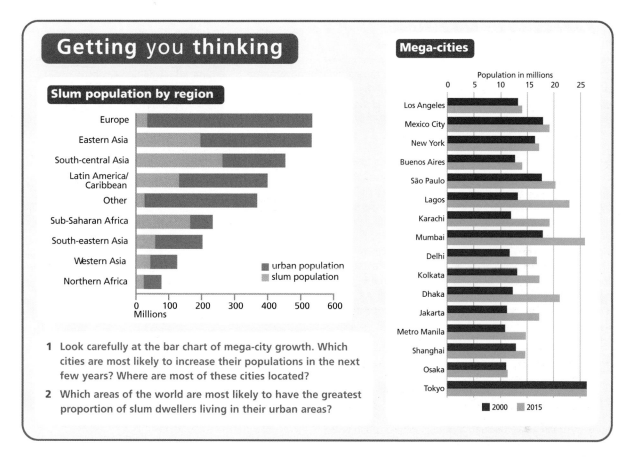
We tend to equate modernity with living in cities. They are the hub of modern life and centres of consumption, with their shopping centres, cinemas, pubs, clubs and supermarkets. Moreover, cities like New York and London are symbols of Western affluence. It is no wonder that people in the developing world aspire to them. Nevertheless, there is a dark side to urban life – all Western cities contain pockets of poverty and miseries, such as crime, suicide and mental illness.

This topic explores the reality of city life in the developing world and why these problems are likely to be heightened for the urban citizens, of say, Mexico City, São Paulo, Lagos and Mumbai. As you may have observed by looking at the bar charts above, these cities in the developing world are rapidly expanding. However, there are grave doubts as to whether they can cope with such rapid growth, and one consequence is the increasing number of people in the developing world who are forced to live in slums.

This topic also examines the related problem of environmental **degradation**. Most countries of the developing world aspire to the economic growth and

wealth experienced by Western nations. However, the evidence suggests that if developing societies ever achieved the West's current level of economic and industrial development, it would put an intolerable strain on the world's resources and ecological stability. There is evidence, too, that present rates of consumption of the world's resources, most of which are consumed (and often wasted) by the urban citizens of Western cities, have contributed to a looming environmental crisis, of which global warming and climate change are likely consequences.

World sociology and urbanization

In 1900, the only country in the world that could be described as 'urban' was Great Britain. The 20th century, however, saw massive migration from the countryside to the towns and cities of both the developed and the developing world. Cohen and Kennedy (2000) note that there were approximately 185 million people living in the towns and cities of the poorer world in 1940. By 1975, this figure had increased to 770 million. Until the 1950s, most of the world's most populated cities were to be found in the developed world. This situation was reversed only 40 years later and now the most populated cities in the world are (in no particular order) Mexico City, São Paulo, Tokyo, Shanghai, New York, Kolkata (Calcutta), Mumbai (Bombay), Beijing, Los Angeles and Jakarta. Note that only three of these cities are in the developed world. Today, there are three times as many city dwellers in the developing world as there are in the developed world.

There were seven cities in 1950 with populations of over 5 million. It is estimated that this number will rise to 93 by 2025 and that 80 of these will be in the developing world. 23 cities are expected to have a population of 10 million by 2015 – 19 of these will be in the developing world. In other words, urban growth will bring another 2 billion people into cities in the developing world. These cities are already growing at a rate of 70 million people per year. This means an overall increase of 180 000 people a day – for example, in Mumbai alone, it is estimated that 300 new people arrive everyday from rural districts. Some 37 per cent of Africans live in cities and this is expected to rise by 50 per cent in the next 25 years. By 2030, Africa will be an urban continent. In contrast, urban growth is actually falling in the developed world as people make the decision to move out of cities.

These trends have been partly caused by rapid population growth in the developing world (see Topic 5), but the 20th century also saw that population gravitating towards urban areas, through a combination of **push** and **pull factors** (see Table 2.8). The fact that urban dwellers in developing societies tend to be younger and consequently more fertile than city populations in the West also contributes to rising urban populations in the poorer countries.

Urbanization and modernization theory

We saw in Topic 2 that modernization theorists such as Rostow and Hoselitz urge developing societies to adopt Western models of economic growth, as well as cultural beliefs, practices and institutions. **Urbanization**, i.e. the trend towards living in cities rather in rural villages, is regarded as a universally positive phenomenon by modernization theorists, because European societies underwent a period of sustained urbanization in the 19th century and developing societies are encouraged to follow the same development path.

On an economic level, cities are seen to help boost growth by giving industrialist–capitalists access to a massive concentrated pool of labour for their factories.

Table 2.8 Push and pull influences on migration to cities in the developing world

Push (from rural areas)	Pull (to the cities)
Poverty	The availability of jobs, especially in transnational factories and services
Displacement by new agricultural technology	The perception that a greater number of waged jobs are available
Loss of land	Access to services such as education and health
Natural disasters, e.g. drought, flood, earthquakes	Perception that urban life offers greater opportunities in terms of living standards, i.e. bright lights and glamour
Disasters caused by poor governance, e.g. war, displaced refugees	Escape from traditional constraints of family, culture and religion
Changes in aspirations among younger people as they access modern media	The perception that urbanization = Westernization = sophistication

The wages paid to city factory workers supposedly filter down to help develop other city services, such as housing, shops and infrastructure.

Very importantly, however, cities are seen to play a central role in promoting cultural change. Cross (1979), for instance, states that 'the city is the nucleus for the cultural penetration of the modernizing society', meaning that the large populations of cities ensure that modern norms and values spread rapidly. Hoselitz argues that cities are catalysts of modernization in that they loosen ties to traditional institutions and value systems by reducing dependency on community and extended kin. As a result, values such as ascription, fatalism and collectivism soon go into decline. The modern person living in the city learns very quickly that the dominant urban values are individualism, achievement, **activism** and meritocracy. Consequently, city life sees the development of modernist values more conducive to progress and development. The result is an entrepreneurial population more prepared to take risks, more receptive to the possibility of geographical and social mobility, and willing to make investments in order to accumulate personal profit.

The critique of modernization theory

The picture of urbanization painted by modernization theory has turned out to be an overly-ideal one, when we consider the actual experience of urbanization in both the developed and developing worlds.

Rapidity of growth and social problems

Urbanization in European and American cities was very gradual – it tended to take place over a period of 100 years – and was largely responsive to employment opportunities. However, the urbanization of developing societies has been much more rapid, and population growth has wildly exceeded the number of jobs available. Urban populations are, therefore, largely unemployed or underemployed, creating grave social problems as people struggle to survive and find themselves in a constant state of poverty.

In 2005, an estimated one billion people were living in slums worldwide. This figure is expected to double by 2030. Most of these were in the developing world. For example, Asia has 60 per cent of the world's slum dwellers whilst Africa has 20 per cent and Latin-America has 14 per cent. In Jakarta, the capital of Indonesia, between 40 and 50 per cent of the population lives in slums, as do at least one third of the populations of Dhaka (Bangladesh), Kolkata (India) and São Paulo (Brazil).

The infrastructure of these cities, e.g. services such as housing, clean water, sanitation, refuse collection and policing, is generally unable to cope with the sheer weight of numbers and, as a result, '**shanty towns**' have developed with shelters constructed out of whatever materials can be found. The standard of living in these towns tends to be very poor and the sorts of classic problems associated with lack of development are very apparent, e.g. high child and maternal mortality, malnutrition, low life expectancy.

For example, in Nairobi (Kenya), the shanty community of Kibera contains between 500 000 and a million people who live without clean running water, sewers or services such as electricity. Some 60 per cent of the people live on just 5 per cent of the land. There is one toilet for every 500 people. Worldwide, an estimated 100 million people have to use the 'wrap and throw' method of getting rid of their faeces. Disease – particularly cholera, typhoid, dysentery and diarrhoea – often kills the residents, especially the children, of shanty towns.

Moreover, slum-dwellers receive little support from the governments of developing countries. In Beijing, shanty towns were bulldozed and an estimated 300 000 people were forcibly removed in preparation for the 2008 Olympic Games. In 2003/4, over 100 000 people were evicted from Jakarta, 150 000 from Delhi (India) and 77 000 from Kolkata.

Moreover, a new set of modern urban problems appear, as some people in these areas turn to illegal or unconventional means to raise their income, such as crime, especially gun crime, drug-dealing, prostitution or begging. Suicide and mental health problems, too, are becoming major problems in these new urban environments. The Commission for Africa notes that Africa's slums are filled with an increasingly youthful population, which is generally unemployed and disaffected. Consequently, Africa's cities are becoming a powder keg of potential political instability and discontent, and a breeding ground for anti-Western sentiment.

Generally, then, the simple cause-and-effect model that modernization theory applies to urbanization (i.e. that people will be attracted to cities because of the pull factor of jobs) does not really apply to the developing world.

Dual-sector economy

The development of shanty town (or *favelas* or *barrios* as they are called in Central and South America) has led to the development of a dual-sector economy in many cities in the developing world. As Peace (2005) notes, in this situation, a minority of people are lucky enough to find work on reasonable pay in a tiny formal sector, consisting of legitimate, regulated and unionized employment, often in the public sector. Many other inhabitants, however, are forced to eke out a meagre living in a bloated informal sector, consisting of unregulated or illegal employment such as sweatshops. These are often exploitative (in terms of the wages paid) and dangerous (in terms of health and safety). The informal sector also includes subsistence forms of economy as the unemployed turn to begging in order to survive. These two sectors often overlap, in that the informal sector may provide the formal sector with a cheap supply of labour.

Environmental problems

The urban haphazard sprawl associated with shanty towns can also create serious environmental problems. Often, these urban centres lack effective public transport, which means overreliance on cheap (and environmentally damaging) cars. Environmentalists note that Mexico City sprawls over 950 square miles (twice the size of Greater Manchester and far more dense) and its residents' three million automobiles emit a total of 12 000 tons of pollutants into the atmosphere every day.

Death of community

Modernization theory may be guilty of looking at Western development, and particularly urbanization, through rose-coloured spectacles. It ignores the widely accepted view that city life in the West has killed the concept of community and that this, in turn, has led to serious social problems in urban areas in the developed world, including social isolation, alienation, crime and drug abuse.

Urbanization and dependency theory

The modernization support for urbanization as the focus for development planning and policy has been criticized by dependency theory. In contrast, dependency theory suggests that urbanization in the developing world is not acting as an effective force for development – rather, it is likely to sustain underdevelopment. Dependency theorists note that modernization theory based its view of urbanization on the European experience. However, European urbanization was a response to industrialization, when people migrated to towns and cities to take work in factories. In developing societies, people have migrated to cities leaving behind land which provided subsistence; however, factory jobs are not available in large numbers, because transnational investment tends to be in highly mechanized forms of production. Cohen and Kennedy (2000) note that the urban poor:

<< have a wide variety of occupations and activities. Religious ascetics, the insane, the physically disabled, micro-traders (selling items like matches or nuts), touts for taxis or rickshaw-pullers, beggars, those seeking work, apprentices and their 'masters' – all these are part and parcel of the rich social landscape in the cities of the poor countries. >> (p.147)

An urban underclass

These migrants to the city end up in the slums, and their existence is so poor that some Marxists argue that they constitute a class below that of the proletariat, i.e. a **lumpen-proletariat** or **underclass**. The hope of Marxists is that this group might demonstrate some revolutionary consciousness as they become aware that the urban elite – the successors of those put into power by colonial rule – own and control a disproportionate share of wealth and monopolize political power in the city. There has, in fact, been little sign of such dissent in these cities. However, local elites have been aware of this possibility and so the cities in the developing world have often been the focus of repressive social controls and human-rights abuses, as these elites see the concentration of the poor and disprivileged as a threat to their power.

The colonial legacy and neo-colonialism

Dependency theorists have argued that the developed world should take some responsibility for the rapid growth of cities in the developing world. It is argued that many of the large urban cities in poorer satellite countries were established under colonialism (such as Kolkata and Mumbai) and were used as the administrative centres for removing capital, raw materials and cash crops to the developed world. These cities tended to have a better infrastructure than the rest of the colony because the colonial administrators resided there, as did the homegrown elites sponsored by the West, who were often the bureaucracy of the colonial state. Shops and services largely developed in the colonial city in response to the wealth of the colonial administration and the bureaucratic elite. Roberts (1978) argues that the neo-colonial cities of the developing world are consequently characterized by historical inequalities:

> « Modern skyscrapers, sumptuous shopping, office and banking facilities coexist with unpaved streets, squatter settlements and open sewerage ... the elegantly dressed are waylaid by beggars and street vendors; their shoes are shined and cars are guarded by urchins from slums.» (quoted by Cohen and Kennedy 2000, p.266)

After independence, these cities remained the centre of these less-developed societies and were seen by the rural poor as symbols of opportunity and potential affluence, leading to mass migration from the countryside. Cohen and Kennedy note that 'the business districts and wealthy parts of these cities are often like islands surrounded by seas of poverty' (p.265).

Dependency theorists argue that cities in developing societies continue to act as staging-posts for neo-colonial exploitation of the labour, raw materials and cash crops of the developing world. Transnational corporations, in particular, act in similar ways to the colonial powers, by establishing their operational headquarters and factories in urban areas. Dependency theorists argue that cities play a key role in ensuring that poorer countries remain in a state of underdevelopment because they monopolize any surplus capital that might be generated by exports or aid. Spare cash or aid investment tends to be largely spent on

the social problems that beset the urban poor in order to avoid social unrest, e.g. feeding the urban poor who do not produce any food for themselves can be very expensive. It has also been spent on expensive vanity projects, such as airports, hotels and conference centres that enhance the look of the city, but only benefit local elites or tourists.

The global city

Cohen and Kennedy note that some cities are perceived to have the characteristics of 'global' or 'world' cities in that they are:

- based in rich industrial countries
- often the corporate headquarters of TNCs, stock exchanges, and major banks, insurance companies and pension funds
- interconnected as sites of global transport, especially air
- often political centres of power
- centres of communications, information, entertainment and news.

Global cities are integrated with one another on the basis of these characteristics. In fact, it can be argued that such cities have more in common with each other than they do with the provincial cities in their own country – for example, London probably has more in common with New York and Hong Kong than it has with Leeds or Manchester.

According to Marxists, global cities are a symbol of the global capitalist economy and are at the centre of the new international division of labour (see Topic 8).

Cohen and Kennedy note that such cities are international and **cosmopolitan** in that they attract international migrants made up of professional workers, entrepreneurs, and unskilled workers who are exploited for their cheap labour in various service industries. They are culturally cosmopolitan, too, in the diversity of languages spoken, the number of religions practised, forms of dress, types of food served and the multicultural lifestyles on display. Suffice to say, no cities in the developing world are considered to have the characteristics that qualify them as global.

World sociology and the environment

In the last 25 years, there has been a rise in interest in the relationship between development and the environment. In particular, there is a growing awareness that environmental degradation cannot continue at its present rate without having major implications for the living standards of people in the developed and developing worlds alike. As Kingsbury et al. (2004) note:

> « Our rush to achieve material development has been predicated on the capacity of the physical environment to support it. In some cases, the environment has been despoiled, and in others, it is simply running out of resources. » (p.266)

Ellwood (2001) agrees:

> *The increasingly global economy is completely dependent on the larger economy of the planet Earth. And evidence is all around us that the planet's ecological health is in trouble.* >> (p.90)

There are concerns about how long current developmental processes can continue before local and global ecological systems collapse. Kingsbury and colleagues point out that environmental degradation does not respect state boundaries and widespread environmental collapse is no longer a case of 'if', but of 'when and where'. Some areas of the world have very limited capacity and are more prone to degradation because of overuse. These areas tend to be in the very poorest parts of the world, such as sub-Saharan Africa.

Environmental pressure points

A number of pressure points have been identified with regard to environmental degradation.

Population

This is covered in some detail by Topic 5, but it is worth briefly revisiting some points of interest here. Neo-Malthusians such as Ehrlich have argued that the earth's resources cannot sustain present levels of population growth. Moreover, the poverty experienced by the bulk of people in the developing world is thought to increase environmental degradation through more desperate use of resources. Neo-Malthusians have, therefore, recommended that population be controlled through state policies. China, India and Indonesia are examples of countries that have taken measures to curb fertility.

However, critics of neo-Malthusians suggest that the world does have the resources to cope with present population growth, but if the standard of living of the populations of the developing world were raised to the standard enjoyed by most people in the West, consumption of natural resources would become unsustainable. The irony here is that we can maintain present levels of natural resources if the poor in developing countries stay in a state of perpetual underdevelopment. There is another way we can sustain the environment and natural resources as well as raising the poor out of their poverty, but this is unpopular in the West because it involves reducing global consumption, and particularly, Western overconsumption and waste of the world's resources. For example, Rees (1996) estimates that about 10 to 14 acres of land are used to maintain the lifetime consumption of the average person in the West, but the total available productive land in the world, if shared out equally, would only come to 4.25 acres per person. The rich world is, therefore, consuming the resources of the poor.

Cohen and Kennedy note that 1.1 billion people in the world constitute a 'consuming class' and most of these live in the developed world.

> *The consuming class eats meat and processed/packaged foods, depends on numerous energy-intensive gadgets, lives in climate-controlled buildings supplied with abundant hot water and travels in private cars and jet aeroplanes. Mostly it consumes*

Key themes ———

Stratification and differentiation

The urban poor

An examination of urbanization in the developing world reveals an extremely unequal distribution of life-chances paralleling that of our own developed world. The urban poor in the shanty town areas of cities in the developing world experience extreme inequalities in access to employment, income, education and healthcare, compared with the elites and foreign expatriates who often enjoy lifestyles comparable to those found in the West. However, it is important to acknowledge that the poor in Western cities are relatively better off, in that their poverty is not usually of the absolute subsistence kind. Note, too, that environmental degradation is caused by rich and poor alike, in that the wealthy in both the developed and developing worlds overconsume and waste natural resources, whilst the poor overuse the marginal resources to which they have access.

> *goods that are soon thrown away when fashions change. In sharp contrast, the 1.1 billion poorest global inhabitants mostly travel on foot, rely on local resources for shelter and possessions (stone, wood, mud, and so on), mainly eat root crops, beans, lentils and rice and frequently drink unsafe water.* >> (p. 326)

Moreover, the 'throwaway economy' created by the consuming class produces vast amounts of waste – much of which is toxic or made of materials and wrapped in packaging that is not eco-friendly, i.e. it may inflict damage on the environment because it does not naturally break down.

Industrial and agribusiness development

There are worrying signs that industrial technology, both in the West and in those countries relatively new to industrialization, has had – and is still having – profound effects on the global environment and climate. For example, carbon dioxide levels in the atmosphere continue to rise because of the burning of fossil fuels, such as coal and oil, in factories, cars, tankers and jet-planes. These fuels result in the emission of greenhouse gases. It is estimated that if China continues on its present path of economic growth, it will contribute 40 per cent of global carbon dioxide emissions by 2050. In addition to these gases, industry worldwide continues to poison rivers and lakes through the massive use of fertilizers and pesticides.

Species extinction

Ellwood (2001) notes that the global extinction crisis is accelerating, with dramatic declines in wildlife. Habitat loss is the major cause of the decline in numbers of many species. In the past 500 years, Ellwood notes that mankind has forced 816 species to extinction:

> *Scientists reckon the normal extinction rate is one species every four years. Today's die-off rate is estimated at 1000 to 10 000 times the natural rate.* >> (p.92)

Deforestation

Kingsbury argues that deforestation may be the world's most significant environmental problem, along with desertification. Deforestation has a number of major implications because rainforests absorb carbon dioxide as well as producing the oxygen upon which all life depends. It is estimated that some of the world's major rainforests, in areas such as Indonesia, Borneo and the Amazon Basin, will be completed deforested within 30 years. At current rates of logging, Chile, which has one-third of the world's temperate rainforest, will be completely deforested by 2022.

This environmental destruction is often motivated by poverty and debt. Brazil cleared 12.5 per cent of rainforest in the Amazon Basin between 1978 and 1996 in an attempt to meet loan repayments to the World Bank and commercial banks in the West. The logging industry mainly exports the hard wood to Europe and the USA for furniture manufacture. Other types of wood are exported to meet the demand from Western culture for newspapers, magazines, etc. Such export earnings, therefore, help pay off Brazil's debts to the West. Ironically, recent IMF insistence that Brazil keep to repayment schedules has led to the cutting of funding for rainforest conservation. There is a human cost, too, as the indigenous Amazon tribes are forced off their land and in some cases, murdered by commercial loggers.

Desertification

It has been estimated that, in 2000, drought and desertification affected 1.2 billion people across 110 countries (peopleandplanet.net 2007). Desertification is mainly the result of the overcultivation and overgrazing of poor-quality land by the poor, who are often forced to keep using unsustainable land in order to survive. The more fertile land in many developing countries is not usually owned or controlled by the poor and is used to grow cash crops for export, such as the cut flowers found in British supermarkets in the winter. Desertification reduces the ability to produce food in some countries, which leads to famine. It has its greatest effect in Africa. Kingsbury *et al.* (2004) point out that desertification is getting worse. In 1970, Africa was self-sufficient in food production, but by 1984, a quarter of Africa's population was being kept alive by food aid and imported grain because of desertification, soil erosion and drought.

Water pollution

Kingsbury notes that the pollution of the world's waterways, e.g. rivers, streams and lakes, for industrial and food purposes has reduced the amount of clean drinking water and seriously threatens the continuing existence of some animal and plant life. In particular, he argues that access to clean drinking water is probably the world's most immediate environmental problem because this has been seriously threatened by the waste products of industrialization, the increased use of pesticides, insecticides and chemical fertilizers, and population growth. Kingsbury estimates that a single person requires up to 20 litres of water a day for drinking, food preparation, sanitation and bathing. However, in 2001, more than a billion people did not have access to piped water or had less than this minimum amount. For example, in Pakistan in 2002, a large majority of the country's 135 million people did not have access to drinkable water.

Why does environmental degradation occur?

Economic necessity

Many of the poor in developing countries have no choice but to use and reuse environmental resources. In other words, this type of behaviour is a matter of economic necessity and survival. As Ellwood argues:

>> *the desperately poor do not make good eco-citizens. Tribal peoples plunder the forest on which they depend for survival; animals are poached and slaughtered by impoverished African villagers for their valuable ivory or their body parts.* >> (p. 95)

Greed

The desire to accumulate wealth, by local elites and international corporations, usually at the expense of others, results in the exploitation and selling-off of environmental resources. At the same time, cost-cutting in order to increase profits may lead to unscrupulous behaviour, such as the illegal dumping of toxic waste.

Western consumer demand

Most developing countries are dependent on relatively few raw materials or cash crops for a large part of their income and in order to pay off their debts. This may result either in overproduction or in the use of production techniques that pay little attention to the environmental costs, because the emphasis is on cutting costs.

Globalization

It is argued that export-led economic growth, i.e. cash-crop production for the world market, and the debt of the developing world have speeded up consumption of the world's natural resources. In particular, in order to pay off their debts, developing countries have expanded their raw material and cash-crop exports. However this oversupply has led to falling prices as natural resources flood the market. Moreover, the emphasis on free markets in World Bank and IMF policy has led to cuts in environmental spending as these organizations insist that developing governments interfere less in their economies.

Sustainable and appropriate development strategies

In the 1980s, there was a move towards introducing more **sustainable** forms of development in order to protect the global environment in the long term. There was an increasing realization amongst agencies such as the World Bank that development had a global dimension, and that it should be targeted at what Korten (1995) calls 'the global threefold human crisis' of deepening poverty, social disintegration and environmental destruction. Development strategies in the 1980s, therefore, focused on ameliorating problems which might otherwise threaten chaos at a global level.

Sustainable development

In 1987, the World Commission on Environment and Development (WCED) concluded that economic development in both the West and the developing world should be compatible with greater responsibility for the global environment. The Commission advocated the policy of sustainable development. A central component of this

idea was the acknowledgement that poverty in the developing countries might be a major cause of global environmental problems such as global warming. The Commission argued that the construction of a more equitable economic relationship between the developed and developing worlds would reduce the need for the developing world to overexploit their environments and thus slow down environmental destruction. Moreover, the WCED argued that rich countries should aim to reduce pollution and put clean air before higher living standards. In the 1990s, 178 UN member states agreed to pursue sustainable development. The United Nations, too, has adopted sustainable development as part of its Millennium Development goals.

Another consequence of sustainable development thinking has been the realization that big aid projects may actually cause great damage to the social and natural environment. For example, in the 1960s and 1970s, $125 billion was spent on large dams in order to provide hydro-electric power, irrigation and antiflooding systems. However, dams have generally failed to be cost-effective and have not generated the expected income that the countries involved need in order to pay off the debt accrued by their construction. Dams have had a terrible human cost, too, in terms of displacing local people – between 40 and 80 million people have been displaced by dam building, about 50 per cent of those in China and India.

After a string of environmental disasters associated with its projects, and years of criticism, the World Bank promised, in the early 1990s, to clean up its act and become a greener funding machine. In 1993, it created an independent Inspection Panel to address environmental and human rights complaints related to aid projects that the bank was funding. In 1995, following the first-ever Inspection Panel investigation, the World Bank dropped its commitment to funding the Arun-III dam in Nepal, a mega-project which would have had disastrous consequences for one of the world's poorest countries.

However, Foster (2004) notes that World Bank-funded projects are still creating environmental problems. For example, in 2003, it invested in an oilfield and pipeline development stretching across Central Asia, known as the Baku-Tbilisi-Ceyhan project. Critics have drawn attention to the possibility that the project may cause serious human-rights abuses, could spark or re-ignite regional wars, may rob local people of their land and livelihoods, and would deliver yet more oil to already saturated Western markets, further contributing to climate change. The Bank justified their funding by arguing that its involvement raised the environmental and social standards of the project. The Bank used similar arguments to justify its financing of Exxon and Chevron for the Chad-Cameroon Oil and Pipeline project in 2000.

Foster notes that the Bank's own policies, which were intended to protect the environment and vulnerable social groups, have been steadily diluted from day one. For example, in 2002, the Bank changed its forest policy to allow it to support logging in tropical forests. Moreover, the Bank adopted a Water Resources Sector Strategy in 2003 that embraces high-risk dam projects and the privatization of water services, a strategy that has been shown to lead to further impoverishment of the poor as the private sector

---

Focus on ...

Sanitation

The business of human waste disposal is a respectable and well-paid profession when conducted by a certified plumber or civil engineer. It was not always thus. Until the automatic installation of

A woman collects excrement in India

flushing toilets in modern European homes, cesspits containing the noisome contents of the 'necessary room' were emptied by a hidden class of workers known as 'nightmen' or 'rakers'. In some parts of the world, such people still exist. The bucket-emptier who passes by under cover of dark in parts of Ghana, or the vyura (Swahili for 'frogman') who empties latrine pits in Dar es Salaam with nothing more than a spade to help him, continue to ply their humiliating trade – often without confessing to it. Gradually, the job of manual shit-shoveller is dying out or being technologically replaced, but far too slowly. In India, large numbers of those working in human waste disposal do what is euphemistically known as 'manual scavenging'. We are not talking about Western-style lavatories here. The women – they are mostly women – who clean shit do so in horrific conditions.

Gowriamma, Narayanamma, Renuka – her name varies from place to place but it always places her as a member of one of the groups in India traditionally known as 'untouchable' because of what they do. Gowriamma might be 25, 35 or 45 – she is never sure. But from the age of 13 onwards, she has cleaned excrement relentlessly from 6.00am to 10.00am every morning. The stench is nauseating, overpowering. These 'dry latrines' or public defecation facilities are enclosed spaces with long, open, shallow drains. Gowriamma's job is to empty the drain. First she sweeps the shit into piles. Then, using two flat pieces of tin, she scoops it up and drops it into a bamboo basket which she carries to a spot where a tractor will arrive to pick it up. No gloves. No water ... it is almost impossible to go through a day's work without some of the shit inadvertently splashing on to her clothes and person.

Source: Mari Marcel Thekaekara (2008) 'A lifetime in muck', *New Internationalist*, August

prices essential services out of their grasp. In the name of poverty alleviation, the Bank has entered into partnership with some of the most notorious producers of hazardous pesticides, again undermining its stated policy commitments to the environment. Personnel exchanges routinely occur between the World Bank and major pesticide companies – companies whose misdeeds have included illegal toxic shipments, chemical dumping and accidents, exposing humans to high levels of toxins and false advertising.

There is some evidence that International Monetary Fund (IMF) activities are also having a negative environmental effect. Loans from the IMF come with strings attached: recipient countries are expected to reduce government spending, raise cash through exports and increase foreign investment – all these pressures have an enormous negative impact on the environment. For example, an IMF loan to Brazil in 1999 led to a 90 per cent cut in the largest official programme for the protection of the Amazon. In the mid-1990s, Cameroon was encouraged by the IMF to cut export taxes on forest products in order to earn cash from exports. By 2000, over 75 per cent of Cameroon's forests had been logged.

Sustainable development has also been undermined by consumption and continual rises in living standards and expectations. As Kingsbury et al. (2004) note:

<< *Technological development has led many and perhaps most of the world's population to, if not expect, then at least to want more, of almost everything, as the developed world has and continues to do.* >> (p.287)

A good example of the negative effect this can have on the environment is the case of China, cheap fridges and chlorofluorocarbons (CFCs). It has long been recognized that CFCs deplete the ozone layer, and in the West, manufacturers of refrigerators (the main producer of CFCs) have converted to non-CFC fridges. However in China,

rises in living standards have led to a demand for cheap fridges produced by Chinese manufacturers. Unfortunately, these happen to be CFC-producing fridges. When the international community protested, China replied that its people could not afford CFC-free fridges and it was not willing to deny them the right to preserve their food.

In addition to China's non-cooperation, the USA (which accounts for 36 per cent of emissions) and Australia (the biggest polluter per capita in the world) have also failed to commit to reducing their emission of industrial pollutants such as carbon dioxide (i.e. greenhouse emissions); this has also seriously undermined the future success of this type of development.

Appropriate development

The concept of sustainable development has been supplemented by the concept of **appropriate development**. This suggests that 'small is beautiful', and that social and ecological outcomes should have precedence over GNP. Moreover, such development should be operated by people in their localities without the need for external (Western) expertise or capital.

A good example of *inappropriate* development would be the provision of diesel-powered electric generators, which rely on both oil and spare parts from the developed world. An example of appropriate development technology that is both sustainable and can be operated using only local expertise might be wind or solar power.

Key terms

Activism the willingness to bring about social change by taking action.

Appropriate development development that prioritizes social and ecological outcomes over GNP, using small-scale technology independent of Western expertise and materials.

Cosmopolitan modern and diverse.

Degradation deterioration.

Lumpen-proletariat see underclass.

Pull factors the attractions of urbanization that draw people to the city.

Push factors those influences, usually negative,

that pressure people into leaving their normal environments.

Shanty towns very poor 'towns' with almost no sanitation, facilities and proper housing that develop outside cities in some developing countries because people are drawn to the city cannot afford anywhere to live there.

Sustainable development aid strategies that address the relationship between poverty and environmental destruction.

Underclass the very poor, who experience subsistence poverty, especially in the cities of the developing world.

Urbanization the growth of towns and cities as people migrate from the countryside.

Check your understanding

1   What were the trends with regard to urbanization during the 20th century?

2   What are the implications of urban dwellers in the developing world being young and fertile?

3   Identify three push factors and three pull factors that attract the rural poor to cities in the developing world.

4   Why does modernization theory see cities as central to development?

5   Why does dependency theory argue that urbanization in the developing world contributes to underdevelopment?

6   What was the relationship between cities in the developing world and colonialism?

7   What is the relationship between population, consumption and environmental degradation?

8   Identify four types of environmental degradation.

9   Identify four reasons why environmental degradation has occurred.

10   Identify two development models which aim to challenge environmental degradation.

'Think global, act local'

Elkington (1999) notes that there is tension between economic development and environmental concerns 'with one side trying to force through new rules and standards, and the other trying to roll them back'. Elkington argues that development should focus on a 'triple bottom line', i.e. economic prosperity, environmental quality and social justice.

The World Bank has recently argued along similar lines, stating that sustainable development should pay attention to five types of 'capital':

- *financial* – i.e. careful planning and money management
- *physical* – i.e. infrastructure
- *human* – i.e. health and education
- *social* – i.e. the quality of interactions
- *natural* – i.e. natural resources, such as water and climate.

The slogan 'think global, act local' is fast becoming the slogan of sustainable development. Elkington argues that if the world does not put environmental and social responsibility on a similar level to economic prosperity, we will run the very real risk of extinction.

Activities

Web.task

Visit **www.newint.org** and use the search facility to find articles on both urbanization and environmental degradation.

An eye on the exam   Urbanization and environment

Item A

Faith in economic growth as the ultimate hope for human progress is widespread. Unfortunately reality shows otherwise. As Ayres argues:

> « *Human economic activity supported by perverse trade policies is well on the way to perturbing our natural environment more and faster than any known event in planetary history. We may well be on the way to our own extinction.* »

Ayres may well be right when he accuses globalization of accelerating the process of global environmental decline. Export-led growth and debt in the developing world have combined to speed up the rapid consumption of the Earth's irreplaceable resources. The persistence of poverty has also spurred environmental decline. In Madagascar, one of the world's most devastated environments, an island once covered in lush forests has turned into a barren wasteland as local people slash-and-burn jungle plots to grow food. In a few short years the land turns to scrub-infested desert, and the people continue their cycle of cutting and burning. Less than a tenth of Madagascar is still tree-covered and the forest is vanishing at a rate of 500 000 acres a year. Poverty is the core of the problem: 70 per cent of the island's 14 million people live on a dollar a day.

Adapted from W. Ellwood (2001) *The No-Nonsense Guide to Globalization*, London: Verso, pp. 93–5

Using information from **Item A** and elsewhere, assess the reasons for environmental degradation in developing countries.

(18 marks)

Grade booster   Getting top marks in this question

You can begin your answer by describing the nature and extent of environmental degradation in developing countries, including desertification, species and habitat loss, deforestation and pollution of water courses. You need to examine the reasons for these processes. You should include poverty and underdevelopment here. Remember to make use of relevant material from the Item in your answer, e.g. to illustrate destruction of rain forest and its relationship to poverty. Consider also the relationship between poverty, population and the environment – poverty may lead to population growth (e.g. the poor may need more family members as security) and this leads to environmental degradation. Other reasons include the activities of TNCs. Consider also the West's contribution to damaging the global environment through its industrialization and carbon economy, consumer demand, globalization and trade policies, IMF development policies, and so on.

Globalization

Getting you thinking

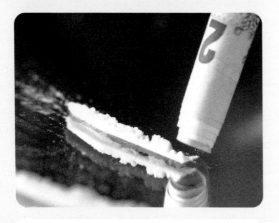

1 **In what ways are the USA's domestic problems, such as crime, tied to global processes?**

2 **What two global processes led to Juan Paredes becoming a coca farmer?**

3 **How would you go about persuading Juan Paredes not to produce coca?**

Americans consume more cocaine than any other industrialized country. Over 22 million say they have tried it, and between two and three million are addicted to it. In 1989, around 2500 Americans died from it. In 1990, one in five people arrested for any crime was hooked on cocaine or crack. Americans spend $110 000 million a year on drugs ($28 000 million on cocaine), more than double the profits of the USA's top 500 companies put together.

Juan Paredes worked as a tin-miner in Bolivia until the late 1980s. In the early 1980s, 79 per cent of his country's export earnings came from tin. However, technological advances in the West meant that large Western companies such as Coke, Pepsi and Heinz switched to substitutes such as aluminium. In October 1985, the worldwide price of tin set by speculators at the London Tin Exchange fell from £8000 to £4000 per ton, putting thousands of miners like Juan out of work. Juan turned to farming instead and managed to obtain the title to four hectares of land. Very soon, he was attracted to the growing of a crop that yielded up to four or five harvests a year, which had a seemingly limitless demand and which earned him far more than tin-mining ever did. That crop was coca. By 1991, Bolivia was the largest producer of the coca leaf in the world and the second ranked producer of refined cocaine.

Adapted from Cohen and Kennedy (2000) and Chrispin and Jegede (2000)

You will probably have realized from doing the exercise above that crime in the USA cannot be analysed in isolation from global processes. The problems faced by the USA in terms of drugs are very much related to economic globalization – especially the fact that countries like Bolivia and Colombia desperately need American dollars to pay their debts to Western banks. However, because their economies are tied up with a single crop or raw material, any fall in demand or price in the global market place is going to result in poverty in this part of the world. This means that poor farmers will be tempted to produce illegal crops in order to survive. The coca leaf is, therefore, a global crop, in that it links the poorest in the poor countries together with the most desperate in the West.

Defining globalization

Cohen and Kennedy (2000) suggest that the function of sociologists today is to provide a 'sociology for one world', i.e. a global sociology that investigates and analyses the increasing interconnectedness and interdependency of the world. Cochrane and Pain (2000) illustrate these ties that bind us together:

« Drugs, crime, sex, disease, people, ideas, images, news, information, entertainment, pollution, goods and money now all travel the globe. They are crossing national boundaries and connecting the world on an unprecedented scale and with previously unimaginable speed. The lives of ordinary people everywhere in the world seem increasingly to be shaped by events, decisions and actions that take place far away from where they live and work. »

Steven (2004), too, notes that:

« Despite huge differences in distance, upbringing and social context, many of us now listen to the same music, read the same books and watch the same films and television. Youth in Soweto listen to LA rap; viewers in southern China's Guangdong province watch pirated tapes of Jackie Chan; Sri Lankan refugee kids in Toronto come home from school to settle down in front of Tamil movies rented from the local grocery store. Teenagers *and their young siblings in almost every place on earth know Bart and Lisa Simpson. I can sit at my home computer downloading the latest communiqués from Mexico's indigenous Zapatista rebels and out of the corner of my eye watch the World Cup live from Korea on the TV in the next room.>>* (pp.16–17)

What Cochrane and Pain, and Steven are describing is 'globalization' – the emergence of a global economic and cultural system which, allegedly, is incorporating the people of the world into a single global society. Cohen and Kennedy argue that globalization needs to be understood as 'a set of mutually reinforcing **transformations**' of the world. These include the following:

1 *Changes in the concept of time and space* – Developments such as the mobile phone, satellite television and the internet mean that global communication is virtually instantaneous, whilst mass travel enables us through tourism to experience a greater range of other cultures.

2 *Economic markets and production in different countries* – These are becoming interdependent because of the growth in international trade, the new international division of labour, the growing influence of transnational corporations and the global dominance of organizations like the World Trade Organization.

3 *Increasing cultural interaction* – Through developments in mass media (especially television, films, music and the transmission of news and international sport), we can now encounter and consume new ideas and experiences from a wide range of cross-cultural sources, in fields such as fashion, literature and food.

4 *Increasingly shared problems* – These may be:

   ● *Economic* – We are becoming much more aware that the economic decisions we make about our lifestyle preferences and leisure pursuits can cause problems such as unemployment, debt and the loss of livelihoods for workers and peasants thousands of miles away. Similarly, the financial problems experienced by the Asian tiger economies in 1998/99 led to unemployment in the UK.

   ● *Environmental* – The Chernobyl nuclear disaster of 1986 demonstrated quite vividly that ecological disasters do not respect national boundaries – today, acres of land in the Lake District and Wales still experience high levels of radiation because of the fall-out from this accident thousands of miles away. Environment degradation is not only caused by Western industry and **consumption**, but also by unwitting damage caused by the poor in the developing world engaging in overcultivation and deforestation. The resulting global climate change has implications for everyone in the world.

   ● *Other common problems* – Include worldwide health problems such as AIDS, international drug-trafficking and the sort of international terrorism committed on 11 September 2001 in New York and 7 July 2005 in London.

Cohen and Kennedy conclude that these transformations have led to 'globalism', a new consciousness and understanding that the world is a single place. Giddens

(1999) notes that most of us perceive ourselves as occupying a 'runaway world' characterized by common tastes and interests, change and uncertainty, and a common fate.

However, as sociologists, we also need to be cautious in our use of the term 'globalization' – as Wiseman (1998) indicates: 'Globalization is the most slippery buzzword of the late 20th century because it can have many meanings and be used in many ways.' We can illustrate this by looking closely at the theoretical interpretations of the concept.

Theories of globalization

Cochrane and Pain (2000) note that three theoretical positions can be seen with regard to globalization:

1 **Globalists** believe that globalization is a fact that is having real consequences for the way that people and organizations operate across the world. They believe that nation-states and local cultures are being eroded by a homogeneous global culture and economy. However, globalists are not united on the consequences of such a process:

   – Hyperglobalists (sometimes called optimists or positive globalists) welcome such developments and suggest globalization will eventually produce tolerant and responsible world citizens.

   – Pessimistic globalists, such as Seabrook (2005), argue that globalization is a negative phenomenon because it is essentially a form of Western (and especially American) imperialism, peddling a superficial and homogeneous mass form of culture and consumption. Such a view focuses on the dangers of what has variously been called the '**McDonaldization**' or 'Coca-Colonization' of the world (see p. 120).

2 **Traditionalists** do not believe that globalization is occurring. They argue that the phenomenon is a myth or, at best, exaggerated. They point out that capitalism has been an international phenomenon for hundreds of years. All we are experiencing at the moment is a continuation, or evolution, of capitalist production and trade.

3 **Transformationalists** occupy a middle ground between globalists and traditionalists. They agree that the impact of globalization has been exaggerated by globalists but argue that it is foolish to reject the concept out of hand. This theoretical position argues that globalization should be understood as a complex set of interconnecting relationships through which power, for the most part, is exercised indirectly. They suggest that the process can be reversed, especially where it is negative or, at the very least, that it can be controlled.

Economic globalization

It is in the area of economic globalization that the debate between traditionalists and hyperglobalists can most obviously be seen. Thompson (2000) notes that the hyperglobalist position claims there has been a rapid and recent intensification of international trade and investment such that distinct national economies have dissolved into a global economy determined by world market-forces. This view has attracted two forms of criticism:

- Neo-Marxists accept that a strong globalization process has occurred, but condemn it as an extension of global capitalist exploitation.
- Traditionalists argue that the international economy has not gained dominance over national economic policies.

The new international division of labour (NIDL)

The neo-Marxist, Frobel, notes that from the 1970s onwards, we have seen substantial movement of industrial capital from the advanced industrialized world to the developing world (Frobel *et al.* 1980). This movement was due to rising labour costs and high levels of industrial conflict in the West, which had reduced the profitability of transnational corporations (TNCs). Many developing nations in the 1970s and 1980s set up export-processing zones (EPZs) or free-trade zones (FTZs), in which transnational companies were encouraged to build factories producing goods for export to the West (see Fig. 2.4). There are now some 800 EPZs or FTZs in the world. Even socialist Cuba has got in on the act! Developments in manufacturing meant that labour could be fragmented into a range of unskilled tasks that could be done with minimal training, whilst computer-controlled technology enabled production to be automatically supervised. Klein (2001) notes that 'to lure the TNCs into their EPZs, the governments of poor countries offer tax breaks, lax health and safety regulations, a low minimum wage and the services of a military willing and able to crush labour unrest. Integration with the local culture and economy is kept to a bare minimum'.

This new international division of labour (NIDL) is thought by hyperglobalists to benefit world consumers by enhancing competition and thus keeping the prices of goods reasonably low. However, Frobel sees the NIDL as merely a new form of neo-colonial exploitation. In addition to exploiting peasants who grow cash crops for Western consumption, he argues that TNCs are now exploiting wage labourers (especially women) in factories throughout the world. Klein agrees and notes that 'entire (developing) countries are being turned into industrial slums and low-wage labour ghettos'.

Pessimistic globalizers share these concerns. They point out that as TNCs relocate production in their search for lower costs and higher profits, so the prospects of employment in the West decline. Wages in the UK will need to be kept sufficiently low so that TNCs see investment in the UK as an attractive option. In the long term, EPZs benefit TNCs rather than developing countries because, today, there are over 70 countries competing to make their EPZ more financially attractive than that of their neighbour. Ellwood (2001) notes:

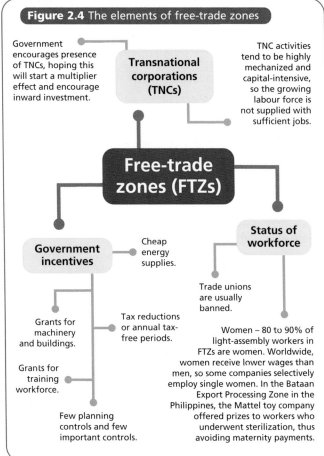

Figure 2.4 The elements of free-trade zones

Government encourages presence of TNCs, hoping this will start a multiplier effect and encourage inward investment.

Transnational corporations (TNCs)

TNC activities tend to be highly mechanized and capital-intensive, so the growing labour force is not supplied with sufficient jobs.

Free-trade zones (FTZs)

Government incentives

Cheap energy supplies.

Grants for machinery and buildings.

Tax reductions or annual tax-free periods.

Grants for training workforce.

Few planning controls and few important controls.

Status of workforce

Trade unions are usually banned.

Women – 80 to 90% of light-assembly workers in FTZs are women. Worldwide, women receive lower wages than men, so some companies selectively employ single women. In the Bataan Export Processing Zone in the Philippines, the Mattel toy company offered prizes to workers who underwent sterilization, thus avoiding maternity payments.

<< *Corporations have the upper hand, trading off one nation against another to see who can offer the most lucrative investment incentives. Tax holidays, interest-free loans, grants, training schemes, unhindered profit remittances and publicly-funded sewers, roads and utilities are among the mix of 'incentives' that companies now expect in return for opening up a new factory or office.* >> (p. 62)

World trade

Another important aspect of economic globalization is the General Agreement on Tariffs and Trade or GATT, which was a set of rules established in 1947 to govern global trade. GATT particularly aimed to reduce trade barriers and competition between nations. In 1994, the World Trade Organization (WTO) was set up to replace GATT. It has 137 member states. The WTO has taken over and extended the GATT agreements on trade in goods, as well as negotiating a new GATT – which covers services such as telecommunications, banking and investment, transport, education, health and the environment. The main impact of these economic rules has been the increase in the flow of global finance from $17.5 trillion in 1979 to over $3000 trillion in 2000. Despite the vast increase in global trade, 90 per cent of global transactions are accounted for by financial flows not directly related to trade in goods and services.

Focus on ...

The WTO and globalization

Phillippe Legrain, former special adviser to the Director-general of the WTO acknowledged four main criticisms of the WTO:

1 It does the bidding of big global companies.
2 It undermines workers' rights and environmental protection by encouraging a 'race to the bottom' between governments competing for jobs and foreign investment.
3 It harms the poor.
4 It is destroying democracy by imposing its approach on the world secretly and without accountability.

However, Legrain defends the WTO and globalization in general by suggesting:

1 The power of global corporations and brands is exaggerated – consumer choice shapes the global marketplace not brands.
2 Global corporations are actually socially responsible – for example, Shell caved in to a handful of Greenpeace activists over the disposal of the Brent Spar oil platform
3 It is misleading to compare the sales revenue of the top corporations with the GDP of countries because these are measuring different things.
4 Inferring from companies' size that they are as powerful as countries is misleading because

companies have to attract workers and capital that are free to go elsewhere, whereas countries can impose taxes and regulations. Governments can – and often do – tame the corporate giants. The European Commission stopped giant General Electric from buying Honeywell. The US government nearly broke up Microsoft, which is still being prosecuted by US states and investigated by the European Commission.
5 Taxes on company profits have steadily risen as a share of rich OECD countries' GDP: from 2.2 per cent in 1965 to 3.3 per cent in 1999.
6 Business has to abide by a battery of government legislation on workers' rights, product liability, health and safety, environmental protection and much else.
7 If global companies are doing so well out of globalization why did US corporate profits fall to 11 per cent in 2000 and 9.3 per cent in 2001 – in line with the average decline over the past 50 years of 10.5 per cent. The figures for Britain show a similar trend.
8 The only 'companies' with powers remotely comparable to those of states are the drug cartels: Colombia's earn billions of dollars a year, control parts of the country, have private armies and operate outside the law.
9 If the corporations are so powerful why is it that every year people start almost two million lawsuits against American companies, which pay out annual damages of around $150 billion.

Source: Legrain, P. (2002) 'Business doesn't rule', *The Guardian*, 9 October

Marxists and global pessimists have criticized the free-trade agenda of the WTO. They claim that global trade rules are unfair and biased against developing countries as these countries are being pressured to open up their economies immediately to Western banks and transnationals, and to abandon tariffs (i.e. taxes) on imports from the West. Organizations such as the World Bank and IMF have tied aid and loans to developing countries to these free-trade conditions. However, under the GATTs, the developed countries are allowed to impose quotas restricting the import of manufactured goods from the developing world. It is argued that such imbalanced rules mean that the WTO is a rich man's club dominated by the developed industrial nations

Transnational corporations (TNCs)

As mentioned earlier, the activities of transnational corporations in the global economy have caused some concern, especially to neo-Marxist traditionalists. TNCs have taken advantage of the relaxation of trade rules brought about by GATT and the WTO, and as Ellwood (2001) notes, they 'have become the driving force behind economic globalization, wielding more power than many nation-states'. Today, 51 of the 100 largest economies in the

world are run by multinationals rather than countries, e.g. Mitsubishi is bigger than Finland whilst General Motors is larger than Denmark (see Table 2.9). The combined annual revenues of the biggest 200 corporations are greater than those of 182 nation-states or 80 per cent of the world's population. This is 18 times the combined annual income of the 1.2 billion poorest people. Moreover, it is estimated that a third of all trade within the global economy is

Table 2.9 Corporate globe straddlers – Largest companies in the world by 2001 revenue, millions $

Company	Country of origin	2001 revenue	Relative to countries
Wal-Mart	USA	219 812	Approx size Sweden
ExxonMobil	USA	191 581	Larger than Turkey
General Motors	USA	177 260	Larger than Denmark
Ford Motor	USA	162 412	Larger than Poland
DaimlerChrysler	Germany	149 608	Larger than Norway
Royal Dutch/Shell	UK/Holland	149 146	Larger than Norway
BP	UK	148 062	Larger than Norway
Mitsubishi	Japan	126 629	Larger than Finland
General Electric	USA	125 913	Larger than Greece

business between branches of the same corporations. Why are these economic trends important? The answer lies in the fact that corporate decision-makers rarely consider the social, environmental and economic consequences of their actions for the people of the developing world.

The trend in transnational business is towards monopoly, and mergers between corporations occur frequently. Concentration is particularly taking place in banking and mass media. Today, for example, the ten largest corporations in the telecommunications industry now control 86 per cent of the global market. Mergers have significant human effects in terms of job losses worldwide. Monopoly also has the effect of increasing both the economic and political power of large corporations over national and regional governments, especially those found in the developing world. In particular, there are concerns that transnationals, along with the World Bank and IMF, are pressurizing smaller, less economically powerful countries to open their economies up to private investment. One particularly worrying contemporary trend has been the attempt by US private healthcare companies to influence the WTO to encourage the privatization of healthcare in developing countries. Water is another resource which transnational companies have recently targeted for private investment.

Another Marxist concern about transnational behaviour has focused on the deregulation of global finance which, together with the revolution in microelectronics (computers, the internet and email) has led to massive movements of money across the globe. In particular, it has resulted in transnational finance corporations engaging in currency speculation for profit. This has resulted in the destabilization of currencies both in the developed and developing worlds, and led to economic suffering for millions in terms of unemployment and loss of savings.

However, it would be a mistake to dismiss all transnational investment in the developing world as exploitative. Although there exist quite legitimate concerns about transnational abuse of power and unethical behaviour, these corporations can bring about positive change. As Ellwood (2001) notes:

<< They are at the cutting edge of technological innovation and they can introduce new management and marketing strategies. It's also true that wages and working conditions are usually better in foreign subsidiaries of multinational firms than in local companies.>> (pp. 61–2).

McDonaldization

The global pessimist, George Ritzer (1993) argues that another aspect of economic globalization is McDonaldization, 'the process by which the principles of the fast food restaurant are coming to dominate more and more sectors of American society as well as the rest of the world'. Ritzer argues that McDonaldization has impacted upon economic production and consumption in four ways:

● *Efficiency* – McDonalds has demonstrated that assembly-line production techniques can be applied to the efficient production of virtually every product and service.
● *Calculability* – McDonalds has demonstrated that maximum quantity (and profit) can be achieved with minimum output in terms of costs such as wages.
● *Predictability* – McDonalds has shown that product, service and environment can all be standardized.
● *Control* – McDonalds has ensured that it has total control over the work process and workforce through the de-skilling and simplifying of tasks and the deployment of technology. This ensures that workers can be trained quickly and effectively. Low wages are paid because jobs are effectively only semi-skilled.

Ritzer sees the process as essentially dehumanizing both for workers and consumers. Moreover, he suggests that it is essentially another form of US economic and cultural imperialism. Spybey (1998), however, rejects this argument and suggests that McDonalds is a true symbol of genuine globalization because the company accommodates local culture and customs wherever it sets up business. Spybey points out that true globalization is actually a combination of global and local influences – there is 'interpenetration' between the two. For example, burgers in McDonalds in India contain no beef or pork products because of local religious beliefs. In this sense, the global McDonalds has an effect upon the local (i.e. by setting up a fast-food outlet), but the local has an effect upon the global too.

The need for global controls

However, the activities of TNCs illustrate a lack of global control by national governments and agencies such as the United Nations. Quite simply, there is no international law in place to regulate the activities of such organizations, despite their blatant and consistent infringement of human rights. This lack of control is not unique to the activities of TNCs.

Globalization also results in opportunities for cross-border crime, which is thought to be worth $500 billion a year. International criminal activity includes people-trafficking for the sex trade, computer fraud, illegal arms-dealing, smuggling, violating patents and copyright

Key themes

Stratification and differentiation

Global consumers or global proletariat?

Marxists argue that globalization is merely an extension of the capitalist stratification system. Exploitation of workers has been globalized in the setting up of a new international division of labour in which the labour power of proletariats in both the developed and developing world are exploited for their surplus value by the agents of global capitalism – transnational companies. On the other hand, postmodernists see globalization as a positive phenomenon because it has created a new class of global consumers with a greater range of choices from which they can construct a hybridized global identity.

agreements, and drug trafficking. The latter is particularly profitable. The world turnover in heroin went up 20 times between 1970 and 1990, whilst cocaine turnover went up 50 times. As described earlier, drug-trafficking is truly a global phenomena as it is linked to the poverty of certain countries, which is a result of their position within the global capitalist system. The international trading system means that poor farmers in countries such as Bolivia, Nepal and Jamaica cannot survive on the income provided by legitimate cash crops and turn instead to the production of coca or poppies (from which heroin can be manufactured).

Globalization also increases the possibility of **white-collar crime** because of more open borders and international computer link-ups. Drug money is also often 'laundered' through legitimate global banking operations.

Finally, violence is also taking on a global dimension as international drug gangs compete with each other for global dominance. Terrorism, too, has also moved beyond national boundaries. Osama Bin Laden's al-Qaeda group has recruited from a range of Arab, Asian and European nations. Moreover, the actions of al-Qaeda have become global actions in their choice of targets (e.g. US and UK embassies around the world, and the hotels, nightclubs and restaurants used by Western tourists), and in their use of media technology (e.g. passing on videos of atrocities to the Al-Jazeera television network, knowing that such images will be transmitted globally, within hours, on television and on the internet).

The globalization of culture

In recent years, the global growth and spread of cultural goods (especially cinema, television, radio, advertising, music and the internet) has been phenomenal. McKay (2000) notes that the total number of television sets in the developing world has grown so rapidly that it has had a globalizing effect on people in the developing world. The Commission for Africa notes a similar phenomenon with regard to mobile phone use in Africa.

Hyperglobalists see the global media as beneficial because it is primarily responsible for diffusing different cultural styles around the world and creating new global hybrid styles in fashion, music, consumption and lifestyle. It is argued that in the postmodern world, such cultural diversity and **pluralism** will become the global norm.

Pessimistic globalists and neo-Marxists, in contrast, are concerned about the concentration of the world's media in the hands of a few powerful media corporations. Media conglomerates, mainly American (such as Disney, Microsoft, Time Warner and AOL) and Japanese (such as Sony) have achieved near monopolistic control of newspapers, film archives, news programmes, television and radio, advertising and satellites. It is suggested that media moguls are able to influence business, international agencies and governments and, consequently, to threaten democracy and freedom of expression.

It is also argued that such media corporations are likely to **disseminate** primarily Western, especially American, forms of culture. For example, most films released by these organizations are produced in Hollywood and so are of a

Here is the statue of Simón Bolívar, who freed Latin America from foreign domination

Source: Allen and Thomas (2001)

What point is this cartoon making about globalization?

certain formulaic (predictable) type. There have been concerns that these Western forms of culture reflect a cultural imperialism that results in the marginalization of local culture. As Steven (2004) argues:

<< For the past century, US political and economic influence has been aided immensely by US film and music. Where the marines, missionaries and bureaucrats failed, Charlie Chaplin, Mickey Mouse and The Beach Boys have succeeded effortlessly in attracting the world to the American way.>>

Mass advertising of Western cultural icons like McDonalds and Coca-Cola has resulted in their logos becoming powerful symbols to people in the developing world (especially children) of the need to adopt Western consumer lifestyles in order to modernize. There is a fear that this may undermine and even destroy rich local cultures and identities. Some commentators refer to this as 'coca-colonization'.

However, transformationalists are critical of cultural-imperialist arguments for three reasons:

1. These arguments make the mistake of suggesting that the flow of culture is one way only – from the West to the developed world. This focus fails to acknowledge how Western culture is enriched by inputs from other world cultures and religions.
2. It assumes that people in the developing world are **consumer dopes**. In fact, their involvement in global culture may result in them accessing a wider range of choices.
3. It underestimates the strength of local culture. As Cohen and Kennedy (2000) observe:

<< On occasions, some inhabitants of Lagos or Kuala Lumpur may drink Coke, wear Levi 501 jeans and listen to Madonna records. But that does not mean they are about to abandon their customs, family and religious obligations or national identities wholesale even if they could afford to do so, which most cannot.>> (p.243)

Focus on ...

The globalization of mobile phones

The use of mobile phones in Africa is increasing much faster than anywhere else in the world (Commission for Africa 2005). Some 75 per cent of all telephones in Africa are mobile. A driving force in their spread has been the need for people to keep in touch with family news, but cellphones are also used to help poor people in remote areas find employment without travelling long distances. This new technology is bringing about many indirect spin-offs.

Mobile servers on motorbikes are now providing telephone connections in rural parts of South Africa. Already, evidence is emerging that data collection via cellphones has the potential to dramatically increase efficiency within health budgets; pilot schemes in Uganda are already showing savings of as much as 40 per cent.

The continent is much ahead of the rest of the world in the use of prepaid phone cards as a form of electronic currency. Africans in the developed world are buying prepaid cards and sending them to their relatives back home, who can then sell the cards to others. Thus the cards have become a form of currency by which money can be sent from the rich world to Africa without incurring the commission charged on more conventional ways of remitting money.

The mobile phone is creating virtual infrastructures and raising the possibility of unthought-of transformations in African culture, infrastructure and politics: studies show that when 20 per cent of a population has the ability to exchange news and ideas through access to cellphones and text messaging, dictatorial or totalitarian regimes find it hard to retain power.

Responses to globalization

Seabrook (2005) notes that, by definition, globalization makes all other cultures local and, by implication, inferior. He suggests that globalization implies a superior, civilized mode of living – it implicitly promises that it is the sole pathway to universal prosperity and security – consequently diminishing and marginalizing local cultures. Seabrook suggests that 'spreading this message of good fortune sweeps aside all other preoccupations, all existing interpretations of the world, the multiple meanings human societies and cultures have derived from or imposed upon their environment'. He argues that integration into a single worldwide economy is a 'declaration of "war" upon other cultures and societies'.

Seabrook notes three principal responses to globalization:

1 *Fatalistic* – we are simply powerless to resist it. Most leaders of the developed world take the position that it is inevitable and irreversible. Seabrook suggests that these leaders are experiencing an 'impotence of convenience' – their confessed powerlessness disguises the fact that the forces of globalization economically advantage their countries.

2 *Welcoming* – Sen (2002) suggests globalization represents hope for all humanity and that a universal techno-scientific culture will liberate people from poverty. Llosa (2000) suggests that much war and conflict is caused by local cultural differences, therefore, the quicker local cultures merge into a single global culture the better. Robertson (1992) notes that the global and the local can work together. He notes that often local people select from the global only that which pleases them, which they modify so that it is adapted to local culture and needs. He calls this 'glocalization'. Cohen and Kennedy agree and refer to this as 'indigenization', i.e. the local 'captures' the global influence and turns it into an acceptable form compatible with local tastes. For example, the Indian film industry in the form of '**Bollywood**' combines contemporary Western ideas about entertainment with traditional Hindu myth, history and culture. There is evidence that this glocalization eventually leads to hybridization – for example, some world music fuses and mixes Western dance beats with traditional styles from North Africa and Asia.

3 *Resistance* – This takes various forms. There is a reassertion of local identities through attempts to preserve local folklore and languages. Seabrook also identifies an increasing trend called 'commodification' – making local cultures 'sellable' abroad and packaging them up for tourism. However, Seabrook also notes that globalization has also seen a 'vehement' reaction in the developing world as people see it as a 'violation of their identity'. He notes that: 'the rise of old nationalisms and the many fundamentalisms of the age – in Iraq and elsewhere – are not arbitrary responses, but the reactions of people under overwhelming pressure'.

Globalization, particularly the pressures of the global economic market, results in profound and painful social and religious disruption. Seabrook suggests too that 'it is not only the economies of countries that are reshaped, but also the minds and sensibility of the people. Their value systems are re-formed in the image of the global market'. This cultural change is interpreted by some sections of developing nations as a form of imperialism – an attempt by the West to spread its supremacy – a colonialism of the mind. Seabrook concludes that 'this is how global terrorism is bred: not by poverty, according to the common wisdom, but as a consequence of the supposed miracle-working, wealth-creating propensities of globalism'. Therefore, some religious and ethnic groups may resist globalization because they interpret the West as having declared an ideological war on local cultures.

Kingsbury *et al.* (2004) note that the idea of a 'global community' means that global norms are interpreted and enforced by a small number of states. The USA, in particular, has set itself up as a 'global policeman' protecting what it argues are global interests. However, some cultures may interpret the pursuit of such interests by the USA, as well as the economic and cultural dominance of US transnationals and brands, as an attack upon the 'purity' of their own cultural or religious beliefs. There is some evidence that this rationale may underpin fundamentalist Islamic attitudes towards the West and the terrorist actions of groups such as Osama Bin Laden's al-Qaeda group.

Finally, some sociologists, such as Giddens (1990) and Beck (2002), have suggested that global communication means that it is now difficult for people to avoid reflecting on world events or acknowledging that we live in a world characterized by 'risks', such as those posed by global warming, war and terrorism. This may result in a broadening of our identities, especially if we choose to champion a particular global cause related to issues such as the environment or debt relief. Such choices may be partly responsible for the rise of new social movements and, in particular, the antiglobalization movement, especially among young people. (See Chapter 4, Topic 5 for more about new social movements – p. 242 onwards.)

Is globalization actually occurring?

The answer to the question in this heading depends on which theoretical position you decide to take. The problem with neo-Marxist and traditionalist views is that they tend to overfocus on economic globalization and neglect the globalization of culture. They also view globalization as a one-way process and as a form of cultural imperialism. Consequently, they tend to see globalization as leading inevitably to **dystopia**.

Pessimistic globalizers, such as Barber and Schulz (1995), fear that we are turning into a 'McWorld' in which cultures and consumption will be standardized. However, the limited evidence we have so far suggests that **hybridity** – cultural borrowing and mixing – rather than uniformity may be the outcome of global cultural change. Cohen and Kennedy (2000) optimistically state that globalization will lead to an extension in human rights, universal access to education and communications, and multicultural understanding. However, we must remember that the phenomenon of globalization is fairly young and, as Cohen and Kennedy soberly note, 'globalization has so

Activities

Research idea

In order to assess the influence of globalization in your own life, construct a questionnaire that operationalizes the concept of cultural globalization in terms of the use of:

- global brands and logos
- transnational services like McDonalds, Burger King and Starbucks
- clothing and trainers
- tastes in film, music and television programmes.

Contact schools abroad via email and ask students to fill in your questionnaire.

Web.task

Visit the Guardian website and research the arguments for and against globalization contained in the special report at:
www.guardian.co.uk/globalisation

This site contains over two dozen links to a range of excellent websites on globalization. Most of them are critical, such as:

- **www.corpwatch.org** – the website of Corporate Watch
- **www.mcspotlight.org/** – aims to track the activities of McDonalds and other transnationals
- **www.nosweat.org.uk/** – looks at companies allegedly running sweatshops in the EPZs
- **www.wdm.org** – an educational and campaigning organization
- **www.iatp.org** – antiglobalization research focusing on sustainable development
- **www.resist.org.uk/** – a site that coordinates the antiglobalization movement.

Key terms

Bollywood Indian film industry based in Bombay.

Consumer dopes people who are easily manipulated into spending their money.

Consumption consuming material and cultural goods and resources.

Disseminate transmit, spread.

Dystopia a future characterized by disaster and negative events.

Globalists those who believe that globalization is occurring.

Hybridity new cultural forms resulting from a mixture of different cultural influences.

Laundered process of transferring money gained illegally into respectable accounts.

McDonaldization a term coined by Ritzer (1993) to describe the process by which the principles of the fast food restaurant are coming to dominate more and more sectors of American society as well as the rest of the world.

Pluralism variety of groups.

Traditionalists in terms of globalization, those who do not believe that globalization is occurring.

Transformationalists theorists who believe that the impact of globalization has been exaggerated by globalists but argue that it is foolish to reject the concept out of hand.

Transformations social changes.

White-collar crime crime committed by the middle and upper classes in the context of corporate life.

far done little to diminish the blight of poverty and wretchedness in which about half of the world's inhabitants is forced to live' (p.372). Kingsbury argues that until globalization challenges such poverty, it is likely that global conflict, especially between East and West, will be a fact for some time to come.

Check your understanding

1 What are the four transformations of the world that have led to globalization according to Cohen and Kennedy?

2 What is globalism?

3 Why are some sociologists like Wiseman sceptical about the use of the term 'globalization'?

4 What is the difference between a positive globalist and a pessimistic globalist?

5 What is meant by the phrase 'coca-colonization of the world'?

6 How does the 'new international division of labour' differ from previous forms of capitalist production?

7 Why are transnationals attracted to EPZs?

8 What is McDonaldization?

9 Identify four criticisms of TNC activity in the developing world?

10 Why are some sociologists anxious about the globalization of culture?

11 What is globalization, according to Marxists?

12 Why might globalization to greater awareness of the world's problems and a desire to change the world for the better among young people?

An eye on the exam Globalization

Item A

Globalization implies that the boundaries between nation-states become less significant in social life. One example of this can be seen in economic life, where world trade is increasingly dominated by transnational corporations and capital can be moved rapidly by investors from one country to another as the international financial markets are connected by computerized technology. Globalization can also be seen in culture, where television programmes, films and books are made for an international market. This cultural globalization can also be seen in the worldwide spread of tastes in foods such as pizzas, burgers and curries.

To many living outside Europe and North America, globalization looks like Westernization or even Americanization, since the USA is now the sole superpower, with a dominant economic, cultural and military position in the global order. Many of the most visible cultural expressions of globalization are American – Coca-Cola, McDonalds, etc. Globalization, some argue, destroys local cultures, widens world inequalities and worsens the lot of the impoverished. It creates a world of winners and losers, a few on the fast track to prosperity, the majority condemned to a life of misery and despair. Some argue that this is less of a global village and more like global pillage.

Adapted from Taylor, P. (1997) *Investigating Culture and Identity*, London: HarperCollins, p.128; and Lecture 1, 'Runaway World', one of the BBC Reith Lectures, BBC Radio 4 given by Anthony Giddens (1999)

Using information from **Item A** and elsewhere, assess the impact of globalization on developing societies.

(18 marks)

Grade booster Getting top marks in this question

You could begin your answer to this question by briefly defining globalization and describing some of the factors that are bringing it about, such as the role of transnational corporations, global media and marketing, and telecommunications. You should look at different aspects of globalization, including both economic and cultural. You should consider different theories of globalization and their implications for whether it is seen as a process controlled by or benefiting the West (or even whether it is actually occurring in the first place). Does it lead to growth, exploitation, or both? Remember to make use of relevant material from the Item in your answer, for example to discuss whether cultural globalization is occurring and responses to it. For instance, does it destroy local cultures, or is there a process of adaptation (e.g. 'glocalization' or hybridity) or resistance?

TOPIC 9

War and conflict in the developing world

Getting you thinking

The Rwandan Genocide was the 1994 mass killing of hundreds of thousands of Rwanda's Tutsis by Hutu militia. In about 100 days, from the assassination of the Prime Minister Juvénal Habyarimana on 6 April up until mid July, at least 500 000 people were killed. Most estimates indicate a death toll between 800 000 and 1 million. Most of the victims were killed in their villages or in towns, often by their neighbours and fellow villagers. The militia members typically murdered their victims by hacking them with machetes, although some army units used rifles. The victims were often found hiding in churches and school buildings, where Hutu gangs massacred them. Ordinary citizens were called on by local officials and government-sponsored radio to kill their neighbours, and those who refused to kill were often killed themselves.

In 2002 a little gang of rebels in the Philippines managed to kidnap some foreign tourists. A French woman among the kidnapped later described how she wrote down their demands for transmission to the authorities. 'What do you want me to write?' she asked. 'A million dollars per tourist' was what they wanted. She wrote it down, then asked, 'Anything else?' A long pause, then a political thought: 'Sack the mayor of Jolo.' The last demand: 'Two divers' wristwatches.' That was the list of 'totally justified' grievances from that particular rebel group. Kidnapping tourists was just an unfortunate necessity to secure social justice. Anyway, the United States refused to pay up but the European governments paid up. This led to a surge of young men wanting to join the rebels. This sort of recruitment to a rebellion is a bit like joining drug gangs in the United States, where young men are willing to work for practically nothing because of the small chance of big money by climbing up the hierarchy of the gang.

Source: Collier, P. (2008), p.21

Blood Diamonds

From 1991 to 2002, the Revolutionary United Front (RUF) waged an insurrection that ravaged the tiny West African nation of Sierra Leone. The conflict created over 2 million refugees and completely destroyed much of the country's infrastructure. Initially, the RUF appeared to be fighting for the country's rural poor, but it quickly lost sight of its founding goals and began a brutal war of terror against ordinary Sierra Leoneans. Villages were burned, women raped, and children gunned down. Many of those who were captured had their hands and feet hacked off by machetes (there were an estimated 100 000 victims of mutilation), and others were forced to work as slaves in the country's diamond mines. Diamonds were critical for the survival of the RUF, which traded them for weapons. The bulk of the mined diamonds were smuggled out of the country through neighbouring Liberia, where warlord and later president, Charles Taylor, supported the rebels. These diamonds eventually found their way into markets around the world.

The film *Blood Diamonds* raises many issues and blames the West for a lot of them. At the core of the film's many messages is the illegal trade of conflict diamonds emanating from Sierra Leone. The film's star, Leonardo DiCaprio has got people talking in Hollywood but admitted to having bought diamonds in the past without realizing the devastating effect the illegal diamond trade had on countries in Africa, with millions of people being displaced and millions of lives lost. He stressed that if he ever bought a diamond again, he would make sure it was a 'conflict-free diamond' and would get it certified by the dealer he bought it from.

1 In your view, what caused neighbours to kill each other in Rwanda?
2 In what way, was the conflict in Sierra Leone linked to globalization?
3 Why might young men be attracted to rebel groups in developing countries?
4 Using the sources above, identify four possible causes of war and conflict in the developing world.
5 How might conflict in the developing world result in increased security risks in the developed world?

The **genocide** in Rwanda, the conflict in Sierra Leone over **blood diamonds** and the kidnapping of foreign tourists by a rebel group in the Philippines have features in common. All three countries are in the developing world and all suffer from extreme inequalities in wealth and income. All three countries have been characterized by **civil war** – localized conflicts that have caused great suffering to their people, especially women and children. You may have speculated that the conflicts mentioned above are related to the possibility of poverty and difference. You would be right to focus on these, although the causes of civil war are often more complex than this. Most importantly, it needs to be realized that civil wars in the developing world cannot be divorced from our world. What happens in Somalia, Sudan or Iraq in this globalized age has repercussions for the Western world, as both 9/11 in the USA and 7/7 in the UK have so graphically illustrated.

Development and conflict

Duffield (2001) notes that, in the early 1990s, the main concern of the international community regarding conflict in the developing world was essentially humanitarian and focused on supporting civilians in war zones. However, the emphasis shifted during the mid-1990s, and the need to address the issue of war and conflict became a central concern within development theory. Duffield notes that:

>> *it is now generally accepted that international organizations should be aware of conflict and its effects and, where possible, gear their work towards conflict resolution and helping to rebuild war-torn societies in a way that will avert future violence. Such engagement is regarded as essential if development and stability are to prevail.* >> (p.1)

He goes on to argue that 'development is ultimately impossible without stability, and, at the same time, security is not sustainable without development' (p.16).

Duffield argues that this new interest in the relationship between development and conflict has been motivated by globalization – specifically the realization that an excluded developing world may encourage international instability through war, criminal activity and terrorism. As Duffield notes, within this new security framework, 'underdevelopment has become dangerous' (p.2).

'Old' wars and 'new' wars

A useful way to begin our analysis of war and conflict in the developing world is to examine Kaldor's (2006) distinction between 'old' wars and 'new' wars. According to Kaldor, 'old' wars, which mainly took place in the first half of the 20th century, have five major characteristics:

1 **Total wars** – They involved a vast mobilization of men and arms by nations.
2 *Public confrontations* – They generally involved battles between opposing armies on battlefields. However, Kaldor notes that the Second World War saw the

privatization of war and conflict – civilians or non-combatants were targeted for the first time through indiscriminate bombing and concentration camps. She argues that the seeds of the genocide that has come to characterize some wars and conflicts in the developing world were sown in this period.

3 *Socially organized and legitimized violence* – Kaldor notes that 'if soldiers are to be treated as heroes and not as criminals, then heroic justification is needed to mobilize their energies, to persuade them to kill and risk being killed'. Consequently, **ideologies** such as patriotism, antifascism, communism and democracy became the justifications for the 'old' wars.
4 *Development of sophisticated technology* – Mass-produced military hardware, such as tanks, ships and aircraft, culminated in atomic and nuclear weapons technology.
5 *Alliances between nations* – Alliances, such as **NATO**, became all-important. Kaldor notes that democracies do not go to war with each other. They are much more likely to cooperate militarily with each other.

Kaldor argues that the wars that have broken out in the developing world differ considerably from 'old' wars, referring to them as 'new' wars. Keen (1995) refers to them as 'privatized' or 'informal' wars because they are not normally focused on attacking other countries but rather they involve internal groups competing for resources and territory. Duffield (1998) calls them 'postmodern' wars because they take advantage of new media technologies such as satellite phones, while Shaw (2000) refers to such wars as 'degenerate' wars because they often have genocidal aspects.

The characteristics of new wars

Kaldor suggests the 'new' wars of the developing world have the following characteristics.

Identity politics

Many of the new wars are focused on identity politics – groups may develop grievances based on national, clan, tribal, religious and linguistic differences. Collier (2008) suggests that the Rwandan civil war in the 1990s (see 'Getting you thinking', p. 125) was caused by tribal differences and resentments. The idea that identity politics underpins civil war in the developing world is also reflected in the fact that many rebel groups are financed by members of their communities who have chosen to live or been exiled abroad (**diaspora communities**), e.g. the Tamil Tigers in Sri Lanka are funded by Canadian Tamils.

Different modes of warfare

The 'new' wars use different modes of warfare, particularly **guerrilla warfare** and **counter-insurgency**. Battles are avoided as far as possible. However, this type of warfare is not aimed at capturing the hearts and minds of the people in order to generate popular support. Rather, territory is captured and controlled through sowing fear and hatred. Kaldor notes that often:

>> the aim is to control the population by getting rid of everyone of a different identity (and indeed of a different opinion) and by instilling terror. Hence, the strategic goal of these wars is to mobilize extremist politics based on fear and hatred. This often involves population expulsion through various means such as mass killing (i.e. **ethnic cleansing**) and forcible resettlement, as well as a range of political, psychological and economic techniques of intimidation. >> (p.9)

This type of violence, then, is mainly aimed at civilians rather than soldiers of the opposing army. It has produced a dramatic increase in the number of refugees and displaced persons. Moreover, widespread human rights abuse is a central feature of today's new wars.

Globalized financing

New wars are financed by a globalized war economy. Rebels finance themselves through plunder, hostage-taking and the black market, or through external assistance – funding from their diaspora, the hijacking of aid, and support from neighbouring governments.

Duffield suggests that war and conflict in the developing world are made worse by the development of economic systems that operate outside the formal, legal, state-regulated economic system. These informal or '**shadow' economies** often interact with the global – e.g. drugs, blood diamonds, ivory and oil may be smuggled or exported to the West with the support of Western multinationals that wish to control the trade in these products. International companies may advance massive amounts of funding to rebel movements in return for resource concessions in the event of a rebel victory. Western arms companies, in all likelihood, will provide the weapons required.

Effect of globalized culture

Kaldor notes that rebel leaders or warlords (see 'Focus on ... warlords and the global economy', right) are often influenced by globalized culture. She argues that 'the effect of television, radio or videos on what often is a non-reading public cannot be overestimated' (p.8). Rebel leaders and their followers often display the symbols of a global mass culture – Mercedes cars, Rolex watches, Ray-Ban sunglasses – combined with the labels that signify their own unique brand of cultural identity.

Poverty and conflict

Duffield argues that there is probably no direct causal relationship between poverty and conflict. There are many poor countries that have never known conflict. However, a study of 34 of the world's poorest countries in 1998 found that two-thirds of these had either recently been involved in a civil war or were currently in one. The existence of poverty is, therefore, a high-risk factor with regard to conflict breaking out.

Collier (2008) argues that civil wars, particularly in Africa, often occur in countries in which state revenues

Focus on ...

Warlords and the global economy

The term '**warlord**' refers to local strongmen who have the military resources to control an area and exploit its resources despite the existence of a state authority.

A good example is Charles Taylor (pictured here), who exercised control over large parts of the African countries of Liberia and Sierra Leone, which he called 'Greater Liberia' or 'Taylorland'. In order to reinforce his control, Taylor established relationships with a number of multinational companies to export timber, agricultural produce and, in particular, diamonds to the West. These multinationals, which included the Firestone tyre company, were essential to Taylor's rule. During the early 1990s, Taylor was France's third largest supplier of tropical hard woods. These exports paid for Taylor's weaponry. Taylor was, therefore, a pioneer in the use of foreign companies as a source of hard currency and, importantly, as a means of physically controlling territory and thereby denying resources to opponents.

Adapted from Duffield, M. (2001) *Global Governance and the New Wars*, London: Zed Books, pp.175–6

have declined because the economy is in decline. Collier notes that low income produces poverty and low economic growth produces hopelessness. Young men, who are the recruits for rebel armies, come cheap in an environment of hopeless poverty. Collier argues that life itself in developing societies is cheap, and joining a rebel movement gives young men a chance of riches.

If the economy is weak, the state is also likely to be weak. The rebel leader, Lauren Kabile, who was involved in a civil war to control the diamond trade in Zaire, told a journalist that rebellion was easy – all you needed was $10 000 and a satellite phone. Everyone in Zaire was so poor that with $10 000 you could hire an army. With a satellite phone, Kabila could strike deals with Western multinational resource extraction companies – it is estimated that he made over $500 million worth of deals with regard to oil and diamond rights.

Collier also highlights the '**coup** trap'. Many governments are more at threat from coups from their military than from rebellion. Moreover, once a country has had a coup it is much more likely to have further coups. Collier argues that Africa is the epicentre of coups because it is so poor.

The criminalization of conflict

It is becoming increasingly accepted within aid policy that there is a connection between conflict and criminality. Duffield (2007) notes that when conflict is triggered by violent and extreme leaders, it easily leads to a self-perpetuating quest for loot. As a result, the borders between legitimate grievance and criminality can become blurred.

Collier (2008) also notes that civil wars in Africa are more likely to occur in countries in which criminality, corruption and inefficiency have spread, and in which the government is weak. **Political legitimacy** in these societies is often non-existent. Moreover, violence becomes 'privatized' – aiming to spreading fear among the civilian population via killing and rape so as to minimize and subdue opposition. Organized crime and human-rights abuses perpetuated by paramilitary groups therefore become common.

Focus on research

Jeremy Weinstein (2006)
Inside rebellion: the politics of insurgent violence

Weinstein's research has looked at the rebel recruitment process in Mozambique and Sierra Leone. He notes that, initially, some recruits to rebel movements are motivated by the fight for social justice. However, others are attracted by the prospect of riches and, because the reality of their daily lives does not usually rise above absolute poverty levels, the rewards do not have to be very high to be attractive. However, Weinstein notes that some people with psychopathic tendencies are attracted by power and the opportunity to strut around with a gun. The key point of Weinstein's research is that in the presence of natural resource wealth – oil, diamonds or perhaps drugs – there are credible prospects of wealth, so that some of the young men who volunteer are motivated by these prospects rather than a mission to right a political wrong. Weinstein concluded that the idealistic rebel leader will find it very difficult to screen these people out. He can try rejecting those who fail to come up with the right slogans, but soon everyone will learn to parrot them. Gradually, the composition of the rebel group will shift from idealists to opportunists and sadists.

Adapted from: Collier, P. (2008) *The Bottom Billion*, Oxford: OUP, pp. 29s

> **Summarize Weinstein's findings about the recruitment of new members of rebel movements.**

Focus on ...

Blood diamonds

The United Nations defines blood diamonds as those that originate from areas controlled by forces or factions opposed to legitimate and internationally recognized governments, and which are used to fund military action in opposition to these governments.

During the 1990s, the rebel group UNITA's ability to wage war in Angola was underwritten by its control of 60 to 70 per cent of Angola's diamond fields and its ability to smuggle these diamonds to the West. Between 1992 and 1998, it is estimated that UNITA made $3.7 billion through illicit diamond sales. However, it is also estimated that 220 000 people have died in Angola in the civil war between the Angolan government and UNITA. The UN attempted to undermine the funding of this conflict by applying sanctions to the production of Angolan rough diamonds, and both the UN and EU now demand an official government certificate of origin for batches of diamonds.

However, the shadow (i.e. illegal) trade in Angolan diamonds has been maintained by two factors. The first is the relative ease with which UNITA and diamond smugglers can obtain certificates from other African countries falsifying the origin of the diamonds. Second, multinational diamond companies have been complicit in this illegal trade. For example, De Beers values and sells 80 per cent of the world's diamonds. In its attempt to maintain a controlling influence on the world diamond trade, De Beers developed a complex organizational structure composed of many foreign-registered subsidiaries. These companies have collaborated with UNITA to make sure that falsely certificated rough Angolan diamonds have found their way to the legitimate market through Antwerp in Belgium and Israel. There is evidence that both the Belgian and Israeli governments have turned a blind eye to these practices. However, De Beers has now cleaned up its act and introduced the Kimberley Process for the certification of diamonds. It will no longer buy diamonds unless they are officially certificated by smart-card technology.

Adapted from Duffield, M. (2001) *Global Governance and the New Wars*, London: Zed Books

The costs of conflict

Collier notes that civil wars are highly persistent. The average international war lasts on average six months but the average civil war is ten times as long.

Duffield notes that civil war violence complicates and deepens poverty. Collier describes civil war as 'development in reverse' because it damages both the country and its neighbours. On average, a civil war reduces economic growth by around 2.3 per cent. A seven-year civil war can mean that a country is 15 per cent worse off in terms of economic growth. A good example of this is the Democratic Republic of Congo, which will need about 50 years of peace in order to get back to the income level it had in 1960.

Economic growth also stagnates because conflict often destroys development assets. Domestic agricultural and industrial production decline dramatically because of physical destruction. War also interrupts normal trade as well as the collection of tax revenue. Education is massively disrupted. For example, Short (1999) notes that the 15-year civil war in Mozambique destroyed 70 per cent of the country's schools. Social capital, too – particularly **social cohesion** – is disrupted by war; families and communities are torn apart by killing and population displacement, as people become refugees, making it difficult for societies to recover. Ethnic groups no longer trust one another. Culture, too, is often destroyed or severely damaged.

Collier observes that war is much worse than just a prolonged economic depression; it kills people. However, it is not active combat that kills – it is disease. Wars create refugees and this mass movement of the population creates the potential for epidemics. The costs of such conflict are often borne by neighbouring countries. Diseases do not respect frontiers. AIDS too spreads through civil war – Collier notes that 'the combination of mass rape and mass migration produce ideal conditions for spreading sexually transmitted disease'.

Often, the end of a war is not the end of the conflict; once a war is over, a conflict is extremely likely to restart. The experience of having been through a civil war roughly doubles the risk of another conflict. Collier estimates that there is only a 50:50 chance of achieving 10 years of peace in developing societies. Low-income countries experience a particularly high risk of relapse. The risk of further war is caused by a legacy of organized killing left by the previous war – violence and extortion prove to be such a profitable way of life that many perpetrators find that life difficult to give up. Killing for the majority of young poor members of rebel groups is the only way they know to earn a living. Moreover, the surplus of cheap guns does not help improve the prospects for a peaceful future in many countries in the developing world.

Collier and Hoeffler (2004) note that the crime rate in post-conflict societies is extremely high – the end of political fighting usually ushers in a boom of homicides. Moreover, this is not normally limited to the immediate geographic region. Conflict countries produce 95 per cent of the world's hard drugs. Because of their lack of state control, and lack of law and order, many of these countries become attractive as bases for terrorism, which may be directed at Western interests.

The effects of armed conflict on children

Children are often recruited by rebel groups as child soldiers during civil war. They are also likely to be the victims of such conflicts. Despite international treaties, thousands of children worldwide fight in armies and paramilitary forces. In 1999, Amnesty International claimed that at least 300 000 children under the age of 18 were actively involved in armed conflict in countries such as Sierra Leone, Liberia, Congo, Sudan, Uganda, Sri Lanka and Burma. The development of smaller, lighter weapons such as the Kalashnikov has made it easier for children to go into combat and to fight alongside adults.

As the 'Focus on research' below illustrates, many child soldiers are involved in conflicts and atrocities involuntarily. They are coerced into violence because of fear that they themselves will be killed. However, some children may be willing volunteers – military action may give them a sense of common purpose, comradeship, loyalty and teamwork that makes up for the poverty that often characterizes their

Focus on research

Child soldiers

Many children who become child soldiers are often abducted and forced to fight against their will as the example of Susan illustrates. Aged 16, Susan was abducted by the Lord's Resistance Army in Uganda:

<< *One boy tried to escape [from the rebels], but he was caught … His hands were tied, and then they made us, the other new captives, kill him with a stick. I felt sick. I knew this boy from before. We were from the same village. I refused to kill him and they told me they would shoot me. They pointed a gun at me, so I had to do it. The boy was asking me, 'Why are you doing this?' I said I had no choice. After we killed him, they made us smear his blood on our arms … They said we had to do this so we would not fear death and so we would not try to escape … I still dream about the boy from my village who I killed. I see him in my dreams, and he is talking to me and saying I killed him for nothing, and I am crying.* >>

Source: Human Rights Watch 2001

communities. However, child soldiers have acquired a reputation in Sierra Leone and Uganda for being excessively brutal in killing or maiming people without pity or mercy. This behaviour is probably caused by knowing nothing but war and violence or by seeing family members killed.

Finally, war and conflict have other effects upon children. They are disproportionately the victims of killing and, alongside women, are disproportionately likely to be displaced from their home and to become refugees. Children are also likely to suffer health consequences as a result of war and may become impoverished and malnourished if they are forced to flee their homes as a result of conflict. Consequently, they may die of diseases, such as measles, that Western children are likely to survive. Similarly, poverty may lead to civil unrest and the potential for uprising, which results in the risk of children being recruited as soldiers or becoming the victims of armed conflict.

The effects of conflict on women

Van Zeijl (2007) argues that sexual violence against women is a norm in many conflicts in developing societies. Feminists such as Brownmiller (2000) and Morgan (2006) argue that rape is inherent in the nature of war: it is never about sex, but about power and the military culture of violence. Amnesty International suggests mass rapes are a weapon of war. In 1998 the United Nations declared the use of rape to suppress women a war crime. However, van Zeijl suggests that the use of rape in the developing world has actually increased in recent years, particularly in Liberia, Sierra Leone, Rwanda, Somalia and Uganda.

Van Zeijl notes that rape is occurring on a massive scale in Darfur in Sudan (see 'Focus on ... Darfur', on p. 104). Van Zeijl claims that rape, used as a weapon of war, can be seen as a gruesome extension of **patriarchal** societies' unequal attitude towards women in peacetime. Women in many parts of the world are still seen as the property of men, rather than their own person – for example, in Sudan, rape within marriage is not seen as a crime – and beating your wife when she 'misbehaves' is widely condoned.

Conclusions

Duffield (2007) notes that globalization has brought great benefits and opportunities. However, it has also brought into existence a 'shrinking and radically interconnected world', in which war and conflict in distant lands, which 20 years ago would have had little relevance to our everyday lives, now directly affect the security of our society and the standard of living we take for granted. As Gordon Brown argued in 2004, 'it is a political imperative – central to our long-term national security and peace – to tackle the poverty that leads to civil wars, failed states and safe havens for terrorists'. In other words, we ignore war and conflict in developing societies at our peril.

Check your understanding

1 What are the key differences between 'old' wars and 'new' wars?

2 How might civil wars in the developing world be caused by identity politics?

3 What is the probable relationship between poverty, civil wars and military coups in the developing world?

4 How might overdependence on one natural resource increase the likelihood of civil war in developing societies?

5 How and why does civil war in the developing world often take on criminal characteristics?

6 Identify four economic consequences of civil war in developing societies.

7 How does civil war in the developing world undermine the power of official aid?

8 Identify four effects that war and conflict in developing societies have on children.

9 What aspects of war in the developing world aim to control the population through the targeting of women?

10 What implications does civil war in the developing world have for developed societies?

Activities

Research idea

Using an atlas and **www.wikipedia.org** or **www.newint.org** work out how many developing countries have experienced civil wars or military coups in the last 20 years.

Web.tasks

1 If you are interested in researching blood diamonds, visit the following websites:

www.stopblooddiamonds.org

www.globalwitness.org

2 There are a number of websites that aim to examine the effect of war and conflict on children:

www.un.org/children/conflict

www.unicef.org/protection

www.watchlist.org

3 Paul Collier's website contains some interesting videos and articles on conflict in Africa and is well worth a visit:

http://users.ox.ac.uk/~econpco/

Key themes

Stratification and differentiation

Child victims

Age is a major source of inequality in the developing world. Warlords are forcing children in conflicts around the world to become killing machines. Some children are kidnapped from their schools or their beds, some are recruited after seeing their parents slaughtered and some may even choose to join the militias as their best hope for survival in war-torn countries from Colombia, across Africa and the Middle East, to south Asia. Once recruited, many are brainwashed, trained, given drugs and sent into battle with orders to kill.

There is no escape for what the United Nations and human rights groups estimate are 250 000 child soldiers today. These children, some as young as 8, become fighters, sex slaves, spies and even human shields. They are easy to manipulate and will do the unspeakable without question or protest, partly because their morals and value systems are not yet fully formed. The journey from boy or girl to killing machine follows a horrifying route of indoctrination, including being forced to execute friends and family.

One girl, Angela, 12, told Human Rights Watch she was told to shoot a friend when she joined Colombia's FARC guerrillas. 'I closed my eyes and fired the gun, but I didn't hit her. So I shot again,' she said. 'I had to bury her and put dirt on top of her. The commander said, "You'll have to do this many more times, and you'll have to learn not to cry".'

Key terms

Blood diamonds diamonds that are mined illegally by rebel groups and sold on the black market to Western dealers.

Civil war localized conflicts that normally involve rebel groups attempting to overthrow a government.

Counter-insurgency a form of rebellion or uprising.

Coups the sudden violent overthrow of a government and seizure of political power, especially by the army.

Diaspora communities a worldwide dispersion of a people, language, or culture that was formerly concentrated in one place.

Ethnic cleansing the violent elimination or removal of people from a country or area because of their ethnic backgrounds, by means of genocide or forced expulsion.

Genocide the systematic killing of all the people from a national, ethnic or religious group, or an attempt to do this.

Guerrilla warfare military or paramilitary operations by rebels rather than armies.

Ideologies sets of ideas which influence the political outlook of millions of people.

NATO the North Atlantic Treaty Organization a military alliance of the USA, Canada and European countries such as the UK and Germany.

Patriarchal male dominated

Political legitimacy the idea that politicians have been elected by the people via elections.

Privatization of war when civilians are deliberately targeted in war

Shadow economies illegal economies, e.g. the 'black market'.

Social cohesion feeling of belonging to a larger entity, e.g. a society.

Total wars wars fought by nations against other nations that use all the resources at their disposal.

Warlord usually a rebel leader, opposed to a government, who controls large amounts of territory through the use of violence and fear.

An eye on the exam — War and conflict

Assess the relationship between war and the development process.

(18 marks)

Grade booster — Getting top marks in this question

You could begin your answer by outlining the different forms that war and conflict can take, for example by distinguishing between 'old' wars and 'new' wars. Focus on the new wars of the developing world and their characteristics, e.g. the role of identity politics, genocide and ethnic cleansing, the role of the media, funding from abroad and the relationship to the global economy of such conflicts. The latter can include the drugs trade as well as supplying commodities and raw materials to western multinationals to pay for arms. You should also examine the two-way relationship between poverty and war in developing countries: how far is poverty a source of conflict and of recruits, and how does war perpetuate poverty? You can also look at how war and conflict affect other aspects of developing societies, such as children (both as victims and as child soldiers) and women.

1 Read **Item A** below and answer parts (a) and (b) that follow.

Item A

Many people argue that we face a 'population time bomb' as the population of less developed societies expands rapidly. However, some sociologists argue that historical evidence on population growth in the West suggests that this is not inevitable. They point to the fact that developing countries are beginning to pass through the same

Stage 1: Pre-industrial society	High birth rate High death rate	Population small but stable
Stage 2: Early industrial society	High birth rate Falling death rate	Rapid population growth
Stage 3: Largely industrialized society	Falling birth rate Low death rate	Population growing more slowly
Stage 4: Mature industrial society	Low birth rate Low death rate	Population large but stable

demographic stages as the ones Western countries have already passed through. The stages that they identify are as shown in the table above.

(a) Identify and briefly explain **three** reasons why today's less developed societies might not pass through the same demographic stages as the West (**Item A**). *(9 marks)*

9/9

Firstly, although death rates are higher in less developed societies (LDCs), they have fallen much more quickly than in the West because of medical advances that were unavailable when the West was developing. A second reason for falling Western birth rates was that industrialization brought greater economic security, so people had less need of large families. Many LDCs cannot industrialize, so people have large families as insurance against poverty. Thirdly, studies show that educated women have more control over their fertility. But in many LDCs, women are denied education, so birth rates remain high.

An examiner comments

Three relevant reasons, all clearly explained – full marks!

This is quite a good answer that looks at a range of possible effects of aid. It deals with some different types of aid (humanitarian, health and education etc), although it could deal with others, e.g. military aid, infrastructure etc. Its main limitation is that it lacks explicit theory – dependency theory would be useful here, while modernization theory and neo-liberalism are also relevant.

(b) Critically examine the effects of aid given by the West to less developed countries. *(18 marks)*

The West can be seen to give aid to LDCs for a number of reasons. Firstly, there is humanitarian aid, such as Band Aid and Live Aid, or money donated to NGOs after a natural disaster such as the tsunami or a famine. This is obviously helpful in dealing with an emergency but it may not be much help in long-term development.

Another reason is to assist in development by providing aid for education, health care etc. However, the aid provided is not always the most appropriate. For example, it may involve giving money to establish a university or hospital in the capital city, when it would be more useful if it were spent on providing primary schools and basic literacy or primary health care clinics in rural areas.

Sometimes the aid comes with 'strings' attached. For example, it may be a condition that the aid money is spent on products from the donor country, which again may not be the best or cheapest, meaning it is less likely to be effective than if the LDC was free to spend it as they wished. It may also be spent paying the salaries of Western experts, aid workers etc, rather than creating jobs for local people. This relates to who controls the aid budget – the Westerners or the locals? This links to kleptocracy, where local politicians syphon off funds from aid budgets, so that the people it was meant for get little or no benefit from it.

Another effect of aid can be that it undermines the local economy. For example, food aid can be useful in an emergency, but there is a danger of it putting local farmers out of business if it is given away, since this will take away their market, perhaps leading them to have to depend on aid too.

12/18

One for you to try

Assess the view that education is the key to development. *(33 marks)*

An examiner comments You need to present different views of the role of education in the development process. Begin with the view of modernization theorists that meritocratic education plays a key role in transmitting the skills and values for development. You should use other approaches to evaluate this view, e.g. you can discuss the dependency theory view that

education plays a role in underdevelopment by transmitting Western ideology, and that it is not meritocratic but only serves pro-Western elites, and excludes the rural poor, women, etc.

Answers to the 'One for you to try' are available free on **www.collinseducation.com/sociologyweb**

CHAPTER 3

The mass media

AQA Specification	Topics	Pages
Candidates should examine:		
The relationship between ownership and control of the mass media.	Covered in Topic 1	134–43
The mass media, globalization and popular culture.	Covered in Topic 2	144–53
The processes of selection and presentation of the content of the news.	Covered in Topic 3	154–66
Media representations of age, social class, ethnicity, gender, sexuality and disability.	Covered in Topics 5 and 6	178–205
The relationship between the mass media, media content and presentation, and audiences.	Covered in Topic 4	167–77
The new media and their significance for an understanding of the role of the media in contemporary society.	Covered in Topic 2	144–53

TOPIC 1

Trends in the ownership and control of the mass media

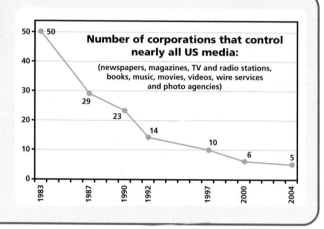

Getting you thinking

1 Explain the main trend in the graph on the right.

2 What effect do you think this trend might have on the content of the media?

3 Are you concerned about the trend shown in the graph? Explain your answer.

Number of corporations that control nearly all US media:

(newspapers, magazines, TV and radio stations, books, music, movies, videos, wire services and photo agencies)

50 — 50
29
23
14
10
6
5

1983 1987 1990 1992 1997 2000 2004

The **mass media** are generally defined as those agencies of communication that transmit information, education, news and entertainment to mass audiences. There are broadly three types of media:

1 *The print media* – newspapers, magazines, comics, books and some forms of advertising – most of these types of media are commercially owned and produced in order to generate profit for the publishing companies that own them.

2 *The audio-visual media* – terrestrial and satellite television, radio, cinema, DVDs and music. Most of these types of media are owned and produced by commercial broadcasters whose main aim is to make profit, usually through subscriptions and/or advertising revenue. However, in the UK, a significant proportion of the audio-visual media is publicly or state-owned, i.e. the BBC is controlled by a board of governors appointed by the government and is funded by a state broadcasting tax (i.e. the television licence). Channel 4, too, is publicly owned and has no shareholders. However, it receives no funding from government but is financed entirely by its commercial activities, e.g. advertising revenue.

3 *The cybermedia or digital media* are relatively new types of media and include the internet or worldwide web – and, in particular, interactive online sites that revolve around social networking, such as Facebook. Other examples of digital media include MP3 players, such as the iPod, and computer game consoles, such as the PS3, Wii and the Xbox.

Ownership and control

Some sociologists have expressed concern about recent trends in media ownership and control. On the surface, the number of media outlets available to the general public has increased dramatically. Thirty years ago, there were only four television channels – today hundreds of television channels are available via digital and satellite services such as Sky and Virgin. The number of national newspapers has remained fairly stable over the last 30 years, but the number of free papers and magazines has grown enormously. Thirty years ago, the internet did not exist.

All these changes in the availability of media seem to imply a greater degree of choice. However, sociologists who have examined recent trends in the ownership of such media suggest that this increased choice may be an illusion. Some even suggest that, despite this media expansion, consumer choice has actually declined. There are a number of trends which are seen as contributing to this contraction of choice.

Concentration of ownership

Bagdikian (2004) points out that, in 1983, 50 corporations controlled the vast majority of all news media in the USA. However, by 1992, 22 companies owned and operated 90 per cent of the mass media – controlling almost all of the USA's newspapers, magazines, TV and radio stations, books, records, movies, videos, wire services and photo agencies. Bagdikian argues that if the USA's media were owned by separate individuals, there would be 25 000 owners; instead, by 2004, media ownership in the USA was concentrated in seven corporations: Time Warner, Disney, News Corp, Sony, Bertelsmann of Germany, Viacom (formerly CBS) and General Electric NBC.

Many of these companies have now started to move into **cybermedia**, which until recently were dominated by four major companies: Microsoft, Apple, Google and Yahoo. We are now seeing concentration in terms of ownership of internet companies, as the traditional media companies compete with cybermedia organizations to control social networking sites, which are extremely lucrative in terms of advertising revenue. For example, NewsCorp now owns MySpace; Time-Warner has bought Bebo; Microsoft now owns a significant stake in Facebook; and Google has bought into YouTube.

The British print media

Curran (2003) suggests that concentration of ownership of British newspapers is not a new phenomenon. In 1937, four men – Lords Beaverbrook, Rothermere, Camrose and Northcliffe, known as the 'press barons' – owned nearly one in every two national and local daily newspapers sold in the UK. Today, seven individuals dominate the ownership and content of UK national daily and Sunday newspapers:

1 News Corp (owned and controlled by the Australian-American Rupert Murdoch and his family) produces *The Times, Sun, News of the World* and *Sunday Times*.
2 Associated Newspapers (owned by Lord Rothermere) owns the *Daily Mail, Mail On Sunday, Metro* and London's biggest selling newspaper, the *Evening Standard*, as well as 54 regional papers.
3 United Newspapers is owned by Richard Desmond and produces the *Daily* and *Sunday Express*, the *Daily Star* and *OK!* magazine.
4 The *Telegraph* group (*Daily* and *Sunday*) is owned by the Barclay Brothers.
5 The *Independent* and *Independent on Sunday* are owned by the Irish entrepreneur, Tony O'Reilly.
6 Viscount Cowdray has a £570 million stake in the Pearson group, which owns the *Financial Times*, Penguin Publishing and *The Economist*.

Only two national newspaper groups are controlled by companies rather than individuals. Trinity Mirror owns the *Daily Mirror, Sunday Mirror, Sunday People* and *Daily Record* (Scotland's biggest selling paper), as well as over 150 regional daily newspapers. The Guardian Media Group is controlled by a board of trustees – the Scott Trust – which owns both the *Guardian* and the *Observer*.

By 2002, just three publishers controlled two-thirds of national newspapers sold in the UK. The top five publishers also controlled 69 per cent of regional evening papers and 75 per cent of free sheets such as *Metro*.

The UK magazine market is dominated by two major companies. Almost two in every three UK women and over 45 per cent of UK men read an IPC magazine, i.e. 27 million UK adults. IPC produces 80 magazines including *What's on TV, Marie Claire, Woman, Nuts* and *Country Life*. IPC is owned by Time Warner. In 2008, the Bauer Publishing Group, controlled by the Bauer family, published 80 magazines including *FHM, Empire, Grazia* and *Elle* with an estimated readership of 26 million.

The broadcasting media

The content of commercial terrestrial television is mainly controlled by one company, ITV plc, which is the result of a merger in 2004 between the two biggest owners of commercial television franchises, i.e. Granada (which controlled most of the regional television stations in the North of England) and Carlton Communications (which controlled most of the terrestrial stations in Southern England and Wales). This company currently owns 11 of the 15 regional commercial television franchises. Channel 5, on the other hand, is owned by three companies – United Business Media, Bertelsmann and Pearson.

Access to satellite, cable and digital television in the UK is generally controlled by two companies – News Corp, which owns BSkyB, and Virgin Media (formerly NTL), owned by Richard Branson.

The British music industry is owned and controlled by six major companies, but only one of these – EMI – is British. In 2007, EMI was acquired by the private equity group Terra Firma controlled by the financier, Guy Hands. The cinema industry is also dominated by American media – three of the five largest cinema owners in the UK, particularly of the multiplexes, are American subsidiaries. Even those chains which are British in origin, e.g. Odeon, Virgin and ABC, are contracted to strong links with US distributors.

The UK media industry is therefore dominated by 13 companies. Ten of these companies are owned and controlled by wealthy and powerful individuals rather than shareholders. Considerable parts of the British media industry are owned and controlled by global corporations.

Horizontal integration

Horizontal integration is also known as **cross-media ownership** and refers to the fact that the bigger media companies often own a diverse range of media. For example, News Corp, in addition to newspapers in Britain and Australia, owns the publisher HarperCollins as well as US interests, including the *New York Post*, Fox TV and 20th Century Fox film studios. It also owns Sky and the biggest Asian satellite channel, Star TV. Associated Newspapers also has stakes in several radio stations, and owns 20 per cent of ITN and 40 per cent of Teletext.

Vertical integration

Some media companies are increasingly trying to control all aspects of their industry in order to maximize their profits, e.g. Time Warner makes its own films and distributes them to its own cinema complexes. News Corp owns television and film studios as well as the satellite television channels that show them. **Vertical integration** therefore gives media companies greater economic control over their operating environment.

Diversification

Diversification is also called 'lateral expansion' and occurs when firms diversify into new business areas in order to spread risk. Losses made in one area may be compensated for by profits in another. Virgin is a good example of a diversified corporation – it has major media interests in music, publishing, cinemas, digital television and internet access. However, it also sells insurance and banking services as well as running an airline and a train service.

Global conglomeration

Media companies have also taken advantage of the erosion of traditional boundaries surrounding media markets. Globalization has opened up national markets and created international competition between media companies. The result is that many of these companies have become **global conglomerations** – transnational corporations with a presence in many countries, operating in a global market. News Corp, for example, owns newspapers in Australia, the UK and USA. Many of these corporations are also conglomerates – business corporations that control dozens of media companies with wide interests across a wide range of products and services.

Synergy

Increasingly, media companies are using their different interests to package their products in several different ways, e.g. *Spiderman 2* was not only a movie – it was a soundtrack album, computer game and ring tone. It was also turned into toy action figures and marketed through fast food outlets, newspaper, radio and television coverage. Often, the media company producing the film will own the companies that produce the music, computer game, etc., or that distribute the franchise (i.e. the licence that lets other companies do it). Another variation on **synergy** is that the media company producing a product often owns newspapers and magazines through which it can be advertised and promoted, e.g. the *Sun* newspaper often promotes Sky products.

Technological convergence

Technological convergence is a fairly new concept and refers to the trend of putting several technologies into one media product – for example, through the personal computer, mobile phones and digital television, we can now access the internet, telecommunication services, games, etc., as well as paying bills, buying films, downloading music and so on. Consequently, companies that normally work in quite separate fields are joining up or converging – for instance, Orange have linked up with Sony to explore ways of improving mobile-phone technology by giving access to media services, such as music, the internet and video.

Why should we study media ownership and control?

Doyle (2002) suggests that we need to study media ownership and control for two reasons:

1   She suggests that there is a need for societies to have a diverse and pluralistic media provision so that all points of view can be heard and abuses of power and influence by elites can be avoided.

2   She notes that ownership and control over the media:

   <<*raise special concerns that do not apply to other sectors of industry.* **Media concentrations** *matter because … media have the power to make or break political careers … Control over a substantial share of the more popular avenues for dissemination of media content can, as politicians are well aware, confer very considerable influence on public opinion.*>> (pp.6–7)

However, Doyle's views have attracted some criticism from those sociologists who call themselves pluralists, who argue that these concerns are exaggerated. They argue that media owners generally manage their media in a responsible fashion, because content is largely determined by the demands of the consumer market and, even if they did not, the professional ethics of journalists and editors, as well as the commonsense of the general public would undermine any attempt by owners to use their media as a mouth piece for their own views.

The pluralist theory of media ownership

From a **pluralist** viewpoint, modern capitalist societies are democratic – all interest groups, whether they are right-wing, centrist or left-wing, are given a platform to express their views to the electorate, and the most persuasive arguments will result in their representatives being voted into power. The mass media are seen to be an essential component of this democratic ideal, because most people obtain their knowledge about politics from newspapers and television. Pluralists, therefore, argue that media owners are objective, responsible and impartial facilitators of this political process.

The economics of media ownership

Moreover, pluralists also point out that the behaviour of media owners is constrained by the market – in free-market economies, media owners compete against each other in order to attract people to their product. Readers, viewers and listeners are the real power-holders because they exercise the right to buy or not to buy. In other words, they have freedom of choice. If they did not like the choices that media owners are making available to them, or if they suspected the media product was biased one way rather than another, the media audience would probably respond by not buying the product and the media company would go out of business. Power, then, according to pluralist thinkers, lies with the consumer or audience rather than with owners. The media, therefore, give the public what the audience wants rather than what the owner decides.

   Pluralists argue that the rationale for media concentration is essentially economic rather than political or ideological. They argue that media products are costly to produce. Concentration of ownership is aimed at the maximization of audience size in order to reduce costs and to attract advertising revenue. The globalization of the media and the conglomerates that have resulted from this are also merely attempts at finding new

Focus on research

The Campaign for Press and Broadcasting Freedom (CPBF)
Media ownership in the age of convergence

In January 2007, the Campaign for Press and Broadcasting Freedom launched its media ownership project to research the changing patterns of ownership in our rapidly converging media, and to develop new policy initiatives.

Long-standing concerns about the power and influence of media moguls in traditional media (film, television, radio, newspapers, books and magazines) remain central to our work on media ownership. The distorting impact of excessive media power on politics is vividly exemplified by Silvio Berlusconi's election victory in Italy and his subsequent actions, or by the global role Rupert Murdoch plays. As the *Wall Street Journal* pointed out when it was still owned by the Bancroft family, Murdoch 'has blurred a line that exists at many other US media companies ... a line intended to keep the business and political interest of owners from influencing the presentation of news'.

We need to develop our analysis to take in the big policy implications of converged media and the transition to multimedia and multiplatform (PC, mobile, interactive TV) systems and the internet. Whereas 'old media' still has some regulatory scaffolding governing programming obligations, new media programme providers and businesses are keen to limit traditional regulation.

Consolidation is occurring at an alarming rate, with $30 billion spent in 2007 in mergers and acquisitions by Microsoft, Time Warner (AOL), Yahoo! and WPP on interactive advertising companies. ... Growing consolidation will also undermine diversity of both content and ownership, and the transformation of the internet from an open, global means of communications into one designed primarily to serve the interests of corporate brands and commercialism.

Privacy also will be eroded as massive databases of information on internet users become more intrusive. For example, the recent Google/DoubleClick merger formed an information colossus that combines information about consumers that Google collects through its search engine with the tracking data that DoubleClick collects about users as they surf the net. Also new ad-targeting systems are being developed which determine users' interests by monitoring the websites they visit.

The outcomes of the Media Ownership project will be to:

● chart the patterns of ownership which span converged communications media
● produce a clear set of relevant policies on media ownership for the UK and Europe
● identify the kind of regulation which is required to protect public service content (news, children's programmes, documentaries, etc.) in the digital age
● produce a chart, popular campaigning pamphlet and book with the facts, arguments and analysis on media ownership
● hold a major conference to launch our polices in autumn 2009
● ensure that in the run-up to the next election our policy proposals are at the centre of political debate.

Source: www.cpbf.org.uk/body.php?subject=media%20ownership

1 List the issues that the CPBF are concerned about in relation to ownership and control of the media.

2 Suggest reasons for the various proposed outcomes of the project.

audiences in order to increase profits, rather than some sort of cultural imperialism.

Vertical and horizontal integration, as well as synergy, reduce costs because media companies no longer have to contract services out to other media companies who might be competing with them. Profits are also enhanced because they are no longer subjected to the fluctuating prices charged by other companies. Moreover, the main rationale for diversification is spreading risk and possible loss, e.g. EMI can afford to sustain losses across its record labels because its music publishing company is so successful.

Pluralists argue that it is practically impossible for owners to interfere in the content of newspapers and television programmes because their businesses are economically far too complex for them to take a regular interest in the content of programmes or newspapers. Whale (1977), for example, argues that 'media owners have global problems of trade and investment to occupy their minds' and so do not have the time to think about the day-to-day detailed running of their media businesses.

Media diversity

Pluralists argue that the range of media products available is extremely diverse and that, as a result, all points of view in a democratic society are catered for. If some viewpoints have a greater range of media representing them, this is not necessarily biased. It merely mirrors what the audience wants or sees as important. For example, if the majority of newspapers raise concerns about young people carrying knifes, they are mirroring the concerns of the majority of citizens. If women's magazines seem to focus disproportionately on features about slimming, beauty, babies and weddings, this is because this is what the majority of women want to read about.

Public service broadcasting

Pluralists point out that a significant share of the media market in the UK is taken up by **public service broadcasters** (PSB), i.e. media outlets controlled by the state, which have a world-wide reputation for impartiality, and which cater for every conceivable taste and opinion. The British Broadcasting Corporation (BBC) is the most obvious example of this, although Channel 4 is also a public service broadcaster.

The BBC was set up by a Royal Charter in 1926, which clearly states that the BBC has a legal obligation to provide specific services – to inform, to educate and to entertain the full audience spectrum (i.e. all social groups in society must be catered for). In 1999, the government outlined what it saw as the functions of the BBC:

- to provide quality programming with particular emphasis on giving the audience access to the 'arts', i.e. drama, opera, classical music
- to protect vulnerable programme types, such as news, documentaries, children's programming and drama
- to accurately and impartially report news
- to educate audiences so that they can make informed decisions about political issues
- to ensure that programming is pluralistic and diverse, and consequently caters for all segments of society
- to protect consumers, especially children, from harmful material.

Pluralists therefore see PSB as the epitome of impartial and objective media and a counterweight to any potential bias in the private sector.

State controls

Pluralists note that the power of media owners is also restricted by state or government controls. For example, in some societies, owners are not allowed to own too much media or different types of media, in order to reduce the possibility that one person's or group's views or products can become too dominant. For example, in the USA, the huge film studios have been prevented from owning film production, film distribution and cinemas at the same time. Many countries have cross-ownership rules preventing companies from owning more than one media form in the same area – for example, you may only be able to own one television station rather than several.

Another state constraint on media ownership is the fact that both the BBC and ITV have some formal legal requirements imposed upon them by a powerful regulator – the Office for Communications (Ofcom) – which was set up in 2003. Ofcom's function is to monitor the content and quality of television and radio output on both the BBC and the commercial channels, and to investigate viewer and listener complaints. Pluralists argue that this combination of audience and regulator prevents unscrupulous media owners imposing biased content upon the general public.

Media professionalism

Pluralists stress the professionalism of journalists and editors, arguing that editors would never allow owners to compromise their independence. They argue that journalists have too much integrity to be biased regularly in favour of one particular perspective. Pluralists also point out that the media have a strong tradition of **investigative journalism**, which has often targeted those in power. For example, two reporters on the *Washington Post* forced the President of the USA – Richard Nixon – to resign after they exposed him for authorizing the bugging of his opponent's offices at Watergate in 1972. Newspapers in the UK have also uncovered corruption in high places and forced politicians to resign from office.

Media audiences

Pluralists also suggest that audiences do not passively accept what is being fed to them. They argue that audiences are selective and often critical of media content. Audiences are very diverse, and interpret and use the media in different ways.

The Marxist critique of media ownership and control

Marxists argue that the economic system of the UK, i.e. capitalism, is deeply unfair because it generally benefits a minority – the capitalist class – at the expense of the majority. Marxists believe that inequalities in wealth and income and, therefore, poverty are the direct result of the way capitalism is organized. They argue that the wealth of the capitalist class is obtained by exploiting the labour power of the working class. Moreover, the capitalist class is able to ensure that class inequality is transmitted down through the generations through inheritance and private education.

The role of ideology

Marxists suggest that the capitalist class uses 'ideology' – i.e. a false but influential set of ideas, values and norms – to make sure that the working class accept capitalism and do not threaten its stability. In order to this, the capitalist class uses its cultural power to dominate institutions such as the education system, religion and the mass media. The role of these ideological agencies is to transmit ruling-class ideology by persuading the majority that capitalist society is meritocratic, i.e. that if people work hard and achieve, they can be materially successful. These agencies, therefore, aim to convince people of the benefits of capitalism. Consequently, working-class people experience '**false class-consciousness**' – they come to believe that capitalism is a fair system which benefits us all equally. They are told that if they fail to get on, it is their fault for not working hard enough to achieve qualifications. Therefore, they fail to see the reality of their situation – that they are being exploited by a system that only benefits a powerful minority.

The media and ideology

Marxists believe that media owners aim to transmit a conservative and conformist ideology in the form of news and entertainment. They argue that the main function of the media is to convince the general public that ruling-class ideology is 'truth' and 'fact'. In other words, as Miliband (1973) argued, the role of the media is to shape how we think about the world we live in. We are rarely informed about important issues such as why people continue to live in poverty. We are never encouraged to be critical of the capitalist system. Marxists argue that owners ensure that we only get a narrow range of 'approved' views and knowledge, with the result that 'alternative', critical points of view are rarely heard. Marxists argue that the media is happy to transmit ruling-class ideology through television and newspapers because media owners are part of the ruling capitalist class and have a vested interest in it not being criticized or dismantled. The last thing they want is equality for all, because this would mean less wealth for them.

Tunstall and Palmer (1991) argue along these lines with regard to government regulation of **media conglomerates**. They suggest that governments are no longer interested in controlling the activities of media owners. Rather 'regulatory favours' are the norm – newspapers owned by a conglomerate will directly support a government or neglect to criticize government policy or even withhold information from the general public in return for governments failing to enforce media regulation or even abolishing it altogether.

Evidence for the ideological nature of ownership and control

The problem with this Marxist account is that it implies that media owners, wealthholders and the political elite are united in some sort of ideological conspiracy to brainwash the population. There is some evidence for this cooperation in other societies – for example, in Italy, it has been demonstrated that Silvio Berlusconi's control of three television stations (which reached 40 per cent of the Italian audience) was instrumental in his party winning the general election in 1994 and Berlusconi becoming Prime Minister. However, on the whole, sociologists generally only have anecdotal evidence to confirm their suspicions that concentration of media ownership is damaging democracy.

However, Curran's (2003) detailed systematic examination of the British press does suggest that the evidence for owner interference in and manipulation of UK newspaper content is strong. He suggests that four distinct periods can be seen with regard to owner intervention and the consequent undermining of journalistic and editorial integrity.

1920 to 1950

Curran notes the rise of the 'press barons' and suggest that proprietorial control was a norm in this period. He notes that Lord Beaverbrook (who owned the *Express* newspaper group) and Lord Northcliffe (who owned Associated Newspapers) exercised detailed control over their favourite newspapers in terms of both content and layout. These owners were quite open in their purpose – Beaverbrook famously said: 'I run the *Daily Express* merely for the purpose of making propaganda and with no other motive.'

However, although false class-consciousness was probably not the ideological motive of the media barons in this period, Curran notes that there was an ideological effect of owner interference in media content:

<< *Their main impact lay in the way in which their papers selectively represented the world. This tended to strengthen the mainly conservative prejudices of their readers and reinforce opposition, particularly within the middle class, to progressive change.*>> (p.47)

1951 to 1974

Curran argues this period was the great pluralist phase in terms of newspaper reporting because there was a greater delegation by owners to editorial authority and autonomy. This period saw investigative reporting (especially into the activities of powerful groups) at its height. Curran argues that a group consensus emerged among journalists and editors that proprietorial influence should be resisted. However, this did not mean that interventionism by owners disappeared; most were still able to insist that their newspaper supported a particular political party.

1974 to 1992

Curran argues that a new type of interventionist proprietorship appeared in this period, as symbolized by Rupert Murdoch – 'a businessman first and foremost' – who acquired both the *Sun* and *The Times*. Murdoch was oriented towards what sold rather than what furthered a party interest or ideological viewpoint. Curran notes that Murdoch shifted his newspapers to the right because he believed that right-wing economic policies were the key to making vast profits.

Murdoch introduced a new personalized style of management to the production of newspapers in the UK – he read proofs, wrote leaders, changed content and layout. Most importantly, he handpicked compliant editors and managing directors. Between 1979 and 1992, Murdoch was a strong supporter of Mrs Thatcher's Conservative government because it pursued economic policies he agreed with and actively encouraged, to such an extent that he was dubbed the 'phantom prime minister'. There is little doubt that this interference produced both overt and covert forms of censorship – for example, during the 1984/5 miners' strike, *Times* journalists found that stories that were critical of the miners' employers were rejected by Murdoch. After a while, self-censorship became the norm as journalists decided there was no point in submitting such stories.

Other proprietors followed suit in this period. For example, Lord Matthews, proprietor of the Express group between 1977 and 1985, said: 'By and large editors will have complete freedom as long as they agree with the policy I have laid down.' Lord Stevens, who succeeded Lord Matthews, said: ' I would not be happy to be associated with a left-wing paper. I suppose the papers echo my political views … I do interfere and say enough is enough'.

1997 to the present day

Curran has noted that media ownership in the past ten years has been based on a 'global conservatism', as British newspaper groups have moved into the global marketplace. The most successful media entrepreneur in this period has been Rupert Murdoch, who Bagdikian dubbed 'lord of the global village'. Curran notes how, in 1997, Murdoch instructed his newspapers to abandon support for the Conservative Party and to support Tony Blair's New Labour. However, this was not due to Murdoch's sudden conversion to social democracy. Rather, it was a hard-nosed business decision because Blair was willing to lift state controls that prevented cross-media ownership. Curran argues that Murdoch was right-wing, but perceived Blair to be 'the only credible conservative worth supporting in 1997. In effect, a tacit deal was made between two power-holders – one a market-friendly politician and the other a pragmatic businessman – in a form that sidelined the public' (p.75). As Curran concludes, 'the Murdoch press thus changed its political loyalty but not its politics' (p.74).

Curran's analysis of British newspapers suggests that both pluralist and Marxist theories may be mistaken in the way they look at media owners. First, the pluralist view that media owners do not intervene in media content is evidently false. Curran argues that the last ten years have seen even greater intervention because owners have undermined newspaper independence and balance in subtle ways by choosing the editors they want and getting rid of editors that 'fail'. As Curran notes:

> « Editors' freedom of action is curtailed by … budgetary controls, management guidelines, and an implicit understanding of how the paper should develop … Journalists tend to be selected in the first place on the grounds that they will 'fit' in. Conforming to hierarchical requirements brings rewards in terms of good assignments, high exposure, promotion and peer group esteem. Resistance invites escalating sanctions. Dissident reporters who do not deliver the goods suffer professional death. » (p.85)

Moreover, there are signs that the general public are well aware that these processes are undermining the pluralist view that journalists are first and foremost the objective seekers of truth. In 1993, only 10 per cent of the general public believed that journalists could be trusted to tell the truth, and in 2002, a Eurobarometer survey conducted across several European nations concluded that the British general public was the least likely to trust the media, particularly the print media.

Curran's analysis also belies the Marxist notion that there is a deliberate capitalist conspiracy to subvert working-class consciousness. There is little evidence of this. Curran suggests media owners are not united in an ideological quest, but are primarily motivated by economics rather than capitalist ideology. Moreover, their actions are not collectivized; they pursue their economic goals in a ruthlessly individualized way in an attempt to obtain a bigger share of the market than their capitalist competitors. For example, Murdoch's instructions to Fox News to be a cheerleader for the Iraq War, and his decision

that Sky News should not cover pro-democracy protests in China were motivated simply by his economic relationships with the USA and China respectively. However, there is sufficient evidence to suggest that the actions of media owners produce media content which in the long term benefits capitalism. In this sense, Curran's analysis fits in with the analysis of the Glasgow University Media Group, which takes a **hegemonic** approach to media ownership and control.

The Glasgow University Media Group

The Glasgow University Media Group (GUMG) suggests that media content does support the interests of those who run the capitalist system but this is an accidental byproduct of the social backgrounds of journalists and broadcasters. These tend to be overwhelmingly White, middle-class and male. A Sutton Trust report in 2006 (see 'Focus on research', p. 141) found that leading news and current affairs journalists are more likely than not to have been to independent schools, which educate just 7 per cent of the population. Of the top 100 journalists in 2006, 54 per cent were independently educated – an increase from 49 per cent in 1986. The Sutton Trust asks the important question: is it healthy that those who are most influential in determining and interpreting the news agenda have educational backgrounds that are so different from the vast majority of the population?

The GUMG claims that these journalists and broadcasters tend to believe in 'middle-of-the-road' (consensus) views and ideas, which are generally unthreatening and which, they believe, appeal to the majority of their viewers, listeners and readers. Such journalists and broadcasters tend to see anyone who believes in ideas outside this media consensus as 'extremist', and consequently such people are rarely invited to contribute their opinion in newspapers or on television. When such alternative views are included in newspapers or television broadcasts, they are often ridiculed by journalists.

Economic pressures

The GUMG argues that this journalistic desire not to rock the boat is mainly motivated by profit. The media is generally a profit-making business – it makes those profits by attracting advertising, and advertisers are attracted to a specific type of media by the number of readers and viewers. If, for some reason, those viewers or readers are put off the television programme or newspaper or magazine because its content is interpreted as offensive, upsetting, etc., then profits decline. Those who commission and plan programmes or decide newspaper or magazine content usually play safe by excluding anything that might offend or upset.

Curran agrees with the GUMG and argues that, at best, journalists are now only a moderating influence. Their objectivity and impartiality has been undermined by the fact that journalists are not immune to the way the labour market has changed in the UK over the past ten years. Curran notes that unemployment has grown considerably

Focus on research

The Sutton Trust: The educational background of leading journalists

As their starting point, the researchers determined who were the 100 leading journalists working in news and current affairs. They did this by consulting senior figures in the media industry. The journalists on their list fell into four categories:

1 newspaper editors
2 newspaper columnists
3 broadcast presenters
4 broadcast editors.

These four groups together shape the news stories presented to the public through newspapers, radio and television – they are the gatekeepers for the news media. The researchers then drew up a list for 1986 in order to track changes over time. As far as possible, the 1986 list comprised the people in the same or equivalent roles to those in 2006, but with some changes to reflect the changing nature of news media (for example, Sky TV's senior journalists appear in the 2006 list but not the 1986 version). On both lists, the organization with the most journalists is the BBC, which,

despite falling shares of viewers and listeners, remains the dominant force in news.

Information on the journalists' backgrounds was gathered by a variety of means: contacting the journalists directly, using official sources such as *Who's Who* and profiles on websites and publications. The schools attended were classified as comprehensive, grammar or private at the time the journalist joined the school. The universities attended were classified into Oxbridge, the Sutton Trust top 13 (those consistently ranked high in the average of major league tables) and other universities.

The researchers also attempted a broader survey into the educational backgrounds of a much wider range of journalists, to see whether the pattern at the top of the profession was constant throughout the profession, and especially for those entering journalism now. However, the response of those approached was unhelpful. Information on the educational background of journalists was requested from the BBC under the Freedom of Information laws, but the BBC said that it would be too time consuming and costly to produce the information. Editors in other news organizations said that such information was not collected.

Finally, the researchers attempted a survey on recruitment procedures, asking a wide range of people, including editors, producers, course directors, students and trainees, how recruitment was carried out.

Source: Blundell, J. and Griffiths, J. (2008) *Sociology since 2000*, Lewes: Connect Publications

1 How did the Sutton Trust identify who were 'leading journalists'?

2 How did the Trust find out about the journalists' educational backgrounds?

3 Why did the Trust try to conduct a broader survey involving a wider range of journalists?

among journalists and there is an increasing tendency for media employers to take on staff on temporary contracts. Compliancy with the ethos of the owner is therefore more likely to secure a journalist a permanent position.

Agenda setting

The result of this journalistic consensus, says the GUMG, is that the media decide what issues should be discussed by society and which ones should be avoided. This is known as '**agenda setting**'. The GUMG argues that the media present us with a fairly narrow agenda for discussion. We talk about the size and shape of a female singer's bottom, but don't often discuss the massive inequalities that exist in society. We are more likely to be outraged by the latest events in Albert Square or Coronation Street than by the number of people living in poverty. In this way, ordinary members of the public never really question the workings of capitalist society. The GUMG consequently argues that we do not get presented with the really important information that would help ordinary members of society

make real choices about how society should be run. Agenda setting therefore results in 'cultural hegemony', with the basic principles of capitalism – private enterprise, profit, the 'free market' and the rights of property ownership – being presented by the media as 'normal' and 'natural'.

The fallacy of choice

We saw earlier that pluralists are keen to focus on public service broadcasters as proof of media integrity. However, a number of commentators have suggested that the BBC is increasingly abandoning its PSB aims because it is losing its audience to commercial and satellite television. As a result, the BBC has become more commercialized and populist in its programming in an attempt to hang on to its audience. Some pluralists argue that this is not a problem because PSB and ITV have had to offer more choices to their audiences in order to compete with Sky and Virgin, e.g. the setting up of the BBC digital channels and an internet news site are a rational response to this increased competition, which pluralists claim can only be good for audiences.

However, critics such as Barnett and Weymour (1999) have argued that the quality of television has been undermined by these commercial pressures. They argue that the main aim of all television companies, including the BBC, is to achieve the largest possible audience. This is because commercial television needs to attract the maximum advertising revenue whilst the BBC needs to justify the licence fee. Large audiences are achieved by targeting the lowest common denominator – content based primarily on entertainment – because this aspect of media is least likely to alienate or bore viewers.

Barnett and Weymour argue that such decisions have had a hegemonic cultural effect in the sense that education, information and news have been increasingly sidelined. They compared television schedules in 1978, 1988 and 1998 and argued that the evidence suggests that television in the UK has been significantly dumbed down. For example, the number of single dramas and documentaries has halved over the last 20 years, while soap operas and cheap reality shows have increased fivefold. We also now get more repeats and cheap American imports. Time allocated to news programming has fallen dramatically, and more time is devoted on serious news programmes to celebrity news and human-interest stories. Barnett and Weymour note that even the BBC is succumbing to these commercial pressures. Furthermore, they conclude that despite hundreds of television channels, we do not have more choice, just more of the same thing. Ironically, the dramatic expansion in the number of television channels may have led to less choice overall.

Curran notes the same pressures in the popular press as the rising costs of newsprint in the 1990s led to a major decrease in serious and political news stories and a corresponding increase in stories with lowest-common-denominator appeal, such as human-interest stories or those focused on celebrities. Curran argues that this led to a fall in journalistic standards because it resulted in intrusive cheque-book journalism and the rise of the paparazzi photographer. In addition, Curran argues that there is little choice for audiences in the printed media. There is no radical alternative to the mainstream newspapers, and the press has failed to reflect the growing diversity of public opinion on issues such as the Euro and the abolition of monarchy.

Conclusion

In conclusion, pluralist theories of media ownership and concentration seem increasingly out of touch with the modern global world. As a theory, it has failed to acknowledge that journalistic or editorial integrity no longer has a great deal of influence in the global marketplace. However, some Marxists are guilty of over-simplifying the relationship of owners both within the media world and with the political elite. Marxist conclusions about the ideological motives of media owners can also be questioned, although the GUMG is probably right to stress that the way the media is organized and

journalists are recruited has resulted in the cultural hegemony of capitalist values and ways of seeing the world. All the indicators suggest this will continue to be the norm and that it is likely to spread even further. The territories of 21st century media owners are no longer restricted by time or space. As Coleridge (1993) notes, as they move into acquiring chunks of the internet and online services, they will have subjugated more territory in a decade than Alexander the Great or Genghis Khan did in their lifetimes.

Check your understanding

1 What types of media are usually thought to make up the mass media?

2 Give examples to illustrate the concentration of ownership in the press and broadcasting media in Britain.

3 What is the difference between horizontal and vertical integration?

4 Why does Doyle argue that it is important to study the ownership and control of the media?

5 What evidence do supporters of the pluralist position use to argue the case that all groups have a voice in the contemporary mass media?

6 How do Marxists use the term 'ideology' to understand the content of the mass media?

7 What is Curran's conclusion about the influence of media owners?

8 Why is the term 'agenda setting' useful when discussing the work of the Glasgow Media Group?

9 How do Barnett and Weymour argue that the quality of television has been undermined?

10 Identify one criticism of Marxist views of ownership and control of the media, and one of pluralist views.

Activities

Research idea

Conduct a small-scale survey to discover to what extent people of different ages and/or ethnic and/or class backgrounds believe that the content of the media reflects the wide variety of views present in British society.

Web.tasks

Use the internet to investigate the synergy in the marketing of the Harry Potter stories.

Key terms

Agenda setting controlling which issues come to public attention.

Cross-media ownership occurs where different types of media – e.g. radio and TV stations – are owned by the same company.

Cybermedia the internet and worldwide web.

Diversification the practice of spreading risk by moving into new, unrelated areas of business.

Global conglomeration the trend for media corporations to have a presence in many countries and operate in a global market.

False class-consciousness coming to believe (wrongly) that capitalism is a fair system which benefits us all equally. Associated with Marxism.

Hegemony domination by consent (used to describe the way in which the ruling class project their view of the world so that it becomes the consensus view).

Horizontal integration also known as cross-media ownership. Refers to the fact that the bigger media companies often own a diverse range of media.

Investigative journalism journalism that aims to expose the misdeeds of the powerful.

Mass media agencies of communication that transmit information, education, news and entertainment to mass audiences.

Media concentration the result of smaller media companies merging, or being bought up by larger companies, to form a small number of very large companies.

Media conglomerate a company that owns various types of media.

Pluralism a theory that society is made up of many different groups, all having more or less equal power.

Public service broadcasting media outlets controlled by the state.

Synergy a mutually advantageous combination of distinct elements, as where two or more related businesses work together, e.g. to promote and sell a film, computer game and toys more effectively than they could individually.

Technological convergence the tendency for once diverse media forms to combine as a result of digital technology.

Vertical integration owning all the stages in the production, distribution and consumption of a product.

An eye on the exam Ownership and control of the mass media

Item A

Some Marxists argue that ownership of the mass media gives the owners direct control of media output. For example, Rupert Murdoch, the owner of News Corporation, is well known for intervening personally in the day-to-day running of his newspapers, as well as in setting their editorial policy himself. Similarly, owners have frequently been known to fire editors who disagree with their political views.

According to this Marxist view, the aim of owners in controlling output in this way is ideological – the function of the media is to turn out pro-capitalist ideology. In any case, the journalists and editors who work for these media barons are usually ideologically in tune with their employers and can be relied upon to adopt the political position the owner wishes them to take.

Using information from **Item A** and elsewhere, assess Marxist explanations of the relationship between ownership and control of the mass media.

(33 marks)

Grade booster Getting top marks in this question

In answering this question, you will need to examine a number of different perspectives on the ownership and control of the media. You should begin your answer with an account of the traditional Marxist view, using information from the Item and elsewhere to illustrate how capitalist owners may directly control media output, and the ideologically and politically conservative stance they usually take. You should go on to evaluate this view in different ways. Consider the hegemonic Marxist approach, focusing on how it sees the relationship between owners and journalists/editors. You should also examine the pluralist view of ownership and control, focusing on consumer demand as the determinant of media content in contrast to the Marxist view that it is capitalist ideology. You can also consider the various legal constraints on capitalist owners controlling output, and the existence of publicly owned media such as the BBC.

New media, globalization and popular culture

Getting you **thinking**

1   How do you think communication and access to information has changed over the last 25 years?

2   What are the advantages of these changes?

3   What are the disadvantages of these changes?

4   Do you think these changes have helped to reduce inequalities or make them worse? Explain your answer.

Defining the new media

The term **new media** generally refers to two trends that have occurred over the past 30 years:

1   *The evolution of existing media delivery systems* – If we examine the media of moving images, we can see that they have been around since the turn of the 20th century, but the way they have traditionally been delivered has been transformed, particularly in the last 20 years. For example, only a decade ago most people received television pictures through aerials and analogue-signal television sets, and there were five terrestrial television channels that could be accessed. Today, however, people are increasingly buying digital, high-definition, flat-screen televisions and subscribing to digitalized satellite and cable television that offer a choice of hundreds of television and radio channels. Moreover, these new television sets offer the consumer a greater set of services, including sending emails, paying bills, shopping and game-playing.

2   *The emergence of new delivery technologies* – Cheap personal computers and mobile-phone technology, and especially texting, are relatively novel forms of communication. However, the most innovative technology that has appeared in the last 20 years is probably the internet or worldwide web – a global multimedia library of information and services in cyberspace made possible by a global system of interconnected computers. Moreover, in the past five years, we have seen the emergence of even newer technology that has improved society's access to the internet, e.g. the introduction of high-capacity broadband wireless networks.

The characteristics of new media

The new media – whether evolved from traditional media delivery systems or new in their own right – share a number of important characteristics in which they differ enormously from the media delivery systems that dominated 20 years ago.

The digital revolution and convergence

The growth of digital technology in the 1990s resulted in changes in the way information is stored and transmitted. The development of digitalization led to the translation of all information, regardless of format (e.g. images, texts, sounds), into a universal computer language. The new media all share this common digital format.

Most importantly, digitalization resulted in the realization that different ways of presenting a variety of types of information – text, photographs, video, film, voices and music – could all be combined into a single delivery system or media. This is known as '**convergence**'. As Boyle (2005) notes, digitalization allows information to be delivered across a range of media platforms; what were once separate and unconnected technologies are 'now part of a converging media landscape that blurs the lines about how we use these technologies'. Theoretically, it is now possible to watch television through a personal computer or on a mobile phone as well as on MP3 players, such as the iPod, to send emails through the television and to download music from the internet.

However, it is important to understand that technological convergence has also produced economic and social convergence. Media and telecommunication industries that had previously produced separate and distinct systems of communication, such as the telephone, television programmes or computers, began to make alliances with each other because digitalization reduced the boundaries between media sectors. This cross-fertilization of ideas and resources underpinned by digitalization produced new forms of multimedia or converged media delivery systems. The mobile phone is an excellent example of this. Jenkins (2008) documents these changes with regard to mobile-phone technology when he observed:

<< *Call me old fashioned. The other week I wanted to buy a cellphone – you know, to make phone calls. I didn't want a video camera, a still camera, an MP3 player, or a game system. I also wasn't interested in something that could show me movie previews, would have customizable ring tones, or would allow me to read novels. I didn't want the electronic equivalent of a Swiss army knife. When the phone rings, I don't want to have to figure out which button to push. I just wanted a phone. The sales clerks sneered at me; they laughed at me behind my back. I was told by company after mobile company that they didn't make single function phones anymore. Nobody wants them. This was a powerful demonstration of how central mobiles* have become to the process of media convergence.>> (pp.4–5)

Cornford and Robins (1999) argued that the digital convergence future would see the emergence of the 'holy grail' of the information age:

<< *... the ubiquitous information appliance that is able to surf the net and interrogate multimedia databases, play music and speech, show films and video, run software, support a telephone conversation and send email.* >> (p.109)

However, Jenkins notes that this is unlikely to happen because convergence refers to a process rather than an endpoint. He argues that there will never be a black box that does everything because our needs are dependent upon different social contexts, e.g. the needs of a teenager may be different from those of an adult. This can be illustrated by the example of mobile-phone technology, in which demands for a converged product are being driven by the needs of young people rather than middle-aged adults.

Jenkins notes that media convergence affects the way we consume media. He observes:

<< *A teenager doing homework may juggle four or five windows, scan the web, listen to and download MP3 files, chat with friends, word-process a paper and respond to email, shifting rapidly among tasks.* >> (p.16)

Jenkins therefore argues that convergence involves both a change in the way media are produced and a change in the way media are consumed. He argues that convergence is, therefore, both a top-down corporate-driven process and a bottom-up consumer-driven process.

Compression

Digital technologies enable the **compression** of signals. This has led to a proliferation of radio and television channels because it means that many signals can be sent through the same cable, telephone line, etc. This has resulted in the development of new markets organized around the concept of 'narrowcasting' – the transmission of particular types of media content to niche or even individualized consumers. For example, digital television providers have attempted to target young audiences by setting up channels aimed at their interests. BBC3 is a good example of this. As Boyle (2007) notes, the focus of many media companies is now on creating a personalized media experience.

Interactivity

The new media are interactive media that are responsive in 'real time' to user input through clicking on links or selecting menu items with a mouse. The internet epitomizes such interactive media because it lets users select the stories that they want to watch, in the order that they want to watch them. They can also mix and match the information they want – for instance, people may access news from several different sources.

Jenkins argues that **interactivity** has been brought about by convergence. He notes that media audiences today will go almost anywhere in search of the kinds of entertainment experiences they want. He suggests that interactivity and convergence have produced a **'participatory culture'**. In other words, media producers and consumers no longer occupy separate roles – they are now participants who interact with each other according to a new set of rules which are constantly evolving. This has produced more control at the user end compared with the past. For example, Jenkins notes that the print fanzine magazines of the 1980s have now migrated to the online digital world of bloggers because these websites have greater accessibility and the speed of feedback is almost instant.

Jenkins also suggests that interactivity has produced a **'collective intelligence'** because consuming new media tends to be a collective process. He notes 'none of us can know everything; each of us knows something; and we can put the pieces together if we pool our resources and combine our skills'. He claims that such collective intelligence can be seen as an alternative source of media power to that of media owners.

The internet provides the main means through which people can interact with each other in a participatory culture and build collective intelligence. They can engage in online discussions or play online live games with each other through mediums such as X-Box Live. They may simply be interested in networking with others through sites such as My Space, Bebo and Facebook. Some of this interactivity will be creative – people may live alternative simulated lives on internet sites, such as Second Life, or they may wish to convey their thoughts, feelings and opinions through the setting up of their own websites or the online diaries known as blogs. They may produce their own films and music and post it on sites such as YouTube and MySpace. User-generated content and information sites, such as Wikipedia and IMDB, are a popular source of knowledge.

Jenkins notes that fans of television programmes have become extremely influential because of the internet – programme makers often take their views into consideration during the production. In this sense, fans have moved from the invisible margins of popular culture and into the centre of current thinking about media production and consumption. Note the recent successful online campaign aimed at persuading Cadbury to bring back their Wispa chocolate bar!

Boyle (2005) sees similar trends in television media because we have now evolved from a system of supply-led television, available free to the whole population, to a demand-led television, organized around the idea that the viewers or subscribers should decide what they want to watch and when. We are no longer restrained by television schedules. The development of Sky+ and Freeview are good examples of how consumers of new media are encouraged to take an active role in the construction of their own television schedules. We can now pause live television. We can interact with particular shows, such as *Strictly Come Dancing* or *Big Brother,* by 'pressing the red button'. If we miss the programme, we can catch up by using our personal computer to access those programmes using BBC iPlayer or 4oD.

Who is using the new media?

A generational divide?

Boyle (2007) notes that new media are often associated with young people. Some sociologists have consequently suggested that there now exists a generational divide in terms of how people use new media. Boyle points out that there is no doubt that the media experience of young people growing up in the UK in 2008 is markedly different from previous generations in terms of access to and familiarity with a wider range of media.

However, Boyle notes that there has always been a generational divide in media use since the emergence of youth cultures in the 1950s. For example, the authorities were extremely unhappy with pop music when it first appeared. Moreover, Boyle argues that 'communication technology has always been used by young people as they assert their particular difference and develop their individual and collective identities through music, sport, media and technology'.

He observes that adult anxieties about the media remain much the same, but the media environment in which these anxieties are expressed has become bigger because there is a larger selection of gadgets, websites and social-networking services available to young people today. Some cultural commentators worry about the influence of easily accessed pornography sites on the internet, or the new forms of bullying that are appearing in mobile-phone text messaging or on social-network sites in cyberspace.

Boyle notes that the key difference in the media that young people use is that it is also a 'now' media – it is significantly different from previous media because of its immediacy and accessibility. Consequently, the ways in which young people access and seek out entertainment and news differ from previous generations. They are more likely to want it all now – and tailored to their specific needs and identities. Boyle notes that the internet is the arena in which this is most likely to happen for young people. It is the central part of the media experience of young people, compared with that of previous generations – young people use the internet for entertainment and social networking through various user-generated sites and other communities on the web. For example, according to Ofcom, 70 per cent of 16 to 24 year olds use sites such as MySpace and Bebo. All these trends mean that children and teenagers today are probably more media-savvy than previous generations.

However, Boyle points out that we must be careful not to exaggerate these generational differences. An Ofcom survey in 2006 indicates that patterns of media consumption are certainly changing. We watched more television than in 2005, made more mobile-phone calls, sent more text messages and spent more time online. Moreover, the 16- to 24-year-old age group spent more time online compared with the 25+ age group; it sent more text messages, and it watched less television. However, 40 per cent of adults use networking sites such as Facebook, whilst the average age of the online gamer is 33 years.

Focus on research

Helen Haste (2005)
Joined-up texting

Helen Haste conducted a survey to investigate the use of mobile phones by young people. She took a random sample of 200 schools and colleges and used self-completion questionnaires to collect data.

Haste found that many young people owned mobile phones for reasons of personal safety and security. Possession of a mobile phone ensured that parents could contact them quickly. Young women and younger children were most concerned with parental concern and personal safety. Some 73 per cent of respondents had used phones in emergencies and nearly a quarter had dialled 999.

Young people used their phones to organize their social lives. A whole range of different rules emerged over the way phones were used in certain situations. Text messaging was most commonly used in seeking information. More complex social negotiations, such as

maintaining or ending relationships, were achieved through a phone conversation. Females were more likely to use a landline for arranging to meet friends. Females were also more likely to use letters to say thank you and to use email to keep in touch with their parents. Males were happy to use a mobile phone conversation to flirt, whereas only 10 per cent of girls were comfortable with this. Females preferred to flirt using text messaging. Serious disagreements were conducted using landline telephones.

Haste, H. (2005) 'Joined-up texting: mobile phones and young people', *Young Consumers*, Quarter 2, 6(3), pp.56–67

1 Identify three ways in which young people used mobile phones.

2 Give two examples of gender differences in the use of mobile phones.

A class divide?

The poor are excluded from the superinformation highway because they lack the material resources to plug into this new media revolution, i.e. they are a digital underclass who cannot afford to keep up with the middle-class technological elite. Some 80 per cent of the richest bracket of households in the UK have internet access, against only 11 per cent of the poorest.

A MORI survey carried out in 2005 also confirms the existence of a digital divide based on gender, employment, class and educational attainment. Men, people aged 16 to 54 who work, come from social classes ABC1, and have a formal educational qualification are more likely to be internet users, the survey found, than women, people aged 55+, those not in work, from social classes C2DE, and people who do not have a formal educational qualification. Boyle notes that about 40 per cent of homes did not have digital TV in 2005. The poor are excluded because they cannot afford digital technology, personal computers, subscriptions to ISPs and wireless broadband. Consequently, a digital divide has opened up between those who have access to this new technology and those who are financially and culturally cut adrift.

A gender divide?

A survey by Ofcom, in 2006, found that girls aged 12 to 15 are more likely than boys to have a mobile phone, use the internet, listen to the radio and read newspapers or magazines. Only when it comes to playing computer and console games do boys overtake girls. Almost all children between 12 and 15 with the internet at home said they

were 'confident' surfing the web and did so on average for eight hours a week. However, girls are more likely than boys to use the web as a communication tool.

Li and Kirkup (2007) found significant gender differences between UK men and women. Men were more likely than women to use email or chat rooms. Men played more computer games than women. Men were more self-confident about their computer skills than women and were more likely to express the opinion that using computers was a male activity and skill.

A global divide?

In 2004, fewer than three out of every 100 Africans used the internet, compared with an average of one out of every two inhabitants of the G8 countries (Canada, France, Germany, Italy, Japan, Russia, the UK and the US). The G8 countries – home to just 15 per cent of the world's population – have almost 50 per cent of the world's total internet users.

On the whole, the USA and Western Europe generate most of the content of the worldwide web. This dominance is reinforced by the fact that an estimated 85 per cent of the web is written in English despite less than 10 per cent of the world's population speaking that language. Moreover, Seaton (2003) points out that the economic and social inequalities of the off-line world mirror the online world. The 6 per cent of the world who regularly use the net are mainly affluent Westerners; they consume websites mainly produced in the Western world and mainly communicate in the language most of the world does not understand.

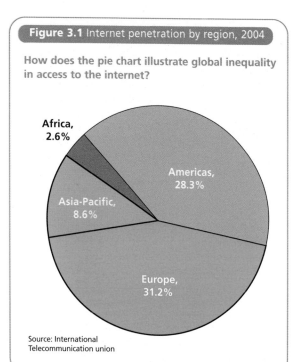

How does the pie chart illustrate global inequality in access to the internet?

Africa, 2.6%
Americas, 28.3%
Asia-Pacific, 8.6%
Europe, 31.2%

Source: International Telecommunication union

Debates about new media

According to Curran and Seaton (2003), two perspectives dominate the debate about the new media in the UK:

1 The '**neophiliacs**' are optimistic about the spread and influence of new media technologies, which they see as offering consumers more choice and the opportunity to participate more interactively and effectively in the democratic process.
2 The '**cultural pessimists**' suggest that new media are not really that new, that interactivity is an illusion because ownership of new media is still overwhelmingly concentrated in the hands of powerful corporations, and that new media content has generally led to a decline in the quality of popular culture.

The neophiliac perspective

Neophiliacs (who are essentially postmodernists – see pp. 266–9) argue that new media is beneficial to society for several reasons, outlined below.

Increased consumer choice

Neophiliacs argue that the convergence, compression and interactivity that characterize media technology and delivery today have increased consumer choice. There are now literally hundreds of entertainment and news channels on television which allow people to see the same events from different angles. It is suggested that the competition between media institutions will result in more quality media output. Moreover, people can choose from a number of media delivery systems, e.g. people may choose to buy music in CD form or to download it from iTunes;

they may listen to it by playing a CD, or through a television, personal computer, an MP3 player or a mobile phone.

An e-commerce revolution

The internet has also led to a revolution in e-commerce in recent years. E-tailers such as Amazon and Play.com have been great economic successes and actually undermined high-street sales of books and music. Most major commercial companies now have their own websites. It is claimed that this e-commerce trend has resulted in more choice to consumers because it increases competition, leads to lower prices and puts consumers in control as they can compare prices from a huge range of products and services.

Revitalizing democracy

It is argued that new media technologies offer opportunities for people to acquire the education and information required to play an active role in democratic societies, and to make politicians more accountable to the people. The internet is a means of communicating information that the giant corporations who own and control the world's traditional media are unlikely to want to report. The internet, in particular, has been highlighted in this respect because it is a public sphere that anybody can access, usually at no or little cost. It provides people with the opportunity to access a wide range of information and alternative interpretations and viewpoints, which are unlikely to be found in the conventional mainstream media that traditionally have set the agenda for debate in wider society. Some commentators have referred to this as 'citizen journalism'.

Seaton notes that many believe that the internet is advancing progressive politics:

>> *Internet technology converts the desk into a printing press, broadcasting station and place of assembly. This enables 'many-to-many communication', which allegedly is changing the way we do politics. In this view, the net is rejuvenating civil society, generating political activism and launching exciting experiments of popular participation in government. Established centres of power and monopolies of communication are being bypassed ... and a process of progressive mobilization is under way that will empower the people.>> (p.264)*

Some media sociologists, therefore, have suggested that the internet can revitalize democracy because it gives a voice to those who would otherwise go unheard. It allows like-minded people to join together and take action which may lead to social change.

Some neophiliacs who are part of the antiglobal-capitalism movement have used the internet to challenge power elites. As Itzoe (1995) argues, the internet is 'a loose and anarchic confederation of millions of users around the world who communicate in perhaps the freest forum of speech in history'. The internet has, therefore, been used in a variety of political ways by these activists:

● to monitor the illegal or immoral activities of big businesses

- to harness mass support for causes such as Make Poverty History
- to coordinate protests and activism ranging from hunt saboteurs and antivivisection to disrupting G8 meetings about climate change and developing countries' debt burden.

Any political point of view, no matter how extreme, can therefore be found on the internet.

The cultural pessimist perspective

Cultural pessimists believe that this revolution in new media technology has been exaggerated by neophiliacs. There are a number of strands to their argument.

'Not-so-new' media

Cornford and Robins (1999) argue that the so-called new media are not that 'new'. 'Old' technology, such as television and telephone landlines, are integral to the use of new media such as computer game consoles (e.g. the Xbox) and broadband and wireless connections to the internet. They suggest, further, that interactivity is not something new because people have written to newspapers and phoned in to radio and television for many years. The only thing that is new about new media is its speed – information, news and entertainment can be accessed in 'real time'. The most convincing example of this is still the plane hitting the second World Trade Center tower. Cornford and Robins suggest that what the new technologies permit is the refinement, extension and embellishment of traditional media. They suggest we might consider the relationship of new media to old as:

>> *being like that between an old Hollywood movie and its re-make: the characters are the same, the story is the same, but the special effects are more spectacular, and the marketing budget is much larger.* >> (p.124)

Domination by media conglomerates

Cultural pessimists criticize the idea that new media are increasing the potential for ordinary people to participate more fully in the democratic process and cultural life. They point to the role of the transnational media conglomerates in the development and control of the new media.

Jenkins (2008) notes that new media developed as a result of investment by the big media corporations. In particular, he argues that the cross-media ownership that began in the 1980s was the first phase of media concentration and technological convergence. Owning different types of media made it more desirable for companies to develop content across a variety of media platforms and delivery system. As Jenkins notes, 'digitalization set the conditions for convergence; corporate conglomerates created its imperative'.

The internet, in particular, is dominated by a small number of media corporations – for example, Microsoft has developed most of the software required for accessing the net as well as being an internet Service Provider (ISP). The USA's main ISP is AOL, which is owned by Time Warner. These ISPs enable people to log on in the first place, direct

users to particular commercial services and play a key role in online advertising. Most of the internet's commercially viable content is, therefore, controlled by, or commissioned by the big entertainment, press, telecommunications, advertising and software companies. These media superpowers had many advantages over individuals in setting up websites – they had back catalogues, funds for investment, technical expertise, close links with the advertising industry, brand visibility and cross-ownership that meant that it was relatively easy for them to cross-promote products – for example, Time Warner produces computer games, websites, films, television, popular music, toys, amusement parks, books, newspapers, magazines and comics. Over three-quarters of the 31 most-visited news and entertainment websites are affiliated with the largest media corporations, according to Curran (2003).

Commercialization

As a result, the internet is now extremely commercialized. Moreover, there have been recent signs that e-commerce has now taken off. Millions of people use the internet to manage their bank accounts, pay bills and buy services, such as insurance and consumer goods. In short, the last five years have seen a major shift in internet activities from educational use to commercial use.

Cornford and Robins agree that these new technologies may produce more choice for the consumer, but there are also some dubious side effects. For example, many companies that sell products and services on the internet engage in consumer surveillance. New technologies, e.g. in the form of cookies, can monitor and process the data generated by interactive media usage so they can segment and target potential future audiences, and thus enhance profits. Some Marxist sociologists have grown alarmed at this commercialization of the internet and other new media, such as mobile phones and digital television, claiming that it encourages materialism, consumerism and false needs, and thereby furthers capitalist domination and control.

Reinforcing elite power

Cornford and Robins are sceptical of the view that new media will lead to a more democratic communications structure that will bring about a new political and social order. They note that through a series of assertive tactics – alliances, mergers, takeovers, licensing deals, patents and copyright restrictions – media corporations seek to monopolize key strategic links within the new media. Jenkins, too, notes that not all the participants in the new media are created equal. Corporations – and even individuals within corporate media – still exert greater power than any individual consumer or even aggregates of consumers. Political elite power-holders too, such as government departments and agencies, political parties, and the security services, have not been slow to see the power of new media delivery systems and have constructed sophisticated and elaborate websites to make sure their view of the world dominates the internet. Media technologies are, therefore, mainly strengthening the power of the existing elites rather than promoting alternative ideas, free speech or democracy. The digital class divide also contributes to this inequality because it is probably those who are unable to access the web who have the most genuine political grievances.

However, Seaton (2003) reports that online political involvement probably mirrors the level of ordinary people's political involvement in the real world. Studies conducted by Hill and Hughes (1997) found that only 6 per cent of webpages were devoted to political issues. They also challenged the view that cyberspace is more likely to contain web content that supports alternative minority political issues or views. Seventy-eight per cent of political opinions expressed on the American websites were mainstream. Seaton remarks 'when the net was a marginal experimental sphere in which counter-cultural movements were especially active, the net had a different significance, but those halcyon days are over' (pp.265–6). Even when the net was used to plan and mobilize the antiglobalization protests, it was only one of a number of strategies used, which included leaflets, posters, graffiti, mainstream news reports and cheap air travel. As the media corporations successfully colonized most of the net with their news, entertainment, business and sport sites, minority political views and civic discourse were shifted to the margins.

Decline in quality of popular culture

Cultural pessimists argue that increased choice of media delivery systems, and particularly the digitalization of television, has led to a decline in the quality of popular culture. Harvey (2008), for example, suggests that digital television may have dramatically increased the number of channels for viewers to choose from, but this has led to a dumbing-down of popular culture as television companies fill these channels with cheap imported material, films, repeats, sport, reality-television shows and gambling. Harvey argues that, increasingly, television culture transmits a 'candy floss culture' that speaks to everyone in general and no one in particular. ITV, especially, underwent a process of 'tabloidization' in the late 1990s in an attempt to compete with Sky. This resulted in a decline in its current affairs and news coverage and an increase in softer crime, human interest and consumer features.

Are endless repeats, on numerous satellite channels, 'dumbing down' popular culture?

A survey conducted by the British Broadcasting Standards Commission (BBSC) in 2003 indicated that television viewers agreed that more channels had led to a decline in the standard of television programmes (Broadcasting Standards Council 2003). Moreover, having to compete with both the commercial television channels, and satellite and cable television, puts pressure on the BBC to fill its schedules with similar content. Consequently, choice becomes more of the same.

Lack of regulation

It is argued by sociologists, politicians and cultural commentators that new media, particularly the internet, is in need of state regulation. All points of view are represented on the net but it is argued that easy access to pornography, and homophobic, racist and terrorism-inciting sites is taking free speech too far. An Ofcom survey in 2006 found that one in six children questioned reported coming across 'worrying' material on the internet, while more than seven out of ten parents of children aged 12 to 15 worried about their offspring seeing inappropriate material.

Some commentators, however, believe that the irresponsible use of the internet is a price worth paying for the free expression and exchange of information that it provides. In any case, the control of information on the web is largely outside the government's control because many ISPs operate outside UK territory. So far, the British government has confined its efforts to monitoring and controlling paedophilia although, in 2008, it announced plans to discuss with ISPs policies that would close down sites that promote race-hate and terrorism.

Conclusions about new media

While neophiliacs are very upbeat about the future role of new media technologies, cultural pessimists remind us that we need to be cautious about how the new media may be employed. Both perspectives probably exaggerate how far the media is being transformed. The last two decades have seen both continuity and, at the extreme, evolutionary rather than revolutionary change. Television is still the most popular medium and the print media, despite fears that it was going to be replaced by the internet, still sells extremely well. A small number of media companies are still very much in control of both traditional and new media.

Postmodernism and the media

It is argued by postmodernist sociologists that UK society has undergone fundamental change in the last decade, so that we are now living in what they call a 'postmodern age'. They argue that this change is caused by a number of economic and social factors:

● Postmodernists have argued that industrialization and the manufacture of goods is in decline in postmodern societies. In the postmodern age, service industries concerned with the processing and transmission of information, and knowledge and servicing consumption, e.g. the mass media, government, finance and retail, have become more important than the factory production of manufactured goods.

- In particular, postmodernist sociologists have argued that the rapid expansion in media technologies in the last decade has led to postmodern societies becoming 'media saturated'.
- As a result, the media – and the popular culture that they generate – now shape our identities and lifestyles much more than traditional influences such as family, community, social class, gender, nation or ethnicity.
- The media has also changed and shaped our consumption patterns by making us more aware of the diversity of choices that exist in the postmodern world. This is because the media provides us with most of our experience of social reality.
- The globalization of media means that we now have more globalized cultural influences available to us in terms of lifestyle choices and consumption.
- Postmodernists argue that the media generally define our lifestyles and identity for us – media such as lifestyle magazines, television documentaries and advertising now shape all aspects of our lives, such as how we should dress and look, how we should organize our homes and gardens, what we should think, how we should be feeling, and so on. If we don't like ourselves, all sorts of media can advise us on how we can 'make over' our bodies or lives.
- The media now inform us that the consumption of images, logos and brands for their own sake (i.e. conspicuous consumption) should be a central aspect of our identities. In other words, fashion, style and image are often more important than substance. We buy the designer *labels* rather than the clothes and goods themselves, with the result that people are no longer judged on the basis of ability, skill or personality but on how 'cool' they look or behave.
- Many people now feel that they no longer belong to real communities – the proto-communities of internet chat-rooms, blogging and online fantasy gaming, such as Second Life, and the imagined communities of television soap operas are increasingly replacing the role of neighbours and extended kin in our lives. We may know the characters from soap operas better than we do the people living in our street.
- In the postmodern world, it is suggested that we no longer look to grand theories or meta-narratives such as science or Marxism to explain the world and its problems. An increasingly media-literate society is now aware that knowledge is underpinned by diversity, plurality and difference and, consequently, all knowledge is relative. All points of view have some relevance.

The critique of postmodernism

Postmodernists have been criticized for exaggerating the degree of social change. Evidence from attitude surveys indicates that many people see social class, ethnicity, family, nation and religion as still having a profound influence over their lives and identities. Media influence is

Millions of people across the world engage in the virtual world of Second Life. But are virtual communities replacing real ones?

undoubtedly important, but it is not the determining factor in most people's lifestyle choices.

There is also a rather naive element to postmodernist analyses, in that they tend to ignore the fact that a substantial number of people are unable to make consumption choices because of inequalities brought about by traditional influences such as unemployment, poverty, racial discrimination and patriarchy. Traditional forms of inequality remain a crucial influence, as access to the internet, digital television and so on is denied to many people in the UK.

The globalization of media

In relation to the mass media, globalization takes a number of forms:

- *Ownership of mass media* – As we have already seen when looking at the ownership and control debate, media companies are no longer restricted by national boundaries. Most Western countries have relaxed ownership controls. As a result, media moguls, such as Rupert Murdoch, and media conglomerates, such as Time Warner, own hundreds of media companies spread throughout the world.
- *Satellite television* – This new medium has opened up the world to the television viewer. You can sit in a hotel anywhere in the world and watch programmes with which you are familiar, on channels such as Sky, Fox, CNN or Al-Jazeera.
- *The internet* – Access to the worldwide web via the internet, global webservers (such as AOL or Google) and new technology (such as wireless broadband) mean that we can access information and entertainment in most parts of the world. However, China (with the help of a Western new-media corporation, Google) forbids the access of its citizens to some parts of the worldwide web, especially sites that it believes support the pro-democracy movement

in China, because the Chinese authorities believe access to such information is politically dangerous.

● *Advertising* – Advertising occurs on a global scale, and particular brands have become global as a result. For example, Coca-Cola, Levis and McDonalds are global household names. Coca-Cola is now the most widely known (and used) consumer product in the world. Its advertising message is simple, its product immediately recognizable wherever you are in the world and its taste the same in every part of the world.

● *Entertainment* – Entertainment has become globalized via satellite television, global marketing and advertising, and the internet. The world's population engages with much the same popular culture – i.e. the same films (mainly Hollywood produced), the same television programmes (e.g. *Friends* was a global phenomenon), and the same music (e.g. Coldplay, Madonna, Britney Spears, etc., are all global icons). Sport has been globalized through global media events such as the Olympic Games, the World Cup and the African Nations Cup.

What are the possible consequences of globalization?

Supporters of globalization, such as postmodernists, suggest that it brings about more choice with regard to identities and lifestyles. They see the global media as a positive influence in that they can inject the developing world with modern ideas and therefore kickstart economic and cultural ideas and behaviour that will help develop those societies. Globalization is also seen as beneficial because it is primarily responsible for diffusing different cultural styles around the world and creating new global hybrid styles in fashion, music, consumption and lifestyle. It is argued that, in the postmodern global world, this cultural diversity and pluralism will become the global norm.

In contrast, Marxists argue that it restricts choice because transnational media companies and their owners, such as Rupert Murdoch, have too much power. Marxists are particularly concerned that local media and cultures may be replaced by a global culture. As Rosenau (1990) observed:

《Coca-Cola, Disney and McDonalds, from Moscow to New York, from Tiananmen Square to Papua, it is the same culture that is present everywhere.》 (p.306).

Cultural pessimists refer to this trend as the 'Disneyfication' of culture because it is claimed that this global culture is overwhelmingly an American entertainment culture, focused on sitcoms, reality television, soap operas, celebrity gossip and consumerism. Kellner (1999) suggests that this global media culture is about sameness and that it erases individuality, specificity and difference.

It is also suggested that global media and culture are 'dumbing down' real and authentic local cultures, and perhaps even killing off the nation state. A good example of this argument is Schiller's (1976) observation of Brazilian television, which, he claims, is a spiced-up copy of Western values, norms and lifestyles. Putnam (1995) argues that one of the side effects of a global culture organized around television and the internet is civic disengagement – people are no longer willing to get involved in their communities. They would rather stay at home and watch television.

However, postmodernists disagree with this Marxist argument. They argue that globalization is good for both the developed and developing worlds because it offers their citizens more choices and opportunities. Postmodernists argue that British cultural identity is now influenced in a positive way by a range of cultures from around the world – for example, fashion and music – brought to us by global media. Postmodernists also argue that local cultures are not swallowed up by global media culture; rather, local culture adapts to global culture. In India, for example, Bollywood films are produced by a local film industry that is organized around both Hollywood and Indian entertainment values. Cohen and Kennedy (2000) suggest that cultural pessimists underestimate the strength of local cultures – they note that people do not generally abandon their cultural traditions, family duties, religious beliefs and national identities because they listen to Madonna or watch a Disney film. Rather, they appropriate elements of global culture, and mix and match with elements of local culture, in much the same way as the citizens of the USA and UK.

Check your understanding

1 How does convergence affect the way we use the media?

2 What, according to Boyle, is the key difference in young people's use of the new media now compared to previous generations?

3 Summarize the differences between men's and women's use of new media.

4 In what ways can it be claimed that there is a 'global divide' in use of the new media?

5 According to 'neophiliacs', what are the main benefits of the new media?

6 What are the main points raised by the 'cultural pessimist' critics of the new media?

7 What role does the media play in postmodern societies?

8 How have postmodern approaches to the media been criticized?

9 Give three examples of ways in which globalization has affected the mass media.

10 List points for and against the argument that globalization is having positive effects on the media and culture.

Key terms

Collective intelligence the way in which users of new media combine skills, resources and knowledge.

Compression the way in which digital technologies can send many signals through the same cable.

Convergence the combination of different ways of presenting a variety of types of information (e.g. text, photographs, video, film, voices and music) into a single delivery system.

Cultural pessimists commentators who are pessimistic about the spread and influence of new media technologies.

Interactivity digital technologies that are responsive in 'real time' to user input.

Neophiliacs commentators who are optimistic about the spread and influence of new media technologies.

New media generally refers to the evolution of existing media delivery systems and the development of new digital communication technologies.

Participatory culture media producers and consumers no longer occupy separate roles; they interact with each other according to a new set of rules.

Activities

Research idea

Design a questionnaire and conduct a survey within your school or college to assess the differences in access to and consumption of the new media in relation to class, gender, ethnicity and age. Consider both household ownership and personal consumption of the various forms of the new media.

Web.task

What skills are required by users of new media? Watch this short film about New Media Literacies (or skills) at **http://uk.youtube.com/watch?v=pEHcGAsnBZE**

An eye on the exam New media, globalization & popular culture

Item A

The trend towards globalization is nowhere more evident than in the sphere of the mass media. Large transnational corporations (TNCs), often based in the United States, produce media output that is disseminated throughout the world. For example, Hollywood blockbusters, MTV and Disney cartoons appear on cinema and television screens on every continent. Some sociologists and campaigners against globalization argue that this is leading to McDonaldization – the Americanization of popular culture and the undermining of local cultures.

Much of the trend towards globalization of the media is due to the development of new technology. For example, the internet, email and mobile phones make distances vanish and turn the world into a single global village.

Using information from **Item A** and elsewhere, assess the impact of the mass media and globalization on popular culture.

(33 marks)

Grade booster   Getting top marks in this question

You could begin your answer with a brief definition of globalization. You should then describe the role of the mass media in the process of globalization. You need to examine different views as to the impact of the global media upon popular culture. You should consider whether the media are undermining and 'Americanizing' local cultures – e.g. you can look at evidence on how much media output in the UK or elsewhere is from US media TNCs. You should also consider the resistance to McDonaldization, e.g. in developing countries, or how far 'local' media output is basically the same as the American material. You can also look at how new technology may be allowing ordinary people and local groups to disseminate their own popular cultures. Remember to make use of relevant material from the Item in your answer.

The selection and presentation of news, and moral panics

Getting you thinking

Which of the following news providers do you trust most and which do you trust least? Explain your answer: Sky, BBC, ITV, broadsheet newspapers, tabloid newspapers.

News is presented in many different forms in the 21st century. However, despite the growth of new media, particularly the internet and 24-hour rolling news channels on satellite television channels, the majority of the population still rely on traditional methods of news coverage. In 2005, 72 per cent of people indicated that television was their primary source of news coverage. In contrast, only 10 per cent relied upon newspapers to obtain their news, and a further 9 per cent relied upon radio.

An Ofcom survey conducted in 2005 indicated that 94 per cent of the UK population believed that it is important for television news to be impartial. Sixty-seven per cent regarded television news as the most trusted news medium and saw it as a 'window on the world' offering the audience fair and unbiased 'evidence' of events as they happened. In contrast, despite sales of about 10 million daily, only 7 per cent saw newspapers in the same light. Most of those surveyed recognized that their newspapers acted as cheerleaders for particular political ideologies and that many newspapers' editorial line identified with a particular political party – the *Daily Mirror* has traditionally

supported Labour, whilst the *Sun, Mail, Express, Times* and *Telegraph* have traditionally supported the Conservatives.

In 2007, most of the news services in the UK were concentrated in the hands of a very small number of organizations. The primary news providers to terrestrial television channels are:

- the BBC – which attracts two-thirds of the UK audience for news
- Independent Television News (ITN) – which provides news to the ITV network as well as Channel 4
- BSkyB – which not only produces its own Sky News and Five News but is also the main conduit (along with FreeView and Virgin) by which people gain access to 24-hour rolling satellite news programmes such as BBC News, CNN, Fox News and Al Jazeera.

The print news media is dominated by those newspapers owned by News Corp (see p. 135), through News International, which, in 2007, had over 50 per cent of the market of daily and Sunday newspaper sales.

In the past ten years, the UK has seen an increase in new ways in which people can access the news, such as satellite television, the internet, blogs and text news to

Table 3.1 UK news provision by television channel		
Channel	News provider	Share of UK news audience
BBC	BBC	64%
ITV1	ITN	22%
Sky News	BSkyB	5%
Channel 4	ITN	5%
Five	BSkyB	3%

Source: Broadcasters' Audience Research Board, May 2006 – April 2007

mobile phones. The internet has been hailed as leading a cultural revolution in terms of giving the population access to alternative sources of news. However, as of 2009, the established television news providers (BBC, ITV, Sky News) and newspaper publishers (e.g. News International, Guardian Media Group) dominated internet 'hits' on their news websites. There is little sign that the alternative news websites or blogs are attracting a significant audience. Couldry *et al.* (2007b) found that 85 per cent of people regularly watched television for news – at least three times a week – as opposed to only 23 per cent of people who used the internet in that way.

However, Couldry *et al.* (2007a) note that newspaper sales, in particular, have fallen dramatically in the last 30 years, whilst young people's viewing of terrestrial channels in general, and their news bulletins in particular, is also in decline. Despite the fact that accessing news websites is still a minority activity, there are signs that online use, especially by the young, may increasingly grow in importance; this may be one of the main reasons why conventional news sources, such as the BBC and newspapers like the *Sun* and the *Guardian,* are spending millions of pounds developing sophisticated news websites.

Television news: a window on the world?

Chandler (1994) suggests that the way television news is presented results in it being regarded as the most reliable source of news by its audience. He notes that:

● Newsreaders are presented as 'neutral' observers in the way they read the scripted news, dress with sober formality and make eye contact with the viewer.
● The body language of newscasters is reduced by seating them behind a desk (which in itself denotes authority) or by having them stand clipboard in hand.
● The content of the news may be far from reassuring, but the newsreader's manner is always friendly, reliable and reassuring. As Peace (1998) argues, this factor creates the idea that the newsreader is the viewer's trustworthy and reliable 'friend'.
● The orderly high-tech studio symbolizes the scientific lengths to which the broadcaster has gone to find the 'truth' and reinforces the image of formal and objective authority.

Overall, then, the presentation of the news by television appears to convey objective truth. Buckingham (1996) carried out research based on interviews and discussions with 12 to 15 year olds about television news, and concluded that the status and credibility of the news was hardly ever challenged by them. Rather, the news was perceived to be an honest and trustworthy reflection of the real world. Moreover, they were happy to accept implicitly the validity of news items that were beyond their own experience. Survey evidence suggests that many mature adults treat their daily diet of television news in precisely the same way. However, sociological critics of the way news is presented suggest that television news actually presents its audience with an *illusion* of objectivity.

The construction of reality in the news

McQuail (1992) argues that 'news' is not objective or impartial. Events happen, but this does not guarantee that they become news – not all events can be reported because of the sheer number of them. The reality is that news is actually a socially manufactured product because it is the end result of a selective process – **gatekeepers** such as editors and journalists, and sometimes proprietors, make choices and judgements about what events are important enough to cover and how to cover them. As McQuail notes, 'news' is not simply a collection of facts that happen, but a special form of knowledge made up of information, myth, fable and morality. In this sense, it is 'loaded' information and often reflects the perspective or interpretation of particular interest groups, particularly powerful groups, rather than being an objective report of events as they occur.

Critics point out that the process of news selection is biased because it is generally dependent upon three broad influences:

1 organizational or bureaucratic constraints/routines
2 the news values held by media organizations
3 ownership, **ideology** and bias.

Organizational or bureaucratic routines

Newspapers and television news programmes do not react spontaneously to world events – news coverage is shaped by the way television news companies and newspapers are organized and which audiences they are aimed at. The logistics of collecting news may bias what news is gathered or how it is actually presented and reported. This can be illustrated in a number of ways.

Sources of news

Many of us rather naively believe that news stories are generated by reporters trekking the streets and interviewing witnesses to particular events. However, this is largely untrue. Many newspapers and TV news producers purchase most of their news items from press agencies such as the Press Association (PA) or Reuters – companies who sell brief reports of world or national news 24 hours per day – because they can no longer afford to employ hundreds of journalists. They also receive press releases from pressure groups, government agencies, public-relations companies, private companies and individuals, all of whom wish to publicize their activities. Many stories appear on the news or in print quite simply because a press agency deems it important or because a spin doctor or public-relations officer wants to plant a positive story about the government or a celebrity.

Financial costs

Sending personnel overseas and booking satellite connections can be very expensive and may result in the BBC or ITN giving us 'news' reports even if very little is actually happening, in order to justify such heavy costs. This is also partly the result of the fact that news organizations will have reporters already stationed in European countries and in the USA, so that when a story arises there is someone there to cover it. However, this often leads to a superficial treatment of events in developing countries because news organizations have very few journalists on duty in Africa or Asia. The last ten years have actually seen a decline in expensive forms of news coverage such as investigative reporting or foreign affairs coverage (apart from conflict in which the UK is involved) because news organizations are cutting costs.

Time or space available

News has to be tailored to fit either the time available for a news bulletin or the column space in a newspaper. For example, the BBC's 9 O'Clock News and ITN's News at Ten contain, on average, 15 items transmitted over a 30-minute period. Similarly, a newspaper has a fixed amount of space for each news category. Sometimes stories are included or excluded merely because they fit or don't fit the time or space available.

Deadlines

Television news has an advantage over newspapers because it can bring us news as it happens, i.e. it is not affected by deadlines, especially now we have 24-hour rolling news on television. A good example of news as it happened was the destruction of the World Trade Center in 2001. On the other hand, newspapers do have deadlines (usually about 10pm, if the news is to be included in the morning edition) and consequently they focus more on yesterday's news. This is why broadsheet newspaper coverage of stories generally tends to be more detailed and analytical than most television news coverage.

Immediacy and actuality

Events are much more likely to be reported, especially on television, if they can be accompanied by sound bites of speech and film footage, especially live background pictures from an actual location. Journalists reporting 'live' from the street are thought to add dramatic actuality; stories that have this footage are therefore more likely to be selected than those that do not.

Recent technological advances in newsgathering – particularly in the form of new media such as internet sites – have also made possible a level of immediacy unimagined a few decades ago. For example, BBC News 24 is now able to inform the UK about news events through live streams, i.e. 'breaking news' on all the BBC websites, by texting to mobile phones and the BBCi digital

A plane crash-lands in the Hudson River in the middle of New York in January 2009. Photos taken on mobile phones by 'citizen journalists' appeared in the news media within minutes. This photo was taken by Janis Krums, a ferry passenger.

interactive service. This new technology has also been used to encourage interaction between news organizations and their audiences/readerships.

Viewers are encouraged to text information or send pictures and video clips of news events direct to the BBC Newsroom on their mobile phones. Pictures and copy of breaking news can therefore reach the newsroom long before professional journalists and camera operators reach the scene, e.g. most of the 'live' pictures from the London bombings of 7/7 came from the mobile phones of '**citizen journalists**'.

Spencer-Thomas (2008) uses Burma to illustrate the growing influence of citizen journalists. He notes that the mass antigovernment demonstrations in Burma in 1988 failed to receive much media attention because the military regime banned overseas journalists from the country. By contrast, the mass demonstration in 2007 received far more attention because civilians themselves had the technology, in the form of modern mobile phones and camcorders, to send instant messages and pictures out of the country to waiting international media such as Reuters, BBC and CNN.

The audience

The content of the news and the style in which news is presented are very much a reaction to the type of audience that is thought to be watching or the social characteristics of a newspaper's readers. For example, Five News is characterized by short, snappy bulletins because it is aimed at a young audience. The Sun is aimed at a working-class youngish readership and so uses simplistic language because it believes this is what its readership wants. It also reflects the educational level of its target audience. Newspapers such as the Guardian, on the other hand, are aimed at the more qualified professional middle classes (as is Channel 4 News).

Who is perceived to be watching a news broadcast at particular times of the day also influences the selection of news. A lunchtime broadcast is more likely to be viewed by women, and so an item relating to a supermarket 'price war' might receive more coverage than it would in a late-evening news bulletin.

News values

Spencer-Thomas (2008) notes that **news values** are general guidelines or criteria that determine the worth of a news story and how much prominence it is given by newspapers or broadcast media. Specifically, they refer to what journalists, editors and broadcasters consider as 'newsworthy', i.e. interesting enough to appeal to and attract a significant readership or audience. What is regarded as newsworthy will vary from newspaper to newspaper because they may be aimed at different types of readership. What television editors and journalists regard as newsworthy may also differ between channels – for example, Channel 4 tends to focus on more social-policy issues than do the BBC or ITV. News values are of crucial importance because news producers are under great commercial pressure to increase their audience or readership in order to generate the advertising revenue that makes up most of a media organization's profit.

One of the best known lists of news values is supplied by Johan Galtung and Marie Holmboe Ruge. Although their research was conducted in 1965, virtually any media analyst's discussion of news values will always refer to their list, which was initially intended for the coverage of international events. Galtung and Ruge (1970) identified the following set of news values used by journalists.

Extraordinariness

Unexpected, rare, unpredictable and surprising events have more newsworthiness than routine events because they are out of the ordinary, e.g. the tsunami that hit South East Asia in 2004 or the unexpected death of Diana, Princess of Wales in 1997. As Charles A. Dana famously put it: 'if a dog bites a man, that's not news. But if a man bites a dog, that's news!'

Threshold

The 'bigger' the size of the event, e.g. war or natural disaster, the more likely it will be nationally reported. There is a threshold below which an event will fail to be considered worthy of attention, and will not be reported. A good example of this is the death of Princess Diana, where we saw almost 24-hour television news coverage of the event being 'filled- out' with items that would not normally reach national television, such as primary schools commemorating her life.

Unambiguity

Events that are easy to grasp are more likely to be reported than those which are open to more than one interpretation, or where understanding of the news depends on first understanding the complex background to the event. A survey of 300 leading media professionals across the USA, conducted by *The Columbia Journalism Review* (2000), revealed that the most regular reason why stories don't appear is that they are 'too complicated for the average person'.

Reference to elite persons

The famous and the powerful – those at the top of the socio-economic hierarchy – are often seen as more newsworthy to the general public than those who are regarded as 'ordinary'. For example, pictures of Prince William on the cover of news magazines can increase sales by tens of thousands. Famous people like Barack Obama therefore get more coverage than your local councillor. If the Queen's finger is nipped by a royal corgi, that is news – for the rest of us it would take a life-threatening savaging by a rabid Rottweiler. Media sociologists have noted that, in the past ten years, the cult of celebrity that exists in the UK has extended our definition of who counts as worthy of public interest, so that celebrity gossip, such as Britney Spears' 'breakdown' is increasingly front-page news, especially in the tabloid newspapers.

On the other hand, members of minority-ethnic groups, the underprivileged, the young – that is, ordinary people living ordinary lives in ordinary towns and cities outside London (where most of the main news centres are located) – are likely to receive limited news coverage, unless they pose a threat to the core values of society.

Reference to elite nations

This relates to cultural proximity, i.e. stories about people who speak the same language, look the same, and share the same preoccupations as the audience receive more coverage than those involving people who do not. Events happening in cultures very different from our own will not be seen as being inherently meaningful to audiences here.

A disaster which involves loss of life will not automatically qualify as important news – its reporting often depends on a kind of sliding scale of importance given to the number of deaths, measured against the country in which they occur. The loss of a few lives in a Western country may achieve recognition, whereas a considerable number of deaths in a developing country would have to occur to achieve similar recognition. This is the so-called 'McLurg's Law', named after a legendary British news editor, who once claimed that 1 dead Briton was worth 5 dead Frenchmen, 20 dead Egyptians, 500 dead Indians and 1000 dead Chinese in terms of news coverage. Consequently, events in distant parts of the world may only be reported when they involve Westerners, e.g. the headline 'Disco Fire in Thailand injures Brits' may be accompanied by an article that reports that 60 other foreigners died in the same fire.

Personalization

Events may be 'personalized' by referring to a prominent individual or celebrity associated with them. Complex events and policies are often reduced to conflict between personalities. This is because journalists and editors believe that their audiences will identify with a story if social events are seen as the actions of individuals. For example, British politics is often presented as a personal showdown between the two party leaders, especially if there is footage of the two engaged in a parliamentary slanging match, complete with cheers and jeers. International affairs, too, are often reported in this way – for example, the invasion of Iraq in 2003 was often presented as Bush and Blair versus Saddam Hussein.

Frequency

This refers to what Dutton (1997) calls 'the time span taken by the event'. Murders, motorway pile-ups and plane crashes happen suddenly and their meaning can be established quickly. However, more long-term structural social trends are often outside the 'frequency' of the daily papers; for example, inflation or unemployment tend to be reported when the government releases figures on them. Therefore, events which occur suddenly and fit in well with the newspaper or news broadcast's schedule are more readily reported than those which occur gradually or at inconvenient times of day or night. Political parties' news-management techniques often take advantage of this news value – for example, in the run-up to an election, they will hold press conferences or arrange photo opportunities at times which do 'fit in'.

Continuity

Once a story has achieved importance and is 'running', it will continue to be covered for some time. This is partly because news teams are already in place to report the story, and partly because previous reportage may have made the story more accessible to the public. **Moral panics** are sometimes the result of such continuity, as journalists and editors enter a cycle of newsworthiness. However, journalistic interest in the story may wane when they assume their audiences are losing interest.

Narrative

Journalists prefer to present news in the form of a story with heroes and villains, and a beginning, middle and end, in order to make it more interesting. If an event can be presented in this way, it is more likely to be reported.

Think about how the Iraq war, for example, has been presented as a newsworthy **narrative**. According to the news narrative, Iraq was being led by a brutal unelected leader who did not care about killing his own people and who was threatening the world with weapons of mass destruction, as well as financing and harbouring terrorist groups. The USA and UK invaded in order to remove the problem, to destroy the weapons of mass destruction and to restore democracy to the people of Iraq. These valiant efforts are currently being disrupted by insurgents, who are a threat to the Iraqi people and need to be removed by the brave efforts of 'our boys' in the army. This narrative forms the basis of much news reporting about Iraq. The 'truth' is a lot more complicated than this, but this narrative underpins much news coverage because it is easier for audiences and readerships to understand.

Negativity

Bad news is regarded by journalists as more exciting and dramatic than good news and is seen as attracting a bigger audience. Generally, good news, e.g. 'there were no murders today', is regarded as less interesting and entertaining than 'three people were shot to death today'. Stories about death, tragedy, bankruptcy, violence, damage, natural disasters, political upheaval or simply extreme weather conditions are therefore always rated above positive stories. Often, journalists will go looking for bad news. For example, Fiske (1987) refers to an American

Use the concept of news values to explain why the death of Princess Diana in a car crash in Paris was the biggest news story of the 1990s.

journalist arriving in the Belgian Congo during the war there, running up to a group of White women waiting for a plane to leave and shouting out: 'Has anyone here been raped and speaks English?'

The threshold for reporting bad news is lower than that for reporting good news because it usually incorporates other news values, i.e. it is often unambiguous; it occurs in a short space of time; it is often unexpected; and it may be big, e.g. a disaster.

Composition

Most news outlets will attempt to 'balance' the reporting of events, so that if for example there has been a great deal of bad or gloomy news, some items of a more positive nature will be added. If there is an excess of foreign news, for instance, the least important foreign story may have to make way for an inconsequential item of domestic news. Balance may also be achieved if news happens to come overwhelmingly from one source over a certain period.

An interesting news story will, therefore, contain some of these news values, but it is unlikely it will contain them all. Research conducted in the USA by Buckley gave 12 television editors 64 news stories, which they were asked to classify for newsworthiness. All classified them in a similar manner and those items with the greatest number of news values made it to the highest position on the list of stories they would have definitely reported.

Ownership, ideology and bias

The implication in many studies of news values seems to be that they are virtually objective factors, to which journalists and editors react reflexively. The gatekeeping process, which leads to the selection of some news stories and the exclusion of others, is seen to be apolitical and unbiased, especially by pluralist sociologists and media professionals themselves.

Neo-pluralism

Pluralists have traditionally argued that journalists are professionals who are disinterested, impartial and objective pursuers of truth. However, some media commentators, who we shall call **neo-pluralists**, suggest that, in the modern world of journalism, these goals are increasingly difficult to attain. Davies (2008) argues that the most basic function of journalism is to check facts. However, he argues that in practice, contemporary journalism has been corrupted by an endemic failure to verify news stories.

Davies was alerted to this practice by what he calls the appearance of 'flat-earth' news stories. This is a type of news story that appears to be and is universally accepted as 'true'. As an example, he cites the millennium bug stories that appeared in 1999, suggesting that there would be a universal breakdown in computerized systems as we entered 2000. Davies concludes that the millions of words written about the bug were written by journalists who had no idea whether what they were writing about was true.

Davies argues that modern-day British journalism is characterized by what he calls '**churnalism**' – the uncritical overreliance by journalists on 'facts' produced by government spin doctors and public-relations experts. He notes that: 'where once journalists were active gatherers of news, now they have generally become mere passive processors of unchecked, second-hand material, much of it contrived by PR to serve some political or commercial interest'. Davies argues they are no longer journalists, but churnalists.

Research by Davies aimed to quantify churnalism in the serious broadsheet press, e.g. *The Times*, plus the *Daily Mail* over a period of two weeks in 1997. He found that 80 per cent of the 2207 stories examined consisted of material which was taken from the PA or public-relations companies. Only 12 per cent of stories were generated by the reporters themselves. He also found that where a story relied on a specific statement of fact, in 70 per cent of them, the claimed fact passed into print without any corroboration at all. Only 12 per cent of 'factual stories' had been thoroughly checked by journalists using investigative techniques.

Davies argues that journalism is forced into churnalism because of commercial pressures that have resulted in more space to fill but with added pressure to do this quickly and at the lowest possible cost. Consequently, facts from official sources are used because they are so cheap. He notes too there are active commercial pressures to pursue stories that tell people what they want to hear, e.g. to give them lots of celebrity stories because this attracts large audiences and therefore advertising revenue. However, he also suggests that journalists today are simply indifferent to the truth and reality. He argues that they prefer to sermonize about the world rather than objectively report it.

However, Davies has attracted some criticisms from Marxist sociologists who suggest that he fails to recognize the role of owners and advertisers in these processes. Edwards and Cromwell (2008), writing on the website Media Lens, argue that newspapers 'are in the business of selling wealthy audiences to advertisers. This is not an apolitical stance. This marketplace naturally favours facts, ideas, values and aspirations that are popular with elite audiences, elite advertisers and elite journalists'. Flat-earth stories underpinned by churnalism provide a cheap supportive environment in order to attract advertising revenue, which makes up most of the profits made by media conglomerates. Monbiot (2004) agrees and notes that 'the falsehoods reproduced by the media before the invasion of Iraq were massive and consequential: it is hard to see how Britain could have gone to war if the press had done its job'.

Marxists are also critical of Davies' view that truth-telling is the primary function of Davies' profession. McChesney (2002) argues that the notion that the media are professional is an ideological myth invented by media owners in order to present the corporate media monopoly as a 'neutral' and unbiased contributor to democracy, so increasing their potential to be profitable. Consequently, some media researchers suggest that news content is manufactured or socially constructed in a way that benefits powerful groups and has negative consequences for the rest of society.

Concentration of ownership of news organizations

Couldry *et al.* (2007a) note that only six corporations operate the majority of major websites, commercial broadcasting/cable casting and newspapers worldwide.

Sociologists have identified a number of ways in which a media owner might influence the editorial priorities, fairness, transparency and impartiality of the news:

- They may issue direct instructions or the media owner may be directly involved in setting the editorial approach or policy of the news media.
- The owner may influence the way in which the news is gathered and presented – in terms of resources available and which stories they consider worthy of investment (e.g. whether to station correspondents in Iraq or to rely on agency coverage).
- The owner's political or business ideology may directly or indirectly impact on the choice of stories pursued by their editors and the way in which those stories are presented. In other words, an owner does not have to exercise day-to-day control – compliant editors who value their jobs know what their employer expects. For example, a number of national newspapers (the *Independent*, the *Guardian*, *Daily Mail*, *Mirror* and *Daily Telegraph*) carried a story on 19 July 2007 concerning Mr Rupert Murdoch's contacts with Mr Blair in the run-up to the Iraq war. The story was not featured at all in either the *Sun* or *The Times*.

Couldry and colleagues note that editors and journalists are subjected to increased commercial pressures in a global multimedia market. This has led to the cutting of newsroom budgets, the undermining of journalistic integrity, and the danger of greater advertiser and sponsor influence over news agenda. Resource pressures mean journalists have to appeal to even bigger audiences and so have to compete with the entertainment sector for consumers. This often leads to the tabloidization of news as it is becomes increasingly underpinned by entertainment values, i.e. coverage of sports, crime, entertainment and celebrity becomes the central focus of news reporting. In contrast, the coverage of political debate and social problems declines because it is not entertaining enough.

Couldry et al. (2007a) argue that these trends have led to a decline in public trust in the media profession, especially among the young and minority audiences. Public opinion polls (for example, Ipsos MORI 2005) put journalists behind doctors, teachers, scientists, business executives and civil servants and on a par with politicians in terms of public esteem and trust. Couldry and colleagues conclude that the general public is aware that, as a result of market forces, the news lacks balance and relevance, and that it generally serves corporate interests rather than society as a whole.

The power elite

Bagdikian (2004), in his critique of the American news media, suggests that almost all media leaders in the USA are part of a wider **power elite** made up of a powerful industrial, financial and political establishment. Consequently, media owners ensure that the content of news is politically conservative and that their news outlets promote corporate values. He notes how such values often imperceptibly permeate news; for example, most newspapers have sections dedicated to business news, which present corporate leaders as heroes or exciting combatants, and they uncritically and frequently report corporate and stock-market information. In contrast, very little attention is paid to ordinary Americans and the economic pressures that they face; for example, the news media seem uninterested in the growing gap between the rich and poor in the USA.

Bagdikian notes that reporters are expected by the public to act like independent, fair-minded professionals. However, he notes that reporters are also employees of corporations that control their hiring, firing and daily management, as well as dictating what stories they can cover and which part of their reporting will be used or discarded. Bagdikian suggests that seeing their journalists as obedient workers on an assembly line has produced a growing incidence of news corporations demanding unethical acts, such as chequebook journalism and intrusion into people's privacy, as symbolized by paparazzi photographers.

Bagdikian also argues that the commercial pressure on journalists has meant the neutralization of information and a reduction in objectivity because of fears that it might offend part of the audience and so reduce circulation. Bagdikian concludes that, as a result of these processes, the news in the USA – and increasingly in the UK – reflects an official, but bland, establishment view of the world.

There is some evidence for Bagdikian's assertions. For example, 274 out of 275 News Corp editors around the world came to exactly the same conclusion as their proprietor, Rupert Murdoch, on the war in Iraq. The only one that did not was in Borneo, a predominantly Muslim country, in which support for the war would have resulted in a major decline in circulation. There is some concern that the recent large BSkyB investment in ITV may have similar effects on ITN (40 per cent of which is owned by

ITV plc), which produces news for all ITV channels and Channel 4. Sky News already produces news for Five. This means that the BBC is the only news broadcaster in the UK not privately owned by a media transnational conglomerate.

The propaganda model of the media

Herman and Chomsky (1988) argue that the media participate in propaganda campaigns helpful to elite interests. They suggest that media performance is largely shaped by market forces and that built into the capitalist system is a range of filters that work ceaselessly to shape media output.

They note that media businesses are profit-seeking businesses, owned by very wealthy companies (or other companies) and they are funded by advertisers who are also profit-seeking entities and who want their advertising to appear in a supportive selling environment. The media are also dependent on government and major businesses as information sources. These overlapping interests mean there is a certain degree of solidarity between government, major media and other corporate businesses. Government and large non-media business firms are also best positioned (and sufficiently wealthy) to be able to pressure the media with threats of withdrawal of advertising or TV licences, and therefore control the flow of information.

However, Herman and Chomsky suggest that the media are also constrained and their content is shaped by the dominant politically conservative ideology, which extols the virtues of free-market capitalism and is critical of any alternative point of view. McChesney (2000) notes that, as a result, the media sees official sources of information as legitimate, but he notes that:

>> *if you talk to prisoners, strikers, the homeless, or protesters, you have to paint their perspectives as unreliable, or else you've become an advocate and are no longer a 'neutral' professional journalist.* >>

Edwards and Cromwell (2006) argue that particular subjects – e.g. US/UK government responsibility for genocide, vast corporate criminality, threats to the very existence of human life – are distorted, suppressed, **marginalized** and ignored by the British mass media. Leaders of developing countries of whom the West disapprove are uncritically demonized whilst the USA is lauded as the champion of democracy and the benign military occupier of Iraq.

The hierarchy of credibility

Stuart Hall (1973) agrees that news is supportive of capitalist interests because those in powerful positions have better access to media institutions than the less powerful. Hall argues that this is a result of the news values employed by most journalists. In particular, most journalists rank the views of politicians, police officers, civil servants and business leaders (Hall calls these groups **'primary definers'**) as more important (or credible) than those of pressure groups, trade unionists or ordinary people. Hall calls this the 'hierarchy of credibility'. News often reports what prominent people say about events rather than the events themselves; indeed, what such

Focus on research

Greg Philo
Bad news from Israel: media coverage of the Middle East conflict

If you don't understand the Middle East crisis, it might be because you are watching it on TV news. This scores high on images of fighting, violence and drama but is low on explanation. The Glasgow University Media Group interviewed 12 small audience groups (a total of 85 people) with a cross section of ages and backgrounds. They were asked a series of questions about the conflict and what they had understood from TV news. The same questions were then put to 300 young people (aged between 17 and 22) who filled in a questionnaire. We asked what came to their mind when they heard the words 'Israeli/Palestinian conflict' and then what was the source of whatever it was. Most (82 per cent) listed TV news as their source and these replies showed that they had absorbed the 'main' message of the news, of conflict, violence and tragedy, but that many people had little understanding of the reasons for the conflict and its origins. Explanations were rarely given on the news and when they were, journalists often spoke in a form of shorthand which assumed quite detailed knowledge of the origins of the conflict. For example, in a news bulletin which featured the progress of peace talks, a journalist made a series of very brief comments on the issues which underpinned the conflict: Journalist: 'The basic raw disagreements remain – the future, for example, of this city Jerusalem, the future of Jewish settlements and the returning refugees.' (ITN 18.30, 16 October 2001)

Adapted from the Glasgow University Media Unit website at www.gla.ac.uk/departments/sociology/units/media

1 How did the Glasgow University Media Group try to achieve a representative sample?

2 Why does Greg Philo write that 'if you don't understand the Middle East crisis it might be because you are watching it on TV news'?

---

people say may constitute an event in itself – powerful people 'make news'.

Some sociologists have drawn attention to the appearance of spin doctors as primary definers of information in recent years. Jones refers to the Labour Government as the 'sultans of spin'. He notes that spinning a story on behalf of the government or other powerful institution is a form of news management aimed at putting a favourable bias on information presented to the general public via the media in order to gain the most support.

The media's focus on primary definers means that minority groups are often ignored by the media or are portrayed negatively as threats to society. Manning (2001) notes that less-powerful groups have to tone down anything extreme or radical in their message in order to get their message heard by the media

The social background of media professionals

However, the Glasgow University Media Group (1981) argue that the way the news is gathered and presented has nothing to do with the rich and powerful. Rather, they argue that news is the product of the social backgrounds of journalists and editors, who are usually White, male and middle-class. The lifestyle that most journalists and editors lead results in them seeing very little wrong with the way society is presently organized (despite inequality) and, as a result, they are rarely critical. They unconsciously side with the powerful and rich quite simply because they have more in common with them, and do not welcome the sorts of radical change proposed by the representatives of the poor and powerless.

Semiotic analysis

The GUMG have studied news broadcasts and have used a technique called **semiotic content analysis** which involves detailed analysis of the language and visual images used by the media. They have found that the language and images used by the media are more sympathetic to the interests of the powerful and often devalue the points of view of less powerful groups. For example, in some news programmes, trade unions are typically presented as 'demanding' whereas management make 'offers'. Fiske (1987) argues that:

>> the word 'offer' suggests its agents ... are generous ... and are comfortably in control, whereas 'demand' suggests that its agents are greedy ... and having to struggle to gain control of the situation. Demand is a disruptive word which places 'demanders' with the negative forces that make news. >> (p.285)

In their analysis of industrial disputes such as strikes, the GUMG discovered that managers were often interviewed in the orderly, calm environment of their offices, whilst strikers were interviewed above the noise of the picket lines. The former were seen as the representatives of order and reason, the latter as shouty and unreasonable.

Individuals may also be labelled by the media as 'scroungers', 'terrorists' or 'extremists' – these labels serve to undermine the credibility of the powerless. In foreign news reports, the media often make the ethnocentric and ideological distinction between 'terrorists', who are seen as disrupting friendly regimes, and 'freedom fighters', who are resisting regimes hostile to the West.

The research of the Glasgow Media Group shows that the media do not just reflect public opinion. They also engage in agenda setting, i.e. they provide the framework (or agenda) in which issues are discussed, so that people think about issues in a way that benefits the ruling class. Certain assumptions are built into news programmes, such as that we all want strikes to end, that we oppose 'extremism' and favour 'moderation', and so on. Agenda setting also refers to the exclusion or marginalization of issues that need to be discussed, such as the causes of inequality and poverty. Hall argues that, over time, news actually creates the illusion that consensus characterizes debate in modern capitalist societies.

Criticisms

However, Schlesinger (1990) is critical of theories that focus on the power of elites or owners because the media do not always act in the interests of the powerful – contemporary politicians are very careful what they say to the media because they are very aware that the media can shape public perceptions of their policies and practices and perhaps influence voting behaviour, as well as putting them under considerable pressure to resign. Media owners too are engaged in competition with each other, as illustrated by newspaper price wars and the fact that some media owners, most notably, Rupert Murdoch and Richard Branson, have engaged in some very public conflicts with each other over matters of media ownership. Schlesinger argues that this does not suggest a unified media, never mind a unified establishment elite.

Pluralists, too, would argue that the news contains many different points of view. They note that certain views may dominate in particular situations, but the direction that bias takes is not consistent, and so there is no overall slant towards the rich and powerful.

Conclusions

The news may not be as impartial as we like to think it is. Critics of news gathering suggest that a range of influences – bureaucratic constraints, news values, churnalism, the concentration of ownership, commercial pressures, primary definers and the social backgrounds of journalists – mean that the news is a socially manufactured product which may end up reflecting the interests and ideology of powerful groups. This may undermine democracy, as audiences are not being exposed to a range of facts and information and, as a result, are unable to make informed choices about how society should be organized or about how to deal with the social and economic inequalities that might eventually destabilize such societies.

Moral panics

An important aspect of news production is the focus on particular types of news that result in moral panics. The media sometimes focus on certain groups and activities and, through the style of their reporting, defines these groups and activities as a problem worthy of public anxiety and official censure and control.

What is a moral panic?

The term 'moral panic' was popularized by Stanley Cohen (1972) in his classic work *Folk Devils and Moral Panics*. It refers to media reactions to particular social groups or particular activities that are defined as threatening societal values and thus create anxiety amongst the general population. This anxiety or panic puts pressure on the authorities to control the problem and discipline the group responsible. However, the moral concern is usually out of proportion to any real threat to society posed by the group or activity.

Cohen focused on the media's reaction to youth 'disturbances' on Easter Monday 1964. He demonstrated how the media blew what were essentially small-scale scuffles and vandalism out of all proportion by using headlines such as 'Day of Terror' and words like 'battle' and 'riot' in their reporting. Little time or interest was paid to what actually happened, which was a series of localized scuffles. Cohen argued that not only were the events overreported, but also the coverage awarded them far outweighed their importance.

He argues that the media tapped into what they saw as a social consensus – they assumed that decent law-abiding members of society shared their concerns about a general decline in the morality of the young symbolized by the growing influence of youth culture. Consequently, mods and rockers were presented and analysed in a distorted and stereotyped fashion as a threat to law and order, and the media attempted to impose a culture of control on them by calling for their punishment.

Goode and Ben-Yehuda (1994) note that the moral panic produces a '**folk devil**' – a stereotype of deviance that suggests that the perpetrators of the so-called deviant activities are selfish and evil, and steps need to be taken to control and neutralize their actions so that society can return to 'normality'. However, the media also engages in a type of social soothsaying – they often adopt a disaster mentality and predict more problems if the problem group is not kept under surveillance or punished. This increases the social pressure on the forces of law and order to stamp down hard on the problem group.

Goode and Ben-Yehuda note the volatility of moral panics – this means they can erupt suddenly, although they usually subside or disappear just as quickly. Some are dormant but reappear from time to time. However, the panic usually has some lasting effect – it may have raised public consciousness and, in extreme cases, may have led to changes in social policy or the law.

However, both the publicity and social reaction to the panic may create the potential for further crime and deviance in the future. Thornton (1995), for example, notes that the 'Just Say No' drug campaign of the early 1990s probably attracted more young people to the use of ecstasy as they realized adult society disapproved of their membership of the e-generation. There is also evidence that the police reaction to illegal rave parties in the 1980s – using riot gear, dogs, horses, etc. – led to young people violently confronting police officers' attempts to close down these parties. Consequently, arrests for violent conduct rose dramatically in those parts of the country where these parties were popular.

Figure 3.2 Stages of a moral panic

Moral panics go through a number of stages, which some sociologists have termed a 'cycle of newsworthiness'.

STAGE 1

The tabloid media report on a particular activity/incident or social group, using sensationalist and exaggerated language and headlines.

STAGE 2

Follow-up articles identify the group as a social problem. They are demonized as 'folk devils', i.e. the media give them particular characteristics, focused particularly on dress and behaviour, which helps the general public and police to identify them more easily.

STAGE 3

The media oversimplify the reasons why the group or activity has appeared, e.g. young people out of control, a lack of respect for authority, a decline in morality.

STAGE 4

Moral entrepreneurs, e.g. politicians and religious leaders, react to media reports and make statements condemning the group or activity; they insist that the police, courts and government take action against them.

STAGE 5

There is a rise in the reporting to the police by the general public of incidents associated with the group or activity as the group or activity becomes more visible in the public consciousness.

STAGE 6

The authorities stamp down hard on the group or activity – this may take the form of the police stopping, searching and arresting those associated with the activity, the courts severely punishing those convicted of the activity or the government bringing in new laws to control the activity and group. Other institutions, e.g. shopping centres may ban the group or activity.

STAGE 7

The group may react to the moral panic, overpolicing, etc., by becoming more deviant in protest, or the activity may go underground where it becomes more difficult to police and control.

STAGE 8

More arrests and convictions result from the moral panic and the statistics are reported by the media, thereby fulfilling the initial media prophecy or prediction that the group or activity was a social problem.

Contemporary examples of moral panics

Ravers and ecstasy use

Redhead (1993) notes that a moral panic in regard to acid house raves in the late 1980s led to the police setting up roadblocks on motorways, turning up at raves in full riot gear and eventually led to the passing of the Criminal Justice Act (1990), which banned illegal parties. Thornton notes that the moral panic that surrounded rave parties in the late 1980s and early 1990s had the effect of attracting more young people to the rave culture, quite simply because it had been labelled deviant by disapproving media coverage.

Refugees and asylum seekers

In 2003, there was a moral panic focused on the numbers of refugees and asylum seekers entering the UK and their motives. Elements of the tabloid press, particularly the *Daily Mail* and the *Sun,* focused on the alleged links between asylum seekers and terrorism to create public anxiety. In the case of asylum seekers, the moral panic of 2003 reduced the motives for people wanting to enter the UK to either terrorism, crime or taking advantage of the UK's generous welfare system. The very complex and genuine reasons why people come to the UK were neglected or ignored altogether.

Binge drinking

Borsay (2007) notes that the moral panic that focused on binge drinking in 2008 is very similar to one that gripped Britain in the early 1700s. He therefore argues that media, public and political concern about problem drinking is not new. He suggests that the parallels between the 18th-century gin craze and contemporary binge drinking are striking. He argues that moral panics characterized both periods, fuelled by pressure groups, the media and perceptions of government complacency. He notes the media-constructed moral panics found in both eras were symbolic of wider anxieties about 'social breakdown'. Borsay notes that the gin craze of the 1700s was finally brought under control with a combination of increased tax and licensing fees, along with restrictions on retail outlets. He concludes that:

<< *no doubt concerted action by the government and police could bring a similar end to binge drinking today, but whether this would produce an overall drop in alcohol consumption and other social problems and a more disciplined and conformist youth remains questionable.* >>

Hoodies

Fawbert (2008) examined newspaper reports about so-called hoodies between 2004 and 2008, and notes that there was only one article in the national papers in 2004 that used the word 'hoodie' to describe a young thug. However, a year later, the Bluewater Shopping Centre caused outrage by banning its shoppers from sporting hoodies and baseball caps. This was followed by Tony Blair vowing to clamp down on antisocial behaviour perpetrated by hoodies. The media seemed to seize on

Table 3.2 Examples of moral panics since the 1950s

Period	Example
Mid-1950s	● teddy boys
1964	● mods and rockers
Late 1960s	● hippies smoking marihuana
	● skinhead violence
Early 1970s	● football hooliganism
	● street crime, i.e. mugging
1976/7	● punk rock
	● heroin addiction
Mid to late 1980s	● homosexuality and Aids (i.e. 'gay plague')
	● illegal acid-house raves
	● hippy peace convoys
	● video-nasties
Early to mid 1990s	● child sex abuse
	● single-parent families, especially teenage mothers
	● ecstasy use (post Leah Betts)
	● children and violence (post Jamie Bulger)
	● dangerous dogs
Mid to late 1990s	● welfare scroungers
	● boys' underachievement in schools
2002/3	● paedophiles
	● Black gun culture
	● asylum seekers
2004–9	● hoodies, knife and gun crime
	● binge drinking

this, and 'hoodies' became a commonly used term, especially between 2005 and 2007, to describe young people involved in crime. He notes that articles would often use the term in the headline, but there would be no reference in the story about whether the young criminal was actually wearing one; it was just presumed. Hoodies suddenly became a symbol of mischief, and sales of the clothing began to soar as young people realized they upset people in authority by wearing them.

Why do moral panics come about?

A reaction to rapid social change

Furedi (1994) argues that moral panics arise when society fails to adapt to dramatic social changes and it is felt that there is a loss of control, especially over powerless groups such as the young. He notes that in the 1950s and 1960s, British society experienced great social change as younger people acquired more economic and cultural power. This period particularly saw the emergence of distinct youth cultures such as teddy boys (1950s) and mods, rockers and hippies (1960s). As a result, the older generation felt they were losing authority and control over the younger generation.

Furedi therefore argues that moral panics are about the wider concerns that the older generation have about the nature of society today – people see themselves (and their families) as at greater risk from a variety of groups. They believe that things are out of control. They perceive, with the media's encouragement, that traditional norms and

values no longer have much relevance in their lives. Furedi notes that people feel a very real sense of loss, which makes them extremely susceptible to the anxieties encouraged by media moral panics.

Cohen and Young (1981) suggest that the media's anxiety about the behaviour of particular social groups originates in the consensual nature of the media in the UK today. Journalists assume that the majority of people in society share common values of reality, especially about what is acceptable and not acceptable. Generally, topics outside these presumed shared ideas are deemed wrong or detrimental. The media's focus on so-called 'problem groups' is seen as newsworthy because journalists, editors and broadcasters assume that like-minded decent people share their moral concerns about the direction that society is taking. In this sense, the media believes that it is giving the public what it wants.

A means of making a profit

Some commentators argue that moral panics are simply the product of news values and the desire of journalists and editors to sell newspapers – they are a good example of how audiences are manipulated by the media for commercial purposes. In other words, moral panics sell tabloid newspapers. However, after a while, news stories exhaust their cycle of newsworthiness and journalists abandon interest in them because they believe their audiences have lost interest too. The social problems, however, do not disappear – they remain dormant until journalists decide at some future date that they can be made newsworthy again and attract a large audience.

Key themes

Crime and deviance
Moral panics

The concept of moral panic has been used by sociologists to help understand a wide variety of social situations where the activities of a group have provoked sensationalized and exaggerated media reaction. This response has resulted in calls for a 'clampdown' by moral entrepreneurs, and the result in many cases has been hasty changes to the law. The effect on the group concerned is often to make them even more committed to their activities – a process known as 'deviance amplification'. Here are some examples you may have come across during your course:

- *Education* – the educational achievement of boys
- *Beliefs in Society* – the activities of some new religious movements (see pp. 26–31)
- *Health* – the relationship between gay men and HIV/Aids
- *Crime and Deviance* – gangs and knife crime
- *Culture and Identity* – various youth subcultures such as skinheads and punks
- *Families and households* – single-parent families.

Serving ruling-class ideology

Marxists such as Stuart Hall see moral panics as serving an ideological function. His study of the moral coverage of black muggers in the 1970s (Hall *et al.* 1978) concluded that it had the effect of labelling all young African-Caribbeans as criminals and a potential threat to White people. This served the triple ideological purpose of:

1 turning the White working class against the Black working class (i.e. 'divide and rule')
2 diverting attention away from the mismanagement of capitalism by the capitalist class
3 justifying repressive laws and policing that could be used against other 'problem' groups.

The notion that moral panics make it easier for the powerful to introduce control legislation that might be rejected by the general public under normal circumstances has attracted some support. For example, the moral panics aimed at the hippy peace convoys and rave culture that existed in the 1980s resulted in a law banning illegal parties and criminalized trespass. The latter law has since been used by the police to prevent demonstrations and workers picketing their place of work. It can also be argued that both the installation of surveillance cameras in our city centres, and greater film and television censorship are the direct consequences of the moral panic that developed out of the murder of the toddler James Bulger by two children.

A reflection of people's real fears

Left realists argue that moral panics should not be dismissed as a product of ruling-class ideology or news values. Moral panics have a very real basis in reality, i.e. the media often identifies groups who are a very real threat to those living in inner-city areas – portraying such crime as a fantasy is naive because it denies the very real harm that some types of crime have on particular communities or the sense of threat that older people feel. In other words, moral panics are probably justified in some cases.

Conclusions

The study of moral panics has drawn our attention to the power of the media in defining what counts as normal and deviant behaviour and the effects of such media labelling on particular social groups. Most importantly, it reminds us continually to question our commonsensical understanding of crime, which is often underpinned by media reporting of crime. However, McRobbie (1999) argues that moral panics are becoming less frequent and harder to sustain today, as those groups labelled as folk devils by the media can now effectively fight back through pressure groups and new social movements.

Check your understanding

1 What evidence is there that the public trust TV news reports more than those in newspapers?

2 Give three reasons why the public regard TV news as a 'window on the world'.

3 Give four examples to illustrate how organizational or bureaucratic routines affect news reporting.

4 Explain how news values are important in the selection of news, providing examples to illustrate the points you make.

5 What evidence does Davies provide to illustrate the importance of what he calls 'churnalism'?

6 How might media owners influence news coverage?

7 Explain how Bagdikian can argue that 'media owners ensure that the content of news is politically conservative and that their news outlets promote corporate values'.

8 How can Hall's idea of a 'hierarchy of credibility' help to explain why news coverage tends to reflect capitalist interests?

9 According to Goode and Ben-Yehuda, what are the effects of:
   (a) 'folk devils'   (b) 'moral panics'?

10 Briefly explain one recent example of a moral panic.

11 Outline three explanations for the existence of moral panics.

Activities

Research ideas

1 List the first ten news items from an edition of the BBC evening news. Do the same for ITN news on the same evening. What are the differences? Can they be explained in terms of 'news values'?

2 Tape one news programme. Analyse the lead story in terms of the sources that are used, e.g. newscaster's script, live film footage, location report from a reporter at the scene, interview – taped, live or by satellite – archive footage (old film), amateur film, etc. Then brainstorm a list of all the people who must have been involved, e.g. reporters, photographers, editors, companies buying and selling satellite time, drivers, outside broadcast crews, film archivists, etc. Discuss how practical problems may have served to structure the story in a particular way.

Web.tasks

1 Look at the websites of the following newspapers on the same day: *Sun, Daily Mail, Daily Telegraph, Guardian*. Compare the presentation of their main stories.

2 Find out about the recent work of the Glasgow University Media Group at **www.glasgowmediagroup.org**

Key terms

'Churnalism' uncritical over-reliance by journalists on 'facts' produced by government spin doctors and public-relations experts.

Citizen journalists members of the public who record news events, for example using mobile-phone cameras.

Content analysis a research method that analyses media content in both a quantitative and qualitative way.

Folk devil stereotype of deviants which suggests that the perpetrators of the so-called deviant activities are selfish and evil and therefore steps need to be taken to control and neutralize their actions so that society can return to 'normality'.

Gatekeepers people within the media who have the power to let some news stories through and stop others, e.g. editors. They therefore decide what counts as news.

Ideology a set of ideas used to justify and legitimate inequality, especially class inequality.

Marginalizing making a group appear to be 'at the edge' of society and not very important.

Moral entrepreneurs politicians, religious leaders, etc., who react to sensational media reports and make statements condemning the group or activity and insist that the police, courts and government take action against them.

Moral panics media reactions to particular social groups or particular activities which are defined as threatening societal values and consequently create anxiety amongst the general population.

Narrativization transforming real events into easily digestible stories with causal agents, (heroes and villains) and a sense of closure.

Neo-pluralism view that journalists are professional, objective pursuers of truth who face obstacles in living up to these principles in the modern world.

News values assumptions about what makes an event newsworthy (i.e. interesting to a particular audience) that guide journalists and editors when selecting news items.

Power elite the wealthy minority who control economic and political power.

Primary definers powerful groups that have easier and more effective access to the media, e.g. the government, the rich and powerful.

Semiotics the sociological study of signs and symbols contained in languages and images such as advertisements. *See also* **content analysis**.

Sociology A2 for AQA

An eye on the exam — The selection and presentation of news, and moral panics

Item A

Many factors affect the production of the news. According to the Glasgow University Media Group, ideological factors play a major part in the way that news is produced. For example, in their studies of industrial conflicts, they found that news reports tend to be selective, dealing with the effects of disputes rather than their causes. They also found that there is biased use of images in TV coverage. For example, during a council workers' strike in Liverpool, images of piles of uncleared rubbish and of unburied dead contributed to the impression that the workers were at fault. Similarly, the language used was biased – for example, strikers were described as 'demanding' while management was described as 'offering'.

In addition to ideological factors, however, news production is also influenced by organizational factors and the culture of journalists and editors.

Using material from **Item A** and elsewhere, critically examine the factors influencing news production.

(18 marks)

Grade booster — Getting top marks in this question

As the Item suggests, you need to examine institutional or organizational factors such as the resources that are available to news organizations and costs of news gathering; the news diary; the time and space available in the newspaper or broadcast (and the time of the broadcast); the news cycle (e.g. frequency of publication) and the nature of the audience. You should also consider the influence of cultural factors upon news production, such as news values (e.g. personalization of news stories), gatekeeping and narrativization. You should examine ideological influences on news production. Here you can make use of relevant information from the Item to look at Marxist views and studies, such as those of the Glasgow University Media Group.

TOPIC 4

The mass media and audiences

Getting you thinking

Still Too Much Violence on TV

A new public opinion poll has found that a clear majority, 64 per cent, of people agree that there is too much violence portrayed in entertainment programmes on television.

Speaking in November 2008, ahead of a major conference on violence in the media, John Beyer, director of mediawatch-uk, said:

'*The results of this independent poll are very significant. It is clear that the majority of people want action taken to reduce screen violence but the crucial question now is how broadcasters, film and game producers will respond to this latest expression of public concern about violence in entertainment. At a time of rising social and criminal violence, manifested in the shocking level of gun and knife crime, we know there is widespread support for standards to be raised generally, especially on television.*'

Source: mediawatch (www.mediawatch.org.uk)

1 **Have you or any of your friends ever played computer games such as Grand Theft Auto? Did you or they enjoy it? What was enjoyable about it?**

2 **Suggest reasons why the director of mediawatch-uk is concerned about screen violence.**

3 **Do you agree with him? Explain your view.**

Many people believe that the media influence behaviour and what we think or believe. Influential psychologists, pressure groups such as mediawatch UK, religious leaders and politicians have suggested that there is a fairly direct causal link between violence in films, television programmes and computer games, and violent real-life crime. It is argued that such media content exerts an overwhelmingly negative effect on mass audiences, and particularly the impressionable young. These beliefs have led to increasing government attempts to control particular types of media, to the extent that many media sociologists believe that Britain is the most heavily censored country in the Western world.

However, sociologists too have argued that media content can have a direct effect upon their audiences and trigger particular social responses in terms of behaviour and attitudes. These sociological contributions to the debate about media effects come from a wide range of perspectives and make for a strange set of bedfellows:

● Some sociologists, e.g. Gerbner *et al.* (1986), have focused on representations of violence in certain types

of media and suggest that these contribute to violent crime and antisocial forms of behaviour in real life, especially that committed by the young.

● Some feminist sociologists, e.g. Dworkin (1990), Morgan (1980) and so on, have suggested that the consumption of pornography, which is easily accessed through newspapers and magazines, and particularly through the internet, is harmful in terms of encouraging sexual violence and negative attitudes towards women.

● Other feminists, e.g. Orbach (1991) and Wolf (1990), have expressed concerns about the representations of young women, particularly size zero models in magazines and newspapers, which they claim may be producing a generation of females who suffer from eating disorders.

● Interactionist sociologists, such as Stanley Cohen (1980) and Jock Young (1981), have pointed to the influence of the media in the creation of moral panics which increase social anxiety and fear among the general population and have even led to changes in social policy and the law (see Topic 3, pp. 162–5).

- Some sociologists have focused on the power of advertising and how it may have an instant effect on the sales of a product, especially if it is promoted by a popular celebrity. A great deal of concern has recently been expressed at advertisements aimed at children which result in 'pester power' and pressure on parents to 'buy' their children's love.
- Feminist critics of the media have focused on the subtle effects of media representations of masculinity and femininity. As Gunter (2008) has noted:

  ≪ *Exposure to individual advertisements showing men promoting cars, and women promoting washing-up liquids might not be regarded as particularly noteworthy. However, repeated over time, such depictions could cultivate the idea that decisions about cars are the preserve of men and decisions about washing-up liquids are best taken by women.* ≫ (p.7)

- Some sociologists, e.g. Norris (1999), claim that media coverage of political issues can influence voting behaviour.
- Some early Marxist commentators, particularly those belonging to the Frankfurt School, such as Marcuse (1964), believed that the media transmitted a 'mass culture' which was directly injected into the hearts and minds of the population making them more vulnerable to ruling-class propaganda. More contemporary Marxists suggest that the way the media is organized and operates in capitalist societies may be influencing sections of the population to believe in cultural values that are a reflection of ruling-class ideology. They argue that media representations of women, ethnic minorities, homosexuality, young people, the elderly, the mentally ill and the disabled may also be creating and reinforcing negative stereotypes of these groups and others.

As we can see, the media effects debate is both complex and crowded. However, this topic intends to focus on two important aspects of this debate:

1 We need to distinguish between effects on *behaviour* and effects on *attitudes*. As we shall see, it is the former that is the most controversial and contested part of the media **effects approach**.
2 The claims that the media have an effect upon its audiences can also be divided into those who assume audiences are passive, **homogeneous** and vulnerable, and those who see audiences as actively interacting with the media and hence evolving into citizens who use media content in a responsible fashion to help them make choices about their identities and lifestyles.

The hypodermic model of media violence

This model believes that a direct **correlation** exists between the violence and antisocial behaviour portrayed in films, on television, in computer games, in rap lyrics, etc., and violence and antisocial behaviour such as drug use and teenage gun/knife crime found in real life. The model suggests that children and teenagers are vulnerable to

In 1993, the tabloid press claimed that watching *Child's Play 3* caused two 10-year-old boys to murder a toddler when there was no evidence that they had even seen it. Why do you think papers like the *Sun* and *Daily Mirror* have taken this view?

media content because they are still in the early stages of socialization and therefore very impressionable. Consequently, they are seen to be in need of protection from this powerful secondary agency of socialization. Believers in this **hypodermic syringe model** point to a number of films which they claim have resulted in young people using extreme violence. The most notorious examples cited in recent years are the Columbine High School massacre and the killing of the Liverpool toddler James Bulger by two young boys.

In April 1999, two students took guns and bombs into their school – Columbine in Colorado – and killed 13 people. A number of media influences have been cited by supporters of the hypodermic syringe model as being primarily responsible for the boys' actions such as playing the computer game *Doom,* listening to the 'violent' lyrics of Marilyn Manson and watching violent videos, most notably *The Basketball Diaries.*

On the 12 February 1993, two 10-year-old boys abducted toddler James Bulger from a shopping mall in Liverpool. They tortured and killed him, according to the tabloid press, by mimicking scenes from a video – *Child's Play 3.* Later that year, the judge, in sentencing the boys, speculated on the significant role that violent videos had played in influencing the boys, although he made no specific reference to *Child's Play 3.* However, tabloid newspapers, particularly the *Sun,* led an emotional campaign to get *Child's Play 3* and other violent films (dubbed 'video nasties') banned. This has been presented by followers of the hypodermic syringe model as a straightforward illustration of the relationship between screen violence and violence in real life. However, the facts are not that simple. The police investigation team stated that there was no evidence at all that either of James's killers had seen *Child's Play 3* or that they had been copying particular scenes. At best, the 'evidence' is speculative.

Imitation or copycat violence

Early studies of the relationship between the media and violence focused on conducting experiments in laboratories. For example, Bandura *et al.* (1963) looked for a direct cause-and-effect relationship between media content and violence. They showed three groups of children real, film and cartoon examples of a self-righting doll ('bobo doll') being attacked with mallets, whilst a fourth group saw no violent activity. After being introduced to a room full of exciting toys, the children in each group were made to feel frustrated by being told that the toys were not for them. They were then led to another room containing a bobo doll, where they were observed through a one-way mirror. The three groups who had been shown the violent activity – whether real, film or cartoon – all behaved more aggressively than the fourth group. On the basis of this experiment, Bandura and colleagues concluded that violent media content could lead to imitation or '**copycat' violence**.

In a similar vein, McCabe and Martin (2005) argued that imitation was a likely outcome of media violence, because the latter is portrayed as an heroic problem-solving exercise that not only goes unpunished but also brings rewards to its perpetrators. Consequently, it is argued that such media violence has a '**disinhibition effect'** – it convinces children that in some social situations, the 'normal' rules that govern conflict and difference can be suspended, i.e. discussion and negotiation can be replaced with violence.

Desensitization

The most influential hypodermic syringe commentator in recent years has been the psychologist, Elizabeth Newson, who, as a consequence of the murder of James Bulger, was commissioned to investigate the effect of violent films and videos. She concluded that sadistic images in films were too easily available and that films too easily encouraged viewers to identify with violent perpetrators rather than victims (Newson 1994). Moreover, she noted that children and teenagers are subjected to thousands of killings and acts of violence as they grow up through viewing television and films. She suggested that such prolonged exposure to media violence may have a 'drip-drip' effect on young people over the course of their childhood and result in their becoming **desensitized** to violence – they become socialized into accepting violent behaviour as normal, especially as a problem-solving device. She concluded that, because of this, the latest generation of young people subscribe to weaker moral codes and are more likely to behave in more antisocial ways than previous generations.

Censorship

Newson's conclusions had a great impact on society and politicians. Her report led directly to increased censorship of the film industry with the passing of the Video Recordings (Labelling) Act 1985, which resulted in videos and DVDs being given British Board of Film Classification (BBFC) age certificates. The BBFC also came under increasing pressure to censor films released to UK cinemas by insisting on the film-makers making cuts relating to bad language, scenes of drug use and violence.

Television too was affected by this climate of censorship. All the television channels agreed on a nine o'clock watershed, i.e. not to show any programmes that used bad language or contained scenes of a sexual or violent nature before this time. Television channels often resorted to issuing warnings before films and even edited out violence themselves or beeped over bad language.

This assumption among the political elite that violent movie content can affect people in real life continues into the 21st century. For example:

- In 2006, an advertising campaign for a film starring the American rapper 50 Cent was criticized for glamorizing gun crime.
- In 2007, the government launched a review of the impact of media violence on children, with the emphasis on the supposedly excessive violence and graphic sexual images found on children's television, on the internet and in computer games such as Grand Theft Auto.
- In 2008, an Ofcom survey of children added to this debate by reporting that two-thirds of their sample of children aged 12 to 15 years claimed that violence in computer games had more impact on their behaviour than violence in film or on television.

A feminist perspective on the hypodermic syringe model

Some feminists see a direct causal link between pornography and sexual violence in real life. Morgan (1980) for example, suggests that 'pornography is the theory, rape is the practice', whereas Dworkin (1990) suggests that pornography trivializes rape and makes men 'increasingly callous to cruelty, to infliction of pain, to violence against persons, to abuse of women' (p.205). Studies by others show that exposure to X-rated material makes both men and women less satisfied with their partners, less supportive of marriage, more interested in emotionless sex, and more accepting of female servitude.

However, there is also evidence that suggests that pornography can be a positive influence on behaviour. For example, a study conducted by Hald in Denmark (2007) concluded that men and women generally considered pornography a positive influence in their lives. They credited it with improving their sex lives, their sexual knowledge, their attitudes toward the opposite gender, and even their general quality of life. Malamuth's American study (1984) found that in certain people who were already inclined to be sexually aggressive, pornography worsened their attitudes and actions towards women. However, for the majority of men, Malamuth found no negative effects.

Critique of the hypodermic syringe model

A number of critiques have developed of the imitation–desensitization model of media effects.

Preventing real-life violence

Some media sociologists claim that media violence can actually prevent real-life violence:

- **Catharsis** – Fesbach and Sanger (1971) found that screen violence can actually provide a safe outlet for people's aggressive tendencies. This is known as catharsis. They looked at the effects of violent TV on teenagers. A large sample of boys from both private schools and residential homes were fed a diet of TV for six weeks. Some groups could only watch aggressive programmes, whilst others were made to watch non-aggressive programmes. The observers noted at the end of the study that the groups who had seen only aggressive programmes were actually less aggressive in their behaviour than the others. It was suggested by Fesbach and Sanger that media violence had had a cathartic effect – watching an exciting film releases aggressive energy into safe outlets as the viewers immerse themselves in the action.

- **Sensitization** – Similarly some media sociologists, such as Jock Young (1981), argue that seeing the effects of violence – and especially the pain and suffering that it causes to the victim and their families – may make us more aware of its consequences and so less inclined to commit violent acts. When filmed in a certain way, (i.e. ever more graphically), violent scenes can be so shocking as to put people off violence. Sensitization to certain crimes therefore may make people more aware and responsible so that they avoid getting involved in violence.

Methodology

The methodology of hypodermic syringe studies, such as Bandura's, have been questioned.

- Gauntlett (2008) notes that most effects studies have been conducted in the artificial context of the laboratory. He argues that this makes their findings questionable because people, especially children, do not behave as naturally under laboratory conditions as they would do in their everyday environment. For example, children's media habits are generally influenced and controlled by parents, especially when they are very young.
- Such studies are not clear how 'violence' should be defined. There exist a number of different types – cartoons; authentic violence as seen in images of war and death on news bulletins; sporting violence, such as boxing, and fictional violence. Moreover, it is often unclear in media effects studies whether these different types of violence have the same or different effects upon their audiences or whether different audiences react differently to different types and levels of violence. The effects model has been criticized because it tends to be selective in its approach to media violence, i.e. it only really focuses on particular types of fictional violence.
- The effects model fails to put violence into context – for example, it views all violence as wrong, however trivial, and fails to see that audiences interpret it according to narrative context. This point is supported by Morrison (1999) who showed a range of clips – including scenes from *Brookside*, news

footage, and excerpts from violent films – to groups of women, young men, and war veterans. All of the interviewees felt that the most violent and disturbing clip was a man beating his wife in *Ladybird, Ladybird*, a film by Ken Loach. It caused distress because of the realism of the setting, the strong language, the perceived unfairness, and also because viewers were concerned about the effect on the child actors in the scene. By contrast, a clip from *Pulp Fiction* – in which a man is killed out of the blue during an innocent conversation, spraying blood and chunks of brain around a car – was seen as 'humorous' and 'not violent', even by women over the age of 60, because there was lighthearted dialogue. Morrison's research, therefore, suggests that the context in which screen violence occurs affects its impact on the audience.

- Many hypodermic syringe model studies tackle social problems like violence backwards. For example, Belson (1978) showed violent teenagers violent videos and claimed that, because they reacted positively to them, this type of viewing had obviously caused the violence in the first place. Gauntlett points out that such studies merely tell us about the viewing preferences of teenage boys rather than the effects of such habits on their behaviour.

Children as sophisticated media users

Some sociologists believe that people, and particularly children, are not as vulnerable as the hypodermic syringe model implies. For example, research indicates that most children can distinguish between fictional/cartoon violence and real violence from a very early age, and generally know that it should not be imitated. Two research studies illustrate this criticism:

- Buckingham (1993) looked at how children interpret media violence. His findings illustrated that children are much more sophisticated in their understanding of media content and much more **media literate** than previous researchers have assumed, e.g. Buckingham's sample could clearly differentiate between fictional violence and real violence.

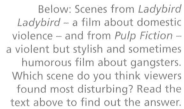

Below: Scenes from *Ladybird Ladybird* – a film about domestic violence – and from *Pulp Fiction* – a violent but stylish and sometimes humorous film about gangsters. Which scene do you think viewers found most disturbing? Read the text above to find out the answer.

- Julian Wood (1993) conducted a small-scale study of boys' use of video. He attended an after-school showing of a horror video in the home of one of the boys whilst the boy's parents were away. Wood describes the boys' comments in detail, and is able to demonstrate that, in this situation, the horror film is used almost as a rite of passage. The boys can prove their heterosexuality to each other, behave in a macho way, swear and, above all, demonstrate their fearlessness. He concludes that this notion of 'terror as pleasure' is not a corrupting influence. Rather, the violence of horror films is merely a part of growing up.

Audiences are not homogeneous

Sociologists are generally very critical of this model because they believe that it fails to recognize that audiences are not homogeneous – they have very different social characteristics in terms of age, maturity, social class, education, family background, parental controls, etc. These characteristics will influence how people respond to and use media content. Active audience research suggests that, because of these characteristics, the audience have a much more active relationship with the media than the hypodermic syringe model assumes. It also suggests that audiences are not the cultural dopes that the hypodermic syringe model makes them out to be.

Scapegoating the media

The hypodermic syringe model focuses almost entirely on media content as the scapegoat for society's ills; it fails to account for other social and psychological factors that may be causing violent or antisocial behaviour, such as peer-group influences, drugs, childhood trauma or mental illness. As Michael Moore points out in his documentary film *Bowling for Columbine*, blaming one cause – the media – for the Columbine massacre makes as much sense as blaming bowling, which both the killers were very keen on!

Conclusions about the hypodermic syringe model

Overall, the evidence claimed for the hypodermic syringe model is really quite weak. For example, most of the studies that have looked at how children are affected when television first arrives in a society have found little change. The last study was in St Helena, a British Colony in the South Atlantic Ocean, which received television for the first time in 1995. Before-and-after studies showed no change in children's social behaviour (Charlton *et al.* 2000).

Guy Cumberbatch (2004) looked at over 3500 research studies into the effects of screen violence, encompassing film, TV, video and more recently, computer and video games. He concluded that:

<< If one conclusion is possible, it is that the jury is still not out. It's never been in. Media violence has been subjected to a lynch mob mentality with almost any evidence used to prove guilt. >>

In other words, there is still *no* conclusive evidence either way that violence shown in the media influences or changes people's behaviour.

Active audience approaches

Active audience approaches see the media as far less influential. They believe that people have considerable choice in the way they use and interpret the media. There are various versions of this view, outlined below.

The two-step flow model

Katz and Lazarsfeld (1965) suggest that personal relationships and conversations with significant others, such as family members, friends, teachers and work colleagues, result in people modifying or rejecting media messages. They argue that social networks are usually dominated by 'opinion leaders', i.e. people of influence whom others in the network look up to and listen to. These people usually have strong ideas about a range of matters. Moreover, these opinion leaders expose themselves to different types of media – newspapers, television news, documentaries, soap operas, etc. – and form an opinion on their content. These interpretations are then passed on to other members of their social circle. Katz and Lazarsfeld suggest that media messages have to go through two steps or stages:

1 The opinion leader is exposed to the media content.
2 Those who respect the opinion leader internalize their interpretation of that content.

Consequently, media audiences are not directly influenced by the media. Rather, they choose to adopt a particular opinion, attitude and way of behaving after negotiation and discussion with an opinion leader. The audience is, therefore, not passive, but active.

However, critics of this model point out two problems:

1 There is no guarantee that the opinion leader has not been subjected to an imitative or desensitizing effect; for example, a leader of a peer group such as a street gang might convince other members that violence is acceptable because he has been exposed to computer games that strongly transmit the message that violence is an acceptable problem-solving strategy.
2 People who may be most at risk of being influenced by the media may be socially isolated individuals who are not members of any social network and so do not have access to an opinion leader who might help interpret media content in a healthy way.

The selective filter model

In his **selective filter model**, Klapper (1960) suggests that, for a media message to have any effect, it must pass through the following three filters:

1 **Selective exposure** – The audience must choose to view, read or listen to the content of specific media. Media messages can have no effect if no one sees or hears them! However, what the audience chooses depends upon their interests, education, work commitments and so on. Hollywood makes specific types of genre film with this in mind – most horror movies are aimed at a teenage audience. Moreover, the BBFC certificate system prevents the access of some audiences to specific types of media content.

2 Selective perception – The audience may not accept the message; some people may take notice of some media content, but decide to reject or ignore others. For example, a heavy smoker may choose to ignore the content of a television programme that stresses the link between smoking and lung cancer. Festinger (1957) argues that people will only seek out information that confirms their existing attitudes and view of the world.

3 Selective retention – The messages have to 'stick' in the mind of those who have accessed the media content. However, research indicates that most people have a tendency to remember only the things they broadly agree with. Berry's (1986) research into knowledgeable, well-motivated, grammar-school sixth formers, found that they only retained 60 per cent of the news information that they were tested on minutes after viewing. Postman (1986) argued that we now live in a 'three-minute culture', i.e. the attention span of the average member of society is only three minutes or less!

Klapper therefore suggests that these three filters involve a degree of active choice on behalf of the audience.

The uses and gratifications model

Blumler and McQuail (1968) and Lull (1995) see media audiences as active; their **uses and gratifications model** suggests that people use the media in order to satisfy particular needs that they have. Blumler and McQuail argue that these needs may be biological, psychological or social. Moreover, these needs are relative – the way the audience use the media to gratify its needs will depend upon influences such as social position, age, gender, ethnicity and so on. For example, Wood (1993) illustrated how teenagers may use horror films to gratify their need for excitement.

Blumler and McQuail identify four basic needs which people use television to satisfy:

1 *Diversion* – As Watson (2008) notes, 'we may use the media to escape from routines, to get out from under problems, to ease worries or tensions'. People may immerse themselves in particular types of media to make up for the lack of satisfaction at work or in their daily lives. For example, women may compensate for the lack of romance in their marriages by reading Mills and Boon romantic novels. Some people even live alternative lives and identities as avatars on websites such as Second Life. With regard to soap opera characters, Watson notes:

<< *These people have become our friends and neighbours. If not friends, they are our companions. What is more, they are our friends' and companions' friends and companions. We go to college or to work, and the topic of conversation may well be what has happened in last night's soap. If you are not a fan you may find yourself an outsider in the dominant social communication of the day.* >> (p.74)

It could be argued today that reality shows such as *Big Brother* may be gratifying similar needs.

2 *Personal relationships* – Watson notes that we often know more about characters in soap operas than we do our own neighbours. The media may, therefore,

Sociology A2 for AQA

Focus on research

Andrea Millwood Hargrave (2003) How children interpret screen violence

Millwood Hargrave found that children (aged 9 to 13) could clearly distinguish between fictional violence and violence that is 'real'. They made clear judgements about the justified use of violence, and this could affect how 'violent' an image was perceived to be in the first place. This research found no evidence of confusion in children's minds between fictional and real-life violence. The children also proved to be very sensitive to cues provided by production techniques: they responded to changes in music, aural cues and visual images to build expectations of how violent a scene might be. Crucially, expectations of violence in various programme genres were clearly differentiated: dramas and soaps were recognized as fictional representations of the 'real' world, while the news was known to be 'real' and always treated seriously. Similarly, clear distinctions were made between cartoon-like film violence – even if the characters were played by actors rather than animated – and film violence that shows human emotions and pain, even though it may be set within a fantastical storyline.

Adapted from Buckingham, D. (2004) *The Media Literacy of Young People: A review of the research literature*, London: Ofcom

Why might the findings of this research reassure those concerned about the effects of media violence on children?

---

provide the means to compensate for the decline of community in our lives. For example, socially isolated elderly people may see soap opera characters as companions they can identify with and worry about in the absence of interaction with family members. Cybercommunities on the web may also be seen by users as alternative families.

3 *Personal identity* – People may use the media to 'make over' or to modify their identity. For example, a teenager who suspects he is gay may use the experience of a gay character in a teenage soap opera such as *Hollyoaks* or *Skins* to help them make decisions about how they might deal with their own sexuality. Sites like Facebook, MySpace and Bebo allow people to use the media to present their particular identities to the wider world in a way that they can control.

4 *Surveillance* – People use the media to obtain information and news about the social world in order to help them make up their minds on particular issues. In recent years, the gratification of this need is increasingly taking on an interactive quality with the growing popularity of online blogging and websites to which people can add their own knowledge, e.g. Wikipedia.

Lull (1995) carried out a participant observation study of families' use of television and agreed with Blumler and McQuail that the audience actively uses the media in a social way. He noted five uses of the media:

1 *Relational* – The media is used as a currency of communication, i.e. it gives people, especially families, something to talk to each other about. This may compensate for the fact that many families no longer sit down together for dinner.
2 *Affiliation* – Television may reinforce family community as some families, parents and children, sit down to watch a popular show that transcends age differences together.
3 *Avoidance* – People may use television to escape from others.
4 *Social learning* – People may use the media to solve problems, to seek guidance, to access information and learning, and to find role models.
5 *Competence dominance* – Members of families, usually the father, may demonstrate their power by controlling the family's access to television – for example, by taking charge of the remote control. An unqualified family member may also gain intellectual validation and status by watching quiz shows and impressing other family members and friends by successfully answering the questions.

However, Watson notes the trend towards children possessing their own privatized new-media technology within the confines of their bedrooms, e.g. iPods, DVD and CD players, televisions, personal computers, access to the internet, mobile phones and games consoles. He argues that this trend may lead to the obsolescence of those social needs relating to social interaction and community because the availability of such gadgets probably means less communication and interaction between family members. The young may see these new forms of media communication as lessening the need for face-to-face forms of communication. A good example of this is the fact that Facebook members do not have to meet someone in person to be their friend.

Marxists are critical of this model because they suggest that needs may be socially manufactured by the media. Marxists argue that the mass media in capitalist societies, especially the advertising industry, promotes the ideology that consumption and materialism are positive goals to pursue. This may mean that people mistake 'false needs' for personal or social needs. The concept of false needs refers to an outcome of media that convinces people that a consumer item is vital to their social wellbeing. For example, people may be persuaded to wear particular brands or logos because these will supposedly make them feel better about themselves.

The reception analysis model

This view suggests that the way people interpret media content differs according to their class, age, gender, ethnic group and other sources of identity. Sociologists who subscribe to this model are interested in analyzing how different groups interpret media content. The **reception analysis model**, therefore, suggests that media content is interpreted in a variety of ways.

Morley's (1980) research into how audiences interpreted the content of a well-known 1970s evening news programme called *Nationwide* examined how the ideological content of the programme (i.e. the messages that were contained in the text and images) were interpreted by 29 groups made up of people from a range of educational and professional backgrounds. Members of these groups were subjected to an in-depth interview in order to see how they had decoded the messages they had received, to see whether they accepted such messages or whether they had modified or rejected *Nationwide's* version (i.e. the preferred reading which media professionals subscribed to) of events and issues relating to strike action taken by a group of workers.

Morley found that audiences were far from passive in their reading of media content; instead, audiences made up their own minds, and there was significant opposition to the views contained in the news programme, both between groups with common characteristics and between people within those groups. Even when the sample agreed with the ideological position of the programme, this was not a result of a blind acceptance that journalists are objective pursuers of truth – rather their acceptance was more to do with personal knowledge and experience.

The reception analysis model concluded that people choose to make one of three readings or interpretations of media content:

1 **Preferred (or dominant) reading** – This is a reading of media content that is based on consensus, i.e. that most people are likely to go along with it because the subject matter is widely accepted as legitimate. For example, the British people generally approve of the Royal Family, so very few people are likely to interpret stories about them in a critical fashion. The dominant reading is also very likely to be shared by journalists and editors, and is likely to underpin news values.
2 **Oppositional reading** – A minority may oppose the views expressed in media content. For example, people who are anti-monarchy or Republicans may be critical of stories about Royal celebrities.
3 **Negotiated reading** – The media audience may reinterpret media content to fit in with their own opinions and values. For example, they may not have any strong views on the Royal Family but enjoy reading about celebrity lives.

Morley suggests all three interpretations or readings of media content can be generated within one social group. For example, let's say the news contains a report about the Glastonbury Festival, focusing on arrests for drug use. A preferred (or dominant) reading might be that young people cannot enjoy themselves without breaking the law. An oppositional reading might be that the police or the media focus on drug-related crime unnecessarily. After all, a few arrests are nothing, considering the thousands who attend. A negotiated reading might be that there is probably a lot of drug use among young people, but that it is mostly cannabis use, which should, in the viewer's opinion, be legalized anyway.

Morley argues that the average person belongs to several subcultural groups and this may complicate a person's reading of media content in the sense that they may not be consistent in their interpretation of it. For example, a young British Jewish person may respond to the Israeli–Palestinian problem in a number of ways:

- As a socially aware, educated person, they may feel that the Palestinians have not been given a fair deal by the Israelis.
- As a British person, they may feel that this conflict has very little impact on them.
- As a Jewish person, they may feel a strong sense of identification with Israel.
- As a young person, they may feel that politics is fairly boring and consequently not show much interest.

These subcultural characteristics are not predictable in the way they influence responses to media content – for example, belonging to a Jewish subculture does not bring about automatic identification with media stories sympathetic to Israel.

The point of reception analysis theory is to suggest that audiences are not passive, impressionable and homogeneous. They act in a variety of subcultural ways and, for this reason, media content is '**polysemic**', i.e. it attracts more than one type of reading or interpretation.

However, Morley did concede that his research could have been compromised by the fact that his sample did not see the *Nationwide* programme in their natural environment. The investigation into the response of the audience to media messages should have been conducted where the audience normally watches television, i.e. in the home, in the company of family members or flatmates.

The cultural effects model

The Marxist **cultural effects model** sees the media as a very powerful ideological influence that is mainly concerned with transmitting capitalist values and norms. There is disagreement about why this process occurs. As we saw in Topic 3, some suggest it is because of the influence of media owners, some suggest that it is due to capitalist market conditions in which the imperative is to make profit, whilst others suggest that it is an accidental byproduct of the social and educational backgrounds of most journalists, who are happy to subscribe to a consensus view of the world.

In its focus on audiences, the cultural effects model, like the reception analysis model, recognizes that the media audience is made up of very different types of people from a variety of social backgrounds who have had very different experiences. This means that they interpret what they see, read and hear in many different ways. For example, a programme about life in an inner-London borough may be interpreted as evidence of racial conflict and deprivation, or as evidence of interesting cultural diversity, depending on who is doing the watching.

However, Marxist cultural effects theory argues that media content contains strong ideological messages that reflect the values of those who own, control and produce the media, whether they be newspapers, magazines, television, pop music or film. Consequently, media

producers expect audiences (who often lack direct experience of an issue) to interpret media content in a particular way, i.e. to agree with their own preferred reading.

The cultural effects model argues that media coverage of particular issues results in most people coming to believe that media perspectives on particular issues are correct – and that these perspectives reflect a consensus perspective that generally fails to challenge or actually reinforces ruling-class ideology. For example, media coverage of unemployment and single-parent families gives the general impression that these situations are often the result of choice and so the claiming of benefits by these groups is probably unjustified. This leads to many people seeing claiming benefits as a form of scrounging. There is evidence that many elderly people are taken in by this media portrayal and that, as a result, they do not claim the benefits that they are rightfully entitled to.

Marxists believe that audiences have been exposed over a long period of time to a 'drip-drip' effect process in which media content has become imbued with ideological values. Cultural effects theory believes that television content, in particular, has been deliberately dumbed down and this has resulted in a decline of serious programmes such as news, documentaries and drama that might made audiences think critically about the state of the world. Instead, reality shows such as *Big Brother* abound, celebrating celebrity, consumption and dubious forms of behaviour.

Curran (2003) argues that the popular tabloid newspapers are also guilty of these ideological practices. He notes that ideological values are embedded in the entertainment features of the tabloid newspaper industry. He notes:

>> *Above all, its greatly enlarged human interest and entertainment content tends to portray tacitly society as a structure of individuals, explain events in individual terms, and to offer individual-moral rather than collective solutions to problems. The press's support for a conservative, 'common-sense' view of the world may have contributed more towards maintaining an inegalitarian and social order than its explicitly political content.* >> (p.103)

Marxists argue that the long-term effect of the preferred reading of media content is that the values of the rich and powerful come to be unconsciously shared by most people – people come to believe in values such as 'happiness is about possessions and money', 'you must look like the models in magazines', 'most asylum seekers are just illegal immigrants', 'black people are potential criminals', 'being a celebrity is really important', etc.

However, it is important to understand that the cultural effects model does not simply suggest that the media is a brainwashing apparatus. Instead it suggests that some media content helps those who manage (and benefit from) capitalist society to obtain the active consent of the majority (who do not particularly benefit from the organization of capitalist society). The cultural effects model recognizes that audiences interpret media messages in different ways but within certain confined limits. As Curran notes above, the frequent reading of particular newspapers means the immersion of the reader into a

Key themes

Socialization, culture and identity

Structure and action

The idea that the media can have a direct effect on the behaviour of its audience is based on an assumption that individuals are the products of the various agencies of socialization that mould their personalities. This kind of structural approach has been criticized by social action theorists, who point out that individuals are active in constructing their 'selves'. People interpret what is going on around them and base their behaviour on these interpretations. As Anthony Giddens (2006) puts it:

>> *Socialization is not a kind of cultural programming in which the child absorbs passively the influences with which he or she comes into contact. Even the most recent newborn infant has needs and demands that affect the behaviour of those responsible for its care: the child is from the beginning an active being.* >>

The 'hypodermic syringe model' of media effects has its origins in structural approaches, while 'active audience' approaches are more associated with social action theory.

---

particular ideological way of seeing and interpreting the world. Consequently, it is argued that this view of the world is bound to affect the reader, who may come to see such ideology as common sense or as a product of their own choices. Cultural effects theory argues that most types of media probably have these ideological effects in the long term.

GUMG research

Research by the Glasgow University Media Group (GUMG) suggests that varied audience groups do have a very clear understanding of the intended ideological message found in media content and a section of that audience often accurately reproduce it in terms of their own attitudes. The GUMG's research into public perceptions of the 1984/5 miners' strike involved giving small groups of people press photographs and asking them to write their own news story. They were then questioned about what they believed about the strike. There were a number of findings:

- The sample quickly recognized the ideological messages contained in the photographs that the strike was violent and that the miners were to blame.
- People who were sympathetic to the miners' cause were weakened in their support by what they saw on the news.
- The majority of the sample who had not directly experienced the strike interpreted it as violent and illegitimate.
- However, some members of the audience rejected the ideological message (although these tended to be in the minority).

Philo (2001), who conducted the research, notes that this version of cultural effects theory shows that, if there is no

direct experience or other knowledge of a particular issue, the ideological power of the media message will be strong and likely to shape an individual's view of the social world. However, alternative sources of knowledge based on direct experience were sometimes used by audiences to evaluate and counter the media message (although they can also be used to justify the acceptance of them). The main point made by Philo and the GUMG is that the cultural effects model needs to be dynamic – internalization or rejection of media messages needs to be understood as a product of the relationship between changing media messages and personal experience.

Criticism of the cultural effects model

However, in criticism of the cultural effects model, it has to be said that these 'cause' and 'effects' are very difficult to operationalize and measure. It also suggests that Marxists are the only ones who can see the 'true' ideological interpretation of media content, which implies that the rest of us are 'cultural dopes'. Pluralists too question the idea that the views of the capitalist elite make up the main constituents of that ideology – they argue that this underestimates the role of professional and objective journalism in constructing media content.

The postmodernist model

Early postmodernists, such as Strinati (1995), have argued that postmodern societies are 'media saturated' and this is having a significant effect upon people's sense of identity. Members of postmodern societies now have a greater range of choices in shaping their identities compared with the past, when identities were mainly shaped by structural forces such as social class. Postmodernists argue that the media today are the main shapers of identity and offer a greater range of consumption choices in terms of identities and lifestyles, informing people how they should dress and look, how they should organize their homes and gardens, what they should think and feel, and so on. Postmodernists argue that a variety of media – lifestyle magazines, television documentaries, advertising, etc. – can advise members of society on how they can alter or 'make over' their bodies, relationships, lives, etc.

Moreover, in the postmodern world, the media transmit the idea that the consumption of signs and symbols for their own sake is more important than the goods they represent. In other words, the media encourage the consumption of logos, designer labels and brands, and these become more important to people's sense of identity than the physical clothes and goods themselves. In other words, people are no longer judged on the basis of ability, skill or personality, but on how 'cool' they look or behave.

The media and globalization

Other postmodernists have examined the effects of the media on globalization and how this in turn has affected local cultures. Thompson (1995) has noted that, in the last ten years, the globalization of communication has become more intensive and extensive, and this has had great significance for local cultures, in that all consumers of the global media are both citizens of the world and of their locality. He argues that such global communication is often domesticated by local cultures to create a hybridized media culture that makes sense within our local communities. Lull (1995), who studied the impact of television in China, notes how television opened up localized ways of thinking and seeing the world and made available new perspectives, lifestyles and ways of thinking and responding to the world. Seeing other global experience allows people to think critically about their own place in the world.

However, Thompson notes that the interaction between global media and local cultures can also create tensions and hostilities. For example, the Chinese authorities have attempted to control and limit the contact that the Chinese people have with global media, whilst some Islamic commentators have used global media to convince their local populations of the view that Western culture is decadent and corrupt.

Postmodernism and reception analysis

Later postmodern perspectives on media content are essentially an extension of reception analysis. Whereas the reception analysis model focuses on how there exist subcultural differences in how audiences might respond to media messages, the postmodern model focuses on how individual members of audiences create their own meanings from a **media text**. As Philo (2001) argues, postmodernists see media content as producing one particular definition of reality, which has the same degree of importance as any other definition of reality.

Moreover, these interpretations of media reality are constantly changing and being modified. They are not fixed. Philo notes that postmodernists argue that:

>> *All definitions of reality are just that – mere definitions which are constantly changing with each new interpretation of what is real or what has occurred. There is, therefore, no 'fixed' way of describing anything – it all depends on what is seen and who is describing it. There is no way of saying that reality is distorted by media images since there is no fixed reality or truth to distort. It is all relative to who is looking; 'truth' and 'reality' are in the eye of the beholder.* >> (p.27)

In other words, rather than seeing the audience as an undifferentiated mass, or as divided into cultural or other groupings, postmodernists argue that generalizations about media effects and audiences are impossible, since the same person may react to the same media message in different ways in different situations.

Conclusions

All of these 'active audience' approaches see the audience as interpreting media messages for themselves and, consequently, this makes it difficult to generalize about the effects of the media. What is apparent is that the media does have the potential power to influence public belief, but the role of audiences in interpreting and modifying media messages cannot be underestimated.

Check your understanding

1 Identify and explain three concerns sociologists have expressed about the effects of the mass media.

2 Explain why the model of media effects described on p. 168 is known as the 'hypodermic syringe model'.

3 In your own words, explain three criticisms of the hypodermic syringe model.

4 What are the 'two steps' in the 'two-step flow' model?

5 In your own words, explain the key ideas of the 'uses and gratifications' model.

6 Give your own example to illustrate Morley's three readings of media content.

7 Give one example of a sociologist who subscribes to cultural effects theory and explain their work.

8 How can the cultural effects model be criticized?

9 According to postmodernists, what has been the effect of the media on globalization?

10 Explain what Philo means by the sentence: 'There is no way of saying that reality is distorted by media images since there is no fixed reality or truth to distort.'

Activities

Research idea

Conduct a content analysis of part of one evening's TV programmes on any one major terrestrial channel. Add up the number of times acts of violence are depicted. After noting down each act of violence, explain the type of programme (e.g. news, cartoon, drama) and the type of violence (e.g. real, humorous).

What do your results tell you about the amount and type of violence on television?

Web.tasks

1 Watch Gerbner talk about violence in the media at http://uk.youtube.com/watch?v=2PHxTr-59hE&feature=related

To what extent do you agree with the views expressed?

2 There is a great deal of concern about lack of regulation of the internet. Search the web using the key words 'internet' and 'censorship' to find out the arguments for and against regulation.

3 Read David's Gauntlett's assessment of the 'effects model' at www.theory.org.uk/effects.htm

Key terms

Active audience approaches theories that stress that the effects of the media are limited because people are not easily influenced.

Catharsis the process of relieving tensions – for example, violence on screen providing a safe outlet for people's violent tendencies.

'Copycat' violence violence that occurs as a result of copying something that is seen in the media.

Correlation a relationship between two or more things, where one characteristic is directly affected by another.

Cultural effects model the view that the media are powerful in so far as they link up with other agents of socialization to encourage particular ways of making sense of the world.

Desensitization the process by which, through repeated exposure to media violence, people come to accept violent behaviour as normal.

Disinhibition effect effect of media violence, whereby people become convinced that in some social situations, the 'normal' rules that govern conflict and difference, i.e. discussion and negotiation, can be replaced with violence.

Effects approach an approach based on the hypodermic syringe model which believes that the media have direct effects on their audience.

Homogeneous the same throughout, undifferentiated.

Hypodermic syringe model the view that the media are very powerful and the audience very weak. The media can 'inject' their messages into the audience, who accept them uncritically.

Media literate an intelligent, critical and informed attitude to the media.

Media text any media output – written, aural or visual, e.g. magazine article, photo, CD, film, TV or radio programme.

Negotiated reading an interpretation of a media text that modifies the intended (preferred) reading so that it fits with the audience member's own views.

Oppositional reading an interpretation of a media text that rejects its intended (preferred) reading.

Polysemic attracts more than one type of reading or interpretation.

Preferred (dominant) reading the intended messages contained within the text.

Reception analysis model the view that individuals make meanings from media messages.

Selective exposure the idea that people only watch, listen or read what they want to.

Selective filter model the view that audience members only allow certain media messages through.

Selective perception the idea that people only take notice of certain media messages.

Selective retention the idea that people only remember certain media messages.

Sensitization the process of becoming more aware of the consequences of violence.

Uses and gratifications model the view that people use the media for their own purposes.

An eye on the exam — The mass media and audiences

Item A

A classic example of the powerful influence of the media was the radio broadcast in 1938 of H.G. Wells's book *The War of the Worlds*. The dramatized adaptation of an invasion of Martians into a rural area of New Jersey, USA, was so convincing that it generated mass hysteria in many American states. Significantly, though, not all of the six million listeners responded in the same way.

Research on the audience response was undertaken by Cantril (1940), who found that several factors affected the extent to which people believed the broadcast to be true. For example, listeners who had not heard the beginning of the programme were more likely to be taken in by it, and those who were not able to check out the story with neighbours, to 'reality test' it, were convinced by the broadcast and reacted accordingly. Radio news was at that time the only source of immediate knowledge about the world at large. As the programme was broadcast in the style of a news programme, listeners were more likely to treat it as real.

Adapted from Haralambos, M. (ed.) (1986) *Sociology: New Directions*, Ormskirk: Causeway Press

Using material from **Item A** and elsewhere, assess the usefulness of the hypodermic syringe model of the mass media.

(33 marks)

Grade booster — Getting top marks in this question

You should begin by giving an account of the hypodermic syringe (HS) model. This should include the idea of a strong media and weak audience, as well as the notion that the media 'inject' messages directly into audiences, who respond immediately and automatically. You should remember to make use of relevant material from the Item in your answer, such as the notion that the broadcast referred to led to instantaneous panic among some listeners. You should evaluate the HS model by reference to other views of the media, such as the cultural effects, selective filter, uses and gratifications or reception analysis or postmodern approaches, explaining how they differ from the HS view. You should also use the Item to develop some points of criticism of the HS model and relate them to other approaches where possible.

Representations of the body: gender, sexuality and disability

Getting you thinking

1. Which of these women are playing stereotypical roles? What are these roles?

2. To what extent do you think that representations of women in the media are changing? Give examples to support your answer.

Bob Connell (1995) argues that cultural expectations about gender roles in the UK in the 20th century were dominated by **hegemonic definitions** of masculinity, femininity and sexuality. These cultural ideas stressed two broad traditional ideas with regard to gender:

1. Paid work was central to men's identity and role. Men were expected to be breadwinners and heads of households responsible for the economic security of their dependants. Masculinity was perceived to be individualistic, competitive, ambitious and aggressive. Men were not expected to openly demonstrate emotion.
2. Females were culturally categorized primarily as home-makers, mothers and carers. Women were confined to a life defined by the family, the home and personal relationships. They were expected to be less rational and more emotional and neurotic than men.

Connell argues that these ideas about gender constituted a patriarchal ideology, which assumed that masculinity was

dominant and femininity was subordinate because males exercised economic, social and physical power over females. This ideology was transmitted from one generation to the next through the process of gender-role socialization that mainly occurred in the family. However, the mass media, a secondary agent of socialization, was also seen as playing a key role in teaching and reinforcing these cultural expectations about how each gender was supposed to operate in the social world. Consequently, a great deal of sociological effort and analysis has been expended in the last 30 years examining media representations of gender roles and how these contributed to the dominance of masculinity and the subordination of femininity. However, media research has also focused on how these representations may be responding to the profound economic and social changes that have occurred in the fields of education and employment, which some argue have transformed the power relationship between males and females.

Almy *et al.* (1984) argue that media representations are important because they enter 'our collective social understandings, constituting our sense of ourselves, the positions we take up in the world, and the possibilities we see for action in it' (p.19). In other words, these media representations not only stereotype masculinity and femininity into fairly limited forms of behaviour, but they also provide role models that members of each gender are encouraged to aspire to.

However, Gauntlett (2008) points out that sociological analysis of media representations need to be cautious, because of the sheer diversity of media that exist in the UK. The mass media constitute a range of audio-visual, written and new media. Moreover, media audiences are also wildly diverse. Gauntlett suggests therefore that it would be folly to assume that the ideological messages that are transmitted reflect similar perspectives on gender. Moreover, it is highly likely that, as a result of media and audience diversity, media messages about gender will be contradictory and possibly irreconcilable.

Traditional media representations of femininity

Limited roles

It is often argued by feminist sociologists that women are generally represented in a narrow range of social roles by various types of media, whilst men are shown performing a full range of social and occupational roles. Tunstall (1987) is typical of this perspective. He argues:

<< The presentation of women in the media is biased because it emphasizes women's domestic, sexual, consumer and marital activities to the exclusion of all else. Women are depicted as busy housewives, as contented mothers, as eager consumers and as sex objects. This does indeed indicate bias for family status because, although similar numbers of men are fathers and husbands, the media has much less to say about these male roles; men are seldom presented nude, nor is their marital or family status continually quoted in irrelevant contexts. Just as men's domestic and marital roles are ignored, the media also ignore that well over half of British adult women go out to paid employment, and that many of their interests and problems are employment-related.>>

Furthermore, feminist analyses often see media representations of working women as a problem in two ways:

1 They are portrayed as unfulfilled, unattractive, possibly unstable and unable to sustain relationships.
2 It is implied that working mothers are guilty of the emotional neglect of their children. Working fathers are rarely portrayed in this way.

Symbolic annihilation

Tuchman *et al.* (1978) used the term '**symbolic annihilation**' to describe the way in which women's achievements are often not reported, or are condemned or trivialized by the mass media. Often their achievements are presented as less important than their looks and sex appeal.

Women (hardly) in the news

Gallagher (1980) reviewed the portrayal of women by the media across different continents and found that the activities of women were rarely seen as newsworthy compared with the activities of men. The Global Media Monitoring Project (GMMP) published a snapshot of gender in news media on one day across 76 countries in 2005 and suggested that little has changed since Gallagher's observations. The GMMP found that women appeared in, or were the subject of British television news stories much less than men: when they did appear they were usually there as celebrities or in some kind of decorative role, and the stories they appeared in tended to be 'softer' news features, e.g. women were interviewed as consumers. There were very few stories about their professional abilities or expertise, and most press coverage continues to rely on men as experts in the fields of business, politics and economics. In 2000, the Association of Women Journalists studied news coverage of women and women's issues in 70 countries. It reported that only 18 per cent of stories quote women, and that the number of women-related stories came to barely 10 per cent of total news coverage. Moreover, Gill (2007) argues that female issues and news are often marginalized by newspapers, in that newspaper editors see the need to have 'women's pages' which focus on women as a special group with special – often emotional – needs.

Coverage of women's sport

A good example of the symbolic annihilation of women's activities is the media coverage of women's sport in newspapers and on television. Research into TV sport presentation shows that what little coverage of women's sport there is tends to sexualize, trivialize and devalue women's sporting accomplishments (Women's Sport and Fitness Foundation 2006). Evidence collected by the Bristol Fawcett Society (2008) suggests this limited coverage is still the case, even in broadsheet quality newspapers such as the *Observer*. Their analysis of the *Observer Sports Monthly* in 2008 found that 177 men were featured, compared with only 13 women.

Duncan and Messner (2005) note that commentators, (97 per cent of whom are men), use different language when they talk about female athletes. Men are described as 'big', 'strong', 'brilliant', 'gutsy' and 'aggressive', whereas women are more often referred to as 'weary', 'fatigued', 'frustrated', 'panicked', 'vulnerable' and 'choking'. Commentators are also twice as likely to call men by their last names only, and three times as likely to call women by their first names only. Furthermore, women in sports are often described as 'girls', whereas males are rarely referred to as 'boys'. Duncan and Messner argue that this reduces female athletes to the role of children, while giving adult status to white male athletes. The media also subject women in sport to the **male gaze** (see p. 180) because female athletes are increasingly photographed in hyper-sexualized poses.

Women's invisibility in the media

Another aspect of symbolic annihilation is the invisibility of women in various parts of the media. Recent studies suggest that the male-to-female ratio in speaking parts in prime-time drama is about 60/40. Even children's television is dominated by males. The Bristol Fawcett Society (2008) analysed a day's output from CBeebies and found that only 30 per cent of main characters were female, all the story narrators were male and a very clear majority of anchors and presenters were also male.

Females are also invisible in new types of media. A content analysis by Dietz (1998) of 33 popular Nintendo and Sega Genesis video games found that there were no female characters in 41 per cent of the games; in 28 per cent of them, females were portrayed as sex objects, while 21 per cent of the games portrayed women as victims of male violence. An Ofcom survey in 2008 found that boys of all ages were more likely than girls to access such games through games consoles. However, on a more positive note, the survey also concluded females were more likely to use social network internet sites that involved creative online activities, particularly those related to communicating or sharing content with other people.

Ideological ideals

Apart from television, the most popular type of media that women mainly access is women's magazines. These magazines have attracted a great deal of attention from feminist sociologists over the last 25 years, who suggest that they strongly encourage women to conform to ideological patriarchal ideals that confirm their subordinate position compared with men.

A cult of femininity?

Ferguson (1983) conducted a content analysis of women's magazines from between 1949 and 1974, and 1979 and 1980. She notes that such magazines are organized around '**a cult of femininity**', which promotes a traditional ideal where excellence is achieved through caring for others, the family, marriage and appearance. She argues that, although modern female magazines, especially those aimed at teenagers, are gradually moving away from these stereotypes, they still tend to focus narrowly on 'him, home and looking good (for him)'. Contemporary evidence suggests that not much has changed. The Bristol Fawcett Society analysed 521 covers of magazines in 2008 that featured people, and discovered that 291 (56 per cent) featured idealized images of men and women, of which 84 per cent were women. The other 44 per cent of magazine covers, which focused on subjects such as sport, politics and music, featured a mere 15 per cent of women.

However, Ferguson's ideas were challenged by Winship (1987), who argued that women's magazines generally play a supportive and positive role in the lives of women. She argues that such magazines present women with a broader range of options than ever before, and that they tackle problems that have been largely ignored by the male-dominated media, such as domestic violence and child abuse.

The sexual objectification of women

Wolf (1990) suggests that the images of women used by the media, especially the print media and advertising, present a particular '**beauty ideal**' through which they transmit the strong ideological message that women should treat their bodies as a project in constant need of improvement. Cumberbatch (2004) found that being 'attractive' fitted the description for nearly two-thirds of females featured in television advertising but only one-quarter of males. He concluded that women generally occupy a passive 'decorative' role in television advertising.

This media beauty ideal, especially when it is found in pornography, national newspapers and lads' magazines such as *Nuts*, essentially views women as **sex objects** to be consumed by what Mulvey (1975) calls the 'male gaze', whereby the camera lens essentially 'eyes up' the female characters, providing erotic pleasure for men. According to Kilbourne (1995), this media representation presents women as mannequins: tall and thin, often size zero, with very long legs, perfect teeth and hair, and skin without a blemish in sight. Kilbourne notes that this mannequin image is used to advertise cosmetics, health products and anything that works to improve the appearance of the body for the benefit of the male gaze (rather than for female self-esteem).

This beauty ideal makes an appearance in a variety of media. Mulvey notes that physical looks, sex appeal and youth seem to be necessary attributes for women to be successful in television and in the cinema. In news presentation, in particular, with its increasingly intimate mode of presentation, good-looking young women are used to improve ratings, employing at times a flirtatious relationship with their more mature male co-presenter.

Slimness = happiness?

Magazines for teenage girls also concentrate heavily on beauty and slimming. For example, content analysis of teenage magazines in the UK indicates that almost 70 per cent of the content and images focus on beauty and fashion, compared with only 12 per cent focused on education or careers.

Some media commentators, such as Orbach (1991), have suggested that such media can create anxieties in young females with regard to their body image and identity. She notes that the media, especially those magazines that focus on fashion and celebrity, as well as the tabloid newspapers, perpetuate the idea that slimness equals success, health, happiness and popularity. She accuses the media of overemphasizing this aspect of the beauty ideal and for encouraging young girls to be unhappy with their bodies. She notes that they create the potential for eating disorders in several ways:

- by constantly exhorting females to be concerned with their weight, shape, size, looks, etc.
- by using pictures of size-zero supermodels to illustrate articles
- by running features that criticize so-called 'overweight' celebrities
- through adverts encouraging dieting and cosmetic surgery.

Orbach argues that exposure to such ideal images coincides with a period in girls' lives where self-regard and self-efficacy is in decline, where body image is at its most fragile because of physical changes of puberty, and where the tendency for social comparison is at its peak.

Hamilton and Waller (1993) take a slightly different view to media effects than Orbach. They suggest that the

Do you think there is a 'causal link between media images of super-thin women and eating disorders in young women'?

media may act as a negative reinforcer of body-size overestimation – the media does not make women feel a need to be thinner *per se*, but the media focus on thinness may assist them in feeling bigger than they already feel themselves to be.

In 2003, *Teen* magazine reported that 35 per cent of girls aged 6 to 12 have been on at least one diet, and that 50 to 70 per cent of normal-weight girls believe they are overweight. Overall, research indicates that 90 per cent of women are dissatisfied with their appearance in some way. Tebbel (2000) reports that women's magazines have ten-and-a-half times more advertisements and articles promoting weight loss than men's magazines do, and over three-quarters of the covers of women's magazines include at least one message about how to change a woman's bodily appearance – by diet, exercise or cosmetic surgery. Television and cinema reinforce the importance of a thin body as a measure of a woman's worth. Fouts (1999) reports that over three-quarters of female characters in television situation comedies are underweight, and only one in 20 are above average in size.

There is no scientific proof of a direct causal link between media images of super-thin women and eating disorders in young women, but all the research points to a direct impact on teenage girls. It is a fact that in societies where there is no established media, there is no culture of thinness and eating disorders are very rare. However, there is evidence that the introduction of Western-style media has led to an increase in eating disorders in several cultures, e.g. Becker *et al.*'s (2003) study of the appearance of eating disorders in Fiji after the introduction of Western television.

Do the modern media empower women?

Gill (2008) argues that the depiction of women in advertising has changed from women as passive objects of the male gaze, to active, independent and sexually powerful agents. She examined advertisements on television, in magazines and on billboards over a ten-year period and suggests that three stereotypes of women can be seen:

1 the young physically toned and smart heterosexual who uses her sexual power to control a man
2 the vengeful heterosexual beautiful woman set on punishing her ex-lover

3 the 'hot lesbian' entwined with another beautiful woman.

However, Gill argues that, although these advertisements claim to **empower** young women, 'the toned, beautiful, heterosexual women featured in these ads come straight out of the most predictable templates of male sexual fantasy, and embody very narrow standards of female beauty and sex appeal'. In other words, the images contained in these advertisements are contradictory. She concludes:

<< *Instead of passive, 'dumb' or unintelligent sex objects, women in advertisements are now active, beautiful, smart, powerful sexual subjects. In some respects, this shift is a positive one, offering modern representations of femininity that give women power and agency, and not exclusively defining women as heterosexual. However, these limited representations of female desire in the media may also be influencing women to feel that they should fit a mould and look and act in a certain way; that they should not only be beautiful, but sexy, sexually knowledgeable and always 'up for it' – and we must question whether this is how women should be represented – and sold to.* >>

In other words, Gill agrees that there are elements of Wolf's beauty ideal in these representations, which may have the negative side-effect of encouraging ordinary women to pursue the impossible. Orbach notes that, as a result, numerous surveys indicate that a majority of young women are constantly dissatisfied with their bodies and likely to be experiencing low self-esteem.

Positive role models?

Other sociologists have noted the increasing number of positive female roles, which, they claim, are emerging especially in television drama and films. It is argued that these reflect the social and cultural changes that females have experienced in the last 25 years, especially the feminization of the economy, which has meant that women are now more likely to have careers and an independent income. Moreover, there has been a fundamental change in women's attitudes – Wilkinson (1994) calls this a 'genderquake' – which means that their aspirations have dramatically changed, with education and career replacing marriage and family as priorities.

These cultural changes started to seep into British television culture through American series such as *Sex in the City*, *Ally McBeal*, *Buffy the Vampire Slayer* and *The X-Files*. Westwood notes how many of these series subverted hegemonic definitions of gender by having female lead characters who were just as confident and powerful as the male character. She also argues that we are now seeing more 'transgressive' (i.e. going beyond gendered expectations) programming on television. Traditional gender roles are constantly being experimented with. She cites the example of *The X-Files*, in which the female character, Scully, represents the 'masculine' world of science, rationality and facts, whilst the male character, Mulder, is emotionally open and vulnerable, i.e. traits normally associated with femininity. There are signs that British television series are now well down this path –

think of the ways in which femininity was represented by the female characters in dramas such as *Dr Who, Prime Suspect* and *Gavin and Stacey.* Some cultural commentators have suggested that soap operas, such as *Coronation Street* and *Eastenders,* also promote independent and assertive female characters compared with weaker male characters. Women often use their sexuality as a source of power over men.

However, Fiske (2003) argues that despite positive changes in media representations of women, there are also contradictions reflecting those faced by women in their attempt to assert feminine values within a society where patriarchal values dominate. Soaps focus on domestic issues – the domestic setting may be regarded as the only legitimate (accepted) area for female authority in patriarchal societies. Therefore, while soap operas do portray women in a more positive way than advertising and other forms of television, they still ultimately respect and conform to hegemonic definitions of femininity. Soaps often show women as having jobs, but rarely pursing their careers, and if they do, more often than not, they are unsuccessful. Thus we can see how even a form of television programming aimed at a majority female audience contains subliminal messages reinforcing the dominant male ideology.

Gauntlett (2008), however, has drawn attention to 21st-century media aimed at young women, which, he claims, differ in character from the media of 20 years ago. He argues that magazines:

> <<are emphatic in their determination that women must do their own thing, be themselves, and/or be as outrageously sassy and sexy as possible. Several recent movies have featured self-confident, tough, intelligent female lead characters. Female pop stars sing about financial and emotional independence, inner strength, and how they don't need a man.>>

This set of media messages from a range of sources suggest that women can be tough and independent whilst 'maintaining perfect make-up and wearing impossible shoes'. He claims that surveys of young women and their lifestyles suggest that these media messages are having a positive and significant impact on the way young women construct their identities today.

Traditional media representations of masculinity

Until fairly recently, there has been little analysis of how the media construct, inform and reinforce cultural expectations about men and masculinity. Tunstall (1987) points out that the media rarely focus on men's marital and domestic roles, or claim that fathers' lack of contact with their children (because of their jobs) leads to social problems such as juvenile delinquency. On the other hand, working and single women are often seen as blameworthy for such problems. Tunstall also observed that men are seldom presented as sex objects in the same way as females or judged by the media in terms of how well

they conform to a feminine definition of an ideal male physical form.

In 1999, the research group Children Now asked boys between the ages of 10 and 17 about their perceptions of the male characters they saw on television, in music videos and in movies (Children Now 1999). Their results indicate that media representations of men do not reflect the changing work and family experiences of most men today. The study found the following:

- On television, most men and boys usually keep their attention focused mostly just on women and girls.
- Many males on TV are violent and angry.
- Men are generally leaders and problem-solvers.
- Males are funny, confident, successful and athletic.
- It is rare to see men or boys crying or otherwise showing vulnerability.
- Male characters on TV could not be described as 'sensitive'.
- Male characters are mostly shown in the workplace, and only rarely at home.
- More than a third of the boys had never seen a man on TV doing domestic chores.

These images support the idea that hegemonic images of masculinity generally continue to dominate mass media coverage of boys and men.

The masculine myth

Easthope (1990) argues that a variety of media, especially Hollywood films and computer games, transmit the view that masculinity based on strength, aggression, competition and violence is biologically determined and, therefore, a natural goal for boys to achieve. He argues that the Hollywood action hero is the embodiment of this view. Easthope argues that, while most men cannot hope to achieve such a masculine image, i.e. it is an ideological myth, they internalize the notion that men have physical, cultural and emotional power and that this is part and parcel of their male identity.

Men and magazines

The 'new man'

The 1980s saw the emergence of a new breed of glossy magazines aimed at middle-class young men, such as *GQ, Maxim* and *FHM.* Interestingly, their content focused on the masculine experience rather than specifically on interests or hobbies. The content of such magazines often suggested that:

- men are emotionally vulnerable
- they should be more in touch with their emotions or feminine side
- they should treat women as equals
- they should care more about their appearance
- active fatherhood is an experience worth having.

These magazines were seen by some commentators as evidence of a new type of masculinity – the 'new man'. Television advertising in the 1980s and 1990s also focused on this phenomenon, presenting us with a series of commercials peopled with caring sharing men.

The 'metrosexual male'

Media representations of this new type of masculinity led to postmodern sociologists speculating that masculinity was responding to the growing economic independence and assertiveness of women. Frank Mort (1988), for example, argued that the rise in men's fashion magazines, and the advertising and consumption of male toiletries and designer-label clothing for men, reflected changes in masculine social attitudes and, in particular, the emergence of the 'metrosexual' male. Rutherford (1998) suggests media images of the new man were an attempt – partly in a response to feminism – to express men's repressed emotions and aimed at revealing a more feminized image. However, Tim Edwards (1997) argues that the new man was quite simply a product of advertisers, who invented the concept in order to sell products to both men and women.

Gauntlett (2008) is particularly supportive of men's magazines such as *FHM*, which, he claims, have an almost obsessive relationship with the socially constructed nature of manhood. He argues that such media are positive because they stress that 'the performance of masculinity can and should be practised and perfected'. His study of the content of *FHM* concludes that the masculine values it transmits are 'fundamentally caring, generous and good-humoured'. Gauntlett argues that these magazines are often centred on 'helping men to be considerate lovers, useful around the home, healthy, fashionable, and funny – in particular, being able to laugh at themselves'.

Retributive masculinity

Collier (1992) notes that men's magazines are often contradictory in their representations of masculinity. He notes that these magazines continue to define success in traditional terms, i.e. in terms of work, salary and materialism, whilst women are objectified in an explicitly sexual fashion. These magazines continue to relegate women to the background. Gauntlett agrees that images of the 'conventionally rugged, super-independent, extra-strong macho man still circulate in popular culture'. Sharples (1999) argues that some of the newer magazines,

Do you agree with Gauntlett that men's magazines have a positive influence on modern men?

such as *Zoo* and *Nuts*, have actually rejected metrosexuality. Rutherford suggests they are symbolic of what he calls '**retributive masculinity**' – an attempt to reassert traditional masculine authority by celebrating traditionally male concerns in their content, i.e. 'birds, booze and football'. Some feminist sociologists have seen these traditional representations as part of an antifeminist backlash. However, as Sharples notes, it is unlikely that these magazines set out to be misogynist – rather they simply promote masculinity in what their editors and journalists see as positive ways. Gauntlett suggests that media sociologists tend to be obsessed with the traditional aspects of men's media and consequently fail to understand that 'men's magazines are not perfect vehicles for the transformation of gender roles, by any means, but they play a more important, complex and broadly positive role than most critics suggest'.

Gary Whannel's observations on David Beckham (2002) note that mass media stories about and images of David Beckham are also contradictory, in that they stress Beckham as representative of both metrosexual and retributive versions of masculinity. Whannel notes that media representations of Beckham are fluid – his good looks, his football skills, competitive spirit and his commitment mark him out as a traditional 'real man'. However, this image has been balanced with alternative media representations that stress his metrosexuality, particularly his emotional commitment to his family and the fact that he spends a great deal of time, effort and money on his image.

There are, then, signs that media representations of masculinity are moving away from the emphasis on traditional masculinity, to embrace new forms of masculinity that celebrate fatherhood and emotional vulnerability. In the past 20 years, the media have also become more accepting of homosexuality, as major celebrities have come out and declared themselves gay. However, as the section on sexuality (pp. 185–9) indicates, there are still contradictions in the media representation of homosexuality. Similarly, it is important not to exaggerate changes in representations of masculinity, as the overall tone of media representations still strongly supports hegemonic versions of what it is to be a man.

Theoretical perspectives and media representations

Feminists are the main sociologists working in this field. They have been very critical of the representations of men and women in the media. However, they differ in their emphasis.

Liberal feminism

Liberal feminists are concerned about media representations because they believe that the mass media plays a major role, alongside the family and education, in the social construction of gender roles, i.e. how children learn to be feminine or masculine. The media emphasis on females as domestic goddesses and sex objects is seen as a problem because it is believed to have a limiting effect on young females' behaviour and aspirations, especially in adolescence.

Liberal feminists believe that media representations are slow to change in response to women's achievements in society. This 'cultural lag' is due to the fact that attitudes and ideas change more slowly than social and economic conditions. Women are still ignored or trivialized by the media, although liberal feminists accept that this is happening to a lesser degree than in the past as the number of female journalists, editors and broadcasters increases.

However, liberal feminists are concerned that women's progress in media professions has considerably slowed. The majority of media owners are male, as are the higher position holders within media conglomerates. For example:

- In 2009, out of 20 national daily and Sunday newspapers, only three editors were female (ironically of tabloid newspapers, the *Sun, Star* and *Sunday Mirror*).
- In 2006, only 26 per cent of the boards of television and film production companies in the UK were women.
- Women made up 50 per cent of the advertising workforce in 2006, but only 26 per cent of managers and 15 per cent of top executives.
- A spot survey carried out by the pressure group Women in Film and Television into 10 prime-time UK dramas during one week's transmissions showed that only 15 per cent of directors and only 25 per cent of writers were female.
- Women continue to dominate areas in the film and television industries such as costume, make-up and hair, which have less status and are paid less than male-dominated technical areas such as camera, sound and lighting.
- In 2002, the BFI analysed UK feature-film productions of the previous two years (including those in production). Out of the total of 350 films, only eight were directed by women.

Socialist and Marxist feminism

Marxist or socialist feminists believe that the roots of the stereotypical images of men and women in the media are economic. They are a by-product of the need of media conglomerates in capitalist societies to make a profit. The male-dominated media aim to attract the largest audience possible, and this leads to an emphasis on the traditional roles of men and women in sitcoms, game shows and soap operas. The alternative images of women encouraged by feminism, e.g. as assertive career women, do not fit easily into this type of media content and consequently such women are ignored, devalued or treated critically.

A great deal of the content of women's magazines is shaped by advertising. These types of media make profits from advertising rather than sales, and therefore it is in the interests of these magazines to promote 'false needs' around beauty, size and shape, etc., in order to attract advertising revenue from the cosmetics, diet and fashion industries. By presenting an ideal difficult to achieve and maintain, the cosmetic and diet product industries are assured of growth and profits. It is estimated that the diet industry alone is worth $100 billion a year in the USA.

Marxists note that another media marketing strategy that encourages women to invest in the beauty market is an increasing emphasis in media content on retaining youth and resisting ageing. Marxists argue that women are therefore not only exploited by the media as mother/housewives and sex objects, but their anxieties about weight and age are also deliberately manipulated by the media so that they can be exploited as consumers of body-related products.

Radical feminism

Radical feminists feel strongly that the media reproduce patriarchy. In patriarchal societies, men dominate positions of power and control and have a vested interest in keeping women in subordinate positions. Radical feminists argue that traditional images are deliberately transmitted by male-dominated media to keep women oppressed into a narrow range of roles.

Radical feminists believe that the media deliberately dupe women into believing in the 'beauty myth', i.e. that they should conform to what is a male image of what it is to be a 'proper' woman in terms of good looks, sexiness, ideal shape, weight, size, etc. Women are strongly encouraged by the media to see these goals as central to their personal happiness, rather than competing with men for positions of power. This creates a form of **false consciousness** in women and deters them from making the most of the opportunities available to them.

Radical feminists claim that men's magazines that celebrate and encourage retributive masculinity are examples of a social backlash directed against the gains made by women because of the feminization of the economy, and attempts to compensate for a 'crisis in masculinity' as men's economic and social power declines. They suggest it is no coincidence that, at the same time as women are achieving greater social, political and professional equality, these magazines symbolically relegate them to subordinate positions as sex objects.

Popular feminism

McRobbie (1999) argues that much of young women's media today constitutes a form of **'popular feminism'** expressed through young women's magazines that promote the concept of 'girl power'. McRobbie argues that young women in the 21st century are promoting a new form of feminism that, on the surface, looks like it is a rejection of the feminism of previous generations that focused on patriarchal forms of exploitation. She argues that:

<< to these young women, official feminism is something that belongs to their mothers' generation. They have to develop their own language for dealing with sexual inequality; and they do this through a raunchy language of 'shagging, snogging and having a good time'. >> (p.122)

McRobbie argues that the key difference in the language used by traditional and popular feminists is that the latter is now in the mainstream of commercial culture, whereas

Girls Aloud: female stereotypes or symbols of popular feminism?

the former was marginalized and often ignored by the mainstream media. Hollows (2000) suggests popular culture in the form of women's magazines is a site of a cultural struggle, in which new forms of femininity and feminism are being defined and negotiated. As Gill (2007) notes: 'the fact that magazines are commercial ventures does not mean that they can not also be spaces for progressive ideas or cultural contestation' (p.204).

Postmodernism

Gauntlett (2008) focuses on the relationship between the mass media and identity. He argues that the mass media today challenge traditional definitions of gender and are actually a force for change, albeit within limits, for encouraging a diversity of masculine and feminine identities. He notes that: 'the traditional view of a woman as a housewife or low-status worker has been kick-boxed out of the picture by the feisty, successful "girl power" icons'. There has also been a new emphasis in men's media on men's emotions and problems, which has challenged masculine ideals such as toughness and emotional reticence. As a result, the media are now providing alternative images and ideas, which are producing a greater diversity of gender identities.

Gauntlett argues that, as far as identity goes, the media provide consumers with a greater degree of choice as they provide the tools for the social construction of identity. However, he also acknowledges the contradictory nature of modern media and notes that, 'like many toolkits, it contains some good utensils and some useless ones'. In particular, Gauntlett suggests that media role-models, alongside parents, friends, teachers, etc., serve as 'navigation points' to assist individuals in making decisions and judgements about their own lifestyles. Gauntlett rejects the view that young men are attracted to magazines that focus on retributive forms of masculinity because they are experiencing a crisis of masculinity. He notes that young men in the 21st century have adapted to the modern world and have grown up with women as their equals. They therefore do not feel threatened or emasculated by the way femininity has changed.

Gauntlett argues that the power relationship between the media and its audience is complex. Both media producers and consumers subscribe to traditional ideas about gender as well as new ideas. However, he notes that in contrast with the past, we now no longer get singular and straightforward media messages that suggest that there is only ideal type of masculinity or femininity. In response, the audience borrows bits and pieces from media content in order to help them to construct their own identities. Gauntlett suggests, therefore, that media content, despite its contradictions, should be seen as resources that people can use to think through their identities and how they might present themselves to the world. The media, in turn, will be influenced by these myriad new forms of identity and lifestyle that result from consuming media messages.

Pluralism

Pluralists claim that critiques of the media representations found in modern media underestimate women's ability to see through gender stereotyping and manipulation. They believe that feminists are guilty of stereotyping females as impressionable and easily influenced. They claim that there is no real evidence that girls and women take any notice of media content or that it profoundly affects their attitudes or behaviour.

Pluralists believe that the media simply reflect social attitudes and tastes – in other words, public demand. They argue that the media are meeting both men and women's needs and that if women were really unhappy at the way they were being represented, they would not buy media products such as women's magazines. However, in criticism of pluralism, the question remains: to what extent are the media actually creating those needs in the first place?

Representations of sexuality

Moral panics and sexuality

The concept of 'moral panic' (explored in Topic 3) is important in understanding media representations of sexuality; the way in which both tabloid newspapers and television news have reported aspects of sexuality have resulted in the social construction of social anxiety or moral panics. Society learns to fear, or to be critical of, particular social groups, i.e. folk devils who are consequently vilified, condemned and discriminated against by society and its social agents. The most obvious example of such a group in recent years have been child sex offenders or paedophiles. However, other groups have also been subjected to the moral hysteria that accompanies a moral panic. For example:

- Homosexuals experience periodic moral panics with regard to their supposedly 'unnatural' practices and, in the 1980s, were actually blamed by the media for the spread of the HIV virus and AIDS – the media even referred to AIDS as a 'gay plague'.
- The 1990s saw a moral panic focused on the alleged promiscuity of teenage girls, who supposedly were getting pregnant in order to obtain benefits and council housing.

Young people's media and representations of sexuality

Batchelor et al. (2004) argue that the mass media have an important role to play in shaping the knowledge and attitudes of young people with regard to sexuality. They carried out a content analysis of media, such as magazines and television programmes consumed by young people, in order to examine how sexuality is represented. They discovered that some aspects of sexuality were represented very positively in terms of publicizing sexual health information, the exploration of issues such as consent and whether couples were 'ready' to have sex. For example, the right of girls to 'say no' was given prominence in several teen dramas and magazines (see 'Focus on research' below). However, Batchelor and colleagues' findings also suggest some limitations in media coverage of young people's sexuality:

- It was assumed in most media texts that young people, if they were aged over 16, were sexually active.
- Contraception and managing 'how far to go' sexually were clearly represented as female responsibilities.

The focus on female responsibility for contraception was emphasized in references to pregnancy and letters to problem pages centred on girls' worries about getting/being pregnant.

- There were no examples of how people might raise concerns such as safer sex, e.g. to avoid STIs.
- There were distinct differences in terms of how young men and women in media texts talked, felt about, and acted, in relation to sex. For example, the study found that female media characters discussed sex with their friends, whereas male characters boasted about their sexual prowess. Girls were portrayed as being more interested in emotions, while male characters were represented as being more interested in sex. The general picture, therefore, both in magazines and in television drama was of boys/men as pursuers and girls/women as the pursued.
- There was a lack of positive images of lesbian and gay teenagers, and a failure to represent sexual diversity.

Read the 'Focus on research' below to discover more about the methods used in Batchelor and colleagues' research.

Focus on research

Batchelor et al. (2004)
Representing young people's sexuality in the 'youth' media

This research examines how sexuality is represented and the level of sexual health information provided in some UK magazines and TV programmes targeted at young people.

The researchers describe how they analysed a cross section of media during a randomly selected week. They examined nine top-selling magazines for young people, ten daily and eight Sunday newspapers (involving 68 newspaper editions over the seven days), and recorded all television programmes between 16:00 and 18:00 on each terrestrial channel (BBC1, BBC2, ITV, Channel 4 and 5). They also recorded a series of programmes that fell outside this time slot, but which have a large teenage audience. These included 'teen dramas' such as *Dawson's Creek* (pictured above) and *Hollyoaks*, as well as a range of soap operas, including *Eastenders* and *Brookside*. The magazine sample consisted of five publications aimed at teenage girls/young women (*Mizz, Sugar, Bliss, J-17* and *19*), two music magazines

(*M8* and *Top of the Pops*), one computer gaming magazine (*PlayStation Plus*) and one 'lad's mag' (*frOnt*).

From the above sample, every item involving sexual content relating to young people was collected. Sexual content was defined as any depiction of sexual behaviours, discussion of sex or sexuality, sexually suggestive behaviour/images/language, sexual health, or sexuality-related issues (e.g. sexual identity). Sexual suggestiveness included flirtatious behaviours (intended to arouse sexual interest in others), sexual innuendoes and double entendres (composed of veiled references to sexual behaviour or sexual organs), and sexualized presentations of the body (such as a woman positioned on her back in a posture of sexual display). Each item was then subject to content analysis. In brief, content analysis is the study of the frequency with which certain identifiable elements occur in a given sample. Each item was coded according to its content, type of discussion and/or reference, and its format (e.g. TV teen drama, magazine editorial, newspaper feature). This quantitative analysis was complemented by qualitative analysis designed to capture the subtleties of the various messages presented, e.g. was the behaviour portrayed as humorous or serious, positive or negative.

Adapted from S.A. Batchelor, J. Kitzinger and E. Burtney (2004) 'Representing young people's sexuality in the 'youth' media', *Health Education Research*, 19(6), pp. 669–76

1 What is the aim of this research?

2 How was the idea of 'sexual content' operationalized?

3 How did the researchers use content analysis in their research?

4 What did they find out about media representations of young people's sexuality?

Representations of homosexuality

Batchelor and colleagues found that being gay was not generally integrated into mainstream media representations. Rather, when it did appear, e.g. in television drama, it was represented mainly as a source of anxiety or embarrassment, or it was seen as a target for teasing and bullying. The study also found that, in mainstream young people's media, lesbianism was completely invisible.

Although homosexuality is no longer illegal and social attitude surveys suggest that society views this form of sexuality as more socially acceptable, it still does not have the same status as heterosexuality. Dyer (2002) observes that 'a major fact about being gay is that it doesn't show … the person's person alone does not show that he or she is gay'. He argues that the media construct stereotypical 'signs of gayness', such as vocal tics, facial expressions, stances and clothing in order to 'make visible the invisible'. Consequently, if a person, whether heterosexual or homosexual, demonstrates these signifiers in the course of their everyday behaviour, they may be labelled as 'gay' and subjected to prejudice and discrimination by others.

Media representations of sexuality in the UK are overwhelmingly heterosexual in character. Gerbner et al. (1986) argues that the media participate in the 'symbolic annihilation' of gays and lesbians by negatively stereotyping them, by rarely portraying them realistically, or by not portraying them at all. Craig (1992) suggests that when homosexual characters are portrayed in the media, e.g. in popular drama, they are often stereotyped as having particular amusing or negative psychological and social characteristics.

1 *Camp* – One of the most widely used gay representations, found mainly in the entertainment media, is the 'camp' character or comedian, e.g. Allan Carr, Julian Clary, 'Sebastian' (Little Britain's aide-de-camp to the Prime Minister). Dyer defines camp as 'a characteristically gay way of handling the values, images and products of the dominant culture through irony, exaggeration, trivialization, theatricalization, and an ambivalent making fun of out of the serious and respectable' (Dyer 1986, cited in Finch, 1990 p.75). Camp characters are generally regarded as extremely colourful and flamboyant figures of fun and, probably for this reason, they are not defined or interpreted as threatening by heterosexual media audiences. However, the camp persona probably does reinforce negative views of gay sexuality by being somewhere in between male and female.

2 *Macho* – Another negative media stereotype that was particularly popularized by the pop group The Village People is the 'macho', which relies on exaggerating masculinity. It is also an openly sexual look, transforming practical male clothing such as safety helmets and police officer's caps into erotic symbols. Research suggests this media representation is regarded as threatening, particularly by men, because it subverts traditional ideas of masculinity.

3 *Deviant* – Gays are often stereotyped as deviants by media representations, i.e. as evil or devious in television drama, as sexual predators or as people who feel tremendous guilt about their sexuality. They are rarely presented in a sympathetic manner, and even when this does occur, plots tend to focus on heterosexual characters' acceptance of their homosexuality. In many cases, gay characters are completely defined by their 'problem', and homosexuality is often constructed to appear morally wrong. Russo, too, notes how Hollywood films have tended to portray gay people as dangerous and psychopathic (Russo 1981).

4 *Gays in the news* – Critics argue that the news media still systematically ignores and distorts the lives and experiences of gays and lesbians. In a 1998 study that analyzed 50 years of coverage of gay and lesbian issues in *Time* and *Newsweek*, Lisa Bennett (2000) found that news media reinforce prejudice and discrimination against gays and lesbians. She observes that gays and lesbians were often linked to deviant or criminal behaviour without evidence to support such claims; and that the media often reprinted offensive and homophobic comments. Bennett concludes that such practices reinforce assumptions that gays and lesbians are inherently inferior to heterosexuals. In the UK right-wing press, homosexuality is often presented as wicked, sinful and unnatural. This section of the news media have often strongly opposed legislation aimed at bringing about social and political equality for gay people such as gay weddings, the adoption of children by gay people and so on.

5 *Coverage of AIDS* – Watney has illustrated how UK news coverage of AIDS in the 1980s stereotyped gay people as carriers of a gay plague. He argues that news coverage of AIDS reflected mainstream society's fear and dislike of the gay community and resulted in unsympathetic accounts that strongly implied – and sometimes, openly stated – that homosexual AIDS sufferers only had their own 'immoral and unnatural' behaviour to blame for their condition or death.

Media sociologists argue that the portrayal of gays and lesbians in soap operas is different to that of other television genres because soap opera narrative is ongoing and viewers are encouraged to interact with the development of particular characters. There is therefore no need for a character's lifestyle to be immediately identifiable to an audience. British soap operas such as *Hollyoaks* and *Eastenders* have featured homosexual and lesbian characters; none of these characters were visually different from the heterosexual characters and their storylines were not restricted to issues of their sexuality. However, there was some stereotyping of homosexuality in that their sexuality was viewed as a moral problem and some of these characters had problems coming to terms with their sexuality. In this sense, the programmes could be said to be reflecting society's concerns about homosexuality.

Gauntlett argues that lesbian, gay and bisexual people are still underrepresented in much of the mainstream media, but things are slowly changing. He notes that television drama is offering prime-time audiences the chance to 'get to know' nice lesbian and gay characters in soap operas, drama series and sitcoms, e.g. Captain Jack in *Torchwood*. Gauntlett argues that tolerance of sexual

Actor John Barrowman, himself gay, plays Captain Jack Harkness, a character in the TV series *Torchwood*, who is portrayed as bisexual and has been shown passionately kissing other men. In what ways does this open portrayal of same-sex attraction challenge media stereotypes?

Sociology A2 for AQA

diversity is slowly growing in society, and the bringing-about of images of diverse sexual identities with which audiences are unfamiliar may assist in making the population generally more comfortable with these alternative sexual lifestyles.

The heterosexual portrayal of homosexuality

Gill (2007) argues that when homosexual images and issues are covered by television, they tend to be sanitized and portrayed in ways that do not challenge heterosexual ideology and – most importantly – do not drive away advertisers and their revenue. Gerbner *et al.* (1986) argues that the commercial structure of the mass media limits the opportunity for representing wildly diverse sexual characters because the television networks shy away from portraying gays and lesbians for fear of alienating or offending advertisers, investors and audiences.

This profit-motivation means that networks are careful in their portrayals of gay and lesbian characters. The hugely popular American comedy *Will & Grace*, which features two openly gay male characters, is a good example of this. There is little or no discussion about gay relationships or romance. The two gay characters are friends, not lovers, and are rarely shown in romantic situations. The primary relationship for both gay men is with the heterosexual female characters. In order to appeal to mass audiences, then, television often desexualizes homosexuality – little reference is made to the very activity that defines them as gay in the first place.

In the past few years, Hollywood has developed a new genre: the gay/straight romance. Films such as *My Best Friend's Wedding*, *The Object of My Affection*, and *The Next Best Thing* all portray a gay man and straight woman as the 'perfect couple'. Some media commentators see this as a good thing, but critics suggest that such representations marginalize the experience of gays and lesbians by suggesting that it is not as important as the heterosexual experience. Other critics suggest that gay characters are only tolerated in television and film drama

because they are used to signify the liberalism and sophistication of heterosexual characters – it is assumed that the heterosexual character is an intelligent and tolerant human being if they have a gay friend.

The popularity of shows such as *Will & Grace* or *Queer Eye for the Straight Guy* suggests that television networks are willing to feature gay characters, so long as the shows attract large audiences and generate profits for advertisers. However, it is argued that Hollywood is still too cautious in its portrayals of gay themes, characters and experiences because its films are designed to appeal to as large an audience as possible. Producers therefore fear that focusing on gay and lesbian themes risks offending a large portion of the audience, as well as potential investors. Gill argues that most media representations of gay people are constructed with the heterosexual audience in mind and so represent little challenge to the existing patriarchal and heterosexist structures of gender and sexuality.

A good example of this caution can be seen when the Americans decided to develop the British gay drama *Queer as Folk*, which Gill (2007) notes was probably the first UK television programme to portray homosexuality in a realistic light and to acknowledge the range of gay sexual practices through a group of characters who were not bland, saintly or desexualized. However, when the American version was in production, fashion houses such as Versace, Prada, Polo, Ralph Lauren and Abercrombie & Fitch refused to allow their brands to appear in the series because they feared that the drama would upset a predominantly heterosexual audience.

Advertising and representation of gay people

The last decade has seen a growing amount of advertising that includes representations of lesbians and gay men. By June 2004, Commercial Closet, a web-based organization that monitors gay-themed adverts, had 1700 adverts from 33 countries in its database. There are probably a number of reasons for this:

1. Some argue that the visibility of gays and lesbians in advertising is an indication of the increased social acceptance of gays and lesbians generally.
2. Others see it as an attempt by advertisers and network executives to access an untapped economic market. The power of the 'pink economy' has now been recognized by advertisers – many gay men and women are professional people with no dependents and large disposable incomes (the so-called 'pink pound') to spend on consumer goods. As a result, companies have actively courted gay and lesbian consumers through gay-positive advertising and marketing campaigns. For example, in 1994, IKEA aired a commercial that depicted two gay men shopping for a dining room set, making the store the first company actively to target gay consumers.
3. Gill suggests that advertising that uses lesbian and gay imagery is actually aimed at the conventional heterosexual audience and actually reflects hegemonic definitions of sexuality. For example, she notes that the increasing numbers of lesbian images in advertising are presented as hypersexual chic rather than as promoting a different sexual identity. She argues that women

shown kissing and touching is a 'kind of eroticized imagery' and 'is a sexualized display designed primarily for heterosexual men because it draws on well-established codes from pornography'. It also allows advertising companies to continue to objectify and sexualize women's bodies and evade charges of sexism. Gill notes that, in contrast to media representations of lesbianism, gay men are rarely portrayed kissing or even touching. This is because male gay identity is presented primarily as a style identity rather than a sexual one. This is symbolized by their attractive bodies and faces and beautiful clothes. Gill points out that gay men in adverts often appear as objects of straight women's desire. A frequent theme is female sexual disappointment at discovering the attractive man she is eyeing up is gay.

In conclusion, critics of mass-media representations of homosexuality worry that after almost 30 years of political struggle, gay and lesbian rights have been reduced to increased consumer choice. They agree that there has been an increase in the number of positive representations of gays and lesbians in commercials, films, and television shows but there is still a long way to go before social and political equality is achieved in society, never mind the mass media.

Representations of disability

There are essentially two broad sociological ways of viewing disability. The first suggests that disabled people are disabled by their physical and/or mental impairments. This view suggests that they need constant care from both medical practitioners and their families. In other words, the disabled are dependent upon the able-bodied.

The second view, held by many disabled sociologists, suggests that the disabled are actually disabled by society, particularly the fact that social institutions, facilities and services are primarily designed and administered with the able-bodied in mind. The disabled therefore have to negotiate a physical environment unsuited to their needs. Moreover, they are also disabled by prejudicial stereotypes and attitudes; these result in discriminatory practices that reinforce the notion that the disabled should be dependent upon able-bodied others or that they should be segregated from the rest of society. The mass media are seen by disabled sociologists like Colin Barnes as partly responsible for the dissemination of these stereotypes and prejudices. As Hevey (quoted in Barnes 1992, p.1) suggests 'the history of the portrayal of disabled people is the history of oppressive and negative representation. This has meant that disabled people have been presented as socially flawed able-bodied people, not as disabled people with their own identities'. This is discussed further in Chapter 7 (see pp. 480–1).

Barnes (1992) identified a number of recurring stereotypes of disabled people, which he claimed regularly appear in media representations of the disabled:

- *As pitiable and pathetic* – Barnes claims that this stereotype has grown in popularity in recent years because of television appeals such as *Children in Need*. He also notes that it is a staple of popular television

drama and news, which often overfocus on children and the possibilities of 'miracle' cures.
- *As an object of violence* – Barnes notes that when disabled people are featured in television drama, they are three times more likely than able-bodied characters to be killed off. This reinforces the notion of the disabled as victims.
- *As sinister and evil* – Disabled people are often portrayed as criminals or monsters. For example, villains in James Bond films often have something physically wrong with them. Morris (1991) notes that disability often becomes a metaphor in drama – 'the writer draws on the prejudice, ignorance and fear that generally exist towards disabled people knowing that to portray a character with a humped back, with a missing leg, with facial scars, will evoke certain feelings in the audience' (p.93).
- *As atmospheric or curio* – Disabled people might be included in drama to enhance an atmosphere of menace, unease, mystery or deprivation. Disabled people are, therefore, used to add visual impact to productions. Television documentaries often see the disabled as curios to be watched in fascination by able-bodied audiences.
- *As super-cripples* – Barnes notes that the disabled are often portrayed as having special powers, e.g. blind people might be viewed as visionaries with a sixth sense or super-hearing. He notes 'super-cripple films' such as *My Left Foot,* in which disabled people (often played by able-bodied actors) overcome their impairments and poverty. In Hollywood films, the impaired male body is often visually represented as a perfect physical specimen in a wheelchair. The BBC's coverage of the Paralympics also fits this category because it involved the BBC celebrating disabled people doing extraordinary things. Ross notes that for disability issues to be reported, they have to be sensational, unexpected or heroic to be interpreted by journalists as newsworthy.
- *As an object of ridicule* – Disabled people are often laughed at in comedies, e.g. *Little Britain*'s Lou and Andy (pictured on p. 481).
- *As their own worst and only enemy* – The media sometimes portray the disabled as self-pitiers who could overcome their difficulties if they would only stop feeling sorry for themselves and think positively.
- *As a burden* – Television documentaries and news features often focus on carers rather than the disabled.
- *As sexually abnormal* – It is assumed by media representations that the disabled do not have sexual feelings or that they are sexually degenerate.
- *As incapable of participating fully in community life* – Barnes calls this the stereotype of omission and notes that disabled people are 'rarely shown as integral and productive members of the community; as students, as teachers, as part of the workforce, or as parents'. He notes that they are conspicuous in their absence from media representations.
- *As ordinary or normal* – Barnes argues that the media rarely portray disabled people as normal people who just happen to have an impairment. They consequently fail to reflect the real, everyday experience of disability.

A qualitative study carried out by Ross (1996) of 384 disabled viewers' attitudes towards media representations of the disabled found that they were overwhelmingly critical of the way in which disabled characters featured on mainstream television. They particularly objected to:

- the infantilization of disabled characters
- the unrealistic and often sanitized portrayal of disability
- the persistent use of wheelchairs, white sticks and guide dogs to signify a disabled character
- the fact that disabled roles were often associated with anger, bitterness or inability to come to terms with disability
- the restricted repertoire of character types
- the lack of first-hand experience of disability by media practitioners
- the failure to present disabled people as capable of running homes, bringing up families, having loving relations, and as ordinary people rather than disabled people.

The effect of telethons

Roper (2003) suggests that mass-media representations of the disabled on telethons' can create problems for the disabled. She suggests that telethons overrely on 'cute' children who are not that representative of the range of disabled people in the UK. They imply that charities rather than governments are responsible for providing funds and services to disadvantaged disabled groups and consequently they very rarely question why people are disadvantaged in the first place. Moreover, Roper argues that these media representations end up creating beggars. She argues that telethons are primarily aimed at encouraging the general public to alleviate their guilt and their relief that they are not disabled, by giving money rather than informing the general public of the facts about disability.

Karpf (1988) argues that there is a need for charities, but that telethons act to keep the audience in the position of givers and to keep recipients in their place as grateful and dependent. She notes that telethons are about entertaining the public rather than helping us to understand the everyday realities of what it is like to be disabled. Consequently, these media representations merely confirm social prejudices about the disabled, e.g. that they are dependent on the help of able-bodied people.

Representations of people with mental disabilities

The Glasgow University Media Group (Philo 1999) found that television and press reporting of people suffering mental disabilities often focuses on violent incidents despite the fact that only a tiny minority of people with mental health impairments are potentially violent. The GUMG concluded that a high proportion of their sample of able-bodied people felt fear and anxiety when in the proximity of people experiencing mental health problems because media coverage convinced them that mental illness was associated with violent behaviour. They also found that this type of media representation could supersede personal experience. One member of the GUMG sample was a person who worked with the

elderly in a hospital. Despite the fact that these patients were neither violent or dangerous, the respondent felt afraid of them because of what she had seen on the television news.

Conclusion

Overall, then, those sociologists who believe that people with impairments are disabled by social attitudes have little faith that media representations of physical and mental disability do justice to the everyday experiences of those who are disabled. They also argue that many able-bodied people's only experience of the disabled is through media representations. Barnes concludes, therefore, that:

> << disabling stereotypes which medicalize, patronize, criminalize and dehumanize disabled people abound in books, films, on television and in the press. They form the bedrock on which the attitudes towards, assumptions about and expectations of disabled people are based. They are fundamental to the discrimination and exploitation which disabled people encounter daily and contribute significantly to their systematic exclusion from mainstream community life.>> (p.19)

Check your understanding

1 Why does Gauntlett argue that sociological analysis of media representations should be 'cautious'?

2 Give two examples of the 'symbolic annihilation' of women.

3 What evidence is there that teenage girls' magazines overconcentrate on beauty and slimness?

4 According to Gill, to what extent are modern women empowered by the increasing number of positive female role-models in the media?

5 Give three pieces of evidence that suggest the depiction of men in magazines is changing.

6 Compare the views of two types of feminism on women's representations in the media.

7 How does Gauntlett argue that 'the power relationship between the media and its audience is complex'?

8 Give three examples of the stereotypical representations of homosexual characters in the media.

9 How does Gauntlett argue that representations of lesbian, gay and bisexual people are changing?

10 Give three examples of:

(a) stereotypes of disabled people identified by Barnes

(b) objections of disabled viewers to media representations of the disabled.

Activities

Research idea

Compare the views of young men and young women about the representations of men and women in the media. You could do this by conducting in-depth interviews or by using a questionnaire. Try showing respondents examples of men's and women's magazines to get them talking.

Web.task

David Gauntlett is the author of *Media, Gender and Identity: An Introduction*. Go to his book's website at **www.theoryhead.com/gender**

Select 'Bonus discussions and interviews' and read his articles and the discussions about men's and women's magazines. To what extent do you agree with Gauntlett's views?

Also, it is well worth exploring some of the 'related features', including links to other websites.

Key terms

Beauty ideal the idea that women should strive for beauty.

Cult of femininity the promotion of a traditional ideal where excellence is achieved through caring for others, the family, marriage and appearance.

Empower make powerful.

False consciousness Marxist term used to describe the way in which people's values are manipulated by capitalism.

Hegemonic definitions the dominant ways of defining something.

Male gaze the camera 'inspecting' women in a sexual way in films and TV.

Popular feminism term used to describe the promotion of 'girl power' in women's magazines.

Retributive masculinity the attempt to reassert traditional masculine authority by the celebration of traditionally male concerns such as football.

Sexual objectification turning into objects of sexual desire.

Symbolic annihilation the way in which women's achievements are often not reported, or are condemned or trivialized by the mass media.

An eye on the exam — Representations of the body: gender, sexuality and disability

Item A

The media put forward representations of many different social groups. However, the picture they offer is not always a fair or accurate one, but rather one that distorts, misrepresents and underrepresents certain groups. For example, Lesley Best's (1993) study of reading schemes for young children showed that females are portrayed in a narrower range of roles than males, and generally portrayed indoors. Similarly, Cumberbatch and Negrine (1992) found that, compared with able-bodied characters, disabled characters in TV drama were more likely to be pitied, patronized, feared, avoided, mocked or abused, and less likely to be respected or shown as attractive. Gays and lesbians too are often portrayed in negative ways. However, the media do not all portray a given group in the same way. For example, women characters in action movies are shown differently from those in soaps. There is also some evidence of change occurring in the way the media portray gender, sexuality and disability.

Using material from **Item A** and elsewhere, assess sociological explanations of the ways in which the mass media represent any two of the following: gender; sexuality; disability. (33 marks)

Grade booster — Getting top marks in this question

You need to deal with two of the areas in the question in a reasonably balanced way. You could begin by describing the patterns of representation, e.g. in terms of negative stereotyping and underrepresentation. You should then examine a range of reasons and explanations for each of the two areas you have chosen. Remember to make use of relevant material from the Item in your answer, both to describe the patterns and also to discuss how far representations are changing. You should also consider both males and females if you choose gender, and both gays and heterosexuals if you choose sexuality. You need to use relevant feminist theories if you choose gender, but Marxism, pluralism and postmodernism can also be applied to all areas.

Representations of ethnicity, age and social class

1   How do you think most people would interpret what is happening in this photograph?

2   Why will they think this?

3   What other possible interpretations can you think of?

According to the 2001 UK Census, ethnic-minority groups represent 7.9 per cent of the UK population. The UK, therefore, is a multicultural society. Moreover, the majority of the main ethnic-minority groups – African-Caribbeans, Pakistanis, Indians and Bangladeshis – are British-born and British citizens. An Ofcom survey conducted in 2008 suggests that members of these ethnic-minority groups are at the forefront in terms of their use of new media such as mobile phones, the internet and multichannel television take-up. For example, members of ethnic minorities in the under-45 age group are more likely to own a mobile phone and access digital TV and the internet than the average person under 45.

Furthermore, adults from ethnic-minority groups are more likely to be confident about using interactive functions on digital devices such as televisions than the general UK population. They are more likely to have downloaded music, video clips, films and television programmes than the UK population as a whole. For example, between 65 and 79 per cent of ethnic-minority groups say that they use the internet to listen to or download music online, compared to 57 per cent of the UK population. Indians and Pakistanis spend more time online than any other adults in the UK (13.5 hours per week compared to the UK average of 12.1 hours per week).

The take-up of media technology among ethnic-minority groups is, therefore, well developed. With this in mind, you might assume that mainstream media institutions and agencies such as newspapers, magazines, advertisers, television, film-makers, record labels and internet providers would be constructing media content that reflected the everyday experiences of all sections of society and bore their media needs in mind. However, this is not the case.

Evidence suggests that media representations of ethnic-minority groups may be problematic because these are shaped by what media professionals believe the majority White audience want to read, see and hear. These media representations may also be contributing to the maintenance – and even reinforcement – of negative racist stereotypes. In this sense, media representations of ethnic minorities may be undermining the concept of a tolerant multicultural society and perpetuating social divisions based on colour, ethnicity and religion.

Representations of ethnic minorities

Evidence suggests that, despite some progress, ethnic minorities are generally underrepresented or are represented in stereotyped and negative ways across a range of media content. In particular, newspapers and television news have a tendency to present ethnic minorities as a problem or to associate Black people with physical rather than intellectual activities, and to neglect and even ignore racism and the inequalities that result from it.

Stereotypical representations

Akinti (2003) argues that television coverage of ethnic minorities overfocuses on crime, Aids in Africa and Black underachievement in schools, whilst ignoring the culture and interests of a huge Black audience, diverse in interests and age, and their rich contribution to UK society. In other words, news about Black communities always seems to be 'bad news'.

Van Dijk (1991) conducted a content analysis of tens of thousands of news items across the world over several decades. He noted that news representations of Black people could be categorized into several types of stereotypically negative types of news, as outlined below.

Ethnic minorities as criminals

Black crime and violence is the most frequent issue found in media news coverage of ethnic minorities. Van Dijk found that Black people, particularly African-Caribbeans, tend to be portrayed as criminals, especially in the tabloid press – and more recently as members of organized gangs that push drugs and violently defend urban territories. Akinti (2003) suggests that television often reflects an inaccurate and superficial view of Black life, focusing almost exclusively on stereotypical issues such as gun crime.

Agbetu (2006) suggests that 'a Black person constructed in the media has three attributes: they are involved in criminality, involved in sports or involved in entertainment'. He suggests that anything that lies outside those classifications is not of interest to the media. He notes that the media frequently focus on Black people as the perpetrators of crime rather than as victims. The word 'Black' is often used as a prefix if an offender is a member of an ethnic minority, e.g. 'a Black youth'. The word 'White' is rarely used in the same way. Furthermore, African-Caribbean people are portrayed as 'only interested in carnival and dancing and, of course, they all come from Jamaica, and they're all yardies'. He argues that 'Black people are troublesome but exciting for the media'. In other words, they are newsworthy because they almost always constitute 'bad news'.

Ethnic minorities and moral panics

Watson (2008) notes that moral panics often result from media stereotyping of Black people as potentially criminal. This effect was first brought to sociological attention by Stuart Hall's classic study of a 1970s moral panic that was constructed around the folk devil of the 'Black mugger' (Hall et al. 1978). Hall argues that some sections of the right-wing newspaper media colluded with the state and its agents, such as the police, to create a moral panic around the criminal offence of 'mugging'. Sensationalist news stories in the tabloid press were based on information fed to them by the police. The result of these stories was the labelling of all young African-Caribbeans as criminals and as a potential threat to White people. Hall claims that this served the ideological purpose of turning the White working class against the Black working class. He argues that this classic 'divide and rule' strategy diverted attention away from the mismanagement of capitalism. Moreover, the subsequent demands from the media and general public for an increased policing of Black communities because of the fear of being mugged led to the introduction of more repressive laws, which eventually ended up restoring ruling-class hegemony, i.e. domination.

Back (2002) notes that the reporting of inner-city race disturbances involving members of ethnic-minority groups in the UK over the last 25 years, often stereotypes them as 'riots'. This implies that such disturbances are irrational and criminal, and conjures up images of rampaging mobs that need to be controlled by justifiable use of police force. Journalists very rarely use the word 'uprising', because this suggests that members of ethnic-minority groups may have a genuine grievance in terms of being the victims of racial attacks, discrimination by employers and police harassment. The idea that people are angry enough to take to the streets because they want to rebel against injustice very rarely forms part of the media coverage of such events.

Moral panics and rap music

Further moral panics have developed around 'Black crime', which is seen by the media as characterized by drugs, gangs and gun culture. In 2003, 'gangsta rap' lyrics came under attack for contributing to an increase in gun crime. Zylinska (2003) notes that this moral panic was initiated by the then Home Secretary, David Blunkett, who announced that he was 'appalled' by some lyrics in rap and hip-hop music, whilst the Culture Secretary, Kim Howells, claimed that the London garage collective So Solid Crew were glorifying gun culture and violence. In 2005, a poster of rapper 50 Cent's film *Get Rich or Die Tryin'* featuring the rapper holding a gun and baby was criticized by the UK Advertising Standards Authority (ASA) for glamorizing gun crime. The ASA noted that 50 Cent had such cultural credibility, especially among young people, that his association with gang culture and criminal behaviour was likely to be seen as glamorizing and condoning the possession and use of guns.

There were also calls for stores in the UK to withdraw 50 Cent's computer game *Bulletproof*, in which players follow 50 Cent from crack-dealing gangsta to superstar by gunning down, stabbing and strangling rivals. Gun-crime campaigners were particularly angered by graphics that allow a bullet's-eye view of a gunshot as it ploughs into a rival's exploding head and the fact that 50 Cent's bullet wounds miraculously heal. More controversy followed 50 Cent's television commercials for Reebok that showed

him counting to nine – the number of times he has been shot.

In 2006, the leader of the Conservative Party, David Cameron, criticized BBC Radio 1 for playing gangsta rap because in its lyrics, such music 'encourages people to carry guns and knives' and consequently become more violent, sexist and intolerant. This is not a new debate. The African-British pressure group Ligali protested at the 2003 Music of Black Origins Awards (MOBO) about the music industry's support, promotion and awarding of artists who promote the ownership of illegal firearms and the ideology of shooting others in order to gain respect, and who have previously engaged in criminal activity and refuse to show remorse for their crimes. Furthermore, Ligali highlighted the **misogynist** nature of rap lyrics and videos, which it claimed devalue, disrespect and damage women by treating them as inanimate objects who exist purely for the purpose of male sexual gratification.

Topic 4 focused on media effects and highlighted how hard it is to determine whether there is a direct causal link between media content and everyday behaviour. However, a number of themes are worth exploring with regard to the relationship between rap/hip-hop and gun crime:

- *A form of cultural identity* – Best and Kellner (1999) argue that rap articulates the experiences and conditions of young Blacks living on the margins in inner-city areas or deprived council estates who feel that they are being stereotyped and stigmatized. They argue that rap provides the means through which they can communicate their anger and sense of injustice. It also shapes their lifestyles and gives them an identity. As Best and Kellner note, 'rap is thus not only music to dance and party to, but a potent form of cultural identity'.

- *Ambivalent effects* – Best and Kellner argue that rap 'is a highly ambivalent cultural phenomenon with contradictory effects'. On a positive note, it highlights racism and oppression, and describes the hopelessness of the inner-city and deprived experience. It is a symbol of Blackness in that it celebrates Black culture, pride, intelligence, strength, style, and creativity. It supplies a voice for people excluded from mainstream society and mass media and enables White people to better understand the everyday experiences of the Black community. However, Best and Kellner note that at its worst, it is 'racist, sexist, and glorifies violence, being little but a money-making vehicle that is part of the problem rather than the solution. Many of its images and models are highly problematic, such as the gangsta rap celebration of the outlaw, pimp, hedonistic pleasure seeker, and drug dealer'. Best and Kellner, therefore, argue that rap music is complex and many-sided with contradictory effects. It attracts a large White audience who can gain some insight into the Black experience. They argue that 'rap music makes the listener painfully aware of differences between Black and White, rich and poor, male and female. Rap music brings to White audiences the uncomfortable awareness of Black suffering, anger, and violence'. However, successful male rap artists undermine this potential awareness by expressing misogyny, violence towards women and homophobia in their lyrics. Ironically, some rappers direct their rage

Sociology A2 for AQA

Focus on ...

Rap music and role models

Grammy Award winner Rhymefest (pictured here) wrote this response to David Cameron's comments on rap music.

<< *I agree that rap music and urban music depicts a life in the inner cities and poor communities that is often violent. I also agree that by glorifying and promoting violence via radio, TV and videos, it does give an acceptance for that behaviour that is then negative for the community. As a Grammy Award-winning artist, who has worked and written with many other rap artists such as Kanye West and ODB, I myself on occasion am guilty of contributing to the culture. I believe that the hip-hop community is definitely in a state of denial about our complicity with the glorification of drugs and violence... However, although I agree with you that we are role models that affect our community and our music does play a role in people's behaviour, beneath the surface there are artists making changes and making the difference and there is more to rap than what you see ...* >>

Do you agree with these comments? Give your reasons.

towards other members of their community, i.e. women and homosexuals, rather than those who are responsible for their oppression and subordination.

- *Negative role models* – In 2007, the REACH report commissioned by the government suggested that violence within the Black community was partly the result of the media's failure to portray the image of Black boys and young Black men positively (REACH 2007). The report suggested that where children are without positive role models, 'they will seek them from the world of fantasy and the media'. Young Black participants in the research specifically cited the negative media portrayals of young Blacks, focused around criminality, guns and gangs as having a detrimental effect on their aspirations. Some even suggested that their teachers give up on them too easily because of these stereotypes. Moreover, these portrayals negatively influenced their self-image, lowered their expectations and resulted in low self-esteem and low confidence.

- *Role of education and family life* – The REACH report does not solely blame the media; it also suggests that the education system and Black family life are also to blame for why some young Black men may turn to negative role models in their communities. Sewell (2004), too, identifies three major risk factors, which he claims are responsible for the relatively high levels of crime among African-Caribbean boys. One of these is media culture, particularly MTV, rap music, advertising, etc., which encourages the idea that status or respect can be achieved by adopting a consumer street culture that views material things such as designer labels, trainers and jewellery (i.e. 'bling') as more important than education. This street culture often takes its lead from deviant or questionable role models, such as 50 Cent, who boast about their sexual conquests and gun-centred lifestyles. However, Sewell also notes that Black family life, especially the absence of fathers and young Black's experience of the White education system, institutional racism and, especially, aggressive policing, are just as important as the media in shaping Black subcultures on the street.

- *Reinforcing capitalist ideology* – Cashmore (1996) suggests that it is not media representations of violence that are responsible for shaping the identities of Black youth, but the lifestyle that is promoted and promised by media culture. Media messages about the lifestyles that can be achieved only reflect the dominant ideology of capitalist societies, which suggests that material success in meritocratic societies is within the reach of anyone if they are intelligent and prepared to work hard. However, the experience of racism convinces young Blacks that legitimate ways of achieving such success are impossible. As Mitchell (2007) argues, the real message that young Blacks pick up from rap is 'that if you're not loaded, you're not happening'. Mitchell argues that the real problem with rap is that far from undermining society's values it's reinforcing them, and the most fundamental of all our society's values at the moment is that 'you are what you own'. The videos show the stars by the swimming pool, in a fast car, wearing designer clothes and jewellery, and surrounded by attractive available young women. Mitchell notes that these images do not do any harm to middle-class youth because they have access to materialism via their parents, higher education and decent jobs and pay. However, he notes:

<<*For working-class youngsters, taught by our culture since the 1970s that they're losers and failures, it's part of a profoundly poisonous cocktail of attitudes. Pride and self-respect are at the heart of this debate and it's the lack of those, or the wrong sort, that's really driving the violence on our streets.* >>

It is probably too simplistic to suggest that rap and hip-hop lyrics are responsible for gun and knife crime in British cities. As Sewell and Cashmore point out, socio-economic factors, are a far more reliable explanation for gang activity than the music teenagers are listening to. In any case, Rhymefest (see 'Focus on ... rap music and role models') and Mitchell point out that hip-hop is about much more than violence – artists rap about a wide spectrum of issues, including politics and race awareness. Also, according to social historians such as Pearson (1983), gang violence existed well before rappers started talking about it. Critics of rap music conveniently ignore the violent content of other music genres, e.g. a moral panic did not arise when the popular Country and Western singer, Johnny Cash sang 'I shot a man just to watch him die'. Finally, some commentators suggest that music, along with films, television and recently computer games have always been a convenient scapegoat to blame for social problems which are both complex and most probably the result of structural inequalities.

Ethnic minorities as a threat

Van Dijk's (1991) content analysis suggested that a common news stereotype was the idea that ethnic minorities are posing a threat to the majority White culture. The concept of 'threat' is central to both news values (i.e. it is an essential component of bad news) and moral panics. In recent years, three groups seem to constitute the greatest threat in the UK, according to newspapers and television. Moral panics have, therefore, been constructed around:

- *immigrants* – who are seen as a threat in terms of their 'numbers', and because of the impact they supposedly have on the supply of jobs, housing and other facilities
- *refugees and asylum seekers* – who are often portrayed as coming to Britain to abuse the welfare state and take advantage of a more successful economy than their own
- *Muslims* – who both before and since 9/11 have been subjected to **Islamophobic** media coverage.

Race, migration and media

Philo and Beattie (1999) argue that moral panics often arise focused on immigrants and asylum seekers. They traced how one such panic developed in the wake of a government trade minister resigning in 1995 because he was unhappy about a lack of European border controls which, he claimed, made the UK vulnerable to mass illegal immigration. Philo and Beattie note that this resignation set off media hysteria about immigration. Television journalists, in particular, presented their stories about immigration in an extremely negative and alarmist way; they focused on borders being 'dangerously' underpoliced, and presented immigration as a 'threat' to the UK way of life, using sensationalist language such as 'flood' and 'tidal wave'. Moreover, the media used the terms 'illegal immigrant' and 'immigrant' interchangeably. Philo and Beattie suggest this coverage also had racist overtones in that journalists focused on illegal immigrants from Africa. Furthermore, the media presented estimates as to the extent of possible immigration as facts.

Philo and Beattie argue that this coverage created fear and concern among the general UK population. No consideration was given by television journalists to the fact that immigrants to the UK had made a substantial contribution to the economy, nor were the complex reasons why people might want to come to the UK explored. The notion that the vast majority of such refugees may be genuinely escaping political persecution, torture and poverty in their home country was neglected or ignored. In fact, it was broadly hinted that immigrants wished to take advantage of the UK's benefit and health systems. Philo and Beattie conclude:

<<*the result was a news which was sometimes xenophobic in tone, which reinforced our identity and their exclusion and, perhaps more importantly, provided a rationale for the apparent need for exclusion.* >> (p.196)

The Information Centre about Asylums and Refugees (ICAR) notes that studies of media coverage of asylum seekers have shown that the media have constructed an image of this group as problems or threats (Greenslade 2005). The ICAR study found the British media often repetitively used certain terms and types of language. Asylum seekers are described as a 'flood' or 'wave' and as 'bogus' or 'fraudulent'. ICAR argues that there is often a link between media coverage and community tensions. They conducted research in London and discovered that unbalanced and inaccurate media images of asylum seekers made a significant contribution to their harassment by local residents.

Media representations of Islam and Muslims

Poole (2000), pre 9/11, argued that Islam has always been demonized and distorted by the Western media. It has traditionally been portrayed as a threat to Western interests. Representations of Islam have been predominantly negative and Muslims have been 'homogenized as backward, irrational, unchanging fundamentalists and misogynists who are threatening and manipulative in the use of their faith for political and personal gain'. Poole's content analysis of broadsheet British newspapers between 1993 and 1996 found that representations of British Muslims suggested that they were a threat to UK security and mainstream values. Patel (1999) suggests that Islam is purposely misrepresented because it commands an allegiance that goes beyond boundaries of wealth, nationality, sex, race or culture and consequently is seen to challenge Western cultural power.

Richardson's (2001) empirical study of representations of British Muslims in the broadsheet press suggests that:

- British Muslim communities are almost wholly absent from the news.
- When they do appear, it is usually in a predominantly negative context.
- British Muslims are very rarely called upon as providers of informed commentary on news events.
- The everyday issues and concerns of Muslim communities in the UK are not being addressed.

In his analysis of Muslims and Islam in the British press, Whitaker (2002) notes the existence of four very persistent stereotypes in news stories and features: Muslims are presented as 'intolerant, misogynistic, violent or cruel, and finally, strange or different' (p.55). Nahdi (2003), too, argues the Western news agenda is dominated by hostile, careless coverage of Islam that 'distorts reality and destroys trust amongst Muslim readerships and audiences'. He argues that the general decline in the standards of Western media and journalism, with the move towards sound bites, snippets and quick and easy stories, has actually legitimized the voice of extremist Islam. Nahdi argues that this way of newsgathering focuses on extreme minority or fringe groups, which represent a very small minority of the Muslim population and which are often unacceptable to other Muslims. Most importantly, it disguises the vast diversity and range of perspectives amongst Muslims and equates the outlook and actions of a few individuals to over one billion people worldwide.

However, positive or balanced stories about Islam and Muslims do exist. Both the BBC and Channel 4 have

Focus on research

Ameli et al. (2007)
The ideology of demonization

Ameli et al. (2007) analysed the mainstream news programmes of *BBC News, Newsnight, ITV News* and *Channel 4 News* before and after the events of 7 July 2005. They particularly examined the language used by journalists to discuss that event. They found that 'asylum-seekers' and 'immigration' were frequently focused on, despite the fact that the suspected bombers were British born and raised. The researchers argue that this had the effect of reinforcing the view that all Muslims are of the same mind and that they should be suspected of being 'others', i.e. not integrated into British society. Moreover, the media also focused on the issues of 'loyalty' and 'belonging' and it was generally accepted that, despite a British upbringing, Muslim youth had the potential to develop extremist views and be led away from 'normality'. They had now become 'the enemy within'. In fact, this media portrayal strongly implied that *any* Muslim, especially any young male, had the potential to become an extremist. Ameli and colleagues conclude that despite the good intentions of these news networks, issues regarding Islam were discussed within a very narrow ideological framework.

Adapted from Ameli, S., Marandi, S., Ahmed, S., Kara, S. and Merali, A. (2007) *The British Media and Muslim Representation: The Ideology of Demonisation*, London: Islamic Human Rights Commission

What evidence does the passage contain to support the researchers' conclusion that 'issues regarding Islam were discussed within a very narrow ideological framework'?

websites that explain Islam in a balanced fashion, whilst the *Guardian, Observer* and *Independent* have sympathetically focused on Muslim Britain. Even the *Sun* ran a two-page editorial in 2005 declaring 'Islam is not an evil religion'. However, despite these positive representations, surveys of the Muslim population in the UK suggest that they see the British media generally as unsympathetic towards Islam. Many media sociologists argue that certain negative images and stereotypes about Islam and Muslims (referred to as Islamophobia) propagated by the British mass media over the past 30 years are now deeply embedded in journalistic practices and the popular consciousness.

Ethnic minorities as abnormal

Sections of the British media may be guilty of creating false cultural stereotypes around the value systems and norms of other cultures. A survey of ethnic-minority audiences conducted by the BBC in 2002 found that Asian audiences were unhappy at the way that the media failed to differentiate between different Asian groups, which have very distinctive cultures. They did not want to be labelled as 'Asian' and they called for their own distinct cultural identities to be shown. They were also concerned that some of their cultural practices were called into question by the media, and were labelled as deviant or abnormal.

Many of the Asian sample felt that the treatment of arranged marriages was often inaccurate and did not reflect the way that the system had changed over time. The distinction between 'forced' marriage – an extremely rare occurrence, strongly disapproved of by Asian communities – and arranged marriage, which is based on mutual consent, is rarely made by the media. A survey of Asian viewers, by the market research company Ethnic Focus (2004), cited the most common complaint 'was that the media divided Asians into two camps; either miserable folk being forced into loveless marriages or billionaires who had come to Britain with nothing and had now made a fortune'.

Ameli et al. (2007) note that media discussion around the issue of the wearing of the hijab and the veil is also problematic, often suggesting that it is somehow an inferior form of dress compared with Western female dress codes – and that it is unnecessary and problematic. It is often portrayed as a patriarchal and oppressive form of control that exemplifies the misogyny of Islam and symbolizes the alleged subordinate position of women in Islam. Ameli and colleagues note that the underlying questions being asked by the media include: 'Why must Muslim women insist on wearing hijab when other women don't?' and 'Why is it that Muslims have so much trouble accepting and adopting our values and dressing accordingly?' As Watson (2008) notes, the general media theme is that the wearing of such apparel symbolizes divisiveness, which Watson argues further encourages suspicion and distrust of Muslim people.

Ethnic minorities as unimportant

Van Dijk (1991) notes that some sections of the media imply that the lives of White people are somehow more important than the lives of non-White people. News items about disasters in other countries are often restricted to a few lines or words, especially if the population is non-White. The misfortunes of one British person tend to be prioritized over the sufferings of thousands of foreigners.

It is argued by the British-African pressure group, Ligali (2006), that Black victims of crime are not paid the same degree of attention as White victims of crime. This view was especially developed after Sir Ian Blair, the Metropolitan police commissioner, claimed that institutionalized racism was present in the British media in the way they reported death from violent crime. He highlighted the discriminatory nature of media coverage given to the murder of the Asian taxi driver Balbir Matharu and that of the White solicitor Tom ap Rhys Pryce on the same day in 2006. He noted 'that the death of the young lawyer was terrible, but an Asian man was dragged to his death, a woman was chopped up in Lewisham, [an African] chap shot in the head in a Trident murder – they got a paragraph on page 97'. A BBC survey of the coverage of the Matharu and Rhys Price murders, showed that Tom ap Rhys Pryce received 87 per cent coverage in the tabloid press compared with 13 per cent for Balbir Matharu. Both the Independent and the Mirror are reported to have not covered the Matharu story at all.

Piers Morgan, editor of the Daily Mirror from 1995 to 2004, described decision-making by newspaper and television editors as influenced by 'subliminal racism':

<< [there is] a perception that the public would be more interested in, for example, five young 'White' teenagers dying in a car crash than they would be if they were five Asian or 'Black' teenagers dying in a car crash, and I remember decisions like that coming along and feeling somehow that we were making the wrong decision here and it was by any sense a racist view to down play one against the other. >>

However, some sections of the media have been very positive in their exposure of problems such as racism. The murder of the Black teenager Stephen Lawrence by White racists in 1993 received high-profile coverage, both on television and in the press. Even the right-wing Daily Mail presented a front-page story highlighting police racism, and attempted to 'name and shame' the racists who had allegedly committed the murder. However, critics suggest that such coverage is actually quite rare. For example, Sir Ian Blair's comments about institutional racism in the media resulted in a hailstorm of media criticism, focusing on his ability rather than engaging with the debate he was attempting to initiate.

Ethnic minorities as dependent

<< Africa is helpless, Africa is poor. Africa is a world of dread and fear. >> Do they know it is Christmas? written by Bob Geldof and Midge Ure

The government report Viewing the World (Glasgow University Media Group 2000) points out that stories about less developed countries tend to focus on a 'coup-war-famine-starvation syndrome'. The implication of such stories, both in newspapers and on television, is that the problems of developing countries are the result of stupidity, tribal conflict, too many babies, laziness, corruption and unstable political regimes. It is implied that the governments of these countries are somehow inadequate because they cannot solve these problems. Such countries are portrayed as coming to the West for help time and time again. Live Aid and Comic Relief are portrayed by the Western media as the only way the people of these countries, which are nearly always African, can survive the calamities and disasters that allegedly characterize their everyday lives.

Pambazuka (2005), an African organization working to increase understanding of African issues makes a number of criticisms of British news coverage of Africa:

● The media constructs myths about Africa, such as Africa's current situation is the fault of African people, which means that people of the West need not feel a sense of responsibility about African issues. Pambuzuka notes a media overemphasis on African corruption and inefficiency and a reluctance to discuss the West's role in keeping some parts of Africa poor by:

- propping up corrupt regimes for political reasons
- failing to give African producers a fair price for their goods
- not controlling the illegal and immoral activities of Western transnational companies.

● Informed African experts are ignored in favour of Europeans who talk from a Eurocentric perspective about African affairs, ultimately to the benefit of their respective nations.

● Media reporting about Africa is too dominated by Western campaigns such as Make Poverty History and Live 8. The agenda of Bob Geldof is highlighted at the expense of Africans themselves.

● There are signs that the media are now suffering from 'Africa fatigue', which reinforces their usual apathy about Africa.

There is some sociological evidence for Pambazuka's observations. The Glasgow University Media Group (2000) found that there has been a drastic reduction in factual programming (i.e. 50 per cent in ten years) about the developing world. A third of media stories about the developing world were focused on bad news, such as war, conflict, terrorism and disasters. Much of the remaining coverage was devoted to sport or visits by Westerners to developing countries – for example, some countries were only featured because Richard Branson's balloon had floated over them! Little time was devoted to analysis of why countries were underdeveloped and poor, and the role of the West with regard to domination of world trade, debt and multinational exploitation was very rarely explored. It can be concluded that British news reporting is ethnocentric, i.e. shaped by the view that British White culture is superior in its values and norms compared with other cultures. As a result, the activities of other cultures are likely to be generally reported as deficient, inferior, strange.

Ethnic minorities as invisible

A survey by the BBC (2002) asked the question: 'Are ethnic minorities better represented on TV than they were 10 years ago?' The answers are shown in Table 3.3. Although the responses were generally positive, members of ethnic-minority groups were less likely to respond positively to the statement. However, since 2002, surveys do indicate that there has been some perceived improvement in the way that television dramas, such as soap operas, deal with race. In 2005, a BBC News Online survey noted that Black and Asian people were better

represented as newscasters and television journalists, as well as in comedy and children's television. However, it was also clearly stated by the same sample that things still have some way to go before the UK's multicultural character is fully represented in the media. A number of problem areas still exist:

1 *Limited roles* – In popular drama, the perception of ethnic-minority audiences is that when actors from ethnic minorities appear, the range of roles they play is very limited and often reflects low status, e.g. Africans may play cleaners or Asians may play shopkeepers. This may reflect the fact that ethnic groups are more likely to be found in low-status, low-paid semi-skilled and unskilled work. It fails to be a true representation of the range of jobs that members of ethnic minorities have, e.g. as successful business people and media professionals.

2 *Cultural irrelevance* – Research carried out by the Open University and British Film Institute (Bennett *et al.* 2006) found that the UK's main ethnic-minority communities do not relate to much of the nation's TV culture and do not identify with television programmes that have strongly White, middle-England associations. A central problem identified by the report was not that minority groups failed to integrate with the national culture, but rather that aspects of the national film and television culture offer little space for ethnic-minority interests or identities.

3 *Invisibility* – One area of the media that has attracted considerable criticism for excluding Black and Asian images, and thus rendering ethnic-minority groups invisible, is the advertising industry, and especially the beauty industry. Gill (2007) has noted that images of feminine beauty in women's media tend to over-emphasize Whiteness. Naomi Campbell has long complained about the relative lack of Black and Asian models. Gill argues this is caused by the assumption that Anglo-Saxon blondes have the ideal feminine look.

4 *Tokenism* – Ethnic-minority audiences are hostile towards **tokenism**, where television programmes, such as soap operas, include characters from ethnic-minority groups purely because they 'should'. The characters themselves are often so unimportant that they are rarely in a series for very long; dramas set in workplaces seem to be a convenient place to include an ethnic-minority actor for cosmetic purpose without being obliged to look at their culture or what happens in their homes. Such tokenism is often the result of positive discrimination or equal opportunities practices by television companies such as the BBC. An ex-BBC executive, Shah (2008) argues that broadcasters overcompensate for the lack of executives, producers, directors and writers from ethnic minorities by putting too many Black and Asian faces on screen regardless of whether they authentically fit the programmes they are in. In this sense, they are 'props'. For example, a Black character will pop up incongruously in a drama like *Emmerdale*, despite the fact that the racial profile of the Yorkshire Dales is overwhelmingly White.

5 *Realism* – Ethnic-minority audiences complain that Black and Asian people are rarely shown as ordinary citizens who just happen to be Black or Asian.

Table 3.3 Responses in BBC survey: Are ethnic minorities better represented on TV than they were 10 years ago?

	Total	White	Black	Asian
Yes	78%	80%	73%	67%
No	8%	7%	12%	16%
Don't know	13%	12%	15%	17%

More often they play 'Black' roles, in which their attitudes, behaviour and interaction with other social groups are shaped by their ethnic identity. Research suggests that ethnic-minority audiences want to see more realistic representation of ethnic-minority people, in areas and situations that occur in their real world, enjoying life in very similar ways to the White majority and facing similar problems often unrelated whatsoever to race.

6 *Ghettoization* – Other critics have suggested that television programmes dedicated to minority issues effectively **ghettoize** such issues by scheduling them at times (i.e. very early or late) or on channels that ensure small audiences. This has two effects. First, it means that White audiences, who may not have direct contact with ethnic-minority groups, are unlikely to access and increase their understanding of minority culture – if programming is labelled as being 'for minorities', the positive representations within them end up simply being preached to the converted. Second, the mainstream media assumes certain issues are being dealt with by minority programming, so mainstream news and documentaries may be less likely and willing to report them.

7 *Media personnel* – Audience research suggests that members of ethnic-minority groups believe that media institutions produce a media content geared to the interests of White people because, as Shah has noted, it is dominated by a metropolitan, liberal, White, male, public-school and Oxbridge-educated, middle-class cultural elite. There has been some acknowledgement of this problem from inside the profession. For example, Greg Dyke, Director-General of the BBC, said in 2002 that the BBC was 'hideously White' in terms of both management and creative types. A survey of media advertising and marketing (Institute of Practitioners in Advertising 2006) found that less than 7 per cent of people working in these fields were from ethnic-minority backgrounds.

Conclusions

Despite these problems, media professionals from ethnic-minority backgrounds have responded to these inequalities and prejudices by developing media institutions and agencies that specifically target the interests and concerns of ethnic-minority audiences. Some have chosen to work within the established system by developing aspects of institutional media, such as the BBC Asian digital network and (despite the risk of ghettoization described above) programmes such as Ebony and Café 21.

Other ethnic-minority media originate from outside the UK, e.g. Bollywood and Asian satellite channels such as Asia TV and Zee TV, that keep people in touch with Indian, Pakistani and Bangladeshi culture and news.

Finally, there is a range of homegrown media agencies that are owned, managed and controlled by ethnic minorities themselves, including:

● newspapers and magazines – e.g. *Eastern Eye, Snoop, The Voice, The Indian Times, New Nation, Desi Xpress*
● radio stations – e.g. Sunrise Radio, Asian FX
● new media websites – e.g. www.brasian.co.uk, www.asianlite.co.uk and www.easterneyeonline.co.uk.

What are the arguments for and against having media agencies that specifically target ethnic-minority groups, as this website does?

How does the media represent social class?

Mass media representations of social classes rarely focus on the social tensions or class conflict that some critical sociologists see as underpinning society. In fact, as previous topics have indicated, some neo-Marxist sociologists suggest that the function of the media is to ensure the **cultural hegemony** of the dominant capitalist class and to ensure that inequality and exploitation are not defined as social problems so that they do not become the focus of social debate and demand for social change.

Representations of the monarchy

Nairn (1988) notes that the monarchy has successfully converted much of the modern mass media to its cause, so that, until fairly recently, it was rare to see any criticism of this institution or the individuals in it.

Nairn argues that this is because, after the Second World War, the monarchy, with the collusion of the media, reinvented itself as a 'Royal Family' with a cast of characters, not unlike our own families, who stood for national values such as 'niceness', 'decency' and 'ordinariness'. Members of this 'family' were presented as 'like us' but 'not like us'; for example, the Queen was just an 'ordinary' working mother doing an extraordinary job. This successful make-over resulted in a national obsession with the Royal Family, reflected in media coverage that has focused positively on every trivial detail of their lives, turning the Queen and her family into an on-going narrative or soap story, but with a glamour and mystique far greater than any other media personality.

Mass-media representations of the Queen are also aimed at reinforcing a sense of national identity, in that she is portrayed as the ultimate symbol of the nation. Consequently, the media regards royal events, such as weddings and funerals, as national events. It was not until the death of Diana, Princess of Wales, in 1997 that the Queen started to receive some criticism from the media for misjudging the popularity of Diana. However, the media's very positive reaction to the Queen's Golden Jubilee in 2002 suggests that the Royal Family has again succeeded in convincing the media and the general public that British identity is wrapped up in the Queen continuing to be the Head of State.

Recent media coverage has continued this process, with Prince William being portrayed as the 'pin-up prince' and Prince Harry as the 'hero prince' after his stint in Afghanistan. Consequently, this royal populism, which is simultaneously created and fed upon by a ravenous tabloid media, celebrity magazines such as *Hello,* and even the BBC and ITV with its 'Royal correspondents', can also engage in damage limitation when members of the Royal Family make mistakes. In 2009, for example, both Prince Harry and Prince Charles were accused of casual racism, but this controversy was quickly defused by a forgiving media, that, only two years previously, had crucified the working-class celebrity, Jade Goody, for similar remarks.

Representations of the upper class and wealth

Neo-Marxists argue that mass-media representations of social class tend to celebrate hierarchy and wealth. Those who benefit from these processes – i.e. the monarchy, the upper class and the very wealthy – generally receive a positive press as celebrities who are somehow deserving of their position. The UK mass media hardly ever portray the upper classes in a critical light, nor do they often draw any serious attention to inequalities in wealth and pay or the overrepresentation of public-school products in positions of power.

Sociological observations of media representations of the upper classes suggest that popular films and television costume drama tend to portray members of this class either in an eccentric or nostalgic way. In films such as *Gosford Park* and *The Queen*, and television costume dramas, a rosy, idealized picture is painted of a ruling elite characterized by honour, culture and good breeding.

Representations of wealth

Reiner (2007) and Young (2007) have recently argued that the media tend to represent the UK as a meritocratic society, in which intelligence, talent and hard work are rewarded. Marxists point out that this is an ideological myth because the evidence suggests wealth is more important than ability in opening up access to Oxbridge and top jobs. Moreover, Cohen and Young (1981) suggest that British culture is a monetary culture characterized by a 'chaos of rewards', whereby top businessmen are rewarded for failure and celebrities are overrewarded for their 'talents'. In contrast, ordinary people in functionally important jobs struggle to get by. However, the media very rarely focus on these issues. Rather, they celebrate celebrity culture and its excesses, and encourage their audiences to engage in a popular culture underpinned by materialism and conspicuous consumption.

Newman (2006) argues that the tabloid media dedicate a great deal of their content to examining the lives of another section of the wealthy elite, i.e. celebrities and their lavish lifestyles. These media representations invite media audiences to admire the 'achievements' of these celebrities. However, very little of this is critical or, if it is, it is superficially focused on issues such as weight or taste.

Newman argues that the media focus very positively on the concerns of the wealthy and the privileged. He notes that the media overfocuses on consumer items such as luxury cars, costly holiday spots and fashion accessories

that only the wealthy can afford. In the UK, the upper class have magazines exclusively dedicated to their interests and pursuits such as *Country Life, Horse and Hound* and *The Tatler*. Newman also notes the enormous amount of print and broadcast media dedicated to daily business news and stock market quotations, despite the fact that few people in the UK own stocks and shares. He notes that 'international news and trade agreements are reported in terms of their impact on the business world and wealthy investors, not on ordinary working people'.

Representations of the middle classes

Some sociologists argue that the middle classes (i.e. professionals, managers, white-collar workers) and their concerns are overrepresented in the media. There is not a great deal of British sociological research in this area, but four broad sociological observations can be made:

1 In general, the middle class are overrepresented on TV (whilst the working class are underrepresented). In dramas, apart from soaps and situation comedies, middle-class families are predominant. They are generally portrayed as concerned about manners, decency and decorum, social respectability, etc.
2 A substantial percentage of British newspapers, e.g. the *Daily Mail* and *Daily Telegraph*, and magazines are aimed at the middle class and their consumption, tastes and interests, such as computers, music, cars, house and garden design, that can only be afforded by those with a good standard of living.
3 The content of newspapers such as the *Daily Mail* suggests that journalists believe that the middle classes of middle England are generally anxious about the decline of moral standards in society and that they are proud of their British identity and heritage. It is assumed that their readership feels threatened by alien influences such as the euro, asylum seekers and terrorism. Consequently, newspapers like the *Daily Mail* often crusade on behalf of the middle classes and initiate moral panics on issues such as video-nasties, paedophilia, asylum seekers and so on.
4 Most of the creative personnel in the media are themselves middle-class. In news and current affairs, the middle classes dominate positions of authority – the 'expert' is invariably middle-class.

Representations of the working class

Finally, it can be argued that some mass-media representations of the working class are also part and parcel of capitalist ideology. Newman notes that there are very few situation comedies, television dramas or films that focus on the everyday lives of the working class, despite the fact that this group constitutes a significant section of society. Newman argues that when working-class people are featured, the media depiction is often either unflattering or pitying. Blue-collar heads of households on prime-time television have typically been portrayed as well-intentioned but dumb buffoons (e.g. Homer Simpson) or as immature macho exhibitionists (e.g. Phil Mitchell in *Eastenders*). Research by Butsch (1992) argued that working-class men were more likely to be portrayed as flawed individuals compared with middle-class individuals.

Moreover, these flaws are highlighted by the portrayal of working-class women as more intelligent, rational and sensible than their husbands.

Newman argues that when news organizations focus on the working class, it is generally to label them as a problem, e.g. as welfare cheats, drug addicts or criminals. Working-class groups, e.g. youth subcultures such as mods or skinheads, are often the subject of moral panics, whilst reporting of issues such as poverty, unemployment or single-parent families often suggest personal inadequacy is the main cause of these social problems, rather than government policies or poor business practices. Studies of industrial relations reporting by the Glasgow University Media Group (2000) suggest that the media portray 'unreasonable' workers as making trouble for 'reasonable' employers.

Other representations are more sympathetic. The 'kitchen-sink' British cinema of the 1960s, represented by films such as *Saturday Night, Sunday Morning* and *Kes*, television drama such as *Our Friends in the North* and films such as *The Full Monty* and *Brassed Off* have portrayed working-class life and problems in a dignified, sensitive and supportive way, and even commented upon and challenged social inequality, class exploitation and racial intolerance.

Curran and Seaton (2003) note that newspapers aimed at working-class audiences assume that they are uninterested in serious analysis of either the political or social organization of UK society. Political debate is often reduced simplistically to conflict between personalities. The content of newspapers such as the *Sun* and the *Star* assume that such audiences want to read about celebrity gossip and lifestyles, trivial human interest stories and sport. Marxists see such media content as an attempt to distract the working-class audience from the inequalities of capitalism (see cultural effects in Topic 4).

Representations of poverty and underclass

Newman argues that when the news media turn their attention to the most destitute, the portrayals are often negative or stereotypical. Often, the poor are portrayed in statistical rather than in human terms by news bulletins that focus on the numbers unemployed or on benefits rather than the individual suffering and personal indignities of poverty. Some sociologists note that the dumbing-down of television has led to a decline in serious dramas and documentaries highlighting the personal costs of poverty and degradation.

A very recent development in media interest in the poor has been the labelling of some sections of the poor as 'chavs' or 'charvers', which Shildrick and MacDonald (2007) suggest is another way of suggesting that the poor are undeserving of public sympathy. As Hayward and Yar (2006) argue, the label 'chav' is now used by newspapers and websites as a familiar and amusing term of abuse for young poor people. Lawler (2005) notes that 'though the term chav/a now circulates widely in Britain as a term of disgust and contempt, it is imposed on people rather than being claimed by them'. He argues that the media use this discriminatory and offensive form of language to vilify what they depict as a peasant **underclass** symbolized by stereotypical forms of appearance (e.g. tracksuits, bling).

This 'dangerous class' is portrayed by the media as consisting of irresponsible parents with 'out of control' children, living in council housing, welfare-dependent and probably criminal. As Webster (2007) argues, these media representations of the poor as 'chavs' define them as 'social scum' and hence neutralize any public concern or sympathy for their social and economic plight.

Swale (2006) notes the conservative social and moral agenda that underpinned some of the media's reporting of the poor in 2005. She notes that newspapers such as the *Sunday Times* started using the term 'Neet' meaning 'Not in Education, Employment or Training' to describe youth whom the paper described as antisocial and feckless. The paper alleged that many of the young poor were responsible for their own poverty because they had dropped out of school, refused work and training when it was offered, and, in the case of girls, become single mothers. Swale argues that this type of coverage negatively stigmatizes sections of the poor as an 'out group', encouraging readers to label those on benefits as the undeserving poor.

McKendrick *et al.* (2008) studied a week's output of mainstream media in 2007 and concluded that coverage of poverty is marginal in the UK media, in that the causes and consequences of poverty were very rarely explored across the news, documentaries or drama. Dramas such as *Shameless* presented a sanitized picture of poverty, despite featuring characters who were economically deprived, whilst family issue-based programmes such as *Jeremy Kyle* treated poverty as an aspect of entertainment (see 'Focus on research', p. 202).

Cohen (2009) argues the UK mass media was so concerned about 'trumpeting the good fortune' of British capitalism that it paid less attention to its 'casualties'. Cohen argues that journalists, entertainers and artists were hopeless at realistically reporting or dramatizing the plight of the poor. He argues that some sections of the media revelled in the suffering of the poor. He notes that:

≪ *Media executives commissioned shows such as* Little Britain *and* Shameless*, in which the White poor were White trash; stupid teenagers who got pregnant without a thought; alcoholic fathers with delinquent children who wallowed in drugs and sex … The poor were the grasping inhabitants of a parasite paradise, scrounging off the … middle classes in television comedy, or freaks to be mocked on the British versions of the* Jerry Springer *Show.* ≫

Little Britain character Vicky Pollard. What stereotypes of poverty and the underclass does this character exemplify?

Focus on research

McKendrick et al. (2008)
The media, poverty and public opinion in the UK

Interviews were conducted with nine key informants involved in producing media coverage of poverty – journalists, editors and press officers. Three aspects of media output were examined. First, a systematic content analysis of news content over a study week (30 July to 5 August 2007) sampled over 150 newspapers, 100 radio news programmes, 75 television news programmes, a selection of news magazines and a range of new media. Second, the varying treatment of six poverty-related news reports was examined across a range of media. Third, interpretive analysis was undertaken of the portrayal of poverty in selected drama, documentary and 'reality TV' broadcasts. To explore audience responses to media coverage, eleven focus groups were conducted with different socio-demographic groups across a range of geographic areas in Britain. The key findings were as follows:

- Coverage of poverty is peripheral in mainstream UK media. The causes of poverty and the consequences of poverty were rarely explored.
- Non-news broadcasts rarely mentioned poverty, although they often featured those experiencing deprivation. Coverage tended to focus on extreme cases, highlighting the inherent 'failings' of undeserving people. Some documentaries explored the inequities of poverty and complex circumstances of those experiencing it, but reached limited audiences.
- In news media, poverty in the developing world received as much coverage as poverty in the UK, but was reported differently. Depictions of extreme poverty outside the UK correspond with and may influence how the public perceive and define poverty.
- Audiences tend to interpret representations of poverty and its causes in accordance with their beliefs and understandings. A key limitation of media coverage is the tendency to marginalize accounts that confront negative public attitudes.

Adapted from McKendrick, J.H., Sinclair, S., Irwin. A., O'Donnell H., Scott, G. and Dobbie, L. (2008) *The Media, Poverty and Public Opinion in the UK*, York: Joseph Rowntree Foundation

1 What do you think the aims of this research were?
2 What three main methods of research were used?
3 Explain why each method was used.
4 What perceptions of poverty are the British public likely to develop?

The media therefore reinforced the popular view that the poor were poor because of their own depravity and weakness. Most importantly, says Cohen, the media failed to see the connection between deprivation and wealth.

Conclusions

Despite the lack of empirical research in this area, it can be argued that media representations of the powerful, i.e. the upper class and the middle class, tend to be more positive than representations of the less powerful working class and poor.

Representations of age

Media representations of different groups of people based on age (i.e. children, adolescents and the elderly), also generalize and categorize people on the basis of stereotypes. The media encourage audiences to assume that specific representations in terms of image and behaviour can be applied wholesale to particular age groups.

Childhood

British children are often depicted in the UK media in fairly positive ways. Content analyses of media products suggest that seven stereotypes of children are frequently used by the media:

1 *As victims of horrendous crimes* (e.g. Madeleine McCann, James Bulger, Holly Chapman and Jessica Wells) – Some critics of the media have suggested that White children who are victims of crime get more media attention than adults or children from ethnic-minority backgrounds. Note, too, that the media ethnocentrically portrays foreign children in quite a different way from British children; for example, African children are often represented as emaciated and dying, whilst 2009 saw many sections of the British media publishing pictures of the dead bodies of Palestinian children in Gaza.
2 *As cute* – This is a common stereotype found in television commercials for baby products or toilet rolls.
3 *As little devils* – Another common stereotype especially found in drama and comedy, e.g. Bart Simpson.
4 *As brilliant* – Perhaps as child prodigies or as heroes for saving the life of an adult.
5 *As brave little angels* – Suffering from long-term or terminal disease or disability.
6 *As accessories* – Stories about celebrities such as Madonna, Angeline Jolie or the Beckhams may focus on how their children humanize them.
7 *As modern* – The media may focus on how children 'these days' know so much more 'at their age' than previous generations of children.

Heintz-Knowles' (2002) study of children on television found that children are often portrayed as motivated primarily by peer relationships, sports, and romance, and least often by community, school-related, or religious issues. They are rarely shown as coping with societal issues such as racism or with major family issues such as child abuse and domestic violence. However, most representations of children are positive and show them engaged in prosocial actions such as telling the truth and helping others. About 40 per cent of television drama depicted children engaged in antisocial actions, such as lying or bullying. However, one very noticeable feature of children's television that has occurred in the last 15 years has been the move to more realistic drama featuring issues from a child's rather than an adult's point of view.

Children are also represented in television commercials in ways that socialize them to become active consumers. They are encouraged by television advertising and film merchandizing to have an appetite for toys and games. Some family sociologists note that this has led to the emergence of a new family pressure: 'pester power', the power of children to train or manipulate their parents to spend money on consumer goods that will increase the children's status in the eyes of their peers. Evans and Chandler (2006) suggest that pester power is creating great anxiety among poorer parents, who will often go into debt to provide for their children's needs.

Youth

There are generally two very broad ways in which young people have been targeted and portrayed by the media in the UK. On the one hand, there is a whole media industry aimed at socially constructing youth in terms of lifestyle and identity. Magazines are produced specifically for young people. Record companies, internet music download sites, mobile telephone companies and radio stations all specifically target and attempt to shape the musical tastes of young people. Networking sites on the internet, such as Facebook, Bebo and MySpace, allow youth to project their identities around the world.

However, as described in Topic 3, youth are often portrayed by news media as a social problem, as immoral or anti-authority, and consequently constructed as folk devils as part of a moral panic. The majority of moral panics since the 1950s have been manufactured around concerns about young people's behaviour, such as their membership of specific 'deviant' subcultures (e.g. teddy boys, hoodies) or because their behaviour (e.g. drug-taking or binge drinking) has attracted the disapproval of those in authority.

Research by Wayne et al. (2007) confirms this overwhelmingly negative portrayal of youth in the UK. Their analysis looked at 2130 news items across all the main television channels during May 2006 and found 286 stories that focused specifically on young people. Of these, 28 per cent focused on celebrities, but 82 per cent focused on young people as either the perpetrators or the victims of violent crime. In other words, young people were mainly represented as a violent threat to society. Wayne and colleagues also found that it was very rare (only 1 per cent) for news items to feature a young person's perspective or opinion. They note that the media only delivers a one-dimensional picture of youth, one that encourages fear and condemnation rather than understanding. Moreover, they argue that it distracts from the real problems young people face in the modern world – such as homelessness, not being able to get onto the housing ladder, unemployment, mental health, etc – that might be caused by society's or the government's failure to take the problems of youth seriously.

The elderly

Research focusing on media representations of the elderly suggests that age is not the only factor that impacts on the way the media portrays people aged 65 and over. For example, Newman (2006) notes that upper-class and middle-class elderly people are often portrayed in television and film dramas as occupying high-status roles as world leaders, judges, politicians, experts, business executives, etc. Leading film stars such as Harrison Ford and Clint Eastwood are well beyond retirement age. Moreover, news programmes seem to work on the assumption that an older male with grey in his hair and lines on his face somehow exudes the necessary authority to impart the news. However, female newscasters, such as Anna Ford, have long complained that these older men are often paired with attractive young females, while older women newsreaders are often exiled to radio. Leading female film and television stars are also often relegated to character parts once their looks and bodies are perceived to be on the wane, which seems to be after the age of 40.

It can be argued that old age is generally devalued by the media industry. This is particularly apparent in the advertising of beauty products aimed at slowing down the ageing process or hiding it altogether. On the whole, however, research into media representations of the elderly shows that the elderly are largely invisible across a range of media and, when they do appear, they are often negatively stereotyped.

Alastair Stewart (born 1952) and Katie Derham (born 1970) were paired by ITN for various news bulletins. How do they illustrate the point made by Anna Ford above?

The invisible elderly

Age Concern (2000) argue that the elderly are under-represented across a variety of mass media. For example, in 2000, 21 per cent of the population was aged 65+, yet only 7 per cent of representations on television were of that age group. Older men constituted 70 per cent of these representations despite making up only 43 per cent of the 65+ population. Landis (2002) conducted an analysis of media representations in popular magazines. She found that in *Family Circle* only 8 per cent of stories and images focused on people aged 55+, whilst in *Good Housekeeping* only 6 per cent of the magazine was focused on the elderly. She found that, in most popular magazines aimed at women, only 9 per cent of features or images were focused on elderly people.

Stereotypes of the elderly

When the elderly do appear in the media, they tend to be stereotyped as having specific characteristics, many of which are negative and one-dimensional:

- *Grumpy* – This stereotype paints elderly women as shrews or busybodies and males as curmudgeons who spend their time waxing lyrical about the past, bemoaning the behaviour of young people and complaining about the modern world, e.g. Victor Meldrew in *One Foot in the Grave*. These characters tend to be portrayed as conservative, stubborn and resistant to social change.
- *Mentally challenged* – This stereotype ranges from those elderly who are forgetful or befuddled to those who are feeble-minded or severely confused, i.e. suffering from senility. This stereotype suggests that growing old involves the loss of or at least, the decline of people's mental functions.
- *Infantile* – Media representations of the elderly portray them as children, who need to be treated as such, or as helpless and dependent on other younger members of the family or society. The 'sweet little old lady' stereotype is typical of this representation.
- *As a burden* – The elderly are portrayed as an economic burden on society (in terms of the costs to the younger generation of pensions and health care) and/or as a physical and social burden on younger members of their families (who have to worry about or care for them).
- *As enjoying a second childhood* – Sometimes films or television show the more affluent elderly attempting to relive their adolescence and engaging in activities that they have always longed to do before they die, as, for example, in the film *The Bucket List*.

Research in the early part of the 21st century generally suggests that the contribution of the elderly to society is not appreciated by media agencies, who rarely consult them as experienced or wise elders with a wealth of experience to pass on to younger members of society. Furthermore, the emphasis in television, film and advertising on youth and beauty imply that ageing should be avoided at all costs, which in itself strongly implies that to be old is a stigmatized identity.

However, recent research suggests that media producers may be gradually reinventing how they deal with the elderly, especially as they realize that this group may have disposable incomes, i.e. extra money to spend on consumer goods.

Lee *et al.* (2007) note that representation of the elderly in advertisements is still fairly low, i.e. 15 per cent, but the majority of these advertisements (91 per cent) portray the elderly as 'golden agers', who are active, alert, healthy, successful and content. However, this research suggests that this stereotype may be unrealistic in that it does not reflect the wide range of experiences that people have as they age, including loss of status, poverty, loneliness and loss of their partner.

Robinson *et al.* (2008) compared how older adults and college students perceived the stereotypes of the elderly found in magazine adverts. They found that the elderly sample liked those adverts that showed them as clever, vibrant and having a sense of humour. Interestingly, neither the elderly nor the student respondents liked those adverts that poked fun at the elderly or presented them as out of touch or as unattractive.

Conclusions

Media representations of age, alongside other agencies of socialization such as family experience and education, are important in shaping our attitudes towards other age groups and perhaps to our own futures as we go through the ageing process. However, research in this field, especially with regard to the very young and the elderly, is fairly limited. Perhaps this fact, too, is illustrative of the low status that society generally accords to these age groups.

Key terms

Cultural hegemony the interests of the ruling class being accepted as 'common sense' by the mass of the population.

Ghettoization in this context, scheduling programmes aimed at minority ethnic groups at times or on channels which ensure small audiences.

Islamophobia fear of Muslims.

Misogyny hatred of women.

Tokenism including a limited number of minority group members only because it is felt that this is expected.

Underclass group below the working class, dependent on benefits and unlikely to secure employment.

Activities

Research idea

Interview a sample of over-60s about their feelings about representations of the elderly in the media. Focus the discussion by showing participants some well-known personalities. To what extent are they concerned about stereotyping in the media?

Web.task

Read the following newspaper article and web column about the links between rap music and gun crime.

http://news.bbc.co.uk/1/hi/entertainment/4578818.stm

www.spiked-online.com/Articles/00000006DBBE.htm

To what extent do you agree with:

1 the Advertising Standards Authority's verdict on the 50 Cent poster?

2 the columnist in 'Spiked'?

Explain your answers.

Check your understanding

1. What evidence is there that 'the take-up of media technology among ethnic minority groups is ... well developed'?

2. According to Agbetu, what are the three attributes of a Black person constructed in the media?

3. How did Hall argue that the moral panic over mugging served an ideological purpose?

4. What are the arguments for and against the view that rap music has a negative influence on young Black men?

5. Give evidence to show how media coverage can represent asylum seekers and refugees as 'a threat'?

6. What evidence is there for Islamophobia in the British media?

7. How has media reporting of less-developed countries been criticized?

8. How do ethnic-minority audiences perceive race issues are dealt with in dramas?

9. How have media professionals from ethnic-minority backgrounds responded to inequalities and prejudices?

10. How has the use of the term 'chav' been criticized by sociologists?

11. Identify and explain three examples of often-used stereotypes of children in the media.

12. In what ways are youth are often represented as a problem in the media?

13. Explain how it can be argued that 'old age' is generally devalued by the media industry.

An eye on the exam — Representations of ethnicity, age and social class

Item A

The media often portray Black people and members of other ethnic minorities in negative and stereotypical ways. In addition, they may suffer 'symbolic annihilation', where they are ignored or under-represented in the media. The poor and the working class often suffer a similar fate – either absent, or presented in a bad light, for example as social security scroungers or incompetents who are responsible for their own poverty. The media also tend to treat different age groups differently. For example, while young people are often portrayed as a threat, the very old are largely ignored or shown as difficult, forgetful or feeble – while representations of them avoid the subject of dying. For Marxists, such stereotypes exist because they play an ideological role for capitalism. By contrast, pluralists see them as a reflection of public views.

Using material from **Item A** and elsewhere, critically examine sociological explanations of mass-media representations of one of the following: ethnicity; age; social class.

(33 marks)

Grade booster — Getting top marks in this question

For this question, don't be tempted to write about a second area, as you will not gain any marks for doing so. Once you have selected one of the areas, you can begin by describing the patterns of representation, both in terms of stereotyping and under- or overrepresentation. Use material from the Item and your own knowledge to do this. If you choose class, you should look at two or more classes (e.g. middle, working, underclass). If you choose ethnicity, look at two or more ethnic groups. If you choose age, look at several age groups. You need to consider a range of reasons and explanations. General theories of the media (e.g. Marxism, pluralism and postmodernism), as well as more specific theories (e.g. deviance amplification), can be applied to all these groups.

1   Read **Item A** below and answer parts (a) and (b) that follow.

Item A

Sociologists see the news as a social construct – that is, they regard it as something that has been created or 'manufactured' by journalists and editors, and not something that is simply out there waiting to be found and reported.

In the manufacturing of the news, bias enters the process, both in terms of which items get selected for reporting (and which ones are rejected) and in the way in which they are presented. Various factors shape the news 'product', in ways that favour some groups at the expense of others. For example, journalists' news values play an important part in deciding whether a story is newsworthy enough to be covered. Similarly, economic factors such as the cost of sending a team abroad may determine whether or not the news organization covers an important event.

(a) Identify and briefly explain **three** possible controls over the ways in which the media portray individuals or groups. *(9 marks)*

(1) Libel laws – newspapers can be sued for publishing false and defamatory things, e.g. falsely accusing someone of being a paedophile. (2) The Race Relations Act makes it a criminal offence to incite racial hatred, so newspapers can be prosecuted for portraying racial groups so as to stir up racist feelings. (3) Advertisers may put pressure on a newspaper media to change the way it portrays potential customers.

(8 / 9)

An examiner comments

The first two points score full marks, but the third needs more explanation - e.g. that negative portrayals of customers will put them off reading that paper and stop them seeing the adverts.

(b) Using information from **Item A** and elsewhere, assess the view that the selection and presentation of the news are biased. *(18 marks)*

According to Marxists such as the Glasgow University Media Group (GUMG), the media are biased in their presentation of the news. For example, in the Arab-Israeli conflict, the news media consistently take the side of the Israelis. GUMG also found similar patterns when looking at industrial disputes. For example, in their coverage of strikes, the language used and images broadcast make it appear to be the strikers' fault. They are portrayed as 'demanding' whereas the employers are 'offering'. Often strikers are interviewed in the street with lots of noise and disorder, whereas the employer is interviewed in a calm, comfortable office, making him look more rational.

Overall, this is a reasonable answer. It focuses on the question of bias in the news and says something about both selection (e.g. economic factors and news values) and presentation (e.g. GUMG), although it doesn't spell this out. It uses the Item and puts the discussion into the context of Marxist theory. It could be improved by reference to other theories of news production, e.g. interactionism, and to other studies.

GUMG argue that this presentation of the news has an ideological function, to discredit anyone who opposes capitalism and prevent them gaining support. This is why news coverage rarely explains the causes of strikes, because this might make the strikers seem to have a just cause. It also makes capitalism look like a reasonable system. In this sense, the news is part of the ideological state apparatus (Althusser).

As Item A says, economic factors are also involved in news production, and these can produce bias. For example, if a TV company has a limited news budget, they may decide not to send teams abroad as this is more expensive, and concentrate on home news instead. However, this has the effect of making it seem that things happening abroad are not worth knowing about, and can contribute to ethnocentrism in the audience.

Item A also mentions 'news values'. These are the ideas journalists use to decide whether it is worth reporting a story. They include things like personalization, stories about elites and stories with negative effects (e.g. disasters). Thus news values are an inbuilt bias that journalists are socialized into, in favour of some kinds of stories and against others.

(13 / 18)

One for you to try

Assess the view that the mass media have only limited and indirect effects on audiences. *(33 marks)*

An examiner comments

You need to examine a range of models of media effects. These should include models supporting the view in the question, e.g. two-step flow, selective filter and uses and gratifications. Describe evidence from studies in support of these models. Evaluate the view by using models that challenge it, e.g. hypodermic syringe. Consider also models that suggest a strong but indirect effect on audiences.

Answers to the 'One for you to try' are available free on www.collinseducation.com/sociologyweb

Power and politics

AQA Specification	Topics	Pages
Candidates should examine:	**Candidates should examine:**	
Different theories of the nature and distribution of power.	Covered in Topics 1 and 2.	208–23
The role of the contemporary state.	Covered in Topic 3.	224–31
The nature of, and changes in, different forms of political participation, including voting behaviour, political action and protest, and membership of political organizations and movements.	Voting behaviour is covered in Topic 4. Other forms of political participation are covered in Topic 5.	232–41 242–52
The role of political parties, pressure/interest groups, new social movements and the mass media in the political process.	Political parties are covered in Topic 4. Pressure and other interest groups are covered in Topic 5.	232–41 242–52
The significance of globalization for an understanding of power and politics in the contemporary world.	Covered throughout the chapter, but see especially the pages listed on the right.	220–21 230

TOPIC 1

Defining power

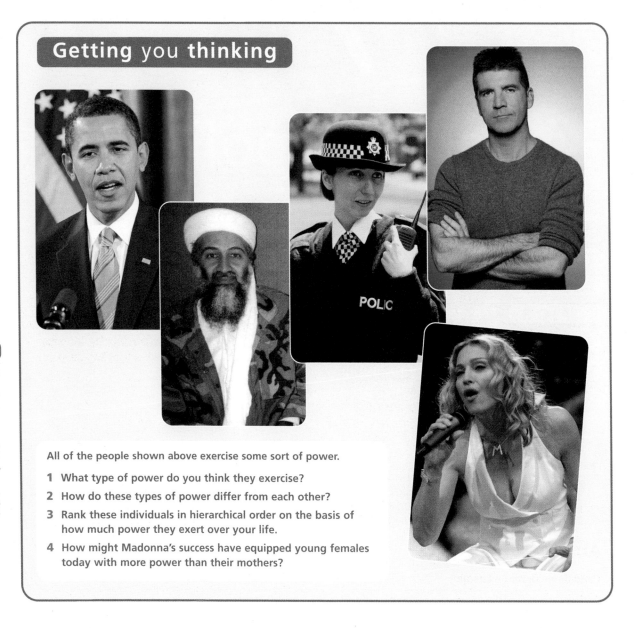

Getting you thinking

All of the people shown above exercise some sort of power.

1 What type of power do you think they exercise?

2 How do these types of power differ from each other?

3 Rank these individuals in hierarchical order on the basis of how much power they exert over your life.

4 How might Madonna's success have equipped young females today with more power than their mothers?

The above exercise should have shown you that power can take several different forms and can be exercised in a number of direct and indirect ways. For example, you are unlikely to meet Barack Obama or Osama Bin Laden, but they still exercise considerable power over your life. For example, the possibility of terrorism on the streets of Britain could be said to depend to a large degree on the policies and actions of these two individuals. In recent years, the power of the police to stop and search you, and even use violence on you, considerably increased as a result of terrorist attacks in London. Similarly, it can be argued that if you are a female, Madonna's success impacts directly on your capacity to exercise power. You exercise more power than your mother because Madonna's career over the years has contributed to an acceptance of a wide range of activities for women that were once considered deviant. Think too about the power Simon Cowell exercises in your life – it can be argued that he has had considerable influence over popular culture, and consequently your tastes and lifestyle.

Max Weber and power

In the most general sense, power refers to any kind of influence exercised by individuals or groups on others. For example, Max Weber defined power as the chance or probability of an individual or group of people imposing their will on others despite resistance, i.e. where A has power over B to the extent that A can get B to do something that B would not otherwise do. This conception of power – the **zero-sum view of power** – implies that the exercise of power involves negative consequences for some individuals and groups because it involves repression, force and constraint. Weber believed that such power could be exercised in a range of social situations.

Focus on research

Max Weber's types of authority

Weber argues that legitimacy can be derived from three sources:

- *Charisma* – Some individuals are able to direct the behaviour of others because they have exceptionally powerful personalities that inspire strong feelings of devotion and loyalty. These may be political leaders such as Adolf Hitler, religious leaders such as Gandhi or the Reverend Jim Jones (see Chapter 1, p. 28) and sporting personalities such as José Mourinho or Sir Alex Ferguson. Note how some of your teachers may use their charisma to motivate you.
- *Tradition* – Power can be derived from historical precedent, such as that embodied in the succession of the Royal Family in the UK. Many people in the UK believe that the Queen has inherited the 'right' to rule and so consider themselves as loyal subjects.
- *Rational–legal* – Most authority in Britain, whether that of the prime minister, a police officer or a teacher, derives from formal rules which often take the form of laws. Such authority is thought to be impartially applied to everyone and enforced without bias. Consequently, people consent to obey this type of power, which is usually administered by a hierarchical **bureaucracy**. Morgan (1999) refers to this as 'the routinization of obedience'. The option of force still exists but it is used only as a final resort.

What types of authority are associated with:

(a) social workers   (b) the Pope

(c) Jesus Christ?

<< *Positions of power can emerge from social relations in a drawing room as well as in the market, from the rostrum of a lecture hall as well as the command post of a regiment, from an erotic or charitable relationship as well as from scholarly discussion or athletics.* >>
(Lukes 1986)

Weber distinguished between two main types of power implied here – coercion and authority:

- Coercion is force, usually in the form of violence or military resources.
- Authority depends upon consent – that is, people believe that the power is **legitimate**. For example, students generally obey their teachers because they accept their authority. This type of power is often wielded by institutions – we accept the power or authority of individuals such as doctors, teachers, judges, tax inspectors, police officers because they belong to an institution which we recognize as having legitimate power. However, as Allen (2000) points out, we also accept authority of which we are not always aware, such as that represented by CCTV which subjects us to daily scrutiny and control, because we accept the idea that the benefits of such a system outweigh the costs. In other words, we accept that the authority of such a surveillance system is legitimate.

Some sociologists have highlighted other forms of power halfway between coercion and authority, such as influence (where people are persuaded to change their minds) and manipulation (where individuals are cynically deceived, perhaps through control over education, knowledge, information and news).

Functionalism and power

Functionalists view power as a positive resource, characterized by consensus and legitimacy. Talcott Parsons (1963) argued that power results from the sharing of resources in order to achieve collective social and cultural goals. If A and B work together, they will both increase their power as well as benefit society. Power is therefore a functional resource working for the benefit of everybody and helping to maintain social order and strengthen social solidarity.

Parsons argued that if power is to be used to pursue collective goals effectively, it needs direction and organization. For this reason, members of society authorize some individuals via democratic elections (namely, politicians) to exercise power on their behalf. Parsons argues that if society is unhappy with the use of that power, members of society simply will not vote for them. In this way, power can never be monopolized and is always used to benefit the greater good. However, this view of power has been criticized as naive, as it fails to acknowledge that power can be accumulated in the hands of individuals with more interest in pursuing their own sectional interests than collective goals or common good.

Marxism and power

Marxists argue that power arises out of the social **relations of production** that characterize the economic system of production found in **capitalist societies** (see Chapter 5, p. 256). These social relations exist between two groups characterized by their access (or lack of access) to economic resources:

- the **bourgeoisie** or ruling class – a minority group who own and control the **means of production**, such as capital, land, factories, technology and raw materials
- the **proletariat** or working class – the majority group who have only their labour power, which they hire out to the bourgeoisie in return for a wage.

This class inequality is further deepened by the bourgeoisie's exploitation of the proletariat's labour power, in that the wealth of the dominant class is increased by the fact that the value of the goods produced by the worker always far exceeds the wage paid. This surplus value is pocketed by the bourgeoisie in the form of profit. Marxists argue, therefore, that inequalities in ownership and control – along with exploitation – lead to economic inequality, and this is the source of political and social power in society. In other words, power derives from class relationships.

Hegemony

Class domination and economic power are maintained through coercion (although this tends to be used as a last resort) and ideological **hegemony** (the control of ideas). Marxists argue that this latter concept is much more effective than force in controlling a proletariat which has the potential to be very disruptive if it decides that the organization of the capitalist infrastructure is unfair and unjust in how income and wealth are distributed. Hegemony or cultural dominance by the ruling class is needed in order to make sure that the working class regard bourgeois power as legitimate, and so reduce the potential for revolutionary protest.

According to Bocock (1986), hegemony occurs when the intellectual and moral ideas of the ruling class provide the dominant cultural outlook for the whole of society. Marxists such as Althusser (1971) argue that the bourgeoisie achieve this cultural dominance by using its economic power to define what counts as knowledge, ideas, art, education, news and so on. Social institutions such as the education system, the legal system, the political system, the mass media and religion, which Marxists see as making up the '**superstructure**' of capitalist society, play an important role in transmitting ruling-class ideology so that it is accepted by the mass of the population as 'normal' or 'natural'.

Westergaard (1996) argues that the result of hegemonic power is that workers fail to understand their own structural position correctly – that is, they fail to realize their true interests as exploited workers. This false class-consciousness means that they rarely realize their potential power for bringing about revolutionary change. The Frankfurt School of Marxism (see Chapter 5,

---

Focus on research

Giddens and power

Leading sociologist Anthony Giddens (1968) is critical of Parsons' view of power. He notes that Parsons fails to understand that the exercise of power is normally used to further particular interests rather than society as a whole.

≪ *What slips away from sight almost completely in the Parsonian analysis is the very fact that power is always exercised over someone! Parsons virtually ignores, quite consciously and deliberately, the hierarchical character of power, and the divisions of interest which are frequently consequent upon it. However much it is true that power can rest upon 'agreement', it is also true that interests of power-holders and those subject to that power often clash.* ≫

Giddens, A. (1968) '"Power" in the recent writings of Talcott Parsons', *Sociology*, 2(3)

1 **Explain Giddens' criticism of Parsons in your own words.**

2 **Giddens argues that all interaction involves power. Explain how power might be involved in:**

   a **a group of friends talking**
   b **a family deciding which TV programmes to watch in the evening**
   c **a doctor–patient interaction**
   d **a parents' evening at school.**

---

pp. 258–9) in a similar analysis argue that the working class has become 'ideologically incorporated' into capitalist society. Marcuse (1964) argued that this incorporation takes the form of encouraging 'one-dimensional thought': the general population is encouraged to indulge in uncritical and sterile forms of entertainment or mass culture that reduce their appetite for critical and creative thought and action that might challenge hegemonic power. Following on from Marcuse, White (2004) argues that Western culture today is dominated by a 'Middle Mind' – a mainstream consensus that is shaped by consumer culture that pleases everyone but moves, challenges or shocks no one. He notes:

≪ *When we accept the Middle Mind as our culture (or, worse yet, when we demand it as consumers), we are not merely being stupid or unsophisticated or 'low brow'. We are vigorously conspiring against ourselves. We murder our own capacity for critique and invention as if we were children saying, 'Can you do this for me?'.>>*

According to Gramsci (1971), hegemony, and the resulting consent of the people, has enabled the ruling class to deal with any threats to its authority without having to use force. However, Gramsci argues that hegemony does not mean that subordinate classes will always lack power or that the power of the dominant class is absolute. He argues that power is potentially available to the subordinate classes if they become sufficiently class-conscious and politically organized to seize or to challenge the control of the means of production. Importantly, Gramsci argues that people in capitalist societies experience 'dual consciousness' – their beliefs are only partly shaped by capitalist ideology because their beliefs are also influenced by their personal day-to-day experiences of society – these sometimes contradict or challenge dominant ideology and so encourage some resistance and opposition to it. This 'resistance' might take an overtly political form (for instance, active campaigning or taking to the streets to oppose G8 talks) or a 'symbolic' form (such as setting out to challenge dominant institutions and beliefs through the use of 'shock', e.g. through fashion statements or simply substituting a hedonistic lifestyle for the 9-to-5 lifestyle demanded by capitalism).

Neo-Marxists such as Stuart Hall (Hall and Jefferson 1976) have developed **relational conceptions of power** – that is, they recognize that power is a process which involves **ideological struggle** between the capitalist class and groups such as working-class youth. The capitalist class is normally able to impose cultural hegemony and so obtain the consent of most of the people to rule. However, pockets of **symbolic resistance** among sections of the working class indicate that power is not a one-way process. Gilroy (1982a) suggests that working-class crime may well be political – a means by which subordinate groups can enjoy some power through hitting back at the symbols of capitalist power such as wealth and property. The work of the Birmingham Centre for Contemporary Cultural Studies similarly suggests that working-class deviant youth subcultures may be symbolically resisting hegemonic definitions of respectability by adopting forms of style and behaviour that set out to shock. For example, the Punk subculture of the late 1970s incorporated conformist symbols, such as the Queen and Union Jack, as well as deviant symbols, such as Nazi insignia, into its dress codes in a deliberately provocative way.

Criticisms of the Marxist theory of power

Michael Mann (1986) takes issue with the Marxist view that all power is rooted in class relationships. He argues that there are two broad types of power:

- *distributional power* – held and exercised by individuals who have the ability to get others to help them pursue their goals
- *collective power* – exercised by social groups over other social groups ranging in size from nation states to families.

Mann notes that power has a number of unique characteristics:

- It can be *extensive* – It can involve the ability to co-opt large numbers of people across huge distances to work together in common interest. For example, some Muslim people, regardless of their nationality or ethnic group, express loyalty first and foremost to their religion.
- It can be *intensive* – It can command extreme loyalty and dedication from followers. For example, the power wielded by some leaders of religious groups, most notably Jim Jones of The People's Temple, has resulted in mass suicide.
- It can be *authoritative* – It can be organized around rules and commands which are largely regarded as legitimate. For example, your head teacher or principal has the power to exclude you from school or college.
- It can be *diffused* – It can result from natural or spontaneous processes rather than an individual or group issuing commands or physically imposing themselves on a subordinate group. For example, a fall in consumer demand for a particular product might force a manufacturer out of business.

Key themes

Stratification and differentiation

Functionalists and Marxists

Functionalists, such as Davis and Moore (1955), see stratification and social inequality as a functional necessity in modern societies, because certain social positions, e.g. occupational roles, are more important than others. In order to attract those with the most talent, high rewards are attached to these positions. Those in the top positions often wield economic power in that they enjoy a superior standard of living. They often make decisions that affect the economic wellbeing of other members of society, e.g. where to locate a new business. They also exercise authority legitimated by both law and state bureaucracy, e.g. head teachers can suspend pupils. Functionalists argue that this power is generally used for the benefit of society and our consent for its use is an important contributor to social order.

Marxists, on the other hand, see social-class inequalities as the natural outcome of the social organization of capitalism. The bourgeoisie control the means of production and exploit the labour power of the working class. The vast profits made by the bourgeoisie give them political power. Consequently, they can use coercion and repression, if they so wish, in order to protect their interests through control of agencies such as the police, the security services and the armed forces. However, Marxists note that in modern capitalist societies, the bourgeoisie are more likely to use cultural and ideological forms of power, through agencies such as education and the mass media, to persuade the subordinate class that society is organized in a just fashion.

Mann agrees with Marxists that economics (or class) is an important source of power but, as the previous examples illustrate, he acknowledges other sources of power:

● World religions often wield ideological power independently of the economic system.
● Military power, particularly in the developing world, may be separate from economic power, as seen in the number of economic elites who have been deposed by military coups.
● The state has political power, which may result from democratic elections in the case of politicians and **meritocracy** in the case of civil servants. Mann notes that political power is not always used in ways which benefit the economically dominant classes – for example, the minimum wage legislation brought in by the Labour Government in 1999 was opposed by big-business interests.

Mann argues that it is rare that any one social group in a single society is able to dominate more than two sources of power, especially as power is increasingly globalized – power networks now extend across the world and consequently no single interest group is able to monopolize power.

Abercrombie et al. (1980) too are dismissive of Marxist claims that a dominant ideology characterizes contemporary society. They make the following arguments:

● Capitalism today is characterized by conflicts between capitalist interests such as small businesses, finance capital, industrialists, multinational companies and state corporations. This conflict undermines the idea that the capitalist class is transmitting strong and unified ideological messages.
● The subordinate class often rejects the so-called dominant ideology – as can be seen in surveys of working-class people who recognize that we live in a class society characterized by inequality. Such workers may express resistance through strikes and membership of trade unions.
● It is the simple fact that workers have to work in order to preserve their standard of living that leads to their cooperation and participation. People conform, not because of ideological hegemony but quite simply because they fear unemployment and poverty.

Poststructuralism and power

Michel Foucault

Foucault (1980) rejects the link between social structure and power. He suggests that power is an inescapable part of everyday life. In particular, power plays a major role in the construction of identity.

According to Foucault, there is a significant relationship between power, knowledge and language. He argued that there exist bodies of knowledge and language which he terms '**discourses**'. These dominate how society sees, describes and thinks about how we should live our lives, in terms of family, sexuality, discipline and punishment,

health and illness, and so on. Our power to behave in certain ways – and the power of others to prevent us behaving in those ways – is dependent upon dominant discourses.

In illustration, Foucault showed how, during the 18th century, there was a shift away from coercive forms of power associated with physical punishment (e.g. execution) to what he calls '**disciplinary power**'. This type of power saw a move to identify and categorize 'normality' and 'deviance' in the form of discourses in the fields of criminality, sexual behaviour and illness. Bauman (1983) notes how this type of power is based on the construction and imposition of surveillance (watching for deviation from normality), routine and regulation. 'It wanted to impose one ubiquitous [i.e. universal] pattern of normality and eliminate everything and everybody which the pattern could not fit.'

Disciplinary power

Foucault's conception of disciplinary power developed from his study of prisons and asylums. Foucault noted that people were no longer simply punished for crimes – rather there was an attempt to judge why people had committed particular crimes, i.e. to categorize them into specific types. A range of expert professions emerged with the power to observe, judge and categorize people's behaviour in terms of 'normality' and 'deviance'. These included psychologists, psychiatrists and social workers. Foucault notes how, over the course of the 20th century, such surveillance and judgement has expanded into institutions such as schools and workplaces. For example, educational psychologists now attempt to explain a range of behaviours exhibited by children in the educational system, ranging from high achievement through to truancy. At the same time, people who choose not to work are dismissed by experts as 'inadequate' or as 'social problems'. Foucault is therefore suggesting that our identity as well as our behaviour patterns are the result of these powerful judgements or discourses about what should count as 'normal' or 'conformist' behaviour.

Bio-power

Foucault identified a second conception of power which he termed '**bio-power**'. Bio-power is concerned with controlling the body and how it is perceived by the general population. Foucault sees bio-power as especially influential in structuring discourses on sexuality and in shaping attitudes and behaviour among the mass of the population towards different types of sexuality. He claims that, from the 19th century onwards, discourse on sexual behaviour rapidly became dominated by professionals working in the fields of psychiatry, medicine and social work. He argues that this discourse on sexual behaviour has power over all of us because it defines what is and what is not 'normal' and 'what is and what is not available for individuals to do, think, say and be' (Clegg 1989).

Foucault suggests that the dominant discourse favours heterosexuality at the expense of homosexuality and other alternative sexualities. This power to impose definitions of 'normality' has become part of institutionalized life and

In 1998, protesters from the gay rights group Outrage! dressed as bishops to protest against what they saw as discrimination by the Church of England. How does this illustrate Foucault's ideas about 'bio-power'?

results in individuals being criticized, treated prejudicially and punished for being different – that is, for indulging in non-heterosexual behaviour or for holding attitudes that challenge the dominant heterosexual discourse. Moreover, Foucault argues that bio-power is extremely influential because it shapes our own sense of identity. For example, if we are attracted to people of the same sex, we may avoid forms of behaviour which other people interpret as 'homosexual' in order to avoid judgement and perhaps prejudice and discrimination. However, Foucault did note that the exercise of such power often leads to some type of resistance and eventually positive social change. He claimed that the de-criminalization of homosexuality was the result of such resistance.

Evaluating Foucault's work

Foucault's work has been criticized for not being empirical in a conventional research sense. He tended to support his arguments with selective historical examples rather than systematically gathered contemporary data. Moreover, his work tended to be overly descriptive at the expense of explanation – for example, it is not entirely clear why disciplinary power and bio-power evolved, nor who exercises these types of power. However, his work has value in that it convincingly explores the relationship between knowledge and power.

Gender and power

Feminists argue that the most important type of power originates in the relationship between men and women. They focus on the concept of '**patriarchy**', which they define as the power that men have over women. Millett (1970) argued that patriarchal power resulted in male dominance and female subordination. She suggests that patriarchy is the most powerful ideology of our culture, arguing that it is more important than social class because

it has been around for a lot longer. Millett argues that patriarchy is the result of a number of factors:

- *Biology* – Males have been able to use their superior physical strength to dominate women. The socialization of children encourages qualities, e.g. aggression, that reinforce the coercion of women.
- *Ideology* – Institutions are dominated by males and consequently these transmit the view that men are better suited than women to high-status jobs and roles.
- *The family* – Millett argues that this institution is the source of patriarchy which it transmits from generation to generation.
- *Caste* – Millett argues that gender is a type of caste that operates independently of class, e.g. she points out that upper-class women are generally regarded as subordinate to men.
- *Education* – Women are not encouraged to study high-status subjects.
- *Economic dependency* – Women are segregated in the job market – they are denied entry to top jobs by a '**glass ceiling**' and often end up in low-paid and low-status women's work.
- *Religion and myth* – Religion often legitimates women's low status in society.

- *Psychology* – Women develop an inferiority complex as a result of the above influences. Many believe that their role is to have children and a family rather than a career.
- *Physical force* – Patriarchy is backed up by force or the threat of it, e.g. domestic violence, rape.

Millett's conception of male power has been criticized. Rowbotham (1982) is sceptical of Millett's claim that all men exploit women and that all men benefit from patriarchy. She points out that this claim is exaggerated because it implies that men and women cannot have loving or friendly relationships without some form of male exploitation being present. Rowbotham suggests that the relationship between men and women is not always characterized by power inequalities.

Westwood and postfeminism

Westwood (2002) notes that feminism saw itself 'as fighting for a reversal of the status quo in which men were seen to be dominant'. However, Westwood argues that this type of approach, symbolized by Millett's ideas, was crude and alienated many women from feminism, because it cast them as powerless subordinates, oppressed and exploited by patriarchal power.

Westwood argues for the development of 'postfeminism', in which sociologists use Foucault's work on discourse to show how women can take control of their lives and identities. She cites Rubin (1998), who argues that females can exercise power through a series of strategies focusing on the microprocesses of power. Women can use their bodies, intuition and control of gestures to gain power and to construct their identities. Westwood uses the example of Diana, Princess of Wales, to demonstrate how the microprocesses of power can be amplified through the media. Westwood concludes that Diana was able to exercise power subtly by presenting herself as a victim of both adultery and institutional power. She made herself highly visible through the media and used her role as the mother of the future king to ensure her voice was heard.

Westwood argues that the Diana story raises many of the issues seen in a Foucauldian reading of power relations. For example, Diana's struggle for power stemmed from her attempts to construct an identity or individuality that was at odds with a discourse that stated that she should be an obedient subject of the monarchy. Such a discourse led to attempts to discipline her and control her behaviour. In her case, this disciplinary power eventually failed because she was able to develop visibility and utilize aspects of the microprocesses of power (especially in the field of sexual politics) that monarchy and society could not ignore.

Check your understanding

1 How does the 'zero-sum of power' model define power?

2 What is the difference between coercion and authority?

3 What type of power is exercised by the prime minister?

4 What is the function of power according to Parsons?

5 Where does political power originate according to Marxists?

6 What is the function of the superstructure in regard to power?

7 According to Gramsci, why might resistance to hegemonic power be possible and what forms might it take?

8 Suggest two ways in which subordinate groups can acquire power according to Marxists.

9 How does Foucault suggest the exercise of power has changed over time?

10 In what way did Princess Diana use her power as a woman according to Westwood?

Activities

Research ideas

1 Construct a spider chart with a box in the centre symbolizing yourself. Draw lines to other boxes containing the names of significant people in your life, e.g. friends, brothers and sisters, parents, other relatives, teachers, employers, workmates. Use a different colour pen to symbolize the type of power relationship you have with these people – for example, if the relationship is based on authority draw a red line, as you would from you to your teacher. Some of your relationships may be based on coercion, persuasion, influence, manipulation, even ideology – use different colour lines to symbolize these. You may have to add categories or adapt existing ones.

2 Ask a small sample of other people (try to include people of different ages, gender, ethnic and class backgrounds) to construct similar diagrams. Compare the diagrams. What similarities and differences do you find?

Web.task

Search the worldwide web for lists of powerful men and/or women in Britain. What is the basis of the power of those who make up these lists?

Criticisms of Westwood

Westwood may be guilty of exaggerating the degree of power that women have in patriarchal societies. It can be argued that women still do not enjoy equal power and status with men in fields such as work, wealth, income and politics. Moreover, Princess Diana's power to resist the will of the monarchy may have been the result of her wealth and social-class position as much as her gender. These gave her the celebrity status that allowed her access to the media in order to promote her version of reality. Diana may also be a unique example in that the mass of ordinary women are unable to use their 'bodies, intuition and gestures' to gain power or get themselves heard.

In fact, the work of Foucault can be used to criticize Westwood's postfeminist position that women can control their own identities. Feminist sociologists have pointed to the way in which dominant discourses about female bodies shape female identity and self-esteem in ways that reinforce female powerlessness. For example, as Bartkey (1992) notes, dominant discourses about femininity celebrate thinness and this results in a strong disciplinary power over women's bodies focusing on weight, shape and appearance. Women, in response, may practise self-discipline by engaging in dieting, slimming, exercise, surgery, and even anorexia and bulimia.

Key terms

what is 'normal' and what is 'deviant'.

Bio-power term used by Foucault to describe concern with controlling the body and its perception.

Bourgeoisie Marxist term describing the ruling (or capitalist) class in capitalist society.

Bureaucracy form of organization associated with modern societies, consisting of a hierarchy of formal positions, each with clear responsibilities.

Capitalist societies where one social class owns the means of production, while another class does the work.

Disciplinary power the power to identify and categorize

Discourse ways of talking and thinking that dominate how society sees, describes and thinks about how we should live our lives.

Glass ceiling work-based situation in which women are prevented from accessing top jobs because of discrimination by male employers.

Hegemony situation where the ideology of the dominant class becomes accepted as the shared culture of the whole of society.

Ideological struggle cultural conflict between the capitalist and subordinate classes.

Legitimate justified and accepted.

Means of production Marxist term referring to the material forces that enable things be produced, e.g. capital, land, factories.

Meritocracy a society in which people are rewarded on the basis of merit, i.e. intelligence and ability, usually via examinations and qualifications.

Patriarchy male power over women.

Proletariat in Marxist terms, the working class, who hire out their labour to the bourgeoisie in return for a wage.

Relational conception of power power seen as a

process that involves ideological struggle between the capitalist class and subordinate groups.

Relations of production Marxist term referring to the allocation of rules and responsibilities among those involved in production.

Superstructure Marxist term used to describe the parts of society not concerned with economic production, such as the media, religion and education.

Symbolic resistance rebellion which takes an indirect form.

Zero-sum view of power idea that power involves one person or group gaining and another person or group losing.

An eye on the exam   Defining power

(a) Identify and briefly explain **three** types of authority. (9 marks)

(b) Identify and briefly explain **three** features of the Marxist view of power. (9 marks)

Grade booster   Getting top marks in this question

For question (a) you could use Max Weber's threefold typology of authority. You can give an example of each type if you wish, but make sure you give a clear definition of each as well. A couple of sentences for each point should be enough provided you stay focused on the question.

For question (b), try to pick out three key ideas or terms from the Marxist view of power. When you explain them, each explanation should contain some explicit reference to power – preferably using the word itself to keep you focused on the question.

The distribution of power

Getting you thinking

Read through the following fictional scenario and then answer the questions that follow.

Imagine you are attending a Public Inquiry into whether a new road should be built between the port of Grimsby and the A1. There are two proposed routes. Route A will cost £210 million and will run straight through the only known habitat in the north of England of the rare wide-mouthed frog. It will also involve the blasting of a tunnel through the Lincolnshire Wolds, an area of outstanding natural beauty. Route B will cost £160 million but will run through the greenbelt around the historic city of Lincoln, as well as involve great disruption to traffic in the area while a bypass is especially built to take traffic away from the city centre. Five groups will give evidence to the Inquiry.

A Lincoln Chamber of Commerce

We favour Route B. The motorway will bring extra business and trade to the city which is good for our members. Hauliers and builders will especially benefit. In particular, it will increase the tourist trade to the city. The motorway will affect the surrounding countryside but there is plenty of it to enjoy that will not be affected. (Report prepared by John Smith of Smith Road Haulage Ltd and Stephen Brook of Brook Building Quarries Ltd.)

B Department of the Environment, Food and Rural Affairs

We approve of Route B for cost reasons. It will also attract foreign investors to the area because of the fast road-links to London. It will increase the status of the area and attract commuters in from London who can take advantage of rail links from Lincoln. Employment opportunities will increase, leading to full employment and higher wages. However, the department is also content with Route A because the Ministry of Defence requires a fast road from the Grimsby area to facilitate the efficient movement of nuclear waste in and out of RAF Binbrook. (This information is highly confidential and should not be disclosed to the Inquiry.)

C Friends of the Earth

We oppose both routes on the grounds that wildlife and the countryside will suffer. We are particularly concerned about the survival of the wide-mouthed frog, which is in danger of extinction across the country. Both roads will be a blot on the landscape. Existing rail services can easily deal with the container traffic from the port of Grimsby.

D North Lincolnshire Ramblers' Association

We oppose both routes. We are concerned that the natural beauty of the area will be ruined. We are concerned about the danger to children from more traffic, especially in terms of accidents and pollution. There may be an influx of new people into the area. Some of these may be undesirables and bring crime to the area. The value of our properties may fall considerably.

E National Farmers' Union

We favour Route A. This route involves less damage to the environment compared with Route B. The danger to the wide-mouthed frog is over-estimated. It can be moved to another habitat. The land around Route B currently attracts about £200 million in EU subsidies – the NFU estimates that we would only receive about £70 million from the Ministry of Transport if the land is compulsorily purchased whereas our members would receive approximately £90 million for the less fertile land around Route A.

1 Look carefully at the five briefs. If you were representing these organizations, what information would you disclose to the Inquiry? What would you hold back and why?

2 What does this exercise tell you about the decision-making process?

The point of this exercise is to demonstrate that decision-making is not a straightforward process. You will have noticed that four of the groups have a vested interest in either one or both routes. Moreover, they probably made decisions not to divulge all of the information they had because it might have prejudiced the Inquiry against them. The Inquiry, then, is basing its conclusions on incomplete information. There are three groups who would benefit enormously whichever road is built. Only one group has nothing to hide. Ironically, this group, Friends of the Earth, is most likely to lose.

What this exercise tells us is that decision-making is not an open process. Rather, there are hidden dimensions to it that we rarely see. It is important to examine the distribution of power if we want to gain insight into the decision-making process in modern societies.

Pluralism

Robert Dahl (1961) carried out an **empirical** study of decision-making in New Haven, USA, on three contentious issues. He employed a range of methods which he believed would precisely measure the exercise of power. These included:

● looking at changes in the socio-economic background of those who occupied influential political positions in the community
● measuring the nature and extent of the participation of particular socio-economic groups
● determining the influence of particular individuals
● randomly sampling community-based activists and voters
● analysing changing voting behaviour.

Dahl's research concluded that:

1 Power in modern societies is **diffused** and distributed among a variety of community elites who represent specific interests in fairly unique areas. No one group exerts influence in general.
2 Each group exercises **countervailing** power – that is, each serves as a check on the others thus preventing a monopoly of power.
3 Power is also **situational**, tied to specific issues. If one group does succeed in dominating one area of policy, it will fail to dominate others.
4 All elites are **accountable** because they rely on popular support and must constantly prove they are working in the public interest rather than in their own.

Dahl concludes, therefore, that societies are characterized by democratic **pluralism**. Power is open to all through political parties and pressure groups. No interest group or individual can have too much of it.

Elite pluralism

Grant (1999) is an elite pluralist, meaning that he accepts that power in the UK is in the hands of **elites** or leaders of pressure groups, political parties and government departments, rather than all members of society having equal access to power. He argues the following:

● Power is widely dispersed between a greater range of pressure groups than ever before.
● Most interest groups in the UK are now represented.
● There now exist multiple arenas in which these pressure groups can influence policy on behalf of their clients, such as Parliament, regional assemblies in Scotland and Wales, the European Union, the mass media and the courts.

As well as lobbying politicians, many of these pressure groups use direct action, such as demonstrations, blockades, advertising, boycotts of consumer goods, internet canvassing and sometimes even violence. Grant acknowledges that some groups have more influence than others, but argues that pressure-group politics is generally a just way of managing the democratic process.

Pluralism: the critique

Dahl was criticized by Newton (1969), who notes that about 50 to 60 per cent of the electorate fail to vote in US presidential elections. It is therefore not enough to assume that inclusion within a community is evidence of sharing in the power process. Newton suggests that Dahl overstates the 'indirect influence' that voters have over leaders for five reasons:

1 Votes are often cast for packages of policies and personnel rather than leaders, and it is extremely difficult for a sociologist to work out what a vote actually stands for. Consider, for example, votes for the Labour Party in the 2005 election. Could the Labour leader, Tony Blair, regard these as support for the Iraq War? Some people voting Labour may have been against the war, but voted the way they did because Labour's other policies – on the economy, poverty, and so on – remained attractive or because they were not attracted to the policies of the other political parties.
2 Indirect influence via the medium of voting assumes voters' interests are similar and that these are clearly communicated to politicians. However, the motives of a stockbroker working in the City of London voting for Labour are going to be different to those of a traditional trade unionist.
3 It is also assumed that voters are represented by selfless politicians. There is a failure to recognize that power may be wielded in self-interest or on behalf of powerful groups that have little in common with the electorate.
4 The needs of groups such as the poor, the unemployed, the young, single mothers and asylum seekers can be ignored because they lack the economic and cultural power to be heard.
5 The power of elected officials may be severely constrained by permanent officials such as civil servants. Ambitious plans to bring about great social change may be slowed down or watered down because of advice and pressure from those responsible for the day-to-day implementation of such policy. The television comedy series Yes, Minister is both a realistic and humorous illustration of this process.

However, in his defence, Dahl did acknowledge that political apathy, alienation, indifference and lack of confidence among the poor and ethnic-minority sections of US society did create obstacles to effective participation in political life.

Second and third dimensions of power

Bachrach and Baratz (1970) note that Dahl only looked at what Lukes (1974) calls the 'first dimension of power' – decisions that can be seen and observed. They argue that Dahl neglected the second dimension of power – the ability to prevent issues from coming up for discussion at all. Power, then, is not just about winning situations but confining decision-making to 'safe' issues that do not threaten powerful interests. In short, power may be expressed through '**non-decision-making**'. Bachrach and Baratz note that non-decision-making can work in two ways:

1 The powerful can ignore the demands of the less powerful. If these demands are put on the political agenda, they can effectively be undermined via fruitless discussion in endless committees and public inquiries.
2 Some issues may not be raised simply because opposition is anticipated.

Lukes takes this critique of Dahl further by identifying a third dimension of power. He suggests some groups exercise power by deliberately manipulating or shaping the desires of less powerful social groups so that they are persuaded that the agenda of the powerful is in their interests. As Faulks (1999) notes, this form of power:

'involves thought control and the creation of a "false consciousness" amongst the powerless, who come to identify with and support what may in reality be the exact opposite of their true interests'.

However, Lukes also acknowledges that powerful groups may pursue policies that they genuinely believe will benefit the whole community, but which in the long term actually benefit the interests of the powerful more than others. He argues, therefore, that we need to identify who benefits in the long term from particular decisions. For example, a couple may make a joint decision that the female will stay at home to raise the children, but the male may benefit in the long term from this decision in terms of career development, income, influence over decision-making, etc. Lukes argues that this third dimension of power is the most potent type of power because it is rarely questioned or challenged.

A study by Saunders (1979) of two policies in a rural community illustrates Lukes' point about the third dimension of decision-making. The two policies were the preservation of the environment and the maintenance of low rates (a form of property tax). These would appear to be in everybody's interests, but the reality was different:

● Preserving the environment ensured that private housing was scarce and expensive, and council house-building was restricted. Farm labourers were forced into tied housing and therefore dependence upon their employers. No new industry was allowed to develop and this resulted in farmers being able to maintain the low wage levels paid to their employees.
● Low rates meant that little was spent on services that would benefit the poor, such as public transport, welfare and education provision.

However, Lukes' concept of the third dimension of power has been criticized by Hay (1997), because it involves making subjective ethical judgements about how power is being used. Lukes is assuming that power should be equally distributed. Hay argues that such a conception of power would make it impossible to construct and administer any political community; for example, the state requires more power than other institutions in order to maintain social order. Moreover, in Lukes' account of power, the uses and consequences of power are interpreted entirely negatively. Hay suggests that these flaws in Lukes' analysis of power indicate that Lukes subscribes to an unrealistic view of human relations.

Hay suggests an alternative model of power which, he argues, has two dimensions:

1 Power involves 'conduct shaping' – in which A directly alters the behaviour of B through coercion or manipulation.
2 Power involves 'context shaping', in which A acts in a way that accidentally and/or indirectly impacts on B's actions. In this sense, moral judgements are removed from the equation of power because we need not blame A for any effect on B because they were never intended. For example, the husband in Lukes' example above, did not intend for his career to benefit from the decision for the couple to have children.

Focus on ...

Pluralism

Abercrombie and Warde (2000) argue that the pluralist view of power in Britain is undermined by four processes:

1 Many interests are not represented by pressure groups and political parties. For example, fewer than half the workforce is represented by trade unions. Sections of society such as the poor, single mothers, women in general, ethnic minorities and young people lack specific groups that represent their interests in the political arena.
2 Some interests (in particular finance capitalism and employers) are overrepresented in terms of powerful interest groups working on their behalf.
3 Many campaigning groups are undemocratically organized and dominated by self-perpetuating **oligarchies**.
4 There is evidence that key institutions in the UK are run by elites who share similar economic, social and educational backgrounds.

What is meant by the pluralist view of power?

Elite theory

Classical elite theory stresses that power is concentrated in the hands of an elite – a closed minority group. Pareto (1935) argued that concentration of power is an inevitable fact of life. In any society, power is exercised by the active few, who are supposedly better suited to such a role than the passive masses because they possess more cunning or intelligence, or because they have more organizational ability. Some elite theorists simply suggest that some elites are 'born to rule'.

Pareto saw power as a game of manipulation between two dominant elites who compete with each other for power:

- the foxes (who used cunning and guile), e.g. politicians and diplomats
- the lions (who exercise power through force), e.g. military dictators.

Pareto argued that all states are run by these elites and all forms of government are forms of elite rule. Political change is merely the replacement of one elite by another, as the elite in power becomes either decadent (soft and ineffective) or complacent (set in their ways). In fact, Pareto argues that history is simply a 'circulation of elites'.

Similarly, Mosca (1939) argued that the masses will always be powerless because they don't have the intellectual or moral qualities to organize and run their societies. He suggested that a minority were more cultured, rational, intellectual and morally superior compared with the masses and were more suited to rule over them. He argued that elections are merely mechanisms by which members of this elite have themselves elected by the masses. Mosca believed in government *for* the people, and dismissed the idea that government could ever be government *by* the people. Mannheim (1960) agreed, but went further, arguing that democracy could not work because the masses were 'irrational', i.e. incapable of rational decision-making. 'Cultured' and 'rational' elites, he claimed, were essential to maintain civilization.

Some critics have suggested that this is a very simplistic view of power and politics because real differences between governments are dismissed. Both socialism and democracy are seen to conceal elites. However, no criteria are provided by which we can measure the so-called superior qualities of elites. It is merely assumed that the masses are inferior and that the elite is superior.

C. Wright Mills: the power elite

The American sociologist C. Wright Mills (1956) regarded the USA as a society characterized by elite rule. He argued that three key elites monopolize power in modern societies like the USA:

1. the economic or business elite, symbolized by the growth of giant corporations controlling the economy
2. the political elite, which controls both political parties and federal and state governments
3. the military elite.

Mills argued that the activities of each elite were interconnected to form a single ruling minority or 'power elite' dominating decision-making in the USA. The cohesiveness of this group is strengthened by their similarity of social background, i.e. White, male, Protestant, urban and sharing the same educational and social-class background. Moreover, there is interchange and overlap between these elites, in that company directors sit on government advisory committees, retired generals chair business corporations, and so on. Such unity, argues Mills, means that power elites run Western societies in their own interests; the bulk of the population is manipulated by the elite through their control of education and, particularly, the newspaper and television news media.

Moore (2001, 2003) and Phillips (2004) have both documented the 'special relationship' between what Phillips calls the 'American dynasty' of the Bush family, the American political **establishment**, economic corporations such as Haliburton and Enron, military incursions in both Afghanistan and Iraq, and an uncritical mass media, especially symbolized by Fox-News. Both authors generally agree that the power elite dominates American politics today and the brand of 'crony capitalism' that it attempts to impose on the rest of the world is alienating vast sections of the world's population, particularly in the Islamic world. Moore's film *Fahrenheit 9/11* is a particularly interesting critique of this power elite.

Focus on research

Hywel Williams (2006)
Power elites in the UK

Williams (2006) is very influenced by C. Wright Mills' concept of the power elite. He identifies three groups of elites in the UK – the political elite, the professional elite and the financial/business elite – and argues they constitute a UK power elite.

Williams argues that democracy in the UK is largely illusory because the ideological differences between political leaders have virtually disappeared and government ministers have tenuous control over an increasingly globalized free market economy. However, he notes that the political elite are 'conduits of power' in that, through mechanisms such as patronage, they are able to appoint members of the professional and financial/business elites to positions of power and influence in government organizations. Moreover, financial/business elites repay this debt by appointing politicians and ex-civil servants to the boards of their companies.

Williams argues that the financial/business elite is the most influential part of the power elite and the political elite often defers to them. In particular, financiers in the City of London shape the economic decisions of governments because their vast wealth is the foundation stone of the British economy and the political elite dare not risk the financial elite moving this wealth abroad.

Williams points out that the power elite has flourished because other sources of power, such as the Church and trade unions, have declined. These may have once acted as a check on the power elite. Williams notes too that the power elite has been successful in manipulating the language of national interest in order to convince society that they are working in all our interests.

Source: Williams, H. (2006) Britain's Power Elites, London: Constable

1 **What sorts of groups do you think make up Williams' professional elite?**

2 **In your opinion, what has been the effect of the worldwide banking crisis on the power elite, and especially their argument that everything they do is in the public or national interest?**

Marxism and the distribution of power

Marxists believe that elites constitute a ruling class whose major aim is the preservation of capitalist interests. Marxists argue that exploitation of the working class has led to the concentration of wealth in the hands of the few. For example, in the UK, the wealthiest 1 per cent of the population own about 22 per cent of total wealth, and the wealthiest 10 per cent own 56 per cent of all wealth – mainly in the form of company shares (Inland Revenue 2004). This economic elite is united by common characteristics, such as inherited wealth and **public school** and **Oxbridge** connections. Marxists argue that the class structure is of central significance because those who own what Abercrombie and Warde (2000) call 'property for power' – the means of production such as **finance capital**, land, technology and factories – are able to exert power over everyone else.

Direct and indirect rule

Miliband (1970) argued that the capitalist class rules both directly and indirectly in the UK:

- *Direct rule* – The capitalist class rules directly by forming Conservative governments. Miliband argued that direct and open rule by the ruling class is common in history, as is their willingness to confront working-class dissent and protest.
- *Indirect rule* – The ruling class also rule indirectly by occupying powerful positions in the **civil service** and **judiciary**. The upper levels of the civil service (responsible for advice and policy) are mainly drawn from the same background as the economic elite. Like other members of this elite, their outlook tends to be conservative and suspicious of change.

Miliband argued that the groups that constitute the political elite (i.e. members of the government, politicians in general, top civil servants, judges and so on) and the economic elite share similar educational backgrounds. Research by the Sutton Trust (2005) reported that 59 per cent of Conservative MPs had attended private schools compared with 18 per cent of Labour MPs. Most importantly, those MPs holding political offices were more likely to have been to public school (42 per cent) compared with MPs on the backbenches (29 per cent), and are also more likely to have attended Oxbridge (34 per cent compared to 24 per cent). In particular, Labour MPs who serve as members of the government are more likely to have been to private school (25 per cent) than Labour backbenchers (16 per cent), and are more likely to have been to Oxbridge (23 per cent compared to 15 per cent). Of officeholders within the Conservative opposition, 62 per cent were from independent schools, and 46 per cent were Oxbridge graduates. No less than 14 Conservative frontbench spokesmen were educated at one school: Eton. In the past 18 years, the proportion of privately educated high court judges has barely shifted: in 1989, it was 74 per cent; in 2007, it was 70 per cent (see Table 4.1). Moreover, of the 10 most senior staff in each armed service, nine out of 10 Army officers, six out of 10 Royal Navy officers, and three out of 10 Royal Air Force officers were educated in independent schools.

Miliband notes this political elite often have family connections and are members of the same London clubs. Moreover, elite members often 'swap' roles. For example, top civil servants on retiring often take up directorships in business, whilst prominent businessmen often appear on government committees. He therefore argues that they are similar enough to constitute a ruling class.

Economic power and ideological power

Marxists also suggest that economic power results in ideological power. The ruling class exerts influence over the ideas transmitted through a range of social institutions. Miliband, for example, focused on the role of the media in promoting the view that the national interest is best served by capitalist interests. This can be seen in advertising campaigns that promote companies such as BP as symbolizing 'security, reliability and integrity'. Television programmes and tabloid newspapers reinforce capitalist values by encouraging people to see the way to fulfilment as being through the acquisition of material goods. Such ideological power leads to hegemony or cultural domination. People accept that the culture of capitalism (based on consumerism, materialism and individualism) is good for them and so consent to power being held by the capitalist class or its representatives, who are seen to manage the economy effectively and thus maintain their standard of living.

Divisions within the capitalist class

Miliband argued that the ruling class rules but does not necessarily govern – instead it rules the government by the fact of common background and hence class interest. If we examine the statistical evidence in regard to social and educational backgrounds, it does seem to support Miliband's argument that those in elite occupations do share characteristics and there is considerable overlap between these groups. Scott (1991) refers to this overlap as 'the establishment' and claims it monopolizes the major positions of power and influence.

However, in criticism of this Marxist argument, other sociologists have pointed out that government economic policy has generally failed to benefit those groups who dominate capitalism. Some actually suggest that the economic elite is characterized by conflict and division. Scott points out that the interests of industrialists may be different from those of finance capital. He notes the existence of 'power blocs' within the capitalist class which form alliances to promote their interests. He notes how different power blocs dominate the political and economic decision-making process at different points in history in Britain. For example, **manufacturing capital** was dominant in the 1950s, while in the 1980s and 1990s, finance capital (i.e. the City) was dominant. It could be argued that power today is dominated by transnational companies and currency speculators, as economics become increasingly globalized. However, Marxists argue that it does not matter which power bloc dominates,

Focus on research

The Sutton Trust: Educational backgrounds of UK's leading people

Table 4.1 Percentages of 500 leading people educated in the UK at different types of schools

	Year	%Ind.	%State	%State selective	%State comp.
Judges	2007	70	30	28	2
	1989	74	26	20	6
Politicians	2007	38	62	27	36
	1974	46	54	32	22
Journalists	2006	54	46	33	14
	1986	49	51	44	6
Medics	2007	51	49	32	17
	1987	51	49	32	17
Chair/CEO of companies, banks, etc.	2007	54	46	26	20
	1987	70	30	20	10
TOTALS	Now	53	47	29	17
	Then	58	42	30	12

Source: Sutton Trust (2007)

Table 4.2 Percentages of 500 leading people who have been to university in the UK educated at Oxbridge

	Year	%Oxbridge		Year
Judges	2007	78	87	1989
Politicians	2007	42	62	1974
Journalists	2006	56	67	1986
Medics	2007	15	28	1987
Chair/CEO of companies, banks, etc.	2007	39	67	1987
TOTALS	Now	47	61	Then

Source: Sutton Trust (2007)

1 Which occupations have experienced the most increase in the percentage of state-educated leaders?

2 How might the trends between 1987 and 2007 support the Marxist contention that there exists a unified capitalist elite which pursues the same interests?

3 Why might critics of the Marxist position be sceptical?

the overlap between them guarantees that capitalist interests are generally promoted before the interests of the rest of society.

Poulantzas: power and the capitalist system

Poulantzas (1973) suggested that the common social background of the ruling class is less important than the nature of capitalism itself. It does not matter whether elite groups rule directly or indirectly because the ruling class will always benefit as long as capitalism exists. Most governments across the world, whether on the right or left of the political spectrum, accept that management of their economies involves the management of capitalism in such a way that they do not lose the confidence of

international investors or the Stock Exchange. Moreover, legislation in favour of subordinate groups, such as pro-trade union or health and safety laws, benefit the capitalist class in the long term because it results in a healthy, fit and possibly more productive workforce.

Poulantzas argued that the capitalist class will always ultimately benefit unless the whole system is dismantled. The capitalist class does not have to interfere directly in decision-making – the fact that the decision-making process is happening within a capitalist framework will always benefit it.

The observations of Abercrombie and Warde (2000) support Poulantzas' argument. They note that no elected government in Britain has ever attempted to abolish or even modify the capitalist economy. In general, British economic policy has been mainly devoted to protecting capitalism by maintaining the strength and value of the pound sterling. No government has seriously tried to reorganize industry so that companies are managed by their workers. There has been little attempt by British governments to extend the welfare state so that it provides adequate provision for everyone from the cradle to the grave. Finally, no government has ever seriously threatened the dominance of the public school system in providing access to top jobs.

Conclusion: pluralism or elitism?

The overall evidence seems to support the view that elites dominate decision-making in both Britain and the USA. There is no doubt that these elites share some elements of a common social background and culture. However, this is not the same as suggesting that these elites constitute a unified ruling class working to promote its own economic and political interests. At best, the evidence for this is speculative (see Topic 3, pp. 226–9).

Key themes

Stratification and differentiation

Meritocracy

Functionalist sociologists see modern stratification systems as meritocratic. In other words, members of society enjoy similar opportunities for upward mobility, and everybody has the potential to have their talents unlocked. In a meritocracy, it should not matter what social background people come from; people are rewarded primarily for having talent, skill, ability and hard work, i.e. merit. However, the concept of meritocracy is seriously undermined by the existence of private education in the UK, especially the existence of the 'great and good' public schools, which charge on average £25 000 for boarding fees. Roughly 7 per cent of children are educated at private schools. However, critics of the functionalist concept of meritocracy suggest private education is the cement in the social-class walls that divide British society. It is also the glue that bonds together members of UK elites or, in Marxist terms, a ruling class.

David Kynaston (2008) argues that most studies of meritocracy recognize that education is the prime engine of social mobility, but he notes the existence of private schools generally reproduce the privileges of the economic elite generation by generation. Empirical evidence supports this view. For example, the Sutton Trust (2007) ranked the success of schools, over a five-year period, at getting their pupils into Oxbridge. Top was Westminster public school, which got 50 per cent of its students into Oxbridge but charges annual boarding fees of £25 956 for the privilege. This means that the wealthy parents of Westminster pupils have an evens chance of their child making it into Oxbridge. Altogether, there were 27 private schools in the top 30; 43 in the top 50 and 78 in the top 100. The Sutton Trust concludes that the 70th brightest sixth-former at Westminster or Eton is as likely to get a place at Oxbridge as the very brightest sixth-formers at a large comprehensive. Kynaston argues that these figures suggest that private education is a 'roadblock on the route to meritocracy'. Only the talents of the children of the wealthy elite are genuinely being unlocked.

Key terms

Accountable those in power can be held responsible for their decisions and actions.

Civil service paid officials who work in government.

Countervailing power an alternative source of power that acts as a balance to the prevailing power source.

Diffused spread widely.

Elite small, closed, dominant group.

Empirical based on first-hand research.

Establishment informal network of the powerful, linked by shared social, economic and educational backgrounds.

Finance capital financial investment institutions.

Judiciary judges.

Manufacturing capital businesses that make products.

Non-decision-making the power to prevent some issues from being discussed.

Oligarchy control by a small elite.

Oxbridge the universities of Oxford and Cambridge.

Pluralism the theory that power is shared amongst a range of different groups in society.

Public school the top private, fee-paying schools, e.g. Eton, Harrow, Roedean.

Situational holders of power vary from issue to issue, no one individual or group is dominant.

Check your understanding

1   What does Dahl mean when he says that power is diffused?

2   What does Lukes identify as the three dimensions of power?

3   What is the most potent type of power, according to Lukes?

4   Outline the contribution of 'foxes' and 'lions' to our understanding of power.

5   What is the power elite?

6   In what ways does a ruling class rule both directly and indirectly, according to Miliband?

7   How does the term 'the establishment' assist an understanding of the distribution of power?

8   Why are the common social backgrounds of elites not that important, according to Poulantzas?

Activities

Research idea

Interview a small sample of teachers about the distribution of power at your school or college. You could ask them to explain one or two recent decisions and how they were taken. To what extent does the evidence you have collected support pluralist or elite theories?

Web.task

Find out the names of the politicians who make up the Cabinet and Shadow Cabinet. Examine the biographical data available on some of these people by looking at their websites. Access can be gained from **www.parliament.uk/directories/hciolists/ alms.cfm** Investigate the educational and occupational backgrounds of the elite to see whether they share any common ground.

An eye on the exam   The distribution of power

Item A

Pluralists believe that the certainty that an election must come, means that a governing party must always conduct itself in a way that will ultimately appeal to the majority of the electorate. There is evidence that widespread retrospective voting does occur. In other words, many voters do in fact remember major features in the overall performance of an administration, and this acts as a check upon it. When the election comes, the government knows that, to win, it must have the backing of a 'majority of minorities'. Thus, no single group can dominate the political process, since neither the governing party, nor any opposition party that wants to become the next government, can win the election without securing a broad base of support from many different groups.

Using material from **Item A** and elsewhere, assess the pluralist view of the distribution of power.

(33 marks)

Grade booster   Getting top marks in this question

In answering this question, remember to make use of relevant information from the Item. You should begin by outlining the pluralist view of the distribution of power – to do this, use both the Item (especially the idea that parties can only win power by representing a range of different interests and groups) and studies such as Dahl. You need to evaluate the pluralist view, so make use of alternative approaches such as elite pluralism, elite theory and Marxism, as well as ideas such as Lukes' three dimensions of power. A good focus for contrasting these different theories with pluralism is how they answer the questions, 'Who rules?' and 'In whose interests do they rule?' For example, do they rule for the benefit of all, or just for a few (e.g. themselves or the ruling class)?

Getting you thinking

Above: the BBC series *Spooks* follows the exploits of a group of fictional MI5 intelligence officers

Above: Home Secretary Jacqui Smith shows off an example of a new identity card (September 2008)

1 What role of the state is implied by this collection of images?

2 How does each of them benefit your daily life?

3 How might you use these images to suggest that the state wields too much power?

4 What state institutions do you come into contact with on a daily basis? Are these contacts mainly beneficial or harmful?

Most of the images in this opening exercise refer to the double-edged means by which the state both controls its citizens and protects them. The security or intelligence services – MI5, MI6 and Special Branch – constitute a secret state that primarily aims to protect British citizens from internal and external threats, such as terrorism. However, these services have been criticized for undermining individual human rights in the pursuit of these goals. The UK has more CCTV cameras per head of population than any other country in the world, and the government is keen to introduce ID cards and perhaps even genetic fingerprinting. The state argues that such developments benefit us all, as do the more conventional state agencies such as the criminal justice system, the NHS, the welfare state and the educational system. However, critics suggest that these security initiatives indicate that the state now has too much power over the lives of its citizens.

What is the state?

Abercrombie and Warde (2000) note that the state is made up of a combination of major social institutions that organize and regulate British society (see Fig. 4.1).

<< *The state consists of that set of centralized and interdependent social institutions concerned with passing laws, implementing and administering those laws, and providing the legal machinery to enforce **compliance** with them. These institutions rest upon the state's monopoly of legitimate force within a given territory, which means that most of the time the laws of Britain are upheld. The powers of the state ultimately rest upon this threat of legitimate force.* >>

A state, then, is a central authority that exercises legitimate control over a given territory. The boundaries of a state are not necessarily identical with its land mass.

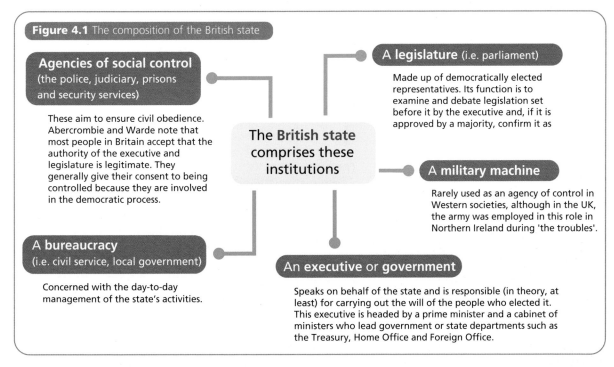

Figure 4.1 The composition of the British state

Agencies of social control (the police, judiciary, prisons and security services)

These aim to ensure civil obedience. Abercrombie and Warde note that most people in Britain accept that the authority of the executive and legislature is legitimate. They generally give their consent to being controlled because they are involved in the democratic process.

The British state comprises these institutions

A legislature (i.e. parliament)

Made up of democratically elected representatives. Its function is to examine and debate legislation set before it by the executive and, if it is approved by a majority, confirm it as

A military machine

Rarely used as an agency of control in Western societies, although in the UK, the army was employed in this role in Northern Ireland during 'the troubles'.

A bureaucracy (i.e. civil service, local government)

Concerned with the day-to-day management of the state's activities.

An executive or government

Speaks on behalf of the state and is responsible (in theory, at least) for carrying out the will of the people who elected it. This executive is headed by a prime minister and a cabinet of ministers who lead government or state departments such as the Treasury, Home Office and Foreign Office.

For example, Britain claims jurisdiction over the air space above the UK and 200 miles of surrounding sea extending beyond its shoreline. The British state also controls territory around the world, including the Falkland Islands in the South Atlantic and Gibraltar. It can use political violence against its own citizens to enforce social order. Moreover, it may use force against other states to protect both its territory and citizens. For example, in 1982, the armed forces of Argentina occupied the Falkland Islands and were expelled by force by the British military.

State power depends on legitimacy as well as the potential for coercion or force. This means that its citizens recognize that the state has the authority or right to exercise power over those who live within the boundaries of its territory. Jones *et al.* (2004) argue that legitimacy is essential because the UK is far too complex a society to be governed by force. Weber's concept of 'rational–legal' legitimacy (see 'Focus on research', p. 209) is often used to explain the origin and nature of state power. This means that, in the exercise of power, both the state and the people agree that rules and procedures must be followed, especially those laws passed by Parliament. As Faulks (1999) notes, in the UK:

≪ *citizens normally expect, as a minimum entitlement, the guarantee of basic civil rights, such as freedom of speech and worship, and normally possess political rights that give them the opportunity to change, through regular competitive elections, the members of the government, which is differentiated from the state as a whole.* ≫

If these expectations are not met, the state cannot demand the obedience of its citizens.

Abercrombie and Warde (2000) argue that the British state is characterized by six significant, far-reaching powers:

1 It has an almost unlimited ability to make and enforce law, although final appeals can now be made to the European Courts.

2 It is able to raise large sums of money via taxation.
3 It employs about one-fifth of the UK's total labour force.
4 It is a major landowner.
5 It controls instruments of economic policy, especially control over currency exchange and interest rates (see Fig. 4.2).
6 It regulates the quality of provision of both services and commodities on behalf of the general public. OFSTED, for example, inspects the quality of schools on behalf of the state.

We can add another power which has increased in recent years: surveillance and recording. Supporters of human rights have become very concerned at the state's ability to observe our behaviour via CCTV, and at its accumulation of information about its citizens through birth, marriage and death registration data, taxation and social security details, criminal records, and so on. Human-rights campaigners are concerned about the proposal, announced by the Labour government in 2003, that all citizens will be required to carry ID cards, linked to a National Identity Database. In 2002, the police announced that all genetic samples taken from citizens, whether guilty of a crime or not, would be kept on police file, although the European Court of Human Rights ruled in 2008 that all DNA samples and fingerprints of people found innocent by the courts must be destroyed.

The British state: a brief history

The state as it is today is the result of a long historical process in which power has been effectively transferred from the monarchy to the people (see Fig. 4.2). The 19th century, in particular, saw the power of the House of Commons increase as the vote was extended to the middle classes. This led to the emergence of distinct political parties with distinct ideologies and high-profile

Figure 4.2 Organizations controlled, regulated and administered by the state

Education

The state finances institutions such as schools, colleges and universities and has played a vital role in defining the content and assessment of the curriculum.

Communications

The BBC is essentially also part of the state. It was set up by Royal Charter. Its political independence is supposedly guaranteed by not being dependent upon the state for its finance, the main bulk of which comes from the licence fee. However, the cost of the licence fee is decided by the state. Parliament must vote on this. Moreover, the executive is responsible for appointing the BBC's Chairman and Governors.

Economic bodies

The Bank of England is part of the state despite its relative autonomy from the Treasury. The state provides a range of economic services to the general public, such as the Post Office, and regulates the economic activities of those industries that were once under state control, such as the railways, gas, electricity and water.

The state controls, regulates and administers the activities of a range of organizations:

Health

The National Health Service (NHS) is the product of the state's decision to take responsibility for the health and welfare of its citizens.

leaders. Elections resulted in the party with the largest share of the vote forming the government and its leader becoming the prime minister. Nineteenth-century governments generally adhered to **laissez-faire** policies (meaning that they were generally reluctant to interfere in the daily social and economic lives of their citizens). Consequently, state policy involved minimal legislation.

During the 20th century, elections became even more important, as the vote was extended to all citizens aged 21 and over in 1928. Political parties produced manifestos of their policies in order to attract voters and, once in power, governments saw it as the state's responsibility to manage the economy and look after the welfare of its citizens.

The post-1945 period saw a massive transformation in the size, range and power of the state. As Abercrombie and Warde (2000) observe:

<< *It has at its disposal enhanced powers of observing, recording and repressing the population (particularly through computer databases). It provides a wide range of services administered by large bureaucracies (both the civil service and local authorities). And it plans and acts on behalf of society as a whole.*>>

For example, the Labour government of 1945–51 extended the role of the state in a number of extraordinary ways:

- It **nationalized** key industries such as the railways, mines, iron and steel.
- It set up the National Health Service (NHS).
- It extended state services in regard to social welfare and the alleviation of poverty.
- The 1944 Education Act extended state control over all aspects of education with the exception of the private sector.

These extensions of state power led to a great expansion in the number of people employed by the civil service, local government and public services.

Up to 1979, a consensus existed between the main political parties on welfare and economic policy. State management by both these parties when in government was remarkably similar. However, after Conservative leader Margaret Thatcher's election victory in 1979, there was a fracturing of this consensus, as the Conservative government committed itself to 'roll back' the frontiers of the state. Nationalized industries were **privatized**, public utilities and council housing were sold, taxation was lowered, and there were attempts, albeit unsuccessful, to reduce the size of the welfare state.

The Labour government that came to power in 1997, after 18 years of Conservative government, committed itself to a so-called '**third way**'. This is usually taken to mean the state taking **paternalistic** responsibility for the '**socially excluded**' while encouraging the general population to take responsibility for their own actions. The 'third way' also extends to the state taking responsibility for maintaining stable economic conditions, although, as we shall see later in this topic, global influences can undermine state actions in this area.

Theories of the modern state

Pluralist theories of the state

As we saw in Topic 2, pluralists like Robert Dahl (1961) argue that modern democratic societies are characterized by power being dispersed between a plurality of elite groups, as represented by political parties and pressure groups. Although these elites share a basic consensus on social values and goals (e.g. they agree that violence is not a legitimate strategy), they are often in conflict with each other. The function of the state, according to pluralist theory, is to act as a neutral, independent referee or 'honest broker', whose role is to reconcile and accommodate competing interests. Aron (1967) saw the state as in the business of compromise. Resources such as power and capital are primarily in the hands of the state, and its role is to distribute such resources to deserving causes on the

Key themes

Crime and deviance

State crimes

What should be defined as 'crime' has always been the subject of fierce debate and this is particularly the case when it comes to 'state crime'. When we watch James Bond assassinate an enemy of the British state, we tend not to think of this action as a 'crime', partly because of the fictional and entertainment context, but also because we interpret Bond's actions as justified in the context of the villain threatening our British way of life. However, there is evidence that employees of the British state have

James Bond: state servant or criminal?

behaved in ways that could be interpreted as 'criminal'. For example, the British state has been alleged to have 'murdered' individuals through assassination and the so-called 'shoot-to-kill' policy in Northern Ireland; in 1988, the SAS killed three unarmed IRA members in Gibraltar; in 2005, controversy raged over the shooting and killing of the innocent Brazilian, Jean Charles de Menezes by the British police at Stockwell tube station.

There has recently been some anxiety about the role of the state with regard to social control and especially, the use of surveillance. It is estimated that there exists one CCTV camera for every 14 people in the UK – an average person can expect to be caught on over 300 cameras every day. Biometrics – fingerprinting, iris scans and DNA profiling – is becoming a common weapon in the state's attempt to control potential criminal and terrorist threats. In 2005, the UK national DNA database contained over 3.4 million DNA profiles. A national identity card is to be introduced in 2012. Critics suggest that the benefits gained by these measures are far outweighed by infringements of civil liberties.

---

basis of public or national interest. The state therefore regulates competing interest groups and operates to ensure that no one group gets its own way all of the time. Aron argued that the state and its servants, such as the civil service, are neutrally serving the needs of all by ensuring that all competing interest groups have some influence on government policy.

However, the pluralist theory of the state has been criticized by Abercrombie and Warde (2000), who point out that many aspects of the state are secret, which makes it is difficult, if not impossible, to assess whether or not the state is an honest broker. They note that civil servants rarely appear in public to explain or to justify their actions. Judges and senior police officers are generally not accountable for their decisions or actions. The security or intelligence services also largely operate outside the law. They note that the elected parts of the state have little idea of the activities of the security services, or of the scale of their operations.

Moreover, some commentators have become concerned with the concentration of political power in the hands of those who manage the state, i.e. the prime minister and a core of close advisers. Many of the latter are not elected officials or civil servants. Tony Blair was criticized for his 'presidential' approach between 1997 and 2005, when the huge majority Labour enjoyed in parliament allegedly led to Labour MPs merely rubber-stamping his executive decisions.

In addition, powerless groups complain that the state ignores or neglects their concerns. Some interest groups representing ethnic minorities have accused the state of **institutional racism**. The immigration laws are the most obvious example, but sociological evidence indicates that institutional racism may be embedded in the everyday practices of the police, the judiciary, the prison service, the NHS – especially the mental-health sector – and in education.

Feminist sociologists, too, argue that the state is patriarchal. State agencies have, until fairly recently, been dominated by male personnel. Feminists argue that state

policy is also patriarchal, especially in the fields of family welfare and in its failure to get to serious grips with gender inequalities.

Marxist theories of the state

Marx and Engels (1848) described the state as a 'committee for managing the affairs of the whole bourgeoisie'. Marxists argue that, while the state gives the illusion of serving the general will of the people, in reality it serves ruling-class interests. Althusser (1971) noted that agencies of the state are essentially ideological apparatuses that function to cultivate a picture of the state as being above any specific interest. However, the reality is that the state serves to reproduce, maintain and legitimate capitalism, ruling-class interests and therefore class inequality.

There are, however, variations in the Marxist approach, outlined below.

Instrumental Marxism

Miliband (1970) and other 'instrumental Marxists' see the state as an instrument controlled directly and indirectly by the ruling class. This view argues that the state is operated and controlled by those representing the interests of capitalism. Miliband argued that the view that the civil service and judiciary are neutral institutions is an ideological one aimed at disguising their true function – to protect the economic interests of the ruling class. Instrumental Marxists argue that political and economic elites are unified by social and educational background and therefore constitute a ruling class.

Structuralist Marxism

Structural Marxists such as Poulantzas (1973) argue that the social backgrounds of those who occupy key positions doesn't really matter. The state is shaped by the economic structure of capitalist society and therefore its actions will always reflect the class relations built into the structure of capitalism. The social relations of capitalism are characterized by class inequality, so the state will always reproduce such inequality unless capitalism is dismantled. However, Poulantzas argued that in order to fulfil its role unchallenged, the state needs to be **relatively autonomous** or free from the direct control of the ruling class. There are a number of reasons for this:

- The bourgeoisie have their own internal conflicts. The state must be free of interference from these in order to represent their interests as a whole.
- The state may need to make concessions to subordinate classes every now and then in order to prevent social disorder. These concessions may not benefit the ruling class in the short term, although they are likely to benefit their objective interests in the long term.
- The state can promote the ideology that it represents the national interest or consensus.

The work of Westergaard (1995) suggests that the state, even when managed by Labour governments, has done very little to challenge the inequality inherent in modern capitalist Britain. Economic inequalities, in terms of the distribution of income and wealth, continue to persist, whilst health inequalities have actually widened in recent years. For example, the incomes of the richest 1 per cent have risen sharply since 1997; the wealthiest 10 per cent of the population now own 56 per cent of the UK's wealth; and the gap in life expectancy between the bottom fifth and the general population has widened by seven to eight years. From a Marxist perspective, these are indications that state social policy is generally benefiting the bourgeoisie. As Hastings (2005) notes:

<< Until the 20th century, disease was no respecter of purses. The wife of a Victorian financial colossus was almost as vulnerable to the perils of childbirth as a maid in his household. The tombstones of the great reveal how many died before their natural spans were exhausted. Today, medical science can do many extraordinary things for people able to pay. There has never been a wider gulf between the remedies available to the rich and those on offer to most of the poor, even in societies with advanced public healthcare systems.>>

Hegemonic Marxism

Hegemonic Marxists point out that the mass of the population consent to the state managing capitalism, despite the fact that it mainly benefits the ruling class rather than society in general. Gramsci (1971) argues that the ruling class are able to manage the state in such a way that hegemony – cultural and ideological domination – is achieved. People accept the moral and political leadership of high-status groups without question because the ruling class control the ideas and beliefs held by members of society, using state agencies and the mass media. However, Gramsci noted that the bourgeoisie was unable to exercise total control over the flow of ideas in any society. Sections of the working class, especially intellectuals amongst them, can gain access to ideas and beliefs that challenge hegemony, giving the proletariat some influence over the policies of the state, e.g. trade-union and welfare-state legislation. However, Westergaard and others have suggested, using Lukes' concept of a third dimension of power (see Topic 2, p. 218), that in the long run such policies have generally benefited the bourgeoisie more than the proletariat.

Hall (Hall and Jefferson 1976) used the concept of hegemony in explaining Margaret Thatcher's victories in three general elections in 1979, 1983 and 1987. He argues that her management of the state was characterized by '**authoritarian populism**'. She was able to use the

Key themes

Stratification and differentiation

Views of the state

The state attracts a great deal of attention with regard to stratification and differentiation. The Marxist theory of social stratification argues that the capitalist class has developed a superstructure of social institutions whose function is to reproduce and legitimate the class inequality found in the economic infrastructure. The superstructure is made up of the state, i.e. its executive (the government), the civil service, the legislature (parliament), the judiciary and laws, agents of social control (such as the police, security services, the armed forces and the BBC) and institutions such as the educational system, the welfare-state and healthcare system, as well as social institutions not directly controlled by the state, such as religion and the mass media. The function of this superstructure is to transmit ruling-class ideology, i.e. capitalist values and beliefs, in order to convince all members of society, but especially the working class, that the way capitalist society is economically and socially organized is natural and just.

The BBC: part of the state's superstructure?

The New Right, too, are sceptical about the power of the state. They argue that state institutions tend to **nanny** members of society and undermine the need for people to stand on their own two feet. They are particularly critical of the welfare state, suggesting that this has led to the emergence of a feckless underclass unwilling to work and pay taxes, and happy to be dependent on state benefits. They argue that the state has made it too easy for people to choose not to work. New Right sociologists therefore see the state as the main cause of inequality.

Sociologists working in the fields of gender, ethnic and disability inequalities have also accused the state of not doing enough to tackle prejudice and discrimination against women, ethnic minorities and the disabled, both in the workplace and wider society. Some have even gone as far as accusing state organizations of institutional sexism, racism and disableism.

ideological apparatus of the media to portray herself as a strong, resolute and moral leader – the Iron Lady – and to convince the general public that a good dose of strong economic medicine, whilst painful, was good for them. She convinced a substantial section of the nation that those who dissented from her vision were the 'enemy within' and threatened the security of the nation, the state and the family. Some Marxists have suggested that this analysis might be useful in explaining the election victory of Tony Blair in 2005, despite the extensive opposition to his decision to join in the invasion of Iraq in March 2003.

Evaluation of the Marxist view

Despite differences of interpretation, all three Marxist positions agree that the state serves the interests of the dominant class. However, as we saw in Topic 2, this is a difficult assertion to prove. We can see economic and social connections between the political elite and members of the economic elite, but this does not necessarily mean that they are using the mechanisms of the state to advance ruling-class interests.

Concepts such as 'ideology' and 'hegemony' are difficult to operationalize and to use as a means of measuring degrees of power. It is also unlikely that hegemony is experienced universally. Over the past 30 years, the state has consistently faced opposition in the form of urban riots by the powerless, strikes, new social movements and terrorism, and it has been forced to use coercion and force on a number of occasions.

The view that the British state is an instrument of the capitalist class can also be criticized because a great deal of economic policy has been unsuccessful. The state has been unable to prevent events such as stock market crashes, devaluation of sterling and the decline of heavy industry and manufacturing. If the state is an agent of the ruling class, its success is far from complete.

Jessop and the workfare state

Jessop (2002) rejects the theories of both Miliband and Poulantzas, although he accepts that capitalism has a powerful effect upon state activities and policies. He argues that the state is not an agent of capitalism. Rather, he argues that the state enjoys 'operational autonomy', meaning that it can operate in ways that can cause damage to capitalist interests, although it generally operates to make sure that capitalism behaves responsibly and for the general good of society. However, he does acknowledge that as a global system, capitalism exerts more influence than the state – it enjoys what he calls 'ecological dominance', in that capitalist investment secures mass employment which is good for society. Moreover, the profit-driven market approach now dominates most areas of social life, including even education and health.

Jessop notes that, over the past 30 years, there has been a change in the way that the state regulates capitalism. Up to the mid-1970s, state regulation was characterized by intervention in the economy aimed at securing full employment and low inflation, as well as welfare-state provision of benefits, housing, training, etc., to those defined as the most in need. Jessop argues that, since the 1980s, the welfare state has been replaced by what he calls the 'workfare state', in which the state works alongside private companies, such as BUPA, in the fields of health, housing and education. Jessop argues that the main aim of this workfare state is to encourage members of society to take more individual responsibility for their welfare and future.

The state in late modernity

Giddens (1994) analyses the role of the state in late modernity. He argues that the products of modern society, such as telecommunications, microcomputers and satellites, have resulted in the citizens of modern states becoming more self-conscious. Consequently, they are more likely to be 'socially reflexive' – they are more aware of the risks and limitations of living in a global society, and are more uncertain of their futures because of threats such as ecological collapse, war, terrorism, etc. This **reflexivity** and uncertainty have a number of political consequences for the state:

- There has been a decline in support for traditional political representation symbolized by the decline in the percentage of the electorate turning out to vote in general elections. Beck (1992) argues that the state has lost credibility because it has failed to protect its citizens from risks it has helped to create, for example, through its alliances with scientists.
- The state cannot bring about positive change if it is underpinned by left-wing or right-wing ideologies because these political belief-systems focus on dated and irrelevant conflicts such as class inequality. Beck argues that the state needs to be underpinned with a 'new scepticism', i.e. self-criticism should permeate all aspects of government.
- This reflexive politics should be free from the influence of political ideologies such as conservatism or socialism, because these only create conflict and so prevent positive social change. Beck believes that the mass media can act as a cheerleader for this new scepticism.

Giddens argues that we need to adopt a 'new politics', i.e. a new type of state based upon the following:

- *Life politics* – The state needs to focus on a politics of lifestyle that would increase its citizens' awareness of how their lifestyles impact on the environment and the world in general.
- *Generative politics* – The state needs to build institutions that nurture both personal freedom and individual responsibility, both to oneself and wider society. For example, welfare systems that are currently concerned with minimizing inequality could be reorganized so that they encourage prevention and precaution, helping citizens to find their own solutions to their plights.
- *Dialogic democracy* – Democracy should encourage what Giddens calls 'active trust', tolerance and diversity. In order to achieve this, the state needs to encourage new social movements and self-help groups to take part in governing society as equal partners.

However, Faulks (1999) is critical of Giddens for a number of reasons.

1 Faulks argues that Giddens overstates **individualization**, i.e. people thinking as individuals rather than as members of social classes. Faulks argues that, because of this, Giddens neglects the structural reasons for inequality and political problems. For example, Faulks notes that class inequality is still extremely important today.

2 Giddens suggests that the state should stay out of most aspects of the life of its citizens, but Faulks argues that the state is essential because it defends and protects its citizens from powerful and potentially exploitative social and economic influences, such as market forces and transnational corporations.

3 Faulks criticizes Beck's notion that the mass media can champion the new scepticism and be a channel of resistance to the state. However, Faulks notes that the media's status as a champion of democracy is also questionable considering the high concentration of media ownership, the lack of minority access to the media and the conservative nature of most editors and journalists.

The state and globalization

Sociologists such as Held (2000) and Sklair (2004) argue that globalization threatens the very existence of the state for four reasons:

1 States find it almost impossible to control the international flow of money which can severely affect exchange rates and undermine economies. Some global currency speculators, such as George Soros, have the power to undermine state economic policy.

2 Transnational economic behaviour can severely disrupt economic policy by shifting investment and therefore employment between countries. It is argued that modern states, especially those in the developing world, are the puppets of global corporations. Such states have to compete with each other for international investment and may even have to compromise some of their policies on taxation and welfare in order to attract it. For example, international organizations such as the International Monetary Fund

(IMF) have insisted they will only give aid if countries agree to change their economic or welfare policies.

3 The global economy means that recession in one part of the world can undermine the economy in another part.

4 Global communications and the internet have made it difficult for states to regulate the flow of information across borders. There are concerns about transnational media influence, **cultural imperialism** and the use of the internet to encourage global dissidence and, especially, terrorism.

It is argued, therefore, that globalization challenges the traditional contexts in which states have operated, because they are less able to resist external events and forces. According to Held and McGrew (2002), there are very few states in the world today (UK included) that can make decisions without reference to other states. For example, British foreign policy is increasingly tied in with that of Europe or the USA, as seen in the joint military operations in Iraq and Afghanistan. The European Union (EU) too has some legal authority over the British state, especially in the fields of economic policy and trade. There are some concerns that this is eroding the power of ordinary people to take part in the democratic process because the agencies of the EU are not elected.

States are also often unable to ignore transnational interests in the form of economic corporations or international organizations such as the United Nations, European Union, NATO, World Bank, World Trade Organization or IMF. Held and McGrew therefore argue that the modern state is undergoing a transformation as its sovereignty is challenged and compromised by these global pressures.

Held and McGrew also argue for new forms of cross-national institutions to assist the state in dealing with global challenges and conflicts in the fields of trade and currency, the environment, security and new forms of communication. They see a bright future in a more democratic EU and the transformation of the United Nations into a world parliament that would deal with global issues such as debt, AIDS, refugees, environmental pollution and famine.

Key terms

Authoritarian populism the view that strong leaders attract popular support.

Compliance conformity.

Cultural imperialism situation where one culture dominates and overrides other cultures. American culture is often accused of cultural imperialism.

Individualization the idea that people now think and reflect on their place in the world as individuals rather than as members of social groups (e.g. social classes).

Institutional racism racism that is built into the routines and practices of an organization.

Laissez-faire to leave alone.

Nanny to provide for people's every need; the New Right criticize the notion of an overprotective 'nanny state'.

Nationalization policy that involved governments taking important industries (e.g. coal) into state (public) ownership.

Paternalistic fatherly, tending to be patronizing.

Privatization selling off previously nationalized industries to the private sector.

Reflexivity the ability to think critically about the effect of your existence on society, as well as the risks caused by society and the state to your continued wellbeing.

Nationalization policy that involved governments taking important industries (e.g. coal) into state (public) ownership.

Relative autonomy term used by Marxists to show that the state can still represent capitalist interests even if it is not made up of capitalists.

Socially excluded those members of the population who are not part of mainstream society because of poverty and lack of opportunity.

Third way political philosophy favoured by New Labour, a middle way between socialism and capitalism.

Check your understanding

1   What is the role of (a) the state executive and (b) the state legislature?

2   In what sense is the BBC a state institution?

3   Identify four ways in which the state was expanded between 1945 and 1951?

4   What is the role of the state according to pluralist theory?

5   Why are Abercrombie and Warde critical of the state?

6   What are the key differences between Miliband and Poulantzas in regard to the role of the state?

7   How has the nature of the British state changed, according to Jessop?

8   Why are Giddens and Beck sceptical about the role of the state?

9   Why is globalization regarded as a threat to the British state?

Activities

Research idea

Take a sample of broadsheet newspapers such as *The Times, Guardian, Independent* and *Daily Telegraph*. Conduct a content analysis to ascertain the influence of the state on our daily lives.

- What proportion of articles are concerned with the state or some agency of the state?
- Is foreign news dominated by accounts of government action?
- Do the articles indicate consent in regard to the role of the state or are they critical of it?

Web.task

Charter 88 is a pressure group that aims to reform the British state, especially in terms of its lack of openness and accountability. Visit their website at **www.charter88.org.uk**

- What issues are they raising about the British state?
- What concerns do they have about the power and openness of government?
- What are they doing about it?

An eye on the exam — The state

Item A

While some sociologists regard the state as an 'honest broker', Marxists by contrast see the state as protecting and serving the interests of the ruling class in society. Rather than acting as a neutral referee in the conflicts of interest that arise in society, it takes the side of the bourgeoisie in their class struggle with the proletariat.

In the view of some Marxists, this is because the ruling class, together with its allies among the higher social groups, actually control the state directly. For example, most key state functionaries come from privileged backgrounds. This means that they are able to use the state to serve capitalist interests

Assess Marxist explanations of the role of the state in today's society.   (33 marks)

Grade booster — Getting top marks in this question

To answer this question, you could begin by outlining the Marxist view of society using concepts such as class conflict and exploitation. From this, use the Item to identify the basic Marxist view of the state as a servant of the capitalist class. You should note that there are different Marxist theories of the state and you can use the Item here to link to Miliband's instrumental Marxist view that the state is directly controlled by the ruling class and its allies. You can use material from Topic 2 on the background of senior civil servants, MPs and judges to illustrate this point. You should also consider Poulantzas' structuralist Marxist view that the state serves capitalism by being relatively autonomous from it. You can evaluate by using alternative views such as pluralism, the power elite and Jessop.

Political parties and voting behaviour

Getting you thinking

Phone voting 'will entice young'

IN A DRIVE to overcome electorate apathy, the inhabitants of two cities are being offered the chance to text-message their votes for the council elections next month. Over six days, as an alternative to trudging to polling stations, Liverpool and Sheffield voters will be able to use pin numbers to cast their votes. An aim of the experiment, which could pave the way for a full range of electronic voting methods in three years, signalling the decline of the traditional polling booth, is to appeal to the disaffected young voters. In St Albans in Hertfordshire about 10,000 electors will be able to vote not through text-messaging but via the internet and phone, on touch-screens in Sainsbury's, and at polling stations. Studies showed that three-quarters were more likely to vote online.

The Guardian, 10 April 2002

YOUNG PEOPLE aged 16 and 17 are able to vote for the first time in forthcoming elections on the Channel island of Jersey in 2008. Derek Gray, a Jersey politician said: '16 and 17 year olds already have a lot of responsibilities like getting married, so it seems logical they should be able to vote'. The Electoral Reform Society agrees and said that 'Children are learning about democracy and citizenship in schools so they should not have to wait two years to participate. They tend to be more idealistic and passionate about issues and it would be great to see this injected into politics.'

The Guardian, 13 October 2008

Jessica Alba strips off to encourage young to vote in US election

Sin City and Fantastic Four actress Jessica Alba is the star of a raunchy US advertising campaign using bondage to encourage America's youth to vote in the 2008 presidential election.

Declare Yourself's pictures show Miss Alba topless, bound and gagged with black tape to emphasize how failing to register to vote stifles people's voices as citizens.

The pictures include the words: 'Only you can silence yourself', and Miss Alba believes they will 'really resonate' with potential young voters.

She said: 'We sign up for MySpace pages and Facebook pages, and download music off the internet. The least people can do is register to vote online, actually making a difference in their world, not just making their lives a little bit cooler. It makes more sense to spend your time making a change in society – and it actually doesn't take that much time. It takes more time to make a music playlist than it does to register to vote.'

Daily Telegraph, 13 September 2008

1 Can Jessica Alba's comments about young people's voting habits and possible solutions to voter apathy in the USA be applied to young people in the UK?

2 Polls of young people suggest that the majority are interested in political issues. What sort of political issues is your peer group interested in and how do these relate to your support for, or apathy towards, conventional political parties?

3 Identify four alternative ways of voting that are being suggested to tackle electoral apathy. How successful do you think these will be?

4 Do you agree that the voting age should be lowered to 16? Explain your view.

5 What would motivate you to go out and vote for a political party?

Sociologists who study voting behaviour have tended to focus on the relationship between voting and social class. However, the last two general elections, in 2001 and 2005, have seen record low turnouts, particularly among young people, and this has prompted interest in other variables, such as age, in an attempt to explain the apathy and indifference that seems recently to have overcome the British voting public.

Political parties

Politics is the site of a struggle between belief systems represented by political parties. In Britain, this struggle has generally been between belief systems or ideologies associated with the 'left' at one extreme (with their emphasis on equality for all and social change) and the 'right' at the other extreme (associated with **individualism**, **free enterprise** and respect for tradition). However, this is an over-simplified view because in the period post-1945 up to the 1970s, **consensus** rather than ideological struggle characterized British politics. In addition, traditional right and left ideologies, as represented by the Conservative and Labour parties respectively, have undergone a political 'make-over' in the last two decades.

The Conservative party

The **right-wing belief** system that characterizes this party is generally focused on preserving tradition and established institutions. Conservatives are particularly concerned with defending the concept of social hierarchy. They believe that inequality is a good thing because it motivates people to adopt **entrepreneurial skills** and work hard. However, Conservatives also believe that one role of government is to provide help for those who are unable to help themselves. This paternalistic streak in Conservative thought led to post-1945 Conservative governments committing themselves to the concept of the welfare state and the maintenance of full employment as an aspect of economic policy.

An ideological struggle amongst the right in the 1970s led to the emergence and dominance of a New Right ideology. This could clearly be seen in practice during the term of Margaret Thatcher's government (1979–90). This government preached minimal state intervention, the promotion of free enterprise and individual choice, and the determination to challenge the power of organizations such as the trade unions. However, after the removal of Margaret Thatcher as Conservative leader in 1990, the emphasis changed again. The Conservative ideology associated with the premiership of John Major (1990–97) shifted back in favour of paternalism. Moreover, under the party's next four leaders, William Hague, Ian Duncan Smith, Michael Howard and David Cameron, Conservative ideology became more **populist** by tapping into people's **nationalist** fears about Europe taking away British sovereignty and the impact of immigration on British identity.

The Labour party

The **left-wing belief** system has also undergone radical change since 1979. From 1945 to the 1970s, the Labour party was generally seen as the party of the working class, and its ideology was predominantly socialist in principle. Nationalization of key industries such as coal, steel and the railways, the setting-up of the welfare state (especially the NHS), and the introduction of the comprehensive system in education, can all be seen as socialist ideology (**socialism**) put into practice.

However, the party reacted to the election defeat of 1979 by embarking on a re-evaluation of its ideology and a revamp of its image. This resulted in Labour jettisoning many of the overtly socialist principles embodied in its constitution and describing itself as a party aiming to work for all sections of the community, rich and poor. Tony Blair's election to the Labour leadership in 1994 saw a major shift to the centre in terms of ideology, as Labour politicians made statements about New Labour being a **social democratic** party rather than a socialist one. Labour presented itself as forging a 'third way' towards a common good. Labour politicians such as Gordon Brown presented themselves as trustworthy and competent, particularly with regard to managing the economy. This rebranding of the Labour party as a 'safe pair of hands' was ultimately successful, as Labour won three successive general elections in 1997, 2001 and 2005.

Voting behaviour

The sociological study of voting behaviour is known as **psephology**. Generally speaking, studies of voting behaviour can be divided into three broad groups of theories dealing with the periods 1952 to 1979, 1979 to 1997, and 1997 onwards.

However, although sociological theories of voting behaviour tend to be focused on these specific time periods, there are common interrelated themes that have been recycled over and over again.

1952 to 1979

Early studies of voting behaviour saw a very strong statistical correlation between social class and voting behaviour. This is known as **class alignment** or **partisan alignment**. Butler and Stokes (1971) studied voting behaviour between 1952 and 1962 and discovered that 67 per cent of their **objective** working-class sample (based on the Registrar-General's classification of occupations) voted for the Labour Party. They noted an even stronger relationship between **subjective class** (based on self-evaluation of respondents) and voting behaviour. They found that where subjective evaluation agreed with objective classification, 80 per cent of their working-class sample voted Labour.

Studies of Conservative voters in this period reached similar conclusions: 75 to 80 per cent of the (objective) middle-class vote went to the Conservative Party. Some sociologists saw these figures as evidence of the institutionalization of class conflict, with the Labour Party

Figure 4.3 Winning parties and prime ministers since 1951

1951	Winston Churchill
1955	Anthony Eden
1959	Harold Macmillan
1963	Resigned 1963 / Alec Douglas-Home
1964	Harold Wilson
1966	Re-elected
1970	Edward Heath
1974	Harold Wilson
1976	Resigned 1976 / James Callaghan
1979	Margaret Thatcher
1983	Re-elected
1987	Re-elected
1990	Resigned 1990 / John Major
1992	Re-elected
1997	Tony Blair
2001	Re-elected
2005	Re-elected
2007	Resigned 2007 / Gordon Brown

Conservative
Labour

and Conservative Party representing the natural interests of the working class and middle class respectively.

Early explanations of voting behaviour focused on the existence of so-called 'deviant voters' – a third of the working class were voting Conservative whilst one-fifth of the middle class were voting Labour. These trends suggested that the relationship between social class and voting behaviour was not so clear cut. McKenzie and Silver's explanation (1968) focused on the working-class **deferential** voter who, they argued, accounted for half of the working-class Conservative vote. They noted that statistically this type of voter tended to be older, have a lower income, be female and reside in rural rather than urban areas. Moreover, attitude surveys of such voters suggested that they subscribed to a world view in which high-status individuals, such as aristocratic landowners, were seen as naturally superior and destined to rule.

McKenzie and Silver argued that many working-class deviant voters were '**secular voters**'. These young, affluent factory workers, like consumers in a supermarket, rationally evaluated the policies of political parties and voted in terms of individual goals rather than class loyalty. Other theories also zoomed in on the idea of 'rational choice' being an alternative variable to class. Butler and Rose (1960), for example, linked the emergence of secular voting to '**embourgeoisement**' – the theory that the increased affluence of the working class in the 1950s was leading them to identify with middle-class values. However, Goldthorpe and Lockwood's (1969) study of affluent workers in Luton found that the working class and middle class actually subscribed to very different value systems.

Goldthorpe and Lockwood further developed the idea of the working-class secular or consumer voter because they discovered very little deep-seated loyalty to the Labour Party among well-paid factory workers. This study was one of the first to note that **class alignment** as a factor in voting behaviour was beginning to waver among large sections of the working class. For example, Goldthorpe and Lockwood's sample voted for Labour not because they were working class but for '**instrumental**' reasons – as a means to an end, as a method of achieving material success.

1979 to 1997

Explanations focusing on working-class instrumentalism in voting became very popular among sociologists in the light of the Conservative election victories in 1979, 1983 and 1987. In particular, the 1983 result was Labour's worst defeat since 1931 in terms of total votes cast (28 per cent). What was evident was that the traditional working-class vote had deserted Labour – little more than half of the manual working class voted for them.

Ivor Crewe and class de-alignment

The work of Ivor Crewe (1984) produced the most extensive research on why a substantial proportion of the working class no longer voted Labour. Crewe argues that the majority of manual workers naturally identified with socialist principles because of their experiences in the workplace and automatically voted for the Labour Party at general elections. However, Crewe argued that the proportion of the workforce who could be described as traditional working-class Labour voters has massively declined because global recession led to the closure of coal mines, steel foundries and factories from the 1970s onwards. Crewe referred to this decline in the numbers of the traditional working class who would always vote Labour as '**class de-alignment**'.

However, Crewe also argued that the working-class has not disappeared. He suggests that both the nature and composition of the working class have undergone radical change because the expansion of the service sector and high-technology manufacturing has led to the emergence of a well-paid and non-unionized 'new working class'. This group is made up of dual-earner families who often own their own homes and who mainly live in the South of England. They do not automatically identify with any political party, but vote for whatever political party is most likely to improve their standard of living, i.e. for instrumental reasons rather than loyalty to a set of political principles. Crewe referred to this trend as '**partisan de-alignment**'.

Crewe identified a number of short-term factors that shaped the instrumentalism of these voters. Margaret Thatcher's Conservative party successfully portrayed itself as the home-owners' party of mortgage tax relief and council-house sales. The Conservatives' promises of tax cuts and reduced public spending (implying further tax cuts) appealed to the material interests of this instrumental working class. Crewe concluded that the Labour vote in the 1980s remained largely working class, but that the working class was no longer largely Labour. Moreover, class was no longer the main variable influencing people's voting habits.

Criticisms of Crewe

If we examine Crewe's work closely, we can see that he was not saying anything radically new. His analysis is essentially a synthesis of 1960s' voting theory. His 'new working-class' is very similar in character to the affluent workers identified by Goldthorpe and Lockwood. Their voting behaviour is instrumentalist and very much based on the notion of 'voter as consumer' making rational choices on the basis of material interests rather than class loyalty. Crewe's theory came under sustained attack from a number of quarters:

- His methodology was regarded as rather suspect. Empirically he was rather vague in the use of the concept 'new working-class'. He distinguished between 'old' and 'new' working class on the basis of such variables as home ownership, trade-union membership and living in the south. It is not clear how these variables operationalize long-term shifts in voting behaviour.
- Butler and Kavanagh (1985) believed that Crewe had underestimated the effects of short-term influences, such as the wave of patriotic fervour that swept the country following the UK's victory over Argentina in the Falklands War in 1982. They point out that opinion polls showed that Margaret Thatcher was at her most

unpopular in the polls prior to Argentina's invasion of the Falklands and the odds were against a Conservative victory. The tabloid media overwhelmingly threw its weight behind Margaret Thatcher because of the Falklands victory. She was portrayed as a resolute, decisive, no-nonsense war leader – the 'Iron Lady' – and Labour leaders were unfavourably compared with her. The Conservative government was able to paint itself as the party of authority while the Labour Party was portrayed as led by weak individuals who could not control in-fighting in their own party, never mind run the country.

- Labour came under sustained attack from the majority of newspapers throughout the 1980s and 1990s until the *Sun* newspaper switched to Tony Blair in 1996. The Glasgow University Media Group (1985) documented that the Labour party was constantly presented as a 'divided' party dominated by **'left-wing loonies'**, who allegedly threatened the national interest. The hegemonic Marxist, Stuart Hall (Hall and Jacques 1983), suggests that media coverage reflected the cultural dominance of the capitalist class, which saw Margaret Thatcher as someone who would protect their interests. Media owners, such as Rupert Murdoch, were happy to sell her brand of 'authoritarian populism' in return for Conservative government support for their dominance of the British media industry.
- The major critique of Crewe's work came from the sociologists Gordon Marshall and Antony Heath. Marshall (1987) argued that Crewe had exaggerated both class and partisan de-alignment. His research suggested that classes had not withered away and that class identities continue to exert a powerful influence on electoral choice. Marshall's survey-based research indicates that manual workers, whether situated in the north or the south, still think in class terms. Marshall argued that Labour had failed to

Key themes

Stratification and differentiation

The working class

Some sociologists have noted that, although social class may be an objective state, subjective interpretations of class often have more meaning for people. The subjective feeling of being 'working-class' or 'middle-class' involves identifying with a cultural and political identity. For example, the evidence suggests that manual workers traditionally saw trade-union membership, a close-knit community and an extended kinship network as essential elements of their working-class identity. Political attitudes too are part of this subjective sense of class identity. Traditional working-class identity was bound up with a 'them (the bosses)-versus-us' type attitude towards employment, along with socialist ambitions for social justice and equality of opportunity. Roberts (2001) argues that this original working class is not completely extinct. There is still an

original working class of trade-union members, living in rented accommodation, who remain in the Labour Party, and who would support a Socialist Labour Party. However, this group is now in the minority. Roberts argues that it has been replaced by two distinct working-class groups:

1. *The new working class* – employees in large unionized firms, with well-paid jobs, who own their own homes and go abroad on their holidays. This group tend to vote for whichever political party best serves their economic interests.
2. *A disorganized and excluded working class* – the unemployed or those in precarious, poorly paid and insecure jobs. Roberts notes that this precarious working class have lost faith in politics. They do not believe that politicians are interested in them, and their experience of politics is limited to poor public services. This group is therefore unlikely to vote because it sees all politicians, Labour and Conservative alike, as failing to offer them and their children a better future.

attract the working-class vote because it had shifted ideologically too far in the direction of the Conservative party. Cynicism and disillusionment had resulted in working voters switching their votes to the Liberal Democrats, or simply not voting at all.

- Heath *et al.* (1991) looked at voting behaviour between 1964 and 1987 and also concluded that Crewe's class de-alignment theories were wrong. Heath and colleagues argued that the main reason Labour had lost four elections in a row between 1979 and 1992 was their record of poor political management during this period (Heath *et al.* 1994). They claim that there was very little change in voting behaviour or social and political attitudes between 1979 and 1992. However, Heath's team does acknowledge that there have been changes in class structure. For example, the changing shape of the class structure because of the decline in primary industries and manufacturing, and the expansion of the service sector, has decreased the Labour vote by 4.5 per cent and increased the Conservative vote by 3.8 per cent (Health .

The 1997, 2001 and 2005 elections

The analysis of the 1997 election result – a Labour landslide – suggests that little has actually changed structurally. Most routine and skilled manual workers, council tenants and trade unionists voted Labour, whilst the **salariat** and the elderly voted Conservative. Most sociologists now agree that structural changes such as class and/or partisan de-alignment had little bearing on this result. Rather, sociologists have focused on the changing political environment as the major explanation. The Conservatives were, quite simply, extremely unpopular after 17 years of continuous rule. The John Major government was interpreted by the electorate as hopelessly divided over issues such as Europe, as incompetent at economic management and tainted by corruption. On the other hand, the public now had greater confidence in Labour. People could see that the party had modernized, that the leadership had distanced themselves from the trade unions and that the internal dissent of the 1980s had largely gone. Most importantly, there was public confidence in the leadership of Tony Blair and Gordon Brown. This confidence in Labour's ability to govern seemed to be confirmed by Labour's victory in 2001, although there were concerns about the turn-out of 60 per cent, which was the lowest since 1935. Voter apathy continued in 2005 when only 61 per cent of the electorate turned out to vote. This election saw a downturn in Labour's fortunes – the government only picked up 36 per cent of the vote and lost 47 seats, although it still commands a majority of over 60 seats.

Social-class alignments

On the basis of these three elections, we can make a number of sociological observations:

- There is some evidence that a large section of the electorate is still committed to fairly stable ideological convictions that reflect the key differences between

Key themes

Crime and deviance

Electoral fraud

In 2008, a report by the Joseph Rowntree Reform Trust Ltd examined the integrity of the electoral system in the UK. The author, Stuart Wilks-Heeg (2008) found the following:

- Experienced election observers have raised serious concerns about how well UK election procedures measure up to international standards.
- There have been at least 42 convictions for electoral fraud in the UK in the period 2000 to 2007.
- Greater use of postal voting has made UK elections far more vulnerable to fraud and has resulted in several instances of large-scale fraud.
- There is widespread, and justifiable, concern about both the comprehensiveness and the accuracy of the UK's electoral registers – the poor state of the registers potentially compromises the integrity of the ballot.
- There is a genuine risk of electoral integrity being threatened by previously robust systems of electoral administration having reached 'breaking point' as a result of pressures imposed in recent years.
- There is substantial evidence to suggest that money can have a powerful impact on the outcome of general elections, particularly where targeted at marginal constituencies over sustained periods of time.
- Outside of ministerial circles, there is a widespread view that a fundamental overhaul of UK electoral law, administration and policy is urgently required.

Wilks-Heeg's research and analysis of convictions for electoral malpractice over the past 15 years suggested 'that there would not appear to be any specific patterns to these convictions; they are not restricted to a single political party, to specific geographical areas or to particular migrant communities'.

working-class and middle-class voters, i.e. the working-class vote is largely loyal to the Labour party whilst the middle-class vote is generally Conservative. For example, in 2005, Labour attracted 45 per cent of the unskilled working-class vote and 43 per cent of the skilled working-class vote compared, with only 28 per cent and 32 per cent respectively for the Conservatives. On the other hand, the upper-middle-class vote mainly went to Conservative candidates. Class-based voting is therefore still important.

- This social-class or partisan alignment is not straightforward, however. Labour, above all other political parties, has recognized this and has had the most success in repositioning itself as a political party occupying the middle ground. Labour politicians have been reluctant to play the 'class card', whilst Tony Blair has made statements such as 'we are all middle class now' to reflect Labour's commitment to society as a whole rather than to narrow sectional working-class interests. Labour has had particular success in attracting a lower-middle-class vote.

- 'Deviant' voters are still central to electoral success. For example, in 2001, more lower-middle-class people voted Labour than Conservative, but Labour lost some support amongst the skilled and unskilled working class. In 2005, almost one third of the skilled working class voted Conservative.

Consumption cleavages

Despite these social-class differences in voting behaviour, some sociologists have argued that '**consumption cleavages**' are more important than social class in shaping voting behaviour. For example, in the 2001 and 2005 elections, more home-owners voted Conservative, although those with mortgages were more likely to vote Labour, while more council tenants and trade unionists voted Labour. Labour's share of the trade-unionist and council-tenant vote actually fell between 1997 and 2005, although Labour still attracted 56 per cent of the council-tenant vote compared with 16 per cent for the Conservatives. Critics of the concept of 'cleavages' suggest that many of the consumption symbols used by these sociologists (such as owning or renting a home, or trade-union membership)

are, in fact, indicators of social-class membership, and, therefore, we should not be surprised that the majority of home owners vote Conservative because these are likely to be members of the middle classes.

Gender

In terms of gender, the evidence up to 2001 suggested that women were more likely than men to vote Conservative, although in 2005 this difference in voting behaviour had almost disappeared. However, the evidence also suggested that young women with children were more likely to vote Labour in 2005 because they believed Labour had managed issues such as childcare, the health service and education effectively. There is also some evidence that the voting preference of females depends on age, in that younger women were more likely to vote Labour whilst older women were more likely to vote Conservative. For example, in the 1997, 2001 and 2005 elections, more women under the age of 45 years voted for Labour, compared with men of the same age-group. However, Childs and Campbell (2008) point out that the opposite was true for older women, who were generally more likely to vote Conservative, compared with men. There is also some evidence that political priorities differ according to gender. Childs and Campbell note that

Focus on research

Rosie Campbell and Kristi Winters (2008)
Gender differences in political attitudes

Campbell and Winters, using single-sex focus groups and a series of internet surveys, aimed to uncover the underlying causes of gender differences in political attitudes and voting habits. The single-sex focus groups took place before the 2005 election and were designed to assess whether there were differences in political thinking between men and women. This part of the research found that women were much more likely than men to raise the particular needs and experiences of friends or family when discussing political issues. Women were much more likely than men to highlight the needs of vulnerable and dependent individuals such as children and the elderly, and to assess the success of political policies on the basis of their effects on people they knew or cared for. Men, on the other hand, tended to be more objective. They preferred to distance themselves from the specific interests and needs of vulnerable individuals or groups.

Campbell and Winters conducted a series of internet surveys in 2007 to test the focus-group findings. The sample was composed of 6000 members of the YouGov panel. In total, 2890 people responded to the survey. The survey questionnaire asked the sample to identify which factors they gave most weight to when thinking about political issues.

The results of the study demonstrated that there are small but significant and consistent areas of difference between the political attitudes of men and women in Britain. For example, women were more likely than men to relate political policies to their own families. Men were more likely than women to state that the national interest was their most important consideration when assessing the success of social policy. Younger women were more likely to feel that only women MPs could properly represent the interests of women. Interestingly, however, the differences in political attitude found in the online surveys were not as large as the differences found in the focus groups.

Campbell, R. and Winters, K. (2008) 'Understanding men's and women's political interests', *Journal of Elections, Public Opinion and Parties*, 18, pp.53–74

1 What problems might arise in using focus groups to research political attitudes?

2 What do you think are the strengths and weaknesses of Campbell and Winters' online surveys?

3 Why do you think the differences found in the online surveys were not as large as those found in the focus groups?

women are generally concerned with spending on health and education whilst men are more concerned with the state of the economy. This parallels the research of Inglehart and Norris (2000) who suggest that, since 1997, younger women have tended to be more 'left-wing' than men. Their evidence suggests that women are more likely than men to support increased taxation if the income gained is spent on welfare policies. Women are much more likely than men to support equal opportunities policies aimed at groups such as women, homosexuals, ethnic minorities and the disabled.

Ethnicity

In terms of ethnicity, voting behaviour has undergone little change, in that Labour has always attracted over 70 per cent of the ethnic-minority vote. For example, in 2001, 84.8 per cent of African-Caribbeans and Asians voted Labour. However, the decision to take the UK into the war in Iraq has had some effect on the Muslim vote in some parts of the country; there were signs in the 2005 election that the Liberal Democrats and independent candidates benefited from Muslims either switching their votes or not turning out at all in protest. The most striking example of this was in Bethnal Green and Bow in East London, a constituency with a significantly large Muslim population, where the antiwar campaigner George Galloway defeated the sitting Labour MP.

Regional differences

Regional differences also now seem to be an important variable in voting behaviour. The Labour vote is mainly found in urban areas, the North, Wales and Scotland, whilst the Conservative vote is largely rural and found mainly in the South. For example, in 1997, the Conservatives did not win a single seat in Wales and Scotland. Again, this may reflect the fact that rural areas and the South are likely to contain large clusters of middle-class voters, although the concept of the 'deferential working-class voter' may still be valid amongst those who work in the countryside.

Political literacy and tactical voting

There is a widespread feeling among political analysts that voters are more politically literate than in the past.

Focus on research

White, Bruce and Ritchie (2000)
Young people's politics

White, Bruce and Ritchie carried out a qualitative study using focus-group interviews. They aimed to explore the alienation that young people feel towards politics, in order to explain their perceived lack of interest in voting and to come up with ways in which to engage them with the political process. The study confirmed a low level of interest in mainstream politics. There were three interconnected reasons for this:

- Young people experienced a lack of knowledge and understanding of politics. Many saw it as 'dull', 'boring' and 'complex', and having little relevance to their everyday lives.

- They lacked faith in politicians, whom they regarded as deceitful and out of touch with the needs and concerns of young people.

- Even those who were politically literate felt there were few opportunities before the age of 18 to get involved with the political process. As a result, they did not actively seek information about politics because they believed they were excluded from this adult world.

White, C., Bruce, S. and Ritchie, J. (2000) *Young People's Politics: Political interest and engagement amongst 14- to 24-year-olds*, York: J. Rowntree Foundation

1 Why might focus group interviews be more suited than questionnaires to this type of topic?

2 On the basis of the findings above, what strategies might be adopted to increase young people's interest in politics?

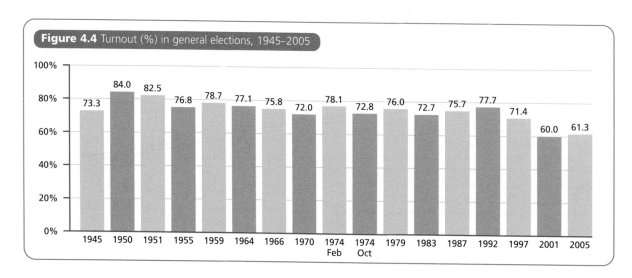

Figure 4.4 Turnout (%) in general elections, 1945–2005

Year	Turnout
1945	73.3
1950	84.0
1951	82.5
1955	76.8
1959	78.7
1964	77.1
1966	75.8
1970	72.0
1974 Feb	78.1
1974 Oct	72.8
1979	76.0
1983	72.7
1987	75.7
1992	77.7
1997	71.4
2001	60.0
2005	61.3

They have more knowledge about the policies of parties and are now more able to make informed judgements about the past and potential future performances of political parties, especially with respect to economic policy and its effect on their standard of living. In 1997 and 2001, so-called middle-class 'deviant voters' used this political knowledge in constituencies where Labour was weak by voting tactically for Liberal Democrat candidates in order to prevent Conservative candidates winning those seats.

Voter apathy

There are signs too that voter apathy is becoming a problem, especially among young people. In 2001 and 2005, only 60 and 61 per cent of the electorate respectively voted, compared with 71 per cent in 1997 (see Fig. 4.4). Some commentators argue that conventional two-party politics are a turn-off, particularly for the younger generation who see very little difference between the messages propagated by the two main parties. For example, in 2001, it is estimated that less than 40 per cent of 18 to 24 year olds voted in the general election.

Some sociologists, particularly Wilkinson and Mulgan (1997), argue that young people now make up a politically disaffected or 'switched-off generation'. There is some evidence for this; Fahmy (2004) notes that young people, compared with older citizens, are less likely to attend party-political rallies, to contact their MP or local councillor, to join a political party or put themselves up for public office. Many studies indicate that young people's political knowledge of both political philosophy and process is poor, whilst surveys indicate that young people are less willing to trust politicians. This last point is important because it suggests that young people are cynical about politics rather than apathetic. Surveys indicate that they believe that politicians and political parties are 'out of touch' with their needs and that their views are not taken seriously anyway. Furlong and Cartmel (1997) also note that the 'life tasks' that engage young people – such as passing exams, leaving home, going to university, getting the first job, establishing intimate relationships – may be more important than political participation.

Park (1999) argues that people's interest in politics develops when they start paying tax, mortgages, household bills etc. Park notes that the gap in voting participation between those aged 18 to 24 years and older

Focus on ...

Reducing the voting age to 16

One opposing argument is that young people are not mature enough, that their personalities are not fully developed and that the process of socialization is not finished at 16. It is argued that young people are not able to comprehend and judge political issues, contexts or relations. There would also be the risk of election campaigns taking place in schools or youth centres. They point out that young people already have the chance to articulate their political views at platforms like youth parliaments, children's parliaments or youth forums, in a proper way.

Proponents argued that the maturity criteria should be rejected in any democratic perspective. The state has to ensure that the flow of information during electoral periods also reaches young people in schools or youth centres. They argue that it is this information that makes the voting decision possible. Advocates also argue that youth forums and parliaments are 'pseudo-institutions' without any real competences in the decision-making process.

Some argue that young people should have a say in shaping the policies that directly affect them; this includes having a vote. Many argue that, as many 16 year olds are in full-time employment and so pay income tax and national insurance contributions, they should be able to vote for the people who set those taxes. Others say that other taxpayers do not have the vote – e.g. those who do not qualify on nationality grounds. Additionally, everyone of whatever age who

spends money is a taxpayer, as most goods and services are subject to VAT. Also, many people who do not pay income tax have the right to vote. So, it could be argued there is no linkage between paying income tax and the right to vote.

Some argue that a lack of maturity could lead to irresponsible voting by 16 year olds. Others, however, argue that irresponsible voting can apply equally to older voters.

Opponents of lowering the voting age argue that, although many important legal rights and responsibilities come into play at 16, many do not do so until 18. Some also argue that there is a trend towards increasing the age at which young people can partake in certain activities; for example, the age at which young people can legally buy tobacco was raised from 16 to 18 in 2007, and there are plans to raise the school leaving age to 18 by 2013 in England. In Austria, Brazil, Cuba and Nicaragua, people are allowed to vote at the age of 16. In East Timor, Indonesia, North Korea, Nauru, Taiwan and Tunisia, people vote at 17.

1 Organize the above arguments into a table listing, on the one hand, the arguments for (i.e. proponents) reducing the voting age to 16 and, on the other hand, the opposing arguments.

2 Which arguments do you agree with and why?

adults got wider in the 1990s. He suggests that the youngest age groups in the 1990s seemed less engaged than first-time voters in 1983. This may mean that even if young people's interest in politics develops with age and responsibility, today's young people could be starting from a much lower base than their pre-1990 peers. In 2002, the University of Manchester carried out a survey on behalf of the Electoral Commission which strongly suggested that the youngest group of voters is more sceptical about party politics than first-time voters were a generation ago.

Fahmy argues, however, that young people are increasingly motivated by single issues relating to protecting the environment, animal welfare, the developing world (e.g. the Make Poverty History campaign in 2005 was very popular in schools and colleges), and/or issues relating to **identity politics**, rather than the more conventional issues of defence, health and education. Certainly, new social movements draw much of their support from the young (see Topic 5).

There is evidence that young people, in particular, reacted against the Iraq war in 2005. Labour attracted 42 per cent of the 18 to 24 age group and 42 per cent of the 25 to 34 age group, but lost 12 per cent of voters in these age brackets to the Liberal Democrats on the issues of Iraq and student tuition fees. However, there is some evidence that Labour lost seats in 2005 because those who voted Labour in 1997 and 2001 decided not to turn out, rather than through defections to the Conservatives or Liberal Democrats. There may be other reasons for this apathy, apart from the war in Iraq, such as possible disillusionment that Labour had not achieved more during its period in office or a perception that the result was a foregone conclusion, so there was no point in voting.

Activities

Research idea

Invite your local MP or a representative from one of the main political parties into your school or college and grill them on how they intend to make politics more young-people friendly.

Web.tasks

1 Use the election website of the Political Science department at Keele University to explore the 2005 general election:
www.psr.keele.ac.uk/area/uk/ge05.htm

2 Access the research of the Birkbeck College research team on the relationship between gender and voting:
www.bbk.ac.uk/polsoc/research/rcampbell voting

3 Access the Youth Citizenship Commission to see their consultation documents on the lowering of the age at which a person can vote:
www.ycc.uk.net

4 To what extent are young people interested in politics? Analyse this issue using the resources at **www.politics.co.uk**

Key terms

Class alignment the idea that social class determines loyalty to political parties and therefore voting behaviour.

Class de-alignment the view that the link between class and voting behaviour has been broken.

Consensus agreement.

Consumption cleavage social divisions based on people's ability to purchase desirable goods and services.

Deferential the feeling that some people are naturally superior and should be looked up to.

Embourgeoisement the view that the working class and middle class were converging in terms of lifestyle, attitude and voting behaviour.

Entrepreneurial skills skills required to identify a market demand and then to set up and run a business to meet that demand.

Free enterprise the idea that the market should determine the success or failure of business.

Identity politics types of political action that focus on the extension of rights to groups which may be socially different from mainstream society.

Individualism putting yourself and your family first.

Instrumental voter a person who votes for a political party because they feel that party will make them better off.

Left-wing beliefs in sympathy with socialism.

'Left-wing loonies' abusive term used by tabloid press to describe some Labour councils in the 1980s.

Nationalist belief that the nation-state is the most important political unit.

Objective class the categorization by government of people into a social-class category, traditionally based on occupation.

Partisan alignment the sense of loyalty to a political party based on awareness of class membership.

Partisan de-alignment the view that the working class no longer see themselves as naturally loyal to the Labour party.

Populist attracting mass support, has popular appeal.

Psephology the sociological study of voting behaviour.

Right-wing beliefs in sympathy with conservatism.

Salariat those who work in white-collar work who are paid a salary rather than a wage.

Secular voters young affluent voters who rationally weigh up political policies in terms of how they will benefit their own standard of living and vote accordingly.

Social democratic the view that social injustices should be addressed and that equal opportunities should be promoted.

Socialism a set of ideas underpinned by belief in a more equal distribution of wealth, income and opportunities.

Subjective class awareness of one's class position.

Check your understanding

1 How did the ideologies of the Conservative and Labour parties diverge after the postwar consensus was fragmented in the late 1970s?

2 What was the main influence on voting behaviour in the 1950s and 1960s according to Butler and Stokes?

3 Identify three characteristics of the deferential voter.

4 In what ways was voting likened to shopping in a supermarket in the 1960s and 1970s?

5 In what ways does Crewe's 'new working class' differ from the traditional working class?

6 How do Butler and Kavanagh challenge Crewe's ideas?

7 How do Marshall and Heath view class and partisan de-alignment?

8 Identify three reasons why Labour won the 1997 general election.

9 What are the main variables influencing voting behaviour in 2001 and 2005?

10 What is the relationship between gender, age and voting behaviour?

An eye on the exam Political parties and voting behaviour

Item A

The rational voter thesis is based on the idea that people have clear knowledge about specific party political policies; that they judge the parties on these policies in an objective and informed way, and then vote. The link is precise and calculating. However, the concept of the voter-consumer engaged in 'rational' voting is flawed in a number of respects. First, there may be no political party that represents an individual's views adequately in terms of its overall package of policies. For example, a voter may agree with the Conservative Party's stance on Europe, but might disagree with its policies on the NHS. Second, the rational voter thesis assumes that the media faithfully reflect the truth. However, the press in many European countries is highly partisan. Research by Golding et al. (2001) suggests that campaigning in the 1997 general election was intensely 'presidential' (rather than issues-based) in style, with the two party leaders (John Major and Tony Blair) dominating the campaign and appearances in the media. Finally, a large proportion of the electorate simply doesn't care about politics. There is no rational response to particular political messages because these are largely ignored.

Adapted from Brynin, M. (1998) 'Why do people support political parties?', *Sociology Review*, November, Oxford: Philip Allan Updates; and Williams, J. (1997) 'Research round-up, Election landslide', *Sociology Review*, September, Oxford: Philip Allan Updates

Using material from **Item A** and elsewhere, assess the claim that voters are rational consumers.

(33 marks)

Grade booster Getting top marks in this question

Remember to make use of relevant information from the Item in your answer. You can use it to help you outline the rational voter theory. Refer to McKenzie and Silver's 'secular' voters, Goldthorpe and Lockwood's concept of 'instrumental' voting, and Crewe's notion of 'partisan de-alignment'. You should examine some of the reasons that underlie this kind of voting, such as changes in the economy and class structure (e.g. the decline of traditional heavy industries and the manual working class). You need to evaluate the rational voter theory. Use the Item to help you (e.g. by considering the role of the media as an ideological force). Use evidence (e.g. Heath and Marshall) to question whether voters still vote on class lines rather than as 'rational individuals'. Also note (using the Item) that there has been an increase in abstentions, suggesting increased voter apathy.

TOPIC 5

Pressure groups and new social movements

Getting you thinking

NFU: A strong rural force

The National Farmers' Union is the democratic organization representing farmers and growers in England and Wales. Its central objective is to promote the interests of those farming businesses producing high-quality food and drink products for customers and markets both at home and abroad.

The NFU takes a close interest in the whole range of rural affairs and works with politicians and officials – both in the UK and internationally – and other groups and organizations to advance rural interests.

Another key aspect of the NFU's work is encouraging a greater understanding of farming and rural life among school children and the wider public.

As well as representing its members' interests, the NFU provides a wide range of services to them including help with legal, planning and taxation matters, marketing and food promotion.

Greenpeace: Mission statement

Greenpeace is an independent, campaigning organization that uses non-violent, creative confrontation to expose global environmental problems, and force solutions for a green and peaceful future. Greenpeace's goal is to ensure the ability of the Earth to nurture life in all its diversity.

Greenpeace does not solicit or accept funding from governments, corporations or political parties. Greenpeace neither seeks nor accepts donations that could compromise its independence, aims, objectives or integrity. Greenpeace relies on the voluntary donations of individual supporters, and on grant support from foundations. Greenpeace is committed to the principles of non-violence, political independence and internationalism. In exposing threats to the environment and in working to find solutions, Greenpeace has no permanent allies or enemies.

Compassion in World Farming

CIWF campaigns to end the factory farming of animals and long-distance transport, through hard-hitting political lobbying, investigations and high profile campaigns.

CIWF was started in 1967 by dairy farmer Peter Roberts. Peter and his wife Anna were becoming increasingly concerned with the animal welfare issues connected to the new systems of intensive factory farming that were becoming popular during the 1960s.

CIWF campaign through peaceful protest and **lobbying** and by raising awareness of the issue of farm animal welfare. We also produce fully referenced scientific reports. Our undercover teams provide vital evidence of the suffering of farm animals.

North West Hunt Saboteurs Association

18th February 2005 saw a day that many decent people had thought to believe may never come – the day that hunting with hounds was relegated to the history books.

The North West Hunt Saboteurs Association (NWHSA), is an organization that is dedicated to the saving of the lives of hunted animals. Whilst 18th February marked a very special day, it did not signal the end of that fight. There is still much work to do to ensure that the hunters do indeed desist with their sick pastime, make the switch to drag hunting, or face the consequences of breaking the law.

The ban is workable, can be enforced and bring an end to hunting as we know it. And this is where the continued role of hunt saboteurs comes in ... We do know that some blatant infringements of the law are taking place. And it's in cases such as these that hunt sabs are possibly best placed to gather evidence, as after all we are the people who have always been in the field with the hunts, know what constitutes illegal hunting and aren't afraid to get in amongst the action to get what is required. This of course doesn't mean that we won't intervene to save the life of the hunted animal – after all, that remains our sole aim as hunt saboteurs.

Animal Liberation

The ultimate struggle. All too often animal liberation is seen, by those who do not understand, as a radical form of animal welfare. It's not about welfare, it's about freedom from oppression, it's about fighting abuses of power and it's about achieving a world in which individuals – irrespective of gender, race or species – are at liberty to be themselves. The state, the establishment and the multinationals seek to control our lives and imprison or kill us when we resist.

They seek to profit from the imprisonment or murder of those from the other species. They seek to own and control the land, the oceans and the skies which should be free to all. Animal Liberation is the struggle – indeed the war – against such tyranny in all its forms. We must fight this tyranny in all its forms. We must fight for the defenceless and the innocent. We must fight for a more compassionate world. We can, we must and we will win the ultimate struggle. When Animal Liberation is achieved, we shall all be free ... free to enjoy the true liberty that has been denied us for far too long!

You will have noticed that the organizations described occupy very different positions on a continuum of political protest. At one extreme are organizations such as the National Farmers' Union (NFU), which work within the existing political system to represent the interests of their members. The NFU is typical of what we call a '**pressure group**'. Two other organizations also operate within the conventional political world – Greenpeace and Compassion in World Farming (CIWF) – but reserve the right to work outside the democratic process in order to draw attention to particular causes. For example, CIWF uses undercover agents in factory-farming enterprises to gather evidence for animal cruelty. Both these organizations qualify as pressure groups, but they can also be classed as part of '**new social movements**', because membership usually involves a type of dedication to a cause which shapes the identity of the member. We can see this more clearly in the case of social movement organizations and groups that lie *outside* the political mainstream. Membership of groups like the Hunt Saboteurs Society and especially the Animal Liberation Front (ALF) involve their members in actively opposing the democratic mainstream. Moreover, the fact of their membership tends to lie at the very heart of the identity of their members – in other words, an Animal Liberationist is likely to see membership of the ALF as a central defining component of their existence.

Pressure groups

Pressure groups are organized bodies that aim to put pressure on decision-makers, such as government ministers, Members of Parliament, representatives in the European Union and local government. This pressure may take the form of mobilizing public opinion and/or lobbying behind the scenes in order to encourage policymakers either to make *no* change to existing policies and practices, or, more likely, to insist on reform and even radical innovation. Pressure groups seek to influence rather than to get elected.

Types of pressure group

It is generally accepted by sociologists that two broad types of pressure group exist:

1 *Interest* or *sectional pressure groups* aim to protect the interests of their members or a section of society. This category would include the following:
   - trade unions representing workers
   - employer and trade associations, such as the Confederation of British Industry (CBI) and Institute of Directors
   - professional associations, such as the British Medical Association and the Law Society
   - even organizations such as the National Trust and Automobile Association.

   All of these protect the interests of particular social groups.

2 *Promotional pressure groups* focus on specific issues or causes that members feel strongly about. Examples would include:
   - Greenpeace and Friends of the Earth, which aim to protect the environment
   - Oxfam, which aims to promote greater understanding and sensitivity towards issues such as poverty and debt in developing countries
   - Gingerbread, which seeks to alleviate the problems and poverty of single-parent families.

However, this distinction is not watertight. For example, some interest pressure groups, such as trade unions, may also pursue causes that are in the wider public interest, such as the need for greater corporate responsibility in terms of health and safety. Professional associations such as the British Medical Association have drawn attention to the need to increase public spending to reduce health risks, such as specific types of cancer.

In addition, Morgan (1999) identifies the following types of pressure groups:

● Ad hoc or 'fire brigade' groups – formed to deal with specific new proposals, such as the building of a motorway. These are often disbanded once their aims and objectives are achieved.

● 'Idea' or think-tank groups – aiming to provide an ideological rationale or to carry out research for the aims and objectives of specific causes or issues. For example, the Fabian Society has provided the intellectual rigour that has underpinned socialism and the actions of trade unions, whilst the Adam Smith Institute has provided much of the New Right philosophy underpinning those organizations in favour of free-market government policies. Groups such as the Joseph Rowntree Foundation often provide the research and evidence in antipoverty campaigns.

- 'Political cause' groups – seeking to change the organization of the political system. For example, Charter 88 aimed to change the nature of democracy in the UK. It can be argued that the Human Rights Act in 2001 was a direct consequence of their campaign.
- 'Latent' groups – those which have not yet fully evolved in terms of organization, representation and influence. There are some social groups, such as the poor and minority ethnic groups, who experience a 'poverty of politics or protest' in that they have no formal organizations to speak out on their behalf. However, their 'representatives' may be consulted by the government or media, especially when moral panics develop around 'problems' perceived to be associated with such groups.

Morgan's typology is by no means comprehensive or watertight. In recent years, we have seen the evolution of the 'celebrity' pressure group, with rock stars such as Sir Bob Geldof, Sting and Bono using their celebrity status to raise the public profile of issues such as famine, the degradation of the Amazonian jungle and debt in the developing world, in order to influence governments to change or modify their policies.

Insider and outsider status

Another useful way to look at pressure groups is to work out whether they have 'insider' or 'outsider' status when it comes to exercising power over the decision-making process.

Insider pressure groups

Pressure groups with insider status are often invited to send representatives to sit on official committees and to collaborate on government policy papers. Civil servants and ministers regularly consult with them. Such groups tend to use 'political brokers' or professional lobbyists who have inside knowledge of how the political process works and/or have official and non-official access to influential politicians and public servants. Such groups prefer to keep a low profile. This is not surprising because, as Duverger (1972) notes, some of these pressure groups, especially those representing the interests of capital, have 'unofficial power' – 'they actually have their own representatives in governments and **legislative bodies**, but the relationship between these individuals and the groups they represent remains secret and circumspect'.

Outsider pressure groups

Outsider groups, on the other hand, do not enjoy direct access to the corridors of power. Such groups attempt to put government under pressure by presenting their case to the mass media and generating public opinion in their favour. Their campaigns are likely to involve demonstrations, boycotts and media campaigns, writing to those with influence and occasionally giving evidence to government committees. Some pressure groups have gone further than this and either disobeyed the law or challenged the law through the courts.

Pressure groups and the distribution of power

Sociological theories of power have generally allocated pressure groups a central role in debates relating to the social distribution of power.

Pluralists see competition between pressure groups for the attention of policymakers as evidence of '**polyarchal democracy**'. In other words, modern democracies like the USA and Britain are seen as being characterized by many sources of power and influence. Pressure groups are seen as part of a diffused power network and are regarded as a force for democracy because they give ordinary people and minority groups an effective voice in the political process. It is suggested that pressure groups increase awareness of issues among the general public and that this prevents complacency among politicians. Moreover, pressure groups monitor government power in order to make sure that the state does not act in unjust or illegal ways. Such pressure may even result in changes in government policy. In this sense, pressure groups are a vehicle for social change which governments dare not ignore if they are to retain public support.

However, this view has been criticized for a number of reasons:

- **Neo-pluralists** suggest that pluralism exaggerates the openness of democratic societies. They argue instead that Britain is a **deformed polyarchy**', meaning that some pressure groups, especially insider groups, have more influence than others because they are strategically better positioned to bargain with policymakers. Their control over scarce resources such as labour, skills, capital and expertise may mean that they always have insider status – they can use threats to withdraw these resources as a way of ensuring substantial influence over decision-making. It was believed that trade unions had such power until the late 1970s, whilst pressure groups representing capital may use their powerful influence over levels of financial investment to shape government economic policy.
- Marxists point out that the influence of some pressure groups may be disproportionate because of the nature of their membership. For example, some groups recruit exclusively from the more powerful and vocal sections of the community, such as the White middle class, and so exercise more power and influence than groups such as the elderly or ethnic minorities. Marxists also argue that powerful capitalist interests, such as finance capital and global corporations, dominate political decision-making and, therefore, competition between pressure groups. However, as we have already seen in Topic 2, it is relatively easy to identify these groups but generally impossible to prove the extent of their influence on the decision-making process. Moreover, analysis of economic government policy over the last 50 years indicates that these economic power blocs have not always benefited from such policy.
- Pressure groups are rarely democratic institutions themselves – members often have little say in the day-to-day running of such organizations.

Table 4.3 Ideal types of old and new social movements

Characteristics	Old social movement – Labour movement	New social movements
Principal objective	Control of state	To change aspects of state policy
Type of movement	Political	Cultural, but redefines the political, e.g. the personal is political
Key issues	Eradication of inequality	Identity, liberation, protection of nature and the maintenance of peace
Organization	Centralized and hierarchical parties and unions	Loose networks of affiliated individuals
Tactics	Participation in elections and industrial action	Sporadic mass demonstrations and protests, cultural expressions of alternative lifestyles and identities
Link to international	International solidarity	Awareness of connections between the global and the local – act local, think global
Main social base	Working class, and socialist intellectuals from other social classes	Middle class, especially professional and public-sector workers, and university-educated working class

Adapted from Faulks, K. (1999) *Political Sociology: A Critical Introduction*, New York University Press

- New Right analysts claim that the existence of pressure groups threatens to destabilize democracy. They argue that there are too many of them vying for political influence. Such **hyperpluralism** makes it increasingly difficult for governments to govern. For example, it is argued that in the 1970s, governments were weakened by competing demands (especially from trade unions), and this led to political stagnation and national decline.

- Recently, there has been concern about the disproportionate influence that global transnational corporations might be exercising over the domestic decision-making of national governments.

New social movements

Recent political sociology has moved away from the study of pressure groups to examine the emergence of new social movements (NSMs).

Hallsworth (1994) defines the term new social movement as:

<< the wide and diverse spectrum of new, non-institutional political movements which emerged or (as in the case of feminism) which re-emerged in Western liberal democratic societies during the 1960s and 1970s. More specifically, the term is used to refer to those movements which may be held to pose new challenges to the established cultural, economic and political orders of advanced (late-20th-century) capitalist society. >>

Storr (2002) notes that NSMs are a form of extra-parliamentary politics, i.e. they tend to operate outside the formal institutions of parliament or government. Faulks (1999) suggests that the most distinctive feature of NSMs is their rejection of the state and their determination to highlight the limitations of a state-centred system of governance.

At this stage, it is useful to distinguish between new social movements and old social movements (OSMs). The term OSM is used to refer to older, more established political organizations, such as the socialist movement, or organizations representing working-class alliances, such as trade unions, or employers' associations. OSMs mainly focus on bringing about economic change and tend to be class-based with formal and centralized organization.

In contrast, Diani (1992) argues that the key characteristics of a new social movement are:

- an informal network of interactions between activist groups, individuals or organizations
- a sense of collective identity
- a sense of opposition to or conflict with mainstream politics with regard to the need for social change.

Using Diani's definition, we can see that NSMs focus on broad issues such as environmentalism, animal rights, antiglobalization, anticapitalism, anarchism, human rights, gay rights, travellers' rights, etc. If we examine the NSM of environmentalism, we can see that it includes a wide diversity of groups and organizations, including pressure groups such as Greenpeace and Friends of the Earth, eco-warriors and anarchist groups such as Reclaim the Streets. The Reclaim the Streets group is also an excellent example of how interconnected NSMs are. The group was originally formed by a group of squatters in protest at the extension of the M11 in East London in the early 1990s, so it was originally an anti-road group. However, its activities have expanded to take in action in support of sacked Liverpool dock workers, organizing global carnivals 'against capital', as well as being heavily involved in antiglobalization protests in cities where the World Trade Organization hold meetings. Reclaim the Streets also protest using environmental actions such as 'guerilla gardening', whereby activists plant trees in unexpected places.

Faulks suggests that the main reason for the appearance of NSMs is disillusionment with the state policies of both left-wing and right-wing governments. NSMs symbolize an awareness, especially among young people, that state solutions have failed and perhaps even worsened problems such as racism and global pollution. They are a reaction to the failure of politicians to achieve social justice and to be accountable for this failure. Moreover, NSMs have also evolved to confront the coercive practices of other social movements that are perceived to be fascist and racist – for example, the anti-Nazi League and Rock Against Racism were part of a NSM that aimed to counter the influence of racist organizations such as the British National Party and Combat 18.

Some sociologists, such as Touraine, have suggested that an NSM can also be composed of ideas and informal networks, rather than a specific organization pursuing particular goals. A good example of this is feminism – it is difficult to identify a particular campaign group or set of influential women that works either defensively or offensively in the pursuit of a feminist or antipatriarchal agenda. Rather there exists a network of female academics who identify themselves as liberal, Marxist or radical feminists, pressure groups such as Gingerbread and the English Collective of Prostitutes, and voluntary groups such as Rape Crisis, that recognize a common theme – that most women in the UK share similar experiences in terms of how a patriarchal society views and treats them.

Types of NSM

Hallsworth (1994) argues that if we examine the ideological values underpinning the activities and philosophy of NSMs, we can see two broad types: defensive NSMs and offensive NSMs.

Defensive NSMs

These are generally concerned with defending a natural or social environment seen as under threat from unregulated industrialization and/or capitalism, impersonal and insensitive forms of state bureaucracy and the development of **risk technology** such as nuclear power or genetically modified (GM) crops. Examples of such organizations include animal-rights groups such as the Animal Liberation Front, environmental groups such as Friends of the Earth and the antinuclear movement. Such groups call for an alternative world order built on forms of **sustainable development** in tune with the natural world, as well as social justice for all.

A variation on defensive NSMs is a form of association that Hetherington (1998) calls the '**Bünde**', made up of vegetarian groups, free-festival goers, dance culture, squatters, travellers, and so on. This social network of groups has characteristics similar to defensive NSMs. They generally resist the global marketplace, are anticapitalist, and oppose the rituals and conventions that modern societies expect their members to subscribe to, such as settling down in one permanent place or abiding by social standards of hygiene. The Bünde therefore create their own spaces, such as 'Teepee valley' in Wales, and gather in 'tribes' at key events and places, such as Stonehenge and Glastonbury, to celebrate symbolically their alternative lifestyles. The Bünde can experience intense hostility from society. For example, the police have been accused of singling out traveller convoys for regular surveillance and harassment.

Offensive NSMs

These aim to defend or extend social rights to particular groups who are denied status, autonomy or identity, or are marginalized and repressed by the state. The concept of difference, therefore, is central to these movements. Hallsworth argues that such NSMs are concerned with

---

Key themes

Stratification and differentiation

Class and social movements

It is useful when looking at the evidence for inequality in all its shapes and forms to consider the role of both old and new social movements.

OSMs such as socialism and trade unionism were very focused on social-class inequalities. They played a major role in the introduction of social policies that tackled poverty and class-based inequality in the UK, such as pensions, welfare benefits, the comprehensive education system and the National Health Service.

NSMs, on the other hand, are more likely to focus on single issues, such as human rights, animal rights, the environment and antiglobalization, as well as identity politics focused on women's rights, disability or sexuality – for example, gay rights have been promoted by groups such as Outrage and Stonewall. Interestingly, NSMs have tended to attract a very middle-class membership. Some sociologists suggest that NSMs are now more

Trade union members marching in the 1980s: an example of an OSM

influential than OSMs because social class has declined as a source of identity in people's lives. However, survey evidence suggests that social class is still perceived by manual workers as the major cause of their low socioeconomic position. Groups representing the poorest in society continue to play a key role in encouraging the government to see the eradication of poverty as a priority.

exposing institutional discrimination and advancing the social position of marginalized and excluded groups such as women, gay men and lesbians, minority ethnic groups, refugees and those denied human rights. They are also involved in bringing about the emancipation of social groups such as women and black people from the ideas promoted by right-wing movements such as pro-family, pro-life and racism.

NSMs and identity

Whether defensive or offensive, NSMs are generally concerned with promoting and changing cultural values and with the construction of identity politics. People involved in NSMs see their involvement as a defining factor in their personal identity. NSMs provide their members with a value system which stresses 'the very qualities the dominant cultural order is held to deny' (Hallsworth 1994). This value system embodies:

- *active participation* – people genuinely feeling that they can help bring about change, as opposed to feeling apathy and indifference towards formal politics
- *personal development* – wanting personal as opposed to material satisfaction
- *emotional openness* – wanting others to see and recognize their stance
- *collective responsibility* – feeling social solidarity with others.

The organization of NSMs

Hallsworth notes that the internal organization of NSMs is often diametrically opposed to that of OSMs. The latter are characterized by high levels of bureaucracy, oligarchic control by elite groups, limited participation opportunities for ordinary members and employment of full-time officials. NSMs, on the other hand, are generally characterized by low levels of bureaucracy, the encouragement of democratic participation at all levels of decision-making for all members and few, if any, full-time officials. Such organizations are usually underpinned by local networks and economic self-help, both of which deliberately aim to distance their activities from traditional political institutions and decision-making. Mainstream politicians are mainly concerned with raising economic standards and improving standards of living. Those actively engaged with NSMs are more likely to be motivated by postmaterialist values – for example, they may wish to improve quality of life for animals and people, or encourage lifestyles that are more in harmony with the environment.

The social characteristics of the members of NSMs

Research into the social basis of support for NSMs suggests that members and activists are typically drawn from a restricted section of the wider community, specifically from the youth sector. Typical members of NSMs are aged 16 to 30 and tend to be middle class in origin; they are likely to be employed in the public and service sector of the economy (teaching, social work, and

Focus on research

Kate Burningham and Diana Thrush (2001)
The environmental concerns of disadvantaged groups

NSMs mainly attract a middle-class clientele, so how do disadvantaged people perceive environmentalism and organizations such as Greenpeace? These researchers carried out focus-group interviews with 89 members of disadvantaged groups in Glasgow, London, North Wales and the Peak District. It found that the poor were more interested in local issues, such as the rundown state of the areas they lived in, rather than national or global environmental concerns. This stemmed from real anxieties about meeting basic economic needs, which left little time for them to think or worry about wider or more abstract concerns. They gave priority to their most immediate problems, and so environmental concerns were viewed as too distant. They knew little about environmental organizations or eco-warriors beyond the media stereotypes, and generally perceived activists as too extreme. No one in the sample belonged to an environmental NSM, although this was put down to the lack of a local presence from such organizations rather than lack of interest. Finally, the sample expressed confusion about green consumerism, particularly about the merits of organic food and non-genetically modified foods. Most felt that buying environmentally friendly food was too expensive anyway.

Burningham, K. and Thrush, D. (2001) *Rainforests Are a Long Way from Here: The Environmental Concerns of Disadvantaged Groups*, York: Joseph Rowntree Foundation

1 **What problems of reliability and validity might arise in the use of focus-group interviewing?**

2 **Using evidence from the above study, explain why working-class people appear to be less interested than middle-class people in the goals of NSMs.**

so on), or born to parents who work in this occupational sector. Other typical members are likely to be peripheral to (i.e. on the margins of) the labour market, such as students and the unemployed. However, Scott (1990) points out that it is difficult to make accurate generalizations about the membership of NSM groups. For example, many of the anti-veal export campaigners at Brightlingsea in Essex in the late 1990s were middle aged or retired.

Cohen and Rai (2000) are critical of those sociologists who distinguish between OSMs and NSMs. They point out that organizations such as Amnesty International, Greenpeace and Oxfam are not that new, and have often used very traditional methods such as lobbying ministers, MPs and civil servants to pursue their interests. Moreover, it is too narrow to say that political parties and trade unions are mainly concerned with class politics or sectional economic interests. Political parties, particularly those of a socialist and liberal tendency, have been involved in identity politics, promoting and protecting the legal and social rights of women, minority ethnic groups, refugees, asylum seekers, and gay men and lesbians, as well as campaigning for human rights and democracy abroad. Both the Green and Liberal Democratic parties have long been involved in environmental campaigns.

Faulks has highlighted the danger of lumping together groups that have very different ideological perspectives, levels of commitment to the 'cause', varied organizational forms and a variety of political as well as cultural objectives. He notes that it may not be appropriate to group together formal groups such as Greenpeace and Friends of the Earth, in which there is very little opportunity for participation by ordinary supporters, with more radical groups such as Earth First and Justice, which promote anarchic activism. For example, these latter groups have been extremely critical of Greenpeace

because it is supposedly too close to the formal political establishment.

However, Cohen and Rai do acknowledge that the way NSMs communicate with their members differs from that of old social movements or pressure groups in two crucial respects:

1   New media technology, particularly the internet and email, have improved the ability of social movements to get their message across to much larger audiences than in the past. This has put greater pressure on politicians to bring about social change.
2   Some social movements have taken advantage of this new media technology to globalize their message. For example, Greenpeace has members in over 150 countries.

NSMs and political action

The type of political action adopted by some NSMs deliberately differs from the activities of OSMs and pressure groups. The latter generally work within the existing framework of politics, and their last resort is the threat of withdrawal of whatever resource they control – for example, labour or capital investment. Many NSMs tend to operate outside regular channels of political action and tend to focus on 'direct action'. This form of political action includes demonstrations, sit-ins, squatting, street theatre, publicity stunts and other obstructive action. Much of this action is illegal, but it often involves fairly mild forms of mass civil disobedience, such as anti-road protestors committing mass trespass in order to prevent bulldozers destroying natural habitats, the Reclaim the Streets movement disrupting traffic in the centre of London, and Greenpeace supporters destroying fields of GM crops. The British gay and lesbian group, Outrage, has involved its supporters in mass gay weddings and 'kiss-ins'.

Key themes

Crime and deviance

Direct action

Various NSMs have engaged in forms of direct action involving criminal behaviour. These organizations claim that such behaviour is political, in that conventional political action has failed to bring about much needed social change. The Animal Liberation Front, in particular, has engaged in what some see as 'terrorism' – using car bombs against scientists who test drugs and cosmetics on animals, and firebombing laboratories that experiment on animals and department stores that sell fur products. The ALF justifies such law-breaking as necessary in order to prevent the 'murder of innocent animals'. Even more mainstream pressure groups, such as Greenpeace, have elected to use criminal action in order to gain mass-media attention for particular causes, e.g. Greenpeace members publicly destroyed a field of genetically modified maize in order to draw attention to the 'dangers' of such crops. The antiglobalization

movement regularly confronts the police in its attempts to disrupt meetings of the World Bank and summits between leaders of the G8 nations. Elements of this movement see criminal damage to symbols of globalization, such as McDonalds outlets, as necessary political action. Sometimes such direct action can show anomalies in existing laws so that politicians will be motivated to change them. For example, Outrage organized a mass gay kiss-in in Piccadilly in the late 1990s to demonstrate how the law discriminated against gay men and lesbians. These types of direct action are useful to illustrate the neo-Marxist idea that some crimes are deliberate and conscious acts aimed at overcoming injustices perpetrated by the current economic and political system.

However, there have been instances of action involving more serious forms of illegal and criminal action – for example, damaging nuclear-weapons installations or military hardware, fire-bombing department stores that sell fur goods, breaking into animal-testing laboratories and attacking scientists with letter and car bombs.

Faulks notes that NSM political action may not look successful but it is all about winning small battles and creating confidence. He notes that supporters of NSMs see the sum of these small battles as eventually transforming society because, bit by bit, they lead to the coercive state being destabilized. Doherty (1998) agrees and argues that the anti-road groups that were set up in the 1980s as a form of environmental protest against the government's road-building programme failed to halt that particular state policy. However, the tactics employed by these eco-warriors, as they called themselves, led to lots of publicity for their cause and great expense for the government in terms of increased security costs. Doherty suggests that these effects led to the Conservative government cutting the size of its road-building programme by two-thirds.

The nature of politics

Many sociologists (e.g. Scott 1990) argue that the emergence of NSMs in the 1960s indicates that the nature of political debate and action has undergone fundamental change. It is suggested that up to the 1960s, both political debate and action were dominated by political parties and pressure groups that sought either to protect or challenge the economic or material order. In other words, politics was dominated by class-based issues. However, the emergence of the women's movement and the civil-rights movement led to a recognition that wider social inequalities were of equal importance and resulted in a concern to protect, and even celebrate, the concept of 'social difference'. It was argued that affluence in Western societies meant than economic issues became subordinated to wider concerns about long-term survival, reflected in increased interest in social movements related to antinuclear technology, peace, the environment and global issues such as debt.

Theories of NSMs

The Marxist Habermas (1979) saw membership of NSMs as arising out of the nature of postcapitalism, in which the majority of people enjoy a good standard of living and are supposedly, therefore, less interested in material things. In such societies, priorities change – economic matters are of less importance than issues such as protecting human rights and democracy from an ever-encroaching state bureaucracy. NSMs, therefore, are a means by which democratic rights are protected and extended.

Touraine (1982), another Marxist, argues that NSMs are a product of a post-industrial society that stresses the production and consumption of knowledge about the state of the world rather than the pursuit of materialism and consumerism. This means that young people are now experiencing longer periods in education and so have the cultural resources to question and criticize traditional sources of knowledge about the world such as science, capitalist enterprise and established political ideologies.

For example, it is no longer taken for granted that science always means progress and benefits for humanklnd. Young people are attracted to NSMs because they are concerned with the promotion of alternative cultural values encouraging quality of life, concern for the environment, anxiety for the plight of the developing world as well as individual freedom of expression and identity. Touraine sees NSMs as being at the heart of a realignment of political and cultural life. He even goes so far as to suggest that they will one day replace political parties as the major source of political identity.

Marcuse (1964) argued that NSMs are the direct result of the **alienation** caused by the capitalist mode of production and consumption. He suggested that capitalism produces a superficial **mass culture** in order to maximize its audience and profits. However, the emptiness of this culture has led some middle-class students, whose education has given them critical insight, to reject materialism. NSMs, therefore, are a form of **counterculture** that encourages people to focus on unselfish needs, such as concern for other people or the environment.

Other writers believe that NSMs are the product of a search for identity rather than the product of common political ideology or shared economic interests. Alberto Melucci (1989) argues that the collective actions and political campaigns associated with NSMs are not organized in a formal sense. It is this looseness that appeals to its membership. This belonging to a vast unorganized network is less about providing its members with a coherent political manifesto or ideology than about providing a sense of identity and lifestyle. In this sense, Melucci argues that NSMs are a cultural rather than political phenomenon. They appeal to the young, in particular, because they offer the opportunity to challenge the dominant rules, while offering an alternative set of identities that focus on fundamentally changing the nature of the society in both a spiritual and cultural way.

Melucci suggests that NSMs have made a significant cultural contribution to society because direct action, even if unsuccessful in conventional terms, reveals the existence of unequal power structures and makes people aware that these require challenging. In fact, Melucci argues 'that to resist is to win' – in other words, the mere fact of a protest action is a kind of success, because it is a challenge to existing power structures. Road protesters might fail to prevent a road being built, but, as Field (quoted in Storr 2002) notes:

<< resistance to road-building is not just about stopping one particular project. Every delay, every disruption, every extra one thousand pounds spent on police or security is a victory: money that is not available to spend elsewhere. 'Double the cost of one road and you have prevented another one being built' is an opinion often expressed by activists. In such an unequal struggle, to resist is to win.>>

Postmodern accounts of NSMs

Postmodernists argue that the meta-narratives that were used to explain the world are in decline, as the modern world evolves into a postmodern world. Meta-narratives are the 'big theories' – science, religions and political philosophies (e.g. socialism, conservatism, nationalism, liberalism and social democracy). The search for truth, self-fulfilment and social progress through these meta-narratives has largely been abandoned as people have become disillusioned by the failure of these belief systems (as seen in the fall of communism) and/or the damage caused by them in terms of war, genocide, environmental destruction and pollution. The postmodern world is characterized by global media technology, which has led to knowledge becoming relative, i.e. accepting that all knowledge has some value. Moreover, the postmodern world is a media-saturated world, in which newspapers, magazines, television, advertising, the internet, etc., provide people with a variety of information and knowledge that they can use to improve and even shape their lifestyles. Postmodernists claim that in traditional industrial societies, structural influences such as social class, patriarchy and ethnicity shaped people's lives and identities. However, the dominance of media-based knowledge in postmodern societies means that people enjoy a greater degree of choice in terms of how they can look, how they conduct their relationships, how they organize their homes, what they can believe, and so on. Postmodernists argue that NSMs also provide society with knowledge that some people will use to make choices about their personal identity. For example, people may construct their identity with reference to NSMs by describing themselves as feminist or vegetarian, as sympathetic to Greenpeace and as active in the antiglobalization movement or the Make Poverty History campaign.

Crook *et al.* (1992) argue that in postmodern society, sociocultural divisions (e.g. differences in consumption and lifestyle) are more important than socioeconomic divisions (e.g. differences between social classes). Consequently, the traditional 'them-versus-us' conflict between employers and the working class has gone into decline and politics is now concerned with more universal moral issues. This has led to the emergence of new political organizations – NSMs that generally appeal to people's moral principles as well as their lifestyles. For example, we may be convinced by the moral arguments advanced by environmental organizations to consume in an ecologically responsible fashion and to dispose of our waste by recycling. Getting involved in NSM activities, therefore, is both a political statement and a lifestyle choice.

Commentators such as Ulrich Beck (1992) and Anthony Giddens (1991) note that in a postmodern world dominated by global media and communications, there is a growing sense of risk – people are increasingly aware of the dangers of the world we live in. In particular, there is a growing distrust of experts such as scientists, who are seen as being responsible for many of the world's problems. Giddens uses the concept of 'increasing **reflexivity**' to suggest that more and more people are reflecting on their place in the world and realizing that their existence and future survival increasingly depend on making sure that key political players, such as governments and global corporations, behave in a responsible fashion.

However, not all sociologists agree that we have entered a postmodern age. Meta-narratives still seem important. Religious meta-narratives, in particular, have re-emerged as important explanations of terrorism and suicide bombings in the UK. Crook and colleagues have

Designer labels: corporate branding or individual choice?

been criticized for overstating the decline of social class, and for suggesting that sociocultural differences in consumption and lifestyle are not connected to socioeconomic differences. As Marxist critics have noted, the poor do not enjoy the same access to cultural consumption or NSMs as other sections of society.

Global social movements

There is evidence that NSMs are becoming increasingly globalized. Klein, in *No Logo* (2001), suggests that global capitalism, with its strategy of **global branding** and marketing, is responsible for the alienation fuelling an emerging global anticorporate movement. She identifies five aggressive branding and marketing strategies adopted by global corporations that have resulted in the superficial mass culture that has led to this alienation:

1 *Logo inflation* – The wearing of logos such as the Nike swoosh or FCUK on clothing has become a universal phenomenon.
2 *Sponsorship of cultural events* – Rock festivals are increasingly sponsored by global corporations. Even the visit of Pope John Paul II to the USA in the late 1990s was sponsored by Pepsi.
3 *Sport branding and sponsorship* – Corporations such as Nike and Adidas have attempted to turn sport into a philosophy of perfection by recruiting sports icons such as Michael Jordan and David Beckham to promote their products.
4 *The branding of youth culture* – Youth trends such as snow-boarding, hip-hop and skate-boarding have been hijacked by corporations in order to make brands 'cool' and 'alternative'.
5 *The branding of identity politics* – Some corporations, most notably Nike and Benetton, have identified their products with liberal issues that young people are likely to identify and sympathize with, e.g. antiracism.

Klein argues that young people are disillusioned with capitalism. This, she claims, is the result of their increasing realization that what counts as youth identity in modern society is often a product of corporate branding rather than individual choice. Moreover, people are beginning to understand that excessive branding has led to corporate censorship – the suppression of knowledge that does not support corporate interests – as well as the restriction of real choice, as two or three corporations dominate particular markets. The antiglobalization social movement has also drawn people's attention to how the activities of global corporations in the developing world sustain debt, subsistence wages and child labour. Consequently, people see governments of all political persuasions as colluding with global corporations or as ineffective in the face of corporate global power. Klein argues that what unites all these people as they join a loose network of anti-globalization groups and organizations is their desire for a citizen-centred alternative to the international rule of these global brands and to the power that global corporations have over their lives. Examples of this alternative in action include consumer boycotts of environmentally unfriendly goods and goods produced by child labour or regimes that regularly engage in human-rights abuse. The global anticorporate movement has also provided networks in which high-profile organizations such as Greenpeace and Oxfam have been able to collaborate and exert pressure on governments and transnational companies.

The social and political significance of NSMs

Faulks (1999) suggests that NSMs have had a significant effect on British politics for several reasons:

- They have mounted a significant challenge to the power of the state.
- They have introduced innovative methods of protest and put new issues on the political agenda, e.g. women's rights, environmental issues, globalization.

- They have helped increase political participation in Europe and the USA among young people who had previously felt alienated by bureaucracy and the increasing similarity of political parties.
- Many of the issues championed by NSMs have been taken up by governments and political parties.
- They have considerably improved sociological understanding of the multifaceted nature of power – in particular, highlighting the ways in which a supposedly neutral state can actually contribute to real inequalities.

However, Faulks does conclude that NSMs have mainly served to highlight the problems of the state rather than significantly diminish its power.

NSMs – the end of class politics?

There has undoubtedly been a huge surge of interest in NSMs in the past 30 years, but it is a mistake to conclude that this indicates the end of class politics. An examination of the distribution of power, studies of voting behaviour and the activities of pressure groups indicate that class and economic interests still underpin much of the political debate in Britain. It is also important not to exaggerate the degree of support that NSMs enjoy. Most people are aware of such movements but are not actively involved in them. However, conventional political parties and pressure groups can still learn a great deal from such movements, especially their ability to attract the educated, articulate and motivated young.

Check your understanding

1 What are the main differences between sectional and promotional pressure groups?

2 What is the difference between an 'insider' and an 'outsider' pressure group?

3 How do pluralists and neo-pluralists differ in their attitudes towards pressure groups?

4 Why are Marxists critical of pressure groups?

5 Identify three differences between old social movements and new social movements.

6 What are the main differences between defensive NSMs and offensive NSMs?

7 In what ways might membership of NSMs be related to anxieties about postindustrial society?

8 How do Marxists like Marcuse explain the emergence of NSMs?

9 How is the notion of 'increasing reflexivity' related to membership of new social movements?

10 What evidence is there that NSMs have become globalized?

Activities

Research idea

Choose an issue, such as vivisection, testing drugs on animals or using animals in testing perfumes, and research one or more of the following:

1 the depth of feeling about the issue in your school or college – find this out either by conducting a brief questionnaire or by asking people in your school or college to sign a petition asking for it to be banned

2 the plans of conventional political parties with regard to the issue

3 what pressure groups and/or social movements exist in regard to your issue and what tactics are they adopting to bring the issue to public attention?

Web.task

www.resist.org.uk/ is the coordinating site for most of the organizations that make up the antiglobalization social movement. Click on their website and go to the 'Links' page. This lists all the organizations/ issues that are affiliated. Choose a sample of organizations and find out their aims and tactics.

Key terms

Alienation an inability to identify with an institution or group to which you might belong.

Bünde term used by Hetherington to describe a new form of association made up of vegetarian groups, free-festival goers, dance culture, travellers, and so on.

Counterculture a culture that is in opposition to authority.

Deformed polyarchy situation where some pressure groups have more influence than others because they are strategically better positioned to bargain with policymakers.

Global branding attempts by global corporations to make their image and products recognizable worldwide.

Hyperpluralism a situation where there are too many pressure groups competing for influence.

Legislative bodies the state, parliament, the judiciary, i.e. agencies that have the power to make laws.

Lobbying a means by which pressure groups and NSMs inform politicians and civil servants of their concerns and/or pass on information that will assist their cause; pressure groups often employ lobbyists to promote their cause in parliament.

Mass culture a superficial entertainment culture propagated by the mass media undermining people's capacity for critical thinking.

New social movements loosely organized political movements that have emerged since the 1960s, based around particular issues.

Neo-pluralists writers who have updated the idea of pluralism.

Polyarchal democracy society in which many sources of power and influence exist.

Pressure group organized body that aims to put pressure on decision-makers.

Reflexivity the ability to reflect on your experiences.

Risk technology technology that poses dangers to society, such as nuclear power.

Sustainable development strategies for modernizing the developing world that result in a fairer distribution of wealth and resources.

An eye on the exam   Pressure groups and NSMs

Item A

It has been suggested that by the late 1960s people had become disillusioned with established political parties and this led to the growth of the NSMs and also of pressure groups. Coxall (1981) argues that the 1960s and 1970s witnessed an explosion of pressure group membership. He cites the examples of Shelter, which by 1969 had more than 220 affiliated branches, and the Child Poverty Action Group, which by 1970 had over 40. In the 1980s, groups such as CND went into decline but others, notably those concerned with the environment and animal welfare, rose to take their place.

A good example of the latter group is the Animal Liberation Front (ALF). Some observers have noted that membership of the ALF is like membership of an extraordinary fundamentalist religion. Since its foundation in 1976, animal rights terrorists have targeted butchers' shops, science laboratories, fur farms, live exports, dog-breeding farms and high-street chemists.

Adapted from Kirby, M. (1995) *Investigating Political Sociology*, London: Collins Educational; and Toolis, K. (2001) 'To the death', *The Guardian*, 7 November

Using material from **Item A** and elsewhere, assess sociological explanations of the rise of new social movements in recent years.

(33 marks)

Grade booster   Getting top marks in this question

You should being by explaining what NSMs are and how they differ from older, more traditional pressure and interest groups, for example in terms of organization, membership, aims and forms of political action. Illustrate your explanation with some examples of NSMs (such as the one in the Item) and distinguish between different types (for example, offensive and defensive or 'Bünde' NSMs). You should examine a range of theories of NSMs. These should include neo-Marxist views (e.g. Habermas, Marcuse) and postmodernism (e.g. Cook *et al.*). You should consider the changing political and social context and how this may have influenced the rise of NSMs. For example, what impact does globalization or the alleged decline of class-based politics have.upon the popularity or impact of NSMs?

1 Read **Item A** below and answer parts (a) and (b) that follow.

> ### Item A
>
> Classical elite theory developed originally in the late nineteenth and early twentieth centuries, as a reaction against Marxism. The Marxist view was that a classless, equal communist society is both possible and inevitable, and that the working-class majority is itself capable of ruling – although it will first have to sweep away the capitalist ruling class by means of a socialist revolution.
>
> By contrast, classical elite theorists such as Pareto and Mosca argued that majority rule was impossible – a minority would always exercise power, even in supposedly egalitarian societies. For example, the former Soviet Union, which came into being following the Russian Revolution of 1917, was supposed to be a communist society of the type that Marx had envisaged, but in reality, critics argue, it was simply another form of minority rule. This seems to support the view that elite rule is inevitable.

(a) Identify and briefly explain **three** reasons for the growth of new social movements in recent years. *(9 marks)*

> There has been an increase in non-class issues outside the traditional class-based interest groups, like the environment. This gives scope for NSMs like Greenpeace to grow.
>
> There is new technology such as the internet. This has made it easier for NSMs to spread their message and organise protest activities, sometimes on a global scale.
>
> There have been changes in the position of women. These have led to the rise of the feminist movement.

An examiner comments

Three relevant reasons. The first two are well explained, but the last should say more how or why the changes gave rise to feminism.

This answer shows knowledge of two versions of elite theory and of Marxism and pluralism, and makes useful evaluation points by contrasting these theories and by drawing a conclusion. However, it could use Item A more, e.g. linking the Soviet example to the final paragraph, and it should also discuss Mills' power elite theory.

(b) Using information from **Item A and elsewhere**, assess the usefulness of elite theory in understanding power. *(18 marks)*

> Elite theorists argue that elite rule is inevitable. Pareto claimed there would always be an elite, either of lions or of foxes. Lions ruled by force, e.g. dictators, while foxes rule by cunning. There was a circulation of elites, with foxes replacing lions and then vice versa, throughout history.
>
> Mosca agreed there would always be elite rule, because elites were better organised and cohesive, and could conspire together. His theory was more sociological than Pareto's, which was based on the psychological characteristics of elites. Neither believed in democracy, but Mosca saw it allowed talented middle-class individuals to move into the elite to renew it.
>
> Pluralists criticise both theories. They argue that no single group can monopolise power in a democracy because rulers have to win support from many different groups. Also, they can be turned out at the next election if they displease too many people.
>
> Marxists also criticise elite theory. As Item A shows, they don't believe minority rule is inevitable, unlike elite theorists. They believe there will ultimately be a classless, equal society without rulers. Marxists see a capitalist ruling class monopolizing power, based on ownership of wealth. This differs from Pareto, who sees rule based on psychological characteristics, and Mosca, who bases it on group cohesion.
>
> Elite theory is useful because it explains why attempts to create equal societies have failed. However, it doesn't fit democratic societies completely, because rulers can be 'sacked' by the electorate.

One for you to try

Assess the view that long-term structural changes in the economy are the main cause of changes in voting behaviour in the last 40 years. *(33 marks)*

An examiner comments

First, outline the main changes in voting behaviour. Discuss the structural changes in the economy, such as the decline of heavy industry. Examine different explanations: partisan and class de-alignment, secular voting and embourgeoisement. Consider also factors such as short-term influences, party images, class alignment, voter apathy, tactical voting, and the impact of NSMs and identity politics

Answers to the 'One for you to try' are available **free** on **www.collinseducation.com/sociologyweb**

CHAPTER 5

Theory and methods

AQA Specification	Topics	Pages
Candidates should examine the following areas, which are also studied at AS Level:		
Quantitative and qualitative methods of research; their strengths and limitations; research design.	Quantitative research in Topic 4 Qualitative research in Topic 5	278–95
Sources of data, including questionnaires, interviews, participant and non-participant observation, experiments, documents, and official statistics; the strengths and limitations of these sources.	Questionnaires and interviews in Topic 7. Participant and non-participant observation in Topic 5. Experiments in Topic 4. Documents and official statistics in Topic 8. Strengths and weaknesses of each in the relevant topics.	278–95 302–15
The distinction between primary and secondary data, and between quantitative and qualitative data.	Detailed discussions in Topics 4 to 8.	278–315
The relationship between positivism, interpretivism and sociological methods; the nature of 'social facts'.	Covered in Topics 4 and 5.	278–95
The theoretical, practical and ethical considerations influencing choice of topic, choice of method(s) and the conduct of research.	Covered throughout the chapter.	
In addition, A2 candidates should examine:		
Consensus, conflict, structural and social action theories.	Covered in Topics 1 and 2.	255–69
The concepts of modernity and post-modernity in relation to sociological theory.	Covered in Topics 1 and 2.	255–69
The nature of science and the extent to which sociology can be regarded as scientific.	Covered in Topic 3.	270–77
The relationship between theory and methods.	Covered in Topics 4, 5 and 6.	278–301
Debates about subjectivity, objectivity and value freedom.	Covered in Topic 9.	316–21
The relationship between sociology and social policy.	Covered in Topic 10.	322–27

TOPIC 1

Modernist sociological theories

Do you feel we are all puppets of society?

Getting you thinking

Use your knowledge from your AS-level studies to match each of the sentences below with the sociological theories they are most closely associated with. Explain your decisions.

1 Society is like a human body – every part of it helps to keep society going.

2 The ruling class benefits in every way from the operation of society while the workers get far less than they deserve.

3 Britain is a patriarchal society. Men generally have more power and prestige than women across a range of social institutions.

4 People do not feel that they are the puppets of society, rather that they have an active role in creating society.

5 Society has experienced such major upheavals from the late 20th century onwards that the old ways of explaining it just won't work any more. We are entering a new sort of society.

If you are not sure, the possible answers are given on the right (upside down). The actual answers to the questions are provided at the end of the topic on p. 261.

Possible answers:
functionalism – feminism –
Marxism – social action
theory or interactionism –
postmodernism

During your AS-level Sociology studies, you will almost certainly have met most of the main sociological theories. The exercise above will have reminded you of some of these. In the first two topics of this chapter, we will be drawing these ideas together and exploring them further.

This topic explores what are known as modernist theories. '**Modernism**' or 'modernity' refers to a period of history in 19th- and 20th-century Western societies that was characterized by major technological, social and political advances. It was within this period and driven by these ideas of rational, progressive thought that sociology was born. The main modernist approaches are Marxism, functionalism and **social action theory (interactionism)**, and these have dominated sociology for much of the subject's existence.

Modernist theories are divided into two main perspectives – **structural approaches** and social action approaches:

- *Structural approaches* attempt to provide a complete theory of society. They begin their analyses from the 'top', by looking first at society as a whole and then working down to the individual parts, and finally to individuals. There are two main structural theories:

Marxism or conflict theory (and its developments, neo-Marxism), and functionalism or consensus theory (and its developments, neo-functionalism). These theories may start from the same position, but they come to very different conclusions.

- *Social action theories* do not seek to provide complete explanations for society; instead they start by looking at how society is 'built up' from people interacting with each other. Quite how far 'up' they arrive is a matter of debate – though one version of social action theory, known as **labelling** theory, does seek to explain the construction of social rules.

Functionalism

Functionalism is closely associated with the work of Talcott Parsons. His work dominated US sociology and vied with Marxist-based approaches in Europe from the 1940s until the 1970s. Today, it still provides us with a useful and relatively simple framework for approaching the study of society.

Parsons' aim was to provide a theoretical framework that combined the ideas of Weber, who stressed the importance of understanding people's actions, and those of Durkheim, who emphasized the necessity of focusing on the structures of societies and how they function.

Parsons' starting point, taken from Durkheim, was the organic analogy – that is, he imagined society as similar to a living being that adapts to its environments and is made up of component parts, each performing some action that helps the living being to continue to exist. In the case of human beings, for example, our organs provide functions to keep us alive – for example, the heart pumps blood. It exists for that purpose and we would not have it if there was no need to pump blood. Other creatures have developed alternative methods of survival – for instance, reptiles do not have hearts as they do not pump blood around the body. Similarly, institutions exist, or don't, because of their functions for the maintenance of society.

Just as our bodies need to resolve certain basic needs in order to survive, so do societies. Parsons (1951) suggests that there are four needs (or **functional prerequisites**) that all societies have to satisfy:

1 *Adaptation* (the economic function) – Every society has to provide an adequate standard of life for the survival of its members. Human societies vary from hunters and gatherers to complex industrial societies.

2 *Goal attainment* (the political function) – Societies must develop ways of making decisions. Human societies vary from dictatorships to democracies.

3 *Integration* (social harmony) – Each institution in society develops in response to particular functions. There is no guarantee that the different institutions will not develop elements that may conflict. For example, in **capitalism** the economic inequalities may lead to possible resentment between groups. Specialist institutions therefore develop that seek to limit the potential conflict. These could include religion, notions of charity and voluntary organizations.

4 *Latency* (individual beliefs and values) – The previous three functional prerequisites all deal with the structure of society. This final prerequisite deals instead with individuals and how they cope. Parsons divides latency into two areas:

– *Pattern maintenance*: this refers to the problems faced by people when conflicting demands are made of them, such as being a member of a minority religious group and a member of a largely Christian-based society. In contemporary sociological terms, we would call this the issue of identity.

– *Tension management*: if a society is going to continue to exist, then it needs to motivate people to continue to belong to society and not to leave or oppose it.

Pattern variables

For a society to exist, it must fulfil the functional prerequisites listed above. However, 'society' is a concept that does not exist in itself, but is rather a term for a collection of people. When Parsons says that a 'society' must resolve certain problems, what he actually means is that *people* must act in certain ways that enable society to

fulfil its needs and ensure its continuation. This is the role of culture, which emphasizes that members of society ought to act in particular ways and, in doing so, ensure that the functional prerequisites are met.

Parsons claims that in all societies there are five possible cultural choices of action. The different answers the cultures provide lead to different forms of social behaviour and thus different ways of responding to the functional prerequisites. It is within these five sets of options that all cultural differences in human societies can be found.

Parsons calls these cultural choices of action **pattern variables**. They are:

● *Affectivity or affective neutrality* – Societies can be characterized either by close interpersonal relationships between people, or by relationships where the majority of interactions are value free. For example, a small rural society may well be based upon personal knowledge of others, whilst in a large, urban society people hardly know each other.

● *Specificity or diffuseness* – The relationships people have can be based on only one link or on many. We may know others simply as a teacher or a colleague, whereas in simpler societies, they may be cousin, healer, ceremonial leader and so on.

● *Universalism or particularism* – In contemporary societies, we believe that rules should apply equally to everyone (even if they don't), yet in many societies rules are not regarded as necessarily being applicable to all. Royalty, ethnic groups, religious leaders may all be able to behave differently.

● *Quality or performance* – This is linked to the previous pattern variable. Should people be treated according to their abilities or by their social position at birth?

● *Self-orientation or collectivity orientation* – Do societies stress the importance of individual lives and happiness or that of the group?

The answers that the culture of a society provides for these five pattern variables determines the way that people behave, which Parsons describes as social roles.

Criticisms within the functionalist approach

Robert Merton (1957) belonged to the same functionalist approach as Parsons. However, Merton was critical of some of Parsons' arguments and proposed two amendments to functionalist theory:

1 Parsons assumed if an institution was functional for one part of society, then it was functional for all parts. But Merton points out that this ignored the fact that some institutions can be both **dysfunctional** (or harmful) for society, as well as functional. In particular, he cites the example of religion, which can both bring people together and drive them apart.

2 Merton suggests that Parsons failed to realize the distinction between manifest (or intended) functions and latent (or unintended) consequences of these actions. Merton says that this makes any analysis of society much more complex than Parsons' simple model.

Pete Saunders (1996)
Do the best reach the top?

Functionalist theory suggests that society is formed as it is because that is functionally the best way of maintaining its existence. This includes inequalities in class and status.

Many critics argue it is not true that the most gifted achieve the top positions, but that success has more to do with inheritance and parental support. Saunders wished to demonstrate that in fact the best do achieve. He used evidence from the *National Child Development Study*, a longitudinal study of 17 000 children born in 1958 to assess their chances of social mobility. In 1991, he had access to information from the study on 6800 individuals in full-time employment, and concluded that occupational status was closely related to ability and effort. His results, therefore, support the functionalist argument.

Saunders, P. (1996) *Unequal but Fair? A study of class barriers in Britain*, London: IEA

In what ways do Saunders' results 'support the functionalist argument'?

Crime and deviance

Merton (1938) famously applied functionalist theory to an understanding of crime and deviance. Merton argued that societies have agreed cultural goals and culturally approved means of achieving these goals. Normally, there is a balance between the goals and the means, and societies remain harmonious. However, under certain circumstances, these means and goals do not mesh adequately together. He argued that the culture of the USA had developed too strong a stress on obtaining the culturally approved goal of financial success, but there were inadequate culturally approved means for a significant proportion of the population to do so. The result was a growth in crime and other forms of deviance.

- Finally, as interactionists point out, human beings in the Parsonian model of society seem rather like puppets having their strings pulled by all-powerful societies via pattern variables. Interactionists, postmodernists and late-modernists all combine to argue that people are much more 'reflexive', making choices and constructing their lives.

Neo-functionalism

Other writers following in the functionalist tradition include Mouzelis (1995) and Alexander (1985). Both these writers argue strongly for the overall systemic approach provided by Parsons. They dispute criticisms of Parsons that suggest he is not interested in how people act, and argue that with some modification Parsonian theory can allow for people to be 'reflexive', making decisions for themselves. These modifications to the theory also help explain social change.

Marxism

The second major sociological perspective that, like functionalism, aims to create a total theory of society by linking individual motivations and wider structural context is the tradition that has developed from Marxism. Marxism derives from the 19th-century writings of Karl Marx (1867/1973), who sought to create a scientific explanation of societies. His starting point was that the economic system of any society largely determined the social structure. The owners of the economic structure are able to control that society and construct values and social relationships that reflect their own interests. Other groups in society, being less powerful, generally accept these values and social relationships, even though they are not in their interests.

Marx began by suggesting that all history can be divided into five periods or epochs, which are distinguished by ever more complex economic

Criticisms outside the functionalist approach

Sharrock *et al.* (2003) argue that there are several main criticisms of functionalism:

- Functionalism overemphasizes the level of agreement or consensus in society. Apart from the simplest of societies, people have different values and attitudes within the same society.
- Parsons suggests that society is rather like an organism, yet this is not true. Organisms actually exist as biological entities, have a natural form and a natural life cycle. Society, on the other hand, is a concept, consisting of the activities of possibly millions of people. There is no natural cycle or natural form.
- Functionalists have real problems explaining social change. If, as Parsons claims, institutions exist to fulfil social needs, then once these needs are fulfilled, there is no reason to change them. Unless, therefore, there are some external changes which impact on the four functional prerequisites, societies should never change in form.
- Parsons seems to ignore differences in power. Yet differences in power can have strong impacts upon the form that society takes and whose interests it reflects.

arrangements. The history of all societies begins with what he entitled 'primitive **communism**' – simple societies, such as hunters and gatherers, where there is no concept of private property and everything is shared. From that point it passes through the ancient societies, such as those of Asia and Rome, through feudalism until it reaches the crucial stage of capitalism. According to Marx, capitalism would inevitably give way to the final stage of history, that of communism.

The Marxist model

Marx developed a theoretical model to describe the development of societies through these epochs. In each of the five epochs there is a particular economic structure (the economic base or **means of production**), which, except in primitive communism, is always controlled by a ruling class. This ruling class then constructs a whole set of social relationships (the **relations of production**) that benefit them and allow them to exploit all others who do not share in the ownership of the means of production. According to Marxist economic theory, the means of production are always advancing, becoming more complex and capable of producing greater wealth – nothing can stop this onward march of technology. However, the values that the ruling group create to benefit themselves tend to move much more slowly. Within each epoch, at the beginning, the values of the ruling class help technology move forward, but over time, because the values do not move as fast, they begin to get in the way of the move forward of technology – in fact, they actually impede it. At this point, a new, challenging group arises with values and ideas that would help the means of production advance, and, after a degree of conflict, they gain control of society and begin to construct their own relations of production. A new epoch has started and the process begins again.

Applying the model to capitalism

Marx believed that contemporary society has reached the stage of capitalism. The majority of his work was about the state of capitalist society and the factors that would, in his opinion, lead on to a communist society.

Within capitalism, there is a ruling class, or 'bourgeoisie', that owns the industry and commerce. All other people who work for a wage, no matter how prestigious or well paid, are members of the working class or proletariat. The bourgeoisie construct relations of production to their own benefit, including concepts of private property, wage labour and the justification of wide inequalities of wealth. The majority of the population accept the inequalities of the system because of the way that dominant institutions, such as religion and education, justify the prevailing economic and social situation. Marx describes this majority as suffering from '**false consciousness**'. However, there is always a degree of conflict between some groups in society who are aware of their exploitation and the bourgeoisie – Marx saw these people as being 'class conscious'. **Class consciousness** manifests itself in terms of strikes and political protest, all examples of **class conflict**.

Over time, capitalism will enter a period of crisis, caused by ever-increasing competition amongst industries, leading to fewer and fewer large employers – who are able to lower the wages on offer to such an extent that the majority of the population live in poverty. At such a point, with a tiny minority of very rich capitalists and a huge majority of relatively poor people, radical social change is inevitable. This change will usher in the final epoch of communism.

Criticisms of Marx

Marx's work has probably been subjected to more critical discussion and straight criticism that any other sociological theory. This is mainly because it is as much a political programme as a sociological theory. However, specific sociological criticisms of Marx's work include the following:

- The description of capitalism and its inevitable move towards a crisis has simply not occurred. Indeed, capitalism has grown stronger and, through globalization, has spread across the world.
- The polarization of people into a tiny rich minority and an extremely poor majority has also not occurred. There is huge inequality, but at the same time there has been a massive growth in the middle classes in society – the very group that Marx predicted would disappear.
- Capitalism changed significantly after Marx's death with the introduction of a wide range of health, pension, housing and welfare benefits, all of which were missing from Marx's analysis.

Neo-Marxism

The basic model of Marxist theory has provided the platform for an entire tradition of writing in sociology. His ideas have been taken up and developed by a wide range of sociologists, keen to show that the model, suitably amended, is still accurate. Neo-Marxists seek to overcome the criticisms listed above.

The extent of writings within the Marxist tradition is too great to cover in any detail, but three versions of neo-Marxism provide us with a fairly representative sample of developments.

The Frankfurt School

The Frankfurt School is associated with the works of three major neo-Marxists: Marcuse, Adorno and Horkheimer, all of whom were originally at Frankfurt University. In separate books, Marcuse (1964/1991), Adorno (1991) and Horkheimer (1974) criticized Marx for being an **economic determinist** – that is for believing society is mainly determined by the economic system. They argued that people's ideas and motivations are far more important than Marx ever acknowledged. Their critique contained three important elements:

1 *Instrumental reason* – According to Adorno, Marx failed to explore people's motivations for accepting capitalism and the consumer goods it offers. Adorno suggests that it was wrong of Marx to dismiss this as simply 'false consciousness'. People work hard to have a career and earn money, but quite why this is their

aim is never explored. Thinking in capitalism is therefore rational, in terms of achieving goals, as long as the actual reasons for having those goals are not thought about rationally.

2   *Mass culture* – Marcuse argued that Marx had ignored the importance of the media in his analysis. Marcuse suggested that the media play a key part in helping to control the population by teaching people to accept their lot and to concentrate on trivial entertainment.

3   *The oppression of personality* – The third element of their critique of Marx focused on the ways that individuals' personality and desires are controlled and directed to the benefit of capitalism. Before capitalism, there was no concept of 'the work ethic'; people did the work that was required and then stopped. Capitalism, and particularly industrial production, needed people who accepted going to work for the majority of their lives and having little leisure. In the early stages of capitalism, therefore, pleasure and desire as concepts were heavily disapproved of – hence the puritan values of Victorian England. But in later capitalism, when it was possible to make money out of desires (and in particular sex), they were emphasized. Sex is now used, for example, to sell a wide range of products. According to the Frankfurt School, therefore, even our wants and desires are manipulated by capitalism in its own interests.

Althusser and the concept of relative autonomy

One of the most sociologically influential neo-Marxist approaches was provided by Althusser (1969), who argued that Marx had overemphasized how much the economic system drove society. Althusser suggested that capitalist society was made up of three interlocking elements:

1   the economic system – producing all material goods
2   the political system – organizing society
3   the ideological system – providing all ideas and beliefs.

According to Althusser, the economic system has ultimate control, but the political and ideological have significant degrees of independence or autonomy. In reality, this means that politics and culture develop and change in response to many different forces, not just economic ones. Althusser used the term **relative autonomy** to describe this degree of freedom of politics and values. This may not at first seem very important, but what it suggests is that society is much more complex and apparently contradictory than in traditional Marxist analysis. So, the march towards a communist state is not clear, but confusing and erratic.

Althusser also used this argument in his analysis of politics and the state. For Marx, the role of politics was simply to represent the interests of the ruling class, but for Althusser, the state was composed of two elements:

1   **repressive state apparatuses** – organizations such as the police and the army
2   **ideological state apparatuses** – the more subtle organizations including education, the media and religious organizations.

Both sets of apparatuses ultimately work for the benefit of capitalism, but there is a huge variation in the way they perform this task, with some contradictions between them.

Althusser's work provided a huge leap forward in neo-Marxist thinking, as it moved away from a naive form of Marxism (rather similar to functionalism), which simply said that everything that existed did so to perform a task for capitalism. Instead, while recognizing this ultimate purpose, Althusser highlighted the massive contradictions and differences between the various institutions of society.

Harvey: a late-modernist approach to Marxism

Some of the most recent and interesting sociological theorizing within neo-Marxism comes from the work of Harvey (1990). Harvey is extremely unusual for a neo-Marxist in that he develops Marxism within a postmodernist framework. As we see in the next topic, postmodernism is a movement that sees a fragmentation of society and a move towards image and superficiality in culture. Harvey argues that this move to postmodernity is the result of economic changes in the 1970s, which led away from manufacturing to commerce, media and retail as the main employers. Coupled with the development of globalization, these changes have presented massive challenges to capitalism.

According to Harvey, capitalism has, however, been clever in its responses to these economic changes, developing new sources of profit through the creation of whole new areas of commerce – what he calls **flexible accumulation** – in particular, through the manipulation of identity, with developments in fashion, travel and new forms of music. Globalization, too, has been utilized to produce cheap goods, which are given added value by being marketed in the more affluent nations.

At the same time, Harvey points out that there have been many real changes that have affected capitalism quite drastically. For example:

●   National governments are less powerful than ever before in modernity, and so change now lies at the global, rather than national, level.
●   Real political discourse within the traditional frameworks of government and political parties has been replaced by image politics, where what *appears* to happen is more important than what *actually* happens.
●   Social class as the dominant form of division between members of societies has been partly replaced by a range of divisions linked to gender, ethnicity, religion and even alternative political movements, such as the green movement.

Social action theories

According to social action theories, the way to understand society is not to start analysis at the top (analysing the structure of society, as Marxism and functionalism do), but to begin from the 'bottom' – analysing the way people interact with each other. Social action theorists do not set

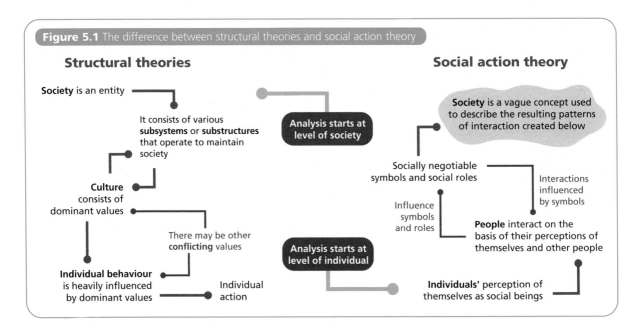

Figure 5.1 The difference between structural theories and social action theory

Structural theories

Society is an entity

It consists of various **subsystems** or **substructures** that operate to maintain society

Culture consists of dominant values

There may be other **conflicting** values

Individual behaviour is heavily influenced by dominant values

Individual action

Analysis starts at level of society

Analysis starts at level of individual

Social action theory

Society is a vague concept used to describe the resulting patterns of interaction created below

Socially negotiable symbols and social roles

Interactions influenced by symbols

Influence symbols and roles

People interact on the basis of their perceptions of themselves and other people

Individuals' perception of themselves as social beings

out to construct a grand theory along the lines of Marxism or functionalism, but are much more content to sketch out the rules of social interaction. These approaches (which are sometimes referred to as 'phenomenological approaches') explore the day-to-day, routine actions that most people perform. Interactionists (social action theorists/ phenomenologists) set out to see how individuals actually *create* society through these routine actions.

Symbolic interactionism

Symbolic interactionism – the full name for interactionism – derives from the writings of Mead (1934) and then Blumer (1962) at the University of Chicago. Both Marxism and functionalism seemed to suggest that people were like marionettes controlled by the 'relations of production' or the 'pattern variables'. Instead, symbolic interactionism sees people as actively working at relationships, creating and responding to symbols and ideas. It is this dynamic that forms the basis of interactionists' studies.

The theory of symbolic interactionism has three core ideas: the symbol, the self, the interaction.

1 *The symbol* – The world around us consists of millions of unique objects and people. Life would be impossible if we treated every separate thing as unique. Instead, we group things together into categories which we then classify. Usually, we then give each group a name (which is a symbol). Examples of symbols include 'trees', 'women', 'gay men', 'terrorists'. You will immediately see that the symbol may evoke some feelings in us; they are not necessarily neutral terms. So, the world is composed of many symbols, all of which have some meaning for us and suggest a possible response or possible course of action. But the course of action that we feel is appropriate may not be shared by everybody.

2 *The self* – In order for people to respond to and act upon the meanings that symbols have for them, they

have to know who they are within this world of symbols and meaning. I cannot decide how I ought to behave until I know who I am and therefore what is appropriate for me to do in certain circumstances. Crucially, this involves us being able to see ourselves through the eyes of others. Blumer suggests that we develop this notion of the self in childhood and, in particular, in games playing. When engaging in a game with others, we learn various social roles and also learn how these interact with the roles of others. This brings us to the third element of interactionism, the importance of the interaction itself.

3 *The interaction* – For sociology, the most important element of symbolic interactionism is actually the point at which the symbol and the self come together with others in an interaction. Each person in society must learn (again through games) to take the viewpoint of other people into account whenever they set out on any course of action. Only by having an idea of what the other person is thinking about the situation is it possible to interact with them. This is an extremely complex business – it involves reading the meaning of the situation correctly from the viewpoint of the other (What sort of person are they? How do they see me? What do they expect me to do?) and then responding in terms of how you see your own personality (Who am I? How do I want to behave?). There is clearly great scope for confusion, error and misunderstanding, so all people in an interaction must actively engage in constructing the situation, reading the rules and symbols correctly.

Goffman and the dramaturgical approach

Erving Goffman (1968) was heavily influenced by symbolic interactionism in his studies of people's interaction in a number of settings. Goffman's work, which has been called the **dramaturgical** approach, is based on similar ideas to symbolic interactionism in that he explores how people perceive themselves and then set out to present an

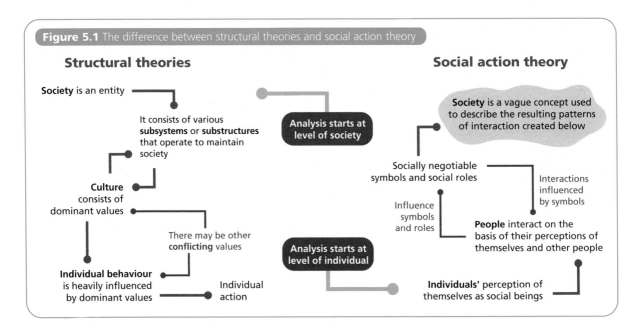

image of themselves to others. Goffman suggests that people work out strategies in dealing with others and are constantly altering and manipulating these strategies. The basis of his ideas is that social interaction can best be understood as a form of loosely scripted play in which people ('actors') interpret their roles.

Evaluation of symbolic interactionism

Interactionism provides a rich insight into how people interact in small-scale situations. However, as a theory it is rather limited in scope and is as much psychological as sociological. Its main weakness lies in its failure to explore the wider social factors that create the context in which symbol, self and interaction all exist and the social implications of this. This means that it has no explanation of where the symbolic meanings originate from. It also completely fails to explore power differences between groups and individuals, and why these might occur.

Some of these criticisms were answered by Becker (1963) and other writers within the labelling perspective. Labelling theory is explored in Chapter 6, *Crime and deviance*, on pp. 352–8, so we will deal with it only very briefly here. An offshoot of symbolic interactionism, labelling theory focuses on explaining why some people are 'labelled' as deviant and how this impacts on both their treatment by others and their perception of themselves. Becker specifically introduces the notion of power into his version of symbolic interactionism and demonstrates how more powerful groups are able to brand certain activities or individuals as deviant, with consequences that are likely to benefit themselves and harm those labelled deviant. One particular study which

combines these is his analysis of the imposition and repeal of the laws on prohibition (making alcohol manufacture and sales illegal) in the USA in the early 20th century. He showed how powerful groups came together, based on a mixture of genuine zeal and self-interest, to introduce the prohibition laws, and he explores the consequences for society. It is, therefore, possible to apply symbolic interactionism to broader social situations and also to include power in the analysis.

Conclusion

In this topic, we have explored a variety of modernist theories, which provide two approaches to understanding society. The first is the structural approach utilized by Marxism and functionalism. This approach starts from the 'top' and works downwards and claims to provide a total theory of society. The second approach starts its analysis from the bottom and works upwards. This is the social action approach utilized by symbolic interactionism. Both approaches have strengths and weaknesses, leading to sociologists taking sides in a debate that lasted more than 20 years. However, changes in society during the 1980s led many sociologists to be dissatisfied with both approaches. We move on to see the results of this dissatisfaction in the next topic.

Answers to 'Getting you thinking'

1 Functionalism
2 Marxism
3 Feminism
4 Social action theory or interactionism
5 Postmodernism

Key terms

Capitalism term used originally by Marx to describe industrial society based on private ownership of property and businesses.

Class conflict in Marxist analysis, the inevitable conflict arising between social classes based on their differing economic interests.

Class consciousness in Marxist analysis, the awareness of belonging to a social class.

Communism term used originally by Marx to describe societies where ownership of land, businesses and so on is shared and not privately owned.

Dramaturgical refers to Goffman's version of interactionism, in which he sees people rather like actors in a play, with some of the script written and some ad-libbed.

Dysfunctional in functionalist theory, activities or institutions which do not appear to benefit society.

Economic determinism belief that the form of society is mainly determined by the economic system.

False consciousness in Marxist analysis, the lack of awareness of being exploited.

Flexible accumulation a term used by the neo-Marxist writer Harvey to explain how capitalism has continued to find new ways of profiting from people.

Functional prerequisites in functionalist theory, societal needs.

Ideological state apparatuses a term used by the neo-Marxist writer Althusser for those institutions which he claims exist to control the population through manipulating values, such as the media.

Interactionism shorthand term for symbolic interactionism.

Labelling a theory developed from symbolic interactionism which was adapted for use in studies of deviance.

Means of production in Marxist analysis, the economic structure of a society.

Modernism (modernity) a period in history characterized by the belief that rational thought can be used to understand and explain the world.

Pattern variables in functionalist theory, cultural choices as 'suggested' by the society.

Relations of production in Marxist analysis, the social relationships in a society.

Relative autonomy a term used by the neo-Marxist writer Althusser to suggest that society is not determined as much as

Marx suggested by the economic base.

Repressive state apparatuses a term used by the neo-Marxist writer Althusser for those institutions which he claims exist to control the population through aggressive means, such as the police.

Social action theory another name for symbolic interactionism; social action theories focus on how society is built up from people interacting with each other.

Structural approaches these attempt to analyse society by looking at it as a whole and then working down to its constituent parts and then to individuals.

Symbolic interactionism a theory associated with G.H. Mead that argues that people constantly work via symbols (language, writing, and so on) to construct society through the process of social interaction.

Check your understanding

1 What is the 'organic analogy'?

2 In your own words identify and briefly explain 'functional prerequisites'.

3 What are the 'means of production' and how do they relate to the 'relations of production'?

4 What does Harvey mean by 'flexible accumulation'?

5 In your own words, explain the key difference between social action theories and structural theories.

6 Explain any one criticism of interactionism.

Activities

Research idea

Conduct a small study of your own in which you explore the nature of symbolic interaction. How do people respond to symbols? Do they respond differently?

Web.task

Add to your notes and depth of knowledge on sociological theory by looking at sections of the following excellent website from Hewett School. Go to: **www.hewett.norfolk.sch.uk/CURRIC/soc/ Theory1.htm2**

An eye on the exam   Modernist sociological theories

Item A

The functionalist method sees any system as having needs or requirements. If the system is to survive, and to continue in more or less its current form, then these needs must be met in some way. The idea of need is quite simple. A human body needs food if it is to survive; it will die without this food.

   How then can functional analysis be used in the study of societies? The first step is to identify the needs of society. A society is assumed to be a relatively self-contained unit. As such it has many internal needs. These include the biological and psychological needs of its members and the need to maintain boundaries and identity. However, many needs can only be met if the society draws on resources from the external environment, for example by producing food – the economic need. Functionalists see social systems as characterized by harmony and consensus. Marx's view, on the other hand, viewed conflict and division as normal features of all societies. Social systems develop over time as a result of contradictions that arise as a result of their economic systems.

Adapted from Fulcher, J. and Scott, J. (2007) *Sociology* (3rd edn), Oxford: OUP

Assess the contribution of functionalism to an understanding of society.   (33 marks)

Grade booster   Getting top marks in this question

Outline the core elements of functionalism, focusing on functional prerequisites and pattern variables, introducing them with the notion of the 'organic analogy'. You should then bring in the whole raft of criticisms made of it, including its overemphasis on consensus; the problem with the organic analogy; its failure to explain social change; the failure to look at power differences; and the way it seems to treat people like puppets. You could point out that Merton did reply to some of these criticisms, talking about dysfunctional institutions and latent functions. Finally, while functionalism is no longer fashionable in sociology, it has contributed to the development of sociological theory, raising the levels of debate and providing a theoretical counterbalance to Marxism.

TOPIC 2

Feminist, late-modern and postmodern sociological theories

Getting you thinking

She's gotta have it

By Polly Vernon

Kate Rainbow, the 31 year old owner of a communications company, says ... 'It's only now becoming obvious, but the market in accessorizing is huge _ Swarovski crystal covers for Blackberries, laptop bags, phone fascias and phone charms. The potential to customize phones and gadgets will grow immensely. People, women in particular, want to make their gadgets individual in some way. Lee agrees: 'Increasingly the lines between jewellery or accessory and gadget are being blurred. You can literally wear your phone or your digital camera around your neck on necklaces designed for that purpose.'

Source: *The Independent Technology Magazine*, Issue 1, 31 July 2005

1 What do you think the text and photo tell us about:
   (a) the changing pace of technology
   (b) the relationship between fashion and technology?

2 Do you think that males and females have different attitudes to modern technology (phones, computers, etc.)? Does this have any impact on what they buy?

3 Can you suggest ways in which the following have brought about social changes:
   (a) mobile phones   (b) the internet?

4 In what ways do you think the developments reflected in the material above affect society? Explain your answer.

iPhone gets faster and sexier – but will UK pay more?

By Martin Hickman, Consumer Affairs Correspondent

APPLE is to sell a new version of its iPhone with faster internet connection speeds and new applications for about £100, slashing the price of the gadget by more than a third.

The device will use Wi-Fi, 3G and Edge networks, automatically switching between them to ensure the fastest download speeds.

Apple said: "The new iPhone 3G also makes it easier to multi-task with simultaneous voice and data communications, so with iPhone 3G you can browse the web, get map directions, or check your email while you are on a call."

Mr Jobs said there would be software upgrades for the phone, on sale in the UK through an exclusive tie-up with the mobile company 02.

"The thing for Apple is to be able to leverage the iPhone for further innovation, or they run the risk of being the next [Motorola] RAZR, which was iconic in its own way, but for which innovation did not come fast enough," said Shiv Bakhshi, director of mobility research for the market research firm IDC.

Source: *The Independent*, 10 June 2008

Topic 1 explored the emergence of sociology during the period of modernity and how the subject was shaped by the dominant ways of thinking of that time. Reflecting the natural sciences, sociology searched for a theoretical perspective that could explain how society was structured, how it functioned and how it changed over time. The theoretical approaches of Marxism and functionalism both claimed to do this, but by the 1970s, sociologists began to accept the fact that these major theoretical approaches simply failed to provide an adequate explanation for the existence of society. It was during this period that social action perspectives became popular, but for most sociologists these had limited value as they never claimed to provide the overarching theoretical frameworks that functionalism and Marxism had claimed. By the 1980s

(and ten years earlier for feminists), sociologists were aware, through their studies of culture, gender, social class and the economy, that enormous changes were taking place. The traditional 'modern' social characteristics of strong social classes, clear gender roles and party-based politics, all linked to an economic system based on industrial production, were no longer an accurate reflection of British (and most other Western) societies. Sociological theory was simply unable to explain these changes. It was in this vacuum that a new breed of theorizing emerged.

One group of writers believed that modernity had moved towards what is now commonly known as '**late modernity**' (or '**high modernity**' according to Giddens (1984)). A separate, much more radical group of theorists argued that society really had totally changed and had moved into a **postmodern** era – hence the term 'postmodernists'.

A third group of sociologists are feminists, who provide the bridge in sociological theorizing from structural and interactionist theories through to postmodern approaches.

Feminism

Gender roles and the issue of patriarchy are explored in a number of units in this book. Feminism as a social and political movement has been concerned to expose the inequalities that exist in the treatment of women in society. However, linked to this movement has been a development in theoretical approaches to explain the situation of women in society.

In many ways, feminism could be seen to be the battering ram that smashed down the closed doors of sociological thinking. Feminism initially emerged from a Marxist theoretical framework, but many feminist writers soon found this approach too constricting and moved beyond this towards more radical theories. Eventually, feminism and one of its offshoots, 'queer theory', began to question some of the very basic concepts upon which sociology was built – in fact, the very notion of male and female came under attack.

For a detailed analysis and evaluation of the various types of feminism, see Chapter 7, pp. 453–7. We recommend that you read that section now (you will certainly need to read it before tackling the 'Eye on the exam' on p. 269).

Late modernity and postmodernity

The distinction between late-modern and postmodern theory

Most students of sociology are understandably confused over the distinction sociologists make between late modernity (or 'high modernity') and postmodernity.

Perhaps the simplest way of dividing the two is that late modernity sees society as having changed and developed new aspects. The task of the late-modernist theory is to adapt more traditional theories of sociology.

Postmodern theorists argue that the whole 'sociological project' was part of a period of history – modernity – in which a particular way of viewing society developed that was closely related to a set of economic and social circumstances. We have now moved into a new set of economic and social circumstances based largely on communication and image, and therefore traditional sociological models have no value at all.

Late or high modernity

In the previous topic on modernism, we saw that the major split between theoretical approaches concerned which 'end' of human society sociologists emphasized. On one side of the argument were 'structural' theorists, such as Marx and Parsons, who, no matter what their differences, stressed that the only way to understand human behaviour was to locate it firmly within a dominant, controlling, structural framework. Their theories suggested that people were manipulated by their cultures. On the other side, however, writers from the social action tradition, such as the interactionists, argued equally passionately that the only way to see society was as an abstract concept consisting of the interaction of individuals and groups. People were actively engaged in defining the world around them and then responding to these definitions.

By the 1980s, most sociologists began to tire of this argument and looked for ways out of it – there had to be a way to combine the two perspectives.

Giddens' structuration theory

The best-known and currently highly influential attempt to resolve the argument can be found in the work of Giddens (1984). Giddens calls his theory **structuration theory**, which, as you can tell from the name, combines the concepts of structure and action.

>> *The difference between society and nature is that nature is not man-made, but society is. While not made by any single person, society is created and recreated afresh, by participants in every encounter. It is indeed only made possible because every member of society is a practical social theorist who draws upon their knowledge and resources, normally in an unforced and routine way.*>> (Giddens 1993)

Structure in Giddens' writings

The starting point for Giddens is that there is such a thing as structure, but only as a way to describe patterns of behaviour of people in society. Structure has no existence beyond this. He therefore rejects the traditional modernist notion of something 'out there' that determines how we behave.

>> *Society only has form, and that form only has effects on people, in so far as structure is produced and reproduced in what people do.* >> (Giddens and Pierson 1998)

The simple way that Giddens himself explains this is by using the example of a language. We all use a series of words and grammatical rules to communicate. We may not know all the words and we may not be aware of what the rules actually are – we just use them. The language therefore exists, but it only does so because we make it exist through our use of it. Giddens calls this 'structure'.

Bearing this in mind, structure consists of two key elements: *rules* and *resources*. Both of these combine to influence how we act:

- Rules are procedures we generally follow in everyday life. They can be formal or informal depending upon the situation and their perceived seriousness. Rules are not fixed and may be changed over time. (Again, think of his analogy with language.)
- People have differing resources – by which he is referring to access to different levels of power. These resources consist of material resources (such as wealth and income), symbolic resources (such as personal or

job-related prestige), biological resources (such as physical attractiveness) and cognitive resources (such as intelligence or skills).

The structure of society, then, consists of people following rules, but different people have different resources to deploy in order to use or amend these rules.

Agency and the duality of structure

If structure is actually only people (or '**agents**' as Giddens calls them) behaving in certain ways, then why is it important? Because, Giddens argues, people draw from society the shared stock of knowledge that they use to guide their actions (that is, 'the rules' above). People therefore make society, but in doing so give themselves the rules and structure to guide them in their actions. This intimate two-way relationship is described by Giddens as the '**duality of structure**'.

Ontological security

Ontology refers to the issues to do with the reality of the world. According to Giddens, humans have a need for a sense of security, provided by rules and resources. As he puts it, people wish to believe that the 'natural and social worlds are as they appear to be'. He describes this situation as '**ontological security**'.

The desire for security and the existence of shared understanding helps people engage in regular patterns of social life. This regularity then helps society to remain stable.

Reflexivity and transformative capacity

In seeking ontological security, people are clearly seeking stability. However, we know that people also seek to bring about social change. You may also recall from your study of functionalism (see Topic 1, pp. 255–7) that there was a real problem with the theory in explaining social change. Giddens says that this change takes place because people are constantly monitoring their situation and their place in society, and assessing whether they match their idea of self-personality – this process is known as 'reflexive monitoring'. If people are unhappy or have an ideal of what they want, then they will actively seek change. Unlike the Marxist or functionalist view, people are not puppets controlled by others. By engaging in **reflexivity**, people have a '**transformative capacity**' to change society.

As a way of illustrating his theory, Giddens points to Willis' *Learning to Labour* (Willis 1977) as an example of structuration, where the young lads' choices of action and the wider structure of society interact to provide an outcome that reflects both. Willis studied a group of 12 working-class boys for 18 months at the end of their schooldays, and then briefly into their first employment. The 'lads' showed little interest in studying, as they knew that their future lay elsewhere in unskilled physical labour. At school, they passed their time by 'having a laff' in lessons and making fun of teachers and the harder-working pupils ('ear 'oles'). Their choice of behaviour in school guaranteed their school failure, thus ensuring that the future that they knew would come about for them actually did come about. When they later entered these unskilled jobs, the skills of 'having a laff' and passing time

enabled them to cope with the work. To summarize, the boys made choices based on their awareness of the wider society and their place in it. It is possible that they could have made other choices, but did not do so. The interaction of their choices and the 'reality' of society resulted in the outcome they predicted.

Criticisms of Giddens

Although Giddens' work is very influential and has attracted much attention, Cuff *et al.* (1990) question how original his ideas actually are. They suggest that these are really just a collection of ideas drawn from a variety of sources. Much of Giddens' work, they suggest, goes little further than the work of some of the founders of sociology. Many would argue that Giddens is merely updating Weber. Despite Giddens claiming the originality of ideas such as 'transformative capacity', sociologists such as Craib (1992) suggest that similar ideas can also be found in Marx, who once wrote that 'men make their own history albeit not in circumstances of their own choosing' or even in Parsons' concept of pattern variables. Cuff and colleagues also suggest that Giddens' theory has rarely been successfully applied, least of all by Giddens himself. Giddens has used the example of Willis' work, yet Willis himself was working from a Marxist perspective.

Beck and the sociology of risk

Another sociologist pushing forward the boundaries of sociology within the 'late modernity' framework is the German sociologist Ulrich Beck. Beck (1992) argues that a central concern for all societies today is that of risk, and this concept has permeated the everyday life of all of us. There are three elements to Beck's thesis: **risk society**, **reflexive modernization** and **individualization**.

Risk society

According to Beck, modernity introduced a range of 'risks' that no other historical period has ever had to face. Note that Beck uses the term 'risk' in a very specific way. Throughout history, societies have had to face a wide range of 'hazards', including famine, plague and natural disasters. However, these were always seen as beyond the control of people, being caused by such things as God or nature. Yet the risks faced by modern societies were considered to be solvable by human beings. The belief was that industrialization, public services, private insurance and a range of other supports would minimize the possibility of risk. Indeed, the very project of sociology began with a desire to control society and minimize social problems.

However, in late modernity (which Beck calls 'advanced or reflective modernization'), the risks are seen as spiralling away from human control. No longer can risks be adequately addressed to the same standards as they were in modernity. Problems such as global warming and nuclear disaster are potentially too complex for societies to deal with.

Reflexive modernization

Late modernity, in which people are reflexive (as outlined in the work of Giddens), leads to their questioning how these risks became uncontrollable – that is, they begin to question the political and technological assumptions of modernity. People begin to be aware of risk and how they as individuals are in danger. They also seek ways of minimizing risk in all spheres of their lives. Risk and risk avoidance become central to the culture of society. This helps explain the growth in control of young children by parents trying to minimize any possible risk to them from cars, paedophiles and the material they watch on television. At the level of politics, there is a huge demand for governments to seek to identify and control every possible risk.

Beck argues that although it is the global political and technological 'system' itself that is the cause of the risk, there has been little attempt to confront the problems at this level; rather, risk avoidance operates at the personal and lower political levels.

Individualization

Beck links the move towards individualization with the move away from 'tradition' as an organizing principle of society. In modern societies, most aspects of people's lives were taken for granted. Social position, family membership and gender roles, for example, were all regarded as 'given'. In late modernity, however, there has been the move towards individualization, whereby all of these are now more open to decision-making. So, the background is of risk and risk awareness, and the foreground is of people making individual choices regarding identity and lifestyle as they plan their lives.

Key themes

Stratification and differentiation

Giddens suggests that in high modernity, social class, though still existing, has changed. He accepts that differences in power and resources exist, but he rejects the notion of social class as consisting of traditional cohesive groups (as suggested by Marxists) and argues that a much more complex pattern of stratification has replaced it. Social classes are no longer clearly hierarchical, but now overlap considerably. Social classes are also highly fragmented within themselves, with different groups existing within each class. Finally, people within classes are aware of the meaning and implication of their claims to belong to a class and are able to amend or change their self-image.

In the UK today, social classes overlap considerably

Criticisms of Beck

Beck has been criticized by a number of writers. Turner (1994) argues that Beck's distinction between 'hazard' and 'risk' is dubious. People have always faced 'risk' and have always sought to minimize this in whatever ways were available at the time, such as religion or some other means that we might now consider of little value. Nevertheless, there was an awareness that something could be done to combat the 'hazard'.

A second criticism derives from Beck's argument that the response to risk was largely individual. Yet a range of political movements have been formed to combat global warming, eradicate poverty in Africa and stop the spread of HIV/AIDS. These are all political movements which are international in scope and which indicate that people do believe that it is possible to control the risks that Beck identifies. In July 2005, a G8 summit took place at which the richest countries in the world committed themselves to seek to resolve poverty in Africa and global warming. A series of rock concerts was also put on across the world to draw attention to the need for the G8 leaders to tackle these issues. However, in defence of Beck, his writings have been so influential that one could equally reply that it is his work that has led people to believe it is possible to challenge global threats.

Elliot (2002) argues that Beck's work fails to recognize differences in power. Beck has suggested that the risk is spread across all groups in society and that differences in power are relatively unimportant. Elliot disputes this, suggesting instead that rich and powerful groups are able to limit risk and to have greater influence on the context in which the risk occurs.

Postmodernism

Postmodernist approaches to sociology emerged in the 1980s, providing a powerful challenge to traditional 'modernist' theories that sought to create an all-encompassing theory to explain society.

Two key postmodernist writers are Baudrillard (1980, 1994) and Lyotard (1984). Although Baudrillard had originally been a Marxist academic and his early works supported a neo-Marxist perspective, he later attacked the 'grand theories' such as Marxism and functionalism. Lyotard and Baudrillard dismissed these as merely **meta-narratives**, or elaborate stories, that effectively gave comfort to people by helping them believe there was some rational, existing basis to society. According to the postmodernists, sociological theory, like science and most other academic subjects, was simply a set of stories or narratives belonging to a specific period in history – the period of modernity, whose roots lie in the 18th-century historical movement known as the Enlightenment. This was the term used by those at the time for an academic movement which applied rational thought to solving scientific, economic, political and social questions. It is difficult for us today to accept that it was really not until then that academics began to believe that the natural and social worlds were governed by forces or laws that could be uncovered through scientific endeavour. The more the laws of economics and science could be uncovered, it was argued, the greater would be the progress in ridding the world of hunger, disease, war and all other problems.

The Enlightenment gave birth, in turn, to modernity, the period of 19th- and 20th-century history characterized by significant technological, social and political advances in Western societies. It was within this period that sociology was born. All of the founders of sociology were very strongly influenced by the idea that societies were progressing from traditional or premodern societies through to modern ones based on science, technology and the industrial process. This belief in scientific and social progress based on the application of rational thought was taken for granted until the 1970s when the postmodernist movement began to emerge.

At their simplest, postmodern theories argue that there cannot be any overarching theoretical explanation of society. This is because society exists only as a reassuring 'narrative'. In order to understand society as it is today, we need to have a deep awareness of the role of the media in creating an image of society that we seek to live out.

Lyotard

Lyotard argues that economic expansion and growth, and the scientific knowledge upon which they are based, have no aim but to continue expanding. This expansion is outside the control of human beings as it is too complex and simply beyond our scope. In order to make sense of this, to give ourselves a sense of control over it and to justify the ever-expanding economic system, grand narratives have been developed. These are political and social theories and explanations that try to make sense of society, which in reality is out of control. Marxism and functionalism and all other sociological theories fall into this category. The role of sociology, therefore, has been to justify and explain, while the reality of life for most people has simply not accorded with the sociological explanations. Lyotard sees contemporary society not as described in sociological theories, but as one that consists of isolated individuals linked by few social bonds.

Baudrillard

Baudrillard is also a critic of contemporary society. Like Lyotard, he sees people as isolated and dehumanized. Lyotard was particularly interested in the notion of knowledge as serving to justify the narratives of postmodern society. He argued that knowledge was a commodity that was bought and sold, and this buying was usually undertaken by big business and government. The result was that what people know about the world (knowledge) was that filtered through business and government. Baudrillard was also interested in the way that knowledge and understanding of the world are created, but his main emphasis was on the media.

The death of the social

Baudrillard notes that, in contemporary societies, the mass of the population expresses a lack of interest in social solidarity and in politics. The hallmark of this postmodern society is the consumption of superficial culture, driven by marketing and advertising. People live isolated lives sharing

Jeff Ferrell (2006)
Empire of Scrounge

In *Empire of Scrounge*, Jeff Ferrell describes how he spent eight months living in Fort Worth, Texas, making a living by collecting and selling articles he found in the 'rubbish' that people left outside their houses to be collected. Ferrell entered a subculture of people who permanently lived off this work, who he describes as 'dumpster divers' or 'trash pickers'. Dumpster divers dress in the clothes they find, sell unwanted articles to second-hand shops or collectors or simply on the streets, and they even eat the food that is left over. Ferrell covered all areas of the city on a scrounged BMX bike he found abandoned.

Ferrell's research demonstrated the extent of inequality in the USA, with people desperate to live off the discarded objects of others. It also demonstrated the development of a 'dumpster diver' subculture where there were, for instance, unwritten rules of etiquette concerning who had the right to collect articles from certain places and who had priority over others when two people were exploring the same batch of discarded 'rubbish'. Finally, it illustrated the fact that the US consumer culture encouraged the disposal of huge quantities of functioning objects because they were no longer 'fashionable'.

Ferrell, J. (2006) *Empire of Scrounge: Inside the urban underground of dumpster diving, trash picking, and street scavenging*, New York: New York University Press

How can Ferrell's research be used to illustrate some of the perspectives described in this topic?

common consumption of the media, through which they experience the world. According to Baudrillard this can best be described as the 'death of the social'.

Media and the experience of the world

The media play a central role in the death of the social. Baudrillard argues that people now have limited direct experience of the world and so rely on the media for the vast majority of their knowledge. As well as gaining their ideas of the world from the media, the bulk of the population are also influenced in how they behave by the same media. Rather than the media reflecting how people behave, Baudrillard argues that people increasingly reflect the media images of how people behave. Of course, at some point, the two move so close together that the media do start once again to mirror actual behaviour, as actual behaviour 'catches up' with the media images.

Sign-objects and the consumer society

In the 21st century, a significant proportion of Western societies are affluent. Members of those societies are able to consume a large number of commodities and enjoy a range of leisure activities. However, Baudrillard argues that this consumption moves people ever further away from social relationships and ever closer to relationships with their consumer lifestyles. Yet the importance of objects in our lives has little to do with their use to us, but much more to do with what meaning they have for us. We purchase items not just because they are functionally useful, but because they signify that we are successful or

fashionable. Consumer goods and leisure activities are, in Baudrillard's terms, '**sign-objects**', as we are consuming the image they provide rather than the article or service itself.

Hyperreality and the simulacrum

Baudrillard argues that, in modern society, it is generally believed that real things or concepts exist and then are given names or 'signs'. Signs, therefore, reflect reality. In postmodern society, however, signs exist that have no reality but themselves. The media have constructed a world that exists simply because it exists – for example, take the term 'celebrity'. A celebrity is someone who is defined as a celebrity, they do not have to have done anything or have any particular talent. It is not clear how one becomes a celebrity nor how one stays a celebrity. Being a celebrity occurs as long as one is regarded as a celebrity. Where a sign exists without any underlying reality, Baudrillard terms it a '**simulacrum**'. He believes

Activities

Key terms

Agents Giddens' term for people.

Duality of structure the notion that people both make society and are strongly influenced by it.

High modernity Giddens' term for late modernity.

Hyperreality the idea that we live in a world that is increasingly perceived and experienced via the media.

Individualization a decline in accepting socially approved roles and an increasing stress on personal choices.

Late modernity a term to describe contemporary society, in which the traditional social groupings, economic organization and culture have all changed so profoundly that traditional sociological explanations no longer hold true.

Meta-narratives a postmodernist term used to refer to the structural theories of Marxism and functionalism.

Ontological security the idea that people want to believe there is some reality beyond them in society, giving them the psychological confidence to engage in interaction.

Postmodern a different perspective on contemporary

society that rejects modernism and its attempts to explain the world through overarching theories. Instead, it suggests that there is no single, shared reality and focuses attention on the significance of the media in helping to construct numerous realities.

Reflexive modernization the idea that risk avoidance becomes a major factor in social organization.

Reflexivity Giddens' term for the ability to perceive yourself as others see you and to create your own identity.

Risk society Beck suggests that contemporary societies are best characterized as ones where people are aware that they face complex risks that are not open to individual control.

Sign-objects Baudrillard's term for the notion that we buy items to express ourselves, not for their function.

Simulacrum (plural 'simulacra') media images that have no basis in reality, but which people increasingly model their behaviour upon.

Structuration theory the term used for Giddens' theory, which seeks to combine both structural and social action theories.

Transformative capacity the ability of people to change society.

Research idea

Ask a sample of young people the extent to which they anticipate being able to control their future. Focus on factors such as choice of partner, higher education, job, friends and family relationships. Use the results to assess the extent of individualization (see p. 265).

Web.task

The site **www.theory.org.uk.** is run by the media sociologist David Gauntlett. Go to the page **www.theory.org.uk/giddens.htm** Make your own notes on at least one aspect of Giddens' thinking as described here.

Then head for
www.theorycards.org.uk/main.htm
Choose three of the theorists mentioned in this topic along with any others you have come across in your Sociology course. Print them out and turn them into playing cards.

An amusing area of his site is the set of 'Lego theorists', including the 'Anthony Giddens in his study' set (shown here),  which shows the sociologist 'composing new works, reading books and discussing ideas in his office at the London School of Economics'. See:
www.theory.org.uk/lego.htm

that the society in which we live is now increasingly based upon simulacra. The fact that so much of our lives are based upon signs that have no basis or reality has led Baudrillard to suggest that we now live in a world of '**hyperreality**' – a world of image.

Criticisms of postmodernism

Postmodernism has been very influential in sociology and can probably claim to have generated the huge growth in the academic subject of media studies. However, its success has been more in pointing to the failure of grand theories rather than in putting anything positive in its place. Of course, postmodernists in reply would argue that that is precisely their point! Baudrillard or Lyotard, though they reject any idea of value-free sociology, do appear to be more critics of society than sociological theorists. Their work is shot through with value-judgements about what is real and what is worthwhile – so their dismissal of contemporary media-based society is less a sociological statement than a political one.

Postmodernists have also been criticized for their failure to accept that not everything is hyperreal. People do live in reality, and some people have much greater access to goods and services than others.

Check your understanding

1 Identify at least three of the social changes that led some sociologists to believe that traditional sociological theory was out of date.

2 Identify the key difference between late-modern and postmodern theory.

3 How does Giddens use the example of language to explain the idea of structure?

4 What does Giddens mean by 'duality of structure'?

5 What piece of research does Giddens use as an example of structuration theory?

6 How has Giddens' work been criticized?

7 What is a 'risk society'?

8 How do postmodernists criticize sociological theory?

9 What does Baudrillard mean by the 'death of the social'?

10 Identify two criticisms of postmodernism.

An eye on the exam   Feminist, late-modern & postmodern theories

Item A

Since the 1970s, feminist theorizing has had a major impact on sociological thinking. It has offered a critique of existing or 'malestream' approaches as excluding women and/or assuming that their experiences are simply the same as men's. It has also guided empirical research in a wide variety of areas within sociology and shed new light on subjects such as families and households, religion, crime and education.

However, it would be wrong to claim that there is a single feminist theory to which all feminist sociologists subscribe. In fact, we can identify a wide range of different feminist approaches, each with its specific strengths and weaknesses.

Adapted from Gauntlett, D. (2002) *Media, Gender and Identity*, London: Routledge

To what extent has feminist theory added to our understanding of society?   (33 marks)

Grade booster   Getting top marks in this question

You could begin with the statement that feminism has added very greatly to our understanding of society and use the Item to indicate some of the ways in which it has done so, including its influence in introducing postmodernist ideas into sociology. Feminism, therefore, has done more than 'just' discuss the role of women. Explain how malestream sociology was before feminism. You should develop the point in the Item that there is a range of different feminist theories, including Marxist feminism, radical feminism, dual systems approach, etc. You also need to add criticisms of feminist theory, particularly the debate about the role of biology and the dispute between those who say that all women share a common position of exploitation and those who point out the significance of differences between them. Finally, you need to say how feminism has also led to a re-examination of male roles and the work of Connell in particular.

TOPIC 3

Sociology and science

Getting you thinking

I RECENTLY TOOK PART in the filming of a TV celebrity game show. I was leading the game, but growing increasingly itchy to escape, so when the cameras were off momentarily, I requested that my fellow contestants vote me off, so I could get out of there as fast as possible.

They complied graciously and I left the set, then settled into the back seat of the Mercedes they'd mercifully sent for me and relaxed into the overwhelming relief at having made my getaway.

However, I suddenly felt ashamed of myself. First, I'd lent my presence and energy to a strain of the culture I abhor and so had gone against my own principles. Secondly, this found me in the position of having to vote someone off, something I found extremely hard. Thirdly, I … should have overridden my

intense restlessness for the sake of winning and stayed the course.

By the time I arrived home, I felt as if I'd prostituted myself. I noticed that with this came a fall in energy levels, a feeling of exhaustion and a drop in my immune system, which triggered the start of a cold. This got my healer's mind working on how to clear shame as quickly as possible when it arises, for while it serves to point out our weaknesses, once these have been noted and acknowledged with a view to self-correction, to indulge it further is merely to beat ourselves up, and hence cause weakness throughout the mind–body–soul complex. So, I started by having a shower to cleanse my soul. Then I did some t'ai chi to rebuild my strength. Then I took some Bach Flower remedy of crab apple, which addresses shame and feeling inwardly dirty. Finally, I forgave

myself for being human, weak and fallible. In addition to this short shame-dissolving routine, as mentioned in a previous column, unresolved shame, according to the Taoist view, resides in your buttocks. Place a palm over each buttock and wobble your buttocks with gusto, as this releases the memories trapped there. If you go for it now, watch for possible shameful memories it may throw up. If any arise, breathe in deeply, as if wrapping the memories into a bundle inside the breath, exhale fully and see the bundle escape into the air and dissolve. Inhale again, say, 'I forgive myself all my transgressions now – by forgiving myself now, I ensure I will not repeat my mistakes', and carry on as you were – except now, hopefully feeling refreshed and renewed.

The Observer, Sunday 11 July 2004

The extract above is taken from a weekly column on alternative health in *The Observer*.

1 What is your initial reaction to the advice given?

2 What reasons can you give for this reaction?

3 If you were suffering from a serious illness and you could choose between the treatment offered by your doctor or that from an alternative practitioner, such as those above, which would you choose. (No, you cannot have both!) Give reasons for your choice.

If you decided to choose conventional Western treatment, you may have done so because modern Western medicine is based on science, and scientific explanations dominate modern societies. Perhaps sociology, too, can provide scientific explanations of the social world.

But there may have been some doubt in your mind. Why should you trust a doctor? Who is to say that other ways of dealing with illness don't work? For sociology, equally, striving to become a 'science' may not be the best path.

Sociology's claim to be a 'social science'

For at least 100 years, sociologists have argued among themselves as to whether or not sociology is a science. For most students coming to the subject for the first time, this seems a fairly pointless debate – after all, who cares how you classify the subject, just get on with it!

But the issue was, and still is, very important. The existence of sociology as an academic subject was for a long time tied up with its acceptance as a science, because both funding and academic prestige are more likely to be gained when subjects are regarded as 'scientific'. This is largely based on the idea that scientific knowledge is superior to other forms of knowledge.

Sources of knowledge

As the introductory exercise showed, we trust some forms of knowledge more than others. However, in daily lives, people mix knowledge from different sources without thinking much about it. Wallace (1971) argues that, in all, there are four sources that we use to gain our knowledge about the world:

1 *Authoritarian sources* derive from a person viewed as a source of true wisdom providing information for us. Because of our belief in this person's wisdom, we accept the explanation as true. This is similar to the way a young child will see their parents as the source of wisdom on most matters.
2 *Mystical sources* refer to somebody claiming an insight into the true nature of the world through some drug-fuelled or religious experience. Regular users of LSD and ecstasy claim that these drugs provide an insight into the real world beyond conventional barriers.
3 *Logico-rational* sources of knowledge are based upon following the rules of logic – essentially, this is 'truth' that emerges from the work of philosophers.
4 Finally, *scientific knowledge* rests upon generating ideas and hypotheses, and then rigorously testing them, through a variety of accepted methodologies.

According to Wallace, scientific knowledge is superior to other sources of knowing in its use of rigorous methods by which others can replicate or refute claims made. He suggests that this is not the case with the other three sources of knowledge. This means, then, that it is really the superior methodology of science that sets it apart from other sources of knowledge. Therefore, the effectiveness and accuracy of methods form the key to science. Any subject, such as sociology, which claims to be a science has therefore to pay great attention to the quality of the methods it uses.

Funding

Subjects receive funding for research from government departments, charities and commerce if they are seen to be 'scientific' and so more likely to produce reliable data that can be useful for these organizations. Subjects that are not seen as being 'scientific' (such as astrology, **parapsychology** and fortune-telling) are much less likely to receive the financial support of these organizations.

Prestige

The prestige of a subject is closely connected with its funding. For well over 200 years, according to Shapin (1995), the status of 'science' as the basis of knowledge, and of scientific methodology as the most effective way of researching, has been the pre-eminent method of understanding and studying the world. This reflects the modernist forms of thought (see Topics 1 and 2), which dominated all forms of thinking and social organization from the 18th century until recently – when it has been challenged by late-modern or postmodern ways of thinking and forms of social organization.

The result of sociology enjoying scientific prestige has been access to research funding, availability of the subject at A-level and university, and academic posts for people to teach it. According to Giddens (1976), much of the story of early sociology (indeed right up to the 1960s) was the promotion of sociology as a science by all the major sociologists, such as Weber, Durkheim, Merton and Parsons.

What is a science?

The modernist approach to science claims that it can be distinguished from other forms of knowledge by the way in which it goes about the process of understanding the world. This modernist approach stresses five key components that distinguish science from other forms of knowledge:

1 *Empirical* – By **empirical** we mean, in the strictest sense, 'knowable through our senses'. In practice, it means that the information can be counted or measured. The tradition comes from the philosopher Locke, who lived and wrote in the 17th century. He was arguing against metaphysical explanations of the world, which relied solely upon assuming that objects and powers existed beyond the 'physical realm'. Magic, some areas of religion and astrology are all metaphysical ways of explaining the world that cannot be proven (or disproved) and so cannot be empirical.
2 *Testable* – This leads us on to a crucial point about the importance of empirical knowledge – that it can be tested and revisited as many times as needed. This means that the knowledge gained is open to **verification** or **refutation** by others. According to Karl Popper (1959), once knowledge is put forward for scrutiny, it should be possible to engage in the process of **falsification** – that is, that the empirical model can be tested with the aim of showing it to be false. Only if all tests have been applied and the knowledge still seems accurate, can scientists assume that it is the best existing explanation.
3 *Theoretical* – Many students comment that good investigative journalism is the same as sociology in that it searches out 'the truth' behind events. This is not an accurate observation, however, because one of the main distinguishing features of sociology, like science, is that of theory construction. A theory seeks to uncover **causal relationships** between phenomena rather than simply describing the phenomena.
4 *Cumulative* – Scientific theory, it is claimed, builds on previous knowledge, so that there is an ever-growing, empirically testable body of such knowledge that moves us forward in our understanding of the world.
5 *Objective* – We discuss the question of objectivity in some detail in Topic 9, but the key issue here is that science blocks out personal prejudices and political views in its search for empirically testable propositions about the world.

The scientific tradition in sociology

As we have seen, traditionally, sociology has sought to be recognized as a science, and one school of sociology – the **positivist** one – has modelled its approach as closely as it can on the physical (or **natural**) **sciences**. The tradition began with the work of Comte and Quetelet, two founding fathers of sociology. They argued that philosophizing about the world was not enough. Statistics needed to be gathered so that cause and effect could be properly proven.

In a similar manner to the way physicists and biologists study the physical world, sociologists adopting the scientific approach seek to uncover general laws and relationships that they believe exist in the social world. Extreme examples of this approach include the work of Durkheim (1952) (for example, his study of suicide – see Chapter 6, Topic 11), and also Karl Marx (1867/1973). Indeed, Marx's work was a lifelong attempt to show that there were laws of economics that would inevitably lead to a communist society.

Much later, the main sociological opposition to Marxist ideas came from Talcott Parsons and the **structural–functionalist school** he founded. Once again, Parsons (1951) was intent upon showing that society existed as a structure and that there were forces and social laws that existed independently of individuals. What is interesting, however, is that though Parsons and Marx were in total opposition, politically and theoretically, they both shared the belief that sociology is a science.

Throughout this and any other textbook of sociology, you will find endless examples of studies that are based on generalized statements about how humans will act in certain circumstances and what factors cause this. Explicitly or not, these approaches support the view of sociology as a science.

The work of Durkheim and Marx combined theory with a search for the evidence to support their ideas. However, another, parallel, approach, which was highly sympathetic to the vision of sociology as a science, was developed in the 19th century through the study of working-class life in Britain. This empirical work, which first emerged in the writings of Mayhew (1851) and Rowntree (1901), formed the basis of the British empirical tradition. (Here, information is gathered about various social phenomena, e.g. the lives of the poor, for its own sake, or to influence social policy.) However, the work never set out to be theoretical. This tradition has remained the most common form of sociological research funded by government and charities. These sorts of empirical studies cover issues such as educational success, crime rates, illegal drug use, and so on.

How do writers justify sociology as a science?

In order to understand this, we need to go back to the elements of science we looked at earlier.

Theoretical

Scientists who are dubious about sociology's claim to scientific status point out that natural objects are predictable because they simply react, whereas people have free will and are, therefore, not predictable. This makes a theoretical statement that involves making a general prediction (if X occurs, then Y will act in this way) impossible in sociology. However, although we cannot predict how individuals will act, we can predict how *groups in general* will act. For example, Durkheim claimed that there are clearly distinguishable patterns of suicide, with certain groups having distinctive rates over a number of years.

Empirical and testable

Natural scientists argue that in the physical world, there are phenomena that exist independently of the scientists, such as such as temperature and density. The scientist merely has to measure these phenomena. In contrast, they argue, society is created by people, and there are no phenomena 'out there' waiting to be measured.

For those sympathetic to the view that sociology is a science, this seems an unfair criticism. They argue that there are a wide range of phenomena that, although ultimately the creation of society, do exist separately from individuals, and that constrain and limit our behaviour (again, a possible answer to critics regarding free will). For example, we are born into a society where a particular language exists and we have to conform to that language. It is, in Durkheim's words, a 'social fact' that exists independently and can be measured in an objective way. Theories can thus be tested to see whether they are true or false.

Cumulative

Again, like all sciences, sociological knowledge is cumulative. Sociologists have built up knowledge over time and accumulated a stock of knowledge about society. It is this cumulative information that forms the current-day sociology that you are studying.

Objective

A major criticism of sociology as a science is that if it deals with issues and concerns about which we all have strong feelings, then how is it possible for sociologists to be objective? Won't their values emerge in their choice of subject and their methods of study? This is a complex subject, so much so that we have devoted the whole of Topic 9 to it. However, positivist sociologists argue that it *is* possible to be value free by adhering rigorously to the methodological process discussed below.

The methodological process in sociology

We saw earlier that there is a traditional process followed by physical scientists. Many of them argue that sociology is simply unable to follow this. We look at this in detail later in Topic 4, which deals with positivism, but critics have particularly concentrated on the difficulty of undertaking experiments in sociology. Sociologists have answered this by arguing that the sociological equivalent of an experiment is the **comparative method** (or multivariate analysis), as used by Weber to explain the emergence of capitalism in Britain and by Durkheim in his study of suicide (see Chapter 6, Topic 11). The comparative method involves comparing societies to find out key differences that might explain different social phenomena.

Sociological criticisms of sociology as a science – and of science as a science!

So far, the dominant voices we have listened to in this topic have been those supporting the notion of sociology as a science. However, since the 1960s, especially with the growth of interactionist and, later, postmodern writings, there has been a range of criticisms from within sociology as to whether it can, or even should, claim to be a science.

Differences between the nature of society and the physical world

The first criticism comes from those who argue that society is not comparable to the natural world and to attempt to transfer the methods and ideas of the natural sciences is mistaken. This argument is less about methods and more about the reality of the world around us. Is there an objective world outside that exists independently of us, or is the world somehow 'constructed' through the ideas and activities of human beings? For Durkheim and all those who have followed his original ideas, the answer is clearly that there is a social structure that exists independently of our feelings and ideas. Therefore, the scientific approach can clearly be used. For many other sociologists, starting with Schutz (1972), there is no social world beyond our existence. Society only has an existence through the activities and beliefs of people and any attempt to study society has to recognize that we start from 'inside' the very thing we are trying to study. For Schutz, and many writers after him, the attempt to separate oneself from society and explore it as an outsider is simply impossible. Schutz sees the role of sociology as being to explore the meanings that people construct – not to look for an external set of explanations.

Inappropriate scientific method

The second set of criticisms is based on the idea that scientific methods actually inhibit sociological research. Billig argues that this methodological straitjacket that scientifically oriented sociologists have imposed upon sociology actually gets in the way of scholarship (Billig *et al.* 1998). Billig claims that, historically, academics read widely across a range of texts and disciplines and then, based upon that, they presented new ideas and insights. Methodology was important, but more important was allowing people freedom to think of new ideas. According to Billig, contemporary sociology that attempts to be scientific actually limits itself within a narrow sphere of thinking and loses the point of the sociological enterprise. This argument reflects the earlier work of C.W. Mills (1959), who argued that the aim of theory and method is to enable what he calls the **sociological imagination** to be freed so that the sociologist can see 'underlying forms and tendencies of society' that others might miss. Being chained to a set of assumptions will block this 'imagination'.

Sociology as a social product of modernity

Bauman (2000) locates the desire to be seen as scientific within the broader context of the dominance of modernity and modernist thinking during the period of sociology's development. Bauman argues that science only held higher prestige because it reflected ways of thinking and social organizations that existed within the historical period known as modernity. Bauman further suggests that the key theme that all the original sociologists from Durkheim, Weber, Marx and even Parsons later in the middle of the 20th century struggled with was the question of *social order*. How was it that society, composed of millions of independently thinking individuals, did not collapse in chaos? This question was actually a central concern of modernity and so sociology was reflecting existing concerns and ideas (or 'paradigms' in Kuhn's terminology 1962/1970); it was not providing brand new insights at all.

Sociology ended up focusing on social class, 'race' and 'the family', thereby reflecting concerns, not innovating. Sociology was driven, therefore, not by some novel insights into human behaviour, but by the desire to reflect wider social concerns.

As late modernity/postmodernity has emerged, however, these structures and this 'doing remarkably similar things in similar circumstances' have weakened and are less important. Instead, people are much more self-aware in terms of image, and self-seeking in terms of identities. The family, for example, is characterized by a range of alternative, more flexible and sexually diverse relationships. In late modernity, according to Bauman, the place of social science is therefore superfluous – and can be replaced by sociological thinking.

Is science a science?

Increasingly, natural science itself has come under fire for not matching the criteria of science discussed above. From the 1960s onwards, a number of sociologists began to put

Focus on research

Rees and Lee (2005)
A scientific survey of young runaways

In 2005, Rees and Lee carried out a survey of 11 000 young people aged 14 to 16 to find out what proportion had run away from home for at least one night, what happened to them and why they had run away.

First, the authors did a full search of previous research in the area of young runaways; their literature search identified a previous study first published in 1999. Rees and Lee therefore decided to use similar methodology, as this would allow them to compare how the situation had changed in the previous seven years.

This study consisted of a representative sample of young people aged 14 to 16, drawn from four or five secondary schools in 16 different areas of the country. Rees and Lee used a questionnaire for the study, which students were asked to complete on their own. In order to ensure that the questionnaire was valid and reliable, they undertook a pilot study with year 10 and 11 groups in three schools and one pupil referral unit. As a result of this, a large number of changes were made.

The questionnaire had six sections and used a 'tick-box' format with space for additional comments. There were a limited number of open-ended questions. The questionnaires were translated into a number of languages reflecting the ethnic background of the students, and there was also large print for partially sighted students.

Rees and Lee took ethical issues very seriously and so provided each school and student with clear statements to explain what the research was about and how it would be used, also explaining that whatever information was obtained would be completely confidential.

Rees, G. and Lee, J. (2005) *Safe and Sound: Still Running II. Findings from the Second National Survey of Young Runaways*, London: The Children's Society

Why might Rees and Lee's research be viewed as scientific?

science itself 'under the microscope'. They found the traditional model of viewing science as a form of superior provider of knowledge was, to say the least, questionable. They suggest that if science itself does not actually fulfil the conditions of being a science, then why should sociology be so obsessed with it?

The paradigm critique

Kuhn (1962/1970) argues that one crucial element of science – that of cumulative progress – cannot be true. Kuhn argues instead that 'normal science' operates within a **paradigm** (or accepted framework of concepts regarding a particular area of knowledge). This framework includes assumptions regarding what is important, the correct procedures, and the right sort of questions to be asking. This paradigm dominates scientific thinking, and traps thought and investigation within it. Any attempt to step outside the accepted conventions is usually ignored and rejected.

Science changes in a series of scientific revolutions that create their own new paradigms, rather than through the accumulation of knowledge. Kuhn suggests that over time there is a gradual build-up of evidence that does not fit into the accepted paradigm and out of this unease emerges a distinctively new explanation that can accommodate the previous inconsistencies. A new paradigm is born and the process begins again. Kuhn calls this the 'process of scientific revolutions'.

Kuhn is himself not free from critics, however. Lakatos (1970), for example, has argued that Kuhn's idea of paradigms is too simplistic and only applies to the past, in relation to the abandonment of ideas regarding the earth being flat, or being the centre of the universe. Modern science is largely open and much more sophisticated in its thinking. Rarely in modern science have central ideas been abandoned.

Antimethodology

Feyerabend (1975) argues that science has developed in an 'anarchic way' and the belief that there has been a gradual, coherent and cumulative advance in knowledge is completely wrong. Instead, he characterizes advances in science as chance, incoherence, sudden leaps forward and dead-ends. The false history that has been created is holding back scientists, as they seek to follow a false set of methodological procedures.

Experiments and open/closed systems

Sayer (1992) has pointed out that the model of the physical sciences presented to the public may be misleading. He argues that we need to distinguish between open and closed systems.

Sciences such as chemistry or physiology operate in closed systems, in which all **variables** can be controlled. This allows experiments to be carried out. However, other physical sciences such as meteorology and **seismology**, operate in open systems, in which the variables cannot be controlled. These sciences recognize unpredictability. Seismology cannot predict when earthquakes will occur, though it does understand the conditions leading to

Key themes

Crime and deviance

The British Crime Survey is a yearly study of the crime levels in England and Wales. Each year, approximately 40 000 people are questioned about the crimes they believe have been committed against them.

Government policy towards combating crime (particularly all the legislation on antisocial behaviour) is strongly influenced by the results of the study. The BCS is fully funded by the government and is regarded as the single most prestigious source of crime statistics. The study rigorously adheres to scientific values, using questionnaires that are devised by eminent criminological researchers who then can spend anything up to a year computing and analysing the findings.

However, there are some significant problems:

- Until 2009, BCS excluded the single largest group of victims of crime – those under 16 years of age. This makes it difficult to compare statistics before and after this year.
- The ways in which the research measures fear of crime has been criticized for exaggerating actual levels of fear, partly by the way the questions are

constructed, but also for the way the survey focuses on the fear.

- The BCS allows people to categorize criminal acts according to their own definitions – not the legal ones. The researchers then reclassify into types of crime according to their views of what the appropriate category is.

Critics therefore claim that this 'scientific study' reflects the interests of the more powerful (older people), and their concerns (fear of crime), whilst excluding the views of the less powerful (people under 16). Finally, the actual classification of statistics are the construction of the sociologists who compute and analyse the findings, rather than those of the victims.

---

earthquakes. Meteorologists can explain the forces producing weather, but the actual weather itself is difficult to predict. Certain sciences, therefore, do not necessarily follow the process which it is claimed is a hallmark of science.

From Sayer's viewpoint (known as **realism**) the social sciences are no different from many physical sciences. Their aim ought to be the uncovering of the relationship between the wider structures that determine the way we relate to other people in everyday life. For example, we can only understand the relationship between a student and teacher by referring to the education system, inequalities of power, the aim of education, and so on.

The feminist critique of science

Feminist sociologists, too, raise doubts on the status accorded to science. Their criticisms are based on three main concerns:

- According to Harding (1986), the (ontological) assumptions science has about society are based upon male perceptions and understandings. Mainstream knowledge is therefore really '**malestream**' knowledge. Women understand and experience the world in different ways from men and so male and female research is intrinsically different.
- Until recently, the majority of sociological studies were based on males – particularly in education, stratification and crime. Thus, as Hart (1989) says, until the 1990s we knew a lot about the lives of men and boys, but relatively little about women and girls.
- Research should not be neutral, but ought instead to be driven by the desire to change the world.

Ramazanoglu (1992) has argued that the role of feminist sociology ought to be transforming gender relationships in such a way as to bring about the equality of females with males. This underlying aim should therefore penetrate the subjects being studied and the methods used.

Modernity, postmodernity and science

Science and modernity have gone hand in hand, according to Rorty (1980), with the belief that rationality, truth, and science are all bound together, and that other ways of knowing the world are inferior.

Postmodernists challenge this view. For Rorty, scientists have simply replaced priests as the sources of truth. We want someone to be the experts and to make sense of the world for us. Science has taken on this role. Yet we now know that, despite the advances in science, there may well be concepts and questions that it can never answer – questions about the origins of the universe, the concept of infinity, and so on.

Lyotard (1984) has also shown that the nature of language limits and channels science because it provides a framework to approach an understanding of the world. Language both opens up possibilities and closes down others since we think within language and are unable to conceive of something that is outside our linguistic framework. This is very similar to Bauman's critique of modernist sociology.

Science and values

We have noted before that sociology has problems in disentangling values from the research process. However, so, too, does science. Scientists do not work in an ideal world. Those who fund their research lead the direction of the work, and not all science necessarily benefits the world. Cigarettes are the result of 'science', yet are the biggest killer of adults in the more affluent societies. Pharmaceutical companies have produced numerous drugs that have been directly harmful to society, including heroin, thalidomide and barbiturates. Beck (1992) has pointed out that science has actually created new and serious risks for society – for example, pollution and global warming.

Sociology and science: the debate in a nutshell

Our discussion so far has suggested the following:

- Sociology has sought scientific status in order to obtain status and acceptance as an academic subject.
- Critics from the traditional sciences have argued that sociology does not meet the criteria of science both in terms of the components (theory, objectivity, etc.) and in terms of the process (**hypothesis**, experiment, etc.)
- One group of sociologists – who have been called positivistic sociologists – have rejected this criticism and have claimed that sociology can and does achieve the criteria to make it a social science.
- However, if we look critically at the nature of science itself, it would appear that the natural sciences also fail the criteria of being a science.
- Postmodernists argue that the whole debate itself is a reflection of outdated notions of a fixed, knowable world out there, waiting to be discovered. They argue instead that all knowledge is relative to the world of those who seek it, and that it is bounded by constraints of language and of culture.

So is sociology a science?

There is no simple answer to this question. According to writers such as Bhaskar (1986) and Sayer (1992), sociology can be as scientific as the natural sciences by adopting certain procedures. At the other extreme, postmodernists such as Rorty (1980) or Bauman (1978) would argue that the real question is why sociology would want to be seen as a science. They go on to say that the whole debate reflects the process of modernity – a period which we are now leaving.

Somewhere in the middle lie the bulk of sociologists who accept that there is a debate over the scientific nature of sociological study, but who get on with their research, attempting to make sense of society in the best and most honest way they can.

Check your understanding

1 Why has it been considered important that sociology should be classified as a 'science'?

2 What are the elements of a science?

3 What do we mean by 'falsification'?

4 What do we mean by the 'British empirical tradition'?

5 What was Kuhn's criticism of the cumulative element of science?

6 Explain the difference between closed and open systems of science.

7 Why is an understanding of modernity and post-modernity relevant to the debate on the nature of science?

Key terms

Causal relationship a relationship between two factors in which one causes the other.

Comparative method a method that involves comparing societies to find out key differences that might explain different social phenomena.

Empirical sociology refers to sociologists who tend to conduct quantitative studies and tend not to theorize.

Falsification the testing of an empirical model with the aim of showing it to be false.

Hypothesis an initial plausible guess concerning the causal relationship between events.

Malestream originally a feminist term implying criticism of traditional sociology for excluding women from the subject both as sociologists and as the subjects of research.

Natural sciences see 'Physical sciences'.

Paradigm a framework of thought that provides the way in which we approach and understand an issue.

Parapsychology a disputed branch of psychology which studies a range of experiences, such as mind-to-mind communication.

Physical sciences the scientific study of the physical world. These include chemistry, physics, biology, botany, etc.

Positivists those advocating an approach that supports the belief that the way to gain knowledge is by following the conventional scientific model.

Realism the view that sociology should aim to uncover the relationship between the wider structures that determine the way we relate to other people in everyday life.

Refutation showing something to be false.

Seismology the study of earthquakes.

Sociological imagination coined by C.W. Mills to suggest that as well as good methodology, sociologists should develop an open and questioning mind.

Structural-functionalist school a version of society that starts by asking what function a social phenomenon performs for a society, e.g. 'What does the family do for society?' Associated with Talcott Parsons.

Variable a social phenomenon that changes in response to another phenomenon.

Verification showing something to be true.

Activities

Research ideas

1. Identify a range of behaviour and beliefs in phenomena that science cannot fully explain. You might think about religious and supernatural beliefs, fortune-telling, astrology, and alternative therapies, for example.

2. Use interviews to discover the extent to which a sample of people believe in or have used these non-scientific approaches. What do your results tell us about trust in science today?

Web.task

Go to The Guardian 'Bad Science' Website, **www.guardian.co.uk/science/series/badscience** where the author Ben Goldacre discusses the issues relating to real or dubious 'scientific research' in the media. Choose any one article to read. What attitude towards scientific research does Ben Goldacre hold? Would all sociologists take issue with him or would they all agree with what he writes?

An eye on the exam — Sociology and science

Item A

The history of science does not just consist of facts and conclusions drawn from those facts. It also contains ideas, interpretations of facts, problems created by conflicting interpretations, mistakes and so on. On closer analysis, we find that science knows no 'bare facts' at all but that the 'facts' that enter our knowledge are already viewed in a certain way and are, therefore, socially created. This being the case, the history of science will be as complex, chaotic, full of mistakes and entertaining as the ideas it contains, and these ideas in turn will be as complex, chaotic, full of mistakes and entertaining as are the minds of those who invented them.

Assess the view that sociology can and should be seen as a science. (33 marks)

Grade booster — Getting top marks in this question

There are two parts to this question – *can* sociology be seen as a science, and *should* it be seen as a science? For the first part, an overview of arguments for and against the scientific status of sociology is required. What constitutes a science? You should discuss issues of theory, empiricism and objectivity. Then add the criticisms of the distinctive nature of the social world and the claim that science itself does not live up to being a science. You could also include feminist and postmodern critiques.

Should sociology be seen as a science? This second part of your answer can be shorter. Arguments for include the idea that, if sociology is presented as a science, then it has a good chance of gaining prestige, of contributing to government policy and of sociologists receiving funding. On the other hand, as Rorty suggests, perhaps this is taking on the role of religion in claiming to be able to uncover 'the truth'. Bauman argues that the role of sociology is to be outside the normal frameworks, providing a critical reflection of society, yet not claiming to have any special scientific status.

TOPIC 4

Positivism and quantitative research methods

Getting you thinking

The extract on the right is from a series that appears in the *Guardian* Saturday Magazine. Each person is asked the simple question 'Are you happy?'

1 What do you mean by happiness? How could you research it?

Design a survey aimed at finding how happy young people are in Britain today.

2 Write down a detailed, step-by-step plan of what you are going to do.

3 How are you going to define and measure happiness?

4 To what extent do you think the results of your survey will give you an accurate picture of the distribution of happiness?

5 What problems are involved in trying to represent concepts such as 'happiness' in figures?

6 Do you think it is possible to measure feelings, beliefs or ideas?

Are you happy?

By Maureen Hills-Jones, former nurse

I STARTED suffering from manic depression after my mother died. It comes and goes. Sometimes I have so much energy, it's ridiculous. I'm extremely happy right now. I undergo periods of extreme excitement followed by a low so deep it feels like grief. It can be a hard thing to explain to my children. The last thing you want to do is inflict it on them.

There are periods of great activity. I buy presents for people and write postcards and letters, even though people don't write letters any more. My kids laugh when they receive them. I talk on the phone. I stay up through the early hours. You can do an enormous amount in the night. I wrote an entire book last year, but then ripped it up. I make the most of these times because I know they're not going to last. It's unpredictable and those around, including my husband, have been very understanding.

I won't take medication. When you do, you're neither happy nor sad – I don't want my life to be like that. I'm open to other solutions to help me, whether that's reflexology or aromatherapy. Manic depression enhances the way you look at the world. When you're in the depression, you plan your funeral, but afterwards it feels as if you've got a new lease of life, a new view of the world – until next time. There will be a next time, but it's best not to dwell on the future. I have learned to live with it.

Source: Craig Taylor, *The Guardian*, Saturday 3 May 2008

We saw in the previous topic that there is considerable debate between sociologists over the scientific status of sociology. However, the fact is that in order to do their job, sociologists have to put this aside and get on with their research. Rather than splitting them into two completely irreconcilable camps, it is perhaps better to think of sociologists as being either more sympathetic to the use of traditional scientific methods (**positivists**) or more sceptical about whether this is the most useful way to proceed (**interpretive sociologists**).

The hypothetico-deductive method

Positivists believe that the scientific tradition is the approach that sociology must follow. Accordingly, they seek to follow the **hypothetico-deductive** research method: a series of steps providing what is regarded as the most scientific method of finding information. By following these steps, the sociologist has the highest chance of generating accurate 'scientific' knowledge. These steps consist of the following:

1 *Background reading and personal experience* – Through study and everyday observation the sociologist uncovers an area of interest.

2 *Formation of a hypothesis* – The sociologist formulates a causal link between two events.

3 *Devising the appropriate form of study to isolate the key variables* – This is usually some form of questionnaire, interview or, less often, observation.

4 *Collecting the data* – There are strict rules governing the way questionnaires and interviews are carried out to ensure **validity** and **reliability**.

5 *Analysing the data* – Statistical models are often used here, such as 'tests of confidence', which allow the sociologist to demonstrate to others how likely their research sampling was to produce accurate results.

6 *Confirming, modifying or rejecting the hypothesis* – this is done by searching for weaknesses as suggested by Popper (see Topic 3).

7 *Theory formation or confirmation* – However, no positivists claim their results are proved by their research, merely that they produce the best explanation until others can improve on it or possibly disprove it. Again, this derives from Popper's argument concerning falsification (see p. 271).

Most real research programmes are rather more complex and overlapping than the classic hypothetico-deductive approach – using some **inductive** features, for example. Nevertheless, it provides the model that positivistic sociologists seek to follow.

We shall look at an example of the hypothetico-deductive model later, but for the moment, in the next section we will examine some of the key **epistemological** issues it raises.

Theoretical approaches linked to positivism and quantitative research methods

The key question here is the nature of society. There are two extreme positions. At one extreme is the claim that society really exists 'out there' and largely determines how we think and act. In this model people can arguably be portrayed as puppets of society. At the other pole is the argument that society only exists through the beliefs and activities of individuals interacting. This model of society sees people as creative actors making society.

Positivists generally support a theoretical model of society that is based on the idea that there is some form of structure that exists independently of individual views, perceptions or desires – sometimes known as the structural model of society. As outlined in Topic 1, there are two main theoretical approaches that are most closely linked to positivism and both base their approaches on the idea of structure: structural functionalism and Marxism.

Structural functionalism

This derives from the work of Parsons (1951) and was heavily influenced by Durkheim and, to a lesser extent by Weber. Functionalism, you will recall, argues that institutions exist in society in the form they do because they contribute to the continuing functioning of society. Underpinning this theoretical model is the acceptance of a social structure that actively guides our actions and beliefs. Durkheim used the term **social facts** to describe the objective 'facts' he claimed existed in society. In his classic study *Suicide: A Study in Sociology* (1897/1952) (see Chapter 6, p. 399), Durkheim believed that he had demonstrated through using statistics on suicide that clear patterns could be uncovered. The 'social facts' were the numbers and types of suicide.

Marxism

Marxist theory or 'dialectical materialism' was based on the belief that economic and social laws exist that govern human behaviour. Marx hoped that by uncovering these laws he would demonstrate that a communist society was the inevitable future. Although people's consciousness and actions play an important part, ultimately the laws are dominant. It is important to remember that although the original model of society devised by Marx was largely based on positivist ideas, most modern Marxist-inspired research is based on a mixture of quantitative and qualitative ideas.

Criticism

We mentioned earlier that there were two conceptions of the nature of society. We have just looked at the way positivism is largely linked to the structural model.

However, this model of society has been strongly attacked by a range of other sociological perspectives, most notably those coming from a social constructionist perspective, such as symbolic interactionism. As mentioned in Topic 1, symbolic interactionism derives from the work of Blumer (1962), and is closely linked to labelling theory.

Symbolic interactionism, labelling theory and ethnomethodology all stress the way that individuals work at making sense of the society around them. According to these approaches, society is created by the activities of people and not the other way around. Positivistic methods are, therefore, inappropriate, with their assumption of some objective reality. Instead (as we shall see in Topic 5), these social constructionist theories try to grasp the rules (if any) that guide people in their daily tasks of creating reality. This usually involves watching people and analysing their conversations and their activities. This takes us back to our earlier point regarding deductive and inductive reasoning. Whereas positivism generally uses a deductive framework, social constructionists start with an inductive one – building up from observations.

We will explore this approach in more detail in Topic 5, where we look at the methods most closely associated with the social constructionist approaches.

Quantitative research: the favoured method of positivists

Positivists believe that there is a social world 'out there', relatively independent of individuals, that can be uncovered by testing hypotheses through using rigorous research-collection techniques. They seek out valid **indicators** to represent the variables under study in order to study them in a reliable way.

This approach strongly favours using quantitative methods such as **surveys**, questionnaires and case studies.

Surveys

A social survey involves obtaining information in a standardized manner from a large number of people. This is done in order to maximize reliability and generalizability (see Topic 7, pp. 304–5). There are two main types of survey – longitudinal and cross-sectional.

Cross-sectional surveys

Cross-sectional surveys are often called 'snapshot' studies as they gather information at one particular time. These are the most common surveys which we are used to reading in newspapers and textbook and are often called 'opinion polls'. This method is very useful for finding out information on a particular topic at one specific moment. If organized properly, these are quick to do, the results can be collated and analysed very quickly and findings are likely to be highly generalizable. However, there are two real difficulties with cross-sectional surveys:

1 The indicators or questions chosen to measure a particular form of attitude must be accurate. If they are not, then the research will not be valid.
2 The surveys provide information for one particular, static moment – they do not provide information over a period of time, so changes in views cannot be measured.

Surveys Aims and weaknesses

Aims

- To uncover straightforward factual information about a particular group of people – for example, their voting intentions or their views on punishment of convicted offenders. This is because a survey allows information to be gathered from a large range and number of people.

- To uncover differences in beliefs, values and behaviour between people, but *only* when these are easily and clearly measurable. If the beliefs and attitudes are complex or it is difficult to find unambiguous indicators for them, then qualitative research may be more appropriate.

- To test a hypothesis, where it is necessary to gain more information to confirm or deny it.

Weakness

The *major weakness of all surveys* is that they cannot easily uncover complex views. This means that there is always an issue regarding the *validity* of quantitative research. Issues of indicators and the **operationalization** of concepts in general are crucial in the research design.

Longitudinal surveys

Longitudinal studies are surveys that take place over a period of time – sometimes years. The cross-sectional survey already mentioned is a very important method and is widely used by sociologists, in particular because of the very high reliability and generalizability of its findings. However, its weakness is that it provides information for one particular moment only. Changes in attitudes or behaviour over time are simply not measured by it, nor are longer-term factors that might influence behaviour. So, when quantitative sociologists are particularly interested in change, they often switch to using a longitudinal survey. By following groups of people over a period of time, sociologists are able to plot the changes that they are looking for. However, longitudinal surveys suffer from some quite serious drawbacks. The biggest of these is the drop-out rate. Answering questions over time and being the object of study can lead to people getting bored or resentful. Separately from this, people move addresses, colleges and friendship groups, so tracking them becomes a complex and expensive task. For both these reasons, longitudinal surveys suffer from low retention.

This is also a problem because the survey will start to lack reliability and generalizability. Quite simply, if the retention rate becomes too low, then the views and behaviour of those who remain may well differ from the views of those who have left the survey.

Such surveys provide us with a clear, ongoing image of changes in attitudes and actions over time. The *British*

Household Panel Survey is a longitudinal study that has studied over 10 000 British people of all ages, living in 5500 households. The interviewing started in 1991 and has continued every year since then. The information obtained covers a vast area, including family change, household finances and patterns of health and caring. It is used by the government to help inform social policies.

Focus on research

Parker *et al.* (1998)
A longitudinal survey

The North-West Longitudinal Study involved following several hundred young people for five years between the ages of 14 and 18. The overall aim of this study was to assess how 'ordinary' young people, growing up in England in the 1990s, developed attitudes and behaviour in relation to the availability of illegal drugs, alongside other options such as alcohol and tobacco.

The main technique was a self-report questionnaire initially administered personally by the researchers (and then by post) to several hundred young people within eight state secondary schools in two, non-inner-city boroughs of metropolitan north-west England.

At the start of the research the sample was **representative** of those areas in terms of gender, class and ethnicity. However, attrition (losing participants) partly reduced this over time with the disproportionate loss of some 'working-class' participants and some from Asian and Muslim backgrounds.

A longitudinal study is able to address issues of validity and reliability far more extensively than one-off snapshot surveys, but in turn must also explain inconsistent reporting that occurs over the years.

In general, the research provides a detailed account of how young people develop attitudes and behaviours through time.

Adapted from Parker, H., Aldrige, J. and Measham, F. (1998)
Illegal Leisure, London: Routledge, pp. 48–9

How does this extract illustrate some of the advantages and disadvantages of longitudinal surveys?

Surveys and response rates

The validity and generalizability of all surveys are dependent on having high response rates. Response rates refer to the proportion of people approached in the survey who actually respond to the questionnaire or interview. The greater the proportion of people who return the questionnaires or agree to be interviewed, the greater the chance the survey has of being valid.

Sampling in quantitative research

One of the main strengths of survey research is that it uses processes that ensure the people in the survey are representative of the whole population. When the people selected are representative, then the results of the survey are likely to be true for the population as a whole and therefore generalizable.

It is very difficult for sociologists to study large numbers of people, as the costs of devising and carrying out the research is just too high. Instead, as we have seen throughout this book, sociologists tend to study a small but representative cross section of the community. If this small sample truly mirrors the bigger population, then the results from studying this chosen group can be said to be true of the larger population too.

Quantitative surveys have two different methods of ensuring that their sample is representative and, therefore, the results are generalizable to the whole population. These two different methods are **probability** (or **random**) **sampling** and **quota sampling**. There are also other forms of sampling – snowball and theoretical – which are more commonly used in qualitative research. (These are discussed in Topic 5, p. 292.)

Key themes

Crime and deviance

Positivistic methods are extremely widely used in research, and are definitely preferred by government departments and most commercial institutions. This is because they are seen as far less likely to be influenced by personal beliefs and as more objective in their findings. It is therefore not surprising that in socially delicate areas, such as crime or ethnic/religious relations, the government will almost always commission positivistic research. Criticisms of the research findings in these controversial areas can be dismissed as biased or sectional views, whereas positivistic and quantitative research is 'scientific'.

An example of positivistic research dealing with a controversial area is the work of Clare Sharp and Tracey Budd (2005), who studied minority ethnic groups and crime rates. The rigorous methods used and the decision to make comparisons to other statistically rigorous studies gives the results a sense of accuracy and objectivity.

Focus on research

The Offending, Crime and Justice Survey (OCJS)
A national survey of young offenders

The Offending, Crime and Justice Survey (OCJS) is a nationally representative, longitudinal, self-report survey which asks young people in England and Wales about their attitudes and experiences of offending. It is commissioned by the Home Office.

Its main aim is to find out the extent of offending, antisocial behaviour and drug use among young people aged from 10 to 25.

The survey had completed five annual 'sweeps' by 2008. (A sweep is a further survey using the same, or similar sample as in a previous survey).

The survey uses a 'panel' (the term panel is often used when the same people are studied for a number of years, as in a longitudinal survey) of about 5000 young people. As some reach the age of 26 and become too old for the survey, other young people aged 10 are added in.

Young people are chosen randomly using the post code address file as a sampling frame.

In order to obtain the information, each young person is interviewed for about one hour in a highly structured way, in which questions are read from a computer and the answer inputted by the interviewer.

More delicate subjects which might cause the young person to lie out of embarrassment are dealt with by giving the young people a laptop with headphones. The young people listen to the questions and answer in private.

The research is particularly useful in providing clear, statistical information on the extent and patterns of offending because of the highly structured nature of the interviewing. Secondly, using a longitudinal survey method allows the researchers to follow up the changing patterns of young people's offending, in a way that a series of surveys to different samples of young people each year, might not.

There are some weaknesses in the design however. The survey rarely provides information on serious crime. First, respondents might well lie as they do not wish to incriminate themselves (or perhaps feel too embarrassed). Second, because of the random nature of the sampling, it is unlikely that significant numbers of serious criminals will be interviewed.

> What evidence is there in the research summary that the methodology used is positivistic and quantitative in approach?

Probability or (random) sampling

Probability or random sampling is based on the same idea as any lottery or ticket draw. If names are chosen randomly, then each person has an equal chance of being selected. This means that those chosen are likely to be a cross section of the population. As we saw earlier, if the sample is representative, the results are likely to be generalizable to the population as a whole.

The sampling frame

In order to make a random sample, sociologists usually prefer to have a **sampling frame**, which is some form of list from which the sample can be drawn. British sociologists typically use Electoral Registers, (which are lists of people entitled to vote) or the Postcode Address File (which is the way that The Post Office links names and addresses to postcodes). However, for smaller studies, sociologists could ask for permission to use the lists of students attending a school, or members of a club that keeps lists of names.

As Bryman (2004) points out, any piece of random sampling can only be as good as the sampling frame, so if this is inaccurate or incomplete then the sampling itself will not be accurate.

The different forms of random sampling

If the names are picked out entirely randomly, then this is known as 'simple random sampling'. However, when given a list of names, it is apparently quite difficult to pick in a truly random way, so very often a method is used whereby every 'nth' name (for example, every fifth or tenth name) on a list is chosen. This is known as **systematic (random) sampling.**

Stratified sampling is a further refinement of random sampling. Here, the population under study is divided according to known criteria (for example, it could be divided into 52 per cent women and 48 per cent men, to reflect the sex composition of the UK). Within these broad strata, people are then chosen at random. In reality, these strata can become quite detailed, with further divisions into age, social class, geographical location, ethnic group, religious affiliation, etc.

The final form of random sampling is known as **cluster sampling** and is used when the people the researcher wishes to interview are in a number of different locations (instead of using postal or email questionnaires). In order to cut costs and save time travelling to many different places, the sociologist simply chooses a number of locations at random and then individuals within these locations. This means that it is possible to generalize for the whole population of Britain by interviewing in a relatively few places. This approach has also been developed into the **multistage cluster sampling**, in which smaller clusters are randomly chosen within the larger cluster.

Random sampling is generally very easy to use and, even if there is no sampling frame, it is possible to stop every 'nth' person in the street or college and question them. It also has the enormous advantage that if certain statistical tests are used, then it is possible to say with a degree of statistical certainty how accurate the results are.

Problems with random sampling

There are a number of problems that can occur with random sampling. First, it is often difficult to obtain a sampling frame, particularly in the last few years since laws restricting access to information held on computers have been introduced.

Where systematic sampling is undertaken, often by asking every 'nth' person in the street or wherever the appropriate location is, it can be extremely difficult for the researcher to maintain the necessary discipline to ask the correct person. If the person looks unpleasant or threatening, then researchers often skip that person and choose the next one! Also, factors such as the time of day or the weather can have an important influence on how representative the people in the street (or college) are. For example, stopping every tenth person in the high street of a town between 9 am and midday, usually results in a high proportion of retired and unemployed people. The sample is not representative and the results are therefore not generalizable.

Non-random (or non-probability) sampling

The main alternative to random sampling in quantitative sociological research is quota sampling.

Quota sampling

For research based on interviews, the main alternative to random sampling, which is commonly used by market research companies, is quota sampling. This can be used in any situation where the key social characteristics of the population under study are already known. For example, census information can give us a detailed picture of the UK population in terms of the proportion of people in each age group, income band, occupational group, geographical location, religious affiliation and ethnicity. There is, therefore, no reason to try to seek a representative sample by random methods. All that has to be done is to select what the key characteristics are and then get the same proportion in the sample as in the main population. Each interviewer is then allocated a quota of people exhibiting the key characteristics. This guarantees that there is a representative coverage of the population.

The main reason for the popularity of quota sampling over random sampling is the very small number of people needed to build up an accurate picture of the whole population (as long as you know what key characteristics to look for). For example, the typical surveys of voting preferences in journals and newspapers use a quota sample of approximately 1200 to represent the entire British electorate.

However, quota sampling has a number of significant drawbacks. The first is that unless the researcher has the correct information on the proportion of people in each key category, then the method is useless. In this situation it is always better to use random sampling. The second drawback is that the statistical tests that can be used with random sampling to ensure that the results of the survey are accurate, cannot be used with quota sampling.

The most important drawback, though, is that quota sampling usually relies upon a researcher choosing people who fall into the quotas they have been given. Relying upon the interviewer's perception of who to interview can lead to all sorts of problems, including the researcher making mistakes in deciding whether people fit into the appropriate categories (for example, thinking people are younger than they are).

Experiments

An **experiment** is a form of research in which all the variables are closely controlled, so that the effect of changing one or more of the variables can be understood. Experiments are often used in the physical sciences, but are much less common in sociology. The reasons for their lack of use in sociology are, first, that it is almost impossible to isolate a social event from the real world around it. This means that researchers cannot control all the variables, which is the essence of an experiment.

Furthermore, experiments usually involve manipulating people in ways that many people regard as immoral.

>> *When natural scientists carry out their research in laboratories, controlling variables is of crucial importance … Experimentation usually involves manipulating one **independent variable** and creating change in the **dependent variable** … What is important is that all other factors are held constant (or controlled) and are not allowed to contribute to any change which might occur.* >> (Moores 1998)

Finally, even if these two problems can be overcome, then what has been found to happen is the problem of the **experimenter effect**, where the awareness of being in an experiment affects the normal behaviour of the participants. Think of your own behaviour when you know you are being photographed, even if you are asked to 'look natural'!

Howell and Frost (1989) conducted a sociological experiment to see which of the three forms of authority identified by Weber (charismatic, traditional and legal-rational – see Chapter 4, p. 209) were most effective in getting tasks done. They found 144 student volunteers and divided them into groups. Each group was given tasks

Key terms

Case study a highly detailed study of one or two social situations or groups.

Cluster sampling the researcher selects a series of different places and then chooses a sample at random from the cluster of people within these areas.

Cross-sectional survey a survey conducted at one time with no attempt to follow up the people surveyed over a longer time.

Dependent variable a social phenomenon that changes in response to changes in another phenomenon.

Epistemological relating to theories of knowledge.

Experiment a highly controlled situation where the researchers try to isolate the influence of each variable. Rarely used in sociology.

Experimenter effect unreliability of data arising as a result of people responding to what they perceive to be the expectations of the researchers.

Field experiment an experiment undertaken in the community or in real life, rather than in a controlled environment.

Hypothetico-deductive model the research process associated with the physical sciences and used by positivists in sociology.

Independent variable the phenomenon that causes the dependent variable to change.

Indicator a measurable social phenomenon that stands for an unmeasurable concept, e.g using church attendance to measure religious belief.

Inductive way of reasoning that starts from the particular and works towards the general. In social research, this might mean identifying patterns and trends, and then developing hypotheses and theories based on them.

Interpretive sociologists those whose approach to sociology and research emphasizes understanding society by exploring the way people see society, rather than following traditional scientific analysis.

Longitudinal survey a survey that is carried out over a considerable number of years on the same group of people.

Multistage cluster sampling where subsamples are taken.

Operationalize to put into practice.

Positivists those sympathetic to the use of traditional scientific methods in sociology.

Probability sampling see Random sampling.

Quantitative research a positivist approach to research, favouring methods that produce statistical data.

Quota sampling where a representative sample of the population is chosen using known characteristics of the population.

Random sampling where a representative sample of the population is chosen by entirely random methods.

Reliability the need for research to be strictly comparable.

Representative a sample is representative if it is an accurate cross-section of the whole population being studied. This allows the researcher to generalize the results for the whole population.

Sampling frame a list used as the source for a random sample.

Social fact a term used by Durkheim to claim that certain objective 'facts' exist in society that are not influenced by individuals. Examples include the existence of marriage, divorce, work, etc.

Stratified sampling where the population under study is divided according to known criteria, such as sex and age, in order to make the sample more representative.

Survey a large-scale piece of quantitative research aiming to make general statements about a particular population.

Systematic sampling where every nth name (for example, every tenth name) on a list is chosen.

Validity the need to show that what research sets out to measure really is that which it measures.

to perform, led by actresses who used different authority methods to undertake the tasks. They concluded that charismatic leadership was the most effective form of authority.

One form of experimental method that has been used more often by sociologists is the **field experiment**. This type of experiment takes place in the real world and involves the social scientist manipulating a real situation and observing the outcomes. Garfinkel (1967) asked his students to behave in unconventional ways in order to uncover the assumptions that lie behind everyday behaviour. For example, when asked 'how are you?', they would enquire what was actually meant by the question and then answer in great detail. As you can imagine, people became quite annoyed by this, thus revealing that everyday social life is governed by many complex rules.

Activities

Research ideas

1   Using the positivist criteria, conduct a small study using what you have learnt to find out what changes students would like to see in your school/college.

2   Carry out a small piece of research into the notion of 'happiness' or another abstract quality.

   ● Separately, ask a small selection of students in your school or college to define what they mean by 'happy' or 'sexy' or 'attractive' (or any other abstract term you wish).

   ● Choose three different definitions and then conduct three parallel surveys, asking people on a scale of 1 to 5 how happy/sexy/attractive they think they are.

   ● Compare and reflect on the result. What problems might your research throw up for positivist research?

Web.tasks

1   Go to **www.mori.co.uk** (the website of MORI, a polling organization). Look through a selection of survey results and and assess the methods of data collection used.

2   The UK government uses positivistic approaches to uncover information about the population. To find out how much information can be obtained, go to: **www.statistics.gov.uk/**

   Click on the 'neighbourhood' heading on the top of the page. Fill in your postcode and explore. The site provides you with detailed information about your area.

Case studies

A **case study** is a detailed study of one particular group or organization. Instead of searching out a wide range of people via sampling, the researcher focuses on one group. The resulting studies are usually extremely detailed and provide a depth of information not normally available. However, there is always the problem that this intense scrutiny may miss wider issues by its very concentration. Case studies are used widely by both quantitative and qualitative researchers. McKee and Bell (1985), for example, studied a small community to explore the impact of high rates of unemployment on family relationships.

The main problem with case studies is that there is never any proof that the particular group chosen to be studied is typical of the population as a whole, therefore it may not be possible to generalize from the findings to other groups.

Check your understanding

1   Explain briefly in your own words the seven stages of the hypothetico-deductive model.

2   What is the difference between 'deductive' and 'inductive' reasoning?

3   What model of society is positivism based upon?

4   Identify two types of random sampling – give one example of when each would be useful.

5   What is 'quota' sampling? What is the main advantage of this method?

6   Give one reason why sociologists tend not to use experiments.

7   What is a case study?

An eye on the exam — Positivism & quantitative research methods

Item A

Despite being widely used and widely respected in the natural sciences, experiments are rarely used in sociology. Some of the reasons for this are ethical, others may be practical. However, some of the techniques of experiments are used in sociology and psychology, though sociologists are unable to have the complete control of variables achieved by scientists. They will always face the problem of wanting to study people in society itself rather than in the false situation of a laboratory.

Assess the view that positivistic methods are inappropriate for understanding society.   (33 marks)

Grade booster — Getting top marks in this question

The key to answering this question lies in how we understand the nature of society. Does it consist of something 'real' that can be explored and mapped, or is it rather an ever-changing interaction in which people create the society through their actions?

You should first define what the positivistic approach to the study of society consists of. Then provide a clear coverage of the methods used in positivism – the hypothetico-deductive method and the use of surveys, statistics and (the weakest link) the experiment. Provide a critique of these, focusing on the failure of positivists to understand the way meaning is constructed and how difficult it is to truly measure a social concept. You may need to discuss 'indicators' here.

A useful conclusion would be that positivistic methods are appropriate in certain situations and not others. For example, they are good for finding out people's attitudes towards migration or their voting intentions, but inappropriate for exploring the activities of a youth 'gang'.

TOPIC 5

Interpretive sociology and qualitative methods

Getting you thinking

≪ Last year I had a brief fling with a friend's boyfriend. I had met him two years previously when he asked me out but rejected him, partly because I was put off by the fact that he was older than me. I became friends with the woman shortly before they became a couple. After they had been together for several months, I spent time alone with him by chance and we got on very well. I became increasingly attracted to him but tried to ignore these feelings. We ended up kissing after several drinks and, although I felt guilty, when he suggested meeting next day I agreed. We met up several times over the following weeks, only sleeping together one night after being close many times. I thought I was in love with him and he with me, but this allowed me to disregard the guilt I felt about my friend. I realise now that I was being naive. Eventually, I realised he was not going to choose between us and any sort of pleasure I had got from the relationship was overshadowed by anxiety about the pain we could cause my friend, so I ended it. I have never told her. We live in different towns but are still in touch. I feel very guilty and don't know whether I should tell her or not. She is still with this man. ≫

What should we do?

Source: *The Guardian*,
8 November 2007

≪ I am a student and have been sharing a house for six months with four other people. We all get on well, but one issue is causing disharmony. It may sound trivial, but one of my housemates keeps piles of dirty plates and cutlery – ours as well as his own – in his room for weeks on end. At times, we have been left with only two clean plates between the five of us. We are reluctant to retrieve things from his room, which is squalid and smells terrible. My housemates have threatened to keep their kitchen stuff locked in their rooms, which he says is ridiculous. He makes us feel as if we are the unreasonable ones. ≫

What should we do?

Source: 'Private Lives', *The Guardian*, 28 February 2008

1 What are your views about these dilemmas?

2 Write down a couple of lines on what you think and then have a group discussion.

3 Do you all agree?

It is likely that the group had quite different views on how best to resolve the dilemmas above. The clear facts have been presented to you and yet different people have interpreted them in different ways and come to different conclusions. Probably this is because you approach the 'facts of the case' from different moral or cultural viewpoints. This is not too dissimilar from sociology, for the theoretical approaches and views on the nature of society that different sociologists favour tend to influence the methods of sociological research they choose.

Essentially, there are two ways to start analysing society. One is to begin by looking at society and how it influences people. To take this starting point reflects the belief that there really is a society 'out there' that is influencing our behaviour and directs us into routine patterns of action.

A second way of starting an analysis is to begin by looking at the individual, and then working up to the social level. In starting here, the researcher sees individual perceptions and ideas as the building blocks of any larger social analysis.

It would be nice if the ideas of those who start at the bottom and work up and those who start at the top and work down met 'in the middle', but, sadly, this is not so. Indeed, the different starting points lead to quite different explanations of what society is like and how it operates.

In the last topic, we looked at the methods used by those who start at the top. These positivistic methods are all based (explicitly in the case of functionalism and Marxism, and implicitly in the case of most quantitative research) on the idea that a society exists in such a way that it can be counted and gauged. In this topic, we are going to look at the methodology of those who believe that analyses ought to start at the bottom – that is, with theories that stress how people perceive the world and interact with one another. These theories include interactionism (and labelling theory, which is a version of it) and there is also an overlap with postmodernism. These various approaches are typically referred to as interpretive or **phenomenological approaches**.

Recently, there has been a move to try to integrate the two levels of theory, most notably in the work of Giddens (1991), but as we said earlier, so far sociologists have found it very difficult to find methods to combine the levels.

Theory and interpretive research

Bryman (2004) has argued that if there is one distinction to be made regarding the different aims of positivist and interpretive research, it is that while positivist research sets out to explain human behaviour through *analysing* the forces that act upon it, interpretive sociology sets out to understand varieties of human behaviour by being able to *empathize* with it.

Weber and *verstehen*

The division between analysis and empathy can be traced back at least as far as Durkheim and Weber. As we have seen in earlier topics, Durkheim's attitude was that society could be treated as a 'thing' that existed beyond the individual and could be explored in a similar way to the physical sciences. For Weber, however, society was very different from an inanimate object. It consisted of thinking, purposeful people who acted as a result of a variety of influences, which could not be understood except by looking through the eyes of the individual actors. Weber used the term '*verstehen*' (similar to the English word 'empathy') to describe the sociological process that looking through the eyes of the individuals involved. In fact, Weber (1947) actually defined sociology as a 'science which attempts the interpretive understanding of social action in order to arrive at causal explanations'.

Symbolic interactionism and labelling theory

As mentioned in earlier topics, symbolic interactionism derives from the writings of Mead, Cooley and Thomas, who were all at the University of Chicago in the 1950s. This theoretical approach informed and developed alongside labelling theory. In the 1960s, Blumer further developed these ideas and gave the name symbolic interactionism to the approach. According to Blumer (1962), societies do not have an existence independent of people's understanding of it. Social objects, events and situations are all interpreted by people in various socially learned ways and then people respond to them in terms of these learned **meanings**. Labelling theory, which is associated with Lemert (1967) and Becker (1963), shares this belief in the importance of symbols (which they call labels), but largely focuses on situations where one group or individual is able to impose its definition of the situation on others – usually with negative consequences for the people being labelled.

Symbolic interactionism and labelling theory tend to use qualitative methods, rejecting the positivist approaches.

Key themes

Crime and deviance

Participant observation is closely associated with the use of the labelling perspective to study deviance.

Howard Becker (1963) conducted a famous participant observational study, using the labelling perspective, in which he investigated the way in which people began to use cannabis and how it gradually became part of their self identity. Becker argues that people who smoke cannabis regularly are not necessarily physically addicted or have some physical or even mental need to use the drug, but instead incorporate the use of their drug into their lifestyle and identity. Their use and understanding of the drug is therefore very different from the view of those who do not smoke cannabis and disapprove of it. By seeing the use of cannabis through the eyes of the users, Becker provided a very different perspective from the dominant approaches of the time, which sought to find the differences between drug users and non-users. However, Becker also clearly has sympathy and liking for the musicians he studied and worked with. Therefore, although the research was a breakthrough in understanding the process by which people learn to use drugs, rather than become 'addicted', it also demonstrates the dangers in participant observation of becoming too close to the people being studied.

Structuration theory

More recently, Giddens has argued in his structuration theory (1984) that there is a form of structure that exists beyond the control of individuals and which does constrain human action. However, Giddens argues that these structures only exist in so far as people make them exist. So, families exist only as long as people choose to stay within the particular set of relationships that define a family. Research, according to Giddens, must therefore understand the motivations and actions of individuals, before it can see how structures can 'exist'.

A good example of the difference between objective facts and perception of facts is Foster's (1995) **ethnographic** study of a housing estate (consisting mainly of blocks of flats) in East London. Objectively, the estate had a high crime rate – at least according to official statistics. However, residents did not perceive the estate to be particularly threatening. Of particular significance was the existence of 'informal social control'. People expected a certain level of crime, but felt moderately secure because the levels were contained by informal controls and by a supportive network. Neighbours looked after each other and they believed that if any trouble should occur, they could rely upon each other for support. Furthermore, because of the degree of intimacy and social interaction on the estate, most people knew who the offenders were, and felt that this knowledge allowed them some degree of protection, because they could keep an eye on the troublemakers.

Official statistics portrayed this estate as having major problems – yet ethnographic research showed that the estate actually provided a secure environment in which most people were happy.

Interpretive approaches and method

Interpretive researchers largely reject the use of quantitative methods (that is, statistical surveys and other positivist approaches) and prefer instead **qualitative research**. Qualitative research methods refer to any approach in sociology that sets out to uncover the meaning of social action rather than measure it through statistics. Interpretive researchers prefer qualitative methods for the following reasons.

Meaning

As we have just noted, qualitative research allows sociologists to search for the meaning for participants of events, situations and actions in which they are involved. This reflects the belief of interpretive approaches that only by understanding how individuals build up their patterns of interaction can a full understanding of society be presented.

Context

Interpretive research usually studies small-scale groups and specific situations. This allows the researcher to preserve the individuality of each of these in their analyses (in contrast with positivistic research which is based on large samples). Interpretive-based research provides the researcher with an understanding of the events, actions and meanings as they are influenced by specific circumstances. It is only within the contexts that action makes sense.

Unanticipated phenomena and influences

Positivistic research tends to fall into a format whereby researchers look for evidence to back up a hypothesis and then amend or reject it. In other words, positivistic researchers tend to anticipate certain outcomes – research does not start in a vacuum, but is based on a fairly clear idea of what should happen if variables react as expected. In qualitative research, the researcher does not necessarily have to have a clear idea of what they are looking for (see 'grounded theory', in the panel on the right) – researchers often start with an interest in a particular area and absolutely no idea of where it might lead. Without the 'blinkers' of the hypothetico-deductive model, researchers are much more open to the unexpected, and to fresh ideas.

Process

Positivistic forms of research are generally interested in outcomes (what happens if), however qualitative research is more interested in the process (what is happening). This reflects a belief by positivists that they are looking for patterns that can be generalized across society – they are not interested necessarily in the details of the actual processes that lead to the outcome. Interpretive sociologists, on the other hand, will be interested in the actual dynamics of the situation – the process.

The differences between **qualitative** and **quantitative** methods

Bryman (2004) suggests that the differences between qualitative and quantitative methods include:

- *Numbers versus words* – Qualitative methods tend to describe social life in words, whilst quantitative research uses far more numbers to paint the sociological picture.

- *Point of view of researcher versus point of view of participants* – In quantitative research the researcher is the one who decides what questions to ask and how to classify the responses. However, in qualitative research, the researcher starts from the point of view of the participants – and writes up what they say, no matter how confusing or contradictory.

- *Researcher is distant versus researcher is close* – In quantitative research, the sociologist usually stays 'outside' and is uninvolved with the participants. The sociologist distributes, collects and analyses the questionnaires or interview results. In qualitative research, sociologists attempting to understand what is going on become heavily involved with the people being researched.

- *Theories tested versus theories emerge* – In quantitative research, sociologists usually have a hypothesis that they wish to test and this forms the basis for the research. In qualitative research, however, the theory may well emerge from the actual process of research. This is known as '**grounded theory**'.

- *Structured versus unstructured* – Quantitative research is usually very well structured as the information needs to be gained in a way that is reliable. Qualitative research, on the other hand, is usually far less structured and is more flexible and open. Incidentally, this does not mean that it is less well organized.

- *Hard reliable data versus rich, deep data* – Quantitative research almost always aims at being **generalizable** and thus is designed to be statistically correct. So, a survey should provide information about the population as a whole. Qualitative research places much greater emphasis on a detailed understanding of the particular group being studied.

Types of qualitative research methods

Qualitative research covers a wide range of methods, but the most common are: observational research (ethnography); focus groups; qualitative interviewing; and secondary sources. In this topic, we will concentrate on just observational research and focus groups, leaving the interviewing and secondary sources to be discussed in the next two topics.

A note on ethnography: We will be using the term *ethnography* quite often in this topic and it can be quite confusing. Ethnography is a general term commonly used by sociologists for participant observation or observation plus in-depth interviewing. So it is best to think of ethnography as a useful term for sociologists immersing themselves in the lives of the people under study, generally joining in as much social activity as possible, so that they can gain an in-depth understanding of the lives of a particular group.

Ethnographic research

Any sociologist undertaking this form of research has quite a number of decisions to make about what is the best form of observational research for their purposes. The key decisions facing the researcher are:

- the extent of involvement with the group under study
- the amount of information that the sociologist gives the group about their research.

The following two examples illustrate the differences between the methods.

Extent of involvement with the group under study

Sociologists can choose the extent of their participation in a group from one extreme of simply being an external observer with no contact with the group whatsoever – this is known as **non-participant observation**, through to the other extreme of complete immersion in the group – in fact, actually becoming a full group member – known as **participant observation**. Of course, in reality, observational research usually falls somewhere in between.

In deciding the extent of their involvement in the group, researchers have to decide what they wish to obtain from their research and weigh up the advantages and disadvantages of the role they adopt. Usually, qualitative researchers ask themselves three questions:

1 *What is possible?* – Is it actually possible to become a member of the group and be accepted? Differences in age, social-class background, gender, lifestyle and education can all have an impact on this.
2 *What is ethically correct?* – Is it acceptable to join a group that is possibly engaging in harmful activities. What harm will come to them by the sociologist's actions? There is also an ethical dimension to the decision. It is one thing to observe a group engaging in immoral or illegitimate activity; it is quite another actually to be involved.
3 *What method will produce the most valid results? Will becoming a full member of the group actually improve the quality of the research?* – The more the researcher becomes involved with the group, the greater their chances of really getting in-depth information. The sociologist is able to see the situation through the eyes of the group being studied and so will be able to emphasize with the group.

On the other hand, by not getting too involved with the group being studied, the sociologist can avoid getting personal feelings mixed up with research perceptions and is much less likely to influence the group in any way (which would ruin the research).

Amount of information the sociologist gives

Sociologists have the choice to be completely honest about the role they are playing – this is known as **overt observation** – or they can tell the participants nothing and pretend to be full members of the group – this is known as **covert observation**.

Once again, the sociologist will make the choice by balancing the three elements:

1 *What is possible?* – Is it actually possible to get away with being a member of the group? Will they find out and the cover be blown. For example, even if the sociologist is young looking and can get accepted by a youth group, how is it possible to hide their job and background?
2 *What is ethically correct?* – Is it acceptable to pretend to be a member of a group without letting them know what is really happening? The ethical guidelines that most sociologists follow insist that informed consent is always obtained. What harm will come to them by the sociologists actions?
3 *What method will produce the most valid results?* – If, by pretending to be a member of a group, the researcher is able to enter groups normally closed to researchers and is able to obtain information that results in greater sociological knowledge, then there is a strong argument for using this form of observation.

By balancing these three issues, in terms of the overt/covert and participant/non-participant decisions, the researcher can then decide exactly what form of observational research role to use.

Gold (1958) has suggested that the result of making these decisions can lead to the researcher taking one of four roles:

- *Complete participant* – A fully functioning member of the group, acting in a covert (hidden) role.
- *Participant as observer* – The researcher joins in as a participant, but is overt (open) about their role.
- *Observer as participant* – The researcher is mainly there to interview and observe.
- *Complete observer* – The researcher simply observes what is going on around them, making no attempt to interview or discuss.

The process of participant observation

Making contact and gaining entry to the group

Participant observational research by its very nature is interested in groups about whom it is difficult to gain information by survey methods. In the majority of cases, it involves studying groups who are marginal to society in some way, very often engaging in deviant behaviour. Most sociologists are not already members of such groups!

The first problem is to make contact and then find some way to gain entry to the group. Most researchers use a contact or gatekeeper who opens the door for them. In Bourgois' (2003) study of East Harlem in the 1990s, it was a local part-time crack dealer, Primo, who befriended him. However, not all groups studied are deviant, and many researchers simply ask their colleagues if they can study them (see 'Convenience sampling' on p. 292), or get a job, or perhaps join a society where they can observe people.

Lee Monaghan, for example, undertook a number of studies involving participant observation. The first one was about the culture of body builders and their use of drugs. Monaghan (1999) joined a gym and used his hobby as a body builder to study those who attended the gym. In a later study (2005), he used these contacts to get a job as a doorman in a club, where he undertook a further participant observational study on this form of employment.

Acceptance by the group

Gaining access and being introduced to a group does not necessarily mean that the group will accept the researcher as a member or observer. The next stage is to work out how one is going to be accepted. This has two elements: role and relationships:

1   *Role* refers to the decision to be covert or overt. Most sociologists take a fairly pragmatic view of what role to take, in the sense that they will adopt the role that gives them the greatest chance of getting the research material they want. The factors limiting that will be relationship issues and ethical issues (see p. 292) about how much harm the researcher may cause by acting covertly.

2   *Relationships* refer to the similarities and differences between the researcher and the group being studied. Age, ethnicity, gender, religion and social class are amongst the wide range of factors that influence the possibility of the researcher getting close to the people being studied and being able to empathize with them.

Recording the activities of the group

Once settled into a group, one of the biggest problems faced by the researcher in participant observation is how to record information. This is particularly problematic for researchers engaged in covert observation. There are a number of answers to the problem of how to keep a **field diary**.

The first is simply to remember as much as possible and then to write this up as soon after the events as possible. This has the enormous advantage of allowing the researcher to pay full attention to what is going on at the time, rather than being distracted by writing notes. Indeed, in covert observation, this is probably the only possible method. But the big problem is that the researcher is bound to forget things, and of course, it may be the things that are forgotten that are the most important.

The second method is to make notes wherever possible as the action is unfolding. This leads to great accuracy, but is almost guaranteed to disrupt normal social interaction, as one person in a group making copious notes of what is going on rather stands out! In Ditton's (1977) study of workplace 'fiddles', he used to go to the toilets to write up his research, using the toilet paper for his notes!

Spotlight on ...

Participant observation

Ethnographers usually live in the communities they study and they establish long-term, close relationships with the people they write about. In other words, in order to collect 'accurate data', ethnographers become intimately involved with the people we study ...

I spent hundreds of nights on the street and in crackhouses observing dealers and addicts. I regularly tape-recorded their conversations and life histories. Perhaps more important, I also visited their families, attended parties and intimate reunions. I interviewed and in many cases befriended, the spouses, lovers, siblings, mothers, grandmothers of the crack dealers featured in these pages.

Adapted from Bourgois, P. (2003) *In Search of Respect* (2nd edn), Cambridge: Cambridge University Press

Non-participant observation

Stephen Moore studied the attitudes of a local community to street drinkers who spent most of their time gathering in the high street of an inner-city area. Members of the community became increasingly punitive in their views and formed action groups to force the local authority and the police to harass the street drinkers. The police and local authority, however, took a much more liberal stance and argued that if the street drinkers were not committing a crime they had the same rights as anyone else to gather.

Moore attended all the meetings called by the action groups and the city council, noting the events as they happened, but did not speak or make his presence too obvious. After the meetings, he talked to various speakers about their attitudes, but only to gain permission to quote what they had said. Similarly, he spent some time with professionals who worked with the street drinkers, but was there simply as an observer.

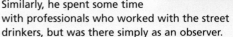

Moore adopted non-participant observation with the community meetings as he did not want to influence what happened. He used the same method when dealing with the street drinkers because the only way to be accepted by them would have been through covert research, and this was practically and ethically difficult.

Moore, S. (2008) 'Street life, neighbourhood policing and the community', in P. Squires *ASBO Nation*, Bristol: Policy Press

Identify differences in the roles taken by the observer in the two pieces of research described above.

Getting at the truth: influencing the group/being influenced by the group

In observational research, it is hard to remain objective. Close contact with the group under study means that the sociologist's feelings almost always slip into their field diaries and research notes at some time. The closer to the group the researcher gets, the more likely it is that bias of some sort will creep in. For example, Bourgois became close friends with some of the crack dealers in his study: 'I interviewed and in many cases befriended, the spouses, lovers, siblings, mothers, grandmothers ... of the crack dealers featured in these pages.'

Not only can the activities of the group influence the researcher, positively or negatively, but the researcher can also influence the group. If the group is small and perhaps less educated than the sociologist, then the researcher's ideas might influence the group – thereby ruining the research. In his classic study of youths in Liverpool, Howard Parker actually gave them legal advice when they were caught by the police for stealing from cars (Parker *et al.* 1998).

Leaving the group

Everyone engaging in participant observation or ethnographic research must, at some time, leave the group.

There are two issues here. The first is, when to leave. Glaser and Strauss (see 'Theoretical sampling', p. 293) argue that the correct time to get out of an ethnographic study is when new information does no more than confirm what the sociologist has already found out. They use the term 'theoretical saturation' to describe this situation.

The second issue is actually how to leave. This can be a very difficult thing. If the researcher likes the group and gets on well with the group being studied, then it might be very emotional to leave and may upset both group members and the researcher. On the other hand, if the researcher is engaged in deviant behaviour, it may actually be very dangerous to leave and so a strategy must be developed. In one classic study of a violent Glasgow youth gang, 'James Patrick' the researcher used a false name to infiltrate the gang, knowing that if they found him after he left, they would get their revenge. Indeed, to this day his real name is not widely known.

Of course, some people never quite leave. Philippe Bourgois (2003) admits to going back regularly to East Harlem in New York and has kept in touch with his principal gatekeeper, Primo. Interestingly, Primo was heavily influenced by Bourgois and turned from a crack user and part-time dealer into a small-time businessman who gave up alcohol and drugs.

Participant observation Advantages and disadvantages

Advantages

- *Experience* – Participant observation allows the researcher to fully join the group and see things through the eyes (and actions) of the people in the group.

- *Generating new ideas* – Often this can lead to completely new insights and generate new theoretical ideas. Also good for validity.

- *Getting the truth* – One of the problems with questionnaires, and to a lesser extent with interviews, is that the respondent can lie. Participant observation prevents this because the researcher can see the person's actual behaviour. This leads to high levels of validity.

- *Digging deep* – Participant observation can create a close bond between the researcher and the group under study, and individuals in the group may be prepared to confide in the researcher. Excellent for validity.

- *Dynamic* – Participant observation takes place over a period of time and allows an understanding of how changes in attitudes and behaviour take place. Again can raise level of validity.

- *Reaching into difficult areas* – Participant observation is normally used to obtain research information on hard-to-reach groups, such as drug users and young offenders.

- Scores very high for validity.

Disadvantages

- *Bias* – The main problem lies with bias, as the (participant) observer can be drawn into the group and start to see things through their eyes. Loses objectivity and therefore validity.

- *Influence of the researcher* – The presence of the researcher may make the group act less naturally as they are aware of being studied, unless the researcher is operating covertly.

- *Ethics* – How far should researchers allow themselves to be drawn into the activities of the group – particularly if these activities are immoral or illegal?

- *Proof* – There is no way of knowing whether the findings of participant observation are actually true or not, since there is no possibility of replicating the research. In other words the results may lack reliability.

- *Too specific* – Participant observation is usually used to study small groups of people who are not typical of the wider population. It is therefore difficult to claim that the findings can be generalized across the population as a whole.

- *Studying the powerless* – Most (participant) observational studies are concerned with the least powerful groups in society. What about the powerful and their activities?

- Scores very low for reliability and generalizability

Causing harm: The ethical dimension of ethnographic studies

Of all forms of research, apart from experiments, participant observation possibly carries the most difficult ethical dilemmas. At virtually any stage in the proceedings, participant observation (particularly covert) can lead to harm to the researcher, to the participants, or to the public.

Even if no harm comes to others, there is still the controversial issue that covert participant observation takes place without the consent of the people being studied. This contradicts one of the bases of all modern research, that those being studied give their informed consent. Holdaway (1983), for example, was a police officer studying his colleagues without their knowledge. He knew that he was leaving the police force to work at a university once his research was completed. When the research, which was critical of his colleagues, was published, some were angry as they felt that he had taken advantage of them.

Sociologists therefore have to be very careful about what they do, and this can lead to many moral dilemmas. This is the last part of the introduction to Bourgois' (2003) study of East Harlem (New York) where he studied crack dealers and users.

>> *Finally, I want to thank my family. I will always be grateful to Charo Chacon-Mendez for coming with me to El Barrio, where we married at the very beginning of the research project. Her help was invaluable. I apologize for imposing so much anxiety on her when I regularly stayed out all night on the street and in crackhouses for so many years. I hope that it is not one of the reasons why we are no longer together. If it is, I regret it profoundly.* >>

Focus groups

A second very common form of qualitative research method is the focus group. A focus group consists of a relatively small number of people, usually less than 12, who are requested to discuss a specific topic. Focus groups ideally are representative of a particular **population** and are obtained through the most appropriate sampling techniques. (These can include both traditional qualitative or quantitative sampling methods.)

Focus groups give researchers an opportunity to hear an issue being discussed, with people being able to discuss and challenge each other's views. Compared with the rather static interview method, focus groups are much more dynamic, with people demonstrating the thought process involved in how they came to their views. In the actual discussions, issues emerge that researchers may never have thought of and so these groups are often innovative. Finally, the focus group members have the power to concentrate more on issues they consider important than on the researcher's priorities. See the panel above for a summary of advantages and limitations of focus groups.

Focus groups Advantages and limitations

Advantages

- Allows researchers to understand *why* people hold certain opinions.
- People can modify and change views, so demonstrating how strongly held their views are.
- Because it is a discussion, the focus group will prioritize issues it thinks are more important. This may be different from the researcher's ideas.
- Focus groups are dynamic, with people probing each other's views and defending their own views.
- Focus groups study group views and interactions.

Limitations

- Researchers have limited control over what happens. The group discussion can veer off into irrelevant (for the researcher) areas.
- Membership of focus groups needs to be carefully run to ensure real discussion, and 'louder' people who dominate discussion need to be controlled.
- Focus groups generate a huge amount of material which is not clearly structured, this means that analysing the material is very difficult.

Sampling in qualitative research

There are three main types of sampling associated with qualitative research: convenience, snowball and theoretical.

Convenience sampling

This refers to any group used for research that is easily available to the researcher. Convenience sampling is very commonly used in ethnography because problems of entry and acceptance by the group being studied are kept to a minimum. Typically, convenience sampling is used for research into occupational groups such as nurses, teachers and students.

Though this is widely used, it can have serious drawbacks. Engaging in covert research can make a person feel like a spy. As seen earlier, where colleagues know and accept the researcher, any results that are critical of them may lead to problems between the researcher and colleagues after the research is over.

Snowball sampling

This is used in all forms of qualitative research, but is most common in studying deviant groups. This method involves finding one person initially who agrees to act as gatekeeper and through them building up an ever bigger network of contacts. The main problem with this form of sampling is

Focus on research

Wilson and Jones (2008)
A qualitative case study

In Topic 4, on p. 285, it stated that a case study that could be either quantitative or qualitative in design. Here is a good example of a largely qualitative case study. David Wilson and Timothy Jones wanted to study the process by which paedophiles move from fantasizing about paedophilia and viewing child pornography to actually engaging in illegal acts.

In order to do this, they decided to undertake a case study of one convicted paedophile currently in prison. This was partly because it is very difficult to gain access to convicted paedophiles. Indeed, the researchers were only given access to this particular prisoner because one of the researchers, David Wilson, had previous contacts with the prison and was trusted by the staff.

The prisoner had volunteered to take part in the study and had given full permission for the publication of the research. However, it was felt that it was important to maintain the anonymity of the prisoner to protect him. 'James' (the pseudonym for the prisoner) was interviewed on four different occasions, with each interview lasting, on average, two hours. All four interviews were unstructured, and James was allowed to lead the interviewer into territory that he felt was important, to explain why he offended.

Wilson and Jones argue that the case study approach allowed a 'richer, deeper understanding to emerge about the relationship between thinking and doing'. James was also encouraged to keep a 'reflective diary' during the twelve months of field research, documenting what was said, and also his thoughts and reactions to these interviews, as well as more general observations about the prison and James's part within it. According to Wilson and Jones, this diary also allowed them to check that what was being said in one interview corresponded with details provided in later interviews.

Wilson, D. and Jones, T. (2008) '"In my own world": A case study of a paedophile's thinking and doing and his use of the internet', *The Howard Journal*, 47(2), pp. 107–20

1 **Use the research above to show how case study research can use a variety of methods.**

2 **How can case study research be criticized?**

that the sample tends to be restricted to one group who have contacts. This may result in a very partial picture of social interaction.

>> *A snowball sample of men and women was built up by making contacts through various institutions such as luncheon clubs, local history groups and other social networks. Many were recommended to us by someone who had already participated, and we were able to interview some members of the same family.*>> (Hood and Joyce 1999)

Theoretical sampling

Theoretical sampling is different from the other types of sampling in that it is closely associated with a particular methodology known as grounded theory. In this approach, instead of starting off with a hypothesis and setting out to prove/disprove it, the researcher chooses an area of interest, begins the research and hopes that ideas will emerge from the process. Glaser and Strauss (1967) developed this approach based on the idea that the source of data collection would have to change as new ideas emerged in the research. At each stage of the research, Glaser and Strauss decided what next group or secondary source was needed to further their research and concentrated their efforts on finding this. When they had reached theoretical saturation (no new ideas are emerging) then it was time to finish.

>> *... but after ten interviews I gradually realized that I needed more interviewees of certain types. For example, initially I found I had only interviewed families with harmonious relationships and so I asked if they could find me families with problems.*>> (Darlington and Scott 2002)

Criticisms of research methods used in interpretive sociology

Positivist sociologists have not been shy in criticizing the methods used by qualitative researchers in the following ways.

Values

Positivists argue that although a value-free sociology may not be possible, there are reasonable limits to observe. Qualitative research is shot through with issues related to value bias, and it is almost impossible to untangle the personal biases of the researcher from the research 'insights' generated. The approach taken by feminists such as Mies (see Chapter 2, p. 103), which commits itself to a particular value approach, is seen as going beyond the acceptable limit. However, the very opposite can occur too. In Lee-Treweek's (2000) study of carers in homes for the elderly, she found that she increasingly disliked the 'carers' she was studying. Their attitudes to the old people so angered her that it was difficult to continue her study in the value-neutral way she wanted.

Transferability/generalizability

Qualitative research is often small scale and specific to a particular group. Positivists claim that it is difficult to transfer the results of research in one specific situation to others – that is, there are problems with results being **transferable**.

Generalizability follows from transferability. To what extent can general statements be made from highly localized and specific studies that aim to uncover the meaning of the interaction of a group in a specific situation?

Interpretive approaches to sociology have generated a range of sophisticated methods that can justifiably claim to provide extremely useful insights into the nature of social action. Interpretive approaches seek, above all else, to understand how people perceive the world about them and how this influences their actions – and the consequences of these actions for both themselves and others. The nature of the questions asked by these approaches therefore leads interpretive sociologists to use qualitative methods, rather than qualitative ones. Whether qualitative approaches are 'better' or 'worse' than qualitative approaches is like asking whether in theory, structural approaches are 'better' or 'worse' than interpretive approaches. There is no simple answer, except to say that each approach asks different questions that need to be studied in different ways.

Lack of transparency

According to Bryman and Burgess (1994), in the qualitative methods associated with interpretive sociology, it is often unclear how conclusions are reached, resting heavily upon the intuition and understanding of the researcher. The reader of the research has to take it on trust that the perception of the situation as described by the interpretive researcher is accurate.

Triangulation (multistrategy research)

In order to be clear about the different research strategies used by sociologists, we have made very clear distinctions between quantitative and qualitative research. In real life research, however, things are rather more complicated. While one group of sociologists is largely in favour of using quantitative methods wherever possible, and other sociologists are largely in favour of using qualitative methods, both groups will dip into the 'other side's' methods if they think it will be useful.

So, quantitative researchers may well back up their work by including some observation or some in-depth, unstructured interviewing, whilst qualitative researchers may well engage in some structured interviewing or draw upon secondary sources in order to strengthen their research. This use of multiple methods is generally known as **triangulation** (though, strictly speaking it is really multistrategy research).

The term 'triangulation' originally referred to the use of different indicators in quantitative research as ways of measuring social phenomena. The aim was to overcome the problem of loss of validity where a faulty indicator was used. However, over time the term has come to mean the use of multiple methods in a particular piece of research, with the aim of improving its validity, reliability and generalizability.

Check your understanding

1 What two ways are there for starting an analysis of society? What terms do sociologists use for these approaches?

2 Explain the meaning of *verstehen* in your own words. Why is it different from Durkheim's approach to sociology?

3 Identify and explain three reasons why interpretive sociologists prefer the use of qualitative methods in research.

4 What advantages does observational research have over quantitative methods?

5 Suggest two examples of research where it would be possible to justify covert observation.

6 Identify two advantages and two disadvantages of focus groups in research.

7 Why do interpretivist-based approaches have a difficulty with generalizability, according to positivist critics?

Activities

Research idea

Design a research strategy using positivist ideas to discover why some young people are attracted to 'clubbing'. Now, design an alternative piece of research using interpretive ideas. How is the research different? How could each piece of research be criticized?

Web.task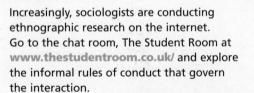

Increasingly, sociologists are conducting ethnographic research on the internet. Go to the chat room, The Student Room at **www.thestudentroom.co.uk/** and explore the informal rules of conduct that govern the interaction.

Key terms

Covert observation where the sociologist does not admit to being a researcher.

Ethnography term used to describe the work of anthropologists who study simple, small-scale societies by living with the people and observing their daily lives. The term has been used by sociologists to describe modern-day observational studies.

Field diary a detailed record of events, conversations and thoughts kept by participant observers, written up as often as possible.

Generalizability the ability to apply the findings of research into one group accurately to other groups.

Grounded theory an approach to theory construction in which theory is generated during research.

Meaning the word used by Blumer to describe the sense people make of a particular situation.

Non-participant observation where the sociologist simply observes the group but does not seek to join in their activities.

Overt observation where the sociologist is open about the research role.

Participant observation where the sociologist joins a group of people and studies their behaviour.

Phenomenological approaches approaches such as interactionism which stress how people perceive the world and interact with one another.

Population the entire group the sociologist is focusing on.

Qualitative research a general term for approaches to research that are less interested in collecting statistical data, and more interested in observing and interpreting the ways in which people behave.

Transferability the ability to transfer the results of research in one specific situation to others.

Triangulation (multistrategy research) a term often used to describe the use of multiple methods (qualitative and quantitative) in research.

Verstehen term first used by Weber in sociology to suggest that the role of sociology is to understand partly by seeing through the eyes of those who are being studied. Similar to 'empathy' in English.

An eye on the exam — Interpretive sociology & qualitative methods

Item A

Firstly, the social world is one which has been given meaning by its constituent actors. Therefore to explore this world, it is necessary to draw upon the concepts that actors themselves use. Consider the difference between the work of a virologist and a sociologist. Viruses do not speak and do not constitute their own behaviour. However, a sociologist who wishes to explore why gay men have unsafe sex must explore what gay men themselves understand by terms like unsafe, protection and sex.

Adapted from Bonnell, C. (1999) 'Gay men: drowning (and swimming) by numbers', in S. Hood, B. Mayall and S. Oliver (eds) *Critical Issues in Social Research*, Buckingham: Open University Press

---

To what extent are sociologists able to explore the meaning and interpretations that people make of the events in their lives?

(33 marks)

Grade booster — Getting top marks in this question

This question is asking you to explore the various qualitative sociological methods which sociologists use to examine society. Begin by briefly stating the two major approaches to research, the quantitative and qualitative, and their merits. Use material from Item A to illustrate the strengths of qualitative research. You should then say how quantitative methods have great difficulties in exploring meaning and interpretations. You should then move on to discuss ethnographic research and focus groups, covering their strengths and weaknesses.

Conclude with a statement that no approach can claim to explore fully the meanings and interpretations people put on their lives, but that increasingly sociologists use triangulation or mixed methods to strengthen the quality of their research.

TOPIC 6

Postmodern and feminist methodologies

Getting you thinking

<< Mass production, the mass consumer, the big city, big-brother state, the sprawling housing estate, and the nation-state are in decline: flexibility, diversity, differentiation, mobility, communication, decentralization and internationalization are in the ascendant. In the process our own identities, our sense of self, our own subjectivities are being transformed. We are in transition to a new era. >>

Source: cited in Callinicos, A. (1989) *Against post-modernism: a Marxist critique*, Cambridge: Polity Press

1 Compare the photos of people and buildings in London in 1950 and today. What differences can you see?

2 What other major social changes affecting contemporary life can you identify?

3 Suggest some explanations for these changes?

4 Briefly think about the major theories of Marxism and functionalism – do you think they are relevant for an understanding of recent social changes?

One of the most exciting developments in sociology over the past 20 years has been the emergence of postmodernism. In many ways this is rather strange, as apparently one of the key messages of postmodernism is that it rejects the very project of understanding society – the aim of sociology itself!

However, some sociologists have enthusiastically taken on board some of its messages and have incorporated them into what they see as a consequently revitalized and radical sociology.

In this topic, we look at the impact of postmodernism on research methods and explore how, by influencing methods, postmodernism has also led sociology into studying new areas previously considered outside its domain.

Postmodernism and the rejection of positivism

Postmodernists, such as Bauman (1990), Lyotard (1984) and Baudrillard (1998), argue that the coherent 'picture' of the social and physical worlds drawn by modernists, is no more 'true' or 'real' than the picture previously painted by the religions that dominated thought processes before **modernity**. Postmodernists see a fragmented, discontinuous world in which the desire for order has led people to impose a framework which ignores those things that do not fit neatly into the classifications and theories that have been constructed.

This idea of artificial structures imposed on a fragmented world has also been applied to sociology itself. Postmodernists argue that the nature of sociological theorizing is rooted in this false idea of structure and order. Not only this, but the methods used by sociologists are also a reflection of the mistaken belief in an organized, structured social world out there.

The postmodern critique of sociological methods has three strands: **relativity,** knowledge as control, and **narrative** and **discourse**.

Relativity

As you know, the assumption underlying positivism is that there is an objective world 'out there' waiting to be uncovered by research. Postmodernists dispute this. They see, instead, many different, competing 'worlds' that exist only in particular contexts and at particular times. There is, quite simply, no objective reality waiting to be discovered. The objective, scientific analysis based upon a scrupulous following of the rules does not produce knowledge about the world – it simply produces another relative version of society . According to Sarap (1993), Lyotard argues that knowledge is only deemed to be true if it is accepted by those who are regarded as the appropriate people to decide upon its worth.

Knowledge as control

Scientists and other professionals and academics are not objective intellectuals engaged in a struggle to find the truth. According to Foucault (1963/1975), they, like any other group in society, are engaged in a struggle to have their concept of knowledge (as opposed to other, competing ones) accepted as reality. The reason for engaging in this struggle is that whoever has control over what is regarded as knowledge, and how to obtain it, gains considerable power in society. Scientists and professionals are therefore not disinterested and objective, but key players in a power struggle. A particularly good example of this can be found in medical knowledge. Despite the fact that about 20% of people in hospital actually contract another illness or are medically harmed in some way by the very 'healing process', doctors have gained control over the task of healing and of defining what is or is not a healthy body. Other ways of dealing with health have been labelled as 'complementary medicine' or 'alternative therapies', and denied equal status on the grounds that they are not scientifically rigorous.

Narrative and discourse

We have seen that, according to postmodernists, sociologists are yet another group seeking to impose their form of knowledge on society, which they do by claiming expert knowledge based on sociology as a form of science.

The outcome of sociological research is the production of explanations or theories that explain social phenomena. Postmodernists call these explanations 'narratives'. The implication is that they are no more than stories, giving a partial account.

Where sociologists have provided large-scale 'grand-theories', which claim to provide a full and complete explanation for human behaviour (e.g. functionalism), the term used by postmodernists is 'meta-narrative'. The reason for the dismissal of these theories is simply that there is no world out there waiting to be explained. All explanation is partial and grounded in the context of people's lives and experiences.

Linked to narrative is the concept of discourse. Discourse can be seen as the framework of language within which discussions about issues occur. Discourse therefore limits and locates discussion.

Postmodernist research

Postmodernism has also been a positive force in three main ways relevant to research:

1 It has introduced new methods and approaches to research.
2 It has introduced different topics to study.
3 It has encouraged people to speak for themselves, thereby allowing their narratives to stand without necessarily interpreting them.

Deconstruction: a new method

Postmodernism argues that all knowledge is relative and that some knowledge is more powerful than others. Postmodernist writers such as Baudrillard (1998) argue that these 'narratives' about what we consider to be knowledge crucially affect how we act. However, they do not influence us in the way that Marxists or functionalists would argue, rather they interact with people to create new and fragmentary patterns of thought and behaviour that alter according to place, time and an unknowable range of other factors. The task of postmodernists is to try to uncover the linkages and possible patterns that underlie these narratives.

Foucault suggests this process of **deconstruction** is like the activities of an archaeologist, in that the sociologist carefully digs down layer after layer to explore the construction of narratives. The postmodern researcher is, however, not concerned to give the 'truth' but to look instead at how particular narratives emerge at different times and in different contexts. Furthermore, they are not seeking to make claims for anything beyond the particular area studied.

One particular area to which deconstruction is applied is the subject of sociology itself, so traditional concepts are taken apart and looked at in new ways.

Transgression: new areas of study

The second innovation that postmodernism brought to research was that of topic areas. Traditionally, sociologists have divided the subject matter of society into various categories and classifications – so we study religion, work, social divisions, crime, and so on. If there is no world out there, and if sociology is just one narrative amongst many others (with no claim of superiority), then we also need to look critically at the sociological enterprise itself. Why do we have these divisions? They don't actually exist and we don't divide ourselves into separate chapters as we live our lives!

Postmodernists suggest that we should **transgress** classification boundaries and think in new ways. Take criminology, for example. Traditionally this studies people who commit crime. But the category 'crime' covers a massive range of actions, which sociologically have little in common. Crimes are just what some people have managed to have declared illegal, no more, no less. A different way of looking at the area is to study why people do harm to others – irrespective of what form that takes. Immediately, torture by the state, low wages, child labour and a million other forms of harmful activity enter the area of study – thus transgressing traditional boundaries.

Furthermore, if all areas of knowledge are equally relative, then how do we know what is more important or relevant than anything else? This has liberated sociologists to study issues such as the body, sexuality, eating and time – all areas which traditionally have been seen as marginal to sociology.

Key themes

Crime and deviance

Recently, postmodern methods have entered the study of crime. In particular, Ferrell (1999) has suggested that crime is increasingly 'framed' by the media, in such a way that although the majority of people will not actually experience serious crime, their perceptions of crime and its impact is derived via media images. Ferrell calls this 'cultural criminology'. Ferrell has also extended this to explore the way that crime is increasingly being defined by the media, so that certain cultural forms are criminalized. He gives the examples of media campaigns against 'performers, producers, distributors and retailers of rap and gangsta rap music'.

Examples of postmodern research

The first thing to say is that, in terms of traditional ideas of research, there are not that many clear examples of postmodern research. Rather, postmodern ideas have percolated throughout sociology, enriching the subject by, on the one hand, providing us with a new way of looking at traditional problems, and, on the other, by giving us new subjects to explore.

Reanalysing sociological concepts

Youth culture

The study of youth culture has been dominated by critical sociologists who have seen it as a form of resistance by young people. The search by these sociologists has been to find the meaning of youth culture and to explain the significance of its clothes and music.

Postmodernists, such as Redhead (1993) have challenged this view and argued that youth culture has 'no meaning' as such but is simply a complex and ever-changing mixture of influences – ranging from resistance, through constructions of what looking good means, to the manipulation of media companies, overlaid with genuine innovation. According to Redhead, to seek the meaning of it all is completely mistaken.

Redhead uses secondary data in his work but also uses the writing of young sociology students, drawing upon their current experiences of clubbing.

New areas of study

Tourism

Urry (1990) has examined tourist attractions and argued that certain places have been constructed so that they are seen and experienced as places of leisure and tourism – rather than for any other characteristics. When people visit, they do so through a 'tourist **gaze**'. This tourist gaze may screen out certain unwanted characteristics and focus solely on the socially constructed tourist image. The Lake District becomes more than a mountainous (and rainy!) place, and instead becomes a place of tranquillity, poetry and beauty. Walkers go there not just to walk, but to experience these additional elements. Spain becomes a place for clubbing, sunshine and beaches, or possibly a retirement dream, rather than a modern, industrialized country with a full range of social problems.

Feminism and methods

Feminist theory and methods are linked in this book to the postmodern movement, mainly because they have contributed importantly to the current fragmentation of sociology. Feminism and postmodernism have provided the most powerful intellectual critiques of traditional sociology and opened up massive new areas for study, as well as new methods to use.

Traditional theoretical and methodological approaches (Marxism, functionalism and even interpretive approaches) assumed that sexual identities, including the role of women, were of no sociological interest. This resulted in females and the female perspective simply being ignored. However, by the 1960s and increasingly in the 1970s, some writers, such as Firestone (1970) and Millett (1970), suggested that knowledge (and methods) are linked to gender. Men and women have different experiences and different starting points from which they construct their knowledge. So, all knowledge is related to gender. Incidentally, this argument has also been extended to different forms of knowledge based on 'ethnicity', religion, disability and sexual identity. Studies of society are then actually studies of male society.

This resulted in a rapid growth of feminist theory, which sought to understand gender relations. We discuss feminist theory in Topic 2 (p. 264) and Topic 9 (pp. 318–19), and in some detail in Chapter 7 (pp. 453–7), but for now the important point is that this emergence of feminist theory was paralleled with the development of different feminist methods of research.

Harding (1987) has suggested that there are three key elements of this feminist methodology, as follows.

1 Women's experiences: a new resource

Harding argues that most research has been devised and conducted by male sociologists and that this has resulted in a concentration on issues of interest to males. Women have different interests and perspectives, which open up new areas for sociological investigation. For example she asks 'Why do men find childcare and housework so distasteful?'

2 New purposes of social science: for women

Harding suggests the purpose of feminist sociological research ought to be to improve the position of women. Traditional social science has been concerned to 'pacify, control and exploit' women, but feminist research is committed and open about its own commitment – unlike the value-free model that has been used as a cover to control women. This commitment is known as a 'feminist **standpoint'**.

3 Locating the researcher in the same critical plane as the subjects

This third element of feminist research aims to bridge the gap between female researchers and female subjects of research. Harding argues that the feminist researcher must examine all her 'assumptions, beliefs and behaviours' and make these clear to both the subjects of research and to the people who read the research. Not only this, but the 'class, race and gender' of the researcher must also be clearly stated. In doing so, the feminist researcher does not appear 'as an invisible, anonymous voice of authority, but as a real, historical individual with concrete, specific desires and interests'. Maynard has added that feminist research should include the perspective of the women being studied, so that research is seen as a joint activity, rather than one in which the sociologist is an expert who studies powerless subjects (Maynard and Purvis 1994).

These ideas have led to in-depth interviewing/discussion and participant observation being particularly favoured in feminist research.

Harding also addresses two other key points which concern feminists – the relative truth of male and female sociologists' accounts of the world, and the question of whether men can ever undertake feminist research. The first question revolves around the problem faced by feminist sociologists that they can sometimes arrive at completely different accounts of society from those of male sociologists. So, who is right? Both? Or only one? Or neither? Harding's reply is quite simple – women are more able to understand society than men and therefore their accounts are to be preferred. The second question concerning men conducting feminist research is one where Harding gives a possibly surprising answer. She believes men can do feminist research – particularly because there are areas, to do with male sexuality and male friendships, where they have greater potential for insight compared with females. However, they would have to follow the three key elements of feminist research mentioned above.

Focus groups

Feminist sociologists routinely use focus groups for their research. Wilkinson (1999) argues that this method fits the ethos of feminism in three ways. First, focus group research is less artificial than other methods because it emphasizes group interaction which is a normal part of social life. As women are able to discuss issues in the company of other women, they are more likely to divulge their true 'lived experiences' than in more artificial interviewing situations. Second, feminist research is concerned to minimize differences in power and status that can occur in research situations, where the more powerful sociological researcher may dominate the interaction. Focus groups tend to even out the power, by giving a group of women the chance to take control over the discussion. Finally, Madriz (2000) has further suggested that where focus groups consist of 'marginalized' women such as 'lower-socioeconomic-class women of colour' then the focus group gives them the sense of solidarity to make sense of their 'experience of vulnerability and subjugation'.

Feminist ethnography

Reinharz (1992) suggests that the most effective way to study women is to use ethnographic methods. She argues that these allow the full documentation of women's lives, especially those aspects that are regarded by males as unimportant (such as domestic tasks). Further, she suggests that ethnography allows researchers to see activities from the viewpoint of women, rather than from the traditional male sociological angle. Finally, Reinharz argues that feminist ethnographic research is less exploitative of the women being studied than traditional male ethnography. For example, Skeggs (2001) points out that in her ethnographic research (see 'Focus on research', p. 300), she was seeking to 'emphasize the words, voices and lives of the women', which fits well with the argument of feminist researchers for a feminist standpoint.

Qualitative interviewing

Feminist sociologists have adopted the in-depth interview as their most used tool of research, according to Bryman (2004). Oakley (1981) argues that traditional structured interviewing is exploitative, offering the interviewee nothing in exchange for their information and reflects a power imbalance between researcher and interviewee, with the researcher deciding what is worth talking about. Therefore feminist unstructured/in-depth interviewing emphasizes that the two women involved are engaged in a discussion based on equality, in which the interviewee is equal in power with the interviewer and has equal right to decide on the direction of the discussion. In her own research interviews on the transition into motherhood, Oakley was asked questions on a range of issues by the respondents and felt that by replying and even advising the women, she was fulfilling the criteria of feminist research methods.

However, feminist writers have had some problems, in that their interpretation of women's responses to their questions do not necessarily square with the respondents'. For example, Millen (1997) interviewed 32 British female scientists about their work. However, her approach, based on feminist ideas, was largely rejected by the respondents. Millen comments:

>> *From my external, academically privileged position vantage point, it is clear that sexism pervades these professions. However, the women did not generally see their careers and interactions with male scientists in terms of gendered social relations. There is therefore a tension between their characterization of their experience and my interpretation of it.* >>

Discussion on feminist methods

This strong approach to the uniqueness and superiority of feminist research has not gone unchallenged.

Mary Maynard, herself a feminist sociologist, disagrees with Harding's arguments. She suggests that the strong position taken by Harding belongs to an early era of feminism when there was a need to stake out its territory and stamp its mark upon sociology (Maynard and Purvis 1994). She also argues that no matter what central themes there are to feminist research, in the end if it is not rigorous and compelling in its accuracy, then it cannot claim to be sociological research.

She argues that the continuing stress on listening to women's experiences, particularly through in-depth interviews, has become political correctness and other forms of research are being prevented. Oakley (1998),

Focus on research

Bev Skeggs (1997) Formations of class and gender

Beverley Skeggs studied 83 White, working-class young women over a period of 12 years using ethnographic measures, involving participant observation and in-depth interviews. The research began with the women enrolling on a health and social care course at a college in the North-West of England and Skeggs followed them through the rest of their education, their employment and their family lives. According to Skeggs, her work was feminist in that she was politically committed to providing a means for 'marginalized' women to express themselves. Furthermore, she wished to show how the young women's perceptions of the society they encountered influenced their actual behaviour.

Skeggs argues that she did not exploit the women for her own career benefits, but that her research gave her 'subjects' a sense of self-worth and that she 'provided a mouthpiece against injustice, particularly with regard to disclosures of violence, child abuse and sexual harassment'.

Skeggs, B. (1997) *Formations of Class and Gender,*
London: Sage Publications

In what ways can Skeggs' research be described as feminist?

Key terms

Deconstruction the breaking down of a taken-for-granted subject to uncover the assumptions within it.

Discourse the linguistic framework within which discussion takes place.

Gaze a postmodern concept which refers to a particular way of seeing an issue, people or place.

Modernity a period in history with specific ways of thinking largely based on rational, scientific thought

applied to both the physical and social worlds.

Narrative an accepted explanation or theory for some occurrence.

Relativity the idea that there is no fixed truth 'out there' waiting to be found. All knowledge is relative to a particular situation.

Standpoint (feminism) the researcher rejects the traditional notion of being neutral and value free, taking the side of the women being researched.

Transgress to cross accepted academic boundaries.

Check your understanding

1   Give two examples of meta-narratives in sociology.

2   Why does the postmodernist stress on the relativity of knowledge imply criticism of positivism?

3   Explain in your own words what is meant by 'discourse'. Give an example.

4   How do postmodernists view experts and professionals?

5   What do postmodernists do when they deconstruct a concept or theory?

6   Give one example of:
    (a) a traditional subject looked at in a new way by postmodernists
    (b) a new subject brought into the domain of sociology by postmodernists.

7   What are the three key elements of feminist methodology, according to Harding?

8   Give one criticism of Harding's approach.

although strongly associated with the use of qualitative interviewing methods, argues that the use of qualitative research methods in feminist studies reflected a desire by feminists to distance their work from the traditional scientific/positivist approaches much favoured by the male sociology 'establishment'. According to Oakley, it is important for feminist researchers to use quantitative as well as qualitative methods in their research. This will allow them access to the prestige, funding and influence on government policy currently enjoyed by those following more positivistic methods. Interestingly, Oakley was one of the first feminist writers to argue for the use of in-depth, qualitative interviews, but clearly she feels that the wheel has turned too far and the total rejection of quantitative methods is harming feminist research.

Activities

Web.task

Search the web for tourist information and images about a particular place. What impression of the place do they create? To what extent do the images and information about the places reflect Urry's idea of the 'tourist gaze'?

An eye on the exam   **Postmodern & feminist methodologies**

Item A

In this study, undertaken from a feminist perspective, the researchers set out to explore the young women's views and experiences of violence. The researchers based much of their methodology on feminist principles. They were open to the subjects about their own feelings, background and belief and sought to answer any questions asked in as honest a way as possible. Furthermore, they sought to eliminate power and status differences between themselves and the young girls. The researchers claim that they accepted that the research had to be led by where the subjects wanted it to go, so it became fully participatory. The researchers eschewed quantitative methods and used a variety of qualitative approaches including in-depth conversations/interviews and simply 'hanging around' with the young women. In fact, Burman and colleagues describe their work as largely 'ethnographic'.

Burman, M.J., Batchelor, S.A. and Brown, J.A. (2001) 'Researching girls and violence: facing the dilemmas of fieldwork', *British Journal of Criminology*, 41, pp. 443–59

Using material from **Item A** and elsewhere, assess the view that feminist research requires its own specific methodology.

(33 marks)

Grade booster   **Getting top marks in this question**

Outline the feminist view of the role of sociological theory as taking women's side, revealing their concerns and providing a voice for them. Explain what kinds of methods feminists have tended to favour and why these might fit with their view of theory. Make use of material from the Item. For example, link the idea of the research being led by the girls in the study to feminist ideas about collaboration between women. Explain what ethnographic methods are, and why feminists might prefer to use ethnographic methods such as in-depth conversations, interviews and 'hanging around' with the girls.

You can criticize the view in the question, for example by using Oakley's views on the value of quantitative as well as qualitative research to feminism.

Questionnaires and interviews in research

Getting you thinking — Which Austen heroine are you?

1 You identify most with:
a Sleeping Beauty
b Cinderella
c Beauty and the Beast
d The wicked queen (in Snow White)
e Tinkerbell
f The Little Mermaid

2 Your favourite movie star is:
a Dark, French and sexily brooding
b George Clooney
c Colin Farrell
d Matthew McConaughey
e Viggo Mortensen
f Harrison Ford

...

10 What do you drink?
a What have you got?
b Champagne
c White wine/spritzers
d The latest trendy cocktail
e Red wine, vodka, and/or brandy
f You don't really drink much.

11 You flirt:
a With anyone who'll flirt back – gender immaterial
b With any good-looking man who crosses your path
c With men you like, but it's more mutual teasing and quick-witted banter than sexual innuendo
d Discreetly. It may feel to you like flirting, but your friends would never call you a flirt
e Yes, but you're uncomfortable if the conversation gets too sexually provocative
f Not really. It's rare that you meet someone you really connect with.

12 You dress:
a Down – jeans, sweaters, trainers
b Classy but sexy – you like to be noticed
c Attractive, but not flashy
d In the latest trends, and you like to show skin – low-rise jeans and a belly-button piercing
e Feminine – skirts, pretty tops, kitten heels
f To express your personality.

This is part of a 15-question quiz about personality types published in *The Times*. The questionnaire and answers are good fun – but if we were serious in asking questions about personality types, what sorts of questions might you ask?

Scoring

Q1	a 2	b 1	c 3	d 4	e 5	f 6
Q2	a 4	b 3	c 5	d 2	e 6	f 1
Q10	a 5	b 4	c 2	d 3	e 6	f 1
Q11	a 4	b 5	c 3	d 1	e 2	f 6
Q12	a 1	b 4	c 3	d 5	e 2	f 6

41–51 You are Elizabeth
(*Pride and Prejudice*) – outgoing, funny and direct. You want a serious relationship, but it's essential for you to find someone you can have fun with or teach to have fun. Your best matches are: Mr Darcy, Henry Tilney, Captain Wentworth ...

64–71 You are Lydia
(*Pride and Prejudice*) – flirty, wild and thoughtless. You're not ready for a serious relationship – what you need is a series of fun flings, and any of these wild boys will do nicely – Henry Crawford, Willoughby, Mr Wickham ...

Source: *The Times*, 29 August 2005

The most common form of research in social science is based on simply asking questions and noting down the answers. Questions, either in questionnaires or interviews, are used equally in both qualitative and quantitative research. In this topic, we will explore the issues linked to the use of questionnaires and interviews and their relationship to particular methodological and theoretical approaches in sociology.

However, not all sociologists agree that just asking questions is enough:

<<Interviews and questionnaires allow access to what people say, but not to what they do. The only way to find out what 'actually happens' in a given situation is through observation.>> (Darlington and Scott 2002)

Questionnaires and interviews in qualitative and quantitative research

Quantitative approaches

Quantitative approaches commonly use one of the following:

● *Questionnaires* – written questions that respondents are requested to complete by themselves. To emphasize this and distinguish them from **structured interviews** (see opposite), quantitative-style questionnaires are often referred to as 'self-completion questionnaires'. This style of questionnaire is likely to contain a majority of **closed questions**, i.e. questions with a very specific answer or with a given set of answers from which the respondent must choose.

- *Structured interviews* – a series of questions read out directly by the researcher to the respondent. No variation or explanation is allowed. There is the possibility of using scripted **prompts**. These are best viewed as oral questionnaires.

Qualitative approaches

Qualitative researchers usually use **semistructured** or **unstructured** interviews. These use a series of questions as a starting point for the in-depth exploration of an issue. Qualitative researchers also use similar discussion techniques in group interviews (more than one person interviewed at the same time) or in focus groups (where a topic is introduced by the researcher and then the group take the discussion where they wish).

Self-completion questionnaires: a quantitative method

Questionnaires are used by sociologists when they are looking for specific information on a topic (often to support a hypothesis). They are extremely useful in surveys as they can reach a large number of people, since the printed questions can be handed out, mailed out, or put on the internet. Even though they are distributed to a large number or a widely dispersed group of people, they are still very easy to administer and can be very quickly organized and distributed. They provide clear information,

which can be converted into statistical data through the use of coding.

In terms of the sorts of questions asked, most questionnaires generally use closed, rather than **open**, questions, as without a researcher present, people may become confused if the questions are complex. Questionnaires are also particularly useful when it comes to asking embarrassing questions, where having an interviewer present may make the respondent feel uncomfortable.

Reliability

Questionnaires are highly standardized, so clearly everyone receives the same questions in the same format. This should make them highly reliable. However, it is never possible to know if everyone interprets the questions in the same way.

Generalizability and representativeness

Questionnaires are widely used in survey work. If the sampling has been correct, then the questionnaire should produce questions that are generalizable to the whole population. However, postal or internet questionnaires are not necessarily answered by the person they were sent to. Anyone in the household or with access to a computer could complete the questionnaire. This throws some doubt on representativeness and generalizability.

The second main problem with all self-completion questionnaires is the low **response rate**. Unfortunately, many people cannot be bothered to reply to questionnaires – unless there is some benefit to them, such as the chance to win a prize. This is a serious drawback of questionnaires in research. A low response rate (that is when only a small proportion of people asked actually replies) makes a survey useless, as you do not know if the small number of replies is representative of all who were sent the questionnaire. Those who reply might have strong opinions on an issue, whereas the majority of people may have much less firm convictions – without an adequate number of replies, you will never know. This often occurs when questions are asked about moral issues such as experiments on animals, or abortion/termination. This is a crucial issue, which impacts on the generalizability of any research using self-completion questionnaires.

Validity

Questionnaires can have high **validity** if they are well designed and seek out answers to relatively simple issues. However, there are a number of problems that they have to overcome to ensure these high levels of validity. People who reply to the questionnaire may interpret the questions in a different way from that which the researcher originally intended. So their replies might actually mean something different from what the researcher believes they mean. Even more problematic than this is the danger of people deliberately lying or evading the truth. There is little that the researcher can do, apart from putting in 'check questions' – which are questions that ask for the same information, but are phrased differently. However, without an interviewer present, the researcher can never really know if the answers are true. Parker *et al.* (1998) used questionnaires to find out what sorts of drugs young people were using over a period of time. Later, in follow-up interviews, one respondent said:

<< The first time we had this questionnaire, I thought it was a bit of a laugh. That's my memory of it. I can't remember if I answered it truthfully or not. … It had a list of drugs and some of them I'd never heard of, and just the names just cracked me up.>>

Designing a good questionnaire

When constructing a questionnaire, the sociologist has to ensure:

- *that the indicators are correct* – so that it asks the right questions, which unearth exactly the information wanted – in sociological terms, 'the concepts have been well operationalized'
- *that there is clarity* – the questions are asked in a short, clear and simple manner that can be understood by the people completing the questionnaire
- *that it is concise* – that it is as short as possible, since people usually cannot be bothered to spend a long time completing questionnaires
- *that it is unbiased* – the respondent is not led to a particular viewpoint or answer.

Collating and analysing self-completion questionnaires

As these are usually closed questionnaires, sociologists use a system known as 'coding'. This consists of allocating each answer a particular number and then putting all the answers into a type of spreadsheet. This spreadsheet can then be interrogated for information. All the different answers to the questions can be summarized and compared against each other. Sociologists have numerous statistical software packages for this.

Structured interviews: a quantitative approach

Quantitative researchers use highly structured interviews, with the interviewer simply reading out questions from a prepared questionnaire. Effectively, they are oral questionnaires in which the researcher writes down the answers. (Hence the use of the term 'self-completion questionnaire' to distinguish it from the highly structured interview.)

Structured interviews are often used in conjunction with quota sampling (see Topic 4, p. 283), as researchers often have to go out in the streets to seek people who fall into the categories allocated to them. Once the person is identified, then the researcher will proceed with the structured interview.

The aim of the structured interview is to increase the reliability of questionnaires; the interviewer's role is deliberately restricted to reading out the questions and recording the answers. In limiting the role of the interviewer to the minimum, the possibility of

interviewer bias is minimized and the possibility of reliability is maximized.

The advantages and disadvantages of structured versus unstructured interviewing are fully discussed in the next section.

Interviews: a mainly qualitative approach

Sociologists generally use interviews if the subject of enquiry is complex, and a self-completion questionnaire would not allow the researcher to explore the issues adequately.

Types of interviews

As we have seen, interviews fall between two extremes: structured and unstructured:

- At their most structured, they can be very tightly organized, with the interviewer simply reading out questions from a prepared questionnaire.
- At the other extreme, interviews can be highly unstructured – more like a conversation, where the interviewer simply has a basic area for discussion and asks any questions that seem relevant.
- In between is the semi-structured interview, where the interviewer has a series of set questions, but may also explore various avenues that emerge by **probing** the respondent for more information.

There are a three further types of specialist unstructured interviews sometimes used by sociologists:

1 *Oral history interviews* – Respondents are asked about specific events that have happened in their lifetimes, but not necessarily to them. These interviews are almost always used to link up with other secondary sources.
2 *Life history interviews* – These are a second form of unstructured interview in which people are asked to recount their lives. Like oral history interviews, this method is almost always linked to secondary sources.
3 *Group interviews* – Interviews are usually conducted on a one-to-one basis, but there are occasions when group interviews are useful and these have similar issues in terms of reliability and validity to focus groups (see Topic 5). Group interviews are commonly used where the researcher wants to explore a 'group dynamic', believing that a 'truer' picture emerges when the group is all together. An example of this is Mairtin Mac an Ghaill's *The Making of Men: Masculinities, Sexualities and Schooling* (1994), in which a group of gay students discuss their experiences of school.

Reliability

Interviews always involve some degree of interaction between researcher and respondent. As in every interaction, there is a range of interpersonal dynamics at work. Differences in age, ethnicity, social class, education and gender, amongst many other things, will impact on the interview. The less structured the interview, the greater the impact of these factors. Reliability levels are, therefore, much lower than for questionnaires and are directly related to the degree of structure of the interview. According to May (2001), the greater the structure, the higher the reliability – as the greater the chance of these variables being excluded and of the different interviews being comparable. However, Brenner *et al.* (1985) argue that 'any misunderstandings on the part of the interviewer and interviewee can be checked immediately in a way that is just not possible when questionnaires are being completed'. So, they believe that reliability is actually greater.

Representativeness and generalizability

Interviews are much more likely to be used in qualitative research, mainly because they allow for greater depth and exploration of ideas and emotions. Qualitative research tends to be more interested in achieving validity than representativeness. There is no reason why interviews should be any less generalizable than questionnaires, but as they are more likely to be used in non-representative studies, interviews have a reputation for being less generalizable. However, there is a much higher response rate with interviews than with questionnaires, as the process is more personal and it is often more difficult to refuse a researcher who approaches politely.

Validity

Interviews, particularly unstructured ones, have high levels of validity. The point of an unstructured interview is to uncover meaning and untangle complex views. Interviewing also has a significant advantage over self-completion questionnaires in that the interviewer is present and can often see if the respondent is lying or not. However, there are some problems ensuring that validity is high in interviewing.

We saw earlier that every interview is a social interaction with issues of class, gender, ethnicity and so on impacting on the relationship between the two people. Not only does this make each interview slightly different, it also means that validity can be affected. In particular, this can lead to the specific issue of interviewer bias – the extent to which the relationship between interviewer and respondent can change the respondents' answers to questions. There is a whole range of possibilities, from respondents wishing to please the interviewer at one extreme, to seeking to mislead at the other.

In fact, there is no reason why people should tell the truth to researchers, and this is particularly true when a sensitive issue is being researched. When questioned about sexual activities or numbers of friends, for example, people may well exaggerate in order to impress the interviewer. This can influence the validity of the research project. So it is rare now for interviews to be used for personal or embarrassing issues, with sociologists preferring self-report questionnaires.

Focus on research

Zoe James (2007)
Policing gypsies and travellers

Zoe James wanted to study groups who have a difficult relationship with the police and who are regarded both by themselves and the majority of people as 'marginal' to the wider society around them.

One part of James' study was on 'New Travellers', sometimes known as 'New Age Travellers'. The study was particularly difficult to do, as New Travellers are suspicious of outsiders and particularly researchers. Her study consisted of 17 in-depth interviews and one focus group with New Travellers living on unauthorized sites throughout the south-west region of England in 2005. Interviews were gained through use of 'snowball' sampling via initial contacts made by a 'gatekeeper'.

The research interviews were carried out in the form of 'guided conversations' (semi-structured interviews) that were not tape recorded, as the New Travellers were very wary of having their views directly recorded. James made notes of the conversations, but also took detailed notes of what she observed on the sites. These notes were 'taken contemporaneously, either in the field (often quite literally), or as soon as possible on leaving the research setting'.

James negotiated with the New Travellers over the form of research methodology and it was only after their full agreement – both as to the methods and the limits of James's research – that they agreed to take part in her work.

James found that despite new laws that provide the police and other enforcement agencies with a range of powers to control and evict travellers from sites, the travellers were determined to continue living their style of nomadic life – even if this meant breaking the law.

James, Z. (2007) 'Policing marginal spaces: Controlling Gypsies and Travellers', *Criminology and Criminal Justice*, 7(4), pp. 367–89

How does the extract above illustrate some of the problems involved in using questioning as a method of data collection?

It is easy for researchers, unknowingly, to slip their values into the research. Usually this happens in questionnaires as a result of the language used. In interviews there is a much wider possible range of influences to bias the research – as well as the language, there is the body language or facial expression of the researcher, or even their class, gender or ethnic background. In particular, interviewers should avoid leading questions.

Loaded words and phrases can also generate bias, i.e. the researchers use particular forms of language that either indicate a viewpoint or may generate a particular positive or negative response. For example, 'termination of pregnancy' (a positive view) or 'abortion' (a negative view); 'gay' or 'homosexual'.

The advantages of interviewing

- Interviewers can pick up non-verbal cues from interviewees.
- The interviewer can see whether the respondent might be lying, by seeing the situation through their own eyes.
- There is a higher response rate than with questionnaires.
- Interviews take place where interviewees feel comfortable.
- The more structured the interview, the higher the chance of replicating it and therefore of high reliability.
- The less structured the interview, the higher the validity as meaning can be explored.

Ethical issues in interviews

There can be significant ethical issues when using interviews in research, as the interviewer can gain considerable information about the interviewee – some of which is potentially embarrassing for the interviewee. Trust needs to be established very early on and the person being interviewed has to have a reassurance that the information will be confidential. Any information that is published will be done in such a way that the interviewee remains anonymous.

Dorothy Scott studied child abuse in a children's home (Darlington and Scott 2002).

<< Confidentiality also proved to be difficult as I became increasingly aware of the difficulty of presenting findings of research based on an intensive analysis of cases without using illustrations which might be recognizable to the staff or the clients.>> (p.38)

Collating and analysing interview data

Interviews are usually recorded and this recording is then **transcribed** (written up) into notes. This is an extremely time-consuming activity. For example. Tizard and Hughes (1991) recorded interviews with students to find out how they went about learning – and every one hour of interview took 17 hours to transcribe and check. However, researchers still prefer to do this, as taking notes at the time of the interview usually interrupts the flow, disrupting the atmosphere. The transcription is then studied for key themes. Increasingly, sociologists use special software that

can be set up to look for key words or phrases and will then collate these into categories. By recording and transcribing interviews, sociologists have independent evidence to support their claims, which they can also provide to other researchers should they wish to replicate the research. This is very important for qualitative sociologists, who are often criticized by quantitative researchers for their failure to provide independent evidence.

Check your understanding

1 Identify and explain three of the key issues in asking questions.

2 What do we mean when we talk about loaded questions and leading questions? Illustrate your answer with an example of each and show how the problem could be overcome by writing a 'correct' example of the same questions.

3 Why are 'response rates' so important?

4 When is it better to use questionnaires rather than interviews?

5 When would it be more appropriate to use unstructured interviews?

6 Give any two advantages of structured interviews compared with unstructured ones.

7 What do we mean by 'transcribing'?

Activities

Research idea

Find out about a sample of young people's experience of schooling. Draft a closed questionnaire to collect this data. Collect and analyse the data quantitatively. Then draft guide questions for an unstructured interview to find out about the same issue. Conduct two or three of these interviews, either taping or making notes of the responses.

Compare the two sorts of data. What differences are there? Why do those differences occur?
Which method do you think was most effective for that particular purpose? Why?

Web.task

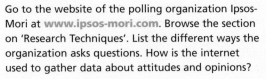

Go to the website of the polling organization Ipsos-Mori at **www.ipsos-mori.com**. Browse the section on 'Research Techniques'. List the different ways the organization asks questions. How is the internet used to gather data about attitudes and opinions?

Key terms

Closed questions questions that require a very specific reply, such as 'yes' or 'no'.

Interviewer bias the influence of the interviewer (e.g. their age, 'race', gender) on the way the respondent replies.

Open questions questions that allow the respondent to express themselves fully.

Probing encouraging the interviewee to expand on an answer, e.g. by asking them directly to expand or simply remaining silent as if expecting more detail from the respondent.

Prompts possible answers to a question.

Response rate the proportion of questionnaires that is returned (could also refer to the number of people who agree to be interviewed).

Semistructured interview where the interviewer has a series of set questions, but may also explore avenues that emerge by probing the respondent for more information.

Structured interview where the questions are delivered in a particular order and no explanation or elaboration of the questions is allowed by the interviewer.

Transcribing the process of writing up interviews that have been recorded.

Unstructured interview where the interviewer is allowed to explain and elaborate on questions.

Validity refers to the problem of ensuring that the questions actually measure what the researcher intends them to.

An eye on the exam — Questionnaires & interviews in research

Item A

<< We set out to compare how crime has been perceived by ordinary working class people at different periods over the last 60 years. We therefore decided to gather testimony from three generations of people. Fifty-four full-length tape-recorded interviews were completed (with 34 men and 20 women). Informants were drawn from various parts of the London Borough of Tower Hamlets. We aimed to find people who could provide testimony which would allow experiences, memories and interpretations of the past. There were obvious problems in interpreting and comparing testimonies about life in the East End over the last 50 years. We recognized that the recalling of images of the past would be affected by a number of factors: selective amnesia, telescoping of events, reinterpretation in the light of previous experiences, suppression of unpleasant memories or exaggeration of one's own involvement. We certainly came across informants who talked of the 'good old days' recounting stories of bed-bug infestation and chronic overcrowding while still insisting that 'life was better then'. >>

Hood, R. and Joyce, K. (1999) 'Three generations: oral testimonies on crime and social change in London's East End', *British Journal of Criminology*, 39(1)

Using material from **Item A** and elsewhere, assess the view that in-depth interviewing is the most useful research method for sociologists.

(33 marks)

Grade booster — Getting top marks in this question

This requires you to define and explain the nature of in-depth interviewing. You should then give a couple of examples of where it is particularly useful. Use material from Item A to illustrate some of your points. However, no one research method is better than any other overall, rather some methods are better than others for particular areas of investigation. For example, in-depth interviewing is excellent for exploring individual beliefs and motivations, but so is a focus group. There are also a number of limitations with in-depth interviewing, for example the high costs, the amount of time the interviews take (therefore precluding a big survey) and the possible influence of the researcher.

You need, therefore, to look at how other methods could be useful in different areas of research. Clearly, you cannot look at all other methods, but some discussion should focus on observational research and some on questionnaires and large-scale surveys.

Secondary data

Getting you thinking

It is beautiful day in September 1944 near the end of the Second World War in a little mountain village in Tuscany, Italy. The United States and British forces are about fifty miles away and slowly advancing and pushing the occupying German forces back.

At the village of Cerpiano, Cornelia Paselli and the rest of the family had been woken early by her father.

"Wake up! Wake up! The Germans are burning houses, it's not safe here. Go and take refuge in the church."

At about 9 o'clock there was a banging on the (church) doors and the German troops shouted at them to come out. The soldiers ushered them down a track ... towards the cemetery and ... told them to get inside.

"A number of the women began to shout and cry and everyone was pushing, she says, forwards, backwards – like a waving mass" says Cornelia.

A German came in with a machine gun and set it up in the left hand corner in front of them and began loading cylinders of ammunition onto and beside the gun.

Suddenly, one woman began to panic. 'I want to go to my daughter!' she shouted, running forward. She was shot dead immediately.

"Then there was a kind of jolt," says Cornelia, "an explosion so intense that I was thrown into the air and landed in the middle of the crowd'. People were shouting and crying, calling out names, others screaming for help and then the machine gun started firing. Bodies started falling on top of her and around her. The she fainted. When she came to again, more bodies were piled around her. She could hear voices and then her mother calling out "Cornelia, Cornelia are you still alive?"

"Mama please be quiet", she whispered back. "Don't talk otherwise they will kill you". But her mother called out for her other daughter. Then a shot rang out.

"Dead bodies are really heavy", she says, "but eventually I managed to free myself". There was no one about except the dead and wounded. She thought to go back to Cerpiano, but she could still see troops and heard shouting from the village and so, instead ran down the valley barefoot through the brambles and scrub.

191 people were killed in the cemetery.

Adapted from: Holland, J. (2008) *Italy's Sorrow: A Year of War 1944–45*, London: Harper Press (pp. 379–81)

1 What are your immediate reactions to the extract above?

2 How do you think the author obtained the information?

3 Do you believe it?

4 Do you think there could be another side to the story (i.e. that of the Germans)?

5 How could we find out?

6 If you wanted to study a topic that happened in 1945, what would you do?

7 Can you think of any problems that might result from using information about an occurrence where you were not present?

In this topic, we explore the way that sociologists can make use of material collected by other people for whatever reason. Because these resources are 'second-hand', when the sociologist comes to examine the data, they are called **secondary data**. However, it is important to remember that they have equal status amongst sociologists with **primary data**, and can be just as difficult to collect and interpret as primary sources. Both qualitative and quantitative researchers make use of secondary sources for a variety of reasons, which we will explore in this topic.

A huge range of material can be considered as secondary data. Bryman (2004) suggests the following categories:

- *Life (personal) documents* – These include diaries, letters, emails, photographs and video recordings. They may be written down, or in visual or aural (i.e. can be heard) form.
- *Official documents* – These derive from the state and include official statistics, government and local authority reports, minutes of government meetings and of Parliament, and the whole range of officially sanctioned publications available.
- *Other documents that derive from organizational sources* – By this, Bryman means the publications of profit-making companies, charities and any other organization that produces some form of formal output.
- *The contents of the mass media* – This is a whole area of study by itself. The mass media refers to all organizations producing information and entertainment for a public audience. This includes radio, television, the internet, newspapers and magazines, and novels.
- *Previous sociological research* – This covers all previously published sociological research and datasets.

Webb *et al.* (1981) also argue for the use of **trace measures** – these are the physical changes produced by human action, such as the number of lager cans left around a building after a group of young people go home after hanging around for the evening.

Approaches to secondary data

Sociologists take different approaches towards analysing and using secondary data. There are four main approaches, outlined below.

Extraction

Extraction simply involves taking statistics or research examples from the original texts. It is commonly used when sociologists examine previous sociological sources and databases.

Content analysis

In **content analysis**, documents and other sources are examined in great detail to see what themes run through them. There are two ways of doing this:

- Qualitative content analysis stresses exploring the meaning and looking for examples to illustrate the themes. This method is particularly commonly used in studies of the mass media.
- On the other hand, quantitative analysis will almost certainly use computer programs, which will count the number of times certain words (which are regarded as indicators of themes) or themes are used.

Semiotics

Semiotics is the study of signs. A sign is something that stands for something other than itself. For example, a Mohican haircut may indicate a rebellious attitude, or a St George's Cross painted on a face signifies support for an England sports team. Semiotics is often used in the study of youth culture, and is apparent in the work of both Marxist cultural studies writers and of postmodernist writers. Both these groups seek to analyse the meaning of the particular clothes, music and 'argot' used by young people. Similarly, sociologists interested in semiotics try to uncover the hidden meaning within the secondary data. It is particularly used in the study of **life documents**, especially photos and in music.

Hermeneutics

The term **hermeneutics** is used for the approach which seeks to analyse the secondary sources from the perspective of the person or organization originally compiling the data. A hermeneutic analysis will look carefully at the political, social and economic context of the secondary data. Again, this is more commonly used in life documents and less commonly in sources from organizations.

Advantages and disadvantages of using secondary sources

Advantages of using secondary sources

All sociological research begins with a **literature search**, or review, of all relevant previous sociological research on the particular topic under investigation. If the information required already exists, even if in a different form, the researcher does not have to repeat the original research. Alternatively, the researcher may use the original data to re-examine previously published data or studies in order to interpret them in a new theoretical light.

Often, sociologists want to look back in history for information but there is no one able to provide a life or oral history. In these cases, the sociologist must use secondary sources, such as **official documents** and letters.

Sometimes, it is impossible for the researcher actually to visit or talk to the group directly. This could be for financial reasons, or because the group may be geographically too distant or scattered. More commonly, the sociologist thinks that studying the group directly would be too obtrusive. This is where trace measures are often used.

For instance, sociologists studying crime and deviance are often faced with situations where direct studies of the group might be considered unethical – a good example is research on children where it may not be possible to get informed consent. Although some sociologists are prepared to engage in participant observational methods, for example, that can involve them in illegal or immoral activities, other sociologists prefer to study these activities with the use of secondary data.

Finally, and overlapping with the previous point, there are groups engaged in activities that they do not want sociologists to study, because they may be illegal, deviant or immoral. For sociologists studying these groups, one of the few ways to gain information is to access any secondary data available.

Disadvantages of using secondary sources

All secondary sources (except trace sources) are created for a reason; this could well create bias and distortion. Government statistics are often neutral, but they are also often constructed in such a way as to throw a positive light on events or statistics. At worst, they can be simple propaganda. Private organizations, such as companies, are concerned to produce a positive image of themselves. They will, therefore, only produce information that promotes this image. This applies equally to charities and any other form of organization.

Life documents, such as a diary, give a very one-sided view of what happened and are almost always bound to be sympathetic to the writer.

Historical sources contain the possibility of bias, which we have already noted for other secondary sources, but there is the even greater problem, according to May (2001), of their being influenced by particular historical events or cultural ways of thinking that the sociologist may not be aware of.

Finally, as we have seen throughout the book, the work of sociologists may contain errors and biases.

Assessing the quality of secondary data

Scott (1990) suggests that there are four criteria to use when judging the usefulness of secondary data to the researcher. These are:

1 *Authenticity* – Is the origin of the data known and does the evidence contained there seem genuine?
2 *Credibility* – Are the data free from error and distortion?
3 *Representativeness* – Is the evidence shown by the data typical of its kind?
4 *Meaning* – Is the evidence clear and comprehensive?

We will use these to guide us through the usefulness of each type of secondary source.

Types of secondary data

Life documents

Life documents include virtually all written, aural and visual material that derives from people's personal lives, including diaries, letters, emails, photographs and video recordings.

Traditionally, the material used by sociologists was written, but, increasingly, there has been a growth in visual material such as photographs and home videos.

Life documents can give sociologists a detailed and very personal look into people's lives; as a way of seeing events through their eyes, it is an unrivalled method. They are also particularly useful when there is no other way to get hold of information, for example if the events happened a long time ago and there is no one to interview. However, the writers may have distorted views of what happened, or they may well be justifying or glorifying themselves in their accounts.

Plummer (2000) suggested that the main forms of life documents include diaries, letters, photographs, film and what he calls '**miscellanea**', which consist of anything else reflecting one's life. We will examine each of these in turn.

Diaries

The key thing about diaries is that they chronicle events as they happen, rather than being filtered by memory or later events, as is the case with autobiographies. Diaries are also very detailed as they cover events day by day. This daily writing is also useful as if gives the sociologist a real idea of the exact timing of when things happened.

However, diaries cannot be relied upon for 'the truth', as people are not objective about their own lives. Instead they filter what happens around them according to their own **biases** and perceptions. It is also important to remember why the diaries were being written, as many politicians and journalists have published diaries that were specifically written for later publication (for example, the diaries of the politician Tony Benn). This would suggest that the contents will be biased to ensure that they come to be perceived by the reader in a positive fashion.

Letters

The most famous example of the use of letters in sociology is Thomas and Znaniecki's *The Polish Peasant* (1918). This is a study of the correspondence of recent immigrants to the United States with their families back in Poland. Thomas and Znaniecki placed an advert in the Chicago newspaper offering to pay for each letter handed to them, and received hundreds of letters. The letters gave them insights into the ordinary lives of immigrants and the issues that concerned them in their new lives in the USA. It also told them about the changes that occurred in family life and relationships as a result of the movement. The letters were divided into various categories by Thomas and Znaniecki, so there were:

- ceremonial letters, which marked formal occasions such as marriages, deaths and birthdays
- informal letters about everyday life
- sentimental letters about love and how family members were missed
- letters asking for and sending money and financial advice.

However, letters are always written with some purpose in mind and to convey a particular image of a person. For example, in Thomas and Znaniecki's work, the immigrant letter writers wanted to demonstrate to the people left in Poland what a success they had made of their lives, and so this 'filter' had to be taken into account when reading the letters.

Visual images

Millions of photographs and images are produced every year by families as the most common form of documenting their lives. Photographs have a very long history in sociology, and in the early days of sociology in America, almost all research was illustrated with photographs. More recently, some sociologists have used photographs to 'capture' images of people's lives as a form of ethnographic study. Jackson (1978) used mainly photographs to explore the lives of prisoners, and Harper (1978) photographed the lives of homeless people. These two sociologists argued that using image rather than text provides a powerful insight into people's lives.

Sutton (1992), however, is very critical of the use of photographs in sociological research. He points out that photographs are almost always taken when groups or families are engaged in holiday or festive occasions and that the photographs are also constructed to reflect a happy image ('Say cheese!'). He conducted a study of visits to Disneyland and concluded that these happy images reinforced the pleasant memories that families had of their visits, helping to forget the more negative experiences. Sutton therefore suggests that to use photographs (and videos) in research has serious drawbacks. However, as Plummer (2000) points out, photographs of events are not restricted to family holidays and occasions, and there is a wide variety of photographic images available which are not necessarily biased.

Miscellanea

Plummer uses this category to include the huge variety of other personal 'documents' that sociologists have used. For example, Schwartz and Jacobs (1979) studied people's suicide notes to try to understand the thoughts and emotion of people in their last hours before death.

However, the same point has to be made regarding miscellanea as for all other life documents. The documents were produced for an effect; they do not necessarily represent the truth or even what people really thought. Taking the example of suicide notes, Schwartz and Jacobs point out that they were often intended to make other people feel guilty and to punish them. They were, therefore, written for an audience and may not necessarily tell their true feelings.

Official publications

Statistics compiled by governments and reputable research organizations are routinely used by sociologists. Governments have entire departments devoted to the production of statistics. In the UK, the Office for National Statistics produces statistics and collates them from other departments. These statistics provide far greater scale and detail than sociologists can generally achieve and offer a source of information that is readily available, comprehensive and cheap to access.

Usually, the government will produce these statistics over a number of years – for example, the government statistical publication *Social Trends* has been published for over 35 years. It is therefore possible to make comparisons at various points in time.

Although these official statistics have many advantages, there are also some problems facing researchers using them. The statistics are collected for administrative reasons and the classifications used may omit crucial information or might classify groupings or activities in a way that is inappropriate for the researcher. A researcher might be interested in the link between religion and income, but the official statistics may be collated on the grounds of ethnic origin or gender and average income.

Official statistics may also be affected by political considerations, as government will always seek to present the statistics in the most positive light. They may also reflect a complex process of interaction and negotiation – as is the case with crime statistics – and may well need to be the focus of investigation themselves!

Reports and government inquiries

The Civil Service and other linked organizations will often produce official reports that investigate important problems or social issues. However, although they draw together much information on these issues, they are constrained by their 'remit', which states the limits of their investigations. The government and other powerful bodies are therefore able to exclude discussion of issues that they do not want to become the centre of public attention. For example, McKie *et al.* (2004) examined official government policy documents on health improvements for families in Britain. They used a particular perspective in their analysis, in that they explored exactly what benefits there would be for women as opposed to other family members. They conclude that there were significant gender inequalities in the official documents, with assumptions about the role of women being to care for other family members.

Documents from other sources

An enormous range of documents is produced by non-governmental organizations (NGOs) – that is, private companies, charities and other social groups. These include annual reports, press releases, advertisements and a range of statistical information about the company's aims and achievements. Increasingly, these are brought into the public domain via the internet.

However, sociologists are even more wary of taking NGOs' materials than they are of taking government ones. Most companies – and even non-profit-making organizations – have a vested interest in ensuring that their public image is positive. It is, therefore, extremely unlikely that negative information will be published by a company about itself. The complexity of using formal information produced by NGOs is illustrated by Forster's (1994) study of career-development opportunities in a large, multinational corporation. The more detail that Forster went into, the more contradictory the information he received:

> << One of the clearest themes to emerge was the apparently incompatible interpretations of the same events and processes amongst the three subgroups within the company – senior executives, HQ personnel and regional personnel managers. These documents were not produced deliberately to distort or obscure events or processes being described, but their effect was precisely to do this. >> (p. 160)

The mass media

The mass media produce an overwhelming amount of information each day, which not only reflects the concerns and values of society but also helps to shape these values. The mass media thus provide fertile ground for sociological researchers.

Content analysis is used by sociologists in order to discover how particular issues are presented. They can do this in two ways:

1   Using quantitative techniques, researchers simply count the number of times a particular activity or term appears in the media being analysed. This helps to prove a particular hypothesis, e.g. regarding the numbers of people from minority-ethnic backgrounds appearing on television. A slightly more sophisticated version of this might be to construct a content analysis grid, where two or more themes can be linked, e.g. the number of times that newspapers run stories that link people from minority-ethnic backgrounds with negative events.

2   In a similar way to the second form of quantitative analysis, researchers may use a qualitative form of content analysis to draw out general themes from the newspapers, film or television. They will, for example, seek to establish not just whether there is a negative association between ethnicity and social problems, but what forms any such association might take.

Quantitative approaches are useful for several reasons:

● They provide clear, unambiguous statistics on the number of times topics appear in the press or are broadcast.

● They can clearly state the criteria they use for the selection of themes.

● They are replicable – other sociologists can return to the original sources and check their accuracy.

However, qualitative approaches have the strength of being able to explore the meaning of the theme or item being researched. Just having the number of times that an item is mentioned in the media does not give a true image of what is being discussed or the importance of the discussion. So, qualitative analyses tend to be more valid but less reliable.

Content analysis is very widely used in sociology because accessing mass-media material and analysing it is simple and relatively cheap. Furthermore, there are no problems in finding a representative sample, as it is possible to obtain a wide variety of newspapers or television programmes. Importantly, it is an unobtrusive method of research – recording a television programme and then analysing it for its content themes does not impact in any way on the making of the programme.

However, Macdonald and Tipton (1993) suggest there is considerable risk of bias and distortion, for two main reasons:

● There are errors of various kinds, most importantly, errors of fact, as the standards of journalists are not as high as those of academics.

● There is distortion of the facts – Newspapers and television programmes have various preferences as to what can be considered news and what 'angle' to approach the news from. The influences include journalistic values, proprietor's values and, perhaps most important in a competitive market, the audience at which the journalists perceive themselves to be aiming the news.

Furthermore, as Cohen (2002) points out, there is no single correct way to 'read' a newspaper's or television programme's hidden meanings. Each sociologist will approach the interpretation of the contents from their own perspective. Therefore, both reliability and validity are low in content-analysis studies.

One final further difficulty sociologists have in content analysis is actually knowing how the viewers or readers interpret the media output. We know from Morley's research (1980) that people approach and understand television programmes from very different perspectives. Sociologists cannot assume that the interpretation they have – even as a group of researchers agreeing on the content's meaning – will be the same as that of the viewer.

Sociological research and data archives

There are a number of **data archives** in Britain where the results of large research studies are stored. These can be accessed and the information reused by other researchers. Many of these can be found at The Data Archive (www.data-archive.ac.uk), based at the University of Essex. This holds over 4000 datasets from government, academic researchers and opinion poll organizations.

The huge advantage of these datasets is that they provide ready-made material. However, the information that the original researchers were seeking may not be the same as what is needed by the researcher using them as secondary data. If the researcher is not careful, it is possible to be led astray by the focus of the original research.

Although we have categorized data sets as purely sociological research, it is worth knowing that some are wholly or part-funded by the government. However, as they tend to collect information that is sociological in character rather than politically sensitive, most sociologists classify government-sponsored datasets as sociological research.

Perhaps the best-known data set is the Census, a survey of all people and households in the country, which takes place every ten years (the last Census was 2001, the next is 2011). All households in Britain are required to complete this by law. It is intended to be the most complete picture of Britain available. In recent years, there has been some concern that not everyone completes the Census – in particular, certain minority-ethnic groups, refugees and asylum seekers, and transient populations such as the homeless and travellers. It may, therefore, underrepresent certain categories of the population.

Other well-known data sets include the longitudinal British Household Panel Survey and the General Household Survey which collects information on:

- housing patterns
- income
- education
- demographic changes
- ownership of consumer items
- household and family information.
- health services usage
- employment
- smoking and drinking

Focus on research

Blanden and Machin (2007)
Intergenerational social mobility

In 2005, Jo Blanden and Stephen Machin investigated what changes have taken place in intergenerational mobility in the UK. In order to do this, they had to rely upon secondary data, which involved comparing the mobility of people born in 1958 compared to 1970.

Blanden and Machin used data that was already available in other surveys, but combined the results and used a slightly different method of categorizing mobility. Specifically, they used information from two very large national surveys: the British Household Panel Survey and the Millennium Cohort Study.

By doing this, they avoided duplicating work already done; they saved time and money and they were able to access historical information (about those born in 1958) which it would have been impossible to obtain – unless they could engage in time-travel!

The study indicated that levels of social mobility have declined recently. Their evidence for this conclusion came from analyses of income similarities between parents and children and also in educational attainment across generations – both pieces of information were obtained from surveys which were originally carried out for very different purposes.

Blanden, J. and Machin, S. (2007) *Recent Changes in Intergenerational Mobility in Britain,* London: The Sutton Trust

Explain why Blanden and Machin used secondary data in their research.

Previous sociological research studies

Previous studies as a starting point

Whenever sociologists undertake a study, the first thing they do is to carry out a literature search – that is, go to the library or the internet and look up every available piece of sociological research on the topic of interest. They can then see the ways in which the topic has been researched before, the conclusions reached and the theoretical issues thrown up. Armed with this information, the researcher can then construct the new research study to explore a different 'angle' on the problem or simply avoid the mistakes made earlier.

Reinterpreting previous studies

Often, sociologists do not want to carry out a new research project, but prefer instead to examine previous research in great detail in order to find a new interpretation of the original research results; the secondary data (that is, the original piece of sociological research) provide all the information that is needed. Sometimes, sociologists might conduct a **meta-analysis**. This is a formal term for the process of looking at the whole range of research on a topic and seeking to identify and draw together common findings.

A good example of how previous sociological work was used as secondary data is provided by Goodwin and O'Connor's (2005) re-examination of a little-known sociological study undertaken in the early 1960s on the lives of young people as they left school and entered work. They compared this with the transition from school to work today. The early work provided them with a detailed and rich database from which they could form hypotheses and make comparisons with contemporary research.

Sometimes, however, there are methodological errors in published research, as well as possible bias in the research findings. There have been many examples of research that has formed the basis for succeeding work and that only many years later has been found to be faulty. A famous piece of anthropological research which was used for 40 years before it was found to be centrally flawed was Mead's *Coming of Age in Samoa* (1928). Mead made a number of mistakes in her interpretation of the behaviour of the people she was studying, but as no one knew this, many later studies used her (incorrect) findings in their work.

Trace measures

One of the problems faced by all sociological researchers is the degree to which their presence and activities actually changes the natural behaviour of the participants. This problem is well recognized in participant observation and experimentation, but also exists to a lesser degree in survey work.

Webb has argued that sociology should use 'unobtrusive measures' in research wherever this is possible, so that this problem is eliminated (Webb *et al.* 1966). He points out that when people interact, they will often leave behind them some physical sign of their activities, the trace measures referred to earlier. According to Webb, there are two types of trace measures:

1 *Erosion measures, which refer to things missing* – The most famous example of erosion measures (and the origin of the term) was the fact that the tiles around a particular exhibit in the Chicago Museum of Science and Industry, which showed real chicks hatching out from their eggs, had to be replaced every six weeks because they became worn out by the sheer numbers of people visiting this exhibit. However, the rest of the museum only needed its tiles replacing after some years.

2 *Accretion measures, which refer to things being added* – They were used by Rathje and Murphy (2002) in their study of rubbish thrown out by households, but they have also been used in studying graffiti in Belfast (to indicate 'ownership' of particular areas) and litter patterns (to demonstrate public use of space).

Check your understanding

1 What are secondary data?

2 What do we mean by the term 'hermeneutics'? Give one other example of ways of approaching the study of documents.

3 Why do sociologists use secondary sources?

4 What are the disadvantages of using secondary sources?

5 What are the advantages and disadvantages of using official statistics and other government documents?

6 What are the advantages and disadvantages of using qualitative secondary data, such as diaries?

7 Give two examples of data archives. How can these be used by sociologists?

8 How can sociologists use trace measures in research?

Activities

Research idea

You can conduct a simple trace measure experiment. Go around your house/garden and look at the objects lying around (anything from a photograph or a scratch in some wood to a CD) and think about the memories that these bring up. Think about the changes in you and your family since these first appeared, and what your feelings are.

Web.task

You are probably a member of a social networking site, such as Facebook. Log on and look through the photos, descriptions, etc., of any friends or other contacts you have on it. What kinds of images do people want to present of themselves? Are there some common themes?

Key terms

Bias where the material reflects a particular viewpoint to the exclusion of others; this may give a false impression of what happened and is a particular problem for secondary sources.

Content analysis exploring the contents of the various media in order to find out how a particular issue is presented.

Data archives where statistical information is stored.

Extraction taking statistics or research examples from the original texts.

Hermeneutics the approach that seeks to understand the mindset of the person writing the original data, by exploring the context in which the document was first created.

Life (personal) documents personal data in written, visual or aural form, including diaries, letters, emails, photographs and video recordings.

Literature search/review the process whereby a researcher finds as much published material as possible on the subject of interest, usually through library catalogues or the internet.

Meta-analysis studying a range of research on a particular topic in order to identify common findings.

Miscellanea a term used by Plummer (2000) to refer to a range of life documents other than letters and diaries.

Official documents publications produced by the government.

Primary data Data collected by the sociologist themselves.

Secondary data data already collected by someone else for their own purposes.

Semiotics the study of the meaning of signs; data are examined for symbolic meaning and reinterpreted in this light.

Trace measures physical changes as a result of human actions.

An eye on the exam · Secondary data

Item A

Sociologists sometimes make use of personal documents in their research. Personal documents include items such as diaries, letters, photo albums, portraits and so on. They can be particularly valuable in situations where it is impossible to interview someone or get them to complete a questionnaire, such as when we want to study the past and there are no survivors from the period we are interested in. For example, Aries studied the emergence of the modern notion of childhood by examining portraits painted of children and adults in the past. Personal documents are particularly useful for sociologists who want to gain insight into a person's life and worldview.

Using material from **Item A** and elsewhere, assess the usefulness of personal documents in sociological research.

(33 marks)

Grade booster · Getting top marks in this question

Personal documents (which we have called 'life documents' in this topic) are one form of secondary data used by sociologists. You should begin by briefly outlining the concept of secondary data and why they are relevant to sociology. Life or personal documents are useful in showing how individuals perceive the world. Illustrate this with reference to material from the Item. For example, you can explain the usefulness of personal documents in studying the past and gaining insight into people's lives.

You should outline the main types of personal documents – diaries, letters, visual images and (to use Plummer's term), miscellanea. Detail the strengths and weaknesses of each. Finally, you could conclude with the clear statement that, subject to the weaknesses you have noted in your answer, personal documents are extremely useful in certain circumstances – in particular, gaining the views of participants in historical or hard-to-access situations (e.g. prisons).

Getting you thinking

1 Do you agree that we should continue to experiment on animals?

2 Do you think that it is acceptable to engage in

   (a) picketing and protests

   (b) illegal, possibly violent activities,

   in order to stop animal testing?

3 Imagine you have been given an opportunity to study scientists working in a lab who actually perform the 'experiments' on the animals.

   (a) What would you like to find out?

   (b) What would the first three questions of your questionnaire be?

   (c) Do you think that you could conduct a series of interviews with the scientists without letting your views come across?

One of the most bitterly contested concepts in sociology has been over the question of the place of personal and political values in theory and research. Three distinct positions can be identified on this issue.

1 At one end of the debate are those sociologists who argue that if sociology wants to make any claim to scientific status then it has to be free of personal and political biases. This is known as **value freedom** or **objectivity**.

2 A second position is that, ideally, our personal values should not intrude into our sociological studies, but that in practice it is simply impossible to keep them out – sociology as **value laden**.

3 At the other extreme from value freedom are those who argue that anyone doing sociology must surely use their studies to improve the condition of those most oppressed in society. Sociology is, therefore, more a tool that helps bring about social change – **committed** sociology – than just an academic subject studying society.

Value-free sociology

As we saw in Topics 3 and 4, there is a significant current of opinion in sociology (deriving from Emile Durkheim) that argues that we should seek to copy the methodology of the physical sciences such as biology or chemistry. One

of the key ideas that these sociologists, or **positivists**, have taken from the physical sciences is that of the importance of objectivity in research.

As discussed earlier, positivists argue that the nature of sociological research is no different from that of the physical sciences – both branches of science (the physical and the social) study a series of phenomena that exist totally independently of the scientists, and which can be measured and classified. On the basis of this, theories can be constructed and tested.

The 'social facts' positivists refer to are the statistics obtained by surveys and, possibly, from official publications. Properly constructed, they claim, these should be a perfect reflection of the subject under study. The evidence to show that surveys are objective and accurate exists in the accuracy of opinion polls on a range of subjects including voting and general elections; market research; extent of drug use and even sexual behaviour.

According to O'Connell Davidson and Layder (1994), personal biases and political opinions of researchers are irrelevant as long as the research is well designed and there is no attempt to distort or alter the findings. Finally, to ensure that no biases have inadvertently intruded, there is the check coming from publication of the research findings, which will include a discussion of methods used. The publication will be read and possibly criticized by other researchers.

Value-laden sociology

This second school of thought believe that whether it is desirable or not, sociology cannot be value free and it is a mistake to see it as such. They further claim that sociologists arguing that sociology is value free are actually doing a disservice to the subject, and they identify a number of issues as evidence in support of their position.

Historical context

Gouldner (1968) has pointed out that the argument for a value-free sociology is partially based in a particular historical context. Weber has traditionally been associated with the idea that personal and political values should be excluded from research. Yet Gouldner claims that Weber was writing at a time when the Prussian (now German) government was making a strong attack on intellectual freedom. According to Gouldner, Weber was merely trying to prevent the government from interfering in sociology by claiming it was value free.

Paying for research

Sociological research has to be financed, and those who pay for the research usually have a reason why they want it done. Sociologists working for British government departments, for instance, usually have to sign an agreement that if the department does not like the ideas or findings, then it has the right to prevent publication.

In *Market Killing*, Philo and Miller (2000) have argued that, increasingly, all sciences are having their critical researchers silenced through a combination of targeted funding by those who only want research undertaken into the topics of benefit to them and by the intrusion of commercial consultancies into research. This means that scientists benefit financially from certain outcomes and lose out if other outcomes are uncovered. They also point out that scientists allow their findings to be manipulated by public-relations companies, operating for the benefit of the funders – even when the findings do not necessarily support the funder's claims.

Career trajectories

As Gouldner (1968) pointed out, all sociologists have personal ambitions and career goals. They want to publish, get promoted, become renowned in their field. These desires can intrude either knowingly or subconsciously into their research activities. According to Kuhn (1962/1970), this involves accepting the dominant 'paradigms' at any particular time within sociology.

Personal beliefs and interests

Sociologists are no different from other people, in that they hold a set of values and moral beliefs. They might set out to eliminate these as best they can, but, ultimately, all our thoughts and actions are based on a particular set of values and it is impossible to escape from these. The best that can be done is to attempt to make these values clear to both ourselves and to the readers of the research.

Similarly, sociologists find certain areas of study 'interesting'. Why are they drawn to these areas in the first place? Often they reflect personal issues and a desire to explore something important to them. This makes it more difficult to extricate personal values from the research process itself. An example of this is the work of Ken Plummer (2000), who has published widely on sexual issues and is a sociologist associated with 'queer theory'. He makes it plain that his own sexual preference encouraged him to become interested in gay issues:

>> *So, in a sense, I was actually exploring my own life side by side with exploring sociological theory. And I suppose that has shaped the way I think about these things today.* >>

Similarly, feminist writers are drawn to subjects of particular interest to women. Indeed, Harding (1986) accuses male sociologists of being biased in their choice of subject matter, and in their selection of 'facts'.

The domain of sociology

Today, sociology does have academic status and has been accepted as a 'social science'. As a subject, it has developed a range of accepted ways of exploring the world, of sensible questions to be asked and reasonable research methods. It has joined other subjects in rejecting other non-orthodox approaches that claim to provide knowledge. For example, Collins and Pinch (1998) studied parapsychology and found that other social scientists believed that parapsychology was simply fantasy, therefore any research conducted by parapsychologists was dismissed out of hand. Any positive outcomes were simply regarded as the result of poor experimental methods or quite simply fraudulent.

The reasons why social scientists have rejected non-orthodox approaches become clear when we consider the work of postmodernists and of Foucault below. A good contemporary example is discussed by Mark J. Smith (2008), who points to the great difficulty that environmental or 'green' sociology has had in getting its concerns about the environment accepted by the sociological 'establishment' – as green concerns are seen as peripheral to the subject.

The postmodern critique

Postmodernists such as Lyotard (1984) and Baudrillard (1998) argue that the whole process of sociological and scientific thinking is itself based on a series of values about the nature of society. As we saw in our discussion of the growth of scientific thinking (Topic 3), science itself is a product of modernist thought.

Postmodernists dispute the assertion that rational thinking based upon verifiable evidence is superior to any other approach to understanding the world. They argue that, in fact, scientific thinking is just one of many possible ways of approaching an understanding of the world and that it is not inherently better – nor does it provide any superior 'truths'. Quite simply, the process of science is based upon a set of values, and all that a sociologist does is derived from a set of values, which are no 'truer' than any other set of values. In writing about their research, postmodernists have adopted two tactics:

1 *Reflexivity* – This involves sociologists including information about themselves and their roles when actually constructing the research, and seeking to show how they may have influenced it.
2 *Narratives* – This is the name given to the different viewpoints and voices that the researcher allows to be heard in the research. Here, the postmodern sociologist is not trying to dominate the account of the research but to put forward different views of the various subjects of the research. Plummer (2000) has used this in his accounts of gay men's life histories.

Foucault

A similar argument is put forward by Foucault (1977) in his analysis of knowledge. He argues that what is considered to be knowledge reflects the ability of more powerful groups to impose their ideas on the rest of society. By gaining control over the production of knowledge (methodology), one also gains control over what is considered knowledge. In an argument similar to that of postmodernists, Foucault therefore argues that the 'value-free' process itself is actually based on a set of values.

Committed sociology

The third approach comes from those who argue that sociology should not be value free but should have some explicit values guiding its approach to study (i.e. it should be committed). The most ardent advocates of this approach are feminist writers and critical (or Marxist) sociologists. It has also been used by writers who are challenging racism and discrimination against people with disabilities. However, it was two sociologists from rather different traditions who started this approach.

Key themes

Crime and deviance

The debate between Howard Becker and Alvin Gouldner described in this topic centres on sociological approaches to the study of deviance. Becker is one of the originators of labelling theory – a theory which, he argues, takes the side of the 'underdogs' in society as it focuses on the ways these groups are labelled as deviant and targeted by the forces of social control. Gouldner disagrees. He believes that labelling theory ends up blaming what he calls the 'middle dogs' – groups such as the police who actually have very little real power. The study of deviance should instead focus on the really powerful groups who actually make the law and give groups like the police their orders.

Whose side are we on?

In the 1970s, a famous debate took place between Howard Becker and Alvin Gouldner. Both sociologists agreed that sociology should not be value free, but the debate that followed went on to ask: 'Well, if we are going to be committed, then what side shall we be on?'

Becker (1970) started the debate by arguing that sociology (or at least the study of deviance, his speciality) had traditionally been on the side of the more powerful, and so had looked at issues from the viewpoint of the police officer, the social worker or the doctor, rather than from those of the criminal, the client or the 'mental patient'. Becker called for sociology to look instead from the viewpoint of the 'underdog'. By examining issues from their perspective, new questions and 'facts' could emerge. This sort of approach is the one that was taken by labelling theorists such as Becker (see Chapter 6, p. 353).

Gouldner (1968) attacked Becker for this argument, claiming that it did not go far enough – and, indeed, merely strengthened the status quo. Gouldner argued that Becker's work still focused on the less powerful. After all, what real power do police officers, social workers and doctors actually have? According to Gouldner, sociology needs to study the really powerful, those who create the structures of oppression of which police officers are merely unimportant agents.

Marxist view

Exactly this sort of argument was taken up by **critical sociologists** or Marxists. Althusser (1969), a writer in the Marxist tradition, has argued that the role of sociology (which he viewed as a science) is to uncover the ways in which the ruling class control the mass of the population. In doing so, sociologists hope to achieve the breakdown of capitalism by exposing the truth of how it operates for the benefit of a few.

A good example of this form of argument comes from the critical (Marxist) criminologists Taylor, Walton and Young who argued in *The New Criminology* (1973) that 'radical criminological strategy … is to show up the law, in its true colours, as the instrument of the ruling class … and that the rule-makers are also the greatest rule-breakers'. Interestingly, however, Young was later to co-found a very different school of sociology, **left realism**, which we explore below.

Feminist view

Feminist writers, such as Spender (1985), would agree with the idea of exposing the workings of an oppressive society, but also argue that the key is to explore how males dominate and control society. Again, the aim is exposing the truth, but the result is to free women from patriarchy.

There are four elements to feminist research, according to Hammersley (1992) – all of which demonstrate a rejection of searching for objectivity:

1 Feminist research starts with the belief that the subordination of women runs through all areas of social life.

2 Rather than seeking to exclude women's feelings and personal experience, these should form the basis of all analysis.

3 The **hierarchical** division between the researcher and the researched should be broken down so that the subjects of research should be drawn in to help interpret the data obtained. This would help the research belong to the women under study.

4 As the overall aim of feminist research is the emancipation of women, the success of research should only be measured in this, not solely in terms of academic credibility.

Feminist writers accuse sociology of traditionally being '**malestream**', that is, interested in male views and concerns, rather than trying to include views of both males and females.

Feminist writers such as Cain (1986) and Smart (1990) also argue that the categorization by sociologists into areas of study (criminology, social class, politics, and so on) has failed to show the pattern of oppression that women face in all these areas – only by transgressing these categories can feminists gain a real view of their situation and of patriarchy.

Left realism

Marxist or critical sociologists saw the role of sociology as uncovering the means by which capitalism oppressed the majority of the population. As we saw earlier, this call to arms was responded to enthusiastically by criminologists such as Taylor, Walton and Young. However, one of these writers, Jock Young, later rejected this approach and helped co-found a very different, and currently influential new school of thought in sociology, now known as 'left realism' (Lea and Young 1984). Left realists argue that rather than wait for a Marxist revolution, it is better to apply sociological research and analysis to social problems as less powerful groups in society experience them, and then to seek ways to resolve these problems. The crucial difference is that this resolution of problems is within capitalism. These left realists are therefore committed, but to improvements within the currently existing political and economic arrangements.

Research ethics

By **ethics**, we refer to the moral dilemmas that sociologists face when undertaking and writing up their research. Research ethics are closely interwoven with the debates over value freedom and objectivity, although there are other distinctive concerns that go beyond the value-freedom debate.

Whatever the view of the researcher regarding the importance of values in research, no sociologist would wish the actual procedure of research to harm those being studied or to produce a piece of research that was not as 'true' to the facts uncovered as possible. Ethical procedure is so important to sociologists that the British Sociological Association – the official body of sociology in Britain – has actually issued a guide to ethics that all researchers are

Key themes

Stratification and differentiation

Those sociologists who take a committed approach argue that sociology should be actively taking the side of disadvantaged groups within society. These groups might be women, minority-ethnic groups, the poor or the disabled. If this is not an active choice then pressure from governments and funding bodies will mean that sociological research will represent the interests of the powerful. The feminist and Marxist approaches described in this topic are examples of committed sociology.

expected to follow. Punch (1994) has summarized the main ethical concerns of sociology as follows:

- *Harm* – Any research undertaken must not cause any harm either directly or indirectly to those being studied (although a further question arises: what should a researcher do if the people under study are going to harm someone else?).
- *Consent* – Any person or group being studied, wherever possible, should give their consent to being the subject of research. This usually involves an honest explanation of the research being undertaken and the future use of the material obtained.
- *Deception* – The researcher should, wherever possible, be clear about their role to those being studied.
- *Privacy and confidentiality of data* – The information obtained should not breach the privacy of the person being studied, and nothing should be published that the person regards as confidential. Research should not, therefore, provide the real name or address of a person being studied.

Dealing with ethical issues

These ethical concerns may seem necessary, but following them can pose great difficulties for sociologists engaged in certain research methods, such as **covert participant observation**. Difficulties also arise in certain areas of research – for example amongst young people, those engaged in criminal or deviant activities, and those with learning difficulties or suffering from mental illness.

An example of both of these fine lines between acting ethically and crossing the boundary can be found in Hobbs' ethnographic study of East End criminals and local CID officers (1988). During his study he found out about many illegal activities committed by both villains and police officers, including acts of violence. Hobbs decided not to pass any information from one group to the other, and despite knowing about criminal activities, he decided that the most 'ethical' thing to do was not to interfere in any way.

Hobbs also mixed overt and covert styles of research with the police. Overtly, he was conducting research through interviews, but covertly he befriended a number of police officers and carefully studied them in their social lives without telling them what he was doing. Hobbs' work can be questioned for its rather dubious ethics in terms of condoning law-breaking behaviour (which was sometimes serious) and in researching the detectives informally without their consent. However, in doing both these activities, he produced a more vibrant and possibly more accurate piece of research than if he had adhered to the 'correct procedures'.

Focus on research

Hobbs (1988)
Studying criminals and policing

Hobbs conducted a famous study of minor criminals and policing in East London. In this study Hobbs needed to spend a large amount of time with police officers in both working and social environments. Indeed, Hobbs became so close to the detectives that he states: 'I often had to remind myself that I was not in a pub to enjoy myself, but to conduct an academic inquiry and repeatedly woke up the following morning with an incredible hangover, facing the dilemma of whether to bring it up or write it up.'

Although Hobbs enjoyed the company of the police officers, he also disapproved of many of the activities which they engaged in – some potentially illegal. He sometimes faced a moral dilemma in that he allowed things to happen that normally he might consider objecting to.

Hobbs, D. (1988) *Doing the Business: Entrepreneurship, the Working Class and Detectives in the East End of London*, Oxford: Oxford University Press

1 When faced with a moral choice which could lead to either the end of the research project or a getting a book published, with the consequent academic prestige, what do you think most sociologists choose?

2 How can sociologists ensure that research is ethical?

Activities

Research idea

Design two questionnaires aiming to discover young women's views on feminism. The first must discover that feminism is still important and relevant to young women, the second that it has gone too far and young women do not support it.

What different questions could you use to get these different results? Could you interpret answers in different ways?

Web.tasks

1 Go to the MORI website at www.mori.co.uk. This contains a wide range of opinion surveys. Take a few examples of their surveys. Check who is sponsoring the research and see if you can identify any evidence of the intrusion of values, for example in the motives for the research and in the sorts of questions asked.

2 The British Sociological Association website lists all ethical issues that sociologists should consider when they undertake research. There is a summary by Punch in the main text, but it is worth exploring the original.

Go to www.britsoc.co.uk and then click on 'Equality and Ethics'. On this page choose 'Statement of Ethical Practice'; finally go through each of the headings on this page.

Based on what you find there, what would you have to do if you wished to interview 14-year-old students in a local comprehensive to find out their views on drug use?

Check your understanding

1 What is meant by 'positivism'?

2 How do positivistic sociologists think the problem of values can be overcome?

3 How can the funding for research influence its content, according to Philo and Miller?

4 Compare the views of Becker and Gouldner on values in sociology.

5 Why do postmodernists see it as impossible to even try to overcome the issue of values?

6 What do we mean by 'committed sociology'? Give two examples.

7 Identify and explain three ethical issues faced by sociologists.

Key terms

Committed where an approach is open in its support of particular values, usually used with reference to Marxist sociologists, feminist sociologists and those wishing to confront racism and discrimination against people with disabilities.

Covert participant observation when the researcher joins a group as a full member, and studies them, but does not tell them that he or she is a researcher.

Critical sociology a term used for sociology influenced by Marxism.

Ethics refers to issues of moral choices.

Hierarchical some people are regarded as more important than others.

Left realism an approach to social problems that argues it is better to cooperate with the authorities to solve social problems, even if fundamental social change is not brought about.

Malestream a feminist term implying criticism of traditional sociology for excluding women from the subject both as sociologists and as the subjects of research.

Objectivity the exclusion of values from research.

Positivism an approach to sociological research which aims to use the rigour and methods of the physical sciences.

Value freedom the exclusion of values from research.

Value laden the belief that sociology cannot be value free and that it is a mistake to see it as such.

An eye on the exam · Values and ethics

Item A

<< Patriarchal knowledge is based on the premise that the experience of only half the human population needs to be taken into account and the resulting version can be imposed on the other half. >>

Spender, D. (1985) *For the Record: The Meaning and Making of Feminist Knowledge*, London: Women's Press

Item B

<< There are numerous points at which bias and the intrusion of values can occur. Values can materialize at any point during the course of research. The researcher may develop an affection or sympathy, which was not necessarily present at the outset of an investigation, for the people being studied. It is quite common, for example, for researchers working within a qualitative research strategy, and in particular when they use participant observation of very intensive interviewing, to develop a close affinity with the people they study to the extent that they find it difficult to disentangle their stance as social scientists from their subjects' perspective. This possibility may be exacerbated by the tendency that Becker identified for sociologists in particular to be very sympathetic to underdog groups. >>

Bryman, A. (2004) *Social Research Methods* (2nd edn), Oxford: OUP

Using material from the **Items** and elsewhere, assess the view that values inevitably enter sociological research in many ways.

(33 marks)

Grade booster · Getting top marks in this question

In answering this question, you need to examine the debate about value-free sociology versus value-laden sociology. You should first examine the argument that it is possible to keep values out of research and achieve objectivity, as positivists claim. Contrast this with the view that the values of those who fund the research inevitably find their way into it, and with the view that researchers' own values, political sympathies and career interests influence their choice of topic, method and findings. You could use Items A and B to illustrate this. You should also consider whether it is even desirable to keep values out of research, or whether sociologists should take the side of those they study, as Becker and others have argued.

TOPIC 10

Sociology and social policy

Getting you thinking

Percentage of people aged 16 and over who smoke cigarettes

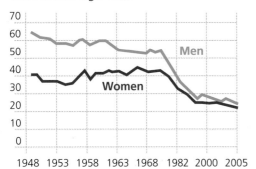

- Smoking costs the NHS £1.7 billion each year.
- Tobacco use causes about 92 000 deaths each year.
- Smoking kills more than 90 per cent of lung cancer patients.

Smoking ban has saved 40,000 lives

By Jeremy Laurance, Health Editor

THE nationwide smoking ban has triggered the biggest fall in smoking ever seen in England, a report says today. More than two billion fewer cigarettes were smoked and 400 000 people quit the habit since the ban was introduced a year ago, which researchers say will prevent 40 000 deaths over the next 10 years.

Smoking was outlawed in all enclosed public spaces in England, including pubs and restaurants, on 1 July 2007.

Source: *The Independent,* 30 June 2008

1 According to this information, what has been the impact of the cigarette smoking ban?

2 How do you think information about individuals' smoking and consumption of alcohol is collected?

3 Explain why it is important to collect information about smoking and alcohol.

You have been asked to research the effects of alcohol on 'fuelling yobbish behaviour'.

4 Explain how you would approach the research including your methods.

5 How would you encourage politicians to take notice of your findings?

Record numbers are treated in hospital for alcohol problems

By Nigel Morris

ALMOST 5000 young people under 18 received emergency treatment for alcohol abuse last year as hospitals admitted record numbers of patients with drink-related problems.

Alarm over levels of binge drinking were reinforced by figures showing twice as many people were suffering mental illness caused by alcohol or liver damage than a decade ago.

As the National Health Service warned that it faced an 'increasing burden' from the effects of alcohol, the Government faced calls to take fresh action against problem drinking.

The number of alcohol-related admissions to NHS hospitals in England rose from 193 637 in 2005/6 to 207 788 in 2006/7, an increase of 7 per cent in just one year. Last year's total was more than double the 93 459 figure for 1995/6, according to the report from the NHS Information Centre for health and social care. More than two-thirds of patients were male, and 4888 of them were under the age of 18.

The culture of binge drinking is a plague on Britain. It causes misery in some of the country's most deprived areas and transforms even the most genteel town centres into no-go areas at weekends. With this bleak context in mind, it is understandable that ministers in Scotland are considering an increase in the legal age for purchasing alcohol from off-licences and supermarkets from 18 to 21. Scotland has one of the fastest growing rates of liver cirrhosis in the world. Does it not make sense to make alcohol harder to get hold of, if only for teenagers?

The answer is no. While one can sympathise with politicians wanting to take radical action to curb binge drinking, the remedy does not lie in simplistic legislative responses.

Source: *The Independent,* 17 June 2008

Sociology is first and foremost an academic subject that sets out to explore the way in which society operates and how it influences our lives – and for many sociologists, that is all they are interested in. For others, particularly those working in universities and research centres, sociological research is undertaken wholly or partly to inform and influence government **social policy**. This is particularly the case where the government or a pressure group provides the funding for the research. The information obtained in research can have quite significant effects on social policy. In fact, so important has this applied branch of sociology become that there has recently been a considerable growth in the academic subject known as social policy, which only concerns itself with studying and influencing how governments respond to social problems.

Applying sociology: the positive view

According to Giddens (2001), there are four practical benefits of studying sociology:

1 understanding social situations
2 awareness of cultural differences
3 assessment of the effects of policies
4 increase in self-knowledge.

These form a useful framework for understanding the relationship between sociology and policy.

Understanding social situations

The most obvious outcome of sociology is that it allows us to understand the world around us, providing us with knowledge and insights. This understanding can take two forms:

● *factual* – providing us with the 'facts', which allow us to form a judgement or develop a theory
● *theoretical* – providing people with an explanation as to why something is happening.

Understanding society and poverty

An example of the way factual and theoretical understanding of social situations can influence social policy is the sociological study of poverty.

Factually

By the late 1960s politicians believed that they had eliminated poverty. The welfare state had been in existence for almost twenty years and everyone was guaranteed a minimum income, some form of housing, and free healthcare; the issue of poverty gradually lost its political importance. However, a series of reports by Townsend (1979) and later by Mack and Lansley (1985) in the 1980s and 1990s showed that poverty remained a huge but hidden problem in Britain, with over 11 million people living in poverty. This research work continues, most notably at the Joseph Rowntree Foundation, which, amongst other things, continuously monitors the issue of poverty.

This research has not only demonstrated the extent of poverty, but also the specific groups at risk of poverty – for example, women and children emerged as the poorest groups. This implied that policies to combat poverty had to look after women and children before anyone else.

Theoretically

The facts on poverty, however, can only be understood in relation to theory. Sociologists uncovered the extent of poverty by devising more sophisticated ways of measuring it. In particular, they brought in a 'relative deprivation' model of poverty (Townsend 1979), proving that poverty can only be understood in terms of what people normally expect to have in a society – even if this was well above the levels of **destitution**. This new way of defining poverty allowed a whole new insight into the nature of poverty in advanced, affluent societies. Furthermore, sociologists were able to put forward a range of possible explanations for poverty based on their research. The result of these researches led indirectly to policies such as the minimum wage, which guaranteed a minimum hourly pay level, and the current system of Tax Credits, which provide additional help for people on low pay

More recently, Room (1995) suggested that seeing poverty as lack of money was too narrow a concept and so the more widely used term 'social exclusion' was introduced. This suggests that 'poor' people experience a much greater range of problems, which effectively cut them off from the wider society. Once again, a theoretical concept pushed forward our understanding of the nature of a social problem. Policy responses to this include targeting healthcare initiatives at the poorest, and providing support for single mothers bringing up children alone, through the Home Start programme, as well as a range of other activities to draw those 'on the margins' back into society.

Awareness of cultural differences

A second important practical benefit, according to Giddens, is the way in which sociology can help people to see others' viewpoint, looking beyond the boundaries of their particular group. Lack of awareness of the activities and beliefs of other groups can lead to prejudice and discrimination. The information that sociology provides therefore allows us to respond to others' views in an informed and relevant way.

An outcome of this is the way that recent governments have tackled discrimination in the areas of disability and race.

Disability

Disabled people often face very significant discrimination as a result of a stereotyping of their potential. They experience particularly high levels of unemployment, are discriminated against in many areas of social life, and are much more likely than the majority of the population to be living in poverty. For example, they are seven times more likely to be unemployed than the average, and over 50 per cent of families with a disabled male adult were living in poverty. This discrimination both ruins the lives of the people involved and, at a political level, costs the government over £100 billion each year in state benefits.

Apart from having a higher chance of living in poverty, disabled people also have to cope with the stigma attached to disability, with people reacting to them in a patronizing or negative manner. Over time, sociological studies have built up a picture of the social and economic exclusion suffered by disabled people leading to groups such as the Disability Alliance, Disablement Income Group and the British Council of Disabled People being set up to demand better treatment. In addition, their work and the work of sociologists has led to a greater public awareness and sympathy, resulting in the 1995 Disability Discrimination Act, which was followed by the Disability Rights Commission Act in 1999. Just as importantly, there has been a gradual shift in public opinion towards acknowledging the rights of disabled people.

Race

Opinion polls over the past 30 years have shown a consistent decline in expressed racism on the part of the majority population. The reasons for this are complex, but certainly one of the contributing factors has been the growth in understanding of the variety of cultures in Britain, and the problems that minority-ethnic groups face. Early sociological studies tended to emphasize the issues causing conflict, but increasingly, sociologists and others have demonstrated the variety and positive nature of the contribution of minority-ethnic groups to British life. 'White' people are more informed and aware of the variety of ethnic groups and are less likely to stereotype them as happened in the past. This awareness, plus the acceptance of a **plural** Britain, has led to the introduction of Race Equality legislation (1976 and 2000) to enforce equality.

Assessment of the effects of policies

Once politicians have recognized that a particular social problem exists, they are then able to develop policies to combat it. If sociological knowledge is used in doing this, then the policies adopted may be those that appear to be most effective in combating the problem. However, it is actually extremely difficult to judge just how effective a policy has actually been, and this leads us to another use of sociology – that of evaluating the effects of a particular policy initiative.

Today, virtually all government initiatives are evidence based – that is, when the government provides funding for new social projects, it requires the people actually running the programme to provide clear evidence that there is some benefit coming from that particular programme. Sociology is the key subject in providing this sort of research into the relevance and effectiveness of policy initiatives.

A good example of evaluation has been the way in which cost–benefit analyses of healthcare have been introduced in the NHS. Much of this work was pioneered by the University of York, where analyses were conducted to find out just how effective certain medical procedures were in terms of better quality of life for patients and cost to the NHS. The government has developed this form of

analysis to pharmaceuticals, and introduced a National Institute for Clinical Excellence which started in 1999 and which dictates what drugs and procedures the NHS is prepared to provide.

Increase in self-knowledge

For many sociologists this is the single most important aim of the subject. Sociology allows people to reflect upon their own experiences of life and in doing so 'liberates' them. Self-knowledge allows people to challenge images of themselves (perhaps currently stereotyped in the media) and to initiate policies that are more sympathetic to them. This is closely linked to Giddens' notion of reflexivity (see Topic 2, p. 265).

Certain groups, such as those with disabilities, minority-ethnic groups and the feminist and gay movements, have all benefited greatly from this aspect of sociology. Sociological research has demonstrated the extent of discrimination against all these groups and this knowledge has empowered them because they are able to show the results to the government and demand action. The result of this has been a wide range of antidiscrimination laws. The publication of research has also allowed groups who have traditionally been discriminated against to become aware of their own shared identities and to take a pride in them. For example, sexual practices surveys showed that sexual activity between same-sex partners was not as infrequent as traditionally believed and opinion polls demonstrated that there was support for equal rights for gay people. This helped the gay community to have the courage to demand equal rights and to feel able to assert their own identities rather than having to hide their sexuality.

Key themes

Stratification and differentiation

Feminists take different positions on the relationship between sociology and social policy. Radical and socialist feminists criticize liberal feminists for their research and close ties with government. Liberal feminists have been content to point out the way in which society discriminates against women in terms of employment, state benefits and within the family. Their aim has been to introduce antidiscrimination legislation and to change the attitudes of men to women. They would argue that they have largely succeeded in this. However, radical and socialist feminists argue that this misses the point – the current patriarchal society is actually based on the exploitation of women and only by dismantling it and bringing about fundamental change can women achieve any form of liberation.

<< *Women appear in a sociology predicated on the universe occupied by men … its methods, conceptual schemes and theories have been based on and built up within the male social universe.*>> (Smith 1973, p. 44)

Sociology and social policy: critical views

The relationship between social policy and sociology has, however, been criticized by a number of writers – in particular, by those who see sociology as having been 'colonized' (i.e. taken over) by governments and thus having its radical potential tamed.

Critical sociology

For those belonging to the critical sociology tradition based on Marxism, the fault with much of sociology is that it has become too closely linked with the capitalist system – which to them is the main cause of the social problems and discrimination. Therefore sociology is not fulfilling its role as a provider of knowledge that could liberate people, but actually serving the interests of powerful groups who could then impose their wishes in even more sophisticated ways.

Postmodernists and policy

Postmodernists such as Bauman (1990) take a position that is radically different from more traditional sociological approaches. They argue that sociology has no contribution to make to policy. Rational, scientific approaches to sociology using surveys or qualitative studies have often been used by government to introduce policies. But postmodernists claim that this is a waste of time; the existence of an orderly and manageable society 'out there' that we can understand and then manipulate is a comforting illusion. They would argue, therefore, that there can be no link between sociology and social policies. For postmodernists the role of sociology is simply to allow people to seek out an understanding of their personal lives within a social context.

> ≪ *Deeply immersed in our daily routines, though, we hardly ever pause to think about the meaning of what we have gone through; even less often have we the opportunity to compare our private experience with the fate of others, to see the social in the individual, the general in the particular; this is precisely what sociologists can do for us. We would expect them to show us how our individual biographies intertwine with the history we share with fellow human beings.* ≫ (Bauman 1990)

Politics and social policy

The assumption underlying much of traditional **empirical sociology** is that if research shows up social problems, then governments will respond by seeking to solve the problems on the basis of the evidence. However, this is not necessarily true for four key reasons.

1 Governments act only when there are groups powerful enough to have their views taken into account by politicians. Gay people are now seen as a potential source of votes and as a group who occupy important positions across society. On the other hand, some of the poorest groups in society have little access to power, and may well be ignored by government.

2 Governments are limited by financial constraints. To eliminate poverty amongst retired people would be simple – raise the state pension by a significant amount. Yet governments regard this as simply too expensive.

3 Some policies will meet too much opposition from entrenched groups. The 'roads lobby', pharmaceutical and cigarette companies have all been very effective in protecting their interests, despite evidence to show that many of their practices are harmful.

4 Governments rarely engage in radical or long-term changes. In a democracy, governments operate within fairly short timetables based on election periods and are more concerned with popularity at the time of an election than introducing longer-term changes. They also are reluctant to commit themselves to very dramatic social change that could lead to upheaval – preferring to operate within the status quo.

Key themes

Crime and deviance

A good example of the critical position in sociology is the debate between **realist** criminologists and critical criminologists (see Chapter 6, pp. 345 and 389). Realist criminologists, such as Lea and Young (1993), argue that sociological surveys indicate that the people who really suffer from crime are the poor and the powerless. It is therefore the duty of the government to introduce policies to prevent crime occurring against these groups, and to improve the quality of their lives. They should do this by better policing, better social conditions and by tackling the social and economic marginalization of the young males who commit most street crime.

Critical criminologists reject this, saying that the approach deals with the symptoms of crime, not the

causes. For writers such as Scraton and Chadwick (1982), it is a mistake to focus on the street crime committed by young men. These people engage in crime precisely because they are marginalized and brutalized by the capitalist system. Critical criminologists argue that realism ignores the very real damage committed by corporations. For them, realists have been caught up in the very system that should itself be attacked.

Focus on research

Hope and Walters (2008)
Funding, research and censorship

In *Critical Thinking about the Uses of Research* (Walters and Hope 2008), Reece Walters claims that: 'We live in a society where Government manipulates and cherry-picks criminological knowledge and produces distorted pictures of the "crime problem".'

The book launches a strong attack on the way that government departments, in particular the Home Office (for England and Wales) and the Scottish Executive fail to fund – or use confidentiality agreements to restrict – research that contradicts some of the favoured policies on crime they wish to put in place. Walters and Hope provide some examples of this claimed censorship of research.

Between 2003 and 2006, Professor Walters researched youth court procedures in Scotland with funding from the Scottish Executive. However, his findings contradicted the positive claims for the youth courts made by The Scottish Executive. The draft report was presented to The Scottish Executive in 2005, but following several months of The Executive questioning content, a final report was submitted in April 2006. Yet it was not until November 2006 that The Executive published the report on its website.

Walters then wrote a critical article in the academic journal *Youth Justice* (Piacentini and Walters 2006). At this point, Walters states that The Executive complained to his employer, Stirling University and also refused to pay the final £15 000 of the research contract.

Walters concludes that despite mounting evidence of censorship, academics are prepared to accept the controls on them in order to obtain funding for their work. He argues this is detrimental to sociology and has called for a boycott of government-funded work. Walters concludes by stating that:

≪ *Like field mice scurrying around a python, to appease university obsession with income generation and with the misguided belief that they will change or influence policy, academic criminologists continue to line the corridors of the Home Office and the Scottish Executive with cap in hand hoping to receive a slice of the government's growing financial pie for criminal justice research.*≫

Hope, T. and Walters, R. (2008) *Critical Thinking about the Uses of Research*, Centre for Crime and Justice Studies, www.crimeandjustice.org.uk

1 **What view does the writer hold on the relationship between research and government funding?**

2 **How might this problem be resolved?**

So, although sociology can uncover the extent of social problems – and also suggest the causes – transferring this into policy does not necessarily happen.

We can see from the discussion above that there is no agreement amongst sociologists about whether sociology ought to be applied or not. For many sociologists, the whole point of the subject is to use the knowledge to improve the quality of life for the majority of the population. However, these sociologists then split into two warring factions. One group argues that it is best to influence government policy to bring about reforms, whilst the other group argues that the insights sociology provides should help us to replace the current political and social system. Finally, there are those who argue that sociology an academic subject and has no need to make any claim beyond its ability to throw light upon the nature of society and its relationship to the lives of individuals.

Key terms

Destitution lacking the minimum resources necessary for food, clothing and housing.

Empirical sociology research based on first-hand investigation.

Plural the fact that British society is now composed of a number of different cultures.

Realist sociology a term used for sociologists broadly sympathetic to the left who wish to influence government policy, particularly in the area of crime.

Social policy has two meanings. It can refer to government policy to solve social problems or the academic subject of studying social problems.

Activities

Research idea

Conduct a survey among sociology students at your school or college to discover which social issues they feel most strongly about.

Have these issues been covered during your course? Are they included in the specifications of your examining board? To what extent has your study of sociology been relevant to the values and experiences of students?

Web.tasks

1 Choose any one of the following government websites: the Home Office, NHS, Department for Education and Skills, Work and Pensions.
Look up the sorts of research being undertaken. What is the aim of research? Do you think that the criticisms of radical sociologists that sociology is 'colonized' are justified?

2 Go to the website of the Joseph Rowntree Foundation at **www.jrf.org.uk/.**
On the opening page, click on 'Read more about what we do'. Check through the research that sociology (or, more accurately, that branch of sociology – social policy) engages in.

Check your understanding

1. Identify Giddens' four links between sociology and policy.

2. Give an example from the text which shows how sociology has influenced policy.

3. How can an awareness of disability issues influence policy?

4. Explain what evidence-based policymaking is.

5. Explain what is meant by sociology having been 'colonized' by government.

6. How do postmodernists view the relationship between sociology and policy?

7. If sociologists provide the 'facts', why don't governments always base their policies upon these facts?

An eye on the exam Sociology and social policy

Item A

One view of the relationship between sociology and social policy is that sociology investigates social problems, identifies their causes and proposes solutions to them. Government then translates the work of sociologists into social policies designed to remedy or alleviate the problem concerned. For example, researchers may discover that poverty and inequality are major causes of ill health, and the government will then devise appropriate policies to tackle the problem, for example by redistributing income.

However, others regard this view as naive and overoptimistic. They argue that politicians normally take little notice of sociologists and their work, and that their arguments and research findings generally have little influence on government policies.

Using material from **Item A** and elsewhere, assess the view that sociological arguments and research findings generally have little influence on the policies of governments. (33 marks)

Grade booster Getting top marks in this question

Begin by looking at the positive view from Giddens that research has practical implications. You should also note the extensive use of research available on government websites (which you will have covered in your webtasks throughout the chapter). Giddens has pointed to the evidence-based policies that government has adopted in a range of areas. Against this, are the views of more critical sociologists who argue that governments are influenced less by evidence than by powerful groups; that financial constraints limit what governments are able to do – they might know what should be done, but cannot do it for lack of funding; and that certain interest groups have enough power to block reforms if their interests are challenged. Finally, governments rarely engage in long-term projects as they are more concerned with popularity at the time of elections.

A final, and perhaps more radical, approach is that of the postmodernists who argue that as there is no ordered society 'out there', it is impossible to change it by introducing policies.

Assess the value of structural perspectives to the understanding of society. *(33 marks)*

There are two types of structural approach – consensus (functionalism) and conflict (Marxism). They see individuals as passive puppets of society. The functionalists see society as made up of institutions working in harmony, socializing individuals into conforming to the value consensus. This makes their behaviour relatively predictable, and so sociologists can discover 'laws' that determine how individuals will behave in given situations. Functionalists see the value consensus as largely preventing change, although they accept gradual change does occur.

Functionalists see society as benefiting everyone. For example, they see the family as meeting the needs of all its members. However, functionalism has been criticized for disregarding conflict and exploitation. For example, feminists argue that they ignore issues such as gender oppression and domestic violence.

The Marxist structural theory also emphasizes conflict. Marxists see society as split into two conflicting classes – the bourgeoisie (capitalists) and proletariat (working class). The conflict between the classes is based on the fact that the bourgeoisie exploits the labour of the proletariat.

Marxists see society as having an economic base made up of the means of production (such as factories and raw materials) plus the two social classes. The capitalists own the means of production and are able to make a profit by exploiting the workers' labour by paying wages worth less than what the workers produce. Above the economic base is the superstructure, which is made up of all the other institutions of society, such as education, religion, the state, family and so on. Althusser divides this into the repressive state apparatus or RSA (e.g. the police and prisons) and the ideological state apparatus or ISA (e.g. the media, education). The function of both is to keep capitalism stable so that the bourgeoisie can continue to exploit the proletariat. For example, the function of religion is seen as keeping the poor, poor by persuading them that there is no point in trying to change society and that their suffering will be rewarded in the afterlife.

A final structural conflict theory is feminism. Feminists are divided into different approaches, but most of them agree that the structure of society is patriarchal, so that all institutions are male dominated and keep women subordinated. Radical feminists see this as being in the interests of all men – the two sexes are like two 'classes', with one exploiting the other. This is especially true of the family, where they see violence and women's servicing of men's domestic and sexual needs, as the basis of their oppression in society. Marxist feminists see women's oppression as being in the interests of capitalism as well as of men. They argue that women are a reserve army of cheap labour that capitalists can make use of and discard as and when they require.

Not all sociologists accept the structural approach. Postmodernists argue that theories such as Marxism are just meta-narratives or 'stories' that do not represent reality. They argue that society is increasingly fragmented and that it is no longer a question of two classes but of many different groups. They also argue that people can now pick and choose their own identity rather than it being shaped by society.

Another approach that rejects the structural theories is interactionism. Interactionists see society as made up of the interactions of individuals, based on the meanings they give to situations. In their view, individuals have free will and can choose how to act, so society cannot control their behaviour.

21/33

An examiner comments This is quite a good answer that shows some accurate knowledge of a range of material relevant to the question. There is a clear understanding of what structural theories are, although there is rather more focus on giving an accurate description of these theories (functionalism, Marxism and feminism) than on discussing their value in understanding society. Appropriate concepts are used in describing the different theories (e.g. value consensus, ISA, exploitation, oppression, meta-narratives).

There is some limited evaluation towards the end, from postmodernist and interactionist perspectives, but this could be developed further. It would also be a good idea to introduce some alternative Marxist views such as Gramsci, and to write a separate conclusion.

One for you to try

Assess the claim that sociology is a science. *(33 marks)*

An examiner comments You should begin your answer by examining the positivist view that sociology can and should be a science. Explain their key ideas, for example that laws of cause and effect are discoverable by following scientific research principles. You can discuss some of the problems of this approach, such as the issue of laboratory experiments in sociology, and how positivists seek to overcome these, for example by the use of official statistics as an alternative. You should also discuss the interpretivists' rejection of the goal of a scientific sociology and their goal of understanding meaningful social action rather than discovering causal laws.

Answers to the 'One for you to try' are available free on www.collinseducation.com/sociologyweb

Crime and deviance

AQA Specification	Topics	Pages
Candidates should examine:		
Different theories of crime, deviance, social order and social control.	These issues stretch across most topics. They are introduced in Topic 1 and explored in Topics 2 to 4. Social control is the subject of Topics 1 and 10.	330–58 392–98
The social distribution of crime and deviance by age, ethnicity, gender, locality and social class, including recent patterns and trends in crime.	Recent patterns and trends are examined in Topic 5. Explanations of these patterns are to be found in the following topics: age (2 and 7), ethnicity (9), gender (7), locality (6) and class (2, 3 and 8).	359–65 338–51 372–91
Globalization and crime in contemporary society; the mass media and crime; green crime; human rights and state crimes.	Globalization, green crime, state crimes and human rights are covered in Topic 8. The relationship between the mass media and deviance is discussed in Topic 4.	378–85 352–58
Crime control, prevention and punishment, victims, and the role of the criminal justice system and other agencies.	Covered in Topic 10. These issues are also discussed in relation to ethnicity in Topic 9.	386–98
The sociological study of suicide and its theoretical and methodological implications.	Covered in Topic 11.	399–404
The connections between sociological theory and methods and the study of crime and deviance.	Connections are made throughout the chapter, especially in the 'Focus on Research' features.	

Deviance and control theories

Getting you thinking

Get tough on the REAL cause of crime

THE CAUSES OF CRIME lie in the widespread and systematic breakdown of all the connections and restraints that create a civilized society. Look at the disempowerment of authority figures such as teachers, who face criminal charges if they lay a hand on a pupil, or the police, who no longer have discretion to hand out warnings if a crime has been committed. Above all, the principal cause is the dismemberment of the traditional family.

It is overwhelmingly those children who are thus abandoned to emotional and moral chaos who are out of control, with parents who are so inadequate that when their children misbehave, they increasingly call in the police.

Family collapse has loaded much more responsibility on to the schools. But these in turn have long stopped transmitting moral values or instilling self-discipline.

Instead, they leave children to make up their own values system, remove all discomfort from them such as intellectual obstacles or failure and, while sentimentalizing self-esteem, abandon the young to find their way in the world without moral or intellectual maps.

Melanie Phillips, *Daily Mail*, 24 April 2006

IT HAS BEEN SAID that a Victorian who fell asleep in 1848 … who woke up in early 21st-century Britain would not only find their country unrecognizable, but would be profoundly shocked by it. They would be astonished obviously by the technical wizardry, but shocked by the change in values – the demise of marriage between heterosexual couples, and the existence of marriage between homosexual and mixed-race couples; the quarter of children living with just one parent; the millions of able-bodied people paid by the state to be idle; the disappearance of deference, even to the monarch; the empty pews on Sundays (and the full mosques on Fridays). Everything they hold most dear – the Christian God-fearing ethos, the family, marriage, the monarch and the value of hard work – would seem decimated.

Values change dramatically over a century, but they also do over decades. Things that caused outrage a generation ago are now celebrated. Until 1967, British men were imprisoned for having sex with other men; forty years later, gay marriage is enthusiastically covered in recently homophobic tabloid newspapers. Attitudes to sexuality, lone-parenthood, marriage, race, welfare benefits, alcohol, drugs and violent crime have all been transformed. People are bound to be confused if the fundamental values they grew up with and internalized as a child, and used to guide their life, are ditched by society when they hit middle age.

Adapted from the Viewpoint 'Has there been a decline in values in British society?' published in 2008 by the Joseph Rowntree Foundation. Reproduced by permission of the Joseph Rowntree Foundation.

1 According to the first extract, what do the causes of crime 'lie in'?

2 According to Melanie Phillips, what is wrong with the family?

3 Do you think this is true of all groups in British society?

4 Look at the second extract. Do you think that British people once shared a common set of values that is now lost?

5 Do you agree with Phillip's analysis of the causes of crime?

6 Do you think that the second extract provides us with any insights into Melanie Phillip's article?

The study of **crime** and **deviance** is arguably the most interesting and dynamic area of sociology. Many of the ideas and debates that have emerged from this branch of sociology have later spread out to influence the study of most other areas of sociology. One debate in particular has profoundly influenced the study of the sociology of health,

of sexuality, of education and of methods, and that is the simple discussion about what is meant by the term deviance, and then the related debate on the relationship between deviance and the law.

Sociologists have suggested two, distinct definitions of deviance: the normative definition and the relativistic.

The normative definition of deviance

The normative definition is perhaps the common-sense one, a version of which most people suggest when they are questioned as to the meaning of deviance. A typical example of a normative definition of deviance would be that it 'refers to actions which differ from the accepted standards of a society' or more sociologically, 'it consists of the violation of social norms'.

The normative definition provides a simple and clear image of a society in which there are shared values and ways of behaving (norms) and the deviant is a person who breaks these shared values. Finding out what the shared values are is relatively easy, as these can be found by various surveys (a good example is The British Attitude Survey, published annually).

Underpinning this definition of deviance is the belief that society is essentially **consensual** – that is, the vast majority of people share similar values. Indeed, it was this approach that was used by Durkheim in his explanation of deviance and its relationship to crime. Durkheim suggests that every society shares a set of core values, which he called the '**collective conscience**'. The more behaviour differed from these core values, the more likely it was to be viewed as deviant. As we see later in our discussion on the relationship between deviance, crime and social control, Durkheim based his explanation for the criminal law on this notion of normative deviance (see p. 335).

This normative definition of deviance has a number of consequences for the study of offending. Perhaps most important is that, if there are core values that most people subscribe to, then the main aim of the sociology of crime and deviance is to explain why some people act in a deviant manner. Therefore, sociologists who accept the normative definition of deviance will often set out to discover what differences there are between people who deviate (including criminals) and people who behave conventionally. Much research goes into exploring how such things as family differences, social-class differences or the influence of the peer group make some people into deviants.

The relativistic approach

The normative definition of deviance starts from the basis that there is a common set of shared values. The relativistic approach argues, instead, that the basis of society is a diversity of values, not a consensus. Societies are just too complex for there to be a clear set of shared values. Sociologists from this perspective point to the conflicts of interest and diversity of beliefs and values that characterize modern societies. The relativistic approach to deviance therefore suggests that there are different sets of competing values that coexist and that are constantly in a state of change, jockeying for positions as the more 'socially valued' values of society. So, the values of society are to be understood less in terms of a consensus of fundamental beliefs and values, and much more as the outcome of some form of dynamic process through which some values become adopted by society at the cost of other values.

There are two main approaches to how this dynamic process works:

1 *the interactionist or labelling approach* – according to which the values that emerge as most highly rated are the result of complex interactions between different groups and individuals in society
2 *the conflict approach* – most commonly associated with Marxists, which argues that the values of society are dominated by, and reflect, the interests of the ruling class, and beneath that the dynamics of the dialectic.

The implications of a relativistic approach, as opposed to a normative approach to understanding deviance, are very important indeed for the study of crime and deviance. Before, we saw that the key question for the normative approach was, 'What is the difference between deviants and conforming people, which makes the deviants act the way they do?'. However, the relativistic approach argues that dominant values are just the outcome of a struggle to get one group's values accepted rather than another's. In this case, studying the personal or social characteristics of deviants is not that important; what is far more important is to ask the question, 'Why do some group's values become the socially accepted ones at the expense of other groups' values?'.

So, the normative definition suggests that the focus of study is to explain the causes of deviant behaviour and the focus of the relativistic definition is to uncover the processes whereby one set of values dominate.

We can see that these two definitions send sociologists in two quite distinct directions and this has particular importance for understanding the relationship between deviance and crime.

The relationship between deviance and crime

A normative-based approach to crime

We have seen that the normative-based approach argues that there are certain values which all people in society agree with and deviant acts are those which conflict with the shared values. The first, and still one of the most valuable, sociological explorations of the relationship between deviance and crime was provided by Durkheim, who identified two different sides of crime and deviance for the functioning of society:

● a *positive* side that helped society change and remain dynamic
● a *negative* side that saw too much crime leading to social disruption.

Positive aspects of crime: social cohesion

According to Durkheim (1895), crime – or at least a certain, limited amount of crime – was necessary for any society. He argued that the basis of society was a set of shared values that guide our actions, which he called the collective conscience. The collective conscience provides a framework with boundaries, which distinguishes between actions that are acceptable and those that are not. The problem for any society is that these boundaries are unclear, and also that they change over time. It is in clarifying the boundaries and the changes that a limited

Focus on research

Definitions of crime and deviance

The American sociologist Marshall B. Clinard (1974) suggested that the term 'deviance' should be reserved for behaviour that is so disapproved of that the community finds it impossible to tolerate. Not all sociologists would accept this definition, but it does describe the area usually covered by studies of deviance. In terms of Clinard's definition, crime and delinquency are the most obvious forms of deviance. 'Crime' refers to those activities that break the law of the land and are subject to official punishment; '**delinquency**' refers to acts that are criminal, or are considered antisocial, which are committed by young people. Social scientists who study crime are often referred to as **criminologists**.

However, many deviant acts that are disapproved of are not defined as criminal. For example, alcoholism and attempted suicide are not illegal in Britain today. Some criminal acts are not even typically seen as deviant. Sometimes, outdated laws are left on the statute books even though people have long since stopped enforcing them. For example, under British law it is technically illegal to make or eat mince pies on Christmas Day and to shout 'taxi' to hail a cab.

Deviance is also relative: there is no absolute way of defining a deviant act. Deviance can only be defined in relation to a particular standard, and no standards are fixed or absolute. As such, what is regarded as deviant varies from time to time and place to place. An act considered deviant today may be defined as normal in the future. An act defined as deviant in one society may be seen as perfectly normal in another. Put another way, deviance is culturally determined, and cultures change over time and vary between societies.

Adapted from Haralambos, M. and Holborn, M. (2004)
Sociology: Themes and Perspectives, London: Collins Education

Give an example of each of the following:

A an act generally disapproved of, but not criminal
B a criminal act often not seen as deviant
C an act likely to be considered deviant in one culture, but not in another
D an act that used to be seen as deviant but is not today.

---

amount of crime has its place. Specifically, Durkheim discussed three elements of this positive aspect:

1 *Reaffirming the boundaries* – Every time a person breaks a law and is taken to court, the resulting court ceremony and the publicity in the newspapers, publicly reaffirms the existing values. This is particularly clear in societies where public punishments take place – for example, where a murderer is taken out to be executed in public or an adulterer is stoned to death.

2 *Changing values* – Every so often when a person is taken to court and charged with a crime, a degree of sympathy occurs for the person prosecuted. The resulting public outcry signals a change in values and, in time, this can lead to a change in law in order to reflect changing values. An example of this is the change in attitude towards cannabis use.

3 *Social cohesion* – Durkheim points out that when particularly horrific crimes have been committed, the entire community draws together in shared outrage, and the sense of belonging to a community is thereby strengthened. This was noticeable, for example, in the UK following the July 2005 London Underground bombings.

The negative aspects of crime: anomie

While a certain, limited amount of crime may perform positive functions for society, according to Durkheim, too much crime has negative consequences. Perhaps his most famous concept was that of '**anomie**', which has been widely used and adapted in sociology. According to Durkheim, society is based on people sharing common values (the collective conscience), which form the basis for actions. However, in periods of great social change or stress, the collective conscience may be weakened. In this situation, people may be freed from the social control imposed by the collective conscience and may start to look after their own selfish interests rather than adhering to social values. Durkheim called this situation anomie. Where a collapse of the collective conscience has occurred and anomie exists, crime rates rocket. Only by reimposing collective values can the situation be brought back under control.

Durkheim's concept of anomie was later developed and adapted by Merton, who suggested Durkheim's original idea was too vague. Merton (1938) argued that anomie was a situation where the socially approved goals of society were not available to a substantial proportion of the population if they followed socially approved means of obtaining these goals. According to Merton, people turn to crime and deviance in this situation. Turn to Topic 2, p. 339 for more details on Merton's theory.

Relativist approaches to crime

Opposed to the normative definition is the relativist approach, which sees crime as the imposition of one group's values into law, over the values of another group.

There are two differing theoretical views within the relativist approach – interactionist and conflict or Marxist.

Interactionism (labelling theory)

(Interactionism is discussed in more detail in Topic 4, pp. 352–8.) Labelling or interactionist theorists, such as Becker, argue that in society there are always different groups who are competing to have their particular values or interests elevated to the position whereby they are passed into law. These values may or may not reflect the views of the bulk of the population. The most important thing is that the group who are promoting their own values, (the moral entrepreneurs) are successful in doing so and thereby have their values made into the law. There are a number of ways in which this can be done, including directly influencing the politicians, but Becker argues that the key role is played by the media who can create a moral panic such that politicians and the public will clamour for the introduction or enforcement of the laws which reflect the interests of the moral entrepreneurs.

Marxism

Marxist approaches too take the position that the law reflects the vested interests of a certain section in society. However, where the interactionist approach sees society as composed of numerous groups competing to have their views adopted, the Marxist view is that there are fundamentally two opposing sets of values – those of the ruling class and those of the proletariat.

According to Marxists, the ruling class successfully imposes its values on society and also laws that reflect its own interests. This is possible because the ruling class has control over the institutions that diffuse values in society, such as the education system and the media, and it also has control over the political process. Those values which are viewed as deviant and those values which are viewed as both deviant and illegal are reflections of the power of the ruling class.

Social control

Deviance is inextricably linked to the concept of social control. As we saw with Durkheim's writings earlier, it is inevitable that a society has some form of boundaries to behaviour that is acceptable. Social control ensures that only a limited number of values and norms are acceptable and in doing so provides predictability, one of the key elements which all societies need. If the behaviour of others was completely unpredictable, then it would be impossible for people to interact. Social control therefore provides the basis for society 'policing the boundaries'; it is the way that societies deal with the deviant and criminal behaviours that we have just been exploring.

There are two forms of social control:

● **Formal social control** is that which is practised by specific social agencies which have the role of maintaining order in society. The most obvious and powerful one is the criminal justice system (consisting of police forces, the judiciary, the probation and prison services).
● **Informal social control** is more subtle and is manifested in the social interaction in which we engage in every day. It pushes us back into conformity

through such things as the comments and the 'looks' of other people around us in our everyday lives. But some social institutions or contexts are more important than others; for example, sociologists have argued that the family, the peer group, the local community and schools are all key institutions in providing the basis for informal social control.

According to functionalist writers (those who emphasize the importance of normative ideas of crime and deviance), it is difficult to study crime and deviance without exploring the processes of social control. This is because most functionalists make the assumption that it is only when social control is *ineffective* that people turn to deviance and crime. If formal and informal social control worked, then no one would be deviant. It is, therefore, only because the institutions of social control we mentioned before do not work that people become deviant. Influenced by this argument, a number of sociologists have looked at why informal social control might not work and might lead certain people into deviance and crime. Perhaps the most famous of these writers is Hirschi.

Informal social control

Individuals and social control

Hirschi (1969) asked the simple question 'Why *don't* people commit crime?' His answer was that deviant or criminal activity occurs when people's attachment to society is weakened in some way. This attachment depends upon the strength of the **social bonds** that hold people to society. According to Hirschi, there are four crucial bonds that bind us together:

1 *Attachment* – To what extent do we care about other people's opinions and wishes?
2 *Commitment* – This refers to the personal investments that each of us makes in our lives. What have we got to lose if we commit a crime?
3 *Involvement* – How busy are we? Is there time and space for lawbreaking and deviant behaviour?
4 *Belief* – How strong is a person's sense that they should obey the rules of society?

Hirschi suggests that increasing attachment to society by improving the factors above will lower the level of crime.

The family and social control

Hirschi's work provides a general theoretical explanation for responding to social control, but the work of Farrington and West links the idea of failure of informal social control to the most important socializing agency – the family. In a now famous and highly influential piece of **longitudinal research**, Farrington and West (1990) studied 411 'working-class' males born in 1953 until their late 30s. The study found that less than 6 per cent of the total sample accounted for over 50 per cent of all convictions, and the research demonstrated that there were consistent **correlations** between family traits and offending. In particular, offenders were more likely to come from homes with poor parenting – especially when the fathers themselves had criminal convictions. Furthermore, offenders were also more likely to come from poorer and single-

Key themes

Socialization, culture and identity

Pampered prisoners

Yvonne Jewkes (2006) carried out a content analysis of British newspapers in order to find out how they reported the activities of inmates in British prisons. Jewkes suggests that there are various 'frames' through which prisoners are viewed. These are: celebrity prisoners, pampered prisoners, sexual relations in prison, lax security and, finally, assaults on prisoners. Of these five frames or themes, four of them involve giving the impression that prisoners lead easy lives in a relatively pleasant environment and only the fifth covers negative aspects of prison life. Jewkes argues that the majority of newspaper readers 'are looking for both confirmation of their existing views – which tend to be punitive – and for further opportunity to be shocked and outraged'. In order to get people to read their articles, therefore, the newspapers will reinforce these views. Jewkes's research is interesting as it partially supports Durkheim's argument that the law-abiding draw together in moral outrage at crime and this helps social cohesion. The newspapers in her study help maintain high levels of moral outrage.

parent families. Farrington and West's research suggests, therefore, that the failure within the family to provide adequate socialization and informal social control can lead to crime and so supports Hirschi's argument.

For some writers, the research of Farrington and West underlined their belief that the family and social control was the key to understanding the causes of crime. Writers such as Dennis and Erdos (1993) argue that the correlation between crime and certain family characteristics is a reflection of a much wider change in society. In particular, the traditional three-generation family structure had provided stability and a place in which moral values and a sense of community belonging had been passed on. However, since the 1960s, a series of changes in the family, in particular the decline in the role and presence of fathers, has weakened the **external patterns of social control** based on families and communities (where community members felt able to restrain extreme behaviour or young offenders) and also undermined the **internalized forms of social control** that had traditionally occurred through family socialization. However, Scraton (2002) rejects Dennis's argument. He accuses Dennis of mixing up a moral argument, reflecting his own views, with a sociological one supported by evidence.

The community and social control

The family may be the most important agency providing socialization to young people, but the family exists within a particular community. Farrington and West's research not only pointed to the importance of the family, but also to the social network in which the family is located.

The close relationship between family, community and offending was taken up by the American writer Charles Murray (1990). He argued that over the previous 30 years, there had been an increase in what he termed 'the **underclass**'. By this, Murray refers to a clearly distinguishable group of young people who:

- have no desire for formal paid employment, preferring to live off benefits and the illegal economy
- have a range of short-term sexual liaisons
- routinely have children born outside serious relationships, so that fathers do not regard their offspring as their responsibility.

The children of these people are brought up with little or no concern for the values of the society in general. The result is that there is now a generation of young people who do not share the values of the wider society and who are much more likely to commit crime. Poorer communities are being destroyed by the underclass, who are driving out the law-abiding majority, and thus the members of the underclass are becoming ever more isolated and confirmed in their behaviour. Dennis and Murray's writings link very closely with the work of the **right realists**, foremost among whom is James Q. Wilson (see p. 393).

Informal social control: a critical perspective

The approaches to informal social control which we have explored so far have suggested that the best way to understand why people commit crime is in terms of a failure of the family or the community to provide adequate socialization and impose sufficient informal social control. The assumption underlying these explanations is essentially consensual and the definition of deviance is a normative one. Critical or Marxist perspectives on social control reject this and emphasize the way that agencies such as the education system and the mass media set out to impose values upon the working class which benefit capitalism, but harm the working class.

However, there is a division between conflict theorists in the way they interpret offending and antisocial behaviour. On the one hand, **critical criminologists** such as Scraton (1997) argue that deviance is an indication of class conflict, reflecting the attempts of the working class to resist the oppression of the ruling class. Ultimately, this is a good thing as it will eventually lead to the collapse of capitalism. On the other hand, **left realists** such as Matthews and Young (1992) see the decline of community controls and the resulting increase in crime and antisocial behaviour as directly harmful for the working class.

Box (1983) has suggested another way of looking at social control and crime. He agrees with the more right-wing writers that it is release from social control that propels people into committing crime. However, his starting point is not that people are basically bad, but that capitalist society controls and exploits workers for its own ends – or, rather, for the benefit of the ruling class. When people are released in some way from direct control, then they are much more likely to commit crime because they see the unfairness of the system.

Box is suggesting, therefore, that control theory can be applied from a left-wing perspective and is not necessarily conservative in its approach.

Formal social control

As we said earlier, most societies tend to have a mixture of informal and formal control mechanisms, but the balance depends upon the type of society. For example, smaller and less complex groups with strongly shared values might rely more upon informal methods, whilst large, complex and multicultural societies may have to rely more upon the use of specific organizations. In this section we explore approaches to understanding formal control in complex, contemporary societies.

The functionalist perspective

Functionalist writers see the criminal justice system as operating to look after the interests of society as a whole. According to this approach, without control and punishment, society would collapse into a state of anomie. As we discussed in some detail earlier, Durkheim (1893) believed that societies could only exist if the members shared certain common, core values, (the collective conscience). However, many other values exist too that have rather less general acceptance (ranging from ones generally accepted to those that are openly in dispute). Thus a system of law exists to mark an unambiguous boundary line, identifying actions that trangress the boundary of acceptance into behaviour generally regarded as so deviant as to be illegal. We also saw how the process of prosecution provides a constant means of checking whether the law reflects the views of the majority of society. The role of the law is therefore crucial both in reflecting a consensus and maintaining social solidarity.

For Durkheim, the type of punishment provided by the formal system of control reflects the type of society. In less complex, **mechanistic societies**, punishment is based on **retribution** – in which savage penalties are imposed upon the wrongdoer in order to demonstrate society's abhorrence at the breaking of the commonly shared values. The punishment will be both public and physical in nature – so people are executed, mutilated and branded.

As societies develop and become more complex (**organic societies**), then the punishment shifts away from public punishment to imprisonment, and the aim of the punishment is more to force the person to make amends for their wrongdoing. He called this 'restitutive law'.

We shall return to explore some of these ideas in Topic 10, in which we examine the current British criminal justice system and, in particular, how they relate to neighbourhood policing and also to restorative justice.

Marxist approaches

Marxist writers, take a very different view of the criminal justice system from functionalists. Writers such as Hall

(Hall *et al.* 1978) and Chambliss (Chambliss and Mankoff 1976) argue that the criminal justice system operates solely for the benefit of the ruling class. The criminal justice system – police, judiciary and prisons – is based on controlling the working class and ensuring that any opposition to capitalism is quashed. Indeed, the law, according to Reiman (2006) is itself based upon outlawing certain acts performed by the working class, yet ignoring possibly more harmful acts performed by the ruling class.

Rusche and Kircheimer (1939) agree with the general Marxist argument that laws reflect the interests of the ruling class. However, they go further and argue that the forms of punishment also reflect their interests. As these interests change, so do the forms of punishment. Rusche and Kircheimer claim, for example, that slavery was an early form of punishment because of the need for manual labour, and that in feudalism the state used physical punishment as there was slightly less need for labour, but the peasants still needed to be repressed. With the arrival of capitalism, the prisons served the useful purposes of, first, training workers in the disciplines of long hours of meaningless work (for example, the treadmill) in poor conditions, and second, of mopping up the unemployed.

To support this argument, they pointed out that in times of high unemployment the prison population expands and then contracts in periods of high employment.

Late-modern perspectives: combining formal and informal control

Late-modern writers provide rather more complex analyses of the criminal justice system and the forms of punishment. Their interests focus more on the changing forms of social control over time. Two writers are particularly well known within this tradition: Foucault and Stanley Cohen.

Foucault

Foucault (1977) uses the term '**discipline**' instead of social control, as his explanation for the changing nature of control combines both informal and formal social control. Foucault argues that there have been key changes in the natures of discipline and punishment over the period of pre-modernity to late-modernity. In pre-modernity, social control was exercised through discipline imposed upon the body – public executions, flogging, cutting limbs and so on. These punishments were performed publicly so that people were frightened by the sheer pain they saw, but also dazzled by the 'majesty of the law' in action. The discipline or nature of formal social control by the state was haphazard and erratic. However, over time, and particularly in late modernity, the nature of discipline and punishment has become much more intertwined and subtle. In particular, Foucault argues, discipline took on two main characteristics:

1 It became extended and diffused throughout society, no longer haphazard and erratic, with more and more agents of social control (police, PCSOs, wardens, antisocial behaviour coordinators, community safety officers, youth offending workers, and so on).
2 It moved from being something physical, imposed via punishment upon individuals, to something subtle

which people internalized in such a way that, increasingly, they police themselves. Instead of a central state seeking to control people through the threat of violence, the state seeks to control through the minds of the population. Examples of this include the cognitive therapy courses prisoners must do on 'controlling offending behaviour' and curbing violence.

Foucault suggests that the effect is such that people always feel that the state is watching them. For Foucault, these ideas are summarized in the design of a prison which was proposed in the mid-19th century (though never built in its pure form) in which prisoners would sit, isolated in their cells in a circular shaped prison which allowed the prison officer sitting in the centre of the prison to watch all the prisoners, but they were unable to see the officer. This meant that they never knew when they were being watched and, consequently, had to ensure that they always behaved as the prison wanted. Foucault called this form of prison the '**panopticon**'.

Cohen

Stan Cohen, writing at about the same time (1985), provided a fairly similar analysis, summarizing his work into a number of key themes which explain the changing nature of formal control in Western societies.

- *Penetration* – Historically, societies had fairly simple forms of control, with the state passing a law which was then haphazardly enforced by whatever authorities existed at the time. However, Cohen argues that increasingly the law is expected to penetrate right through society, and that conformity and control are part of the job that schools, the media and even private companies are supposed to engage in. Social control has extended throughout society and is performed by many more agencies than in the past. Today, the police are only one of a wide range of 'enforcement agencies'. This leads to his second point.

- *Size and density* – Cohen points out the sheer scale of the control apparatuses in modern society, with literally hundreds of thousands of people working for the state and other organizations involved in imposing control – and over a period of time, millions having that control imposed upon them. For example, approximately one-third of all males under 30 have been arrested for a criminal offence. Cohen points out that the range of control agencies is increasing and 'processing' ever larger numbers of people. Furthermore, the criminal justice system is constantly extending its reach into the population by devising new 'social problems' which require ever more control by the state. A good example of this was the construction of the term 'antisocial behaviour' at the turn of 21st century. This drew a wide range of unrelated acts – such as young people hanging around, noisy neighbours, dropping litter, and prostitution – under the umbrella of antisocial behaviour. A new profession was then introduced to police these acts, that of the antisocial behaviour coordinator and each local authority is required by the government to have at least one of these officials.

- *Identity and visibility* – Cohen argues that control and punishment used to be public and obvious, but more recently there has been a growth in subtle forms of control and punishment. Closed-circuit TV (CCTV), tagging, legally enforceable drug routines for the

Key terms

Anomie term, first used by Durkheim, to describe a breakdown of social expectations and behaviour. Later used by Merton to explain reactions to situations where socially approved goals were impossible for the majority of the population to reach by legitimate means.

Collective conscience a term used by Durkheim to describe the core, shared values of society.

Consensual where the vast majority of people share similar values

Correlation a statistical relationship between two or more social events.

Crime activities that break the law of the land and are subject to official punishment

Criminologists social scientists who study crime.

Critical criminology work of criminologists influenced by Marxist thinking.

Delinquency criminal or antisocial acts committed by young people.

Deviance behaviour that is different from the normal expectations of a society and is viewed as 'wrong' or bad'.

Discipline a term used by Foucault, merging the notions of formal and informal social control.

External patterns of social control social control imposed by people on potential or actual offenders.

Formal social control the process whereby laws and rules are enforced by agencies that have been created specifically for this purpose, such as the police.

Informal social control the process whereby individuals are encouraged or coerced by people they mix with into conforming with what are perceived as appropriate values.

Internalized forms of social control social control that people impose upon themselves via their conscience, which is, in turn, largely the result of their upbringing.

Left realism a Marxist-derived approach to criminology that argues that crime hurts the most vulnerable in society rather than the rich and powerful, and so more resources need to be spent on helping and protecting these poorer victims of crime.

Longitudinal research sociological research method involving studying a group over a long period of time.

Mechanistic societies technologically and socially simple societies, in which people are culturally very similar.

Organic societies culturally and technologically complex societies, in which people are culturally different from each other.

Panopticon a design of prison in which the prisoners can be observed at all times, but never know whether or not they are being observed. The term is now used as a means of describing a society where this happens.

Restitutive a model of law based upon trying to repair the damage done to society.

Retributive a model of law based upon revenge.

Right realism approach to crime deriving from the right-wing theories of James Q. Wilson and emphasizing 'zero tolerance'.

Social bond in control theories, the forms of social control preventing people acting in a deviant way.

Underclass term used by Charles Murray to describe a distinctive 'class' of people whose lifestyle involves taking what they can from the state and living a life involving petty crime and sexual gratification.

'mentally ill' and curfews are all part of an ever-growing and invisible net of control. He also notes that the state has handed over part of its monopoly of controlling people to private organizations. So there has been a growth in private security companies, doorstaff at nightclubs and even private prisons. All of whom exist to police people, but are not members of the police force.

Conclusion

In this introductory topic, we have explored the concepts of deviance and informal social control. What emerges is a profound division between the various sociological perspectives on crime and deviance, which have their starting points in the differing definitions of the basis of deviance. If one takes the view that the basis of society is a consensus on fundamental values, then the role of sociology is to explain why some people fail to conform and this leads to exploration of issues such as lack of socialization and poor informal control.

On the other hand, those sociologists who see society as based on conflicting values have limited interest in exploring why people do not conform. The interest in this approach is how certain values come to dominate, and the related question is why should anyone conform to these dominant values if they are not in their interests?

Check your understanding

1 Identify and briefly explain the two views on defining 'deviance' supported by sociologists.

2 Explain how crime could be negative for society.

3 Give two examples of different ways sociologists have interpreted the relationship between deviance and the law.

4 What correlations did Farrington and West find between the family and criminal behaviour?

5 What do sociologists mean by informal social control? Give one example.

6 Explain the meaning of formal social control. Give two examples of agencies of social control.

7 Why is Foucault's approach to social control significantly different from other sociological explanations?

8 What changes in social control does Cohen suggest have occurred?

Activities

Research idea

Identify two small samples, one of over-40 year olds and one of 16 to 19 year olds. Write a short questionnaire to find out what each group sees as the main social problems in Britain today and how best these should be addressed. Compare the answers of the two groups. What do they tell you (if anything) about changing values?

Web.task

Your local authority will have a Community Safety Partnership detailing the activities your area is engaging in to tackle crime. Visit it and see what initiatives are being carried out. You can find the address at **www.homeoffice.gov.uk/crime/**.

Find out what you can about Family Intervention Projects – how can you link these to the ideas of Foucault and Cohen?

An eye on the exam   Deviance and control theories

Examine the role of formal and informal social control in controlling individuals' behaviour.   (12 marks)

Grade booster   Getting top marks in this question

For this question, you should start your answer with a brief definition of each type of social control, noting that social control is exercised over both criminal and non-criminal forms of deviant behaviour. You should give some examples of each type – for instance, imprisonment or fines, and being 'sent to Coventry' or 'grounded' by parents. You should examine some of the different social institutions that exercise social control, such as education, the family, police and prisons. You need to consider different sociological perspectives on the question of social control, such as functionalist and Marxist views, as well as 'late-modern' approaches such as those of Foucault or Stan Cohen. You could also link your discussion of some of the institutions, such as the family, to perspectives such as functionalism or the New Right.

TOPIC 2

Strain and subcultural theories

Getting you thinking

Youngsters 'turning to gangs instead of parents'

Gangs are the new families for many youngsters. One in three teenagers do not consider their parents to be role models, according to a survey.

The Prince's Trust youth charity found that young people were turning instead to gangs and 'youth communities' for support: 58 per cent of young people claimed that finding a sense of identity is a key reason for joining a gang; 22 per cent said young people were looking for role models in gangs, with 55 per cent citing friends and peers as role models.

Martina Milburn, chief executive of The Prince's Trust, said: 'All the threads that hold a community together – a common identity, role models, a sense of safety – were given by young people as motivations to join gangs. Our research suggests that young people are creating their own "youth communities" and gangs in search of the influences that could once have been found in traditional communities.'

It found that young people with a problem were twice as likely to turn to a friend for advice as to a parent.

Last month, South Wales Chief Constable Barbara Wilding warned that gangs based on drugs and violence had replaced traditional families for many youths.

'In areas of extreme deprivation there are almost feral groups of very angry young people. Many have experienced family breakdown, and in place of parental and family role models the gang culture is now established.

'Tribal loyalty has replaced family loyalty, and gang culture based on violence and drugs is a way of life.'

www.dailymail.co.uk/news/article-1042760/
Youngsters-turning-gangs-instead-parents.html

1 Who do you turn to for advice over difficult or embarrassing issues, your parents or friends?

2 Do you 'hang around' most evenings with your friends?

3 Are there any 'gangs' in your area?

4 Define what you mean by a 'gang'.

You may well feel that your friends exert a considerable influence on your life. Sometimes, groups of friends develop norms and values that are unconventional and may encourage deviant acts. **Subcultural theories** share the common belief that people who commit crime usually share different values from the mass of law-abiding members of society. However, crime-committing people do not live in complete opposition to mainstream values, rather they have 'amended' certain values so that this justifies criminal behaviour – hence the term '**subculture**'. (The relationship between offending and subculture is illustrated in Fig. 6.1.) **Strain** is a term that is used to refer to explanations of criminal behaviour that argue that crime is the result of certain groups of people being placed in a position where they are unable, for whatever reason, to conform to the values and beliefs of society. Many sociologists use the term interchangeably with 'subculture'. Although, strictly speaking, they are not the same thing (for example, Merton is a 'strain' theorist and does not really discuss subculture), we have put them together here because of the degree of overlap between the two approaches.

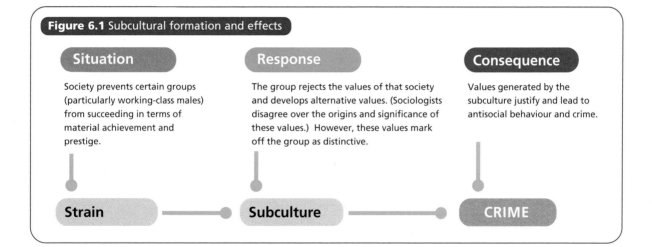

Figure 6.1 Subcultural formation and effects

Situation

Society prevents certain groups (particularly working-class males) from succeeding in terms of material achievement and prestige.

Response

The group rejects the values of that society and develops alternative values. (Sociologists disagree over the origins and significance of these values.) However, these values mark off the group as distinctive.

Consequence

Values generated by the subculture justify and lead to antisocial behaviour and crime.

Strain ———● **Subculture** ———● **CRIME**

The origins of subculture

Subcultural theories derive from two different schools of sociology – and if you think carefully about each of the approaches we discuss later, you will probably be able to tell which school of thought they derive from.

Appreciative sociology

The first parent-school is that of the University of Chicago, which developed in the early part of the 20th century in response to the dramatic social change that was taking place in US cities at that time. Chicago sociologists were determined to appreciate the wide variety of different cultures and lifestyles in Chicago that existed as a result of the huge influx of migrants arriving from all over Europe and southern USA. Chicago sociologists pioneered the use of participant observation in their research. They simply wanted to observe and note down the sheer variety and dynamism of urban life. Integral to this was the study of deviant groups, with Frederic Thrasher's *The Gang* (1927) and Whyte's *Street Corner Society* (1943) demonstrating that deviant groups in society had clear norms and values of their own that justified their different behaviour.

Strain theory

In the 1930s, Robert Merton (1938), tried to locate deviance within a functionalist framework. For Merton, crime and deviance were evidence of a poor fit (or a strain) between the socially accepted goals of society and the socially approved means of obtaining those desired goals. The resulting strain led to deviance.

Merton argued that all societies set their members certain goals and, at the same time, provide socially approved ways of achieving these goals. Merton was aware that not everyone shared the same goals; he pointed out that, in a stratified society, the goals were linked to a person's position in the social structure. Those lower down had restricted goals. The system worked well as long as there was a reasonable chance that a majority of people were able to achieve their goals. However, if the

majority of the population were unable to achieve the socially set goals, then they became disenchanted with society and sought out alternative (often deviant) ways of behaving. Merton used Durkheim's term anomie (see p. 332), to describe this situation.

The following five different forms of behaviour could then be understood as a strain between goals and means:

1 *Conformity* – The individual continues to adhere to both goals and means, despite the limited likelihood of success.
2 *Innovation* – The person accepts the goals of society but uses different ways to achieve those goals; criminal behaviour is included in this response.
3 *Ritualism* – The means are used by the individual, but sight of the actual goal is lost, e.g. the bureaucrat or the police officer blindly enforcing the letter of the law without looking at the nature of justice.
4 *Retreatism* – The individual rejects both goals and means. The person dependent upon drugs or alcohol is included in this form of behaviour.
5 *Rebellion* – Both the socially sanctioned goals and means are rejected and different ones substituted. This is the political activist or the religious fundamentalist.

Criticism of Merton

Merton has been criticized by Valier (2001), amongst others, for his stress on the existence of common goals in society. Valier argues that there are, in fact, a variety of goals that people strive to attain at any one time.

Illegitimate opportunity structure

The idea of strain between goals and means had a very significant impact on the writings of Cloward and Ohlin (1960), who owed much to the ideas of Merton.

They argued that Merton had failed to appreciate that there was a parallel opportunity structure to the legal one, called the **illegitimate opportunity structure**. By this they meant that for some subcultures in society, a regular illegal career was available, with recognized illegal means of obtaining society's goals. A good example of this is given in Dick Hobbs' book *Bad Business* (1998). Hobbs interviewed successful professional criminals and demonstrated how it is possible to have a career in crime, given the right connections and 'qualities'.

According to Cloward and Ohlin, the illegal opportunity structure had three possible adaptations or subcultures:

1 *Criminal* – There is a thriving local criminal subculture, with successful role models. Young offenders can 'work their way up the ladder' in the criminal hierarchy.
2 *Conflict* – There is no local criminal subculture to provide a career opportunity. Groups brought up in this sort of environment are likely to turn to violence, usually against other similar groups. Cloward and Ohlin give the example of violent **gang** 'warfare'.
3 *Retreatist* – This tends to be a more individual response and occurs where the individual has no opportunity or ability to engage in either of the other two subcultures. The result is a retreat into alcohol or drugs.

Evaluation of Cloward and Ohlin

This explanation is useful and, as Hobbs' work shows, for some people there really is a criminal opportunity structure. But the approach shares some of the weaknesses of Merton's original theory:

● It is difficult to accept that such a neat distinction into three clear categories occurs in real life.
● There is no discussion whatsoever about female deviancy.

Status frustration

Writing in the mid 1950s, Albert Cohen (1955) drew upon both Merton's ideas of strain and also on the **ethnographic** ideas of the Chicago school of sociology. Cohen was particularly interested in the fact that much offending behaviour was not economically motivated, but simply done for the thrill of the act. (This is as true today as it was in the 1950s, for vandalism typically accounts for about 18 per cent of current crime recorded by the British Crime Survey.)

According to Cohen, 'lower-class' boys strove to emulate middle-class values and aspirations, but lacked the means to attain success. This led to **status frustration** – that is, a sense of personal failure and inadequacy. The result was that they rejected those very values and patterns of 'acceptable' behaviour that they could not be successful within. He suggests that school is the key area for the playing out of this drama. Lower-class children are much more likely to fail and so feel humiliated. In an attempt to gain status, they 'invert' traditional middle-class values by behaving badly and engaging in a variety of antisocial behaviours.

Criticisms of Albert Cohen

● There is no discussion of females. His research is solely about males.

● The young 'delinquents' need to be brilliant sociologists to work out what are middle-class values and then invert them!
● Cohen fails to prove that school really is the key place where success and failure are demonstrated.

Focal concerns

In the late 1950s, Walter Miller developed a rather different approach to explaining the values of crime when he suggested that deviancy was linked to the culture of lower-class males. Miller (1962) suggested that working-class males have six '**focal concerns**' that are likely to lead to delinquency:

1 *Smartness* – A person should both look good and also be witty with a 'sharp repartee'.
2 *Trouble* – 'I don't go looking for trouble, but ...'.
3 *Excitement* – It is important to search out thrills (see Katz, Topic 7, p. 375).
4 *Toughness* – Being physically stronger than others is good. It is also important to be able to demonstrate this.
5 *Autonomy* – It is important not to be pushed around by others.
6 *Fate* – Individuals have little chance to overcome the wider fate that awaits them.

According to Miller, then, young lower-class males are pushed towards crime by the implicit values of their subculture.

Evaluation of Miller

Miller provides little evidence to show that these are specifically lower-class values. Indeed, as Box (1981) pointed out, they could equally apply to males right across the class structure.

Key themes

Sociological theories and methods

Participant observation

Subcultural theories are almost always based upon using observational methods. A famous example of participant observation is Howard Parker's book *View from the Boys* (1992). Parker studied a group of young males in Liverpool who stole car radios to fund their lifestyle, which involved cannabis use, heavy drinking and fighting. Parker joined in some of these activities and admits that he got so involved that he actually kept watch while they stole the radios. Towards the end of his study, when the 'Boys' were being prosecuted for their activities, they turned to him for support and advice. There are moral issues here about how far sociologists should get involved with those they are studying, but also methodological issues about the extent of bias in such studies.

Applying subcultural theory: the British experience

The studies we have looked at so far have mainly been American ones. However, subcultural studies were being undertaken in Britain too – though with a variety of results. Howard Parker (1974) successfully applied Miller's focal concerns in his study of working-class 'lads' in inner-city Liverpool (see 'Key themes'), although he could probably have applied these equally successfully to rugby-playing students at Liverpool University.

On the other hand, studies by David Downes (1966) of young working-class males in London could find no evidence of distinctive values. Instead, Downes suggested that young working-class males were 'dissociated' from mainstream values, by which he meant that they were concerned more about leisure than their long-term future or employment, and were more likely to engage in petty crime. So, in the UK, evidence of distinctive subcultures has been fairly difficult to obtain.

Subterranean values

One consistent criticism of subcultural theories was that there was little evidence to demonstrate a distinct set of antisocial values. Even if there were subcultures, were they a response to middle-class values or to a distinctive set of working-class values?

Matza put these criticisms together to make a strong attack upon subcultural theory (Matza and Sykes 1961). Matza argued that there were no distinctive subcultural values, rather that all groups in society used a shared set of **subterranean values**. The key thing was that, most of the time, most people control these deviant desires. They only rarely emerge – for example, at the annual office party, or the holiday in Agia Napa. But when they do emerge, we use **techniques of neutralization** to provide justification for our deviant actions (see Fig. 6.2). The difference between a persistent offender and a law-abiding citizen is simply how often and in what circumstances the subterranean values emerge and are then justified by the techniques of neutralization.

Matza's critique of subculture is quite devastating. He is saying that all of us share deviant, 'subcultural values', and that it is not true that there are distinctive groups with their own values, different from the rest of us.

Subculture: the paradox of inclusion

In his book *On the Edge*, Carl Nightingale (1993) studied young Black youth in an inner-city area of Philadelphia. For Nightingale, subculture emerges from a desire to be part of, rather than to reject, mainstream US society that has rejected and marginalized them. Nightingale notes the way that Black children avidly consume US culture by watching television with its emphasis on consumerism and the success of violence – yet at the same time they are excluded economically, racially and politically from participating in that mainstream US culture. The response is to overcompensate by identifying themselves with the wider culture by acquiring articles with high-status trade names or logos. Once again, drawing upon Merton's ideas, the subculture reflects the belief that it is not so much how these high-status goods are obtained, rather the fact of possessing them. In the USA, these are often obtained through violence, expressed in violent gangs and high crime rates.

Similarly, Philip Bourgois' study of El Barrio (2002) looks at the lives of drug dealers and criminals in this deprived area of New York and finds that they, too, believe in the 'American Dream' of financial success. The values of their 'subculture' are really little different from mainstream values, the only difference being that they deal drugs in order to get the money to pursue an all-American lifestyle.

So, both Nightingale's and Bourgois' versions of subculture take us back to the strain theory of Merton, and Cloward and Ohlin, emphasizing that the desire to be included leads, paradoxically, to the actions that ensure that they are excluded from society.

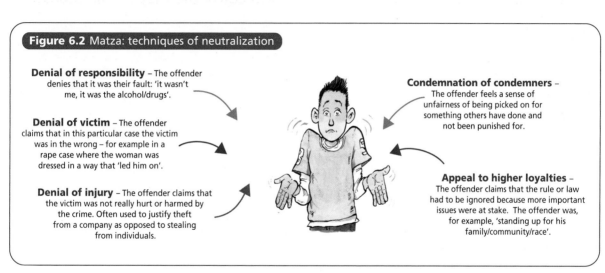

Figure 6.2 Matza: techniques of neutralization

Denial of responsibility – The offender denies that it was their fault: 'it wasn't me, it was the alcohol/drugs'.

Denial of victim – The offender claims that in this particular case the victim was in the wrong – for example in a rape case where the woman was dressed in a way that 'led him on'.

Denial of injury – The offender claims that the victim was not really hurt or harmed by the crime. Often used to justify theft from a company as opposed to stealing from individuals.

Condemnation of condemners – The offender feels a sense of unfairness of being picked on for something others have done and not been punished for.

Appeal to higher loyalties – The offender claims that the rule or law had to be ignored because more important issues were at stake. The offender was, for example, 'standing up for his family/community/race'.

Key themes

Socialization, culture and identity

Subcultures

Subculture as a concept is not solely related to crime and deviance; it is widely used throughout sociology to explain just why particular groups behave in ways that are different from the rest of society. These applications of the idea of subcultural theory are also often shot through with value judgements on the part of sociologists. In schools, for example, numerous sociologists, notably Willis, have uncovered antischool subcultures where the students oppose the values of the school and get pleasure from being disruptive. In Willis' study there seems a degree of admiration for the lads.

Murray has used the term in a much broader and more negative sense to claim the existence of an 'underclass' of people who prefer to live off state benefits and petty crime. The females are likely to have early pregnancies and are single parents, while the males will father a number of children by different partners, but are unlikely to support their children financially. Murray's arguments are strongly contested by other sociologists however. Whereas, Murray writes disapprovingly about the underclass, Stacey writes supportively about the development of gay and lesbian families. Stacey identifies a new subculture emerging of gays and lesbians rejecting the dominant values regarding the importance of heterosexuals as the only people able to have a family with children.

sharing a set of values. He suggested that it was much better to think of subcultures in terms of 'fluidity, occasional gatherings and dispersal'. Neo-tribes then referred more to states of mind and lifestyles that were very flexible, open and changing. Deviant values are less important than a stress on consumption, suitably fashionable behaviour and individual identity that can change rapidly.

Masculinity

Subcultural theory is overwhelmingly male subcultural theory. The assumptions underlying the vast bulk of the writings we have looked at within this tradition have been discussing masculine behaviour. However, as Collison (1996) points out, they may well have missed the significance of this. In order to explain male offending behaviour, it is important to explain the nature of being male in our society and the links masculinity itself has to crime. The work of Connell (1995) is particularly interesting here, in that he sees the existence of a hegemonic masculinity which males both conspire with and aspire to. The emphasis of this hegemonic masculinity is very similar in values to Miller's early work on 'lower-class values'. However, Winlow (2004) argues that the values are best seen within the context of a changing economic social structure. Winlow suggests that the traditional (working-class) male values fitted physical work undertaken by men in industrial settings. These have now gone and the values are inappropriate for contemporary employment. He suggests, too, that the problem may be even greater for those young men excluded completely from employment.

Contemporary alternatives to subculture

Postmodernism

Most of the approaches we have looked at here, as well as the Marxist subcultural approaches described in Topic 3, seek to explain deviant behaviour by looking for some rational reason why the subculture might have developed. Recent postmodern approaches reject this explanation for behaviour. Katz (1988), for example, argues that crime is seductive – young males get drawn into it, not because of any process of rejection but because it is thrilling. In a similar manner, Lyng (1990) argues that young males like taking risks and engaging in '**edgework**' as he puts it. By edgework, he means going right to the edge of acceptable behaviour and flirting with danger.

Neo-Tribes

Maffesoli (1996) introduced a postmodernist innovation in understanding subcultures, with his argument for the existence of neo-tribes. Maffesoli was unhappy with the idea that the idea of subculture had been transformed from a concept based on values more into one of a group

Goths: subculture or neo-tribe?

Gangs and subcultures

Despite the widespread media coverage of youth gangs, which give the impression of widespread gang membership, only about 6 to 9 per cent of young people claim to belong or to have ever belonged to a 'gang', and just 2 per cent claim to carry or ever carry a knife, according to research by YouGov (2008).

Indeed researchers suggest that the idea of a gang is defined differently by different young people. This has led Marshall *et al.* (2005) to suggest that there are three distinct categories of youth groupings, which vary in the degree of seriousness of offending behaviour, but which are often mixed together under the term 'gang':

1   *Peer groups or 'crews'* – These are unorganized groups of young people who tend to hang around together in a particular place. Any offending behaviour is incidental and does not reflect any great estrangement from society.
2   *Gangs* – Youth gangs in Britain tend to have similar characteristics to peer groups or crews, but instead have a focus on offending and violence. These are the sorts of youth gangs that the majority of the theoretical models of subculture in this topic were intended to explain.
3   *Organized criminal groups* – These are the most serious types of groups, who are heavily involved in serious crime. The age of the members vary and there is a clear hierarchy. For the gang members, the illegal activities comprise their occupation. These are the sorts of gangs to which Cloward and Ohlin's analysis can most easily be applied.

Key terms

Edgework derives from Lyng. Refers to activities of young males which provide them with thrills derived from the real possibility of physical or emotional harm (e.g. stealing and racing cars; drug abuse).

Ethnographic form of observational research in which researcher lives amongst, and describes activities of, particular group being studied.

Focal concerns term used by Miller to describe key values.

Gang term applied to a wide variety of youth groups, but should only be used for organized groups that regularly engage in offending.

Illegitimate opportunity structure an alternative, illegal way of life that certain groups in society have access to.

Status frustration according to Cohen, this occurs

when young men feel that they are looked down upon by society.

Strain term used by Merton and other functionalists to describe a lack of balance and adjustment in society.

Subculture a distinctive set of values that provides an alternative to those of the mainstream culture.

Subcultural theories explanations of crime and deviance focusing on the idea that those who deviate hold different values to the majority.

Subterranean values a set of deviant values that exist alongside the socially approved values, but are usually kept hidden or under control. They may emerge in certain social situations, such as at parties or after drinking alcohol.

Techniques of neutralization justifications for our deviant actions.

Focus on research

Smith and Bradshaw (2005)
Gang membership and teenage offending

Smith and Bradshaw undertook a longitudinal research study to explore gang membership and youth offending. The project used a wide range of research methods including self-report questionnaires with young people conducted in annual sweeps to identify any changes and patterns. This was followed by semistructured interviews, for depth of detail, with a subsample of the young people. At the same time, a sample of teachers and parents completed questionnaires. The researchers also examined the records of social work reports and children's hearings (a type of youth court).

A variety of schools were used as the basis for the research, which included 23 state secondary schools, eight independent schools and nine special schools. However, there is a problem with these as a sampling frame, as the research only reached young people in education.

In terms of findings, Smith and Bradshaw concluded that rates of gang membership fell with age, with 20 per cent of respondents reporting that they were members of a 'gang' at age 13, falling to 5 per cent at age 17, suggesting that young people mature out of gang membership.

They found that rates of membership were higher in more deprived neighbourhoods, among respondents from manual households and among one-parent families. They also found that there was a 'close association' between gang membership and offending, and also drug use.

Smith, D.J. and Bradshaw, J. (2005) *Gang Membership and Teenage Offending*, Edinburgh: Edinburgh University, Centre for Law and Society

1   Why is a longitudinal study useful in explaining why people join (and leave) gangs?

2   What problems can you see in using self-report studies about gang membership, offending and drug use?

3   What advantages do semistructured interviews have compared to structured ones?

4   Can you indentify one problem with this research?

Check your understanding

1. What is meant by 'appreciative sociology'?

2. How does Merton use the idea of anomie to explain deviance?

3. How, according to A. Cohen, does school failure lead to the formation of subcultures?

4. How does the idea of 'techniques of neutralization' undermine some subcultural arguments?

5. What do we mean by the 'paradox of inclusion'?

6. Why is the idea of 'masculinity' relevant to understanding criminal behaviour?

Activities

Research idea

Check the graffiti in your area – are there any tags of particular groups which appear regularly? What does this suggest?

Web.task

www.law.ed.ac.uk/cls/esytc/findings/digest8.pdf
This is part of an extensive research project about young people in Edinburgh. If you work in groups, you can divide the study into themes; each group can work on a theme and then present a poster summarizing the main points of your theme to the rest of the class. For example, you could use the themes: context to the research; methodology; gang membership; offending; drug use, and so on.

An eye on the exam — Strain and subcultural theories

Item A

In his book, *In Search of Respect*, Philippe Bourgois studied criminal groups in a large US city. Bourgois rejected the idea that these gang members were significantly different from other Americans in their aspirations. He claimed that it was a mistake to imagine they lived in a subculture with separate values and beliefs from the rest of US society.

>> *I want to place drug dealers and street level criminals into their rightful positions with the mainstream of US society. They are not 'exotic others' operating in an irrational netherworld. On the contrary, they are 'made in America'. Highly motivated, ambitious inner-city youths have been attracted to the rapidly expanding, multi-billion dollar drug economy precisely because they believe ... [in] the American Dream.*

> *In fact, in their pursuit of success, they are even following the minute details of the classical yankee model for upward mobility. They are aggressively pursuing careers as private entrepreneurs: they take risks, work hard and pray for good luck.* >>

Bourgois, P. (2002) *In Search of Respect* (2nd edn), Cambridge: Cambridge University Press

Using material from **Item A** and elsewhere, examine strain theories as an explanation of crime and deviance in contemporary society.

(12 marks)

Grade booster — Getting top marks in this question

You need to describe the main features of strain theories, such as Merton's. You should, therefore, explain what is meant by 'strain' and include the five different possible responses to strain that Merton identifies. Make sure you use some of the material in the Item. For example, try to link ideas about the American Dream, motivation, hard work, upward mobility, and so on, to the key ideas of strain theories. To evaluate strain theories, you could draw upon subcultural theories, such as those of Cloward and Ohlin, and Albert Cohen, identifying the deficiencies they see in Merton's approach and considering whether they offer a better explanation of crime and deviance than do strain theories.

TOPIC 3

Critical criminologies

Getting you thinking

Today, more than 350 million children, aged from 5 to 17, are at work. They can be differentiated on the basis of their age, the effect that working has on their basic rights and, in particular, the extent to which their work causes them harm.

More than 140 million of the total are old enough to be working under international standards. Nevertheless, getting on for half of these – 60 million – suffer harm because they are involved in the abuse of the 'worst forms' of child labour, from which they should be protected. The remaining 80 million have reasonable jobs, either in industrialized or developing countries.

Out of approximately 211 million working children under 15, more than half (over 120 million) are involved in the 'worst forms'. So, together with older adolescents, almost 180 million young people below 18 are involved in the 'worst forms', approximately 1 in every 12 children in the world today. The vast majority of these, more than 170 million, are engaged in work that is hazardous, posing a health risk and, in some cases, even threatening their lives.

www.unicef.org.uk/publications/pdf/ECECHILD2_A4.pdf

Look at the photos of the children working. Although it would be illegal in the UK for them to work like this, it is legal in their countries. The girls making the fluffy toys work up to 12 hours each day in a factory in south-east Asia and earn a pittance. The boy works in a battery recycling factory in Bangladesh, spending the day breaking up batteries to get reuseable parts and metal out of them.

1 Do you think it is wrong? Do you think it should be made illegal (as it is in the UK) or do you think that each country should be left to sort out its own laws?

2 Suggest why an act should be made illegal.

3 Using your own ideas, can you find any examples of activities that you think ought to be crimes, but are not? Can you suggest why they are not crimes?

<< I wake up at the first cockcrow, I clean the house and the kitchen, I collect kindling, which we sell in bundles at the market and we survive thanks to the money it brings in. I do the cooking and washing. I go to the market, I chop wood. My aunt's children go to school and I stay home to do everything. I only eat once a day ... If I happen not to sell enough oranges they tell me I am cursed and 'good for nothing'. And if I'm ever unlucky enough to lose any, I have to pay them back out of the little money that my parents give me whenever they stop by to visit. I want to go back to my parents ... I often have headaches. At night I tremble, I'm so tired.>>

Matou, a 12-year-old in Guinea, working for a woman 85 kilometres away from her home. When Matou's parents learnt about her suffering, they urged her employer to send her to school. Her employer promised she would, but nothing has come of it.

Recorded for UNICEF, 2003

The activity on the previous page should have alerted you to the possibility that laws, and the way they are applied, may favour certain groups – in most cases, the rich and powerful. This is the starting point for Marxist and neo-Marxist approaches – often referred to as critical criminology.

The traditional Marxist approach

Karl Marx himself wrote very little about crime, but a Marxist theory of crime was first developed by Bonger as early as 1916 and then developed by writers such as Chambliss (1975). The overall background to this approach was based on the Marxist analysis of society, which argues that society is best understood by examining the process whereby the majority of the population are exploited by the owners and controllers of commerce and industry. Marxists argue that this simple, fundamental fact of exploitation provides the key to unlock the explanations for the workings of society.

The key elements of the Marxist or critical criminological approach include:

- the basis of criminal law
- the dominant **hegemony** of the ruling class
- law enforcement
- individual motivation
- crime and control.

The basis of the criminal law

The starting point for Marxist analysis is that all laws are essentially for the benefit of the ruling class, and that criminal law reflects their interests. For example, concern with the laws of property ownership largely benefit those with significant amounts of property. For those who are poor, there is little to steal. Personal violence is dangerous, and the ruling class wish to control the right to use violence in society through their agents – the police and the army. Criminal law therefore operates to protect the rich and powerful.

Law creation and the dominant hegemony

In capitalist societies, the ruling class impose their values – that is, values that are beneficial to themselves – upon the mass of the population. They do this through a number of agencies, such as the education system, religion and the mass media. (This concept of ruling-class values being imposed upon the population is commonly known as 'hegemony'.)

This dominant set of values forms the framework on which laws are based in a democracy. However, we have just seen that, according to Marxists, the set of values is actually 'forced' on the people. Thus, what they believe they are agreeing to as a result of their own beliefs is, in reality, in the interests of the ruling class.

Law enforcement

Despite the fact that the law-making process reflects the interests of the ruling class, many of these laws could provide benefits for the majority of the population if they were applied fairly. However, even the interpretation and enforcement of the law is biased in favour of the ruling class, so that the police and the judicial system will arrest and punish the working class, but tend not to enforce the law against the ruling class.

Individual motivation

Marxist theory also provides an explanation for the individual motivation underlying crime. Bonger (1916), the very first Marxist writer on crime, pointed this out. He argued that capitalism is based upon competition, selfishness and greed, and this formed people's attitudes to life. Therefore, crime was a perfectly normal outcome of these values, which stressed looking after oneself at the expense of others. However, Bonger also said that in many cases, poor people were driven to crime by their desperate conditions

Crime and control

As we saw in Chapter 5 (see pp. 257–9, 'Marxism'), the ruling class in capitalism constantly seeks to divert the attention of the vast majority of the population away from an understanding of the true causes of their situation, and to impose their values through the mass media, religious organizations and the education system. These institutions provide alternative accounts of reality justifying the capitalist system as the natural and best economic system. Crime plays a significant part in supporting the ideology of capitalism, as it diverts attention away from the exploitative nature of capitalism and focuses attention instead on the evil and frightening nature of certain criminal groups in society, from whom we are only protected by the police. This justifies heavy policing of working-class areas, 'stop and searches' of young people, and the arrests of any sections of the population who oppose capitalism.

An example of the traditional Marxist approach

William Chambliss' study of British vagrancy laws provides an illustration of the ways in which laws may be directly related to the interests of the ruling class. The first English vagrancy laws appeared in 1349, one year after the outbreak of the Black Death plague that was to kill more than one-third of the country's entire population. One result of the catastrophe was to decimate the labour force, so that those who were left could ask for high wages – and many people did this, moving from village to village in search of high pay. To combat this, the vagrancy laws were introduced, requiring every able-bodied man on the road to accept work at a low, fixed wage. The law was strictly enforced and did produce a supply of low-paid labour to help the workforce shortage. For almost 200 years the laws remained unchanged, but in 1530, changes were introduced which altered the emphasis of the laws to protect the concerns of an increasingly powerful merchant class from the many highway robbers who were preying on the traffic of goods along major highways. The vagrancy laws were amended so that they could be used to punish anyone on the road without a job, who was presumed to be a highwayman.

In both cases, the law was introduced and imposed in such a way as to benefit the ruling class – whilst apparently being concerned with stopping vagrants from travelling around England.

Criticisms of the traditional Marxist approach

1 The victims of crime are simply ignored in this analysis. The harm done by offenders is not taken into account. This is particularly important, as the victims are usually drawn from the less well-off sections of the population.
2 The explanation for law creation and enforcement tends to be one dimensional, in that all laws are seen as the outcome of the interests of the ruling class – no allowance is made for the complexity of influences on law-making behaviour.

The New Criminology

Partly as a result of these criticisms of what was a fairly crude Marxist explanation of crime, and partly as a result of the influence of interactionism (see Topic 4), Taylor, Walton and Young attempted to produce a fully social theory of deviance in *The New Criminology* (1973). This became an extremely influential book – possibly because it was a fairly successful fusing of Marxism and interactionism, the two most prominent theories of that time.

The new criminologists argued that in order to understand why a particular crime took place, it was no use just looking at the individual's motivation (e.g. alcohol or jealousy) and obvious influences (e.g. family background), which is what traditional positivist sociology might do. A Marxist perspective must be taken, looking at the wider capitalist society that is helping generate the circumstances of the crime and police response to it. It is also important to use interactionist ideas to see how the behaviour of victim, offender, media and criminal justice system all interact to influence how the situation develops.

Ideology and the New Criminology

A further element of the New Criminology was that, apart from the actual analysis that is suggested, it also argued that any sociology of crime and deviance had to be critical of the established capitalist order. This meant that instead of accepting the capitalist definition of

crime and seeking to explain this, its role ought to be to uncover and explain the crimes of the rich. There was no attempt to be unbiased; rather, the approach looked critically at the role of the police, the media and the criminal justice system in general – pointing out how they serve the needs of the ruling class.

Part of this critical approach to crime and criminal justice was to look in a fresh way at the ordinary criminal, who should best be seen as someone who is angry at capitalism and mistakenly expresses this anger through crime, rather than politics. This later led to debates between '**left realists**', who seek to work within the current system, and those who remained true to the ideas of critical criminology.

A good example of critical criminology is the work of Stuart Hall *et al.* (1978) in *Policing the Crisis: The State and Law and Order*. In the 1970s, London witnessed a growth in 'muggings' – assault and robbery of people in the streets. The media focused on this crime and a wave of publicity forced the problem to the top of the political and policing agenda. Although Hall did not exactly follow the model put forward in *The New Criminology*, the general critical criminological framework was used – see Table 6.1.

What a fully social theory of deviance must cover, according to Taylor *et al.* (1973)	**Table 6.1** The New Criminology Application of these ideas in Hall *et al.* (1978)
The wider origins of the deviant act	The 1970s was a period of considerable social crisis in Britain, the result of an international downturn in capitalist economies.
The immediate origins of the deviant act	This turmoil was shown in a number of inner-city riots, conflict in Northern Ireland and a high level of strikes. The government was searching for a group that could be **scapegoated**, to draw attention onto them and away from the crisis.
The actual act	Mugging – which according to the police was more likely to be carried out by those from African-Caribbean backgrounds.
The immediate origins of social reaction	Media outrage at the extent of muggings, linked to racism amongst the Metropolitan Police.
The wider origins of social reaction	The need to find scapegoats and the ease with which young men from African-Caribbean backgrounds could be blamed.
The outcome of social reaction on the deviants' further action	A sense of injustice amongst ethnic minorities and a loss of confidence by ethnic-minority communities in the criminal justice system.
The nature of the deviant process as a whole	The real causes of crime were not addressed and were effectively hidden by the criminal justice system.

Criticisms of the New Criminology

Traditional Marxists such as Hirst (1975) argued that the New Criminology strayed too far from the Marxist tradition. Others, such as Rock (1988), who were concerned directly in combating crime, argued that it gave far too romantic a view of criminals (in later writings, Young echoed this criticism and suggested it was one of the reasons for his development of left realism). Feminist criminologists, such as Pat Carlen (1988), pointed out that there was absolutely no specific discussion of the power of patriarchy in the analysis, which simply continued the omission of women from criminological discussion.

Methodologically, it has always been extremely difficult to apply this perspective, as it is so complicated. In fact, no sociologist has actually managed to use this approach and so it remains more as an interesting model than an approach that guides research – as we saw earlier, the nearest attempt was made by Hall.

Marxist subcultural theory

A second strand of thought that developed from Marxism, was a specific explanation for the existence of subcultures amongst the working class. According to The Centre for Contemporary Cultural Studies (a group of writers at Birmingham University), capitalism maintains control over the majority of the population in two ways:

- ideological dominance through the media
- economic pressures – people want to keep their jobs and pay their mortgages.

Key themes

Socialization, culture and identity

'The lads'

Paul Willis's *Learning to Labour* (1977) is a study of working-class boys in a secondary school. They realize early on the sorts of jobs they are going to get and reject the school and its concerns. They develop their own subculture, which Willis calls 'the lads'. This subculture is based on 'having a laff' and on rejecting school rules, teachers and work. However, their very rejection of school ensures that they are going to fail – thus making their belief come true – but, of course, they have been instrumental in their own failure.

Figure 6.3 A subcultural analysis of skinheads

Skinheads: a 'magical' attempt to rediscover the working-class community

'Skinheads' football violence reflected a concern with their territory – linked to the redevelopment of traditional working-class communities in London in the '60s.'

'Skinheads' clothes were closely linked to the style of a traditional manual worker.'

Based on Cohen, P. (1972) *Knuckle Sandwich: Growing up in the working-class city*, Harmondsworth: Penguin

Only those groups on the margins of society are not 'locked in' by ideology and finance, and thus are able to provide some form of resistance to capitalism. The single largest group offering this resistance is working-class youth.

According to Brake (1980), amongst others, this resistance is expressed through working-class youth subcultures. The clothes they wear and the language they use show their disdain of capitalism and their awareness of their position in it. Brake argues that this resistance, however, is best seen as **'magical'**. By magical, he means that it is a form of illusion that appears to solve their problems, but in reality does no such thing. According to him, each generation of working-class youth face similar problems (dead-end jobs, unemployment, and so on), but in different circumstances – that is, society changes constantly so that every generation experiences a very different world, with the one constant being that the majority will be exploited by the ruling class.

Each generation expresses its resistance through different choice of clothes, argot (slang and patterns of speech), music, and so on. But each will eventually be trapped like their parents before them.

Criticism of the Marxist subcultural approach

Methodological Problems

Stan Cohen (1980) pointed out that these writers were simply biased in their analysis. They wanted to prove that working-class youth cultures were an attack on capitalism, and therefore made sure that they fixed the evidence to find this. He pointed out, for example, that there were many different ways to interpret the subcultural style of the groups, and that the interpretation that the Marxist writers had imposed was just one of many possibilities. The researchers using this method knew what they wanted (signs of subcultural resistance) when they started looking at youth culture, and so they extracted what they needed to prove their theory and ignored what did not fit it.

Theoretical problems

Blackman (1995) points out that the emphasis on the working-class basis of subcultural resistance ignores the huge variation of subcultures based on variations in sexual identity, locality, age, 'intellectual capacity' and a range of other social factors. Thornton (1995) argues that there is simply no 'real' social-class basis to youth subcultures at all; these are, in fact, creations of the media.

Crimes of the state

Critical criminology makes a close link between the criminal law and the interests of the state. It argues that the law reflects the interests of the ruling class. Despite this, some critical criminologists have argued that where deemed 'necessary', the state will actually break its own laws and even international laws. According to Ross (2000), it may do this in order to protect itself or the interests of major capitalist corporations. Ross distinguishes three types of **crimes of the state**:

1 between crimes committed within a particular country and those by one country on another
2 between direct and indirect actions of the state apparatus
3 between crimes of commission and omission.

Within one country, Ross distinguishes between the apparatus of the state being *indirectly* involved in crime, through agencies that are not directly controlled by it, such as the police, and criminal acts committed *directly*, by failing to undertake activities (omission) which lead to grave consequences for its citizens. An example of an indirect crime might be the shooting of the innocent Brazilian Jean Charles de Menezes by police in London in 2005, while an example of a direct crime would be the failure to provide flood protection or to enforce laws that prevent housing collapsing in the event of an earthquake.

States may also be directly involved in crimes (commission), by failing to provide the full facts on events, by disinformation or by covering up activities that would be deemed illegal if found out.

Ross suggests that both direct and indirect crimes of the state benefit the ruling class.

In terms of crimes being committed by one country against another, Barak (1991) has explored how states commit crimes in other countries (or against other countries) in ways that would benefit the major economic organizations of the aggressor nation. In particular, Barak pointed to the way that the USA had interfered in the political processes of Central and South American countries to ensure that the interests of large US corporations would be safeguarded. The activities of the US government involved supporting rebel groups in hostile countries and support for right-wing, repressive governments in friendly countries. US agencies were directly involved in torture and murders. More recently, Whyte (2007) has critically examined the role of the US in Iraq and claims that:

Tombs and Whyte (2003)
State and corporate crime

Jean Charles de Menezes: a victim of state crime?

Tombs and Whyte set out to explore why so little attention has been paid by British criminologists to state and corporate crime. They pointed out that out of 298 articles published in the *British Journal of Criminology* over a ten-year period, only one article discussed crimes of the state and six discussed corporate crime. Tombs and Whyte suggest that there are three reasons for this silence on the matter:

1 Research in Britain is increasingly 'policy oriented', with the government, local authorities and other state agencies asking for very specific pieces of research on particular policies. In effect, these agencies set the research agenda and they are simply not interested in paying for sociologists to criticize them. This has had the effect of limiting research into wider, more critical areas.

2 Even if research is done, it is difficult to get the conclusions widely distributed. For example, the government often makes researchers sign agreements that they can only publish their research if they are given permission from the government.

3 It is extremely difficult to gain access to the more powerful groups in society. They have the power to deny access to information and to refuse to be interviewed. This leaves the sociologists who research these areas struggling to obtain evidence. Without evidence, criticisms of the role of the state can easily be refuted.

One final point that Tombs and Whyte make is that sociologists in non-democratic countries may well face threats if they seek to research areas which might threaten the interests of the powerful.

Tombs, S. and Whyte, D. (2003) *Unmasking the Crimes of the Powerful: Scrutinizing States and Corporations*, New York: Peter Lang

1 In your own words, explain why sociologists rarely publish articles on the crimes of the state and of the powerful.

2 Do critical criminologists believe that a 'value-free' sociology is possible? Explain your answer.

3 What methods could sociologists use to uncover the 'crimes of the powerful'?

In August 2005, storm surges caused by Hurricane Katrina broke through the flood defences of New Orleans, and 80 per cent of the city was flooded. How could this be seen as a direct crime of the state?

<< As the US government-appointed auditor has subsequently established, an unknown proportion of Iraqi oil revenue has disappeared into the pockets of contractors and fixers in the form of bribery, overcharging, embezzlement, product substitution, bid rigging and false claims. At least $12 billion of the revenue appropriated by the coalition regime has not been adequately accounted for. This neoliberal strategy of economic colonization was facilitated by major violations of the international laws of conflict and by unilaterally granting immunity from prosecution to US personnel.>> (p.177)

Problems in studying crimes of the state

According to Green and Ward (2004), however, there are considerable problems in studying the issue of crimes by state. The first problem is that states themselves define what is criminal within their own boundaries. For example, observers from outside a particular country may argue that repressive activities happening inside that country constitute a 'crime', but this can only be a viewpoint, not a statement of fact, as crimes are defined by the criminal code of a particular country. If the state says that an action is not a crime – then it is not.

Green and Ward suggest that the way around this is to use the standard of 'human rights', as defined by the United Nations. If the laws of a country break internationally agreed 'human rights', then the state can be accused of 'crimes of the state'.

Earlier, we saw that Ross argued states can commit crime by *not* doing things, which could than lead to grave consequences for its population, e.g. by failing to provide flood protection or to enforce laws that prevent housing collapsing in the event of an earthquake. However, once

the idea of 'human rights' is brought into the debate, then the issue of crimes of the state becomes even more complex. Barak (1991) has argued, for example, that the failure of the US government to provide adequate social-security payments for the poor and the lack of a federal healthcare system in America can be viewed as a breach of human rights and, therefore, a state crime.

A separate and quite distinctive problem faced by sociologists in studying crimes of the state, according to Tombs and Whyte (2007), is that states are able to prevent sociologists actually studying the whole issue. In democracies, this is done by restricting access to information and by refusing to fund such research. In non-democratic states, threats can be used to dissuade researchers.

An overview of Marxist or critical criminological approaches

Critical criminology has provided a very powerful counterbalance to explanations of crime and deviance that focus on the individual, their family or the community in which they live. Critical criminology has forced sociologists to explore the wider social, economic and political factors which shape society. Perhaps most of all, they point out that crimes can only happen when people break the law, but that the law itself reflects differences in power between groups. Powerful groups, they claim, can ensure

Check your understanding

1   How does the ruling class impose its values on others?

2   According to Marxists, how neutral is the law?

3   What is Bonger's explanation of individual motivation for crime?

4   How does Chambliss' research on vagrancy support a Marxist view of crime?

5   In what ways does the New Criminology utilize both Marxism and interactionism?

6   Why is it convenient for capitalism to find scapegoats?

7   How do Marxists explain the development of working-class subcultures?

8   How do working-class subcultures resist capitalism?

9   In what way is their resistance 'magical'?

10 How have different Marxist approaches to crime and deviance been criticized?

that the law, and the enforcement of the law, reflects their interests.

However, Marxism as a significant theoretical perspective in sociology has been on the wane for a number of years. The questions it raises remain as important, but the answers provided by critical criminologists have been less influential in the subject.

Key terms

Crimes of the state actions performed, or permitted to be performed, by the government that harm groups within society and breach their human rights.

Hegemony the ideas and values of the ruling class that dominate thinking in society.

Left realist a development from Marxist criminology which argues that it is better to work within capitalism to improve people's lives, than to attempt wholesale social change.

'Magical' illusory; in this context, something that appears to solve problems, but in reality does not.

Scapegoats groups in society (usually relatively powerless) who are blamed by the powerful for the problems of society, thus drawing attention away from the real causes of crime.

Activities

Research idea

Get hold of a copy of *Private Eye* magazine and read its investigations on corruption in commerce and of the way that the presentation of news is influenced by the media:

www.private-eye.co.uk

Web.tasks

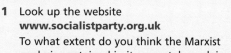

1   Look up the website
    www.socialistparty.org.uk
    To what extent do you think the Marxist analysis contained in it accurately explains today's problems?

2   Using the worldwide web, look up newspaper reports and background information about any recent terrorist or criminal event. See if you can apply the 'New Criminology' framework of Taylor, Walton and Young to interpret the event.

An eye on the exam   Critical criminologies

Item A

The criminal law is thus not a reflection of custom, but a set of rules laid down by the state in the interests of the ruling class, and resulting from the conflicts arising in class-structured societies; criminal behaviour is, then, the inevitable expression of class conflict resulting from the exploitative nature of economic relations.

Criminality is simply not something that people have or don't have; crime is not something some people do and others don't. Crime is a matter of who can pin the label on whom, and underlying this socio-political process is the structure of social relations determined by capitalism.

Adapted from: Chambliss, W.J. (1975) 'Towards a Political Economy of Crime', *Theory and Society*, Vol. 2 (abridged)

Using material from **Item A** and elsewhere, assess the usefulness of Marxist approaches to an understanding of crime and deviance.

(21 marks)

Grade booster   Getting top marks in this question

You should outline some of the main Marxist and neo-Marxist approaches to crime and deviance. These include sociologists such as Chambliss, Bonger, the new criminologists and Marxist subcultural theorists such as Brake. You should consider issues such as law making and enforcement in relation to class interests, ideology and crime, and crime as resistance. You can assess Marxist approaches from the standpoint of other perspectives, such as feminism. You could also use the criticisms made by Stan Cohen of Marxist analyses of youth subcultural styles. In assessing the strengths and weaknesses of Marxist approaches, make sure you use relevant material from Item A. For example, you could use it to begin a discussion of why Marxists believe capitalism and class conflict inevitably produce criminal behaviour.

TOPIC 4

Labelling theory

Getting you thinking

The government has introduced a range of laws concerning 'antisocial behaviour'. The official definition of antisocial behaviour is 'behaviour which causes or is likely to cause harassment, alarm or distress'. This has caused considerable problems for the police, as one person's sense of harassment, alarm or distress may well be different from another's.

Crackdown on young drinkers

UNDERAGE drinkers are being targeted in a police crackdown. Officers have stepped up evening patrols in the trouble hotspots of Littleport to make sure youngsters behave themselves. Letters have been written to parents of children caught drinking alcohol.

Police have also broken up gangs of up to 10 teenagers in recent weeks after complaints from residents who felt intimidated by them.

Pc Dave Bishop, community beat manager for Littleport, said: "We have ongoing action plans for underage drink and noise complaints, particularly in the old medical centre area.

"I was out recently with my sergeant and moved on a group of 10 youths. There were small groups gathered over the Christmas period, but I wouldn't call them 'gangs'.

"We have increased patrols in the evenings as there are isolated groups around the place. However, if they are hanging around the play area, I don't think that's a problem, provided they are behaving themselves."

The increased police presence follows a raft of complaints to police about antisocial behaviour in Littleport in the past few months.

"Elderly people are terrified of leaving their homes after dark because of these gangs and if you see a police car after dark it's a rarity.

"I've seen gangs of 15–20 youths hanging around, so it's no wonder people feel so threatened. Many of them are very abusive, but they know they will get away with it."

Cambridge Evening News, 15 January 2008

1 Do you think that young people hanging around are engaging in antisocial behaviour?

2 The article above states that people are 'terrified' of the 'gangs'. Do you think this is a reasonable reaction? Explain your answer.

3 What behaviour do you consider is antisocial – give one example that annoys you and you would like to see the police 'crack down' on?

4 Do you think the official definition of antisocial behaviour means that young people are more likely to be labelled as troublemakers and picked on by the police?

Understanding deviance: reaction not cause

Most approaches to understanding crime and deviance (with the exception of Marxist approaches) accept that there is a difference between those who offend and those who do not. On the basis of this assumption, they then search for the key factors that lead the person to offend.

However, since the early 1950s, one group of sociologists influenced by **symbolic interactionism** have questioned this approach, arguing that it is mistaken in its fundamental assumption that lawbreakers are somehow different from the law-abiding. **Labelling theory**, derived from symbolic interactionism, suggests, instead, that most people commit deviant and criminal acts, but only some people are caught and stigmatized for it. So, if most people commit deviant acts of some kind, it is pointless trying to search for the differences between deviants and non-deviants – instead the stress should be upon understanding the reaction to and definition of deviance rather than on the causes of the initial act. As Howard Becker (1963) puts it:

>> *Deviancy is not a quality of the act a person commits but rather a consequence of the application by others of rules and sanctions to an 'offender'. Deviant behaviour is behaviour that people so label.* >>

This is a radically different way of exploring crime; in fact, it extends beyond crime and helps us to understand any deviant or **stigmatized** behaviour. Labelling theory has gradually been adopted and incorporated into many other sociological approaches – for example, Taylor, Walton and Young (1973) have used it in their updating of Marxist criminology, while postmodernist approaches also owe much to it.

The best-known exponent of 'labelling theory' is Howard Becker. In *The Outsiders*, Becker gives a very clear and simple illustration of the labelling argument, drawing upon an anthropological study by Malinowski (1948/1982) of a traditional culture on a Pacific Island.

Malinowski describes how a youth killed himself because he had been publicly accused of **incest**. When Malinowski had first inquired about the case, the islanders expressed their horror and disgust. But, on further investigation, it turned out that incest was not uncommon on the island, nor was it really frowned upon provided those involved were discreet. However, if an incestuous affair became too obvious and public, the islanders reacted with abuse, the offenders were ostracized and often driven to suicide.

Becker, therefore, argues the following:

1   Just because someone breaks a rule, it does not necessarily follow that others will define it as deviant.
2   Someone has to enforce the rules or, at least, draw attention to them – these people usually have a vested interest in the issue. (In the example of the incestuous islanders, the rule was enforced by the rejected ex-lover of the girl involved in incest.)
3   If the person is successfully labelled, then consequences follow. (Once publicly labelled as deviant, the offender in Malinowski's example was faced with limited choices, one of which was suicide.)

Responding to and enforcing rules

Most sociological theories take for granted that once a person has committed a deviant or criminal act, then the response will be uniform. This is not true. People respond differently to deviance or rule-breaking. In the early 1960s, when gay people were more likely to be stigmatized than now, John Kitsuse (1962) interviewed 75 heterosexual students to elicit their responses to (presumed) sexual advances from people of the same sex. What he found was a very wide range of responses from complete

tolerance to bizarre and extreme hatred. One told how he had 'known' that a man he was talking to in a bar was homosexual because he had wanted to talk about psychology! The point of Kitsuse's work is that there was no agreed definition of what constituted a homosexual 'advance' – it was open to negotiation.

In Britain today, British Crime Survey statistics show that young Black males are more likely to be stopped for questioning and searching than any other group. This is a result of the police officers' belief that this particular social group is more likely to offend than any other; for this reason, they are the subjects of 'routine suspicion'.

Criticism

Akers (1967) criticized labelling theorists for presenting deviants as perfectly normal people who are no different from anyone else until someone comes along and slaps a label on them. Akers argues that there must be some reason why the label is applied to certain groups/individuals and not to others. As long as labelling fails to explain this, then it is an incomplete theory.

The consequences of rule enforcement

As we have just seen, being labelled as a deviant and having laws enforced against you is the result of a number of different factors. However, once labelled as a deviant, various consequences occur for the individual.

The clearest example of this is provided by Edwin Lemert, who distinguished between '**primary**' and '**secondary**' **deviance** (Lemert 1972). Primary deviance is rule-breaking, which is of little importance in itself, while secondary deviance is the consequence of the responses of others, which is significant. To illustrate this, Lemert studied the coastal **Inuits** of Canada, who had a long-rooted problem of chronic stuttering or stammering. Lemert suggested that the problem was 'caused' by the great importance attached to ceremonial speech-making. Failure to speak well was a great humiliation. Children with the slightest speech difficulty were so conscious of their parents' desire to have well-speaking children that they became overanxious about their own abilities. It was this very anxiety, according to Lemert, that led to chronic stuttering. In this example, chronic stuttering (secondary deviance) is a response to parents' reaction to initial minor speech defects (primary deviance).

The person labelled as 'deviant' will eventually come to see themselves as being bad (or mad). Becker used the term '**master status**' to describe this process. He points out that once a label has successfully been applied to a person, then all other qualities become unimportant – they are responded to solely in terms of this master status.

Rejecting labels: negotiability

The process of being labelled is, however, open to 'negotiation', in that some groups or individuals are able to reject the label. An example of this is Reiss' (1961) study of young male prostitutes. Although they had sex with other men, they regarded what they did as work and maintained an image of themselves as being 'straight'.

Deviant career

These ideas of master status and negotiability led Becker to devise the idea of a '**deviant career**'. By this, he meant all the processes that are involved in a label being applied (or not) and then the person taking on (or not) the self-image of the deviant.

Creating rules

Once labelling theorists began the process of looking at how social life was open to negotiation and that rule enforcement was no different from other social activities, then attention shifted to the creation of rules and laws. Why were they made? Traditionally, sociologists had taken either a Marxist perspective (that they were made in the interests of the ruling class) or a functionalist/pluralist perspective (which argued that laws in a democracy reflected the views of the majority of the population). Becker (1963) doubted both these accounts and argued instead that:

> ≪ *Rules are the products of someone's initiative and we can think of the people who exhibit such enterprises as '***moral entrepreneurs***'.* ≫

So, labelling theorists argue that laws are a reflection of the activities of people (moral entrepreneurs) who actively seek to create and enforce laws. The reasons for this are either that the new laws benefit the activists directly,

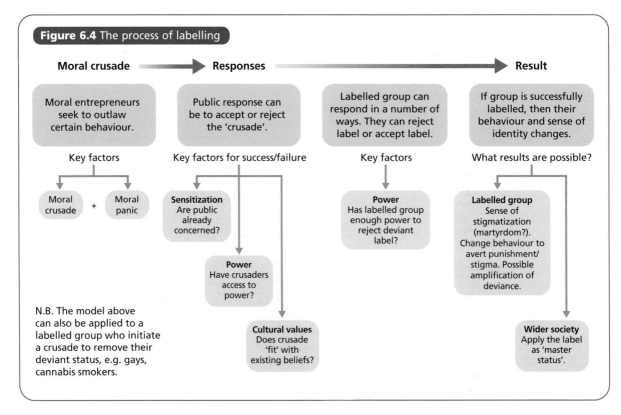

Figure 6.4 The process of labelling

Moral crusade ➡ **Responses** ➡ **Result**

Moral crusade	Responses		Result
Moral entrepreneurs seek to outlaw certain behaviour.	Public response can be to accept or reject the 'crusade'.	Labelled group can respond in a number of ways. They can reject label or accept label.	If group is successfully labelled, then their behaviour and sense of identity changes.

Key factors — Moral crusade + Moral panic

Key factors for success/failure:
- **Sensitization** Are public already concerned?
- **Power** Have crusaders access to power?
- **Cultural values** Does crusade 'fit' with existing beliefs?

Key factors:
- **Power** Has labelled group enough power to reject deviant label?

What results are possible?
- **Labelled group** Sense of stigmatization (martyrdom?). Change behaviour to avert punishment/stigma. Possible amplification of deviance.
- **Wider society** Apply the label as 'master status'.

N.B. The model above can also be applied to a labelled group who initiate a crusade to remove their deviant status, e.g. gays, cannabis smokers.

Key themes

Sociological theories and methods

Teacher expectations

Teachers claim to treat all pupils alike, but every child in the classroom knows the teacher's favourites and every class knows its reputation with the teachers. These pupils' awareness of their place in the eyes of teachers can affect their behaviour. This is commonsense knowledge in the classroom, but it is also how labelling theory is played out in the educational system.

Rosenthal and Jacobson's (1968) study, which involved telling teachers that some students were especially gifted – even though, unknown to the teachers, the pupils had been chosen entirely at random – resulted in the teachers having raised expectations of those pupils. As a result of this, the academic attainment of those pupils improved.

Mac An Ghaill's (1998, 1992) work on race and achievement also found that the students in his study believed that teachers have expectations of (sixth-form) students based on 'racial' labelling. Black students believed that teachers had higher expectations of, and aspirations for, Asian and White students.

or these activists believe that the laws are truly to the benefit of society.

Becker's most famous example is his study of the outlawing of cannabis use in the USA in 1937. Cannabis had been widely used in the southern states of the USA. Its outlawing was the result of a successful campaign waged by the Federal Bureau of Narcotics which, after the repeal of the prohibition laws (that had banned alcohol), saw cannabis as a growing menace in society. Through a press campaign and lobbying of senior politicians, the Bureau was successful in outlawing the growing and use of the drug. However, Becker points out that the campaign was only successful because it 'plugged in' to values commonly held in the USA which included:

1 the belief that people ought to be in control of their actions and decisions
2 that pleasure for its own sake was wrong
3 that drugs were seen as addictive and, as such, 'enslaved' people.

The term Becker used to describe the campaign was **'moral crusade'**, and it is this terminology (along with the

concept of moral entrepreneurs) that sociologists use to describe movements to pass laws (see Fig. 6.4).

Criticisms

The idea that there are those who seek to pass laws or to impose rules upon others has been accepted by most sociologists. However, Marxist writers, in particular, have pointed out that there is a wider framework within which this is placed. Are all laws just the product of a particular group of moral entrepreneurs? If so, then what are the conditions under which some groups succeed and others fail? Labelling theory does not really answer this issue very well; in fact, labelling theory does not have a coherent theory of power, as it argues that more powerful groups are able to impose their 'definition of the situation' on others, yet does not explain why some groups have more power than others and are more able to get laws passed and enforced that are beneficial to them. In defence of labelling theory, Becker (1970) does suggest in a famous article ('Whose side are we on?') that there are differences in power and that it is the role of the sociologist to side with the underdog. However, no overall theory of differences in power is given.

Labelling and values

We have just mentioned a famous article by Becker, in which he argues that labelling theory has a clear value position – that is, it speaks up for the powerless and the underdog. Labelling theorists claim to provide a voice for those who are labelled as deviant and 'outsiders'.

However, Liazos (1972) criticizes labelling theorists for simply exploring marginally deviant activities as, by doing so, they are reinforcing the idea of pimps, prostitutes and mentally ill people as being deviant. Even by claiming to speak for the underdog, labelling theorists hardly present any challenge to the status quo.

Gouldner (1968) also criticizes labelling theorists for their failure to provide any real challenge to the status quo. He argued that all they did in their studies was to criticize doctors, psychiatrists and police officers for their role in labelling – and they failed ever to look beyond this at more powerful groups who benefit from this focus on marginal groups. Gouldner is putting forward a Marxist argument, by claiming that labelling theorists draw attention away from the 'real crime'.

Crime, labelling and the media

Labelling theory alerts us to the way in which the whole area of crime depends upon social constructions of reality – law creation, law enforcement and the identities of rule breakers are all thrown into question. The media play a key role in all three of these processes, as most people's perceptions of crime are actually created – or at least informed – by the media.

Labelling theory has contributed two particularly important concepts to our understanding of the relationship between the media and crime: deviancy amplification and **moral panics**.

Deviancy amplification

The term '**deviancy amplification**' was coined by the British sociologist Leslie Wilkins to show how the response to deviance, by agencies such as police and media, can actually generate an increase in deviance. According to Wilkins (1964), when acts are defined as deviant, the deviants become stigmatized and cut off from mainstream society. They become aware that they are regarded as deviants and, as a result of this awareness, they begin to develop their own subculture. This leads to more intense pressure on them and further isolation, which further confirms and strengthens them in their deviance.

Jock Young (1971) used this concept in his study of drug use in North London. He showed that increased police activity led to drug use being 'driven underground'. This had the effect of isolating users into a drug subculture, with 'a distinctive style of dress, lack of workaday sense of time, money, rationality and rewards', thus making re-entry to regular employment increasingly difficult – which, of course, made it difficult for them to afford the drugs. The scarcity of drugs drove the price up and this drew in professional criminals who regarded it as worthwhile entering the illicit drug business; criminal rings developed and the competition between them led to violence. It also led to the use of dangerous substitutes and adulterants in drugs by suppliers, interested only in

maximizing profits, thus creating a situation where users no longer knew the strength of drugs and were consequently more likely to overdose. The process described here caused wide public concern which spurred the police to intensify their clampdown even further, which only served to accelerate the spiral of this 'amplification' process.

Moral panics

The idea of moral panics both overlaps with and complements the concept of deviancy amplification. The term was first used in Britain by Stan Cohen in a classic study (1972) of two youth subcultures of the 1960s – 'mods' and 'rockers'. Cohen showed how the media, for lack of other stories, built up these two groups into **folk devils**. The effect of the media coverage was to make the young people categorize themselves as either mods or rockers. This actually helped to create the violence that took place between them, which also confirmed them as troublemakers in the eyes of the public.

The concept of moral panic and the role of the media in helping to create them, has been widely used in sociology since Cohen's original British work – though perhaps the best adaptation of this is the study by Hall and colleagues of 'mugging' (see Topic 3, p. 347).

Moral panics: an outdated idea?

McRobbie and Thornton (1995) argue that 'moral panics', as described by Cohen in the 1960s, are outdated and

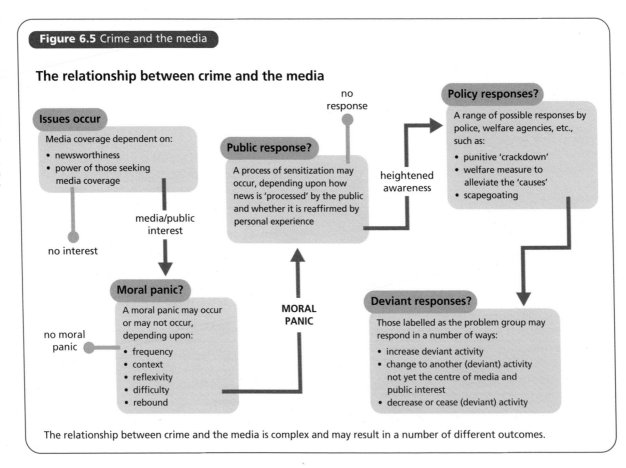

Figure 6.5 Crime and the media

The relationship between crime and the media

Issues occur

Media coverage dependent on:
- newsworthiness
- power of those seeking media coverage

no interest

media/public interest

Moral panic?

A moral panic may occur or may not occur, depending upon:
- frequency
- context
- reflexivity
- difficulty
- rebound

no moral panic

MORAL PANIC

Public response?

A process of sensitization may occur, depending upon how news is 'processed' by the public and whether it is reaffirmed by personal experience

no response

heightened awareness

Policy responses?

A range of possible responses by police, welfare agencies, etc., such as:
- punitive 'crackdown'
- welfare measure to alleviate the 'causes'
- scapegoating

Deviant responses?

Those labelled as the problem group may respond in a number of ways:
- increase deviant activity
- change to another (deviant) activity not yet the centre of media and public interest
- decrease or cease (deviant) activity

The relationship between crime and the media is complex and may result in a number of different outcomes.

have to be seen in the context of the development of the media and the growing sophistication of the audiences. McRobbie and Thornton make the following points:

- *Frequency* – There has been an increasing number of 'moral panics' – they are no longer rare or particularly noteworthy.
- *Context* – Whereas moral panics would scapegoat a group and create 'folk devils' in the 1960s, today there is no single, unambiguous response to a panic as there are many different viewpoints and values in society.
- *Reflexivity* – As moral panics as a concept are so well known, many groups try to create them for their own benefit. However, the same knowledge means that the media know this and do not necessarily wish uncritically to start a moral panic over an issue.
- *Difficulty* – Moral panics are much more unlikely to start in society because it is far less clear today what is unambiguously 'bad'. Society is too fragmented and culturally pluralistic.
- *Rebound* – People are more wary about starting moral panics as there is the possibility of it rebounding on them. Politicians who start a campaign about family values or drugs have to be very careful about their own backgrounds.

Labelling has been very important in helping to understand the role of the media. However, if what McRobbie and Thornton say is true, then by their very success, sociological concepts such as moral panic have gradually filtered into the wider society, so that journalists and politicians are now aware of them and use them in their decisions about what actions to take.

Focus on research

Heckert and Best (1997)
The stigmatization of red hair

Heckert and Best conducted a study into the impact of having ginger hair. For some years there has been a negative image promoted about ginger-haired people and the researchers argued that people with ginger hair are negatively labelled and are treated as deviants. They interviewed 20 ginger-haired people in all, nine males and eleven females, using open questions. They found that ginger-haired people were viewed as having all or some of the following characteristics – hot tempered, clownish, weird, wild (women) or wimpy (men). They were typically treated more negatively in childhood and as a result had low levels of self-esteem. Interestingly, both researchers were ginger-haired!

Heckert, D.N. and Best, A. (1997) 'Ugly Duckling to Swan: Labeling Theory and the Stigmatization of Red Hair', *Symbolic Interaction*, 20(4), pp. 365–84

1 How might the researchers' own ginger hair have influenced respondents?

2 Evaluate the reliability and representativeness of this research.

Check your understanding

1 Instead of looking at the cause of crime, what does labelling theory focus on?

2 What theoretical approach does labelling theory derive from? How?

3 Explain and give one example of what labelling theorists mean when they say that the response to lawbreaking is variable.

4 Explain the importance of the term 'master status' in understanding deviance.

5 In what way does the labelling approach to the introduction of laws differ from the Marxist approach?

6 How has labelling theory been criticized?

7 Explain the importance of the idea of 'deviancy amplification'.

8 What criticisms have been made of the term 'moral panic'?

Activities

Research idea

Conduct a survey to discover young people's perceptions of the elderly. Do their views represent particular labels and stereotypes?

Then interview a small number of elderly people. Are they aware of stereotypes and labels? How do they feel about these labels? Do they affect them?

Be sensitive in your interviewing technique, following the usual ethical guidelines.

Web.task

Search the worldwide web for newspaper and other information about any moral panic of your choice (e.g. concern over film violence, drugs such as ecstasy, underage sex). To what extent can you identify the key features of a moral panic, such as media exaggeration, the creation of 'folk devils', the activities of moral entrepreneurs, and so on?

Key terms

Deviancy amplification when the action of the rule enforcers or media in response to deviance brings about an increase in the deviance.

Deviant career the various stages that a person passes through on their way to being seen as, and seeing themselves as, deviant.

Folk devils groups associated with moral panics

who are seen as troublemakers by the media.

Incest sex between close members of a family (other than man and wife).

Inuits previously known as 'eskimos'.

Labelling theorists a theory developed from **symbolic interactionism**, adapted for use in studies of deviance

Master status when people are looked at by others solely on the basis of one type of act

(good or bad) which they have committed; all other aspects of that person are ignored.

Moral crusade the process of creating or enforcing a rule.

Moral entrepreneur person or group which tries to create or enforce a rule.

Moral panic outrage stirred up by the media about a particular group or issue.

Primary deviance the act of breaking a rule.

Secondary deviance the response to rule breaking, which usually has greater social consequences than initial rule-breaking.

Stigmatized labelled in a negative way.

Symbolic interactionism a theory derived from social psychology which argues that people exist in a social world based on symbols that people interpret and respond to.
Labelling theorists tend to substitute the term 'label' for 'symbol'.

An eye on the exam — Labelling theory

Item A

Labelling theory – with its rejection of so-called positivistic criminology – was closely allied to the development of the sociology of deviance. This sociology not only changed the theoretical base for the study of criminals, but also brought in its wake a dramatic restructuring of empirical concerns. Sociologists turned their interests to the world of expressive deviance; to the twilight marginal worlds of tramps, alcoholics, strippers, dwarfs, prostitutes, drug addicts, nudists; to taxi-drivers, the blind, the dying, the physically ill, the handicapped and even to a motley array of problems of everyday life. It opened up the field of inquiry so that it was possible to discuss a range of areas hitherto neglected – thereby enabling the foundations for a formal theory of deviance and a method for understanding the routine and the regular through the eyes of the powerless.

Adapted from Carrabine, E., Iganski, P. , Lee, M., Plummer, K. and South, N. (2004) *Criminology: A Sociological Introduction*, London: Routledge, p. 74

Using material from **Item A** and elsewhere, assess the usefulness of labelling as an approach to the study of crime and deviance.

(21 marks)

Grade booster — Getting top marks in this question

You will need to outline the key ideas of the labelling approach to crime and deviance, explaining how it differs from other approaches in focusing on the process and consequences of labelling rather than on the causes of the deviant behaviour itself. Remember to make use of relevant material from the Item. For example, you can link it to any studies with which you are familiar of the kinds of groups it mentions (e.g. Becker on cannabis users) as well as using other labelling-oriented studies, such as Cohen on mods and rockers or Lemert on stuttering. You can also consider in what ways labelling 'changed the theoretical base for the study of criminals' (Item A) as compared with previous approaches to the topic.

In evaluating, bring in criticisms of individual studies or concepts involved in the labelling process (e.g. McRobbie and Thornton's criticisms of moral panics).

TOPIC 5

Patterns of crime

Getting you thinking

1 Have you had any crime (no matter how minor) committed against you in the last year? What was it? Did you report it to the police? Explain the reasons for you reporting/not reporting it.

2 Which of the three people in the photographs is most likely to be the victim of an attack at night on the streets? Explain the reasons for your answer.

3 Which car is more likely to be stolen: a smart new BMW or a 15-year-old Vauxhall Astra? Explain your answer.

4 Is bullying a crime? Please explain the reasons for your answer.

5 At school/college, how does the institution deal with bullying, cannabis use and 'minor' thefts? What implications does this have for official statistics?

Our commonsense ideas about crime do not always match the picture revealed by statistics. Many of us believe that crime is something committed by the less wealthy against the more wealthy and more vulnerable sections of the community. This view may well have influenced your answers to the questions above. However, police figures indicate that poorer areas have higher crime rates than wealthy areas, that young men are more likely to be the victims of crime than old ladies, and that battered Ford Fiestas are more likely to be stolen than the latest executive BMW. But are these figures accurate, and how can we use statistics about crime to help us understand why some people commit crimes?

In order to understand why people commit crime, we need first to find out who commits crime and what sorts of crimes are committed. Sociologists use three different ways to build up this picture of crime. Each method provides us with particular information, but also has a number of weaknesses that need to be identified if our picture is to be accurate. The three methods of collecting information are: police-recorded statistics, victim surveys and self-report studies.

Police-recorded statistics

Police-recorded statistics are drawn from the records kept by the police and other official agencies, and are published every six months by the **Home Office**.

The **official statistics** are particularly useful in that they have been collected since 1857 and so provide us with an excellent historical overview of changing trends over time. They also give us a completely accurate view of the way that the criminal justice system processes offenders through arrests, trials, punishments, and so on.

Police-recorded statistics as social constructions

Police-recorded statistics are **social constructions** – they cannot be taken simply at their face value because they only show crimes that are reported to and recorded by the police. When we dig a little deeper, a lot of hidden issues are uncovered.

Reporting crime

Police-recorded statistics are based on the information that the criminal justice agencies collect. But crimes cannot be recorded by them if they are not reported in the first place, and the simple fact is that a high proportion of 'crimes' are not reported to the police at all. According to the **British Crime Survey**

(Home Office 1998), we know that individuals are less likely to report a 'crime' to the police if they regard it as:

- too trivial to bother the police with
- a private matter between friends and family – in this case they will seek redress directly (get revenge themselves) – or one where they wish no harm to come to the offender
- too embarrassing (e.g. male rape).

Other reasons for non-reporting of crimes are that:

- the victim may not be in a position to give information (e.g. a child suffering abuse)
- they may fear reprisals.

On the other hand, people are more likely to report a crime if:

- they see some benefit to themselves (e.g. an insurance claim)
- they have faith in the police ability to achieve a positive result.

Recording of crimes

When people do actively report an offence to the police, you would think that these statistics at least would enter the official reports. Yet in any one year, approximately 57 per cent of all crimes reported to the police fail to appear in the official statistics. Figure 6.6 below shows the proportion of the crimes committed that are reported to the police and the proportion recorded by the police.

The role of the police

Clearly, the police are filtering the information supplied to them by the public, according to factors that are important to them. These factors have been identified as follows:

- *Seriousness* – They may regard the offence as too trivial or simply not a criminal matter.
- *Social status* – More worryingly, they may view the social status of the person reporting the matter as not high enough to regard the issue as worth pursuing.
- *Classifying* – When a person makes a complaint, police crimes officers must decide what category of offence it is. How they classify the offence will determine its

Focus on research

The British Crime Survey

The British Crime Survey (BCS) was first introduced in 1982, heavily influenced by a similar type of survey which had been undertaken in the USA since 1972 (funded by the US Department of Justice). Originally, the UK studies were every two years, but since 2000, they have been carried out every year. The sample size is enormous, with almost 40 000 people being interviewed. The idea behind the study is that by asking people directly what crimes have been committed against them, the problems of crime reporting and police recording are avoided. Supporters of the survey suggest that it is more 'valid' than the police statistics.

The sampling technique is based on (a) all households in England and Wales and then (b) anyone over 16 living in these households. The households are selected using the Postcode Address File, developed by the Post Office to recognize all households in Britain. Interviews last 50 minutes and each person is asked if they have been the victim of a list of selected crimes. There is then a smaller 'sweep' (a subsample), who are asked to answer questions on selected (sometimes sensitive) issues directly into a laptop computer.

Is the BCS more accurate than the police-recorded statistics? The answer provided by Maguire (2002) is that the BCS is neither better nor worse, but simply provides an alternative, overall picture of crime which helps fill in some gaps in the police-recorded statistics.

1 What steps does the BCS take to maximize the representativeness of the survey?

2 Can you identify any groups who may still be left out of the survey?

3 Why do you think respondents in the smaller subsample are asked to input their answers directly into a laptop computer?

Figure 6.6 Comparing a victim survey (BCS) and crimes recorded to the police

Kershaw, C., Nicholas, S. and Walker, A. (2008) *Crime in England and Wales 2008*, Home Office RDS/Ministry of Justice

Compare these two pie charts which show the differences in the image of 'crime rates' between the two methods of collecting information.

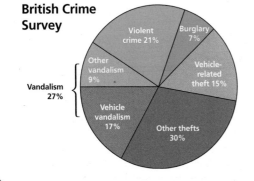

British Crime Survey

Violent crime 21%
Burglary 7%
Other vandalism 9%
Vehicle-related theft 15%
Vandalism 27%
Vehicle vandalism 17%
Other thefts 30%

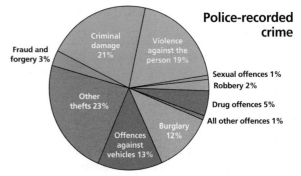

Police-recorded crime

Criminal damage 21%
Fraud and forgery 3%
Violence against the person 19%
Sexual offences 1%
Robbery 2%
Other thefts 23%
Drug offences 5%
All other offences 1%
Burglary 12%
Offences against vehicles 13%

seriousness. So, the police officer's opinion determines the category and seriousness of crime (from assault, to aggravated assault for example).

- *Discretion* – Only about 10 per cent of offences are actually uncovered by the police. However, the chances of being arrested for an offence increase markedly depending upon the 'demeanour' of the person being challenged by a police officer (that is, their appearance, attitude and manner). Anderson *et al.* (1994) show that youths who cooperate and are polite to police officers are less likely to be arrested than those regarded as disrespectful.
- *Promotion* – Police officers, like everyone else, have concerns about career and promotion. This involves trying to impress senior officers. However, at work they also need to get on with other colleagues, who do not like officers who are too keen (as this makes more work for everyone). Arrests reflect a balance between comradeship and a desire for promotion (Collison 1995).

The role of the courts

Official statistics of crimes committed and punished also reflect the decisions and sentences of the courts. However, these statistics, too, are a reflection of social processes.

British courts work on the assumption that many people will plead guilty – and about 75 per cent of all those charged actually do so. This is often the result of an informal and largely unspoken agreement whereby the defence will try to get the charges with the lightest possible punishment put forward by the prosecution. (In the USA, this bargaining is far more open than in Britain, and is known as **plea-bargaining**.) The result is an overwhelming majority of pleas of guilty, yet these pleas are for less serious crimes than might 'really' have been committed. The statistics will reflect this downgrading of seriousness.

The role of the government

What is considered to be a crime changes over time, as a result of governments changing the law in response to cultural changes and the influence of powerful groups. Any exploration of crime over a period is therefore fraught with difficulty, because any rise or fall in the levels of crime may reflect changes in the law as much as actual changes in crime. A good example of this is the way that attitudes to cannabis use have shifted – while there has been an increase in the numbers of people possessing and using cannabis (both of which are a crime), the number of arrests for its possession has actually declined, as the police respond to public opinion. The police statistics might make it look as if cannabis use is actually declining, when it is not.

Victim surveys

A second way of estimating the extent and patterns of crime is by using **victimization** (or **victim**) **surveys**. In these, a sample of the population, either locally or nationally, is asked which offences have been committed against them over a certain period of time.

Strengths of victim surveys

This approach overcomes the fact that a significant proportion of offences are never recorded by the police. It also gives an excellent picture of the extent and patterns of victimization – something completely missing from official accounts. The best known victimization study is the British Crime Survey which is now collected every year and has been in operation since 1982 (see 'Focus on research', opposite).

Weaknesses of victim surveys

- The problem of basing statistics on victims' memories is that recollections are often faulty or biased.
- The categorization of the crimes that has been committed against them is left to the person filling in the questionnaire – this leads to considerable inaccuracy in the categories.
- Victim surveys also omit a range of crimes, such as fraud and corporate crime, and any crime where the victim is unaware of or unable to report a crime.
- Despite victim surveys being anonymous, people appear to underreport sexual offences.

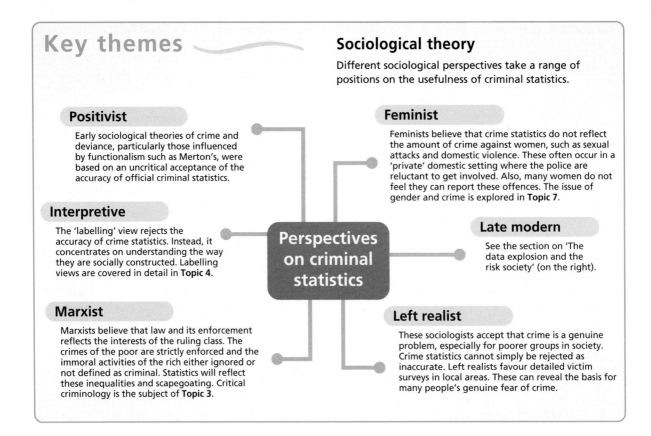

Key themes

Sociological theory

Different sociological perspectives take a range of positions on the usefulness of criminal statistics.

Perspectives on criminal statistics

Positivist

Early sociological theories of crime and deviance, particularly those influenced by functionalism such as Merton's, were based on an uncritical acceptance of the accuracy of official criminal statistics.

Interpretive

The 'labelling' view rejects the accuracy of crime statistics. Instead, it concentrates on understanding the way they are socially constructed. Labelling views are covered in detail in **Topic 4**.

Marxist

Marxists believe that law and its enforcement reflects the interests of the ruling class. The crimes of the poor are strictly enforced and the immoral activities of the rich either ignored or not defined as criminal. Statistics will reflect these inequalities and scapegoating. Critical criminology is the subject of **Topic 3**.

Feminist

Feminists believe that crime statistics do not reflect the amount of crime against women, such as sexual attacks and domestic violence. These often occur in a 'private' domestic setting where the police are reluctant to get involved. Also, many women do not feel they can report these offences. The issue of gender and crime is explored in **Topic 7**.

Late modern

See the section on 'The data explosion and the risk society' (on the right).

Left realist

These sociologists accept that crime is a genuine problem, especially for poorer groups in society. Crime statistics cannot simply be rejected as inaccurate. Left realists favour detailed victim surveys in local areas. These can reveal the basis for many people's genuine fear of crime.

- The BCS itself suffers from the problem of not collecting information from those under 16, although this is not necessarily a problem of victim surveys as such. The British Youth Lifestyles Survey (2000), for example, was carried out specifically to obtain detailed information on crimes against younger people.

Local victim surveys

The BCS is a typical cross-sectional survey, and as such may contain some errors – certainly, it does not provide detailed information about particular places. This has led to a number of detailed studies of crime, focusing on particular areas. These provide specific information about local problems.

The most famous of these surveys were the **Islington Crime Surveys** (Harper *et al.* 1986 and Jones *et al.* 1995). These showed that the BCS underreported the higher levels of victimization of minority ethnic groups and domestic violence.

The media and sensitization

Victim surveys are dependent upon people being aware that they are victims. This may seem obvious, but in fact this depends very much on the 'victim' perceiving what happens to them as being a crime. The media play a key role in this as they provide illustrations of 'crimes' and generally heighten sensitivity towards certain forms of behaviour. This is known as **sensitizing** the public towards (certain types of) activity that can be seen as a crime worth reporting. A positive example of this has been the change in portrayal of domestic violence from a family matter to being a criminal activity.

Self-report studies

The third method for collecting data is that of **self-report studies**. These are surveys in which a selected group or cross-section of the population are asked what offences they have committed. Self-report studies are extremely useful as they reveal much about the kind of offenders who are not caught or processed by the police. In particular, it is possible to find out about the ages, gender, social class and even location of 'hidden offenders'. It is also the most useful way to find out about victimless crimes, such as illegal drug use.

Weaknesses of self-report studies

- The problem of validity – The biggest problem is that respondents may lie or exaggerate, and even if they do not deliberately seek to mislead, they may simply be mistaken.
- The problem of representativeness – Because it is easy to study them, most self-report surveys are on young people and students. There are no such surveys on professional criminals or drug traffickers, for example!
- The problem of relevance – Because of the problem of representativeness, the majority of the crimes uncovered tend to be trivial.

Nevertheless, the only information that we have available of who offends, other than from the official statistics of people who have been arrested, comes from self-report studies, and they have been very widely used to explore such issues as crime and drug use. Figure 6.7 summarizes the processes and problems involved in different methods of finding out about patterns of crime.

The data explosion and the risk society

Maguire (2002) has pointed out that since the 1970s there has been a huge increase in the amount of statistics gathered on crime and 'antisocial behaviour'. Before then, the main source of information was the government publication *Criminal Statistics*, which relied solely upon criminal justice agencies for the figures. Since the 1970s, information has come to be gathered on wider aspects of crime:

● *Unreported and unrecorded offences* – Information is collected through the BCS.
● Specialist subcategories of crime – There are now literally hundreds of crime categories that official statistics record.
● *Hidden crime* – Information on sexual offences, domestic violence, white-collar crime and, most recently, corporate crime has started to be gathered.
● *Victim perspectives* – Possibly the most recent innovation has been the collection of information from the victims of crime.

Garland (2001) suggests that it is not just an expansion of knowledge for its own sake that has driven the explosion of statistical information. He suggests, instead, that the answer can be found within the concerns of late modernity. During modernity, governments took upon themselves the task of controlling crime and punishing criminals. According to Garland, most people believed that the government had crime control in hand. Garland suggests that in late modernity, there is a much greater sense of uncertainty and risk, and governments are no longer believed to catch and punish all criminals. Instead, the government engages in **risk management** – it gathers statistics on crime so that it can better assess and manage this risk. Garland has also introduced the notion of **'responsibilization'** – part of risk management is to push responsibility for avoiding becoming victims of crime back onto individuals. The statistics are part of this process of informing individuals how best to avoid becoming victims of crime.

Patterns of offending

Using the three methods of gathering information, sociologists have managed to construct an interesting picture of offending and victimization patterns.

Types of offences

● *Property crime* – According to the British Crime Survey, 62 per cent of crime in 2000 was accounted for by some form of property theft, with burglary and vehicle theft forming the bulk of these.
● *Violent crime* – All forms of violence account for approximately 20 per cent of BCS-reported crime, but the huge majority of these acts of violence – about 68 per cent – consisted only of very minor physical hurt (at most slight bruising). In fact, only about 5 per cent of violent crimes reported involved more than trivial injury.

Types of victims

● *Victims of violence* – Young males, in particular the unemployed and low-waged, have a particularly high chance of being victims (see Fig. 6.8). Interestingly, in about 88 per cent of cases of violence, the victim and perpetrator know each other.

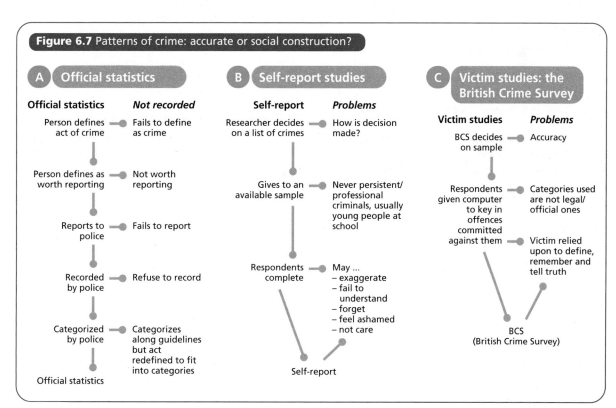

Figure 6.7 Patterns of crime: accurate or social construction?

A   Official statistics

Official statistics	Not recorded
Person defines act of crime	Fails to define as crime
Person defines as worth reporting	Not worth reporting
Reports to police	Fails to report
Recorded by police	Refuse to record
Categorized by police	Categorizes along guidelines but act redefined to fit into categories
Official statistics	

B   Self-report studies

Self-report	Problems
Researcher decides on a list of crimes	How is decision made?
Gives to an available sample	Never persistent/ professional criminals, usually young people at school
Respondents complete	May ... – exaggerate – fail to understand – forget – feel ashamed – not care
Self-report	

C   Victim studies: the British Crime Survey

Victim studies	Problems
BCS decides on sample	Accuracy
Respondents given computer to key in offences committed against them	Categories used are not legal/ official ones
	Victim relied upon to define, remember and tell truth
BCS (British Crime Survey)	

- *Victims of property crime* – Victims of property crime are most likely to be low-income households living in poorer areas.
- *Repeat victimization* – Victim surveys demonstrate not only that some people are more likely than others to be victims in the first place, but that a proportion of the victims are likely to be targeted more than once (**repeat victimization**) – see Fig. 6.8. Of all households burgled, 20 per cent experienced repeat burglaries, and one tiny group has a disproportionately high chance of being victimized: 0.4 per cent of householders accounted for 22 per cent of all burglaries.

The statistics suggest that crime does not happen to everyone – it targets the poorer and less powerful groups in society more than the affluent. They also tell us that violent crime tends to happen between people who know each other, even live together.

Types of offenders

According to both official statistics and self-report studies, offenders are most likely to be young and male. The peak age of offending for males is about 18, and for females about 14. The next four topics attempt to explain why some of the patterns identified here exist. They focus on crime and locality, gender, class and ethnicity respectively.

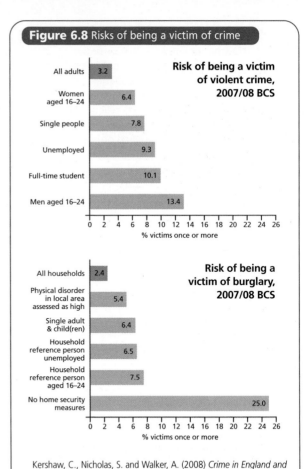

Figure 6.8 Risks of being a victim of crime

Risk of being a victim of violent crime, 2007/08 BCS

	% victims once or more
All adults	3.2
Women aged 16–24	6.4
Single people	7.8
Unemployed	9.3
Full-time student	10.1
Men aged 16–24	13.4

Risk of being a victim of burglary, 2007/08 BCS

	% victims once or more
All households	2.4
Physical disorder in local area assessed as high	5.4
Single adult & child(ren)	6.4
Household reference person unemployed	6.5
Household reference person aged 16–24	7.5
No home security measures	25.0

Kershaw, C., Nicholas, S. and Walker, A. (2008) *Crime in England and Wales 2008*, Home Office RDS/Ministry of Justice

Sociology A2 for AQA

Check your understanding

1. Explain why official statistics give a completely accurate picture of the workings of the criminal justice system.

2. Explain why official statistics do not give an accurate picture of the number and types of crimes committed.

3. Why might official statistics give a more accurate picture of the amount of car theft than the amount of domestic violence?

4. How might a person's 'demeanour' affect their likelihood of arrest?

5. Explain why so many people plead guilty in court.

6. Do reductions in arrests for possession of cannabis reflect a decrease in the use of the drug? Explain your answer.

7. Suggest three crimes that you think people might be willing to admit to being victims of when questioned in a victimization study.

8. Why might some people exaggerate the amount of crime that they have committed in a self-report study?

9. Suggest two reasons why young males might make up the majority of victims of violence.

10. Explain why repeat victimization may occur.

Key terms

British Crime Survey annual victimization survey carried out by the Home Office.

Home Office government department responsible for criminal justice matters.

Islington Crime Surveys famous local victimization studies focusing on one area of North London.

Official statistics statistics released by government agencies.

Plea-bargaining where there is an informal (sometimes unspoken) agreement that if an accused person pleads guilty to a lesser crime than that of which he or she is accused, the prosecution will agree.

Repeat victimization where people are victims of the same crime more than once.

Responsibilization Garland suggests this is the shift towards blaming people for becoming victims of crime, by suggesting they have not taken adequate precautions.

Risk management the process whereby governments stop trying to prevent all crime and instead see it as their job to limit the risk of crime for the population.

Self-report studies where people are asked to note down the crimes they have committed over a particular period.

Sensitizing refers to the extent of disorder or minor criminal activity that people will accept.

Social construction in this case, refers to the fact that statistics represent the activities of the people constructing the statistics rather than some objective reality.

Victimization (or victim) surveys where people are asked what crimes have happened to them over a particular period.

Activities

Research ideas

1 The table below is based on a national sample of people aged 16 and over, who were asked to indicate what the greatest problem in their area was.

	Very/fairly big problem (%)	Very/fairly common (%)
Teenagers hanging around	32	51
Rubbish and litter	31	42
Vandalism	32	34
Drug use/dealing	33	31
Run-down homes	13	15
Noisy neighbours	9	14
Abandoned cars	13	14
Racial attacks	7	5
People sleeping rough	4	3

Conduct a small pilot survey of 14 to 16 year olds using the categories in the table. Do your results reflect the results here? Why do you think there may be differences?

2 Carry out interviews with a small sample of people of different ages and genders to discover the factors that influence public reporting of crime. Does it depend on seriousness, whether the crime has a victim or other factors? Does likelihood of reporting correlate with variables such as age or gender?

Web.tasks

1 Go to **www.homeoffice.gov.uk/rds/soti.html**

Then click on 'Interactive Maps of Crime Data at local authority level link'. On the map that loads on your computer, explore crime rates in your local-authority area.

2 Find the site of the Home Office at **www.homeoffice.gov.uk**

Go to the section on Research Development Statistics. Try to find figures about the amount and type of crime using official statistics, self-report studies and victim studies. What similarities and differences can you find? Try to explain the patterns you find.

An eye on the exam — Patterns of crime

Item A

The predominant focus on recorded crime is at best partial and at worst hopelessly ideological. Since the British Crime Survey started to be produced in the early 1980s, it has been clear that police-recorded crime figures provide a far from accurate picture of crime levels. Moreover, a whole range of crimes, from white-collar fraud and business crime to environmental crimes and state crimes, rarely if ever figure in police-recorded crime statistics. However, using victim surveys produces no better results, as, in the first place, the victims are generally unaware that they are victims.

Adapted from Carrabine, E. *et al.* (2004) *Criminology: A Sociological Introduction*, London: Routledge

Using material from **Item A** and elsewhere, examine the usefulness of victim surveys for an understanding of patterns of crime.

(12 marks)

Grade booster — Getting top marks in this question

You need to explain first what a victim survey such as the British Crime Survey (BCS) involves, and how the statistics derived from it differ from those produced by the police. You should look at both the advantages and the disadvantages of using victim surveys in studying patterns of crime. What are the problems associated with police figures, and can victim surveys overcome these problems? Do they cover all kinds of crime and all kinds of victim? You could also distinguish between national victim surveys (e.g. BCS) and local ones (e.g. Islington). Remember to make use of material from the Item in your answer. For example, why are people sometimes unaware that they are victims of crime, and what effect does this have on the data produced by victim surveys?

TOPIC 6

Environmental approaches: the criminology of place and time

This topic explores the relationship of crime to places and times. This link is hardly an original idea – since the earliest recorded history, people have been warned against going to dangerous places, particularly at night-time. Sociologists have taken this basic idea and explored the links between where people live, work and have their leisure, and crime patterns. We examine the explanation under two groupings:

● locating offenders
● exploring the location of offences.

Explaining offenders

Chicago sociology

The pattern

In the late-19th and early-20th centuries, one of the fastest growing cities in the USA was Chicago. The city also possessed one of the new university departments of sociology, and two of its researchers, Shaw and McKay (1931) began plotting the location of the addresses of those who committed crimes in the city. The results showed that, if they divided the city into **concentric zones**, each of the five zones they identified had different levels of offenders, with zone two (which was nearest the city centre) showing the highest rates.

This was interesting in itself, but they also found that because of rapid social change, the population living in zone two was changing regularly, so that although the various zones maintained their different levels of offenders over time, they were different offenders. This meant that there was something about the zones, rather than individuals who lived there, that was linked to crime rates.

The explanation: social disorganization

Shaw and McKay suggested that as each successive wave of immigrants arrived in the city, they were moved into the cheapest and least desirable zones – that is, the **zone of transition**. Over time, some were successful and they moved out to the more affluent suburbs, while the less successful remained. The places of those who had moved on were taken by newer immigrants, and so the process started again. This pattern of high population turnover created a state of **social disorganization**, where the informal mechanisms of social control that normally hold people back from criminal behaviour were weak or absent.

Cultural transmission

In their later writings, Shaw and McKay (1942) altered the meaning of 'social disorganization' to refer to a distinct set of values that provided an alternative to those of the mainstream society. This amended approach came to be known as **cultural transmission** theory. They argued that amongst some groups in the most socially disorganized and poorest zones of the city, crime became culturally acceptable, and was passed on from one generation to the next as part of the normal socialization pattern. Successful criminals provide role models for the next generation by demonstrating both the normality of criminal behaviour and that a criminal career was possible.

Differential association

One criticism of Shaw and McKay and other members of the Chicago School of Criminology was that their theories were too vague and difficult to prove.

In response, Sutherland and Cressey (1966) introduced the concept of **differential association**. This states that someone is likely to become criminal 'if they receive an excess of definitions favourable to violation of law over definitions unfavourable to violation of law'. This simply means that if people interact with others who support lawbreaking, then they are likely to do so themselves.

Further tightening his approach in order to avoid criticisms of vagueness, Sutherland suggested that these definitions vary in frequency, duration, priority, and intensity:

● *frequency* – the number of times the definitions occur
● *duration* – over what length of time
● *priority* – e.g. at what stage in life (childhood socialization is more important than other periods)
● *intensity* – the status of the person making the definition (e.g. family member rather than a stranger).

Housing policies

Most British research failed to reproduce the clear pattern of concentric circles that the Chicago School had identified. Crime rates certainly varied by areas, but in more complex patterns.

One early study by Morris in 1957 found no evidence that people in areas of high delinquency held a coherent set of values that was any different from that of mainstream society. Morris suggested that a key factor in the concentration of delinquents in certain areas was linked to the local council's housing policies. For example, in his study of Croydon, the local council's policy of housing problem-families together meant that these areas became, almost by definition, high-crime areas.

The impact of local-authority housing decisions was clarified much later by the work of Baldwin and Bottoms (1976), who compared two similar local-authority housing estates, separated by a dual carriageway. One of the estates 'Gardenia' had a 300 per cent higher number of offenders and a 350 per cent higher level of crimes than the other 'Stonewall'. The difference according to him was the result of a process that he named '**tipping**'.

Tipping

Most estates consist of a mixture of people from different backgrounds and with different forms of behaviour. Informal social control imposed by the majority of residents limits the offending behaviour of the antisocial minority. However, if for whatever reason (such as local-authority housing policies), the antisocial minority grow in number, their behaviour drives away some of the law-abiding families. Those who wish to enter the estate tend to be relatives of the antisocial families and this leads to a speed up in the law-abiding residents leaving. The estate has 'tipped' and becomes increasingly regarded as a problem estate. Those who are able to flee, do so. In Baldwin and Bottom's analysis, Gardenia had tipped, whilst Stonewall had not.

Disorder

W.G. Skogan (1990) in the USA has fleshed out this idea of tipping. He suggests that social control breaks down when, for example, there is a combination of physical deterioration in local buildings and parks, and an increase in social disorder in the form of public alcohol and drug use. This leads to a situation of disorder, which has three consequences:

1 It undermines the mechanisms of informal social control and leads people to withdraw, thus undermining the bonds between people.
2 It generates worries about neighbourhood safety, so that people avoid going out at night, thus making it easier for street crime to be committed.
3 It causes law-abiding people who can afford it to move out of the area, and leads to a decrease in property values and the growth of housing to let.

Key themes

Sociological theories and methods

Ethical issues

Newspapers set out to produce colourful stories about people and places that the people who buy the papers want to read about. Journalists go to great lengths to uncover the names and addresses of deviants, publishing these in 'the public good'. The outcome is that both guilty and innocent people have been hounded out of their homes and neighbourhoods. Media campaigns which highlight negative aspects of a particular housing development will mean that people will be frightened to move into the area and those already living there may well feel even more fearful.

Sociologists, too, are interested in deviants and areas with social problems, but they are committed by their code of ethics to minimize the negative impact of their studies on people and areas they research. Before any research programme, the sociologist has to obtain ethical approval from the university. Above all, they must demonstrate that no harm will occur to the people being studied. This is why virtually all studies since the 1980s use pseudonyms for individuals in the study, altering the names of schools, organizations and neighbourhoods where the research has taken place, so that no one will be able to trace the participants. In the study by Baldwin and Bottoms above, for example, the names 'Gardenia' and 'Stonewall' were used, while Stephen Ball (1981), in his study of a comprehensive school, talks about 'Beachside Comprehensive'.

Social capital

Social disorganization explains crime and deviance by a lack of common, shared values, although there is relatively little evidence to support this. However, more recently, there has been a shift back to understanding the role of values. In Topic 1, we explored Putnam's concept of **social capital**, in which he argues that there has been a decline in the extent to which people are linked into family and friendship networks. The result is that individuals feel more alone and less confident about engaging in community activity. According to Putnam, this results in a weak community unable to impose social control on those who engage in offending.

In the USA, William Julius Wilson (1996) has adapted a version of this approach to explain the high levels of offending in deprived neighbourhoods. He argues that there is a high level of social interaction between people, so that it is not true that people are isolated. There are, however, low levels of social control. Wilson suggests that this comes from a sense of powerlessness and a lack of integration into the wider society. People in deprived areas do interact, but not in a way that provides social controls or positive social models for young people, as the adults themselves feel isolated from the broader society.

A study by Sampson *et al.* (1997) of inner-city Chicago provides support for Wilson's model. They found considerable social interaction between people, but little community organization – which they call '**collective efficacy**'. Areas with higher levels of collective efficacy had lower rates of crime than those without, no matter how much personal social interaction occurred.

Explaining offences

So far we have been exploring theories that look at where offenders live and why they have higher levels of offending. However, other approaches have looked at where offences take place and why they occur in these places and not others.

This distinction has been highlighted in Wilkstrom's (1991) study of crime patterns in Stockholm. This is particularly important as it demonstrates that the types and extent of offences vary across neighbourhoods. At its simplest, city centres, poorer districts and affluent areas adjacent to poorer districts have higher rates of crime. Within this, crimes of violence are more likely in the poorer districts, while burglary was more likely in the affluent areas adjacent to poorer districts. This observation shifted environmental theories towards explanations of these different patterns of offences.

Cognitive maps

P.J. and P.L. Brantingham (1991) argue that we all hold **cognitive maps** of the towns and cities where we live, so some parts of our local town are familiar to us and other parts much less known. In particular, we know the routes from our homes to where we study or work, and where we go for entertainment. According to the Brantinghams, offenders are most likely to commit offences where opportunities (e.g. houses to burgle) link with 'cognitively

known' areas, and conversely that places that are less 'cognitively known' are less likely to be burgled (see Fig. 6.9). This provides an explanation for the patterns of crime we noted earlier, such as for burglary.

Opportunity theory

If crimes are most likely to be committed in areas that offenders know, then the next question must be why, within these areas, are some properties or people chosen and others are not? Clarke (1995) seeks to explain this with **opportunity theory**. Opportunity consists of two elements:

- how *attractive* the target is – for example, how much can be gained by committing a crime against this particular place or person and, if it is property, how easy it is to carry away and to sell afterwards
- how *accessible* the target is – for example, how easy it is to commit the crime.

Routine activities

These ideas of cognitive maps and opportunity were further developed by Cohen and Felson (1979) in their concept of **routine activities**. They argue that crimes are more likely to occur where the day-to-day activities of victims and offenders are likely to coincide, and where there is little in the way of formal or informal control to prevent an offence taking place. Cohen and Felson have introduced two new issues into the discussion with their definition:

1. Crimes are likely to occur where there is no 'capable guardian', such as a police officer, neighbours or informal social control engendered by a sense of community.
2. It is not just place that is important, but also time. For example, the person who is more likely to be 'mugged' is the person returning from work, walking along a quiet street, in the evening. We will explore this issue of time later.

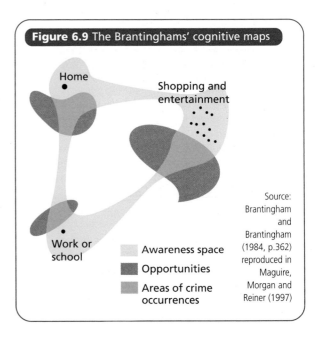

Figure 6.9 The Brantinghams' cognitive maps

Home

Shopping and entertainment

Work or school

- Awareness space
- Opportunities
- Areas of crime occurrences

Source: Brantingham and Brantingham (1984, p.362) reproduced in Maguire, Morgan and Reiner (1997)

Situational crime prevention

The work of Clarke (opportunity theory), and Cohen and Felson (routine activities) were based on the idea that most crime occurs when the offender thinks that the advantages of committing the crime outweigh the disadvantages of capture and punishment. According to these theorists, the easier it is for a person to commit a crime and the greater the resulting benefit, then the greater the chance of a crime being committed. Separately, Clarke and Felson have argued that if society wishes to limit crimes, it is more effective to make the 'costs' of committing the crime higher rather than to study the social 'causes' of crime. Their arguments led to the development of **'situational crime prevention'**. This approach involved making the costs higher:

● *for theft* – by making it more difficult to steal (e.g. by using locks, having Neighbourhood Watch Schemes) and making it more difficult to sell stolen goods (e.g. by marking valuable articles with identifiable codes which show they are stolen)

● *for violence* – by limiting opportunities, such as having plastic glasses in pubs at night and having security staff to maintain order.

However, while it might lower certain types of minor crime, it is irrelevant for the 'crimes of the powerful' and it also fails in the basic task of any sociological theory of offering an explanation of why someone would want to offend in the first place.

The privatization of public space

Sociologists have always been aware of the distinction between public space (where anyone can go) and private space (where entry is controlled by the owner), and its importance for the levels and types of offending. For example, as long ago as the 1960s, Stinchcombe (1963) used the term 'the institution of privacy' to illustrate how policing tended to be against deviant activities carried out in public, with much less stress placed on violence and abuse in the home.

However, in recent years, the issue of private and public space has re-emerged as an important debate for sociologists, as changes have taken place in the nature of urban life.

Shearing and Stenning (1983) pointed to the growth of shopping centres and leisure complexes, which are both public, in that they are spaces where (most) people are welcomed, and private, in that they are privately owned and the owners have the power to exclude those they define as undesirable. In housing, too, there has been the growth of gated communities – housing estates where only residents and guests are allowed.

Focus on research

Bernasco and Nieuwbeerta (2005)
How burglars choose their targets

Bernasco and Nieuwbeerta conducted a detailed study of burglary patterns in The Hague, in the Netherlands. They obtained information on 548 residential burglaries and from 290 (arrested) burglars across the city over a period of one year. They concluded that there were some very clear patterns of burglary. The affluence of the neighbourhood was not very important; instead, homes were more likely to be broken into if they were relatively near to where the offender lived and if there was perceived to be limited 'guardianship', meaning people keeping an eye on the property. Other factors were the high rate of burglary in areas of the city where there were mixed ethnic groups and a high proportion of single-parent families. Bernasco and Nieuwbeerta did not find any evidence for concentric zones where crimes were more likely.

Bernasco, W. and Nieuwbeerta, P. (2005) 'How do residential burglars select target areas?', *British Journal of Criminology*, 45(3)

1 To what extent do the methods used by the authors provide a representative picture of burglary?

2 Summarize the factors that appeared to make some houses vulnerable to burglary.

Key themes

Socialization, culture and identity
The decline of community

The move towards late modernity and the linked stress on the importance of the individual as opposed to the family or community, have had a significant impact on a wide variety of social issues. Some sociologists suggest that decline of informal social control by the family and community has helped contribute to the increase in offending rates. Others have pointed to the way that the decline of traditional working-class communities has impacted on voting patterns. The Labour Party, which once could rely on the solid support of equally solid working-class inner-city communities, is now aware that voting is based on a much wider range of issues, of which the interests of the individual are important. The claimed decline in community not only reflects the increase in divorce rates, but also contributes to increased levels of divorce and marital instability in that the pressures placed on couples to remain together have declined significantly. However, if the decline in community has occurred for the majority White population, for many ethnic groups the sense of community has not shown similar levels of decline.

Shearing and Stenning argue that the owners of these private 'public' spaces have taken over the responsibility for policing them – using CCTV and security guards – and this has led to the **privatization of public space**. The police have been increasingly confined to the more peripheral areas of the city and to the poorer (particularly 'problem') housing estates. The exclusion of undesirable groups (young people, known offenders, beggars) from these private 'public' areas, has simply displaced crime to the less affluent public areas.

Time: the night-time economy

Earlier, we noted the implication in Cohen and Felson's routine activities theory, that time is a crucial and neglected element in understanding crime. If different places have varying levels of crime and different styles of control, then so do different times. The busy city centre, filled with families shopping during the day, becomes the location for the young seeking pleasure at night. The same location, therefore, changes its meaning and possibilities with the closing of the shops and the coming of the darkness.

An interesting example of the significance of time is what Hobbs *et al.* (2000) call the '**night-time economy**'. They point out that in the last 15 years, there has been a huge growth in pubs and clubs, as Britain's younger people have increasingly embraced the leisure society. This involves, in Britain at least, going out at the weekend to clubs and pubs to consume alcohol (and possibly also drugs) and to enjoy oneself. In 2003, for example, there were over 210 million club admissions to the value of £2.5 billion. Investment in the night-time economy totals around £1 billion a year and is growing at an annual rate of 10 per cent.

The sheer scale of the leisure industry means that there are now huge numbers of young people who come together within a very narrow time-band and in a relatively restricted area, in order to engage in the search for pleasure. Almost three-quarters of all violent incidents in urban areas occur during the weekend between 9 pm and 3 am, usually by and between groups of young males fuelled by drink and/or drugs. Hobbs (2003) illustrates this by pointing out that, in Manchester, an average of 75 000 people are out visiting the clubs, pubs and bars on Friday and Saturday evenings. There are only about 30 police officers to control them, but over 1000 door staff and 'bouncers'. So, the control of the night-time economy has largely been passed from the police to private security companies.

A similar thing is happening in other British towns and cities. The high rates of violent crime occurring within this framework of time and space illustrate the three elements referred to by Cohen and Felson: offenders, targets (victims), and lack of guardians.

The night-time economy and the global economy

Taylor (1999) has added a global perspective to discussions about the nocturnal economy and crime. His argument is that the development of the nocturnal economy is bound up with the process of globalization and its impact upon the British economy, in particular the impact on inner cities. According to Taylor, the impact of the global economy on Britain has been a huge decrease in manufacturing and the associated loss of traditional working-class employment. The consequent effects have been that many traditionally industrial towns have seen a significant decline in their local economies. This is reflected in a decline in town centres and the manufacturing

Activities

Research idea

Undertake a small survey of fear of crime in your area. Choose a local shopping centre (e.g. near/on a social-housing estate) or the town centre. Ask a small random selection of people about their fear of being victims of crime. Ask them about whether they go out in the evening and, if so, do they have greater concerns than during the day. What differences, if any, emerge?

(You should ask permission from your college before you undertake this. You must always work in small groups of two or three, and one person in each group must have a mobile phone.)

Web.task

The government has promised to provide a neighbourhood crime map for every neighbourhood in England and Wales. At the time of writing, this was still not available nationally – but it is worth googling the term 'neighbourhood crime map'.

However, the Metropolitan Police have already created one. Go to **http://maps.met.police.uk/** to explore crime in London. Go to the FAQs section to learn more about 'crime mapping'.

Check your understanding

1   Shaw and McKay suggested two explanations for the behaviour of the people in the zones they identified. What are these explanations?

2   Explain, in your own words, what is meant by the term 'tipping'.

3   According to the Brantinghams, where are offences most likely to take place?

4   What information do 'cognitive maps' and 'routine activities theory' tell us about where and who are more likely to be targeted by offenders?

5   Briefly explain how the privatization of public space 'displaces' crime.

6   Why is the crime rate likely to rise during the hours of 9 pm and 3 am?

districts, with shops and manufacturing premises closing down, and also in an increase in the numbers of people unemployed or in irregular work. Clearly, different cities have been affected differently, so that the North-East of England has been hit far harder than the South. However, in all cities, the leisure industry referred to above has taken over a number of the derelict buildings for clubs and bars, whilst providing a limited number of jobs in these services and in security. Taylor suggests that where the levels of unemployment have remained highest (yet the leisure facilities are still provided), there are likely to be the highest levels of disorder and crime, and in those cities where the unemployment has not risen, there is less crime – or at least a slower growth in crime.

Key terms

Cognitive maps a personal map of a town based on an individual's daily activities.

Collective efficacy the ability of a community to achieve their aims (which usually include limiting crime).

Concentric zones widening circles.

Cultural transmission values are passed on from one generation to the next.

Differential association the theory that deviant behaviour is learned from, and justified by, family and friends.

Night-time economy refers to the way that a leisure industry has developed at night, which provides the location of many offences.

Opportunity theory crime occurs when there is an opportunity; stop the opportunity and crime is less likely to occur.

Privatization of public space the way that public areas are increasingly being owned and controlled by companies, who police it in such a way as to exclude undesirables.

Routine activities the normal activities of daily life provide the cognitive maps and opportunities for crime.

Situational crime prevention an approach to crime which ignores the motivation for offending and instead concentrates on making it more difficult to commit crime.

Social capital the extent of social networks.

Social disorganization a city area that does not have a shared culture.

Tipping the process by which an area moves from being predominantly law-abiding to predominantly accepting antisocial behaviour.

Zone of transition the cheapest, least desirable zones of the city, into which immigrants are moved.

An eye on the exam Environmental approaches

Item A

Situational crime prevention (SCP) involves intervening in the immediate situations in which crime takes place in order to reduce its likelihood or seriousness. It often involves designing crime out of products, services and environments, for example by use of anticlimb paint, CCTV and security guards in shops, better street lighting, metal detectors at airports, neighbourhood watch schemes and the redesigning of housing estates.

SCP does not rely on intervening in children's socialization to prevent them becoming criminals later, or on the threat of punishments to deter current criminals. Instead, it makes specific changes aimed at influencing the decision or ability of offenders to commit particular crimes in particular situations. Like rational choice theory, SCP sees criminals as acting rationally. By making certain crimes less rewarding, more risky or needing greater effort, SCP makes criminals less likely to choose to commit them.

Examine the effectiveness of situational crime prevention as a means of reducing the impact of crime on society (**Item A**).

(12 marks)

Grade booster Getting top marks in this question

Remember to use the Item to help you identify some of the different situation crime prevention techniques that exist, such as anticlimb paint, CCTV, security guards and metal detectors. Add others if you can. How far do these measures actually work? For example, do they just result in displacement of crime onto 'softer' targets? Do criminals act rationally in choosing their course of action, as rational choice theory suggests? Try to link your points about crime prevention techniques to sociological concepts and theories. You could evaluate the approach in the Item by contrasting it with views that seek to explain criminal behaviour in terms of social background or labelling by law enforcers.

TOPIC 7

Gender issues and offending

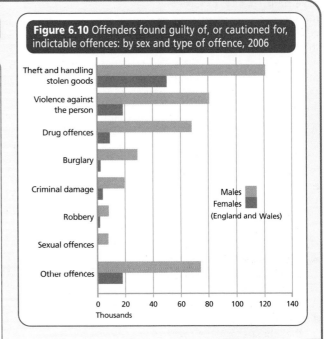
In this topic, we want to explore the relationship that gender has to offending. Official records show an overwhelming predominance of males compared with females committing crime. Self-report studies, too, show a noticeable, if less marked, difference between the offending levels of males and females. Given this, there has to be something in the different construction of femininity and masculinity that can help us to explain these differences. We will try to unravel some of the strands of explanation offered.

Before we do so, however, we need to explain why, surprisingly perhaps, there has been relatively little research that explicitly sets out to explain the links between gender and offending. It seems that most sociologists have started off with the assumption that males commit more crime, and have then moved on to explore why it is that only

some males commit crime. Explanations offered by sociologists have, therefore, concentrated mainly on comparing offending males with non-offending males, without explaining why males are more likely to offend in the first instance.

The topic falls into two main areas of discussion:

● the issue of women and crime
● male gender roles and crime.

First, we ask why women have been ignored in the sociology of crime and delinquency, before turning to examine the explanations for lower rates of female offending. In the second part of the topic, we turn things on their head and ask what lessons the exploration of gender roles might have for male offending. The answers we arrive at may be rather surprising, for it seems that the opening-up of criminology by feminists provides us with clues as to why males have such high rates of offending. Indeed, so significant are these insights that much contemporary criminology is heavily influenced by them.

Invisible female offenders

Anyone studying the sociology of crime and deviance will notice after a while that it is mainly about male offending. In fact, it would not be unfair to call it the sociology of male crime and deviancy. Although it is true that the majority of offenders are male – comprising about 80 per cent of all official statistics on offenders – it is surprising that 20 per cent of all offenders are simply ignored.

Frances Heidensohn (1989) has criticized the male dominance of the subject (known as **malestream** criminology) and has suggested that there are four reasons why it is so:

- *Male dominance of offenders* – As the majority of offenders are male, for many sociologists it was therefore most appropriate to study them, rather than the minority of female offenders.
- *Male domination of sociology* – Although the majority of sociology students are women, it has always been the case that the majority of academics have been male. According to Heidensohn, sociological topics of investigation reflect a male view and male interests.
- *Vicarious identification* – This follows from the previous point. Men study what interests them, and, applied to crime, this is most often the lives of the marginal and the exciting, i.e. **vicarious identification**.
- *Sociological theorizing* – Male sociologists constructed their theories without ever thinking about how they could be applied to females. Most traditional theories are 'gender blind'; in effect, that means they ignore the specific viewpoint of women.

Explaining female crime: women's roles

Most theories that explain crime, as we saw earlier, implicitly accept that males are more likely than females to commit crime. In the process, criminologists have omitted to explain what it is that makes males more likely than females to commit crime. There have, however, been a number of exceptions to this and we explore these approaches in this section. Three major approaches to explaining the relationship between women and offending are:

1 biological explanations
2 sex-role theory
3 changing role or 'liberationist' perspective.

Biological explanations

This approach has been used by different writers to explain why the vast majority of women do not offend and, conversely, why a small minority do. It starts from the belief that women are innately different from men, with a natural desire to be caring and nurturing – neither of them values that support crime. 'Normal' women are therefore

less likely to commit crime. On the other hand, some women writers, such as Dalton (1964), have claimed that hormonal or menstrual factors can influence a minority of women to commit crime in certain circumstances.

Sex-role theory

Sex-role theory argues that women are less likely to commit crime than men because there are core elements of the female role that limit their ability and opportunity to do so. There are a number of different versions of this theory, all of which can fit quite comfortably together.

Socialization

According to this approach, girls are socialized differently to boys. The values that girls are brought up to hold are those that simply do not lead to crime. Talcott Parsons (1937) argues, for instance, that as most child-rearing is carried out by mothers, girls have a clear role model to follow that emphasizes caring and support. Evidence to support this differential socialization was provided by Farrington and Painter (2004) in their longitudinal study of female offenders. They uncovered different patterns of socialization between offenders and non-offenders. In particular, they found that female offenders were much more likely to have had harsh or erratic parenting, and to have had little support or praise from their parents for their achievements at school and in their community.

Social control

Females are less likely to commit crime because of the closer levels of supervision that they are subjected to at home in childhood. This control carries on throughout life, with the role of women being more constrained that that of males. Heidensohn (1996), for example, says:

> << An examination of female criminality and unofficial deviance suggests that we need to move away from studying infractions and look at conformity instead, because the most striking thing about female behaviour is how notably conformist to social mores women are. >>

Heidensohn points to the wide range of informal sanctions to discourage women from straying from 'proper' behaviour, including gossip, ill repute and the comments of male companions. Hagan (1987) studied child-raising patterns in Canada and argued that there was significantly greater informal control of daughters' activities in families compared to sons.

Marginalization

In order to commit crime, a person needs to have the opportunity to do so. The narrower range of roles that women are allowed to have limits their opportunities to commit crime, as they are more confined by their socialization and social control than men.

The result of these three influences on the lives of females, is to deflect them away from offending and towards conformity.

The changing role or 'liberationist' perspective

So far, we have characterized female sex-roles as being more passive and less aggressive than those of males. However, a number of writers, including Adler (1975), have suggested that the increasing rates of female crime are linked to their freedom from the traditional forms of social control, discussed earlier, and their acceptance into more 'masculine' roles. More recently, Denscombe (2001) has argued that changing female roles over the last ten years mean that, increasingly, females are as likely as males to engage in risk-taking behaviour. In his research into self-images of 15 to 16 year olds in the East Midlands, in which he undertook in-depth interviews as well as focus groups, he found that females were rapidly adopting what had traditionally been male attitudes. This included such things as 'looking hard', 'being in control' and being someone who can cope with risk-taking. This provides theoretical support for the fact that female crime levels are rising much more quickly than male ones, not just in terms of numbers but also in terms of seriousness of crimes committed.

Westwood (1999) develops similar ideas when she argues that identities are constantly being reconstructed and reframed. The concept of a fixed female identity has limited our understanding of crime, so we need to understand how women are reconfiguring their identity in a more confident, forceful way, and the possible link to the growth of female crime. However, Heidensohn (2002) disputes this argument, citing evidence from a number of other studies which show that convicted offenders tend to score highly on psychological tests of 'femininity', indicating, according to her, that they have not taken on male roles.

Transgression: A postmodernist critique

The various explanations of female crime put forward were not popular with feminist sociologists, as they felt that they were not really adequate explanations for the differences between male and female causes for offending. Pat Carlen (1992) argued, for example, that these were theoretically weak and represented a sort of 'bolt-on' to existing male criminology.

It was in response to the need for a feminist version of criminology – one that answered the concerns of women – that Carol Smart (1990) introduced the idea of a **transgressive criminology**. By this, Smart was suggesting that criminology itself as a discipline was tied to male questions and concerns and that it could never offer answers to feminist questions. Instead of trying to produce a feminist criminology by asking the question, 'What can feminism offer criminology?', feminists should be arguing, 'What can criminology offer feminists?' The answer to this question lay in looking at a whole range of activities (both legal and illegal) that actually harm women, and asking how these came about and how they could be changed. The term 'transgressive', in this context then, meant to go beyond the boundaries of

Focus on research

Stephen Jones (2008)
The influence of men on female offenders

One of the current explanations for the rise in female offending is that it reflects the increased freedom of women from male control. This decline in male social control has allowed women to make choices to offend in the same way that men do. Increasing autonomy for women leads to increasing offending by women. However, this has been criticized by other sociologists, who suggest that women offend precisely because they are under the control of men.

Stephen Jones decided to test the extent to which female offending was of their own choosing or whether they were influenced by men. He did this by interviewing women who had been found guilty of an offence for which they had been charged jointly with a male (the co-defendant) and asking them how much they had been influenced by their male co-defendant. This is how he describes his research methods:

<< *Between December 2004 and December 2005, all sentenced women aged 21 or over who passed through one English prison were given a letter inviting them to be interviewed about their experience with a co-defendant. It was usually possible for the letters to be delivered by the researcher in person and this proved valuable as it enabled the women to ask questions about the research ... Fifty women with co-defendants agreed to be interviewed. These were conducted in private and tape-recorded. The interviews were of a semistructured nature. Having been asked several background questions about themselves and their co-defendants, the women were then engaged in a more general conversation about the relationship they had with these people and how they came to commit offences together.* >>

Jones, S. (2008) 'Partners in crime: a study of the relationship between female offenders and their co-defendants,' *Criminology and Criminal Justice*, 8

1   Explain the aims of this research and the reason why it was conducted.

2   Why do you think the interviews were conducted in the way described above?

criminology. This did lead to feminists (and sympathetic male sociologists) looking more closely at things such as:

- the way women stayed in at night for fear of becoming victims
- domestic violence
- how women were treated by the law in issues of rape and harassment (where they form the overwhelming bulk of the victims).

Transgression is a good example of the postmodern influence in sociology, when the traditional boundaries of sociology and the categories used to classify issues are abandoned, and new ways of thinking are introduced.

Explaining male crime: male roles and masculinity

Smart's idea of transgressive criminology, linked to the growing importance of postmodern analysis, began to feed back into mainstream criminology. Some sociologists began to go beyond traditional confines and to revisit the issue of why most crime is male crime.

Normative masculinity

The analysis of masculinity began with the Australian sociologist, Bob Connell (1995). He argued that there were a number of different forms of masculinity, which change over time – in particular, he identified the concept of hegemonic masculinity (see Topic 2, p. 342). Although crime was not central to his analysis, the idea of multiple, constructed masculinities was taken up by Messerschmidt (1993).

Connell argues that a '**normative masculinity**' exists in society, highly valued by most men. Normative masculinity refers to the socially approved idea of what a 'real male' is. According to Messerschmidt, it 'defines masculinity through difference from and desire for women'. Normative masculinity is so prized that men struggle to live up to its expectations. Messerschmidt suggests then that masculinity is not something natural, but rather a state that males only achieve as 'an accomplishment', which involves being constantly worked at.

However, the construction of this masculinity takes place in different contexts and through different methods depending upon the particular male's access to power and resources. So, more powerful males will accomplish their masculinity in different ways and contexts from less powerful males. Messerschmidt gives examples of businessmen who can express their power over women through their control in the workplace, while those with no power at work may express their masculinity by using violence in the home or street. However, whichever way is used, both types of men are achieving their normative masculinity.

So, it is achieving masculinity that leads some men to commit crime – and, in particular, crime is committed by those less powerful in an attempt to be successful at masculinity (which involves material, social and sexual success). The idea that masculinity is the actual basis of crime is reflected in the writings of a number of writers.

Katz: seductions of crime

A postmodern twist on the idea of masculinity is the work of Katz (1988), who argues that what most criminology has failed to do is to understand the role of pleasure in committing crime. This search for pleasure has to be placed within the context of masculinity, which stresses the importance of status, control over others and success.

Key themes — Sociological theories and methods

Although male sociologists have largely ignored female offending, feminist writers from the various strands within feminism have all sought to include criminological analyses within their approaches.

Feminist perspectives on crime and deviance

Liberal feminism

This approach to feminism is based on the idea that by bringing women onto the agenda and by demonstrating how women have been ignored in research, there will be greater understanding of female deviance. In particular, new theories can be developed that will cover both males and females.

Radical feminism

Radical feminists argue that the only way to understand crime is to see it through a female perspective – and research should be based on the assumption that all men are prepared to commit crimes against women if given the chance. Women should construct their own unique approaches to explaining crime and deviance, and this should incorporate the threat from men.

Socialist feminism

This approach stresses that the position of men and women in general – and with reference to crime in particular – can only be understood by locating males and females within the context of societies divided by both sexism and by capitalism.

Postmodern feminism

The work of Smart (1990) and Cain (1986) is particularly important, since they argue that the very concerns of criminology (burglary/street crime, etc.) are actually a reflection of male concerns, and that women should be looking beyond these to study how harm comes to women in the widest sense possible. Feminist criminology should not accept the (male) boundaries of criminology, but should look at the way women are harmed by a whole range of processes.

Katz claims that crime is always explained with reference to background causes, but rarely attempts to look at the pleasure that is derived from the actual act of offending. Doing evil, he argues, is motivated by the quest for a 'moral self-transcendence' in the face of boredom. Different crimes provide different thrills, that can vary from the 'sneaky thrills' of shoplifting, to the 'righteous slaughter' of murder.

Katz argues that by understanding the emotional thrills that transgression provides, we can understand why males commit crime. Katz gives the example of robbery, which is largely undertaken, he claims, for the chaos, thrill and potential danger inherent in the act. Furthermore, in virtually all robberies 'the offender discovers, fantasizes or manufactures an angle of moral superiority over the intended victim', such that the robber has 'succeeded in making a fool of his victim'. This idea of the thrill of crime has been used to explain the apparent irrational violence of football 'hooligans', and also the use of drugs and alcohol.

Katz's work is clearly influenced by the earlier work of Matza (1964) (see Topic 2), who has argued that constructing a male identity in contemporary society is difficult. Most youths are in a state of **drift** where they are unsure exactly who they are and what their place in society is. For most young males, this is a period of boredom and crisis. It is in this period of life that any event that unambiguously gives them a clear identity is welcomed, and it could equally be an identity of offender as much as employee. Committing offences provides a break from boredom, pleasure and a sense of being someone – for example, a gang member or a 'hard man'.

Key themes

Education

One of the most obvious points about crime is that the overwhelming majority of offenders are male. However, it wasn't really until the rise of feminist writings in the 1970s that sociologists began to look at the possible relationship between crime and the values of being a 'real' male. Ideas about subculture began to be replaced with notions of how masculinity was created and the impact this had on how men, and particularly young men, behaved. Once the idea of masculinity emerged, sociologists realized that it could explain a lot about the behaviour of young men in general. One especially fruitful area of study was of the educational experiences of young males. Over the past 20 years, there has been a huge shift in the comparative success rates of males and females at school, with girls having significantly better exam success than boys, and also exhibiting far less poor behaviour in the classroom. The reason for these differences in behaviour appears to be that the accepted notion of what a young male ought to be in society (or dominant hegemonic model of masculinity) contradicts the role required in the school of an obedient, hard-working pupil. Masculinity, as portrayed in the media, means being tough, possibly aggressive, sexually active and a person of action. None of this fits easily with the role of a school student.

Lyng: edgework

A linked argument can be found in the work of Lyng (1990), who argues that young males search for pleasure through risk-taking. According to Lyng, the risk-taking can best be seen as 'edgework', by which he means that there is a thrill to be gained from acting in ways that are on the edge between security and danger.

This helps explain the attractiveness of car theft and 'joy riding', and of searching for violent confrontations with other groups of males. By engaging in this form of risk-taking, young men are, in Messerschmidt's terms, 'accomplishing masculinity', and also proving that they have control over their lives.

Masculinities in context

The work of Connell (via Messerschmidt) and the arguments of Katz and Lyng have been very influential in contemporary criminology. However, they have all been criticized for not slotting the notion of masculinities into a context. So, Winlow (2004) has asked questions about the conditions in which men demonstrate their aggressiveness, and why it is that young, working-class males are more

Activities

Research idea

Devise a simple 'self-report' questionnaire (see Topic 5) with a maximum of ten questions. The offending behaviour or deviant acts should be fairly minor, but common (e.g. starting a fight, drinking alcohol under age).

Either working in groups or individually, divide your questionnaires into two sets. Give out one set of questionnaires to be completed anonymously (but devise a way of ensuring you know the gender of the person completing each one). Use the other set with interview techniques to complete the questionnaire directly.

1 Are there different results between the two methods?
2 Are there any differences between males and females?

Web.tasks

1 Go to the Home Office Research and Statistics Publications site. You will find a report on domestic violence, sexual assault and stalking at **www.homeoffice.gov.uk/rds/pdfs04/hors276.pdf**

What does this report tell you about the relationship between gender and these crimes?

2 Visit the Fawcett Society (an organization to promote the rights of women) at the address below and then click on the heading 'Women and Justice'. Explore the up-to-date statistics on women's experience of the criminal justice system.

www.fawcettsociety.org.uk/index.asp?PageID=721isit

likely to be violent. The answers, he argues, lie in the changing nature of the economy in late modernity. For generations, working-class masculinity has been linked to manual employment in manufacturing industry. With the huge changes in the economy, most notably the decline in manual work and the increase in low-level, white-collar employment, a significant proportion of the male working-class population has been excluded from the possibilities of regular employment. According to Wilson (1996), this has resulted in the development of an urban underclass who manifest a range of violent and antisocial behaviours. The masculinity they exude, therefore, can only be understood within the context of the changing economic structure of the UK.

Key terms

Drift term used by Matza to describe a state where young men are unsure about their identity and their place in society.

Malestream a term used to describe the fact that male ways of thinking have dominated criminology.

Normative masculinity the socially approved idea of what a real male is. According to Messerschmidt, it 'defines masculinity through difference from and desire for women'.

Sex-role theory explanations based on the restricted roles women are claimed to have in society.

Transgressive criminology feminist theorists use this term to suggest a need to 'break out' of the confines of traditional criminology.

Vicarious identification when people obtain a thrill by putting themselves in the place of another person.

Check your understanding

1   Why did criminology traditionally ignore female crime?

2   Give three examples of sex-role theory.

3   How is the idea of 'transgression' relevant to the debate about gender and crime?

4   In your own words, explain the term 'normative masculinity'. How does it help us to understand crime?

5   What is 'moral transcendence'?

6   Suggest three examples of 'edgework'.

7   What implication for the level of female crime is there as a result of the changing role of women in recent years?

An eye on the exam   Gender issues and offending

Item A

Messerschmidt argues that much of male offending reflects the desire of young men to meet the culturally ideal form of dominant masculinity. Jefferson is critical of this explanation, however, arguing that this form of explanation tells us little about why it is that only a minority of young men from a given ethnic group or social class choose to 'accomplish' masculinity by 'doing crime' while the majority do not. He follows Katz in noting that criminological knowledge has repeatedly failed to recognise the pleasure that is involved in 'doing masculinity' and 'doing crime'.

Adapted from Hopkins Burke, R. (2001) *An Introduction to Criminological Theory*, Cullompton: Willan

Using material from **Item A** and elsewhere, assess explanations for apparent gender differences in involvement in crime.

(21 marks)

Grade booster   Getting top marks in this question

You could begin by outlining the different patterns of recorded crime for males and females – e.g. differences and similarities in the kinds of offences committed, proportion of males and females in the official statistics. When assessing explanations you need to look at both male and female patterns. You can assess explanations of female patterns, such as sex-role theory (e.g. the informal social control of females reduces opportunities), and the marginalization versus women's liberation explanations. Make sure you use relevant material from Item A in assessing explanations of males. For example, it hints at class and ethnicity as important variables, and it offers a criticism of Messerschmidt's explanation, which you could develop, as well as ideas about thrill seeking, masculinity and crime.

Occupational, corporate and environmental crime

Getting you thinking

Cotton accounts for 16 per cent of global insecticide releases – more than any other single crop. Almost 1.0 kilogram of hazardous pesticides is applied for every hectare under cotton. Between 1 and 3 per cent of agricultural workers worldwide suffer from acute pesticide poisoning, with at least 1 million requiring hospitalization each year, according to a report prepared jointly for the FAO, UNEP and WHO. These figures equate to between 25 million and 77 million agricultural workers worldwide.

Andhra Pradesh, India: Rangamma Harrijana and her family weep at the grave of her son Mallesh, who died after spraying pesticide on cotton crops

Three-quarters of counterfeit items seized here last year came from factories in China, 'staffed' by children paid as little as £10 a week and working up to 18 hours a day. Since their fingers are small, they are better at the intricate stitching that makes fake designer items look so convincing.

Read the two passages on the left and look at the pictures:

1 Should we refuse to buy cotton goods made with cotton where pesticide is used? Would other countries do the same? Should we make it a crime to use chemicals? But who would pass the law? How could we enforce it?

2 Do you (or any of your relatives/friends) buy fake goods, such as bags, watches and clothes? What do you think about it now?

3 Each year, small children die in Britain because of accidents resulting from playing with unsafe, cheap imitations of more expensive toys. Who is to blame? The children? The parents? The manufacturers? Or are these just unfortunate accidents?

What is meant by 'occupational crime' and 'corporate crime'?

The study of **occupational crime** and **corporate crime** developed from the original work of Sutherland in the 1940s. Sutherland used the term '**white-collar**' **crime** to refer to crime committed by people who worked in offices. However, Sutherland's work overlaps with the interests of Marxist writers who were interested in the

'crimes of the powerful'. Both approaches share the concern that traditional research into crime centres on such things as robbery and burglary, and in doing so focuses on working-class offenders. People committing offences such as fraud, who tend to be at the other end of the class structure, are generally ignored.

Although there has been general agreement with Sutherland's argument that crime committed by the powerful needed studying, there remains considerable debate between sociologists about exactly what should be studied under this term. Sutherland (1940) originally defined white-collar crime as 'crime committed by a person of respectability and high social status in the course of his occupation'.

The definition is unfortunately very vague and includes within it two, quite different activities: on the one hand, it means crimes against the organization for which the person works, and on the other, crimes for the benefit of the organization for which the person works or which they own.

Occcupational and corporate offending: the problem of law

There is one more problem in the debate about what occupational/corporate crime actually is. Very often, when sociologists talk about white-collar or corporate crime, they may actually not be discussing actions that are illegal – that is, if the company or person is 'caught', no one is likely to go in front of a judge and face the possible personal risk of going to jail. Instead, the crime studied may actually be the breaking of supervisory codes (as in financial services) or technical standards (chemical content of consumer goods), or may refer to a whole range of actions that are, it could be argued, harmful and may even lead to death, but are not strictly speaking illegal – low safety standards at work, but that meet minimum legal criteria, for example. In fact, as Nelken (2002) points out, the debate about corporate crime is as much about corporate practices and sociologists' biases about what is morally wrong, as it is about breaking the law.

Some writers, such as Pearce and Tombs (1998), argue that corporate crime ought to extend to the manufacture of cigarettes and alcohol – both of which are linked to illness and death. Others point out that transnational companies that manufacture in poorer nations, where safety standards are negligible, are engaging in human-rights violations and are therefore committing crime – even if they are acting in a perfectly legal way according to the laws of the country where they are manufacturing.

So, much of the debate about occupational or corporate 'crime' goes beyond the limits of the law and looks at actions that have harmful consequences – and, in doing so, takes us beyond the limits of conventional criminology, opening up debates about what the sociology of crime and deviance ought to study.

The distinctions between occupational and corporate crime

This has led to two confusing and overlapping traditions:

- Studies of *occupational crime* – How and why people steal from companies and the public in activities associated with their jobs; for example, the employee who claims false expenses from the company or who overcharges customers and keeps the additional amount.
- The study of *corporate crime* – Much more important as a field of study in sociology, this is crime by corporations or businesses that has a serious physical or economic impact on employees, consumers or the general public. Corporate crime is motivated by the desire to increase profits.

Occupational crime

The impact of occupational crime

Theft by employees is a major source of crime in Britain – though whether the action of depriving an employer of goods, services or money is actually defined as theft is a real issue. Ditton (1977) and Mars (1982) have both studied theft by employees and found that in the range of industries they studied – from workers in the tourist industry to bakery delivery drivers – minor theft was regarded as a legitimate part of the job and redefined into a 'perk' or a 'fiddle'. Indeed, according to Mars, fiddling was part of the rewards of the job. For their part, according to Clarke (1990), management generally turned a blind eye to fiddles, accepting them as part of the total remuneration of the job and taking these into account in determining wage structures.

Levi (2007) estimates that direct losses from fraud in Britain total £12.98 billion. Fraudulent health and unemployment benefit claims total about £3 billion and frauds within the NHS are estimated at a possible £6 billion.

Practices of occupational crime extend into the professions too. Functionalist writings on the reason for the existence of the professions (Parsons 1964) stress that the key difference between professionals and most other workers is the degree of trust placed in them by their clients/patients. According to Nelken (2002), however, there is a considerable body of evidence pointing to fraudulent claims made by doctors and dentists against insurance companies in the USA and, to a smaller extent, against the NHS in Britain.

Barclay and Tavares (1999) found that theft by shop staff amounts to £350 million each year, which is about 25 per cent of all retail losses.

In an earlier study by Levy (1987), he found that 75 per cent of all frauds on financial institutions such as banks and building societies were by their own employees. Of 56 companies he surveyed, over 40 per cent had experienced fraud of over £50 000 by employees that year. However, employers were very reluctant to prosecute as they feared that by doing so, they could attract negative publicity.

Corporate crime

The impact of corporate crime

Many sociological approaches – particularly that of left realists – have pointed out the enormous costs of conventional crime to society, as well as the damage it does to the quality of people's lives. Those interested in studying corporate crime argue, however, that the costs of conventional crime are dwarfed by those of corporate crime. There are no clear calculations of the costs of corporate crime in Britain, but one contemporary study in the USA suggests that the annual cost to American society is in the region of $400 billion. This compares to an annual cost of $13 billion for all forms of other crime combined.

The 'costs' of corporate crime are not just economic, however. Tombs and Whyte (2007) point out that in the

UK, Great Western Trains were fined £1.5 million for its role in a train crash in London in 1999, when seven people were killed and 150 injured. In 2006, Balfour Beatty was fined £10 million for four deaths and 150 injuries caused by their failure to maintain the railway lines adequately.

We pointed out earlier the way that corporate 'crime' can transgress the boundaries of crime through acts that may not actually be illegal, but are regarded by sociologists as morally reprehensible and often a violation of certain human rights. Mokhiber (1988) points out that, in the USA, 800 people die each day from smoking related diseases; 8000 a day die from asbestos-related cancers and 85 000 cotton textile workers suffer breathing problems from dust related to their jobs.

Corporate crime: an invisible issue

Corporate crime is clearly a major problem for society and actually costs economies more than conventional crimes. What is particularly interesting is just how little attention is paid to it and how sanctions against those engaged in this form of crime are relatively minor.

The invisibility has been explained in several ways:

- *Differences in power* – Marxist-influenced writers, such as Pearce (1976), argue that the laws governing corporate crime, as well as the enforcement of these laws, reflect the inequalities in power of a capitalist society. The owners of the corporations are members of the ruling class, and they ensure that the law and its enforcement reflect their interests. However, it is not just Marxist writers who stress differences in power; most other sociologists exploring this area, such as Braithwaite (2000) and Tombs (2002), also suggest that the way the laws are defined and enforced are a reflection of the economic and political influence of large corporations. They can be distinguished from Marxist writers in that they do not see a coherent ruling class that manipulates power to its own ends.
- *Media representations of crime* – Tombs and Whyte (2003) have pointed out that corporate crimes are rarely considered newsworthy, partly because the crimes are often too complex to summarize in an article, or are too dull or have no clear victims. Often, when such crime is reported, media coverage is less about it being a crime than a 'scandal' or 'abuse' or even an 'accident'.
- *The policing of corporate crime* – According to Braithwaite (2000), business and finance tend to be controlled through 'regulation' rather than policing, and a different set of terms are used in the policing of corporations: agencies are developed by government to 'oversee' the activities of companies. A good example of this is the financial sector in Britain, which is meant to be controlled by the Financial Services Authority and the Bank of England. However, these agencies rarely call in the police if they find violations of procedure (the term 'lawbreaking' is rarely used); companies are advised or educated. They are generally negotiated with and, at the most extreme, they receive sanctions, which usually take the form of a company fine.

Key themes

Sociological theories and methods

Fiddles

The problem with studying any area of deviance is how to get information about the activities of those people involved. It is possible to ask questions about deviant and possibly illegal activity, but, understandably, the majority of people engaged in illegal acts are not too keen to provide the researcher with completely true answers! Studying crime at work, for example, illustrates this difficulty for sociologists in a very real way. It is well known that in many jobs people engage in minor acts of theft, which can be as minor as stealing pens or using the telephone for private calls. For many workers, these are not really regarded as acts of theft, but are perks of the job.

Very often employers turn a blind eye to these activities, but if they are brought to their attention, then usually the employee is sacked.

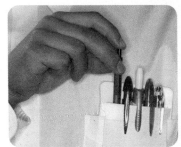

Jason Ditton decided to study these minor perks or fiddles in a large bakery, using participant observational methods. The main issue he had to face was whether to be open with his co-workers or to engage in covert studies. He decided the best method in this case was to use covert methods. Covert methods have the advantage over overt methods, in that the researcher has a greater chance of actually studying deviant behaviour and, once in the group, there is no awareness by the group members of being researched, so they are more likely to act normally. However, a number of problems are recognized in using covert participant observation. These include the difficulty of making notes, and the fact that the researcher, for obvious reasons, cannot conduct interviews/focus groups or give out questionnaires. Above all else is the ethical issue that covert research does not get informed consent from the people being studied.

- *Lack of research* – As Tombs (2007) points out, each year the British government spends considerable effort in finding out how many 'crimes' are committed through the British Crime Survey (see p. 360), yet nothing similar is attempted to find out the extend of corporate crime. (However, Hopkins (2002) has noted that, in recent years, the government has become very active funding research into crimes *against* businesses.) Even academic research into this area is relatively limited, with sociologists having limited access to large corporations and little expertise in business methods.

State–corporate crime

There is a close relationship between large corporations and governments. At its simplest, governments rely upon large corporations for tax revenues and to provide employment. Corporations rely upon governments for a sympathetic and organized environment in which they can engage in their activities. They are therefore mutually dependent.

It has been suggested that this can lead to a situation in which 'serious harms' can result from the interaction between them. An example of this is Kramer's (2006) research into the circumstances surrounding the US space shuttle *Challenger*, which exploded soon after take off in 1986, killing all its crew. Kramer argues that the explosion was actually a result of political decisions by NASA to maintain the space exploration programme but with large budgetary cuts. This resulted in one large corporation being pressured to provide components for the space shuttle that were known to be potentially dangerous. The corporation agreed to continue providing the parts, as they were influenced by the high level of profits and the need to fulfil contractual obligations. The executives of the corporation did this even though, Kramer argues, they knew what the possible consequences of component failure might be.

Before the launch of the space shuttle, both NASA (the government space agency) and the company MTI knew the potential dangers. However, the explosion was described at the time as an 'accident'.

Globalization and crime

Giddens (1964) defines **globalization** as 'the intensification of worldwide social relations which link distant localities in such a way that local happenings are shaped by events occurring many miles away and vice versa'. By this, Giddens means that modern forms of communication have made distance and national borders far less important than barriers between social groups. What happens in one society can quickly impact on other societies – anywhere in the world.

The importance of globalization on crime cannot be overestimated. According to the United Nations Development Programme (1999), the result of globalization has been a massive growth in the following forms of crime:

- dealing in illicit drugs
- illegal trafficking in weapons
- iillegal trafficking in human beings
- corruption
- violent crimes, including terrorism
- war crimes.

The importance of this can be seen by the fact that the total value of transnational organized crime is estimated by the United Nations to be approximately £1 trillion per year.

Ian Taylor is interested in how the broader effects of globalization have impacted upon crime. Taylor (1999) suggests that the impact of globalization on economies provides fertile soil for the growth of transnational crime.

Taylor's analysis is extensive and complex, but two examples from his work illustrate the very diverse ways that globalization can generate new forms of crime:

1 The ability to move finance around the world with limited controls enables a whole range of financial crimes, from tax evasion and insider trading to the laundering of profits from illegal activities such as drugs production and distribution.
2 Cheap international transport and effective communication systems have allowed companies to shift production to countries where production costs are lowest. This generally involves moving from high-tax countries, such as those of Western Europe, with decent welfare provision and health and safety laws, to low-tax countries with no welfare provision or employment laws – typically in South East Asia. The resulting decline in employment and income levels in Western European countries has led to increased levels of crime and social disorder.

Ruggiero (1996) points to a further consequence of this shift in production. He argues that the decline in employment encourages the growth of small firms in Western Europe that avoid labour laws and operate outside the formal economy. Furthermore, these countries will employ the cheapest labour they can find, often focusing their recruitment on illegal immigrants.

However, the impact of globalization can also be felt in the way that even normal transnational companies can engage in practices that are either illegal or morally discreditable. According to Michalowski and Kramer (1987), modern transnational corporations can practise a policy of **law evasion**, for example setting up factories in countries that do not have pollution controls or adequate safety legislation, rather than producing in countries with stricter standards. They may sell goods to poorer countries when the goods have been declared unsafe in the more affluent countries (a fairly common procedure with pharmaceuticals). Box (1983) has claimed that multinationals dump products, plants and practices illegal in industrialized countries onto undeveloped or underdeveloped countries. They are able to do this because the poorer countries do not have the resources to control the large companies and also because officials are likely to accept bribes.

Organized crime

Globalization has also brought about the growth of transnational organized crime. The same ease of communication that has enabled legal industries to develop production and distribution around the world has also allowed the growth of organized crime groupings. Organized crime is involved in a number of activities including:

- *The drugs trade* – According to the United Nations Office on Drugs and Crime (UNODC 2005), the value of the illegal drugs trade is $13bn at production level, $94bn at wholesale level and $332bn based upon retail prices.

Pearce and Tombs (1998) argue that the manufacture of cigarettes should be regarded as a corporate crime. What do you think?

● *Human trafficking* – According to Raymond (2002), this is worth about $5 to 7 billion, with 4 million persons moved from one country to another and within countries. This includes about 500 000 a year to Western Europe alone, for use in the sex industry

Both these are closely linked to money laundering. According to the International Monetary Fund, it is estimated to involve between $800 billion and $1.5 trillion dollars per year (about 2 to 5 per cent of world GDP).

Environmental or green crimes

One form of crime that links globalization, corporations and organized crime is **environmental** (or '**green**') **crime**. Environmental or green criminology refers to crimes committed against the environment. Like the other issues discussed in this topic, there is dispute about exactly what constitutes a 'crime', with writers such as Situ and Emmons (1999) arguing that 'an environmental crime is an action that breaks the national or international laws'. A second, more radical approach explores other actions that may not currently be defined as 'crimes', but which are, according to criminologists such as Chunn and Menzies (2003), equally harmful to the environment.

The differences in definition are carried over to understanding the causes of environmental crime. For example, in 1984 in Bhopal, India, an explosion in a factory run by a US firm, Union Carbide, released a gas which has since killed up to 20 000 people, according to some estimates. The differing approaches were used to explain this event. The first, associated with Situ and Emmons, is that local health and safety laws were broken, which caused the events. The second, associated with Chunn, is that Union Carbide and firms like this deliberately locate their plants in countries where health and safety laws are weak and where there is much less concern for the environment.

Environmental or green criminology is still in its early stages and it is unclear where its boundaries lie. Nigel

South (2004) has suggested a twofold framework for understanding environmental or green crimes:

1 primary environmental crimes
2 environmental law breaking.

Primary crimes are currently legal under international law, but South argues that the extent of the environmental damage should see them come under the analysis of criminologists. At present, they tend to be examined as simply 'environmental issues'. South's primary crimes cover such things as air and water pollution, deforestation and species decline. Walters (2008) gives the example of commercial growing of genetically modified crops in the UK despite the 'ecological harm and uncertainties that have been widely documented'. He argues that the reason they are being allowed is the commercial benefits that genetically modified crops will bring to the companies that produce them. Thornton and Beckwith (2004) claim that 24 000 people die prematurely each year because of air pollution, yet much of the pollution is not illegal and is based on a model of self-regulation. Even where pollution is illegal, it is rarely enforced and the maximum fine is £20 000.

The second part of South's framework covers actions that are already illegal under international law, but these laws may not be enforced. These illegal acts include the dumping of hazardous waste and unauthorized pollution through the discharge of waste. According to Walters (2007), the British nuclear industry has illegally disposed of thousands of barrels of radioactive waste in the seas around the Channel Islands and reportedly 'lost' 30 kgs of plutonium from Sellafield nuclear power station.

The Environmental Justice Foundation (2007) estimates that up to 3.2 million cubic metres of timber sold in the UK is stolen from the Amazon rainforest and other protected habitats.

South's distinction between primary crimes and the flouting of rules does provide a means of linking two distinct traditions, which can help form the basis of a 'green criminology'.

Genetically modified crops: a sign of progress or an environmental crime? What do you think?

Explaining occupational and corporate crime

Sociologists have sought to incorporate occupational and corporate crime into existing theories – though with varying degrees of success. The approaches include:

- differential association and subcultural theory
- emotion-based approaches
- labelling theory
- anomie
- Marxist explanations.

Differential association and subcultural theory

Sutherland (1940), who initiated the sociological discussion of white-collar crime, argued that his theory of differential association (see Topic 6, p. 367) helped account for why business executives committed such enormous amounts of crime benefiting themselves and their organizations. Sutherland claimed that the culture of the organization might well justify committing illegal or dubious acts in order to achieve the organization's goals. Geis (1967), for example, examined the evidence given to congressional hearings into illegal price-fixing agreements of companies in the USA. He found that people taking up posts in organizations tended to find that price-fixing was an established practice and they would routinely become involved in it as part of the learning process of their jobs.

As early as 1952, Aubert studied how rationing procedures had been subverted during World War II by officials and members of food organizations, so that favouritism was shown to some groups and individuals (including themselves). Aubert (1952) found that these 'white-collar criminals' had an 'elaborate and widely accepted ideological rationalization for the offences'. In fact, criminal practices were quite normal. Evidence that such practices continue to this day comes from Braithwaite's (1984) study of the pharmaceutical industry, where bribing health inspectors was regarded as a perfectly normal part of business practice.

Emotion-based approaches

More recently, the interest in emotions and the meaning of masculinity has spilled over into explaining occupational and organizational crime. Often, when studying these forms of crime, the researcher is puzzled that people who earn huge incomes or who have enormous power, put themselves at risk either by seeking further personal gain, or more surprisingly perhaps, leading the company into illegal activity with limited personal benefits. According to Portnoy (2003), the answer could lie in the search for thrills and excitement. This is no different from the explanations offered for other forms of crime by writers such as Katz and Lyng (see Topic 7, pp. 375–6). Portnoy describes a world of excitement and thrill-seeking in the world of high finance, where the excitement is as valued by the executives as are the financial benefits.

In a similar manner, Punch (1996) argues that high finance is a world of 'power struggles, ideological debate, intense political rivalry, manipulation of information buffeted by moral ambiguity'. For these writers, then, crimes by companies and by individuals are explicable by thrill-seeking. Interestingly, this also links to ideas of masculinity, as the majority of people in senior positions are male, with high-risk 'macho' attitudes regarded positively by the culture of big business.

Labelling theory

According to Mars (1982), labelling theory provides the most appropriate avenue for understanding occupational crime and how employers respond to it. Employees build up expectations about what they deserve and what is an appropriate or 'fair' payment for the job; if they do not receive this, will engage in illegal practices to reach the 'fair' salary.

Mars, in his study of the catering industry (1982), explains theft by employees and sharp practice by restaurant owners by referring to the conflicting values of capitalism:

> << There is only a blurred line between **entrepreneuriality** and flair on the one hand and sharp practice and fraud on the other. >>

How this is labelled by the person and the company employing them will determine the outcome of the label – criminal, 'overstepping the mark' or simply 'sharp practice'. Nelken (2002) looked at the workings of the English Family Practitioner Panels, which examine the cases of NHS professionals accused of not having complied with their NHS contracts – in other words, accused of defrauding the NHS by overclaiming. His conclusion was that 'everything possible was done to avoid the impression that potentially criminal behaviour is at issue' – thus where 'misconduct' (theft) was proved, the NHS professional had income withheld, but nothing else. Nelken notes that on one occasion where the dentist involved admitted to 'fraud', the Panel 'pleaded with him to retract his admission' so that it would not pass on for criminal prosecution. Nelken therefore argues that crime committed by professionals is rarely defined as such.

On a broader scale, labelling theory can help explain corporate crime in a rather different way. Labelling theory argues that negative labels are applied to certain groups or organizations when other, more powerful groups are able to impose that label. According to Nelken (2002), much of corporate crime can be explained by this. Legislation making some forms of activity legal or illegal is 'fought over' by various interest groups and the resulting law will reflect the views and interests of the more powerful.

Anomie

Merton's anomie approach has also been applied to explain both occupational and corporate crime. Anomie theory states that every society has culturally approved goals as well as the means to achieve these goals; if people are unable to obtain the goals by the culturally approved means, then they will develop alternatives. Box, who straddles a number of theoretical perspectives, used the idea of Merton's version of anomie (see Topic 2, p. 339) to help explain why organizations break the law.

Box (1983) argues that if an organization is unable to achieve its goals using socially approved methods, then it may turn to other, possibly illegal, methods of achieving its goal of maximizing profit.

The idea of anomie was also developed in a wider way by Braithwaite (1984), who argued that corporate crime could be seen as 'an illegitimate means of achieving any one of a wider range of organizational and personal goals when legitimate means are blocked'. In his study of the pharmaceutical industry, he found that scientists were willing to fabricate their results in order to have their products adopted by their companies. The motivation for this was often not solely financial greed, but the desire for scientific prestige.

Similarly, in the high-pressure world of business, individuals who perceive themselves as failing may turn to various alternative modes of behaving, including occupational crime, according to Punch (1996).

However, Nelken (2002) is sceptical about the worth of anomie theory. He points out that anomie theory fails to explain why some individuals and companies choose illegal responses and others legal. Nelken suggests that until this is made clear, then the explanation is just too vague.

Marxist explanations

Perhaps the theoretical approach that has most enthusiastically adopted the study of corporate crime is the Marxist tradition. Corporate crime fits the critical criminological view that the real criminals are the rich and powerful. Critical criminologists argue that despite the fact that the powerful are able to use their dominance of society to avoid having the majority of their activities defined as illegal, they will still break the law where it conflicts with their interests. Furthermore, if they are actually caught, then they are less likely to be punished.

Swartz (1975) argues that as capitalism involves the maximization of corporate profits, then 'its normal functioning produces deaths and illnesses'. Business crime is, therefore, based upon the very values and legitimate practices of capitalism. Box (1983) has pointed out the success that the powerful have had in promoting the idea that corporate crime is less serious and less harmful than the range of normal street crimes, violence and burglary. Box describes this as a deliberate process of 'mystification' that has helped keep corporate crime a minor object of study in criminology.

This theme was taken up by Frank Pearce (1976) who was interested in why there were so few prosecutions against corporations and senior business people. He concluded that they were so rare because otherwise there would be an undermining of the belief that the vast majority of crime is carried out by the working class. If the true pattern of crime came to be known by the bulk of the population, then it would create a crisis of legitimacy for the ruling class.

Slapper and Tombs (1999) claim that their research into the behaviour of large transnational companies in developing countries demonstrates the Marxist case that illegal and immoral practices are normal under capitalism. These companies routinely sell unsafe products, pay low wages and provide dangerous working conditions.

However, Carrabine et al. (2004) have criticized the Marxist position on corporate crime, by pointing out that the provision of poor working conditions, pollution of the environment and low pay are not restricted to capitalist societies. Until the collapse of the Soviet Union, some of the most dangerous and lowest-paid work was under a communist regime. They point, as well, to the Chernobyl nuclear plant in the Ukraine, which overheated, causing a large area of the country to be irradiated and caused a range of radiation-based diseases for generations to come. Nelken (2002) also points out that there are numerous laws controlling businesses in capitalist societies, when a simple Marxist perspective would suggest that the power available to the ruling class would limit such legislation to a minimum.

Activities

Research ideas

Visit your local market and/or a car boot sale.

- What proportion of the goods on sale do you think are fake?
- Are there different types of fakes? How can you tell they are fakes?
- How many stalls have the same fakes? What does this suggest?

Warning: It is important that you do not question stall holders. What they are doing is illegal and they may not be too happy talking about their activities to you!

Find out the extent of counterfeiting by going to **www.supebrand.com/index.php**

Web.tasks

1 Visit the Serious Fraud Squad website at **www.sfo.gov.uk/publications**

   Go to the annual review for last year. What does this tell you about the number of cases of fraud under investigation and how many were actually prosecuted? In your view, what proportion of government resources is devoted to combating serious fraud?

2 Corporate Watch is a website packed with examples of corporate irresponsibility: **www.corporatewatch.org**

   Prepare a report on one or two examples.

3 Visit the websites below and explore some of the examples of green 'crime' they uncover in their reports:

   www.ejfoundation.org – Environmental Justice Foundation for information on environmental issues

   www.unodc.org/unodc/en/data-and-analysis/WDR.html – Value of Drugs United Nations Report

Key terms

Corporate crime crimes committed by companies against employees or the public.

Entrepreneuriality qualities of people with original ideas for making money.

Environmental ('green') crime crimes and/or forms of harm perpetrated on the environment.

Globalization better methods of communication allow goods, knowledge and services to cross distances and national borders easily.

Law evasion acting in such a way as to break the spirit of laws while technically conforming to them.

Occupational crime crimes committed against a company by an employee.

Primary crimes environmentally damaging acts that are currently legal in some or all countries, but have very harmful consequences for the planet.

Transnational crime crime that is organized and committed across national boundaries.

White-collar crime a term originally used by Sutherland for both occupational and corporate crime.

Check your understanding

1. Explain the difference between corporate and occupational crime.

2. Which costs society more, white-collar crime or 'conventional' crime? Illustrate your answer with figures.

3. What do we mean by state–corporate crime?

4. What do we mean by the term 'globalization', and give one example of how this relates to crime?

5. Why are Marxists particularly interested in studying corporate crime?

6. What two elements are there in South's framework for a green criminology?

An eye on the exam — Occupational, corporate and environmental crime

Item A

Reiman (2003) shows how the poor are arrested and charged, out of all proportion to their numbers, for the kinds of crimes that poor people generally commit: burglary, robbery, assault and so forth. Yet when we look at the kinds of crimes poor people almost never have the opportunity to commit, such as stock market fraud, industrial safety violations, embezzlement and serious tax evasion, the criminal justice system shows an increasingly benign and merciful state. The more likely it is for a particular form of crime to be committed by middle- and upper-class people, the less likely it is that it will be treated as a criminal offence. Yet when the public are questioned about crimes committed against them, as in the British Crime Survey, few, if any, see themselves as victims of corporate or white-collar crimes, and fewer still of environmental crimes.

Source: Carrabine, E., Iganski, P., Lee, M., Plummer, K. and South, N. (2004) *Criminology: A Sociological Introduction*, London: Routledge

Examine some of the reasons for the patterns described in **Item A**. (21 marks)

Grade booster — Getting top marks in this question

For this question, first of all you need to identify the relevant patterns described in the Item. These include the following: the poor are arrested and charged for 'street' crimes such as burglary; crimes by the middle and upper classes are often not treated as crimes; the public are unaware that they are victims of corporate or environmental crimes. Try to give reasons for each of these patterns. For example, the poor are more likely to be criminalized because of selective law enforcement by the police; the powerful can afford lawyers to get them off the hook; white-collar and corporate crime often have no specific individual victim (e.g. tax evasion); environmental crimes such as pollution may be hard to detect, or its source hard to trace.

Ethnicity and crime

Getting you thinking

Gang warfare on the streets of London as Asian and Black youths battle outside Julie Christie's house

A WARM LATE summer afternoon on a leafy street in an area colonised by fashionable cafes and shops came to an abrupt end when the peace was shattered by a raw, terrifying eruption of gang violence this week. Armed with spades, screwdrivers, bars and sticks, two gangs clashed and sent locals fleeing into shops for safety.

This running battle between Black and Asian youths – a sickening example of brutal Britain today – was captured by a photographer who had been waiting in the street to take a photo of the actress Julie Christie, who lives nearby.

Daniel Martin & Niall Firth, *The Daily Mail*, 5 Sept 2008

The silenced majority

Constant media stories about gang crime create a depressing and unbalanced picture of Black youngsters. So why are their positive achievements ignored?

SINCE JANUARY, the term 'knife crime' has been used more than 1,500 times by the national press – and it is a fair bet that most media images associated with these figures will be of young Black men. Unsurprisingly, this is leading to a growing sense of frustration among Black community leaders, academics and, not least, Black youngsters themselves, over what they see as blatant misrepresentation.

Black youths who fit this media stereotype represent a tiny fraction of the young Black population as a whole, they argue, and while negative stories about Black teenagers are almost guaranteed headlines, the positive achievements of Black youth go largely ignored.

This trend has consequences beyond creating an unbalanced picture. Numerous studies have shown a clear link between media furore and draconian policy-making, says Kjartan Sveinsson, the author of a Runnymede Trust report on the ways in which popular understandings of race and crime influence media reporting, and vice versa. 'The tragedy is this can increase racial tension on the street and do little to stem the violence,' he says. Which in turn, of course, leads to further reports of violence, and the circle continues.

Eric Allison, *The Guardian*, 25 Aug 2008

1 Do you agree with the argument that Black youths only get negative news coverage?

2 Do you think that Black or Asian youths are portrayed differently from White youths in the media?

3 How do you think this could be changed?

A recurring theme in media reporting of street crime since the mid-1970s has been the disproportionate involvement of young African-Caribbean males. It has partly been on this crime–race linkage that the police has justified the much greater levels of **stop and search** of young, Black males, than of White males.

Images of Asian criminality have, until recently, portrayed the Asian communities as generally more law-abiding than the majority population. However, after the attack on the World Trade Center in New York in 2001 and, more significantly, the bombings in 2005 on the London Underground, a new discourse has emerged regarding Muslim youths. The newer image is of them as being potentially dangerous – a threat to British culture.

Just discussing the relationship between criminality and race is itself a difficult task, and some sociologists argue that making the subject part of the A-level specifications actually helps perpetuate the link. After all, there are no discussions on 'White people and crime'! Despite these reservations, sociologists have set out to examine the argument that there is a higher rate of crime by certain ethnic minorities, and the counterclaim that the criminal justice system is racist.

Offending, sentencing and punishment

Offending

There are three ways of gathering statistics on ethnicity and crime: official statistics, victimization studies and self-report studies.

Official statistics

According to Home Office statistics (Ministry of Justice 2008), about 9.5 per cent of people arrested were recorded as 'Black' and 5.3 per cent as 'Asian'. This means that, relative to the arrest rates of the population as a whole, Black people were over three times more likely than White people to be arrested. Asian people's rates were similar to those for White people.

Official statistics tell us the numbers of people arrested by the police. However, they are not necessarily a reflection of offending rates, as they could be seen, equally, as a comment on the actions of the police. If, as some sociologists argue, the actions of some police officers are partly motivated by racism, then the arrest rates reflect that, rather than offending rates by ethnic-minority groups.

A second point to remember is that offenders are most likely to be young males aged between 14 and 25. Any ethnic group with a high proportion of this age group within it will have relatively high arrest rates. The British 'Black' population does, in fact, have a high proportion of young males in this age group and we would therefore expect arrest rates to be higher. A similar demographic profile is emerging amongst 'Asian' British youth.

Finally, the more economically disadvantaged a particular social group is, the higher the crime rates. Once again, young Black British youths tend to be in worse-paid jobs and more likely to be unemployed than White or Asian youths.

Victimization studies

Victim-based studies (such as the British Crime Survey) are gathered by asking victims of crime for their recollection of the ethnic identity of the offender. According to the British Crime Survey, the majority of crime is **intraracial**, with 88 per cent of White victims stating that White offenders were involved, 3 per cent claiming the offenders were Black, 1 per cent Asian and 5 per cent 'mixed'.

About 42 per cent of crimes against Black victims were identified as being committed by Black offenders and 19 per cent of crimes against Asians were by Asian offenders. The figures for White crimes against ethnic minorities are much higher – about 50 per cent, though this figure needs to be seen against the backdrop of 90 per cent of the population being classified as White.

Like official statistics, asking victims for a description of who committed the crimes is shot through with problems. For a start, only about 20 per cent of survey-recorded crimes are personal crimes (such as theft from the person), where the victims might actually see the offender. Bowling and Phillips (2002) argue that victims are influenced by

Focus on research

Waddington *et al.* (2004)
Race, the police, & stop and search

Waddington, Stenson and Don were concerned at the way it has become accepted that members of minority-ethnic groups are unfairly stopped by the police. They therefore undertook research in Reading and Slough, two towns to the west of London. The researchers used a variety of methods. These included:

- direct non-participant observation of police officers, including watching CCTV footage
- detailed analysis of the official records of stop and search
- interviews with police officers about their stop and search activities.

The researchers argue that the evidence suggests that police officers do stop a proportionately high number of young members of ethnic-minority groups (and of White groups), but that these figures are in direct proportion to their presence in the central city areas and their likelihood to be out at night. Those groups who are most likely to be out in the evening in high crime areas are most likely to be stopped and, in these areas, young people – and particularly young members of ethnic-minority groups – are most likely to be out. They conclude that police stop and searches in the area they researched reflected the composition of people out on the streets, rather than any ethnic bias.

Waddington, P.A.J., Stenson, K. and Don, D. (2004) 'In proportion – race, and police stop and search', *British Journal of Criminology*, 44(6)

1 Comment on the range of methods used by the researchers. Are there any other groups that might have been interviewed?

2 Explain how the researchers reached their conclusion that 'police stop and searches in the area they researched reflected the composition of people out on the streets, rather than any ethnic bias'.

(racial) stereotypes and 'culturally determined expectations' as to who commits crime. Certainly, research by Bowling (1999) indicates that where the offender is not known, White people are more likely to ascribe the crime to those of African-Caribbean origin.

Self-report studies

Self-report studies use an anonymous questionnaire to ask people what offences they have committed. Graham and Bowling's study (1995) for the Home Office of 14 to 25 year olds found that the self-reported offending rates were more or less the same for the White, Black and Asian respondents. However, those from Black British backgrounds are 3.6 times more likely to be arrested (Jones and Singer 2008).

Sentencing

After arrest, those of African-Caribbean backgrounds are slightly more likely to be held in custody and to be charged with more serious offences than Whites. But they are more likely than average to plead, and to be found, not guilty. However, if found guilty, they are more likely to receive harsher sentences – in fact, those of African-Caribbean backgrounds have a 17 per cent higher chance of imprisonment than Whites. Those of Asian origin are also more likely than average to plead not guilty, but more likely than average to be found guilty, yet have an 18 per cent lesser chance of being imprisoned.

Sociologists are divided as to whether these statistics mean that members of ethnic-minority groups are discriminated against. Bowling and Phillips (2002) summarize the 'patchy' knowledge of sociologists, by saying that the research indicates that both direct and indirect discrimination (types of charges laid, access to bail, etc.) against members of ethnic-minority groups does exist.

Punishment

According to Jones and Singer (2008), the proportion of nationals of Black British background in prison was 7.4 per 1000 population compared to 1.4 per 1000 for Whites. The rate for people from Asian groups was 1.7 per 1000. Black British prisoners form about 19 per cent of the total prison population, about seven times higher than would be expected in terms of their presence in the population.

Policing and ethnic minority groups

We have already seen that there are considerable differences between the arrest rates for members of ethnic-minority groups and those for Whites, with those of African-Caribbean origins having a four-times higher rate of arrest than Whites. Sociologists are split between those who argue that this reflects real differences in levels of offending and those who argue that the higher arrest rates are due to the practices of the police.

A reflection of reality?

Sociologists all reject the idea that there is an association between 'race' and crime, in the sense that being a member of a particular ethnic group in itself has any importance in explaining crime. However, a number of writers (Mayhew et al. 1993) argue that most crime is performed by young males who come from poorer backgrounds. This being so, then there would be an overrepresentation of offenders from minority ethnic groups, quite simply because there is a higher proportion of young males in the ethnic-minority population than in the population as a whole. It is also a well-researched fact that minority ethnic groups overall are likely to have lower incomes and poorer housing conditions. These sociologists would accept that there is evidence of racist practices by certain police officers, but that the arrest rates largely reflect the true patterns of crime.

Phillips and Brown's (1998) study of ten police stations across Britain found that those of African-Caribbean origin accounted for a disproportionately high number of arrests. However, they found no evidence that they were treated any differently during the arrest process, with about 60 per cent of both Blacks and Whites and about 55 per cent of Asians eventually being charged.

Racist police practices?

A second group of sociologists see the higher arrest rates as evidence of police racism. Within this broad approach there are a number of different explanations.

Reflection of society approach

This approach, often adopted by the police, is that there are some individuals in the police who are racist, and once these 'bad apples' are rooted out, the police force will not exhibit racism. This approach was suggested by **Lord Scarman** (1981) in his inquiry into the inner-city riots of 1981. According to Scarman, the police reflect the wider society and therefore some racist recruits may join.

Canteen culture

The 'canteen (or working) culture' approach (see Topic 10, p. 396) argues that police officers have developed distinctive working values as a result of their job. Police officers have to face enormous pressures in dealing with the public: working long hours, facing potential danger, hostility from significant sections of the public, and social isolation. In response, they have developed a culture that helps them to deal with the pressures and gives them a sense of identity. The 'core characteristics' of the culture, according to Reiner (1992), include a thirst for action, cynicism, conservatism, suspicion, isolation from the public, macho values and racism.

Studies by Smith and Gray (1985), Holdaway (1983) who was himself a serving police officer at the time, and Graef (1989), all demonstrated racist views amongst police officers who, for example, held stereotypical views on the criminality of youths of African-Caribbean origin. Most importantly, it led them to stop and search these youths to a far greater extent than any other group. In fact, African-Caribbean people are six times more likely than Whites to be stopped and searched by the police.

Institutional racism

After the racist murder of a Black youth, Stephen Lawrence, in 1993, and after very considerable pressure from his parents, the **Macpherson Inquiry** was set up to look at the circumstances of his death and the handling of the situation by the police. Sir William Macpherson concluded that the police were characterized by **institutional racism**. By this he meant that the police have 'procedures, practices and a culture that tend to exclude or to disadvantage non-White people' (cited in Bowling and Phillips 2002).

The key point about institutional racism is that it is not necessarily intentional on the part of any particular person in the organization, but that the normal, day-to-day activities of the organization are based upon racist ideas and practice. This means that police officers might not have to be racist in their personal values, but that in the course of their work, they might make assumptions about young Black males and the likelihood of their offending that influence their attitudes and behaviour as police officers.

Theorizing race and criminality

Left-realist approach

Lea and Young (1993), leading writers in the left-realist tradition, accept that there are racist practices by the police. However, they argue that, despite this, the statistics do bear out a higher crime rate for street robberies and associated 'personal' crimes by youths of African-Caribbean origin. They explain this by suggesting that British society is racist and that young ethnic-minority males are economically and socially **marginalized**, with lesser chances of success than the majority population. Running alongside this is their sense of relative deprivation. According to Lea and Young, the result is the creation of subcultures, which can lead to higher levels of personal crime as a way of coping with marginalization and relative deprivation (see Topics 2 and 3 for a discussion of subcultures).

Capitalism in crisis

A study by Hall *et al.* (1978) of street crime ('**mugging**') illustrates a particular kind of Marxist approach. According to Hall, the late 1970s were a period of crisis for British capitalism. The country was undergoing industrial unrest, there was a collapse in the economy and the political unrest in Northern Ireland was particularly intense. When capitalism is in crisis the normal methods of control of the population may be inadequate, and it is sometimes necessary to use force. However, using obvious repression needs some form of justification. It was in these circumstances that the newspapers, basing their reports on police briefings, highlighted a huge increase in 'mugging' (street robberies).

According to Hall, the focus on a relatively minor problem, caused by a group who were already viewed negatively, served the purpose of drawing attention away from the crisis and focusing blame on a scapegoat – young African-Caribbean males. This 'moral panic' (see 'Key themes' above) then justified increased numbers of police on the streets, acting in a more repressive manner.

Hall's analysis has been criticized for not making any actual effort to research the motivations and thinking of

young African-Caribbean males. What is more, the association between 'criminality and Black youth', made by the police and the media, has continued for over 25 years, and so it seems unlikely that this can be explained simply by a 'crisis of capitalism'.

Cultures of resistance

A third approach overlaps with the Marxist approach just outlined. According to this approach, linked with Scraton (1987) and Gordon (1988), policing, media coverage and political debates all centre around the issue of 'race' being a problem. Minority ethnic groups have been on the receiving end of discrimination since the first migrants arrived, leaving them in a significantly worse socioeconomic position than the White majority.

In response to this, **cultures of resistance** have emerged, in which crime is a form of organized resistance that has its origins in the **anticolonial** struggles. When young members of minority ethnic groups commit crimes, they are doing so as a political act, rather than as a criminal act.

There are a number of criticisms of this approach. Lea and Young (1993) have been particularly scathing, pointing out that the majority of crimes are actually 'intraracial', that is 'Black on Black'. This cannot, therefore, reflect a political struggle against the White majority. Second, they accuse writers such as Scraton of 'romanticizing' crime and criminals, and thereby ignoring the very real harm that crime does to its victims.

Exclusion and alternative economies

This approach integrates the previous approaches and relates quite closely to the work of Cloward and Ohlin (1960) (see pp. 339–40). A good example of this sort of argument is provided by Philippe Bourgois' study (2002) of El Barrio, a deprived area in East Harlem, New York. Bourgois spent seven years living and researching the street life and economy of El Barrio, whose inhabitants were overwhelmingly Puerto Ricans, illegal Mexican immigrants and African-Americans. Bourgois argues that the economic exclusion of these minority ethnic groups, combined with negative social attitudes towards them, has forced them to develop an 'alternative economy'. This involves a wide range of both marginally legal and clearly illegal activities, ranging from kerbside car-repair businesses to selling crack cocaine. Drug sales are by far the most lucrative employment: 'Cocaine and crack … have been the fastest growing – if not the only – equal-opportunity employers of men in Harlem'.

Running alongside this informal economy has developed a distinctive (sub)culture, which Bourgois calls 'inner-city street culture' – as he puts it:

>> this 'street culture of resistance' is not a coherent, conscious universe of political opposition, but rather a spontaneous set of rebellious practices that in the long term have emerged as an oppositional style. >>

This subculture causes great damage because the illegal trade in drugs eventually involves its participants in lifestyles of violence, substance abuse and '**internalized rage**'. Many of the small-scale dealers become addicted and drawn into violence to support their habit. Furthermore, their behaviour destroys families and the community. The result is a chaotic and violent 'community', where the search for dignity in a distinctive culture leads to a worsening of the situation.

Although this is an extreme lifestyle, even for the USA, elements of it can help us to understand issues of race and criminality in the UK. Exclusion and racism lead to both cultural and economic developments that involve illegal activities and the development of a culture that helps resolve the issues of lack of dignity in a racist society. But both the illegal activities and the resulting culture may lead to an involvement in crime.

Statistical artefact approach

The **statistical artefact** approach suggests that the higher levels of involvement of young males from an African-Caribbean background in crime is more a reflection of how the statistics are interpreted than of a genuinely higher level. Fitzgerald et al. (2003) researched ethnic-minority street crime in London, comparing crime rates against a wide range of socioeconomic and demographic data. They also interviewed a cross section of young, ethnic-minority offenders and their mothers, as well as running focus groups of 14 to 16 year olds in schools. The outcomes of the study were complex, but they throw light upon a number of the other explanations we have discussed so far. They reached the following conclusions:

● Street crime is related to levels of deprivation in an area, as well as to a lack of community cohesion, as measured by a rapid population turnover. This reflects crime levels in Britain as a whole, as we know amongst all ethnic groups that the higher the levels of deprivation in an area, the higher the levels of crime.
● The high rates of ethnic-minority offending were directly linked to the numbers of young, ethnic-minority males. Once again, all statistics point to young males as the highest offending group in the population, whatever their ethnic background. As there are higher proportions of young, ethnic-minority males in the population as a whole, and in London in particular, then we would expect there to be higher rates of crime committed by ethnic-minority males – if only as a reflection of the high percentage they form of all young males.
● There was a statistical link between higher crime levels and lone-parent families. African-Caribbean households are more likely to be headed by a lone parent, so there would be a statistical link here too.
● A subculture had developed amongst certain ethnic-minority children that provided justification for crime. This was very closely linked with school failure and alienation from school. However, similar views were held by White school-age students who were doing

Check your understanding

1 What different interpretations are there concerning the arrest rates of members of ethnic-minority groups?

2 What do we mean when we say that the majority of crime is 'intraracial'?

3 Identify any two problems with the statistics derived from 'victimization studies'.

4 What are self-report studies? Do they confirm the statistics derived from the arrest rates?

5 What two general explanations have sociologists put forward for the higher arrest rates of members of minority ethnic groups?

6 Explain the significance of the terms 'canteen culture' and 'institutional racism' in explaining the attitudes and behaviour of the police towards minority ethnic groups.

7 How do 'left-realist sociologists' explain the relationship between ethnicity and crime?

8 What is the relationship between crises in capitalism and police action against 'muggers'?

9 What does the term 'culture of resistance' mean?

poorly at school or who were no longer attending. A disproportionate amount of all crime is performed by young, educationally disaffected children of all backgrounds.

In conclusion, therefore, Fitzgerald and colleagues suggest that there is no specific set of factors that motivates young, ethnic-minority offenders – they are exactly the same ones that motivate White offenders. However, the overrepresentation of young males from African-Caribbean backgrounds is partly the result of their sheer numbers in the age band in which most offending takes place.

Activities

Research idea

Your local police force will have an ethnic-minority liaison officer (or similar title). Ask the officer to come to your institution to talk about their work and, in particular, stop and search. Before the talk, get into small groups and sort out a list of questions – ideally, you should then email these to the officer to base their talk on.

Web.tasks

1 The Ministry of Justice produces an online publication *Race and the Criminal Justice System*, which contains a wide range of up-to-date statistics. Explore the site and make your own mind up about the way that ethnic minorities interact with the criminal justice system. **www.justice.gov.uk/publications/raceandcjs.htm**

2 At the beginning of the topic, we discussed the image of Black youth presented by the media. Visit some of the websites of the main national newspapers. In the 'Search' box, key in terms such as 'Black youth', 'Asian youth', 'White Youth', 'Gangs', 'Knife crime'. What picture emerges?

Key terms

Anticolonial struggles historically, Black resistance to Western attempts to control and exploit Black people.

Cultures of resistance the term used to suggest that ethnic-minority groups in Britain have developed a culture that resists the racist oppression of the majority society.

Institutional racism racism that is built into the normal practices of an organization.

Internalized rage term used by Bourgois to describe the anger and hurt caused by economic and social marginalization.

Intraracial within a particular ethnic group.

Lord Scarman in 1981 there were serious inner-city disturbances, particularly in Brixton in London. Lord Scarman led a government inquiry into the causes of these 'riots'.

Macpherson Inquiry Sir William Macpherson led an inquiry into the events surrounding the murder of Stephen Lawrence (allegedly) by White racists, and the subsequent police investigation.

Marginalized a sociological term referring to those who are pushed to the edge of society in cultural, status or economic terms.

Mugging a term used to describe street robbery. It has no status as a specific crime in England and Wales.

Statistical artefact the 'problem' emerges from the way that the statistics are collected and understood.

Stop and search police officers have powers to stop and search those they 'reasonably' think may be about to, or have committed, a crime; this power has been used much more against ethnic-minority youths than White youths.

An eye on the exam Ethnicity and crime

Assess the usefulness of conflict theories for an understanding of the relationship of ethnic-minority youth to crime.

(21 marks)

Grade booster Getting top marks in this question

For this question, you need to consider two or more conflict theories, such as left realism and Marxism (e.g.Hall). You can consider the role of the mass media in stereotyping Black youth as criminals and creating media panics about them. You can also link unemployment to denial of opportunity (e.g. in education, housing and the labour market) and consider how far the resulting material deprivation leads to higher crime rates. You should also consider how far police action and prejudice lead to higher arrest and conviction rates for Black youth. Note that the question refers to ethnic-minority youth, not just Black youth, so you should consider crime rates among different ethnic groups in your answer. Victimization and self-report studies can be used to question the patterns of crime seen in the official statistics.

The criminal justice system: prevention, policing and punishment

Getting you thinking

1 What do you think about DNA testing – do you think that it is an attack on our civil liberties or a useful way to catch criminals?

2 Would you willingly give your DNA profile to be stored by the police?

3 Do you think that the government intrudes too much into our lives?

4 What is your view of the police –do you think they pick on some groups more than others?

Big Brother UK: Police now hold DNA 'fingerprints' of 4.5m Britons

MORE THAN one million people's genetic fingerprints have been added to the police DNA database in only ten months. The 'Big Brother' system, already the biggest in the world, now permanently stores the details of more than 4.5 million individuals. The rise is the equivalent of 150 new entries every hour. The database now covers one in 13 of the population – around 7.5 per cent. In total, 6.5 million people are on the police fingerprint database

Although the database is a crime-fighting tool, producing around 3000 matches a month with samples taken from crime scenes, around a third of all the DNA stored is taken from individuals who were not charged with any offence, and have no criminal record.

Campaigners also fear unscrupulous government agencies could use the database to track political protesters, find out who they are related to, or to refuse jobs or visas to anyone considered 'undesirable'. They have demanded tougher safeguards including time-limits on storing data and an independent regulator.

The Home Office has repeatedly claimed the innocent have 'nothing to fear' from the growth of the database, which police cite as a key tool in modern crime-fighting. But critics fear the Government will eventually link the database to its plans for ID cards, and eventually move to make DNA sampling universal – an approach which civil liberties campaigners view as a nightmare scenario.

At this rate of growth, the database will double in size by 2011, with almost 10 million profiles stored.

Shami Chakrabarti, director of civil rights group Liberty, said: 'The DNA database has become a national disgrace, stuffed with innocent children and a disproportionate number of Black people.'

Daily Mail, 5 November 2007

In the first topic in this chapter, we discussed the ways in which certain forms of behaviour come to be viewed as deviant and then, within that range of behaviour, how a narrower range is actually made illegal. We also saw that people are dissuaded from committing deviant and illegal acts through the process of social control.

In this topic, we will revisit social control, looking in some detail at the contributions sociologists have made to our understanding of the criminal justice system.

The topic is divided into three parts:

1 We explore the ways in which the criminal justice system sets out to limit crime amongst the population at large and the ways in which this relates to a growing body of sociological theory.

2 We look at policing and what influences how the police operate.

3 Finally, we explore the parts of the criminal justice system that judge and punish offenders.

Crime prevention and community safety

Situational crime prevention

Crime prevention, in the formal sense, developed from the writings of a group of criminologists, such as Clarke (1992) who focused on what has become known as '**situational crime prevention**'.

Clarke based his ideas on the deceptively simple notion that people will commit offences when the costs of offending (economic or social) are less than the benefits obtained from offending. However, unlike most previous criminologists who argued that the way to make the costs outweigh the benefits was to increase punishment, he argued that it was better to make it more difficult to steal or attack someone. For policy makers, this presented a range of new possibilities and they combined Clarke's ideas with those of an earlier writer, Oscar Newman. As early as the 1970s, Newman (1972) had introduced the idea of '**defensible space**', arguing that, by changing the design of streets and housing estates, it was possible to make them safer.

Situational crime prevention as a policy led to a wide range of initiatives. These included '**target hardening**', which involved making sure that it was more difficult to steal things, for example by improving locks on houses and windows, and by marking valuable objects with owners' postcodes in indelible ink, so that should they be stolen, they would be more difficult to sell. At the same time, areas with high levels of crime would have physical changes made in order to limit the opportunities for crime or benefits from it.

Critics of this approach, such as Garland (2001), have argued that it ignores the *causes* of crime, dealing only with limiting its extent and impact. Furthermore, critics argue, it leads to **crime displacement**, in which the type of crime, or the times of crimes or the place of crimes might all shift in response to the new measures. For example, CCTV may limit crime in areas where it is introduced, but crimes may rise outside this area.

Community safety/crime reduction

Although situational crime prevention continues to be very influential, since the mid-1990s a rather broader approach, known as **community safety** (or **crime reduction**), has developed. This approach argues that alongside crime prevention measures, two other actions must happen:

1 *Intervention* – It is important to identify the groups most at risk of committing crime and to put into action forms of intervention to limit their offending.
2 *Community* – It is important to involve the local community in combating crime.

Intervention

As we saw earlier with situational crime prevention, policy makers were not interested in the broader causes of crime, but rather with what worked to stop offending. The concept of 'what works' came to dominate thinking on offending in Britain and the USA.

In Britain, the work of the Cambridge School of Criminology, for example Farrington (1995) and West (and Farrington 1973), was particularly influential. They took a **positivistic** research approach, using longitudinal studies in which they compared the backgrounds of young males who offended with those young males without any police record. They found clear differences between the two groups. Some of the main '**risk factors**' which were linked to early offending were:

- low income and poor housing
- living in run-down neighbourhoods
- high degree of 'impulsiveness and hyperactivity'
- low school attainment
- poor parental supervision with harsh and erratic discipline
- parental conflict and lone-parent families.

The implications of the research were that intervening to change some or all of these risk factors would lead to lower levels of crime. The importance of this was underlined by the claimed success of the Perry Pre-School Project in Michigan, USA. Two groups of African-American children aged 3 or 4 from disadvantaged backgrounds were chosen. One group was given pre-school educational support and the family received weekly visits from social workers. The results were dramatic. By the age of 27, members of the group which received the interventions had half the number of arrests of the group that did not receive interventions.

This risk-based model of offending has been – and still is – extremely influential. Governments in both the USA and Britain decided where possible to identify the children at risk of offending and to put various interventions in place. Indeed, it has been argued (Rodgers 2008) that many of the social policy interventions that have been introduced since 1998 – to combat poverty, to redevelop run-down housing estates, to improve schools and to support families – can be seen to be as much anticrime measures as social policies to improve the lives of the poor and marginalized.

Community

Running parallel to the risk-based interventions are other policies that emphasize the importance of drawing upon the influence of the community.

Community approaches to crime reduction have been heavily influenced by the **broken windows theory** of Wilson and Kelling (1982). They argued that high levels of crime occur in neighbourhoods where there has previously been a loss of informal social control over minor acts of antisocial behaviour. They claim that if low-level antisocial behavior can be prevented (such as littering, noise, or youths blocking the pavements), then the escalation to more serious criminal acts can, in turn, be stopped. The analogy that Wilson and Kelling use is of an abandoned building. The point out that once one window gets broken, then all the windows soon get smashed. So, by preventing the breaking of the first window, all the rest are more likely to be saved. In a similar way, stop the minor crimes and the major ones are much less likely to happen.

The policy implications were that the government should find ways of strengthening local communities to 'fight' crime and antisocial behaviour. The ways chosen have been to introduce a range of legal powers through which the police and local authorities can issue antisocial behaviour orders, curfews, street drinking bans and dispersal orders (where you must leave a designated area of a town if a police officer tells you to do so). Exactly what is to be targeted as 'antisocial behaviour' depends upon local crime and antisocial perception surveys that local authorities have to carry out.

Theoretical perspectives on community safety/crime reduction

Managing crime in the culture of control

Garland (2001), in *The Culture of Control,* argues that the development in crime prevention and community safety just described is part of much wider shifts in the nature of the criminal justice system in late-modern societies. He provides a theoretical framework to explain these changes.

He suggests that the traditional method of dealing with crime, which he calls **penal welfarism**, has been overtaken by a much more complex model that is less concerned about *preventing* crime than *managing* crime by reassuring communities. Penal welfarism is the term Garland uses to describe how the criminal justice system in Britain sought to catch and punish offenders, but also to rehabilitate them so that they could be reintegrated in society. According to Garland, this approach has been seen as a failure by policy makers, as more than 60 per cent of those sent to prison reoffend.

Replacing this traditional model is the new '**culture of control**', which has two elements: adaptive and expressive. The point of both elements is to change society's attitude to crime and the role of the state in combating offending:

1 *The adaptive response* leads governments to identify certain groups that represent a danger to society and then to intervene in their lives at an early stage in order to change the way these risk groups think and act. Examples of this include Home Start, where volunteers help parents who are deemed to have problems, and family intervention projects where experts work with 'problem families'.
2 *The expressive strategy*, according to Garland, represents a complete change in the way that crime is viewed by society. Increasingly, he argues, crime has come to be seen as central to politics and to winning elections. It is more important to politicians to create the *perception* that crime is declining than to effect any real changes in the levels of crime. Therefore, much government intervention centres on changing perceptions rather than effective measures to limit crime.

Actuarialism

Feeley and Simon (1992) have developed a similar analysis to that of Garland. They argue that a 'new penology' has developed in crime control. The criminal justice no longer operates on the basis of catching offenders in order to punish or rehabilitate them, but instead seeks to 'identify and manage unruly groups'. Feeley and Simon call this **actuarialism**. The term derives from the insurance industry, where the people who work out the chances of a particular event happening (and therefore the price to charge for insurance) are known as actuaries. Feeley and Simon argue that, in contemporary society, the stress of social control has changed from controlling deviant behaviour, to controlling potentially deviant people. Therefore, agencies of social control work out who is likely to pose the greatest risk of deviance and then act against them. The police patrol working-class and ethnic-minority areas, while the private security companies police the shopping developments, monitor people who enter and exclude the potential troublemakers – defined as the poor, the young and the homeless.

Penetration into society

The final theoretical approach to understanding the growth of community safety has been provided by Foucault (1977) and, separately, by Stanley Cohen (1985).

(We have discussed these theorists already in Topic 1.) According to Foucault and to Cohen, community safety policy is just one example of the way that governments seek to diffuse their power throughout the community. Public concern over crime allows governments to intervene in an ever-broader range of social activity, as new areas of social life, such as the family, the community and the school, are redefined as potential causes of crime.

Davis: control of space

Davis, in the very influential book, *City of Quartz* (1990), studied Los Angeles and pointed out that there is an increasing division between the affluent, living in segregated and (privately) protected areas, and the areas lived in by the poorer majority. The role of the police is to contain the poor, segregating them in their ghettos.

The police

The main agency responsible for the enforcement of social control is the police force. This is the arm of the state whose role is to maintain public order and to enforce the law. In recent years, there have been considerable changes in the styles of policing.

Styles of uniformed policing in Britain

Traditional 'beat' policing, in which one officer had a geographical area to control, was phased out in the 1960s and replaced by officers in cars who responded to reports of incidents. During the 1980s, on top of ordinary patrol cars, the police introduced a new form of policing in urban areas that involved larger groups of police officers in minibuses ready to respond to disturbances. By the turn of

Key themes

Socialization, culture and identity

Social control

Policing and forms of social control have been examined closely by neo-Marxist sociologists, who are interested in finding out the ways that capitalist society controls the proletariat. Althusser (1971) argues that the police are part of the 'state apparatus' that seeks to control the population by repressive methods. He also argues that other agencies are involved in social control, performing the same task, but using a more positive approach, e.g. education, religion and the media. Therefore, rather than seeing the police as being a distinctive control group, they should be seen as a part of a broad spread of 'repressive state apparatuses'.

In a similar manner, Hall *et al.* (1978) argue that most people provide little trouble to capitalism as they are sucked into it through employment, mortgages and consumption. The role of the police is to deal with those on the margins of society – young people, ethnic minorities, street-life people and such like – who pose a threat because they are not bonded into capitalism.

the century, these methods of policing were largely replaced by two approaches – neighbourhood policing and reactive policing:

- *Neighbourhood policing* – Dedicated teams of police and community support officers work in a geographical area. The aim is to get to know members of the community and to respond to their specific concerns. In reality, this means dealing with issues of antisocial behaviour.
- *Reactive policing* – Police respond to emergency calls from the public for help.

The relationship of the police to society

Although, there would appear to be relatively little controversy about these styles of policing, the changes over time have been explored theoretically by different sociological approaches. There are three main positions in understanding the relationship of the police to society: the consensual approach, the conflict approach and the late-modern approach.

The consensual approach

A consensual approach sees the police as having a close relationship with the local area, and the role of the police force being to represent the interests of the majority of law-abiding people, defending them against the minority of offenders. Officers are drawn from the community and reflect its characteristics. Individual offenders are caught as a result of complaints made by the community. Neighbourhood and reactive policing reflect the balance of police work, which is responding to the specific and emergency needs of local communities.

The conflict approach

A very different view of the police is provided by Scraton (1985), who argues that the police can best be seen as an occupying force, imposed upon working-class and ethnic-minority communities. Police officers largely patrol working-class and ethnic-minority areas, where they impose the law and order that reflects the interests of the more powerful groups.

According to Reiner (1997), those who are stopped and searched, or questioned in the street, arrested, detained in the police station, charged and prosecuted, are disproportionately young men who are unemployed or casually employed, and from discriminated-against minority ethnic groups. The police themselves recognize that their main business involves such groups, and their mental social maps delineate them by a variety of derogatory epithets: 'assholes', 'pukes', 'scum', 'slags', 'prigs'.

The late-modern approach

This approach is the one we discussed earlier when we explored the changes in the development of community safety. Writers like Garland, Foucault, Cohen, and Feeley and Simon would all argue that the shift towards neighbourhood policing represents an extension of control over the population, with the police, as representatives of the state, integrating themselves in local communities.

Discretion, policing and the law

It is the job of the police to enforce the law. However, there are so many laws that could be applied in so many different circumstances that police officers need to use their **discretion** in deciding exactly which laws to apply and in what circumstances. Sociologists have been particularly interested in studying the nature of such discretion, and in seeing the implications for different groups in society. Discretion can also provide evidence to support one or other of the (consensual or conflict) styles of policing we have just discussed.

Reiner (1992) has suggested three ways of explaining the basis of police discretion: individualistic, cultural and structural.

Individualistic

The explanation for police discretion is that a particular police officer has specific concerns and interests, and thus interprets and applies the law according to them.

Focus on research

Hough and Roberts (2004)
Perceptions of youth crime

Mike Hough and Julian Roberts conducted research on the public's attitudes to youth offending and the punishment of young people. They inserted additional questions into the Office of National Statistics Omnibus Survey (the ONS is a government department) which takes place every month (on a variety of subjects). Researchers have to buy a block of questions and Hough and Roberts bought a block of 30 questions. Government-trained interviewers then conducted interviews with 1692 people aged over 16. The block of questions took about 15 minutes to complete. The response rate was 67 per cent.

Hough and Roberts found that people have negative perceptions about youth and the youth justice system. People believe that **offending rates** are higher than they are in reality and that young people are unlikely to be punished.

Hough, M. and Roberts J.V. (2004) *Youth Crime and Youth Justice Public Opinion in England and Wales*, Oxford: Blackwell

Suggest reasons why respondents believed that offending rates are higher than they really are.

Key themes

Sociological theories and methods

Studying 'canteen culture'

There have been numerous studies of the police from both quantitative and qualitative perspectives. It has been relatively easy to get hold of statistics showing the rates of arrest of criminals, or the numbers of stops and searches of people in the streets. However, these sorts of studies have rarely given an insight into how the police actually operate on a day-to-day basis. In order to do this, sociologists have generally resorted to using some form of participant observation. But the culture of police officers – the 'canteen culture' – is a closed one, so that anybody from outside the force trying to study police officers is usually forced into using covert participant observation. Two famous studies are by Holloway (1983) and Hobbs (1998): in both, the researchers felt that the only way to uncover the reality of policing was not to declare their research interests openly. In fact, when Holloway undertook his research, he was a serving policeman. The result of their work was a detailed insight into the lives of police officers. However, although the research makes great reading, it is never possible to say for certain that the research is accurate or generalizable, as covert participant observational research is almost impossible to replicate.

Colman and Gorman (1982) found some evidence for this in their study of police officers in inner London. In particular, they noted individual racist police officers who would apply the law more harshly on certain ethnic minorities.

Cultural

New recruits enter a world that has a highly developed culture – evolved from the particular type of job that police officers must do. Police officers are overwhelmingly White and male. They work long hours in each other's company and are largely isolated from the public. The result of this is the development of a very specific occupational culture – sometimes referred to as a '**canteen culture**'. According to Skolnick (1966), this has three main components – and we can add a fourth suggested by Graef (1989): that of masculinity.

1 *Suspiciousness* – As part of their job, police officers spend much of their time dealing with people who may have committed a criminal offence. As part of their training, therefore, they are taught to discriminate between 'decent people' and 'potential troublemakers'. According to Reiner (1992), they categorize and stereotype certain people as 'police property'. This involves regarding young males, and particularly youths from ethnic minorities, as potential troublemakers.
2 *Internal solidarity and social isolation* – We have just noted how police officers spend large amounts of time in the company of their peers, isolated from the public. They also rely upon each other in terms of support in times of physical threat and when denying accusations from the public.
3 *Conservatism* – Those who join the police in the first place are rarely politically radical, and while the actual job of policing emphasizes a non-political attitude – police officers must uphold the law – it also upholds traditional values and the very nature of the state. Added to the factors of social isolation and the majority recruitment from White males, this generates a strong sense of conservative values.
4 *Masculinity* – Most police officers are male and drawn from the working class. The culture of police officers very much reflects traditional working-class values of heavy drinking, physical prowess and heterosexuality. Racial stereotyping is also heavily emphasized and linked with assuming the role of a police officer.

Structural

A third approach, derived from Marxist theory, stresses that the very definition of law is biased in favour of the powerful groups in society and against the working class. Therefore, any upholding of the law involves upholding the values of capitalist society. Police officers' definition of crime in terms of street crimes and burglary (as opposed to white-collar or corporate crime) derives from their role as agents of control of a capitalist society. Their internal values simply reflect the job they have been given to do.

Evidence for this view can be found in Tarling's (1988) study, which showed that over 65 per cent of police resources are devoted to the uniformed patrolling of public space – particularly poorer neighbourhoods and central-city areas. The result is that, as Morgan and Russell (2000) found, about 55 per cent of prisoners in police custody were unemployed, and of the rest, 30 per cent were in manual, working-class jobs. Most detainees were young, with 60 per cent being under 25, and 87 per cent of all those arrested being male. Finally, over 12 per cent were from African or African-Caribbean backgrounds – despite these groups forming less than 3 per cent of the population (see Topic 9 for more on ethnicity and crime).

The courts

Once a person has been caught by the police, the decision to press charges will be made by the Crown Prosecution Service and the person will then be taken to court. Less serious offences are judged in magistrates courts (presided over by magistrates) and serious crimes in Crown Courts (presided over by judges).

Magistrates courts

Magistrates are volunteers drawn from the local community and are meant to be representative of it. However, when Morgan and Russell (2000) explored the background of the magistrates, they found that, although there was an equal balance from either sex and that, overall, the magistrates reflected the ethnic divisions in the country, 40 per cent of magistrates were over retirement age and 70 per cent held, or had previously held, professional or managerial positions.

When it comes to the more senior judges, their background is overwhelmingly male, White and educated at Oxford or Cambridge Universities. However, for the last 10 years, there has been a significant increase in the proportion of female and ethnic-minority-background judges appointed. Nevertheless, in 2007, of all 3544 judges, 81 per cent were male, 19 per cent were female and 3.5 per cent came from an ethnic-minority background (Hansard 2008). Although the backgrounds of magistrates and judges do not have to reflect the population as a whole, critics have argued that, as they are drawn from such a narrow band of social backgrounds, they are unable to understand the situation of those they are judging – as offenders are overwhelmingly socially marginalized males, with a disproportionate number drawn from the ethnic minorities.

Trends in sentencing

Apart from fines – the most common form of punishment – there are only two main types of punishment: community punishment and custodial punishment (prison). There were 83 714 people in custody in October 2008, an increase in 2 per cent over the previous year and one of the highest figures ever. The single biggest category of offence for which people were imprisoned was violence, followed by drug offences. There were just under 79 000 males in prison and just under 4000 female prisoners, a ratio of 20:1. There were 12 700 British nationals from ethnic-minority backgrounds. In 2008, there were approximately 112 000 people serving community sentences, supervised by probation.

It is very difficult to prove which form of punishment is more effective in stopping offending. Approximately 50 per cent of those who undertake community punishment reoffend, but about the same percentage of those imprisoned go on to reoffend after release.

Punishment

Punishment is the key component of formal social control. It has therefore been an area of great interest to sociologists, as it reflects upon changes in the wider society. We have already explored this in Topic 1. Durkheim was the first sociologist to take the issue seriously, by suggesting that the nature of social solidarity in society is closely reflected in the form and severity of punishment. Less complex societies or **mechanistic societies** are held together by the similarity of their members, who share a narrow range of beliefs. People who offend in these societies are likely to be severely punished, in particular through violent means. However, modern, socially complex or **organic societies** are more loosely held together by mutual economic need, or as Durkheim puts it, through the division of labour. Punishment in complex societies is far less vicious and Durkheim argued that the idea of the prison emerged in order to rehabilitate offenders and bring them back into society.

Max Weber was also interested in the development of punishment and saw the prison and other modern forms of punishment as reflecting the changing nature of authority in society. Weber argued that as societies developed, so the form of authority that people obeyed changed from that of a charismatic ruler, or of the

traditional chief, to a legal authority based on bureaucracies that were set up to achieve certain rational aims. One of these bureaucracies was the criminal justice system, which attempted in a dispassionate way to get people to follow the law. Therefore, the criminal justice system, based on agreed, value-neutral procedures, replaced violence and the irrational desire for revenge.

Norbert Elias (1978), in *The Civilizing Process*, examined punishment as key element of what he called 'the civilizing process'. Elias' overall argument is that modern society has only become possible as people have learned to self control and developed agreed ways of acting. A major part of self-control has been to control anger and the desire to inflict violence on others. This move away from the impulse to violence had an impact on responses to crime. In a similar argument to that of Weber, Elias saw a gradual move away from inflicting horrendous

Check your understanding

1 Give two examples of crime prevention.

2 Briefly explain what is meant by the term 'community safety'.

3 What does Garland mean when he writes about the 'culture of control'?

4 Explain the term 'actuarialism'. Why is it different from traditional policing practices?

5 Identify the components of the police occupational culture.

6 Why is an understanding of police discretion important?

Activities

Research ideas

1 Contact your local police and ask if an officer will come in to discuss policing in the local area. Prepare some questions based on the material in this topic.

2 Conduct a small-scale survey at your school or college aiming to find out students' attitudes towards the police.

Web.task

Learn about the Criminal Justice System by going to: **www.cjsonline.gov.uk/**

Go to the website of the Judiciary for England and Wales. There are a number of learning resources there. Try 'The Crime Survey Quiz' (and explain why it is biased), 'The Myth Busting Quiz' and 'Lifeline of Joe X' **www.judiciary.gov.uk/learning_resources/index.htm**

punishment, to the development of a criminal justice system including a form of punishment which was intended to develop self-control. Interestingly, a number of the most commonly used psychological courses that prisoners are expected to attend in contemporary prisons are ones which focus on maintaining self-control and not giving in to anger.

The final, and most important writer on punishment, Foucault, has been referred to throughout this topic and in Topic 1. For Foucault, the prison, community punishment and community safety initiatives can all be combined as part of the process of the state extending its tentacles of discipline and control throughout society.

Key terms

Actuarialism Feeley and Simon's view that modern governments look for risk factors and then focus all their energies on the group(s) identified as most likely to commit crime (*see* Risk factors).

Broken windows theory the idea that if less serious crimes are allowed, more serious ones are likely to occur later.

Canteen culture a term which refers to the occupational culture developed by the police.

Community safety refers to any preventive measure designed to stop crime from happening.

Crime displacement where effective crime prevention in one place has the unfortunate result of moving it elsewhere or onto different victims.

Crime reduction *see* **Community safety**.

Culture of control Garland claims that modern governments have given up trying to stop crime; they now merely wish to manage it and to manage people's attitudes towards it.

Defensible space architectural design that makes it more difficult to commit crime.

Discretion the fact that the police have to use their

judgement about when to use the force of the law.

Mechanistic societies technologically and socially simple societies, as identified by Durkheim, in which people are culturally very similar.

Offending rates statistics referring to the number of crimes committed, and by whom.

Organic societies culturally and technologically complex societies, as identified by Durkheim, in which people are culturally different from each other.

Penal welfarism Garland's name for the traditional

approach of the criminal justice system, which sought to punish and rehabilitate offenders.

Postitivistic using natural-scientific methods, adapted to sociology.

Risk factors the family and social factors which are statistically most likely to predict future offending.

Situational crime prevention: making it more difficult to commit crime and to benefit from it.

Target hardening ways of making objects more difficult to steal and people less likely to be victims.

398

Sociology A2 for AQA

An eye on the exam — Prevention, policing and punishment

Item A

Studies of policing and crime prevention show that the police tend to concentrate more of their attention on particular neighbourhoods. In terms of their efforts – as measured by the number of officers on patrol and other interventions made at local level – certain areas receive a disproportionately high level of police interest and activity. For example, council-housing estates, especially the more run-down or 'sink' estates, and neighbourhoods with a high proportion of Black and other ethnic-minority populations, together with areas where young people congregate, all tend to be policed more heavily compared with other areas.

Examine the reasons why the police concentrate their attention on particular neighbourhoods (**Item A**).

(12 marks)

Grade booster — Getting top marks in this question

Use the Item to give you some clues, for example about the types of neighbourhood that police focus on. You should consider a number of possible reasons for the patterns shown in the Item. These could include individual officers, preferences (e.g. racist or prejudiced officers), as well as the various factors relating to police culture (so-called 'canteen culture'), such as suspiciousness, internal solidarity and social isolation, conservatism and masculinity. You can relate these to the social composition of the police force (mainly White males) and to their occupational socialisation (e.g. how to distinguish between law-abiding citizens and troublemakers). You can also look at Marxist ideas about the role of the police force in capitalist society and how this is reflected in which groups they are most likely to arrest.

Suicide

> You may find the subject matter of this topic distressing or disturbing. If you do, please talk to your teacher. Alternatively, you can talk in confidence to the Samaritans on 08457 90 90 90.

Getting you thinking

Welsh town hit by suicides

THE WELSH town of Bridgend has been rocked by a spate of over 15 suicides of young people.

Phillip Walters, the coroner for the town of Bridgend fears that teenage sites such as Bebo play a part in the spate of mystery deaths. Mr Walter said: 'I shall be looking at these networking sites myself to see if there is a link between them and the growing number of youngsters committing suicide. But in the meantime I want to warn youngsters about the possible dangers these websites can pose.'

The Assistant Chief Constable of South Wales Police said: 'What we have found is that these are vulnerable young people, and taking one's own life may be becoming an acceptable option to young people for issues that they are facing.' He pointed to a variety of factors that might have influenced these young people to take their own lives. These included relationship break-ups, friendship issues and family problems.

The security guard who found one body said: 'They need to talk to people like their family, not spend all their time on computers or watching television. I feel so sad for her and her family.'

Ruth Coombs of the mental health charity Mind Cymru said: 'There are particular issues for different communities in Wales. In rural areas, problems with depression and feelings of isolation are big.'

Adapted from articles in the Daily Mail, Jan/Feb 2008

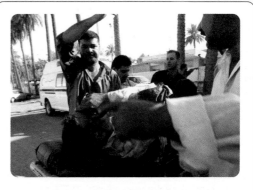

Female suicide bombers leave 50 dead, 250 injured on day of carnage to Iraq

SUICIDE BOMBERS struck the Iraqi cities of Baghdad and Kirkuk leaving 50 people dead and scores injured. Three female suicide bombers killed 28 people and wounded 92 when they blew themselves up among Shi'ites walking through the streets of Baghdad on a religious pilgrimage on Monday, Iraqi police said.

And in the northern oil city of Kirkuk a suicide bomber killed 22 people and wounded 150 at a protest against a disputed local elections law, Iraqi health and security officials said.

One security official said the bomber may also have been a woman.

Daily Mail 28 July 2008

1 List the various explanations for suicide given in the two articles.

2 Which, if any, of the explanations listed strike you as being most likely to be true?

3 Committing suicide is generally believed to be an individual decision, so what possible explanations can you suggest as to why some places have higher suicide rates than others?

4 What similarities and differences can you find between the suicides described in the two articles?

5 What light might your answers to the previous question throw onto the argument that suicide can only be understood as a result of an individual decision?

You may have already developed some theories of your own as to why people commit suicide and why patterns of suicide exist. Suicide is, arguably, the ultimate deviant act, as it goes against all ideas of self-preservation and is extremely difficult for most people to comprehend.

Yet suicide was relatively understudied by sociologists until the 1960s. This was because one major piece of work, by Durkheim in 1897, had so dominated sociological thought that it was believed there was little more to say. Yet, when newer interpretations did come along, they carried with them some profound attacks on some of the pillars of theory and research upon which sociology had founded its very claim to be a social science.

So, in this topic, we study suicide not just because the subject matter is interesting for society, but also as a case study in how applying different theories and methods to the same problem can provide very different and contradictory explanations. In particular, we can see the deep divisions between the **positivists**, who believe in following the methods of the natural sciences wherever possible, and the **interpretive sociologists**, who prefer to explore the way society is constructed through people's interactions.

Suicide: a scientific approach

Durkheim's study of suicide

Durkheim (1897) chose suicide as a subject of study, not just because it was interesting in itself, but in an attempt to prove that the (then) new subject of sociology could provide an explanation for an act that seemed to be the very opposite of what could be considered as 'social'. By proving that sociology had something useful to say in explaining suicide, Durkheim hoped to secure the status of sociology amongst the newly emerging sciences.

This attempt to locate sociology as a science, with its adherence to more social-scientific methods of research, is crucial in understanding how Durkheim tackled the issue. Durkheim's chosen method, now called '**multivariate analysis**', consisted in comparing the incidence of various social factors with the known incidence of a particular event – in this case, suicide. He therefore studied the statistics of suicide that he collected from death certificates and other official documents and found that there were a number of clear patterns.

Over a period of 20 years, it could be seen that suicide rates were consistently different across countries, and regions within countries, across different religions, and across the married and unmarried. These regularities immediately supported Durkheim's argument that there was a social explanation for suicide, for if suicide was an entirely individual matter, based on individual decisions, no such patterns should emerge.

To explain these patterns, Durkheim returned to the theme of shared values and **social cohesion**. He argued that people are naturally selfish and do not concern themselves with the problems faced by others, unless, that is, society can force them to do so. Society achieves this by finding ways of making people aware of their social bonds to others. The greater the level of **social integration**, the more harmonious a society. In fact, society achieves this form of social control by drawing people together on the basis of common values taught primarily through the family and reinforced by religion. (It is important to remember that religion was much more influential 120 years ago than it is today.)

Durkheim suggested that the individuals who feel most closely integrated into society are those with close family relationships. It follows that those without close family ties

are the least bonded to society. We shall see the importance of this later.

Religion operated on a broader level, providing people with a moral underpinning for shared values. However, different religions do place varying amounts of stress on individual fulfilment. At one extreme, Protestant versions of Christianity give considerable importance to individual fulfilment, while religions such as Hinduism and Roman Catholicism stress the importance of the group, and consider the search for personal happiness relatively unimportant.

The outcome of the significance of the family and religion in different societies resulted in varying levels of social integration, with Protestant-based societies being less integrated and Catholic/Hindu ones being more integrated. Furthermore, individuals in society vary in their degree of social integration into society, depending upon their membership of family networks.

Durkheim's categorization of societies

It was Durkheim's hypothesis that suicide is directly related to the levels of social integration in a society or group within society. He placed societies into four categories, depending upon their levels of social integration.

Egoistic

In egoistic societies, individual rights, interests and welfare are heavily stressed and allegiance to the wider group is weak, with people being encouraged to look after themselves and those particularly close to them at the expense of the wider society. As a result, social bonds are weak and there is a low level of social integration. Egoistic societies are closely related to Protestantism, a strand of Christianity that stresses the responsibility of individuals to make their own decisions and to accept the consequences of doing so. Culturally, individual failure or unhappiness are viewed as acceptable grounds for people to take their

Key themes

Sociological theories and methods

The realist approach

Taylor (1990) argues that Durkheim uses a 'realist' methodological approach in his study of suicide. Realists, like positivists, believe that scientific methods drawn from the natural sciences are appropriate for analysing society. Realists, such as Bhaskar (1998), argue that the natural sciences often have to use 'indicators' for things that are known to exist, but which are not directly observable in themselves, e.g. subatomic fields and 'quarks'. Natural scientists must therefore use some other indicator that is measurable and (theoretically) is an accurate representation of the unmeasurable concept. Sociologists have developed this idea in the study of society and argue that, although many things are not directly observable, they still exist; furthermore, there are indicators that can be used to measure them. The indicators that Durkheim uses are the official suicide rates.

own lives – **egoistic suicide**. This is typical of contemporary European and North American societies.

However, within this form of society, there are social institutions that counteract the wider egoistic values of society and provide a sense of belonging. These include the family and other forms of religion, such as Catholicism, that stress the importance of an individual's responsibility to the wider church. Durkheim also noted that, in times of war or some other form of threat, societies draw together.

Durkheim concluded that there are likely to be relatively high rates of suicide in societies with low levels of social integration, but that, within those societies, people integrated in families or religious groups that provide greater levels of social integration are less likely to take their own lives. For example, married people are less likely to commit suicide than single people.

Altruistic

In altruistic societies, the welfare of individuals is viewed as far less important than that of the group. Individual choice or happiness is simply not a high priority. Durkheim therefore argued that there was insufficient motivation for members to commit suicide – with one exception. **Altruistic suicide** occurs when the individual is expected to commit suicide on behalf of the wider society – rather than in egoistic societies where the suicide takes place because of individual unhappiness. A contemporary example of altruistic suicide might be suicide bombers prepared to sacrifice themselves for their political or religious cause.

Anomic

Durkheim believed people are naturally selfish and will only look after their own interests unless society restricts their actions. According to Durkheim, societies develop cultural and social mechanisms that provide a clear framework of what is acceptable behaviour. However, if these restraints are weakened, for whatever reason, then

1945: Japanese kamikaze pilots pose for a final photograph before setting out on their suicide mission: to crash their planes deliberately into Allied ships. Which of Durkheim's types of suicide best describes the deaths of these men?

some people may revert to their natural selfishness, whilst others may simply become bewildered. Social restraints on behaviour are most likely to weaken in periods of dramatic social change (for example, during an economic or political crisis). Durkheim, therefore, linked increases in suicide levels to periods of rapid social change – **anomic suicide**.

Fatalistic

This final form of suicide reflects the fact that in extremely oppressive societies, people may lose the will to live and prefer to die. Durkheim considered such **fatalistic suicide** a fairly uncommon occurrence, but it could be argued that it accounts for the very high levels of suicide in prisons, for example.

Internal criticisms of Durkheim

Durkheim's analysis of suicide was used for over 70 years as an excellent example of how to undertake positivistic sociological analysis. During that time, however, there was a degree of criticism of his approach from those who basically agreed with it. These criticisms are known as 'internal criticisms':

- Durkheim's analysis depends upon the concept of social cohesion, for he argues that suicide rates vary as it varies. Yet, he never provides a clear, unambiguous definition of it, nor is there any obvious method of measuring it.
- He claimed that social integration was linked most closely to religion and family membership. But Durkheim provides no explanation of exactly how this can be verified or falsified. As we see in Chapter 5, Topic 3, 'Sociology and science', a key element of science is the ability to carry out some form of research activity that can either prove or disprove a theory. Durkheim's methodology fails this test.

Key themes

Sociological theories and methods

Statistics: truth or social construction?

The debate over suicide between different branches of sociology – in particular, between those who believe that statistics provide us with a reflection of reality and those sociologists who see statistics as simply a social construction – has implications for a wide range of sociological areas of study. These include such things as:

- religious belief and attendance
- the extent of aid to the developing nations
- voting patterns
- the existence of social class
- the extent of wealth and poverty.

Beyond this, the debate also reflects profoundly on theory and method. In theory, it illustrates the contribution of social-action theories to our understanding of everyday life; in methods, it is a perfect example of positivism versus constructionism as approaches to researching the social world.

- Durkheim relied largely upon official statistics – yet official statistics are open to dispute – in particular, in Catholic-dominated countries and regions, suicide was regarded with great stigma and doctors were very reluctant to certify this as being the reason for death.

Interpretive criticisms of the scientific approach

However, a second group of writers have criticized Durkheim's analysis as fundamentally flawed. They argue that, rather than being an excellent example of sociological methodology, the research ought to be used as an example of why the use of traditional scientific methods in sociology is a mistake. These are known as 'interpretive criticisms'.

Interpretive approaches stress the way that society operates through people interacting on the basis of sharing meanings. Interpretive sociologists have paid great attention to exploring the way that these meanings are constructed and how they influence individual behaviour. As we have pointed out elsewhere in the book, interpretive sociologists reject the idea that society can be studied with methods borrowed from the physical sciences – precisely the approach most favoured by Durkheim.

Two writers in this tradition, Douglas and Atkinson, have been particularly effective in their criticism of Durkheim's explanation.

Douglas – the meanings of suicide

Douglas (1967) argued that defining suicide simply by referring to the physical fact of killing oneself misses the central issue, which is that suicide has different meanings to those who take their own lives, and their motives vary too.

If this is the case, and we can only understand society by studying the meanings through which people understand and interpret the world, then suicide needs much greater exploration as to its meaning than Durkheim provided.

Douglas suggested that those who commit suicide may define their action in at least four ways:

1 *Transforming the self* – A person commits suicide as a means of gaining release from the cares of the world.
2 *Transforming oneself for others* – The suicide tells others how profound their feelings are on a particular issue.
3 *Achieving fellow feeling* – The person is asking for help or sympathy; this includes 'suicide' attempts, in that the person hopes to be found.
4 *Gaining revenge* – The person believes they have been forced into a position where they have to commit suicide.

So, there is no single act that can be termed 'suicide'. Since the meanings that individuals place upon their acts are so different, it is mistaken to categorize them as the same phenomenon. The only thing they have in common is death. The devastating conclusion, if this argument is accepted, is that Durkheim's statistical comparisons are worthless.

Focus on research

Jacobs (1967) Suicide notes

Jacobs studied 112 suicide notes written by both adults and young people who had committed suicide in Los Angeles. The primary aim of the research had actually been to study suicide attempts by young people, but during the research process, Jacobs gained access to the notes of 'successful' suicides as well. On

Singer Kurt Cobain, who committed suicide in 1994, leaving a long suicide note (see Webtask 3 on p. 404)

reading these, Jacobs was struck by just how sensible and rational the arguments put by the note-writers were. He then spent some time engaging in what he calls a phenomenological analysis of the notes – which involved thinking about the 'conscious deliberation that takes place before the individual is able to consider and execute the act of suicide'. Jacobs was able to categorize the notes into six clear groups, reflecting different reasons and intentions. For example, one group of people committed suicide because they were ill and no longer wanted to carry on; within these, there were people who asked for forgiveness for their act and those who did not. Jacobs' research does suggest a clarity and reasoned intent behind suicide – if one accepts that it is possible to put oneself (as he did) in the mind of the person committing suicide.

Jacobs, J. (1967) 'A phenomenological study of suicide notes', *Social Problems*, 15, pp. 60–72)

1 Assess the extent to which suicide notes might provide a representative sample of those who take their own lives.

2 In what way does Jacobs' research challenge the idea that suicide is an irrational act?

Atkinson – the social construction of suicide

Atkinson (1971) further developed this criticism that Durkheim failed to understand that categories such as 'suicide' are really socially constructed. In Britain, for example, before a death can be classified as suicide, a **coroner** must carry out an inquest and, on the basis of this, the death is classified as suicide or not. Atkinson argues that the official statistics therefore reflect coroners' decisions rather than any underlying 'reality'.

In order to make a decision, the coroner must piece together a series of 'clues' and then decide whether or not these point to suicide. Atkinson suggests that the following clues are particularly important:

- *Suicide notes* – In about 30 per cent of suicides, a note is found, although more may have been written but the family have destroyed them because of the accusations contained in them.
- *Mode of death* – Some types of death are seen as more typical of suicide than others.
- *Location and circumstances of death* – Coroners believe that suicides are committed in places and circumstances where they will not be discovered and where the person is sure the outcome will be successful.
- *Life history and mental condition* – Coroners believe that suicide is often related to depression caused by significant events in the deceased's life. So coroners search for evidence of such events.

Integrating positivistic and interpretive approaches

The criticisms made by writers such as Douglas and Atkinson have generally been accepted by sociologists as a useful corrective to the more positivistic approach of Durkheim.

Taylor (1990), however, has suggested that both Durkheim and his critics have missed the significance of **parasuicides**, as in the majority of cases, people who attempt suicide do not die. Taylor points out that, when questioned, it seems most attempts at suicide are less a definite decision to finish with life and more of a gamble, in which people leave the outcome in the hands of fate. If they survive, then they were not meant to die; if they die, then that was what fate or God intended.

Taylor suggests that parasuicide allows us to widen the discussion of suicide into one of 'risk-taking'. Developing the analysis of Durkheim further, he suggests that successful parasuicides could be categorized into 'ordeal' suicides, which can be related to a profound sense of anomie, and the more purposive suicides, similar to Durkheim's fatalism. Taylor also supports Durkheim's belief

that suicide is more likely in individuals too detached from others in society (egoistic suicides) and those overattached (altruistic suicide).

The point of Taylor's argument is that it is possible to pull together the wider social factors that Durkheim emphasized with the sense of meaning that Douglas stressed; the two approaches are not necessarily exclusive. Indeed, much of contemporary sociology has been the search for ways of integrating the two traditions.

Focus on research

Case 1

A man ingested barbiturates and went to sleep in his car, parked outside his estranged wife's house. A note he had written to her was pinned on his chest, indicating his expectation that she would notice him when she returned from her date with another man. This possibility of being rescued, however, was obliterated by a dense fog that descended around midnight.

Case 2

A woman had become depressed after her marriage of 15 years broke up and was being prescribed antidepressants. One morning at work she began swallowing the tablets one by one. A colleague at work noticed what she was doing and reported it to a senior. The company doctor was called in and he summoned an ambulance. She was unconscious on arrival at hospital but survived, after intensive medical treatment. She later said that she was unsure about her intentions at the time she was taking the tablets.

1 Read the two cases above. What term is used by Taylor to describe this form of behaviour?

2 How do the cases illustrate the problem of treating official suicide statistics as 'social facts'?

Key terms

Altruistic suicide Durkheim's term for suicide in societies where people see their own happiness as unimportant.

Anomic suicide Durkheim's term for suicide in societies where rapid change is occurring (see Topic 1, p. 332 for more discussion of 'anomie').

Coroners officials who decide on cause of death.

Egoistic suicide Durkheim's term for suicide in societies where people regard their individual happiness as very important.

Fatalistic suicide Durkheim's term for suicide in extreme, usually oppressive, situations where people lose the will to live.

Interpretive sociologists those whose approach to sociology stresses the need to study the way that society is

based on socially constructed meanings.

Multivariate analysis a method of gathering statistics from different societies and comparing the patterns to help explain social differences between the societies.

Parasuicide a term used by Taylor for suicide attempts where the person is not certain whether they want to die or not, and 'gambles' with their life.

Positivism belief that sociology should use the same approaches to research as the natural sciences, such as physics.

Social cohesion the extent to which a society is held together by shared culture and values.

Social integration the extent to which people feel they 'belong' to a society or social group.

Check your understanding

1 What do we mean by 'positivism'?

2 What approach to the study of suicide was used by Durkheim?

3 How is social integration linked to suicide?

4 Explain the term 'anomic suicide'.

5 Give any one 'internal criticism' of Durkheim's analysis of suicide.

6 Why is Douglas' criticism significant?

7 Give two examples of how coroners decide whether a death is suicide or not.

8 What does Taylor mean by 'parasuicide'? Why is the term important?

Web.tasks

1 Go to the government's statistics site at **www.statistics.gov.uk/default.asp** and search for 'suicide'. What patterns can you find? Which areas have the highest and lowest suicide rates? Suggest reasons for differences.

2 Search the worldwide web for suicide statistics (The National Library for Electronic Health is a useful starting point). What statistics can you find? What is their source? What possible explanations are there for the patterns shown? How might they be interpreted by positivists and interpretive sociologists?

3 Go to **www.well.com/~art/suicidenotes.html** and choose a cross section of these suicide notes. What different interpretations would Durkheim, Douglas, Atkinson and Taylor place on these notes?

An eye on the exam   Suicide

Item A

Durkheim established correlations between suicides and other sets of social facts. He found that suicide rates were higher in predominantly Protestant countries than in Catholic ones. Jews had a low suicide rate, lower even than Roman Catholics. Generally, married people were less prone to suicide than those who were single, although married women who remained childless for a number of years ended up with a high suicide rate. Durkheim also found that a low suicide rate was associated with political upheaval. War also reduced the suicide rate.

Adapted from Haralambos, M. and Holborn, M. (2004) *Sociology: Themes and Perspectives* (6th edn): London: Collins Education

Using material from **Item A** and elsewhere, examine some of the reasons why there might be 'correlations between suicides and other sets of social facts'.   (12 marks)

Grade booster   Getting top marks in this question

You could begin your answer by briefly explaining what a correlation is, and outlining a few correlations from the Item and elsewhere (for example, what is the correlation between suicide and religion or suicide and marriage?). You need to consider a range of reasons for these correlations. As the Item is about Durkheim, you should consider moral regulation and social integration, linking them to his four types of suicide. You also need to examine one or two alternative reasons for these correlations, such as those put forward by Douglas and Atkinson. For example, how do the meanings and interpretations of coroners and others help us to understand the kind of correlations Durkheim identifies? Lastly, does Taylor's approach offer an explanation of any of the correlations?

1   Read **Item A** below and answer parts (a) and (b) that follow.

Item A

When we look at the official crime statistics as recorded by the police, females and males seem to have different patterns of criminal behaviour. For example, males seem much more likely to commit crime in the first place: for every one female convicted of a criminal offence, about four males are convicted. And when we look at imprisonment, the gender gap is even greater.

The lower rate of imprisonment for women may, in turn, be a reflection not just of their lower rate of offending in the first place; it may also reflect differences in the nature and seriousness of the crimes that males and females commit. Females tend to have a higher rate of conviction for mainly petty crimes against property, such as shoplifting, handling stolen goods, benefit fraud and forgery. By contrast, males have higher conviction rates for offences involving violence against the person and sexual offences, as well as for more 'aggressive' property offences such as burglary and criminal damage.

(a)   Examine some of the reasons why females and males seem to have different patterns of criminal behaviour (**Item A**). *(12 marks)*

An examiner comments

> A reasonable point, but the reference to victims doesn't focus the paragraph very well on the question.

Women are often seen as victims rather than criminals. Feminists argue that this is because most sociologists are men, so they are not interested in studying female crime. Others believe men's crimes are focused on because they are more serious.

> This shows some knowledge of the chivalry theory, but it should identify it as such. There is some brief evaluation of it (women police officers).

One explanation for why women are not seen as the offender is that as many police officers are men, brought up to act as 'knights in shining armour' to protect women. However, this view could be outdated, as there are more female officers today.

> This is reasonable as a description, but it needs to examine possible reasons for these patterns.

It also depends on the type of crime being committed. With petty crimes such as shoplifting, men are likely to be penalized more harshly, whereas women tend to get off lightly. However, when the crimes are more serious, e.g. murdering a child, women often get tougher sentences.

> A reasonable point that explains differences in crime and sentencing in terms of ideas about gender stereotypes and gender roles – but should refer to these concepts explicitly.

One explanation for this is that it is more acceptable for a man to be violent or 'macho', whereas women are supposed to have a caring nature. Women also often avoid a jail sentence if they have young children to look after, because this fits their stereotypical role.

Gender differences in crime have been changing over time. A female sociologist showed that, with the women's liberation movement, it was now more acceptable for women to commit serious crimes. She argued that crime statistics for men and women in different societies shows that women committing crimes such as armed robbery, violence, etc., was increasing more rapidly than men committing them. She believed women's crime would continue increasing and until it reached a par with men's. This was due to changes in women's position and greater gender equality.

> A reasonable account of the 'liberation' explanation, but it should identify the sociologist (Adler) and offer some evaluation of it.

Overall, we can see that the main perception of females is that they are victims. However, this is changing and in one sense it may now be more 'normal' for women to commit crimes.

$\frac{6}{12}$

> A relevant but brief conclusion – but it needs a more general one for the answer as whole.

> Overall, a reasonable answer that recognizes some possible reasons for apparent gender differences in crime, such as the chivalry theory, the liberation theory and stereotypes about gender roles. However, it would benefit from identifying these explanations and related concepts (e.g. patriarchy, socialization), and should also try to evaluate some of these reasons. For example, critics argue that the 'liberation' view would lead us to expect liberated middle-class women to be committing more crimes, whereas it is poorer women whose crime rates have increased. Also, this answer focuses mostly on females; it should look at males too – e.g. at theories of masculinity and crime.

(b)   Assess the functionalist explanation of deviance and social control. *(21 marks)*

> A reasonable start showing understanding of the functionalist view, but too brief.

Functionalism is a consensus theory of crime and deviance, which sees members of society as sharing the same norms and values. Crime and deviance are the breaking of these norms and values.

It is important to recognize the difference between crime and deviance. Crime is behaviour that goes against the criminal law, such as murder or burglary. It is a form of deviant behaviour, but not all forms of deviant behaviour are against the law. For example, homosexuality might be seen by some (e.g. the New Right) as deviant, but it is not against the law in Britain. However, homosexuality was a criminal act in the past, and still is in societies such as Iran today. This shows that deviance is relative to time and culture.

Functionalists such as Durkheim argue that there is a collective conscience in society that crime goes against. However, despite breaking society's norms, crime does perform important functions according to Durkheim. When it is punished, crime reinforces the collective conscience because the majority of society is so shocked at the crime that people draw closer together, which strengthens social solidarity.

According to functionalists, most members of society are socialized to conform to the norms and values of society, not to break them. Therefore, social control is not always necessary, because people usually behave as they are expected to. However, not everyone is socialized perfectly, and so there will always be some deviance in society. Also, in complex societies, there are different subcultures that socialize their members in different ways and this creates deviance.

This links to another functionalist idea on deviance – that it can bring about social change. If everybody was socialized perfectly, no one would ever behave differently or do anything new, so society would stagnate. According to Durkheim, all social change begins as deviance, since to do something new is to go against established norms.

Overall, therefore, functionalists argue that crime can have positive functions for society. However, too much crime can be a threat to social stability. According to Durkheim, it can result in anomie, where the norms of society become unclear and society begins to disintegrate because no one is clear about how to behave.

> No need to distinguish between crime and deviance unless you link it to the functionalist explanation.

> Good point about strengthening social solidarity – though it would be good to mention social control too.

> Quite a good paragraph that analyses some of the reasons for deviance from a broadly functionalist viewpoint.

> A good account of one of the functions of deviance.

> A good point about anomie – but an abrupt end to the answer.

12/21

Overall, this answer shows a good knowledge of the functionalist view. Several functions of crime are identified, such as reinforcement of social solidarity and promoting social change. These are quite well analysed and explained. On the other hand, there are several weaknesses. First, there is little evaluation. It would be useful to introduce one or more other perspectives (e.g. Marxism) as an alternative view. Second, other functionalist views, e.g. Merton or Cohen, would be useful. Third, there is a wasted second paragraph that loses focus on the question. Finally, it lacks a conclusion.

406

Sociology A2 for AQA

One for you to try

This question requires you to **apply** your knowledge and understanding of sociological research methods to the study of this issue in crime and deviance.

2 Read **Item B** and answer the question that follows.

Item B

According to the official statistics on crimes recorded by the police, members of some minority ethnic groups are more likely to be arrested, charged and convicted than the population at large. In particular, Black people are over-represented in the crime statistics in relation to their numbers in the overall population. For example, in 2005, approximately 9 per cent of people arrested were recorded as 'Black'; this means that their chance of being arrested was three times higher than that of White people. Asian people made up 5 per cent of those arrested.

However, it may be that these patterns just reflect the behaviour of the police in relation to ethnic minorities, which some sociologists would argue is sometimes racist. For example, there is said to be a 'canteen culture' in the police force of which racism is an element. This may lead to disproportionate targeting of Black people, especially young males.

Using information from **Item B** and elsewhere, assess the strengths and limitations of using official statistics for the study of ethnic groups and crime. *(15 marks)*

An examiner comments

Here, you need to know what the main features of official statistics are, and that you need to be able both to outline and to evaluate the advantages and disadvantages of official statistics. These include practical, ethical and theoretical issues such as time, cost, reliability and validity. You need to apply these advantages and disadvantages to the study of ethnic groups and crime. For example, official statistics might be useful in providing us with a free source of data about the activities of the police and courts in relation to ethnic groups but, because of police racism (Item B), they may not necessarily give us a valid picture of the real patterns of crime in relation to ethnicity.

Answers to the 'One for you to try' are available **free** on **www.collinseducation.com/ sociologyweb**

Stratification and differentiation

AQA Specification	Topics	Pages
Candidates should examine:		
Different theories of stratification, including stratification by social class, gender, ethnicity and age.	Theories of class stratification are covered in Topic 2, gender stratification in Topic 6, ethnic stratification in Topic 7, and age stratification in Topic 8	416–23 449–77
Dimensions of inequality: class, status and power; differences in life-chances by social class, gender, ethnicity, age and disability.	Social-class differences in life-chances are the focus of Topic 3, gender differences Topic 6, ethnic differences Topic 7, age differences Topic 8, and disability Topic 9	424–32 449–85
The problems of defining and measuring social class; occupation, gender, and social class.	The problems of defining and measuring social class are covered in Topic 1.	408–15
Changes in structures of inequality, and the implications of these changes.	Changes in the class structure and the implications of these changes are covered in Topic 4.	433–40
The nature, extent and significance of patterns of social mobility.	Covered in Topic 5.	441–48
The connections between sociological theory and methods and the study of stratification and differentiation.	Connections are made in the 'Focus on research' and 'Key themes' features throughout both this chapter and Chapter 5, *Theory and methods*.	

Defining and measuring social class

Getting you thinking

1 Look at the photo on the right. All these children enjoy equal access to education, but does this mean that they will enjoy similar lifestyles when adults?

2 What social factors may create barriers for them?

3 Look at the two photographs below. What ways of measuring class do they indicate?

4 How do the photographs below relate to the criteria listed in the table?

5 Which of the criteria suggested in the table would you use to judge a person's social class and why?

When a random group of respondents were asked to identify the criteria they would use to assess a person's class, the results were as shown in the table below (figures are %).

Neighbourhood	36
How they talk	17
Job	31
What they wear	15
Pay	29
Parental background	13
Educational background	27
Use of leisure time	11
Wealth (assets such as property and **material** goods)	22
Political party support	11

Adapted from Hadford, G. and Skipworth, M. (1994) *Class*, London: Bloomsbury, p.19

It is generally believed that modern societies provide their citizens with the opportunities to better themselves. We all enjoy access to education and the chance to obtain formal qualifications; we all have access to a job market that offers decent incomes and promotion opportunities; we all enjoy the possibility of acquiring wealth. Or do we? The exercise above suggests that these opportunities may not exist for all social groups, or if they do, that some social groups have greater or easier access to these opportunities. In other words, inequalities between social groups are a fact of life in modern societies. The job of sociologists working in the field of stratification is to identify which social groups enjoy unfettered access to economic and social opportunities, and which are denied them, and why.

Differentiation and stratification

All societies **differentiate** between social groups – men and women, the young and the old, the working class and the middle class, and ethnic groups such as Whites, Asians and African-Caribbeans are often perceived to be socially different in some way. When these differences lead to greater status, power or privilege for some over others, the result is **social stratification**. This term – borrowed from geology – means the layering of society into strata, from which a hierarchy emerges reflecting different ranks in terms of social influence and advantage. The degree to which a society has a fixed hierarchy is determined by the degree of opportunity its members have to change their social position.

The sociological term for a person's social importance is **social status**. Status can be gained in two ways:

- **Ascribed status** is given at birth either through family (e.g. the Queen was 'born to rule') or through physical, religious or cultural factors (e.g. in some societies, women and girls are regarded as second-class citizens simply because they are female) – see Table 7.1 below.
- **Achieved status** is the result of factors such as hard work, educational success, marriage, special talent or sheer good fortune (e.g. winning the lottery).

Societies that allow for and reward achievement are called **open societies**, whereas those that ascribe social position are known as **closed societies**. Politicians tend to see the degree of openness in society as a measure of the freedoms they have helped to create, but they often overemphasize the extent to which society is open. Modern Britain, for example, may have free education for all up to the age of 18 or 19, but, as we shall see in Topic 3, those who are rich enough to attend a top public school have significant advantages in life.

In reality, few societies are totally open or closed and each could be placed somewhere along a continuum (see Fig. 7.1). Traditional societies tend to be more closed because of the greater influence of religion and tradition, which means that people can only play a limited range of roles and these tend to be fixed at birth. Modern societies, which seem more fluid and open, may actually experience significant levels of closure, in that some groups face social barriers and obstacles when attempting to improve themselves.

> **Figure 7.1** Open or closed: the continuum of social status
>
> All societies can be placed somewhere along this line.
>
> Openness ———————————— Closure
>
> | Lots of opportunities to change social position | Equal amount of restrictions and opportunities | No opportunities to change social position |

Table 7.1 Examples of traditional societies based on ascribed status

	The caste system	The feudal estate system
Place and time	Although officially banned in India today, the Hindu **caste system** of stratification is still enormously influential.	The **feudal estate system** was found in medieval Europe.
Structure	There are four basic castes or layers, ranging from the Brahmins (religious leaders and nobles) at the top, to the Sudras (servants and unskilled manual workers) at the bottom. 'Untouchables' exist below the caste system and are responsible for the least desirable jobs, such as sewage collection.	The king owned all the land and, in return for an oath of loyalty and military support, he would allocate the land to barons who, in turn, would apportion parts of it to knights. The majority (95%) were peasants or serfs who had to work the knight's land and, in return, were offered protection and allowed to rent land.
Restrictions	People are born into castes and cannot move out of them during the course of their lives. There are strong religious controls over the behaviour of caste members – for example, you cannot marry a member of another caste, nor can you do certain jobs because these are assigned exclusively to certain castes.	Feudal societies, too, were mainly closed societies – people's positions were largely ascribed and it was rare for people to move up. Marriage between groups was rarely allowed and feudal barons even restricted the geographical movement of the peasants.
Possibility of social mobility	The system is based upon religious purity – the only way people can be promoted to a higher caste is by living a pure life and hoping that they will be reincarnated (reborn) as a member of a higher caste.	On rare occasions, exceptional acts of bravery could result in a gift of land.

Social class

Social class is the stratification system found in modern industrial societies such as Britain. **Social classes** are groups of people who share a similar economic position in terms of occupation, income and ownership of wealth. They are also likely to have similar levels of education, status and power. Class systems are different from previous systems in the following ways:

- They are not based on religion, law or race, but on economic factors such as occupation and wealth.
- There is no clear distinction between classes – it is difficult to say where the working class finishes and the middle class begins, for example.
- All members of society have equal rights irrespective of their social position.
- There are no legal restrictions on marriage between the classes.
- Social-class societies are generally open societies – you can move up or down the class structure through jobs, the acquisition of wealth or marriage.
- Such systems are usually **meritocratic** – that is, people are not born into ascribed roles. Individuals are encouraged to better themselves through achievement at school and in their jobs, by working hard and gaining promotion.

Just how meritocratic social-class societies really are, and the extent to which factors such as race, gender and age can affect access to opportunity, will be a key focus of this chapter.

Measuring social class

Question 3 in the 'Getting you thinking' on p. 408 should have shown that measuring social class is not an easy exercise. People define social class in different ways and some even deny its existence altogether.

Why is there a need to measure class?

Various groups, such as sociologists, advertisers and government agencies, have vested interests in **operationalizing** and measuring the concept of social class in a consistent way for a number of reasons:

- Sociologists want to address class differences in all areas of social life in order to identify reasons why inequalities come about.
- Advertisers want to target particular social groups in order to maximize sales.
- Governments need to formulate social policies in order to address inequalities and future trends.

Each interest group has tended to operationalize the concept of social class in a different way. For example, governments and sociologists tend to approach social class as an objective reality that results in observable patterns of behaviour and inequality in areas such as health, life expectancy and education. Advertisers are more interested in how people subjectively interpret their class position, because this may affect their consumption patterns and their leisure pursuits.

Occupation as an indicator of social class

The single most objective measurable factor that corresponds best with social class is occupation. It is something that the majority of the population has in common. It also governs other aspects of their life, such as income, housing and level of education. Occupation, therefore:

- shapes a significant proportion of a person's life
- is a good indicator of income and consequently wealth and lifestyle
- is a good indicator of similar educational (i.e. skill and knowledge) levels
- is an important influence on a person's sense of identity.

However, this approach to social class still leaves out those who do not work, such as the extremely rich and the long-term unemployed. While such objective measures using occupation have enabled social class to be measured statistically, getting such measures right has proved to be more of a problem. The various occupational scales that have been constructed have all been criticized for failing to present a true picture of the class structure.

Scales of social class

The Registrar General's scale

This occupational scale was used by the government from 1911 until 2000 and involved the ranking of thousands of jobs into six classes based on the occupational skill of the head of household:

- Class I: Professional, e.g. accountants, doctors
- Class II: Lower managerial, professional and technical, e.g. teachers
- Class IIINM: Skilled non-manual, e.g. office workers
- Class IIIM: Skilled manual, e.g. electricians, plumbers
- Class IV: Semi-skilled manual, e.g. agricultural workers
- Class V: Unskilled manual, e.g. labourers, refuse collectors.

This scheme differentiated between middle-class occupations (non-manual jobs were allocated to classes I to IIINM) and working-class occupations (manual jobs were allocated to classes IIIM to V). The Registrar General's scheme has underpinned many important social surveys and sociological studies, particularly those focusing on class differences in educational achievement and life expectancy.

Criticisms of the Registrar General's scale

The Registrar General's scale was the main way in which class was measured in official statistics. Most sociological research conducted between 1960 and 2000 uses this classification system when differentiating between different classes. However, it does have disadvantages:

- Assessments of jobs were made by the Registrar General's own staff – Hence, there was a bias towards seeing non-manual occupations as having a higher status than manual occupations. However, as we shall see later in this chapter, Marxists argue that the working conditions of some white-collar workers, particular those found in workplaces such as call-centres, is remarkably similar to that of manual workers employed in factories.

- It failed to recognize those people who do not work – The unemployed were classified according to their last job. However, the number of never-employed unemployed has dramatically increased and undermined the idea that jobs underpin social class.
- Feminists criticized the scale as sexist – The class of everyone in a household was defined by the job of the male head of household. Women were assigned to the class of their husbands (or their fathers, if unmarried).
- It glossed over the fact that workers allocated to the same class often had widely varying access to resources such as pay and promotion.
- It failed to distinguish between the employed and self-employed – This distinction is important because evidence shows that these groups do not share similar experiences. For example the **black economy** is much more accessible to the self-employed – they can avoid paying tax and VAT by working at a cheaper rate 'for cash', which cannot be traced through their accounts, or by not fully declaring all the work they do.

The Hope-Goldthorpe scale

Sociologists were often reluctant to use government-inspired scales as they lacked sufficient sociological emphasis. In order to study **social mobility** (see Topic 5), John Goldthorpe created a more sociologically relevant scale that has proved very popular with social researchers. Goldthorpe recognized the growth of middle-class occupations – and especially the self-employed – and based his classification on the concept of **market position**, i.e. income and economic **life-chances**, such as promotion prospects, sick pay and control of hours worked. He also took account of **work** or **employment relations**, i.e. whether people are employed or self-employed, and whether they are able to exercise authority over others. The Hope-Goldthorpe scale also acknowledged that both manual and non-manual groups may share similar experiences of work and, for this reason, Goldthorpe grouped some of these together in an **intermediate class**. Instead of the basic non-manual/manual divide used by the Registrar General's scale, Goldthorpe introduced the idea of three main social divisions into which groups sharing similar market position and work relations could be placed: he referred to these as the **service class**, the intermediate class and the working class (see Table 7.2).

Goldthorpe's scale was first used in studies conducted in 1972, published in 1980. The scale more accurately reflected the nature of the British class system, but it was still based on the male head of household. He defended this position by claiming that, in most cases, the male worker still determines the market situation and lifestyle of a couple, i.e. the male is still the main breadwinner. However, many feminists remained unconvinced by this argument. They argued that scales based on the idea of a male 'head of household':

- overlook the significance of dual-career families, where the joint income of both partners can give the family an income and lifestyle of a higher class
- ignore situations where women are in a higher-grade occupation than their husbands
- overlook the significance of the increasing number of single working women and single working parents, who were classified by Goldthorpe according to the occupation of their ex-partners or fathers.

A feminist alternative: the Surrey Occupational Class Schema

This scale was developed by the feminist sociologists Arber, Dale and Gilbert (1986) in an attempt to overcome what they saw as the **patriarchal** bias inherent in the Hope-Goldthorpe scale. In this scheme, women are classified on the basis of their own occupations, whether they are married or not. The gendered nature of work in contemporary society, especially the growing service sector of the economy, is also taken into account. This is most evident in class 6 which is divided into 6a (sales and personal services – female dominated) and 6b (skilled manual – overwhelmingly male) (see Table 7.3 on p. 412).

However, the inclusion of women in such occupational classifications does present some difficulties because women's relationship to employment is generally more

Table 7.2 The Hope-Goldthorpe Scale

Service class

1. Higher professionals
   High-grade administrators; managers of large companies and large proprietors

2. Lower professionals
   Higher-grade technicians; supervisors of non-manual workers; administrators; small-business managers

Intermediate class

3. Routine non-manual (clerical and sales)

4. Small proprietors and self-employed artisans (craftspersons)

5. Lower-grade technicians and supervisors of manual workers

Working class

6. Skilled manual workers

7. Semi-skilled and unskilled manual workers

Source: Goldthorpe, J.H. (1980) *Social Mobility and Class Structure in Modern Britain*, Oxford: Clarendon Press

varied than that of men. More women work part time or occupy jobs for short periods because of pregnancy and childcare. It is, therefore, difficult to know whether the class assigned provides a meaningful insight into their life experience as a whole or whether it merely reflects a short-term or temporary experience that has little impact on lifestyle and life-chances.

A new scale for the 21st century: the National Statistics Socio-Economic Classification (NS-SEC)

The NS-SEC scale, which essentially is a variation on the Hope-Goldthorpe scale, fully replaced the Registrar General's scale for government research and statistics, and was used for the first time to classify data from the 2001 census (see Table 7.4).

Key themes

Sociological theories and methods

Indicators of social class

We can see from this topic that defining and measuring social class is a major problem for sociologists. This is because social class is an abstract social concept that needs to be operationalized. In other words, indicators of what identifies the social class of individuals must be identified. Most sociologists and civil servants faced with this problem have tended to use occupation and level of educational achievement as the indicator, although in his study of educational inequality, Boyland (cited in Gold 2003) also chose to use as his indicators receipt of free school meals alongside occupation. However, not all sociologists agree with these indicators. Goldthorpe actually acknowledges that a person's job is made up of a complex interplay of factors, while the NS-SEC (see below) focuses on a range of indicators related to work, such as authority over others, pay, autonomy over working practices and promotion potential. Finally, the debate about how to measure social class is complicated by the fact that people's subjective awareness of their class position and identity can differ from objective definitions. However, Pawson (1989) notes that, while people may be able to place themselves within class categories, these may not mean a great deal to them. Evans (1992) has demonstrated that people's attitudes towards inequality, for example, often have very little to do with their awareness of their class position.

Table 7.4 The National Statistics Socio-Economic Classification (NS-SEC)

	Occupational classification	% of working population	Examples
1	Higher managerial and professional	11.0	Company directors, senior civil servants, doctors, barristers, clergy, architects
2	Lower managerial and professional	23.5	Nurses, journalists, teachers, police officers, musicians
3	Intermediate	14.0	Secretaries, clerks, computer operators, driving instructors
4	Small employers and self-accountable workers	9.9	Taxi drivers, window cleaners, publicans, decorators
5	Lower supervisory, craft and related	9.8	Train drivers, plumbers, printers, TV engineers
6	Semi-routine	18.6	Traffic wardens, shop assistants, hairdressers, call-centre workers
7	Routine	12.7	Cleaners, couriers, road sweepers, labourers
8	Long-term unemployed or the never-worked		

Source: Rose, D. and Pevalin, D. (with K. O'Reilly) (2001) *The National Statistics Socio-economic Classification: Genesis and Overview*, London: ONS

Like the Hope-Goldthorpe scale, the NS-SEC is based on:

- employment relations – whether people are employers, self-employed or employed, and whether they exercise authority over others
- **market conditions** – salary scales, promotion prospects, sick pay, how much control people have over the hours they work, and so on.

Strengths of the NS-SEC

- It no longer divides workers exclusively along manual and non-manual lines. Some categories contain both manual and non-manual workers.
- The most significant difference between the Hope-Goldthorpe scale and the NS-SEC is the creation of Class 8, i.e. the long-term unemployed and never-employed unemployed. Some sociologists, most notably from New Right positions, have described this group of unemployed as an 'underclass' (see Topic 4, p. 438).
- Feminist arguments have been acknowledged and women are now recognized as a distinct group of wage earners. They are no longer categorized according to the occupation of their husbands or fathers.

Potential weaknesses of the NS-SEC

- The scale is still based primarily on the objective criteria of occupation. This may differ from what people understand by the term 'social class' and their subjective interpretation of their own class position.
- Those who do not have to work because of access to great wealth are still not included.
- Some argue that the scale still obscures important differences in status and earning power, e.g. headteachers are in the same category as classroom teachers.
- Some critics have suggested that ethnicity and gender may be more important in bringing about social divisions and shaping identity.

Subjective measurements of social class

Social surveys suggest there is often a discrepancy between how objective measurements of social class classify jobs and how people who actually occupy those jobs interpret their social status or class position. For example, many teachers like to describe themselves as working-class despite the fact that both the Registrar-General's classification of occupations and the NS-SEC objectively class them as middle-class. This is because many teachers have experienced upward mobility through educational qualifications from working-class origins and feel that their perspective on the world is still shaped by working-class values and experience. This subjective awareness of class position often conflicts with official objective interpretations.

Focus on research

Savage, Bagnall and Longhurst (2001)
Class identities

Mike Savage and his colleagues carried out in-depth interviews with 178 people living in four sites in and around Manchester. They identified three groups of people in terms of subjective class identity:

- First, there was a small minority of their sample who strongly identified themselves as belonging to a specific class. These were often graduates who had the cultural confidence to express their class position in an articulate fashion.
- The second group was also well educated, but did not like to identify with a particular class position. Rather, this group tended either to reject the notion of social class, because they saw themselves as individuals rather than a product of their social-class background, or they preferred to debate the nature of social class rather than acknowledge their belonging to any particular group. Some felt happier differentiating themselves from other social classes rather than focusing on their own membership of a particular social class.
- The third group, which made up the majority of the respondents, actually identified with a social class, but did so in an ambivalent, defensive and uncommitted way. Some of this group prefaced their 'belonging' with remarks such as 'I suppose I'm ...' or 'Probably, I'm ...'.

Savage and colleagues concluded that identification with the concepts of 'working class' and 'middle class' for this part of their sample was based on a simple desire to be seen as normal and ordinary, rather than any burning desire to be flag-wavers for their class. They conclude that, in general, the notion of class identity was 'relatively muted'.

Savage, M., Bagnall, G. and Longhurst, B. (2001) 'Ordinary, ambivalent and defensive class identities in the North West of England', *Sociology*, 35(4),

1 Suggest reasons why Savage's research team used in-depth interviews in this study.

2 Explain how the findings of Savage and colleagues led them to conclude that class identity is 'relatively muted' (i.e. unclear, muffled).

More important, it is the subjective interpretation of class position that is responsible for the sharp boundary lines that exist between the social classes in the UK. In other words, there is some evidence (which will be explored in more detail in later sections) that those people who interpret themselves as 'working-class', 'middle-class' and 'upper-class' have very clear ideas about what characteristics people who 'belong' to their class should have. Moreover, they tend to have very strong views about the characteristics of other social classes. These subjective interpretations may have little or nothing in common with official and objective attempts to construct broad socioeconomic classifications based on employment. Reay (1998) agrees with these observations and argues that class analysis should move away from the large-scale quantitative analyses of the past based on occupational classifications. He suggests that small-scale **ethnographic** studies of how class is 'lived' and experienced alongside gender and ethnicity may give us greater insight into class position and inequality.

Studies of subjective class identities confirm Reay's observation. Marshall *et al.* (1988) found that 53 per cent of their sample saw themselves as 'working-class' despite the fact that the majority of their sample were in white-collar, non-manual jobs. However, Savage *et al.* (2001) are not convinced that identification with such class categories has any real meaning beyond the need to feel normal and ordinary. They argue that people identify with the term 'middle-class' because they see it as the least **loaded** of the terms offered to them by sociologists. In fact, Savage and colleagues argue that, by saying they are middle-class, people are actually saying they are typical,

ordinary people, who are neither particularly well off nor particularly badly off. Bradley (1999) notes, too, that when people identify themselves as working-class, this does not involve a strong sense of group or collective loyalty or attachment to traditional working-class institutions such as trade unions. Again, it is more likely to indicate a claim to be an ordinary and typical working person. In other words, subjective interpretations of social class may have very little to do with the characteristics allocated to social class by objective official classifications.

Activities

Research ideas

1   Imagine you are conducting sociological research on social class at a horse-racing track or a cricket match, using observation only – you are not allowed to distribute questionnaires or conduct interviews. What sorts of things might you listen or look out for that might give you clues as to a person's social class?

2   Undertake a piece of research using a structured interview to measure the class distribution of students on various school or college post-16 courses. Pilot it with a random sample of ten students across the institution. After each interview write down any issues that may affect the validity, representativeness or reliability of the evidence gathered.
    For example:

    ● Did respondents understand the questions, answer truthfully or exaggerate aspects of lifestyle/income?
    ● Did they find the questions too intrusive or personal? Were they confused by the terminology you used?
    ● Identify the main problems you encountered in trying to operationalize social class.
    ● Did you note any differences between people's subjective interpretations of their social class position and how the NS-SEC ranks them?
    ● What, if any, conclusions can you draw from your findings?

Web.task

1   Search the worldwide web to find out about the caste system in India. How did it work and how influential is it today? Does it have influence in the UK?

2   Use a careers service on the worldwide web – such as www.prospects.ac.uk – to compare occupations in different social classes. Find out about pay, working conditions and the skills and qualifications needed. Can these explain differences in their position on social-class scales?

Check your understanding

1   What is the difference between social differentiation and social stratification?

2   Why might those at the bottom of the caste system accept their lot?

3   What determined a person's position in the hierarchy in the feudal estate system?

4   Why are most modern societies more open than most traditional societies?

5   Why is occupation considered to be the most defining characteristic for the measurement of social class?

6   What problems are created by using occupation as the key indicator of social class?

7   What were the strengths and weaknesses of each of the scales used before 2000?

8   How does the NS-SEC scale address the weaknesses of the other scales?

9   How might the NS-SEC scale still be said to be lacking?

Key terms

Achieved status the degree of social honour and prestige accorded to a person or group because of their achievements or other merits.

Ascribed status the degree of social honour and prestige accorded a person or group because of their origin or inherited characteristics.

Black economy illegal ways of increasing income.

Caste system Hindu system of stratification, now officially banned in India but still influential.

Closed societies societies with no social mobility.

Differentiation perceived social differences between people, e.g. along lines of gender, age or race.

Employment relations see 'Work relations'.

Ethnographic research which focuses on the everyday life of the group being studied, usually using observation and/or unstructured interviews.

Feudal estate system stratification system of medieval Europe.

Intermediate class according to Goldthorpe, a lower grouping of the middle class containing those with poorer work and market situations than the service class, e.g. clerical workers.

Life-chances opportunities for achieving things that provide a high quality of life, such as good housing, health and education.

Loaded questions that suggest or encourage a particular answer.

Market position or conditions income and economic life-chances, such as promotion prospects, sick pay, and control over hours worked and how work is done.

Material physical, often economic, things such as money and consumer goods.

Meritocratic rewarding hard work or talent, rather than inherited wealth or position.

Open societies societies with a high degree of social mobility, where status is usually allocated on the basis of achievement and merit.

Operationalize define something in such a way that it can be measured.

Patriarchal male-dominated.

Service class according to Goldthorpe, those with the highest work and market

situations: the upper-middle class, e.g. large proprietors as well as administrators, managers and professionals.

Social class hierarchically arranged groups in modern industrial societies based on similarities in status, wealth, income and occupation.

Social mobility the movement of individuals up or down the social scale.

Social status degree of social honour, prestige and importance accorded to a person or group.

Social stratification the hierarchical layering of a society into distinct groups with different levels of wealth, status and power.

Work relations whether people are employed or self-employed, and are able to exercise authority over others.

An eye on the exam — Defining and measuring social class

Item A

Both the Registrar-General's and Goldthorpe's class schemes have been useful in highlighting class-based inequalities, such as those related to health and education, as well as reflecting class-based dimensions in voting patterns, political outlooks and general social attitudes. However, such schemes suffer from several significant limitations.

Occupational class schemes are difficult to apply to the economically inactive. Such schemes are also unable to reflect the importance of property ownership and wealth to social class. The rapid economic transformations occurring in industrial societies have made the measurement of class even more problematic. New categories of occupations are emerging; there has been a general shift away from factory production towards service and knowledge work, and an enormous number of women have entered the workforce in recent decades.

Adapted from Giddens, A. (2001) *Sociology*, Cambridge: *Polity Press*, pp. 288–90

Using material from **Item A** and elsewhere, examine some of the problems involved in operationalizing the idea of social class.

(12 marks)

Grade booster — Getting top marks in this question

First, explain what it means to 'operationalize' a concept – i.e. define it so that it can be measured. Focus on the problems of operationalizing social class – don't write about the advantages of different ways of doing so. Make use of material from the Item to help you identify some of these problems. For example, what does 'the economically active' mean and which groups does it refer to? Does the increase in women working mean we may have to classify husbands' and wives' class positions separately? Might the changes in the nature of occupations also cause problems of classification? Item A is about occupational schemes, but you can also talk about the problems of operationalizing property or status based on ideas of class. You can also consider the problems of trying to use subjective rather than objective classifications of class.

TOPIC 2

Theories of stratification

Getting you thinking

Look at the photo of a richer and a poorer person.

1 Using your knowledge of sociological theory, suggest how the following perspectives might explain the relative class position of the people in the picture:

    (a) Marxism

    (b) functionalism.

2 What do you think are the advantages and disadvantages for societies of having:

    (a) a high level of social inequality?

    (b) a low level of inequality?

In the broadest terms, you may have been able to work out that Marxists explain class differences in terms of exploitation – the rich owners of large businesses pay as little as possible to their workers, while benefiting from the existence of a group of poor and unemployed people, who help keep the general level of wages low and who can do some low-paid work when necessary. For functionalists, however, inequality can actually benefit society by motivating people to work hard and fulfil their potential. It is this latter view that we consider first.

Functionalism

The founding father of functionalism, Emile Durkheim (1858–1917), argued that class stratification existed because it was functional or beneficial to social order. He saw modern societies as characterized by a specialized occupational **division of labour**, in which people have very different jobs, skills and abilities. Some of these jobs are more beneficial to society than others. Consequently, they attract more rewards. This is the origin of social divisions. However, Durkheim argued that members of society are happy to take their place within this division of labour because they believe in its moral worth, i.e. there is common agreement or consensus about how society and its institutions, such as work, should be organized. This **value consensus** also means that members of society accept that stratification, and therefore inequality, are good for society. They consequently accept that occupations should be graded in terms of their value to society and that those occupying the more functional or valued positions should receive greater rewards for their

efforts. Durkheim, therefore, saw the stratification system as a moral classification system embodying and reflecting common values and beliefs.

He also argued that stratification is beneficial because it sets limits on competition and people's **aspirations**, in that it clearly links criteria such as skills and qualifications to particular roles so that people do not become overly ambitious and therefore disappointed and resentful if they fail or don't do as well as they had hoped. Rather, because the system is regarded as fair and just, members of society are relatively contented with their lot, and thus social order is the norm.

Durkheim did acknowledge some potential problems with this system that might cause conflict and, therefore, possible breakdown in social order. He noted that if people are unable to compete freely for jobs or roles – if they are forced into certain types of work – then moral consensus and solidarity could break down. Durkheim believed that ascription (the arrangement whereby roles are allocated on the basis of fixed inherited criteria such as gender and ethnicity) could lead to conflict because those allocated to particular roles or jobs would have had no choice in the matter. On the other hand, Durkheim believed that the possibility of acquiring skills and qualifications, which is normally found in open societies, gave people an element of choice and so reaffirmed their moral commitment to society. However, he also believed that this moral order could be disturbed by sudden shifts in a society, such as economic recession or the accumulation of too much power in the hands of one individual or group, because these shifts could destabilize what people expected from the stratification system. For example:

- Recession could lead to a rapid and sudden rise in unemployment and deflation in wages.
- A dictatorship could lead to people being put into functionally important and highly rewarded roles on the basis of **patronage** rather than ability, thus fuelling resentment and potential conflict.

Talcott Parsons (1902–79) saw stratification as a ranking system based on moral evaluation – that is, based on respect, prestige, social honour, social approval and disapproval. He argued that modern class stratification reflects a **normative** consensus about what society values. For example, with regard to kinship, society agrees that parents should have more status than children. Society also values personal qualities such as beauty and intelligence, achievement such as qualifications and skills, and possessions such as consumer goods and designer labels. We also look up to authority (the ability to influence others because of a particular status, e.g. we all obey our doctor's orders) and power (the ability of some people to get their way regardless of resistance).

Parsons noted that achievement and skills are the most highly valued qualities in contemporary Western societies. Parsons argues that stratification is therefore the outcome of general agreement in society about how jobs should be ranked in terms of their functional importance or value to society. Those most highly valued are consequently more highly rewarded. As Bottero notes (2005):

<< People have little choice but to accept the general value placed on the different positions in a hierarchy. They may not like it, but – if they want to get on – they have to live with it and play by the rules. >> (p.49)

Durkheim's and Parson's theories of stratification were built upon by Davis and Moore in the 1950s. Table 7.5 below outlines both their views and those of their critics.

Is stratification really good for society?

A similar view to that of Davis and Moore has been proposed by the New Right thinker, Peter Saunders (1996). He points out that economic growth has raised the standard of living for all members of society, and social inequality is thus a small price to pay for society as a whole becoming more prosperous. Saunders is influenced by Hayek (1944), who argued that capitalism is a dynamic system that continually raises everybody's standards of living, so the poor in society today are much better off than they were in the past. Moreover, **capitalist societies** offer incentives to those with talent and enterprise in the form of material wealth. If these incentives did not exist, Saunders argues, then many of the consumer goods that we take for granted today, such as cars, ballpoint pens, computers and iPods, would not exist, because talented people would not have been motivated to produce them. However, this perspective, like functionalism, downplays the argument that the social and economic inequality may create resentment and dissatisfaction that could lead to deviance, disaffection and social disorder.

Marxism

According to Marx (1818–83), the driving force of virtually all societies is the conflict between the rich and powerful minority who control the society, and the powerless and

Table 7.5 The functionalist theory of stratification	
Davis and Moore (1955)	**Criticisms**
All societies have to ensure that their most important positions are filled with the most talented people. They therefore need to offer such people high rewards.	Does this really happen? Lots of occupations can be seen to be essential to the smooth running of society but are not highly rewarded, such as nurses. There are also plenty of idiots in high places!
Class societies are meritocracies – high rewards in the form of income and status are guaranteed in order to motivate gifted people to make the necessary sacrifices in terms of education and training. Educational qualifications (and hence the stratification system) function to allocate all individuals to an occupational role that suits their abilities. People's class position is a fair reflection of their talents.	Some groups may be able to use economic and political power to increase their rewards against the will of the majority. High rewards sometimes go to people who play no functionally important roles but who simply live off the interest generated by their wealth. Do the three to five years of training at college and/or university merit a lifetime of enhanced income and status? Isn't higher education a privilege in itself?
Most people agree that stratification is necessary because they accept the meritocratic principles on which society is based.	There is a substantial level of resentment about the unequal distribution of income and wealth, as illustrated by the controversy over 'fat-cat' levels of pay. Unequal rewards may be the product of inequalities in power.
Stratification encourages all members of society to work to the best of their ability. For example, those at the top will wish to retain their advantages whilst those placed elsewhere will wish to improve on their position.	The **dysfunctions** of stratification are neglected by Davis and Moore. For example, poverty is a major problem for people and negatively impacts on mortality, health, education and family life.

poor majority who survive only by working for the rich and powerful. These two classes are always in conflict as it is in the interests of the rich to spend as little as possible in paying their workers.

Causes of conflict

The heart of this class conflict is the system of producing goods and services – what Marx called the **mode of production**. This is made up of two things:

- the **means of production** – the resources needed to produce goods, such as capital (money for investment), land, factories, machinery and raw materials
- the social **relations of production** – the ways in which people are organized to make things, i.e. the way in which roles and responsibilities are allocated among those involved in production.

Marx described modern Western societies as capitalist societies and suggested that such societies consist of two main classes:

- the **bourgeoisie** – the capitalist or ruling class, who own the means of production; they are the owners or, today, the large shareholders in businesses, and control decisions about employment, new investment, new products, and so on.
- the **proletariat** – the working or subordinate class, who sell their ability to work (labour power) to the bourgeoisie; most people make a living by working for a profit-making business, but they have no say in business decisions or how they are put to work, and rely on the success of the company they work for.

Marx argued that the social relations of production between the bourgeoisie and proletariat are unequal, exploitative and create class conflict. Capitalism's relentless pursuit of profit means that wages are kept as low as possible and the bourgeoisie pockets the difference between what they pay their workers and the value of the goods produced by workers. This '**surplus value**' forms the basis of their great wealth. Moreover, workers lose control over their jobs as new technology is introduced in order to increase output and therefore profits. Workers become **alienated** by this process and are united by a shared exploitative class experience. This common class experience means that the working class is a **class-in-itself**.

So, according to Marx, capitalism is a pretty dreadful kind of society. However, if this is the case, why do most people happily accept it – even believing it to be superior to other kinds of societies? Marx had an answer for this, too. Workers very rarely see themselves as exploited because they have been 'duped' by **ideological apparatuses**, such as education and the media, into believing that capitalism is fair and natural. The working class are consequently 'suffering' from **false class consciousness**.

Marx believed that the conflict inherent in the capitalist system would come to a head, because the increasing concentration of wealth would cause the gap between rich and poor to grow and grow, i.e. to become **polarized**, so that even the most short-sighted members of the proletariat would see that the time for change had come.

Marx predicted that, eventually, the proletariat would unite, overthrow the bourgeoisie, seize the means of production for themselves and establish a fairer, more equal society – known as **communism**. For Marx, then, radical social change was inevitable as the working class was transformed from a class-in-itself into a revolutionary **class-for-itself**.

Evaluation of Marx

Marx's ideas have probably been more influential than those of any other political thinker and have had a huge impact in the 20th century. They inspired communist revolutions in many countries, such as China and Russia. However, his ideas have also come in for a great deal of criticism, especially since the communist regimes of Eastern Europe crumbled in the 1990s.

- Marx is accused of being an economic **determinist** or **reductionist**, in that all his major ideas are based on the economic relationship between the bourgeoisie and proletariat. However, many contemporary conflicts, such as those rooted in nationalism, ethnicity and gender, cannot be explained adequately in economic terms.
- Marx is criticized for underestimating the importance of the middle classes. He did recognize a third (in his view, relatively minor, class) made up of professional workers, shopkeepers and clerks, which he called the **petit-bourgeoisie**. However, being outside the system of production, they were deemed unimportant to the class struggle. In his view, as the two major camps polarized, members of this class would realign their interests accordingly with either one. Some **neo-Marxists** have argued that the upper middle class have aligned themselves with the bourgeoisie in that they act as agents for that class in their role of managers and professionals – in other words, the service class 'service' their employers by managing their businesses. Other Marxists, most notably Braverman (1974), argue that white-collar workers have more in common in terms of their working conditions with the proletariat. These issues are explored further in Topics 3 to 5.
- In particular, Marx's prediction that the working class would become 'class conscious' because they would experience extreme misery and poverty, and therefore seek to transform the capitalist system, has not occurred. As we saw in Topic 1, the class identity of working-class people today is probably limited. Most people who see themselves as working-class do so not because they recognize their exploited status but because they wish to claim their typicality in terms of being working people. Furthermore, although Western capitalist societies may have problems such as poverty and homelessness, they do have a reasonably good record in terms of democracy and workers' rights. Moreover, the living standards of the working class have risen. It may be, then, that working-class people are sensibly reconciled to capitalism rather than being 'falsely conscious'. In other words, they appreciate the benefits of capitalism despite being aware of the inequalities generated by it.

Neo-Marxism

Neo-Marxists have tended to focus on the relationship between the **infrastructure** (i.e. the capitalist economy and particularly the social relationships of production characterized by class inequality, exploitation and subordination) and the **superstructure** (i.e. all the major social institutions of society, such as education, the mass media, religion, the law and the political system). Neo-Marxists argue that the function of the superstructure is the reproduction and legitimation of the class inequality found in the infrastructure. In other words, the superstructure exists to transmit ruling-class **ideology** and, in particular, to make sure that the mass of society subscribes to ruling-class ideas about how society should be organized and does not complain too much about the inequality that exists, e.g. in income and wealth. The function of the superstructure, therefore, is to encourage acceptance of class stratification and to ensure that false class consciousness continues among the working class.

Education is seen by neo-Marxists as a particularly important ideological apparatus working on behalf of the capitalist class. Marxists, such as Althusser (1971), suggest that education transmits the idea that capitalist society is a meritocracy – i.e. that ability is the major mechanism of success. However, this disguises the reality of the stratification system: that those born into ruling- or middle-class backgrounds are much more likely to achieve, because what goes on in the educational system, in terms of both the academic and **hidden curriculum**, is the product of bourgeoise values. The **cultural capital** of the children of the upper and middle class (along with the material advantages they enjoy, such as private education) ensure that class inequality is reproduced in the next generation. The children of the working class, on the other hand, lack this cultural capital and so are condemned to a life of manual work, as they are ejected from the educational system at the age of 16. However, these working-class children rarely blame the capitalist system for their 'failure'. Rather, the ideology of meritocracy ensures that they blame themselves, with the consequence that the working class rarely challenge the organization of capitalism or see stratification and inequality as a problem.

Other neo-Marxists have focused on the ideological power of the mass media and how the bourgeoisie might be using this to their advantage. The Frankfurt School of Marxists, for example, writing since the 1930s, have focused on the role of the media in creating a popular culture for the masses that has diverted working-class attention away from the unequal nature of capitalism towards consumerism, celebrity culture and trivia. Marcuse (1964), for example, noted that capitalism has been very successful in bedazzling the working class with what he saw as 'false needs' to buy the latest consumer goods. Neo-Marxists argue that the latest soap storylines, and the lifestyles of the rich and famous, are now given more priority by the media, especially the tabloid newspapers and commercial television, than political and economic life. As Lawrence Friedman (1999) argues, the lifestyle of the rich and famous is now the modern **opium** of the masses.

Consequently, the mass of society is now less knowledgeable about how society is politically and economically organized. The result of this ideological barrage is that the working class is less united than ever, as people compete with each other for the latest material goods. As a result, stratification and class inequality are rarely challenged. This has led to Reiner (2007) arguing that the 'class war' has been won to devastating effect by the capitalist class.

However, in criticism of neo-Marxism, Saunders (1990) argues that such writers suffer from the same two problems:

● How is it that they know the truth when it is hidden from everybody else? The answer, says Saunders, smacks of arrogance. He points out rather sarcastically

---

Key themes

Socialization, culture and identity

Education and the mass media

It is worth thinking through the roles of agencies such as the mass media and education with regard to stratification. Functionalist theories stress the central role of value consensus and agencies of socialization in preparing people to take their role voluntarily in the specialized division of labour and to accept that the organization of this system benefits all sections of society. Education obviously plays a major positive role in this process by socializing us into key values, such as achievement, competition and individualism. The mass media reaffirm our commitment to a meritocratic society by positively reporting on individual success and by celebrating values such as wealth, hard work and equal opportunity.

Marxists, on the other hand, argue that conflict and inequality lie at the heart of a deeply divisive capitalist society. They see agencies such as education and the mass media functioning in an ideological way to convince those groups at the bottom of the socio-economic order that inequality is fair, just and deserved. Both education through the hidden curriculum and the mass media (by stressing entertainment at the expense of serious news) work to hide the real facts of inequality in capitalist societies from the working class. See Chapter 3, pp. 134–42, for a more detailed discussion of ideology and the media.

Sociologists who have been influenced by Weber generally agree with this Marxist analysis.

Feminists who argue that women generally occupy a lower status position than men, even when occupying the same class position, often complain that both education and media generally operate in favour of males. See Chapter 3, pp. 178–85, for a more detailed discussion of the media and gender.

Finally, postmodernists see both education and especially the globalization of mass media as partly responsible for the death of social class as a primary source of identity. Postmodernists argue that education and mass media have made many more choices available to us and consequently our identities are a mixture of different influences.

'Marxists know the true situation because Marxist theory is true' (p.19).

- Marxist theory does have the unfortunate habit of dismissing what working-class people say and think about their situation as the product of ideology and false class consciousness. As Parkin (1972) notes, there is a haughty assumption in Marxist ideology theory that the working class cannot ever appreciate the reality of their situation because they are experiencing a kind of collective brain damage.

Max Weber

Another classical theorist, Max Weber (1864–1920), disagreed with Marx's view on the inevitability of class conflict. Weber also rejected the Marxist emphasis on the economic dimension as the sole determinant of inequality. Weber (1947) saw 'class' (economic relationships) and 'status' (perceived social standing) as two separate but related sources of power that have overlapping effects on people's life-chances. He also recognized what he called **'party'** as a further dimension. By this, he meant the political influence or power an individual might exercise through membership of pressure groups, trade unions or other organized interest groups. However, he did see class as the most important of these three interlinking factors.

Like Marx, Weber saw classes as economic categories organized around property ownership, but argued that the concept should be extended to include 'occupational skill' because this created differences in life-chances (income, opportunities, lifestyles and general prospects) among those groups that did not own the means of production, namely the middle class and the working class. In other words, if we examine these two social classes, we will find status differences within them. For example, professionals are regarded more highly than white-collar workers, whilst skilled manual workers are regarded more highly than unskilled workers or the long-term unemployed. These differences in status lead directly to differences in life-chances and therefore inequality.

The significance of status in inequality

People who occupy high occupational roles generally have high social status, but status can also derive from other sources of power such as gender, race and religion. Weber noted that status was also linked to consumption styles (how people spend their money). For example, some people derive status from conspicuous consumption – e.g. from being seen to buy expensive designer products. This idea has been taken further by postmodernists, who suggest that in the 21st century, consumption and style rather than social class will be the biggest influence on shaping people's identity.

Weber defined social classes as clusters of occupations with similar life-chances and patterns of mobility (people's opportunities to move up or down the occupational ladder). On this basis, he identified four distinct social classes:

1. those privileged through property or education
2. the petty-bourgeoisie (the self-employed, managers)
3. white-collar workers and technicians (the lower middle class)
4. manual workers (the working class).

Weber's ideas have influenced the way in which social class is operationalized by sociologists such as Goldthorpe (1980) and by the government through the recent NS-SEC scale – see Topic 1. Goldthorpe's concepts of market situation and work relations are based on the notion that status differences (and, therefore, life-chances) exist between particular occupational groups.

Weber was sceptical about the possibility of the working class banding together for revolutionary purposes – i.e. becoming class conscious – because differences in status would always undermine any common cause. Social classes were too internally differentiated, and this undermined any potential for group identity and common action.

The concept of 'status groups' rather than social classes is central to Weber's theory of stratification. Weber noted that people often make positive and negative judgements about other people's standing and esteem, and these can affect a person's life-chances. These judgements tend to focus on qualities which are shared by groups. Therefore, we might make judgements about people's education ('they are brilliant' or 'thick'; 'they went to university'), their religion ('they are extremists' or 'they treat women negatively'), their age ('they cannot cope with responsibility'), their ethnicity ('they are all muggers or drug users'), their gender ('they are too emotional') and even their bodies ('they are too thin, too fat, ugly, beautiful'). Status groups, then, are those who share the same status position, as well as a common awareness of how they differ from other status groups. In other words, their identity is bound up with their exclusiveness as a group, and this will shape their lifestyle in terms of how they interact with others – for instance, they may only socialize with people like themselves.

Evaluation of Weber

Class, status and wealth

Marxists argue that Weber neglected the basic split between capitalists and workers, and argue that class and status are strongly linked – after all, the capitalist class has wealth, high status and political power. Weber recognized that these overlap, but suggested that a person can have wealth but little status – like a lottery winner, perhaps – or, conversely, high status but little wealth – such as a church minister. He suggested that it is very rare that high-status groups allow wealth alone to be sufficient grounds for entry into their status group. He noted that such groups may exclude wealthy individuals because they lack the 'right' breeding, schooling, manners, culture, etc. This practice of 'social closure' will be explored in more depth in later topics. Conversely, someone may be accepted as having high status by the wealthy, despite being relatively poor in comparison, such as the aristocrat who has fallen on hard times. Weber rightly points out that high status and political power can sometimes be achieved without great economic resources.

Party

Party or power plays a role in this too. Weber saw this third type of inequality as deriving from membership of any formal or informal association that sets out to achieve particular goals. Such associations might include political parties, trade unions, the freemasons, old boy networks and even sports clubs. Membership of these can influence the social status a person has in the community. For example, membership of the freemasons might increase a person's potential to make social and business contacts, and, therefore, their wealth, whilst many middle-class men may be keen to join the local golf club because of the prestige that such membership may confer on them.

Gender and ethnicity

Weber's analysis helps explain why some groups may share economic circumstances but have more or less status than others, for example, due to gender or ethnic differences. Weber saw gender and ethnicity as status differences which have separate and distinct effects on life-chances compared with social class. In other words, the working class might have less status than the middle class, but working-class Black people and working-class women may have less status than working-class White men.

Status and identity

However, Savage *et al.* (2001) take issue with the importance of 'status' in terms of shaping people's identity or giving us insight into the nature of inequality. Savage notes that people rarely make status claims, and suggests that they are wary of 'appearing to demonstrate openly their cultural superiority'. Savage's research suggests that people are more concerned with stressing how ordinary or how mainstream they are. Very few social groups assert that they are a special case. However, Savage does acknowledge that as a general rule, class, status and party do go together. As Bottero (2005) notes:

> ≪ The rich tend to be powerful, the powerful to be wealthy, and access to high-status social circles tends to accompany both. ≫ (p.41)

Conflict and stability

Bottero concludes that Weber provides an adaptable 'history-proof' model of stratification which may be more valid than Marxism in analyzing the variety of stratification arrangements that exist across the world. However, she notes that both Marx and Weber fail to explain why societies organized around conflict or difference are so stable, orderly and reasonably free of major conflict between the social groups who occupy them.

Interpretive sociology

Most of the accounts that we have examined – especially functionalism and Marxism – are **structural theories**. This type of stratification theory is often accused of over-determinism: reducing all human behaviour to a reaction

Gate Gourmet supplies in-flight meals for airlines. Its workers went on strike in August 2005, disrupting British Airways flights. Many of its workers at Heathrow Airport are from ethnic minorities – in particular, the West London Sikh community. Discuss the Gate Gourmet workers in terms of Weber's categories of class, status and party.

to either social or economic structure, and presenting people as puppets of society, unable to exercise any choice over their destiny. Interpretivist sociologists suggest that the social actions of individuals are more important than the social structure of society. Interpretivists argue that how people subjectively view the world and their place in it is important because such interpretations make us aware that we have choices in how we behave. For example, we might decide that our ethnicity is more important to us than our social class and act accordingly.

However, Bottero notes that this focus on **agency** or action assumes that social life is patternless. She argues that interpretivists often ignore the very real constraints on people's behaviour caused by structured social inequalities in income, wealth, education, ethnicity, gender, etc. She notes that the organization of society still sets 'substantial limits on choice and agency for all and creates situations in which some are more free to act than others' (p.56). She notes that Marx recognized the role of choice and agency when he stated that 'men make their own history', but he also recognized that social structure shaped action when he said that 'they do not make it under circumstances chosen by themselves'.

Giddens and structuration

Giddens (1973) attempted to combine structure and action in his theory of structuration, in which he argued that individuals create structural forces, such as social class, by engaging in particular actions. For example, he noted that class advantages can be passed on to the younger generations through family interaction. He also noted that consensus about the status or standing of occupations, as well as our acceptance that some people have the authority to tell us what to do at work, creates a hierarchy of occupations and, therefore, a stratification system based on social class. Giddens also notes that we judge people by the type of house or area they live in, by the car they drive, by the clothes or logos they wear, by the consumer goods they buy. He argues that this consensus about consumption also contributes to stratification and therefore inequality.

Key terms

Agency social action.

Aspirations ambitions.

Alienation lack of fulfilment from work.

Bourgeoisie the ruling class in capitalist society.

Capitalist societies societies based on private ownership of the means of production, such as Britain and the USA.

Class-for-itself a social class that is conscious of its exploited position and wishes to change its situation.

Class-in-itself a social group that shares similar experiences.

Communism system based on communal ownership of the means of production.

Cultural capital attitudes, ways of thinking, knowledge, skills, etc., learnt in middle-class homes that give middle-class children advantages in education.

Determinist or reductionist the view that phenomena can be explained with reference to one key factor.

Division of labour the way the job system is organized.

Dysfunctions the negative effects of social actions, institutions and structures.

False class consciousness where the proletariat see the society in a way that suits the ruling class and so pose no threat to them.

Grand narratives postmodernist term for big structural theories, such as functionalism and Marxism.

Hidden curriculum the rules and regulations that underpin schooling in order to produce conformity.

Ideological apparatuses social institutions that benefit the ruling class by spreading the ideas that help maintain the system in their interests, e.g. the mass media, education system.

Ideology set of beliefs underpinning any way of life or political structure. Used by Marxists and neo-Marxists to refer specifically to the way powerful groups justify their position.

Infrastructure in a Marxist sense, the capitalist economic system that is characterized by class inequality.

Means of production the material forces that enable things to be produced, e.g. factories, machinery and land.

Mode of production economic base of society that constitutes the entire system involved in the production of goods.

Neo-Marxists those who have adapted Marx's views.

Normative accepted by all, taken for granted.

Opium a popular drug of the 19th century that supposedly helped people forget their troubles.

Party term used by Weber to describe political influence.

Patronage giving jobs or positions of power/privilege to reward loyalty or membership of kinship or political groups.

Petit-bourgeoisie term used by Marx to describe the small middle class sandwiched between the proletariat and bourgeoisie.

Polarization at opposite ends of the spectrum.

Proletariat the working class in capitalist societies.

Relations of production the allocation of roles and responsibilities among those involved in production.

Structural theory those explanations that generally see the organization of society as more important than individual actions.

Superstructure social institutions such as education, mass media, religion, which function to transmit ruling-class ideology.

Surplus value term used by Marx to describe the profit created by the work of the proletariat but taken by capitalists.

Value consensus moral agreement.

However, in 1990, Giddens decided social class was no longer as significant as it had been in the past. Rather, he argued that the major social division in society was between the employed and the unemployed or socially excluded. Social class inequalities no longer constrained the activities and lifestyle of a whole mass of people such as the working class or poor – it was now individuals and families that experienced constraints and opportunities. Moreover, Giddens set himself on the postmodernist road when he argued that lifestyle and taste were now more significant than social class in the construction of identity.

Postmodernism

Postmodernists reject what they see as the **grand narratives** of the stratification theories discussed so far. They focus instead on the concepts of 'identity' and 'difference'. They argue that the increasing diversity and plurality found in postmodern social life has led to the break-up of collective social identity, and especially class identity. It is argued that the group categories of 'social class', 'ethnicity', and 'gender' no longer exist in an homogeneous form. Subjective individual identity is now more important than objective collective identity. Best (2005) argues that, for postmodernists, 'the problem of identity is one of avoiding a fixed identity and keeping one's options open, avoiding long-term commitments, consistency and devotion'.

Check your understanding

1. Why is social stratification acceptable, according to Durkheim?

2. In what circumstances might stratification be dysfunctional to society, according to Durkheim?

3. Why, according to Davis and Moore, do some people deserve more rewards than others?

4. Why do functionalists like Davis and Moore see social stratification as good for society?

5. What, according to Marx, determines a person's social class?

6. What is false class consciousness and how does it aid stratification?

7. Marx is accused of being an economic reductionist – what does this mean?

8. What is the role of the superstructure with regard to stratification?

9. What three sources of inequality does Weber identify as important in modern societies?

10. How does the concept of status help explain gender and ethnic differences?

11. How do postmodernists view class identity?

Postmodernists, such as Waters (1995), argue that social class is in terminal decline as a source of identity and that consumption – how we spend our money – is now central in terms of how we organize our daily lives. As Best notes, 'we are all cast into the roles of consumers'. Postmodernists argue that increasing affluence and standards of living have led to individuals being faced with a variety of consumer choices about their lifestyle rather than being forced into particular forms of cultural behaviour by forces beyond their social control, such as social class. In particular, they argue that people now use a variety of influences, particularly those stemming from globalization and popular mass media culture, to construct personal identity. For example, Waters suggests that, as a result, postmodern stratification and inequality are about lifestyle choices, fragmented association (we never belong to or identify with one group for very long), being seduced into conspicuous consumption by advertising, and constant change in terms of what we are supposed to be interested in, the choices available to us and how we are supposed to feel.

Topic 3 examines social class and its relationship to future life-chances and identity and, consequently, it is recommended that you use the evidence from that section to judge the validity of this postmodernist view of the influence of social class.

Activities

Research idea

Conduct a piece of research to discover how young people explain inequality. Design an interview schedule to assess the ways in which your sample explain inequality. Do they take a functionalist position and see inequality as beneficial, motivating and meritocratic? Alternatively, do they agree with Marxists that inequality is damaging, unfair and demotivating?

Web.task

Go to the following sites and investigate the writings on class of the classical sociologists:

- www.intute.ac.uk/socialsciences/sociology/ – use the search engine on this marvellous site to access archives on Durkheim and Marx as well as Verstehen – Max Weber's Home Page
- www.anu.edu.au/polsci/marx/marx.htm – an Australian website with some excellent materials on Marx.

An eye on the exam Theories of stratification

Item A

The Marxian analysis revolves around the concept of class, and Marx's great insight was to see the exploitation of the working class by the factory owners as the determining factor in social division. People's behaviour is determined by the class grouping in which they find themselves.

According to Marxian analysis, the state is an institution that helps to organize capitalist society in the best interests of the bourgeoisie. The legitimacy of the capitalist system is maintained by ideology; working-class people are victims of a false consciousness. In other words, working-class people are said to hold values, ideas and beliefs about the nature of inequality that are not in their own economic interests to hold. Working-class people have their ideas manipulated by the media, schools and religion, for example, and regard economic inequality as fair and just.

Adapted from Best, S. (2005) *Understanding Social Divisions*, London: Sage, p.14

Assess the usefulness of the Marxist view of stratification (**Item A**).   (21 marks)

Grade booster Getting top marks in this question

You could begin by summarizing the key features of the Marxist view. Make use of material from the Item to get you started on issues such as exploitation, economic determinism, ruling-class ideology and the state. You should also mention key ideas such as the two-class model, class conflict and revolution. Remember that, for this question, you need to show your evaluation skills, and not just your knowledge. You could do this by drawing on alternative theories of stratification such as Weber, feminism and postmodernism. Consider issues such as non-class aspects of stratification (gender, ethnicity, status, power, etc.) and how far these overlap with, or cut across, class divisions; the question of how many classes there are; whether Marx's two classes have fragmented; and whether revolution is inevitable.

TOPIC 3

Life-chances and social class

Getting you thinking

GIVENCHY

1 Look at the photographs. How do they show that consumption and lifestyle may be becoming increasingly important as sources of identity?

2 How available are the lifestyle choices illustrated here to all social groups? Who may be denied access and why?

You may have concluded from the exercise above that **consumption**, especially of designer goods and labels, is increasingly important to lifestyle in 21st-century Britain. As we saw in Topic 2, some sociologists have seen these trends as evidence that the UK is no longer a class society, and that our occupational status and the market rewards attached to it are no longer the main source of identity and inequality today. Rather, these sociologists note that social divisions such as those between neighbourhoods, regions and ethnic groups, are now far more important. Other sociologists do not accept the validity of this picture of the United Kingdom. They argue instead that, although the nature of social class in the UK is changing, it is still the most important influence on all aspects of our lives.

Social exclusion and inclusion

Savage (2000) argues that since 1979, when it suffered the first of four successive election defeats, the Labour party has deliberately avoided talking about class and has focused instead on the concept of '**social exclusion**'. Consequently, political debate has focused on the idea that groups such as the long-term unemployed, single mothers

and the residents of socially deprived areas are somehow excluded from the living standards that most of us take for granted. In response, social policy has been devised in the fields of education, training and welfare with the concept of '**social inclusion**' in mind – that is, it has aimed to target these groups so that they can become part of mainstream society again.

However, Savage argues that the concepts of 'social exclusion' and 'social inclusion' are deliberately 'bland and inoffensive' – they reflect the New Labour or **Blairite** view that social-class divisions are no longer important because we allegedly now live in a society 'where most social groups have been incorporated into a common social body, with shared values and interests'. It has been argued by Labour politicians that Britain in the 21st century is a classless society, or if social class is to be acknowledged at all, a society in which the vast majority of us share in middle-class lifestyles and aspirations – as Tony Blair once said, 'we are all middle-class now'.

Sociologists have also taken up this baton of classlessness. New Right sociologists such as Peter Saunders, as well as postmodernists such as Pakulski and Walters, have argued that social class is no longer important as a source of personal identity for people in the

21st century. These sociologists, despite their theoretical differences, have suggested that consumption patterns and 'cleavages' are far more important than social class in shaping lifestyle and life-chances today.

Is the UK a meritocracy?

In order to assess whether social class has any relevance in modern Britain today, it is useful to examine the concept of meritocracy. Many of those who argue that social class as a source of inequality no longer matters base this idea on the view that the UK is a meritocracy, i.e. that social origin and background are no longer important in shaping educational and occupational success. They argue that meritocratic institutions such as education and businesses are only interested in rewarding individual merit – hard work, effort, talent, ability, achievement, and so on. In a meritocracy, then, success and failure, and hence inequality, are the product of the individual and not their social-class background.

Sociologists such as Giddens and Diamond (2005) and Labour politicians who argue in favour of meritocracy have become known as the '**new egalitarians**'. They suggest that Britain is a fair and open society in which all social groups are given the potential to unlock their talents and to realize material rewards. However, sociologists such as Roberts, Bottero and Young and research organizations such as the Sutton Trust – who we can collectively call the '**new traditionalists**' – suggest that Britain is still a class society in which social background and structural inequalities in income, wealth, power, education and health mean that working-class people rarely have their talents unlocked and, consequently, experience great inequality in material rewards and life-chances.

The new egalitarian view

Giddens and Diamond (2005) argue that social class is no longer an important source of inequality or identity in the 21st century. They suggest that the UK is a meritocratic society in that **equality of opportunity** is now the norm, i.e. all members of society are objectively and equally judged on their talent and ability. Social background, and therefore social class, is now less important than ever before. Consequently, if people fail to achieve, the implication is that this must be due to an individual failing, e.g. they are not motivated enough or they have been demotivated by, for example, an overgenerous welfare benefit system to work hard.

They argue that the decline of class and the associated rise in meritocracy are the result of a number of social changes that have taken place over the past 30 years, such as:

● The decline of the primary and secondary sectors of the economy has led to a dramatic decline in the number of traditional manual workers and the identity politics associated with them, such as trade union membership. Moreover, the Labour party, which was traditionally seen as the party of the working class, has moved to distance itself from such class-based politics in recent years.

● The service sector of the economy – the public sector, financial services, retail and personal services – has greatly expanded. Many of the jobs in this sector are better paid and more secure than manual work. Furthermore, many workers in this sector, especially women who dominate these jobs in terms of numbers, have been upwardly mobile from the working class. They are now able to invest in a better lifestyle, e.g. owning their own home, and as a result this has undermined traditional patterns of class identification and loyalty.

● The majority of young people in Britain now experience further education, and the opportunities for going into higher education have increased tremendously for all social groups.

● Work contexts are less likely to be socially exclusive, i.e. made up of people from similar class backgrounds, because young people often combine education with work and take longer to establish their careers. As Furlong et al. (2006) note, in call centres, students often work, temporarily, next to same-age peers who lack advanced qualifications.

Giddens and Diamond conclude that these trends have resulted in the working class becoming just one more group among many that may be experiencing some type of economic and social deprivation in the UK. They argue that there exist a number of distinctive cleavages or disparities between the social experiences of particular social groups that require addressing by social policy, such as:

● between different types of families, i.e. single-parent families do not experience the same opportunities as dual-career families

● between homeowners and those who live in council housing

● between those living in neighbourhoods with high levels of crime and antisocial behaviour, and little community spirit, and those living in ordered and integrated communities

● between those with secure well-paid jobs and those in insecure casual or temporary low-paid work and those who are long-term unemployed. Hutton (1996) argues that society is now divided into segments (he also avoids the use of the term 'social class'!) based on inequalities in income and wealth. He argues that the top 40 per cent of society comprises all those with secure jobs, whilst the bottom 30 per cent comprises the disadvantaged – the unemployed and the poor. The middle 30 per cent comprises the **marginalized** – those workers who are not well paid and who often occupy insecure jobs

● between the disabled and the able-bodied

● between ethnic groups

● between the elderly and younger members of society

● between male pupils and female pupils – female pupils consistently do better at school than male pupils at key stages 1–3 as well as GCSE. Some new egalitarians, therefore, suggest that the talents of boys are not being unlocked compared with girls.

Giddens and Diamond, therefore, reject the notion of an overarching class inequality and argue instead that 'social exclusion' is a more accurate term for 'the range of deprivations' (e.g. low wages, child poverty, lack of educational and training opportunities, low levels of community belonging, and the lack of integration into a unified national identity) that prevent a diverse range of groups from taking their 'full part in society'.

They argue that such deprivations can only be tackled if the following conditions are met:

1   The economy is dynamic, competitive, flexible and efficient – They consequently reject the idea of increasing taxation on the wealthy entrepreneurs whose companies dominate the economy because they argue that the UK can only attract the best businessmen and managers in the world and, therefore, produce a healthy economy if salaries and rewards are attractive. In addition, high rewards encourage talented people to have high aspirations and to work hard to achieve them. As Hazel Blears, the Labour cabinet minister said in 2008, 'an attack on wealth and income distribution is an attack on aspiration'. However, new egalitarians do acknowledge that some of the practices of the very wealthy, such as tax avoidance, tax evasion and irresponsible corporate behaviour, need to be addressed in order to bring about a fairer society.

2   The excluded are provided with educational and training opportunities, tax breaks and minimum wages so that their talents and abilities can be more effectively unlocked – this should enable them to take meritocratic advantage of the jobs being created by the expansion of the global economy and, therefore, to experience upward social mobility and greater economic rewards.

3   The welfare state is reformed so that those who currently do not want to work can be 'encouraged' to unlock their potential through compulsory training schemes and employment.

Giddens and Diamond argue that there are four indicators or measures of social exclusion which the Labour government has adopted since 1997:

1   the number of people not in employment, education or training

2   the number of those earning below 60 per cent of the average wage

3   the number of those experiencing low levels of social interaction

4   the number of those who believe that they live in an area characterized by high crime, vandalism or material dilapidation.

Using these indicators, Giddens and Diamond argue that less than 1 per cent of the UK population experience social exclusion on all four counts. They also conclude that deprivation affects a very diverse range of disconnected groups. Often, the only thing these groups have in common is one of the above indicators of social exclusion and deprivation. Consequently, they do not constitute a working-class group as a whole.

Giddens and Diamond conclude that social class in the UK has been undermined by a process of 'individualization', meaning that the experiences of young people, in particular, have become more varied and no longer predictable on the basis of social class. They now have access to a diverse set of pathways, making it harder to identify groups of individuals who have the same set of experiences. Class identity and inequality are, therefore, dismissed as things of the past that have very little influence on people's experiences and life-chances in the modern UK.

The traditionalist view

The 'new traditionalists' are sociologists who argue that class divisions and conflict are still the key characteristics of British society today. They believe that New Labour politicians have abandoned their commitment to equality and social justice for those exploited by the organization of capitalism, namely the working class. These 'traditionalists' believe that New Labour has betrayed its working-class roots because it has done nothing to redistribute wealth and income from rich to poor, nor to address the fundamental flaws that they see as inherent in the capitalist system. Traditionalists accuse the government of tinkering with policies under the banner of social exclusion that raise the opportunities of groups such as the poor and single parents without addressing what traditionalists see as the main cause of their inequality: the concentration of vast amounts of wealth in the hands of an obscenely rich few. They suggest that the concept of social exclusion has three consequences:

1   It implies that the cause of deprivation lies in several factors unrelated to the economic organization of society.

2   By implying that individual effort is the key to economic success, little is done to change existing structural arrangements that have traditionally benefited the economic elite.

3   It shifts the blame for inequality, poverty, etc., very firmly onto the shoulders of those on the bottom rungs of society.

So, who is correct: the traditionalists or the new egalitarians? We need to examine the evidence in more detail before we can come to any firm conclusions.

Trends in income, wealth and poverty

A number of observations can be made about the distribution of income, wealth and poverty between 1945 and now.

Income

Between 1979 and 1997 (during an unbroken period of Conservative government), income inequality between the rich and poor in Britain widened until it was at its most unequal since records began at the end of the 19th century. No other Western industrialized country, apart from the USA, had experienced this level of inequality.

Average income rose by 36 per cent during this period, but the top 10 per cent of earners experienced a 62 per cent rise, whilst the poorest 10 per cent of earners experienced a 17 per cent decline. In 2000, those in the service class (professional, managerial and administrative employees) earned well above the average national wage, whereas every group of manual workers (skilled, semi-skilled and unskilled) earned well below the national average. In 2002/03, the richest 10 per cent of the population received 29 per cent of total disposable income (compared with 21 per cent in 1979), whilst the poorest 10 per cent received only 3 per cent (compared with 4 per cent in 1979).

Since 1997, when Labour took power, income inequality has widened even further: in 2007, the top 0.1 per cent (47 000 people in all) received 4.3 per cent of all income – this was three times greater than their share in 1979. The top 10 per cent of individuals in the UK now receive 40 per cent of all personal income (21 per cent in 1979), whilst the poorest 10 per cent still received only 3 per cent (4 per cent in 1979). The Institute for Fiscal Studies study of 2007 tax records concluded that income inequality between the rich and the poor is now at its highest level since the late 1940s (Brewer *et al.* 2008).

Income inequality and market forces

Roberts (2001) notes that the new egalitarian explanation for income inequality is market forces. It is argued that income inequalities have widened because skill requirements have been rising, and workers with the right skills, most notably finance professionals working in the City of London, have benefited. New egalitarians, such as Giddens and Diamond, suggest that the economically successful often bring benefits to the wider society in terms of drive, initiative and creativity, and should not be penalized in the form of excessive taxes. However, Roberts notes that the facts do not support the market-forces view. He points out that pay rarely corresponds with labour shortages or surpluses. Roberts shows that universities today produce more graduates compared with 30 years ago and, logically, average graduate pay should have fallen. However, in practice, graduate pay has actually risen – pay differentials between graduates and non-graduate employees have widened.

Roberts also argues that only class theory can explain income inequalities. He notes that upper-middle-class occupations, such as company executives and senior managers, generally fix their own salaries. They also often supplement their salaries with other financial incentives, such as being given stock options, bonuses and profit-sharing deals, as they have overall day-to-day operational control over corporations and, in some cases, actually own the majority of shares in the company. The reduction in tax rates for top earners from 83 per cent to 40 per cent in 1979 enormously benefited this group. Roberts notes that whilst some middle-class professionals can negotiate their salaries, the vast majority of lower-middle-class and working-class occupations either have to negotiate collectively as part of trade unions or they are told how much they will earn.

Corporate moral responsibility

In recent years there been some concern about the salaries of so-called 'fat-cat' executives. It has been suggested that corporations should be more morally responsible in the context of a society in which poverty, deprivation and debt is a norm for many people. For example, in October 2005, Philip Green, the chief executive of Arcadia, was criticized for being greedy in paying himself £1.4 billion in salary. Moreover, there are signs that society is increasingly unhappy because top executives are not only rewarded for success, but seemingly also for failure, in that many executives are paid off with 'golden goodbyes' often totalling hundreds of thousands of pounds. Orton and Rowlingson (2007) conducted a survey into public attitudes to wealth inequality and found deep social unease, especially about the pay of the highest earners. In addition, people were more likely to think that people at the top of the pay scale are paid too much rather than people at the bottom are paid too little.

Poverty

These arguments about corporate moral irresponsibility and executive greed become more acute when we consider that the Low Pay Unit estimated in 2000 that 45 per cent of British workers (overwhelmingly semi-skilled and unskilled workers) were earning less than two-thirds of the average wage. Furthermore, many low-paid workers are often caught in a **poverty trap**. This means they earn above the minimum level required to claim benefits, but

Key themes

Socialization, culture and identity

Educational achievement

This topic has outlined the statistical patterns and facts of class inequalities. You should be willing to explore those sociological theories and studies that focus on social class factors in their explanations of educational inequalities.

With regard to educational achievement, there are essentially four ideas worth exploring:

1   Cultural deprivation theory focuses on the deficiencies of working-class culture in terms of parental interest, childrearing and language use. Such sociologists imply that middle-class family socialization better prepares children for success in education.
2   **Material deprivation**, such as low income and fear of debt, can also be an obstacle to working-class educational success.
3   Marxists blame the hidden curriculum, which they see as part of a middle-class-dominated educational system, and the fact that the working class, through no fault of their own, are denied access to the cultural capital required for educational success.
4   Marxist interpretivists such as Paul Willis argue that working-class kids choose to 'fail' at school because the middle-class goals of schools have little to do with their aspirations.

the deduction of tax, etc., takes them below it. Similarly, many on benefits actually end up worse off if they take low-paid work because they are no longer eligible for state support.

Low pay has particularly impacted on levels of poverty. While levels of absolute poverty have fallen in the UK, especially since 1997, relative poverty has continued to rise steeply. As Savage (2000) notes, relative poverty in 1997 was twice the level it reached in the 1960s and three times what it had been in the late 1970s. Children have been particularly affected. Forty per cent of children are born into families in the bottom 30 per cent of income distribution. Treasury figures in March 1999 estimated that up to 25 per cent of children never escape from poverty and that deprivation is being passed down the generations by unemployment and underachievement in schools.

Feinstein et al. (2007), in a study of 17 000 children born in 1970, found that a child born to a labourer was six times more likely to suffer extreme poverty by the age of 30 than one born to a lawyer. The study also showed that, despite billions of pounds of government funding to cut child poverty, the gap between the poorest and richest children is probably wider today than it was three decades ago. Feinstein points out that the three most influential factors in predicting poverty at the age of 30 were parental occupation, low income and housing – all prime symbols of social-class position.

Wealth

The 20th century did see a gradual redistribution of wealth in the UK. In 1911, the most wealthy 1 per cent of the population held 69 per cent of all wealth, yet by 1993, this had dropped to 17 per cent. However, this redistribution did not extend down into the mass of society. Rather it was very narrow – the very wealthy top 1 per cent distributed some of its wealth to the wealthy top 10 per cent via trust funds in order to avoid paying taxes in the form of death duties. The result of this redistribution within the economic elite is that in 2003, the top 1 per cent and top 10 per cent owned 18 per cent and 50 per cent of the nation's wealth respectively. The wealth of the most affluent 200 individuals and families doubled by 2000. This polarization of wealth in the UK has also been encouraged by a soaring stock market (investments in stocks and shares) and property values, which as Savage notes 'have allowed those who were already wealthy to accumulate their wealth massively'. In contrast, half the population shared only 10 per cent of total wealth in 1986, and this had been reduced to 6 per cent by 2003.

Things look even worse if property ownership is removed from this wealth analysis and the focus is exclusively on wealth in the form of cash, stocks and shares, art and antiques, etc. In 2003, the top 1 per cent of the population owned 34 per cent of all personal wealth, whilst the bottom 50 per cent owned just 1 per cent.

The privatization of public utilities such as British Telecom and British Gas in the 1980s widened share ownership, so that by 1988, 21 per cent of people owned shares. However, the evidence suggests this was a short-term phenomenon as people who had never owned shares before sold their shares quickly as their value rose. Today,

although about 17 per cent of all people own shares, the richest 1 per cent of the population still own 75 per cent of all privately owned shares. As Roberts (2001) notes:

>> We are certainly not all capitalists now. In 1993, the least wealthy half of the population owned just 7 per cent of all personally-held wealth; around 30 per cent of adults do not own the dwellings in which they live; a half of all employees do not have significant occupational pensions. In fact, a half of the population has near-zero assets, and many are in debt when account is taken of outstanding mortgages, bank overdrafts, hire-purchase commitments, loans on credit cards, store cards and all the rest. It is only roughly a half of the population that has any significant share in the country's wealth. >> (pp.178–9)

The fact that nearly half the population have a share in the country's wealth may sound impressive, but Roberts points out that most of these people will liquidate assets such as savings and pension funds in old age in order to safeguard the standard of living they have enjoyed in the latter half of their life. As Roberts notes, it is only the extremely wealthy who can expect to die with most of their wealth intact. A lot of wealth that people have is also tied up with property in which people live. Homeowners can make money out of their property but this is not the main reason most people buy their houses. Most people own one house, whilst the extremely wealthy may own several houses as well as land bought for its future investment value. Finally, Roberts notes that the proportion of the population with enough wealth that they do not have to work for others is still less than 1 per cent. This elite group employ others to work for them. On the other hand, the life-chances of the vast majority of the population depend on the kinds of jobs they can obtain. Roberts concludes:

>> Despite the spread of wealth, this remains a clear class relationship and division. It is, in fact, the clearest of all class divisions, and it still splits the population into a tiny minority on the one side, and the great mass of the people on the other. >> (p.180)

Health

Bottero (2005) claims that 'social inequalities are written on the body' and 'hierarchy makes you sick'. She notes that if illness was a chance occurrence, we could expect to see rates of **morbidity** (i.e. illness and disease) and **mortality** (i.e. death) randomly distributed across the population. However, it is clear from Department of Health statistics that the working class experience a disproportionate amount of illness. In general, health across the population has improved over the last 30 years but the rate of improvement has been much slower for the working class. Generally, the working class experience worse mortality rates and morbidity rates than the middle classes. For example, 3500 more working-class babies would survive per year if the working-class infant mortality rate was reduced to middle-class levels. Babies born to professional fathers have levels of infant mortality half that of babies born to unskilled manual fathers.

Focus on research

Andy Furlong et al. (2006)
Social class in an 'individualized' society

The research aimed to identify the main routes that describe the transitions of young people from school into work. Using data from a longitudinal study carried out in the west of Scotland, the research studied the experiences of over 1000 young people aged between 15 and 23. The research identified eight transitional routes:

1. long higher education – university
2. short higher education – shorter courses such as HND
3. enhanced education – highers (equivalent to A-levels), then employment
4. direct job – leave school at 16 to go to work
5. assisted – on government training schemes
6. unemployment
7. domestic – time out of the labour market to have and/or care for children
8. other – usually made up of chronically sick or disabled people.

Furlong and colleagues found that these transitional routes can largely be predicted on the basis of educational achievement, which, in turn, is predicted by social class. Some 58 per cent of those following the long higher education route had parents in the professional and managerial classes (i.e. classes 1 and 2). Only 18 per cent of children from this class had taken the assisted route, 16 per cent the unemployed route and 14 per cent the domestic route. In contrast, only 9 per cent from semi-skilled and unskilled backgrounds had made it through the higher education route. However, 27 per cent from these backgrounds had taken the assisted route, 27 per cent the unemployed route and 24 per cent had taken the domestic route. Furlong and colleagues conclude that although the social experiences of young people may appear to be more fluid today, concepts such as social class still help sociologists to understand the distribution and persistence of socioeconomic inequalities.

Furlong, A., Cartmel, F., Biggart, A., Sweeting, H. and West, P. (2006) 'Social class in an 'individualised' society', *Sociology Review*, 15(4), pp.28-32

Explain how the research described above shows that inequalities are persistent. Use examples from the research in your answer.

Class and death rates

If we examine death rates we can see that, between 1972 and 1997, death rates for professionals fell by 44 per cent, but fell by only 10 per cent for the unskilled. Bartley *et al.* (1996) note that men in Social Class I (using the old RG scale) had only two-thirds the chance of dying between 1986 and 1989 compared with the male population as a whole. However, unskilled manual workers (Social Class V using the old RG scale) were one-third more likely to die compared with the male population as a whole. Despite the NHS providing free universal health care to all, men in Social Class V were twice as likely to die before men in Social Class I.

Bottero notes that:

≪ *There is a strong socio-economic gradient to almost all patterns of disease and ill-health. The lower your socio-economic position, the greater your risk of low birthweight, infections, cancer, coronary heart disease, respiratory disease, stroke, accidents, nervous and mental illnesses.* ≫ (p.188)

Moreover, she points out that there are specific occupational hazards linked to particular manual jobs which increase the risk of accidental injury, exposure to toxic materials, pollution, etc. Poor people are more likely to live in areas in which there are more hazards, such as traffic and pollution, and fewer safe areas to play. Consequently, poor children are more likely to be run over and to suffer asthma.

The health gradient

Some studies have suggested that there exists a **health gradient**, in that at every level of the social hierarchy, there are health differences. Some writers, most notably Marmot *et al.* (1991), have suggested that social position may be to blame for these differences. They conducted a study on civil servants working in Whitehall, i.e. white-collar staff, and concluded that the cause of ill health was being lower in the hierarchy. Those low in the hierarchy had less social control over their working conditions, greater stress and greater feelings of low self-esteem. These psychosocial factors triggered off behaviour such as smoking and drinking, poor eating habits and inactivity. The net result of this combination of psychosocial and lifestyle factors was greater levels of depression, high blood pressure, increased susceptibility to infection and build-up of cholesterol. If we apply Marmot's findings to society in general, it may be the fact that working-class occupations are the lowest in the hierarchy that may be causing their disproportionate levels of morbidity and mortality.

Other sociologists, most notably Wilkinson (1996), argue that the health gradient is caused by income inequality. He argues that relative inequality affects health because it undermines **social cohesion** – the sense that we are all valued equally by society, which affirms our sense of belonging to society. Wilkinson argues that inequality disrupts social cohesion because it undermines self-esteem, dignity, trust and cooperation, and increases feelings of insecurity, envy, hostility and inferiority, which lead to stress. As Wilkinson notes:

<< To feel depressed, cheated, bitter, desperate, vulnerable, frightened, angry, worried about debts or job and housing insecurity; to feel devalued, useless, helpless, uncared for, hopeless, isolated, anxious and a failure; these feelings can dominate people's whole experience of life, colouring their experience of everything else. It is the chronic stress arising from feelings like these which does the damage. It is the social feelings which matter, not exposure to a supposedly toxic environment. >> (p.215)

Wilkinson notes that egalitarian societies have a strong community life, in that strong social ties and networks exist in the wider society to support their members. In other words, members of these societies have access to **'social capital'** – social and psychological support from others in their community which helps them stay healthy. It is argued that in societies characterized by extreme income inequality, social capital in the form of these networks is less likely to exist and health inequalities continue to grow. We can see this particularly in the UK in residential areas characterized by high levels of council housing.

Housing

In 1979, there were 8 million council houses with 4 million tenants with low incomes. By 2000, there were only 5 million council houses with the same number of low-income tenants. Council estates, therefore, have large concentrations of people on income support, such as the unemployed, single mothers, the elderly, the low paid and asylum seekers. According to the General Household Survey (2001), 51 per cent of single-parent families are council tenants, compared to 15 per cent of the general population. In 2001, it was estimated that 45 per cent of tenants in publicly owned housing were on state benefits of one type or another. This trend has created less desirable residential areas and pockets of deprivation, with dysfunctional communities, failing schools and a disproportionate level of social problems such as crime. For example, it is estimated that 42 per cent of all burglaries happen to the homes of those belonging to the poor and single parents, the vast majority of whom are living on council estates.

Council estates are generally poorly resourced in terms of shops, recreational facilities, public transport and healthcare services such as GPs and hospitals. Very importantly, there is evidence of low social cohesion on these estates, and as a result, there may be high rates of depression, isolation, hostility and anxiety. As Wilkinson notes, social capital in the form of supportive formal and informal social networks is also likely to be absent because of family breakdown, economic cutbacks in council services and a lack of community spirit fostered by people constantly moving in and out of the area, a high crime rate, fear of crime, antisocial behaviour and intensive policing.

Education

Kynaston (2008) argues that most studies of meritocracy recognize that education is the prime engine of social mobility. However, he points out that meritocracy in the UK is undermined by the existence of private schools, which generally reproduce the privileges of the economic elite, generation by generation. Only about 7 per cent of all children are educated at private schools, but these pupils take up 45 per cent of Oxbridge places and a disproportionate number at other top UK universities. As ex-Labour leader Neil Kinnock once observed, public schools are the 'very cement in the walls that divide British society'.

Empirical evidence supports this view. For example, The Sutton Trust (2007) ranked the success of schools, over a five-year period, at getting their pupils into Oxbridge. Top was Westminster public school, which got 50 per cent of its students into Oxbridge and which charges annual boarding fees of £25 956 for the privilege. This means that the wealthy parents of Westminster pupils have a 50/50 chance of their child making it into Oxbridge. Altogether, there were 27 private schools amongst the top 30 schools with the best Oxbridge record; 43 in the top 50; and 78 in the top 100. The Sutton Trust concluded that the 70th brightest sixth-former at Westminster or Eton is as likely to get a place at Oxbridge as the very brightest sixth-formers at a large comprehensive school. Kynaston concludes that these figures suggest that private education is a 'roadblock on the route to meritocracy'. Other Sutton Trust studies show quite clearly that those in high-status jobs, such as senior politicians, top business leaders, judges, etc., are often privately and Oxbridge educated. Moreover, the 'old school tie' network ensures important and valuable social contacts for years to come, particularly in the finance sector of the economy. This is, almost certainly, still the most influential pathway to the glittering prizes of top jobs and super-salaries. This educational apartheid means that only the talents of the children of the wealthy elite are genuinely being unlocked.

Cultural capital

The evidence suggests that middle-class children are more advantaged than working-class children. Studies show that they benefit from living in better areas (with better schools). This, of course, is assisted by the better incomes earned by their parents, which means they can afford to buy into areas which have schools with good league-table standings. Income increases educational choices, so, for instance, parents can choose to send their children to private schools or to hire personal tutors. Middle-class parents are also able to use their knowledge, expertise, contacts and greater confidence in expressing themselves and in dealing with fellow professionals – their cultural capital – to ensure that their children are well served by the educational system. All of these factors undermine the view that the UK is a meritocracy.

The underachievement of working-class children

Working-class children perform much worse in education than all other social groups at all levels of the education system. For example, more working-class children leave school at the age of 16 with no qualifications than middle-class 16 year olds, and while the number of working-class

18 year olds entering university has increased, the number of middle-class undergraduates still far exceeds them. Moreover, Furlong and Cartmel (2005) found that children from disadvantaged backgrounds were more likely to be found in the 'new universities' rather than elite institutions and they were less likely to secure graduate jobs on leaving. Moreover, as Savage and Egerton (1997) found, ability does not wipe out class advantage. For example, their study found that less than half of the 'high-ability' working-class boys in their study made it into the service class (compared with three-quarters of the 'high-ability' boys with service-class fathers). Furthermore, 65 per cent of their 'low-ability' service-class boys were able to avoid dropping down into manual work.

Feinstein (2007) suggests that class inequalities are a significant influence on the underachievement of working-class children. Feinstein notes that the children of skilled manual workers may not do as badly at school as the children of welfare dependants or unskilled workers, but they still underachieve and there are many more of them. Children from these backgrounds have already fallen behind their more advantaged peers by the age of 3. This process continues throughout childhood, and it operates both ways: less-able and initially low-achieving middle-class children generally improve their position, but the position of initially high-achieving working-class children generally declines. Consequently, more than half of the children from skilled working-class homes (45 per cent of the child population) who are in the top 25 per cent in reading skills at the age of 7 will fall out of this top quarter by age 11. By contrast, if a child from a professional home is in the top quarter at 7 years, he or she is highly likely still to be there four years later. Hirsch (2006) argues that many working-class children

fall behind because their homes – however loving and well-intentioned – don't and often can't provide the same support for formal learning as more affluent homes because they lack the material resources, such as income, computers, internet access and so on.

Conclusions

The new egalitarians are undoubtedly correct in drawing our attention to the fact that a diversity of social groups, such as the long-term unemployed, single mothers and asylum-seekers, are socially excluded from mainstream society and so experience a range of social and economic deprivations. However, their reluctance to acknowledge the role of social class and its indicators (such as inequalities in income, wealth, housing, health and education) is incomprehensible given the weight of the evidence available. As Savage (2000) concludes:

<< *In recent years, whatever people's perceptions of their class might be, there is no doubting that class inequality has hardened. People's destinies are as strongly affected and perhaps more strongly affected, by their class background than they were in the mid-20th century.* >>

The evidence in this section also challenges the postmodernist view that social class has ceased to be the primary shaper of identity and that people exercise more choice about the type of people they want to be,

Activities

Research idea

Get an A to Z of your local area. Enlarge a residential area that you know to be a high-demand area. Similarly, enlarge an area in low demand. Annotate each as far as possible to highlight differences in facilities/resources. Conduct a survey of residents in each area to discover the level of services and facilities on offer there.

Compare and contrast the two areas to test the extent to which people in low-demand areas suffer a variety of social exclusions.

Web.task

Go to the government statistics site at www.statistics.gov.uk

Select Neighbourhood statistics. Choose your own postcode or the district or postcode where your school or college is situated. You will be able to investigate a variety of indicators of wealth and deprivation. How does your area compare with other parts of the region or with Britain as a whole?

Check your understanding

1. What groups are typically socially excluded according to the new egalitarians?

2. What is the main difference between new egalitarians and new traditionalists?

3. What is the new egalitarian attitude towards the rich?

4. Why have income inequalities widened in the UK over the last thirty years?

5. What have been the main trends with regard to wealth redistribution in the UK over the past 30 years?

6. Give three statistical examples of health differences between classes.

7. What effect has the health gradient had on the social make-up of some residential areas?

8. What evidence is there that council housing is becoming increasingly the domain of the socially deprived?

9. What problems do those living on council estates face?

10. How do educational inequalities support the view that social class may still be important?

especially in terms of lifestyle and consumption. Postmodernists and New Right thinkers, such as Saunders, neglect the fact that lifestyle choices and consumption depend on educational qualifications, the jobs we have and the income we earn. Unfortunately, members of the working class are less likely to qualify on all three counts for the postmodern lifestyle. Moreover, they are well aware that it is their social class more than any other social factor that is holding them back from making the sorts of choices that are taken for granted by social classes above them.

Key terms

Blairite ideas uniquely associated with Tony Blair or New Labour.

Cleavage a term used by Saunders to describe differences in the spending patterns of social groups.

Consumption spending on goods and services.

Equality of opportunity the view that all members of society should have the same opportunities to succeed.

Health gradient the fact that the chances of dying or becoming ill progressively increase or decline the lower or higher you are on the occupational hierarchy.

Marginalization powerlessness, i.e. the inability to overcome social and economic injustices.

Material deprivation the lack of physical resources needed in order to lead a full and normal life.

Morbidity rate reported ill health per 100 000 of population.

Mortality rate number of deaths per 100 000 of population.

New egalitarians a group of sociologists and politicians who believe that social-class divisions are in decline and that policies to socially include deprived groups are working.

New traditionalists sociologists who argue that class divisions and conflict are still the key characteristics of British society today.

Poverty trap the fact that after taxation and national insurance contributions, the wages paid by some jobs fall below the official poverty line.

Social capital social relationships that benefit people, e.g. in finding a job.

Social cohesion the idea that people feel a sense of belonging to society because they feel valued and wanted.

Social exclusion the fact that some people are excluded from what everyone else takes for granted, usually because of poor educational, family or economic circumstances.

Social inclusion being part of the mainstream because of the opportunities offered by government policies, e.g. training, education.

An eye on the exam — Life-chances and social class

Item A

Functionalists would argue that we are now living in a meritocratic society, in which our status is achieved as the fair reward for our efforts and abilities as individuals. However, there is strong evidence that our status is ascribed to a large extent by the social class into which we are born.

In other words, our class of origin has a powerful influence upon our life-chances across a whole range of areas. For example, working-class babies are more likely than their middle-class counterparts to die before they reach their first birthday. Similarly, there are inequalities in educational opportunity that systematically disadvantage working-class children. From a Marxist perspective, such inequalities arise from the nature of capitalist society and the exploitation of one class by another.

Assess the evidence for the view that social class remains the major influence upon individuals' life-chances.

(21 marks)

Grade booster — Getting top marks in this question

Begin by explaining what is meant by the term 'life-chances'. Then go on to examine some of the relevant evidence for the view in the question. You should consider a range of different areas, such as income and wealth, housing, education and health chances. What are the trends – for example, has the class gap in relative life-chances narrowed or widened? Use appropriate concepts, such as social exclusion, the health gradient, the poverty trap and cultural capital Make use of Item A, for example to discuss how far we are living in a meritocracy – are those with ability better able to improve their life-chances nowadays, e.g. through educational opportunity? Evaluate by putting your answer into a theoretical context; for example, what would functionalists and Marxists say about the influence of social class on life-chances? You could also refer to the influence of ethnicity and/or gender upon life-chances.

TOPIC 4

Changes in the class structure

Getting you thinking

1 What do you think are the main differences between the people in the photographs above?

2 Which would you call 'posh' and why?

3 Why do you think Victoria Beckham was often referred to as 'Posh' when she performed with the Spice Girls?

4 With which social class do you most associate the Beckhams? Explain your answer.

5 What do the terms 'working class', 'middle class' and 'upper class' mean to you?

6 What factors other than class affect the way people are perceived today?

Your answers to the above questions may demonstrate that class is a difficult thing to define nowadays and that status is no longer a matter of being on the right side of the class divide. The old idea of the class structure was that it comprised a triangular shape, with numbers increasing towards the base, which was composed of a vast number of unskilled manual workers providing a strong industrial-based manufacturing sector. This model implied a strict hierarchy, with higher levels of income, status and power towards the top. Although this was never actually the true shape (because manufacturing jobs have never accounted for the majority of the workforce), there has been a dramatic shift in Britain's industrial structure, with only about 18 per cent of the population working in manufacturing today. At the same time, numbers of those working in **tertiary** or **service-sector jobs** (those providing services such as transport, retailing, hotel work, cleaning, banking and insurance) have increased dramatically from 25 per cent to 75 per cent.

The upper class

It has been argued that the upper class (the extremely wealthy, property-owning elite who need not work in order to maintain their lifestyle), especially the aristocratic and traditional rich, have declined in wealth, power and influence over the course of the 20th century. In particular, it has been argued by Roberts (2001) that high death duties (now called 'inheritance tax') have resulted in a substantial number of upper-class families losing their family seats (the country houses where their family lived for generations) and experiencing downward social mobility. Some have even been forced to take up salaried employment in the service sector. In other words, it is argued that the upper class is in danger of being assimilated into the upper-middle class. But how true are these assertions? A number of observations can be made on the basis of the evidence available.

Inherited wealth

The upper class is still very wealthy. We saw earlier how the top 1 per cent have got 'poorer', but only because they have made real efforts to avoid inheritance tax by transferring their wealth via trust funds to the top 10 per cent. Moreover, the top 10 per cent still own about one-half of the country's wealth.

The evidence also suggests that we should talk about wealthy families rather than wealthy individuals. In this context, inheritance is very important. In general, individuals or families are wealthy because their fathers were also rich. Inheritance is responsible for most of the inequality in the distribution of wealth.

Positions of economic leadership

Scott (1982) argues that there now exists a unified propertied class which has actively used its wealth to maintain its privileged position at the top of the socio-economic structure. He argues that the core of the upper class – the richest 0.1 per cent (between 25 000 and 50 000 people) – occupy positions of leadership in manufacturing, banking and finance. He suggests that this core is made up of three groups:

- entrepreneurial capitalists, who own (or mainly own) businesses founded by their family
- internal capitalists, the senior executives who head the bureaucracies that run the big companies
- finance capitalists, who usually own or run financial institutions such as merchant banks and firms of stockbrokers.

It can be argued that the traditional landed gentry, mainly aristocratic in character, has managed since the turn of the 20th century, through investment and marriage to business and financial leaders, to become an integral part of the three groups that make up the core of the modern upper class.

Networks and social closure

The upper class is also supported by networks that permeate throughout that class. These may be based on marriage or kinship. For example, there is a tendency for members of the upper class to marry other upper-class individuals. This obviously gives the class a unity based on marriage and kinship, and is instrumental in strengthening business and financial ties between families.

Membership of the upper class is strengthened by **social closure** – the ability to control mobility into upper-class circles. This is partly achieved by networking and being part of an 'in crowd'. Another major means of ensuring social closure is the emphasis on public-school education. Generation after generation of upper-class children have been educated at fee-paying schools, such as Eton, Harrow, Winchester, Westminster, Charterhouse and Rugby. The large movement of such pupils into the elite universities of Oxford and Cambridge reinforces such students' belief in their 'difference' from the rest of society. The 'old-boy network', based very much on common schooling, is a type of networking that financially benefits members of the upper class and reinforces self-recruitment to the upper class. This means that current members of the upper class are likely to be the offspring of wealthy individuals who attended the same schools and universities. Their sons and daughters are very likely to follow the same route.

A good example of the power of social closure can be seen if we examine the current political establishment. Despite the fact that only 7.3 per cent of the UK population attend private fee-paying schools, ex-private-school pupils were disproportionately represented among top politicians in 2008 and included:

- nearly a third of Labour government ministers
- 59 per cent of Conservative MPs
- 17 out of 27 members of David Cameron's shadow cabinet.

In addition:

- 14 members of the Conservative opposition frontbench attended Eton College, including the Conservative leader, David Cameron
- the Conservative mayor of London, Boris Johnson, was educated at Eton
- the two leading Liberal Democrats in 2008, Nick Clegg and Chris Huhne, both attended Westminster School.

The 'Establishment'

Scott argues that the upper class's influence is not confined to business. There is overwhelming evidence that those in top positions in politics, the civil service, the church, the armed services and the professions come disproportionately from upper-class families. Scott refers to this group as the 'establishment' – a coherent and self-recruiting body of men with a similarity of outlook who are able to wield immense power. However, exactly how this group interacts and whether they do so for their own benefit is extremely difficult to prove.

Although the basis of the wealth of the upper class is no longer primarily land, this class still retains many of the characteristics it possessed 50 years ago, especially the emphasis on public-school education, thus helping to ensure that social closure continues unchallenged.

The middle classes

The expansion of the middle classes

In 1911, some 80 per cent of workers were in manual occupations. This number fell to 32.7 per cent in 1991 and is approximately 25 per cent today. Non-manual workers (traditionally seen as middle-class) have now become the majority occupational group in the workforce. As Savage (1995) points out, there are now more university lecturers than coal miners in the UK.

Reasons for the expansion

The number of manual jobs in both **primary** and **secondary industries** has gone into decline since the 1970s as a result of a range of factors, including new technologies, the oil crisis and globalization (i.e. the same raw materials and goods can be produced more cheaply in developing countries). The tertiary or service sector of the economy that is organized around education, welfare, retail and finance has expanded hugely in the past 20 years. Mass secondary education and the expansion of both further and higher education have ensured the existence of a well-educated and qualified workforce. The service sector is made up of a mainly male professional workforce at its top end but, as a result of changes in women's social position, the bulk of workers in this sector are female.

The boundary problem

Studying the middle classes can be problematic because not all sociologists agree who should be included in this category. This is the so-called '**boundary problem**'. Traditionally, differentiating between the middle class and working class was thought to be a simple task involving distinguishing between white-collar, or non-manual, workers on the one hand and blue-collar, or manual, workers on the other. Generally, the former enjoyed better working conditions in terms of pay, holidays and promotion possibilities. Today, however, this distinction is not so clear cut. Some sociologists, notably Braverman, argue that some **routine white-collar workers** no longer fit neatly into a middle-class category.

A fragmented middle class

The term 'middle class' covers a wide range of occupations, incomes, lifestyles and attitudes.

Roberts et al. (1977) argued that the middle class was becoming fragmented into a number of different groups, each with a distinctive view of its place in the stratification system. They suggest that we should no longer talk of the middle class, but of the 'middle classes'. Savage et al. (1992) agree that it is important to see that the middle class is now divided into strata, or '**class fractions**', such as higher and lower professionals, higher and middle managers, the petit bourgeoisie and routine white-collar workers.

Professionals

Savage and colleagues argue that higher and lower professionals mainly recruit internally – in other words, the sons and daughters of professionals are likely to end up as professionals themselves. The position of professional workers is based on the possession of educational qualifications. Professionals usually have to go through a long period of training – university plus professional examinations before they qualify. Savage argues that professionals possess both **economic capital** (a very good standard of living, savings, financial security) and cultural capital (seeing the worth of education and other cultural assets such as taste in high culture), which they pass on to their children. Moreover, they increasingly have social capital (belonging to networks that can influence decision-making by other professionals such as head teachers). Professionals also have strong occupational associations, such as the Law Society and the British Medical Association, that protect and actively pursue their interests (although the lower down the professional ladder, the weaker these associations/unions become). The result of such groups actively pursuing the interests of professionals, especially those in the state sector in areas such as the NHS, is high rewards, status and job security.

Savage concludes that professionals are aware of their common interests and quite willing to take industrial action to protect those interests. In this sense, then, professionals have a greater sense of class identity than other middle-class groups. However, there is a slight danger that as the state sector becomes increasingly privatized, many professionals will face an increased threat of redundancy and reduced promotional opportunities as a result of de-layering (a reduction in the number of 'tiers' of management in an organization).

Managers

Savage and colleagues suggest that managers have assets based upon a particular skill within specific organizations. Such skills (unlike those of professionals) are not easily transferable to other companies or industries. They note that many managers have been upwardly mobile from the routine white-collar sector or the skilled working class. Many have worked their way up through an organization which they joined at an early age. They consequently often lack university degrees. Their social position, therefore, is likely to be the result of experience and reputation rather than qualifications. Savage notes too that most managers do not belong to professional associations or trade unions. Consequently, they tend to be more individualistic in character and are less likely to identify a common collective interest with their fellow managers – whom they are much more likely to see as competitors. Savage argues that managers actively encourage their children to pursue higher education because they can see the benefits of a professional career. However, managers, despite being well paid, are less likely to have the cultural or social capital possessed by professionals.

Savage argues that job security differentiates professionals from managers – managers, particularly middle managers such as bank managers, are constantly under threat of losing their jobs because of recession, mergers and **downsizing**. They are consequently more likely to be potentially downwardly mobile.

However, some sociologists have noted that, in the past 20 years, a super-class of higher executives has appeared who run companies on a day-to-day basis and who are on spectacular salaries and often have share options worth millions. The Income Data Services showed that nearly half of all senior executives of Britain's 350 largest public companies made more than £1 million a year, with eight directors on packages of £5+ million (Cohen 2005). Adonis and Pollard (1998) claim that this 'super-class' or salariat now makes up approximately 15 per cent of middle-class occupations. According to Adonis and Pollard, the lifestyle of this super-class revolves around nannies and servants, second homes, private education for their children, private health schemes, exotic foreign holidays and investment in modern art. The super-class tends to live on private urban estates patrolled by private security companies. Some sociologists have suggested that this super-class is no longer middle-class because it has more in common with the unified property elite that now makes up most of the upper class.

The self-employed

Between 1981 and 1991, the number of people **self-employed**, referred to by Marx as the '**petit-bourgeois**', rose from 6.7 per cent of the workforce to over 10 per cent. Research by Fielding (1995) examined what the self-employed in 1981 were doing in 1991. He showed that two-thirds of his sample constituted a relatively stable and secure part of the workforce in that they remained self-employed over this ten-year period. However, he noted that the character of the self-employed has undergone some change. The number of managers who prefer to work for themselves (for example, as consultants) rose considerably in the 1980s, especially in the finance and computer industries. Some writers argue that many firms now prefer to contract services to outside consultants rather than employ people themselves because it is cheaper and they have fewer legal obligations to such workers.

Routine white-collar workers

Marxists such as Harry Braverman (1974) argue that routine white-collar workers are no longer middle class. Braverman argues that they have been subjected to a process of **proletarianization**. This means that they have lost the social and economic advantages that they enjoyed over manual workers, such as superior pay and working conditions. Braverman argues that, in the past 20 years,

employers have used technology, especially computers, to break down complex white-collar skills, such as book-keeping, into simplistic routine tasks. This process is known as '**de-skilling**' and is an attempt to increase output, maximize efficiency and reduce costs. Control over the work process has, therefore, been removed from many non-manual workers.

These developments have been accompanied by the parallel development of the feminization of the routine white-collar workforce (especially in the financial sector and call centres), because female workers are generally cheap to employ and are seen by employers as more adaptable and amenable to this type of work. Braverman concludes that de-skilling means that occupations that once were middle class are today in all respects indistinguishable from those of manual workers.

However, Marshall et al. (1988) have challenged the idea of proletarianization. In a national random sample of female workers, they found that it was mainly manual workers who claimed that their work had been de-skilled. Over 90 per cent of non-manual workers felt that little had changed, and most identified with the middle class rather than the working class. Finally, they were also more likely to vote Conservative than Labour. Marshall and colleagues therefore concluded that proletarianization among routine white-collar workers was not taking place.

New-technology workers

In further contrast to Braverman, however, Clark and Hoffman-Martinot (1998) highlight the growth of a technological elite of 'wired workers' – new professionals who are as productive as entire offices of routine non-manual workers because of their use of technology, and who spend most of their days behind computers working in non-hierarchical settings. They enjoy considerable **autonomy**, are paid extremely well, often working flexibly, sometimes from home and are engaged in dynamic problem-solving activities. Such workers can be found in a wide range of new occupations regarded as part of the 'infotech sector' – areas such as web design, systems analysis, e-commerce, software development, graphic design and financial consultancy. At the lower end of this sector, however, are growing numbers of casual workers who spend all day on the telephone in front of a VDU, often working in very poor conditions in call-centres.

In conclusion, then, the middle classes are an important and vibrant part of the class structure. What was once a minority group, perceived as a class apart from the working class in terms of income, lifestyle, status, and culture, has become a much larger, more heterogeneous (diverse) body.

The working class

Changes in class solidarity

Fulcher and Scott (1999) point out that, until the late 20th century, the working class had a strong sense of their social-class position. Virtually all aspects of their lives, including gender roles, family life, political affiliation and

Focus on research

Simon Charlesworth
A phenomenology of working-class experience

Simon Charlesworth's study focuses on working-class people in Rotherham in Yorkshire, the town where he grew up. Charlesworth based his study on 43 unstructured, conversational interviews, although he also clearly spoke to large numbers of people whom he knew socially. Many of the people to whom he spoke were male, but at least a third were female.

Charlesworth finds class seeping into all aspects of life in Rotherham. Generally, he finds that the lives of people are characterized by suffering and depression. The loss of a man's job, for instance, has a physical consequence because it can lead to fear and panic because of loss of earnings. Older people, in particular, are faced with the difficulties of learning to cope with a changing world. One of his main findings is that miserable economic conditions cause people to feel both physically and psychologically unhealthy.

Many of the unemployed workers experienced a lack of identity and a sense of being devalued because of the loss of status which normally accompanies paid work. However, the culture of the working-class lad demands respect and consequently this was pursued by committing crime and antisocial behaviour.

Other working-class lads saw no point in working at education or qualifications because even if they acquired them, they were not able to obtain decent work. There were further problems for those who did get to university or college, as they felt out of place and excluded from the culture because they were no longer fully part of it.

Charlesworth concludes that changes in the social climate have left people without a sense of belonging to their 'communities' or an understanding of how the world is developing. They have little hope for their future and they worry for their children. He claims that the socially excluded and deprived of Rotherham (which the locals called 'Deadman's Town') feel rage and suffering. The culture that develops out of unemployment and poverty is one of having to make do and buy only what is necessary and cheap. It is therefore marked by social and spiritual decay.

Adapted from Blundell, J. and Griffiths, J. (2002) *Sociology since 1995*, Vol 2, Lewes: Connect Publications

1 Identify two criticisms that might be made of Charlesworth's methods as described in the passage above.

2 What factors have caused working-class culture in Rotherham to be marked by a 'social and spiritual decay'?

---

leisure, were a product of their keen sense of working-class identity. Lockwood's (1966) research found that many workers, especially in industrial areas, subscribed to a value system he called '**proletarian traditionalist**'. Such workers felt a strong sense of loyalty to each other because of shared community and work experience, and so were mutually supportive of each other. They had a keen sense that capitalist society was characterized by inequality and unfairness. Consequently, they tended to see society in terms of conflict – a case of 'them' (their employers who were seen as exploiting them) versus 'us' (the workers united in a common cause and consciousness).

Later research has claimed that this type of class identity is in decline because the service sector of the economy has grown more important as the traditional industrial and manufacturing sectors have gone into decline. Recession and unemployment linked to globalization have undermined traditional working-class communities and organizations such as trade unions. However, Cannadine (1998) argues that this idea – that once upon a time the working class subscribed to a collective class consciousness and an adversarial view of society – is exaggerated and the evidence lacking. He argues that the history of the working class suggests no clear consistent pattern of class consciousness – collectivism only emerges at particular times and in particular contexts, and even then, is rarely universally shared.

Middle-class lifestyles?

In the 1960s, Zweig (1961) argued that a section of the working class – skilled manual workers – had adopted the economic and cultural lifestyle of the middle class. This argument became known as the '**embourgeoisement** thesis' because it insisted that skilled workers had become more like the middle class by supporting bourgeois values and the Conservative party, as well as enjoying similar income levels.

This view was investigated in Goldthorpe and Lockwood's famous study of a car factory in Luton (1969). They found little evidence to support Zweig's assertion. Economically, whilst wages were comparable to those of members of the middle classes, they did not enjoy the same working conditions or fringe benefits, such as expense accounts,

Key themes

The underclass

Families and households

The concept of 'underclass' is a useful tool to use to construct synoptic links. The New Right see the growth of a criminal and antisocial underclass as fuelled by the rise in numbers of single teenage mothers, who are failing to control their delinquent children. Combined with the decline of marriage, and the growth of divorce and cohabitation, this group is seen as a threat to the stability of the nuclear family and social order.

Education

In terms of education, the underclass is also seen by the New Right as mainly responsible for problems such as poor classroom discipline, exclusion, truancy and poor levels of achievement in state schools in inner-city areas. It is argued that the poor attitude held by parents in the underclass towards education is more important than poverty or other forms of material deprivation in explaining educational underachievement.

Crime and deviance

The underclass are seen by the New Right as constituting a criminal class, in that, for them, the benefits of crime far outweigh the costs because they lack the normal range of controls that law-abiding people have in their lives.

Wealth, poverty and welfare

In the field of welfare and poverty, the New Right suggest that members of the underclass 'choose' to be poor and are happy to be dependent on welfare benefits.

company car, sick pay or company pensions. They had to work longer hours and had less chance of promotion. They did not readily mix with members of other classes, either inside or outside work, and 77 per cent of their sample voted Labour. Goldthorpe and Lockwood did, however, argue that there were signs of **convergence** between working-class and middle-class lifestyles, but concluded that, rather than an increase in the middle class, what had emerged was a new working class.

The privatized new working class

Goldthorpe and Lockwood identified a new trend, the emergence of the 'privatized instrumentalist' worker who saw work as a means to an end rather than as a source of identity. These affluent workers were more home-centred than traditional working-class groups; they were also less likely to subscribe to the notion of working-class community and 'them-versus-us' attitudes. However, Fiona Devine (1992) undertook a second study of the Vauxhall

plant at Luton in the late 1980s, in which she argued that Goldthorpe and Lockwood's study may have exaggerated the degree of working-class privatization. She found that workers retained strong kinship and friendship links, and had a reasonably developed working-class identity in that they were critically aware of class inequalities such as the unequal distribution of wealth and income.

Although the concept of embourgeoisement is now rarely used, it is frequently argued that the working class have fragmented into at least two different layers:

- the traditional working class, in decline and typically situated in the north of England
- a new working class found in the newer manufacturing industries, mainly situated in the south, who enjoy a relatively affluent lifestyle but still see themselves as working-class.

False consciousness?

However, Marxists reject the view that there is a fragmented working class. They argue that there is still a unified working class made up of manual workers – both Black and White, male and female, and routine white-collar workers. They would argue that the sorts of divisions discussed above are the product of ruling-class ideology, which attempts to divide and rule the working class. The fact that some groups do not see themselves as working class is dismissed by Marxists as false class-consciousness. They would argue that in relation to the means and social relations of production, all so-called 'class fractions' are objectively working class because they are alienated and exploited by the ruling class, whether they realize it or not.

The underclass

The concept of the **underclass** has entered everyday speech to describe those living at the margins of society, largely reliant on state benefits to make ends meet. However, the concept has been rejected by many sociologists due to its negative and sometimes politically charged connotations. Members of the political right, such as Charles Murray (1994) in the USA, in particular, have focused on the cultural 'deficiencies' of the so-called underclass, blaming them for their situation, and accusing them of being welfare-dependent (i.e. relying on benefits). It is also argued that they supplement their income through petty crime, or compensate for deprivation through excessive drug and alcohol abuse. Murray identifies a Black underclass which, he alleges, is to be found in most American cities. Similar points have been made about members of non-working groups in deprived areas of Britain, particularly single-mothers living in inner-city areas or on deprived council estates (Dennis and Erdos 1993).

A matter of choice?

Many New Right commentators (such as Saunders 1995) suggest that a large number of the poor see 'poverty' as a choice, as a way of life preferable to work. Young single mothers are often cited as examples of this – for example, by having a second child in order to secure a flat that will be paid for by the state. However, various studies such as those by Morris (1993) and Gallie (1994) have examined the extent to which the poor possess cultural differences that may account for their situation. They found that there is little evidence of an underclass culture and that the most disadvantaged groups actually have a greater commitment to the concept of work than many other groups.

Marxists are also sceptical about the existence of an underclass. They point out that capitalist economies produce large numbers of poorly skilled and insecure workers who are constantly at risk of falling into poverty because capitalism is an unstable and inconsistent economic system. Bottero (2005) notes:

> ≪ In highly unequal labour markets there is always someone at the bottom, but this does not mean that the lowest brick is any different from the other bricks in the pile. The underclass are simply elements of the working class who have been hit by adverse life-course events or economic recession. ≫ (p.226)

Rather than blaming the cultural deficiencies of the poor, critics of the underclass thesis prefer to use the concept of social exclusion to explain poverty. Social exclusion can take many forms, the accumulated effects of which can lead to extreme poverty. Consider the current refugee 'crisis' concerning Eastern European immigrants to Britain: these people are excluded from gaining anything but casual low-paid work; they may be ineligible for state benefits; they have language barriers to contend with and may also be socially excluded because of xenophobic attitudes and racism.

Some sociologists have noted that social exclusion may build resentment that can lead to other social ills such as crime or increased suicide rates. Jock Young (1999) suggests that crime rates may be reflecting the fact that a growing number of people do not feel valued or feel that they have little investment in the societies in which they live. Young (2007) suggests that there exists a contradiction between culture that strongly encourages the acquisition of money and material goods and structural exclusion, and this has produced 'social bulimia'. Members of society are strongly encouraged to subscribe to the meritocratic ideal, but society's failure to deliver the material success promised by this has resulted in widespread feelings of **anomie** expressed through a sense of unfairness, relative deprivation and crises of identity that can only be resolved by crime.

Does class identity still exist?

Postmodernists argue that class identity is no longer relevant as a collective group identity and has now fragmented into numerous separate and individualized identities. Social identity is now more pluralistic, individualistic and diverse. Pakulski and Waters (1996) argue that people now exercise more personal choice about what type of people they want to be, rather than have their identity shaped by their membership of a social class. They argue that gender, ethnicity, age, region and family role interact and impact with consumption and media images to construct postmodern culture and identity.

However, postmodern ideas may be exaggerated as recent surveys indicate that social class is still a significant source of identity for many (e.g. Marshall *et al.* 1988). Members of a range of classes are still aware of class differences and are happy to identify themselves using class categories. On the other hand, according to Savage, class identities have declined in importance because of changes in the organization of the economy (for example, the decline of primary industries and factory work, the expansion of white-collar work as well as the rise of more insecure forms of manual and non-manual work), which he argues have largely dissolved the boundaries between social classes. Consequently, class is rarely viewed as an issue by most people, despite its continuing objective influence on people's social experience and life-chances, as seen clearly in Topic 3.

Key terms

Anomie a breakdown in, absence of or confusion about social norms, rules, etc.

Autonomy freedom to choose one's own actions.

Boundary problem the constantly shifting nature of work makes it more difficult to draw boundaries between classes of workers.

Class fractions the recognition that the main social classes are fragmented into competing and often conflicting internal groups or fractions.

Convergence coming together, e.g. of working-class and middle-class lifestyles.

De-skilling reducing the skill needed to do a job.

Downsizing reducing the size of the permanent workforce.

Economic capital money in shares (and so on) which generates more money.

Embourgeoisement the idea that the working class is adopting the attitudes, lifestyle and economic situation of the middle classes.

Primary industries those involved in extraction of raw materials, e.g. mining, agriculture, fishing.

Proletarianization a tendency for lower-middle-class workers to become de-skilled and hence to share the market position of members of the working class.

Proletarian traditionalist members of the working class with a strong sense of loyalty to each other because of shared community and work experience.

Routine white-collar workers clerical staff involved in low-status, repetitive office work.

Secondary industries those involved in producing products from raw materials.

Self-employed/petit-bourgeois owners of small businesses.

Social closure the process by which high-status groups exclude lower-status groups from joining their ranks.

Tertiary or service sector jobs providing services such as transport, retailing, hotel work, cleaning, banking and insurance.

Underclass termed used by Charles Murray to describe those living at the margins of society, largely reliant on state benefits to make ends meet.

Activities

Research ideas

1 Ask a sample of adults across a range of occupations how 'flexible' their work is. Ask them about their job security, the sort of tasks they do, their working hours, how much freedom they have, and so on.

2 Conduct a survey of your peers in casual part-time employment to find out the conditions of work they experience.

Web.task

Channel 4's History site contains a quiz about social class. Once you've had a go, click on 'Find out more' to access a list of interesting books and films about class.

www.channel4.com/history/microsites/H/history/c-d/classquiz.html#30

Check your understanding

1 How has the structure of the upper class changed in the last 50 years?

2 What is the 'establishment'?

3 Why do some writers suggest that we should no longer talk of the middle class but of the 'middle classes'?

4 How do managers differ from professionals?

5 Why do Marxists see white-collar workers as experiencing proletarianization?

6 What was the 'embourgeoisement thesis' and how was it challenged?

7 How do Marxists challenge the view that the working class has fragmented?

8 What happened to class identity, according to postmodernists such as Pakulski and Waters?

9 What is an 'underclass'?

10 How does the New Right view of the underclass differ from the Marxist view?

An eye on the exam — Changes in the class structure

Item A

Many sociologists have argued that there have been major changes in the class structure in the last half-century or so. For example, Goldthorpe and Lockwood have argued that the working class has split into a traditional and a new working class, each with its own distinctive features. Similarly, the middle class may also be becoming increasingly fragmented, so that some argue we must now talk of the middle classes in the plural, rather than the middle class. This increasing fragmentation of the class structure – if this is what it is – may have serious implications for people's behaviour and sense of group identity.

Assess the view that Britain's class structure is increasingly fragmented today.   (21 marks)

Grade booster — Getting top marks in this question

In your answer, look at evidence and arguments for and against the view. Use material from Item A on the working class and middle class – e.g. develop the account of Goldthorpe and Lockwood's traditional and new working class, and outline the different groups that have been described as middle class. Consider also whether the class position of routine non-manual workers is changing. You should also go beyond the Item to look at the upper class and the underclass.

Put your answer into a theoretical context – e.g. contrast the Marxist view that there remain only two classes, with postmodernist or other views that emphasize increasing fragmentation. You can also evaluate by questioning whether the class structure really is *increasingly* fragmented (some argue it has always been fragmented). You could also consider the implications of fragmentation for people's behaviour and identity – e.g. voting, trade-union membership, class-consciousness and solidarity.

TOPIC 5

Social mobility

Getting you thinking

A north–south divide?

National statistics showing overall improvement may actually mask regional inequalities. The average household in Britain spent £359 per week in 1999/2000. However, a London household spent about £400, whereas in the North East it was £290.

Adapted from: Denscombe, M. (2001)
Sociology Update, Leicester: Olympus

Some argue that dehumanizing, exploitative, monotonous jobs have disappeared and working life has improved significantly for most of the working class.

1 Look at the two photos of people doing different jobs. Are they evidence for or against the view expressed above? Explain your answer.

2 What does the extract tell us about increasing opportunities in Britain?

The movement of individuals up or down the social scale is known as social mobility. We only need to look around us or to talk to older people to see that the population nowadays is generally more affluent and enjoys better working conditions – in other words, there appears to have been considerable upward social mobility. However, as the exercise above may have shown, the picture is far less simple once we start taking into account variations caused by factors such as region, ethnicity or gender. These difficulties have not prevented sociologists from attempting to measure social mobility and using their results to comment on the extent to which society is becoming more open or closed.

There are two main ways of looking at social mobility:

● **Intergenerational** mobility refers to movement between generations, e.g. a son moving further up the social scale than his father.

● **Intragenerational** mobility refers to the movement of an individual within their working life. An individual may start off as an office junior and work their way up to office manager, win the lottery or marry someone wealthy.

Problems of measuring social mobility

The use of occupation as an indicator of social class creates many problems (as discussed in Topic 1, pp. 410–12). The earliest studies of social mobility used the Registrar General's scale which, as we have seen, considered an individual's social class solely in terms of the occupation of the male head of household. In fact, this indicator of class persisted well beyond the period for which it had any relevance, mainly because of the comparative nature of social mobility studies. After all, how can you draw any conclusions about the nature of social movement if it is not possible to compare like with like?

Another key problem is that mobility studies focus on the working population and say nothing about the very rich and the very poor – important groups in society, both of whom are unlikely to work, albeit for different reasons. Most importantly, the economic gap between these two groups appears to be increasing.

Social mobility studies

The Oxford (Nuffield) Mobility Study (OMS) 1972

This large-scale study in 1972 led by John Goldthorpe (1980) found high rates of what is known as **absolute mobility**. Absolute mobility refers to the overall numbers (in percentages) of individuals from specific origins reaching particular class destinations. The Oxford Mobility Study (OMS), using the Hope-Goldthorpe scale of measuring social class, compared sons with fathers in their sample and discovered much greater numbers of people from working-class origins being upwardly mobile into the service class compared with the 1950s and 1960s. Over two-thirds of the service class had started off either in the intermediate or working classes. For example, 16 per cent of working-class sons had risen into middle-class occupations by 1972, whilst 15 per cent of middle-class sons had experienced downward mobility into working-class jobs. Further data taken from the National Child Development Study (NCDS) in 1991 confirms these trends – according to its data, 26 per cent of working-class sons had experienced upward social mobility into middle-class jobs.

Why has absolute mobility increased?

Goldthorpe points out that an increase in absolute mobility is not necessarily the product of meritocracy or evidence that society has become more open in terms of its opportunities. He suggests three reasons for the increase:

1   There have been changes in the economy and, therefore, the occupational structure, i.e. the job market. The proportion of the working population in the service class (middle-class jobs with good pay and prospects) is increasing, while the intermediate class (lower white-collar jobs) and working class (manual work) are decreasing in size. For example, between 1901 and 1961, the proportion of working-class jobs as part of the working population declined from 75 per cent to 38 per cent, whilst the percentage of professionals and managers increased from 8 per cent to 34 per cent. In particular, the service class has more than doubled in numbers since the 1950s because of the expansion in government jobs in areas such as the welfare state. This led to a greater demand for professionals and administrators in the fields of education, welfare and health. Furthermore, the financial service sector, in particular, has expanded whilst heavy industry, which mainly employs manual workers, has gone into serious decline. These trends mean that the sons of those working in 1960 have significantly more chance of getting into the service class than their fathers.
2   There have been differences in the fertility rate of social classes and consequently in the number of children being born. The fertility rate of the service class has been too low to cope with the growth of service-sector jobs. This sector therefore had no choice but to recruit from other social classes.
3   Education has dramatically expanded since the Second World War. In particular, the introduction of free secondary education in 1944 and the expansion of higher education made recruitment into the service class easier because, for the first time, people from working-class backgrounds had access to educational qualifications.

The significance of relative mobility

On the face of it, it would appear that there has been a significant amount of social mobility across the generations. However, what such data masks is the relative chance that a person from a particular class has of moving upwards or downwards. This is known as **relative mobility**. By comparing the relative mobility chances of different generations, it is possible to determine whether the class structure has become more open. The data from the OMS suggests that there is little evidence of this. Rather, the OMS discovered that boys from the service class were four times more likely to obtain a service-class job than boys from the working class and twice as likely as boys from the intermediate class. The OMS dubbed this '**the 1–2–4 rule of relative hope**' and argued that, while there was more room at the top indicated by absolute mobility levels, there was little sign that this was accompanied by greater equality in opportunities for all social classes to get there.

The Scottish Mobility Study (SMS)

This study by Payne (1987) noted that the potential for social mobility was also dependent upon age and region. For example, the data noted that social mobility was more likely to occur in the south-east of England, especially London. Young people living in this region were more likely to enjoy both job and promotion opportunities that propelled them upwards compared with their parents. However, in contrast, people living in the North of England and Scotland, especially those belonging to an older age profile, were significantly less likely to experience job and promotion opportunities that would help them to escape the social class of their parents (see Table 7.6).

Such mobility patterns may lead to a growing heterogeneous (mixed) middle class, based largely in the south-east of England, underpinned by an increasingly homogeneous (similar) working class and underclass, located mainly in the north of England and Scotland. Some sociologists have suggested that members of the underclass, particularly young people, may engage in disruptive behaviour, such as inner-city rioting, as a form of protest at the lack of opportunity in the deprived areas in which they live.

Table 7.6 The Scottish Mobility Study's Findings

	Age	Location	Region
Associated with high mobility	Young	Urban	South of England
Associated with low mobility	Older	Rural	North and Scotland

The Essex University Mobility Study (EUMS)

This study by Marshall *et al.* (1988) largely confirmed the findings of the OMS. The EUMS found that someone starting in the service class had a seven times greater chance of ending up in the service class than someone from a working-class background. Marshall argues that these relative rates tell us that we are still far from being an equal-life-chance society. Moreover, Marshall argues that the evidence suggests that the expansion of service-class jobs has slowed down and will soon end, so blocking opportunities for those outside the service class.

Why have changes in absolute mobility not been accompanied by changes in relative mobility?

New egalitarian politicians are fond of portraying the UK as a society in which people have the opportunity to better themselves – i.e. as a meritocratic society in which all social groups are treated fairly. However, as we have seen, data from the OMS and EUMS, in particular, contradict this view, indicating simply that the service sector has expanded, rather than that any revolution in equality has taken place. In fact, the OMS and EUMS go further and strongly suggest that equality is unlikely to occur in the near future because of the existence of class barriers and social closure (see Topics 3 and 4 for evidence of this) that prevent bright working-class people, in particular, from getting ahead.

However, these views of the UK are not universally shared. The New Right sociologist, Peter Saunders claims the stress on relative mobility by Goldthorpe and Marshall indicates a deliberate desire by left-wing sociologists to obscure the fact that capitalism works reasonably well as a meritocratic system. He argues that absolute levels of mobility are more important than relative levels. A number of theories have evolved out of this debate.

Key themes

Sociological theories and methods

Studying social mobility

Social mobility studies suffer a number of methodological problems that can undermine the reliability of their research tools and the validity of their findings:

● There has not been universal agreement on how to operationalize social class (see Topic 1) across all mobility studies. The earliest studies used the Registrar General's classification, which takes occupation as the primary indicator of social class. In the 1970s and 1980s, this was generally replaced by the Hope-Goldthorpe scale with its emphasis on market situation and employment conditions. However, this scale was particularly rejected by feminist sociologists because it classed women as economic appendages of either their husbands or fathers. To complicate matters further, this scale became the government's new classification – the NS-SEC – in 2000, and included women on the basis of their jobs, independently from men. All these factors mean that comparative analysis of data from different mobility studies is extremely difficult.

● Such classifications very rarely keep up with contemporary developments. For example, employment conditions are constantly evolving and, as we see from the example of call-centres, occupations that might be classed as middle-class may have more in common with manual occupations in terms of job security, satisfaction and status.

● Some studies – notably, Saunders (see below), and Savage and Egerton (see p. 444) – have used the same data from the NCDS, but have interpreted this data in quite different ways. For example, Saunders sees such data as evidence that inequality is decreasing, whereas Savage and Egerton see the same data as evidence that inequality is still a major problem.

Intelligence theory

Saunders (1995), using data from the NCDS, argues that there is a genetic base to social mobility. He suggests that people with middle-class jobs are generally brighter than those with working-class jobs. He claims that, like height and weight, there is a genetic base to most of the abilities and intelligence that people develop. Bright parents, therefore, have bright children. Saunders argues that the best predictor of where we end up in terms of occupations and social class is **innate** ability or merit, which he claims is twice as important as social-class background. He also suggests that middle-class parents are better at motivating their children. He further concludes that private schooling, cultural capital, material conditions in the home and parental contact with schools are only a minor influence on a child's future destination. Saunders concludes that 'in the end what matters most is whether you are bright, and whether you work hard' (p.72).

Saunders argues that absolute mobility is more important than relative mobility because it has had a profound effect on how people think about their social status and class position, and how they judge what is fair in modern society. In particular, Saunders argues that absolute mobility has had a crucial effect upon people's attitudes towards the future – it has resulted in the working class becoming more aspirational and seeing upward mobility as a very real possibility for their children. Moreover, their experience of upward social mobility and the improvements in living standards that accompany it means that they have greater expectations about consumption compared with previous generations. Payne (1992) makes a similar point when he notes:

<< *Manual workers in this country now expect to own a car, and a television, to occupy a dwelling of several rooms in good physical condition, to take a holiday abroad, to have several sets of clothing. Such a lifestyle would in 1950 have been associated with the middle or upper classes, who made up about one quarter of society. In less than a single lifetime, manual workers have in consumption terms been upwardly mobile.>>* (p.220)

Saunders argues that absolute mobility data is convincing evidence that capitalism has opened up new opportunities for advancement and brought fantastic benefits to the working class.

However, Saunders' methodology has come under sustained attack. Roberts (2001) is critical of Saunders' use of intelligence tests and argues that it is impossible to measure raw innate ability. He notes 'performance in intelligence tests, the construction of these tests, and what we mean by ability, are all socially contaminated' (p.219). Best (2005) notes that Saunders' sample was biased towards the middle class because he excluded part-time workers, housewives and the unemployed. Moreover, other research has clearly shown that some teachers often label working-class pupils negatively, thereby affecting their motivation. These classroom practices may lead to a self-fulfilling prophecy of low achievement. Apparent low ability and motivation may, therefore, be the product of class in the sense that working-class children may not receive the same degree of positive attention from teachers as middle-class children.

Savage (2000) argues that the claim that middle-class children are brighter is an ideological myth. He states:

<< *It is quite plausible – indeed likely – that those who fill these (middle-class) jobs will be deemed to be 'brighter' than those who do not. However, in this case, 'brightness' does not cause mobility, it is simply the filter that distinguishes those who are upwardly mobile from those who are not.>>* (p.77)

Neo-Marxist theory

Marxists argue that social mobility is a myth because class societies such as the UK are essentially concerned with **social reproduction**, i.e. ensuring that inequalities in wealth and income are reproduced generation by

generation by their children and their children's children, and so on.

Marxists argue that inequalities in relative mobility therefore reflect wider social-class inequalities that are a natural consequence of the exploitative social relations of production that exist under capitalism. Bourdieu (1977), for example, argues that the economically dominant classes are able to construct educational systems that reflect their cultural values. Moreover, the educational environment benefits middle-class children because their home experience and upbringing have equipped them with the knowledge and skills (cultural capital) that fits the requirements of teachers and both the academic and the hidden curriculum. Working-class children, on the other hand, are disadvantaged because their knowledge, skills and experiences are often dismissed as unimportant by the educational system. Marxists, therefore, argue that the economic and social advantages enjoyed by middle-class children in education are responsible for their upward social mobility.

Marxists are interested in the ideological effects of social mobility. For example, they argue that the few working-class people who do achieve upward mobility are used to create the myth that capitalist societies are truly open and meritocratic. They also argue that sections of the lower middle class, particular white-collar workers working in call-centres, have experienced a decline in status, career prospects and relative income, and therefore, downward intragenerational mobility. Marxist sociologists argue that employment conditions in call-centres are not that dissimilar to the factory floor and assembly line. As Denscombe (1999) notes, such workers 'receive low pay and there is little opportunity for contact with other workers. There is little or no opportunity for creativity in their work, sticking as they do to a prepared script and having their calls monitored'. Marxists also suggest that the very high level of staff turnover in these jobs indicates high levels of alienation, i.e. workers do not like doing these jobs.

Marxists note that, although reforms have widened the educational opportunities of working-class children and improved their attainment levels, it is the middle or service class that has taken most advantage of the expansion of educational opportunities in the UK, especially the expansion of higher education. For example, 80 per cent of middle-class children go into higher education, compared with less than 15 per cent of children from the unskilled working class. There is evidence, too, that because of cultural and social capital, people from middle-class origins are more likely to be promoted at work than those from working-class backgrounds. As Roberts (2001) comments:

<< *Connections are useful – knowing people who will put in a word at the right time. Then there is the matter of having the right kind of accent, tastes and dress sense to be regarded as the right type of person.>>* (p.217)

Savage and Egerton (1997), using the same NCDS data as Saunders, argue that people from working-class backgrounds need to have more intelligence and more qualifications to reach the same positions as their middle-class peers. They note that both the ruling class and the service class are able to find ways of preventing even their less 'able' sons from moving down the social ladder. They found that low-ability children with service-class fathers had much more chance of staying in the service class than ending up in other classes. Furthermore, 75 per cent of high-ability sons of service-class fathers ended up in the service class compared to only 45 per cent of the high-ability sons of working-class fathers. This disparity was even greater for working-class, high-ability girls who, it seems, had less than half the chance of their service-class counterparts of ending up in that class. Savage and Egerton concluded that working-class girls need to have higher levels of ability than working-class males if they are to progress into the service class.

Savage and Egerton argue that Saunders' focus on innate ability serves to justify inequality because the idea that some people are 'naturally' less intelligent hides the real cause of their inequality: their social-class position. However, neo-Marxist theory does not escape criticism. New Right sociologists have asked whether there really is such a match between what goes on in middle-class homes and the culture of education. They argue that if the system so benefits the economically dominant, members of the middle class would not experience downward mobility. However, Marxists point out that the numbers of downwardly mobile members of the middle class are extremely low compared with the numbers of working-class people who experience no upward social mobility.

Rational action theory

Goldthorpe (1996) argues that inequalities in relative levels of social mobility may be the result of the fact that people are '**rational actors**' who calculate the relative costs and benefits of trying to reach occupational destinations. However, Goldthorpe argues that these costs and benefits will differ in value depending on where in the socio-economic order a person starts. As Roberts (2001) notes:

<< *Supporting a child through higher education will be a greater burden on a working-class family, relative to its resources, than for a middle-class family. A working-class child who achieves an intermediate-class position is likely to be regarded as successful, whereas a middle-class family will view this as a failure and might well do everything possible to secure a better outcome.*>> (p.222)

Evaluating theories of social mobility

Social mobility studies tend to work using fairly broad structural categories, such as working class, intermediate class and service class. However, such studies often do not recognize that these categories are made up of occupations that have undergone profound changes in their conditions in recent years, possibly affecting the status and job security of workers and, therefore, experience of mobility. For example, many middle-class jobs are no longer permanent. Rather, flexible working arrangements and contracts are becoming the norm, so that a white-collar worker or professional might job-share,

Focus on research

Geoff Payne and Judy Roberts (2002) Male social mobility

Payne and Roberts used data from the 1987, 1992 and 1997 British Election Survey, in combination with OMS data from 1972 and 1983, to examine rates of absolute and relative mobility. In terms of absolute mobility, they found that the proportions of men being mobile between 1972 and 1997 had increased – for example, 55 per cent of men were in a different social class from the one in which they had been born. They also found that over half the men born into the manual class were upwardly mobile in 1992, compared with 39 per cent in 1972. As regards relative rates of mobility, Payne and Roberts argued that the gates of equality opened quite wide between 1972 and 1992, in that a service-class child only had twice the odds of returning to the service class compared with a working-class child making it to the service class. This finding was obviously an improvement on the 1–2–4 rule of relative hope set out by the OMS in 1972. However, their 1997 data shows these gates closing again for two reasons: the service sector has stopped growing, i.e. there are fewer middle-class jobs to be upwardly mobile into, and the odds of working-class people making it into these jobs has increased again back to 1972 levels.

Adapted from Payne, G. and Roberts, J. (2002) 'Opening and closing the gates: recent developments in male social mobility in Britain', *Sociological Research Online*, 6(4), Feb 2002

1　**What problems can you see in the methodology used by Payne and Roberts?**

2　**How might their data for 1972 to 1992 support that of Peter Saunders?**

3　**How might their 1997 data support the work of Savage or Marshall?**

work part time, be a temporary worker (e.g. a supply teacher) or be on a fixed-term contract. Although Marxist theories have focused on call-centre employment, most mobility studies do not recognize the sometimes precarious nature of these new middle-class occupations. In many ways, it can be argued that such employment conditions reflect downward mobility as far as security and job satisfaction are concerned.

Women and social mobility studies

Feminist sociologists have long complained that women have been neglected in social-mobility studies. The major mobility studies have tended to compare sons' with fathers' occupations. There seem to be three reasons for this:

- Surveys that included women would involve larger samples and so would be more expensive and time consuming.
- The focus on men in previous studies means it is easier to compare all-male samples.
- The nature of men's and women's work is different. For example, women are more likely to be employed part-time and many women are full-time housewives.

Goldthorpe (1983) claimed that there was no need for any independent study of female mobility since most women take their class from their husband/father. He noted that whether a woman chooses to work or not largely depends upon her husband's performance as a breadwinner. He states that 'the status a woman derives from her man, or that she acquires herself, is more significant than the status she shares with other women'. However, Abbott (1990) disagrees with this view. She argues that there is a need to study female mobility because women's experience of work is different from that of men. Consequently, men and women experience different absolute-mobility rates. Abbott argues that the limited mobility prospects of women actually enhance men's opportunities. For example, if women find it difficult to enter the service class, men's chances of filling these jobs obviously improves.

Women's social mobility patterns

Studies of female mobility have come to several conclusions:

- There is considerable mobility from all social classes into lower white-collar work. However, this reflects the fact that most women who work are concentrated in this type of work. In contrast, few women experience downward social mobility into manual work, simply because few women are employed in this sector.
- The EUMS (which attempted to overcome sexism by using the term 'chief childhood supporter') found that women were much more likely to experience downward social mobility compared to their fathers. Even when their male and female samples had the same qualifications, the eventual destinations of women were less advantageous compared with men.
- Kay (1996) concluded that women were more likely to be downwardly mobile than men because of career interruptions such as pregnancy and childcare. Divorce and the likelihood of being head of a single-parent family also impede upward mobility.

However, recent studies of female social mobility, aspirations and educational performance indicate the probability of positive change. Roberts (2001) argues as follows:

<< Recent school-leaving cohorts have been the first waves of young women in modern times whose mothers worked for the greater part of their adult lives and during their daughters' (and sons') childhoods. These mothers (and fathers) have encouraged their daughters to aim for decent jobs – not to be left in the typing pools or at the supermarket check-outs.>>

Studies by Wilkinson (1994), and Roberts and Chadwick (1991) indicate what Wilkinson calls a '**genderquake**' in female attitudes. Females now regard future occupational careers as an important lifestyle choice. There has been a remarkable improvement in female educational performance in the last ten years in so far as females outperform males at all levels of the British educational system. The evidence suggests that if women postpone marriage and parenthood, or if they do have children, take maternity leave rather than give up work altogether, and invest in high-quality childcare, they are likely to be highly qualified, to be in middle-class jobs, and their career prospects are likely to remain more or less in line with those of men.

However, research does indicate class inequality in female patterns of social mobility. A study by the Economic and Social Research Council, *Twenty-Something in the 90s* (1997), looked at a group of 26 year olds who were born in 1970. It confirmed that class of origin was still a major factor affecting mobility for both men and women. The study noted, however, that middle-class women were just as likely as middle-class men to go to university and from there into well-paid jobs. Unskilled women were 30 times less likely to work full-time compared with professional women. In spite of this, the study found that women's career development opportunities are still influenced by discrimination from male employers, and by the fact that society expects their primary responsibility to be domestic work and childcare, which forces them to downplay their careers.

Ethnic-minority social mobility patterns

Roberts argues that all non-White minorities experience an 'ethnic penalty' with regard to social mobility, in that occupational and educational outcomes are lower and the risks of unemployment are higher compared with White people with similar qualifications. The only ethnic group that does not experience this ethnic penalty are Indians. The ethnic group which seems to experience the greatest inequality in terms of social mobility are African-Caribbeans. This group is most likely to underperform in education and is most likely to be unemployed.

Platt (2005) notes that many immigrants to the UK in the 1950s experienced downward mobility, in that well-qualified Asians were forced to take jobs in manual work. Platt conducted a study of second- and third-generation Asians and African-Caribbeans and compared job destinations with parents, who were often immigrants. She found that 35 per cent of her Indian sample and 22 per cent of her African-Caribbean sample had service-class jobs, compared with 38 per cent of her White control sample. However, like the OMS before her, she concludes that this is due to the expansion of the service class and contraction of the working class rather than any significant change in equal opportunities. She also noted that the children of African-Caribbeans employed in the service class were less likely than Indians to stay in that class. They were more likely than any other group to experience downward social mobility to the working class. Platt concludes that, in the face of institutional racism and economic deprivation, social class may be weak in protecting ethnic-minority groups against the possibility of downward social mobility.

Recent studies of social mobility

The social mobility study of Blanden *et al.* (2005) looked at children born in 1970 and classified them into four income 'quartiles' on the basis of family income at the time they were born and what they were earning as adults. They discovered that 37 per cent of children in Britain born into the lowest income group remained there and would probably do so for the rest of their lives. Only an extremely small number of children from the bottom quartiles were able to use educational qualifications in order to make it into the top quartiles. In contrast, children from the highest income group were most likely to be earning high incomes as adults regardless of educational qualifications.

However, Blanden and colleagues are criticized because of weaknesses in their research methodology and in their interpretation of their data. Gorard (2008) points out that they only used families that had both a father and a son with a known earned income. They ignored all women, most single-parent families and the unemployed. Gorard notes: 'strangely, neither a professional daughter born to a working-class family, nor a professional son born to an unemployed father, would be counted as examples of social mobility in this study' (p.28). Moreover, Gorard suggests that they focused only on the bad news and

ignored the good news that 63 per cent of children born into the bottom quartile moved out of it in terms of income earned as adults.

However, Goldthorpe and Jackson's (2007) study of mobility patterns is just as pessimistic as that of Blanden and colleagues. They suggest that there is unlikely to be a return to the generally rising rates of upward mobility that characterized the middle decades of the 20th century. They argue that the growth of the service sector has peaked and that opportunities for short-range upward mobility within the working class has been restricted by a sharp decline in skilled manual jobs. They conclude that the growth in social mobility promised by Labour's emphasis on unlocking the talents of those at the bottom of society can only occur at the expense of middle-class downward mobility.

Conclusions

Social mobility studies can be a little confusing and contradictory. This is because they often do not compare like with like in terms of samples and definitions of social class. However, this does not mean that we cannot come up with some conclusions about social mobility and meritocracy.

What we can see is that the children of the working class are experiencing greater opportunities than 50 years ago, but so are the children of the middle class. Working-class upward mobility probably had little to do with educational expansion, despite the fact that most

Check your understanding

1　Why do sociologists study social mobility?

2　What is the difference between absolute and relative mobility?

3　Why has absolute social mobility increased?

4　What is the 1–2–4 rule of relative hope?

5　What social problems might arise as a result of the lack of opportunity for upward social mobility?

6　How does Saunders explain differences in relative mobility?

7　Why does Saunders think absolute mobility is more important than relative mobility?

8　What do absolute mobility levels tell us about capitalism according to Saunders?

9　How does Savage and Egerton's work challenge Saunders' claims?

10　Why have women been excluded from mobility studies for so long?

11　What are the main reasons for the patterns in women's mobility?

12　How does ethnic-minority social mobility compare with social mobility in general?

Activities

Research ideas

1　Ask your parents what their parents did at the height of their working lives. Note down answers, keeping each gender separate. Consider what you realistically expect you will be doing by the time you are 30. Collate your results with those of other students in your class. Quantify the extent of mobility for males and for females. Compare your results with some of the studies discussed in this topic.

2　Interview a small number of workers (both male and female) in some of the newer jobs in the service sector of the economy: office work, call-centre work, and so on. Ask them about job satisfaction, pay and conditions of work. To what extent are these jobs preferable to manual work?

Web.task

Go to the government statistical service website: www.statistics.gov.uk

Find out about low pay, the distribution of employment, regional variations in income and expenditure and gender differences in employment. What do they tell us about social mobility?

educational social policy has been aimed at improving working-class opportunity. It has more to do with economic changes, especially the expansion in the service sector and decline in manual work. There are also signs that females are now beginning to experience improved social mobility. The signs, however, are not great for ethnic minorities. Whilst Indians are experiencing some upward mobility, most other groups, especially African-Caribbeans are stuck at the bottom of the socio-economic hierarchy.

Overall, we can conclude that upward social mobility does not depend on luck, as Jencks *et al.* (1972) once suggested. Rather, the evidence suggests that, as John Scott (2005) argues, 'class structures are self-reproducing'. Roberts (2001) notes that, despite meritocratic education systems, most Western societies experience similar differences in relative mobility. He suggests that it is unlikely that these differences will ever disappear, despite government attempts to eradicate them. Scott agrees and notes that in modern Britain:

> << *your chances of throwing a six in the life-game of snakes and ladders are significantly affected by your class of origin: those in the highest classes have a far better chance of securing the opportunities for upward mobility and for avoiding downward mobility.*>> (p.21)

This observation has led Roberts to note that policy makers only try to equalize opportunities because the ruling class 'need to be seen to be making all possible efforts to ensure that success is open to all the talents' (p.223) when, in reality, it is not.

Key terms

1–2–4 rule of relative hope the OMS finding in regard to relative mobility that children from the service class are four times more likely and children from the intermediate class twice as likely as children from the working class to reach service-class jobs.

Absolute mobility the total amount of movement between social classes.

Genderquake a revolution in women's attitudes which has led to them seeing education and careers rather than marriage and motherhood as their priority.

Innate inherited at birth.

Intergenerational between generations (fathers and sons, for example).

Intragenerational within a generation (your progress within a career, for example).

Rational actors people who calculate the costs and benefits of actions before carrying them out.

Relative mobility the chance one class has of moving up or down relative to another.

Social reproduction the transmission of inequalities in wealth and income from one generation to another.

An eye on the exam — Social mobility

Item A

There have been a number of sociological studies of social mobility in Britain since the 1940s. However, the picture of mobility that emerges from these studies is not wholly clear or consistent. For example, there is evidence from some studies of an increase in absolute rates of social mobility, while at the same time there has been little or no increase in relative mobility.

Much of the research has focused only on the intergenerational mobility of men, and we know less about women's mobility, although the evidence suggests that there are significant gender differences here. For instance, women seem more likely to experience downward intergenerational mobility when we compare their occupations with those of their fathers.

Examine the extent of social mobility in Britain today (**Item A**).   (12 marks)

Grade booster — Getting top marks in this question

You need to outline the patterns of social mobility in Britain today. Make use of the Item to help you do so. For example, you should define absolute and relative mobility and consider the evidence for the extent of each of these. Similarly, you need to use some relevant studies to examine gender differences in social mobility (e.g. the EUMS).

To develop evaluation, put your answer into the context of a debate. For example, do the patterns of mobility support the claim that Britain is becoming more meritocratic, as functionalists claim, or simply that opportunities for mobility have come largely from changes in the occupational structure? Make use of recent studies (e.g. Blanden *et al.* and Gorard), not just ones from the 1970s and 80s.

TOPIC 6

Gender and stratification

Getting you thinking

Table 7.7 Occupations 2004

Employees and self-employed aged 16 and over (Great Britain)

Selected occupations	Women (%)	Men (%)
Receptionists	95	5
Educational assistants	93	7
Nurses	88	12
Care assistants & home carers	88	12
Primary & nursery teachers	87	13
Cleaners and domestics	80	20
Secondary teachers	54	46
Chefs and cooks	46	54
Retail & wholesale managers	35	65
Marketing & sales managers	26	74
IT managers	18	82
Software professionals	17	83
Production, works & maintenance managers	9	91

Adapted from ONS (2004) *Labour Force Survey Spring 2004*

Table 7.8 Full-time earnings by sector 2005

Mean earnings of employees on adult rates (UK)

Industry sectors	Women (£ / hour)	Men (£ / hour)	Gender pay gap*
Banking, insurance & pension provision	13.98	23.86	41.4
Health & social work	11.54	17.03	32.2
Real estate, renting & business activities	12.70	16.66	23.8
Wholesale, retail & motor trade	9.02	11.54	21.8
Public admin. & defence	11.62	14.44	19.5
Manufacturing	10.38	12.89	19.5
Hotels & restaurants	7.12	8.55	16.7
Construction	10.83	12.35	12.3
Education	13.87	15.68	11.5
Transport, storage & communication	11.02	12.09	8.9
Public sector	13.18	15.20	13.3
Private sector	10.65	13.75	22.5
All sectors**	11.67	14.08	17.1

* 100 – (women's full-time earnings as a percentage of men's full-time earnings)
** Including sectors not shown separately.

Adapted from ONS (2005) *Annual Survey of Hours and Earnings, 2005*

1 Identify the main patterns in each of the tables on this page.

2 Using ideas you have developed from studying your Sociology course, suggest explanations for each of these patterns.

Table 7.9 'Sex and power' 2008 index

Women in selected 'top jobs' over a five-year period

Industry	2003	2004	2005	2006	2007
Members of Parliament	18.1	18.1	19.7	19.5	19.3
Cabinet Ministers	23.8	27.3	27.3	34.8	26.1
Directors of the top 100 UK companies	8.6	9.7	10.5	10.4	11.0
Local authority chief executives	13.1	12.4	17.5	20.6	19.5
Senior police officers	7.5	8.3	9.8	12.2	11.9
Senior judges	6.8	8.3	8.8	9.8	9.6
Top civil servants	22.9	24.4	25.5	26.3	26.6
Top health service execs	28.6	27.7	28.1	37.9	36.9
Secondary school heads	30.1	31.8	32.6	34.1	30.0

Adapted from Equality and Human Rights Commission (2008) *Sex and Power, 2008* (www.equalityhumanrights.com)

You will probably have noted patterns in each of the tables on the previous page and realized that, despite all the improvements in the social position of women, gender differences in paid work are still very noticeable. You should also have been able to offer some explanations drawn from your past study of the subject. These may well match up with some of those introduced later in this topic, which examines gender inequality in the UK, focusing particularly on paid work. There are many other aspects of gender inequality in British society – you should pay particular attention to gender differences and inequalities in poverty, health, education, and crime and deviance.

Gender inequality in employment

During the past 30 years, the number of female workers in the UK has risen by 2.45 million, whereas the number of male workers has only risen by 0.5 million. There are a similar number of men and women in work in 2008 – 13.6 million of each sex – compared with 1985, when men filled two million more jobs than women. However, there are still significant differences in the distribution of male and female workers throughout the occupational structure. Catherine Hakim (1979) refers to these differences as 'occupational segregation' because in the UK 'men and women do different kinds of work, so that one can speak of two separate labour forces, one male and one female, which are not in competition with each other for the same jobs'. She suggests that there are two types of occupational segregation:

- **Horizontal segregation** – Men and women are concentrated in different types of jobs in different sectors of the economy.
- **Vertical segregation** – Women occupy the lower levels of pay and status in particular jobs.

Horizontal segregation

Table 7.7 on p. 447 gives us an insight into how occupations are gender segregated. In the public sector, women are mainly employed in health and social work and in education, where they made up 79 per cent and 73 per cent of the workforce respectively in 2006. In the private sector, women are overconcentrated in clerical, administrative, retail and personal services, such as catering, whereas men are mainly found in the skilled manual and upper professional sectors (EOC 2006).

According to the Office of National Statistics (ONS), in 2008 men and women were still likely to follow very different career paths. Men were ten times more likely than women to be employed in skilled trades (19 per cent compared with 2 per cent) and were also more likely to be managers and senior officials. A fifth of women in employment do administrative or secretarial work, compared with 4 per cent of men. Women are also more likely than men to be employed in personal services and in sales and customer services. Men are more likely to be

self-employed than women. Nearly three quarters of the 3.8 million self-employed people in 2008 were men, a proportion that has remained the same since early 1997.

There is some evidence that horizontal segregation may be in decline because there has been a decline in men's work, such as that found in the primary (e.g. engineering, coal-mining) and secondary sectors (e.g. car manufacturing) of the economy. Increasing female educational success, especially in higher education, has resulted in more women entering areas of work previously dominated by men, such as the medical, legal and financial sectors of the economy. For example, in 2005, according to the Women and Work Commission, 75 per cent of pharmacists, nearly 40 per cent of accountants and about 50 per cent of solicitors were women.

Vertical segregation

Skill and status

The evidence suggests that, within occupational groups, women tend to be concentrated at the lower levels. When women do gain access to the upper professional or management sector, the evidence suggests that they encounter a '**glass ceiling**' – a situation in which promotion appears to be possible, but restrictions or discrimination create barriers that prevent it. For example, 66 per cent of full-time secondary school teachers in 2007 in England were female, but only 30 per cent of secondary school heads were. In 2007, male primary school teachers were three times more likely than female primary teachers to become head teachers.

In 2008, women made up only 11 per cent of directors of the top 100 British companies, a quarter of NHS consultants, 10 per cent of high court judges and just two out of 17 national newspaper editors.

The Equality and Human Rights Commission noted in 2008 that women lack access to the most powerful jobs in society, and that it will take 55 years at the current rate of progress for women to achieve equal status with men at senior levels in the judiciary, and 73 years for equality to be achieved in top management jobs in Britain's top 100 companies.

Pay

Generally, men are better paid. In 1975, women only earned about 71 per cent of the average full-time male wage. This gap has narrowed over the last 30 years, but the gap between men's pay and women's pay was 17 per cent in 2007. However, the government claims that the gap is lower – 12.6 per cent – if calculated in terms of median pay, i.e. comparing men and women who are in the middle of their respective pay ranges, rather than average pay. The ONS argue that the problem with using average pay to calculate the gender gap is that a few men who are exceptionally well paid (i.e. the top 10 per cent of individuals in the UK, who now receive 40 per cent of all personal income) can artificially inflate the average and therefore distort the true pay gap between men and women. However, whatever method is used, significant differences still exist between men and women.

Key themes

Sociological methods

Scott MacEwen (1994) notes that there are two ways of measuring segregation. The first is an objective and scientific measure using survey or census data to calculate the numbers of women and men in an occupation. This is precise but measures broad occupations only, rather than specific jobs. However, it is at the level of specific jobs that segregation is most extreme. For example, the occupation 'cleaner' obscures the fact that it is mainly men who are 'street cleaners' and women who are 'office cleaners'. Similarly, the occupation 'teacher' glosses over the fact that the vast majority of primary teachers are female.

The second method is to measure occupational segregation subjectively. Here, interviews or questionnaires are used to ask people whether their type of job is done exclusively or mainly by men or women, or shared equally. This method does have its problems – for example, it relies on the judgement of the respondent – but it does focus more directly on individual jobs

Adapted from Pilcher, J. and Whelehan, I. (2004) *50 Key Concepts in Gender Studies*, London: Sage

Hourly pay statistics are also only one aspect of the inequality women experience in pay. If specific occupations are examined, the gap is much greater than 12.6 per cent. It rises to 22.3 per cent in the private sector, although it is only 13.4 per cent in the state sector. For example, the difference in earnings in 2006 between men and women in health and social work jobs was 32 per cent, and in banking and insurance it was 41 per cent.

Even women who have managed to reach top positions are not immune from pay inequality. In 2008, the Chartered Management Institute (CMI) showed that the average female executive is earning £32 614 a year, £13 655 less than the average male executive, who earns £46 269 a year. The CMI estimate it will not be until 2195 that women's pay begins to outstrip that of men. Moreover, according to a TUC report in 2008, young women earn 26 per cent less than young men for apprenticeships, and dominate the lowest-paid sectors such as hairdressing and childcare. It is estimated by Trevor Phillips, who chairs the Equality and Human Rights Commission, that women who work full time will earn on average £330 000 less than a man over their working lives and, at the current rate, it will take at least another two decades to close the pay gap.

When annual earnings are examined, the gap between men and women increases quite dramatically. In 2006, the annual earnings gap between men and women was 27.1 per cent. The weekly income gap between males and females increases even further to 44 per cent when all economic activity is considered, i.e. full-time, part-time and self-employment, unemployment and other benefits and pensions. The income gap is widest in retirement, at 47 per cent in 2006. While retired men got nearly half their income from non-state or occupational pensions, retired women got only a quarter of their income from this source.

Work situation

Women are more likely than men to be employed in part-time work. In 2005, 42 per cent of female employees worked part time, compared with only 9 per cent of male employees. Part-time work tends to have worse working conditions, less job security and fewer promotion prospects than full-time work. In 1999, women in part-time work earned, on average, 60 per cent of the average hourly pay of male full-time employees. By 2005, this situation had slightly improved – part-time female employees earned 61.6 per cent of men's average full-time earnings.

What about men?

Whilst men generally enjoy a greater range of work opportunities, more status and more pay, there is evidence of change in the experience of work for some men, particularly working-class men. This change has been mainly caused by economic recession which has led to unemployment in traditional industries and manufacturing. In parts of the country, women may even have replaced men as the main breadwinner in some families. Some writers suggest that this has led some men to feel frustrated at their inability to fulfil their traditional role as breadwinner and protector. Mac an Ghaill (1996) suggests these men are experiencing a 'crisis in masculinity'. This may threaten marital stability and play some part in causing higher divorce rates in such areas.

Willott and Griffin (1996) have explored this so-called 'crisis'. They researched a group of long-term unemployed men in the West Midlands. Their respondents typified the kinds of men most likely to be marginalized because they had little hope of finding steady employment. However, while their role as provider was undermined, their other masculine characteristics (in particular their sense of authority over their families) remained. Willot and Griffin reject the thesis that men are experiencing a crisis in masculinity. Rather, they suggest that there is merely a weakening of certain elements of traditional masculinity.

Sociological explanations of gender stratification in employment

Functionalism and human capital theory

You should be familiar with the functionalist position associated particularly with the work of Talcott Parsons in the mid-20th century. Parsons felt that separate gender roles for men and women were helpful to societies. He claimed that women were more suited to what he called 'expressive roles' – those emphasizing caring and emotions – while men were the ideal candidates for 'instrumental roles' – those that required qualities of competition, aggression and achievement. This view implies that men are more suited to paid employment and women are more suited to domesticity. The implications of Parsons' view are that women will be less motivated and less suited to the labour market than men. Therefore, he suggests that it is not surprising that they will, on average, be paid less.

Some economists have gone on to suggest that the pay gap between men and women is justified because it reflects the fact that men have more '**human capital**' than women because of their greater orientation to paid work. It is suggested that women are less committed to paid work and are more likely to take career breaks or to opt for part-time work in order to continue to care for their families. Men, however, will be able to build up their skills, qualifications and experience because they are in receipt of more education and training and their employment is not interrupted by family commitments.

Human capital theory has been criticized by Olsen and Walby (2004). They used data from the longitudinal British Household Panel Survey to investigate the causes of pay differences between men and women. They accept that pay differentials partly reflect the fact that women tend to experience less full-time employment than men and take more career breaks, but they argue that the main cause of women's low pay is 'systematic disadvantage in acquiring human capital'. For example, pay is lower in occupations where there are high concentrations of women. This could well be because these jobs provide less training and promotion prospects than those jobs in which men are in the majority. Furthermore, human capital theory assumes that experience of employment increases wages, yet experience of part-time work (which is mainly taken up by women) is actually associated with a slight reduction in wages.

Dual labour-market theory

Many sociologists have looked for explanations for gender stratification within the structure of the labour market as a whole. Barron and Norris (1976) argue that a **dual labour-market** exists, i.e. the labour market is divided into two sectors:

1 a primary sector consisting of secure, well-paid jobs with good prospects
2 a secondary sector characterized by poor pay, insecurity and no ladder of promotion.

It is very difficult to move from the secondary to the primary sector. Barron and Norris argue that women are more likely to be found in the disadvantaged secondary sector for three reasons.

1 Women's 'unsuitability'

There is some evidence that employers may hold stereotypical beliefs about the 'unsuitability' of women for primary-sector roles. Studies by West and Zimmerman (1991) and Hartnett (1990) both noted that employers in the 1990s subscribed to myths and negative stereotypes about women workers such as:

● Male workers do not like working for a female manager – employers are therefore reluctant to promote females to management positions.
● Women are less dependable because they often take time off work to deal with family commitments.
● Women are financially dependent on their husbands and so are either not as committed to work as male breadwinners or they have less need of pay rises/promotion.
● Women will stop work when they marry and have children, so there is little point investing in their long-term training.
● Children are psychologically damaged by their mothers spending long periods of time at work rather than spending quality time with them. In order to protect children, women should not be given management jobs because these involve long and unsociable hours.

2 Disrupted career development

Jobs with good promotion prospects often recruit people at a young age and require several years of continuous service. It is difficult in most jobs to take long periods of time out of work and return to a similar position. However, social pressure to have a family often leads to women taking extensive time out of employment. Consequently, they lack experience compared with men and often miss out on promotion when they do return to the workplace. Abbott and Wallace (1997) argue that women's continuous employment is also undermined by the fact that the husband's career and pay is often regarded as more important. Therefore, if his job requires a move to another part of the country, wives are often forced to interrupt their careers and give up their jobs.

Key themes

Gender, life-chances and stereotyping

Education

Although girls now outperform boys in terms of numbers of GCSEs and A-level qualifications, there are clear differences in subjects studied. In 2005, 71 per cent of entries for English Literature A-level and 69 per cent of Sociology A-level entries were female, whilst 76 per cent of A-level Physics entries were male. In vocational training in 2005, gender differences were even more marked, with females heavily dominating early-years care and hairdressing (97 per cent and 91 per cent respectively), while plumbing, electrical work and construction were 99 per cent male.

Power and politics

Although women make up 46 per cent of the workforce, they are underrepresented in many jobs with power and influence. For example, only 19 per cent of MPs, 12 per cent of senior police officers and 9.6 per cent of top judges are women.

Mass media

Women constituted only 13.6 per cent of editors of national newspapers and 10.5 per cent of the chief executives of large media companies in 2005. The media are a continuing source of conventional gender stereotyping. Toy manufacturers also develop and market toys specifically for girls or boys. Not only are they stereotyped, but many boys' games and toys are noticeably violent and aggressive.

Family

Even before birth, expectations based on gender may affect how a child is perceived by its parents. Some parents, especially fathers, hope their firstborn will be a son in order to continue the family name and to be a protector to any younger (girl) children that follow. Once a child is born, it is treated in gendered ways, and studies have shown that a mother will react differently to a baby depending on whether they are told that it is a girl or a boy.

More examples of gender stereotyping from the topics you have studied can be found throughout this book and its AS-level companion.

Adapted from *Sex and Power* by the Equality and Human Rights Commission (2008), and various pamphlets and *Facts About Women and Men In Great Britain* by the Equal Opportunities Commission (2006)

3 Weak legal and political framework supporting women

Both the Equal Pay and Sex Discrimination Acts are ineffective because they fail to protect women's employment rights. Coussins (1976) described the Sex Discrimination Act as 'feeble', because it does not apply to many areas of employment. Further, she doubted the commitment of governments to eliminate gender inequality. She noted that the government has done little to promote free or cheap nursery care and encourage employers to provide crèche facilities for their workers who are mothers. However, recent changes in the legal position of part-time workers have benefited women considerably and some attempt has been made to recognize that men, too, have some responsibility for childrearing, with the introduction of recent legislation to allow unpaid leave for either partner.

Evaluation of dual labour-market theory

Dual labour-market theory has two strengths as an explanation of vertical segregation:

1   It stresses that the social organization of work in Western societies is essentially **patriarchal**, with men in positions of power making gendered discrimination and women's subordinate status at work seem 'normal' and 'natural'.
2   It undermines the popular assumption that better qualifications and increased ambition for women – what Wilkinson calls the 'genderquake' – would automatically dismantle gender divisions in employment. Women with the same qualifications as

men will continue to be disadvantaged as long as these two sectors exist and continue to be underpinned with patriarchal stereotypical assumptions about the role of women.

However, Bradley (1996) points out that the theory fails to explain inequalities in the same sector. For example, teaching is not a secondary labour-market occupation yet, as we saw above, women are less likely than men to gain head-teacher posts.

Feminism

Perhaps the most significant contributions to understanding gender stratification have come from the range of perspectives classified as feminist. Here, we focus on the ways feminists have explained the position of women in employment.

Liberal feminism

Liberal feminists argue that traditional forms of gender-role socialization found in the family, but also in education and the mass media, are responsible for reproducing a sexual division of labour in which masculinity is largely seen as dominant and femininity as subordinate. For example, parents continue to see a boy's education as more important than a girl's, whilst schools continue to channel boys and girls into stereotypical subject choices which impact in the long term on university and career choices.

Ann Oakley (1974) argues that the main reason for the subordination of women in the labour market is the continuing dominance of the mother–housewife role for women. She argues that patriarchal ideology stresses the view that a woman's major function is to raise children and that family rather than career should be the main focus of their lives. The fact that female professional workers are three times more likely not to be married than their male counterparts also supports this view, as does the fact that being childless increases a woman's chances of becoming a director of a major company.

In the 1990s, some liberal feminists suggested that these processes were coming to an end. Sue Sharpe's work on the attitudes of teenage girls (1994) suggests that education and careers are now a priority for young women. Females have also enjoyed greater educational success than males in recent years. Liberal feminists, therefore, have an optimistic view of the future for women. In the family, they see evidence of both partners accepting equal responsibility for domestic work and childrearing. They also argue that dual-career families in which both partners enjoy equal economic status are becoming the norm. Legislators too are beginning to recognize male responsibility for childcare with the recent increases in paternity rights.

However, liberal feminism has been subject to some criticisms:

● Although there is evidence that masculinity and femininity are socially constructed, it does not explain why this leads to men dominating and women being oppressed.
● It implies that people passively accept their gender identities, underestimating the degree to which women may resist society's expectations of them.
● It fails to acknowledge that women's experiences differ according to social class and race.
● In seeing gender equality as simply a matter of time, real obstacles to progress are being overlooked. During World War II, when women were required to work in munitions factories, for example, free crèche places were made available. Over half a century later, only a small percentage of workplaces provide this facility.

Marxist feminism

Marxist feminists are heavily influenced by Marxist sociological theory. They argue that the subordination of women to men is directly linked to their position within a capitalist society. According to Margaret Benston (1972), women benefit capitalism in two important ways:

1   Women provide free domestic labour, which functions to make male workers more effective. She notes that women were excluded from paid employment in the early to mid-19th century. Thereafter, the major role of women became the mother-housewife role. Benston argues that if the woman is a full-time housewife, the male wage actually ends up paying for both the labour power of the male and the domestic labour power of the woman. The housewife, by providing a comfortable home, meals, etc., provides emotional and domestic support for her husband so that he can return to work as a healthy and efficient worker.

Women have returned to the labour market in large numbers since the 1980s, but it can be argued from a Marxist-feminist perspective that domestic labour is still important because surveys indicate that women in relationships with men still take most of the responsibility for housework and childcare.

2   Women are also responsible for raising the future labour force at no extra cost to the capitalist class. This raising of the next generation of waged workers is referred to as the 'reproduction of labour power'.

According to Ansley (1976), women in relationships with men also function to soak up the male worker's frustration with his paid work (e.g. low pay, low status, little power) in the form of domestic violence.

Other Marxist feminists see women as part of '**reserve army of labour**', which is only hired by prosperous firms in times of rapid economic expansion and fired when recession sets in. Marxists argue that women are more vulnerable to trends such as economic recession, downsizing and mergers, and therefore constitute a more disposable part of the workforce for a number of reasons:

● They change jobs more frequently than men because of pregnancy and childcare, or because their job is secondary to that of their partner, i.e. they may be forced to change jobs if their partner is relocated to another part of the country.
● They are generally less skilled, often part time and less likely to be members of trade unions. As a result, it is easier for employers to sack them.
● Capitalist ideologies are generally patriarchal and so mainly locate women in the home. The idea that married women have less right to a job than men is common among management, unions and even among women themselves. Therefore, when women lose their jobs an ideology of domesticity comes into play which suggests that women are more generally suited to the home and childcare rather than work or a career, 'justifying' discrimination against them in the labour market.

Marxist feminists have been criticized for being tautological, in that the starting point of their argument is also their conclusion. Marxist feminists believed that there had to be a reason why women were excluded from the workforce and why they undertook domestic labour for men. Marxists explained this in terms of its benefits to capitalism. They therefore looked for the benefits to capitalism of women working at home and came to the conclusions that we have seen above. Walby (1986) is critical of this approach because, as she points out, it could quite as easily have been argued that women staying at home harmed capitalism because women competing with men for jobs would probably lower wages and increase profits. Women who earn also have superior spending power, which boosts capitalism.

The reserve army of labour theory has been criticized, too, because it does not explain why male and female labour are put to different uses. In other words, it fails to explain why there are men's jobs and women's jobs. It also fails to explain why women ended up with responsibility for domestic labour, especially considering that historical evidence suggests that in the pre-industrial period, this was the responsibility of children and older adults of both sexes rather than exclusively female.

Marxist feminism can also be criticized for overlooking the fact that patriarchy can be as influential in its own right, the implication being that once capitalism is abolished, gender inequality will disappear. However, there is no guarantee of this. According to Ellwood (1982), in the communist Soviet Union, women could fly to the moon but they still had to do the ironing once they got home.

Radical feminism

Radical feminists argue that gender inequality is more important than class inequality. They argue that society is divided into two fundamental gender classes – men and women – whose interests are opposed. Modern societies are patriarchal societies in which women are exploited and oppressed by men in all aspects of social life. Culture, government, tradition, religion, law, education and the media all reflect patriarchal leadership and power.

According to radical feminists, all these types of patriarchal inequality originate not in wider society, but in the intimacy of personal relationships, in sexual partnerships, and in families and households of various kinds. From a radical feminist perspective, all personal relationships are 'political', in that they are based upon different and unequal amounts of power, which are determined by sex and which are reinforced by every aspect of the wider society. Radical feminists particularly focus on the power relationships that are experienced in private – above all, the significance of sexuality and men's use of domestic and sexual violence. Radical feminists note that patriarchal definitions of women's sexuality are used to control women for the benefit of men. Women are told how to look, dress and behave. When patriarchal ideology fails, then women are constantly under the threat of male violence and sexual aggression, which limits their capacity to live as free and independent beings.

However, radical feminism has been criticized for failing to acknowledge historical change, e.g. the fact that women now experience the same rights as men. Radical feminists also fail to take account of divisions between women themselves, caused by class and ethnicity. Black feminists have been particularly critical of the **ethnocentricity** of most feminist approaches, which have assumed that all women experience patriarchy in the same way. Black feminists point out that different forms of inequality actually interact with each other. Bhavani (2000) puts the following question: 'When comparing racism to sexism, which is more fundamental?' In her view, racism and sexism shape each other and both, in turn, are influenced by social class.

Dual systems approach

Delphy (1977) takes a slightly different approach, emphasizing, like the radical feminists, the key role of the family. Like Marxists, however, she argues that the

Explain the radical feminist argument that 'all personal relationships are political'

household is an important and underrated place of work. Indeed, she refers to 'housework' as 'the domestic mode of production' and argues that the work performed by women is highly productive. However, she notes that men dominate households because they have more economic power than women. As a result, the views and wishes of men prevail within families. Some support for this position comes from studies of family poverty (Joseph Rowntree Foundation 1995), which indicate that women rather than men experience the consequences of poverty within families because men are more likely than women to spend money on themselves rather than the family unit.

Walby on patriarchy

Sylvia Walby (1990) suggests that the radical-feminist and Marxist approaches could be combined. She argues that capitalism and patriarchy work alongside each other to exploit women. Walby argues that patriarchy has evolved from 'private patriarchy', in which women were limited to the domestic sphere, to 'public patriarchy', in which women have entered the public arenas of employment, politics and so on, but are still disadvantaged. She notes that 'women are no longer restricted to the domestic hearth, but have the whole society in which to roam and be exploited'.

Walby argues that patriarchy intersects with capitalism and racism to produce a modern form of gender stratification underpinned by six key patriarchal social structures:

1 *The area of paid work* – Women experience discrimination from employers and restricted entry into careers because of the ideology that 'a woman's place is in the home'; when they enter work they experience low pay, low status, etc.

2. *The household* – Female labour is exploited in the family
3. *The state* – This acts in the interests of men rather than women in terms of taxation, welfare rules, the weakness of laws protecting women at work, etc.
4. *Cultural institutions such as the mass media* – These represent women in a narrow set of social roles, such as sex objects and as mother–housewives or wives and girlfriends, rather than people in their own right. (This is covered in depth in Chapter 3, *Mass media*, see pp. 179–82.)
5. *Sexuality* – A double standard persists in modern society that values multiple sexual partners for men but condemns the same behaviour in women
6. *Violence against women* – Sexual assault, domestic violence and the threat of violence are used by men to control the behaviour of women.

Walby acknowledges that inequalities between men and women vary over time and in intensity. For example, young women are now achieving better educational qualifications than men and, as a result, the intensity of patriarchy has to some extent lessened. Nevertheless, women continue to be disadvantaged. Walby notes that the most powerful positions in all aspects of society continue to be held by men. She concludes that patriarchy continues to exist but that different **gender regimes** affect groups of women differently. For example, the experience of White single mothers is likely to be different to the experience of Asian women or White female professionals.

Criticisms of feminist theory

Feminist theory has not gone uncriticized. A huge amount of debate has been generated by the approaches just explored.

- There does not seem to be much agreement between feminists about how patriarchy should be defined, what its causes are and the forms that it takes in modern societies.
- Some feminists have suggested that if patriarchy is universal, i.e. found in all societies, then, its origin may be biological. It has been suggested that whilst women are in the stages of advanced pregnancy, childbirth and childrearing, they are more likely to be dependent on men. Patriarchy may therefore be the product of women's reproductive role rather than culture or capitalism.
- Delamont (2001) has pointed out that feminist writers seem to assume that women share a common position of exploitation. She suggests that there are many divisions between women on grounds of income and social class, ethnicity and religion.
- Feminists often fail to take into account the changing nature of modern societies, which has resulted in women rapidly acquiring social, legal, educational and economic benefits. It is argued that if modern societies were truly patriarchal, women would remain fixed into a subordinate position. This is obviously not the case in the UK today.

Preference theory

Catherine Hakim (2000) has examined data about gender and work from across the world. She argues that reliable contraception, equal-opportunities legislation, the expansion of white-collar and part-time jobs, and the increase in lifestyle choices give women in modern societies more choices than ever before. However, women do not respond to these choices in the same ways. She identifies three main types of work–lifestyle preferences that women may adopt:

1. *Home-centred* – 20 per cent of women prefer not to be in employment because family life and children are their main priorities.
2. *Adaptive* – The majority of women (about 60 per cent) are those who want to combine family and paid work in some way.
3. *Work-centred* – 20 per cent of women see careers or other involvement in public life as their priority. Childless women are concentrated in this category.

Hakim argues that this choice of preferences creates conflict between different groups of women – the policies and practices that suit one group may not necessarily work in the interests of the others. Men, on the other hand, are much more alike in their preferences – most fit into the 'work-centred' category. This is one reason for the continuation of male dominance or patriarchy.

Hakim's ideas seem to be supported by Scott, who found that support for gender equality appears to be declining across Britain because of concerns that women who play a full role in the workforce do so at the expense of family life (Scott *et al.* 2008). She found that both women and men are becoming more likely to believe that both the mother and the family will suffer if a woman works full time. In 1994, 51 per cent of women in Britain and 52 per cent of men said they believed family life would not suffer if a woman went to work. By 2002, those proportions had fallen to 46 per cent of women and 42 per cent of men. There was also a decline in the number of people thinking the best way for a woman to be independent is to have a job. As Scott notes:

> ≪ It is conceivable that opinions are shifting as the shine of the 'super-mum' syndrome wears off, and the idea of women juggling high-powered careers while also baking cookies and reading bedtime stories is increasingly seen to be unrealisable by ordinary mortals. ≫

However, Scott also found that there was a continuing decline in the proportion of women and men who think 'it is the husband's job to earn income and the wife's to look after the children'. In 1987, 72 per cent of British men and 63 per cent of British women agreed with this proposition, but by 2002, the proportion had fallen to 41 per cent of men and 31 per cent of women.

The Fawcett Society, which campaigns for equal rights for men and women, said the study showed that work and family were still patriarchal institutions. Workplaces –

and, in particular, the culture of long working hours and the lack of flexible working – are still made by men for the benefit of men. Moreover, women still shoulder the bulk of caring and housework at home. Women are therefore often presented with impossible choices – they are forced to choose between caring for a family at home or either maximizing their career opportunities or bringing much needed income into the home.

Hakim's work has provoked much opposition from feminists. For example, Ginn et al. (1996) point out that all too often it is employer attitudes rather than women's work orientation that confine women to the secondary labour market or the home.

Postmodern or 'difference' feminism

Postfeminism has two strands. The first asserts that feminism is no longer necessary because women have largely won equality. Faludi (1992) suggests that feminism went too far in criticizing men, the family and femininity, and this has created a male backlash which has undermined the power of the feminist message. Consequently, few girls see themselves as 'feminists' today. She notes how politicians, business leaders and advertisers among others have, on the one hand, recognized women's equality, whilst on the other hand, they have highlighted its cost to women. Magazines in the USA, for example, claim that professional women are more prone to alcoholism, hair loss and infertility, whilst women without children suffer more hysteria and depression.

The second strand abandons the feminist grand theories to adopt a more postmodern position. Brooks (1997) argues that there needs to be a shift from the old debates about equality to debates about difference. Postmodern feminists suggest that terms like 'patriarchy' and 'women' overgeneralize because male ideology does not affect all women in the same way and so all women do not experience oppression in the same way. Postmodern feminists believe that there exist a range of masculinities and femininities; consequently, they reject the idea that some characteristics should be preferred over others. They particularly concentrate on differences between women and how these might affect choices and lifestyles, especially with regard to inequalities in consumption and how women construct their identity.

Conclusion: which is more important, gender or class?

Feminists, particularly radical feminists, have pointed to the importance of gender inequalities in society. For many of these writers, despite cosmetic improvements to the position of women, gender is still the most significant social division in modern societies.

For many years, when sociologists talked about social inequality, they meant social class. However, Pilcher and Whelehan (2004) identify three key developments since

the 1970s that have threatened the predominance of class analysis:

1   *Social and economic changes* – There has been a major shift from heavy industry and manufacturing to an economy dominated by service jobs in retail, finance and the public sector. Some sociologists have seen this feminization of the economy and workplace as a sign that gender may now be more important than social class in shaping our experience of work, inequality, etc.
2   *Feminists,* such as Walby (1990), have pointed out that much conventional sociology has either ignored gender or failed to recognize the importance of gender in structuring other forms of inequality.
3   *Postmodern perspectives* have directed attention towards diversity, difference and choice, which has undermined the traditional focus on large social and economic groupings such as classes (see pp. 422 and 439).

Today, most sociologists would argue that social class, gender and ethnicity combine to shape our experience of society and social consequences, such as inequality. For example, Skeggs' (1997) research on a group of White, working-class women leads her to conclude that class cannot be understood without gender and vice versa. Similarly, Anthias (2001) argues that class, gender and ethnicity each involve distinctive features, but together create the conditions we live in and the opportunities we have.

Check your understanding

1   Using your own words, explain the difference between horizontal and vertical segregation.

2   What is the relationship between vertical segregation and the glass ceiling?

3   How can dual labour-market theory be used to explain vertical segregation?

4   Why have some sociologists argued that a 'crisis of masculinity' exists?

5   How does human capital theory justify the gender pay gap? How can it be criticized?

6   How does Walby use the concept of patriarchy to explain gender stratification?

7   According to Hakim, why are women now able to have different 'preferences' for their work/lifestyle balance?

8   What does Faludi mean by the 'male backlash'?

9   How does postmodern feminism differ from other forms?

10 Why is class analysis less popular with sociologists than 50 years ago?

Key terms

Dual labour-market theory see Key Terms in Topic 7.

Ethnocentricity the view that your own culture is 'normal' and all others 'abnormal'.

Gender regimes term used by Walby to illustrate how patriarchy continues to exist but affects different groups of women in different ways.

Glass ceiling invisible barrier preventing women from gaining high-status positions in employment.

Horizontal segregation gender division in the workplace whereby men and women work in different jobs in different occupational sectors.

Human capital education, training and employment experience believed to give some employees pay advantages.

Patriarchy system of male domination.

Postfeminism recent views on gender influenced by postmodernism.

Reserve army of labour Marxist concept used to describe an easily exploitable pool of workers drawn from vulnerable groups, who can be moved in and out of the labour market as it suits capitalists.

Vertical segregation gender division in the workplace whereby women occupy the lower levels of pay and status in particular jobs.

Activities

Research ideas

1 Try to get hold of a staff list from your school or college. Find out which of the staff are in which positions. To what extent does the institution you are studying in reflect vertical segregation?

2 Interview a sample of younger and older women about feminism. What meaning do they give to feminism? To what extent do their views reflect different types of feminism?

Web.tasks

1 Find out the range of feminist views on a series of different issues by exploring the site: **www.feminism.com**

2 Find the latest statistics on the position of men and women in British society at the websites of the Equality and Human Rights Commission and the government's Women's Equality Unit.

An eye on the exam   Gender and stratification

Item A

During her lifetime, a woman will earn over a quarter of million pounds less than the average man – and this is without taking motherhood into account, which adds another £140 000! The pay gap is not only disastrous for women, but for everyone, because it reduces family incomes. But why are women earning less than men?

First, women work in low-paid sectors of the economy, such as retail and caring. Second, the existence of the 'glass ceiling' – men predominate in management, with women clustered in the lower-paid roles of organizations. Pay discrimination – inequality and lack of transparency in pay systems – discriminates against women. Finally, women still take the major responsibility for caring and domestic duties, leaving them unable to have real choices about their working lives.

Adapted from Equal Opportunities Commission (2005) *Equal Pay Year* brochure, EOC

Using material from **Item A**, assess sociological explanations of gender inequality in today's society.

(21 marks)

Grade booster   Getting top marks in this question

Make use of Item A to identify and outline some of the gender inequalities in today's society, including those in the workplace (e.g. pay, promotion, employment in different sectors from men) and in the home (childcare and housework). You need to consider a range of different sociological explanations in your answer, such as the different varieties of feminism (liberal, Marxist, radical and difference), human capital theory and dual labour-market theory. In discussing explanations, make use of relevant concepts, such as patriarchy, reserve army of labour, primary and secondary labour markets, and horizontal and vertical segregation. You can develop evaluation by considering evidence for or against different views as well as by using one view to argue against another.

Ethnicity and stratification

Getting you thinking

JANE ELLIOTT, a junior school teacher in the USA, began her crusade against racism and discrimination one day after the assassination of Dr Martin Luther King, Jr in 1968. She wanted her students to experience actual racism, so she told the blue-eyed students they were smarter, nicer, cleaner and deserved more privileges than the students with brown eyes. The day became a life-changing experience for the children and for Elliott. On the second day of the experiment, Elliott reversed the situation. What she discovered was amazing. Whoever was on top was not only better-behaved, but also more likely to learn. One dyslexic boy even learned how to read for the first time.

Elliott believed that all people are racists, whether they choose to believe it or not. She was frequently interviewed on TV chat shows as her experiment quickly caught the media's attention. 'I am a racist,' she said. 'If you want to see another racist, turn to the person on your right. Now look at the person on your left.'

Elliott stressed that the world didn't need a colour-blind society, but rather a society that recognizes colour. She said people are conditioned to the myth of White superiority. 'Differences are very valuable', she said. 'Start recognizing them and appreciating them.

They are what make up our world.'

The experiment is commonly used today to raise awareness of discrimination issues with students around the world. The following comments were made by an older group of Dutch students in 1998:

'Today, I have learned what it is to be seen by others as a minority. I did not expect that it would be so humiliating! In the end, I really had the feeling that I was a bit inferior. I was against racism and discrimination already, but now I understand what it really is.'

'I was one of the blue-eyes today, and I did not find that funny. I felt greatly discriminated against because we (the blue-eyeds) had to shut our mouth and stand still. The brown eyes were treated well. I really understand that people who are discriminated against must feel very angered, like I felt today. It was very much worth it.'

'When you feel day by day what I today as a blue-eye felt (especially in the beginning of the day) then your life is rotten... Racism is so very easy to do. Before you realize it happens. As a person, you are powerless, it makes more sense to revolt together.'

Source: Magenta Foundation (a web-based antiracist educational organization based in the Netherlands) © 1999 Amsterdam. www.magenta.nl

1 Why does Jane Elliott believe that all people are racists?

2 Is it racist to treat people differently on the basis of characteristics over which they have no control?

3 Should people have to control their social or cultural characteristics to conform to the requirements of the dominant culture?

4 To what extent can it be argued that it is racist to treat all people in the same way?

Your discussion may have concluded that racism has several dimensions, and that it is racist both to treat people negatively on the basis of their perceived physical or cultural differences and, ironically, to ignore such difference. Both aspects can also be seen to operate when examining racism sociologically.

It is important to understand that the terms '**race**' and '**ethnicity**' are potentially problematic for a number of reasons. First, the concept of 'race' was once used to

suggest biological differences between groups, but has since been discredited in that sense and abandoned in favour of the term 'ethnicity' or 'ethnic minority'. However, Kenyatta and Tai (1999) argue that the concept of 'race' is a superior concept because it focuses attention on power differences, economic exploitation, inequality and conflict. They argue that sociological discussions of 'ethnicity' tend to be focused on culture, religion and identity rather than inequality. However, with regard to inequalities in employment, education and health, most sociological literature focuses on differences between the ethnic majority, i.e. Whites, and ethnic minorities. This chapter will generally do the same.

The term 'ethnic minority' is also problematic. There are literally hundreds of different ethnic groups living in the modern UK. However, the sociological literature tends to focus on those who make up about 7 per cent of the UK population, i.e. people from Asian backgrounds who make up about 5 per cent of British society and people from African-Caribbean backgrounds who make up about 2 per cent. However, the terms 'Asian' and 'African-Caribbean' are also problematic. The term 'Asian' does not refer to people from the wider Asian continent – rather it refers only to those people who are from or related to people from the Indian subcontinent, particularly India, Pakistan and Bangladesh, although a large number of Asians came to the UK in the 1970s from East Africa, particularly Uganda and Kenya. Chinese people, therefore, are treated as a separate category. However, the term 'Asian' disguises national, regional and, particularly, religious differences and conflicts between Asian groups. Many sociologists believe that insufficient attention is paid to the specific origins and experience of people of Asian origin in the UK. As Bhopal et al. (1991) point out:

>> The term 'Asian' is applied to people who have come to Britain from many different parts of the world, most notably India, Pakistan, Bangladesh, Uganda, Kenya and Tanzania, and from peasant or urban middle class backgrounds; they are also differentiated in their religion, language, caste, kinship obligations, diet, clothing, health beliefs, and birth and burial practices, and yet there is an inbuilt assumption through the use of the term that they all share a common background and experience.>>

The term 'African-Caribbean' is also fraught with problems. People from African-Caribbean backgrounds originally came from a dozen or so islands that were ex-colonies of the UK and scattered across thousands of miles of ocean. These islands have their own very distinctive and cultural identities and consequently people from them have very little in common apart from the colour of their skin and perhaps support for the West Indies cricket team.

Another problem with using terms like 'ethnic minorities', 'Asians', 'Blacks', etc., is that they imply that people from these backgrounds are recent immigrants and that they have very little in common with British culture. However, it is important to understand that we are now on the third generation of people in the UK from Asian or African-Caribbean origin. Most people from these backgrounds are young British citizens rather than recent migrants.

Finally, the term 'Muslim' has recently taken on an emotional meaning for White people because of the appearance of Islamic terrorism in the UK. This emotional response may have reinforced divisions between the White population and the Muslim minority. However, Samad (2006) notes that such divisions disguise the fact that most Muslims share a great deal in common with White people – especially working-class Whites – in terms of educational attainment, uncertain labour market futures, social exclusion and marginalization.

Racism

Miles (1989) has argued that a key factor in the fact that ethnic-minority groups are more likely than Whites to be found at the bottom of the stratification system is **racism**. This is a system of beliefs and practices that exclude people from aspects of social life on the grounds of racial or ethnic background.

Racism can be seen to have three key elements: **prejudice**, **racial discrimination** and institutional discrimination.

Prejudice

Racial prejudice is a type of racism that is expressed through opinion, attitude or fear rather than action, i.e. many prejudiced people do not act upon their beliefs (although some do). Prejudice is a way of thinking that relies heavily on stereotypes or prejudices that are usually factually incorrect, irrational, exaggerated and distorted. These are used to legitimate hostility and mistrust towards members of ethnic groups who are perceived to have negative characteristics.

According to Heath and Rothon (2003), the authors of the 2003 British Social Attitudes survey, in 1983, 35 per cent of adults described themselves as prejudiced against people of other races. This rose to a peak of 39 per cent in 1987 before falling steadily to 25 per cent in 2000 and 2001. However, in 2002, the proportion claiming to be racially prejudiced jumped to 31 per cent, the highest figure since 1994.

Connolly and Keenan (2000) in a survey of Northern Ireland found that a quarter of all their respondents were unwilling to accept either an African-Caribbean, Chinese or South Asian person as a resident in their local area. Similarly, over two out of every five people also stated that they were unwilling to accept a member of any of these three groups as a close friend. Fifty-four per cent of respondents stated that they were unwilling to accept a person of South Asian origin as a relative by way of marriage.

In 2006, a Channel 4 survey, 'How racist is Britain?', into the attitudes of 1000 White Britons towards people from different cultures found that the vast majority (84 per cent) said they were not prejudiced at all and only 1 per cent admitted to being 'very prejudiced'. However, the survey found that people subscribe to very contradictory views on race. Many of the sample were very prejudiced on some issues and very suspicious of unfamiliar cultures. On the other hand, they were also extremely tolerant, e.g. many of them were antiracist and welcomed diversity. The oldest and youngest parts of the sample were the most open-minded about mixing with ethnic-minority people. The most racist were members of the 45 to 65 age group.

Prejudice is part of a society's culture and passed from generation to generation through agencies of socialization such as the family and mass media. Rothon and Heath note that increasing levels of education are responsible for Britain being less racially prejudiced compared with 30 years ago. Their evidence suggests that educated people are the least likely to be racially prejudiced. Less than one

Focus on research

Adam Rutland (2005)
The development and regulation of prejudice in children

Rutland (2005) tested 155 White children aged between 6 and 16, assessing their responses to stories to discover the extent of their conscious and unconscious racial prejudice. The children were then split into groups according to how acceptable they thought it was to discriminate against Black children. Some children were told that they were being videotaped and that the material would be kept as a record of their answers, whilst others were shown that the cameras in their rooms were not working. In subsequent tests, children who believed they were being recorded and would be judged on the views they expressed toned down their racist opinions and presented more positive reactions to Black people than they had before. In Rutland's words, 'this suggests that they were controlling their explicit ethnic bias in line with what is generally regarded as acceptable. Racially prejudiced White teenagers are simply very skilful at repressing their attitudes'

Previous research has suggested that children show signs of racial prejudice as early as 3 years of age, that these attitudes peak around the ages of 7 and 8 and decrease in adolescence. However, Rutland's study indicates that rather than becoming more enlightened and tolerant in their racial attitudes, racially prejudiced White teenagers are simply very skilful at hiding their racial prejudice when they feel it is in their interests to do so.

Dr Rutland points to the impact his research should have on the work schools need to do to manage relationships between White and ethnic-minority students if they are to be more successful in eliminating racial discrimination among them.

Source: Rutland, A. (2005) *The Development and Regulation of Prejudice in Children*, London: ESRC research

1 **What methods were used by Rutland and how might their reliability be questioned?**

2 **What implications do Rutland's findngs have for race relations in the UK?**

in five graduates (18 per cent) admit to being prejudiced compared with more than a third (35 per cent) of those with no qualifications. Rothon and Heath note that younger people are more tolerant and therefore less racially prejudiced than older people. However, research by Rutland (2005) questions this assumption. His data found that rather than becoming more enlightened and tolerant in their racial attitudes, racially prejudiced White teenagers are aware that racial prejudice is not acceptable and consequently they very skilfully hide their prejudicial attitudes because they feel that it is in their interests to do so (see 'Focus on research', left).

Rothon and Heath argue that the rise in prejudice since 2001 has been fuelled by hostile newspaper coverage of immigration and asylum seekers. Barker (1982) agrees and argues that mass media representations of ethnic minorities are symbolic of a new type of prejudice which is the product of New Right politicians and journalists. This type of prejudice highlights 'cultural difference' and suggests that traditional White British/English culture is under threat from ethnic-minority culture because ethnic minorities are allegedly not committed to integration with their White neighbours. The mass media, especially tabloid newspapers, such as the *Sun* and *Daily Mail*, reinforce these prejudices by portraying Black people, Muslims, refugees and migrants from Eastern Europe as a 'problem'. They are often represented as scrounging off welfare benefits, as criminals and as a threat to the British way of life. Barker notes that these media representations play down the problem of White prejudice towards ethnic minorities. Instead, they strongly imply that the fault lies with the 'reluctance' of ethnic minorities to adopt a British way of life.

Rothon and Heath note that although many UK newspapers urged readers not to link Islam and terrorism, numerous articles have made such a connection. They suggest that this may have resulted in a rise in 'Islamophobia' – unfounded hostility and prejudice towards Islam, and therefore fear or dislike of Muslims.

The Runnymede Trust (1997) identified a number of components that they believe make up Islamophobia and make anti-Muslim hostility seem natural and normal:

● Islam is seen as a monolithic bloc, static and unresponsive to change.
● Islam is seen as inferior to the West. Specifically, it is seen as barbaric, irrational, primitive and sexist.
● Islam is seen as violent, aggressive, threatening, supportive of terrorism and engaged in a 'clash of civilizations'.

Racial discrimination

Racial discrimination is racial prejudice put into practice. It can take many forms.

Racist name-calling and bullying

On an everyday level, racial discrimination may take the form of racist name-calling. Connolly and Keenan's survey found that 21 per cent of respondents stated that their friends had called someone a name to their face because of their colour or ethnicity. They also note that because of the sensitivity of the issue, this figure is likely to be an underestimation of the true incidence of racist name-calling.

Research sponsored by the Department for Education and Skills (2002) found that 25 per cent of pupils from minority-ethnic backgrounds in mainly White schools had experienced racist name-calling within the previous seven days. A third of the pupils of minority-ethnic backgrounds reported experiences of hurtful name-calling and verbal abuse either at school or during the school journey, and for about a half of these (one in six overall) the harassment was continuing or had continued over an extended period of time.

A survey conducted by Mirza (2007) found that nearly 100 000 racist incidents in schools have been recorded by education authorities between 2002 and 2006. Cities such as Leeds, Manchester and Birmingham have seen great increases in reported racism in the classroom. Education authorities suggest such increases are the product of more efficient and robust reporting methods, but Mirza suggests that the problem suffers from underreporting because of embarrassment and fear of further racist bullying.

Racial attacks

Discrimination may take the form of racial attacks and street violence. According to the Institute of Race Relations, between 1991 and 1997 there have been over 65 murders in Britain with a suspected or known racial motive. Although some of these victims have been White, the overwhelming majority of victims have been Asian, African-Caribbean, African or asylum seekers.

The Crime and Disorder Act created a number of new 'racially aggravated offences' in 1998. It stated that, for crimes such as assault, harassment and wounding, if there was an additional racial element to the offence, punishments should be increased. Racist chanting at football grounds was also made a criminal offence. More than 61 000 complaints of racially motivated crime were made in 2006/07, a rise of 28 per cent in just five years, with increases reported by most police forces in England and Wales. Officers classified 42 551 of the complaints as racially or religiously aggravated offences. Nearly two thirds were offences of harassment, 13 per cent wounding, 12 per cent criminal damage and 10 per cent assault.

However, the number of racial attacks reported to the police may still only be a fraction of the actual attacks that take place. According to the British Crime Survey, those at greatest risk of racially motivated attacks are Pakistani and Bangladeshis at 4.2 per cent, followed by Indians at 3.6 per cent and Black people at 2.2 per cent. This compared with only 0.3 per cent for White people.

A study of racial harassment conducted by Chahal and Julienne (1999) found that the experience of racism had become part of the everyday experience of Black and minority-ethnic people. Being made to feel different in a variety of social situations and locations was largely seen as routine and in some instances expected. Racist abuse was the most common form of everyday racism. The study found that there was limited support for victims of racist harassment and they generally felt ignored, unheard and unprotected.

Employer racism

In 2004, a BBC survey showed ethnic-minority applicants still face major discrimination in the job market. CVs from six fictitious candidates – who were given traditionally White, Black African or Muslim names – were sent to 50 well-known firms covering a representative sample of jobs by Radio Five Live. All the applicants were given the same standard of qualifications and experience, but their CVs were presented differently. White 'candidates' were far more likely to be offered an interview than similarly qualified Black or Asian 'names'. Almost a quarter of applications by two candidates given traditionally 'White' names – Jenny Hughes and John Andrews – resulted in interview offers. But only 9 per cent of the 'Muslim' applications, by the fictitious Fatima Khan and Nasser Hanif, prompted a similar response. Letters from the 'Black' candidates, Abu Olasemi and Yinka Olatunde, had a 13 per cent success rate.

In 2007, the Commission for Racial Equality reported that they had received 5000 complaints from ethnic-minority workers during the first half of 2007 and that 43 per cent of these were related to employment. The most common complaints focused on workplace bullying, lack of career progression and being unable to secure interviews. Employer racism may be partly responsible for the fact that in 2007 the unemployment rate for ethnic minorities was over 11 per cent – twice the national average. The Office for National Statistics have estimated that a Black person is three times more likely to be out of work than a White person. Research from the Joseph Rowntree Foundation suggests that, even when they are in work, people from ethnic-minority groups do not receive the same rewards as people from White backgrounds with similar qualifications. In 2004, White men were paid an average of £1.80 per hour more than ethnic-minority men.

Institutional racism

Some sociologists argue that racism is a basic feature of the rules and routines of Britain's social institutions, such as the police and courts, the immigration service, central and local government, the mass media, the education system, and the employment and housing markets. Racism is taken for granted and is so common that it is not even recognized as racism. This is known as '**institutional racism**'.

Policing

Lord Macpherson's 1998 report into the murder of the Black teenager Stephen Lawrence by White youths in 1993 concluded that the London Metropolitan Police were guilty of 'institutional racism', which was defined as 'unwitting prejudice, ignorance, thoughtlessness and racial stereotyping which disadvantaged minority-ethnic groups'. For example, when the police arrived at the scene, they initially failed to understand that Stephen had been murdered because he was Black and they also assumed that all Black people near the site of the killing (including Stephen's best friend, who had witnessed the attack) were suspects rather than witnesses. The Macpherson report denounced the Metropolitan Police as fundamentally racist for its handling of the investigation into Stephen's death. No one has been convicted of the crime.

Despite Macpherson's criticisms, chief constables have recently been accused of being complacent about the amount of racial prejudice among police officers. Studies by Holdaway (2005) and by Bowling and Phillips (2007) suggest that there exists an occupational police culture in which some officers take for granted that Black people are 'naturally' more criminal than White people. Such officers as a matter of routine use derogatory language and jokes when discussing ethnic minorities with their fellow officers. A *Panorama* investigation into cadets training to be police officers in Manchester in 2005 suggested that little was being done to prevent recruits with racist tendencies from joining the police. Holdaway's most recent research suggests that ethnic-minority officers experience racist bullying and banter from their fellow White officers. The London Metropolitan's Black Police Officer's Association actually advised Black and Asian people not to join the police in 2008 because of these experiences.

Home Office statistics on police stop and search of Black people support the view that the police may be guilty of racial stereotyping. They reveal that, in 2007, Black people were seven times more likely to be searched than White people, and Asians twice as likely.

Immigration

Britain's immigration laws are often cited as an example of institutional racism. The laws restrict the entry of Black people, while allowing White migrants easier entry.

There is also evidence that immigration rules have been implemented in a racist manner. For example, Black visitors are more likely than foreign White visitors to be stopped for questioning by immigration control. The Home Office conceded in 1999 that such practices are institutionally racist.

It is important to understand that institutional racism is not conscious nor intentional. Not all members of key institutions are necessarily racist – they may or may not be. However, it is the manner in which some institutions operate that has racist outcomes. Teachers, for example, may be committed to antiracist education but schools still expel four times as many Black pupils as White.

Another aspect of institutional racism is the failure to recognize that ethnic-minority cultures may differ in key respects from White culture, such as failing to recognize special dietary or religious needs if a Muslim or Hindu is admitted to hospital, or not providing female medical professionals to deal with female members of religious groups.

One way of tackling institutional racism is to increase the numbers of ethnic-minority employees working in key institutions, especially in higher-status positions. The monitoring of the number of ethnic-minority people in key institutions can highlight imbalances that can then be addressed through equal-opportunities strategies. However, these strategies, particularly positive discrimination, may create the potential for resentment among sections of the White population.

Key themes

Health

- Infant mortality is 100 per cent higher among the children of African-Caribbean or Pakistani mothers than among children of White mothers.
- Pakistani and Bangladeshi people are five times more likely to be diagnosed with diabetes and 50 per cent more likely to have coronary heart disease than White people.
- People from African-Caribbean backgrounds experience high levels of strokes compared with other social groups.

Education

- Pakistani and Black pupils achieve less than other pupils at all stages of compulsory education. In 2006, only 51 per cent of Pakistani pupils and 48 per cent of Black pupils achieved 5 or more GCSEs at grades A* to C, compared with 58 per cent of White pupils and 72 per cent of Indian pupils.
- Male ethnic-minority pupils perform particularly badly. 52 per cent of White boys achieved five or more GCSE grades A* to C in 2006 compared with 38 per cent of African-Caribbean boys and 45 per cent of Pakistani boys.
- 46 per cent of 18-year-old Whites achieved one or more AS-levels compared with 40 per cent of Blacks and 37 per cent of Pakistanis/Bangladeshis.
- Modood (2006) notes that ethnic minorities make up

16 per cent of undergraduates at UK universities, which is nearly double their share of the population. However, he also points out that they are more likely to enter the less prestigious new universities, they are more likely to drop out and they are less likely to finish their degree.

- African-Caribbean pupils are over four to six times more likely to be excluded than White pupils, and three times more likely to be excluded permanently. Many of those excluded are of higher or average ability, although the schools see them as underachieving.
- Ethnic-minority children from poor families measured by receipt of free school meals do better than poor White children, e.g. only 20 per cent of White children with FSM status achieved five or more GCSE grades A* to C compared with 34 per cent of African-Caribbean children, 43 per cent of Bangladeshi children and 35 per cent of Pakistani children.

Wealth, poverty and welfare

- 70 per cent of all people from ethnic minorities live in the 88 most deprived local authority districts, compared with 40 per cent of the general population.
- Some ethnic-minority groups are more likely to live in poor housing. 30 per cent of Bangladeshi and 22 per cent of Pakistani households live in overcrowded housing compared with 2 per cent of Whites.

Ethnic minorities and life-chances: empirical evidence

Ethnic minorities are disadvantaged in many areas of social life. Like the White poor, they experience multiple deprivations. However, it is very important to be aware of the significant differences between various minorities, and of the way inequalities also link with gender and class differences. For example, the majority of Muslim immigrants entered Britain at the bottom of the socio-economic ladder. Many (mostly Pakistanis and Bangladeshis) are still concentrated in semi-skilled and unskilled sectors of industry. These communities suffer from unemployment, poor working conditions, poverty, overcrowded housing, poor health, and low educational qualifications. In many ways, they share the experiences of the White urban poor. On the other hand, people from Indian and Chinese backgrounds tend to do reasonably well both in the education system and the labour market.

The 2001 disturbances in Oldham, Burnley and Bradford highlighted how multiple social deprivation can lead to deep disaffection, alienation and frustration. The areas most affected suffered from relatively high levels of youth unemployment, inadequate youth facilities, and a lack of a strong civic identity and shared social values that could have united these diverse local communities. Instead, these communities were strongly polarized along ethnic, cultural, religious and economic lines. A feeling of 'us' and 'them' developed between White and Muslim communities, enabling divisive racist organizations such as the British National Party (BNP) to exploit anti-Muslim feelings among many White people.

Key themes

Jobs, pay and poverty

- In 2004, Whites had the lowest unemployment rates at 5 per cent. The highest unemployment rates were among Black Caribbean men (14 per cent) and men from Black African, Mixed and Bangladeshi groups (each 13 per cent). Unemployment rates were slightly lower for Pakistani and Chinese men (11 per cent and 10 per cent respectively). Indian men had the lowest unemployment rates among the ethnic-minority groups at 7 per cent. In 2004, 37 per cent of Bangladeshis aged 16 to 24 and 35 per cent of Pakistanis were unemployed compared with 11 per cent of White young people.
- Differences can also be seen when unemployment rates are compared by religion. In 2004, the unemployment rate among economically active Muslim men (13 per cent) was twice the rate of Sikh (7 per cent) or Hindu (5 per cent) men. Christian men had the lowest unemployment rates (4 per cent)
- Research by The Joseph Rowntree Foundation (Clark and Drinkwater 2007) found that men from ethnic minorities in managerial and professional jobs earn up to 25 per cent less than their White colleagues. Black African and Bangladeshi men were most likely to face the greatest pay discrimination. Indian men were the least likely to be discriminated against, but they were still earning less than White men doing the same job.
- Research by the Joseph Rowntree Foundation in 2007 showed that 40 per cent of ethnic-minority communities live in poverty –

double the poverty rate of the White British communities – and are most likely to live in London, parts of the north and the Midlands than elsewhere in the UK. Half of all ethnic-minority children in the UK live in poverty.
- Ethnic-minority men were less likely than White men in 2004 to be employed in skilled trades (12 per cent compared with 20 per cent) and more likely than White men to be employed in unskilled 'elementary occupations' (16 per cent compared with 12 per cent).
- An African-Caribbean graduate is more than twice as likely to be unemployed as a White graduate, while an African is seven times as likely.
- Ethnic-minority men are overrepresented in the service sector. The distribution industry (including restaurants and retail businesses) is the largest single source of service-sector jobs for men from ethnic-minority groups, employing 70 per cent of Bangladeshi and 58 per cent of Chinese men. In contrast, only 17 per cent of White and 19 per cent of Black men work in this industry (Labour Market Trends 2000).
- However, it is important to acknowledge that a degree of upward social mobility exists within British Asian communities. For example, 47 per cent of Indian men were professional, managerial and technical workers in 2000, compared with 41 per cent of Whites.

Power and politics: the legal system

- In 2006, 86 per cent of male prisoners were White, 11 per cent were Black and 5 per cent were Asian.
- 14 per 1000 of the White population are subject to police stop and searches compared with 93 per 1000 of the Black population and 29 per 1000 of the Asian population. Black people are therefore nearly seven times and Asian people over twice as likely to be stopped and searched as White people.

Sources: ONS *Labour Market Surveys* (2002–05), *The Guardian, Social Trends* 38 (2007) and *Ethnic Minorities Factfile* (CRE 2002).

Explanations of racism and racial inequality

Cultural explanations

Racist stereotyping probably originates in a number of diverse cultural sources:

- *Britain's colonial past* – Britain's imperial power exercised during the 19th and 20th centuries clearly saw Black and Asian people as subordinate to and heavily dependent upon White people. The teaching of Britain's imperial history in schools may reinforce stereotypes of ethnic minorities picked up during family socialization and in the media.
- *Language* – Language often contains implicit cultural messages. For example, some socio-linguists have noted that words associated with Black people – e.g. 'things are looking black', accident blackspot, black sheep of the family – are negative. Black is also symbolic of evil and wrong-doing. Whiteness, on the other hand, is associated with innocence, purity, goodness, etc. The use of this type of language may, therefore, reinforce racist stereotypes passed down through socialization.
- *The mass media* – A number of degrading unsympathetic or negative stereotypes of ethnic minorities are common across the media. Van Dijk (1991) conducted a content analysis study of tens of thousands of news items across the world over several decades. He found that Black crime and violence is one of the most frequent issues in ethnic coverage. Ethnic minorities are often portrayed as a threat to the White monopoly of jobs and housing. Moreover, ethnic-minority cultures are often represented as abnormal in terms of their values and norms, and thus as undermining the British way of life. The *Big Brother* racism scandal in 2007, in which the Indian actress, Shilpa Shetty, was racially abused by White housemates, originated in the fact that they regarded her culture and accent as strange and alien.
- *Family* – People may pick up these stereotypes in the course of normal socialization from their parents and other family members.

The host–immigrant model or assimilation theory

A sociological approach that also stressed the importance of culture was Patterson's (1965) theory – the host–immigrant model – which shares many of the assumptions of functionalist sociology. Patterson depicted Britain as a basically stable, homogeneous and orderly society with a high degree of consensus over values and norms. However, she claims that this equilibrium was disturbed by the arrival of immigrant 'strangers' in the 1950s who subscribed to different cultural values. Patterson argues that this resulted in a culture clash between West Indians (who were regarded as boisterous and noisy) and their English hosts (who valued privacy, quiet and 'keeping oneself to oneself'). Patterson argued that these clashes reflected understandable fears and anxieties on the part of the host community. She claimed that the English were not actually racist – rather they were unsure about how to act towards the newcomers.

She therefore suggested that there were three causes of racial prejudice, discrimination and racial inequality:

- the host culture's (White people's) fear of strangers, cultural difference and social change
- the host culture's, particularly the working class's, resentment at having to compete with ethnic minorities for scarce resources such as jobs and housing
- the failure of ethnic minorities to assimilate, i.e. to become totally British and integrate – they tended to live in segregated communities rather than socially mixing.

Patterson's theory is implicitly critical of the insistence of ethnic minorities that they should retain their own cultural values and practices because these allegedly make White people anxious. However, she was reasonably optimistic about the future of race relations in the UK and argued that ethnic minorities would eventually move toward full cultural assimilation by shedding their 'old' ethnic values and taking on English or British values.

There are signs that the Labour government elected in 1997 has been very influenced by this assimilationist model. Government ministers have implied that racial tensions and inequality are the result of a supposed Asian desire and choice for residential self-segregation – to live in 'comfort zones' with 'their own kind'. Labour has suggested that this self-segregation of areas has led to school segregation; in some primary and secondary schools, Asian pupils have become the majority, and the affluent White middle-class have consequently responded by moving elsewhere – this has become known as 'White flight'. However, the White poor get left behind and have to compete for the same jobs and housing, which has led to racial tensions in areas like Lancashire as some areas allegedly have become no-go areas for White people.

Labour has responded by introducing 45-minute multiple-choice nationality or citizenship tests. In order to get British citizenship, immigrants to the UK must successfully answer questions on aspects of British culture and swear an oath of allegiance to the Queen. Some commentators have suggested that this Britishness test should have a language component to ensure all potential citizens can speak and write English. Critics have suggested that Labour believes that racism, racial inequality, racial tensions and the alienation of Muslim youth can only be tackled by ethnic minorities doing more to assimilate – the ideological message quite simply is: embrace British culture and become 'more like us'.

Criticisms

The evidence from areas in which racial tensions spilled over into riots in 2002, such as Oldham and Burnley, collected by the Commission for Racial Equality (CRE) suggests segregation was a product of discrimination rather than choice. Estate agents in Oldham promoted residential segregation by steering White and ethnic-minority populations into different areas. The CRE also

How is the Labour government's introduction of citizenship tests influenced by the assimilationist model?

noted evidence that suggests council officers allocated Asians to the most deprived council estates compared with Whites. Despite Whites and Asians suffering similar levels of economic and social deprivation, this policy did not promote social mixing. This segregation also made it easier for the British National Party (BNP) to stir up rumours and resentment among the White population. The BNP claimed that Asians were being allocated superior council housing despite the fact that 25 per cent of the White population lived in council housing compared with only 9 per cent of Pakistanis. The CRE also point out that Whites are responsible for White flight rather than Asians, because the White middle classes do not want to mix socially with Asians. Being able to afford to move out of an area because ethnic minorities are moving in is a type of racism.

Critics of this assimilationist host–immigrant approach point out that African-Caribbeans are the most assimilated of all ethnic-minority groups – they speak English as a first language at home, they intermarry into the White population, their children mix freely and easily with White children and they are usually Christian. There are no cultural barriers preventing them from assimilating into British cultural life. However, the economic, social and educational position of African-Caribbean people is no better than it was 50 years ago. They are still more likely to be unemployed and in poverty than Whites and their children are still most likely to fail academically or be excluded from school.

Patterson can be criticized because she failed to acknowledge that the UK is a multicultural society and that the concept of assimilation is ethnocentric – it fails to recognize that no one culture is superior and that all cultures, British and ethnic minority, have similar value. The host–immigrant model also focuses so much on culture that it tends to end up 'blaming the victim' or scapegoating them, by attributing racism and racial inequality to their 'strange' cultures.

Finally, racial hostility has not declined as predicted by Patterson. The basic structure of British society remains unchanged, and the struggle over scarce jobs, housing and money between groups of urban poor, Whites, Asians and African-Caribbeans continues to fuel racial tensions.

Weberian explanations

The work of Max Weber (1864–1920) has had a significant influence on explanations for racial discrimination and inequality. He noted that modern societies are characterized by a class struggle for income and wealth. In this sense, he would agree with Marxists. However, he also notes that modern societies are also characterized by status inequality. Status and power are in the hands of the majority-ethnic group, thereby making it difficult for ethnic-minority groups to compete equally for jobs, housing, etc. Ethnic minorities who do manual jobs are technically part of the working class, but they do not share the same status as the White working class. This is because they are likely to face prejudice and discrimination from the White working class who see them as in competition for the same scarce resources, e.g. jobs. Ethnic minorities therefore suffer from status inequality as well as class inequality. Even middle-class Asians doing professional jobs may experience status inequality in the form of prejudicial attitudes held by members of both the White middle and working classes.

Organization of the job market

Such prejudice and discrimination can be seen in the distribution of ethnic minorities in the labour force. The **'dual labour-market theory'** of Barron and Norris focuses on ethnic inequalities as well as gender inequalities in employment. They suggest that there are two labour markets:

- *the primary labour sector* – characterized by secure, well-paid jobs, with long-term promotion prospects and dominated by White men
- *the secondary labour sector* – consisting of low-paid, unskilled and insecure jobs.

Barron and Norris (1976) point out that women and Black people are more likely to be found in this secondary sector. They argue that Black people are less likely to gain primary-sector employment because employers may subscribe to racist beliefs about their unsuitability and even practise discrimination against them, either by not employing them or by denying them responsibility and promotion.

Furthermore, Barron and Norris point out that the legal and political framework supporting Black people is weak. Trade unions are generally White dominated and have been accused of favouring White workers and being less interested in protecting the rights of Black workers. The Race Relations Act 1976 (which was introduced to protect Black people from discriminatory practices) was generally thought to be weak and was rarely used in practice.

However, the recent amendment to the Race Relations Act, which came into force in 2001, increases the need for greater clarity concerning the meaning and status of race. It 'places a general duty on public authorities to work towards the elimination of unlawful discrimination and promote equality of opportunity and good relations between persons of different racial groups'. The modern Race Relations Act, therefore, aims to have a much greater and wider impact – it seeks to ensure that racial discrimination is outlawed throughout the public sector and places a duty on all public bodies and authorities to promote good race relations. However, it is too early to say whether this amendment is having any real impact.

Underclass

Another Weberian approach is that of Rex and Tomlinson (1979), who argue that ethnic-minority experience of both class and status inequality can lead to poverty, which is made more severe by racism. They believe that a Black underclass has been created of people who feel marginalized, alienated and frustrated. Another aspect of status inequality is that some young Blacks may feel both socially excluded from the standard of living most other members of society take for granted and experience policing as harassment. These feelings may occasionally erupt in the form of inner-city riots.

However, there is considerable overlap between the White and Black population in terms of poverty and unemployment, although the constant threat of racism does suggest that some members of the White working class do not recognize the common economic situation they share with Black and Asian workers. The concept of status inequality may therefore help to explain the apparent divisions between the White and ethnic-minority working class and the outbreaks of racial conflict between White and Asian people in some northern towns in 2001.

Marxist explanations

Marxists such as Castles and Kosack (1973) argue that ethnic minorities are generally part of the exploited working class and it is this that determines their fate in capitalist society. Marxists see racial conflict, discrimination and inequality as symptoms of some deeper underlying class problem. They see these symptoms as deliberately encouraged by the capitalist class for three ideological reasons:

1. *Legitimization* – Racism helps to justify low pay and poor working conditions because ethnic-minority workers are generally seen as second-class citizens undeserving of the same rights as White workers. Capitalist employers benefit from the cheap labour of ethnic minorities in terms of profits made. Some Marxists note that ethnic minorities, like women, are a **reserve army of labour** that is only taken on in large numbers during periods of economic boom but whose jobs are often the first to be lost in times of recession. However, the existence of racism means that the plight of ethnic minorities in the job market is rarely highlighted.
2. *Divide and rule* – If ethnic minority and White workers unite in a common economic interest, they are in a stronger position to campaign for better wages and conditions. Castles and Kosack argue that racism benefits employers because it divides the workforce.

The White workforce will fear losing their jobs to the cheaper labour of ethnic-minority workers. Employers play on these fears during pay negotiations to prevent White workers from demanding higher wages or going on strike.

3. *Scapegoating* – When a society is troubled by severe social and economic problems, then widespread frustration, aggression and demands for radical change can result. However, instead of directing this anger at the capitalist class or economic system, White people are encouraged by racist ideology and agents such as the mass media to blame relatively vulnerable groups such as ethnic minorities for unemployment, housing shortages and inner city decline, e.g. 'they have come over here and stolen our jobs, taken over all our corner shops'. Ethnic minorities become the scapegoats for the social and economic mismanagement of capitalism. This process works in the interest of the wealthy and powerful capitalist class because it protects them from direct criticism and reduces pressure for radical change.

However, some Marxists such as Miles (1989) have been influenced by the Weberian argument that the concept of 'status' should be used alongside the concept of 'class' to explain racism and racial inequality. Miles argues that the class position of ethnic minorities is complicated by the fact that they are treated by White society as socially and culturally different, and consequently they have become the victims of racist ideologies that prevent their full inclusion into UK society. At the same time, ethnic minorities too set themselves apart from the White majority by stressing and celebrating their unique cultural identity. Miles suggests that, as a result of these two processes, ethnic minorities are members of **racialized class fractions**'. He argues that the White working class stress the importance of their ethnicity and nationality through prejudice and discrimination, whilst ethnic minorities react to such racism by stressing their ethnicity in terms of their observance of particular religious and cultural traditions.

Miles acknowledges that some ethnic minorities may be economically successful and become part of the middle classes. These professionals and owners of businesses may see their interests lying with capitalism. For example, recent statistics suggest there are currently over 5000 Muslim millionaires in Britain. Furthermore, their ethnicity may be a crucial influence in their business practices and financial success. However, the fact of their ethnicity probably makes it difficult for them to be fully accepted by the White middle class. They are, therefore, a racialized class fraction within the middle class.

Recent approaches

It would be a mistake to think that all ethnic minorities are disadvantaged in UK society. Owen and Green (1992) note that Indians and Chinese are two ethnic groups that have made significant economic progress in the British labour market since the 1980s. Recent figures indicate that their average earnings are very similar to those of White workers. More generally, evidence suggests that increasing numbers from these ethnic minorities are entering the ranks of the professional middle class. Sociologists are also starting to notice the growth of ethnic-minority businesses and the spread of self-employment among ethnic-minority groups, particularly Asians. However, it is important to note that although groups such as Indians are moving into white-collar and professional work, they may experience a 'glass ceiling' as White professionals and managers fill the higher-status positions within this sector.

Some sociologists have also questioned whether self-employment is really such a privileged sector of the economy. The high rate of self-employment among ethnic minorities may be a reaction to the racial discrimination that prevents them from getting employment. In other words, self-employment may be forced upon them. Sometimes, these businesses are precarious ventures in extremely competitive markets (e.g. taxi-driving) and offer small rewards for long hours. Often, the owners of such businesses only manage to survive because they are able to use cheap family labour.

Postmodernist approaches

Postmodernists, such as Modood (1992), reject Weberian and Marxist explanations that seek to generalize and offer blanket explanations for ethnic groups as a whole. Postmodernists argue that ethnic-minority groups in the UK are characterized by difference and diversity. They point out that the experience of racism is not the same: different groups may have different experiences. For example, police stop-and-search tactics focus on African-Caribbeans rather than other ethnic-minority groups.

Postmodernists point out that there are also different ethnic-minority cultural responses to racism.

However, postmodernists tend to focus on 'culture and identity' issues rather than racial inequality. They suggest that both White and ethnic-minority identities are being eroded by globalization and consumption, and so members of such groups are less likely to have their identity shaped by membership of their ethnic group. Postmodernists suggest that in the 21st century, the young, in particular, have begun to 'pick and mix' their identity from a new globalized culture that interacts with both White British culture and the ethnic-minority subcultures that exist in the UK. This process has produced new **hybrid identities**. As a result, racial or ethnic differences are not fixed and imposed by membership of an ethnic group. Instead, identity has become a matter of choice. The implication of these trends is that as ethnicity and race are reduced in importance and influence, so racism and racial disadvantage will decline.

Postmodernists argue that the extent and impact of racism differ from one person to another as identities are chosen and interact. They argue that once identity is better understood, ethnic disadvantage can be targeted and addressed. For example, if we know that Jamaican boys not born in Britain living in a particular area are more

Activities

Research ideas

1 Carry out a piece of research to explore local people's knowledge of ethnic differences. Do they understand the distinctions between the various Asian groups? Do they understand the significance of particular festivals? Do they know of prophets or holy books? Can they point on a world map outline to the countries of origin of the various groups?

2 Assess the extent to which an organization such as your school or college might be deemed to be institutionally racist. Look at the distribution of ethnic groups on the various courses. Try to acquire statistics on exclusions, achievement rates and progression. What problems might you encounter in your research and how might you overcome them?

Web.tasks

1 Go to the guardianunlimited website at **www.guardianunlimited.co.uk**. Search the archive by typing in 'race equality'. Read the articles highlighting a range of issues from institutional racism, social policy reform to rural racism and racial harassment.

2 The website of the Commission for Racial Equality, at **www.cre.org.uk**, contains a range of research findings and factsheets. Select one or two and write summaries.

Check your understanding

1 How can it be argued that the term 'race' has more explanatory value than the term 'ethnicity'?

2 Where does racial prejudice come from? Give examples to back up your arguments.

3 Explain why members of organizations deemed 'institutionally racist' may not necessarily be racist individuals.

4 How can institutional racism be tackled?

5 What is wrong with early functionalist explanations of ethnic inequality?

6 How has the Labour government's policy towards race relations been influenced by assimilation theory?

7 Briefly summarize three Weberian accounts of ethnic inequality in the workplace.

8 How do Marxists argue that racism benefits capitalism?

9 Why do postmodernists reject Weberian and Marxist explanations of ethnic inequality?

likely to drop out of school, then something meaningful can be done to address this problem.

In criticism of postmodernism, evidence from studies of ethnic identity suggest that ethnic and religious identity often overlap, and that through agencies such as the family, community, places of worship and faith schools, ethnic identity is imposed rather than chosen. Such processes are often reinforced by the experience of unemployment, poverty, poor housing, inner-city deprivation and the constant fear of racial harassment. In conclusion, we can argue that postmodern ideas have greatly exaggerated the capacity of both White and ethnic-minority people to resist cultural influences and that they unrealistically play down the social and economic factors, such as everyday racism, that impact on the life-chances of ethnic-minority groups compared with Whites.

Key terms

Dual labour-market theory the view that two labour markets exist: the first has secure, well-paid jobs with good promotion prospects, while the second has jobs with little security and low pay; vulnerable groups such as women, the young, elderly and ethnic minorities are concentrated in this second sector.

Ethnicity cultural heritage shared by members of a particular group.

Hybrid identities new identities created by ethnic mixing.

Institutional racism where the sum total of an organization's way of operating has racist outcomes.

Prejudice/Cultural attitudes a style of thinking that relies heavily on stereotypes that are factually incorrect, exaggerated or distorted.

Race variation of physical appearance, skin colour and so on between populations that confers differences in power and status.

Racial discrimination racial prejudice put into practice, for example by denying someone a job on the basis of their skin colour or membership of a different ethnic group.

Racialized class fractions term used by Miles to describe splits in the working class along racial lines.

Racism systematic exclusion of races or ethnic groups from full participation in society.

Reserve army of labour Marxist concept used to describe an easily exploitable pool of workers drawn from vulnerable groups such as women, ethnic minorities, the old and the young.

An eye on the exam — Ethnicity and stratification

Item A

The 'host–immigrant' model is a functionalist approach to ethnic and race relations. It assumes that immigrants are entering a society that is based on a set of shared values. The need for value consensus means that a group with different values and beliefs is likely to be seen as both strange and inferior. If this group is also physically distinct from the host community, then racial inequality develops. Although functionalists accept the need for *social* inequality, they see *racial* inequality as dysfunctional, since it prevents talented individuals from minority groups achieving their full potential and society is less efficient as a result. Similarly, racial conflict disrupts the smooth functioning of the social system. However, functionalists are optimistic that minorities will be gradually integrated into a shared value system and that this, along with measures to guarantee equal opportunity, will result in an end to racial conflict and inequality.

Using material from **Item A**, assess the host–immigrant model of race relations.   (21 marks)

Grade booster — Getting top marks in this question

Use material from Item A to identify and summarize key features of the host–immigrant model of race relations and link it to features of the functionalist perspective such as value consensus and absence of fundamental conflicts.

You need to evaluate the model, and a good way to do so is to draw upon alternative perspectives. These include structural approaches, such as the Marxist explanations of Castles and Kosack and Miles, as well as Rex and Tomlinson's Weberian views and postmodernism. Make sure you use their key concepts such as reserve army of labour, racialized class fractions and the underclass. You should also use empirical evidence on the life-chances of different ethnic groups, e.g. in areas such as employment, education and housing, to see whether ethnic inequality is narrowing, since this would be an expectation of the host–immigrant model.

TOPIC 8

Age and stratification

Getting you thinking

- Young people are not allowed to watch films with too much sex or violence in them until the age of 18.
- The legal minimum age to stand for Parliament is 18 years.
- To become a judge, a person needs to have practised law for a minimum of 7 years.
- A person must be 13 years old to register on Facebook, Bebo and MySpace.
- Magistrates must retire at the age of 70.
- A third of job-seekers between the age of 50 and 65 are unable to find work.
- An analysis of fictional representations of the elderly in television drama and sit-coms found that 46 per cent of elderly characters were portrayed as grumpy, interfering, lonely, stubborn and sexless.
- Only 16 per cent of pensioners have a car compared with 77 per cent of all households.

Source: Ray and Sharp (2006) *Ageism: A Benchmark of Public Attitudes in Britain*, Policy Unit, Age Concern England

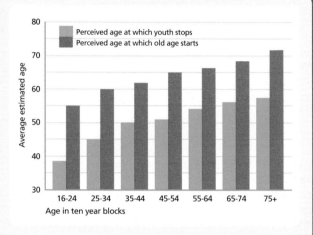

Study the figure above and the points on the left, and then answer the following questions:

1 What does the bar chart tell you about attitudes towards youth and old age?

2 What do the listed facts about age tell you about the treatment of the young and the elderly in UK society?

3 In your opinion, why are the elderly in particular subjected to such negative treatment in the UK?

Age cultures: a natural or social creation?

Ageing is a physical process that all human beings experience. However, in most societies, age is divided up into significant periods – childhood, youth or adolescence (i.e. being a teenager), young adulthood, middle age and old age. These periods have different social meanings attached to them with regard to social expectations about behaviour and lifestyle, responsibilities to others, independence and dependence, and so on. These social meanings are relative to culture and time.

In many pre-industrial and tribal societies, for example, the period of youth is notably absent, because at puberty children go through 'rites of passage' – often involving physical ordeal – that transform them into adults with much the same responsibilities as other adult members of the society. The term 'elder' in these societies symbolizes great wisdom, dignity and authority. The elderly are treated with great respect and consequently have a great deal of status. Vincent (2001) notes that what constitutes 'old

age' varies cross-culturally, although how age is defined and treated differs within our own society too. It can be argued that young people and the elderly have a great deal in common in that they both experience low status. The transition to adulthood, however, is celebrated at 18 with a social event whilst those reaching their 100th birthday are regarded as so special they get a message of congratulation from the Queen.

These age categories, or **age strata**, are not 'natural' but created by society. That is, they are **social constructions**. You may have noticed from the exercise above that different age groups have different subjective interpretations of what counts as 'young' and as 'old' – what you see as 'old' may be quite different from how the 'objectively old' (official definitions see 65 years – the age of retirement – as the beginning of old age) view themselves. However, the consequences of these constructions are that members of different age groups will experience differing degrees of social status, self-esteem and prejudice. These, in turn, will produce different experiences of inclusion and exclusion, and often marginalization and inequality.

The elderly – the demographic picture

The decline in the death rate, the increase in life expectancy and a decline in the birth rate over the last 50 years have led to an ageing of the UK population. There are increasing numbers of people aged 65 and over and declining numbers of children under 16. Between 1971 and 2004, the number of people aged under the age of 16 declined by 18 per cent while the number of people aged over 65 increased by 29 per cent. Consequently, in 2008, about 18 per cent of the population, i.e. approximately 11 million people, were over retirement age. Davidson (2006) points out that, in 2002, in the UK population over the age of 60, for every 100 men there are 127 women; over the age of 80, this ratio increases to 100 : 187. Altogether, over 65 per cent of the elderly are women.

Age and inequality

Bradley (1996) refers to old age as the most neglected and hidden dimension of social stratification and hence inequality – for example, pensioners are one of the most significant groups that make up the poor. The annual Spotlight report by Help the Aged (2008) suggests that in 2005/6, 11 per cent of UK pensioners, i.e. 1.2 million people, were living in severe poverty on less than half of average earnings. Nearly double that number – 21 per cent, or 2.2 million people – were classified as living in poverty, with incomes less than 60 per cent of average earnings. These figures suggest that nearly a third of the elderly are in poverty. The Spotlight report claims that such poverty is having a negative effect on the health of the elderly – one in four of the elderly poor suffered illness as a direct result of poverty.

There is some evidence that, in 2007, an additional 200 000 pensioners were experiencing 'fuel poverty', meaning that they were spending at least 10 per cent of their income on electricity, gas and coal just to stay warm. The numbers of pensioners likely to be experiencing fuel poverty by 2010 is estimated at 1.2 million.

Age, gender, ethnicity and social class

Age interacts with social class and gender to bring about inequality. People who are poor in old age are most likely to be those who have earned least in their working lives, i.e. women and those employed in manual jobs. This can be seen especially with regard to pension rights. Many of those working in professions such as teaching and finance can supplement their state pension with a company or private pension. However, many manual occupations fail to provide this extra.

Davidson notes that the majority of those people who are not eligible for – or who cannot afford the contributions required for – participation in private occupational pension schemes are female. This is because they are more likely to have their careers interrupted by pregnancy and childcare, and are more likely to be employed in low-paid, part-time work for a significant period of their lives. Oppenheim and Harker (1996) found

that 73 per cent of male employees receive company pensions, compared with only 68 per cent of female full-time employees and only 31 per cent of female part-time workers. Consequently, women are more likely in later life to be dependent on a husband's occupational pension or on a state pension supplemented by benefits. Mordaunt et al. (2003) report that as a result twice as many elderly women compared with men rely on benefits and one in four single (never married, widowed or divorced) women pensioners in the UK live in poverty.

Davidson notes that the proportion of ethnic-minority elders reaching retirement is higher now than ever before. She argues that interrupted work patterns, low pay and racial discrimination mean that ethnic-minority workers also have less opportunity to pay into private occupational pension schemes. They also have less economic potential to save and invest for old age. Ethnic-minority women are further disadvantaged. Davidson suggests their old age may be underpinned by race, gender and age discrimination.

Scase and Scales (2000) argue that the elderly are likely to be split between affluent early retirees and those who are on or close to the breadline. This latter group may have to continue working beyond retirement age in order to avoid severe poverty, especially as the value of state pensions relative to earnings has been declining since the early 1990s. Ray et al. (2006) also note that the retirement age often differs according to social class and status. For example, senior business executives and political leaders have the power to resist the official legal retirement requirement, and consequently they may avoid the potential poverty and negative connotations associated with being elderly or retired.

The effects of ageism

Robert Butler (1969) defined ageism as a process of negative stereotyping and discrimination against people purely on the grounds of their chronological age. The elderly have mainly been the victims of this discrimination. For example, Butler argued that ageism is about assuming all older people are the same, despite their different life histories, needs and expectations, but Best (2005) also notes that the young, especially youth, can be victims of ageism too. Moral panics which negatively focus on the activities and cultural habits of young people are cited as evidence of such ageism. However, it can argued that ageism practised against the elderly has greater negative consequences than that practised against the young, in terms of self-esteem and social well-being.

Butler suggested that ageism was composed of three connected elements:

1 prejudicial attitudes towards older persons, old age and the ageing process
2 discriminatory practices against older people
3 institutional practices and policies that perpetuate stereotypes about older people.

He argued that ageism leads to the elderly experiencing fundamental inequalities in the UK in terms of their access to jobs and services, their income and how they are viewed by younger members of society.

Focus on research

Milne et al. (1999)
Grey power

A study of elderly people in Britain (Milne et al. 1999) found evidence of two distinct 'worlds'. In one world, composed of people in the early years of retirement who live in a shared household with an occupational pension, there is a reasonably comfortable lifestyle.
In the second world, made up of those over 80 who live alone with few savings, people can suffer acute poverty.

The former grouping, comprising relatively affluent older people, is much sought after by manufacturers all over the industrialized world, where the term 'grey power' is sometimes used to refer to the consumption habits and patterns of those over 65. Of course, the term cannot be applied to all older people. First, social-class differences continue into retirement. Lifestyle and taste differences, and the impact of different occupations as well as different forms of housing tenure, persist. Second, ill health is also gendered, with men more likely to experience it at an earlier age. The jobs people did also affect their income in old age; ex-professional and managerial workers have more income than ex-manual workers. Finally, older men have generally higher incomes than older women.

Adapted from Abercrombie, N. and Warde, A. (2000) *Contemporary British Society* (3rd edn), Cambridge: Polity Press

1 Why is it that the term grey power 'cannot be applied to all older people'?

2 What might be the circumstances which lead to an older person belonging to either of the 'worlds' described above?

Institutional ageism

Greengross (2004) agrees with Butler and argues that ageism is deeply embedded and very widespread in UK society. Moreover, it is often unconscious, which makes it difficult to tackle. She notes that arbitrary age barriers set by the state mean older citizens cannot participate in many voluntary and civic activities – for example, the age limit for being a juror is 65 years whilst all judges and magistrates have to retire at 70 years. In 2006, the government implemented the UK's first age discrimination legislation. This covered all higher and further education, but excluded unpaid voluntary and civic work. Despite this

legislation, employers are still able to force workers to retire at the age of 65. In 2008, Age Concern unsuccessfully challenged the compulsory retirement age in the European courts. However, the government has stated that it will eventually move away from insisting on a compulsory legal retirement age.

Greengross argues that the National Health Service (NHS) is guilty of institutional ageism because older patients in the NHS are treated differently from the young. Older people are subjected to discrimination in that they are often omitted from clinical trials or are denied particular treatment or operations on the basis of their chronological age. Greengross notes that these decisions are usually based on prejudiced views of what a 'good innings' is or is based on the view that the interventions are not worth pursuing because a person is 'too old'. There is some evidence that trainee medical professionals may be avoiding specializing in geriatric medicine because it is regarded as a low-status sector of the NHS.

Ray et al. (2006) argue that there is a subtle difference between age-discriminatory state practices, e.g. the ageist policies practiced by the NHS as outlined above, and age-differentiated state practices, e.g. protective legislation, positive stereotyping and special treatment. The latter policies and practices are designed to benefit rather than harm the elderly. For example, having an age at which a person becomes eligible for a state pension helps to ensure an adequate income in retirement, whilst concessions on a range of services, such as free or reduced public transport, free NHS prescriptions and free television licences for those over 75, help to reduce the financial burden on the old.

However, Ray and colleagues argue that some of these practices can prove just as harmful for older people as more overtly negative forms of discrimination. For example, the types of concessions mentioned above can reinforce ageist stereotypes of older people as needy and dependent and, by doing so, exclude them from choices and opportunities.

Greengross also notes that the elderly experience ageism with regard to services other members of society take for granted. For example, ageism practiced by financial services may mean older people may have difficulty in hiring a car, getting insurance, getting a credit card or negotiating a loan.

Ageism and the mass media

Another type of institutional ageism is found in the mass media. Featherstone and Wernick (1995) point out that birthday cards in particular indicate the distaste widely held about the ageing process. Representations of men and women in the UK media tend to focus on the 'body beautiful', and television and advertising encourage women in particular to see their bodies as 'projects' in needs of constant care and improvement. Ageing – and its outward signs, such as wrinkles, grey hair, etc. – is often presented as the greatest threat to our well-being, one that needs to be resisted at all costs. Carrigan and Szmigin (2000) argue that the advertising industry either ignores older people or presents them as negative stereotypes – physically unattractive, mentally deficient, senile, cranky, grumpy, cantankerous or difficult. They conclude that advertisers fail to reflect the elderly in any authentic way.

Older people portrayed on television are often marginalized, comical or based on inaccurate stereotypes. Genuine older people are generally underrepresented on television. These stereotypes are often the only experience younger people have of old age. These negative images may, therefore, create perceptions of a future old age as a time of dependency, poor health, poverty and vulnerability, even though this may bear little relationship to the lived experience of many older people.

The 'demographic timebomb'?

Another aspect of ageism is the debate about the so-called '**demographic timebomb**'. It is predicted that in 2014, people aged over 65 years will outnumber people aged under 16 for the first time, and that the gap will widen thereafter. The number of people over retirement age in 2021 is projected to be 12.2 million. New Right thinkers have assumed, almost without question, that these elderly people are going to be dependent on younger people, that they are going to put intolerable strain on services such as health care, and that they will be a drain on the economy because of the disproportionate costs of the health care, social services and housing assistance they will supposedly need. Generally, then, this demographic timebomb is seen as likely to lead to a potential crisis for the welfare state, family and economy.

However, the concept of a demographic timebomb is based on a number of ageist assumptions that do not stand up to scrutiny:

- One such assumption is that elderly people are likely to be dependent because of poor physical and mental health. Whilst ageing is associated with some biological decline in physical and mental abilities, there is little evidence that this has a significant effect on the lifestyle of the elderly. For example, only one in 20 people over 65 and one in five people over 80 experience dementia. Ray and colleagues argue that overall, research has failed to prove a link between declining health and capability, and ageing.
- In terms of physical health, some authors suggest that there is a 'medical myth' that unfairly suggests ageing is synonymous with disease. However, decline in terms of illness may be due to prolonged and life-long exposure to an unhealthy environment and lifestyle, rather than to the ageing process itself.
- There is also an assumption that the elderly are incapable of doing paid work because the ageing process makes them incompetent. However, Ray and colleagues note that research findings indicate that younger workers are no better at their jobs than older workers, despite the widespread perception that this is the case. In experiments, it has been shown that there is no significant difference between the abilities of younger and older workers, with each group performing particularly well or poorly in different areas. Increasingly, because of the prospect of poverty and inadequate state pensions, the elderly are already returning to work post-retirement in fairly large numbers despite discrimination in the workplace. Over 1 million people are already voluntarily working beyond the state pension age, and research by the Prudential insurance company in 2005 estimated that figure could rise to 2.5 million by the end of the decade because many people won't be able to afford to retire.
- Taylor-Gooby (1996) points out that the number of pensioners increased from 6.5 million in 1951 to 10 million in 1991 without causing any major economic or social problems.

Ageist attitudes

It can be argued that all these ageist practices result in negative stereotypes underpinning social attitudes about the elderly in the modern UK, so dehumanizing members of this group. The elderly have already lost a major source of status, respect, identity and economic security – work – when they have been forced to retire. However, the sorts of ageist practices and stereotypes outlined above result in their association, particularly by the young, with dependence, vulnerability and disability. The elderly are generally seen as making little or no contribution to society and/or as a burden on society. The ascribed characteristics of age therefore serve to exclude many elderly people from full involvement in society.

The research of Ray and colleagues found that ageism is common in the UK but, despite its negative consequences, it does not have a malicious character. They note that it exists in the form of what they call 'benevolent prejudice', in that the elderly are generally viewed as moral and admirable. Most people in their survey agreed that they should be valued and cherished. However, the sample also generally saw the elderly as 'incompetent, less intelligent but dear dodderers'. Ray and colleagues suggest that disadvantages can arise from both these positive and negative attitudes which can result in the continued socio-economic

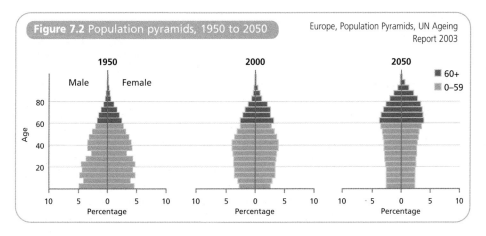

Figure 7.2 Population pyramids, 1950 to 2050

Europe, Population Pyramids, UN Ageing Report 2003

exclusion of the elderly. At an individual level, they claim that the elderly are infantilized, ignored and treated in a patronizing and disrespectful fashion. It can also lead to conflict if the elderly person fails to live up to these social expectations – for example, they may be treated preferentially when being given a seat on a bus, but may be criticized as selfish for spending their savings on a holiday when they should be looking to provide an inheritance for their families.

At an institutional level, Ray and colleagues claim that ageism can mean exclusion from the workplace and positions of power or decision-making because employers assume lower competence. It might also lead to a failure to offer the elderly choices in health and social care, and to the assumption that older people might not want the sorts of life-chances that younger people do. Finally, it might be assumed that it is natural for older people to have lower expectations and reduced choice and control. Consequently, less account is taken of their views. Ray and colleagues conclude that ageism, and therefore age inequality, can only be tackled if older people are regarded by the state and society as active participants in decisions about their future, rather than as passive victims.

The young

Like the elderly, the young also make up a large subgroup of the poor. A quarter of children live in households receiving less than 60 per cent of the average median income. In addition, many young people of working age face social deprivation caused by low pay, student loans and, in some cases, ineligibility for benefits and unemployment. In 2005, the unemployment rate for those under 25 was over 18 per cent. However, the increase in those on training schemes masks the true figure. Again, this is affected by other factors, such as ethnicity – for example, twice as many African-Caribbean males are unemployed compared with Whites.

Furthermore, the extended transitions into adulthood that characterize the experience of young people in advanced industrial societies often bring with them extended periods of relative deprivation and reduced social standing. There are now more likely to be intermediate stages between leaving school and entry into the labour market, between living in the parental home and having a home of one's own, and (perhaps) between being a child in a family and being a parent or partner in one, as Table 7.10 demonstrates. Each of these stages is, however, potentially problematic.

Declining opportunities for those in vulnerable groups has led to increases in homelessness and financial hardship amongst the young, especially in run-down urban areas. Beatrice Campbell in *Wigan Pier Re-visited* (1985) and *Goliath* (1993) referred to adaptations some young people make in the absence of access to the mainstream routes to adult status. She suggests that some young women use having a baby as a means of acquiring adult status in a society which has increasingly closed down other options for them. Young men, on the other hand, with little prospect of work, turn to daring crimes such as car theft and joyriding as alternatives which offer the opportunity to show off their skills. Both motherhood and car theft become public ways of achieving status.

Young people at work

Most young workers earn relatively little, and are given less responsibility and status in almost every occupational sector. Currently, some 227 000 18- to 20-year-old workers earn the minimum wage (Bulman 2003). Young workers are central to many industries, but are generally subjected to the worst pay and conditions and required to be the most 'flexible'. This is particularly evident in retail and catering. More than two-thirds of McDonalds' staff are aged under 20, while the Restaurateurs' Association says that in the commercial sector of the hospitality industry, 31 per cent of staff are aged 16 to 24. Of the nearly two million young people aged between 16 and 24 in full-time education, 40 per cent are also in paid employment. Two-thirds of Pizza Hut's 'crew' staff are in full-time education, as are one-fifth of Sainsbury's store staff (Sachdev and Wilkinson 1998).

There is some evidence that ageism that can affect the young too. Vincent notes that young job applicants may be passed over in favour of older and more mature workers. He notes that reverse discrimination – in which older workers are offered dead-end jobs because it is assumed that younger workers are more ambitious – also takes place.

Table 7.10 Extended transitions to adulthood

Childhood	Youth	Adulthood
School	College or training scheme	Labour market
Parental home	Intermediate household, living with peers or alone	Independent home
Child in family	Intermediate statuses, including single parenthood, cohabiting partner	Partner–parent
More secure housing	Transitional housing in youth housing market, e.g. furnished flats and bedsits	More secure housing
'Pocket money' income	'Component' or partial income, e.g. transitional NMW (National Minimum Wage)	Full adult income
Economic 'dependence'	Economic semi-dependence	Economic 'independence'

Source: Jones, G. (2002) *The Youth Divide – Diverging Paths to Adulthood*, York: Joseph Rowntree Foundation

Theoretical explanations of age inequality

Functionalism

Functionalists such as Parsons (1977) considered age to be of increasing importance in modern societies. In pre-industrial society, Parsons argued, age did not really matter because family determined one's place in society. However, since industrialization, people have been more socially and geographically mobile, and age groups have become more important. Parsons argued that they provide **role sets** that create a link between the kinship group and the wider society. For example, Pilcher (1995) suggests youth is a stage of transition that connects childhood (which is mainly experienced as dependency upon adults in families and schools) to adulthood (which is mainly experienced as independence at work and in relationships that might lead to the setting-up of our own families). In this sense, age is important as a mechanism of social integration – it allows people to move from one social institution to another without too much social disturbance or conflict. However, critics note that there is a strong possibility that such social order might be undermined by unemployment, low pay, the expensive housing market, the lengthening of education and higher education costs. All these trends are likely to lead to more dependence on the family. The difficulties in this transition to economic independence are having a knock-on effect in other areas of social life, e.g. young mothers are marrying later.

Functionalists, such as Cummings and Henry (1961), suggest that the way society treats the old has positive benefits for society. The ageing process and the social reaction to it is part of a mutual process in which the elderly, either by voluntary choice or legal compulsion, are encouraged to abandon their occupational roles within the specialized division of labour. The implication here is that the ageing process inevitably leads to social incompetence. This process of 'social disengagement' functions to allow younger members of society to take the place of the old in the specialized division of labour with minimum disruption to both social order and economic efficiency. However, critics of **disengagement theory** point out that retirement from work and society is often not voluntary. Moreover, this disengagement also has negative consequences for the self-esteem of the elderly in terms of ageism. Critics of functionalism point out that disengagement often leads to the neglect of the experience, skills and talents of older members of society which could still be of great benefit to society. Furthermore, disengagement theory ignores the fact that many old people continue to be active participants in society.

Marxism

According to Marxists, the young provide a cheap pool of flexible labour that can be hired and fired as necessary. They tend not to have dependants and so are willing to work for low wages. In terms of full-time employment, their lack of experience legitimates low pay, and competition for jobs keeps wages low.

Marxists, such as Phillipson (1982), suggest that the logic of capitalism, which is about exploiting workers and

---

Focus on research

Bynner et al. (2002)
Young people's changing routes to independence

Several studies funded by the Joseph Rowntree Foundation have explored the different patterns of transition from school to work. Some have found that new divisions are appearing among young people entering adulthood and, according to the research, there are winners and losers in the system. The ways in which young people make their domestic transitions to adulthood are polarizing into the majority, whose transitions are extended over many years, and a minority, whose transitions are rapid, stigmatized and potentially problematic. According to Bynner et al. (2002), this polarization is increasing. They identify a 'widening gap between those on the fast and the slow lanes to adulthood'. What was previously a middle-class pattern of slow transition is becoming more widespread among the more affluent working class, and is now a majority pattern. This trend may be due to people choosing to marry and have children later in their lives, or because lack of resources and the demands of mortgages and expensive lifestyles cause them to postpone family building. At the other end of the scale, there is a continuation of the working-class pattern of early childbirth, which has become more problematic as the support structures of marriage, extended kinship networks, job security and formal welfare systems have become eroded. In the fast lane, early partnership formation and parenthood is usually followed by partnership breakdown and lone parenthood.

> « Teenage motherhood ... epitomizes the problem: early school leaving, no qualifications, poor job or youth training, pregnancy and childbirth, poor prospects of ever getting a decent job leading to family poverty. » (Bynner et al. 2002)

These slow-track and fast-track patterns are closely linked to socio-economic background and educational level. Working-class and female transitions tend to be more condensed and earlier, while middle-class and male transitions tend to be more protracted and later.

Bynner, J., Elias, P., McKnight, A., Pan, H. and Pierre, G. (2002) *Young People's Changing Routes to Independence*, York: Joseph Rowntree Foundation

1 What has caused the affluent working class to merge with the 'majority pattern of slow transition'?

2 Why is the fast track to adulthood increasingly problematic for the less affluent?

consumers for profit, is incompatible with the needs of the elderly. The elderly, despite their greater needs, are neglected by the capitalist system because they no longer have the disposable income or spending power which is so attractive to capitalists. Moreover, as Kidd (2001) notes, because their labour-power is no longer of any use to capitalism, the elderly are seen as a drain on its resources through their use of welfare and health provision. Consequently, then, in capitalist societies such as the UK, early retirement and increasing life expectancy mean that the elderly have little or no status because they are likely to possess little economic power. Cultural and ideological stereotypes of the elderly help justify this state of affairs. As a result, the elderly are more likely to be in poverty and to experience ill-health as an aspect of that poverty.

However, some old people, particularly those from an upper-middle-class background have more power and status because their earning power during their working lives was greater and they were able to accumulate savings and wealth. The relationship this group has with capitalism is beneficial. This privileged sector of the elderly has the economic power to consume services, such as private health schemes, and they therefore enjoy greater life expectancy and better health.

Labelling theory

Ray et al. (2006) generally take a social action or interactionist approach to the treatment of the elderly. They note that there is evidence that the mental capability and wellbeing of the elderly can be negatively affected by exposure to stereotypical labels and experiences of ageism. Their labelling theory suggests that a self-fulfilling prophecy may be the result of exposure to ageism, which can cause a person to behave in a way which confirms these beliefs. They note that research has shown that the use of 'baby talk' or infantilized language causes older people to accept the inference that they are no longer independent adults, thus causing them to behave in a passive and dependent manner. In addition, research has shown that the linguistic expression of pity, particularly from medical professionals, conveys the idea that older people are helpless. Some older people may internalize this message and, as a result, increase their dependence on others.

Ray and colleagues argue that negative stereotypes can also impact on older people in other ways. For example, it can affect the way a person reacts to ageing themselves. Negative labels about ageing and the discrimination that follows can cause negative age-related changes to worsen, as the older person sees their life as a downward spiral and therefore takes no counter action. Evidence from the Age Concern and Mental Health Foundation Inquiry into Mental Health and Wellbeing in Later Life found that older people themselves said that the most effective way to improve mental health and wellbeing would be to improve public attitudes to older people.

Postmodernist theory

Postmodernists such as Blaikie (1999) argue that chronological age, ageism and age-determined inequality are less likely to shape people's life experience in the 21st century. He suggests that UK society has undergone a social transformation from social experiences based on collective identities originating in social class and generation to an increasingly individualized and **consumerist** culture in which old age can be avoided by investing in a diverse choice of youth-preserving techniques and lifestyles.

Key terms

literally damage society in an explosive way.

Age stratum (pl. strata) an age layer in society experiencing differential status and market situation relative to other age groups or layers.

Consumerism emphasis on lifestyle and purchasing patterns.

Demographic timebomb a population trend so potentially grave in its consequences that it could

Disengagement theory the proposition that society enhances its orderly operation by disengaging people from positions of responsibility once they reach old age.

Role set a group sharing similar characteristics of whom a particular set of roles are expected.

Social constructions social categories arising from shared meanings held by members of social groups.

Check your understanding

1 'Age is an ascribed characteristic but is also socially constructed.' Explain this statement and give an example of another characteristic that can be understood in this way.

2 Give examples which show how some members of both the young and elderly may suffer disadvantages relative to the majority of the population.

3 (a) Why do some commentators suggest that the increasing numbers of elderly people constitute a 'demographic timebomb'?
  (b) How can this view be criticized?

4 What sort of pressures may be put on families as a result of the 'demographic timebomb'?

5 What evidence is there that young people experience inequality?

6 Why might extended transitions into adulthood become problematic?

7 (a) What is an age stratum?
  (b) Which age strata would you say enjoy the highest status and market position in the contemporary UK? Why?

8 Why, according to Marxists, are both the young and old marginalized in capitalist society?

9 What evidence is there of increasing opportunities for consumerism among the elderly?

Featherstone and Hepworth (1991) argue that age is no longer associated with some events and not with others. For example, as Kidd notes, the elderly who were regarded as non-sexual only ten years ago are now seen to be able to experience sex and to have an active sexuality.

However, Vincent (2001) suggests that global capitalism is still the major determinant of age-related inequality. He argues that decreasing labour-market stability and rapidly changing employment patterns have increased uncertainty. As a result, the UK is experiencing the growth of a 'fragmented society in which some have been able to use market-position (earnings-related pensions and property-related windfalls) to secure good (i.e. not much reduced) material conditions in old age, while others have missed out. Those who miss out are those with poor market opportunities' (p.5).

Conclusions

To conclude, it is difficult to generalize about people's experiences of age. This is because these experiences will vary according to other aspects of stratification, such as class, gender and ethnicity. Social class, for example, probably plays a great part in determining people's level of income in old age. Consequently, theories of age which fail to take this into account can never be wholly convincing.

Activities

Research idea

Ask a sample of your peers to come up with phrases commonly used to describe the elderly (e.g. 'dirty old man', 'little old lady'). Analyse your results and try to formulate a range of ageist terms highlighting the social exclusion of the elderly in society.

Web.tasks

1 Visit the 'Age concern' website at **www.ageconcern.org.uk/**

- Use the search facility and type 'statistics'. Download the most recent statistics on inequalities currently faced by the elderly.
- Type 'How ageist is Britain?' to locate their comprehensive study of ageism in 2004.

2 Bearing in mind that 'Youth' is defined by the United Nations as denoting people between the ages of 15 and 24, get a global perspective on issues facing young people and download the 'World Youth Report 2003' via the link: **www.un.org/esa/socdev/unyin/wyr03.htm**

An eye on the exam   Age and stratification

Item A

Age and gender are social categories through which members of society define and identify individuals and groups. They are a central part of how we see ourselves and how others see us. Age and gender act as important bases for structuring inequality, giving or denying individuals access to power, status, material resources and opportunities. However, while nowadays there is equality before the law between men and women in societies such as Britain, age still remains significant in determining individuals' citizenship rights and duties.

AQA exam paper, June 2004

Examine the importance of age as a form of stratification (**Item A**).   (12 marks)

Grade booster   Getting top marks in this question

You need to examine some of the ways in which age differences are a basis for inequality. For example, develop the point in the Item that age is a basis for distributing legal rights unequally – for instance, the right to vote, serve on a jury, consume alcohol, have sex and claim various benefits are all age related. Examine different age groups, not just (for example) the old. Use concepts such as ageism and the social construction of age – e.g. old age as enforced dependency. Remember that not all members of an age group share the same status or life-chances; class, gender and ethnicity interact with age (e.g. young girls are less likely to be allowed out alone than young boys; working-class pensioners are more likely than middle-class ones to be in poverty). Use perspectives such as Marxism and functionalism to provide contrasting explanations of age stratification.

Getting you thinking

Imagine a world in which wheelchair-users and able-bodied people live completely segregated lives. The wheelchair-users develop their own society to meet their needs and construct a village which, in its design and everyday activity, reflects the fact that everybody uses a wheelchair. Able-bodied people do not often visit the village and the wheelchair-users control all aspects of their lives. They make the goods that they sell in their shops with special aids; they work the machines that clean the street, run their own schools, banks, post offices, and the transport system of the village, and so on. For the villager, being in a wheelchair is normal because everybody else they meet is also in a wheelchair. They see wheelchair-users on television and hear them on the radio. Able-bodied people, however, are rarely seen and little understood.

The wheelchair-users design the buildings in the village to suit their physical situation. Because everyone is always in wheelchairs, there is no need to have ceilings at 9 feet 6 inches high or door heights at 7 feet 2 inches. Soon it becomes standard practice to build doors to a height of 5 feet and ceiling or rooms to a height of 7 feet 4 inches. Everyone is happy in the village because all the buildings and environment are truly in tune with the needs of the wheelchair-users.

However, one day a few able-bodied people, through no choice of their own, come to live in this village. Naturally, one of the first things they notice is the heights of the doors and ceilings. They notice this directly, by constantly knocking their heads on the door frames. Soon all the able-bodied members of the village are marked by the dark

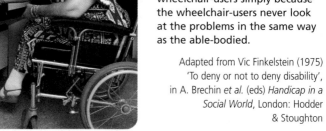

bruises they carry on their foreheads and develop painful back problems by constantly having to bend down. They go to see the village doctors, who are, naturally, also wheelchair-users. The doctors produce learned reports, which say their problems are caused by the handicap of their physical size. This handicap causes a disadvantage that makes them disabled in this society. Special aids are designed by the wheelchair-user doctors for the able-bodied disabled members of the village. All the able-bodied are given special toughened helmets (provided free by the village) to wear at all times.

However, the able-bodied disabled cause many problems. When they seek jobs, no one will employ them because of prejudice and discrimination, and as a result they fall into poverty. Charities are created by the wheelchair users to collect money for the able-bodied poor, and many shops and pubs have an upturned helmet placed on the counters for customers to leave their small change. Painted on the helmets are the words 'Help the able-bodied disabled'. One day, however, when the able-bodied are sitting together and discussing their problems, they realize that they have never been consulted by the wheelchair-users about the way the village is designed and run. They realize that there are solutions to their problems that have never occurred to the wheelchair-users simply because the wheelchair-users never look at the problems in the same way as the able-bodied.

Adapted from Vic Finkelstein (1975) 'To deny or not to deny disability', in A. Brechin *et al.* (eds) *Handicap in a Social World*, London: Hodder & Stoughton

1 **What problems were experienced by the able-bodied when they moved into the village?**

2 **What additional problems not mentioned in the text might have been experienced by the able-bodied in this wheelchair-user-friendly environment?**

3 **What point is Finkelstein making about the experience of the disabled in UK society?**

According to the Department of Work and Pensions, in 2006 there were 10.1 million people living in the UK who were classed as 'disabled'. This official definition includes those people who have been medically defined as suffering a longstanding illness, disability or infirmity, which causes them significant difficulty with their day-to-day activities. Of this disabled population, 9.5 million are adults, with 4.6 million being over retirement age, whilst 700 000 are children.

What these figures suggest is that 17 per cent of the population of the UK are disabled, which is significantly higher than the number of people in the UK who belong to ethnic-minority groups. However, if we examine the content of Sociology textbooks over the past ten years, we will find plenty of material on ethnicity, race and racism, but very little on disability. As Tim Davies (1994) notes, most sociological research in this field has been carried out by disabled sociologists. Able-bodied sociologists, in comparison, have shown little interest in how society stratifies by disability, how mental and physical ability affects our everyday functions and why the disabled experience discrimination, exclusion and inequality.

Davies suggests that there are three reasons for the lack of sociological interest in the relationship between disability, stratification and inequality:

1 Few sociologists themselves are disabled.
2 Disability provokes complex emotional responses in the non-disabled, which Davies describes as a 'mixture of guilt, fear, revulsion, anxiety, pity and embarrassment'. He suggests that the easiest way of dealing with these feelings is avoidance of studying disability.
3 Most importantly, Davies notes that most sociologists have mistakenly dismissed disability as a medical rather than as a sociological problem worthy of social research. Sociologists have tended to see disability as a result of individual circumstances rather than as a product of the social organization of society or as a social issue.

Defining disability

A great deal of the literature on disability tends to use the two related concepts of **impairment** and **disability** interchangeably. Impairment refers to any psychological, physical or anatomical loss or abnormality that affects how a person functions on an everyday basis. Disability refers to the resulting disadvantages experienced by people with impairments that make it difficult for them to perform their 'normal' roles and which may result in inequality compared with non-disabled people.

The medical model

The idea that disability is determined by impairment is the product of the **medical model** – an approach that sees disabled people as needing constant care from medical personnel. This model takes an individualistic approach in that it treats disability as a property of individuals who, because of their impairment, are unable to take advantage of the opportunities enjoyed or taken for granted by able-bodied people. According to Shakespeare (1996): 'Medical approaches consider negative self-identity to be an outcome of physical impairment, and focus on the need for adjustment, mourning, and coming to terms with loss.'

The medical model explains the economic disadvantages experienced by the disabled (and therefore their position at the bottom of the stratification system) in terms of individual impairment. This perspective drives the official emphasis on rehabilitation and retraining that can be seen in state policy towards the disabled. Hyde (2001) notes that health, housing, employment, educational and welfare policies aimed at providing services for the disabled overwhelmingly focus on individual limitations.

However, critics such as Davies note that this model ignores the wider social influences that impact on the individual over which they have no control. For example, the medical model fails to recognize social barriers that prevent the disabled from fully participating in society. Davies argues that impairment is only a partial explanation of the social disadvantages experienced by the disabled. Davies also suggests that the medical model endorses government policies, which are ineffective in promoting full social participation and, at worst, reinforce disadvantage and social exclusion. For example, employment policy has focused on individual rehabilitation rather than getting rid of the discriminatory barriers that employers put up, which, Davies argues, are mainly responsible for holding the disabled back.

The social model

Davies's critique of the medical model is typical of the alternative **social model** of disability, which argues that sociologists need to focus on the society in which the individual disabled person is located.

The social model takes issue with the term 'disability'. Shearer (1981) argues that 'disability' is something imposed on disabled people by the patterns and social expectations of a society organized by and for the non-disabled. This is the theme of Finkelstein in the 'Getting you thinking' activity opposite. Disabled sociologists, such as Barnes (1992), suggest that 'impairment' should be used to refer to physical, intellectual, sensory and hidden limitations, whereas 'disability' should refer to the loss or limiting of opportunities that prevent the disabled from taking part in the normal life of the community on an equal basis with others *because of physical and social barriers*.

The social model, therefore, argues that disabled people are actually disabled and stratified by society rather than by their impairment. In particular, the social model highlights two major social barriers that prevent the disabled from participating fully in society:

1 Social institutions act in a discriminatory fashion that undermines disabled people's potential for independence.
2 The attitudes and beliefs (i.e. prejudices and stereotypes) that non-disabled people hold about disabled people portray them in a negative light and consequently oppress them.

Thompson (1993) argues that there exists a combination of social forces, cultural values and personal prejudices that marginalize the disabled and produce a type of inequality which he calls '**disableism**'.

Disableism comes in many shapes and forms. For example, the social environment in which we live and work is often inaccessible to the disabled. Hyde notes that transport systems are a good example of this – he points out that disabled people are often prevented from travelling to work, not by their inability to use buses but because public transport has been designed for the exclusive use of people without impairments.

Marxist theory of disability

The Marxist theory of disability strongly sympathizes with the position that the social model takes. Oliver (1990) suggests that the marginalization and oppression of disabled people takes a unique form in Western capitalist societies. He argues that in pre-industrial, agricultural society, most people worked either on the land or in the textile trade as spinners, weavers, etc. Moreover, they lived in small, tight-knit communities. He suggests that attitudes and practices in regard to the disabled were very different – they often played a key role in the economic life of such communities.

Oliver argues that industrialization and the factory system transformed economic life by introducing a more intensive labour process, such as assembly-line production, and as a result the worth of individuals came to be assessed according to their economic value – efficient, quick work was seen as immensely profitable. Paid employment, especially in factories, became the main source of identity and status. As Hyde (2001) notes, the dominant ideology of capitalism was 'competitive individualism' and those among the working-class who were not employed – the chronically sick and disabled – were therefore seen to have an inferior social status compared with waged workers.

Oliver argues that the social exclusion of the disabled from economic life was reinforced by state policy in the 19th century, which had two main social consequences for the disabled:

1   The state transferred their responsibility for the assessment, treatment and care of the disabled to medical professionals. This resulted in the ideological dominance of the medical model of disability.
2   Disabled people were increasingly committed to long-stay hospitals and asylums – in other words, treatment of the disabled often resulted in institutionalization in what Goffman called '**total institutions**'. Such institutions treated the disabled by stripping them of their identity. Cure often involved disabled people having to accept an identity that was imposed upon them by the institution, which was often organized around 'learned helplessness'. In other words, disabled people learned that they were the problem and that they needed to be dependent in order to be 'cured'.

Disability, inequality and stratification

Both the social model and Marxism suggest that the notion that the UK is a meritocracy is clearly false with regard to the opportunities experienced by disabled people. They argue that the disabled are deliberately and often unconsciously restricted from enjoying the same potential for upward mobility as the non-disabled. In other words, like people from ethnic minorities and young people, the disabled are stratified at the bottom of the social system and, consequently, experience the same sorts of problems as the urban poor. Social-model sociologists, such as Hyde, argue that disableism and the inequality that results can clearly be seen in the antidisabled prejudice that underpins everyday beliefs, language and mass-media representations of disabled people. Moreover, Hyde argues that disableism takes institutional forms too and can be clearly seen in the routine practices found in educational, commercial, welfare, health, legal and political systems.

Prejudice

Ryan and Thomas (1980) argue that disabled people are primarily seen in terms of what is 'wrong' or 'abnormal' about them, rather than in terms of the characteristics they share with non-disabled people. Morris (1992), too, argues that prejudicial attitudes towards disabled people revolve around the view that disabled people do not belong and so should be segregated from non-disabled society. He suggests that the disabled are often stigmatized. Davies notes that they are often seen as possessing **discrediting** characteristics – for example, wheelchair-users are often stereotyped as ugly, **asexual**, intellectually impaired, unable to speak for themselves ('does he take sugar?'), bitter and dependent. Furthermore, they are most often portrayed as deserving of our pity.

Language and mass-media representations

Davies argues that our everyday use of language is a fairly efficient way of transmitting prejudice about disabled people. He notes that 'language doesn't simply reflect the world, it constructs the world for us by the meanings it conveys'. So, in learning a language, we learn to see the world in a particular way. Hyde argues that the everyday language used to describe the disabled is often derogatory and abusive, as the poem on the opposite page indicates. He argues that such language tends to dehumanize and objectify disabled people.

Media representations, too, reinforce prejudicial attitudes towards the disabled in two ways:

1   Barnes (1992) notes the existence of negative stereotypes on television and in the print media. He suggests that the disabled are often portrayed as pitiable, pathetic, sinister and evil.
2   Barnes argues that even what most people might regard as positive images are actually stereotypical assumptions. For example, stories about the 'extraordinary heroism' or 'remarkable courage' of disabled people present the disabled as 'super-cripples', whilst television appeals such

as 'Children in Need' reinforce the notion that the disabled should be the recipients of our pity and charity. Shakespeare (1996) suggests such representations encourage the disabled to become 'professional cripples' and dependent on charity.

Barnes notes that we rarely see media images of the disabled that reflect the real-life experience of disabled people. Research by Cumberbatch and Negrine (1992) suggests that, as far as most of the media are concerned, disabled people are largely invisible – only 0.5 per cent of fictional characters in television dramas are disabled in any way. However, there are signs of positive change. For example, the BBC dedicated a substantial amount of screen time to the 2008 Paralympics live from China.

Davies argues that such stereotyping is immensely powerful for two reasons:

1   It results in social segregation. Non-disabled people have very little contact with disabled people. This isolation from society further reinforces prejudice against the disabled because the non-disabled are never in a position to see the everyday lived experience of disabled people and therefore understand their point of view.
2   Disability often acts as a **master status**, in that disabled people are often seen exclusively in terms of their impairment. Oliver and Barnes (1998) note that 'to become 'disabled' is to be assigned a new identity indicating membership of a separate tribe or species'. Davies argues that it is taken for granted by society that the label of 'disabled' defines those with

impairments as people who are deserving of low status. Furthermore, this creates the potential for a self-fulfilling prophecy as the disabled learn that dependency and helplessness are expected of them. Hyde notes that the disabled have very few role models to aspire to. Consequently, disabled people develop a negative self-identity. They lack self-confidence and self-esteem and passively accept discrimination, exclusion and disadvantage.

Institutional forms of discrimination

Hyde (2001) argues that the disabled experience institutional forms of discrimination because many organizations and public bodies have failed in terms of their everyday rules, routines and services to provide for them. He argues that discriminatory practices are commonplace; for example, disabled people's access to services like shops, public transport or leisure facilities is steadily improving, but there is still widespread inaccessibility, which can actively restrict disabled people's opportunities. Hyde suggests that the disabled are still often excluded from mainstream social activities by the leisure and retail industries as well as transport systems.

Oliver (1990) argues that 'disableism' underpins social or state policies in such areas as housing (which is often built with the able-bodied rather than the disabled in mind), education, healthcare and welfare, e.g. social security. Oliver notes how many of the services for the disabled are largely delivered by able-bodied professionals who fail to take account of the unique needs and preferences of disabled people.

A 2008 report by the disability campaigning group Leonard Cheshire Disability (Parckar 2008) suggested that 89 per cent of disabled people surveyed felt that there was discrimination and prejudice towards disabled people in the UK, and that this is a key factor in the poverty of expectation and poverty of opportunity that disabled people experience.

How do images in the mass media such as these reinforce or challenge stereotypes?

Focus on research

Angela Neath (2003)
Applying a social model

The purpose of this study was to examine the experiences of six visually impaired servicemen aged between 20 and 30 years old, returning from recent conflicts, i.e. the Falklands war, Northern Ireland and the first Gulf War. Neath carried out detailed semi-structured interviews with the servicemen. Her questions focused on their lives before the incident that caused their sight loss, particularly their jobs and relationships, and how these had been affected since the onset of their blindness. She guaranteed anonymity and confidentiality.

Neath found that the men had endured a number of negative experiences that lend support to the social model of disability. She notes that blindness has traditionally been regarded as a negative social identity associated with helplessness, irrationality, hopelessness and darkness – often generating pity from the sighted. Consequently, her sample reported that patronizing social attitudes were deemed to be the greatest oppressive factor in their lives because such attitudes attempted to impose a disabled identity upon them that conflicted with their own self-perception. For example, one respondent reported 'people definitely see me as blind rather than as a person', whilst another said 'it is not only physical limitations that restrict us to our homes ... It is the knowledge that each entry into the public world will be dominated by stares, by condescension, by pity and by hostility'. Another remarked 'people need educating so that they can understand, yes, we're disabled but we've got some brain up here'.

Neath also found evidence of institutional discrimination. As servicemen, all the men had a strong sense of their masculinity but this was undermined by their blindness and the way they were treated after the onset of that blindness by their employers. None of the sample were given appropriate support by their employers in finding suitable work after their sight loss. Neath points out that work gives people a positive self-identity as productive and economically self-sufficient. However, the armed services made little attempt to find them jobs in the service. As Neath notes, 'their jobs had made them who they were and that had been lost to them'. As a result, they felt forced into a negative self-identity that involved being vulnerable, incapable and dependent.

One of the respondents compensated for these negative experiences by spending all his time on his hobby of talking to people around the world on his amateur radio transmitter. As he noted of the people he talked to, 'they're like you, they can't see you. I can't see them, so we're all the same'.

Angela Neath (2003) Unpublished MA dissertation, Dept of Sociology and Social Policy, The University of Leeds

1 Identify two reasons why the guarantee of anonymity and confidentiality probably increased the validity of Neath's interview data.

2 Identify two methodological problems of Neath's research design.

3 How do the first-hand accounts quoted above support the social model of disability?

Education

In his examination of the provision of education for disabled children in the UK, Hyde notes that large numbers of children and young people with impairments continue to be educated in special schools. He argues that this segregation from mainstream education reinforces cultural prejudice and discrimination. Moreover, even when disabled children are educated in mainstream schools, many receive their education in Special Education Needs (SEN) classes. Hyde notes that educational policy and spending does not see SEN as a high priority, and disabled children experience inadequate provision in terms of resources, facilities and teaching. Consequently, they experience lower levels of educational achievement.

The Leonard Cheshire Disability campaigning group found that, in 2007, disabled people still faced substantial disadvantage in the education system – 25 per cent of disabled people of working age had no qualifications, compared to 11 per cent of non-disabled people. These poor skills have a greater impact on disabled people: only

20 per cent of unqualified disabled people are in work, compared to 60 per cent of unqualified non-disabled people. Even worse, disabled adults are less likely to take part in apprenticeships or skills development that might change this or aid their career progression. At 16, young disabled people were twice as likely not to be in any form of education, employment or training as their non-disabled peers (15 per cent as opposed to 7 per cent). These entrenched inequalities often drive down the aspirations of disabled people and compound their disadvantages.

Employment

In 2005, there were 6.8 million disabled people of working age, i.e. one in five of the UK's working population. However, only 50 per cent of the disabled were in employment compared with 81 per cent of the non-disabled. Furthermore, disabled workers were nearly four times more likely than the non-disabled to be unemployed, i.e. 47 per cent of disabled workers were unemployed in 2005. Disabled workers were also more likely to be in part-time work and manual jobs compared with non-disabled workers.

Low pay is another aspect of the institutional discrimination experienced by the disabled in employment. In 2005, disabled workers received average gross hourly pay that was 10 per cent less than that received by non-disabled workers. Research also suggests that disabled applicants for jobs are six times more likely to be refused an interview than non-disabled applicants, even when they have suitable skills and qualifications. Furthermore, employers are often reluctant to adapt their working environments to the needs of disabled workers.

Hyde notes that statutory employment policy has reinforced the economic disadvantages experienced by the disabled and failed to provide an adequate response to the vocational needs of disabled people. The 1944 Disabled Person's (Employment) Act required employers to hire a 3 per cent quota of disabled workers, but this legislation was often ignored by employers and weakly enforced by the government. The Disability and Discrimination Act (1995) provides disabled people with a right not to be discriminated against. However, this legislation only applies to a minority of employers, i.e. those with 15 or more employees. Furthermore, the government relies on voluntary compliance despite, as Hyde notes, extensive research showing employer prejudice and even hostility towards disabled people. Consequently, disabled people have to take jobs in companies specifically set up for the disabled, such as Remploy.

Poverty

This economic exclusion and disadvantage has implications for the living standards of the disabled during retirement because it means that disabled people are in a weaker position than the non-disabled to accumulate savings and adequate occupational pension entitlements. Consequently, disabled people have a higher risk of ending up in poverty.

Albert *et al.* (2002) note that being poor is a major factor in transforming impairment into disability. They argue that disability exacerbates poverty, while having an impairment makes being poor more difficult. They suggest that poverty, disability and impairment are clearly linked 'in a deadly embrace'.

A report by Leonard Cheshire Disability estimated that up to 3 million disabled people were trapped in poverty in 2007 (Parckar 2008). The report notes that disabled people are twice as likely to live in poverty as non-disabled people, i.e. 16 per cent of non-disabled people live in relative poverty compared with 30 per cent of disabled people. This is because, compared with the able-bodied, disabled people face extra costs related to managing their impairment, such as paying for adaptations to the home, social-care support, mobility aids or communication aids. When these extra costs of disability are taken into account, the report estimates that about 50 per cent of disabled people are living below or around the official poverty line, set at 60 per cent of average national income.

Focus on research

ESRC Society Today
Disability statistics

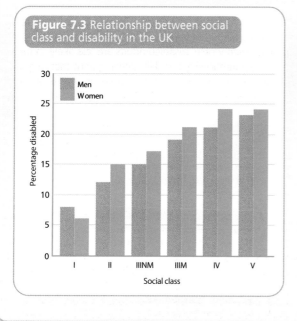

Figure 7.3 Relationship between social class and disability in the UK

Table 7.11 Percentage of GDP spent on disability benefits in different European countries

	1994	1998	2002
Spain	1.7	1.6	1.5
France	1.7	1.7	1.7
Italy	1.8	1.5	1.5
Ireland	0.8	0.7	0.8
Netherlands	4.1	3.2	3.0
Germany	1.8	2.2	2.3
Finland	4.9	3.8	3.4
Sweden	4.1	3.8	4.3
UK	2.9	2.6	2.5
European average	2.2	2.2	2.2

Source: www.esrcsocietytoday.ac.uk, Facts and figures

1 Describe the relationship between social class, gender and disability shown in Fig. 7.3.

2 Suggest possible explanations for the relationship between disability and social class.

3 Suggest possible explanations for the relationship between gender and disability

4 Look at Table 7.11. Suggest possible explanations of why some countries spend a larger percentage of GDP on disability benefits than others.

Leonard Cheshire Disability argues that the government has generally neglected the plight of the disabled poor because of its focus on reducing child poverty and that experienced by the elderly. The non-working disabled therefore have to rely on welfare benefits that are not sufficient to lift them out of poverty. This leaves people with little or no chance of escaping poverty other than through charity, or support from family and friends. Moreover, the report argues that poor decision-making in the benefit system can drive people into debt and push people further into poverty.

The political process

Oliver (1990) notes that the disabled are excluded from the formal political process. They are often not invited to take part in official discussions about their rights and needs. Legislation aimed at the disabled is often made by able-bodied politicians and civil servants, who have a poor understanding of what disabled people need. Inappropriate services are often the result. Even the charities and pressure groups that represent the interests of the disabled often fail to provide the disabled with a voice in their management.

Many disabled people have responded to this lack of political representation by embarking on what has been described as the 'last great civil rights battle'. These disabled activists are critical of the pressure groups for the disabled because they are often run by non-disabled people. It is argued by disabled political activists that these organizations perpetuate the general public's view that disabled people are dependent on charity.

Hyde notes that these disabled critics have challenged negative stereotypes by becoming self-organized. The disabled people's movement, which is very much based on the social model of disability, is aimed at transforming official responses to the needs of disabled people and developing a positive disabled identity. Hyde argues that this collective action has already had success in that it resulted in the introduction of the Disability Discrimination Act and programming specifically aimed at the disabled on television.

Evaluation of the social model of disability

There are signs that official bodies are now more willing to address the criticisms of services and facilities made by the social model of health. For example, the government's Department of Health website says that it 'subscribes to the social model of disability; that disability is defined as the disadvantage experienced by an individual as a result of barriers (attitudinal, physical, etc.) that impact on people with impairments and/or ill health'.

However, criticisms of the social model and the disabled people's movement have appeared from within the ranks of the disabled themselves. It is suggested that the social model is weakened by its lack of reference to the role of impairment in restricting their participation in social activities. For example, Davies (1994) notes that people with serious mental impairments may find it impossible to

Check your understanding

1. Why does Davies think that sociologists have avoided studying disability?

2. How do sociologists such as Davies and Barnes define impairment and disability?

3. What approach is taken to the disabled by the medical model?

4. What criticisms are made of the medical model of disability by those sociologists who sympathize with the social model of disability?

5. What does the social model mean when it states that disabled people are 'disabled by society'?

6. Using employment, transport systems and education as your examples, illustrate the concept of 'disableism'.

7. What were the effects of industrialization on the disabled according to Marxist sociologists?

8. How do the prejudicial stereotypes about the disabled found in everyday speech and in the mass media affect the way many of the disabled see themselves?

9. How have some disabled people reacted to disableism?

10. What criticisms can be made of the social model of health's emphasis on disableism?

Activities

Research idea

Ask a sample of your peers to come up with phrases commonly used to describe the disabled. Analyse your results and try to formulate a range of prejudicial and stereotypical terms highlighting the social exclusion of the disabled in society.

Web.tasks

1. Visit the site www.poverty.org.uk and gather the latest statistics on the relationship between the disabled, low income, welfare benefits and old age.

2. In what way do the representations of the disabled found on websites such as
   www.paralympics.org.uk
   www.remploy.co.uk
   www.lcdisability.org.uk
   suggest that the social model of disability is winning its argument?

take part in everyday activities, however those activities are defined and organized. Morris (1992) argues that:

<< there is a tendency within the social model of disability to deny the experiences of our bodies, insisting that our physical differences and restrictions are entirely socially created. While environmental barriers and social attitudes are a crucial part of our experience of disability – and do indeed disable us – to suggest that this is all there is to it is to deny the personal experience. >>

Shakespeare and Watson (1997) agree, arguing that the social model only partially addresses the lived experience of disabled people. They argue that it overstresses the importance of social factors because social activists fear that any discussion about the effects of physical or intellectual impairment will dilute the message that the disabled are discriminated against.

Barnes and Mercer (2003) are critical of the disabled people's movement because they claim it is not representative of disabled people as a whole. They maintain that the 'positive disabled identity' associated with collective political action is enjoyed disproportionately by people with physical and sensory impairments because people with these types of impairments dominate the movement. Those disabled people with intellectual impairments are often unable to participate; as a result, their interests are underrepresented, and they experience greater levels of exclusion and disadvantage. They truly are at the bottom of the stratification system.

Key terms

Asexual not having an interest in sex.

Disability the types of economic, social and cultural disadvantages experienced by disabled people that result in inequality compared with able-bodied people.

Disableism the everyday prejudice and discrimination that disabled people face from both people in general and from institutions that fail to provide for their needs.

Discrediting negative labelling or stereotyping that implies low status.

Impairment the physical, intellectual, sensory and hidden limitations experienced by disabled people.

Master status one aspect of a person's appearance or identity that dominates the way others perceive them.

Medical model an approach that focuses almost exclusively on impairment and consequently sees the difficulties experienced by the disabled as a product of their physical or mental condition.

Social model an approach that focuses on how the difficulties and disadvantages experienced by the disabled may be the product of prejudicial attitudes and discriminatory practices.

Total institutions a concept, associated with Goffman, used to describe organizations such as prisons and asylums in which inmates have to surrender their individuality to the routine of the organization.

An eye on the exam Disability and stratification

Item A

Disabled people face considerable disadvantages in the United Kingdom today. They are more than twice as likely to have left school without qualifications than the non-disabled population. They face a greater risk of being unemployed than able-bodied people: half the disabled are unemployed, compared with only a fifth of the non-disabled. If they are in employment, disabled people are more likely to experience low pay. As a result of these factors, the disabled are more likely to experience poverty. Furthermore, the experience of poverty is likely to be made worse because of their impairment, because disabled people face higher living costs than do able-bodied people – for example, the cost of transport and mobility, or of special diets, is greater.

Examine the reasons for the disadvantages faced by disabled people in the UK today (Item A). (12 marks)

Grade booster Getting top marks in this question

You need to consider a range of possible reasons for the disadvantages faced by disabled people. In your answer, you should draw upon some of the material in the Item to help you. For example, you could consider why disabled people are more likely to leave school without qualifications, to face unemployment or to experience low pay. To examine the reasons behind such disadvantages, you need to make use of sociological concepts and explanations. You should consider the role of stereotyping, prejudice and discrimination, for example by the media and employers, as well as the role of government policy, e.g. in employment law, housing and transport. Use the distinction between disability and impairment, and the debate between medical and social models of disability, to provide a framework for your answer.

1   Read **Item A** below and answer parts (a) and (b) that follow.

Item A

Inequality between males and females pervades every area of social life. For example, in most societies, women outlive men; on the other hand, they are more likely to report illness than men. In the United Kingdom today, girls achieve more in school than do boys.

On the other hand, women perform a bigger share of housework and childcare while increasingly taking on a double burden of domestic labour and paid employment. In developing countries, women's burden is, if anything, even greater than in the UK. For example, one study found that women do 60 to 80 per cent of all agricultural work.

Similarly, in the field of politics, women are underrepresented among MPs and ministers in virtually all countries of the world. The same applies in other branches of the state, where women are in a small minority among senior civil servants, judges and the top ranks of the military.

(a) Examine some of the reasons for gender inequality in society
    (**Item A**). *(12 marks)*

An examiner comments

As Item A shows, there is great inequality between males and females. One reason for this is patriarchy and sexism, where women are discriminated against in areas such as employment, preventing them from reaching the top because of a 'glass ceiling' that blocks their promotion. This could explain why there are so few women judges and senior civil servants. Employers fear that they will leave to have children or that their domestic responsibilities will come before loyalty to the company. For example, studies show that women are more likely to move if their husband gets a job elsewhere than vice versa, and when children are sick, it is the women who take time off to care for them.

> A promising start. The answer identifies some important concepts and applies them to the area of employment, as well as drawing on the Item for the point about judges and senior civil servants.

There may also be prejudice based on stereotyped ideas about men and women. For example, women are seen as caring and men as tough, which may explain why there are few women in the top ranks of the army (Item A).

> Good use of the Item, linked to the concept of stereotyping.

In Third World countries, there seems to be greater gender inequality. In some countries there is legal discrimination – e.g. in Saudi Arabia, women are not allowed to drive or to go out unaccompanied by a male relative. Modernization theorists argue that these inequalities will disappear as these societies modernize. However, when we look at industrialized countries, we find women performing a dual burden, so this claim may not be valid.

> Shows knowledge of patterns of inequality as well as a possible explanation, which is also evaluated.

Feminists argue that gender inequality is fundamental and that women are oppressed in all societies. However, they disagree about the causes of women's oppression and the solutions. For example, liberal feminists believe it can be ended by reforms such as equal pay legislation and changes in socialization, whereas Marxist feminists believe it will require the overthrow of capitalism.

$\frac{10}{12}$

> Overall, this is a very good answer to the question. It makes good use of the Item at several points – such as gender and employment, in developing countries, and in the state. It deals with several reasons for gender inequality, including employers' attitudes, legal discrimination, modernization theory and types of feminism. However, there is still room for some improvement; for example, it could explore the different feminist positions in a little more detail. It could also consider areas where females do better than males, such as educational achievement and life expectancy.

(b) Assess the usefulness of functionalist approaches in explaining structured social inequality. *(21 marks)*

> A reasonable start to the essay that identifies the key functionalist idea that inequality is functional. However, it doesn't really link this to the paragraph's second idea, that of value consensus.

The functionalist view of stratification is that it is beneficial and functional to society. For example, according to Emile Durkheim, social inequality is based on society's value consensus, where all members of society agree that the different occupations should be ranked according to their value to society.

Talcott Parsons shares this view. He argues that the value consensus of society ranks different occupations in a hierarchy of value to society. He goes on to argue that this is why some occupations have higher status and rewards than others. For example, society values doctors more highly than it values street sweepers and so we give doctors more 'social honour' or status than street sweepers and pay them more. Because all societies value some roles or occupations more than others, inequality is inevitable – some will always be valued and rewarded more highly.

> This shows some relevant knowledge of Parsons' views, especially the idea that inequality is inevitable.

Two other functionalists, Davis and Moore, have developed Parsons' ideas. They argue that it is important for all societies to have the most able people performing the most important roles. For example, we would not want someone to be a surgeon or pilot without showing they had the necessary ability to do the job. Davis and Moore go on to argue that this is why society offers higher rewards to such jobs. This is in order to encourage everyone to go after them, thus ensuring competition for these posts. People will be willing to strive for educational qualifications needed to enter these occupations, and will make the necessary sacrifices to do so (e.g. spending a long time in education when they could be out earning).

The result is that the most talented and hardest working will win through, getting the best qualifications and the most important jobs. For functionalists, this is beneficial for everyone, not just the successful ones who make it to the top, because society will have the most able people doing the jobs it values most highly. Therefore inequality is functional and beneficial.

> Two very good paragraphs explaining Davis and Moore's ideas clearly and accurately, and linking them back to the set question.

However, functionalist approaches have come in for heavy criticism, especially from conflict sociologists. They argue that Davis and Moore are wrong to assume that the most able always get to the top. For example, able but poor students may be forced to drop out of education because of their family's material deprivation. There is also the problem that Davis and Moore's argument is circular. How do we know which occupations are more important? Answer: they are the ones with the highest rewards (e.g. doctors). Why do they get the highest rewards? Answer: because they are the most important occupations!

> Two good evaluation points here, both explained clearly.

In general, functionalism is useful because it tries to explain why inequality seems to be found in all known societies. In their view, it exists everywhere because it is necessary and beneficial. However, other sociologists reject the idea that it is functional for society or individuals.

14/21

> Overall, this answer shows a good understanding of several functionalist approaches to social inequality, and explains them clearly (especially Davis and Moore). However, the very important concept of meritocracy needs introducing into the account of functionalism. The last two paragraphs introduce some relevant evaluation points into the answer and the final paragraph also attempts a general conclusion. However, evaluation could be developed further, both in terms of the possible dysfunctions of meritocracy and by presenting rival explanations of inequality such as Marxism.

One for you to try

This question requires you to **apply** your knowledge and understanding of sociological research methods to the study of this issue in stratification and differentiation.

2   Read **Item B** and answer the question that follows.

Item B

The life chances of the different social classes vary significantly. Members of the manual working class have a shorter life expectancy and experience more ill health than the middle and upper classes. Similarly, they are much more likely to live in overcrowded housing conditions or to experience homelessness, while their children generally do less well at school, are more likely to leave education earlier and take up less-skilled, lower-paid jobs.

The lifestyles of the social classes also differ considerably from one another, though perhaps not so much now as was the case a few generations ago. More recently, the impact of the mass media and other forms of commercial leisure and entertainment have reduced some of the differences between the social classes. However, it is still unlikely that we will find unskilled manual workers at the ballet or opera, at the polo match or on the grouse moor.

Using information from **Item B** and elsewhere, evaluate the advantages and disadvantages of using structured interviews to study social-class differences. *(24 marks)*

An examiner comments

Remember that you need to know what the main features are of the method, and you need to be able both to outline and to evaluate the advantages and disadvantages of structured interviews. These include practical, theoretical and ethical factors, such as time, cost, reliability and validity. You need to apply these to the study of class differences For example, this method might be useful in showing the class patterns in leisure patterns for example, but without giving much insight into what these leisure pursuits mean to members of the different classes.

Answers to the 'One for you to try' are available **free** on **www.collinseducation.com/ sociologyweb**

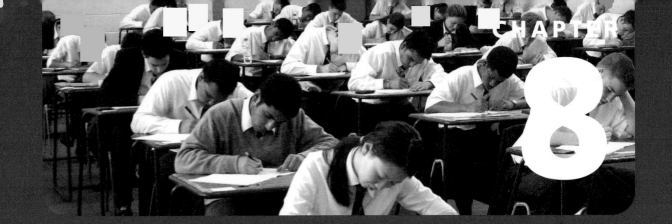

CHAPTER 8

Preparing for the AQA A2 exam

TOPIC 1

Preparing for the AQA A2 exam

What will I study?

Aim/rationale of the course

The AQA specification at A2 builds on the knowledge and skills of the AS level. It offers you the opportunity to acquire deeper knowledge and understanding of key aspects of sociological thought, a sound introduction to sociological research methods, and the opportunity to study a number of different areas of social life in depth.

The A2 course allows choice of topic areas within Units 3 and 4. It also ensures a thorough coverage of sociological perspectives and of the two 'core themes':

- Socialization, culture and identity
- Social differentiation, power and stratification.

These 'core themes' are required elements of any A2-level Sociology specification.

The knowledge and skills acquired in this course should enable you to take a more informed and critical look at many aspects of society and how they relate to people's lives, while at the same time enabling you to develop and practise the skills of informed debate and critical analysis. The skills acquired in a sociology course can be of life-long benefit.

Units of study and assessment

The AQA A2 course is divided into two units of study, which lay out what you should know (see Table 8.1 below). (They are numbered 3 and 4 because the AS level covers 1 and 2.)

- Unit 3 contains *four* topic areas, and each topic area forms the basis of a question in the written examination 'unit of assessment'. You must choose *one* topic area.
- Unit 4 contains *three* topic areas. You must choose *either* Crime and deviance *or* Stratification and

differentiation, plus a compulsory question on Theory and methods.

Both units are synoptic. That is, you must make links between the topic in question and other topics you have studied.

How will I be assessed?

Skills

The skills you will acquire and develop in your A2 course are tested in the examination by two 'Assessment Objectives': AO1 counts for 40 per cent and AO2 counts for 60 per cent of the available marks.

Assessment Objective 1 (AO1): Knowledge and understanding

This requires you to demonstrate your knowledge and understanding of the chosen topic area that forms the basis of the assessment. It covers knowledge and understanding of relevant sociological theories and perspectives, concepts, studies and social policies. You should also be able to make reference to relevant issues and events. Also included in AO1 is the skill of 'Communication'. While this is not assessed separately, and therefore does not carry a particular mark weighting, it is an important skill, as poor communication will prevent you from showing the examiner what you mean.

Assessment Objective 2 (AO2): Application, analysis, interpretation and evaluation

This range of skills together counts for 60 per cent of the available marks.

- The skill of interpretation covers your ability to work out and respond to what the question is requiring you to do, and to interpret different types of evidence, including research studies and statistical data, by discussing what they can tell us.

Table 8.1 Units of study and assessment		
Unit	Subjects covered	Form of assessment
3	• Beliefs in society • Global development • Mass media • Power and politics	Written examination of one hour 30 minutes. Data-response section with two questions, and one essay from a choice of two per topic area.
4	• Crime and deviance • Stratification and differentiation • Theory and methods	Written examination paper of two hours. Two data-response sections with two questions in each, and one essay on theory and methods.

The questions are likely to include the following words: 'identify', 'explain', 'examine', 'assess' and 'evaluate'.

- *Identify* – Name whatever you have been asked for; for example, in answer to the question, 'Identify a system of social stratification', you could refer to the caste system or the class system.
- *Explain* – Pick out distinguishing features of a named phenomenon and say why they are important, e.g. the role of religious beliefs in the caste system.
- *Examine* – Look at the advantages and disadvantages of a theory, or look at the evidence for and against a statement or theory.
- *Assess* – Look at all sides, or all theories that relate to the topic, and come to a conclusion.
- *Evaluate* – Similar to assess, look at all sides and weigh up the evidence for and against them all, and come to a conclusion.

- *Application* involves the ability to apply what you know to the set question in an appropriate way.
- Good *analysis* is shown by presenting an informed, detailed and accurate discussion of a particular theory, perspective, study or event, and also by the ability to present your arguments and evidence in a clear and logical manner.
- *Evaluation* refers to your ability to recognize and discuss the strengths and weaknesses of theories, perspectives, studies, sociological methods and data presented in a variety of forms.

Units of assessment/exams

The basic structure of the units of assessment is shown in Table 8.1; the question structure is discussed in more detail in the next section. The weighting given to each of the two A2 Units is given in Table 8.2, which shows you the percentage of the marks allocated to each unit in terms of the full A-level.

How can I do well in the written exams?

Question style and structure

A2 questions vary from paper to paper, but both papers include 'data-response' sections. These sections usually consist of one piece of data and two questions.

The Items at A2 level are there to prompt your thoughts and point you in the right direction when answering the questions in that section. They may prompt ideas that you can use in the essay, but this is more likely to be a happy accident than a result of careful design.

- In Unit 3, each question is marked out of 60. The data-response section is worth 27 marks and the essay is worth 33 marks.
- In Unit 4, 90 marks are available. There are two data-response sections. The first is worth 33 marks and focuses on your chosen topic. The second is worth 24 marks and focuses on applying sociological methods to that topic. The final question is a 33-mark essay on Theory and methods.

For each unit, you should distribute your time between the different sections and questions according to how many marks they are worth. Don't forget to leave yourself time to read the Items, plan your answers and read it all through at the end.

Exam tips

- Throughout A2 there is more emphasis on the AO2 skills than at AS, so the examiner is looking at how you use the knowledge and how you analyse and evaluate it. While some description will be necessary, do not spend too long on this, as your use of that evidence is more important than demonstrating the detail. You can assume that the examiner has also read the study to which you are referring.
- Read both the Item and the whole question very carefully before you begin to answer. The Item will contain information that is essential, helpful, or both, and reading the whole question will give you an understanding of which aspects of the topic have been covered. If you find you are trying to use the same material twice, make sure you have fully understood the questions, as the examiner strives to prevent duplication of material.
- Keep an eye on the time, as it is very important that you allow enough time for each question. Do not spend too long on the shorter questions.
- Where a question is divided into sections, plan all the sections of your answer before you start to write.
- In all your answers, refer to appropriate theories, perspectives, studies and evidence to support and inform your response. Where possible, bring in examples of recent or current events or social policies to illustrate the points you are making. Make quite sure that you have given sufficient demonstration of the AO2 skills, particularly analysis and evaluation.
- Finally, make sure that you answer the question that the examiner has set, rather than the one that you wished for. This is a serious point – many candidates fail to achieve marks because they have not kept to the focus of the question. No question is likely to ask you simply to 'Write everything you know about ...', and yet this is what some students do. However, it is better to write something than to sit there doing nothing. Leaving a blank means you cannot score any marks, but if you write something, it could be correct enough or relevant enough to pick up some marks.

REFERENCES

Abbott, P. (1990) 'A re-examination of "Three theses re-examined"', in Payne, G. (ed) *The Social Mobility of Women*, London: Routledge

Abbott, P. and Wallace, C. (1997) *An Introduction to Sociology: Feminist Perspectives*, London: Routledge

Abercrombie, N. and Warde, A. (2000) *Contemporary British Society* (3rd edn), Cambridge: Polity Press

Abercrombie, N., Hill, S. and Turner, B.S. (1980) *The Dominant Ideology Thesis*, London: Allen and Unwin

Adamson, P. (1986) 'The rich, the poor, the pregnant', *New Internationalist*, 270

Adler, I. (1975) *Sisters in Crime*, New York: McGraw-Hill

Adonis, A. and Pollard, S. (1998) *A Class Act: the Myth of Britain's Classless Society*, Harmondsworth: Penguin

Adorno, T.W. (1991) *The Culture Industry: Selected Essays on Mass Culture*, London: Routledge

Agbetu, T. (2006) *Institutional Racism and the British Media*, www.ligali.org

Age Concern (2000) *How Ageist is Britain*, www.ageconcern.org.uk

Ahmed, L. (1992) *Women and Gender in Islam: Historical Roots of a Modern Debate*, New Haven and London: Yale University Press

Akers, R.L. (1967) 'Problems in the sociology of deviance: social definitions and behaviour', *Social Forces* 46 (4)

Akinti, P. (2003) 'Captivate us', *Guardian*, 21 Feb

Akthar, T. (2005) '(Re)turn to religion and radical Islam', in T. Abbass (2005) *Muslim Britain: Communities under Pressure*, London: Zed Books

Albert, B., McBride, R. and Seddon, D. (2002) *Perspectives on Disability, Poverty and Technology*, Norwich: University of East Anglia

Aldridge, A. (2000) *Religion in the Contemporary World: A Sociological Introduction*, Cambridge: Polity Press

Alexander, J. (1985) *Neo-Functionalism*, London: Sage

Alibhai-Brown, Y. (2005) quoted in *Africans on Africa: Colonialism*, www.news.bbc.co.uk

Allen, J. (2000) 'Power: its institutional guises (and disguises)', in G. Hughes and R. Fergusson (eds) *Ordering Lives: Family, Work and Welfare*, London: The Open University/Routledge

Allen, T. and Thomas, A. (2001) *Poverty and Development in the 21st Century*, Oxford: OUP

Almy, M. *et al.* (eds) (1984) *Difference: On Representation and Sexuality*, New York: The New Museum of Contemporary Art

Althusser, L. (1969) *For Marx*, Harmondsworth: Penguin

Althusser, L. (1971) *Lenin and Philosophy and Other Essays*, London: New Left Books

Ameli, S., Marandi, S., Ahmed, S., Kara, S. and Merali, A. (2007) *The British Media and Muslim Representation: The Ideology of Demonisation*, London: Islamic Human Rights Commission

Anderson, S., Kinsey, R., Loader, I. and Smith, C. (1994) *Young People, Crime and Policing in Edinburgh*, Aldershot: Avebury

Ansley, F. (1976) quoted in J. Bernard, *The Future of Marriage*, Harmondsworth: Penguin, p.233

Anthias, F. (2001) 'The concept of social division and theorising social stratification: looking at ethnicity and class', *Sociology*, 35(4), pp.835–54

Arber, A., Dale, S. and Gilbert, N. (1986) 'The limitations of existing social class classification of women', in A. Jacoby (ed.) *The Measurement of Social Class*, Guildford: Social Research Association

Archer, L. (2003) *Race, Masculinity and Schooling: Muslim boys and education*, Maidenhead: Open University Press

Armstrong, K. (1993) *The End of Silence: Women and the Priesthood*, London: Fourth Estate

Aron, R. (1967) 'Social class, political class, ruling class' in R. Bendix and S.M. Lipset (eds) *Main Currents in Sociological Thought*, Vols 1 and 2, Harmondsworth: Penguin

Ashworth, J. H. and Farthing, I. (2007) *Churchgoing in the UK: A research report on church attendance in the UK*, Middlesex: Tearfund

Atkinson, J.M. (1971) 'Social reactions to suicide: the role of coroners' definitions', in S. Cohen (ed.) *Images of Deviance*, Harmondsworth: Penguin

Aubert, V. (1952) 'White collar crime and social structure', *American Journal of Sociology*, 58

Aune, K., Sharma, S. and Vincett, G. (eds) (2008) Women and Religion in the West: Challenging Secularization, Aldershot: Ashgate

Bachrach, P. and Baratz, M.S. (1970) *Power and Poverty: Theory and Practice*, Oxford: OUP

Back, L. (2002) 'Youth, "race" and violent disorder', *Sociology Review*, 11(4), April

Badawi, I. (1994) 'Islam', in J. Holm and J. Bowker (eds), *Women in Religion*, London: Pinter

Bagdikian, B. (2004) *The New Media Monopoly*, Boston: Beacon Press

Bainbridge, W.S. (1978) *Satan's Power*. Berkley: University of California Press

Bakan, J. (2004) *Corporation: The Pathological Pursuit of Profit and Power*, London: Constable and Robinson

Baldwin, J. and Bottoms, A.E. (1976) *The Urban Criminal*, London: Tavistock

Ball, S.J. (1981) *Beachside Comprehensive: A Case-Study of Secondary Schooling*, Cambridge: CUP

Bandura, A., Ross, D. and Ross, S.A. (1963) 'The imitation of film mediated aggressive models', *Journal of Abnormal and Social Psychology*, 66(1), pp. 3–11

Barak, G. (ed.) (1991) *Crimes by the Capitalist State: An introduction to state criminality*, Albany: State University of New York Press

Baran, P. (1957) *The Political Economy of Growth*, New York: Monthly Review Press

Barber, B.R. and Schulz, A. (eds) (1995) *Jihad vs McWorld*, New York: Ballantyne Books

Barclay, G. and Tavares, C. (1999) *Information on the Criminal Justice System in England and Wales Digest 4*, London: Home Office

Barker, E. (1984) *The Making of a Moonie*, Oxford: Blackwell

Barker, P. (1982) *The Other Britain: A New Society Collection*, London: Routledge & Kegan Paul

Barnes, C. (1992) *Disabling Imagery and the Media: an exploration of the principles for media representations of disabled people*, Halifax: British Council of Organisations of Disabled People and Ryburn Publishing

Barnes, C. and Mercer, G. (2003) *Disability*, Cambridge: Polity Press

Barnett, S. and Weymour, E. (1999) *A Shrinking Iceberg Slowly Travelling South: Changing Trends in British Television*, London: Campaign for Quality Television

Barron, R.G. and Norris, G.M. (1976) 'Sexual divisions and the dual labour market', in D.J. Barker and S. Allen (eds) *Dependence and Exploration in Work and Marriage*, London: Longman

Bartkey, S.C. (1992) 'Reevaluating French feminism', in N. Fraser and S.C. Bartkey (eds) *Critical Essays in Difference, Agency and Culture*, Bloomington: Indiana University Press

Bartley, M., Carpenter, L., Dunnell, K. and Fitzpatrick, R. (1996) 'Measuring inequalities in health: an analysis of mortality patterns using two social classifications', *Sociology of Health and Illness*, 18(4) pp.455–74

Batchelor, S.A., Kitzinger, J. and Burtney, E. (2004) 'Representing young people's sexuality in the 'youth' media', *Health Education Research*, 19(6), pp. 669–76

Bates, S. (2006) 'Devout Poles show Britain how to keep the faith', *Guardian*, 23 Dec, pp.12–13

Baudrillard, J. (1980) *For a Critique of the Political Economy of the Sign*, New York: Telos Press

Baudrillard, J. (1994) *The Illusion of the End*, Cambridge: Polity Press

Baudrillard, J. (1998) *Selected Writings* (M. Poster ed.), Cambridge: Polity Press

Bauer, P.T. (1981) *Equality, the Third World, and Economic Delusion*, London: Methuen

Bauman, Z. (1978) *Hermeneutics and Social Sciences: Approaches to Understanding*, London: Hutchinson

Bauman, Z. (1983) 'Industrialism, consumerism and power', *Theory, Culture and Society*, 1(3)

Bauman, Z. (1990) *Thinking Sociologically*, Oxford: Blackwell

Bauman, Z. (1992) *Intimations of Postmodernity*, London: Routledge

Bauman, Z. (1997) *Postmodernity and Its Discontents*, Cambridge: Polity Press

Bauman, Z. (2000) 'Sociological enlightenment – For whom, about what?', *Theory, Culture and Society*, 17(2), pp.71–82

BBC (2002) BBC Race Survey, http://news.bbc.co.uk/hi/english/static/in_depth/uk/2002/race/results_full.stm#Television

Beck, U. (1992) *Risk Society: Towards a New Modernity*, London: Sage

Beck, U. (2002) 'A life of one's own in a runaway world: individualisation, globalisation and politics', in U. Beck and E. Beck-Gernsheim, *Individualisation*, Sage, London

Becker, A. *et al.* (2003) 'Binge eating and binge eating disorder in a small-scale, indigenous society: the view from Fiji', published online in Wiley InterScience (www.interscience.wiley.com)

Becker, H. (1950) *Through Values to Social Interpretation: Essays on Social Contexts, Actions, Types and Prospects*, California: Duke University Press

Becker, H. (1963) *The Outsiders: Studies in the Sociology of Deviance*, New York: Free Press

Becker, H. (1970) 'Whose side are we on?', in H. Becker, *Sociological Work*, New Brunswick: Transaction Books

Beckford, J.A. (1985) *Cult Controversies*, London: Routledge

Beckford, R. (2000) 'Dread and Pentecostal: A political theology for the Black church in Britain', London: SPCK

Bellah, R.N. (1970) 'Civil religion in America', in *Beyond Belief: Essays in Religion in a Post-traditional World*, New York: Harper & Row

Bellah, R.N. (1987) 'Introduction: America's Cultural Conversation', in R.N. Bellah, R. Madsen, R., W.M. Sullivan, A. Swidler and S.M. Tipton (eds) *Individualism and Commitment in American Life: Readings on the Themes of Habits of the Heart*, New York: Harper & Row

Belson, W. (1978) *Television Violence and the Adolescent Boy*, Farnborough: Teakfield

Bennett, A., Savage, M., Silva, E., Warde, A., Gayo-Cal, M. and Wright, D. (2006) *Media Culture: The Social Organisation of Media Practices in Contemporary Britain: A Report for The British Film Institute*, London: British Film Institute

Bennett, L. (2000) 'Fifty years of prejudice in the news', *Gay and Lesbian Review Worldwide*, 7(2), pp.30–5

Benston, M. (1972) 'The political economy of women's liberation', in N. Glazer-Mahlbin and H.Y. Wahrer (eds) *Women in a Man-made World*, Chicago: Rand McNally

Berger, A.L. (1997) *Children of Job: American Second Generation Witnesses to the Holocaust*, New York: NY State University Press

Berger, P. (1967) *The Sacred Canopy: Elements of a Sociological Theory of Religion*, New York: Anchor Books

Berger, P. (1971) *A Rumour of Angels*, Harmondsworth: Penguin

Berger, P. (1973) *The Social Reality of Religion*, Harmondsworth: Penguin

Bergesen, A. (1990) 'Turning world-system theory on its head', in M. Featherstone (ed.) *Global Culture: Rationalism, Globalisation and Modernity*, London: Sage

Berry, C. (1986) 'Message misunderstood', *The Listener*, 27 Nov

Best, L. (1993) 'Dragons, dinner ladies and ferrets; sex roles in children's books', *Sociology Review*, Feb

Best, S. (2005) *Understanding Social Divisions*, London: Sage

Best, S. and Kellner, D. (1999) **'**Rap, Black rage, and racial difference', *Enculturation*, 2(2), Spring

Bhaskar, R. (1986) *Scientific Realism and Human Emancipation*, London: Verso

Bhaskar, R. (1998) *The Possibility of Naturalism: A Philosophical Critique of the Contemporary Human Sciences* (3rd edn), New York and London: Routledge

Bhavani, K. (2000) *Feminism and Race*, Oxford: OUP

Bhopal, R., Phillimore, P. and Kohli, H.S. (1991) 'Inappropriate use of the term "Asian": an obstacle to ethnicity and health research', *Journal of Public Health Medicine*, 13, pp.244–6

Billig, M., Condor, S., Edwards, D., Gane, M., Middleton, D. and Radley, A.R. (1988) *Ideological Dilemmas*, London: Sage Publications

Bilton, T., Bonnett, K., Jones, P., Lawson, T., Skinner, D., Stanworth, M. and Webster, A. (2002) *Introductory Sociology* (4th edn), Basingstoke: Macmillan

Bird, J. (1999) *Investigating Religion*, London: HarperCollins

Black, M. (2002) *The No-Nonsense Guide to International Development*, London: Verso

Blackman, S. (1995) *Youth: Positions and Oppositions, Style, Sexuality and Schooling*, Aldershot: Avebury

Blaikie, A. (1999) *Ageing and Popular Culture*, Cambridge: CUP

Blanden, J., Gregg, P. and Machin, S. (2005) *Intergenerational Mobility in Europe and North America*, London: London School of Economics, Centre for Economic Performance

Blumer, H. (1962) 'Society as symbolic interaction', in N. Rose (ed.) *Symbolic Interactionism*, Englewood Hills, NJ: Prentice-Hall

Blumler, J.G. and McQuail, D. (1968) *Television in Politics: Its Uses and Influence*, London: Faber & Faber

Bocock, B.J. (1986) *Hegemony*, London: Tavistock

Bonger, W. (1916) *Criminality and Economic Conditions*, Chicago: Little Brown

Borsay P. (2007) 'Binge drinking and moral panics: historical parallels?', History & Policy website, www.historyandpolicy. org/papers/policy-paper-62.html

Boserup, E. (1970) *Women's Role in Economic Development*, London: Earthscan

Bottero, W. (2005) *Stratification: Social Division and Inequality*, London: Routledge

Bourdieu, P. (1977) 'Cultural reproduction and social reproduction', in J. Karabel and A.H. Halsey (eds) *Power and Ideology in Education*, New York: OUP

Bourgois, P. (1995, 2002/3 [2nd edn]) *In Search of Respect*, Cambridge: CUP

Bowling, B. (1999) *Violent Racism: Victimisation, Policing and Social Context* (revised edn), Oxford: OUP

Bowling, B. and Phillips, C. (2002) *Racism, Crime and Justice*, Harlow: Pearson

Bowling, B. and Phillips, C. (2007) 'Disproportionate and discriminatory: reviewing the evidence on stop and search', *Modern Law Review*, 70, pp.936–61

Box, S. (1981) *Deviance, Reality and Society* (2nd edn), Eastbourne: Holt Rheinhart Wilson

Box, S. (1983) *Crime, Power and Mystification*, London: Tavistock

Boyle, R. (2005) 'Press the red button now: television and technology', *Sociology Review*, Nov

Boyle, R. (2007) 'The "now" media generation', *Sociology Review*, Sept

Bradley, H. (1996) *Fractured Identities: Changing Patterns of Inequality*, Cambridge: Polity Press

Bradley, H. (1999) *Gender and Power in the Workplace*, Basingstoke, Macmillan

Braithwaite, J. (1984) *Corporate Crime in the Pharmaceutical Industry*, London: Routledge

Braithwaite, J. (2000) *Regulation, Crime and Freedom*, Aldershot: Ashgate

Brake, M. (1980) *The Sociology of Youth and Youth Subcultures*, London: Routledge

Brantingham, P.J. and Brantingham, P.L. (1984) *Patterns of Crime*, New York: Macmillan

Brantingham, P.J. and Brantingham, P.L. (1991) *Environmental Criminology* (revised edn), Prospect Heights: Waveland Press

Braverman, H. (1974) *Labour and Monopoly Capitalism*, New York: Monthly Press

Brenner, M., Brown, J. and Canter, M. (1985) *The Research Interview: Uses and Approaches*, London: Academic Press

Brewer, M., Sibetia, L. and Wren-Lewis, L. (2008) *Racing Away; Income Inequality and the Evolution of High Incomes*, IFS Briefing Notes, BN76, Institute for Fiscal Studies

Brierley, P. (2002) *Reaching and Keeping Tweenagers*, London: Christian Research

Brierley, P. (2006) *Pulling Out of the Nose Dive: A Contemporary Picture of Churchgoing; What the 2005 English Church Census Reveals*, London: Christian Research

Brierley, P. (ed.) (1979, 1989, 1999, 2000, 2001) *Christian Research Association, UK Christian Handbook, Religious Trends* 1979, 1989, 1999, 2000, 2001, London: HarperCollins

Bristol Fawcett Society (2008) *Representation, Misrepresentation, No Representation: Women in the Media*, Bristol Fawcett Society/Bristol Feminist Network

British Attitude Survey, www.statistics.gov.uk/STATBASE/Source.a sp?ComboState=Show+Links&More=Y&v lnk=619&LinkBtn.x=26&LinkBtn.y=14

British Youth Lifestyles Survey (2000) Home Office Research Study 209

Broadcasting Standards Council (2003) *Content and Analysis, of public opinion and content on issues of taste and decency in broadcasting*, Briefing Update No.7, www.ofcom.org.uk

Brooks, A. (1997) *Postfeminisms: Feminisms, Cultural Theory and Cultural Forms*, London: Routledge

Brown, C.G. (2001) *The Death of Christian Britain: Understanding Secularization 1800–2000*, London: Routledge

Brownmiller, S. (2000) *Against Our Will: Men, Women and Rape*, New York: Fawcett Books

Bruce, S. (1995) *Religion in Modern Britain*, Oxford: OUP

Bruce, S. (1996) *Religion in the Modern World: From Cathedrals to Cults*, Oxford: OUP

Bruce, S. (2001) 'The social process of secularisation' in R.K. Fenn (2004) *The Blackwell Companion to the Sociology of Religion*, Oxford: Blackwell

Bruce, S. (2002) *God is Dead: Secularization in the West*, Oxford: Blackwell

Bryman, A. (2004) *Social Research Methods* (2nd edn), Oxford: OUP

Bryman, A. and Burgess, A. (1994) *Analysing Qualitative Data*, London: Routledge

Buckingham, D. (1996) *Moving Images: Understanding Children's Emotional Responses to Television*, Manchester: Manchester University Press

Buckingham, D. (ed.) (1993) *Reading Audiences: Young People and the Media*, Manchester: Manchester University Press

Bulman, J. (2003) 'Patterns of pay: results of the 2002 New Earnings Survey', *Labour Market Trends*, London: HMSO

Burchill, J. (2001) *Guardian*, Sat 18 Aug

Burkey, S. (1993) *People First*, London: Zed Books

Butler, C. (1995) 'Religion and gender: young Muslim women in Britain', *Sociology Review*, 4(3), Oxford: Philip Allan

Butler, D. and Kavanagh, D. (1985) *The British General Election of 1983*, London: Macmillan

Butler, D. and Rose, R. (1960) *The British General Election of 1959*, London: Frank Cass

Butler, D. and Stokes, D. (1971) *Political Change in Britain*, London: Macmillan

Butler, R. (1969) 'Ageism: another form of bigotry', *The Gerontologist*, 9, p.243

Butsch, R. (1992) 'Class and gender in four decades of television situation comedy', *Critical Studies in Mass Communication*, 9, pp.387–99

Cain, M. (1986) 'Realism, feminism, methodology and law', *International Journal of the Sociology of Law*, 14

Calderisi, R. (2006) *The Trouble with Africa*, New Haven: Yale University Press

Campbell, B. (1985) *Wigan Pier Re-visited*, London: Virago Press Ltd

Campbell, B. (1993) *Goliath: Britain's Dangerous Places*, London: Methuen

Cannadine, D. (1998) *Class in Britain*, London: Yale University Press

Cantril, H. (1940) *The Invasion from Mars: A study in the psychology of panic*, Princeton, NJ: Princeton University Press

Caplan, L. (ed.) (1987) *Studies in Religious Fundamentalism*, London: Macmillan

Caplow, T. (1954) *The Sociology of Work*, New York: McGraw-Hill

Cardoso, F.H. (1972) 'Dependency and development in Latin America', *New Left Review*, 74, July/Aug

Carlen, P. (1988) *Women, Crime and Poverty*, Milton Keynes: OU Press

Carlen, P. (1992) 'Criminal women and criminal justice: the limits to and potential of feminist and left realist perspectives', in R. Matthews and J. Young (eds) *Issues in Realist Criminology*, London: Sage

Carmen, R. (1996) *Autonomous Development: Humanising the Landscape*, London: Zed Books

Carnell, B. (2000) Article titled 'Paul Ehrlich' dated 17 May 2000 downloaded from www.overpopulation.com

Carrabine, E., Iganski, P., Lee, M., Plummer, K. and South, N. (2004) *Criminology: A Sociological Introduction*, London: Routledge

Carrigan, M. and Szmigin, I. (2000) 'The ethical advertising covenant: regulating ageism in UK advertising', *International Journal of Advertising*, 19(4), pp.509–28

Cashmore, E. (1996) *Dictionary of Race and Ethnic Relations*, London: Routledge

Castles, S. and Kosack, G.C. (1973) *Immigrant Workers and Class Structure in Western Europe*, Oxford: OUP

Catley-Carlson, M. (1994) 'Population policies and reproductive rights – always in conflict?', in B. Hartmann (ed.) *Reproductive Rights and Wrongs: the Global Politics of Population Control*, Boston MA: South End Press

Chahal, K. and Julienne, L. (1999) *We Can't All Be White*, York: Joseph Rowntree Foundation

Chambliss, W.J. (1975) 'Towards a political economy of crime', *Theory and Society*, Vol. 2 pp.149–70

Chambliss, W.J. and Mankoff, M. (1976) *Whose Law? What Order?*, New York: John Wiley & Sons

Chandler, D. (1994) *Notes on the Construction of Reality in TV News Programmes*, www.aber.ac.uk/media/Modules

Charlton, T., Gunter, B. and Hannan, A. (2000) *Broadcast Television Effects in a Remote Community*, Hillsdale, NJ: Lawrence Erlbaum

Chase-Dunn, C. (1975) 'The effects of international economic dependence on development and inequality: a cross national study', *American Sociological Review*, 40, Dec

Children Now (1999) *Boys to Men: Entertainment Media Messages about Masculinity*, Oakland, CA: Children Now

Childs, S. and Campbell, R. (2008) 'Is politics gendered', *Sociology Review*, Nov

Choudhury, T. (2007) *The Role of Muslim Identity Politics in Radicalization (a study in progress)*, London: Department for Communities and Local Government

Chrispin, J. and Jegede, F. (2000) *Population, Resources and Development*, London: HarperCollins

Christian Research (2004) 'Home Office Citizenship Survey', Quadrant, Sept 2004: 4

Christian Research (2006) 'Three new churches a week', press release, London: Christian Research, 23 Feb

Chunn, D. and Menzies, R. (eds) (2003) *Toxic Criminology – Environment, Law and the State in Canada*, Toronto: Fernwood Books

Clark, K. and Drinkwater, S. (2007) *Ethnic Minorities in the Labour Market: Dynamics and Diversity*, York: Joseph Rowntree Foundation

Clark, T.N. and Hoffman-Martinot, V. (eds) (1998) *The New Political Culture*, Boulder CO: Westview

Clarke, M. (1990) *Business Crime: Its Nature and Control*, Bristol: Policy Press

Clarke, R.V.G. (1995) 'Situational crime prevention', in M. Tonry and D. Farrington (eds) *Building a Safer Society*, Chicago: University of Chicago

Clarke, R.V.G. (ed.) (1992) *Situational Crime Prevention*, New York: Harrow & Heston

Clegg, S.R. (1989) *Frameworks of Power*, London: Sage

Clinard, M.B. (1974) *Sociology of Deviant Behavior*, New York: Holt, Rhinehart & Winston

Cloward, R. and Ohlin, L. (1960) *Delinquency and Opportunity*, London: Collier Macmillan

Cochrane, A. and Pain, K. (2000) 'A globalising society' in D. Held (ed.) *A Globalising World: Culture, Economics and Politics*, London: Routledge

Cohen, A. (1955) *Delinquent Boys*, New York: The Free Press

Cohen, L.E. and Felson, M. (1979) 'Social change and crime rate trends: a routine activities approach', *American Sociological Review*, 44

Cohen, N. (2005) 'Capital punishment', *The Observer*, 6 Nov

Cohen, N. (2009) *Waiting for the Etonians: Reports from the Sickbed of Liberal England*, London: Fourth Estate

Cohen, R. and Kennedy, P. (2000) *Global Sociology*, Basingstoke: Macmillan

Cohen, R. and Rai, S. (eds) (2000) *Global Social Movements*, Athlone: Continuum International Publishing Group

Cohen, S. (1972, 1980 [2nd edn]) *Folk Devils and Moral Panics*, London: Paladin

Cohen, S. (1985) *Visions of Social Control*, Cambridge: Polity

Cohen, S. (2002) 'Moral panics as cultural politics', (New introduction), in *Folk Devils and Moral Panics: The Creation of the Mods and Rockers* (3rd edn), London: Routledge

Cohen, S. and Young, J. (1981) *The Manufacture of News: Deviance, Social Problems and the Mass Media* (2nd edn), London: Constable

Coleridge, N. (1993) *Paper Tigers: The Latest, Greatest Newspaper Tycoons and How They Won the World*, London: Heinemann

Collier, P. (2008) *The Bottom Billion*, Oxford: OUP

Collier, P. and Hoeffler, A. (2004) 'Aid, policy and growth in post-conflict societies', *European Economic Review*, 48, pp.1125–45

Collier, R. (1992) 'The New Man: Fact or Fad?', *Achilles Heel*, 14, Winter

Collins, H. and Pinch, T. (1998) *The Golem: What You Should Know About Science* (2nd edn) Cambridge: CUP

Collison, M. (1995) *Police, Drugs and Community*, London: Free Association Books

Collison, M. (1996) 'In search of the high life', *British Journal of Criminology*, 36(3), pp.428–44

Colman, A. and Gorman, L. (1982) 'Conservatism, dogmatism and authoritarianism amongst British police officers', *Sociology*, 16(1)

Columbia Journalism Review (2000) 'Self-censorship', *Columbia Journalism Review*, May/Jun

Commission for Africa (2005) *Our Common Interest*, London: Penguin

Conklin, J.E. (1977) *Illegal but not Criminal: Business Crime in America*, Englewood Cliffs, NJ: Prentice Hall

Connell, R.W. (1995) *Masculinities*, Cambridge: Polity Press

Connolly, P. and Keenan, M. (2000) *Racial Attitudes and Prejudice in Northern Ireland* (Report 1), Belfast: Northern Ireland Statistics and Research Agency

Cornford, J. and Robins, K. (1999) 'New media', in J. Stokes and A. Reading (eds) *The Media in Britain: Current debates and developments*, London: MacMillan

Couldry, N., Curran, J. et al. (2007a) *Media Ownership and the News*, Submission to House of Lords Select Committee on Communications, Goldsmiths Media Research Group

Couldry, N., Livingstone, S., and Markham, T. (2007b) *Media Consumption and Public Engagement: Beyond the Presumption of Attention*, London: Palgrave Macmillan

Coussins, J. (1976) *The Equality Report*, NCCL Rights for Women Unit: London

Coxall, W.N. (1981) *Parties and Pressure Groups*, London: Longman

Craib, I. (1992) *Anthony Giddens*, London: Routledge

Craig, S. (ed.) (1992) *Men, Masculinity and the Media*, Newbury Park, CA: Sage

Crewe, I. (1984) 'The electorate: partisan de-alignment ten years on', in H. Berrington (ed.) *Change in British Politics*, London: Frank Cass

Croall, H. (2001) *Understanding White-collar Crime*, Milton Keynes: OU Press

Crook, S., Pakulski, J. and Waters, M. (1992) *Postmodernisation: Change in Advanced Society*, London: Sage

Cross, M. (1979) *Urbanisation and Urban Growth in the Caribbean*, Cambridge: CUP cited in M. O'Donnell (1983) *New Introductory Reader in Sociology*, London: Nelson Harrap

Cuff, E.C., Sharrock W.W. and Francis, D.W. (1990) *Perspectives in Sociology*, London: Routledge

Cumberbatch, G. (2004) *Video Violence: Villain or Victim?* Report for the Video Standards Council

Cumberbatch, G. and Negrine, R. (1992) *Images of Disability on Television*, London: Routledge

Cummings, E. and Henry, W. (1961) *Growing Old: The Process of Disengagement*, New York: Basic Books

Curran (2003) 'Press history', in J. Curran and J. Seaton (2003) – see next entry

Curran, J. and Seaton, J. (2003) *Power without Responsibility: the press, broadcasting, and new media in Britain* (6th edn), London: Routledge

Dahl, R. (1961) *Who Governs: Democracy and Power in an American City*, New Haven: Yale University Press

Dalton, K. (1964) *The Pre-menstrual Syndrome and Progesterone Therapy*, London: Heinemann Medical

Daly, M. (1973) *Beyond God the Father*, Boston, MA: Beacon Press

Daly, M. (1978) *Gyn/Ecology: The Meta-ethics of Radical Feminism*, Boston, MA: Beacon Press

Darlington, Y. and Scott, D. (2002) *Qualitative Research in Practice: Stories from the Field*, Milton Keynes: OU Press

Davidman, L. (1991) *Religion in a Rootless World: Women turn to Orthodox Judaism*, Berkeley: University of California Press

Davidson, K. (2006) 'Gender and an ageing population', *Sociology Review*, 15(4), Apr

Davie, G. (1994) *Religion in Britain 1945–1990, Believing Without Belonging*, Oxford: Blackwell

Davie, G. (1995) 'Competing fundamentalisms', *Sociology Review*, 4(4), Oxford: Philip Allan

Davies, C. (2004) *The Strange Death of Moral Britain*, Edison, NJ: Transaction Publishers

Davies, N. (2008) *Flat Earth News*, London: Chatto & Windus

Davies, T. (1994) 'Disabled by society', *Sociology Review*, 3(4), April

Davis, K. and Moore, W.E. (1955) 'Some principles of stratification', in Bendix, R. and Lipset, S.M. (eds) *Class, Status and Power* (2nd edn 1967), London: Routledge & Kegan Paul

Davis, M. (1990) *City of Quartz*, London: Vintage

Day, A. (2007) 'Believing in belonging: religion returns to sociology mainstream', *Network*, British Sociological Association, Summer 2007

de Beauvoir, S. (1953) *The Second Sex*, London: Jonathan Cape

Deacon, D.N., Golding, P. and Billig, M. (2001) 'Press and broadcasting: "real issues" and real coverage', in P. Norris (ed) *Britain Votes 2001*, Oxford: OUP

Delamont, S. (2001) *Changing Women: Unchanged Men: Sociological Perspectives on Gender in a Post-Industrial Society*, Buckingham: OU Press

Delphy, C. (1977) *The Main Enemy*, London: Women's Research & Resources Centre

Dennis, N. and Erdos, G. (1993) *Families without Fatherhood*, London: IEA

Denscombe, M. (1999) *Sociology Update*, Leicester: Olympus Books

Denscombe, M. (2001) 'Uncertain identities and health-risking behaviour: the case of young people and smoking in late modernity', *British Journal of Sociology*, 52, March

Department for Education and Skills (DfES) (2002) *Minority Ethnic Pupils in Mainly White Schools*, DfES research report 365, London: DfES

Devine, F. (1992) *Affluent Workers Revisited*, Edinburgh University Press: Edinburgh

Diani, M. (1992) 'The concept of social movement', *Sociological Review*, 40, pp.1–25

Dietz, T. (1998) 'An examination of violence and gender role portrayals in video games: Implications for gender socialization and aggressive behavior', *Sex Roles*, 38, pp.425–42

Ditton, J. (1977) *Part-time Crime: An Ethnography of Fiddling and Pilferage*, Basingstoke: Macmillan

Doherty, B. (1998) 'Opposition to road building', *Parliamentary Affairs*, 51(3), pp.370–83

Douglas, J.D. (1967) *The Social Meaning of Suicide*, Princeton, N.J: Princeton University Press

Downes, D. (1966) *The Delinquent Solution*, London: Routledge

Doyle, G. (2002) *Media Ownership*, London: Sage

Drane, J. (1999) *What is the New Age Saying to the Church?*, London: Marshal Pickering

Drury, B. (1991) 'Sikh girls and the maintenance of an ethnic culture', *New Community*, 17(3), pp. 387–99

Duffield, M. (1998) 'Post-modern conflict: warlords, post-adjustment states and private protection', *Civil Wars*, Spring 1(1), pp.65–102

Duffield, M. (2001) *Global Governance and the New Wars*, London: Zed Books

Duffield, M. (2007) *Development Security and Unending War; Governing the World of Peoples*, Cambridge: Polity

Duncan, M.C. and Messner, M.A. (2005) *Gender in Televised Sports: News and Highlights Shows, 1989–2004*, Los Angeles: Amateur Athletic Foundation of Los Angeles

Durkheim, E. (1893/1960 reissue) *The Division of Labour in Society*, Glencoe: Free Press

Durkheim, E. (1895/1982 reissue) *The Rules of Sociological Method* (ed. S. Lukes), London: Macmillan

Durkheim, E. (1897/1952 reissue) *Suicide: A Study in Sociology*, London: Routledge Kegan Paul

Durkheim, E. (1912/1915/1961 reissue) *The Elementary Forms of Religious Life*, London: Allen & Unwin

Dutton, B. (1997) *The Media*, London: Longman

Duverger, M. (1972) *Party Politics and Pressure Groups*, London: Nelson

Dworkin, A. (1990) *Pornography: Men Possessing Women*, New York: E.P. Dutton

Dwyer, C. (1999) 'Contradictions of community: questions of identity for young British Muslim women', *Environment and Planning A*, 31(1), pp.53–68

Dyer, R. (2002) *The Matter of Images: Essays on Representation*, London: Routledge

Easthope, A. (1990) *What a Man's Gotta Do: The Masculine Myth in Popular Culture*, Boston, MA: Unwin Hyman

Economic and Social Research Council (1997) *Twenty-Something in the 90s: Getting on, Getting by, Getting Nowhere*, Research Briefing, Swindon: ESRC

Edwards, C. (1992) 'Industrialisation in South Korea', in T. Hewitt, H. Johnson and D. Wield (eds) *Industrialisation and Development*, Oxford: OUP

Edwards, D. and Cromwell, E. (2006) *Guardians of Power: The myth of the liberal media*, London: Pluto Press

Edwards, D. and Cromwell, E. (2008) *Flat Earth News – The Inside View – Part 1*, www.medialens.org/alerts/08/080305_flat_earth_news.php

Edwards, T. (1997) *Men in the Mirror: Fashion, Masculinity and Consumer Society*, London: Cassell

Ehrlich, P. (1968) *The Population Bomb*, New York: Ballantyne

El Sadaawi, N. (1980) *The Hidden Face of Eve: Women in the Arab World*, London: Zed Books

Elias, N. (1978) *The Civilizing Process: The History of Manners*, Oxford: Blackwell Publishing

Elkington, J. (1999) *Cannibals With Forks: The Triple Bottom Line of 21st Century Businesses*, Oxford Capestone

Elliot, A. (2002) 'Beck's sociology of risk: a critical assessment', *Sociology*, 36(2), pp.293–315

Ellwood, W. (1982) 'Two steps forward, one step back', *New Internationalist*, 118

Ellwood, W. (2001) *The No-Nonsense Guide to Globalisation*, London: Verso

Elson, D. and Pearson, R. (1981) 'The subordination of women and the internationalisation of factory production', in K. Young et al. (eds) *Of Marriage and the Market: Women's Subordination in International Perspective*, London: CSE Books

Environmental Justice Foundation (2007) statement in the 'Impact Report' on the website www.ejfoundation.org/

Equal Opportunities Commission (2006) *Facts about Women and Men in Great Britain*, EOC

Erixon, F. (2005) *Why Aid Does Not Work*, www.news.bbc.co.uk

Escobar, A. (1995) *Encountering Development: The Making and Unmaking of the Third World*, Princeton: Princeton University Press

ESRC Society Today (2006) 'Pentecostals overtake Methodists in England', press release, Swindon: Economic and Social Research Council, 19 Dec

Esteva, G. (1992) 'Development' in W. Sachs (ed.) *The Development Dictionary: A Guide for Knowledge and Power*, London: Zed Books

Esteva, G. and Austin, J.E. (1987) *Food Policy in Mexico: the Search for Self-Sufficiency*, Ithaca: Cornell University Press

Ethnic Focus (2004) quoted in I. Burrell, 'Terrestrial TV either ignores Asians or casts them in stereotypical roles', *Independent*, 17 Aug

Evans, J. and Chandler, J, (2006) 'To buy or not to buy: family dynamics and children's consumption', *Sociological Research Online*, 11(2) www.socresonline.org.uk

Evans, G. (1992) 'Is Britain a class-divided society? A re-analysis and extension of Marshall et al.'s study of class consciousness', *Sociology*, 26(2), pp.233–58

Evans, P. (1979) *Dependent Development: The Alliance of Multinational, State and Local Capital in Brazil*, Princeton: Princeton University Press

Fahmy, E. (2004) *Encouraging Young People's Political Participation in the UK*, London: Routledge,

Faludi, S. (1992) *The Undeclared War against Women*, London: Chatto & Windus

Farrington, D.P. (1995) 'The development of offending and anti-social behaviour from childhood: key findings from the Cambridge Study in Delinquent Development', *Journal of Child Psychology and Psychiatry*, 36, pp.929–64

Farrington, D.P. and Painter, K.A. (2004) *Gender Differences in Offending: Implications for risk focussed prevention*, Home Office Online Report 09/04

Farrington, D.P. and West, D.J. (1990) 'The Cambridge Study in Delinquent Development: a long-term follow-up of 411 London males', in H.J. Kerner and G. Kaiser (eds) *Criminality; Personality, Behaviour and Life History*, Berlin: Springer-Verlag

Faulks, K. (1999) *Political Sociology: A Critical Introduction*, New York University Press

Fawbert, J. (2008) 'Hoodies: Moral Panic or Justifiable Concern', www.beds.ac.uk/news/2008/feb/080214-hoodies

Featherstone, M. and Hepworth, M. (1991) 'The mask of ageing and the postmodern life course', in M. Featherstone, M. Hepworth and B.S. Turner (eds) *The Body: Social Process and Cultural Theory*, London: Sage

Featherstone, M. and Wernick, A. (1995), *Images of Ageing: Cultural Representations of Later Life*, London & New York: Routledge

Feeley, M. and Simon. J. (1992) 'The new penology: notes on the emerging strategy of corrections and its implications', *Criminology*, 30(4), pp.449–74

Feinstein, L. et al. (2007) *Reducing Inequalities*, London: National Children's Bureau

Fenn, R.K. (ed.) (2004) 'Feminism and the sociology of religion: from gender blindness to gendered difference', in *The Blackwell Companion to the Sociology of Religion*, London: Blackwell

Ferguson, M. (1983) *Forever Feminine: Women's Magazines and the Cult of Femininity*, London: Heinemann

Ferrell, J. (1999) 'Cultural criminology', *Annual Review of Sociology*, 25(1)

Fesbach, S. and Sanger, J.L. (1971) *Television and Aggression*, San Francisco: Jessey-Bass
Festinger, L., Riecken, H., and Schachter, S. (1956) *When Prophecy Fails*, Minneapolis: University of Minnesota Press
Festinger, L.A. (1957) *A Theory of Dissonance*, Stanford, CA: Stanford University Press
Feyerabend, P. (1975) *Against Method*, London: New Left Review Editions
Fielding, A. (1995) 'Migration and middle-class formation in England and Wales', in T. Butler and M. Savage (eds) *Social Change and the Middle Class*, London: UCL
Finch, M. (1990) 'Sex and address in *Dynasty*', in M. Alvarado and J.O. Thompson (eds) *The Media Reader*, London: BFI
Firestone, S. (1970) *The Dialectic of Sex*, New York: Bantam Books
Fiske, J. (1987) *Television Culture*, London: Methuen
Fiske, J. and Hartley, J. (2003) *Reading Television*, London: Methuen
Fitzgerald, M., Stockdale, J. and Hale, C. (2003) *Young People's Involvement in Street Crime*, London: Youth Justice Board
Forster, N. (1994) 'The analysis of company documentation', in C. Cassell and G. Symon (eds) *Qualitative Methods in Organizational Research*, London: Sage
Foster, J. (1995) 'Informal social control and community crime prevention', *British Journal of Criminology*, 35
Foster, P. (2004) 'Globalising Greenwash', *New Internationalist*, March
Foster-Carter, A. (1985) *The Sociology of Development,* Ormskirk: Causeway Press
Foster-Carter, A. (1993) 'Development', in Haralamabos, M. (ed.) *Developments in Sociology*, Vol 9, Ormskirk: Causeway Press
Foucault, M. (1963/1975) *The Birth of the Clinic*, New York: Vintage Books
Foucault, M. (1977) *Discipline and Punish: The Birth of the Prison,* London: Allen Lane
Foucault, M. (1980) *Power/Knowledge: Selected Interviews and Other Writings 1972–77* (ed. C. Gordon), Brighton: Harvester Press
Fouts, G. (1999) quoted on www.mediaawareness.ca/english/issues/stereotyping/women_and_girls/women_beauty.cfm
Frank, A.G. (1971) *The Sociology of Development and the Underdevelopment of Sociology*, London: Pluto Press
Frazer, J.G. (1922, originally 1890) *The Golden Bough*, London: Macmillan
Friedman, L.M. (1999) *The Horizontal Society*, New Haven: Yale University Press
Frobel, F., Heinrichs, J. and Kreye, O. (1980) *The New International Division of Labour*, Cambridge: CUP
Fulcher, J. and Scott, J. (1999, 2007 [3rd edn]) *Sociology*, Oxford: OUP
Furedi, F. (1994) 'A plague of moral panics', *Living Marxism,* 73, Nov
Furlong, A. and Cartmel, F. (1997) *Young People and Social Change*, Buckingham: OU Press
Furlong, A. and Cartmel, F. (2005) *Vulnerable Young Men in Fragile Labour Markets: Employment, unemployment and the search for long-term security*, York: Joseph Rowntree Foundation
Furlong, A., Cartmel, F., Biggart, A., Sweeting, H. and West, P. (2006) 'Social class in an 'individualised' society', *Sociology Review*, 15(4), pp.28–32
Galeano, E. (1992) *Open Veins of Latin America*, New York: Monthly Press Review
Gallagher (1980) quoted in L. Van Zoonen (1996) *Feminist Media Studies,* London: Sage
Gallie, D. (1994) 'Are the unemployed an underclass: some evidence from the Social Change and Economic Life Initiative', *Sociology*, 28
Galtung, J. and M. H. Ruge (1970) 'The structure of foreign news', in J. Tunstall (ed.) *Media Sociology: A Reader*, London: Constable
Garfinkel, H. (1967) *Studies in Ethnomethodology*, Englewood Hills, NJ: Prentice-Hall
Garland, D. (2001) *The Culture of Control: Crime and Social Order in Contemporary Society*, Chicago: University of Chicago Press
Gauntlett, D. (2008) *Media, Gender and Identity: An Introduction* (2nd edn), London: Routledge
Geis, G. (1967) 'The heavy electrical equipment anti-trust cases of 1961', in M.B. Clinard and R. Quinney (eds) *Criminal Behaviour Systems*, New York: Holt, Rhinehart & Winston
General Household Survey (2001) London: ONS, HMSO
George, S. (1993) 'The debt boomerang', *New Internationalist*, 243, May
Gerbner, G., Gross, L., Signorielli. N. and Morgan, M. (1986) *Television's Mean World: Violence profile No. 14–15*, Philadelphia: Annandale School of Communications, University of Pennsylvania
Gereffi, G. (1994) 'Rethinking development theory: insights from East Asia and Latin America', in A. Douglas-Kincaid and A. Portes (eds) *Comparative National Development: Society and Economy in the New Global Order*, North Carolina: University of North Carolina Press
Giddens, A. (1964) *Structuration and Related Theories of Social Life and Communication*, London: Routledge
Giddens, A. (1973) *The Class Structure of the Advanced Societies,* London: Hutchinson
Giddens, A. (1976) *The New Rules of Sociological Methods*, London: Hutchinson
Giddens, A. (1984) *The Constitution of Society: Outline of the Theory of Structuration*, Cambridge: Polity Press
Giddens, A. (1990) *The Consequences of Modernity*, Cambridge: Polity
Giddens, A. (1991) *Modernity and Self-Identity*, Cambridge: Polity Press
Giddens, A. (1993) *New Rules of Sociological Method : A positive critique of interpretative sociologies* (2nd edn), Cambridge: Polity Press.
Giddens, A. (1994) *Beyond Left or Right*, Cambridge: Polity Press
Giddens, A. (1999) *A Runaway World? The BBC Reith Lectures*, London: BBC Radio 4, BBC Education
Giddens, A. (2001) *Sociology* (4th edn), Cambridge: Polity Press
Giddens, A. (2006) *Sociology* (5th edn), Oxford: Polity Press
Giddens, A. and Diamond, P. (2005) *The New Egalitarianism*, Cambridge: Polity
Giddens, A. and Pierson, C. (1998) *Conversations with Anthony Giddens: Making Sense of Modernity*, Cambridge: Polity Press
Gill, R. (2007) *Gender and the Media*, Cambridge: Polity Press
Gill, R. (2008) 'Empowerment/sexism: figuring female sexual agency in contemporary advertising', *Feminism and Psychology*, 18(1), pp.35-60
Gilroy, P. (1982a)'Steppin' out of Babylon: race, class and autonomy', in *The Empire Strikes Back: Race and Racism in Britain*, London: CCCS/Hutchinson
Ginn, J., Arber, S., Brannen, J., Dale, A., Dex, S., Elias, P., Moss, P., Pahl, J., Roberts, C. and Rubery, J. (1996) 'Feminist fallacies: a reply to Hakim on women's employment', *British Journal of Sociology*, 47
Glaser, B.G. and Strauss, A.L. (1965) *Awareness of Dying*, Chicago: Aldine
Glasgow University Media Group (1981) *Bad News*, London: Routledge
Glasgow University Media Group (1985) *War and Peace News*, Milton Keynes: OU Press
Glasgow University Media Group (2000) *Viewing the World: News Content and Audience Studies*, London: Department for International Development
Glasner, P. (1977) *The Sociology of Secularisation*, London: Routledge & Kegan Paul
Glass, D.V. (1954) *Social Mobility in Britain*, London: RKP
Glendinning, A. and Bruce, S. (2006) 'New ways of believing or belonging: is religion giving way to spirituality?', *British Journal of Sociology*, 57(3), pp.399–414
Glock, C.Y. and Stark, R. (1969) 'Dimensions in religious commitment', in R. Robertson (ed.) (1969) *The Sociology of Religion*, Harmondsworth: Penguin
Goffman, E. (1968) *Asylums*, Harmondsworth: Penguin
Gold, K. (2003) 'Poverty is an excuse', *Times Educational Supplement*, 7 March
Gold, R. (1958) 'Roles in sociological field investigation', *Social Forces*, 36, pp.217–23.
Goldthorpe, J. (1975) *The Sociology of the Third World*, Cambridge: CUP
Goldthorpe, J. (1980) *Social Mobility and the Class Structure in Modern Britain*, Oxford: Clarendon Press
Goldthorpe, J. (1983) 'Women and class analysis: in defence of the conventional view', *Sociology*, 17(4)
Goldthorpe, J. (1996) 'Class analysis and the reorientation of class theory', *British Journal of Sociology*, 47(3), pp.481–505
Goldthorpe, J. and Jackson, M. (2007) 'Intergenerational class mobility in contemporary Britain: political concerns and empirical findings', *The British Journal of Sociology*, 58(4), Dec
Goldthorpe, J. and Lockwood, D. (1969) *The Affluent Worker in the Class Structure* (3 vols), Cambridge: CUP
Goode, E. and Ben-Yehuda, N. (1994) *Moral Panics: The Social Construction of Deviance*, Oxford: Blackwell
Goodwin, J. and O'Connor, H. (2005) 'Exploring complex transitions: looking back at the golden age of from school to work', *Sociology*, 39(2), pp.201–20
Goody, J. (1961) 'Religion and ritual: the definitional problem', *British Journal of Sociology*, 12, pp.142-64
Gorard, S. (2008) 'Researching social mobility', *Sociology Review,* 18(1), Sept
Gordon, P. (1988) 'Black people and the criminal law: rhetoric and reality', *International Journal of the Sociology of Law*, 16
Gouldner, A.W. (1968) 'The sociologist as partisan: sociology and the welfare state', *The American Sociologist*, May
Graef, R. (1989) *Talking Blues: The Police in Their Own Words,* London: Collins Harvill
Graham, J. and Bowling, B. (1995) *Young People and Crime*, Home Office Research Study 145, London: Home Office
Gramsci, A. (1971) *Selections from the Prison Notebooks*, London: Lawrence and Wishart
Grant, W. (1999) *Pressure Groups and British Politics*, Basingstoke: Palgrave
Greeley, A. (1972) *Unsecular Man*, New York: Schocken Books, Inc
Greeley, A. (1992) *Sociology and Religion: A Collection of Readings*, New York: HarperCollins Publishers
Green, P. and Ward, A. (2004) *State Crime: Governments, Violence and Corruption*, London: Pluto Press
Greengross, S. (2004) 'Why ageism must be eradicated', *BBC News*, 7 Dec
Greenslade, R. (2005) *Seeking Scapegoats: The coverage of asylum in the UK press*, Information Centre about Asylums and Refugees (ICAR)
Gross, R.M. (1994) 'Buddhism', in J. Holm and J. Bowker (eds) *Women in Religion*, London: Pinter
Gunter, B. (2008) 'Why study media content', *Sociology Review*, Nov
Habermas, J. (1979) *Communication and the Evolution of Society*, London: Heinemann
Hadden, J. and Bromley, D. (1993) *Religion and the Social Order: The Handbook on Cults and Sects in America*, Greenwich, CT: JAI Press
Haddon, J.K. and Long, T.E. (eds) (1993) *Religion and Religiosity in America*, New York: Crossroad Publishing Company
Hagan, J. (1987) *Modern Criminology: Crime, Criminal Behaviour and its Control*, New York: McGraw-Hill
Hakim, C. (1979) *Occupational Segregation*, Department of Employment Research Paper no.9, London: HMSO
Hakim, C. (2000) *Work–Lifestyle Choices in the 21st Century*, Oxford: OUP
Hald, G.M. (2007) *Pornography Consumption: A study of prevalence rates, consumption patterns, and effects*, Aarhus, Denmark: Psykologisk Institut, Aarhus Universitet
Halevy, E. (1927) *A History of the English People in 1815*, London: Unwin
Hall, S. (1973) *Encoding and Decoding in the Television Discourse*, Birmingham: University of Birmingham, Centre for Contemporary Cultural Studies
Hall, S. (1978) *Policing the Crisis,* London: Macmillan
Hall, S. (1985) 'Religious ideologies and social movements in Jamaica', in R. Bocock and K. Thompson (eds) *Religion and Ideology*, Manchester: Manchester University Press
Hall, S. and Jacques, M. (1983) *The Politics of Thatcherism*, London: Lawrence & Wishart
Hall, S. and Jefferson, T. (1976) *Resistance through Rituals*, London: Hutchinson
Hall, S., Critcher, C., Jefferson, A., Clarke, J. and Robert, B. (1978) *Policing the Crisis: Mugging, the State and Law and Order,* London: Palgrave Macmillan
Hallsworth, S. (1994) 'Understanding New Social Movements', *Sociology Review*, 4(1), Oxford: Philip Allen
Hamilton, K. and Waller, G. (1993) 'Media influences on body size estimation in anorexia and bulimia: an experimental study', *British Journal of Psychiatry*, 162, pp.837–40.
Hamilton, M. (2001) *The Sociology of Religion* (2nd edn) London: Routledge
Hammersley, M. (1992) 'By what criteria should ethnographic research be judged?', in M. Hammersley, *What's Wrong with Ethnography?*, London: Routledge
Hancock, G. (1989) *Lords of Poverty*, New York: Atlantic Monthly Press
Hansard (2008) www.publications.parliament.uk/pa/cm200708/cmhansrd/cm080610/text/80610w0027.htm
Hanson, E. (1997) *Decadence and Catholicism*, Cambridge, Mass: Harvard University Press
Harding, S. (1986) *The Science Question in Feminism*, Ithaca & London: Cornell University Press

Harding, S. (1987) *Feminism and Methodology*, Bloomington, IN & Buckingham: Indiana University Press & OU Press
Harper, D. (1978) 'At home on the rails: ethics in a photographic research project', *Qualitative Sociology*, 1, pp.66–77
Harper, P., Pollak, M., Mooney, J., Whelan, E. and Young, J. (1986) *The Islington Crime Survey*, London Borough of Islington
Harris, G. (1989) *The Sociology of Development*, London: Longman
Harrison, P. (1990) *Inside the Third World: The Anatomy of Poverty* (2nd edn), Harmondsworth: Penguin
Hart, A. (1989) 'Gender and class in England', *New Left Review*, 1/175
Hartnett, O. (1990) 'The sex role system', in P. Mayes (ed.) *Gender*, Longman: London
Harvey, D. (1990) *The Condition of Modernity*, Blackwell: Oxford
Harvey, S. (2008) *Maintaining and Strengthening Public Service Broadcasting: The Limits of Competition. A response to Ofcom's Second Review of Public Service Broadcasting, Phase Two: Preparing for the Digital Future*, London: AHRB Centre for British Film and Television Studies
Haste, H. (2005) 'Joined-up texting: mobile phones and young people', *Young Consumers*, Quarter 2, 6(3), pp.56–67
Hastings, M. (2005) 'They've never had it so good', *Guardian*, 6 Aug
Hay, C. (1997) 'Divided by a common language: political theory and the concept of power', *Politics*, 17(1), pp.45–52
Hayek, F.A. (1944/1986) *The Road to Serfdom*, London: Routledge
Hayter, T. (1981) *The Creation of World Poverty* (2nd edn), London: Pluto Press
Hayward, K.J. and Yar, M. (2006) 'The "Chav" phenomenon: consumption, media and the construction of a new underclass', *Crime, Media, Culture*, 2(1), pp.9–28
Heath, A. (1991) *Understanding Political Change: The British Voter, 1964–87*, Oxford: Butterworth Heinemann
Heath, A. and C. Payne (1999) *Twentieth Century Trend in Social Mobility in Britain*, University of Oxford Centre for Research into Elections and Social Trends, Working Paper No. 70
Heath, A. and Rothon, C., (2003) *British Social Attitudes: the 20th Report: Continuity and Change over Two Decades*, National Centre for Social Research
Heath, A., Evans, G., Field, J. and Witherspoon, S. (1991) *Understanding Political Change: The British Voter 1964–1987*, Oxford: Pergamon
Heath, A., Jowell, R. and Curtice. J. (1994) 'Can Labour win?', in A. Heath, R. Jowell, J. Curtice with B. Taylor (eds) *Labour's Last Chance?*, Aldershot: Dartmouth Publishing
Heelas, P. (1996) *The New Age Movement*, Cambridge: Polity Press
Heelas, P., Woodhead, W., Seel, B., Tusting, K. and Szerszynski, B. (2004) *The Spiritual Revolution: Why Religion Is Giving Way to Spirituality*, Oxford: Blackwell
Heidensohn, F. (1989, 1996 [2nd edn]) *Women and Crime*, London: Macmillan
Heidensohn, F. (2002) 'Gender and crime', in M. Maguire, R. Morgan and R. Reinder, *The Oxford Handbook of Criminology* (3rd edn), Oxford: OUP
Heintz-Knowles, K. (2002) *The Reflection on the Screen: Television's Image of Children*, Oakland, CA: Children Now
Held, D. (ed.) (2000) *A Globalising World: Culture, Economics, Politics*, London: Routledge
Held, D. and McGrew, A. (2002) *Globalization and Anti-Globalization*, Cambridge: Polity Press
Help the Aged (2008) *Spotlight Report 2008: Spotlight on older people in the UK*, Help the Aged
Herberg, W. (1960) *Protestant – Catholic – Jew* (revised edn), New York: Anchor Books
Herman, E. and Chomsky, N. (1988) *Manufacturing Consent*, New York: Pantheon Books
Hetherington, K. (1998) *Expressions of Identity: Space, Performance, Politics*, London: Sage
Hill, K.A. and Hughes, J.E. (1997) 'Computer-mediated political communication: The Usenet and political communities', *Political Communication*, 14, pp.3-14
Hirsch, D. (2006) *Experiences of Poverty and Educational Disadvantage*, York: Joseph Rowntree Foundation
Hirschi, T. (1969) *Causes of Delinquency*, Berkeley, CA: Univ. of California Press
Hirst, P.Q. (1975) 'Radical deviancy theory and Marxism: a reply to Taylor, Walton and Young', in E. Taylor, P. Walton and J. Young (eds) *Critical Criminology*, London: Routledge
Hobbs, D. (1988) *Doing the Business, Entrepreneurship, the Working Class and Detectives in the East End of London*, Oxford: OUP
Hobbs, D. (1998) *Bad Business: Professional Crime in Britain*, Oxford: OUP
Hobbs, D. (2003) *The Night-time Economy*, London: Alcohol Research Forum Papers
Hobbs, D., Lister, S., Hadfield, P. and Winlow, S. (2000) 'Receiving shadows: governance and liminality in the night-time economy', *British Journal of Sociology*, 51(4) pp.682–700
Holdaway, S. (1983) *Inside the British Police*, Oxford: Blackwell
Holdaway, S. (2005) 'The challenge of creating a multi-racial police force', *ESRC Society Today*
Holden, A. (2002) *Jehovah's Witnesses: Portrait of a Contemporary Religious Movement*, London/New York: Routledge
Hollows, J. (2000) *Feminism, Femininity and Popular Culture*, Manchester: Manchester University Press
Holm, J. and Bowker, J. (eds) (1994) *Women in Religion*, London: Pinter
Home Office (1998) *British Crime Survey*, Research and Statistics Directorate of the Home Office
Hood, R. and Joyce, K. (1999) 'Three generations: oral testimony of crime and social change in London's East End', *British Journal of Criminology*, 39(1), pp.136–60
Hoogvelt, A. (2001) *Globalisation and the Post Colonial World* (2nd edn), Basingstoke: Palgrave
Hook, S. (1990) *Convictions*, New York: Prometheus Books
Hopkins, M. (2002) 'Crimes against businesses', *British Journal of Sociology*, (42)4, pp.782–97
Hopkins, N. and Kahani-Hopkins, V. (2004) 'Identity construction and political activity: beyond rational actor theory', *British Journal of Social Psychology*, 43(3), pp.339–56
Horkheimer, M. (1974) *Eclipse of Reason*, New York: OUP
Hoselitz, B. (1960) *Sociological Aspects of Economic Growth*, Chicago: Chicago Free Press
Howell, J.M. and Frost P.J. (1989) 'A Laboratory Study of Charismatic Leadership',*Organizational Behavior and Human Decision Processes*, 43, pp.243–69
Hunt, J. (2004b) 'Gender and development', in D. Kingsbury, J. Remenyi, J. McKay and J. Hunt (eds) *Key Issues in Development*, Basingstoke: Palgrave
Hunt, S. (2005) *Religion and Everyday Life*, London: Routledge
Hunter, J.D. (1987) *Evangelism: The Coming Generation*, Chicago: University of Chicago Press
Huntington, S.P. (1993) 'The clash of civilisations', *Foreign Affairs*, 72
Hutton, W. (1996) *The State We're In*, London: Vantage
Hyde, M. (2001) 'Disabled people in Britain today: discrimination, social disadvantage and empowerment', *Sociology Review*, 10(4), April
Inglehart, R. and Norris, P. (2000) 'The developmental theory of the gender gap: women's and men's voting behaviour in global perspective', *International Political Science Review*, 21(4), pp.441–63
Inkeles, A. (1969) 'Making modern men: on the causes and consequences of individual change in six developing countries', *American Journal of Sociology*, 75
Inland Revenue (2004) Distribution of Personal Wealth – www.hmrc.gov.uk/stats/personal_wealth/menu.htm
Institute of Practitioners in Advertising (2006) quoted in *Guardian*, 25 Jan
Itzoe M.A. (1995) *A Regulatory Scheme for Cyberporn*, University of Indiana
Jackson, B. (1978) 'Killing time: life in the Arkansas penitentiary', *Qualitative Sociology*, 1 pp.21 –32
Jencks, C., Smith, M., Acland, H., Bane, M.J., Cohen, D., Gintis, H., *et al.* (1972) *Inequality: A reassessment of the effect of family and schooling in America*, New York: Basic Books.
Jenkins, H. (2008) *Convergence Culture: Where Old and New Media Collide*, New York: New York University Press
Jessop, B. (2002) *The Future of the Capitalist State*, Cambridge: Polity Press
Jewkes, Y. (2006) 'Creating a stir? Prisons, popular media and the power to reform', in P. Mason (ed.) *Captured by the Media: Prison Discourse in Media Culture*, Cullompton: Willan
Johal S. (1998) 'Brimful of Brasia', *Sociology Review*, 8(1)
Jones, A. and Singer, L. (2008) *Statistics on Race and the Criminal Justice System 2006/7*, London: Ministry of Justice
Jones, B., Kavanagh, D., Moran, M. and Norton, D. (2004) *Politics UK* (5th edn), London: Pearson Longman
Jones, T., Maclean, B. and Young, J. (1995) *The Second Islington Crime Survey*, London Borough of Islington
Joseph Rowntree Foundation (1995) *Income and Wealth: Report of the JRF Inquiry Group*, York: JRF
Kaldor, M. (2006) *New and Old Wars: Organized Violence in a Global Era* (2nd edn), Cambridge: Polity Press
Karpf, A. (1988) 'Give us a break, not a begging bowl', *New Statesman*, 27 May
Katz, E. and P. Lazarsfeld (1965). *Personal Influence*, New York, Free Press
Katz, J. (1988) *Seductions of Crime: Moral and Sensual Attractions in Doing Evil*, New York: Basic Books
Kaur-Singh, K. (1994) 'Sikhism', in J. Holm and J. Bowker (eds) *Women in Religion*, London: Pinter
Kautsky, K. (1953) *Foundations of Christianity*, New York: Russell
Kay, T. (1996) 'Women's work and women's work': implications of women's changing employment patterns', *Leisure Studies*, 15, pp.49–64
Keen, D. (1995) 'When war itself is privatised', *Times Literary Supplement*, Dec
Kellner, D. (1999) in B. Smart (ed.) *Resisting McDonaldisation*, London: Sage,
Kenyatta, M.L. and Tai, R.H. (1999) *Critical Ethnicity: Countering the Waves of Identity Politics*, Oxford: Rowman and Littlefield
Kepel, G. (1994) *The Revenge of God: The Resurgence of Islam, Christianity and Judaism in the Modern World*, Cambridge: Polity Press
Kidd, W. (2001) 'Time to think about age', *Sociology Review*, 10(3), Feb
Kilbourne, J. (1995) 'Beauty and the beast of advertising', in G. Dines and M. Humez (eds) *Gender, Race and Class in Media*, Thousand Oaks: Sage Publications
Kilby, P. (2001) quoted in D. Kingsbury, J. Remenyi, J. McKay and J. Hunt (eds) *Key Issues in Development*, Basingstoke: Palgrave
Kingsbury, D., Remenyi, J., McKay, J. and Hunt, J. (eds) (2004) *Key Issues in Development*, Basingstoke: Palgrave
Kitsuse, J. (1962) 'Societal reaction to deviant behaviour', *Social Problems*, (9) Winter
Klapper, J.T. (1960) *The Effects of Mass Communication*, New York: Free Press
Klein, N. (2001) *No Logo*, London: Flamingo
Knott, K. and Khokher, S. (1993) 'Religious and ethnic identity among young Muslim women in Bradford', *New Community*, 19(4), p.593–610
Korten, D. (1995) 'Steps towards people-centered development: vision and strategies', in N. Heyzer, J.V. Ricker and A.B. Quizon (eds) *Government–NGO Relations in Asia: Prospects and Challenges for People-centred Development*, Basingstoke: Palgrave
Kramer, R. (2006) 'The Space Shuttle *Challenger* explosion', in R. Michalowski and R. Kramer (2006) *State-Corporate Crime: Wrongdoing at the intersection of business and government*, New Brunswick, NJ: Rutgers University Press
Kuhn, T.S. (1962/1970) *The Structure of Scientific Revolutions* (2nd edn), Chicago: University of Chicago Press
Kynaston, D. (2008) 'The road to meritocracy is blocked by private schools', *Guardian*, 22 Feb
Lakatos, I. (1970) 'Falsification and the methodology of scientific research programmes', in I. Lakatos and A. Musgrave (eds) *Criticism and the Growth of Knowledge*, Cambridge: CUP
Landes, D. (1998) *The Wealth and Poverty of Nations*, London: Little Brown and Company
Landis (2002) quoted on www.tc.umn.edu/~rbeach/teachingmedia/module5/9.htm
Langone, M.D. and Martin, P. (1993) 'Deprogramming, exit counselling, and ethics: clarifying the confusion', *Cult Observer*, 10(4)
Lappe, F. and Collins, J. (1977) *Food First*, Boston: Houghton Miflin
Lawler, S. (2005) 'Introduction: class, culture, identity', *Sociology* 2005, 39(5)
Lea, J. and Young, J. (1984, 1993 revised edn) *What is to be Done about Law and Order?*, Harmondsworth: Penguin
Leach, E. (1988) *Culture and Communication*, Cambridge: CUP
Lee, M.M., Carpenter, B. and Meyers, L.S. (2007) 'Representation of older adults in television adverts', *Journal of Ageing Studies*, 21, pp.23–30
Lee-Treweek, G. (2000) 'The insight of emotional danger: research experiences in a home for the elderly', in G. Lee-Treweek and S. Lingogle (eds) *Danger in the Field: Risk and Ethics in Social Research*, London: Routledge

Lemert, E. (1967/1972) *Human Deviance, Social Problems and Social Control*, Englewood Cliffs, NJ: Prentice-Hall

Lemert, E. (1972) *Human Deviance, Social Problems and Social Control*, Englewood Cliffs, NJ: Prentice-Hall

Lenin (1965) *Collected Works*, Vol. 10, Moscow: Progress Publishers

Leonard, M. (1992) 'Women and Development', *Sociology Review*, Sept

Lerner, D. (1958) *The Passing of Traditional Society*, Glencoe: Free Press

Levi, M. (1987) *Regulating Fraud*, London: Tavistock

Levi, M., Burrows, J., Fleming, J. and Hopkins, M. (2007) *The Nature, Extent and Economic Impact of Fraud in the UK*, London: ACPO

Levine, E. (1980) 'Deprogramming without tears', *Society*, 17 (March), pp.34–8

Li, N. and Kirkup, G. (2007) 'Gender and cultural differences in Internet use: a study of China and the UK', *Computers and Education*, 48(2), Feb

Liazos, A. (1972) 'The poverty of the sociology of deviance: nuts, sluts and perverts', *Social Problems*, 20

Ligali (2006) www.ligali.org/

Llosa, M.V. (2000) 'The culture of liberty', *Foreign Policy*, 5, pp.66–72

Lockwood, D. (1966) 'Sources of variation in working-class images of society', *Sociological Review*, 14

Lukes, S. (1974) *Power: A Radical View*, London: Macmillan

Lukes, S. (1986) 'Domination by economic power and authority', in S. Lukes (ed.) *Power*, Oxford: Blackwell

Lull, J. (1995) *Media, Communication, Culture: A global approach*, New York: Columbia University Press.

Lyng, S. (1990) 'Edgework: a social psychological analysis of voluntary risk-taking', *American Journal of Sociology*, 95(4), pp.851–6

Lyon, D. (2000) *Jesus in Disneyland: Religion in Postmodern Times*, Cambridge: Polity Press

Lyotard, J.-F. (1984) *The Post-Modern Condition: A Report on Knowledge*, Manchester: University of Manchester Press

Lyotard, J.-F. (1984) *The Post-Modern Condition: A Report on Knowledge*, Manchester: University of Manchester Press

Mac an Ghaill, M. (1988) *Young, Gifted and Black*, Milton Keynes: OU Press

Mac an Ghaill, M. (1992) 'Coming of age in 80s England: reconceptualising black students' educational experience', in D. Gill, B. Mayor and M. Blair (eds) *Racism and Education: Structures and Strategies*, London: Sage

Mac an Ghaill, M. (1994) *The Making of Men: Masculinities, Sexualities and Schooling*, Milton Keynes: OU Press

Mac an Ghaill, M. (ed.) (1996) *Understanding Masculinities: Social Relations and Cultural Arenas*, Buckingham: OU Press

McCabe, K.A. and Martin, G.M. (2005) *School Violence, the Media, and Criminal Justice Responses*, York: Peter Lang Publishing

McChesney, R. (2002) in K. Borjesson (ed.) *Into the Buzzsaw: Leading Journalists Expose the Myth of a Free* Press, Amherst, NY: Prometheus

Macdonald, K. and Tipton, C. (1993) 'Using documents', in N. Gilbert (ed.) *Researching Social Life*, London: Sage

MacGuire, M.B. (1981) *Religion: The Social Context*, California: Wadsworth Publishing

Mack, J. and Lansley, S. (1985) *Poor Britain*, London: Allen & Unwin

McKay, H. (2000) 'The globalisation of culture', in D.Held (2000) *A Globalising World? Culture, Economics, Politics*, London: Routledge

McKay, J. (2004) 'Reassessing development theory: "modernization" and beyond', in D. Kingsbury, J. Remenyi, J. McKay and J. Hunt (eds) *Key Issues in Development*, Basingstoke: Palgrave

McKee, L. and Bell, C. (1985) 'Marital and family relations in times of male unemployment', in B. Roberts, R. Finnegan and D. Gallie (eds) *New Approaches to Economic Life*, Manchester: Manchester University Press

McKendrick, J.H., Sinclair, S., Irwin. A., O'Donnell H., Scott, G. and Dobbie, L. (2008) *The Media, Poverty and Public Opinion in the UK*, York: Joseph Rowntree Foundation

McKenzie, R.T. and Silver, A. (1968) 'The working class Tory in England', in P. Worsley *Angels in Marble*, London: Heinemann

McKie, L., Bowlby, S. and Gregory, S. (2004) 'Starting well: gender, care and health in the family context', *Sociology*, 38(3), pp.593–611

McQuail, D. (1992) *Mass Communication Theory* (5th edn), London: Sage

McRobbie, A and Thornton, S. (1995) 'Rethinking "moral panic" for multi-mediated social worlds', *British Journal of Sociology*, 46(4), pp.559–74

McRobbie, A. (1999) *In the Culture Society: Art, Fashion and Popular Music*, London: Routledge

Madriz, M. (2000) 'Focus groups in feminist research', in N.K. Denzin and Y.S. Lincoln (eds) *Handbook of Qualitative Research* (2nd edn), Thousand Oaks, CA: Sage

Maduro, O. (1982) *Religion and Social Conflicts*, New York: Orbis Books

Maffesoli, M. (1996) *The Time of the Tribes*, London: Sage

Maguire, M. (2002) 'Crime statistics: the data explosion and its implications', in M. Maguire, R. Morgan and R. Reiner (eds) *The Oxford Handbook of Criminology* (3rd edn), Oxford: OUP

Maguire, M., Morgan, R. and Reiner, R. (eds) (1997) *The Oxford Handbook of Criminology* (2nd edn), Oxford: OUP

Malamuth, N.M. (1984) 'Debriefing effectiveness following exposure to pornographic depictions', *The Journal of Sex Research*, 20(1), pp.1–13

Malinowski, B. (1954/1982 reissue) *Magic, Science and Religion and Other Essays*, New York: Anchor Books

Mamdani, M. (2004) *Good Muslim, Bad Muslim: America, the Cold War and the Origins of Terror*, New York: Pantheon

Mann, M. (1986) *The Sources of Social Power*, Vol. 1, Cambridge: CUP

Mannheim, K. (1960) *Ideology and Utopia*, London: Routledge

Manning, P. (2001) *News and News Sources: A Critical Introduction*, London: Sage

Marcuse, H. (1964/1991) *One Dimensional Man: Studies in the Ideology of Advanced Industrial Societies*, London: Routledge

Marmot, M.G., Smith, G.D., Stansfeld, S., Patel, C., North, F., Head, J., White, I., Brunner, E. and Feeney, A. (1991) 'Health inequalities among British civil servants: the Whitehall II study', *The Lancet*, 337, pp.1387–93

Mars, G. (1982) *Cheats at Work: An Anthropology of Workplace Crime*, London: George Allen & Unwin

Marshall, B., Webb, B. and Tilley, N. (2005) *Rationalisation of Current Research on Guns, Gangs and Other Weapons: Phase 1*, London: Jill Dando Institute of Crime Science, University College London

Marshall, G. (1982) *In Search of the Spirit of Capitalism: Max Weber and the Protestant Ethic Thesis*, London: Hutchison

Marshall, G. (1987) 'What is happening to the working class?', *Social Studies Review*, Jan

Marshall, G., Newby. H., Rose, D. and Vogler, C. (1988) *Social Class In Modern Britain*, London, Hutchinson

Martin, D. (1978) *A General Theory of Secularisation*, Blackwell: Oxford

Marx, K. (1844) *Selected Writings* (2000 edn), Oxford: OUP

Marx, K. (1845) 'The German Ideology', extract in T. Bottomore and M. Rubel (eds, 1963 edn) *Karl Marx: Selected Writings in Sociology and Social Philosophy*, Harmondsworth: Penguin

Marx, K. (1848) *The Communist Manifesto* (2002 edn), Harmondsworth: Penguin

Marx, K. (1867/1973) *Capital: A Critique of Political Economy*, Harmondsworth: Penguin

Marx, K. and Engels, F. (1848, reissued 2002) *Manifesto of the Communist Party*, North Charleston, SC: BookSurge

Marx, K. and Engels, F. (1957) *On Religion*, Moscow: Progress Publishers

Marx, K. and Engels, F. (1975) 'On the history of early Christianity', in *Collected Works of Karl Marx and Frederick Engels*, Vol. 27, Moscow: Progress Publishers

Matthews, R. and Young, J. (eds) (1992) *Issues in Realist Criminology*, London: Sage

Matza, D. (1964) *Delinquency and Drift*, New York: Wiley

Matza, D. and Sykes, G. (1961) 'Juvenile delinquency and subterranean values', *American Sociological Review*, 26(5), pp.712–19

May, T. (2001) *Social Research: Issues, Methods and Process*, Buckingham: OU Press

Mayhew, H. (1851) *London Labour and the London Poor* (republished 1985), Harmondsworth: Penguin

Mayhew, P., Aye Maung, N. and Mirrlees-Black, C. (1993) *The 1992 British Crime Survey*, Home Office Research Study 111, London: Home Office

Maynard, M. and Purvis, J. (eds) (1994) *Researching Women's Lives from a Feminist Perspective*, London: Taylor & Francis

Mayo, R. (2005) *'Nazareth Project: second draft Monday Feb 14th 2005', unpublished paper.*

Mead, G.H. (1934) *Mind, Self and Society* (ed. C. Morris) Chicago: University of Chicago

Mead, M. (1928) *Coming of Age in Samoa*, New York: Morrow

Melucci, A. (1989) *Nomads of the Present*, London: Hutchinson

Merton, R.K. (1938) 'Social structure and anomie', *American Sociological Review*, 3

Merton, R.K. (1949; revised and expanded, 1957 and 1968) *Social Theory and Social Structure*, New York: The Free Press

Messerschmidt, J. (1993) *Masculinities and Crime*, Lanham, MD: Rowman & Littlefield

Metcalf, H., Modood, T. and Virdee, S. (1996) *Asian Self-Employment*, London: Policy Studies Institute

Michalowski, R. and Kramer, R. (1987) 'The space between laws: the problem of corporate crime in a transnational context', *Social Problems*, 34

Miles, R. (1989) *Racism*, London: Routledge

Miliband, R. (1970/1973) *The State in Capitalist Society*, London: Quartet

Millen, D. (1997) 'Some methodological and epistemological issues raised by doing feminist research on non-feminist women', *Sociological Research* Online www.socresonline.org.uk/socresonline/2/3/3.html

Miller, A.S. and Hoffman, J.P. (1995) 'Risk and religion: an explanation of gender differences in religiosity', *Journal for the Scientific Study of Religion*, 34, pp.63–75

Miller, W.B. (1962) 'Lower class culture as a generating milieu of gang delinquency', in M.E. Wolfgang, L. Savitz and N. Johnston (eds) *The Sociology of Crime and Delinquency*, New York: Wiley

Millett, K. (1970) *Sexual Politics*, New York: Doubleday

Mills, C.W. (1959) *The Sociological Imagination*, Oxford: OUP

Millwood Hargrave, A. (2003) *How Children Interpret Screen Violence*, London: BBC/BBFC/BSC/ITC

Milne, A., Hatzidimitradou, E. and Harding, T. (1999) *Later Lifestyles: A Survey by Help the Aged and Yours Magazine*, London: Help the Aged

Ministry of Justice (2008) *Statistics on Race and the Criminal Justice System – 2006/7*, www.justice.gov.uk/docs/stats-race-criminal-justice.pdf

Mirza (2007) quoted in 'Revealed: Racism in Schools', *Channel4 News*, 24 May

Mitchell, D. (2007) 'You are what you own', *Guardian*, 29 Aug

Modood, T. (1992) *Not Easy Being British: Colour, Culture and Citizenship*, Runnymede Trust and Trentham Books

Modood, T. (2006) 'Ethnicity, Muslims and higher education entry in Britain', *Teaching in Higher Education*, 11(2), pp.247–50

Modood, T., Beishon, S. and Virdee, S. (1994) *Changing Ethnic Identities*, London: Policy Studies Institute

Mohanty, C. (1997) 'Under western eyes: feminist scholarship and colonial discourse', in, N. Visuanathan, L. Duggan, L. Nisonoff and N.Wiergersma (eds), *The Women, Gender and Development Reader*, London: Zed Books

Mokhiber, R. (1988) *Corporate Crime and Violence*, San Francisco: Sierra Club

Molyneux, M. (1981) 'Women in socialist societies: problems of theory and practice', in K.Young *et al.* (eds) *Of Marriage and the Market: Women's Subordination in International Perspective*, London: CSE Books

Monaghan, L. (1999) 'Creating "the perfect body": a variable project', *Body and Society*, 5(2–3), pp.267–90

Monaghan, L. (2005) 'Get ready to duck: bouncers and the realities of ethnographic research on violent groups', *British Journal of Criminology*, 41, pp.536–48

Monbiot, G. (2004) 'Our lies led us into war', *Guardian*, 20 Jul

Moore, M. (2001) *Stupid White Men*, London: Penguin

Moore, M. (2003) *Dude, Where's My Country?*, London: Penguin

Moores, M. (1998) 'Sociologists in white coats', *Sociology Review*, 7(3)

Mordaunt, S., Rake, K., Wanless, H. and Mitchell, R. (2003) *One in Four*, Age Concern

Morgan, I. (1999) *Power and Politics*, London: Hodder & Stoughton

Morgan, R. (1980) 'Theory and practice: pornography and rape', in L. Lederer (ed.) *Take Back the Night: Women on Pornography*, New York: William Morrow

Morgan, R. (2006) 'Rape, murder, and the American GI', Alternet, 17 Aug, www.alternet.org/waroniraq/40481/

Morgan, R. and Russell, N. (2000) *The Judiciary in the Magistrates' Courts*, Home Office and LCD Occasional Paper 66, London: Home Office/LCD

Morley, D. (1980) *The Nationwide Audience*, London: BFI

Morris, J. (1991) *Pride Against Prejudice: Transforming Attitudes to Disability*, London: The Women's Press

Morris, J. (1992) *Disabled Lives: Many Voices, One Message*, BBC Education

Morris, L. (1993) *Dangerous Classes: The Underclass and Social Citizenship*, London: Routledge

Morris, T.P. (1957) *The Criminal Area: A study in Social Ecology*, London: Routledge

Morrison, D.E. (1999) *Defining Violence: The Search for Understanding*, Luton: University of Luton Press

Mort, F. (1988), 'Boy's own? Masculinity, style and popular culture', in R. Chapman and J. Rutherford, *Male Order: Unwrapping Masculinity*, London: Lawrence & Wishart

Mosca, G. (1939) *The Ruling Class*, New York: McGraw Hill

Mouzelis, N. (1995) *Sociological Theory: What Went Wrong?*, London: Routledge

Mulvey, L. (1975) 'Visual pleasures and narrative cinema', *Screen*, 16(3)

Murray, C. (1990) *The Emerging British Underclass*, London: Institute of Economic Affairs, Health and Welfare Unit

Murray, C. (1994) *The Crisis Deepens*, London: IEA

Myrdal, G. (1968) *Asian Drama: An Enquiry into the Poverty of Nations*, New York: The Twentieth Century Fund

Nahdi, F. (2003) 'Doublespeak: Islam and the media', *Open Democracy*, 3 Apr

Nairn, T. (1988) *The Enchanted Glass. Britain and its Monarchy*, London: Radius

Nelken, D. (2002) 'White collar crime', in M. Maguire, R. Morgan and R. Reiner, *The Oxford Handbook of Criminology* (3rd edn), Oxford: OUP

Nelson, G.K. (1986) 'Religion', in M. Haralambos (ed.) *Developments in Sociology*, Vol. 2, Ormskirk: Causeway Press

New Internationalist (1986) 'Fly Me to the Moon', Issue 169

New York Times (1993) 'African land frees ex-emperor and all criminals', *New York Times*, 2 Sept

Newman, D. (2006) *The Architecture of Stratification: Social Class and Inequality*, London: Sage

Newman, O. (1972) *Defensible Space: Crime prevention through urban design*, New York: Collier

Newson E. (1994) *Video Violence and the Protection of Children*, Report of the Home Affairs Committee, London: HMSO

Newton, K. (1969) 'A Critique of the Pluralist Model', *Acta Sociologica*, 12

Niebuhr, H.R. (1929) *The Social Sources of Denominationalism*, New York: The World Publishing Company

Nightingale, C. (1993) *On the Edge*, New York: Basic Books

Norris, P. (1999) *On Message: Communicating the Campaign*, London: Sage

Oakley, A. (1974) *Housewife*, London: Allen Lane

Oakley, A. (1981) 'Interviewing women: a contradiction in terms', in H. Roberts (ed.) *Doing Feminist Research*, London: Routledge

Oakley, A. (1998) 'Gender, methodology and people's ways of knowing: some problems with feminism and the paradigm debate in social science', *Sociology*, 32, pp.707–31

O'Beirne, M. (2004) *Religion in England and Wales: Findings from the 2001 Home Office Citizenship Survey*, Home Office Res. Study 274, London: HMSO

O'Connell Davidson, J. and Layder, D. (1994) *Methods, Sex and Madness*, London: Routledge

Oliver, M. (1990) *The Politics of Disablement*, Basingstoke: Macmillan

Oliver, M. and Barnes, C. (1998) *Disabled People and Social Policy: From Exclusion to Inclusion*, Harlow: Addison Wesley Longman

Olsen, W. and Walby, S. (2004) *Modelling Gender Pay Gaps*, Manchester: Equal Opportunities Commission

Oppenheim, C. and Harker, L. (1996) *Poverty: The Facts* (3rd edn), London: CPAG

Orbach, S. (1991) *Fat is a Feminist Issue*, London: Hamlyn

Orton, M. and Rowlingson, K. (2007) *Public Attitudes to Economic Inequality*, York: Joseph Rowntree Foundation

O'Toole, R. (1984) *Religion: Classic Sociological Approaches*, Toronto: McGraw Hill

Owen, D.W. and Green, A.E. (1992) 'Labour market experience and occupational change amongst ethnic groups in Great Britain', *New Community*, 19, pp.7–29

Pakulski, J. and Waters, M. (1996) *The Death of Class*, London: Sage

Pambazuka (2005) 'African British perspective on the politics of Live 8, G8 and the UK media', *Pambazuka News*, 20 Oct

Parckar, G. (2008) *Disability Poverty in the UK*, London: Leonard Cheshire Disability

Pareto, V. (1935) *The Mind and Society*, New York: Dover

Park, A. (1999) 'Young people and political apathy', in R. Jowell, J. Curtice, A. Park, K. Thomson and L. Jarvis (eds) *British Social Attitudes: the 15th Report*, Ashgate: Aldershot

Parker, H. (1974, 1992 [2nd edn]) *View from the Boys*, Aldershot: Ashgate

Parker, H., Aldridge, J. and Measham, F. (1998) *Illegal Leisure: the Normalization of Adolescent Recreational Drug Use*, London: Routledge

Parkin, F. (1972) *Class Inequality and Political Order*, St. Albans: Paladin

Parsons, T. (1937) *The Structure of Social Action*, New York: McGraw-Hill

Parsons, T. (1951) *The Social System*, New York: Free Press

Parsons, T. (1963) 'On the concept of political power', *Proceedings of the American Philosophical Society*, 107

Parsons, T. (1964) *Essays in Social Theory*, New York: The Free Press

Parsons, T. (1964a) 'Evolutionary universals in society', *American Sociological Review*, 29 June

Parsons, T. (1965) 'Religious perspectives in sociology and social psychology', in W.A. Lessa and E.Z. Vogt (eds) *Reader in Comparative Religion: An Anthropological Approach* (2nd edn), New York: Harper & Row

Parsons, T. (1977) *The Evolution of Societies*, J. Toby (ed.), Englewood Cliffs, NJ: Prentice-Hall

Patel, S. (1999) 'The media and its representation of Islam and Muslim women', in J. Waghorn (ed.) *Young Women Speak: A Message to the Media*, London: The Women's Press

Patterson, S. (1965) *Dark Strangers*, Harmondsworth: Penguin

Pawson, R. (1989) *A Measure For Measures*, London: Routledge

Payne, G. (1987) *Economy and Opportunity*, Basingstoke: Macmillan

Payne, G. (1992) 'Competing views of contemporary social mobility and social divisions', in R. Burrows and C. Marsh (eds) *Consumption and Class*, Basingstoke: Macmillan

Peace, M. (1998) *The Construction of Reality in Television News*, www.aber.ac.uk/~ednwww/Undgrad/ED3 0520/mbp701.html

Peace, M. (2005) quoted on www.sociologystuff.com

Pearce, F. (1976) *Crimes of the Powerful: Marxism, Crime and Deviance*, London: Pluto

Pearce, F. and Tombs, S. (1998) *Toxic Capitalism: Corporate Crime and the Chemical Industry*, Aldershot: Ashgate

Pearson, G. (1983) *Hooligan: A History of Respectable Fears*, Basingstoke: Palgrave

Pearson, R. (2001) 'Rethinking gender matters in development' in T. Allen and A. Thomas (2001) *Poverty and Development in the 21st Century*, Oxford: OUP

peopleandplanet.net (2007) 'Desertification and degraded land', 14 Dec, www. peopleandplanet.net/doc.php?id=348

Pew Global Attitudes Project (2002) www.pewglobal.org

Pew Global Attitudes Survey (2006) *The Great Divide: How Westerners and Muslims View Each Other*, Washington, DC: Pew Research Center

Phillips, C. and Brown, D. (1998) *Entry into the Criminal Justice System: A Survey of Police Arrests and their Outcomes*, Home Office Research Study 185, London: Home Office

Phillips, K. (2004) *American Dynasty; Aristocracy, Fortune and the Politics of Deceit in the House of Bush*, London: Penguin

Phillipson, C. (1982) *Capitalism and the Construction of Old Age*, Basingstoke: Macmillan

Philo, G. (1999) *Message Received*, Glasgow University Media Group, London: Longman

Philo, G. (2001) 'Media effects and the active audience', *Sociology Review*, 10(3), Feb

Philo, G. and Beattie, L. (1999) 'Race, migration and media', in G. Philo (ed) *Message Received: Glasgow Media Group Research 1993-1998*, Harlow: Longman

Philo, G. and Glasgow University Media Group (1982) *Really Bad News*, London: Writers and Readers

Philo, G. and Miller, D. (2000) *Market Killing: What the Free Market Does and What Social Scientists Can Do About It*, Harlow: Longman

Piacentini, L. and Walters, R. (2006) 'The politicization of youth crime in Scotland and the rise of the "Burberry Court"', *Youth Justice*, 6, pp.43-59

Pilcher, J. (1995) *Age and Generation in Modern Britain*, Oxford: OUP

Pilcher, J. and Whelehan, I. (2004) *50 Key Concepts in Gender Studies*, London: Sage

Platt, L. (2005) 'The intergenerational social mobility of minority ethnic groups', *BSA Publications*, Volume 39(3), pp.445–61

Plummer, K. (2000) *Documents of Life*, Thousand Oaks, CA: Sage

Poole, E. (2000) 'Media representation and British Muslims', *Dialogue Magazine*, Apr

Popper, K. (1959) *The Logic of Scientific Discovery*, London: Hutchinson

Porritt, J. (1985) *Seeing Green: The Politics of Ecology*, Oxford: Blackwell

Portnoy, F. (2003) *Infectious Greed: How Deceit and Risk Corrupted the Financial Markets*, New York: Times Books

Postman, N. (1986) *Amusing Ourselves to Death*, London: Methuen

Poulantzas, N. (1973) *Political Power and Social Classes*, London: New Left Books

Pryce K. (1979) *Endless Pressure*, Harmondsworth: Penguin

Punch, K.F. (1998) *Introduction to Social Research*, London: Sage

Punch, M. (2005) 'Politics and ethics in qualitative research', in N.K. Denzin and Y.S. Lincoln (eds) *Handbook of Qualitative Research*, Thousand Oaks, CA: Sage

Punch, M. (1996) *Dirty Business: Exploring Corporate Misconduct*, London: Sage

Putnam, R. (1995) 'Bowling alone: America's declining social capital', *Journal of Democracy*, (6)1, Jan pp. 65-78

Ramazanoglu, C. (1992) 'On feminist methodology: male reason versus feminist empowerment', *Sociology*, 26(2), pp.213–18

Rankin, P. (2005) *Buried Spirituality*, Salisbury: Sarum College Press

Rathje, W.L. and Murphy, C. (2002, originally 1992) *Rubbish! The Archaeology of Garbage*, Phoenix: University of Arizona Press

Ray, S., Sharp, E. and Abrams, D. (2006) *Ageism: A benchmark of public attitudes in Britain*, London: Age Concern England/University of Kent

Raymond, G. J. (2002) *A Comparative Study of Women Trafficked in the Migration Process: Patterns, Profiles and Health: Consequences of Sexual Exploitation in Five Countries*, New York: UN

REACH (2007) *An independent report to Government on raising the aspirations and attainment of Black boys and young Black men*, London: Department for Communities and Local Government www.communities.gov.uk/publications/co mmunities/reachreport

Reay, D. (1998) 'Rethinking social class: qualitative perspectives on gender and social class', *Sociology*, 32(2), pp.259–75

Redhead, S. (1993) *Rave Off: Politics and Deviance in Contemporary Youth Culture*, Aldershot: Ashgate

Redhead, S. (ed.) (1993) *Rave off: Politics and Deviance in Contemporary Youth Culture*, Aldershot: Avebury

Rees, W. (1996) quoted in M. Wackernagel and W. Rees, *Our Ecological Footprint: Reducing Human Impact On Human Health*, Gabriola Island, BC: New Society Publishers

Reiman, J. (2003 [7th edn], 2006 [8th edn]) *The Rich Get Richer and the Poor Get Poorer: Ideology, Class and Criminal Justice*, Harlow: Allyn & Bacon / Pearson Longman

Reiner, R. (1992) *The Politics of the Police*, Hemel Hempstead: Wheatsheaf

Reiner, R. (1997) 'Policy on police', in M. Maguire, R. Morgan, R. Reiner (eds) *The Oxford Handbook of Criminology* (2nd edn), Oxford: OUP

Reiner, R. (2007) *Law and Order, An Honest Citizen's Guide to Crime and Control*, Cambridge: Polity

Reinharz, S. (1992) *Feminist Methods in Sociological Research*, New York: OUP

Reiss, A.J. (1961) 'The social integration of queers and peers', *Social Problems*, 9(2), p.102–20

Remenyi, J. (2004) 'What is development', in D. Kingsbury, J. Remenyi, J. McKay and J. Hunt (eds) *Key Issues in Development*, Basingstoke: Palgrave

Rex, J. and Tomlinson, S. (1979) *Colonial Immigrants in a British City*, London: Routledge & Kegan Paul

Richardson, J. (2001) 'British Muslims in the broadsheet press: a challenge to cultural hegemony?', *Journalism Studies*, 2(2)

Riddell, R.C. (2007) *Does Foreign Aid Really Work?*, Oxford: OUP

Ritzer, G. (1993) *The McDonaldisation of Society*, Thousand Oaks, California: Pine Forge Press

Robbins, T. (1988) *Cults, Converts, and Charisma*, London: Sage

Roberts, B. (1978) *Cities of Peasants: The Political Economy of Urbanisation in the Third World*, London: Edward Arnold

Roberts, K. (2001) *Class in Modern Britain*, Basingstoke: Palgrave

Roberts, K. and Chadwick, C. (1991) *Transitions into the Labour Market: The New Routes of the 1980s*, Youth Cohort Series 16, Research and Development Series 65, Sheffield: Employment Department

Roberts, K., Cook, F.G., Clark, S.C. and Semeonoff, E. (1977) *The Fragmentary Class Structure*, London: Heinemann

Robertson, R. (1992) *Globalisation: Social Theory and Global Culture*, London: Sage

Robey, B, Rutstein, S.O. and Morris, L. (1993) 'The Fertility Decline in Developing Countries', *Scientific American*, 269(6), pp.60–7

Robinson, T., Gustafson, B. and Popovich, M. (2008) 'Perceptions of negative stereotypes of older people in magazine adverts: comparing the perceptions of older adults and college students', *Ageing and Society*, 28, pp.233–51

Rock, P. (1988) 'The present state of British criminology' in *The British Journal of Criminology*, 28(2)

Rodgers, J. (2008) *Criminalising Social Policy: Its Nature and Consequences*, London: Sage

Room, G. (1995) *Beyond the Threshold: The measurement and analysis of social exclusion*, Bristol: The Policy Press

Roper, L. (2003) *Disability in Media*, www.mediaed.org.uk/posted_documents/DisabilityinMedia.htm

Rorty, R. (1980) *Philosophy and the Mirror of Nature*, Oxford: Blackwell

Rosenau, J.N. (1990) *Turbulence in World Politics: A Theory of Change and Continuity*, Princeton: Princeton University Press,

Rosenthal, R. and Jacobson, L. (1968) *Pygmalion in the Classroom*, New York: Holt, Rinehart & Winston

Ross, J.I. (ed.) (2000) *Varieties of State Crime and Its Control*, Monsey, NJ: Criminal Justice Press

Ross, K. (1996) 'Disability and the media: a suitable case for treatment?', http://archive.waccglobal.org/wacc/publications/media_development/archive/1998_2/disability_and_the_media_a_suitable_case_for_treatment

Rostow, W.W. (1971) *The Stages of Economic Growth*, Cambridge: CUP

Rowbotham, S. (1982) 'The trouble with patriarchy', in M. Evans (ed.) *The Woman Question*, London: Fontana

Rowntree, B.S. (1901) *Poverty: A Study of Town Life*, London: Macmillan

Rubin, H. (1998) *The Princessa: Machiavelli for Women*, London: Bloomsbury

Ruggiero, V. (1996) *Organized and Corporate Crime in Europe: Offers That Can't Be Refused*, Aldershot: Dartmouth

Runnymede Trust (1997) *Islamophobia: A Challenge For Us All*, Runnymede Trust, London: The Runnymede Trust

Rusche, G. and Kircheimer, O. (1939) *Punishment and Social Structure*, New York: Columbia University Press

Russo, V. (1981) *The Celluloid Closet: Homosexuality in the Movie*, New York: Harper & Row

Rutherford, J. (1988) 'Who's that man?', in R. Chapman and J. Rutherford (eds) *Male Order: Unwrapping Masculinity*, London: Laurence & Wishart

Rutland, A. (2005) *The Development and Regulation of Prejudice in Children*, London: ESRC research

Ryan, J. and Thomas, F. (1980) *The Politics of Mental Handicap*, Harmondsworth: Penguin

Sachdev, S. and Wilkinson, F. (1998) *Low Pay and the Minimum Wage*, Institute of Employment Rights

Sachs, J. (2005) *Why Aid Does Work*, www.news.bbc.co.uk

Sachs, W. (1992) 'Where all the world's a stooge', *Guardian*, 29 May

Sahlins, M. (1997) 'The original affluent society' in M. Rahnema and V. Bawtree (eds) (1997) *The Post Development Reader*, London: Zed Books

Said, E. (2003) *Orientalism: Western Conceptions of the Orient*, Harmondsworth: Penguin

Samad, Y. (2006) 'Muslims in Britain today', *Sociology Review*, 15(4)

Samad, Y. (2006) *Sociology Review*, 15(4), April 2006

Sampson, R.J., Raudenbusch, S.W. and Earls, F. (1997) 'Neighbourhoods and violent crime: a multi-level study of collective efficacy', *Science*, 277, pp.918–24

Sanderson, T. (1999) 'UK Church offers atheists "baby blessing"', BBC News online article, 14 July

Sankara, T. (1988) *Thomas Sankara Speaks: The Burkina Faso Revolution 1983–1987*, New York: Pathfinder Press

Sarap, M. (1993) *An Introductory Guide to Post-structuralism and Postmodernism*, Hemel Hempstead: Harvester Wheatsheaf

Saunders, P. (1979) *Urban Politics*, Harmondsworth: Penguin

Saunders, P. (1990) *Social Class and Stratification*, London: Routledge

Saunders, P. (1995) *Capitalism – A Social Audit*, Buckingham: OU Press

Saunders, P. (1996) *Unequal but Fair? A Study of Class Barriers in Britain*, London: Institute of Economic Affairs

Savage, M. (1995) 'The middle classes in modern Britain', *Sociology Review*, 5(2), Oxford: Philip Allan

Savage, M. (2000) *Class Analysis and Social Transformation*, Buckingham: OU Press

Savage, M. and Egerton, M. (1997) 'Social mobility, individual ability and the inheritance of class inequality', *Sociology*, 31(4)

Savage, M., Bagnall, G. and Longhurst, B. (2001) 'Ordinary, ambivalent and defensive class identities in the North West of England', *Sociology*, 35(4), pp.875–92

Savage, M., Barlow, J., Dickens, P. and Fielding, I. (1992) *Prosperity, Bureaucracy and Culture: Middle-class Formation in Contemporary Britain*, London: Routledge

Sayer, A. (1992) *Method in Social Science: A Realist Approach* (2nd edn), London: Routledge

Scarman, Lord (1981) *The Scarman Report*, Harmondsworth: Penguin

Scase, R. and Scales, J. (2000) *Fit and Fifty*, Swindon: Economic and Social Research Council

Scharf, E.R. (1970) *The Sociological Study of Religion*, London: Hutchinson University Library

Schiller, H. (1976) *Communication and Cultural Domination*, Armonk, NJ: International Arts and Sciences Press

Schlesinger, P. (1990) 'Rethinking the sociology of journalism: source strategies and the limits of media-centrism', in M. Ferguson (ed.) *Public Communication: the new imperatives*, London: Sage

Schutz, A. (1972) *The Phenomenology of the Social World*, London: Heinemann

Schwartz, H. and Jacobs, J. (1979) *Qualitative Sociology: A Method to the Madness*, London: Collier-Macmillan

Scott MacEwen, A. (1994) 'Gender segregation and the SCELI research', in A. Scott MacEwen (ed.) *Gender Segregation and Social Change*, Oxford: OUP

Scott, A. (1990) *Ideology and The New Social Movements*, London: Unwin Hyman

Scott, J. (1982) *The Upper Classes: Poverty and Privilege in Britain*, London: Macmillan

Scott, J. (1991) *Who Rules Britain?*, Cambridge: Polity Press

Scott, J. (2005) 'Social mobility: occupational snakes and ladders', *Sociology Review*, 15(2), Nov

Scott, J., Dex, S and Joshi, H. (2008) *Women and Employment: Changing Lives and New Challenges*, Cheltenham: Edward Elgar Publishing

Scraton, P. (1985) *The State of the Police*, London: Pluto

Scraton, P. (1987) *Law, Order and the Authoritarian State: Readings in Critical Criminology*, Milton Keynes: OU Press

Scraton, P. (1997) 'Whose "childhood"? What "crisis"?', in P. Scraton (ed.) *'Childhood' in 'Crisis'?*, London: UCL Press

Scraton, P. (2002) 'Defining "power" and challenging "knowledge": critical analysis and resistance in the UK', in K. Carrington and R. Hogg (eds) *Critical Criminology: Issues, debates, challenges*, Cullompton: Willan Publishing

Scraton, P. and Chadwick, K. (1982) 'The theoretical and political priorities of critical criminology', in G. Mars, *Cheats at Work, an Anthropology of Workplace Crime*, London: Allen & Unwin

Seabrook, J. (2005) 'Globalization: a war on local cultures', *Sociology Review*, 15(2), Nov

Seager, J. (2003) *The Penguin Atlas of Women in the World: Completely Revised and Updated*, New York: Penguin Books

Seaton, J. (2003) 'Broadcasting futures', in J. Curran and J. Seaton (2003) *Power without Responsibility: the press, broadcasting, and new media in Britain* (6th edn), London: Routledge

Sen, A. (1987) *Hunger and Entitlements*, Helsinki: World Institute for Development Economics Research

Sen, A. (2002) 'Does globalization equal Westernisation?', *The Globalist*, 25 March

Sewell, A. (2004) 'Where white liberals fear to tread', *Guardian*, 30 Mar

Shah, S. (2008) 'Too many black and Asian faces on TV', *Guardian*, 26 Jun

Shakespeare, T. (1996) 'Disability, identity, difference', in C. Barnes and G. Mercer (eds) *Exploring the Divide*, Leeds: Disability Press

Shakespeare, T. and Watson, N. (1997) 'Defending the social model', in L. Barton and M. Oliver (eds) *Disability Studies: Past, Present and Future*, Leeds: The Disability Press

Shapin, S. (1995) 'Here and everywhere: sociology of scientific knowledge', *Annual Review of Sociology*, 21

Sharp, C. and Budd, T. (2005) Minority Ethnic Groups and Crime: Findings from the Offending, Crime and Justice Survey 2003 (2nd edn), London: Home Office

Sharpe, S. (1994) *Just Like a Girl: How Girls Learn to be Women – From the Seventies to the Nineties*, Harmondsworth: Penguin

Sharples, J. (1999) *Men's Magazines: Good For Men*, www.theory.org.uk

Sharrock, W., Hughes, J. and Martin, P. (2003) *Understanding Modern Sociology*, London: Sage

Shaw, C.R. and McKay, H.D. (1931) *Social Factors in Juvenile Delinquency*, Washington, DC: Government Printing Office

Shaw, C.R. and McKay, H.D. (1942) *Juvenile Delinquency and Urban Areas*, Chicago: University of Chicago Press

Shaw, M. (2000) 'War and globality: the role and character of war in the global transition', in Ho-Won Jeong (ed.) *Peace and Conflict: A New Agenda*, Aldershot: Ashgate

Shearer, A. (1981) *Disability: Whose Handicap?* Oxford: Blackwell

Shearing, C. and Stenning, P. (1983) 'Private security: implications for social control', *Social Problems*, 30(5), pp.493–506

Shildrick, T. and MacDonald, R. (2007) 'Class, consumption and prejudice: contemporary representations of "the social scum"', ESRC research seminar series on identities and consumption, University of Teesside

Shiner, L. (1967) 'The concept of secularization in empirical research', *Journal for the Scientific Study of Religion*, 6, pp.207–20

Shiva, V. (1989) *Staying Alive: Women, Ecology and Development*, London: Zed Books

Short, C. (1999) House of Commons Hansard Written Answers, 23 Nov

Simon, R.J. and Nadell, P.S. (1995) 'In the same voice or is it different? Gender and the clergy', *Sociology of Religion*, 56(1)

Situ, Y. and Emmons, D. (1999) *Environmental Crime: The Criminal Justice System's Role in Protecting the Environment*, London: Sage

Skeggs, B. (1997) *Formations of Class and Gender*, London: Sage

Skeggs, B. (2001) 'Feminist ethnography', in P. Atkinson, A. Coffey, S. Delamont, J. Lofland and L. Lofland (eds) *Handbook of Ethnography*, London: Sage

Sklair, L. (2004) *Globalization: Capitalism and its Alternatives*, Oxford: OUP

Skogan, W.G. (1990) *Disorder and Decline: Crime and the Spiral of Decay in American Neighbourhoods*, New York: Free Press

Skolnick, J. (1966) *Justice without Trial*, New York: Wiley

Slapper, G. and Tombs, S. (1999) *Corporate Crime*, Harlow: Longman

Smart, C. (1990) 'Feminist approaches to criminology; or postmodern woman meets atavistic man', in L. Gelsthorpe and A. Morris (eds) *Feminist Perspectives in Criminology*, Milton Keynes: OU Press

Smith, C. (2005) *Soul Searching: The religious and spiritual lives of American teenagers*, Oxford: OUP

Smith, D. (1973) 'Women's perspective as a radical critique of sociology', *Sociological Inquiry*, 44

Smith, D.J. and Gray, J. (1985) *People and Police in London*, London: Gower

Smith, M.J. (2008) *Environment and Citizenship: Integrating Justice, Responsibility and Civic Engagement*, London: Zed Publications

South, N. (2004) in Carrabine, E., Iganski, P., Lee, M., Plummer, K. and South, N. (2004) *Criminology: A Sociological Introduction*, London: Routledge

Southwold, M. (1978) 'Buddhism and the definition of religion', *Man* (NS), 13, pp.362–79

Spencer-Thomas, O. (2008) *What is Newsworthy?*, www.btinternet.com/~owenst/index.html

Spender, D. (1985) *Man Made Language*, London: Routledge

Spybey, T. (1998) 'Globalisation or imperialism', *Sociology Review*, Feb

Stark, R. and Bainbridge, W. (1985) *The Future of Religion: Secularisation, Revival and Cult Formation*, Berkeley: California University Press

Steinem, G. (1995) 'Words and Change', *Ms Magazine*, Sept/Oct

Steven, P. (2004) *The No-Nonsense Guide to Global Media*, London: Verso

Stinchcombe, A. (1963) 'Institutions of privacy in the determination of police administration', *American Journal of Sociology*, 69

Storr, M. (2002) 'Sociology and social movements: theories, analyses and ethical dilemmas', in P. Hamilton and K. Thompson (eds) *The Uses of Sociology*, Oxford: The OU/Blackwell

Strinati, D. (1995) *An Introduction to Theories of Popular Culture*, London: Routledge

Sutherland, E.H. (1940) 'White-collar criminality', *American Sociological Review*, 5, pp.1–12

Sutherland, E.H. and Cressey, D. (1966) *Principles of Criminology* (revised edn), Chicago: University of Chicago Press

Sutton Trust (2005) *The Educational Backgrounds of Members of the House of Commons and House of Lords*, London: Sutton Trust

Sutton Trust (2007) *The Educational Backgrounds of the UK's 500 Leading People,* London: Sutton Trust

Sutton, R.I. (1992) 'Feelings about a Disneyland visit: photography and the reconstruction of bygone emotions', *Journal of Management Enquiry*, 1, pp.278–87

Swale, J. (2004) 'Education: A World Perspective', *Sociology Review*, 14(1), Sept

Swale, J. (2006) 'Meet the "Neets": media accounts of the underclass debate', *Sociology Review*, 15(3), Feb

Swartz, J. (1975) 'Silent killers at work', *Crime and Social Justice*, 3, pp.15–20

Tarling, R. (1988) *Police Work and Manpower Allocation*, Paper 47, London: Home Office

Taylor, I. (1999) *Crime in Context: A Critical Criminology of Market Societies*, Cambridge: Polity Press

Taylor, J., Walton, P. and Young, J. (1973) *The New Criminology*, London: Routledge

Taylor, S. (1990) 'Beyond Durkheim, sociology and suicide', *Social Studies Review*, Nov

Taylor-Gooby, P. (with Vic George) (1996) *Welfare Policy: Squaring the Welfare Circle*, Basingstoke: Macmillan

Tebbel, C. (2000) *The Body Snatchers: How the Media Shapes Women*, New South Wales: Finch Publishing

The Sutton Trust (2007) *Entry to Leading Universities*, Sutton Trust

Thomas, W.I. and Znaniecki, F. (1918) *The Polish Peasant in Europe and America*, Chicago: University of Chicago Press

Thompson, D. (1996) *The End of Time: Faith and Fear in the Shadow of the Millennium*, London: Sinclair Stevenson

Thompson, G.F. (2000) 'Where do MNCs conduct their business activity and what are the consequences for national systems' in S. Quack, G. Morgan and R. Whitely (eds) *National Capitalisms, Global Competition and Economic Performance*, Amsterdam: John Benjamins

Thompson, I. (1986) *Sociology in Focus: Religion*, Harlow: Longman

Thompson, J.B. (1995) *The Media and Modernity: A Social Theory of the Media*, Cambridge: Polity

Thompson, N.(1993) *Antidiscriminatory Practice*, Basingstoke: MacMillan

Thornton, J. and Beckwith, S. (2004) *Environmental Law* (2nd edn), London: Sweet & Maxwell

Thornton, S. (1995) *Club Cultures: Music, Media and Subcultural Capital*, Cambridge: Polity

Thrasher, F. (1927) *The Gang,* Chicago: University of Chicago Press

Timmons Roberts, J. and Hite, A. (2000) *From Modernisation to Globalization*, Oxford: Blackwell

Tizard, B. and Hughes, M. (1991) 'Reflections on young people learning', in G. Walford (ed.) *Doing Educational Research*, London: Routledge

Tombs, S. (2002) 'Understanding regulation: a review essay', *Social and Legal Studies*, 11(1), p.111–31

Tombs, S. (2007) 'A political economy of corporate killing ', *Criminal Justice Matters*, 70(1), Winter, pp.29–30

Tombs, S. and Whyte, D. (2003) *Unmasking the Crimes of the Powerful: Scrutinizing States and Corporations,* New York: Peter Lang

Tombs, S. and Whyte, D. (2007) *Safety Crimes*, Cullompton: Willan

Tonnies, F. (1887, reissued 1957) *Community and Society: Gemeinschaft und Gesellschaft* (trans. & ed. C.P. Loomis), Detroit: The Michigan State University Press

Touraine, A. (1982) *The Voice and The Eye*, Cambridge: CUP

Toussaint, E. (2008) *The World Bank: A Critical Primer*, London: Pluto Press

Townsend, P. (1979) *Poverty in the United Kingdom*, Harmondsworth: Penguin

Troeltsch, E. (1931/1976) *The Social Teachings of the Christian Churches*, Chicago: University of Chicago Press

Tuchman, G., Kaplan Daniels, A. and Benit, J. (eds) (1978) *Hearth and Home: Images of Women in the Mass Media*, NY: OUP

Tunstall, J. (2000) *The Media in Britain*, London: Constable

Tunstall, J. and Palmer, M. (1991) *Media Moguls*, London: Routledge

Turner, B. (1983) *Religion and Social Theory*, London: Sage

Turner, B.S. (1994) 'From regulation to risk', in B.S. Turner (ed.) *Orientalism, Postmodernism and Globalism*, London: Routledge

Tylor, E.B. (1903, originally 1871) *Primitive Culture*, London: Murray

United Nations Development Programme (UNDP) (1999) *Human Development Report 1999*, New York/Oxford: OUP. http://hdr.undp.org/en/reports/global/hdr 1999/

United Nations Office on Drugs and Crime (UNODC) (2005) *World Drugs Report* www.unodc.org/pdf/WDR_2005/volume_ 1_web.pdf

Urry, J. (1990) *The Tourist Gaze*, London: Sage

Valier, C. (2001) *Theories of Crime and Delinquency,* Harlow: Longman

Van der Gaag, N. (2004) *The No-Nonsense Guide to Women's Rights*, London: Verso

van Dijk, T. (1991) *Racism and the Press*, London: Routledge

van Zeijl, F. (2007) 'War against women', *New Internationalist*, 401, June

Vincent, J. (2001) 'The life course and old age', *Sociology Review*, 11(2), Nov

Voas, D. and Crockett, A. (2005) 'Religion in Britain: neither believing nor belonging', *Sociology*, 39(1), pp.11–28

Walby, S. (1986) *Patriarchy at Work*, Cambridge: Polity Press

Walby, S. (1990) *Theorizing Patriarchy*, Oxford: Blackwell

Walker, A. and Aune, K. (eds) (2003) *On Revival: A Critical Examination*, Carlisle: Paternoster Press

Wallace, W. (1971) *The Logic of Science in Sociology*, Chicago: Aldine-Atherton

Wallerstein, E. (1979) *The Rise and Future Demise of the World Capitalist System: Concepts for Comparative Analysis from the Capitalist World-economy*, Cambridge: CUP

Wallis, R. (1984) *The Elementary Forms of New Religious Life*, London: Routledge

Walters, R. (2007) 'Crime, regulation and radioactive waste', in P. Beirne and N. South (eds) *Issues in Green Criminology: Confronting harms against humanity, animals and nature*, Cullompton: Willan

Walters, R. (2008) *Eco Crime and Genetically Modified Food*, London: Cavendish Routledge

Warner, R.S. (1993) 'Work in progress toward a new paradigm for the sociological study of religion in the United States', *American Journal of Sociology*, 98(5), pp.1044–93

Waters, M. (1995) *The Death of Class*, London: Sage

Watson, H. (1994) 'Women and the veil: personal responses to global process', in A. Ahmed and H. Donnan (eds) *Islam, Globalisation and Postmodernity*, London: Routledge

Watson, J. (2008) *Media Communication: An Introduction to the Theory and Process* (3rd edn), Basingstoke: Palgrave

Wayne, M. (2007) 'The media and young people – hyping up the new folk devils', *Socialist Worker*, 2069, 22 Sep

Webb, E., Campbell, D., Schwartz, R. and Sechrest, L. (1981) *Nonreactive Measures in the Social Sciences* (2nd edn), Boston: Houghton Mifflin

Weber, M. (1905/1958) *The Protestant Ethic and the Spirit of Capitalism*, London: Unwin

Weber, M. (1920/1963) *The Sociology of Religion*, Boston, Mass: Beacon Press

Weber, M. (1947) *The Theory of Social and Economic Organisation*, New York: Free Press

Webster, A. (1990) *Introduction to the Sociology of Development*, Basingstoke: Palgrave

Webster, C. (2007) *Understanding Race and Crime*, Buckingham: OU Press

West, C. and Zimmerman, D.H. (1991) 'Doing gender', in J. Larber and S.A. Farrell (eds) *The Social Construction of Gender*, London: Sage, pp.13–37

West, D.J. and Farrington, D.P. (1973) *Who Becomes Delinquent?*, London: Heineman

Westergaard, J. (1995) *Who Gets What: The hardening of class inequality in the late 20th century*, Cambridge: Polity Press

Westergaard, J. (1996) 'Class in Britain since 1979; facts, theories and ideologies', in D. Lee and B. Turner (eds) *Conflicts about Class: Debating Inequality in Later Industrialisation*, Harlow: Longman

Westwood, S. (1999) 'Representing gender', *Sociology Review*, Sept

Westwood, S. (2002) *Power and the Social*, London: Routledge

Whale, J. (1977) *The Politics of the Media*, London: Fontana

Whannel, G. (2002) 'David Beckham, identity and masculinity', *Sociology Review*, 11, pp.2–4

Whitaker, B. (2002) 'Islam and the British press after September 11', www.al-bab.com/media/articles/bw020620.htm

White, C. (2004) *The Middle Mind: Why Consumer Culture is Turning Us Into The Living Dead*, London: Penguin

Whyte, D. (2007) 'The crimes of neo-liberal rule in occupied Iraq', *British Journal of Criminology*, 47, pp.177–95

Whyte, W.F. (1943) *Street Corner Society: The Social Structure of an Italian Slum*, Chicago: University of Chicago Press

Wilkins, L. (1964) *Social Deviance: Social Policy, Action and Research*, London: Tavistock

Wilkinson, H. (1994) *No Turning Back: Generations and the Genderquake*, London: Demos

Wilkinson, H. and Mulgan, G. (1997) 'Freedom's children and the rise of generational politics', in G. Mulgan (ed.) *Life After Politics: New Thinking for the Twenty-first Century*, London: Fontana

Wilkinson, R. (1996) *Unhealthy Societies: The Afflictions of Inequality*, Routledge: London

Wilkinson, S. (1999) 'Focus groups: a feminist method', *Psychology of Women Quarterly*, 23, pp.221–44

Wilks-Heeg, S. (2008) *Purity of Elections in the UK: Causes for Concern*, York: The Joseph Rowntree ReformTrust Ltd

Wilkstrom, P.H. (1991) *Urban Crime, Criminals and Victims: the Swedish Experience in an Anglo-American Comparative Perspective*, New York: Springer-Verlag

Williams, W.M. (1956) *The Sociology of an English Village: Gosforth*, London: Routledge & Kegan Paul

Willis, P. (1977) *Learning to Labour: How Working-class Kids get Working-class Jobs*, Farnborough: Saxon House

Willott, S.A. and Griffin, C.E. (1996) 'Men, masculinity and the challenge of long-term unemployment', in M. Mac An Ghaill (ed.) *Understanding Masculinities: Social Relations and Cultural Arenas*, Buckingham: OU Press

Wilson, B. (1982) *Religion in Sociological Perspective*, Oxford: OUP

Wilson, B.R. (1966) *Religion in a Secular Society*, London: B.A. Watts

Wilson, J.Q. and Kelling, G. (1982) 'Broken windows: the police and neighbourhood safety', *Atlantic Monthly*, March, pp.29–38

Wilson, W.J. (1996) *When Work Disappears: The World of the New Urban Poor*, New York: Albert Knopf

Winlow, S. (2004) 'Masculinities and crime', *Criminal Justice Matters*, 55(18)

Winship, J. (1987) *Inside Women's Magazines*, London: Pandora Press

Wiseman, J. (1998) *Global Nation? Australia and the politics of globalisation*, Cambridge/Melbourne, CUP

Wolf, N. (1990) *The Beauty Myth*, London: Vintage

Women's Sport and Fitness Foundation (2006) *Playing Catch-Up*, London: Women's Sport and Fitness Foundation

Wood, J. (1993) 'Repeatable pleasures: notes on young people's use of video', in D. Buckingham (ed.) *Reading Audiences: Young People and the Media*, Manchester: Manchester University Press

Woodhead, L. (2004) 'Feminism and the sociology of religion: from gender blindness to gendered difference', in R.K. Fenn (ed.) *The Blackwell Companion to the Sociology of Religion*, London: Blackwell

Woodhead, L. (2005) *Christianity: A Very Short Introduction*, Oxford: OUP

Woodhead, L. (2007) cited in R. Pigott 'Lifting the veil on religion and identity', *The Edge*, Spring 2007, pp.16–20

Woodhead, L. and Heelas, P. (2000) *Religion in Modern Times: An Interpretive Anthology*, Oxford: Blackwell

Wright Mills, C. (1956) *The Power Elite*, Oxford: OUP

Yinger, M. (1970) *The Scientific Study of Religion,* London: Routledge

YouGov (2008) *The Culture of Youth Communities*, London: The Princes Trust

Young, J. (1971) *The Drug Takers*, London: Paladin

Young, J. (1999) *The Exclusive Society: Social Exclusion, Crime and Difference in Late Modernity*, London: Sage

Young, J. (2007) *The Vertigo of Late Modernity*, London: Sage

Zweig, E. (1961) *The Worker in an Affluent Society*, London: Heinemann

Zylinska, J. (2003) 'Guns n' rappers: moral panics and the ethics of cultural studies', *Culture Machine*, www.culturemachine.tees.ac.uk

INDEX

covert participant observation 319, 320, **321**, 380, 396
creationism 5
credibility hierarchy 160–1
Crewe, Ivor 234–6
crime **336**
   British Crime Survey 275, 353, 359–60, 363, **364**
   capitalism 346, 389
   community safety 392–4
   corporate/occupational 378–81, 383–4
   definitions 332
   deviance relationship 331–3
   displacement 393, **398**
   elites 219
   environmental 366–71, 382
   ethnicity 193–5, 386–91
   functionalist theory 257
   gender issues 372–7
   globalization 120–1, 381–2
   justice system 335–6, 347, 392–8
   labelling theory 355–7
   masculinity 375–7
   new social movements 248
   normative approach 331–2
   offending patterns 363–4
   participant observation 287
   police-recorded statistics 359–61
   positivism 281
   power 213
   prevention 369, 392–4
   racial theories 389–91
   relativist approaches 332–3
   religion 11, 28
   self-report studies 362–3
   state crime 227, 349–50, 381
   underclass 438
   victim surveys 361–2
   see also deviance; offending
criminality 193–5, 320
criminology 325, 326, 332, **336**
   critical 334, 345–51
   environmental 366–71
   transgressive 374–5
Criswell, Rev. W. A. 18
critical criminology 334, **336**, 345–51
critical sociology 318, **321**, 325
cross-media ownership 135, **143**
cross-sectional surveys 280, **284**
crystals 29, **31**
Cuba 61
cults 21, 24
   apologists 29, **31**
   characteristics 28
   cultic milieu 29, **31**, 49
   femininity **191**
   women 36
culture
   capital 419, **422**, 430
   control 394, **398**
   development 67, **71**
   differences 323–4
   effects model 174–5, **177**
   globalization 121–2
   hegemony 199, **204**
   hybridity 42, **43**
   imperialism 67, **71**, 121, 122, 230, **230**
   pessimist perspective 148, 149–50, **153**
   resistance cultures 389–90, **391**
   transmission 366–7, **371**
   zones 70
culture-specific development 67, **71**
Curran, J. 139–41, 142
cybermedia 134, 135, **143**

Dahl, Robert 217–18
dams 113
Darfur 104
data archives 313, **315**
Davies, N. 159
Davis, M. 394
de Beavoir, Simone 33
de-skilling 77, **79**, 120, 436
death rate 428, 432
debt 84–6
   developing countries 80
   repayments 83, 84, 95
   women 103
decision-making process 216–18
deconstruction 297, **300**
defensible space 393, **398**
defensive new social movements 246
deference **24**, 234
deforestation 91, **97**, 112
deformed polyarchy 244, **252**
delinquency 332, **336**
democracy 61, **63**, 148–9, 219
demography 90, 91, **97**
   timebomb 473, **476**
   see also population
denominations 20–1
dependency **79**
   neo-colonialism 73–5
   origins 72–3
   solutions 75
dependency theory 72–9
   aid 75, 82, 84, 85
   criticisms 76–7, 78
   debt 84
   population 93–6
   urbanization 109–10
dependent development 75
dependent variables 283, **284**
deregulation of global finance 120
desacrilization 46, **51**
desensitization 169, **177**
desertification 91, **97**, 112
destitution 55, 323, **326**
determinism 418, **422**
developing countries
   aid 81–4
   capitalism 68
   characteristics 56
   commodities 73, 74, 86
   conflict 125–31
   debt 80, 84–6
   exploitation 76–7
   fertility rate 94–5
   gender 98–106
   geography 55
   local elites 74, 76
   media representations 197–8
   neo-colonialism 73–4
   patriarchy 101
   population 90
   transnational corporations 76
   urbanization 67
   Western perceptions 54, 64
   Westernization 61
   women 99–102, 104–6
   see also development
development 54–63
   conflict 126
   culture 69–70
   environment 110–11
   gender 103
   globalization 62
   measurement 57–9
   modernization theory 64–71
   people-centred 61–2
   post-development school 62
   processes 65–6

social damage 68
sustainability 59
terminology 55–6
Western values 60–1, 68–9
see also developing countries
deviance
   amplification 164, 356, **358**
   control theories 330–7
   crime relationship 331–3
   definitions 331, 332
   deviant career 354, **358**
   labelling theory 318, 352–3
   modernization theory 68
   red-haired people 357
   religion 11, 28
   research methods 380
   see also crime; offending
Diana, Princess of Wales 157, 214, 215
diaries 290, 295, 310
diaspora communities 126, **131**
differential association 367, **371**, 383
differentiation 409, **415**
diffusion 217, **222**
digital technologies 134, 145
digital underclass 147
direct action 248–9
direct rule 220
disability 323–4, **487**
   media representations 189–90
   stratification 480–7
   theoretical models 481–2
disableism 482, 483–6, **487**
discipline 335, **336**
   power 212, **215**
discourses 212, **215**, 297
discrediting 482, **487**
discretion 395–6, **398**
discrimination 323–4, 459, 461–2, 483–6
disease 95
disengagement 46–7, **51**
   theory 475, **476**
disinhibition effect 169, **177**
'Disneyfication' 152
Disneyland 47
disorder 367
dissemination 121, **123**
distributional power 211
diversification 135–6, **143**
division of labour 416, **422**
DNA profiling 227
doctor/patient ratio 95
dominant reading 173, **177**
donor countries (aid) 87
Douglas, J. D. 402
downsizing 436, **439**
dramaturgical approach 260–1, **261**
drift 376, **377**
drugs
   trafficking 85, 116, 121, 381
   use 287, 343
dual labour-market theory 452–3, 466, **469**
dual systems approach 455–6
dual-sector economy 109
duality of structure 265, **268**
dumpster diver subculture 267
Durkheim, Émile 3
   crime 331–2
   modernization theory 64
   punishment 335
   religion 8–9, 10
   scientific approach 273
   society 287
   stratification 416–17
   suicide 400–3

dysfunctionality 256, **261**
dysfunctions **422**
dystopias **123**

e-commerce 148, 149
eco-feminism 103, **105**
eco-warriors 249
ecological limits 68, **71**
economic capital 435, **439**
economic determinism 258, **261**
economic development 57–8, 59–60
economic exclusion 390
economic globalization 117–21, 127
economic leadership 434
economic power 221
ecumenical movement 47, **51**
edgework 342, **343**, 376
education 430–1
   disability 484
   ethnicity 463
   gender 453
   girls 99, 101
   labelling theory 355
   masculinity 376
   modernization theory 66
   occupations 221
   social class 427
   stratification 419
   underclass 438
   women 92–3, 104
effects approach 168, **177**
egoistic suicide 400–1, **403**
El Barrio (New York) 390
El Sadaawi, N. 33
elderly people 46, 203–4, 471–4
elections 236, 238, 239
elites **222**
   education 221
   mass media 157, 160
   new media 149–50
   pluralism 217
   theory 219
Elliott, D. R. 76
embourgeoisement 234, **240**, 437
emergency aid 81
emotion-based crime 383
empirical sociology **276**, 325, **326**
empiricism **71**, 217, **222**, 271, 272
employees' theft 379
employment
   disability 484–5
   ethnicity 464
   gender 450–3
   men 451–2
   racism 462
   stratification 452–3
   women 99, 102, 104, 452–3
   young people 474
   see also unemployment
empowerment 35, **36**
Engels, Friedrich 11
Enlightenment 4–5, **6**
enquiry methods 93
entrepreneurialism 15, **19**, 233, **240**
entrepreneuriality 383, **385**
environment 110–15
   cities 109
   crime 366–71, 382, **385**
   degradation 103, 107, 111–12, **114**
   developing countries 59, 68, 85
environmentalism 247
epistemology 279, **284**
equality of opportunity 425
equality of outcome **432**
Erlich, Paul 91, 93, 94

501

Index

Sociology A2 for AQA